1998
BROOKMAN

UNITED STATES, UNITED NATIONS & CANADA
STAMPS & POSTAL COLLECTIBLES

FEATURING

SPECIALIZED LISTINGS

OF

STATE DUCK & INDIAN RESERVATION STAMPS
PLATE NO. COILS & UNEXPLODED BOOKLETS
U.S. SOUVENIR CARDS • PAGES • PANELS

UNITED STATES FIRST DAY COVERS

Plus

Confederate States
U.S. Possessions
U.S. Trust Territories
Canadian Provinces
U.N. First Day Covers

ILLUSTRATED/GRADING GUIDE

SUBJECT INDEX, IDENTIFIER & BIBLIOGRAPHY

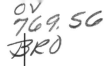

1998
BROOKMAN

TERMS AND INFORMATION

CONDITION - We price United States stamps issued prior to 1890 in two grades - Average and Fine. From 1890 to present we list a price for F-VF and VF quality. **FOR INFORMATION ON GRADING SEE PAGE vii.**

GUM AND HINGING

Original Gum (O.G.)

Prior to 1882, Unused stamps may have partial or no gum. If you require o.g., add the percentage indicated in ( ). **Example** (OG + 25%). From 1882 to present, o.g. can be expected, but stamps may have been hinged or have hinge remnants.

Never Hinged

Most issues are priced in F-VF, Never Hinged condition. Premiums for Average, NH usually run about half the F-VF premium. Prices for Never Hinged stamps on issues prior to 1882 will be quoted upon request.

SPECIAL PRICING INSTRUCTIONS

Average - From 1890-1934 **Average hinged perforated** stamps, when available, will be priced at 60-70% of the F-VF Hinged price depending upon the general quality of the issue.

Average hinged imperforate stamps, when available, will be priced at 70-75% of the F-VF Hinged price depending upon the general quality of the issue.

From 1935 to present, average quality, when available, will be priced at 20% below the F-VF price.

Very Fine NH, 1935-Date

VF NH singles, plate blocks, line pairs, etc. are available (unless specifically priced at the following premiums: Add 10¢ to any item priced under 50¢. Add 20% to any item priced at 50¢ and up. Unless priced as Very Fine, sets are not available Very Fine and stamps should be listed individually with appropriate premium.

Very Fine Unused O.G. Plate Blocks & Line Pairs

Very Fine Unused Plate Blocks and Line Pairs prior to #749 & 723 (and selected Back-of-the-Book Issues) are generally available at the respective F-VF NH price.

Very Fine Used

From 1847-1934, Very Fine Used stamps, when available, are priced by adding the % indicated to the appropriate Fine or F-VF price. **Example** (VF + 50%). From 1935 to date, the premiums are the same as for VF NH copies.

MINIMUM ORDER OF $20 - Present day costs force us to require that mail orders total a minimum of $20.00. Send payment with order.

PRICES - Every effort will be made to maintain these prices throughout the life of this edition. However, prices are subject to change if market conditions require. We are not responsible for typographical errors.

Edited By David S. Macdonald
First Day Covers Contributing Editors
Robert G. Driscoll
James McCusker

Back Cover Photos Courtesy Of Shreves Philatelic Galleries and Brookman/Barrett & Worthen

TABLE OF CONTENTS

STAMPS

INDEX TO ADVERTISERS

We wish to thank the advertisers who through their patronage help to keep the Brookman Price Guide available at the lowest possible price. We urge you to support our advertisers and let them know their ads were helpful to you in your philatelic pursuits.

BROOKMAN GRADING GUIDE

The following guide is a simplified approach to stamp grading designed to help you better understand the quality you can expect to receive when you order a specific grade. All grades listed below are for undamaged stamps free of faults such as tears, thin spots, creases, straight edges, scrapes, etc. Stamps with those defects are considered "seconds" and sell for prices below those listed. The stamps you receive may not always match the criteria given since each stamp must be judged on its own special merits such as freshness, color, cancellation, etc. For example: a well centered stamp may be graded only as "Average" because of a very heavy cancellation. Grading stamps is an art, not a science, and frequently the cliche "beauty is in the eye of the beholder" applies. Stamps offered throughout this price list fall into the "Group A" category unless the heading contains a (B) or (C).

GROUP A - WELL CENTERED ISSUES

| Average | Average | Average | Average |

| F-VF | F-VF | F-VF | F-VF |

| Very Fine | Very Fine | Very Fine | Very Fine |

GROUP A	AVERAGE	F-VF	VERY FINE
PERFORATED STAMPS	Perforations touch or barely clear of design on one or two sides.	Perforations well clear of design on all sides.	Design very well centered within perforations.
IMPERFORATE STAMPS	One edge may touch design.	All four edges are clear of design.	Four edges are well clear of and well centered around design.
COILS AND BOOKLET PANES	Perforated and imperforate edge may touch design on one or two edges.	Perforated and imperforate edges are clear of the design.	Design very well centered within perforated and imperf. edges.

NOTE: Stamps of poorer centering than "Average" grade are considered seconds.

"EXTREMELY FINE" is a grading term used to descibe stamps that are almost "Perfect" in centering, color, freshness, cancellations, etc. This grade, when available, is priced substantially higher than Very Fine quality.

GROUP B - MEDIAN CENTERED ISSUES

| Average | Average | Average | Average | Average |

| F-VF | F-VF | Very Fine | Very Fine | Very Fine |

GROUP B	AVERAGE	F-VF	VERY FINE
PERFORATED STAMPS	Perforations touch or barely cut into design on one or two sides.	Perforations clear of design on all four sides.	Design well centered within perforations.
IMPERFORATE STAMPS	One or two edges may touch or barely cut into design.	All four edges are clear of design as in "A".	Four edges are well clear of and well centered around design as in "A".
COILS AND BOOKLET PANES	Perforated and imperforate edge may touch or barely cut into design.	Perforated and imperforate edges are clear of design as in "A".	Design well centered within perforated and imperforated edges.

GROUP C - POORLY CENTERED ISSUES

| Average | Average | Average | Average | Average |

| Fine | Fine | Very Fine | Very Fine | Very Fine |

GROUP C	AVERAGE	FINE	VERY FINE
PERFORATED STAMPS	Perforations may cut into design on one or more sides.	Perforations touch or just clear of design on or more sides.	Perforations will clear design on all four sides.
IMPERFORATE STAMPS	One or more edges may cut into design.	One or more edges touch the design.	All four edges clear of the design.
COILS AND BOOKLET PANES	Perforated and imp. edge may cut into design on one or more sides.	Perforated and imperforate edges may touch or just clear design.	Perforated & imperforated edges well clear of design on all four sides.

Welcome to Stamp Collecting!

Challenge...information...friendships... and just plain fun are part of "the World's Most Popular Hobby," stamp collecting! For more than 150 years, stamp collecting has been the hobby choice of royalty, movie stars, sports celebrities, and hundreds of thousands of other people. Why do so many different types of people like stamps? One reason is, the hobby of stamp collecting suits almost anybody -- it's very personal. You fit the hobby to yourself, instead of forcing yourself to fit rules, as with many hobbies. There's not much free choice about how to play golf or softball or square dance -- there are many rules.

But stamp collecting can be done in a very simple way using stamps you find on your everyday mail and place on plain paper in a three-ring binder. Or you can give a "want list" to a stamp dealer. He will pull the stamps you want from his stock, and you mount them in the correct spaces in a custom-made album that you bought.

Or you can go to stamp shows or stamp shops and spend hours looking through boxes of stamps and envelopes in search of a particular stamp with a certain postal marking or a special first-day cover that has a meaning to suit your own interests.

Stamp collecting is a special mix of the structured and the unstructured, and you can make it a personal hobby that will not be like anyone else's. It's a world all its own, and anyone can find a comfortable place in it.

"Stamp Collector" or "Philatelist"?

Some people think that a "philatelist" (fi-LAT-uh-list) means someone who is more expert or serious than someone who is a "stamp collector." That's not true! But one advantage of using the word "philately" (fi-LAT-uh-lee) is that it includes all areas of the hobby -- not just stamps -- such as postal markings, postal history, postal stationery, and the postal items from the time before there were stamps, such as folded letters.

Finding Material for Your Collection

You can easily find everything for your stamp hobby by mail. Stamps, other philatelic material, catalogues, albums, and so on are easy to get by mail order. The philatelic press carries advertising for all of these hobby needs, and stamp shows in your area also will have dealers there. If you are lucky, you also may have a retail stamp store nearby.

Stamp shows may be small one- or two-day events in your local area, or very large events in big-city convention halls lasting several days and featuring hundreds of dealers and thousands of pages of stamp exhibits to see. Stamp shows also provide chances to meet other collectors, some of whom you may have "met" only by mail before.

How to Learn About Your New Hobby

Organizations, publications, and other collectors can help you grow in the hobby. The hobbies/recreation section of your local library may have basic books about stamp collecting, and the reference department may have a set of catalogs.

If your local library has no books on stamp collecting, you can borrow some from the huge collection of the American Philatelic Research Library through interlibrary loan or by becoming a member of the American Philatelic Society.

The APS/APRL are the largest stamp club and library in the United States and offer many services to collectors, including a 100-page monthly magazine, insurance for stamp collections, and a Sales Division through which members can buy and sell stamps by mail among themselves. The APS/APRL are at P.O. Box 8000, State College, PA 16803, or call (814) 237-3803.

There also are many newspapers and magazines in the stamp hobby, including Linn's Stamp News, Stamp Collector, Scott Monthly Journal, Mekeel's, Global Stamp News, and Stamps. Some can be found on large newsstands.

Taking Care of Your Collection

Paper is very fragile and must be handled with care. Stamp collectors use special tools and materials to protect their collectibles. Stamp tongs may look like cosmetic tweezers, but they have special tips that will not damage stamps, so be sure to buy your tongs from a stamp dealer and not in the beauty section at the drugstore!

Stamp albums and other storage methods (temporary file folders and boxes, envelopes, etc.) should be of archival-quality acid-free paper, and any plastic used on or near stamps and covers (postally-used envelopes of philatelic interest) also should be archival -- as used for safe storage by museums. Plastic that is not archivally safe has oil-based softeners that can leach out and do much damage to stamps. In recent years philatelic manufacturers have become more careful about their products, and it is easy now to find safe paper and plastic for hobby use.

Never use cellophane or other tapes around your stamps. Even so-called "magic" tape will cause damage that cannot be undone. Stamps should be put on pages either with hinges (small rectangles of special gummed paper) or with mounts (little self-adhesive plastic envelopes in many sizes to fit stamps and covers). Mounts keep stamps in the condition in which you bought them. Also available are pages with strips of plastic attached to them; these are "self-mounting" pages, meaning all you have to do is slip your stamp into the plastic strip.

Other hobby tools include gauges, for measuring the perforations on stamps, and watermark fluid, which makes the special marks in some stamp papers visible momentarily. "Perfs" and watermarks are important if you decide to do some types of specialized collecting.

A Stamp Is a Stamp?

Not really -- a stamp can be many things: a feast for the eye with beautiful design and color and printing technique...a study in history as you find out about the person, place, or event behind the stamp...a mystery story, as you try to find out how and why this stamp and envelope traveled and received certain postal markings. Collectors who enjoy postal history always want the stamp with its envelope, which is one reason why you should not be quick to soak stamps off their covers. If you find an old hoard of

envelopes, get some advice before you take the stamps off!

Some collectors enjoy the "scientific" side of the hobby, studying production methods and paper and ink types. This also might include collecting stamps in which something went wrong in production: errors, freaks, and oddities. Studying watermarks takes special fluids and lighting equipment, also needed to study the luminescent inks used on modern stamps to trigger high-tech canceling equipment in the post office.

Other branches of collecting include first-day covers (FDCs), which carry a stamp on the first day it was sold with that day's postmark. Some FDCs have a cachet (ca-SHAY), which is a design on the envelope that relates to the stamp and adds an attractive quality to the cover. Some clubs, catalogues, and dealers specialize in FDCs.

Clubs, etc.

It is possible to collect for a lifetime and never leave home -- get everything you need by mail -- but a lot of enjoyment can be added if you join a club or go to stamp shows and exhibitions, and meet other collectors like yourself. Local clubs usually have a general focus, have meetings, and may organize stamp shows as part of their activities. Specialty-collecting groups, which may focus on stamps of one country or one type of stamp, will have a publication as the main service to members, but may have other activities and occasional meetings at large stamp shows. The American Philatelic Society, "America's Stamp Club," is the oldest and largest stamp organization in the United States and has served hundreds of thousands of collectors since 1886.

Again, Welcome to Stamp Collecting!

The more you know about it, the more you will like it -- Happy Collecting!

This introduction was prepared by the American Philatelic Society, the oldest and largest national stamp organization in the United States. Information on membership benefits and services is available from APS, P.O. Box 8000, State College, PA 16803; telephone 237-3803.

COMMEMORATIVE, SPECIAL ISSUE & AIR MAIL IDENTIFIER

COMMEMORATIVE, SPECIAL ISSUE & AIR MAIL IDENTIFIER

x.

DEFINITIVE ISSUE IDENTIFIER

The purpose of these listings is to aid the novice and intermediate collector in identifying U.S. definitive issues.

The first step in identification should be to note the stamp's denomination, color, and subject and then locate it on the list below. If that step does not provide you with a definitive Scott No., you will have to do some additional work.

If the identification can only be made by determining the stamp's "type", grill size or press from which the stamp was printed, it will be necessary to check the appropriate pages of the Brookman or Scott catalogs for this information.

If the identification can only be made by determining the stamp's perf measurements or watermark, you will then have to use your perf gauge and/or watermark detector. If you do not own these "tools," contact your favorite dealer.

* With few exceptions, this list features major Scott Nos. and omits Reprints, Re-issues and Special Printings.
* Watermark and Press notations are not listed when they do not contribute to the stamp's identification.
* Scott nos. followed by "**" were also issued Bullseye Perf. 11.2
* Scott nos. followed by a "*" were issued both Untagged and Tagged.
* All bklt. singles are perforated on two or three sides only.

| 803 | 1030 | 5/40 | 63/92 | 134/206 |
| Prexie Issue | Liberty Issue | | | |

Den.	Color	Subject	Type / Comment	Press	Perf.	Wmk.	Scott #
½¢	olive brn	N. Hale		F	11		551
½¢	olive brn	N. Hale		R	11x10.5		653
½¢	dp orng	B. Franklin	1938 Prexie Issue		11x10.5		803
½¢	rd orng	B. Franklin	1954 Liberty Issue		11x10.5		1030
1¢	blue	B. Franklin	Ty I		Imperf		5
1¢	blue	B. Franklin	Ty Ib		Imperf		5A
1¢	blue	B. Franklin	Ty Ia		Imperf		6
1¢	blue	B. Franklin	Ty II		Imperf		7
1¢	blue	B. Franklin	Ty III		Imperf		8
1¢	blue	B. Franklin	Ty IIIa		Imperf		8A
1¢	blue	B. Franklin	Ty IV		Imperf		9
1¢	blue	B. Franklin	Ty I		15		18
1¢	brt. bl	B. Franklin	Ty I, reprint, w/o gum		12		40
1¢	blue	B. Franklin	Ty Ia		15		19
1¢	blue	B. Franklin	Ty II		15		20
1¢	blue	B. Franklin	Ty III		15		21
1¢	blue	B. Franklin	Ty IIIa		15		22
1¢	blue	B. Franklin	Ty IV		15		23
1¢	blue	B. Franklin	Ty V		15		24
1¢	blue	B. Franklin			12		63
1¢	blue	B. Franklin	"Z" Grill		12		85A
1¢	blue	B. Franklin	"E" Grill		12		86
1¢	blue	B. Franklin	"F" Grill		12		92
1¢	buff	B. Franklin	Issue of 1869 "G grill"		12		112
1¢	buff	B. Franklin	w/o grill, original gum		12		112b
1¢	buff	B. Franklin	Re-iss/wht crackly gum		12		123
1¢	buff	B. Franklin	Same, soft porous paper		12		133
1¢	brn. orng.	B. Franklin	Same, w/o gum		12		133a
1¢	ultra	B. Franklin	hard paper, w/grill		12		134
1¢	ultra	B. Franklin	Same, w/o grill		12		145
1¢	ultra	B. Franklin	Same, w/Secret mark		12		156
1¢	dk. ultra	B. Franklin	Soft porous paper		12		182
1¢	gray bl.	B. Franklin	Same, re-engraved		12		206
1¢	ultra	B. Franklin			12		212
1¢	dull bl.	B. Franklin	w/o Triangles		12		219
1¢	ultra	B. Franklin	w/ Tri. in Top corners		12	NW	246
1¢	blue	B. Franklin	w/ Tri. in Top corners		12	NW	247
1¢	blue	B. Franklin	w/ Tri. in Top corners		12	DL	264
1¢	dp. grn	B. Franklin	w/ Tri. in Top corners		12	DL	279
1¢	blue grn	B. Franklin	"Series 1902"		12	DL	300
1¢	blue grn	B. Franklin	"Series 1902"		Imperf	DL	314
1¢	blue grn	B. Franklin	"Series 1902" B. Pn./6		12	DL	300b
1¢	blue grn	B. Franklin	"Series 1902" Coil		12 Hz	DL	316
1¢	blue grn	B. Franklin	"Series 1902" Coil		12 Vert	DL	318
1¢	green	B. Franklin			12	DL	331
1¢	green	B. Franklin	Blue Paper		12	DL	357
1¢	green	B. Franklin			12	SL	374
1¢	green	B. Franklin			Imperf	DL	343
1¢	green	B. Franklin			Imperf	SL	383
1¢	green	B. Franklin	Bklt. Pn. of 6		12	DL	331a
1¢	green	B. Franklin	Bklt. Pn. of 6		12	SL	374a
1¢	green	B. Franklin	Coil		12 Hz	DL	348
1¢	green	B. Franklin	Coil		12 Hz	SL	385
1¢	green	B. Franklin	Coil		12 Vert	DL	352
1¢	green	B. Franklin	Coil		12 Vert	SL	387
1¢	green	B. Franklin	Coil		8.5 Hz	SL	390
1¢	green	B. Franklin	Coil		8.5 Vert	SL	392
1¢	green	Washington			12	SL	405
1¢	green	Washington			10	SL	424
1¢	green	Washington		F	10	NW	462
1¢	green	Washington		R	10	NW	543
1¢	green	Washington		F	11	NW	498
1¢	gray grn	Washington	Offset	F	11	NW	525
1¢	green	Washington	19mm x 22.5mm	R	11	NW	544
1¢	green	Washington	19.5-20mm x 22mm	R	11	NW	545
1¢	gray grn	Washington	Rossbach Press		12.5	NW	536
1¢	green	Washington		R	11x10	NW	538
1¢	green	Washington		R	10x11	NW	542
1¢	green	Washington			Imperf	SL	408
1¢	green	Washington			Imperf	NW	481
1¢	green	Washington	Offset		Imperf	NW	531
1¢	green	Washington	Bklt. Pn. of 6		12	SL	405b

Den.	Color	Subject	Type / Comment	Press	Perf.	Wmk.	Scott #
1¢	green	Washington	Bklt. Pn. of 6		10	SL	424d
1¢	green	Washington	Bklt. Pn. of 6		10	NW	462a
1¢	green	Washington	Bklt. Pn. of 6		11	NW	498e
1¢	green	Washington	Bklt. Pn. of 30		11	NW	498f
1¢	green	Washington	Coil		8.5 Hz	SL	410
1¢	green	Washington	Coil		8.5 Vert	SL	412
1¢	green	Washington	Coil	F	10 Hz	SL	441
1¢	green	Washington	Coil	R	10 Hz	SL	448
1¢	green	Washington	Coil	R	10 Hz	SL	441
1¢	green	Washington	Coil	R	10 Hz	NW	486
1¢	green	Washington	Coil	F	10 Vert	SL	443
1¢	green	Washington	Coil	R	10 Vert	SL	452
1¢	green	Washington	Coil	R	10 Vert	NW	490
1¢	deep grn	B. Franklin		F	11		552
1¢	green	B. Franklin	19¾ x 22¼mm	R	11		594
1¢	green	B. Franklin	19¼ x 22¾mm	R	11		596
1¢	green	B. Franklin		R	11x10		578
1¢	green	B. Franklin		R	10		581
1¢	green	B. Franklin		R	11x10.5		632
1¢	green	B. Franklin		F	Imperf		575
1¢	deep grn	B. Franklin	Bklt. Pn. of 6	F	11		552a
1¢	green	B. Franklin	Bklt. Pn. of 6	R	11x10.5		632a
1¢	green	B. Franklin	Coil	R	10 Vert		597
1¢	yel. grn.	B. Franklin	Coil	R	10 Hz		604
1¢	green	B. Franklin	Kansas Ovpt.		11x10.5		658
1¢	green	B. Franklin	Nebraska Ovpt.		11x10.5		669
1¢	green	Washington	1938 Prexie Issue		11x10.5		804
1¢	green	Washington	Bklt. Pn. of 6		11x10.5		804b
1¢	green	Washington	Coil		10 Vert		839
1¢	green	Washington	Coil		10 Hz		848
1¢	dk green	Washington	1954 Liberty Issue		11x10.5		1031
1¢	dk green	Washington	Coil		10 Vert		1054
1¢	green	A. Jackson			11x10.5		1209*
1¢	green	A. Jackson	Coil		10 Vert		1225*
1¢	green	T. Jefferson			11x10.5		1278
1¢	green	T. Jefferson	Bklt. Pn. of 8		11x10.5		1278a
1¢	green	T. Jefferson	B.Pn./4 + 2 labels		11x10.5		1278b
1¢	green	T. Jefferson	Coil		10 Vert		1299
1¢	dk blue	Inkwell & Quill			11x10.5		1581
1¢	dk blue	Inkwell & Quill	Coil		10 Vert		1811
1¢	black	Dorothea Dix			11		1844**
1¢	violet	Omnibus	Coil		10 Vert		1897
1¢	violet	Omnibus	Coil, re-engraved		10 Vert	B	2225
1¢	brnish verm	Margaret Mitchell			11		2168
1¢	multi	Kestrel	No "¢" Sign		11		2476
1¢	multi	Kestrel	'¢' sign added		11		2477
1¢	multi	Kestrel	Coil		10 Vert		3044
1¼¢	turquoise	Palace of Governors			10.5x11		1031A
1¼¢	turquoise	Palace of Governors	Coil		10 Hz		1054A
1¼¢	lt. grn	Albert Gallatin			11x10.5		1279
1½¢	yel brn	W.G. Harding		F	11		553
1½¢	yel brn	W.G. Harding		R	10		582
1½¢	yel brn	W.G. Harding		R	11x10.5		633
1½¢	brown	W.G. Harding	"Full Face"	R	11x10.5		684
1½¢	yel brn	W.G. Harding		F	Imperf		576
1½¢	yel brn	W.G. Harding		R	Imperf		631
1½¢	brown	W.G. Harding	Coil		10 Vert		598
1½¢	yel brn	W.G. Harding	Coil		10 Hz		605
1½¢	brown	W.G. Harding	"Full Face," Coil		10 Vert		686
1½¢	brown	W.G. Harding	Kansas Ovpt.		11x10.5		659
1½¢	brown	W.G. Harding	Nebraska Ovpt.		11x10.5		670
1½¢	bstr brn	M. Washington			11x10.5		805
1½¢	bstr brn	M. Washington	Coil		10 Vert		840
1½¢	bstr brn	M. Washington	Coil		10 Hz		849
1½¢	brn carm	Mount Vernon			10.5x11		1032
2¢	black	A. Jackson			12		73
2¢	black	A. Jackson	"D" Grill		12		84
2¢	black	A. Jackson	"Z" Grill		12		85B
2¢	black	A. Jackson	"E" Grill		12		87
2¢	black	A. Jackson	"F" Grill		12		93
2¢	brown	Horse & Rider	Issue of 1869 "G grill"		12		113
2¢	brown	Horse & Rider	w/o grill, original gum		12		113b
2¢	brown	Horse & Rider	Re-iss/wht crackly gum		12		124
2¢	red brown	A. Jackson	Hard paper, w/grill		12		135
2¢	red brown	A. Jackson	Hard paper,w/o grill		12		146
2¢	brown	A. Jackson	Same, w/secret mark		12		157
2¢	vermillion	A. Jackson	Yellowish wove (hard)		12		178
2¢	vermillion	A. Jackson	Soft porous paper		12		183
2¢	red brown	Washington			12		210
2¢	pl rd brn	Washington	Special Printing		12		211B
2¢	green	Washington			12		213
2¢	lake	Washington	w/o Triangles		12		219D
2¢	carmine	Washington	w/o Tri.		12		220

Left table:

Den.	Color	Subject	Type / Comment	Press	Perf.	Wmk.	Scott #
2¢	pink	Washington	Ty I Tri. in Top corners		12	NW	248
2¢	carm. lake	Washington	Ty I Tri. "		12	NW	249
2¢	carmine	Washington	Ty I Tri. "		12	NW	250
2¢	carmine	Washington	Ty I Tri. "		12	DL	265
2¢	carmine	Washington	Ty II Tri. "		12	NW	251
2¢	carmine	Washington	Ty II Tri. "		12	DL	266
2¢	carmine	Washington	Ty III Tri. "		12	NW	252
2¢	carmine	Washington	Ty III Tri. "		12	DL	267
2¢	red	Washington	Ty III Tri. "		12	DL	279B
2¢	carm rose	Washington	Ty III Tri. "		12	DL	279Bc

319/322	332/393	406/546	554/671
"Shield"	"TWO" Cents	"2" Cents	

Den.	Color	Subject	Type / Comment	Press	Perf.	Wmk.	Scott #
2¢	red	Washington	Bklt. Pn. of 6		12	DL	279Be
2¢	carmine	Washington	"Series 1902"		12	DL	301
2¢	carmine	Washington	"Series 1902" B.Pn./6		12	DL	301c
2¢	carmine	Washington	"Shield" Design, Die I		12	DL	319
2¢	carmine	Washington	"Shield", Die II		12	DL	319i
2¢	carmine	Washington	"Shield", B.Pn./6, Die I		12	DL	319g
2¢	carmine	Washington	"Shield", B.Pn./6, Die II		12	DL	319h
2¢	lake	Washington	"Shield", B.Pn./6, Die II		12	DL	319q
2¢	carmine	Washington	"Shield" Design		Imperf	DL	320
2¢	lake	Washington	"Shield" Design		Imperf	DL	320a
2¢	carmine	Washington	"Shield" Coil		12 Hz	DL	321
2¢	carmine	Washington	"Shield" Coil		12 Vert	DL	322
2¢	carmine	Washington	"TWO CENTS" Design		12	DL	332
2¢	carmine	Washington	"TWO..." Blue Paper		12	DL	358
2¢	carmine	Washington	"TWO..."		12	SL	375
2¢	lake	Washington	"TWO..."		12	SL	375v
2¢	carmine	Washington	"TWO..."	F	11	DL	519
2¢	carmine	Washington	"TWO..."		Imperf	DL	344
2¢	carmine	Washington	"TWO..."		Imperf	SL	384
2¢	dark carm	Washington	"TWO..."		Imperf	SL	384v
2¢	carmine	Washington	"TWO..." Bklt. Pn. of 6		12	DL	332a
2¢	carmine	Washington	"TWO..." Bklt. Pn. of 6		12	SL	375a
2¢	carmine	Washington	"TWO..." Coil		12 Hz	DL	349
2¢	carmine	Washington	"TWO..." Coil		12 Hz	SL	386
2¢	carmine	Washington	"TWO..." Coil		12 Vert	DL	353
2¢	carmine	Washington	"TWO..." Coil		12 Vert	SL	388
2¢	carmine	Washington	"TWO..." Coil		8.5 Hz	SL	391
2¢	carmine	Washington	"TWO..." Coil		8.5 Vert	SL	393
2¢	carmine	Washington	"2 CENTS" Design		12	SL	406
2¢	lake	Washington	"2..."		12	SL	406v
2¢	carmine	Washington	"2..."		10	SL	425
2¢	carmine	Washington	"2..."		10	NW	463
2¢	pf carm rd	Washington	"2..."		11	SL	461
2¢	carmine	Washington	"2..." Ty I	F	11	NW	499
2¢	carmine	Washington	"2..." Ty Ia	F	11	NW	500
2¢	carmine	Washington	"2..." Offset Ty. IV		11	NW	526
2¢	carmine	Washington	"2..." Offset Ty. V		11	NW	527
2¢	carmine	Washington	"2..." Offset Ty. Va		11	NW	528
2¢	carmine	Washington	"2..." Offset Ty. VI		11	NW	528A
2¢	carmine	Washington	"2..." Offset Ty. VII		11	NW	528B
2¢	carm rose	Washington	Ty III (Coil Waste:)	R	11	NW	546
2¢	carm rose	Washington	Ty II	R	11x10	NW	539
2¢	carm rose	Washington	Ty III	R	11x10	NW	540
2¢	carmine	Washington	"2 CENTS"	F	Imperf	SL	409
2¢	carmine	Washington	"2..."	F	Imperf	NW	482
2¢	carm rose	Washington	"2..." Offset Ty IV		Imperf	NW	532
2¢	carmine	Washington	"2..." Offset Ty V		Imperf	NW	533
2¢	carmine	Washington	"2..." Offset Ty Va		Imperf	NW	534
2¢	carmine	Washington	"2..." Offset Ty VI		Imperf	NW	534A
2¢	carmine	Washington	"2..." Offset Ty VII		Imperf	NW	534B
2¢	carmine	Washington	"2..." Bklt. Pn. of 6		12	SL	406a
2¢	carmine	Washington	"2..." Bklt. Pn. of 6		10	SL	425e
2¢	carmine	Washington	"2..." Bklt. Pn. of 6		10	NW	463a
2¢	carmine	Washington	"2..." Bklt. Pn. of 6	F	11	NW	499e
2¢	carmine	Washington	"2..." Bklt. Pn. of 30	F	11	NW	499f
2¢	carmine	Washington	"2 CENTS" Coil		8.5 Hz	SL	411
2¢	carmine	Washington	"2..." Coil		8.5 Vert	SL	413
2¢	carmine	Washington	"2..." Coil Ty I	F	10 Hz	SL	442
2¢	red	Washington	"2..." Coil Ty I	R	10 Hz	SL	449
2¢	carmine	Washington	"2..." Coil Ty III	R	10 Hz	NW	487
2¢	carmine	Washington	"2..." Coil Ty III	R	10 Hz	SL	450
2¢	carmine	Washington	"2..." Coil Ty III	R	10 Hz	NW	488
2¢	carmine	Washington	"2..." Coil Ty I	F	10 Vert	SL	444
2¢	carm red	Washington	"2..." Coil Ty I	R	10 Vert	SL	453
2¢	red	Washington	"2..." Coil Ty II	R	10 Vert	SL	454
2¢	carmine	Washington	"2..." Coil Ty II	R	10 Vert	NW	491
2¢	carmine	Washington	"2..." Coil Ty III	R	10 Vert	SL	455
2¢	carmine	Washington	"2..." Coil Ty III	R	10 Vert	NW	492
2¢	carmine	Washington	"2..." Hz Coil Ty I	R	Imperf	SL	459
2¢	deep rose	Washington	"2..." Hz Coil Ty Ia/ Shermack Ty III Perfs	F	*	NW	482A
2¢	carmine	Washington		F	11		554
2¢	carmine	Washington	19¾ x 22¼ mm	R	11		595

Right table:

Den.	Color	Subject	Type / Comment	Press	Perf.	Wmk.	Scott #
2¢	carmine	Washington	19¾ x 22¼ mm	R	11x10		579
2¢	carmine	Washington	Die I	R	11x10.5		634
2¢	carmine	Washington	Die II	R	11x10.5		634A
2¢	carmine	Washington		R	10		583
2¢	carmine	Washington		F	Imperf		577
2¢	carmine	Washington	Bklt. Pn. of 6	F	11		554c
2¢	carmine	Washington	Bklt. Pn. of 6	R	10		583a
2¢	carmine	Washington	Bklt. Pn. of 6	R	11x10.5		634d
2¢	carmine	Washington	Coil		10 Vert		599
2¢	carmine	Washington	Coil Die II		10 Vert		599A
2¢	carmine	Washington	Coil		10 Hz		606
2¢	carmine	Washington	Kansas Ovpt.		11x10.5		660
2¢	carmine	Washington	Nebraska Ovpt.		11x10.5		671
2¢	rose carm	J. Adams			11x10.5		806
2¢	rose carm	J. Adams	Bklt. Pn. of 6		11x10.5		806b
2¢	rose carm	J. Adams	Coil		10 Vert		841
2¢	rose carm	J. Adams	Coil		10 Hz		850
2¢	carm rose	T. Jefferson			11x10.5		1033
2¢	carm rose	T. Jefferson	Coil		10 Vert		1055*
2¢	dk bl gray	Frank Lloyd Wright			11x10.5		1280
2¢	dk bl gray	Frank Lloyd Wright	B. Pn. of 5 + Label		11x10.5		1280a
2¢	dk bl gray	Frank Lloyd Wright	Booklet Pn. of 6		11x10.5		1280c
2¢	red brn	Speaker's Stand			11x10.5		1582
2¢	brn black	Igor Stravinsky			10.5x11		1845
2¢	black	Locomotive	Coil		10 Vert		1897A
2¢	black	Locomotive	Coil, "Re-engraved"		10 Vert	B	2226
2¢	brt blue	Mary Lyon			11		2169
2¢	multi	Red-headed Woodpecker			11.1		3032
2.5¢	gray bl	Bunker Hill			11x10.5		1034
2.5¢	gray bl	Bunker Hill	Coil		10 Vert		1056

10/26a	64/94	136/214	221	253/268

Den.	Color	Subject	Type / Comment	Press	Perf.	Wmk.	Scott #
3¢	orng brn	Washington	Ty I		Imperf		10
3¢	dull red	Washington	Ty I		Imperf		11
3¢	rose	Washington	Ty I		15		25
3¢	dull red	Washington	Ty II		15		26
3¢	dull red	Washington	Ty IIa		15		26a
3¢	pink	Washington			12		64
3¢	pgn bld pink	Washington			12		64a
3¢	rose pink	Washington			12		64b
3¢	rose	Washington			12		65
3¢	lake	Washington			12		66
3¢	scarlet	Washington			12		74
3¢	rose	Washington	"A" Grill		12		79
3¢	rose	Washington	"B" Grill		12		82
3¢	rose	Washington	"C" Grill		12		83
3¢	rose	Washington	"D" Grill		12		85
3¢	rose	Washington	"Z" Grill		12		85C
3¢	rose	Washington	"E" Grill		12		88
3¢	rose	Washington	"F" Grill		12		94
3¢	ultra	Locomotive	"G grill"		12		114
3¢	ultra	Locomotive	w/o grill, Original gum		12		114a
3¢	green	Washington	Hard paper, w/grill		12		136
3¢	green	Washington	Same, w/o grill		12		147
3¢	green	Washington	Same, w/secret mark		12		158
3¢	green	Washington	Same, Soft porous paper		12		184
3¢	blue grn	Washington	Same, re-engraved		12		207
3¢	vermillion	Washington			12		214

302	333/541	720/722	12/30A	67/95

Den.	Color	Subject	Type / Comment	Press	Perf.	Wmk.	Scott #
3¢	purple	A. Jackson	w/o Triangles		12		221
3¢	purple	A. Jackson	w/ Tri. in Top corners		12	NW	253
3¢	purple	A Jackson	w/ Tri. in Top corners		12	DL	268
3¢	violet	A. Jackson	"Series 1902"		12	DL	302
3¢	dp violet	Washington		F	12	DL	333
3¢	dp violet	Washington	Blue paper	F	12	DL	359
3¢	dp violet	Washington		F	12	SL	376
3¢	dp violet	Washington		F	10	SL	426
3¢	violet	Washington		F	10	NW	464
3¢	lt violet	Washington	Ty I	F	11	NW	501
3¢	dk violet	Washington	Ty II	F	11	NW	502
3¢	violet	Washington	Ty III Offset		11	NW	529
3¢	purple	Washington	Ty IV Offset		11	NW	530
3¢	violet	Washington	Ty II Coil Waste	R	11x10	NW	541
3¢	dp violet	Washington		F	Imperf	DL	345
3¢	violet	Washington	Ty I	F	Imperf	NW	483

DEFINITIVE ISSUE IDENTIFIER

Den.	Color	Subject	Type / Comment	Press	Perf.	Wmk.	Scott #
3¢	violet	Washington	Ty II	F	Imperf	NW	484
3¢	violet	Washington	Ty IV Offset		Imperf	NW	535
3¢	lt violet	Washington	B. Pn. of 6, Ty I	F	11	NW	501b
3¢	dk violet	Washington	B. Pn. of 6, Ty II	F	11	NW	502b
3¢	dp violet	Washington	Coil "Orangeburg"	F	12 Vert	SL	389
3¢	dp violet	Washington	Coil	F	8.5 Vert	SL	394
3¢	violet	Washington	Coil, Ty I	F	10 Vert	SL	445
3¢	violet	Washington	Coil, Ty I	R	10 Vert	SL	456
3¢	violet	Washington	Coil, Ty I	R	10 Hz	NW	489
3¢	dp violet	Washington	Coil, Ty I	R	10 Vert	NW	493
3¢	dull violet	Washington	Coil, Ty II	R	10 Vert	NW	494
3¢	violet	A. Lincoln		F	11		555
3¢	violet	A. Lincoln		R	10		584
3¢	violet	A. Lincoln		R	11x10.5		635
3¢	violet	A. Lincoln	Coil		10 Vert		600
3¢	violet	A. Lincoln	Kansas Ovpt.		11x10.5		661
3¢	violet	A. Lincoln	Nebraska Ovpt.		11x10.5		672
3¢	dp violet	Washington	Stuart Portrait		11x10.5		720
3¢	dp violet	Washington	Stuart B. Pn. of 6		11x10.5		720b
3¢	dp violet	Washington	Stuart Coil		10 Vert		721
3¢	dp violet	Washington	Stuart Coil		10 Hz		722
3¢	dp violet	T. Jefferson			11x10.5		807
3¢	dp violet	T. Jefferson	Bklt. Pn. of 6		11x10.5		807a
3¢	dp violet	T. Jefferson	Coil		10 Vert		842
3¢	dp violet	T. Jefferson	Coil		10 Hz		851
3¢	dp violet	Statue of Liberty			11x10.5		1035*
3¢	dp violet	Liberty	Bklt. Pn. of 6		11x10.5		1035a
3¢	dp violet	Liberty	Coil		10 Vert		1057*
3¢	violet	F. Parkman			10.5x11		1281
3¢	violet	F. Parkman	Coil		10 Vert		1297
3¢	olive	Early Ballot Box			11x10.5		1583
3¢	olive grn	Henry Clay			11x10.5		1846
3¢	dark grn	Handcar	Coil		10 Vert		1898
3¢	brt blue	Paul D. White MD			11		2170
3¢	claret	Conestoga Wagon	Coil		10 Vert		2252
3¢	multi	Bluebird			11		2478
3¢	multi	Eastern Bluebird			11.1		3033
(3¢)	multi	Dove	ABN		11x10.8		2877
(3¢)	multi	Dove	SVS		10.8x10.9		2878
3.1¢	brn (yel)	Guitar	Coil		10 Vert		1613
3.4¢	dk blsh grn	School Bus	Coil		10 Vert		2123
3.5¢	prpl (yel)	Weaver Violins	Coil		10 Vert		1813
4¢	**blue grn**	**A. Jackson**			**12**		**211**
4¢	carmine	A. Jackson			12		215
4¢	dk brn	A. Lincoln	w/ Triangles		12		222
4¢	dk brn	A. Lincoln	w/ Tri. in Top corners		12	NW	254
4¢	dk brn	A. Lincoln	w/ Tri. in Top corners		12	DL	269
4¢	rose brn	A. Lincoln	w/ Tri. in Top corners		12	DL	280
4¢	brown	U.S. Grant	"Series 1902"		12	DL	303
4¢	brown	U.S. Grant	Coil, Shermack Ty III		*	DL	314A
4¢	orng brn	Washington		F	12	DL	334
4¢	orng brn	Washington	Blue Paper	F	12	DL	360
4¢	brown	Washington		F	12	SL	377
4¢	brown	Washington		F	10	SL	427
4¢	orng brn	Washington		F	10	NW	465
4¢	brown	Washington		F	11	NW	503
4¢	orng brn	Washington		F	Imperf	DL	346
4¢	orng brn	Washington	Coil	F	12 Hz	DL	350
4¢	orng brn	Washington	Coil	F	12 Vert	DL	354
4¢	orng brn	Washington	Coil	F	8.5 Vert	SL	395
4¢	brown	Washington	Coil	F	10 Vert	SL	446
4¢	brown	Washington	Coil	R	10 Vert	SL	457
4¢	orng brn	Washington	Coil	R	10 Vert	NW	495
4¢	yel brn	M. Washington		F	11		556
4¢	yel brn	M. Washington		R	10		585
4¢	yel brn	M. Washington		R	11x10.5		636
4¢	yel brn	M. Washington	Coil		10 Vert		601
4¢	yel brn	M. Washington	Kansas Ovpt.		11x10.5		662
4¢	yel brn	M. Washington	Nebraska Ovpt.		11x10.5		673
4¢	brown	W.H. Taft			11x10.5		685
4¢	brown	W.H. Taft	Coil		10 Vert		687
4¢	red violet	J. Madison			11x10.5		808
4¢	red violet	J. Madison	Coil		10 Vert		843
4¢	red violet	A. Lincoln			11x10.5		1036*
4¢	red violet	A. Lincoln	Bklt. Pn. of 6		11x10.5		1036a
4¢	red violet	A. Lincoln	Coil		10 Vert		1058
4¢	black	A. Lincoln			11x10.5		1282*
4¢	black	A. Lincoln	Coil		10 Vert		1303
4¢	rose mag	"Books, etc."			11x10.5		1584
4¢	violet	Carl Schurz			10.5x11		1847
4¢	rdsh brn	Stagecoach	Coil		10 Vert		1898A
4¢	rdsh brn	Stagecoach	Coil, re-engr.	B	10 Vert		2228
4¢	bl violet	Father Flanagan			11		2171
4¢	claret	Steam Carriage	Coil		10		2451
4½¢	**dark gray**	**White House**			**11x10.5**		**809**
4½¢	dark gray	White House	Coil		10 Vert		844
4½¢	blue grn	The Hermitage			10.5x11		1037
4½¢	blue grn	The Hermitage	Coil		10 Hz		1059
4.9¢	brn blk	Buckboard	Coil		10 Vert		2124
5¢	**rd brn**	**B. Franklin**			**Imperf**		**1**
5¢	rd brn	B. Franklin	Bluish paper (reprint)		Imperf		3
5¢	rd brn	T. Jefferson	Ty I		Imperf		12
5¢	brick red	T. Jefferson	Ty I		15		27
5¢	rd brn	T. Jefferson	Ty I		15		28
5¢	brt rd brn	T. Jefferson	Ty I		15		28b
5¢	Indian red	T. Jefferson	Ty I		15		28A
5¢	brown	T. Jefferson	Ty I		15		29
5¢	orng brn	T. Jefferson	Ty II		15		30
5¢	brown	T. Jefferson	Ty II		15		30A
5¢	buff	T. Jefferson			12		67
5¢	red brn	T. Jefferson			12		75
5¢	brown	T. Jefferson			12		76
5¢	brown	T. Jefferson	"A" Grill		12		80
5¢	brown	T. Jefferson	"F" Grill		12		95
5¢	blue	Z. Taylor	Yellowish wove (hard)		12		179
5¢	blue	Z. Taylor	Soft Porous Paper		12		185
5¢	yel brn	J. Garfield			12		205
5¢	indigo	J. Garfield			12		216
5¢	choc	U.S. Grant	w/o Triangles		12		223
5¢	choc	U.S. Grant	w/ Tri. in Top corners		12	NW	255
5¢	choc	U.S. Grant	w/ Tri. in Top corners		12	DL	270
5¢	dk blue	U.S. Grant	w/ Tri. in Top corners		12	DL	281
5¢	blue	A. Lincoln	"Series 1902"		12	DL	304
5¢	blue	A. Lincoln	"Series 1902"		Imperf	DL	315
5¢	blue	Washington			12	DL	335
5¢	blue	Washington	Blue Paper		12	DL	361
5¢	blue	Washington			12	SL	378
5¢	blue	Washington			10	SL	428
5¢	blue	Washington			10	NW	466
5¢	blue	Washington			11	NW	504
5¢	blue	Washington			Imperf	DL	347
5¢	blue	Washington	Coil		12 Hz	DL	351
5¢	blue	Washington	Coil		12 Vert	DL	355
5¢	blue	Washington	Coil		8.5 Vert	SL	396
5¢	blue	Washington	Coil	F	10 Vert	SL	447
5¢	blue	Washington	Coil	R	10 Vert	SL	458
5¢	blue	Washington	Coil	R	10 Vert	NW	496
5¢	carmine	Washington	Error of Color		10	NW	467
5¢	rose	Washington	Error of Color		11	NW	505
5¢	carmine	Washington	Error of Color		Imperf	NW	485
5¢	dk blue	T. Roosevelt		F	11		557
5¢	blue	T. Roosevelt		R	10		586
5¢	dk blue	T. Roosevelt	Coil	R	10 Vert		602
5¢	dk blue	T. Roosevelt		R	11x10.5		637
5¢	dp blue	T. Roosevelt	Kansas Ovpt.		11x10.5		663
5¢	dp blue	T. Roosevelt	Nebraska Ovpt.		11x10.5		674
5¢	brt blue	J. Monroe			11x10.5		810
5¢	brt blue	J. Monroe	Coil		10 Vert		845
5¢	blue	J. Monroe			11x10.5		1038
5¢	dk bl gray	Washington			11x10.5		1213*
5¢	dk bl gray	Washington	Bklt. Pn. of 5 + "Mailman" Label		11x10.5		1213a
			"Use Zone Nos." Label		11x10.5		1213a*
			"Use Zip Code" Label		11x10.5		1213a*
5¢	dk bl gray	Washington	Coil		10 Vert		1229*
5¢	blue	Washington			11x10.5		1283*
5¢	blue	Washington	Re-engr. (clean face)		11x10.5		1283B
5¢	blue	Washington	Coil		10 Vert		1304
5¢	henna brn	Pearl Buck			10.5x11		1848
5¢	gray grn	Motorcycle	Coil		10 Vert		1899
5¢	dk olv grn	Hugo Black			11		2172
5¢	carmine	Luis Munoz Marin			11		2173*
5¢	black	Milk Wagon			10 Vert		2253
5¢	red	Circus Wagon	Coil Engraved		10 Vert		2452
5¢	carmine	Circus Wagon	Coil Gravure		10 Vert		2452B
5¢	brown	Canoe	Coil Engraved		10 Vert		2453
5¢	red	Canoe	Coil Gravure		10 Vert		2454
5.2¢	carmine	Sleigh	Coil		10 Vert		1900
5.3¢	black	Elevator	Coil		10 Vert		2254
5.5¢	dp mag	Star Rt Truck	Coil		10 Vert		2125
5.9¢	blue	Bicycle	Coil		10 Vert		1901
6¢	**ultra**	**Washington**	**"G" Grill**		**12**		**115**
6¢	carmine	A. Lincoln	hard wh paper, w/grill		12		137
6¢	carmine	A. Lincoln	Same, w/o grill		12		148
6¢	dull pink	A. Lincoln	Same, secret mark		12		159
6¢	pink	A. Lincoln	Same, sft porous pap		12		186
6¢	rose	A. Lincoln	Same, re-engraved		12		208
6¢	brn red	A. Lincoln	Same, re-engraved		12		208a
6¢	brn red	J. Garfield	w/o Triangles		12		224
6¢	dull brn	J. Garfield	w/ Tri. in Top corners		12	NW	256
6¢	dull brn	J. Garfield	w/ Tri. in Top corners		12	DL	271
6¢	dull brn	J. Garfield	w/ Tri. in Top corners		12	USIR	271a
6¢	lake	J. Garfield	w/ Tri. in Top corners		12	DL	282
6¢	claret	J. Garfield	"Series 1902"		12	DL	305
6¢	rd orng	Washington			12	DL	336
6¢	rd orng	Washington	Blue paper		12	DL	362
6¢	rd orng	Washington			12	SL	379
6¢	rd orng	Washington			10	SL	429
6¢	rd orng	Washington			10	NW	468
6¢	rd orng	Washington			11	NW	506
6¢	rd orng	J. Garfield		F	11		558
6¢	rd orng	J. Garfield		R	10		587
6¢	rd orng	J. Garfield		R	11x10.5		638
6¢	rd orng	J. Garfield	Kansas Ovpt.		11x10.5		664
6¢	rd orng	J. Garfield	Nebraska Ovpt.		11x10.5		675
6¢	dp orng	J. Garfield	Coil		10 Vert		723
6¢	red orng	J.Q. Adams			11x10.5		811
6¢	red orng	J.Q. Adams	Coil		10 Vert		846
6¢	carmine	T. Roosevelt			11x10.5		1039
6¢	gray brn	F.D. Roosevelt			10.5x11		1284*
6¢	gray brn	F.D. Roosevelt	Bklt. Pn. of 8		11x10.5		1284b
6¢	gray brn	F.D. Roosevelt	Bklt. Pn. of 5 + Label		11x10.5		1284c
6¢	gray brn	F.D. Roosevelt	Coil		10 Hz		1298
6¢	gray brn	F.D. Roosevelt	Coil		10 Vert		1305
6¢	dk bl,rd & grn	Flag & White House			11		1338

DEFINITIVE ISSUE IDENTIFIER

Den.	Color	Subject	Type / Comment	Press	Perf.	Wmk.	Scott #
6¢	dk bl,rd & grn	Flag & White House			11x10.5		1338D
6¢	dk bl,rd & grn	Flag & White House	Coil		10 Vert		1338A
6¢	dk bl gray	D.D. Eisenhower			11x10.5		1393
6¢	dk bl gray	Eisenhower	Bklt. Pn of 8		11x10.5		1393a
6¢	dk bl gray	Eisenhower	Bklt. Pn of 5 + Label		11x10.5		1393b
6¢	dk bl gray	Eisenhower	Coil		10 Vert		1401
6¢	orng verm	Walter Lippmann			11		1849
6¢	multi	Circle of Stars	Bklt. Single		11		1892
6¢	red brn	Tricycle	Coil		10 Vert		2126
6.3¢	brick red	Liberty Bell	Coil		10 Vert		1518
7¢	**vermilion**	**E.M. Stanton**	**Hard wh paper, w/grill**		**12**		**138**
7¢	vermilion	E.M. Stanton	Same, w/o grill		12		149
7¢	orng verm	E.M. Stanton	Same, w/secret mark		12		160
7¢	black	Washington			12	SL	407
7¢	black	Washington			10	SL	430
7¢	black	Washington			10	NW	469
7¢	black	Washington			11	NW	507
7¢	black	Wm. McKinley		F	11		559
7¢	black	Wm. McKinley		R	10		588
7¢	black	Wm. McKinley		R	11x10.5		639
7¢	black	Wm. McKinley	Kansas Ovpt.		11x10.5		665
7¢	black	Wm. McKinley	Nebraska Ovpt.		11x10.5		676
7¢	sepia	A. Jackson			11x10.5		812
7¢	rose carm	W. Wilson			11x10.5		1040
7¢	brt blue	B. Franklin			10.5x11		1393D
7¢	brt carm	Abraham Baldwin			10.5x11		1850
7.1¢	lake	Tractor	Coil		10 Vert		2127
7.4¢	brown	Baby Buggy	Coil		10 Vert		1902
7.6¢	brown	Carreta	Coil		10 Vert		2255
7.7¢	brn (brt yl)	Saxhorns	Coil		10 Vert		1614
7.9¢	carm (yl)	Drum	Coil		10 Vert		1615
8¢	**lilac**	**W.T. Sherman**	**w/o Triangles**		**12**		**225**
8¢	violet brn	W.T. Sherman	w/ Tri. in Top corners		12	NW	257
8¢	violet brn	W.T. Sherman	w/ Tri. in Top corners		12	DL	272
8¢	violet brn	W.T. Sherman	w/ Tri. in Top corners		12	USIR	272a
8¢	violet blk	M. Washington	"Series 1902"		12	DL	306
8¢	olive grn	Washington			12	DL	337
8¢	olive grn	Washington	Blue Paper		12	DL	363
8¢	olive grn	Washington			12	SL	380
8¢	pl olv grn	B. Franklin			12	SL	414
8¢	pl olv grn	B. Franklin			10	SL	431
8¢	olv grn	B. Franklin			10	NW	470
8¢	olv grn	B. Franklin			11	NW	508
8¢	olv grn	U.S. Grant		F	11		560
8¢	olv grn	U.S. Grant		R	10		589
8¢	olv grn	U.S. Grant		R	11x10.5		640
8¢	olv grn	U.S. Grant	Kansas Ovpt.		11x10.5		666
8¢	olv grn	U.S. Grant	Nebraska Ovpt.		11x10.5		677
8¢	olv grn	M. Van Buren			11x10.5		813
8¢	dk viol bl & carm	Statue of Liberty		Flat	11		1041
		Statue of Liberty		Rotary	11		1041B
		Statue of Liberty Redrawn		Giori	11		1042
8¢	brown	Gen. J.J. Pershing		R	11x10.5		1042A
8¢	violet	Albert Einstein			11x10.5		1285*
8¢	multi	Flag & Wh House			11x10.5		1338F
8¢	multi	Flag & Wh House	Coil		10 Vert		1338G
8¢	blk,rd & bl gry	Eisenhower			11		1394
8¢	dp claret	Eisenhower	Bklt. sgl./B.Pn. of 8		11x10.5		1395a
8¢	dp claret	Eisenhower	Bklt. Pn. of 6		11x10.5		1395b
8¢	dp claret	Eisenhower	Bklt. Pn. of 4 + 2 Labels		11x10.5		1395c
8¢	dp claret	Eisenhower	Bklt. Pn. of 7 + Label		11x10.5		1395d
8¢	multi	Postal Service Emblem			11x10.5		1396
8¢	dp claret	Eisenhower	Coil		10 Vert		1402
8¢	olive blk	Henry Knox			10.5x11		1851
8.3¢	green	Ambulance	Coil		10 Vert		2128
8.3¢	green	Ambulance	Coil Precan.	B	10 Vert		2231
8.4¢	dk bl (yel)	Grand Piano	Coil		10 Vert		1615C
8.4¢	dp claret	Wheel Chair	Coil		10 Vert		2256
8.5¢	dk pris grn	Tow Truck	Coil		10 Vert		2129
9¢	**salmn rd**	**B. Franklin**			**12**	**SL**	**415**
9¢	salmn rd	B. Franklin			10	SL	432
9¢	salmn rd	B. Franklin			10	NW	471
9¢	salmn rd	B. Franklin			11	NW	509
9¢	rose	T. Jefferson		F	11		561
9¢	rose	T. Jefferson		R	10		590
9¢	orng red	T. Jefferson		R	11x10.5		641
9¢	lt rose	T. Jefferson	Kansas Ovpt.		11x10.5		667
9¢	lt rose	T. Jefferson	Nebraska Ovpt.		11x10.5		678
9¢	rose pink	W.H. Harrison			11x10.5		814
9¢	rose lilac	Alamo			10.5x11		1043
9¢	slate grn	Capitol Dome			11x10.5		1591
9¢	slate grn	Capitol Dome	Bklt. Single		11x10.5		1590
9¢	slate grn	Capitol Dome	Bklt. Single		10		1590a
9¢	slate grn	Capitol Dome	Coil		10 Vert		1616
9¢	dark grn	Sylvanus Thayer			10.5x11		1852
9.3¢	carm rose	Mail Wagon	Coil		10 Vert		1903
10¢	**black**	**Washington**			**Imperf**		**2**
10¢	black	Washington	Bluish paper (reprint)		Imperf		4
10¢	green	Washington	Ty I		Imperf		13
10¢	green	Washington	Ty II		Imperf		14
10¢	green	Washington	Ty III		Imperf		15
10¢	green	Washington	Ty IV		Imperf		16
10¢	green	Washington	Ty I		15		31

| | | | | | 13/35 | 62B/96 | 17/36b | 69/97 |

Den.	Color	Subject	Type / Comment	Press	Perf.	Wmk.	Scott #
10¢	green	Washington	Ty II		15		32
10¢	green	Washington	Ty III		15		33
10¢	green	Washington	Ty IV		15		34
10¢	green	Washington	Ty V		15		35
10¢	dark grn	Washington	Premier Gravure, Ty I		12		62B
10¢	yel grn	Washington	Ty II		12		68
10¢	green	Washington	"Z" Grill		12		85D
10¢	green	Washington	"E" Grill		12		89
10¢	yel grn	Washington	"F" Grill		12		96
10¢	yellow	Eagle & Shield	"G" Grill		12		116
10¢	brown	T. Jefferson	w/grill, Hard wh paper		12		139
10¢	brown	T. Jefferson	Same, w/o grill		12		150
10¢	brown	T. Jefferson	Same, w/secret mark		12		161
10¢	brown	T. Jefferson	Soft porous paper:				
			w/o secret mark		12		187
			w/secret mark		12		188
10¢	brown	T. Jefferson	Soft paper, re-engr.		12		209
10¢	green	D. Webster	w/o Triangles		12		226
10¢	dark grn	D. Webster	w/ Tri. in Top corners		12	NW	258
10¢	dark grn	D. Webster	w/ Tri. in Top corners		12	DL	273
10¢	brown	D. Webster	Ty I "		12	DL	282C
10¢	orng brn/brn	D. Webster	Ty II "		12	DL	283
10¢	pl rd brn	D. Webster	"Series 1902"		12	DL	307
10¢	yellow	Washington			12	DL	338
10¢	yellow	Washington	Blue Paper		12	DL	364
10¢	yellow	Washington			12	SL	381
10¢	yellow	Washington	Coil		12 Vert	DL	356
10¢	orng yel	B. Franklin			12	SL	416
10¢	orng yel	B. Franklin			10	SL	433
10¢	orng yel	B. Franklin			10	NW	472
10¢	orng yel	B. Franklin			11	NW	510
10¢	orng yel	B. Franklin	Coil	R	10 Vert	NW	497
10¢	yel orng	J. Monroe		F	11	NW	562
10¢	yel orng	J. Monroe		R	10	NW	591
10¢	orange	J. Monroe		R	11x10.5	NW	642
10¢	orange	J. Monroe	Coil	R	10 Vert	NW	603
10¢	orng yel	J. Monroe	Kansas Ovpt.		11x10.5	NW	668
10¢	orng yel	J. Monroe	Nebraska Ovpt.		11x10.5	NW	679
10¢	brn red	J. Tyler			11x10.5		815
10¢	brn red	J. Tyler	Coil		10 Vert		847
10¢	rose lake	Indep. Hall			10.5x11		1044*
10¢	lilac	A. Jackson			11x10.5		1286*
10¢	red & bl	Crossed Flags			11x10.5		1509
10¢	red & bl	Crossed Flags	Coil		10 Vert		1519
10¢	blue	Jefferson Mem.			11x10.5		1510
10¢	blue	Jefferson Mem.	Bklt. Pn. of 5 + Label		11x10.5		1510b
10¢	blue	Jefferson Mem.	Bklt. Pn. of 8		11x10.5		1510c
10¢	blue	Jefferson Mem.	Bklt. Pn. of 6		11x10.5		1510d
10¢	blue	Jefferson Mem.	Coil		10 Vert		1520
10¢	multi	"Zip Code"			11x10.5		1511
10¢	violet	Justice			11x10.5		1592
10¢	violet	Justice	Coil		10 Vert		1617
10¢	prus bl	Richard Russell			10.5x11		1853
10¢	lake	Red Cloud			11		2175
10¢	sky blue	Canal Boat	Coil		10 Vert		2257
10¢	green	Tractor Trailer	Coil Intaglio		10 Vert		2457
10¢	green	Tractor Trailer	Coil Gravure		10 Vert		2458
10.1¢	slate blue	Oil Wagon	Coil		10 Vert		2130
10.9¢	purple	Hansom Cab	Coil		10 Vert		1904
11	**dark grn**	**B. Franklin**			**10**	**SL**	**434**
11¢	dark grn	B. Franklin			10	NW	473
11¢	light grn	B. Franklin			11	NW	511
11¢	lt bl/bl grn	R.B. Hayes		F	11		563
11¢	light blue	R.B. Hayes		R	11x10.5		692
11¢	ultra	J.K. Polk			11x10.5		816
11¢	carm & dk viol bl	Statue of Liberty			11		1044A*
11¢	orange	Printing Press			11x10.5		1593
11¢	dk blue	Alden Partridge			11		1854
11¢	red	RR Caboose	Coil		10 Vert		1905
11¢	dk green	Stutz Bearcat	Coil		10 Vert		2131
12¢	**black**	**Washington**			**Imperf**		**17**
12¢	black	Washington	Plate 1		15		36
12¢	black	Washington	Plate 3		15		36b
12¢	black	Washington			12		69
12¢	black	Washington	"Z" Grill		12		85E
12¢	black	Washington	"E" Grill		12		90
12¢	black	Washington	"F" Grill		12		97
12¢	green	S.S. Adriatic	"G grill"		12		117
12¢	dull violet	H. Clay	Hard wh paper, w/grill		12		140
12¢	dull violet	H. Clay	Same, w/o grill		12		151
12¢	blksh viol	H. Clay	Same, w/secret mark		12		162
12¢	claret brn	B. Franklin			12	SL	417
12¢	claret brn	B. Franklin			10	SL	435

DEFINITIVE ISSUE IDENTIFIER

Den.	Color	Subject	Type / Comment	Press	Perf.	Wmk.	Scott #
12¢	copper rd	B. Franklin			10	SL	435a
12¢	claret brn	B. Franklin			10	NW	474
12¢	claret brn	B. Franklin			11	NW	512
12¢	brn carm	B. Franklin			11	NW	512a
12¢	brn violet	G. Cleveland		F	11		564
12¢	brn violet	G. Cleveland		R	11x10.5		693
12¢	bright viol	Z. Taylor			11x10.5		817
12¢	red	B. Harrison			11x10.5		1045*
12¢	black	Henry Ford			10.5x11		1286A*
12¢	rd brn (bge)	Liberty Torch	Coil		10 Vert		1816
12¢	dk blue	Stanley Stmr	Ty I Coil		10 Vert		2132
12¢	dk blue	Stanley Stmr	Ty II Coil, precanc.		10 Vert		2132b
12.5¢	olive grn	Pushcart	Coil		10 Vert		2133
13¢	purp blk	B. Harrison	"Series 1902"		12	DL	308
13¢	blue grn	Washington			12	DL	339
13¢	blue grn	Washington	Blue Paper		12	DL	365
13¢	apple grn	B. Franklin			11	NW	513
13¢	green	B. Harrison		F	11		622
13¢	yel grn	B. Harrison		R	11x10.5		694
13¢	bue grn	M. Fillmore			11x10.5		818
13¢	brown	J.F. Kennedy			11x10.5		1287*
13¢	brown	Liberty Bell			11x10.5		1595
13¢	brown	Liberty Bell	Bklt. Pn. of 6		11x10.5		1595a
13¢	brown	Liberty Brll	Bklt. Pn. of 7 + Label		11x10.5		1595b
13¢	brown	Liberty Bell	Bklt. Pn. of 8		11x10.5		1595c
13¢	brown	Liberty Bell	Bklt. Pn of 5 + Label		11x10.5		1595d
13¢	brown	Liberty Bell	Coil		10 Vert		1618
13¢	multi	Eagle & Shield	Bullseye Perfs		11x10.5		1596
13¢	multi	Eagle & Shield	Line Perfs		11		1596d
13¢	dk bl & rd	Flag Over Indep. Hall			11x10.5		1622
13¢	dk. bl & rd	Flag Over Indep. Hall			11		1622c
13¢	dk bl & rd	Flag Over Indep. Hall	Coil		10 Vert		1625
13¢	bl & rd	Flag Over Captl	Bklt. Single		11x10.5		1623
13¢	bl & rd	Flag Over Captl	Bklt. Single		10		1623b
13¢	bl & rd	Flag Over Captl	B. Pn. of 8 (7 #1623 (13¢) + 1 # 1590 (9¢))		11X10.5		1623a
13¢	bl & rd	Flag Over Capt	B. Pn. of 8 (7 #1623b (13¢) + 1 #1590a (9¢))		10		1623c
13¢	brn & bl (grn bistr)	Indian Head Penny			11		1734
13¢	lt maroon	Crazy Horse			10.5x11		1855
13¢	black	Patrol Wagon	Coil		10 Vert		2258
13.2¢	slate grn	Coal Car	Coil		10 Vert		2259
14¢	blue	American Indian		F	11		565
14¢	dk blue	American Indian		R	11x10.5		695
14¢	blue	F. Pierce			11x10.5		819
14¢	gray brn	Fiorello LaGuardia			11x10.5		1397
14¢	slate grn	Sinclair Lewis			11		1856
14¢	sky blue	Iceboat	Coil, overall tag		10 Vert		2134
14¢	sky blue	Iceboat, Ty II	Coil, block tag	B	10 Vert		2134b
14¢	crimson	Julia Ward Howe			11		2176
15¢	black	A. Lincoln			12		77
15¢	black	A. Lincoln	"Z" Grill		12		85F
15¢	black	A. Lincoln	"E" Grill		12		91
15¢	black	A. Lincoln	"F" Gril		12		98
15¢	brn & bl	Landing of Columbus:	Ty I Frame, "G grill"		12		118
			Same, w/o grill, o.g.		12		118a
			Ty II Frame, "G grill"		12		119
			Ty III, wh crackly gum		12		129
15¢	orange	D. Webster	Hard wh paper, w/grill		12		141
15¢	brt orng	D. Webster	Same, w/o grill		12		152
15¢	yel orng	D. Webster	Same, w/secret mark		12		163
15¢	red orng	D. Webster	Soft porous paper		12		189
15¢	indigo	H. Clay	w/o Triangles		12		227
15¢	dk blue	H. Clay	w/ Tri. in Top corners		12	NW	259
15¢	dk blue	H. Clay	w/ Tri. in Top corners		12	DL	274
15¢	olive grn	H. Clay	w/ Tri. in Top corners		12	DL	284
15¢	olive grn	H. Clay	"Series 1902"		12	DL	309
15¢	pl ultra	Washington			12	DL	340
15¢	pl ultra	Washington	Blue Paper		12	DL	366
15¢	pl ultra	Washington			12	SL	382
15¢	gray	B. Franklin			12	SL	418
15¢	gray	B. Franklin			10	SL	437
15¢	gray	B. Franklin			10	NW	475
15¢	gray	B. Franklin			11	NW	514
15¢	gray	Statue of Liberty		F	11		566
15¢	gray	Statue of Liberty		R	11x10.5		696
15¢	blue gray	J. Buchanan			11x10.5		820
15¢	rose lake	John Jay			11x10.5		1046*
15¢	maroon	O.W. Holmes			11x10.5		1288
15¢	dk rse clrt	O.W. Holmes	Type II		11x10.5		1288d
15¢	dk rse clrt	O.W. Holmes	Bklt. sgl./B.Pn. of 8		10		1288Bc
15¢	gray, dk bl & red	Ft McHenry Flag			11		1597
15¢		Ft McHenry Flag	Bklt. sgl./B. Pn. of 8		11x10.5		1598a
15¢		Ft McHenry Flag	Coil		10 Vert		1618C
15¢	multi	Roses	Bklt. sgl./B. Pn. of 8		10		1737a
15¢	sepia (yel)	Windmills	Bklt. Pn. of 10		11		1742a
15¢	rd brn & sepia	Dolley Madison			11		1822
15¢	claret	Buffalo Bill Cody			11		2177
15¢	violet	Tugboat	Coil		10 Vert		2260
15¢	multi	Beach Umbrella	Bklt. sgl./B. Pn. of 10		11.5x11		2443a
16¢	black	A. Lincoln			11x10.5		821
16¢	brown	Ernie Pyle			11x10.5		1398
16¢	blue	Statue of Liberty			11x10.5		1599
16¢	blue	Statue of Liberty	Coil		10 Vert		1619
16.7¢	rose	Popcorn Wagon	Coil		10 Vert		2261
17¢	black	W. Wilson		F	11		623
17¢	black	W. Wilson		R	10.5x11		697
17¢	rose red	A. Johnson			11x10.5		822
17¢	green	Rachel Carson			10.5x11		1857
17¢	ultra	Electric Auto	Coil		10 Vert		1906
17¢	sky blue	Dog Sled	Coil		10 Vert		2135
17¢	dk bl grn	Belva Ann Lockwood			11		2178
17.5¢	dk violet	Racing Car	Coil		10 Vert		2262
18¢	brn carm	U.S. Grant			11x10.5		823
18¢	violet	Dr. Elizabeth Blackwell			11x10.5		1399
18¢	dark bl	George Mason			10.5x11		1858
18¢	dark brn	Wildlife Animals	Bklt. Pn. of 10		11		1889a
18¢	multi	Flag/Amber Waves...			11		1890
18¢	multi	Flag/Sea to...Sea	Coil		10 Vert		1891
18¢	multi	Flag/Purple Mtns...	Bklt. Single		11		1893
18¢	multi	Flag/Purple Mnts...	Bklt. Pn. of 8 (7 #1893 (18¢) + 1 #1892 (6¢))		11		1893a
18¢	dk brn	Surrey	Coil		10 Vert		1907
18¢	multi	Washington & Monument	Coil		10 Vert		2149
19¢	brt violet	R.B. Hayes			11x10.5		824
19¢	brown	Sequoyah			10.5x11		1859
19¢	multi	Fawn			11.5x11		2479
19¢	multi	Fishing Boat	Coil Type I		10 Vert		2529
19¢	multi	Fishing Boat	Coil Type III		9.8 Vert		2529C
19¢	multi	Balloon	Bklt. sgl./B. Pn. of 10		10		2530,a
20¢	ultra	B. Franklin			12	SL	419
20¢	ultra	B. Franklin			10	SL	438
20¢	lt. ultra	B. Franklin			10	NW	476
20¢	lt. ultra	B. Franklin			11	NW	515
20¢	carm rse	Golden Rose		F	11		567
20¢	carm rse	Golden Gate		R	10.5x11		698
20¢	brt bl grn	J. Garfield			11x10.5		825
20¢	ultra	Monticello			10.5x11		1047
20¢	dp olive	George C. Marshall			11x10.5		1289*
20¢	claret	Ralph Bunche			10.5x11		1860
20¢	green	Thomas H. Gallaudet			10.5x11		1861
20¢	black	Harry S. Truman			11		1862**
20¢	blk, dk bl & red	Flag/Supreme Court			11		1894
20¢		Flag/Sup. Ct.	Coil		10 Vert		1895
20¢		Flag/Sup. Ct.	Bklt. sgl./Pns. of 6 & 10		11x10.5		1896,a,b
20¢	vermilion	Fire Pumper	Coil		10 Vert		1908
20¢	dk blue	Rocky Mtn. Bighorn	Bklt. sgl./Pn. of 10		11		1949a
20¢	sky blue	Consumer Ed.	Coil		10 Vert		2005
20¢	bl violet	Cable Car	Coil		10 Vert		2263
20¢	red brown	Virginia Agpar			11.1x11		2179
20¢	green	Cog Railway	Coil		10 Vert		2463
20¢	multi	Blue Jay	Bklt. Sgl./B. Pn. of 10		11x10		2483,a
20¢	multi	Blue Jay	Self-adhesive		Die-Cut		3048
20¢	multi	Blue Jay	Coil		11.6 Vert		3053
20.5¢	rose	Fire Engine	Coil		10 Vert		2264
21¢	dull blue	Chester A. Arthur			11x10.5		826
21¢	green	Amadeo Giannini			11x10.5		1400
21¢	bl violet	Chester Carlson			11		2181
21¢	olive grn	RR Mail Car	Coil		10 Vert		2265
21.1¢	multi	Envelopes	Coil		10 Vert		2150
22¢	vermilion	G. Cleveland			11x10.5		827
22¢	dk chlky bl	John J. Audubon			11		1863**
22¢	bl rd blk	Flag/Capitol			11		2114
22¢	bl rd blk	Flag/Capitol	Coil		10 Vert		2115
22¢	bl rd blk	Flag/Capitol/"of the People"	Bklt. Sgl.		10 Hz		2116
22¢	bl rd blk	Flag/Capitol/"of the People"	B. Pn. of 5		10 Hz		2116a
22¢	blk & brn	Seashells	Bklt. Pn. of 10		10		2121a
22¢	multi	Fish	Bklt. Pn. of 5		10 Hz		2209a
22¢	multi	Flag & Fireworks			11		2276
22¢	multi	Flag & Fireworks	Bklt. Pn. of 20		11		2276a
23¢	purple	Mary Cassatt			11		2181
23¢	dk blue	Lunch Wagon	Coil		10 Vert		2464
23¢	multi	Flag & Presorted First Class	Coil		10 Vert		2605
23¢	multi	USA & Flag Presort First Cl	Coil		10 Vert	ABNC	2606
23¢	multi	USA & Flag Presort First Cl	Coil		10 Vert	BEP	2607
23¢	multi	USA & Flag Presort First Cl	Coil		10 Vert	SVS	2608
24¢	gray lilac	Washington	"Twenty Four Cents"		15		37
24¢	red lilac	Washington	"24 Cents"		12		70
24¢	brn lilac	Washington			12		70a
24¢	steel blue	Washington			12		70b
24¢	violet	Washington			12		70c
24¢	grayish lil	Washington			12		70d
24¢	lilac	Washington			12		78
24¢	grayish lil	Washington			12		78a
24¢	gray	Washington			12		78b
24¢	blkish viol	Washington			12		78c
24¢	gray lilac	Washington	"F" Grill		12		99
24¢	grn & viol	Decl. of Indep.	"G grill"		12		120
24¢	grn & viol	Decl. of Indep.	w/o grill, original gum		12		120a
24¢	purple	Gen'l. W. Scott	Hard wh paper, w/grill		12		142
24¢	purple	Gen'l. W. Scott	Same, w/o grill		12		153
24¢	gray blk	B. Harrison			11x10.5		828
24¢	red (blue)	Old North Church			11x10.5		1603
24.1¢	dp ultra	Tandem Bicycle	Coil		10 Vert		2266
25¢	yel grn	Niagara Falls		F	11		568
25¢	blue grn	Niagara Falls		R	10.5x11		699
25¢	dp rd lil	Wm. McKinley			11x10.5		829
25¢	green	Paul Revere			11x10.5		1048
25¢	green	Paul Revere	Coil		10 Vert		1059A*
25¢	rose	Frederick Douglass			11x10.5		1290*
25¢	orng brn	Bread Wagon	Coil		10 Vert		2136
25¢	blue	Jack London			11		2182
25¢	blue	Jack London	Bklt. Pn. of 10		11		2182a
25¢	blue	Jack London	Bklt. Sgl./B. Pn. of 6		10		2197,a
25¢	multi	Flag & Clouds			11		2278
25¢	multi	Flag & Clouds	Bklt. Sgl./B. Pn. of 6		10		2285Ac
25¢	multi	Flag/Yosemite	Coil		10 Vert		2280

DEFINITIVE ISSUE IDENTIFIER

Den.	Color	Subject	Type / Comment	Press	Perf.	Wmk.	Scott #
25¢	multi	Honeybee	Coil		10 Vert		2281
25¢	multi	Pheasant	Bklt. Sgl./B. Pn. of 10		11		2283,a
25¢	multi	Pheasant	Same, w/o red in sky		11		2283b,c
25¢	multi	Grossbeak	Bklt. Single		10		2284
25¢	multi	Owl	Bklt. Single		10		2285
25¢	multi	Grossbk & Owl	Bklt. Pn. of 10 (5 ea.)		10		2285b
25¢	multi	Eagle & Shield	Self-adhesive		Die cut		2431
25¢	dk rd & bl	Flag	Self-adhesive		Die cut		2475
28¢	brn (bl)	Ft. Nisqually			11x10.5		1604
28¢	myrtle grn	Sitting Bull			11		2183
29¢	blue (bl)	Sandy Hook Lighthouse			11x10.5		1605
29¢	blue	Earl Warren			11		2184
29¢	dk violet	T. Jefferson			11		2185
29¢	multi	Red Squirrel	Self-adhesive		Die cut		2489
29¢	multi	Rose	Self-adhesive		Die cut		2490
29¢	multi	Pine Cone	Self-adhesive		Die cut		2491
29¢	blk & multi	Wood Duck	Bklt. sgl./B. Pn. of 10		10		2484,a
29¢	red & multi	Wood Duck	Bklt. sgl./B. Pn. of 10		11		2485,c
29¢	multi	African Violet	Bklt. sgl./B. Pn. of 10		10x11		2486,a
29¢	bl,rd,clar	Flag/Rushmore	Coil, Engraved		10		2523
29¢	bl,rd,brn	Flag/Rushmore	Coil, Gravure		10		2523A
29¢	multi	Tulip			11		2524
29¢	multi	Tulip			12.5x13		2524a
29¢	multi	Tulip	Coil	Roulette	10 Vert		2525
29¢	multi	Tulip	Coil		10 Vert		2526
29¢	multi	Tulip	Bklt. sgl./B. Pn. of 10		11		2527,a
29¢	multi	Flag/Rings	Bklt. sgl./B. Pn. of 10		11		2528
29¢	multi	Flags on Parade			11		2531
29¢	blk,gld,grn	Liberty/Torch	Self-adhesive		Die cut		2531A
29¢	multi	Flag & Pledge	blk. denom Bklt. sgl., Bklt. Pn. of 10		10		2593,a
29¢	multi	Flag & Pledge	red denom., Bklt. sgl., Bklt. Pn. of 10		10		2594,a
29¢	brn,multi	Eagle & Shield	Self-adhesive		Die cut		2595
29¢	grn,multi	Eagle & Shield	Self-adhesive		Die cut		2596
29¢	red,multi	Eagle & Shield	Self-adhesive		Die cut		2597
29¢	multi	Eagle	Self-adhesive		Die cut		2598
29¢	blue,red	Flag/White House	Coil		10 Vert		2609
29¢	multi	Liberty	Self-adhesive		Die cut		2599
30¢	orange	B. Franklin	Numeral at bottom		15		38
30¢	orange	B. Franklin	Numerals at Top		12		71
30¢	orange	B. Franklin	"A" Grill		12		81
30¢	orange	B. Franklin	"F" Grill		12		100
30¢	bl & carm	Eagle, Shield & Flags,	"G" Grill		12		121
			w/o grill, original gum		12		121a
30¢	black	A. Hamilton	Hard wh paper, w/grill		12		143
30¢	black	A. Hamilton	Same, w/o grill		12		154
30¢	gray blk	A. Hamilton	Same		12		165
30¢	full blk./grnish blk	A. Hamilton	Soft porous paper		12		190
30¢	orng brn	A. Hamilton			12		217
30¢	black	T. Jefferson			12		228
30¢	orng red	B. Franklin			12	SL	420
30¢	orng red	B. Franklin			10	SL	439
30¢	orng red	B. Franklin			10	NW	476A
30¢	orng red	B. Franklin			11	NW	516
30¢	olive brn	Buffalo		F	11		569
30¢	brown	Buffalo		R	10.5x11		700
30¢	dp ultra	T. Roosevelt			11x10.5		830
30¢	blue	T. Roosevelt			11x10.5		830 var
30¢	dp blue	T. Roosevelt			11x10.5		830 var
30¢	black	R.E. Lee			11x10.5		1049
30¢	red lilac	John Dewey			10.5x11		1291*
30¢	green	Morris School			11x10.5		1606
30¢	olv gray	Frank C. Laubach			11		1864**
30¢	multi	Cardinal			11		2480
32¢	blue	Ferryboat	Coil		10 Vert		2466
32¢	multi	Peach	Booklet Single		10x11		2487
32¢	multi	Peach	Self-adhesive		Die cut		2493
32¢	multi	Peach	Self-adhesive Coil		Die cut		2495
32¢	multi	Pear	Booklet Single		10x11		2488
32¢	multi	Pear	Self-adhesive		Die Cut		2494
32¢	multi	Pear	Self-adhesive Coil		Die cut		2495A
32¢	multi	Peach & Pear	Bklt. Pane of 10		10x11		2488a
32¢	multi	Peach & Pear	Self-adhesive Pane		Die cut		2494a
32¢	multi	Pink Rose	Self-adhesive		Die cut		2492
32¢	red-brown	James K. Polk			11.2		2587
32¢	multi	Flag over Porch			10.04		2897
32¢	multi	Flag over Porch	Coil	BEP	9.9 Vert		2913
32¢	multi	Flag over Porch	Coil	SVS	9.9 Vert		2914
32¢	multi	Flag over Porch	Self-adhesive Coil		Die cut 8.7		2915
32¢	multi	Flag over Porch	Self-adhesive Coil		Die cut 9.7		2915A
32¢	multi	Flag over Porch	Self-adhesive Coil		Die cut 11.5		2915B
32¢	multi	Flag over Porch	Self-adhesive Coil		Die cut 10.9		2915C
32¢	multi	Flag over Porch	Self-adhesive Coil		Die cut 9.8		2915D
32¢	multi	Flag over Porch	Bklt.Sgle./P.Pn. of 10		11x10		2916a
32¢	multi	Flag over Porch	Self-adhesive		Die-cut 8.8		2920,20b
32¢	multi	Flag over Porch	Self-adhesive		Die-cut 11.3		2920d
32¢	multi	Flag over Porch	Self-adhesive		Die-cut 9.8		2921a
32¢	multi	Flag over Porch	Linerless SA Coil		Die-cut		3133
32¢	multi	Flag over Field	Self-adhesive		Die cut		2919
32¢	brown	Milton S. Hershey			11		2933
32¢		Cal Farley			11		2934
32¢	multi	Yellow Rose	Self-adhesive		Die-cut		3049
32¢	multi	Statue of Liberty			Die-cut		3122
32¢	multi	Citron, Moth	Self-adhesive		Die-cut		3126,28a
32¢	multi	Flowering Pineapple, Cockroaches	Self-adhesive		Die-cut		3127,29a
35¢	gray	Charles R. Drew M.D.			10.5x11		1865

Den.	Color	Subject	Type / Comment	Press	Perf.	Wmk.	Scott #
35¢	black	Dennis Chavez			11		2186
37¢	blue	Robert Millikan			10.5x11		1866
39¢	rose lilac	Grenville Clark			11		1867**
40¢	brn red	J. Marshall			11x10.5		1050
40¢	bl black	Thomas Paine			11x10.5		1292*
40¢	dk grn	Lillian M. Gilbreth			11		1868**
40¢	dk blue	Claire Chennault			11		2187
45¢	brt blue	Harvey Cushing, MD			11		2188
45¢	multi	Pumpkinseed Fish			11		2481
46¢	carmine	Ruth Benedict			11		2938
50¢	orange	T. Jefferson	w/ Tri. in Top corners		12	NW	260
50¢	orange	T. Jefferson	w/ Tri. in Top corners		12	DL	275
50¢	orange	T. Jefferson	"Series 1902"		12	DL	310
50¢	violet	Washington			12	DL	341
50¢	violet	B. Franklin			12	SL	421
50¢	violet	B. Franklin			12	DL	422
50¢	violet	B. Franklin			10	SL	440
50¢	lt violet	B. Franklin			10	NW	477
50¢	rd violet	B. Franklin			11	NW	517
50¢	lilac	Arlington Amph		F	11		570
50¢	lilac	Arlington Amph		R	10.5x11		701
50¢	lt rd viol	W.H. Taft			11x10.5		831
50¢	brt prpl	S.B. Anthony			11x10.5		1051
50¢	rose mag	Lucy Stone			11x10.5		1293*
50¢	blk & orng	Iron "Betty" Lamp			11		1608
50¢	brown	Chester W. Nimitz			11		1869**
52¢	purple	Hubert Humphrey			11		2189
55¢	green	Alice Hamilton			11		2940
56¢	scarlet	John Harvard			11		2190
65¢	dk blue	"Hap" Arnold			11		2191
75¢	dp mag	Wendell Wilkie			11		2192
78¢	purple	Alice Paul			11.2		2943
90¢	blue	Washington	"Ninety Cents"		15		39
90¢	blue	Washington	"90 Cents"		12		72
90¢	blue	Washington	Same, "F" Grill		12		101
90¢	carm & blk	A. Lincoln	"G grill"		12		122
90¢	carm & blk	A. Lincoln	w/o grill, o.g.		12		122a
90¢	carmine	Com. Perry	Hard wh paper, w/grill		12		144
90¢	carmine	Com. Perry	Same, w/o grill		12		155
90¢	rose carm	Com. Perry	Same		12		166
90¢	carmine	Com. Perry	Soft porous paper		12		191
90¢	purple	Com. Perry	Soft porous paper		12		218
90¢	orange	Com. Perry			12		229
$1.00	black	Com. Perry	Ty I		12	NW	261
$1.00	black	Com. Perry	Ty I		12	DL	276
$1.00	black	Com. Perry	Ty II		12	NW	261A
$1.00	black	Com. Perry	Ty II		12	DL	276A
$1.00	black	D.G. Farragut			12	DL	311
$1.00	violet brn	Washington			12	DL	342
$1.00	violet brn	B. Franklin			12	DL	423
$1.00	violet blk	B. Franklin			10	DL	460
$1.00	violet blk	B. Franklin			10	NW	478
$1.00	violet brn	B. Franklin			11	NW	518
$1.00	deep brn	B. Franklin			11	NW	518b
$1.00	violet blk	Lincoln Memorial			11		571
$1.00	prpl & blk	W. Wilson			11		832
$1.00	prpl & blk	W. Wilson			11	USIR	832b
$1.00	rd viol & blk	W. Wilson	Dry Print, smooth gum		11		832c
$1.00	purple	P. Henry			11x10.5		1052
$1.00	dl purple	Eugene O'Neill			11x10.5		1294*
$1.00	dl purple	Eugene O'Neill	Coil		10 Vert		1305
$1.00	brn,orng&yel (tan)	Rush Lamp & Candle Holder			11		1610
$1.00	dk prus grn	Bernard Revel			11		2193
$1.00	dk blue	Johns Hopkins			11		2194
$1.00	bl & scar	Seaplane	Coil		10 Vert		2468
$1.00	gold,multi	Eagle & Olympic Rings			11		2539
$1.00	blue	Burgoyne			11.5		2590
$2.00	brt blue	J. Madison	w/ Tri. in Top corners		12	NW	262
$2.00	brt blue	J. Madison	w/ Tri. in Top corners		12	DL	277
$2.00	dk blue	J. Madison	"Series 1902"		12	DL	312
$2.00	dk blue	J. Madison	"Series 1902"		10	NW	479
$2.00	orng rd & blk	B. Franklin			11		523
$2.00	carm & blk	B. Franklin			11		547
$2.00	dp blue	U.S. Capitol			11		572
$2.00	yel grn&blk	W.G. Harding			11		833
$2.00	dk grn&rd (tan)	Kerosene Table Lamp			11		1611
$2.00	brt viol	William Jennings Bryan			11		2195
$2.00	multi	Bobcat			11		2482
$2.90	multi	Eagle			11		2540
$2.90	multi	Space Shuttle			11x10½		2543
$3.00	multi	Challenger Shuttle			11.2		2544A
$5.00	dk green	J. Marshall	w/ Tri. in Top corners		12	NW	263
$5.00	dk green	J. Marshall	w/ Tri. in Top corners		12	DL	278
$5.00	dk green	J. Marshall	"Series 1902"		12	DL	313
$5.00	lt green	J. Marshall	"Series 1902"		10	NW	480
$5.00	dp grn & blk	B. Franklin			11		524
$5.00	carm & bl	Freedom Statue/Capitol			11		573
$5.00	carm & blk	C. Coolidge			11		834
$5.00	rd brn & blk	C. Coolidge			11		834a
$5.00	black	A. Hamilton			11		1053
$5.00	gray blk	John Bassett Moore			11x10.5		1295*
$5.00	rd brn,yel&orng (tan)	RR Conductors Lantern			11		1612
$5.00	copper rd	Bret Harte			11		2196
$5.00	slate grn	Washington & Jackson			11.5		2592
$8.75	multi	Eagle & Moon			11		2394
$9.35	multi	Eagle & Moon	Bklt. sgl./B. Pn. of 3		10 Vert		1909,a
$9.95	multi	Eagle			11		2541
$9.95	multi	Moon Landing			10.7x11.1		2842

Den.	Color	Subject	Type / Comment	Press	Perf.	Wmk.	Scott #
$10.75	multi	Eagle & Moon	Bklt. sgl./B. Pn. of 3		10 Vert		2122,a
$10.75	multi	Endeavor Shuttle			11		2544A
$14.00	**multi**	**Spread winged Eagle**			**11**		**2542**
* (4¢)	gold,carm	Text only	Make-up rate		11		2521
(5¢)	multi	Butte	Coil		9.8 Vert		2902
(5¢)	multi	Butte	Self-adhesive Coil		Die-cut 11.5		2902B
(5¢)	multi	Mountain	Coil	BEP	9.8 Vert		2903
(5¢)	multi	Mountain	Coil	SVS	9.8 Vert		2904
(5¢)	multi	Mountain	Self-adhesive Coil		Die-cut 11.5		2904A
(5¢)	multi	Mountain	Self-adhesive Coil		Die-cut 9.8		2904B
(10¢)	multi	Automobile	Coil		9.8 Vert		2905
(10¢)	multi	Automobile	Self-adhesive Coil		Die-cut 11.5		2907
(10¢)	multi	Eagle & Shield	Coil "Bulk Rate, USA"		10 Vert		2602
(10¢)	multi	Eagle & Shield	Coil "USA Bulk Rate"		10 Vert	BEP	2603
(10¢)	multi	Eagle & Shield	Coil "USA Bulk Rate"		10 Vert	SVS	2604
(10¢)	multi	Eagle & Shield	Self-adhesive Coil		Die-cut 11.5		2906
A (15¢)	**orange**	**Eagle**			**11**		**1735**
A	orange	Eagle	Bklt. Sgl./Pn. of 8		11x10.5		1736,a
A	orange	Eagle	Coil		10 Vert		1743
(15¢)	multi	Auto Tail Fin	Coil	BEP	9.8 Vert		2908
(15¢)	multi	Auto Tail Fin	Coil	SVS	9.8 Vert		2909
(15¢)	multi	Auto Tail Fin	Self-adhesive Coil		Die-cut 11.5		2910
B (18¢)	**violet**	**Eagle**			**11x10.5**		**1818**
B	violet	Eagle	Bklt. sgl./Pn of 8		10		1819,a
B	violet	Eagle	Coil		10 Vert		1820
C (20¢)	**brown**	**Eagle**			**11x10.5**		**1946**
C	brown	Eagle	Coil		10 Vert		1947
C	brown	Eagle	Bklt. sgl./Pn. of 10		11x10.5		1948,a
D (22¢)	**green**	**Eagle**			**11**		**2111**
D	green	Eagle	Coil		10 Vert		2112
D	green	Eagle	Bklt. sgl./Pn. of 10		11		2113,a
E (25¢)	**multi**	**Earth**			**11**		**2277**
E	multi	Earth	Coil		10 Vert		2279
E	multi	Earth	Bklt. sgl./Pn. of 10		10		2282a
(25¢)	multi	Juke Box	Coil	BEP	9.8 Vert		2911
(25¢)	multi	Juke Box	Coil	SVS	9.8 Vert		2912
(25¢)	multi	Juke Box	Self-adhesive Coil		Die-cut 11.5		2912A
(25¢)	multi	Juke Box	Self-adhesive Coil		Die-cut 9.8		2912B
(25¢)	multi	Juke Box	Linerless SA Coil		Die-cut		3132
F (29¢)	**multi**	**Tulip**			**13**		**2517**
F	multi	Tulip	Coil		10		2518
F	multi	Tulip	Bklt. Stamp	BEP	11 bullseye		2519
F	multi	Tulip	Bkt. Stamp	KCS	11		2520
F	blk,dk bl,red	Flag	Self-adhesive		Die cut		2522
G (20¢)	**multi**	**FlagBlack "G"**		**BEP**	**11.2x11.1**		**2879**
G (20¢)	multi	Flag Red "G"		SVS	11x10.9		2880
G (25¢)	multi	Flag, Black "G"	Coil	SVS	9.8 vert.		2888
G (32¢)	multi	Flag, Black "G"		BEP	11.2x11.1		2881
G (32¢)	multi	Flag, Red "G"		SVS	11x10.9		2882
G (32¢)	multi	Flag, Black "G"	Bklt. Stamp	BEP	10x9.9		2883
G (32¢)	multi	Flag, Blue "G"	Bklt. Stamp	ABN	10.9		2884
G (32¢)	multi	Flag, Red "G"	Bklt. Stamp	SVS	11x10.9		2885
G (32¢)	multi	Flag	Self-adhesive		Die cut		2886,87
G (32¢)	multi	Flag, Black "G"	Coil	BEP	9.8 vert.		2889
G (32¢)	multi	Flag, Blue "G"	Coil	ABN	9.8 vert.		2890
G (32¢)	multi	Flag, Red "G"	Coil	SVS	9.8 vert.		2891
G (32¢)	multi	Flag, Red "G"	Coil	Roulette	9.8 vert.		2892

Adventures in Topicals

(Second of a *Brookman Times* series)
By George Griffenhagen
Editor of *Topical Time*

There is much more to topical stamp collecting than accumulating postage stamps picturing something or someone associated with a theme. To experience the adventure of topical collecting, you need to expand your horizons by including a variety of philatelic elements in your collection. As promised in the last installment of this series, we will review the variety of philatelic elements that awaits your discovery.

To most people, a postage stamp is something they stick on an envelope to mail a letter. However, stamp collectors know that postage stamps come in a variety of forms. There are Definitives (most 19th century stamps were definitives); Commemoratives (they made their appearance at the close of the 19th century); Semi-Postals (also called charity stamps); Provisionals (to fill and urgent need); and Locals (for use in a limited geographical area). The stamp design is generally limited to a single stamp, but Composites are those in which the design extends over two or more stamps have become popular. Se-tenants consist of two or more adjacent stamps differing in design or denomination, while Tete-beche is a term describing adjacent stamps, one of which is inverted.

Any of the above stamps can include Surcharges (inscriptions that change the face value) or Overprints (inscriptions that change the purpose of a stamp); a classical example of the latter is the 1928 U.S. George Washington stamp with an overprint for MOLLY PITCHER, Revolutionary War heroine.

Perfins and Watermarks offer interesting philatelic elements. Among the thousands of Perfins (named for PERforated INSignia), topical collectors can find designs for anchors, bells, coffee grinders, dancers, eagles, fish, flags, spinning wheels, swans, and windmills. Watermarks (patterns impressed into the paper during manufacture) also come in a variety of images including anchors, birds, coats-of-arms, flowers, lions, moons, posthorns, pyramids, stars, swans, and trees.

Marginal inscriptions frequently include more than plate numbers or other post office inscriptions. Designs on tabs and margins (selvage) of stamps and souvenir sheets often supplement a theme as much as the design of the stamp itself. Equally interesting are the tabs and marginal advertisements attached to postage stamps.

The introduction of postage stamp booklets in 1895 offered opportunities for governmental promotional messages and commercial advertising on covers, interleaves, and labels required to make the total face value of the booklet a convenient multiple of the local currency. Commercial advertising was introduced into the stamp booklets during the first decade of the 19th century. By the 1920s, entire stamp booklets were devoted to advertisements of a single firm.

There are, of course, many stamps that are not postage stamps. Revenues (also called fiscals or tax stamps) are stamps indicating the payment of a fee or collection of a tax. They predate postage stamps by several centuries, having been used in The Netherlands as early as 1627 and in Spain as early as 1637. Even though revenues are not postage stamps, they lay claim to being the "most historic stamps of all time." It was a 1765 revenue stamp imposing a tax on legal documents in the British colonies in America which ignited the American Revolutionary War. Cinderellas are virtually any item that looks like a postage stamp but is not a postage stamp. They include such material as advertising seals, bogus stamps, charity seals, fantasy stamps, food rationing stamps, political seals, poster stamps, and propaganda seals. There are even Test Stamps issued by various postal administrations for use in developing stamp vending machines.

Covers (envelopes that have passed through the mail bearing appropriate postal markings) were used centuries before the introduction of the postage stamp. Today they are classified either as Commercial or Philatelic. Many adventures lies ahead for the collector who searches for a particular stamp that belongs in a topical collection. By the second half of the 19th century, envelopes were imprinted with a wide range of colorful advertisements (called Corner Cards referring to the return address). Patriotic Cover became popular during the American Civil War, and Mourning Covers (with their black borders) were widely used during the Victorian era. Other interesting covers include Balloon Mail (which preceeded First Flight Covers), Paquebots (mail posted on ther high seas), Crash/Wreck Covers, Free Frank Covers, and Censored Covers. First Day Covers (FDCs) comprise the major portion of philatelic covers.

Postal Stationery includes all forms of stationery bearing a printed stamp (indicium). Pre-stamped letter sheets were used as early as the 17th century, but it was the British Mulready which was introduced in 1840 that popularized postal stationery. The first Postal Card bearing an indicium was issued in Austria in 1869, and the Aerogramme (air letter) led to the subsequent use of the British Airgraph and the American V-Mail during World War II.

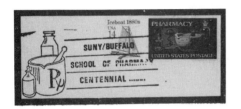

Cancellations (called postmarks when they include date and place of posting) come in a variety of forms. The most desirable for the topical collector are Fancy Cancels applied by obliterators made of cork or wood. The rarest were produced in Waterbury, Connecticut, from 1865 to 1869. With the introduction of rapid cancelling machines, Slogan Cancels, Pictorial Cancels, and First Day of Issue cancels were created. The introduction of the postage meter in the early 20th century also led to a variety of advertising slogans.

Other philatelic elements of interest to the topical collector are Maximum Cards (introduced around 1900); Autographs on stamps and covers; and the Telephone Card (which was used as early as the 1880s to prepay telephone calls). The scope of material for the topical collector is limited only by one's imagination.

For a detailed review of philatelic elements, obtain your copy of the all-new American Topical Association (ATA) handbook entitled Adventures in Topical Stamp Collecting which is available for $22.00. $40.00 brings you a copy of Adventures plus a full year membership in the world's largest society devoted to topical collecting and six issues of Topical Time. Join the most popular area of stamp collecting now by contacting ATA at P.O. Box 65749, Tucson, AZ 85729.

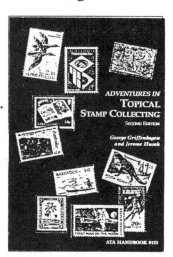

SELECTED and ANNOTATED BIBLIOGRAPHY

The volumes listed below are recommended for the library of any collector who wishes to gain more knowledge in the areas covered by the *1996 Brookman*. While the main emphasis is on stamps, many of these volumes contain good postal history information. Check with your favorite dealer for availability and price. (To conserve space, some bibliographic notations have been abbreviated).

19th & 20th Century

Cummings, William W., ed., *Scott 1995 Specialized Catalogue of U.S. Stamps*
This annual publication offers a treasure trove of information on virtually every area of the postage and revenue stamps of the US, UN & US Possesstions. A "must have."

Sloane, George B., *Sloane's Column*, arr. by George Turner, 1961, (BIA 1980)
A subject by subject arrangement of Sloane's 1350 columns which appeared in "STAMPS" magazine from1932-1958 covering virtually every facet of U.S. philately.

White, Roy, *Encyclopedia of the Colors of U.S. Postage Stamps*, Vol 1-5, 1981, 86.
The first four volumes cover US stamps from 1847-1918 plus a few selected issues. Volume five covers the US Postage Dues from1879-1916. They are the finest available works for classifying the colors of U.S. postage stamps.

19th Century
General

Brookman, Lester G., *The United States Postage Stamps of the 19th Century*, 3 vol., 1966. (Reprinted in 1989 by D.G.Phillips Co.)
This is the finest and most informative work on 19th Century issues. Each stamp, from the 5¢ Franklin of 1847 thru the $2 Trans-Mississippi of 1898, is given separate, and often in-depth treatment. This is a must for any collector.

Luff, John N., *The Postage Stamps of the United States*, 1902.
While much of Luff's information has been superseded by Brookman, his treatment of Postmaster Provisionals and several Back-of-the-book sections make this a worthwhile volume. (The "Gossip Reprint", 1937, is more useful and recommended.)

Perry, Elliot, *Pat Paragraphs*, arr by George Turner & Thomas Stanton, BIA, 1981.
A subject by subject arrangement of Perry's 58 pamphlets which were published from 1931-1958. The emphasis is on the 19th century classics as well as carriers & locals.

Baker, Hugh J. and J. David, *Bakers' U.S. Classics*, 1985
An annotated compilation of the Bakers' columns from "STAMPS" magazine which appeared from 1962-1969. This major work provides extensive coverage of nearly all aspects of U.S. and Confederate philately.

By Issue or Subject

Ashbrook, Stanley B., *The United States One Cent Stamp of 1851-57*, 2 vol, 1938.
Although most of stamp and plating information in Volume 1 has been superseded by Mortimer Neinken's great work, Vol. 2 features an indispensible amount of information on the postal history of the period.

Neinken, Mortimer L., *The United States One Cent Stamp of 1851 to 1861*, 1972.
United States, The 1851-57 Twelve Cent Stamp, 1964.
The One cent book supplements and updates, but does not replace, Ashbrook's study. The Twelve cent booklet deals almost exclusively with the plating of this issue. Both are fundamental works.

Chase, Dr. Carroll, *The 3¢ Stamp of the U.S. 1851-57 Issue*, Rev. ed., 1942.
This outstanding work provides the most comprehensive information available in one place on this popular issue. (The Quarterman reprint, 1975, contains a new forward, corrections, additions and a selected bibliography of articles.)

Hill, Henry W., *The United States Five Cent Stamps of 1856-1861*, 1955.
This extensively illustrated volume is the only work dealing exclusively with this issue. It includes studies on stamps, plating, cancels, and postal history.

Neinken, Mortimer L., *The United States Ten Cent Stamps of 1855-1859*, 1960.
This work not only provides an indispensable amount of stamp and plating information, but it also reprints Chapters 50-53 from Ashbrook Vol. 2 dealing with California, Ocean and Western Mails.

Cole, Maurice F., *The Black Jacks of 1863-1867*, 1950.
A superb study of the issue with major emphasis on postal history.

Lane, Maryette B., *The Harry F. Allen Collection of Black Jacks, A Study of the Stamp and it's Use,* 1969
The title says it all. This book beautifully complements, but does not replace, Cole.

Ashbrook, Stanley B., *The U.S. Issues of 1869, Preceded by Some Additional Notes on "The premieres Gravures of 1861"*, 1943
This work concentrates on the design sources and production of the 1869 issue. Ashbrook concludes with his "Addendum" attacking Scott for listing the Premieres.

Willard, Edward L., *The U.S. Two Cent Red Brown of 1883-1887*, 2 vol., 1970.
Volume I deals with the background, production and varieties of the stamp. Vol. II deals exclusively with the cancellations found on the stamp. A good Banknote intro.

20th Century
General

King, Beverly S. and Johl, Max G. *The United States Postages Stamps of the Twentieth Century*, Vol. 1 revised, Vol. 2-4, 1934-38.
These volumes are still the standard work on 20th Century U.S. postage stamps from 1901 to 1937. (The 1976 Quarterman reprint contains only the regular issue, air mail and Parcel Post sections from the original volumes. It is highly recommended.)

By Issue or Subject

Armstrong, Martin A., *Washington-Franklins, 1908-1921*, 2nd Edition, 1979.
Armstrong, Martin A., *US Definitive Series, 1922-1938*, 2nd Edition, 1980.
Armstrong, Martin A., *United States Coil Issues, 1906-38*, 1977
Each of these volumes not only supplements the information found in Johl, but expands each area to include studies of essays, proofs, booklet panes, private perfs, Offices in China and the Canal Zone. One major plus is the wealth of illustrations, many of rare and unusual items, which were not included in Johl's work due to laws restricting the publication of stamp pictures prior to 1938.

20th Century
By Issue or Subject (cont.)

Schoen, DeVoss & Harvey, *Counterfeit Kansas-Nebraska Overprints on 1922-34 Issue plus First Day Covers of the Kansas-Nebraska Overprints*, 1973.
A fine pamphlet covering K-N varieties, errors and First Day covers, plus important information pointing out the differences between genuine and fake overprints.

Datz, Stephen, *U.S. Errors: Inverts, Imperforates, Colors Omitted*, 1992 Ed., 1991.
This volume does a superb job covering the subjects listed in its title, It is extensively illustrated and provides price, quantity and historical information.

Air Mail & Back-of-the-Book

Amercian Air Mail Society, *American Air Mail Catalog*, Fifth Ed., 5 vols + 1990 Pricing Supplement, 1974-1990.
Virtually everything there is to know about air mail stamps and postal history.

Arfken, George B., *Postage Due, The United States Large Numeral Postage Due Stamps, 1879-1894*, 1991.
A Comprehensive study of virtually every aspect of these interesting stamps. Additionally, about half the book is devoted to their extensive usage which helps to clarify some of the more complex markings and routings found on "Due" covers.

Gobie, Henry M. *The Speedy, A History of the U.S. Special Delivery Service*, 1976
Gobie, Henry M., *U.S. Parcel Post, A Postal History*, 1979.
Each of these volumes includes information on the stamps, but their main thrust is on the postal history of the respective services. Official documents and Postal Laws & Regulations have been extensively reproduced and numerous covers illustrating the various aspects of the services are pictured.

Markovits, Robert L., *United States, The 10¢ Registry Stamp of 1911*, 1973.
This pamphlet provides a superb blueprint for the formation of specialized collection around a single stamp. It is extensively illustrated and concludes with an extensive bibliography which touches upon a multitude of additional subjects.

McGovern, Edmund C., ed, *Catalog of the 19th Century Stamped Envelopes and Wrappers of the United States*, USPSS 1984

Haller, Austin P., ed., *Catalog of the 20th Century Stamped Envelopes and Wrappers of the United States*, USPSS 1990

Beachboard, John H., ed., *United States Postal Card Catalog*, USPSS 1990
Each of the three previous volumes contains the finest available information in their respective fields. They are indispensable to the postal stationery collector.

First Day Covers & Related Collectibles

Planty, Dr. Earl & Mellone, Michael, *Planty's Photo Encyclopedia of Cacheted FDCs, 1923-1939*, Vol. 1-10, 1976-1984

Mellone, Mike, *Specialized Catalog of First Day Covers of the 1940's (2nd ed.), 1950's and 1960's*, 2 vol., 2 vol., 3 vol. respectively, 1983-1985.

Pelcyger, Dr. Scott, *Mellone's Specialized Catalog of First Day Ceremony Programs & Events*, 1989
Each of these volumes illustrates virtually every known cachet and ceremony program for the stamps listed within. They each provide an invaluable resource.

Radford, Dr. Curtis D., *The Souvenir Card Collectors Society Numbering System for Forerunner and Modern Day Souvenir Card*, 1989.
The most informative work on this popular collecting area.

Revenues

Toppan, Deats and Holland, *'An Historical Reference List of the Revenue Stamps of the United States...",* 1899.
The information in this volume, while almost 100 years old, still provides the collector with much of the basic knowledge available today on US Revenues and "Match and Medicines" from 1862-1898. (The "Gossip" reprint is recommended.)

Confederate States

Dietz, August, *The Postal Service of the Confederate States of America*, 1929
This monumental work has been the "Bible" for Confederate collectors. Covering virtually every aspect of Confederate philately, its content remains useful, even after 60+ years. (A 1989 reprint makes this work more affordable for the average collector.)

Skinner, Gunter and Sanders, *The New Dietz Confederate States Catalog and Handbook*, 1986.
This volume makes an effort to cover every phase of Confederate philately and postal history. Despite the presence of some flaws, it is highly recommended.

Possessions

Plass, Brewster and Salz, *Canal Zone Stamps*, 1986.
Published by the Canal Zone Study Group, this outstanding well written and extensively illustrated volume, is now the "bible" for these fascinating issues.

Meyer, Harris, et. at, *Hawaii, Its Stamps and Postal History*, 1948.
After 45 years, this volume, which deals with virtually every facet of Hawaiian stamps and postal history, remains the finest work written on the subject.

Palmer, Maj. F.L., *The Postal Issues of the Philippines*, 1912
An ancient, but still useful study, with interesting information on the U.S. overprints.

British North America

Boggs, Winthrop S., *The Postage Stamps and Postal History of Canada*, 2 vol., 1945. (Quarterman reprint, One vol., 1975)
For above 50 years this remains the standard work on Canadian stamps and postal history. One of the "must have" books. (The reprint omits most of the Vol. 2 appendices.)

Lowe, Robson, *The Encyclopedia of British Empire Postage Stamps, Vol. 5, North America*, 1973
This work continues the fine tradition of Robson Lowe's earlier volumes dealing with the British Empire. Covering all of BNA, it is an essential tool for the collector.

1847 General Issue, Imperforate VF + 50% (C)

1,3,948a   2,4,948b

Scott's No.		Unused Fine	Ave.	Used Fine	Ave.
1	5¢ Franklin, Red Brown	2250.00	475.00	300.00	
1	5¢ Red Brown, Pen Cancel	...	250.00	175.00	
2	10¢ Washington, Black	11000.00	1100.00	675.00	
2	10¢ Black, Pen Cancel	...	600.00	425.00	
3	5¢ Red Brown, 1875 Repro	750.00	550.00	...	...
4	10¢ Black, 1875 Reproduction	900.00	675.00	...	...

NOTE: SEE #948 FOR 5¢ BLUE AND 10¢ BROWN ORANGE.

1851-1856 Issue, Imperf "U.S. Postage" at Top (VF, OG+100%, VF+50%, OG+50%) (C)

5A-9   10-11   12   13-16   17

Scott's No.		Unused Fine	Ave.	Used Fine	Ave.
5A	1¢ Franklin, Blue, Type Ib	...		3500.00	2000.00
6	1¢ Blue, Type Ia	...		5500.00	3250.00
7	1¢ Blue, Type I	500.00	300.00	110.00	65.00
8	1¢ Blue, Type III	...		1600.00	975.00
8A	1¢ Blue, Type IIIa	2500.00	1400.00	675.00	400.00
9	1¢ Blue, Type IV	400.00	240.00	95.00	57.50
10	3¢ Wash., Orange Brown, Ty. I	1500.00	900.00	55.00	32.50
11	3¢ Dull Red, Type I	135.00	80.00	7.50	4.50
12	5¢ Jefferson, Red Brown, Ty. I	...		850.00	500.00
13	10¢ Wash., Green, Type I	...		600.00	350.00
14	10¢ Green, Type II	1750.00	1050.00	190.00	135.00
15	10¢ Green, Type III	1750.00	1050.00	190.00	135.00
16	10¢ Green, Type IV	...		1350.00	800.00
17	12¢ Washington, Black	...	1500.00	250.00	150.00

1857-61 Same Design as Above but Perf. 15 (VF, OG+150%, VF+100% OG+50%) (C)

18-24   25-26   37   38   39

Scott's No.		Unused Fine	Ave.	Used Fine	Ave.
18	1¢ Franklin, Blue, Type I	700.00	425.00	350.00	200.00
19	1¢ Blue, Type Ia	...	...	...	2000.00
20	1¢ Blue, Type II	475.00	275.00	160.00	95.00
21	1¢ Blue, Type III (Plate 4)	3500.00	1200.00	1200.00	700.00
22	1¢ Blue, Type IIIa	675.00	400.00	300.00	175.00
23	1¢ Blue, Type IV	3000.00	1800.00	350.00	200.00
24	1¢ Blue, Type V	100.00	55.00	25.00	15.00
25	3¢ Washington, Rose, Type I	1175.00	675.00	45.00	27.50
26	3¢ Dull Red, Type II	50.00	27.50	3.75	2.25
27	5¢ Jefferson, Brick Red, Type I	5500.00		650.00	400.00
28	5¢ Red Brown, Type I	1500.00	900.00	300.00	170.00
28A	5¢ Indian Red, Type I	...	1650.00		1050.00
29	5¢ Brown, Type I	975.00	525.00	200.00	120.00
30	5¢ Orange Brown, Type II	675.00	400.00	850.00	500.00
30A	5¢ Brown, Type II	750.00	450.00	160.00	95.00
31	10¢ Wash., Green, Type I	4750.00		500.00	290.00
32	10¢ Green, Type II	2275.00	1300.00	180.00	110.00
33	10¢ Green, Type III	2275.00	1300.00	180.00	110.00
34	10¢ Green, Type IV	...		1475.00	795.00
35	10¢ Green, Type V	180.00	95.00	52.50	32.50
36	12¢ Wash., Black, Plate I	425.00	225.00	115.00	67.50
36b	12¢ Black, Plate III	375.00	200.00	110.00	62.50
37	24¢ Washington, Gray Lilac	675.00	375.00	190.00	110.00
38	30¢ Franklin, Orange	875.00	500.00	275.00	160.00
39	90¢ Washington, Blue	1200.00	750.00	...	...

NOTE: #5A THROUGH 38 WITH PEN CANCELS USUALLY SELL FOR 50-60% OF LISTED
USED PRICES. USED EXAMPLES OF #39 SHOULD ONLY BE PURCHASED WITH, OR
SUBJECT TO, A CERTIFICATE OF AUTHENTICITY.

#40-47 ARE 1875 REPRINTS OF THE 1857-60 ISSUE.

IMPORTANT NOTICE

PRIOR TO 1882 `UNUSED' PRICES ARE FOR STAMPS THAT MAY HAVE NO GUM
OR PART GUM. FOR ORIGINAL GUM ADD % INDICATED !

1861 New Designs, Perf. 12, Thin Paper (VF, OG+150%, VF+75% OG+50%) (C)

Scott's No.		Unused Fine	Ave.	Used Fine	Ave.
62B	10¢ Wash., Dark Green	...	...	450.00	250.00

1861-62 Modified Designs, Perf. 12 (VF, OG+150%, VF+100% OG+50%) (C)

63   73   65   67,75-76   68

69   77   70,78   71   72

		Unused Fine	Ave.	Used Fine	Ave.
63	1¢ Franklin, Blue	140.00	80.00	16.50	10.00
64	3¢ Washington, Pink	...	2200.00	425.00	250.00
64b	3¢ Rose Pink	300.00	175.00	80.00	45.00
65	3¢ Rose	80.00	43.50	1.50	.90
67	5¢ Jefferson, Buff	5000.00		425.00	240.00
68	10¢ Wash., Yellow Green	300.00	165.00	33.50	19.75
69	12¢ Washington, Black	525.00	315.00	60.00	33.75
70	24¢ Wash., Red Lilac	800.00	450.00	80.00	45.00
70b	24¢ Steel Blue	...	3000.00	300.00	160.00
70c	24¢ Violet, Thin Paper	...	3500.00	550.00	315.00
71	30¢ Franklin, Orange	625.00	335.00	75.00	43.50
72	90¢ Washington, Blue	1375.00	750.00	225.00	125.00

1861-66 New Vals. or Designs, Perf. 12 (VF, OG+150%, VF+100% OG+50%) (C)

		Unused Fine	Ave.	Used Fine	Ave.
73	2¢ Jackson, Black	165.00	85.00	25.00	12.50
75	5¢ Jefferson, Red Brn.	2150.00	1200.00	260.00	150.00
76	5¢ Brown	500.00	300.00	70.00	42.50
77	15¢ Lincoln, Black	650.00	375.00	75.00	45.00
78	24¢ Washington, Lilac/Gray Lilac	425.00	240.00	52.50	30.00

1867 Designs of 1861-66 with Grills of Var. Sizes (VF, OG+150%, VF+100%OG+50%) (C)

Grills consist of small pyramids impressed on the stamp and are classified by area,
shape of points and number of rows of points. On Grilled-All-Over and "C" Grills, points thrust
upward on FACE of stamp; on all other grills points thrust upward on BACK of stamp. Points of
"Z" grill show horizontal ridges (-); other grills from "D" through "I" show vertical (I) ridges or
come to a point. It is important to see a Scott catalog for details of these interesting stamps.

1867 "A" Grill (Grill All Over)

		Unused Fine	Ave.	Used Fine	Ave.
79	3¢ Washington, Rose	...	1500.00	525.00	300.00

1867 "C" Grill 13 x 16mm Points Up

		Unused Fine	Ave.	Used Fine	Ave.
83	3¢ Washington, Rose	3250.00	1700.00	475.00	265.00

1867 "D" Grill 12 x 14mm Points Down

		Unused Fine	Ave.	Used Fine	Ave.
84	2¢ Jackson, Black	...	5500.00	1375.00	800.00
85	3¢ Washington, Rose	2750.00	1550.00	385.00	225.00

1867 "Z" Grill 11 x 14mm

		Unused Fine	Ave.	Used Fine	Ave.
85B	2¢ Jackson, Black	2850.00	1650.00	425.00	240.00
85C	3¢ Washington, Rose	...	3000.00	1250.00	750.00
85E	12¢ Washington, Black	4000.00	2350.00	600.00	350.00

1867 "E" Grill 11 x 13mm

		Unused Fine	Ave.	Used Fine	Ave.
86	1¢ Franklin, Blue	1100.00	625.00	240.00	140.00
87	2¢ Jackson, Black	525.00	300.00	67.50	37.50
88	3¢ Washington, Rose	375.00	200.00	12.00	6.95
89	10¢ Washington, Green	1800.00	1050.00	175.00	100.00
90	12¢ Washington, Black	2000.00	1200.00	200.00	115.00
91	15¢ Lincoln, Black	3950.00	2100.00	395.00	225.00

1867 "F" Grill 9 x 13mm

		Unused Fine	Ave.	Used Fine	Ave.
92	1¢ Franklin, Blue	485.00	300.00	90.00	50.00
93	2¢ Jackson, Black	200.00	110.00	25.00	13.50
94	3¢ Washington, Red	165.00	95.00	3.50	1.95
95	5¢ Jefferson, Brown	1400.00	775.00	325.00	200.00
96	10¢ Wash., Yellow Green	1150.00	625.00	110.00	65.00
97	12¢ Washington, Black	1275.00	700.00	125.00	75.00
98	15¢ Lincoln, Black	1350.00	750.00	160.00	90.00
99	24¢ Washington, Gray Lilac	2000.00	1100.00	375.00	235.00
100	30¢ Franklin, Orange	2600.00	1500.00	365.00	225.00
101	90¢ Washington, Blue	4000.00	2250.00	835.00	475.00

#102-11 ARE 1875 RE-ISSUES OF THE 1861-66 ISSUE.

2

1869 Pictorial Issues-"G" Grill 9½ mm. (VF,OG+125%, VF+75%, OG+25%) (C)

| 112,123,133 | 113,124 | 114 | 115 | 116 |

| 117 | 119 | 120 | 121 | 122 |

Scott's		Unused		Used	
No.		Fine	Ave.	Fine	Ave.
112	1¢ Franklin, Buff	250.00	140.00	65.00	37.50
113	2¢ Horse & Rider, Brown	210.00	125.00	25.00	14.00
114	3¢ Locomotive, Ultramarine	150.00	85.00	6.75	3.75
115	6¢ Washington, Ultramarine	925.00	535.00	95.00	55.00
116	10¢ Shield & Eagle, Yellow	950.00	550.00	85.00	50.00
117	12¢ "S.S. Adriatic", Green	875.00	500.00	95.00	55.00
118	15¢ Columbus, Brn & Blue,Ty.I	2500.00	1450.00	325.00	195.00
119	15¢ Brown & Blue, Type II	1000.00	575.00	150.00	85.00
120	24¢ Decl. of Indep., Grn & Vio	2800.00	1600.00	425.00	240.00
121	30¢ Shield, Eagle & Flags	2650.00	1500.00	275.00	160.00
122	90¢ Lincoln, Carm. & Black	4500.00	2500.00	1100.00	700.00

1875 and 1880 Re-issues, without Grill (VF,OG+125%, VF+75%, OG+20%) (C)

123	1¢ Buff, Hard White Paper	290.00	165.00	200.00	115.00
124	2¢ Brown, Hard White Paper	325.00	175.00	295.00	165.00
133	1¢ Buff, Soft Porous Paper (1880)	175.00	100.00	140.00	77.50
133a	1¢ Brown Orange, w/o gum	160.00	110.00	125.00	70.00

#126-32 ARE 1875 RE-ISSUES OF THE 1869 ISSUE.

1870-71 Nat'l Print-Grilled-Hard Paper (VF,OG+125%, VF+75%, OG+25%) (C)

| 134/206 | 135/183 | 136/214 | 179,185 | 137/208 |

| 138,149,160 | 139/209 | 141/189 | 143/217 | 144/218 |

134	1¢ Franklin, Ultramarine	795.00	485.00	60.00	33.50
135	2¢ Jackson, Red Brown	475.00	250.00	40.00	22.50
136	3¢ Washington, Green	325.00	180.00	12.50	7.00
137	6¢ Lincoln, Carmine	1850.00	1050.00	275.00	165.00
138	7¢ Stanton, Vermilion	1300.00	750.00	225.00	135.00
139	10¢ Jefferson, Brown	2000.00	1150.00	425.00	250.00
140	12¢ Clay, Dull Violet		...	...	1100.00
141	15¢ Webster, Orange		1500.00	650.00	375.00
143	30¢ Hamilton, Black	3500.00	900.00	525.00	
144	90¢ Perry, Carmine	...	4000.00	875.00	500.00

1870-71 Same as above but without Grill (VF,OG+125%, VF+75% OG+25%) (C)

145	1¢ Franklin, Ultramarine	185.00	110.00	8.00	4.75
146	2¢ Jackson, Red Brown	150.00	85.00	5.00	3.00
147	3¢ Washington, Green	150.00	85.00	.85	.50
148	6¢ Lincoln, Carmine	285.00	160.00	12.50	7.25
149	7¢ Stanton, Vermilion	350.00	195.00	55.00	30.00
150	10¢ Jefferson, Brown	325.00	180.00	13.50	8.00
151	12¢ Clay, Dull Violet	675.00	375.00	65.00	38.50
152	15¢ Webster, Bright Orange	650.00	365.00	80.00	47.50
153	24¢ Scott, Purple	650.00	365.00	80.00	47.50
154	30¢ Hamilton, Black	1600.00	900.00	100.00	60.00
155	90¢ Perry, Carmine	1575.00	900.00	165.00	95.00

PRIOR TO 1882, UNUSED PRICES ARE FOR STAMPS WITH PARTIAL OR NO GUM, FOR ORIGINAL GUM, ADD % PREMIUM INDICATED IN ( ).

1870-71 National Print - Without Secret Marks

| 1¢ | 2¢ | 3¢ | 6¢ | 7¢ | 10¢ | 12¢ |

Arrows point to distinguishing characteristics: 1¢ ball is clear; 2¢ no spot of color; 3¢ light shading; 6¢ normal vertical lines; 7¢ no arcs of color cut around lines; 10¢ ball is clear; 12¢ normal 2.

1873 Continental Print-White Hard Paper (VF,OG+100%,VF+75%OG+20%)(C)
Same designs as preceding issue but with secret marks as shown below.

Arrows point to distinguishing characteristics: 1¢ dash in ball; 2¢ spot of color where lines join in scroll ornaments; 3¢ under part of ribbon heavily shaded; 6¢ first four vertical lines strengthened; 7¢ arcs of color cut around lines; 10¢ a crescent in the ball; 12¢ ball of 2 is crescent shaped.

Scott's		Unused		Used	
No.		Fine	Ave.	Fine	Ave.
156	1¢ Franklin, Ultramarine	110.00	67.50	2.00	1.15
157	2¢ Jackson, Brown	185.00	105.00	10.75	6.25
158	3¢ Washington, Green	67.50	37.50	.28	.18
159	6¢ Lincoln, Dull Pink	235.00	130.00	10.75	6.25
160	7¢ Stanton, Org. Vermilion	500.00	275.00	50.00	27.50
161	10¢ Jefferson, Brown	325.00	190.00	12.00	7.25
162	12¢ Clay, Blackish Violet	825.00	465.00	65.00	37.50
163	15¢ Webster, Yellow Orange	800.00	450.00	62.50	35.00
165	30¢ Hamilton, Gray Black	950.00	550.00	60.00	32.50
166	90¢ Perry, Rose Carmine	1350.00	775.00	160.00	95.00

1875-Continental Print-Yellowish Hard Paper (VF,OG+100%, VF+75% OG+20%) (C)

178	2¢ Jackson, Vermilion	180.00	105.00	5.50	3.25
179	5¢ Taylor, Blue	230.00	135.00	9.00	5.00

1879 American Prtg. - Continental Design, Soft Porous Paper (VF,OG+100%, VF + 75% OG + 20%) (C)

Soft porous paper is less transparent than hard paper. When held to the light it usually appears mottled, somewhat like newsprint.

182	1¢ Franklin, Dark Ultramarine	135.00	75.00	1.60	.95
183	2¢ Jackson, Vermilion	70.00	40.00	1.60	.95
184	3¢ Washington, Green	55.00	31.50	.22	.15
185	5¢ Taylor, Blue	275.00	135.00	8.75	5.00
186	6¢ Lincoln, Pink	465.00	265.00	12.50	7.50
187	10¢ Brown (no secret mark)	925.00	500.00	17.50	10.75
188	10¢ Brown (secret mark)	700.00	400.00	16.50	10.00
189	15¢ Webster, Red Orange	170.00	95.00	16.50	10.00
190	30¢ Hamilton, Full Black	500.00	275.00	37.50	21.75
191	90¢ Perry, Carmine	1150.00	675.00	150.00	85.00

#166-77,180-81,192-204 ARE 1875-80 RE-ISSUES.

| 212 | 210,213 | 211,215 | 205,216 |

1882 New Design (VF NH+75%, VF OG & Used+50%) (C)

Scott's		NH	Unused,OG		Used	
No.		Fine	Fine	Ave.	Fine	Ave.
205	5¢ Garfield, Yel. Brn.	210.00	130.00	75.00	4.75	2.75

1881-82 Re-engraved Designs (VF NH+75%, VF OG & Used+60%) (C)

206	1¢ Franklin, Gray Blue	55.00	35.00	20.00	.50	.30
207	3¢ Washington, Blue Grn	65.00	42.50	25.00	.28	.18
208	6¢ Lincoln, Rose (1882)	395.00	250.00	140.00	45.00	25.00
208a	6¢ Brown Red (1883)	350.00	225.00	125.00	52.50	30.00
209	10¢ Jefferson, Brown (1882)	135.00	85.00	50.00	2.50	1.40
209b	10¢ Black Brown	265.00	165.00	95.00	14.75	8.75

1883-88 New Designs or Colors (VF NH+75%, VF OG & Used + 60%) (C)

210	2¢ Washington Red Brn	47.50	30.00	17.50	.22	.15
211	4¢ Jackson, Blue Green	210.00	135.00	75.00	6.50	3.75
212	1¢ Franklin, Ultramarine (1887)	90.00	57.50	30.00	.80	.50
213	2¢ Washington, Green (1887)	37.50	23.50	13.50	.27	.18
214	3¢ Wash., Vermilion (1887)	65.00	42.50	25.00	30.00	18.50
215	4¢ Jackson, Carmine (1888)	210.00	135.00	70.00	11.50	7.00
216	5¢ Garfield, Indigo (1888)	210.00	135.00	70.00	6.50	3.75
217	30¢ Hamilton, Orange Brn('88)	475.00	300.00	180.00	65.00	35.00
218	90¢ Perry, Purple (1888)	1100.00	725.00	425.00	140.00	80.00

#205C, 211B and 211D are Special Printings

1890-1893 No Triangles (VF Used + 50%) (C)

| 219 | 219D,220 | 221 | 222 | 223 |

| 224 | 225 | 226 | 227 | 228 |

Scott's No.		VF	NH F-VF	Unused VF	F-VF	Used F-VF
219	1¢ Franklin, Dull Blue	37.50	21.50	22.50	15.00	.20
219D	2¢ Washington, Lake	315.00	185.00	190.00	125.00	.50
220	2¢ Carmine	30.00	19.00	19.50	13.00	.20
220a	2¢ Cap on left "2"	90.00	55.00	57.50	37.50	1.50
220c	2¢ Cap on both "2's"	260.00	160.00	165.00	110.00	10.00
221	3¢ Jackson, Purple	115.00	70.00	67.50	45.00	4.50
222	4¢ Lincoln, Dark Brn	115.00	70.00	67.50	45.00	1.75
223	5¢ Grant, Chocolate	115.00	70.00	67.50	45.00	1.75
224	6¢ Garfield, Brn Red	125.00	75.00	72.50	47.50	13.50
225	8¢ Sherman, Lilac (1893)	85.00	50.00	55.00	35.00	8.50
226	10¢ Webster, Green	215.00	135.00	140.00	90.00	2.10
227	15¢ Clay, Indigo	310.00	195.00	200.00	130.00	14.75
228	30¢ Jefferson, Black	515.00	300.00	315.00	200.00	17.00
229	90¢ Perry, Orange	715.00	450.00	450.00	300.00	80.00

1893 Columbian Issue (VF Used + 50%) (B)

| 230 | 231 | 232 |

| 237 | 239 | 245 |

230	1¢ Blue	42.50	27.50	27.50	17.50	.35
231	2¢ Violet	40.00	25.00	26.00	16.50	.20
231v	2¢ Violet, "Broken Hat" 3rd person to left of Columbus has a triangular "cut" in his hat	130.00	75.00	80.00	50.00	.50
232	3¢ Green	100.00	60.00	65.00	40.00	11.75
233	4¢ Ultramarine	150.00	90.00	95.00	57.50	5.50
234	5¢ Chocolate	160.00	100.00	110.00	65.00	6.00
235	6¢ Purple	150.00	90.00	100.00	57.50	17.00
236	8¢ Magenta	120.00	77.50	75.00	50.00	7.00
237	10¢ Black Brown	235.00	140.00	150.00	92.50	5.50
238	15¢ Dark Green	425.00	250.00	250.00	160.00	47.50
239	30¢ Orange Brown	550.00	325.00	350.00	215.00	65.00
240	50¢ Slate Blue	900.00	550.00	525.00	350.00	120.00
241	$1 Salmon	2500.00	1600.00	1600.00	1000.00	435.00
242	$2 Brown Red	2600.00	1650.00	1650.00	1050.00	395.00
243	$3 Yellow Green	4200.00	2600.00	2500.00	1675.00	725.00
244	$4 Crimson Lake	5500.00	3500.00	3500.00	2250.00	975.00
245	$5 Black	6500.00	4150.00	4000.00	2650.00	1100.00

1894 Issue - Triangles - No Watermark (VF Used + 75%) (C)

| 246/279 | 252/279B | 253,268 | 254,269,280 | 255,270,281 |

| 256,271,282 | 258/283 | 259,274,284 | 261,276 | 262,277 |

Scott's No.		VF	NH F-VF	Unused VF	F-VF	Used F-VF
246	1¢ Franklin, Ultramarine	45.00	27.00	27.50	18.00	3.25
247	1¢ Blue	100.00	65.00	67.50	45.00	1.75
248	2¢ Wash., Pink, Tri. I	35.00	21.00	21.00	14.00	2.50
249	2¢ Carmine Lake, Tri. I	225.00	135.00	135.00	90.00	1.75
250	2¢ Carmine, Triangle I	40.00	26.00	25.00	17.00	.30
251	2¢ Carmine, Triangle II	325.00	210.00	210.00	140.00	2.75
252	2¢ Carmine, Triangle III	200.00	120.00	125.00	80.00	3.00
253	3¢ Jackson, Purple	160.00	92.50	90.00	60.00	6.50
254	4¢ Lincoln, Dark Brown	195.00	115.00	110.00	72.50	3.00
255	5¢ Grant, Chocolate	160.00	92.50	90.00	60.00	3.65
256	6¢ Garfield, Dull Brown	240.00	160.00	150.00	100.00	16.50
257	8¢ Sherman, Violet Brn	215.00	135.00	130.00	87.50	11.00
258	10¢ Webster, Dark Grn	340.00	215.00	210.00	140.00	7.75
259	15¢ Clay, Dark Blue	415.00	270.00	275.00	175.00	35.00
260	50¢ Jefferson, Orange	650.00	395.00	400.00	260.00	70.00
261	$1 Perry, Black, Type I	1350.00	850.00	825.00	550.00	200.00
261A	$1 Black, Type II	3500.00	2200.00	2150.00	1450.00	425.00
262	$2 Madison, Bright Blue	4500.00	2800.00	2700.00	1800.00	625.00
263	$5 Marshall, Dark Green	6250.00	4000.00	4000.00	2650.00	1150.00

Triangle Varieties on the 2¢ Stamps

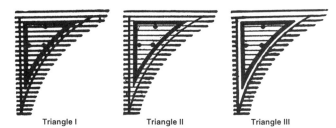

| Triangle I | Triangle II | Triangle III |

TRIANGLE I - The horizontal background lines run across the triangle and are of the same thickness within the triangle as the background lines.
TRIANGLE II - Horizontal lines cross the triangle but are thinner within the triangle than the background lines.
TRIANGLE III - The horizontal lines do not cross the triangle and the lines within the triangle are as thin as in Triangle II.

Circle Varieties on the $1 Stamps

| Type I | Type II |

Types of $1.00 stamps. Type I, the circles enclosing "$1" are broken where they meet the curved lines below "One Dollar." Type II, the circles are complete.

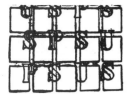

This illustration shows a block of 15 with the Double Line watermark. Since only 90 letters were used per 100 stamps, they appear in various positions on the stamps.

1895 Same Designs - Double Line Wmk. (VF Used + 50%) (C)

Scott's No.		VF	NH F-VF	Unused VF	F-VF	Used F-VF
264	1¢ Franklin, Blue	11.50	7.25	7.00	4.75	.20
265	2¢ Wash., Carmine, Tri.I	50.00	32.00	31.50	21.00	.70
266	2¢ Carmine, Triangle II	45.00	28.50	27.50	18.75	2.75
267	2¢ Carmine, Triangle III	8.50	5.50	5.50	3.65	.20
268	3¢ Jackson, Purple	60.00	38.75	38.50	25.75	.90
269	4¢ Lincoln, Dark Brown	57.50	38.00	38.00	25.00	1.25
270	5¢ Grant, Chocolate	60.00	38.75	38.50	25.75	1.50
271	6¢ Garfield, Dull Brown	125.00	80.00	77.50	52.50	3.75
272	8¢ Sherman, Violet Brn	90.00	57.50	57.50	37.50	1.00
273	10¢ Webster, Dark Green	115.00	72.50	72.50	47.50	1.20
274	15¢ Clay, Dark Blue	335.00	215.00	210.00	140.00	8.50
275	50¢ Jefferson, Orange	435.00	280.00	275.00	185.00	17.50
276	$1 Perry, Black, Type I	1000.00	650.00	635.00	425.00	52.50
276A	$1 Black, Type II	2000.00	1300.00	1250.00	850.00	120.00
277	$2 Madison, Bright Blue	1700.00	1150.00	1125.00	750.00	250.00
278	$5 Marshall, Dark Green	3500.00	2300.00	2250.00	1500.00	350.00

1898 NEW Colors - Double Line Wmk. (VF Used + 50%) (C)

No.		VF	F-VF	VF	F-VF	Used
279	1¢ Franklin, Green	16.50	10.75	10.50	7.00	.20
279B	2¢ Wash., Red, Tri.III	16.50	10.75	10.50	7.00	.20
279Bc	2¢ Rose Carmine, Tri. III	350.00	230.00	225.00	150.00	90.00
279Bd	2¢ Orange Red, Tri. III	17.75	11.75	11.50	7.50	.25
279Be	2¢ Bklt. Pane of 6, Tri. III	675.00	450.00	475.00	315.00	...
280	4¢ Lincoln, Rose Brown	52.50	32.50	32.50	21.75	.80
281	5¢ Grant, Dark Blue	57.50	37.50	38.00	25.00	.70
282	6¢ Garfield, Lake	77.50	50.00	48.50	32.50	2.00
282a	6¢ Purplish Lake	110.00	70.00	67.50	45.00	2.75
282C	10¢ Webster, Brn., Type I	295.00	190.00	185.00	125.00	2.25
283	10¢ Orange Brn., Type II	190.00	120.00	115.00	75.00	1.80
284	15¢ Clay, Olive Green	265.00	170.00	165.00	110.00	6.50

1898 Trans-Mississippi Issue (VF Used + 50%) (B)

285   286   288

290   292   293

285	1¢ Marquette, Green	47.50	30.00	31.50	21.00	4.65
286	2¢ Farming, Copper Red	42.50	26.50	27.00	18.00	1.15
287	4¢ Indian, Orange	235.00	145.00	150.00	100.00	17.50
288	5¢ Fremont, Dull Blue	235.00	145.00	150.00	100.00	16.50
289	8¢ Wagon Train, Vio. Brn.	300.00	200.00	195.00	130.00	32.50
290	10¢ Emigration, Gray Vio.	300.00	200.00	195.00	130.00	17.50
291	50¢ Mining, Sage Green	1150.00	700.00	675.00	450.00	130.00
292	$1 Cattle in Storm, Black	2300.00	1500.00	1400.00	950.00	400.00
293	$2 Bridge, Orange Brn.	3900.00	2500.00	2300.00	1600.00	650.00

1901 Pan-American Issue VF Used + 50% (B)

294   295   297   299

294-99	Set of 6	885.00	585.00	565.00	385.00	95.00
294	1¢ Steamship, Grn. & Blk.	35.00	22.50	22.50	15.00	2.75
295	2¢ Train, Carmine & Blk.	35.00	22.50	22.50	15.00	.85
296	4¢ Auto, Choc. & Blk.	150.00	100.00	90.00	65.00	13.00
297	5¢ Bridge, Ultra & Black	165.00	110.00	110.00	75.00	12.50
298	8¢ Canal, Brn. Vio & Blk.	220.00	150.00	140.00	95.00	45.00
299	10¢ Steamship, Brn. & Blk.	325.00	215.00	210.00	140.00	22.50

1902-03 Issue Perf. 12 VF Used + 50% (C)

300   301   302   304   306

308   310   312,479   313,480   319

Scott's No.		VF	NH F-VF	Unused VF	F-VF	Used F-VF
300	1¢ Franklin, Blue Green	13.50	9.00	8.75	6.00	.18
300b	1¢ Booklet Pane of 6	900.00	600.00	625.00	425.00	...
301	2¢ Washington, Carmine	18.00	12.00	12.50	8.25	.18
301c	2¢ Booklet Pane of 6	850.00	575.00	585.00	395.00	...
302	3¢ Jackson, Bright Violet	80.00	52.50	55.00	35.00	2.25
303	4¢ Grant, Brown	90.00	57.50	57.50	37.50	1.00
304	5¢ Lincoln, Blue	90.00	57.50	57.50	37.50	1.15
305	6¢ Garfield, Claret	105.00	70.00	67.50	45.00	2.00
306	8¢ M. Wash., Violet Black	65.00	42.50	42.50	28.50	1.60
307	10¢ Webster, Red Brown	90.00	60.00	60.00	40.00	1.15
308	13¢ B. Harrison, Purp. Black	65.00	42.50	42.50	28.50	6.50
309	15¢ Clay, Olive Green	225.00	150.00	150.00	100.00	4.50
310	50¢ Jefferson, Orange	650.00	425.00	415.00	275.00	20.00
311	$1 Farragut, Black	1100.00	750.00	750.00	500.00	45.00
312	$2 Madison, Dark Blue	1600.00	1075.00	1050.00	700.00	140.00
313	$5 Marshall, Dark Green	4250.00	2800.00	2800.00	1850.00	525.00

1906-08 Same Designs, Imperforate VF Used + 30% (B)

314	1¢ Franklin, Blue Green	37.50	27.50	25.00	18.50	14.50
315	5¢ Lincoln, Blue	650.00	525.00	500.00	350.00	450.00

* Genuinely used examples of #315 are rare. Copies should have contemporary cancels and be purchased with, or subject to, a certificate of authenticity.

1903 Shield Issue, Perforated 12 VF Used + 50% (C)

319	2¢ Carmine, Die I	8.50	5.75	5.50	3.75	.15
319g	2¢ Booklet Pane of 6, D.I	200.00	135.00	140.00	95.00	...
319f	2¢ Lake, Die II	16.50	10.50	10.50	7.00	.40
319h	2¢ Booklet Pane of 6, D.II	285.00	200.00	210.00	140.00	...

1906 Shield Issue, Imperforate VF Used + 30% (B)

320	2¢ Carmine, Die I	35.00	26.50	24.00	18.00	13.50
320a	2¢ Lake, Die II	100.00	70.00	65.00	47.50	35.00

1904 Louisiana Purchase Issue VF Used + 50% (B)

323   325   327

323-27	Set of 5	635.00	425.00	425.00	280.00	69.50
323	1¢ Livingston, Green	45.00	30.00	30.00	20.00	3.50
324	2¢ Jefferson, Carmine	42.50	27.50	27.50	18.50	1.25
325	3¢ Monroe, Violet	135.00	90.00	90.00	60.00	25.00
326	5¢ McKinley, Blue	165.00	105.00	110.00	70.00	17.50
327	10¢ Map, Brown	285.00	190.00	185.00	125.00	25.00

1907 Jamestown Issue VF Used + 75% (C)

328   329   330

328-30	Set of 3	300.00	185.00	195.00	120.00	27.50
328	1¢ John Smith, Green	45.00	26.50	30.00	17.50	3.00
329	2¢ Jamestown, Carmine	57.50	35.00	37.50	22.50	2.75
330	5¢ Pocahontas, Blue	215.00	130.00	140.00	85.00	22.50

PLATE BLOCKS

Scott #	NH VF	NH F-VF	Unused F-VF	Scott #	NH VF	NH F-VF	Unused F-VF
294 (6)	400.00	275.00	180.00	319 (6)	120.00	80.00	55.00
295 (6)	400.00	275..00	180.00	320 (6)	300.00	235.00	170.00
300 (6)	230.00	150.00	110.00	323	240.00	160.00	115.00
301 (6)	275.00	185.00	125.00	324	250.00	165.00	120.00
314 (6)	250.00	185.00	125.00	328 (6)	365.00	225.00	160.00
				329 (6)	525.00	315.00	225.00

1908-09 Wash-Franklins Double Line Wmk. - Perf. 12 VF Used + 50% (B)

| 331,357,374 | 332/519 | 333/541 | 338/381 | 342 |

Scott's No.	VF	NH F-VF	Unused VF	F-VF	Used F-VF
331	1¢ Franklin, Green	13.50	8.75	8.50	5.50	.15
331a	1¢ Booklet Pane of 6	250.00	175.00	195.00	130.00	...
332	2¢ Washington, Carmine	12.50	8.00	7.75	5.00	.15
332a	2¢ Booklet Pane of 6	240.00	150.00	170.00	115.00	...
333	3¢ Deep Violet	52.50	35.00	35.00	23.50	2.15
334	4¢ Orange Brown	65.00	42.50	42.50	27.50	.90
335	5¢ Blue	80.00	52.50	51.50	35.00	1.75
336	6¢ Red Orange	95.00	65.00	62.50	42.50	4.50
337	8¢ Olive Green	75.00	50.00	48.50	32.50	2.25
338	10¢ Yellow	120.00	80.00	77.50	52.50	1.25
339	13¢ Blue Green	77.50	50.00	48.50	32.50	17.50
340	15¢ Ultramarine	105.00	70.00	67.50	45.00	5.00
341	50¢ Violet	500.00	350.00	325.00	225.00	15.00
342	$1 Violet Brown	850.00	535.00	525.00	350.00	65.00

1908-09 Series, Double Line Wmk. - Imperf. VF Used + 30% (B)

		VF	NH F-VF	Unused VF	F-VF	Used F-VF
343	1¢ Franklin, Green	9.75	7.50	7.50	5.50	3.50
344	2¢ Washington, Carmine	12.00	9.50	9.50	7.00	2.75
345	3¢ Deep Violet	26.50	20.00	20.00	15.00	16.50
346	4¢ Orange Brown	45.00	33.50	33.75	25.00	19.50
347	5¢ Blue	66.50	51.50	51.50	38.50	28.75

PLATE BLOCKS

Scott #	VF	NH F-VF	Unused F-VF	Scott #	VF	NH F-VF	Unused F-VF
331 (6)	95.00	65.00	45.00	343 (6)	85.00	65.00	45.00
332 (6)	95.00	65.00	45.00	344 (6)	135.00	100.00	75.00
333 (6)	400.00	275.00	195.00	345 (6)	265.00	210.00	160.00

1908-10 Coils, Double Line Wmk. - Perf. 12 Horiz. VF Used + 50% (C)

		VF	NH F-VF	Unused VF	F-VF	Used F-VF
348	1¢ Franklin, Green	40.00	28.50	30.00	20.00	10.50
349	2¢ Washington, Carmine	75.00	52.50	52.50	35.00	7.00
350	4¢ Orange Brown	180.00	120.00	125.00	80.00	65.00
351	5¢ Blue	200.00	135.00	135.00	90.00	80.00

(#348-351 Pairs are valued at 2.3 x the single price.)

1909 Coils, Double Line Wmk. - Perf. 12 Vert. VF Used + 50% (C)

		VF	NH F-VF	Unused VF	F-VF	Used F-VF
352	1¢ Franklin, Green	97.50	65.00	67.50	45.00	27.50
353	2¢ Washington, Carmine	95.00	62.50	65.00	42.50	7.00
354	4¢ Orange Brown	220.00	150.00	150.00	100.00	47.50
355	5¢ Blue	235.00	160.00	165.00	110.00	65.00
356	10¢ Yellow	...	2000.00	2250.00	1500.00	P.O.R.

(#352-356 Unused Pairs are valued at 3 x the single price.)
(#348-56, 385-89 should be purchased with, or subject to, a certificate of authenticity.)

LINE PAIRS

Scott #	VF	NH F-VF	Unused F-VF	Scott #	VF	NH F-VF	Unused F-VF
348	335.00	220.00	150.00	352	675.00	465.00	325.00
349	525.00	365.00	260.00	353	675.00	465.00	325.00

1909 "Blue Papers", Double Line Wmk., Perf. 12 VF Used + 60% (B)

		VF	NH F-VF	Unused VF	F-VF	Used F-VF
357	1¢ Franklin, Green	190.00	115.00	120.00	75.00	75.00
358	2¢ Washington, Carmine	180.00	110.00	115.00	70.00	65.00
359	3¢ Deep Violet	...	2250.00	2500.00	1450.00	...
361	5¢ Blue	...	5000.00	...	3350.00	...
362	6¢ Red Orange	...	1500.00	1850.00	1075.00	950.00
364	10¢ Yellow	...	1750.00	2150.00	1250.00	1000.00
365	13¢ Blue Green	...	3000.00	...	2150.00	...
366	15¢ Pale Ultramarine	...	1400.00	1700.00	1000.00	900.00

* Blue Papers, which were printed on experimental paper with approximately 35% rag content, actually have a grayish appearance which can best be observed by looking at the stamps from the gum side. Additionally, the watermark is more clearly visible than on the stamps printed on regular paper (#331-340). The stamps are also noted for having carbon specks imbedded in the texture of the paper.

* Blue Papers should be purchased with, or subject to, a certificate of authenticity. Genuinely used Blue Papers, other than the 1¢, 2¢ & 13¢ values, are extremely rare. Examples should have contemporary cancels.

NOTE: PLATE BLOCKS, AND OTHER BLOCKS, ARE ALL BLOCKS OF 4 UNLESS OTHERWISE INDICATED IN ( ).
NOTE: VF UNUSED PLATE BLOCKS AND LINE PAIRS ARE GENERALLY AVAILABLE AT THE RESPECTIVE F-VF NH PRICE.

1909 Commems. (Used) Perf. VF + 40% - Imperf. VF + 30% (B)

| 367,369 | 370 | 372 |

Scott's No.	VF	NH F-VF	Unused VF	F-VF	Used F-VF
367	2¢ Lincoln, Perf. 12	10.50	7.25	7.00	4.75	1.60
368	2¢ Lincoln, Imperf.	40.00	30.00	30.00	22.50	17.50
369	2¢ Bluish Paper, Perf. 12	375.00	260.00	265.00	175.00	175.00
370	2¢ Alaska-Yukon, Perf. 12	15.00	10.75	10.75	7.00	1.50
371	2¢ Alaska-Yukon, Imperf.	57.50	42.50	40.00	30.00	21.50
372	2¢ Hudson-Fulton, Perf. 12	20.00	14.50	13.50	10.00	3.25
373	2¢ Hudson-Fulton, Imperf.	65.00	50.00	47.50	35.00	21.50

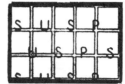

1910-11 Single Line Wmk. Perf 12 VF Used + 50% (B)

(Same designs as 1908-1909 Series)

This illustration shows a block of 15 stamps with the Single Line Watermark. The watermark appears in various positions on the stamps.

		VF	NH F-VF	Unused VF	F-VF	Used F-VF
374	1¢ Franklin, Green	12.00	7.50	8.25	5.50	.18
374a	1¢ Booklet Pane of 6	235.00	150.00	165.00	110.00	...
375	2¢ Washington, Carmine	11.00	7.00	7.50	5.25	.18
375a	2¢ Booklet Pane of 6	200.00	130.00	140.00	95.00	...
376	3¢ Deep Violet	31.50	20.00	20.00	13.75	1.35
377	4¢ Brown	45.00	29.50	30.00	20.00	.45
378	5¢ Blue	45.00	29.50	30.00	20.00	.45
379	6¢ Red Orange	62.50	39.50	39.50	26.50	.75
380	8¢ Olive Green	190.00	125.00	130.00	85.00	11.00
381	10¢ Yellow	185.00	120.00	130.00	80.00	3.50
382	15¢ Pale Ultramarine	425.00	280.00	300.00	200.00	13.50

1911 Single Line Wmk., Imperf. VF Used + 30% (B)

		VF	NH F-VF	Unused VF	F-VF	Used F-VF
383	1¢ Franklin, Green	5.25	4.00	3.50	2.75	2.50
384	2¢ Washington, Carmine	8.75	6.50	6.00	4.75	2.75

PLATE BLOCKS

Scott #	VF	NH F-VF	Unused F-VF	Scott #	VF	NH F-VF	Unused F-VF
367 (6)	180.00	130.00	90.00	374 (6)	125.00	85.00	60.00
368 (6)	285.00	215.00	160.00	375 (6)	125.00	85.00	60.00
370 (6)	325.00	250.00	165.00	376 (6)	250.00	175.00	120.00
371 (6)	365.00	275.00	210.00	377 (6)	300.00	210.00	140.00
372 (6)	450.00	335.00	225.00	378 (6)	375.00	260.00	175.00
373 (6)	425.00	335.00	250.00	383 (6)	70.00	52.50	40.00
				384 (6)	175.00	140.00	100.00

1910 Coils S. Line Wmk. - Perf. 12 Horiz. VF Used + 50% (C)

		VF	NH F-VF	Unused VF	F-VF	Used F-VF
385	1¢ Franklin, Green	42.50	28.50	29.50	19.50	12.00
386	2¢ Washington, Carmine	77.50	52.50	52.00	35.00	14.50

1910-11 Coils S. Line Wmk. - Perf. 12 Vert. VF Used + 50% (C)

		VF	NH F-VF	Unused VF	F-VF	Used F-VF
387	1¢ Franklin, Green	180.00	120.00	120.00	80.00	32.50
388	2¢ Washington, Carmine	1100.00	750.00	850.00	550.00	225.00
389	3¢ Washington, Deep Violet	...	...	USED FINE		6750.00

(Examples of #388 and 389 must be purchased with, or subject to, a certificate of authenticity.)

1910 Coils S. Line Wmk. - Perf. 8½ Horizontally VF Used + 50% (B)

		VF	NH F-VF	Unused VF	F-VF	Used F-VF
390	1¢ Franklin, Green	9.00	6.25	6.25	4.25	4.50
391	2¢ Washington, Carmine	57.50	38.75	39.50	26.50	9.50

1910-13 Coils S. Line Wmk. - Perf. 8½ Vertically VF Used + 50% (B)

		VF	NH F-VF	Unused VF	F-VF	Used F-VF
392	1¢ Franklin, Green	38.75	26.50	26.50	17.50	17.50
393	2¢ Washington, Carmine	77.50	52.50	52.50	35.00	7.50
394	3¢ Deep Violet	95.00	65.00	65.00	45.00	45.00
395	4¢ Brown	95.00	65.00	65.00	45.00	45.00
396	5¢ Blue	95.00	65.00	65.00	45.00	45.00

Unused Coil Pairs are valued as follows:

#385, 387 @ 3 x a single, #386, 388 @ 3.5 x a single, #390-396 @ 2.5 x a single.

LINE PAIRS

Scott #	VF	NH F-VF	Unused F-VF	Scott #	VF	NH F-VF	Unused F-VF
385	485.00	325.00	225.00	392	215.00	145.00	100.00
386	895.00	575.00	395.00	393	320.00	225.00	150.00
387	675.00	450.00	300.00	394	425.00	325.00	225.00
390	47.50	32.00	22.50	395	425.00	325.00	225.00
391	295.00	200.00	135.00	396	425.00	325.00	225.00

1913 Panama-Pacific, Perf. 12 VF Used + 50% (B)

397,401	398,402	399,403	400,400A,404

Scott's No.	NH VF	NH F-VF	Unused VF	Unused F-VF	Used F-VF
397-400A Set of 5	695.00	475.00	475.00	330.00	41.50
397	1¢ Balboa, Green	30.00	20.00	20.00	13.50	1.25
398	2¢ Panama Canal, Carmine	30.00	20.00	21.00	14.00	.40
399	5¢ Golden Gate, Blue	125.00	82.50	82.50	55.00	8.00
400	10¢ San Fran., Orange Yel.	215.00	145.00	150.00	100.00	20.00
400A	10¢ Orange	335.00	230.00	225.00	165.00	15.00

1914-15 Panama-Pacific, Perf. 10 VF Used + 50% (B)

Scott's No.	NH VF	NH F-VF	Unused VF	Unused F-VF	Used F-VF
401-04 Set of 4	1875.00	1275.00	1300.00	925.00	70.00
401	1¢ Balboa, Green	45.00	30.00	30.00	20.00	5.25
402	2¢ Panama, Carmine (1915)	130.00	87.50	85.00	57.50	1.40
403	5¢ Golden Gate, Blue(1915)	260.00	175.00	180.00	120.00	13.50
404	10¢ San Fran.,Orange(1915)	1500.00	1050.00	1075.00	750.00	55.00

1912-14 Single Line Wmk. - Perf. 12 VF Used + 50% (B)

405/545	406/546	337/380	419/515	423/518

NOTE: THE 1¢ TO 7¢ STAMPS FROM 1912-21 PICTURE WASHINGTON. THE 8¢ TO $5 STAMPS PICTURE FRANKLIN.

Scott's No.	NH VF	NH F-VF	Unused VF	Unused F-VF	Used F-VF
405	1¢ Washington, Green	10.50	6.75	6.75	4.50	.18
405b	1¢ Booklet Pane of 6	125.00	87.50	90.00	60.00	...
406	2¢ Carmine	9.75	6.25	6.00	4.00	.18
406a	2¢ Booklet Pane of 6	130.00	87.50	90.00	60.00	...
407	7¢ Black (1914)	135.00	90.00	90.00	60.00	7.50

1912 Single Line Wmk. - Imperf. VF Used + 30% (B)

		NH VF	NH F-VF	Unused VF	Unused F-VF	Used F-VF
408	1¢ Washington, Green	2.10	1.60	1.40	1.10	.55
409	2¢ Carmine	2.35	1.80	1.65	1.25	.55

PLATE BLOCKS

Scott #	NH VF	NH F-VF	Unused F-VF	Scott #	NH VF	NH F-VF	Unused F-VF
397 (6)	225.00	150.00	100.00	405 (6)	100.00	70.00	50.00
398 (6)	350.00	240.00	175.00	406 (6)	135.00	90.00	65.00
401 (6)	450.00	295.00	210.00	408 (6)	30.00	22.50	15.75
				409 (6)	50.00	39.50	27.50

1912 Coils Single Line Wmk. - Perf. 8½ Horiz. VF Used + 50% (B)

		NH VF	NH F-VF	Unused VF	Unused F-VF	Used F-VF
410	1¢ Washington, Green	11.00	7.50	7.75	5.25	4.25
411	2¢ Carmine	15.00	10.00	10.50	7.00	4.25

1912 Coils Single Line Wmk. - Perf. 8½ Vert. VF Used + 50% (B)

		NH VF	NH F-VF	Unused VF	Unused F-VF	Used F-VF
412	1¢ Washington, Green	45.00	29.50	29.50	20.00	5.75
413	2¢ Carmine	75.00	50.00	48.50	32.50	1.10

(#410-413 Unused Pairs are valued at 2.5 x the single price.)

LINE PAIRS

Scott #	NH VF	NH F-VF	Unused F-VF	Scott #	NH VF	NH F-VF	Unused F-VF
410	55.00	36.50	25.00	412	160.00	110.00	75.00
411	75.00	50.00	33.50	413	325.00	210.00	150.00

1912-14 Franklin Design. Single Line Wmk. - Perf. 12 VF Used + 50% (B)

		NH VF	NH F-VF	Unused VF	Unused F-VF	Used F-VF
414	8¢ Franklin, Olive Green	70.00	45.00	45.00	30.00	1.20
415	9¢ Salmon Red (1914)	90.00	57.50	60.00	40.00	11.75
416	10¢ Orange Yellow	75.00	46.50	47.50	31.50	.35
417	12¢ Claret Brown (1914)	85.00	53.50	55.00	36.50	3.95
418	15¢ Gray	135.00	90.00	90.00	60.00	3.50
419	20¢ Ultramarine (1914)	315.00	200.00	200.00	135.00	14.50
420	30¢ Orange Red (1914)	230.00	150.00	150.00	100.00	14.75
421	50¢ Violet (1914)	700.00	475.00	485.00	325.00	17.50

* #421 usually shows an offset on the back; #422 usually does not.

1912 Franklin Design. Double Line Wmk. - Perf. 12 VF Used + 50% (B)

		NH VF	NH F-VF	Unused VF	Unused F-VF	Used F-VF
422	50¢ Franklin, Violet	500.00	325.00	315.00	210.00	17.50
423	$1 Violet Brown	875.00	585.00	600.00	400.00	55.00

1914-15 Flat Press Single Line Wmk., Perf. 10 VF Used + 50% (B)

Scott's No.	NH VF	NH F-VF	Unused VF	Unused F-VF	Used F-VF
424	1¢ Washington, Green	6.00	3.75	3.75	2.50	.18
424d	1¢ Booklet Pane of 6	7.75	5.25	5.25	3.50	...
425	2¢ Rose Red	5.00	3.00	3.00	2.00	.15
425e	2¢ Booklet Pane of 6	45.00	30.00	29.50	20.00	...
426	3¢ Deep Violet	27.50	17.50	17.50	11.50	1.50
427	4¢ Brown	62.50	40.00	40.00	27.50	.60
428	5¢ Blue	55.00	36.50	38.50	25.00	.55
429	6¢ Red Orange	90.00	60.00	60.00	40.00	1.50
430	7¢ Black	160.00	100.00	100.00	67.50	4.50
431	8¢ Franklin, Olive Green	70.00	46.50	46.50	31.50	1.65
432	9¢ Salmon Red	95.00	57.50	57.50	38.50	9.00
433	10¢ Orange Yellow	90.00	56.50	56.50	37.50	.35
434	11¢ Dark Green (1915)	41.50	26.50	27.50	18.50	7.50
435	12¢ Claret Brown	52.50	32.50	32.50	21.50	3.85
435a	12¢ Copper Red	57.50	37.50	37.50	25.00	4.25
437	15¢ Gray	215.00	140.00	145.00	97.50	7.50
438	20¢ Ultramarine	375.00	240.00	250.00	165.00	3.75
439	30¢ Orange Red	475.00	295.00	325.00	210.00	18.50
440	50¢ Violet (1915)	1050.00	750.00	700.00	495.00	18.50

PLATE BLOCKS

Scott #	NH VF	NH F-VF	Unused F-VF	Scott #	NH VF	NH F-VF	Unused F-VF
424 (6)	70.00	45.00	30.00	428 (6)	550.00	365.00	275.00
425 (6)	47.50	30.00	20.00	429 (6)	650.00	435.00	300.00
"COIL STAMPS" Impt. & Pl.# Blk. / 10				431 (6)	750.00	525.00	375.00
424 CS (10)	200.00	140.00	95.00	434 (6)	385.00	260.00	180.00
425 CS (10)	230.00	160.00	110.00	435 (6)	435.00	290.00	215.00
426 (6)	285.00	200.00	140.00	435a (6)	500.00	350.00	250.00
427 (6)	800.00	550.00	400.00				

1914 Coils Flat Press S.L Wmk. - Perf. 10 Horiz. VF Used + 50% (B)

		NH VF	NH F-VF	Unused VF	Unused F-VF	Used F-VF
441	1¢ Washington, Green	2.15	1.50	1.60	1.10	1.10
442	2¢ Carmine	17.50	11.75	11.50	8.00	7.50

1914 Coils Flat Press S.L Wmk. - Perf. 10 Vert. VF Used + 50% (B)

		NH VF	NH F-VF	Unused VF	Unused F-VF	Used F-VF
443	1¢ Washington, Green	44.50	29.50	29.00	19.50	6.25
444	2¢ Carmine	62.50	42.00	42.50	28.50	1.50
445	3¢ Violet	425.00	280.00	300.00	200.00	110.00
446	4¢ Brown	250.00	170.00	160.00	110.00	42.50
447	5¢ Blue	90.00	60.00	62.50	42.50	30.00

(#441-447 Unused Pairs are valued at 2.5 x the single price.)

The two top stamps are Rotary Press while the underneath stamps are Flat Press. Note that the designs of the Rotary Press stamps are a little longer or wider than Flat Press stamps. Flat Press stamps usually show spots of color on back.

Perf. Horizontally	Perf. Vertically

1915 Coils Rotary S.L. Wmk. - Perf. 10 Horiz. VF Used + 50% (B)

		NH VF	NH F-VF	Unused VF	Unused F-VF	Used F-VF
448	1¢ Washington, Green	14.00	9.00	9.00	6.00	3.75
449	2¢ Red, Type I	...	...	3000.00	1800.00	300.00
450	2¢ Carmine, Type III	22.00	14.00	14.00	9.50	3.75

1914-16 Coils Rotary S.L. Wmk. - Perf. 10 Vert. VF Used + 50% (B)

		NH VF	NH F-VF	Unused VF	Unused F-VF	Used F-VF
452	1¢ Washington, Green	21.50	13.50	13.50	9.00	2.25
453	2¢ Carm. Rose, Type I	210.00	140.00	140.00	95.00	3.75
454	2¢ Red, Type II (1915)	175.00	120.00	120.00	80.00	9.50
455	2¢ Carmine, Type III (1915)	21.00	13.00	13.50	9.00	.95
456	3¢ Violet (1916)	450.00	300.00	325.00	210.00	95.00
457	4¢ Brown (1916)	52.50	35.00	37.50	25.00	16.75
458	5¢ Blue (1916)	59.50	40.00	42.50	28.50	16.75

(#448,450,452-58 Unused Pairs are valued at 2.5% x the single price.)

LINE PAIRS

Scott #	NH VF	NH F-VF	Unused F-VF	Scott #	NH VF	NH F-VF	Unused F-VF
441	13.50	9.00	6.00	452	125.00	85.00	57.50
442	90.00	60.00	40.00	453	925.00	625.00	425.00
443	240.00	170.00	115.00	454	850.00	575.00	375.00
444	365.00	230.00	155.00	455	100.00	67.50	45.00
447	425.00	280.00	185.00	457	265.00	175.00	120.00
448	75.00	52.50	35.00	458	315.00	210.00	140.00
450	110.00	75.00	50.00				

NOTE: VF UNUSED PLATE BLOCKS AND LINE PAIRS ARE GENERALLY AVAILABLE AT THE RESPECTIVE F-VF NH PRICE.

1914 Imperf. Coil Rotary Press S.L. Wmk. - VF Used + 30% (B)

Scott's No.	NH VF	NH F-VF	Unused VF	Unused F-VF	Used F-VF
459 2¢ Washington, Carmine	650.00	500.00	450.00	350.00	700.00

* Genuinely used examples of #459 are rare. Copies should have contemporary cancels and be purchased with, or subject to, a certificate of authenticity.

1915 Flat Press Double Line Wmk. - Perf. 10 VF Used + 75% (B)

	NH VF	NH F-VF	Unused VF	Unused F-VF	Used F-VF
460 $1 Franklin, Violet Black	1350.00	975.00	975.00	675.00	75.00

1915 Flat Press S. Line Wmk. - Perf. 11 VF Used + 100% (B)

	NH VF	NH F-VF	Unused VF	Unused F-VF	Used F-VF
461 2¢ Pale Carmine Red	250.00	135.00	165.00	90.00	195.00

(Counterfeits of #461 are common. Purchase with, or subject to, a certificate.)

1916-17 Flat Press, No Wmk. - Perf. 10 (VF Used + 50%) (B)

	NH VF	NH F-VF	Unused VF	Unused F-VF	Used F-VF
462 1¢ Washington, Green	13.00	8.25	8.25	5.50	.30
462a 1¢ Booklet Pane of 6	20.00	12.50	13.50	9.00	...
463 2¢ Carmine	9.00	5.50	5.00	3.75	.25
463a 2¢ Booklet Pane of 6	160.00	110.00	100.00	75.00	...
464 3¢ Violet	150.00	90.00	90.00	60.00	12.50
465 4¢ Orange Brown	85.00	52.50	55.00	37.50	1.75
466 5¢ Blue	140.00	87.50	90.00	60.00	1.75
467 5¢ Carmine ERROR	1050.00	750.00	750.00	500.00	650.00
467 5¢ Single in Block of 9	1350.00	950.00	950.00	700.00	...
467 5¢ Pair in Block of 12	2500.00	2000.00	1450.00	1375.00	...
468 6¢ Red Orange	175.00	110.00	110.00	72.50	7.00
469 7¢ Black	215.00	135.00	135.00	90.00	10.00
470 8¢ Franklin, Olive Green	100.00	67.50	72.50	47.50	5.75
471 9¢ Salmon Red	110.00	65.00	67.50	45.00	13.50
472 10¢ Orange Yellow	200.00	125.00	125.00	82.50	1.10
473 11¢ Dark Green	65.00	42.50	45.00	30.00	17.50
474 12¢ Claret Brown	90.00	55.00	57.50	38.50	5.00
475 15¢ Gray	340.00	215.00	220.00	150.00	9.75
476 20¢ Ultramarine	440.00	275.00	275.00	190.00	10.75
477 50¢ Light Violet (1917)	1825.00	1295.00	1250.00	895.00	55.00
478 $1 Violet Black	1175.00	850.00	850.00	575.00	15.00

1917 Flat Press, No Wmk.-Perf. 10, Designs of 1902-3 VF used 35% (B)

	NH VF	NH F-VF	Unused VF	Unused F-VF	Used F-VF
479 $2 Madison, Dark Blue	625.00	425.00	425.00	300.00	40.00
480 $5 Marshall, Light Green	475.00	335.00	325.00	225.00	45.00

NOTE: #479 & 480 have the same designs as #312 & 313

1916-17 Flat Press, No Wmk. - Imperforate VF Used + 30% (B)

	NH VF	NH F-VF	Unused VF	Unused F-VF	Used F-VF
481 1¢ Washington, Green	1.50	1.20	1.10	.90	.80
482 2¢ Carmine, Type I	2.35	1.80	1.65	1.30	1.20
483 3¢ Violet, Type I (1917)	21.00	17.00	16.50	13.00	7.50
484 3¢ Violet, Type II (1917)	17.00	14.00	12.00	10.00	4.75

*3¢ Type I, the 5th line from the left of the toga rope is broken or missing;
3¢ Type II, the 5th line is complete. See Scott for more details.

PLATE BLOCKS

Scott #	NH VF	NH F-VF	Unused F-VF	Scott #	NH VF	NH F-VF	Unused F-VF
462 (6)	270.00	180.00	120.00	481 (6)	19.50	15.75	11.50
463 (6)	225.00	150.00	100.00	482 (6)	33.50	27.00	20.00
473 (6)	575.00	400.00	275.00	483 (6)	185.00	150.00	115.00
474 (6)	1025.00	700.00	475.00	484 (6)	155.00	125.00	90.00

PLATE BLOCKS

1916-19 Coils Rotary, No Wmk. - Perf. 10 Horiz. VF Used + 40% (B)

	NH VF	NH F-VF	Unused VF	Unused F-VF	Used F-VF
486 1¢ Washington, Green (1918)	1.50	1.10	1.00	.75	.20
487 2¢ Carmine, Type II	29.50	20.00	19.50	13.75	4.25
488 2¢ Carmine, Type III (1919)	5.85	4.00	3.90	2.75	1.50
489 3¢ Violet, Type I (1917)	9.00	6.00	5.50	4.00	1.35

1916-22 Coils, Rotary, No Wmk. - Perf. 10 Vert. VF Used + 40% (B)

	NH VF	NH F-VF	Unused VF	Unused F-VF	Used F-VF
490 1¢ Washington, Green	1.20	.80	.75	.55	.20
491 2¢ Carmine, Type II	...	...	2300.00	1500.00	750.00
492 2¢ Carmine, Type III	18.00	12.00	11.50	8.00	.20
493 3¢ Violet, Type I (1917)	32.50	24.00	22.50	16.00	2.75
494 3¢ Violet, Type II (1918)	20.00	14.00	14.00	10.00	1.00
495 4¢ Orange Brown (1917)	20.75	14.50	13.75	9.75	3.75
496 5¢ Blue (1919)	6.50	4.50	4.50	3.25	1.00
497 10¢ Franklin, Orng.Yel.(1922)	35.00	25.00	24.50	17.50	10.75

(#486-90, 492-97 Unused Pairs are valued at 2.3 x the single price.)

LINE PAIRS

Scott #	NH VF	NH F-VF	Unused F-VF	Scott #	NH VF	NH F-VF	Unused F-VF
486	7.50	5.25	3.75	493	200.00	150.00	110.00
487	235.00	160.00	110.00	494	105.00	75.00	55.00
488	42.50	25.00	17.50	495	120.00	90.00	65.00
489	60.00	40.00	27.50	496	46.50	33.50	23.50
490	8.25	5.50	3.75	497	215.00	155.00	110.00
492	100.00	72.50	47.50				

NOTE: PRIOR TO 1935, TO DETERMINE VERY FINE USED PRICE, ADD VF% AT BEGINNING OF EACH SET TO THE APPROPRIATE FINE PRICE. MINIMUM 10¢ PER STAMP.

FOR INFORMATION CONCERNING VERY FINE SEE PAGE II

1917-19 Flat Press, No Watermark - Perf. 11 VF Used + 50% (B)

Scott's No.	NH VF	NH F-VF	Unused VF	Unused F-VF	Used F-VF
498 1¢ Washington, Green	.90	.60	.65	.45	.20
498e 1¢ Booklet Pane of 6	5.25	3.50	3.75	2.50	...
499 2¢ Carmine, Ty. I	.85	.55	.55	.40	.20
499e 2¢ Booklet Pane of 6	9.75	6.50	6.50	4.35	...
500 2¢ Deep Rose, Ty. Ia	375.00	285.00	275.00	190.00	160.00
501 3¢ Light Violet, Type I	22.00	14.50	15.00	10.00	.20
501b 3¢ Booklet Pane of 6	115.00	80.00	82.50	55.00	...
502 3¢ Dark Violet, Type II	29.00	19.00	19.50	13.00	.35
502b 3¢ Booklet Pane of 6 (1918)	85.00	57.50	62.50	45.00	...
503 4¢ Brown	22.50	15.00	15.00	10.00	.25
504 5¢ Blue	17.50	12.00	12.00	8.00	.25
505 5¢ Rose ERROR	725.00	525.00	525.00	375.00	450.00
505 5¢ ERROR in Block of 9	950.00	700.00	750.00	550.00	...
505 5¢ Pair in Block of 12	1650.00	1200.00	1250.00	900.00	...
506 6¢ Red Orange	26.50	17.00	16.50	11.50	.35
507 7¢ Black	52.50	35.00	35.00	23.50	1.00
508 8¢ Franklin, Olive Bistre	24.00	16.00	16.00	11.00	.80
509 9¢ Salmon Red	27.50	18.00	18.50	12.50	2.00
510 10¢ Orange Yellow	35.00	23.00	24.00	15.75	.18
511 11¢ Light Green	18.00	12.00	11.00	8.25	2.75
512 12¢ Claret Brown	18.00	12.00	11.00	8.25	.50
513 13¢ Apple Green (1919)	21.50	14.50	14.75	9.75	5.75
514 15¢ Gray	72.50	45.00	47.50	32.50	1.00
515 20¢ Light Ultramarine	95.00	62.50	65.00	42.50	.35
516 30¢ Orange Red	77.50	50.00	50.00	33.50	1.00
517 50¢ Red Violet	125.00	85.00	87.50	60.00	.70
518 $1 Violet Brown	110.00	72.50	75.00	50.00	1.60
518b $1 Deep Brown	...	1600.00	1500.00	1000.00	675.00

PLATE BLOCKS

Scott #	NH VF	NH F-VF	Unused F-VF	Scott #	NH VF	NH F-VF	Unused F-VF
498 (6)	28.50	19.00	13.50	509 (6)	240.00	170.00	120.00
499 (6)	28.50	19.00	13.50	510 (6)	310.00	210.00	150.00
501 (6)	165.00	110.00	75.00	511 (6)	195.00	135.00	100.00
502 (6)	230.00	155.00	110.00	512 (6)	195.00	135.00	100.00
503 (6)	230.00	155.00	110.00	513 (6)	215.00	150.00	110.00
504 (6)	210.00	140.00	100.00	514 (6)	825.00	575.00	425.00
506 (6)	275.00	190.00	135.00	515 (6)	950.00	650.00	475.00
507 (6)	400.00	280.00	200.00	516 (6)	950.00	650.00	475.00
508 (6)	250.00	170.00	120.00				

1917 Same Design as #332, D.L. Wmk. - Perf. 11 VF Used + 100% (C)

	NH VF	NH F-VF	Unused VF	Unused F-VF	Used F-VF
519 2¢ Washington, Carmine	575.00	350.00	385.00	250.00	425.00

(* Mint and used copies of #519 have been extensively counterfeited. Examples of either should be purchased with, or subject to, a certificate of authenticity.)

523,547   524   537

1918 Flat Press, No Watermark, Perf. 11 VF Used + 40% (B)

	NH VF	NH F-VF	Unused VF	Unused F-VF	Used F-VF
523 $2 Franklin,Orng. Red & Blk.	1150.00	850.00	850.00	600.00	190.00
524 $5 Deep Green & Black	450.00	310.00	295.00	210.00	29.50

1918-20 Offset Printing, Perforated 11 VF Used + 40% (B)

	NH VF	NH F-VF	Unused VF	Unused F-VF	Used F-VF
525 1¢ Washington, Gray Grn.	3.50	2.60	2.50	1.75	.65
526 2¢ Carmine, Type IV (1920)	45.00	32.50	30.00	22.50	3.75
527 2¢ Carmine, Type V (1920)	28.00	20.00	18.00	13.50	.95
528 2¢ Carmine, Type Va (1920)	15.00	10.50	10.50	7.50	.25
528A 2¢ Carmine, Type VI (1920)	80.00	60.00	57.50	40.00	1.25
528B 2¢ Carmine, Type VII (1920)	33.75	25.00	22.50	16.00	.30
529 3¢ Violet, Type III	5.50	3.75	3.35	2.50	.25
530 3¢ Purple, Type IV	2.25	1.60	1.50	1.15	.18

1918-20 Offset Printing, Imperforate VF Used + 30% (B)

	NH VF	NH F-VF	Unused VF	Unused F-VF	Used F-VF
531 1¢ Washington, Green (1919)	15.00	12.50	11.00	9.00	8.00
532 2¢ Carmine Rose, Type IV (20)	50.00	42.50	38.50	32.50	27.50
533 2¢ Carmine, Type V (1920)	290.00	240.00	210.00	175.00	75.00
534 2¢ Carmine, Type Va (1920)	18.00	15.00	13.50	10.75	7.00
534A 2¢ Carmine, Type VI (1920)	50.00	42.50	36.50	30.00	20.00
534B 2¢ Carmine, Type VII (1920)	1850.00	1650.00	1350.00	1000.00	525.00
535 3¢ Violet, Type IV	14.50	11.50	11.00	8.00	5.00

1919 Offset Printing, Perforated 12½ VF Used + 75% (B)

	NH VF	NH F-VF	Unused VF	Unused F-VF	Used F-VF
536 1¢ Washington, Gray Grn	27.50	17.50	18.75	12.50	15.00

PLATE BLOCKS

Scott #	NH VF	NH F-VF	Unused F-VF	Scott #	NH VF	NH F-VF	Unused F-VF
525 (6)	28.50	20.00	15.00	530 (6)	25.00	17.75	13.75
526 (6)	325.00	230.00	170.00	531 (6)	110.00	85.00	60.00
527 (6)	225.00	160.00	115.00	532 (6)	450.00	365.00	265.00
528 (6)	115.00	85.00	...	534 (6)	130.00	100.00	75.00
528A (6)	595.00	450.00	325.00	534A (6)	465.00	385.00	275.00
528B (6)	235.00	180.00	125.00	535 (6)	97.50	67.50	52.50
529 (6)	70.00	50.00	35.00	536 (6)	260.00	175.00	125.00

DALE Enterprises, Inc.
P.O. Box 539-BG
Emmaus, PA 18049-0539
U.S.A.

Offers you 'lots'
to choose from.

For monthly Price List &
Mail Sales Send this card or
call (610) 433-3303 or
FAX (610) 965-6089

For a free sample magazine and
information about membership
in America's national philatelic
society send the attached card
or contact:

**American Philatelic Society
P.O. Box 8000, Dept. TB
State College, PA 16803
Phone: (814) 237-3803
FAX: (814) 237-6128**

SEND FOR YOUR FREE COPY!

TO REALLY
ENJOY STAMP
COLLECTING!

YES! Please send a FREE sample copy of *The American Philatelist* and an illustrated membership brochure describing APS member services. The sample is yours absolutely free - nothing to cancel! You may apply for membership, including a magazine subscription, only by completing the membership application. **PLEASE PRINT:**

Name _____

Address _____

_____

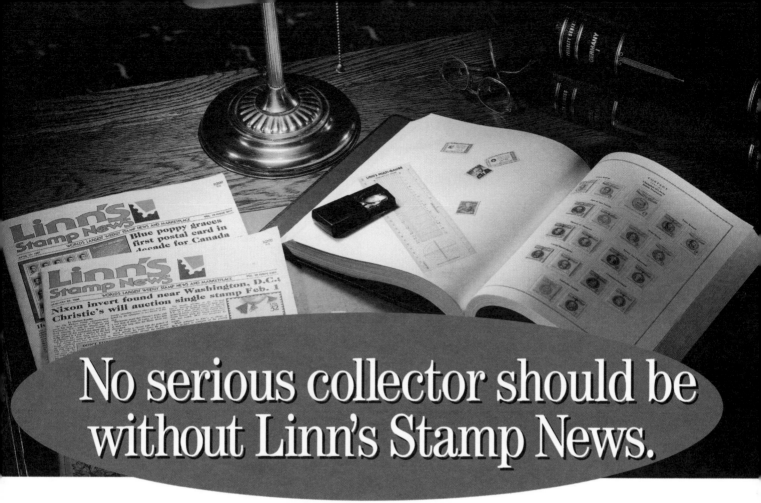

No serious collector should be without Linn's Stamp News.

Miss an issue of Linn's and you miss plenty:

- All the latest-breaking news from Linn's exclusive national and international sources.

- In-depth analysis from top authors on all aspects of collecting, including pricing trends, values, news issues, forgeries, security and more.

- Regular features you can't afford to miss — *Stamp Market Index, Stamp Market Tips* and *Tip of the Week, Collectors' Forum, Editor's Choice, Readers' Opinions, Postmark Pursuit, Collectors' Workshop, Refresher Course* and much more

- The world's largest stamp marketplace. Listings of events, auctions and sales. Classified ads and readers' notices for buying, selling and trading.

Right now you can receive Linn's at the special introductory rate of only $9.95... plus get a bonus refresher manual to help jump start your own collection. Linn's *Stamp Collecting Made Easy...* is yours **FREE** with your paid, introductory subscription.

Your **FREE** refresher course will take you on a simplified tour of the techniques, terms and intricacies of stamp collecting. We'll show you how to buy stamps, how to sort, soak, catalog, store and mount them.

We'll explain terms like roulette, souvenir sheet, overprint and surcharge. You'll learn the right way to use a perforation gauge.

Linn's is researched, written and published by stamp collectors like you. And we understand you want to get the most fun and satisfaction from your collecting.

Mail the card on the left and receive the special introductory rate of 13 issues for $9.95. You'll save over 60% off the regular price plus get our money back guarantee. We'll also send you FREE, Linn's 96-page, all illustrated: *STAMP COLLECTING MADE EASY* with your paid order.

P.O. Box 29, Sidney, OH 45365

Guarantee: Receive a complete refund if you are not completely satisfied at any time.

1919 Victory Issue VF Used + 50% (B)

Scott's No.	NH VF	NH F-VF	Unused VF	Unused F-VF	Used F-VF
537 3¢ Violet	20.00	12.50	11.50	7.50	3.00
537a 3¢ Deep Red Violet	700.00	475.00	500.00	335.00	125.00
537c 3¢ Red Violet	80.00	52.50	55.00	37.50	12.75

1919-21 Rotary Press Printing - Various Perfs. VF Used + 75% (C)

	NH VF	NH F-VF	Unused VF	Unused F-VF	Used F-VF
538 1¢ Wash. Perf. 11x10	19.50	11.00	11.50	7.50	7.50
538a 1¢ Vert. Pr. Imperf. Horiz.	85.00	57.50	67.50	45.00	100.00
539 2¢ Car. Rose, Ty. II, Pf. 11x10	...	...	...	2500.00	...
540 2¢ Car. Rose,T.III, Pf.11x10	23.50	13.50	13.50	9.00	8.00
540a 2¢ Vert. Pr., Imperf. Horiz.	85.00	57.50	67.50	45.00	100.00
541 3¢ Violet, Perf. 11x10	72.50	42.50	42.50	27.50	29.50
542 1¢ Green, Perf. 10x11 (1920)	25.00	15.00	15.00	9.50	.95
543 1¢ Green, Perf. 10 (1921)	1.20	.70	.75	.45	.20
544 1¢ Perf. 11 (19x22½ mm) (1922)	...	...	...	...	2400.00
545 1¢ Pf.11 (19½x22 mm) (21)	295.00	165.00	175.00	110.00	115.00
546 2¢ Carmine Rose, Pf.11 (21)	195.00	115.00	125.00	75.00	100.00

1920 Flat Press, No Watermark, Perf. 11 VF Used + 40% (B)

	NH VF	NH F-VF	Unused VF	Unused F-VF	Used F-VF
547 $2 Franklin, Carm. & Blk.	375.00	260.00	250.00	175.00	35.00

1920 Pilgrim Issue VF Used + 40% (B)

548 549 550

	NH VF	NH F-VF	Unused VF	Unused F-VF	Used F-VF
548-50 Set of 3	82.50	60.00	61.50	42.75	15.75
548 1¢ Mayflower, Green	7.00	5.00	4.85	3.50	2.40
549 2¢ Landing, Car. Rose	10.75	7.75	7.50	5.25	1.75
550 5¢ Compact, Deep Blue	67.50	48.50	50.00	35.00	12.00

PLATE BLOCKS

Scott #	NH VF	NH F-VF	Unused F-VF	Scott #	NH VF	NH F-VF	Unused F-VF
537 (6)	170.00	110.00	70.00	542 (6)	250.00	175.00	120.00
538	150.00	95.00	67.50	543 (4)	22.50	15.00	10.00
538a	1050.00	800.00	600.00	543 (6)	50.00	36.50	25.00
540	160.00	100.00	70.00	548 (6)	67.50	47.50	35.00
540a	900.00	675.00	500.00	549 (6)	85.00	62.50	45.00
541	500.00	350.00	235.00	550 (6)	675.00	515.00	365.00

1922-25 Regular Issue, Flat Press, Perf. 11 VF Used + 40% (B)

551,653   553/633   556/636   562/642   566,696

567,698   570,701   572   573

	VF	F-VF	Unused VF	Unused F-VF	Used F-VF
551 ½¢ Hale, Olive Brn ('25)	.35	.25	.30	.20	.15
552 1¢ Franklin, Green ('23)	2.70	2.00	1.90	1.35	.15
552a 1¢ Booklet Pane of 6	13.00	9.00	9.00	6.50	...
553 1½¢ Harding, Yel. Brn. ('25)	5.50	3.85	3.50	2.50	.25
554 2¢ Wash. Carmine ('23)	3.65	2.50	2.40	1.70	.15
554c 2¢ Booklet Pane of 6	16.50	12.00	11.00	7.75	...
555 3¢ Lincoln, Violet ('23)	33.50	24.75	22.75	16.50	1.00
556 4¢ M. Wash., Yel. Brn. ('23)	33.50	24.75	22.75	16.50	.25
557 5¢ T. Roosevelt, Dk. Blue	33.50	24.75	22.75	16.50	.18
558 6¢ Garfield, Red Orange	56.50	42.50	41.50	30.00	.75
559 7¢ McKinley, Black ('23)	15.00	11.00	10.50	7.50	.65
560 8¢ Grant, Ol.Grn. ('23)	75.00	55.00	50.00	37.50	.20
561 9¢ Jefferson, Rose ('23)	28.75	21.50	20.75	15.00	1.10
562 10¢ Monroe, Orange ('23)	42.50	29.50	27.50	19.50	.20
563 11¢ Hayes, Greenish Blue	2.70	2.00	1.90	1.35	.40
564 12¢ Cleveland, Br. Vio. ('23)	15.00	11.00	10.00	7.25	.20
565 14¢ Indian, Blue ('23)	9.00	6.25	6.00	4.25	.70
566 15¢ Liberty, Gray	43.50	30.00	29.75	21.75	.20
567 20¢ Golden Gate,C.Rose ('23)	43.50	30.00	29.75	21.75	.20
567 25¢ Niagara Falls, Yel. Grn.	35.00	26.50	25.00	17.50	.65
569 30¢ Buffalo, Ol Brown ('23)	62.50	45.00	42.50	30.00	.45
570 50¢ Amphitheater, Lilac	105.00	75.00	70.00	50.00	.20
571 $1 Lincoln, Vio. Blk. (1923)	80.00	58.50	56.50	42.50	.50
572 $2 Capitol, Blue (1923)	185.00	140.00	135.00	97.50	9.50
573 $5 Carmine & Blue (1923)	350.00	260.00	250.00	195.00	12.50

1922-25 Regular Issue, Flat Press, Perf. 11

PLATE BLOCKS

Scott #	NH VF	NH F-VF	Unused F-VF	Scott #	NH VF	NH F-VF	Unused F-VF
551 (6)	8.00	5.75	4.00	561 (6)	240.00	175.00	130.00
552 (6)	30.00	22.50	16.50	562 (6)	275.00	200.00	140.00
553 (6)	45.00	32.50	22.50	563 (6)	40.00	29.50	21.50
554 (6)	31.00	22.50	16.50	564 (6)	130.00	100.00	75.00
555 (6)	240.00	170.00	120.00	565 (6)	80.00	60.00	45.00
556 (6)	240.00	170.00	120.00	566 (6)	350.00	275.00	200.00
557 (6)	270.00	190.00	135.00	567 (6)	350.00	275.00	200.00
558 (6)	525.00	385.00	275.00	568 (6)	300.00	225.00	160.00
559 (6)	100.00	70.00	50.00	569 (6)	400.00	300.00	200.00
560 (6)	825.00	600.00	425.00	571 (6)	625.00	450.00	335.00

1923-25 Flat Press - Imperforate VF Used + 25% (B)

Scott's No.	NH VF	NH F-VF	Unused VF	Unused F-VF	Used F-VF
575 1¢ Franklin, Green	12.00	9.00	9.00	7.00	4.00
576 1½¢ Harding, Yel. Brn. (1925)	2.50	2.00	1.80	1.40	1.30
577 2¢ Washington, Carmine	2.50	2.00	2.00	1.40	1.35

1923 Rotary Press, Perforated 11 x 10 VF Used + 75% (C)

	NH VF	NH F-VF	Unused VF	Unused F-VF	Used F-VF
578 1¢ Franklin, Green	160.00	95.00	110.00	65.00	100.00
579 2¢ Washington, Carmine	125.00	70.00	87.50	50.00	90.00

1923-26 Rotary Press, Perforated 10 VF Used + 50% (B)

	NH VF	NH F-VF	Unused VF	Unused F-VF	Used F-VF
581-91 Set of 11	270.00	190.00	190.00	130.00	16.50
581 1¢ Franklin, Green	15.00	10.00	10.00	7.00	.90
582 1½¢ Harding, Brown (1925)	7.50	5.00	5.25	3.50	.90
583 2¢ Wash., Carmine (1924)	3.75	2.50	2.50	1.75	.25
583a 2¢ Booklet Pane of 6	140.00	100.00	95.00	65.00	...
584 3¢ Lincoln, Violet (1925)	40.00	26.50	26.50	18.50	2.25
585 4¢ M. Wash., Yel Brn (1925)	26.50	18.00	18.50	12.50	.70
586 5¢ T. Roos., Blue (1925)	26.50	18.00	18.50	12.50	.30
587 6¢ Garfield, Red Or. (1925)	12.50	8.25	8.50	5.75	.60
588 7¢ McKinley, Blk. (1926)	18.00	12.50	12.75	8.50	6.00
589 8¢ Grant, Ol. Grn. (1926)	40.00	26.50	27.50	18.50	3.75
590 9¢ Jefferson, Rose (1926)	8.50	5.75	5.95	4.00	2.25
591 10¢ Monroe, Orange (1925)	90.00	65.00	65.00	45.00	.30

PLATE BLOCKS

Scott #	NH VF	NH F-VF	Unused F-VF	Scott #	NH VF	NH F-VF	Unused F-VF
575 (6)	110.00	90.00	65.00	584	300.00	210.00	150.00
576 (6)	26.50	21.00	15.00	585	250.00	175.00	125.00
577 (6)	37.50	27.00	22.50	586	225.00	165.00	115.00
579	850.00	500.00	350.00	587	110.00	77.50	55.00
581	140.00	97.50	67.50	588	120.00	85.00	60.00
582	52.50	35.00	25.00	589	280.00	200.00	140.00
583	31.50	21.75	15.00	590	57.50	40.00	27.50
				591	650.00	450.00	315.00

1923 Rotary Press, Perforated 11 VF Used + 100% (C)

	NH VF	NH F-VF	Unused VF	Unused F-VF	Used F-VF
594 1¢ Franklin, Green	...	...	FINE	USED	3850.00
595 2¢ Washington, Carmine	450.00	250.00	300.00	175.00	225.00

1923-29 Rotary Press Coils, VF Used + 30% (B), (599A VF Used + 75%)

	NH VF	NH F-VF	Unused VF	Unused F-VF	Used F-VF
597-99,600-06 Set of 10	25.95	18.50	18.75	13.95	1.80

Perforated 10 Vertically

	NH VF	NH F-VF	Unused VF	Unused F-VF	Used F-VF
597 1¢ Franklin, Green	.55	.40	.40	.30	.15
598 1½¢ Harding, Brown (1925)	1.10	.85	.85	.65	.20
599 2¢ Washington, Car. Type I	.70	.55	.50	.40	.15
599A 2¢ Carmine, Type II (1929)	225.00	135.00	150.00	100.00	11.00
599A 2¢ Average Quality		80.00	...	60.00	6.75
600 3¢ Lincoln, Violet (1924)	9.50	7.00	6.50	5.00	.25
601 4¢ M. Washington, Yel. Brn	6.50	4.75	4.75	3.50	.40
602 5¢ T. Roos., Dk. Blue (1924)	2.50	1.90	1.75	1.35	.20
603 10¢ Monroe, Orange (1924)	5.95	4.25	4.25	3.15	.20

Perforated 10 Horizontally

	NH VF	NH F-VF	Unused VF	Unused F-VF	Used F-VF
604 1¢ Franklin, Green (1924)	.45	.35	.35	.25	.18
605 1½¢ Harding, Brown (1925)	.45	.35	.35	.25	.20
606 2¢ Washington, Carmine	.45	.35	.35	.25	.20

NOTE: Type I, #599, 634 - No heavy hair lines at top center of head.
Type II, #599A, 634A - Three heavy hair lines at top center of head.

(597-606 Unused Pairs are valued at 2.2 x the single price.)

LINE PAIRS

Scott #	NH VF	NH F-VF	Unused F-VF	Scott #	NH VF	NH F-VF	Unused F-VF
597	3.25	2.40	1.90	601	53.50	40.00	30.00
598	10.00	7.50	5.75	602	17.75	12.95	9.75
599	2.75	2.00	1.60	603	35.00	27.00	21.50
599A	975.00	650.00	500.00	604	5.00	3.75	2.80
599,599A	1100.00	775.00	600.00	605	4.25	3.25	2.50
600	50.00	36.50	27.50	606	3.00	2.25	1.80

NOTE: STAMP ILLUSTRATIONS INDICATE DESIGNS. PERFORATIONS AND TYPES MAY VARY.

1923 Harding Memorial (#610 VF Used + 30%, #612 VF Used + 50%)
Imperf. VF Used + 20% (B)

610-612   614   616

Scott's No.		NH		Unused		Used
		VF	F-VF	VF	F-VF	F-VF
610-12	Set of 3....................	38.50	27.50	28.50	20.00	6.00
610	2¢ Black, Flat Press, Perf. 11	.95	.75	.70	.55	.20
611	2¢ Black, Flat Press Imperf......	11.50	9.00	8.75	6.50	4.50
612	2¢ Black, Rotary, Perf. 10........	28.50	19.50	20.00	14.50	1.75

1924 Huguenot - Walloon Issue VF Used + 30% (B)

614-16	Set of 3................................	63.50	48.50	44.50	33.50	18.00
614	1¢ "New Netherlands"................	5.00	3.65	3.65	2.75	2.75
615	2¢ Fort Orange................	9.00	6.85	6.65	5.00	2.00
616	5¢ Ribault Monument..............	52.50	39.50	36.50	27.00	13.75

617   618   619

1925 Lexington - Concord Issue VF Used + 30% (B)

617-19	Set of 3.............................	56.50	42.50	41.00	31.00	18.00
617	1¢ Cambridge	5.15	3.75	3.65	2.75	2.50
618	2¢ "Birth of Liberty"	9.00	6.85	6.65	5.00	3.50
619	5¢ "Minute Man"	45.00	33.50	32.50	24.50	13.00

PLATE BLOCKS

Scott #		NH	Unused	Scott #		NH	Unused
	VF	F-VF	F-VF		VF	F-VF	F-VF
610 (6)	29.50	22.50	16.50	616 (6)	450.00	335.00	250.00
611 (6)	135.00	110.00	80.00	617 (6)	65.00	50.00	37.50
612	425.00	290.00	200.00	618 (6)	105.00	80.00	60.00
614 (6)	52.50	385.00	28.50	619 (6)	400.00	300.00	225.00
615 (6)	95.00	70.00	52.50				

620   621   622,694   623,697

1925 Norse American VF Used + 30% (B)

620-21	Set of 2....................................	32.75	24.75	24.50	18.50	13.95
620	2¢ Sloop, Carmine & Blk.	7.50	5.50	5.35	4.00	3.00
621	5¢ Viking Ship, Blue & Black ...	27.50	19.75	19.50	15.00	11.50

1925-26 Designs of 1922-25, Flat Press, Perf. 11 VF Used + 40% (B)

622	13¢ Harrison, Green (1926).....	22.50	16.50	17.00	12.00	.55
623	17¢ Wilson, Black	29.50	21.00	20.00	15.00	.30

627   628   629,630

1926 Commemoratives VF Used + 30% (B)

627	2¢ Sesquicentennial	4.25	3.25	3.25	2.50	.45
628	5¢ Ericsson Memorial	10.50	8.00	8.00	5.75	2.50
629	2¢ Battle of White Plains	3.75	2.75	2.65	2.00	1.40
630	2¢ White Plains, Phil. Exhib. Souvenir Sheet of 25	625.00	525.00	500.00	400.00	425.00
630v	2¢ "Dot over S" Var. Sheet	650.00	550.00	525.00	425.00	450.00

1926 Rotary Press, Imperforate VF Used + 20% (B)

631	1½¢ Harding, Brown	3.50	2.80	2.65	2.10	1.85
631v	1½¢ Vert. Pair, Horiz. Gutter	8.50	7.00	6.50	5.50	...
631h	1½¢ Horiz. Pair, Vert. Gutter	8.50	7.00	6.50	5.50	...

FOR INFORMATION CONCERNING VERY FINE SEE PAGE II

PLATE BLOCKS

Scott #		NH	Unused	Scott #		NH	Unused
	VF	F-VF	F-VF		VF	F-VF	F-VF
620 (8)	300.00	230.00	180.00	627 (6)	60.00	47.50	35.00
621 (8)	900.00	700.00	550.00	628 (6)	125.00	95.00	70.00
622 (6)	240.00	170.00	120.00	629 (6)	60.00	47.50	37.50
623 (6)	280.00	210.00	150.00	631	85.00	72.50	52.50

1926-1928 Rotary. Pf. 11x10½, Same as 1922-25 VF Used +30%
(634A VF Used +75%)

Scott's No.		NH		Unused		Used
		VF	F-VF	VF	F-VF	F-VF
632-34,635-42	Set of 11...........	28.75	22.50	22.50	18.00	1.60
632	1¢ Franklin, Green (1927)...........	.35	.25	.30	.20	.15
632a	1¢ Booklet Pane of 6	8.75	6.50	6.75	5.25	...
633	1½¢ Harding, Yel. Brn. (1927)...	3.00	2.30	2.25	1.75	.20
634	2¢ Wash., Carmine, Ty. I	.35	.25	.30	.20	.15
634d	2¢ Booklet Pane of 6 (1927)	2.75	2.10	2.15	1.65	...
634A	2¢ Carmine, Type II (1928)	575.00	350.00	325.00	200.00	12.50
635	3¢ Lincoln, Violet (1927)...........	.70	.55	.55	.45	.18
636	4¢ M. Wash., Yel. Brn. (1927)...	4.25	3.25	3.25	2.50	.18
637	5¢ T. Roos., Dk. Blue (1927)......	3.25	2.50	2.50	2.00	.18
638	6¢ Garfield, Red Or. (1927).......	3.25	2.50	2.50	2.00	.18
639	7¢ McKinley, Black (1927).........	3.25	2.50	2.50	2.00	.18
640	8¢ Grant, Ol. Grn. (1927)..........	3.25	2.50	2.50	2.00	.18
641	9¢ Jefferson, Or. Red (1927)	3.25	2.50	2.50	2.00	.18
642	10¢ Monroe, Or. (1927)	6.00	4.65	4.85	3.75	.20

PLATE BLOCKS

Scott #		NH	Unused	Scott #		NH	Unused
	VF	F-VF	F-VF		VF	F-VF	F-VF
632	3.00	2.25	1.75	637	26.50	20.00	15.00
633	120.00	90.00	65.00	638	26.50	20.00	15.00
634 (4)	2.75	2.25	1.75	639	26.50	20.00	15.00
634 EE (10)	7.50	5.75	4.50	640	26.50	20.00	15.00
635	14.50	11.00	8.00	641	26.50	20.00	15.00
636	120.00	90.00	67.50	642	42.50	31.50	25.00

1927-28 Commemoratives VF Used + 30% (B) (#646-648 VF Used + 50%)

643   644   645   649

643	2¢ Vermont Sesqui	2.00	1.60	1.50	1.20	.90
644	2¢ Burgoyne Campaign	6.25	4.65	4.50	3.50	2.25
645	2¢ Valley Forge (1928)	1.65	1.30	1.25	1.00	.45
646	2¢ "Molly Pitcher" ovpt. (on #634)	2.00	1.35	1.50	1.00	1.00
647	2¢ "Hawaii" ovpt. (on #634)	9.00	6.25	6.75	4.50	4.25
648	5¢ "Hawaii" ovpt. (on #637)	25.00	16.50	18.50	12.50	12.00
649	2¢ Aeronautics (1928)...............	1.95	1.50	1.45	1.10	.90
650	5¢ Aeronautics (1928)...............	8.50	6.50	6.50	5.00	3.00

651   654-656   657   663

1929 Commemorative VF Used + 30% (B)

651	2¢ George Rogers Clark..............	.90	.70	.70	.55	.50

1929 Rotary, Perf. 11x10½, Design of #551 VF Used + 30% (B)

653	½¢ Hale, Olive Brown	.35	.25	.30	.20	.15

1929 Commemoratives VF Used + 30% (B)

654	2¢ Edison, Flat, Perf. 11	1.35	1.00	.95	.75	.65
655	2¢ Edison, Rtry, Perf. 11x10½ ...	1.40	.95	.95	.70	.25
656	2¢ Edison Coil, Perf. 10 Vert	22.50	16.50	16.50	12.50	1.50
657	2¢ Sullivan Expedition	1.20	.90	.90	.70	.60

NOTE: VF UNUSED PLATE BLOCKS AND LINE PAIRS ARE GENERALLY AVAILABLE AT THE RESPECTIVE F-VF NH PRICE.

13

1927-1929 Commemorative & Regular Issues

PLATE BLOCKS & LINE PAIRS

Scott #	NH VF	NH F-VF	Unused F-VF	Scott #	NH VF	NH F-VF	Unused F-VF
643 (6)	58.50	45.00	37.50	650 (6)	95.00	72.50	52.50
644 (6)	60.00	46.50	37.50	651 (6)	17.00	13.50	10.50
645 (6)	46.50	35.00	25.00	653	2.10	1.60	1.20
646	47.50	33.50	25.00	654 (6)	47.50	36.50	27.50
647	200.00	135.00	95.00	655	60.00	45.00	32.50
648	400.00	270.00	200.00	656 Ln. Pr.	100.00	75.00	57.50
649 (6)	22.00	18.00	13.50	657 (6)	38.75	30.00	23.50

KANSAS - NEBRASKA ISSUES

1929 "Kans." Overprints on Stamps #632-42 VF Used + 60% (C)

Scott's No.		VF	NH Fine	Unused VF	Unused Fine	Used Fine
658-68	Set of 11	385.00	250.00	265.00	175.00	130.00
658	1¢ Franklin, Green	3.85	2.50	2.95	1.90	1.50
659	1½¢ Harding, Brown	5.25	3.50	4.00	2.75	2.25
660	2¢ Washington, Carmine	5.25	3.50	4.00	2.75	.80
661	3¢ Lincoln, Violet	30.00	21.00	21.50	14.50	10.00
662	4¢ M. Washington, Yel. Brn	30.00	21.00	21.50	14.50	7.00
663	5¢ T. Roosevelt, Deep Blue	25.00	16.00	18.00	11.00	8.25
664	6¢ Garfield, Red Orange	50.00	32.50	33.50	22.50	13.50
665	7¢ McKinley, Black	50.00	32.50	33.50	22.50	18.00
666	8¢ Grant, Olive Green	145.00	95.00	97.50	65.00	55.00
667	9¢ Jefferson, Light Rose	24.00	16.00	16.50	11.00	9.50
668	10¢ Monroe, Orng. Yel	40.00	26.50	27.00	18.00	10.00

1929 "Nebr." Overprints on Stamps #632-42 VF Used + 60% (C)

Scott's No.		VF	NH Fine	Unused VF	Unused Fine	Used Fine
669-79	Set of 11	475.00	315.00	335.00	220.00	110.00
669	1¢ Franklin, Green	4.75	3.25	3.25	2.25	1.85
670	1½¢ Harding, Brown	4.75	3.25	3.25	2.25	2.00
671	2¢ Washington, Carmine	4.25	2.85	2.85	2.00	.95
672	3¢ Lincoln, Violet	21.00	14.00	15.00	10.00	7.75
673	4¢ M. Washington, Brn	29.50	20.00	23.00	15.00	9.50
674	5¢ T. Roosevelt, Deep Blue	25.00	17.00	18.50	12.50	11.50
675	6¢ Garfield, Red Orange	75.00	49.50	50.00	33.50	16.50
676	7¢ McKinley, Black	40.00	27.00	28.50	18.50	12.50
677	8¢ Grant, Olive Green	56.50	37.50	37.50	25.00	17.00
678	9¢ Jefferson, Light Rose	67.50	45.00	45.00	29.50	20.00
679	10¢ Monroe, Orng. Yel	175.00	115.00	125.00	80.00	16.50

NOTE: IN 1929, SOME 1¢-10¢ STAMPS WERE OVERPRINTED "Kans." AND "Nebr." AS A MEASURE OF PREVENTION AGAINST POST OFFICE ROBBERIES IN THOSE STATES, THEY WERE USED ABOUT ONE YEAR, THEN DISCONTINUED. Genuine unused, o.g. K-N's have either a single horiz. gum breaker ridge or two widely spaced horiz. ridges (21 mm apart). Unused, o.g. stamps with two horiz. ridges spaced 10 mm apart have counterfeit ovpts. Unused stamps without ridges are regummed and/or have a fake ovpt.

PLATE BLOCKS

Kansas | Nebraska

Scott #	NH VF	NH Fine	Unused Fine	Scott #	NH VF	NH Fine	Unused Fine
658	57.50	40.00	30.00	669	57.50	40.00	30.00
659	85.00	55.00	40.00	670	85.00	55.00	40.00
660	72.50	48.50	35.00	671	50.00	35.00	25.00
661	295.00	200.00	135.00	672	250.00	165.00	110.00
662	295.00	200.00	135.00	673	360.00	240.00	165.00
663	230.00	155.00	110.00	674	370.00	245.00	170.00
664	650.00	450.00	315.00	675	735.00	485.00	350.00
665	700.00	500.00	350.00	676	475.00	315.00	225.00
666	1250.00	850.00	650.00	677	650.00	435.00	325.00
667	315.00	210.00	140.00	678	715.00	475.00	350.00
668	525.00	350.00	250.00	679	1450.00	1000.00	750.00

1929-1930 Commemoratives VF Used + 30% (B)

680   681   682   683

Scott's No.		VF	NH F-VF	Unused VF	Unused F-VF	Used F-VF
680	2¢ Battle of Fallen Timbers	1.25	.95	1.00	.75	.70
681	2¢ Ohio River Canal	.85	.65	.65	.50	.60
682	2¢ Mass. Bay (1930)	1.10	.85	.75	.60	.45
683	2¢ Carolina-Charleston ('30)	2.00	1.50	1.40	1.10	1.00

1930 Regular Issues, Rotary Press VF Used + 30% (B)

684,686   685,687   688   689   690

Scott's No.		VF	NH F-VF	Unused VF	Unused F-VF	Used F-VF
684	1½¢ Harding, Brn., Pf. 11x10½	.40	.30	.35	.25	.15
685	4¢ Taft, Brn., Pf. 11x10½	1.30	1.00	1.00	.80	.15
686	1½¢ Brown, Coil, Pf. 10 Vert	2.50	1.95	1.95	1.50	.20
687	4¢ Brown, Coil, Pf. 10 Vert.	5.25	3.95	3.50	2.70	.65

1930-31 Commemoratives VF Used + 30% (B)

		VF	NH F-VF	Unused VF	Unused F-VF	Used F-VF
688	2¢ Braddock's Field	1.60	1.20	1.25	.90	.85
689	2¢ Baron Von Steuben	.80	.60	.60	.45	.45
690	2¢ General Pulaski (1931)	.38	.28	.32	.22	.20

PLATE BLOCKS & LINE PAIRS

Scott #	NH VF	NH F-VF	Unused F-VF	Scott #	NH VF	NH F-VF	Unused F-VF
680 (6)	43.50	33.50	25.00	688 (6)	52.50	40.00	30.00
681 (6)	30.00	23.50	18.00	689 (6)	32.50	25.00	20.00
682 (6)	43.50	33.50	25.00	690 (6)	18.75	15.00	12.00
683 (6)	67.50	52.50	40.00	Line Pairs			
684	3.75	2.75	2.10	686	13.50	9.50	7.00
685	17.50	12.50	10.00	687	28.75	21.00	16.00

1931 Rotary Press, Pf. 11x10½ or 10½x11 VF Used + 30% (B) Designs of #563-70, 622-23

Scott's No.		VF	NH F-VF	Unused VF	Unused F-VF	Used F-VF
692-701	Set of 10	165.00	122.50	127.50	95.00	2.10
692	11¢ Hayes, Light Blue	4.50	3.35	3.35	2.50	.18
693	12¢ Cleveland, Brown Violet	10.00	7.25	7.50	5.50	.18
694	13¢ Harrison, Yel. Grn	3.50	2.60	2.65	2.00	.20
695	14¢ Indian, Dark Blue	6.50	4.75	5.00	3.75	.45
696	15¢ Liberty, Gray	13.00	9.50	10.00	7.50	.20
697	17¢ Wilson, Black	8.50	6.35	6.50	5.00	.25
698	20¢ Golden Gate, Car. Rose	16.00	11.75	12.00	9.00	.20
699	25¢ Niagara Falls, Blue Green	17.50	12.75	13.00	10.00	.20
700	30¢ Buffalo, Brown	26.50	20.00	21.00	16.00	.20
701	50¢ Amphitheater, Lilac	67.50	50.00	52.50	39.50	.20

PLATE BLOCKS

Scott #	NH VF	NH F-VF	Unused F-VF	Scott #	NH VF	NH F-VF	Unused F-VF
692	20.00	15.00	12.00	697	41.50	31.00	24.00
693	45.00	33.75	26.50	698	75.00	57.50	45.00
694	21.00	16.00	12.50	699	77.50	60.00	47.50
695	31.75	23.75	18.50	700	125.00	95.00	75.00
696	57.50	42.50	33.75	701	325.00	240.00	190.00

702   703   704   715

1931 Commemoratives VF Used + 30% (B)

		VF	NH F-VF	Unused VF	Unused F-VF	Used F-VF
702	2¢ Red Cross	.35	.25	.30	.20	.18
703	2¢ Battle of Yorktown	.55	.45	.45	.35	.30

1932 Washington Bicentennial VF Used + 40% (B)

Scott's No.		VF	NH F-VF	Unused VF	Unused F-VF	Used F-VF
704-15	Set of 12	39.50	28.75	29.95	22.75	2.35
704	½¢ Olive Brown	.35	.25	.30	.20	.15
705	1¢ Green	.35	.25	.30	.20	.15
706	1½¢ Brown	.70	.50	.55	.40	.18
707	2¢ Carmine Rose	.35	.25	.30	.20	.15
708	3¢ Deep Violet	.85	.60	.70	.50	.18
709	4¢ Light Brown	.50	.40	.40	.30	.18
710	5¢ Blue	2.65	2.00	2.10	1.60	.20
711	6¢ Red Orange	6.00	4.50	4.75	3.50	.20
712	7¢ Black	.50	.40	.40	.30	.20
713	8¢ Olive Bistre	5.00	3.75	4.00	3.00	.65
714	9¢ Pale Red	4.35	3.15	3.25	2.50	.20
715	10¢ Orange Yellow	20.00	14.50	15.00	11.50	.18

NOTE: VF USED STAMPS ARE PRICED AT A MINIMUM OF 10¢ PER STAMP MORE THAN THE F-VF PRICE.

1931-1932 Commemoratives
PLATE BLOCKS

Scott #	NH VF	F-VF	Unused F-VF	Scott #	NH VF	F-VF	Unused F-VF
702	3.35	2.50	2.00	708	25.00	19.00	15.00
703 (4)	4.25	3.25	2.50	709	11.00	8.25	6.75
703 (6)	5.75	4.50	3.50	710	31.50	23.00	18.50
704-15	**565.00**	**425.00**	**335.00**	711	100.00	75.00	60.00
704	6.50	4.75	3.75	712	11.50	8.25	6.75
705	6.25	4.75	3.75	713	100.00	75.00	60.00
706	30.00	23.00	18.00	714	67.50	50.00	40.00
707	3.25	2.50	1.90	715	200.00	150.00	120.00

1932 Commemoratives VF Used + 30% (B)

716   717   718   720-22   723

Scott's No.		VF	NH F-VF	Unused VF	F-VF	Used F-VF
716	2¢ Winter Olym., Lake Placid	.65	.50	.50	.40	.25
717	2¢ Arbor Day	.35	.25	.30	.20	.15
718	3¢ Summer Olympics	2.50	1.90	1.95	1.50	.20
719	5¢ Summer Olympics	3.50	2.75	2.80	2.15	.30

1932 Regular Issues, Rotary Press VF Used + 30% (B)

720	3¢ Washington, D. Violet	.35	.25	.30	.20	.15
720b	3¢ Booklet Pane of 6	72.50	52.50	47.50	35.00	...
721	3¢ D. Violet, Coil, Pf. 10 Vert.	3.00	2.25	2.25	1.75	.20
722	3¢ D. Violet, Coil, Pf. 10 Hor.	1.60	1.20	1.25	.95	.65
723	6¢ Garfield, Orange, Coil, Perf. 10 Vertically	15.00	12.00	11.75	9.00	.30

1932 Commemoratives VF Used + 30% (B)

724   725   726   727,752

724	3¢ William Penn	.50	.40	.40	.30	.20
725	3¢ Daniel Webster	.60	.45	.45	.35	.30

1933 Commemoratives VF Used + 30% (B)

726	3¢ Georgia, Oglethorpe	.50	.40	.40	.30	.25
727	3¢ Peace, Newburgh	.35	.25	.30	.20	.15

PLATE BLOCKS & LINE PAIRS

Scott #	NH VF	F-VF	Unused F-VF	Scott #	NH VF	F-VF	Unused F-VF
716 (6)	20.00	15.00	11.50	726 (6)	22.50	18.00	13.50
717	11.00	8.50	6.75	726 (10)"cs"	27.50	22.50	17.50
718	23.50	18.00	14.00	727	8.75	6.75	5.50
719	42.50	32.50	25.75	**Line Pairs**			
720	2.00	1.50	1.20	721	8.75	6.75	5.50
724 (6)	18.00	14.50	10.50	722	7.00	5.25	3.95
725 (6)	32.50	25.00	20.00	723	72.50	55.00	40.00

1933 Commemoratives VF Used + 30% (B)

728,730a,	729,731a,	732	733,735a,	734
766a	767a		753	

728	1¢ Chicago, Ft. Dearborn	.35	.25	.30	.20	.15
729	3¢ Chicago, Fed. Bldg.	.35	.25	.30	.20	.15
730	1¢ Chicago, Imperf S/S of 25	...	...	...	35.00	32.50
730a	1¢ Single Stamp from sheet	...	...	.70	.60	.50
731	3¢ Chicago, Imperf. S/S of 25	...	...	...	30.00	27.50
731a	3¢ Single Stamp from Sheet	...	...	.65	.55	.50
732	3¢ Natl. Recovery Act	.35	.25	.30	.20	.15
733	3¢ Byrd. Antarctic Exp	.80	.65	.65	.50	.60
734	5¢ Gen. Kosciuszko	.95	.75	.75	.60	.35
735	3¢ Byrd, Imperf S/S of 6	...	...	...	17.50	16.50
735a	3¢ Single Stamp from sheet	...	...	3.00	2.75	2.65

NOTE: #730, 731 AND 735 WERE ISSUED WITHOUT GUM.

1934 Commemoratives VF Used + 30% (B)

736   737,738,754   739,755

Scott's No.		VF	NH F-VF	Unused VF	F-VF	Used F-VF
736	3¢ Maryland Tercentary	.35	.25	.30	.20	.18
737	3¢ Mother's Day, Rotary, Perf. 11x10½	.35	.25	.30	.20	.15
738	3¢ Mother's Day, Flat Press, Perf. 11	.35	.25	.30	.20	.20
739	3¢ Wisconsin Tercentenary	.35	.25	.30	.20	.15

PLATE BLOCKS

Scott #	NH VF	F-VF	Unused F-VF	Scott #	NH VF	F-VF	Unused F-VF
728	4.25	3.25	2.65	734 (6)	52.50	42.50	35.00
729	5.00	4.00	3.00	736 (6)	16.00	12.50	10.00
732	2.75	2.20	1.80	737	1.85	1.50	1.25
733 (6)	25.00	20.00	16.50	738 (6)	7.50	6.00	5.00
				739 (6)	6.50	5.00	4.00

1934 National Parks Issue - Perf. 11 VF Used + 30% (B)

740,756   744,760   747,763   749,765

741,757   742,758   743,759

745,761   746,762   748,764

740-49	Set of 10	15.00	12.50	12.75	9.95	6.25
740	1¢ Yosemite, Green	.35	.25	.30	.20	.15
741	2¢ Grand Canyon, Red	.35	.25	.30	.20	.15
742	3¢ Mt. Rainier, Violet	.35	.25	.30	.20	.15
743	4¢ Mesa Verde, Brown	.65	.50	.50	.40	.35
744	5¢ Yellowstone, Blue	1.35	1.10	1.10	.90	.70
745	6¢ Crater Lake, Dk. Blue	1.85	1.50	1.50	1.25	1.00
746	7¢ Acadia, Black	1.25	1.00	1.00	.80	.70
747	8¢ Zion, Sage Green	2.85	2.25	2.25	1.80	1.75
748	9¢ Glacier, Red Orange	3.00	2.35	2.35	1.85	.75
749	10¢ Great Smoky, Gray Blk.	4.95	3.95	3.95	3.25	1.25

NATIONAL PARKS PLATE BLOCKS

Scott #	NH VF	F-VF	Unused F-VF	Scott #	NH VF	F-VF	Unused F-VF
740-49	**180.00**	**140.00**	**115.00**	745 (6)	28.75	22.50	18.00
740 (6)	2.10	1.65	1.35	746 (6)	18.50	15.00	12.00
741 (6)	2.65	2.10	1.65	747 (6)	28.75	22.50	18.00
742 (6)	3.00	2.50	2.00	748 (6)	31.00	24.50	20.00
743 (6)	12.50	10.00	8.00	749 (6)	48.75	37.50	30.00
744 (6)	14.50	11.50	9.25				

1934 National Parks Souvenir Sheets

750	3¢ Parks, Imperf. Sheet of 6	...	50.00	...	40.00	30.00
750a	3¢ Single Stamp from Sheet	5.75	5.25	5.00	4.50	3.75
751	1¢ Parks, Imperf. Sheet of 6	...	16.00	...	13.50	12.00
751a	1¢ Single Stamp from Sheet	2.25	1.90	1.80	1.60	1.60

NOTE: PRICES THROUGHOUT THIS LIST ARE SUBJECT TO CHANGE WITHOUT NOTICE IF MARKET CONDITIONS REQUIRE. MINIMUM MAIL ORDER MUST TOTAL AT LEAST $20.00.

1933-1934 Souvenir Sheets

730,766

731,767

735,768

750,770

751,769

VERY FINE COPIES OF #752-DATE ARE AVAILABLE FOR THE FOLLOWING PREMIUMS:
ADD 10¢ TO ANY ITEM PRICED UNDER 50¢. ADD 20% TO ANY ITEM PRICED AT 50¢ & UP.
UNLESS PRICED AS VERY FINE, SETS ARE NOT AVAILABLE VERY FINE AND STAMPS
SHOULD BE LISTED INDIVIDUALLY WITH APPROPRIATE PREMIUM.

1935 Farley Special Printing Issue

These stamps were issued imperforate (except #752 & 753) and without gum.
For average quality on #752 and 753, deduct 20%. Horiz. and Vert. Gutter or
Line Blocks are available at double the pair price.
NOTE: #752, 766A-70A HAVE GUTTERS INSTEAD OF LINES.

Horizontal Pairs   **Vertical Pair**
Vertical Gutters   **Horizontal Line**

Cross Gutter Block   **Arrow Block**

Scott's No.		F-VF Plate Blocks	Hz. Pair Vert.Line	Vert. Pr. Hz.Line	Singles Unused	Used
752-71	Set of 20	...	127.50	85.00	27.50	25.00
752	3¢ Newburgh, Pf.10½x11	16.50	7.00	4.00	.20	.18
753	3¢ Byrd, Perf. 11 .... (6)	17.50	39.50	1.75	.50	.45
754	3¢ Mother's Day, Imperf ... (6)	18.50	1.65	2.10	.55	.55
755	3¢ Wisconsin, Imperf. .... (6)	18.50	1.65	2.10	.55	.55

National Parks, Imperforate

756-65	Set of 10 .... (6)	285.00	41.50	39.50	14.50	13.95
756	1¢ Yosemite................... (6)	6.50	.55	.45	.20	.18
757	2¢ Grand Canyon .... (6)	7.50	.60	.65	.22	.20
758	3¢ Mt. Rainier .... (6)	17.50	1.25	1.60	.50	.45
759	4¢ Mesa Verde .... (6)	21.50	2.50	3.00	1.10	1.10
760	5¢ Yellowstone .... (6)	27.50	5.25	4.25	1.75	1.75
761	6¢ Crater Lake............... (6)	39.50	6.00	6.75	2.25	2.10
762	7¢ Acadia...................... (6)	36.50	4.50	5.00	1.80	1.75
763	8¢ Zion.......................... (6)	45.00	6.50	5.00	1.80	1.80
764	9¢ Glacier..................... (6)	47.50	5.75	6.00	2.00	1.85
765	10¢ Great Smoky.......... (6)	52.50	12.00	10.00	3.75	3.50

Singles And Pairs From Souvenir Sheets, Imperforate

766a-70a	Set of 5........................	...	36.50	32.75	9.75	8.50
766a	1¢ Chicago....................	...	7.50	6.00	.90	.60
767a	3¢ Chicago....................	...	8.50	6.50	.90	.60
768a	3¢ Byrd	...	7.50	6.75	3.00	2.75
769a	1¢ Park	...	4.75	4.25	1.65	1.60
770a	3¢ Park	...	10.00	11.00	3.75	3.65

Airmail Special Delivery, Imperforate (Design of CE1)

771	16¢ Dark Blue.............. (6)	69.50	6.00	7.75	2.50	2.40

FARLEY SPECIAL PRINTING
POSITION BLOCKS
All stamps are F-VF and without gum as issued

Scott's No.	Center Line Block	T or B Arrow Block	L or R Arrow Block	Scott's No.	Center Line Block	T or B Arrow Block	L or R Arrow Block
752-71	450.00	...	...	762	18.50	10.00	11.25
752	50.00	15.00	8.50	763	22.50	14.00	11.50
753	90.00	85.00	3.75	764	20.00	12.50	13.50
754	9.50	3.50	4.50	765	35.00	25.00	21.00
755	9.50	3.50	4.50	766a-70a	83.75	...	...
756-65	160.00	92.50	87.50	766a	15.00	...	...
756	4.50	1.25	1.00	767a	17.50	...	...
757	5.00	1.40	1.50	768a	18.50	...	...
758	7.00	2.90	3.60	769a	10.75	...	...
759	12.50	5.50	6.50	770a	23.50	...	...
760	18.50	11.50	9.50	771	77.50	13.00	16.75
761	22.50	13.50	15.00				

772   773   775

774   784   777

778

776   782   783

1935 Commemoratives

Scott's No.		Mint Sheet	Plate Block	F-VF NH	F-VF Used
772-75	**Set of 4**.....................................	...	...	**.70**	**.55**
772	3¢ Connecticut............................	9.95	1.90	.20	.15
773	3¢ California-Pacific....................	9.00	1.40	.20	.15
774	3¢ Boulder Dam...........................	8.50	(6) 2.10	.20	.15
775	3¢ Michigan Centenary................	8.25	1.50	.20	.15

1936 Commemoratives

		Mint Sheet	Plate Block	F-VF NH	F-VF Used
776-78,782-84	**Set of 6**..................	...	...	**3.70**	**3.40**
776	3¢ Texas Centennial....................	8.75	1.50	.20	.15
777	3¢ Rhode Island..........................	9.00	1.50	.20	.15
778	3¢ TIPEX Souv. Sht. of 4............	...	...	2.85	2.50
778a	3¢ Conn., Imperforate................	...	...	.70	.60
778b	3¢ Calif., Imperforate..................	...	...	.70	.60
778c	3¢ Mich., Imperforate.................	...	...	.70	.60
778d	3¢ Texas, Imperforate................	...	...	.70	.60
782	3¢ Arkansas Cent	8.75	1.50	.20	.15
783	3¢ Oregon Territory	8.75	1.40	.20	.15
784	3¢ Susan B. Anthony..............(100)	17.50	1.00	.20	.15

1936-1937 Army - Navy Series

785   786   787

788   789

1936-1937 Army - Navy Series

790   791   792

793   794

Scott's No.		Mint Sheet	Plate Block	F-VF NH	F-VF Used
785-94	**Set of 10**.....................................	195.00	47.50	**3.65**	**1.60**
785-94	**Very Fine Set of 10**....................	...	56.50	**4.65**	**2.40**
785	1¢ Army-Wash. & Greene............	5.75	1.10	.20	.15
786	2¢ Army-Jackson & Scott (1937) .	6.50	1.10	.20	.15
787	3¢ Army-Sherman, Grant. Sheridan (37)	14.50	1.50	.30	.15
788	4¢ Army-Lee & Jackson (1937) ...	35.00	11.00	.50	.25
789	5¢ Army-West Point (1937)	45.00	12.00	.80	.30
790	1¢ Navy-Jones & Barry................	5.75	1.10	.20	.15
791	2¢ Navy-Decatur & MacDonough (37)	7.00	1.10	.20	.15
792	3¢ Navy-Farragut & Porter (1937)	14.50	1.50	.30	.15
793	4¢ Navy-Sampson, Dewey, Schley (37)	27.50	11.50	.40	.25
794	5¢ Navy-U.S. Naval Academy (37)	45.00	12.00	.80	.30

1937 Commemoratives

795   796   798   799

797

800   801   802

Scott's No.		Mint Sheet	Plate Block	F-VF NH	F-VF Used
795-802	**Set of 8**......................................	...	...	**2.15**	**1.50**
795	3¢ Ordinance of 1787	8.00	1.50	.20	.15
796	5¢ Virginia Dare ....(48)	17.50	(6) 8.25	.25	.20
797	10¢ SPA Souvenir Sheet.............	...	...	.75	.65
798	3¢ Constitution Signing...............	10.75	1.60	.22	.15
799-802	Territorials Set of 4......................	33.75	5.75	.75	.50
799	3¢ Hawaii Territory......................	8.75	1.50	.20	.15
800	3¢ Alaska Territory......................	8.75	1.50	.20	.15
801	3¢ Puerto Rico Territory...............	8.75	1.50	.20	.15
802	3¢ Virgin Is. Territory..................	8.75	1.50	.20	.15

NOTE: FROM 1935 TO DATE, WITH FEW LISTED EXCEPTIONS, UNUSED PRICES ARE FOR NEVER HINGED STAMPS. HINGED STAMPS, WHEN AVAILABLE, ARE PRICED AT APPROXIMATELY 15% BELOW THE NEVER HINGED PRICE.

1938 Presidential Series

803

804,839,848 805,840,849 806,841,850 807,842,851

808,843 809,844 810,845 811,846 812

813 814 815,847 816 817

818 819 820 821 822

823 824 825 826 827

828 829 830 831

832 833 834

Scott's No.		Mint Sheet	Plate Block	F-VF NH	F-VF Used
803-34	Set of 32	...	815.00	180.00	14.50
803-34	Very Fine Set of 32	...	985.00	215.00	18.00
803-31	Set of 29 (½¢-50¢)	...	180.00	36.95	5.25
803-31	Very Fine Set of 29	...	220.00	43.50	7.75
803	½¢ Franklin ....(100)	6.50	.50	.20	.15
804	1¢ Washington ....(100)	9.00	.50	.20	.15
804b	1¢ Booklet Pane of 6, 2½ mm (1942)	...	...	2.00	...
804bv	Same, 3 mm Gutter (1939)	...	...	5.95	...
805	1½¢ Martha Washington ....(100)	9.00	.50	.20	.15
806	2¢ John Adams ....(100)	11.50	.50	.20	.15
806	2¢ Electric Eye Plate	...	(10) 7.50	...	...
806b	2¢ Booklet Pane of 6, 2½ mm (1942)	...	...	5.75	...
806bv	Same, 3 mm Gutter (1939)	...	...	8.95	...
807	3¢ Jefferson ....(100)	12.00	.50	.20	.15
807	3¢ Electric Eye Plate	...	(10) 25.00	...	...
807a	3¢ Booklet Pane of 6, 2½ mm (1942)	...	...	8.25	...
807av	Same, 3 mm Gutter (1939)	...	...	14.95	...
808	4¢ Madison ....(100)	110.00	4.50	1.00	.15
809	4½¢ White House ....(100)	25.00	1.30	.22	.15
810	5¢ Monroe ....(100)	28.00	1.20	.25	.15
811	6¢ John Quincy Adams........(100)	35.00	1.40	.30	.15
812	7¢ Jackson ....(100)	45.00	1.90	.40	.15
813	8¢ Van Buren ....(100)	50.00	2.10	.45	.15

Scott's No.		Mint Sheet	Plate Block	F-VF NH	F-VF Used
814	9¢ William H. Harrison ....(100)	60.00	2.25	.50	.15
815	10¢ Tyler.....................(100)	55.00	1.95	.45	.15
816	11¢ Polk.....................(100)	67.50	4.25	.70	.15
817	12¢ Taylor...................(100)	125.00	6.00	1.35	.18
818	13¢ Fillmore ....(100)	210.00	9.50	2.25	.18
819	14¢ Pierce ....(100)	105.00	5.75	1.10	.18
820	15¢ Buchanan ....(100)	75.00	2.85	.60	.15
821	16¢ Lincoln..................(100)	110.00	6.00	1.20	.55
822	17¢ Andrew Johnson ....(100)	115.00	6.00	1.20	.18
823	18¢ Grant....................(100)	225.00	10.00	2.30	.22
824	19¢ Hayes ....(100)	190.00	9.25	2.00	.60
825	20¢ Garfield ....(100)	120.00	4.95	1.10	.15
826	21¢ Arthur ....(100)	215.00	10.00	2.25	.20
827	22¢ Cleveland ....(100)	145.00	12.00	1.50	.75
828	24¢ Benjamin Harrison ....(100)	425.00	18.50	4.25	.35
829	25¢ McKinley ....(100)	100.00	4.75	1.10	.15
830	30¢ Theodore Roosevelt.........(100)	485.00	22.50	5.00	.18
831	50¢ Taft.....................	...	38.50	8.50	.18
832	$1 Wilson, Purple. & Black	...	45.00	10.00	.20
832b	$1 Wtmk. "USIR" (1951)	...	1750.00	300.00	65.00
832c	$1 Dry Printing,Red Vlt/Blk(1954)	...	40.00	9.00	.20
833	$2 Harding	...	135.00	27.50	4.75
834	$5 Coolidge.................	...	500.00	115.00	4.50

1938 Commemoratives

835 836 837 838

		Mint Sheet	Plate Block	F-VF NH	F-VF Used
835-38	Set of 4	...	...	1.00	.50
835	3¢ Constitution Ratification	24.00	4.50	.45	.15
836	3¢ Swedish-Finnish Terr...........(48)	9.50	(6) 3.25	.20	.15
837	3¢ Northwest Territory ....(100)	25.00	10.50	.20	.15
838	3¢ Iowa Territory	18.50	7.50	.25	.15

1939 Presidential Coils

Scott's No.		Line Pairs NH	F-VF NH	F-VF Used
839-51	Set of 13	132.50	31.50	5.00
839-51	Very Fine Set of 13.........	160.00	38.00	6.25

Perforated 10 Vertically

839	1¢ Washington	1.30	.30	.15
840	1½¢ M. Washington.........	1.35	.30	.15
841	2¢ John Adams	1.50	.30	.15
842	3¢ Jefferson	1.75	.50	.15
843	4¢ Madison	30.00	6.75	.65
844	4½¢ White House	5.00	.60	.50
845	5¢ Monroe	27.50	5.50	.40
846	6¢ John Q. Adams	7.00	1.00	.25
847	10¢ Tyler........................	46.50	11.00	.80

Perforated 10 Horizontally

848	1¢ Washington	2.25	.75	.20
849	1½¢ M. Washington.........	4.00	1.30	.60
850	2¢ John Adams	6.00	2.40	.70
851	3¢ Jefferson	5.50	2.25	.70

1939 Commemoratives

852 853 854 857

855 856 858

Scott's No.		Mint Sheet	Plate Block	F-VF NH	F-VF Used
852-58	Set of 7	...	...	4.15	.95
852	3¢ Golden Gate Expo	10.00	1.60	.20	.15
853	3¢ N.Y. World's Fair	10.50	2.10	.20	.15
854	3¢ Washington Inaugural	47.50	(6) 5.50	.95	.18
855	3¢ Baseball Centennial	110.00	11.00	2.25	.20
856	3¢ Panama Canal	24.50	(6) 4.00	.45	.18
857	3¢ Printing	10.00	1.40	.20	.15
858	3¢ 4 States to Statehood	10.00	1.40	.20	.15

1940 Famous Americans Series

863   868   873   878

883   888   893

Scott's No.		Mint Sheet	Plate Block	F-VF NH	F-VF Used
859-93	Set of 35	2575.00	425.00	34.75	16.95
859-93	Very Fine Set of 35....................	...	500.00	41.75	20.95
859/91	1¢,2¢,3¢ Values (21)	...	30.75	3.95	2.50
	Authors				
859	1¢ Washington Irving...............(70)	8.75	1.25	.20	.15
860	2¢ James F. Cooper ....(70)	10.00	1.25	.20	.15
861	3¢ Ralph W. Emerson................(70)	10.50	1.25	.20	.15
862	5¢ Louisa M. Alcott ....(70)	40.00	11.75	.40	.25
863	10¢ Samuel L. Clemens ....(70)	175.00	45.00	2.10	1.75
	Poets				
864	1¢ Henry W. Longfellow............(70)	8.75	2.00	.20	.15
865	2¢ John G. Whittier ....(70)	10.75	1.85	.20	.15
866	3¢ James R. Lowell ....(70)	14.50	2.65	.20	.15
867	5¢ Walt Whitman ....(70)	40.00	11.50	.45	.25
868	10¢ James W. Riley..................(70)	185.00	49.50	2.10	1.75
	Educators				
869	1¢ Horace Mann ....(70)	15.00	2.65	.20	.15
870	2¢ Mark Hopkins ....(70)	8.75	1.25	.20	.15
871	3¢ Charles W. Eliot..................(70)	16.50	2.65	.22	.15
872	5¢ Frances E. Willard ....(70)	40.00	12.00	.40	.30
873	10¢ Booker T. Washington ....(70)	185.00	41.50	2.50	1.65
	Scientists				
874	1¢ John James Audubon ....(70)	7.75	1.30	.20	.15
875	2¢ Dr. Crawford W. Long ....(70)	9.50	1.10	.20	.15
876	3¢ Luther Burbank ....(70)	10.50	1.20	.20	.15
877	5¢ Dr. Walter Reed ....(70)	37.50	7.75	.50	.20
878	10¢ Jane Addams.....................(70)	105.00	31.50	1.50	1.40
	Composers				
879	1¢ Stephen C. Foster...............(70)	6.50	1.10	.20	.15
880	2¢ John Philip Sousa ....(70)	11.00	1.20	.20	.15
881	3¢ Victor Herbert.....................(70)	10.75	1.25	.20	.15
882	5¢ Edward A. MacDowell ....(70)	50.00	12.50	.60	.30
883	10¢ Ethelbert Nevin ....(70)	325.00	47.50	4.75	2.00
	Artists				
884	1¢ Gilbert C. Stuart..................(70)	6.00	1.00	.20	.15
885	2¢ James A. Whistler................(70)	7.00	1.00	.20	.15
886	3¢ Augustus Saint-Gaudens.....(70)	9.50	1.15	.20	.15
887	5¢ Daniel Chester French.........(70)	52.50	10.75	.65	.30
888	10¢ Frederic Remington ....(70)	165.00	35.00	1.95	1.65
	Inventors				
889	1¢ Eli Whitney..........................(70)	11.00	2.00	.20	.15
890	2¢ Samuel F.B. Morse ....(70)	9.00	1.15	.20	.15
891	3¢ Cyrus H. McCormick............(70)	23.75	2.00	.35	.15
892	5¢ Elias Howe ....(70)	105.00	16.50	1.25	.40
893	10¢ Alexander Graham Bell......(70)	1000.00	85.00	14.50	3.25

1940 Commemoratives

894   895   896   897

				F-VF NH	F-VF Used
894-902	Set of 9	...	...	2.10	1.30
894	3¢ Pony Express.......................	19.00	3.50	.35	.18
895	3¢ Pan American Union..............	18.75	4.25	.30	.18
896	3¢ Idaho Statehood	13.50	2.50	.22	.15
897	3¢ Wyoming Statehood	12.50	2.10	.22	.15

NOTE: FROM #752 TO DATE, AVERAGE QUALITY STAMPS, WHEN AVAILABLE, WILL BE PRICED AT APPROXIMATELY 20% BELOW THE APPROPRIATE FINE QUALITY PRICE. VERY FINE COPIES OF #752 - DATE ARE AVAILABLE FOR THE FOLLOWING PREMIUMS: ADD 10¢ TO ANY ITEM PRICED UNDER 50¢. ADD 20% TO ANY ITEM PRICED AT 50¢ & UP. UNLESS PRICED AS VERY FINE, SETS ARE NOT AVAILABLE VERY FINE AND STAMPS SHOULD BE LISTED INDIVIDUALLY WITH APPROPRIATE PREMIUM.

1940 Commemoratives (cont.)

898   899   900   901   902

Scott's No.		Mint Sheet	Plate Block	F-VF NH	F-VF Used
898	3¢ Coronado Expedition	10.75	1.75	.20	.15
899	1¢ Defense, Liberty..................(100)	9.50	.55	.20	.15
900	2¢ Defense, Anti-Aircraft..........(100)	9.50	.55	.20	.15
901	3¢ Defense, Torch....................(100)	15.00	.80	.20	.15
902	3¢ Thirteenth Amendment	20.00	3.85	.35	.20

1941-1943 Commemoratives

903   904   905

906   907   908

		Mint Sheet	Plate Block	F-VF NH	F-VF Used
903-08	Set of 6......................................	...	...	1.50	.90
903	3¢ Vermont Statehood................	13.75	2.10	.22	.15
904	3¢ Kentucky (1942).....................	10.00	1.40	.20	.15
905	3¢ Win the War (1942).............(100)	15.00	.70	.20	.15
906	5¢ China (1942).........................	35.00	12.00	.55	.28
907	2¢ United Nations (1943).........(100)	7.50	.50	.20	.15
908	1¢ Four Freedoms (1943)........(100)	7.50	.60	.20	.15

1943-44 Overrun Nations (Flags)

909   910   911

912   913   914

		Mint Sheet	Plate Block	F-VF NH	F-VF Used
909-21	Set of 13....................................	175.00	64.50	2.95	2.40
909-21	Very Fine Set of 13....................	...	75.00	3.95	3.25
909	5¢ Poland.................................	13.00	7.25	.20	.18
910	5¢ Czechoslovakia.....................	12.50	4.00	.20	.18
911	5¢ Norway.................................	9.00	1.75	.20	.15
912	5¢ Luxembourg	9.00	1.75	.20	.15
913	5¢ Netherlands..........................	9.00	1.75	.20	.15
914	5¢ Belgium................................	9.00	1.75	.20	.15
915	5¢ France.................................	9.00	1.75	.20	.15
916	5¢ Greece	30.00	15.00	.50	.35
917	5¢ Yugoslavia	22.50	8.00	.30	.22
918	5¢ Albania................................	22.50	8.00	.30	.22
919	5¢ Austria.................................	17.00	5.25	.27	.22
920	5¢ Denmark	18.00	6.25	.27	.22
921	5¢ Korea (1944)........................	13.00	5.25	.20	.22
921v	5¢ "KORPA" Variety (1 per sheet)	45.00	...	26.50	...

(On #909-21, the country name rather than a plate number appears in the margin.)

1944 Commemoratives

922   923   924

925   926

Scott's No.		Mint Sheet	Plate Block	F-VF NH	F-VF Used
922-26	Set of 5	...	...	1.00	.65
922	3¢ Transcontinental Railroad	16.00	1.65	.30	.15
923	3¢ Steamship "Savannah"	8.00	1.70	.20	.15
924	3¢ Telegraph	7.50	1.00	.20	.15
925	3¢ Corregidor, Philippines............	8.50	1.25	.20	.15
926	3¢ Motion Pictures	9.50	1.10	.20	.15

1945 Commemoratives

927   928   929

930   931   932

933   934   935

936   937   938

Scott's No.		Mint Sheet	Plate Block	F-VF NH	F-VF Used
927-38	Set of 12	...	...	1.95	1.40
927	3¢ Florida Statehood....................	7.00	.70	.20	.15
928	5¢ United Nations Conference	8.00	.70	.20	.15
929	3¢ Iwo Jima (Marines)	9.00	.80	.20	.15
930-33	Set of 4	21.00	2.15	.70	.50
930	1¢ Roosevelt, Hyde Park	2.50	.50	.20	.15
931	2¢ Roosevelt, Warm Springs	4.50	.50	.20	.15
932	3¢ Roosevelt, White House..........	5.75	.55	.20	.15
933	5¢ Roosevelt, Map (1946)............	9.00	.80	.20	.15
934	3¢ Army	7.00	.65	.20	.15
935	3¢ Navy	7.00	.65	.20	.15
936	3¢ Coast Guard	7.00	.65	.20	.15
937	3¢ Alfred E. Smith .... (100)	11.00	.55	.20	.15
938	3¢ Texas Statehood	5.50	.55	.20	.15

1946 Commemoratives

939   940   941

942   943   944

Scott's No.		Mint Sheet	Plate Block	F-VF NH	F-VF Used
939-44	Set of 6	...	...	.90	.70
939	3¢ Merchant Marine	6.50	.55	.20	.15
940	3¢ Honorable Discharge ....(100)	11.00	.55	.20	.15
941	3¢ Tennessee Statehood.............	5.50	.55	.20	.15
942	3¢ Iowa Centennial	5.50	.55	.20	.15
943	3¢ Smithsonian Institution...........	5.50	.55	.20	.15
944	3¢ Santa Fe, Kearny Expedition..	5.50	.55	.20	.15

1947 Commemoratives

945   946   947

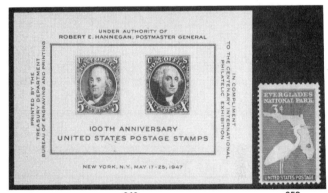

948   952

949   950   951

Scott's No.		Mint Sheet	Plate Block	F-VF NH	F-VF Used
945-52	Set of 8	...	...	1.80	1.35
945	3¢ Thomas A. Edison ....(70)	7.50	.55	.20	.15
946	3¢ Joseph Pulitzer	5.50	.55	.20	.15
947	3¢ Postage Centenary	5.50	.55	.20	.15
948	5¢ & 10¢ CIPEX Souv. Sheet......	...	...	.75	.65
948a	5¢ Franklin, Blue	...	...	.30	.25
948b	10¢ Wash., Brown Orange	...	...	.45	.30
949	3¢ Doctors....................................	7.00	.80	.20	.15
950	3¢ Utah Settlement Centennial....	6.50	.70	.20	.15
951	3¢ Frigate Constitution.................	5.50	.55	.20	.15
952	3¢ Everglades Park	5.50	.55	.20	.15

953   954   955

956   957   958

959   960   961

962   963   964

965   966   967   969

968   970   971

972   973   974

975   976   977

978   979   980

Scott's No.		Mint Sheet	Plate Block	F-VF NH	F-VF Used
953-80	Set of 28	...	...	4.25	3.00
953	3¢ George W. Carver................(70)	7.50	.55	.20	.15
954	3¢ California Gold Rush..............	5.50	.55	.20	.15
955	3¢ Mississippi Territory	5.50	.55	.20	.15
956	3¢ Four Chaplains......................	5.50	.55	.20	.15
957	3¢ Wisconsin Centennial	5.50	.55	.20	.15
958	5¢ Swedish Pioneers	7.50	.70	.20	.15
959	3¢ Progress of Women	5.50	.55	.20	.15
960	3¢ William A. White..................(70)	7.50	.60	.20	.15
961	3¢ U.S. - Canada Friendship	5.50	.55	.20	.15
962	3¢ Francis Scott Key....................	5.50	.55	.20	.15
963	3¢ American Youth	5.50	.55	.20	.15
964	3¢ Oregon Territory....................	5.50	.55	.20	.15
965	3¢ Harlan F. Stone ....(70)	7.50	.70	.20	.15
966	3¢ Palomar Observatory ....(70)	7.50	1.00	.20	.15
967	3¢ Clara Barton, Red Cross.........	6.00	.60	.20	.15
968	3¢ Poultry Industry.....................	5.50	.60	.20	.15
969	3¢ Gold Star Mothers..................	5.50	.60	.20	.15
970	3¢ Fort Kearny, Nebraska............	5.50	.60	.20	.15
971	3¢ Volunteer Firemen.................	6.00	.60	.20	.15
972	3¢ Indian Centennial	5.50	.60	.20	.15
973	3¢ Rough Riders	5.50	.60	.20	.15
974	3¢ Juliette Low, Girl Scouts	5.50	.60	.20	.15
975	3¢ Will Rogers, Humorist ....(70)	7.50	.60	.20	.15
976	3¢ Fort Bliss, Texas ....(70)	9.00	1.20	.20	.15
977	3¢ Moina Michael, Educator	5.50	.55	.20	.15
978	3¢ Gettysburg Address	8.50	.80	.20	.15
979	3¢ Turners Society.....................	5.50	.55	.20	.15
980	3¢ Joel Chandler Harris ....(70)	7.50	.60	.20	.15

1949 Commemoratives

981   982   983

984   985   986

981-86	Set of 6	...	...	.90	.65
981	3¢ Minnesota Territory	5.50	.55	.20	.15
982	3¢ Washington & Lee University..	5.50	.55	.20	.15
983	3¢ Puerto Rico Election	5.50	.55	.20	.15
984	3¢ Annapolis Tercentenary..........	5.50	.55	.20	.15
985	3¢ Grand Army of the Republic ...	5.50	.55	.20	.15
986	3¢ Edgar Allan Poe, Writer ....(70)	7.50	.65	.20	.15

NOTE: WE HAVE ESTABLISHED A MINIMUM PRICE OF .20 FOR UNUSED STAMPS AND .15 PER USED STAMP. THIS INCLUDES THE VALUE OF THE STAMP PLUS THE COST INVOLVED IN PROCESSING. YOU CAN USUALLY SAVE SUBSTANTIALLY WHEN PURCHASING COMPLETE SETS.

NOTE: PRICES THROUGHOUT THIS LIST ARE SUBJECT TO CHANGE WITHOUT NOTICE IF MARKET CONDITIONS REQUIRE. MINIMUM MAIL ORDER MUST TOTAL AT LEAST $20.00.

1950 Commemoratives

987   988   990

991   989   992

993   994   995

996   997

Scott's No.		Mint Sheet	Plate Block	F-VF NH	F-VF Used
987-97	Set of 11	...	...	1.65	1.25
987	3¢ Bankers Association	5.50	.55	.20	.15
988	3¢ Samuel Gompers, Labor ..... (70)	7.25	.55	.20	.15
989-92	National Capitol, Set of 4............	27.50	2.40	.65	.50
989	3¢ Freedom Statue, Capitol.........	6.00	.60	.20	.15
990	3¢ Executive Mansion	7.50	.65	.20	.15
991	3¢ Supreme Court	6.50	.60	.20	.15
992	3¢ U.S. Capitol	9.00	.80	.20	.15
993	3¢ Railroad Engineers	6.50	.60	.20	.15
994	3¢ Kansas City Centenary...........	5.50	.55	.20	.15
995	3¢ Boy Scouts	6.50	.60	.20	.15
996	3¢ Indiana Territory	5.50	.55	.20	.15
997	3¢ California Statehood	5.75	.55	.20	.15

1951 Commemoratives

998   999   1000

1001   1002   1003

998-1003	Set of 6....................................	...	...	.90	.60
998	3¢ Confederate Veterans	6.75	.60	.20	.15
999	3¢ Nevada Settlement Centennial	5.50	.55	.20	.15
1000	3¢ Landing of Cadillac, Detroit	5.50	.55	.20	.15
1001	3¢ Colorado Statehood................	5.50	.55	.20	.15
1002	3¢ Chemical Society	5.50	.55	.20	.15
1003	3¢ Battle of Brooklyn	6.00	.60	.20	.15

VERY FINE COPIES OF #752-DATE ARE AVAILABLE FOR THE FOLLOWING PREMIUMS:
ADD 10¢ TO ANY ITEM PRICED UNDER 50¢. ADD 20% TO ANY ITEM PRICED AT 50¢ & UP.
UNLESS PRICED AS VERY FINE, SETS ARE NOT AVAILABLE VERY FINE AND STAMPS
SHOULD BE LISTED INDIVIDUALLY WITH APPROPRIATE PREMIUM.

1952 Commemoratives

1004   1005   1006

1007   1008   1009   1011

1010   1012   1013

1014   1015   1016

Scott's No.		Mint Sheet	Plate Block	F-VF NH	F-VF Used
1004-16	Set of 13.....................................	...	...	1.95	1.35
1004	3¢ Betsy Ross	6.00	.55	.20	.15
1005	3¢ 4-H Clubs..............................	5.50	.55	.20	.15
1006	3¢ B & O Railroad.......................	6.00	.55	.20	.15
1007	3¢ Amer. Automobile Assoc	5.50	.55	.20	.15
1008	3¢ N.A.T.O.............................(100)	10.50	.55	.20	.15
1009	3¢ Grand Coulee Dam.................	5.50	.55	.20	.15
1010	3¢ Marquis de Lafayette	5.75	.55	.20	.15
1011	3¢ Mt. Rushmore Memorial	6.00	.55	.20	.15
1012	3¢ Civil Engineers Society...........	5.50	.55	.20	.15
1013	3¢ Service Women	6.00	.55	.20	.15
1014	3¢ Gutenberg Bible.....................	5.50	.55	.20	.15
1015	3¢ Newspaper Boys	5.50	.55	.20	.15
1016	3¢ Int'l. Red Cross	5.50	.55	.20	.15

1953 Commemoratives

1017   1018   1019

1020   1021   1022

1017-28	Set of 12....................................	...	...	1.80	1.35
1017	3¢ National Guard.......................	5.75	.55	.20	.15
1018	3¢ Ohio Statehood...............(70)	7.25	.55	.20	.15
1019	3¢ Washington Territory	5.50	.55	.20	.15
1020	3¢ Louisiana Purchase	5.50	.55	.20	.15
1021	5¢ Opening of Japan, Perry........	7.95	.75	.20	.15
1022	3¢ American Bar Association	6.50	.75	.20	.15

1953 Commemoratives (cont.)

| 1023 | 1024 | 1025 |

| 1026 | 1027 | 1028 |

Scott's No.		Mint Sheet	Plate Block	F-VF NH	F-VF Used
1023	3¢ Sagamore Hill, T. Roosevelt...	5.50	.55	.20	.15
1024	3¢ Future Farmers	5.50	.55	.20	.15
1025	3¢ Trucking Industry	5.50	.55	.20	.15
1026	3¢ General George S. Patton	7.50	.65	.20	.15
1027	3¢ New York City	5.50	.55	.20	.15
1028	3¢ Gadsden Purchase	5.50	.55	.20	.15

1954 Commemoratives

| 1029 | 1060 | 1061 |

| 1062 | 1063 |

				F-VF NH	F-VF Used
1029,1060-63	Set of 5...............................	...	...	.75	.55
1029	3¢ Columbia University...............	5.50	.55	.20	.15

1954-1968 Liberty Series (B)
(Sheets of 100)

| 1030 | 1031,1054 | 1031A,1054A | 1032 | 1033,1055 |

| 1034,1056 | 1035,1057 | 1036,1058 | 1037,1059 | 1038 |

| 1039 | 1040 | 1041,1041B | 1042 | 1042A |

		Mint Sheet	Plate Block	F-VF NH	F-VF Used
1030-53	Set of 28...................................	...	510.00	117.50	11.50
1030-53	Very Fine Set of 28	...	615.00	140.00	14.00
1030-51	½¢-50¢ Values only (26)	...	60.95	14.00	2.40
1030	½¢ Franklin, Wet ('55)	6.00	.55	.20	.15
1030a	½¢ Dry Printing ('58)	5.50	.50	.20	.15
1031	1¢ Washington, Dry ('56)	5.00	.50	.20	.15

1954-1968 Liberty Series (B)
(Sheets of 100)

Scott's No.		Mint Sheet	Plate Block	F-VF NH	F-VF Used
1031b	1¢ Wet Printing ('54)	6.00	.55	.20	.15
1031A	1¼¢ Palace of Governors ('60).....	6.00	.55	.20	.15
1032	1½¢ Mount Vernon (1956)...........	7.75	1.60	.20	.15
1033	2¢ Jefferson	7.00	.50	.20	.15
1034	2½¢ Bunker Hill (1959)	9.00	.65	.20	.15
1035	3¢ Statue of Liberty, Dry	10.00	.55	.20	.15
1035f	3¢ Booklet Pane of 6, Dry Printing	...	...	6.50	2.50
1035b	3¢ Tagged, Dry Printing (1966)....	37.50	9.75	.32	.30
1035e	3¢ Wet Printing	12.50	.60	.20	.18
1035a	3¢ Booklet Pane of 6, Wet Printing	...	...	5.50	...
1036	4¢ Abraham Lincoln, Dry	11.50	.55	.20	.15
1036a	4¢ Booklet Pane of 6 (1958)	...	...	2.85	2.25
1036b	4¢ Tagged, Dry Printing (1963)....	80.00	13.95	.70	.65
1036c	4¢ Wet Printing	13.75	.70	.20	.20
1037	4½¢ The Hermitage (1959)	13.00	.75	.20	.15
1038	5¢ James Monroe	15.00	.65	.20	.15
1039	6¢ T. Roosevelt, Dry (1955)	35.00	1.50	.40	.15
1039a	6¢ Wet Printing	45.00	2.00	.50	.18
1040	7¢ Woodrow Wilson (1956)	32.50	1.50	.35	.15
1041	8¢ St. of Liberty, Original, Flat	34.50	3.00	.35	.15
1041B	8¢ Liberty, Original, Rotary	34.50	3.00	.35	.15
1042	8¢ St. Lib., Redrawn (1958)	31.50	1.35	.32	.15

#1041,1041B: Torch Flame between "U.S." and "POSTAGE".
#1042: Torch Flame goes under "P" of "POSTAGE".

| 1042A | 8¢ J.J. Pershing ('61) .... | 32.50 | 1.50 | .33 | .15 |

| 1043 | 1044 | 1044A | 1045 | 1046 |

| 1047 | 1048,1059A | 1049 | 1050 | 1051 |

| 1052 | 1053 |

1043	9¢ The Alamo ('56)	55.00	2.10	.55	.15
1044	10¢ Indep. Hall ('56)	37.50	1.35	.35	.15
1044b	10¢ Tagged (1966)	400.00	60.00	3.75	3.00
1044A	11¢ St. of Liberty ('61).................	40.00	1.75	.40	.15
1044Ac	11¢ Tagged (1967)	325.00	55.00	3.00	2.50
1045	12¢ Ben. Harrison ('59)	55.00	2.25	.55	.15
1045a	12¢Tagged (1968)	80.00	5.00	.80	.25
1046	15¢ John Jay ('58)	110.00	4.75	1.10	.15
1046a	15¢ Tagged (1966)	200.00	14.00	2.10	.50
1047	20¢ Monticello ('56)	80.00	3.75	.80	.15
1048	25¢ Paul Revere ('58)	150.00	6.75	1.50	.15
1049	30¢ Robert E. Lee, Dry (1957).....	190.00	8.50	1.95	.15
1049a	30¢ Wet Printing (1955)...............	265.00	11.50	2.75	.25
1050	40¢ John Marshall, Dry (1958)	275.00	12.75	2.85	.15
1050a	40¢ Wet Printing (1955)...............	375.00	17.50	3.75	.25
1051	50¢ S.B. Anthony, Dry (1958)	195.00	8.25	1.80	.15
1051a	50¢ Wet Printing (1955)...............	250.00	9.75	2.25	.25
1052	$1 Patrick Henry, Dry (1958)	575.00	25.00	5.50	.15
1052a	$1 Wet Printing (1955)...............	695.00	31.50	7.00	.25
1053	$5 Alex Hamilton ('56)	...	450.00	100.00	8.50

NOTE: USED STAMPS ARE OUR CHOICE OF WET OR DRY, TAGGED OR UNTAGGED.

1954-80 Liberty Series Coil Stamps, Perf. 10 (B)

		Line Pairs	F-VF NH	F-VF Used
1054-59A	**Set of 8 ....**	**28.50**	**3.65**	**2.25**
1054-59A	**Very Fine Set of 8 ....**	**34.75**	**4.35**	**3.00**

#1054A and #1059 are Perforated Horizontally.

1054	1¢ Washington, Dry, Large Holes ('57)	3.50	1.50	.20
1054s	1¢ Dry, Small Holes (1960)................	1.10	.25	.15
1054c	1¢ Wet Printing (1954)	3.00	.70	.20
1054A	1¼¢ Pal.of Governors, Sm.Holes ('60)	2.50	.20	.15
1054AI	1¼¢ Large Holes	375.00	19.50	.50
1055	2¢ Jefferson, Dry, Large Holes (1957)	1.65	.20	.15
1055s	2¢ Dry, Small Holes (1961)................	3.00	.70	.20
1055a	2¢ Tagged, Shiny Gum (1968)	.40	.20	.15
1055av	2¢ Tagged, Dull Gum........................	2.25	.25	...
1055d	2¢ Wet Printing, Yellow Gum (1954) ..	4.25	.75	.20
1055dw	2¢ Wet Printing, White Gum.............	32.50	4.25	...

NOTE: SETS INCLUDE OUR CHOICE OF LARGE OR SMALL HOLES.

1954-80 Liberty Coils (cont)

		Line Pairs	F-VF NH	F-VF Used
1056	2½¢ Bunker Hills, Large Holes ('59)...	3.50	.22	.20
1056s	2½¢ Sm. Holes, Bureau Precancel ('61)	...	...	.35
1057	3¢ Liberty, Dry, Large Holes (1956) ...	3.25	.45	.20
1057s	3¢ Dry Printing, Small Holes (1958)...	.60	.20	.15
1057b	3¢ Tagged, Small Holes (1967)..........	37.50	2.00	1.00
1057c	3¢ Wet Printing,Large Holes (1954)...	5.00	.70	.20
1058	4¢ Lincoln, Dry, Large Holes (1958)...	15.00	1.10	.20
1058s	4¢ Dry Printing, Small Holes	.75	.20	.15
1059	4½¢ Hermitage, Large Holes (1959)..	16.50	1.65	1.10
1059s	4½¢ Small Holes	395.00	22.50	...
1059A	25¢ Paul Revere (1965)	3.25	.85	.30
1059Ab	25¢ Tagged, Shiny Gum (1973)	2.25	.80	.25
1059Ad	25¢ Tagged, Dull Gum (1980)	4.50	1.65	...

1954 Commemoratives (see also No.1029)

Scott's No.		Mint Sheet	Plate Block	F-VF NH	F-VF Used
1060	3¢ Nebraska Territory.................	5.50	.55	.20	.15
1061	3¢ Kansas Territory	5.50	.55	.20	.15
1062	3¢ George Eastman .... (70)	7.50	.55	.20	.15
1063	3¢ Lewis & Clark Expedition........	5.50	.55	.20	.15

1955 Commemoratives

1064   1065   1068

1066   1067   1069

1070   1071   1072

				F-VF NH	F-VF Used
1064-72	**Set of 9........................**	...	...	1.50	.95
1064	3¢ Penn. Academy of Fine Arts...	5.50	.55	.20	.15
1065	3¢ Land Grant Colleges.............	5.50	.55	.20	.15
1066	8¢ Rotary International	16.00	1.95	.32	.15
1067	3¢ Armed Forces Reserves........	5.50	.55	.20	.15
1068	3¢ Old Man of the Mtns, NH	6.50	.55	.20	.15
1069	3¢ Soo Locks Centennial.............	5.50	.55	.20	.15
1070	3¢ Atoms for Peace	5.75	.55	.20	.15
1071	3¢ Fort Ticonderoga, NY	5.75	.55	.20	.15
1072	3¢ Andrew Mellon.................... (70)	7.25	.55	.20	.15

1956 Commemoratives

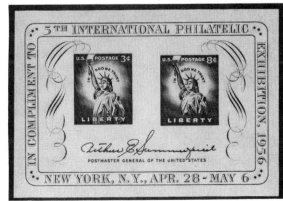

1075

1073   1074   1076

Scott's No.		Mint Sheet	Plate Block	F-VF NH	F-VF Used
1073-85	**Set of 13....................................**	...	...	3.95	3.25
1073	3¢ Franklin 250th Anniv	5.75	.55	.20	.15
1074	3¢ Booker T. Washington	5.50	.55	.20	.15
1075	3¢ & 8¢ FIPEX Souv. Sheet	...	...	2.25	2.15
1075a	3¢ Liberty Single	...	...	1.00	.90
1075b	8¢ Liberty Single	...	...	1.25	1.15
1076	3¢ FIPEX Stamp	5.50	.55	.20	.15

1077   1078   1079

1080   1081   1082

1083   1084   1085

1077	3¢ Wildlife - Wild Turkey..............	5.50	.55	.20	.15
1078	3¢ Wildlife - Antelope..................	5.50	.55	.20	.15
1079	3¢ Wildlife - King Salmon	5.50	.55	.20	.15
1080	3¢ Pure Food & Drug Act	5.50	.55	.20	.15
1081	3¢ Wheatland, Buchanan	5.50	.55	.20	.15
1082	3¢ Labor Day	5.50	.55	.20	.15
1083	3¢ Nassau Hall, Princeton	5.50	.55	.20	.15
1084	3¢ Devils Tower, Wyoming...........	5.50	.55	.20	.15
1085	3¢ Children's Issue	5.50	.55	.20	.15

1957 Commemoratives

1086   1087   1088

1089   1090   1091

1092   1093   1094

1095   1096   1097

1098   1099

Scott's No.		Mint Sheet	Plate Block	F-VF NH	F-VF Used
1086-99	Set of 14	...	...	2.25	1.50
1086	3¢ Alexander Hamilton	5.50	.55	.20	.15
1087	3¢ Polio, March of Dimes............	5.50	.55	.20	.15
1088	3¢ Coast & Geodetic Society.......	5.50	.55	.20	.15
1089	3¢ Architects Institute	5.50	.55	.20	.15
1090	3¢ Steel Industry........................	5.50	.55	.20	.15
1091	3¢ Naval Review, Jamestown......	5.75	.55	.20	.15
1092	3¢ Oklahoma Statehood..............	5.50	.55	.20	.15
1093	3¢ School Teachers....................	8.50	.70	.20	.15
1094	4¢ 48-Star U.S. Flag	6.50	.55	.20	.15
1095	3¢ Shipbuilding Anniv ....(70)	7.50	.55	.20	.15
1096	8¢ Ramon Magsaysay ....(48)	10.75	1.10	.24	.15
1097	3¢ Birth of Lafayette....................	6.00	.55	.20	.15
1098	3¢ Wildlife - Whooping Crane......	5.50	.55	.20	.15
1099	3¢ Religious Freedom.................	5.50	.55	.20	.15

1958 Commemoratives

1100   1104   1105

1106   1107   1108

1100,1104-1123	Set of 21	...	...	3.50	2.10
1100	3¢ Gardening-Horticulture............	5.50	.55	.20	.15
1104	3¢ Brussels World Fair	5.50	.55	.20	.15
1105	3¢ James Monroe ....(70)	7.50	.55	.20	.15
1106	3¢ Minnesota Centennial	5.50	.55	.20	.15
1107	3¢ Geophysical Year	5.50	.55	.20	.15
1108	3¢ Gunston Hall, Virginia	5.50	.55	.20	.15

1109   1110   1112

Scott's No.		Mint Sheet	Plate Block	F-VF NH	F-VF Used
1109	3¢ Mackinac Bridge, MI	5.50	.55	.20	.15
1110	4¢ Simon Bolivar ....(70)	8.50	.60	.20	.15
1111	8¢ Simon Bolivar ....(72)	17.50	1.60	.25	.15
1112	4¢ Atlantic Cable Centennial	6.25	.60	.20	.15

1113   1114   1115

1116   1118   1119

1120   1121

1122   1123

1958-59 Lincoln Commemoratives

1113-16	Set of 4	30.00	3.00	.85	.50
1113	1¢ Beardless Lincoln ('59)	2.50	.45	.20	.15
1114	3¢ Bust of Lincoln ('59)...............	6.25	.60	.20	.15
1115	4¢ Lincoln-Douglas Debates	8.50	.85	.20	.15
1116	4¢ Statue of Lincoln ('59)............	14.00	1.25	.30	.15

1958 Commemoratives (continued)

1117	4¢ Lajos Kossuth ....(70)	8.50	.60	.20	.15
1118	8¢ Lajos Kossuth ....(72)	17.50	1.30	.25	.15
1119	4¢ Freedom of Press	6.75	.60	.20	.15
1120	4¢ Overland Mail	6.50	.60	.20	.15
1121	4¢ Noah Webster ....(70)	8.50	.60	.20	.15
1122	4¢ Forest Conservation	6.25	.60	.20	.15
1123	4¢ Fort Duquesne, Pittsburgh......	6.25	.60	.20	.15

1959 Commemoratives

| 1124 | 1126 | 1127 | 1134 |

| 1128 | 1129 | 1130 |

| 1131 | 1132 | 1133 |

| 1135 | 1136 | 1137 | 1138 |

Scott's No.		Mint Sheet	Plate Block	F-VF NH	F-VF Used
1124-38	Set of 15....................................	...	...	2.35	1.60
1124	4¢ Oregon Statehood	6.25	.60	.20	.15
1125	4¢ Jose San Martin.............. (70)	8.75	.60	.20	.15
1126	8¢ Jose San Martin.............. (72)	16.50	1.25	.25	.15
1127	4¢ 10th Anniv. N.A.T.O....... (70)	8.75	.60	.20	.15
1128	4¢ Arctic Explorations.................	6.25	.60	.20	.15
1129	8¢ World Peace & Trade	11.50	1.00	.25	.15
1130	4¢ Silver Discovery.....................	6.25	.60	.20	.15
1131	4¢ St. Lawrence Seaway.............	6.25	.60	.20	.15
1132	4¢ 49-Star Flag	6.25	.60	.20	.15
1133	4¢ Soil Conservation	6.25	.60	.20	.15
1134	4¢ Petroleum Industry	6.25	.60	.20	.15
1135	4¢ Dental Health.........................	10.00	.90	.22	.15
1136	4¢ Ernst Reuter .... (70)	8.50	.60	.20	.15
1137	8¢ Ernst Reuter .... (72)	16.50	1.25	.25	.15
1138	4¢ Dr. Ephraim McDowell........(70)	8.75	.65	.20	.15

1960 Commemoratives

| 1139 | 1140 | 1141 |

| 1142 | 1143 | 1144 |

		Mint Sheet	Plate Block	F-VF NH	F-VF Used
1139-73	Set of 35....................................	...	...	5.50	3.75
1139-44	Set of 6	43.50	4.25	1.00	.65
1139	4¢ Washington Credo	6.50	.65	.20	.15
1140	4¢ Franklin Credo	6.50	.65	.20	.15
1141	4¢ Jefferson Credo	6.50	.65	.20	.15
1142	4¢ F.S. Key Credo	6.50	.65	.20	.15
1143	4¢ Lincoln Credo	9.50	.90	.22	.15
1144	4¢ Henry Credo (1961)................	9.50	.90	.22	.15

1960 Commemoratives (cont.)

| 1145 | 1146 | 1147 | 1151 |

| 1149 | 1150 | 1152 |

| 1153 | 1154 | 1155 |

Scott's No.		Mint Sheet	Plate Block	F-VF NH	F-VF Used
1145	4¢ Boy Scout Jubilee...................	8.75	.90	.20	.15
1146	4¢ Winter Olympics	6.75	.60	.20	.15
1147	4¢ Thomas G. Masaryk .... (70)	8.50	.60	.20	.15
1148	8¢ Thomas G. Masaryk .... (72)	16.50	1.10	.25	.15
1149	4¢ World Refugee Year	6.25	.60	.20	.15
1150	4¢ Water Conservation	6.25	.60	.20	.15
1151	4¢ Southeast Asia Treaty .... (70)	8.50	.60	.20	.15
1152	4¢ American Woman	6.25	.60	.20	.15
1153	4¢ 50-Star Flag	6.25	.60	.20	.15
1154	4¢ Pony Express Centennial	7.25	.70	.20	.15
1155	4¢ Employ the Handicapped	6.25	.60	.20	.15

| 1156 | 1157 | 1158 | 1159 |

| 1161 | 1162 | 1163 | 1167 |

1156	4¢ World Forestry Congress........	6.25	.60	.20	.15
1157	4¢ Mexican Independence...........	6.25	.60	.20	.15
1158	4¢ U.S. - Japan Treaty................	7.25	.65	.20	.15
1159	4¢ Ignacy J. Paderewski.......... (70)	8.50	.60	.20	.15
1160	8¢ Ignacy J. Paderewski.......... (72)	16.50	1.10	.25	.15
1161	4¢ Robert A. Taft .... (70)	8.50	.60	.20	.15
1162	4¢ Wheels of Freedom	6.25	.60	.20	.15
1163	4¢ Boys' Club of America	6.25	.60	.20	.15
1164	4¢ Automated Post Office............	6.25	.60	.20	.15

1960 Commemoratives (continued)

1164   1165   1169

1170   1171   1172   1173

Scott's No.		Mint Sheet	Plate Block	F-VF NH	F-VF Used
1165	4¢ Gustaf Mannerheim .... (70)	8.50	.60	.20	.15
1166	8¢ Gustaf Mannerheim .... (72)	16.50	1.10	.25	.15
1167	4¢ Camp Fire Girls	6.25	.60	.20	.15
1168	4¢ Guiseppe Garibaldi .... (70)	8.50	.60	.20	.15
1169	8¢ Guiseppe Garibaldi .... (72)	16.50	1.10	.25	.15
1170	4¢ Walter F. George .... (70)	8.50	.60	.20	.15
1171	4¢ Andrew Carnegie .... (70)	8.50	.60	.20	.15
1172	4¢ John Foster Dulles .... (70)	8.50	.60	.20	.15
1173	4¢ "Echo I" Satellite	11.50	1.00	.24	.15

1961 Commemoratives

1174   1175   1176   1177

1178   1179   1180

1181   1182   1183

1174-1190	Set of 17	...	...	4.50	1.75
1174	4¢ Mahatma Gandhi .... (70)	8.50	.60	.20	.15
1175	8¢ Mahatma Gandhi .... (72)	16.50	1.20	.25	.15
1176	4¢ Range Conservation	7.00	.60	.20	.15
1177	4¢ Horace Greeley .... (70)	8.50	.60	.20	.15

1961-1965 Civil War Centennial

1178-82	Set of 5	90.00	9.25	2.00	.55
1178	4¢ Fort Sumter (1961)	16.50	1.65	.35	.15
1179	4¢ Battle of Shiloh (1962)	11.50	1.10	.25	.15
1180	5¢ Gettysburg (1963)	17.50	1.75	.40	.15
1181	5¢ Wilderness (1964)	15.00	1.50	.35	.15
1182	5¢ Appomattox (1965)	34.75	3.75	.80	.15

1961 Commemoratives (cont.)

1184   1185   1186

1187   1188   1189   1190

Scott's No.		Mint Sheet	Plate Block	F-VF NH	F-VF Used
1183	4¢ Kansas Statehood	6.50	.60	.20	.15
1184	4¢ George W. Norris	6.25	.60	.20	.15
1185	4¢ Naval Aviation	6.75	.65	.20	.15
1186	4¢ Workmen's Compensation	6.25	.60	.20	.15
1186v	Plate Number Inverted	6.75	.95	...	...
1187	4¢ Frederic Remington	6.50	.65	.20	.15
1188	4¢ Republic of China, Sun Yat-sen	9.50	.85	.20	.15
1189	4¢ Basketball - James Naismith ..	12.00	1.00	.25	.15
1190	4¢ Nursing	16.75	1.50	.35	.15

1962 Commemoratives (See also 1179)

1191   1192   1193

1195   1194   1196

1197   1198   1199

1191-1207	Set of 17	...	...	2.60	1.85
1191	4¢ New Mexico Statehood	6.25	.60	.20	.15
1192	4¢ Arizona Statehood	7.00	.60	.20	.15
1193	4¢ Project Mercury	7.50	.80	.20	.15
1194	4¢ Malaria Eradication	6.25	.60	.20	.15
1195	4¢ Charles Evans Hughes	6.25	.60	.20	.15
1196	4¢ Seattle World's Fair	6.25	.60	.20	.15
1197	4¢ Louisiana Statehood	6.25	.60	.20	.15
1198	4¢ Homestead Act	6.25	.60	.20	.15
1199	4¢ Girl Scouts 50th Anniversary ..	6.50	.60	.20	.15

1962 Commemoratives (cont.)

1200   1201

1202   1203   1205

1206   1207

Scott's No.		Mint Sheet	Plate Block	F-VF NH	F-VF Used
1200	4¢ Brien McMahon	6.25	.60	.20	.15
1201	4¢ Apprenticeship Act	6.25	.60	.20	.15
1202	4¢ Sam Rayburn	6.25	.60	.20	.15
1203	4¢ Dag Hammarskjold...............	6.25	.60	.20	.15
1204	4¢ Hammarskjold "Error"...........	7.00	1.30	.20	.15
1205	4¢ Christmas Wreath.............. (100)	12.50	.60	.20	.15
1206	4¢ Higher Education	6.50	.65	.20	.15
1207	4¢ Winslow Homer Seascape	7.50	.65	.20	.15

1962-1963 Regular Issues

1208   1209,1225   1213,1229

1208	5¢ Flag & Wh. Hse. ('63) .... (100)	14.50	.65	.20	.15
1208a	5¢ Flag Tagged (1966)............. (100)	35.00	2.50	.35	.25
1209	1¢ Andrew Jackson (1963)..... (100)	5.50	.45	.20	.15
1209a	1¢ Tagged (1966) .... (100)	7.50	.50	.20	.18
1213	5¢ George Washington .... (100)	14.50	.65	.20	.15
1213a	5¢ Pane of 5 "Mailman", Slog. I...	...	...	6.00	2.25
1213a	5¢ Pane of 5 "Use Zone", Slog. II	...	...	25.75	9.50
1213a	5¢ Pane of 5 "Use Zip Code", Slog. III	...	...	3.00	2.25
1213b	5¢ Tagged (1963) .... (100)	32.50	8.00	.65	.50
1213c	5¢ Pane of 5 "Zone" Tagged, Slog. II	...	...	80.00	...
1213c	5¢ Pane of 5 "Zip" Tagged, Slog. III	...	...	1.35	...
1225	1¢ Jackson Coil	Line Pr.	2.75	.20	.15
1225a	1¢ Coil, Tagged (1966)...............	Line Pr.	.70	.20	.18
1229	5¢ Washington Coil	Line Pr.	2.75	.95	.15
1229a	5¢ Coil, Tagged (1963)...............	Line Pr.	8.95	1.50	.25

NOTE: USED STAMPS ARE OUR CHOICE OF TAGGED OR UNTAGGED.

1963 Commemoratives (See also 1180)

1230   1231   1232

1230-41	Set of 12	...	...	2.15	1.20
1230	5¢ Carolina Charter	7.00	.65	.20	.15
1231	5¢ Food for Peace	7.00	.65	.20	.15
1232	5¢ West Virginia Statehood..........	7.00	.65	.20	.15

1963 Commemoratives (cont.)

1233   1234   1235

1236   1237   1238

1239   1240   1241

Scott's No.		Mint Sheet	Plate Block	F-VF NH	F-VF Used
1233	5¢ Emancipation Proclamation....	8.00	.85	.20	.15
1234	5¢ Alliance for Progress	7.00	.65	.20	.15
1235	5¢ Cordell Hull	7.00	.65	.20	.15
1236	5¢ Eleanor Roosevelt	7.00	.65	.20	.15
1237	5¢ The Sciences.........................	7.00	.65	.20	.15
1238	5¢ City Mail Delivery	7.00	.65	.20	.15
1239	5¢ Int'l. Red Cross Centenary	7.00	.65	.20	.15
1240	5¢ Christmas Tree .... (100)	14.00	.65	.20	.15
1240a	5¢ Tagged .... (100)	67.50	7.50	.65	.50
1241	5¢ Audubon-Columbia Jays	8.75	.80	.20	.15

1964 Commemoratives (See also 1181)

1243   1242   1244

1245   1246   1247

1242-60	Set of 19	...	...	3.95	1.85
1242	5¢ Sam Houston.........................	7.50	.85	.20	.15
1243	5¢ Charles M. Russell	7.50	.85	.20	.15
1244	5¢ N.Y. World's Fair	7.50	.85	.20	.15
1245	5¢ John Muir, Naturalist...............	7.50	.85	.20	.15
1246	5¢ John F. Kennedy Memorial.....	18.50	1.85	.40	.15
1247	5¢ New Jersey Tercentenary.......	7.50	.65	.20	.15

FOR INFORMATION CONCERNING VERY FINE SEE PAGE II

1248   1249   1250   1251

1252   1254-57   1253

1258   1259   1260

Scott's No.		Mint Sheet	Plate Block	F-VF NH	F-VF Used
1248	5¢ Nevada Statehood	7.00	.65	.20	.15
1249	5¢ Register and Vote	7.00	.65	.20	.15
1250	5¢ William Shakespeare	7.00	.65	.20	.15
1251	5¢ Doctors Mayo	16.50	1.50	.35	.15
1252	5¢ American Music	8.75	.85	.20	.15
1253	5¢ Homemakers, Sampler	8.75	.85	.20	.15
1254-7	5¢ Christmas, attached ....(100)	27.50	1.35	1.10	1.10
1254-7	5¢ Set of 4 Singles	...	...	1.00	.60
1254-7a	5¢ Christmas Tagged, attd...(100)	75.00	8.75	3.00	2.95
1254-7a	5¢ Set of 4 Singles	...	...	2.65	2.40
1258	5¢ Verrazano-Narrows Bdg	7.00	.65	.20	.15
1259	5¢ Fine Arts - Stuart Davis	7.00	.65	.20	.15
1260	5¢ Amateur Radio	9.00	.90	.20	.15

1965 Commemoratives

1262   1261   1263

1265   1264   1266

Scott's		Mint Sheet	Plate Block	F-VF NH	F-VF Used
1261-76 Set of 16		...	...	2.95	2.00
1261	5¢ Battle of New Orleans	7.00	.65	.20	.15
1262	5¢ Physical Fitness - Sokol	7.00	.65	.20	.15
1263	5¢ Crusade Against Cancer	7.00	.65	.20	.15
1264	5¢ Churchill Memorial	7.50	.65	.20	.15
1265	5¢ Magna Carta	7.00	.65	.20	.15
1266	5¢ Int'l. Cooperation Year, U.N.	7.00	.65	.20	.15

1267   1268   1269   1270

1271   1272   1273

1274   1276   1275

Scott's No.		Mint Sheet	Plate Block	F-VF NH	F-VF Used
1267	5¢ Salvation Army	7.00	.65	.20	.15
1268	5¢ Dante Alighieri	7.00	.65	.20	.15
1269	5¢ Herbert Hoover	7.00	.65	.20	.15
1270	5¢ Robert Fulton	7.00	.65	.20	.15
1271	5¢ 400th Anniv. of Florida	7.00	.65	.20	.15
1272	5¢ Traffic Safety	7.00	.65	.20	.15
1273	5¢ John S. Copley Painting	7.00	.65	.20	.15
1274	11¢ Telecommunication Union	25.00	5.50	.45	.30
1275	5¢ Adlai Stevenson	7.00	.65	.20	.15
1276	5¢ Christmas Angel ....(100)	13.50	.65	.20	.15
1276a	5¢ Christmas, Tagged ......(100)	65.00	8.75	.65	.35

1965-79 Prominent Americans Series

(Sheets of 100)

1278,1299   1279   1280   1281,1297   1282,1303

		Mint Sheet	Plate Block	F-VF NH	F-VF Used
1278-88,1289-95 Set of 20		...	105.00	22.50	4.95
1278-88, 1289-95 Very Fine Set of 20		...	125.00	26.75	6.95

NOTE: OUR SETS WILL CONTAIN OUR CHOICE OF TAGGED OR UNTAGGED.

		Mint Sheet	Plate Block	F-VF NH	F-VF Used
1278	1¢ Thomas Jefferson (1968)	6.00	.45	.20	.15
1278a	1¢ Booklet Pane of 8	...	...	.95	.95
1278ae	1¢ Pane of 8, Dull Exp. Gum	...	...	1.25	...
1278b	1¢ Booklet Pane of 4 (1971)	...	...	.70	.65
1279	1¼¢ Albert Gallatin (1967)	12.50	8.25	.20	.15
1280	2¢ Frank Lloyd Wright (1968)	6.50	.45	.20	.15
1280a	2¢ Booklet Pane of 5 (S4 or S5) ('68)	...	...	1.10	1.00
S4 is "Mail Early", S5 is "Use Zip Code"					
1280c	2¢ Booklet Pane of 6 ('71)	...	...	1.00	.95
1280ce	2¢ Pane of 6, Dull Exp. Gum	...	...	.90	...
1281	3¢ Francis Parkman ('67)	8.50	.50	.20	.15
1282	4¢ Abraham Lincoln	14.00	.65	.20	.15
1282a	4¢ Lincoln, Tagged	12.00	.55	.20	.15

1283,1304   1283B,1304C   1284,1298   1285   1286

		Mint Sheet	Plate Block	F-VF NH	F-VF Used
1283	5¢ Washington, Dirty Face ('66)	18.75	.75	.22	.15
1283a	5¢ Washington, Tagged	15.00	.65	.20	.15
1283B	5¢ Washington,Clean Face ('67)	13.50	.65	.20	.15

Scott's No.		Mint Sheet	Plate Block	F-VF NH	F-VF Used
1283Bd	5¢ Clean Face, Dull Gum............	42.50	3.25	.45	...
1284	6¢ F.D.Roosevelt (1966).............	23.00	1.10	.24	.15
1284a	6¢ F.D.R., Tagged	20.00	.85	.20	.15
1284b	6¢ Booklet Pane of 8 (1967)	...	...	1.60	1.50
1284c	6¢ Pane of 5 (S4 or S5) (1968)....	...	...	1.50	1.35
1285	8¢ Albert Einstein (1966)	28.50	1.40	.30	.15
1285a	8¢ Einstein, Tagged	22.50	1.15	.25	.15
1286	10¢ Andrew Jackson (1967)	28.50	1.35	.30	.15

1286A   **1287**   **1288/1305E**   **1289**   **1290**

1291   **1292**   **1293**   **1294,1305C**   **1295**

1286A	12¢ Henry Ford (1968)	34.50	1.50	.35	.15
1287	13¢ John F. Kennedy (1967)	62.50	2.85	.65	.15
1288	15¢ O.W. Holmes, Die I (1968)....	42.50	1.95	.45	.15
1288d	15¢ Holmes, Die II (1979)	95.00	13.50	1.00	.20
1288B	15¢ Bklt. Single, Pf. 10 Die III	...	...	.45	.15
1288Bc	15¢ Bk. Pane of 8, Die III (1978)..	...	...	3.50	3.50
1289	20¢ George C. Marshall (1967)	72.50	3.25	.75	.15
1289a	20¢ Marshall, Tagged (1973)	57.50	2.50	.60	.15
1289ad	20¢ Dull Gum	97.50	6.00	1.00	...
1290	25¢ Frederick Douglass (1967)....	97.50	4.25	1.10	.15
1290a	25¢ Douglass, Tagged (1973)	85.00	3.50	.85	.15
1290ad	25¢ Dull Gum	115.00	6.75	1.20	...
1291	30¢ John Dewey (1968)..............	100.00	4.65	1.05	.15
1291a	30¢ Dewey, Tagged(1973)	80.00	3.75	.85	.15
1292	40¢ Thomas Paine (1968)	125.00	5.95	1.35	.15
1292a	40¢ Paine, Tagged (1973)	100.00	4.75	1.10	.15
1292ad	40¢ Dull Gum	145.00	7.75	1.50	...
1293	50¢ Lucy Stone (1968)................	165.00	7.50	1.75	.15
1293a	50¢ Stone, Tagged (1973)	140.00	6.25	1.50	.15
1294	$1 Eugene O'Neill (1967)	325.00	14.50	3.50	.15
1294a	$1 O'Neill, Tagged (1973)	275.00	12.50	3.00	.15
1295	$5 John B. Moore (1966)	...	72.50	16.50	2.95
1295a	$5 Moore (1973)	...	57.50	13.00	2.75

#1288 and 1305E: Die I top bar of "5" is horiz., tie touches lapel.
#1288d and 1305Ei: Die II top bar of "5" slopes down to right, tie does not touch lapel.
#1288B and 1288Bc: Die III booklets only, design shorter than Die I or II.

1305   **1306**   **1307**

1966-81 Prominent Americans, Coils, Perf. 10

1297-1305C	Prominent Am. Coils (9) ...		12.95	4.65	1.75
1297-1305C	Very Fine Set of 9		15.75	5.60	2.50
1297	3¢ Parkman (1975)	Line Pr.	.50	.20	.15
1297b	3¢ Bureau Precancel	Line Pr.	2.75	.25	.20
1297d	3¢ Dull Gum	Line Pr.	5.00	.50	...
1298	6¢ F.D. Roosevelt, Pf. Hz. ('67) ...	Line Pr.	1.40	.20	.15
1299	1¢ Jefferson (1968)	Line Pr.	.40	.20	.15
1299a	1¢ Bureau Precancel	Line Pr.	.60	.20	.18
1303	4¢ Lincoln	Line Pr.	.60	.20	.15
1303a	4¢ Bureau Precancel	Line Pr.	185.00	10.00	1.00
1304	5¢ Washington, Original..............	Line Pr.	.50	.20	.15
1304a	5¢ Bureau Precancel...................	Line Pr.	200.00	11.75	1.00
1304d	5¢ Dull Gum	Line Pr.	8.50	1.25	...
1304C	5¢ Redrawn ('81)	Line Pr.	1.80	.22	.15
1305	6¢ F.D.Roosevelt, Pf. Vert. ('68)	Line Pr.	.75	.25	.15
1305b	6¢ Bureau Precancel	Line Pr.	300.00	16.00	1.50
1305E	15¢ Holmes, Die I (1978)	Line Pr.	1.25	.45	.15
1305Ed	15¢ Die I, Dull Gum	Line Pr.	6.50	1.60	...
1305Ef	15¢ Bureau Precancel	Line Pr.	...	42.50	3.95
1305Ei	15¢ Holmes, Die II (1979)	Line Pr.	1.80	.60	.25
1305C	$1 O'Neill (1973)	Line Pr.	6.75	3.00	.75
1305Cd	$1 Dull Gum	Line Pr.	7.75	3.50	...

NOTE: F.VF, NH Bureau Precancels have full original gum and have never been used.

1966 Commemoratives

1306-22	Set of 17			3.25	1.85
1306	5¢ Migratory Bird Treaty	7.50	.65	.20	.15
1307	5¢ Humane Treatment Animals ...	7.00	.65	.20	.15

1308   **1309**   **1310**   **1312**

1313   **1314**   **1315**

1316   **1317**   **1318**

1319   **1320**   **1321**   **1322**

Scott's No.		Mint Sheet	Plate Block	F-VF NH	F-VF Used
1308	5¢ Indiana Statehood...................	7.00	.65	.20	.15
1309	5¢ American Circus (Clown)........	9.50	.90	.20	.15
1310	5¢ SIPEX Stamp........................	7.00	.65	.20	.15
1311	5¢ SIPEX Souvenir Sheet	...	...	.20	.20
1312	5¢ Bill of Rights.........................	7.50	.65	.20	.15
1313	5¢ Polish Millenium....................	7.00	.65	.20	.15
1314	5¢ National Park Service	8.50	.80	.22	.15
1314a	5¢ Parks, Tagged	16.50	2.00	.35	.30
1315	5¢ Marine Corps Reserve............	7.00	.65	.20	.15
1315a	5¢ Marines, Tagged....................	16.50	2.00	.35	.25
1316	5¢ Fed. of Women's Clubs...........	7.00	.65	.20	.15
1316a	5¢ Women's Clubs, Tagged.........	16.50	2.00	.35	.25
1317	5¢ Johnny Appleseed	7.00	.65	.20	.15
1317a	5¢ Appleseed, Tagged	16.50	2.00	.35	.25
1318	5¢ Beautification of America	8.00	.75	.20	.15
1318a	5¢ Beautification, Tagged............	16.50	2.00	.35	.25
1319	5¢ Great River Road....................	7.50	.65	.20	.15
1319a	5¢ Great River, Tagged	16.50	2.00	.35	.25
1320	5¢ Savings Bond - Servicemen ...	8.00	.75	.20	.15
1320a	5¢ Savings Bonds, Tagged..........	16.50	2.00	.35	.25
1321	5¢ Christmas, Madonna and Child by Hemming ....(100)	13.50	.65	.20	.15
1321a	5¢ Christmas, Tagged ....(100)	32.50	1.90	.35	.25
1322	5¢ Mary Cassatt Painting............	8.00	.75	.20	.15
1322a	5¢ Cassatt, Tagged	16.50	2.00	.35	.30

1967 Commemoratives

1323   **1324**   **1325**

1967 Commemoratives (cont.)

1326   1327   1328

1329   1330   1333   1334

1331-32   1338/1338D

1335   1336   1337

1968 Commemoratives (cont.)

1342   1343   1344

1345   1346   1347

1348   1349   1350

1351   1352   1353

1354   1355   1356

Scott's No.		Mint Sheet	Plate Block	F-VF NH	F-VF Used
1323-37	Set of 15	...	...	4.30	1.65
1323	5¢ National Grange	8.00	.65	.20	.15
1324	5¢ Canada Centenary	7.00	.65	.20	.15
1325	5¢ Erie Canal	7.00	.65	.20	.15
1326	5¢ Search for Peace - Lions	8.00	.80	.20	.15
1327	5¢ Henry David Thoreau	7.50	.65	.20	.15
1328	5¢ Nebraska Statehood	7.50	.65	.20	.15
1329	5¢ Voice of America	7.00	.65	.20	.15
1330	5¢ Davy Crockett	9.00	.85	.20	.15
1331-2	5¢ Space Twins, Attached	44.75	4.50	1.95	1.50
1331-2	Set of 2 Singles	...	...	1.10	.35
1333	5¢ Urban Planning	7.00	.65	.20	.15
1334	5¢ Finnish Independence	7.00	.65	.20	.15
1335	5¢ Thomas Eakins Painting	7.00	.65	.20	.15
1336	5¢ Christmas, Madonna	7.00	.65	.20	.15
1337	5¢ Mississippi Statehood	7.75	.75	.20	.15

1968-71 Regular Issues

1338	6¢ Flag & White House (100)	17.50	.75	.20	.15
1338D	6¢ Same, Huck Press ('70) (100)	17.00 (20)	3.50	.20	.15
1338F	8¢ Flag & White House ('71) (100)	21.50 (20)	4.50	.24	.15
1338A	6¢ Flag & W.H.-Huck Coil ('69) Full Line Pr.	2.25		.20	.15
1338A	6¢ Flag & W.H.-Huck Coil ('69) Partial Line Pr.	.90		...	...
1338G	8¢ Flag & W.H.-Huck Coil ('71) Partial Line Pr.	1.75		.24	.15

NOTE: #1338 is 19mm x 22mm, #1338D is 18¼mm x 21 mm.

1968 Commemoratives

1339   1341   1340

1339-40,42-64	**Set of 25**	...	...	**6.35**	**4.15**
1339	6¢ Illinois Statehood	8.25	.85	.20	.15
1340	6¢ Hemis Fair '68, San Antonio	8.25	.85	.20	.15

1968 Airlift to Servicemen

1341	$1 Eagle Holding Pennant	150.00	12.75	3.00	1.75

Scott's No.		Mint Sheet	Plate Block	F-VF NH	F-VF Used
1342	6¢ Support Our Youth - Elks	8.25	.85	.20	.15
1343	6¢ Law and Order	16.50	1.60	.35	.15
1344	6¢ Register and Vote	8.25	.85	.20	.15

1968 Historic American Flags

1345-54	Hist. Flag, Strip/10	16.75 (20)	7.50	3.50	4.00
1345-46	Plate Blk. of 4	...	1.50	...	...
1345-54	Set of Singles	...	...	2.75	2.50
1345	6¢ Fort Moultrie	...	...	.45	.30
1346	6¢ Fort McHenry	...	...	.45	.30
1347	6¢ Washington Cruisers	...	...	.25	.24
1348	6¢ Bennington	...	...	.25	.24
1349	6¢ Rhode Island	...	...	.35	.28
1350	6¢ First Stars & Stripes	...	...	.35	.28
1351	6¢ Bunker Hill	...	...	.25	.24
1352	6¢ Grand Union	...	...	.25	.24
1353	6¢ Philadelphia Light Horse	...	...	.25	.24
1354	6¢ First Navy Jack	...	...	.30	.28

1968 Commemoratives (continued)

1355	6¢ Walt Disney	22.50	2.10	.50	.15
1356	6¢ Father Marquette	8.50	.85	.20	.15

NOTE: UNUSED YEAR SETS HAVE SE-TENANTS ATTACHED, USED SETS HAVE SINGLES.

1968 Commemoratives (cont.)

1357	1358	1359

1360	1361	1362

1363	1364

Scott's No.		Mint Sheet	Plate Block	F-VF NH	F-VF Used
1357	6¢ Daniel Boone	8.25	.85	.20	.15
1358	6¢ Arkansas River Navigation	8.25	.85	.20	.15
1359	6¢ Leif Erikson	8.25	.85	.20	.15
1360	6¢ Cherokee Strip	9.75	1.10	.22	.15
1361	6¢ John Trumbull Painting	9.50	.90	.20	.15
1362	6¢ Waterfowl Conservation	12.75	1.10	.25	.15
1363	6¢ Christmas, Angel Gabriel	8.25 (10)	1.95	.20	.15
1363a	6¢ Christmas, Untagged	14.75 (10)	3.25	.30	.25
1364	6¢ American Indian - Joseph	12.75	1.10	.27	.15

1969 Commemoratives

1365-68

1369	1370	1371	1373

1365-86	**Set of 22 (no precancels)**	...	...	**7.95**	**2.95**
1365-8	6¢ Beautification, attached	25.00	2.50	2.25	2.15
1365-8	Set of 4 Singles	...	...	1.35	.65
1369	6¢ American Legion	8.25	.85	.20	.15
1370	6¢ Grandma Moses Painting	8.50	.85	.20	.15
1371	6¢ Apollo 8 Mission	14.00	1.30	.30	.15
1372	6¢ W.C. Handy	8.75	.90	.20	.15
1373	6¢ California Settlement	8.25	.85	.20	.15

1969 Commemoratives (cont.)

1372	1374	1375

1376-79

1381	1380	1382

1383	1385	1386

1384	1384 Precancel

Scott's No.		Mint Sheet	Plate Block	F-VF NH	F-VF Used
1374	6¢ John Wesley Powell	8.25	.85	.20	.15
1375	6¢ Alabama Statehood	8.25	.85	.20	.15
1376-9	6¢ Botanical Congress, att'd	29.50	2.75	2.50	2.50
1376-9	Set of Singles	...	...	1.60	.65
1380	6¢ Dartmouth College	9.50	.95	.20	.15
1381	6¢ Professional Baseball	55.00	4.95	1.20	.15
1382	6¢ College Football	20.00	1.85	.45	.15
1383	6¢ D.D. Eisenhower Memorial .. (32)	5.75	.85	.20	.15
1384	6¢ Christmas, Winter Sunday	8.25 (10)	1.95	.20	.15
1384a	6¢ Precancelled (Set of 4 Cities) .	175.00 (10)	85.00	2.75	1.60
1385	6¢ Crippled Children	8.25	.85	.20	.15
1386	6¢ William M. Harnett Painting . (32)	5.75	.85	.20	.15

NOTE: UNUSED YEAR SETS HAVE SE-TENANTS ATTACHED, USED SETS HAVE SINGLES.

NOTE: PRICES THROUGHOUT THIS LIST ARE SUBJECT TO CHANGE WITHOUT NOTICE IF MARKET CONDITIONS REQUIRE. MINIMUM MAIL ORDER MUST TOTAL AT LEAST $20.00.

1970 Commemoratives

1387-90

1391   1392

1405   1406   1407

1408   1409   1419

1410-13

Scott's No.	Mint Sheet	Plate Block	F-VF NH	F-VF Used
1387-92,1405-22 Set of 24 (no prec.)	...	...	6.75	2.80
1387-90 6¢ Natural History, attached ...(32)	7.25	1.00	.90	.90
1387-90 Set of 4 Singles	...	...	.85	.60
1391 6¢ Maine Statehood....................	9.50	1.00	.22	.15
1392 6¢ Wildlife Conserv. - Buffalo	9.50	1.00	.22	.15

1970-74 Regular Issue

1393,1401   1393D   1394/1402   1396

1397   1398   1399   1400

	Mint Sheet	Plate Block	F-VF NH	F-VF Used
1393-94,1396-1400 Set of 8....................	...	...	2.90	.90
1393 6¢ Eisenhower ....(100)	16.50	.85	.20	.15
1393v 6¢ Dull Gum...........................(100)	39.50	4.00	.40	...
1393a 6¢ Booklet Pane of 8	...	...	1.60	1.50
1393ae 6¢ Pane of 8, Dull Exper. Gum....	...	...	1.40	...
1393b 6¢ Bklt. Pane of 5, (S4 or S5) ('71)	...	...	1.25	1.25
1393D 7¢ Benjamin Franklin ('72) .... (100)	19.50	.95	.22	.15
1393Dv 7¢ Dull Gum...........................(100)	39.50	2.75	.40	...
1394 8¢ Ike, Multicolored ('71)....(100)	22.50	1.00	.24	.15
1395 8¢ Ike, Deep Claret, Bklt. Single..	...	...	.25	.15
1395v 8¢ Booklet Single, Dull Gum........	...	...	.30	...
1395a Booklet Pane of 8 (1971)............	...	...	2.25	2.10
1395b Booklet Pane of 6 (1971)............	...	...	1.75	1.75
1395c Booklet Pane of 4 Dull('72)	...	...	1.70	1.60
1395d Booklet Pane of 7, Dull (S4) (1972)	...	...	3.25	2.75
1395d Booklet Pane of 7, Dull (S5) (1972)	...	...	1.95	1.80
S4 is "Mail Early", S5 is "Use Zip Code"				
1396 8¢ U.S. Postal Service ('71).....(100)	21.50 (12)	3.00	.24	.15
1396 8¢ U.S. Postal Service...................	... (20)	4.75	...	...
1397 14¢ Fiorello La Guardia ('72) ...(100)	37.50	1.75	.40	.15
1398 16¢ Ernie Pyle ('71) ....(100)	42.50	1.85	.45	.15
1399 18¢ Dr. Eliz. Blackwell ('74) .....(100)	67.50	3.00	.65	.15
1400 21¢ Amadeo P. Giannini ('73)..(100)	62.50	2.75	.65	.15
1401 6¢ Eisenhower Coil, Perf. Vert. ...	Line Pr.	.50	.20	.15
1401a 6¢ Bureau Precancel	Line Pr.	150.00	8.50	1.00
1401d 6¢ Dull Gum	Line Pr.	2.75	.45	...
1402 8¢ Ike Coil, Perf. Vert. ('71)	Line Pr.	.60	.25	.15
1402b 8¢ Bureau Precancel	Line Pr.	130.00	6.50	1.00

NOTE: #1395 ONLY EXISTS WITH ONE OR MORE STRAIGHT EDGES SINCE IT COMES FROM BOOKLET PANES.

1414   1414a   1420

1415-18   1421-22

Scott's No.	Mint Sheet	Plate Block	F-VF NH	F-VF Used
1405 6¢ Edgar Lee Masters - Poet.......	8.25	.85	.20	.15
1406 6¢ Women Suffrage	8.25	.85	.20	.15
1407 6¢ South Carolina Founding	8.25	.85	.20	.15
1408 6¢ Stone Mountain Memorial	12.00	1.10	.25	.15
1409 6¢ Fort Snelling, Minnesota	8.25	.85	.20	.15
1410-13 6¢ Anti-Pollution, Attached	14.50 (10)	3.50	1.35	1.35
1410-13 Set of 4 Singles........................	...	...	.95	.65
1414 6¢ Christmas, Nativity, Ty. I.........	8.25 (8)	1.50	.20	.15
1414a 6¢ Christmas, Nativity, Precncl....	9.50 (8)	2.50	.20	.15
1414d 6¢ Type II, Horiz. Gum Breakers .	40.00 (8)	8.50	.85	.30
1414e 6¢ Type II, Precancelled	47.50 (8)	12.50	1.00	.35
1415-18 6¢ Christmas Toys, attd.............	25.00 (8)	5.00	2.35	2.25
1415-18 Set of 4 Singles	...	...	1.65	.60
1415a-18a 6¢ Toys, Precan., attached....	37.50 (8)	7.50	3.50	3.50
1415a-18a Set of 4 Singles....................	...	...	2.20	.80
1419 6¢ United Nations 25th Anniv	8.25	.85	.20	.15
1420 6¢ Landing of the Pilgrims	8.25	.85	.20	.15
1421-22 6¢ DAV - Servicemen, attd	8.25	1.30	.42	.40
1421-22 Set of 2 Singles.......................	...	...	.40	.30

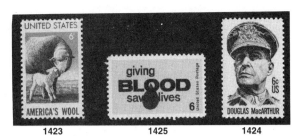

1423   1425   1424

1427-30

1426   1432   1431

1433   1434-35

1436   1437   1438   1439

1440-43

1444   1445   1446   1447

Scott's No.		Mint Sheet	Plate Block	F-VF NH	F-VF Used
1423-45	**Set of 23**............................	...	...	5.50	2.85
1423	6¢ American Wool Industry	8.25	.85	.20	.15
1424	6¢ Gen. Douglas MacArthur........	8.25	.85	.20	.15
1425	6¢ Blood Donor...........................	8.25	.85	.20	.15
1426	8¢ Missouri Sesquicentennial......	11.75 (12)	3.25	.26	.15
1427-30	8¢ Wildlife, attached .... (32)	8.75	1.20	1.10	1.00
1427-30	Set of 4 Singles	...	...	1.00	.70
1431	8¢ Antarctic Treaty.....................	10.75	1.00	.24	.15
1432	8¢ Bicentennnial Emblem............	11.00	1.10	.24	.15
1433	8¢ John Sloan Painting...............	10.75	1.00	.24	.15
1434-5	8¢ Space Achievement, attd........	12.75	1.15	.55	.50
1434-5	Set of 2 Singles	...	...	.50	.30
1436	8¢ Emily Dickinson	10.75	1.00	.24	.15
1437	8¢ San Juan, Puerto Rico............	10.75	1.00	.24	.15
1438	8¢ Prevent Drug Abuse	10.75 (6)	1.50	.24	.15
1439	8¢ CARE.....................................	10.75 (8)	1.95	.24	.15
1440-3	8¢ Historic Preservation, attd ... (32)	8.75	1.20	1.10	.95
1440-3	Set of 4 Singles	...	...	1.00	.70
1444	8¢ Christmas, Adoration	10.75 (12)	2.95	.24	.15
1445	8¢ Christmas, Partridge..............	10.75 (12)	2.95	.24	.15

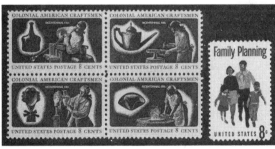

1448-51
1454
1452
1453

1456-59   1455

1446-74	**Set of 29**...................................	...	...	6.85	3.75
1446	8¢ Sidney Lanier..........................	10.75	1.00	.24	.15
1447	8¢ Peace Corps...........................	11.75 (6)	1.60	.25	.15
1448-54,C84	Parks Set of 8	58.50	5.65	1.40	1.10
1448-51	2¢ Cape Hatteras, attached... (100)	6.75	.60	.45	.45
1448-51	Set of 4 Singles	...	...	.44	.44
1452	6¢ Wolf Trap Farm......................	8.25	.85	.20	.15
1453	8¢ Old Faithful .... (32)	7.50	1.00	.24	.15
1454	15¢ Mt. McKinley.........................	21.00	1.90	.45	.25
	See #C84 for 11¢ City of Refuge National Park Issue				
1455	8¢ Family Planning	10.75	1.10	.24	.15
1456-9	8¢ Colonial Craftsmen, attd.........	11.50	1.25	1.00	.85
1456-9	Set of 4 Singles	...	...	.90	.60

| 1460 | 1461 | 1462 |

| 1463 | 1464-67 |

| 1469 | 1468 | 1470 |

| 1471 | 1472 | 1473 | 1474 |

Scott's No.		Mint Sheet	Plate Block	F-VF NH	F-VF Used
1460-62,C85	Olympics Set of 4	57.50	12.95	1.30	.70
1460	6¢ Olympics - Bicycling	9.00 (10)	2.10	.20	.15
1461	8¢ Olympics - Bobsledding	11.75 (10)	2.75	.24	.15
1462	15¢ Olympics - Running	23.50 (10)	5.25	.50	.35
	See #C85 for 11¢ Olympics				
1463	8¢ Parent Teacher Assn..............	10.75	1.00	.24	.15
1463r	8¢ P.T.A. Error Plate # Reversed	11.00	1.10	...	...
1464-7	8¢ Wildlife Conserv., attd.......... (32)	7.50	1.10	1.00	.90
1464-7	Set of 4 Singles	...		.90	.60
1468	8¢ Mail Order Business	10.75 (12)	3.00	.24	.15
1469	8¢ Osteopathic Medicine	10.75 (6)	1.60	.25	.15
1470	8¢ Tom Sawyer	10.75	1.10	.25	.15
1471	8¢ Christmas Angel	10.75 (12)	3.00	.24	.15
1472	8¢ Christmas, Santa Claus	10.75 (12)	3.00	.24	.15
1473	8¢ Pharmacy	20.00	1.75	.42	.15
1474	8¢ Stamp Collecting .... (40)	8.50	1.00	.24	.15

1973 Commemoratives

| 1475 | 1476 | 1477 |

1475-1508	Set of 34	...	...	8.25	4.25
1475	8¢ Love.....................................	10.75 (6)	1.50	.24	.15
1476-79	Communications in Colonial America(4)	39.75	3.85	.95	.50
1476	8¢ Printers and Patriots	10.75	1.00	.24	.15
1477	8¢ Posting a Broadside	10.75	1.00	.24	.15

| 1478 | 1479 | 1488 |

| 1480-83 | 1484 |

| 1485 | 1486 | 1487 |

1489-98

Scott's No.		Mint Sheet	Plate Block	F-VF NH	F-VF Used
1478	8¢ Postrider...............................	10.75	1.00	.24	.15
1479	8¢ Drummer	10.75	1.00	.24	.15
1480-83	8¢ Boston Tea Party, attd	12.00	1.15	1.00	.90
1480-83	Set of Singles	...	...	.90	.60
1484-87	Arts Set of 4................................	32.75	11.95	.95	.50
1484	8¢ Arts - George Gershwin.......... (40)	9.00 (12)	3.25	.25	.15
1485	8¢ Arts - Robinson Jeffers........... (40)	8.50 (12)	3.00	.24	.15
1486	8¢ Arts - Henry Tanner................ (40)	8.50 (12)	3.00	.24	.15
1487	8¢ Arts - Willa Cather .... (40)	8.50 (12)	3.00	.24	.15
1488	8¢ Nicolaus Copernicus	11.50	1.10	.25	.15

1973 Postal Service Employees

1489-98	8¢ Postal Employees, attd	13.00 (20)	5.50	2.50	2.50
1489-98	8¢ Set of Singles	...	...	2.40	1.50

VERY FINE COPIES OF #752-DATE ARE AVAILABLE FOR THE FOLLOWING PREMIUMS:
ADD 10¢ TO ANY ITEM PRICED UNDER 50¢. ADD 20% TO ANY ITEM PRICED AT 50¢ & UP.

1500   1499   1501

1502   1503   1504

1505   1506   1507   1508

Scott's No.		Mint Sheet	Plate Block	F-VF NH	F-VF Used
1499	8¢ Harry S Truman .... (32)	7.75	1.10	.25	.15
1500-2,C86	Electronics Set of 4	52.50	4.95	1.15	.70
1500	6¢ Electronics - Marconi	8.25	.85	.20	.15
1501	8¢ Electronics - Transistors	10.75	1.00	.24	.15
1502	15¢ Electronics - Inventions	19.50	1.85	.45	.35
See #C86 for 11¢ Electronics					
1503	8¢ Lyndon B. Johnson .... (32)	8.25 (12)	3.50	.28	.15
1504	8¢ Rural America - Cattle	10.75	1.00	.24	.15
1505	10¢ Rural America - Tent ('74)	13.50	1.30	.30	.15
1506	10¢ Rural America - Wheat ('74)	13.50	1.30	.30	.15
1507	8¢ Christmas, Madonna	10.75 (12)	3.00	.24	.15
1508	8¢ Christmas, Needlepoint	10.75 (12)	3.00	.24	.15

1509,1519   1510,1520   1511   1518

1973-1974 Regular Issues

1509	10¢ Crossed Flags .... (100)	28.50 (20)	6.50	.30	.15
1510	10¢ Jefferson Memorial .... (100)	28.50	1.35	.30	.15
1510b	Booklet Pane of 5	...	...	1.95	1.95
1510c	Booklet Pane of 8	...	...	2.50	2.25
1510d	Booklet Pane of 6 (1974)	...	...	7.50	5.00
1511	10¢ Zip Code (1974) .... (100)	28.00	(8) 2.50	.30	.15
1518	6.3¢ Liberty Bell Coil ('74) ....Line Pr.		.60	.20	.15
1518a	6.3¢ Bureau Precancel ....Line Pr.		1.20	.30	.20
1519	10¢ Crossed Flags Coil Line Prs./Full	4.75	Part 1.50	.35	.15
1520	10¢ Jeff. Memorial Coil ....Line Pr.		.70	.30	.15
1520a	10¢ Bureau Precancel ....Line Pr.		130.00	6.50	1.00

1525   1526   1527

1528   1529

1530-37

1538-41   1542

Scott's No.		Mint Sheet	Plate Block	F-VF NH	F-VF Used
1525-52	Set of 28......................................	...	...	8.50	3.95
1525	10¢ Veterans of Foreign Wars........	13.50	1.30	.30	.15
1526	10¢ Robert Frost............................	13.50	1.30	.30	.15
1527	10¢ Expo '74, Spokane................ (40)	13.00 (12)	4.25	.35	.15
1528	10¢ Horse Racing..........................	13.50 (12)	3.75	.30	.15
1529	10¢ Skylab I.................................	13.50	1.30	.30	.15
1530-37	10¢ U.P.U. Centenary Set, attd. (32)	11.50 (10)	3.50	2.75	2.50
1530-37	Same, Plate Block of 16...............	...	(16) 5.95		
1530-37	Set of Singles	...	...	2.65	2.00
1538-41	10¢ Mineral Heritage, attd .... (48)	14.00	1.30	1.20	1.00
1538-41	Set of Singles	...	...	1.10	.60
1542	10¢ Kentucky Settlement................	13.50	1.30	.30	.15

1974 Commemoratives (cont.)

1543-46

1547   1548   1549

1551   1550   1552

Scott's No.	Mint Sheet	Plate Block	F-VF NH	F-VF Used
1543-46 10¢ First Continental Congress, attd	15.00	1.40	1.30	1.10
1543-46 Set of 4 Singles	...	...	1.20	.60
1547 10¢ Energy Conservation	13.50	1.30	.30	.15
1548 10¢ Sleepy Hollow	13.50	1.30	.30	.15
1549 10¢ Retarded Children..................	13.50	1.30	.30	.15
1550 10¢ Christmas, Angel	13.50 (10)	3.25	.30	.15
1551 10¢ Christmas, Currier & Ives........	13.50 (12)	3.75	.30	.15
1552 10¢ Christmas, Peace on Earth, Self-adhesive	13.50 (20)	6.25	.30	.25
1552 Same - Plate Block of 12	...	(12) 3.75	...	...

NOTE: MOST COPIES OF #1552 ARE DISCOLORED FROM THE ADHESIVE. PRICE IS FOR DISCOLORED COPIES.

1975 Commemoratives

1553   1555   1554

1556   1557   1558

1553-80 Set of 28..................................	...	...	7.95	3.75
1553-55 American Arts Issue				
1553 10¢ Benjamin West Portrait..........	13.50 (10)	3.25	.30	.15
1554 10¢ Paul Laurence Dunbar - Poet .	13.50 (10)	3.25	.30	.15
1555 10¢ D.W. Griffith	14.00	1.30	.30	.15
1556 10¢ Space Pioneer - Jupiter	14.00	1.30	.30	.15
1557 10¢ Space Mariner 10	14.00	1.30	.30	.15
1558 10¢ Collective Bargaining..............	13.50 (8)	2.50	.30	.15

1975 Commemoratives (cont.)

1559   1560   1561

1562   1563   1564

1565-68   1569-70

Scott's No.	Mint Sheet	Plate Block	F-VF NH	F-VF Used
1559-62 Contributors to the Cause (4)	59.75	14.50	1.30	.75
1559 8¢ Sybil Ludington	10.75 (10)	2.50	.24	.20
1560 10¢ Salem Poor............................	13.50 (10)	3.25	.30	.15
1561 10¢ Haym Salomon	13.50 (10)	3.25	.30	.15
1562 18¢ Peter Francisco.....................	25.00 (10)	6.25	.55	.35
1563 10¢ Lexington-Concord .... (40)	11.00 (12)	3.75	.30	.15
1564 10¢ Battle of Bunker Hill .... (40)	11.00 (12)	3.75	.30	.15
1565-68 10¢ Military Uniforms, attd............	14.50 (12)	4.25	1.30	1.10
1565-68 Set of 4 Singles	...	...	1.20	.60
1569-70 10¢ Apollo Soyuz, attd.............. (24)	7.25 (12)	4.00	.65	.50
1569-70 Set of 2 Singles	...	...	.60	.30

1571   1572-75

1571 10¢ Int'l. Women's Year................	13.50 (6)	1.90	.30	.15
1572-75 10¢ Postal Service Bicent., attd....	14.50 (12)	4.25	1.30	1.10
1572-75 Set of Singles	...	...	1.20	.60

NOTE: UNUSED YEAR SETS HAVE SE-TENANTS ATTACHED, USED YEAR SETS HAVE SINGLES.

| 1576 | 1577-78 |

| 1579 | 1580 |

Scott's No.	Mint Sheet	Plate Block	F-VF NH	F-VF Used
1576	10¢ World Peace through Law	14.50	1.35	.30	.15
1577-78	10¢ Banking Commerce, attd.... (40)	12.00	1.50	.65	.50
1577-78	Set of 2 Singles	...	...	.60	.30
1579	10¢ Christmas, Madonna and				
	Child by Ghirlandaio	13.50 (12)	3.75	.30	.15
1580	10¢ Christmas Card, Perf. 11.2......	13.50 (12)	3.75	.30	.15
1580b	10¢ Christmas (P. 10½ x 11)..........	50.00 (12)	20.00	.85	.50

1975-1981 Americana Issue (Perf. 11 x 10½)

| 1581,1811 | 1582 | 1584 | 1585 |

| 1590/1616 | 1592,1617 | 1593 | 1594,1816 |

| 1595,1618 | 1596 | 1597/1618C | 1599,1619 |

| 1603 | 1604 | 1605 | 1606 |

| 1608 | 1610 | 1611 | 1612 |

1975-1981 Americana Issue (continued)
(Sheets of 100)

Scott's No.	Mint Sheet	Plate Block	F-VF NH	F-VF Used
1581-85,91-94,96-97,99-1612 Set of 19		132.50	27.95	5.75
1581	1¢ Ability to Write (1977)	5.00	.50	.20	.15
1581v	1¢ Dry Gum	6.00	.60	.20	...
1582	2¢ Freedom/Speak Out ('77)	7.50	.50	.20	.15
1582v	2¢ Dry Gum, white paper.................	29.50	1.75	.30	...
1582b	2¢ Dry Gum, cream paper (1981)...	11.50	.60	.20	...
1584	3¢ Cast a Free Ballot ('77)..............	11.00	.50	.20	.15
1584v	3¢ Dry Gum	12.00	.90	.20	...
1585	4¢ Public That Reads ('77)	12.50	.60	.20	.15
1585v	4¢ Dry Gum	23.75	1.50	.25	...
1590	9¢ Assem., Bklt.Sngl Pf.11x10½ ('77)	...	...	.65	.60
1590 & 1623 attached Pair (from 1623a)......		...	...	.95	.95
1590a	9¢ Booklet Single, Perf. 10	...	...	26.50	22.50
1590a & 1623b attd. Pair (from 1623c).........		...	...	28.50	...
1591	9¢ Assemble, Large Size................	25.00	1.25	.27	.15
1591v	9¢ Dry Gum	97.50	7.95	1.00	...
1592	10¢ Right to Petition ('77)	28.50	1.40	.30	.15
1592v	10¢ Dry Gum	33.75	1.60	.35	...
1593	11¢ Freedom of Press	29.00	1.35	.30	.15
1594	12¢ Freedom of Conscience ('81) ..	33.50	1.85	.35	.15
1595	13¢ Liberty Bell, Bklt. Single...........	...	...	.40	.15
1595a	13¢ Booklet Pane of 6	...	...	2.50	2.00
1595b	13¢ Booklet Pane of 7	...	...	2.65	2.50
1595c	13¢ Booklet Pane of 8	...	...	2.75	2.65
1595d	13¢ Booklet Pane of 5 (1976).........	...	...	2.00	1.85
1596	13¢ Eagle & Shield, Bullseye Perfs.	38.50 (12)	5.00	.40	.15
1596d	13¢ Line Perfs * ....(12)	595.00	40.00	...
1597	15¢ McHenry Flag, Pf. 11 ('78)......	42.50 (20)	9.50	.45	.15
1598	15¢ McHenry Flag, Bklt. Sgl. ('78) ..	...	...	.55	.15
1598a	15¢ Booklet Pane of 8	...	...	5.00	2.50
1599	16¢ Statue of Liberty (1978)	47.50	2.25	.50	.20
1603	24¢ Old North Church....................	65.00	3.25	.70	.20
1604	28¢ Fort Nisqually (1978)	75.00	3.75	.80	.20
1604v	28¢ Dry Gum	140.00	13.50	1.50	...
1605	29¢ Lighthouse (1978)	85.00	4.00	.90	.65
1605v	29¢ Dry Gum	180.00	17.50	1.80	...
1606	30¢ Schoolhouse (1979).................	85.00	4.00	.90	.15
1608	50¢ Iron "Betty" (1979)	140.00	6.50	1.50	.30
1610	$1 Rush Lamp (1979)...................	275.00	12.00	2.75	.30
1611	$2 Kerosene Table Lamp ('78)	535.00	23.00	5.50	.60
1612	$5 Railroad Lantern (1979).............	1300.00	60.00	13.75	2.25

* #1596 Bullseye Perforations line up perfectly where horiz. and vertical rows
meet. Pf 11.2   #1596d Line Perfs. do not meet evenly. Perforated 11:

1975-79 Americana Coil Issues - Perf. 10 Vert.

| 1613 | 1614 | 1615 | 1615C |

Scott's No.	Line Pair	F-VF NH	F-VF Used
1613-19,1811-16 Americana Coils (12) .... (11)	11.50	3.25	1.85
1613	3.1¢ Guitar (1979)................	.75	.20	.15
1613a	3.1¢ Bureau Precancel	5.50	.20	.18
1614	7.7¢ Saxhorns (1976)	1.10	.25	.20
1614a	7.7¢ Bureau Precancel	3.75	.70	.35
1615	7.9¢ Drum (1976)	.75	.25	.20
1615a	7.9¢ Bureau Precancel	3.00	.35	.20
1615v	7.9¢ Dry Gum	3.00	.40	...
1615va	7.9¢ Bureau Precancel, Dry Gum	3.50	.45	...
1615C	8.4¢ Steinway Grand Piano (1978)	2.25	.28	.20
1615Cd	8.4¢ Bureau Precancel	2.75	.45	.30
1616	9¢ Right to Assemble (1976)	.80	.28	.15
1616b	9¢ Bureau Precancel	9.95	.65	.35
1617	10¢ Right to Petition (1977)	.95	.30	.15
1617a	10¢ Bureau Precancel	2.75	.35	.25
1617v	10¢ Dry Gum	1.50	.33	...
1618	13¢ Liberty Bell	1.00	.35	.15
1618a	13¢ Bureau Precancel	...	6.50	.50
1618v	13¢ Dry Gum	1.75	.50	...
1618va	13¢ Bureau Precancel, Dry Gum..................	26.50	1.40	...
1618C	15¢ Fort McHenry Flag (1978).....................	...	.45	.15
1619	16¢ Statue of Liberty (1978)	1.40	.50	.35
1619a	16¢ Block Tagging	...	.90	.55

1975-77 Regular Issue

| 1622,1625 | 1623 |

1975-77 Regular Issues

Scott's No.		Mint Sheet	Plate Block	F-VF NH	F-VF Used
1622	13¢ Flag/Ind. Hall, Pf. 11x10½ (100)	35.00 (20)	8.25	.38	.15
1622c	13¢ Perf. 11 (1981)............. (100)	175.00 (20)	90.00	1.10	.95

* Plate Blocks of #1622 have Pl. #'s at Top or Bottom.
* Plate Blocks of #1622c have Pl. #'s at Left or Right.

1623	13¢ Flag over Capitol, Bklt. Sgl.				
	Pf. 11 x 10½ (1977)	...	...	.38	.20
1623a	13¢ & 9¢ Bklt. Pn./8 (7#1623,1#1590)			2.75	2.75
1623b	13¢ B. Sgl., Pf. 10 (1977)			.60	.55
1623c	13¢ & 9¢ B.P./8 (7#1623b,1#1590a)			29.75	18.50
1625	13¢ Flag over Ind. Hall, Coil ....(Partial Line)	2.50	.40	.15

1976 Commemoratives

1629-31		1632

		Mint Sheet	Plate Block	F-VF NH	F-VF Used
1629-32,83-85,90-1703	Set of 21	...	...	8.95	2.85
1629-31	13¢ Spirit of '76, attd......................	18.50 (12)	5.00	1.20	.90
1629-31	Set of Singles	...	...	1.10	.45
1632	13¢ Interphil '76, Philadelphia	17.50	1.60	.38	.15

1633	1635	1654

1976 State Flags Issue

		Mint Sheet	Plate Block	F-VF NH	F-VF Used
1633-82	13¢ State Flags attd	21.50 (12)	5.25	...	...
1633-82	13¢ Set of Singles	...	...	20.00	14.50
1633-82	13¢ Individual Singles	...	...	.55	.35

1633	DE	1646	VT	1659	FL	1671	ND
1634	PA	1647	KY	1660	TX	1672	SD
1635	NJ	1648	TN	1661	IA	1673	MT
1636	GA	1649	OH	1662	WI	1674	WA
1637	CT	1650	LA	1663	CA	1675	ID
1638	MA	1651	IN	1664	MN	1676	WY
1639	MD	1652	MS	1665	OR	1677	UT
1640	SC	1653	IL	1666	KS	1678	OK
1641	NH	1654	AL	1667	WV	1679	NM
1642	VA	1655	ME	1668	NV	1680	AZ
1643	NY	1656	MO	1669	NE	1681	AK
1644	NC	1657	AR	1670	CO	1682	HI
1645	RI	1658	MI				

1976 Commemoratives (continued)

1683	1684	1685

1686-89

1976 Commemoratives (continued)

Scott's No.		Mint Sheet	Plate Block	F-VF NH	F-VF Used
1683	13¢ Telephone Centennial	17.50	1.60	.38	.15
1684	13¢ Commercial Aviation...............	17.50 (10)	4.35	.38	.15
1685	13¢ Chemistry	17.50 (12)	4.70	.38	.15

1976 American Bicentennial Souvenir Sheets

		Mint Sheet	Plate Block	F-VF NH	F-VF Used
1686-89	Set of Four Souvenir Sheets	...	...	26.50	25.00
1686	13¢ Surrender of Cornwallis	...	...	4.25	4.00
1686a-e	Any Single			.95	.90
1687	18¢ Decl. of Independence.............	...	...	6.00	5.75
1687a-e	Any Single			1.35	1.30
1688	24¢ Washington Crossing Del........	...	...	8.25	8.00
1688a-e	Any Single			1.80	1.70
1689	31¢ Washington at Valley Forge	...	...	10.75	10.50
1689a-e	Any Single			2.25	2.15

1976 Commemoratives (continued)

1691-94

1699	1690	1700

1695-98

1701

1702

		Mint Sheet	Plate Block	F-VF NH	F-VF Used
1690	13¢ Ben Franklin and Map	17.50	1.60	.38	.15
1691-94	13¢ Dec. of Independence, attd	24.50 (16)	11.00	2.50	1.25
1691-94	Set of 4 Singles	...	...	2.40	.60
1695-98	13¢ Winter Olym. Games, attd	22.50 (12)	6.50	1.90	1.50
1695-98	Set of 4 Singles	...	...	1.80	.60
1699	13¢ Clara Mass .... (40)	16.95 (12)	5.75	.45	.15
1700	13¢ Adolph S. Ochs.................. (32)	11.00	1.60	.38	.15
1701	13¢ Christmas, Nativity	17.50 (12)	4.75	.38	.15
1702	13¢ Christmas Winter Pastime,				
	Andriotti Press	17.50 (10)	3.95	.38	.15
1703	13¢ Same, Gravure-Intaglio	17.50 (20)	7.75	.38	.15

#1702: Andriotti Press, lettering at Base is Black, No Snowflakes in Sky.
#1703: Intaglio-Gravure, lettering at Base is Gray Black, Snowflakes in Sky.

1704   1706-09

1705   1710   1711

1712-15   1716

1717-20   1721

1725

1722   1723-24   1726

1727   1728   1729   1730

Scott's No.		Mint Sheet	Plate Block	F-VF NH	F-VF Used
1722	13¢ Herkimer at Oriskany .... (40)	14.00 (10)	3.95	.38	.15
1723-24	13¢ Energy Conservation, attd. (40)	15.00 (12)	5.00	.80	.60
1723-24	Set of 2 Singles	...	...	.75	.30
1725	13¢ Alta California Settlement	17.50	1.60	.38	.15
1726	13¢ Articles of Confederation	17.50	1.60	.38	.15
1727	13¢ Talking Pictures	17.50	1.60	.38	.15
1728	13¢ Surrender at Saratoga .... (40)	14.00 (10)	4.00	.38	.15
1729	13¢ Christmas, Washington at Valley Forge........................ (100)	34.50 (20)	8.00	.38	.15
1730	13¢ Christmas - Mailbox............ (100)	33.50 (10)	4.00	.38	.15

1731   1732-33   1734   1735

1737   1738-42

1978 Commemoratives

		Mint Sheet	Plate Block	F-VF NH	F-VF Used
1731-33,44-69	Set of 29	...	...	14.25	5.75
1731	13¢ Carl Sandburg, Poet	17.50	1.60	.38	.15
1732-33	Captain Cook, attached................	17.50 (20)	8.00	.95	.75
1732	13¢ Captain Cook Portrait	...	1.60	.38	.15
1733	13¢ Hawaii Seascape....................	...	1.60	.38	.15

1978-80 Regular Issues

		Mint Sheet	Plate Block	F-VF NH	F-VF Used
1734	13¢ Indian Head Penny .... (150)	55.00	1.70	.38	.15
1735	(15¢) "A" & Eagle, Perf. 11 .... (100)	42.50	1.90	.45	.15
1735c	(15¢) Bullseye Perf. 11.2 .... (100)	60.00	3.25	.65	.35
1736	(15¢) "A" & Eagle, Perf. 11x10½ Booklet Single...............................	...	...	.42	.15
1736a	15¢ Booklet Pane of 8	...	...	3.00	2.75
1737	15¢ Roses, Perf. 10, Bklt. Single....	...	...	.45	.15
1737a	15¢ Booklet Pane of 8	...	...	3.50	3.00
1738-42	15¢ Windmills, Strip of 5 (1980) ...	...	...	2.50	2.00
1738-42	15¢ Set of 5 Singles.....................	...	...	2.40	.75
1742a	15¢ Booklet Pane of 10 (2 ea. #1738-42) (1980)................	...	...	4.95	4.50
1743	(15¢) "A" & Eagle, Coil, Pf. Vert. ....Line Pr.	1.10		.45	.15

NOTE: Modern booklet panes are glued into booklets and prices listed are for panes without selvedge and, usually, folded. Limited quantities exist unfolded with full selvedge—these are usually priced anywhere from 1½ to 4 times these prices when available.

Scott's No.		Mint Sheet	Plate Block	F-VF NH	F-VF Used
1704-1730	**Set of 27 ....**	...	...	**10.00**	**3.10**
1704	13¢ Washington at Princeton...... (40)	14.00 (10)	3.95	.38	.15
1705	13¢ Sound Recording..................	17.50	1.60	.38	.15
1706-09	13¢ Pueblo Art, attd .... (40)	15.75 (10)	4.50	1.65	1.25
1706-09	Set of 4 Singles.............................	...	...	1.50	.60
1710	13¢ Lindbergh's Flight....................	17.50 (12)	4.75	.38	.15
1711	13¢ Colorado Sthd., Line Perfs......	17.50 (12)	4.75	.38	.15
1711c	Bullseye Perfs	65.00 (12)	24.50	1.35	1.10
	#1711 Perforated 11, #1711c Perf. 11.2				
1712-15	13¢ American Butterflies, attd.......	18.50 (12)	5.50	1.65	1.25
1712-15	Set of 4 Singles............................	...	...	1.50	.60
1716	13¢ Lafayette's Landing........... (40)	14.00	1.60	.38	.15
1717-20	13¢ Revolutionary War Civilian Skills, attd.........................	18.50 (12)	5.50	1.65	1.25
1717-20	Set of 4 Singles............................	...	...	1.50	.60
1721	13¢ Peace Bridge 50th Ann.	17.50	1.60	.38	.15

1978 Commemoratives (continued)

1744   1745-48

1749-52   1753

1754   1755   1756

1757

Scott's No.		Mint Sheet	Plate Block	F-VF NH	F-VF Used
1744	13¢ Harriet Tubman........................	23.50 (12)	6.50	.50	.15
1745-48	13¢ Quilts, attd .... (48)	19.00 (12)	5.50	1.65	1.25
1745-48	Set of 4 Singles	...	...	1.50	.60
1749-52	13¢ American Dance, attd .... (48)	19.00 (12)	5.50	1.65	1.25
1749-52	Set of 4 Singles	...	...	1.50	.60
1753	13¢ French Alliance .... (40)	14.00	1.60	.38	.15
1754	13¢ Cancer Detection,Pap Test.....	21.00	2.10	.45	.15
#1755-56 Performing Arts					
1755	13¢ Jimmie Rodgers Commemorative..	17.50 (12)	5.00	.38	.15
1756	15¢ George M. Cohan	21.50 (12)	5.75	.45	.15

1978 CAPEX Souvenir Sheet

Scott's No.		Mint Sheet	Plate Block	F-VF NH	F-VF Used
1757	13¢x8 ($1.04) CAPEX				
	Souvenir Sheet .... (6)	17.00	...	2.95	2.50
1757	S.Sh. with Plate No......................	...	3.25	...	...
1757a-h	Set of 8 Singles...........................	...	...	2.85	1.50
	Strip of Four (a-d).....................	...	...	1.50	1.25
	Strip of Four (e-h).....................	...	...	1.50	1.25
	Block of 8, attached	...	...	3.50	3.25

1978 Commemoratives (continued)

1758   1759   1760-63

1764-67   1768   1769

1758	15¢ Photography........................ (40)	15.75 (12)	5.75	.45	.15
1759	15¢ Viking Mission to Mars............	20.00	2.25	.50	.15
1760-63	15¢ American Owls, attd..............	21.00	2.00	1.80	1.65
1760-63	Set of 4 Singles...........................	...	...	1.70	.60
1764-67	15¢ American Trees, attd .... (40)	17.50 (12)	6.00	1.80	1.65
1764-67	Set of 4 Singles...........................	...	...	1.70	.60
1768	15¢ Christmas Madonna............. (100)	39.50 (12)	5.50	.42	.15
1769	15¢ Christmas Hobbyhorse .... (100)	39.50 (12)	5.50	.42	.15

1979 Commemoratives

1770   1771   1772

1770-1802 Set of 33...................................		...	...	14.85	4.15
1770	15¢ R.F. Kennedy .... (48)	18.50	1.80	.42	.15
1771	15¢ Martin Luther King, Jr.............	20.00 (12)	6.25	.50	.15
1772	15¢ Int'l. Year of the Child............	19.50	1.80	.42	.15

NOTE: PRICES THROUGHOUT THIS LIST ARE SUBJECT TO CHANGE WITHOUT NOTICE IF MARKET CONDITIONS REQUIRE. MINIMUM ORDER MUST TOTAL AT LEAST $20.00.

1774   1775-78   1773

1795-98

1799

1800

1801   1802

Scott's No.		Mint Sheet	Plate Block	F-VF NH	F-VF Used
1787	15¢ Seeing Eye Dog	19.50 (20)	9.00	.42	.15
1788	15¢ Special Olympics	19.50 (10)	4.50	.42	.15
1789	15¢ John P. Jones, Perf. 11x12.	19.50 (10)	4.50	.42	.15
1789a	15¢ Perf. 11	32.50 (10	8.25	.70	.25
1790	10¢ Olympics - Decathalon	14.50 (12)	4.50	.32	.20
1791-94	15¢ Summer Olympics, attd	21.00 (12)	6.50	2.10	1.75
1791-94	Set of 4 Singles	...	...	1.95	.60
1795-98	15¢ Winter Olympics, Perf. 11 x 10½, attd. (1980)	21.00 (12)	6.50	2.10	1.50
1795-98	Set of 4 Singles	...	...	1.95	.60
1795-98a	15¢ Perf. 11 attd	47.50 (12)	14.00	4.00	3.95
1795-98a	Set of 4 Singles	...	...	3.75	3.60
1799	15¢ Christmas Madonna	(100) 39.50 (12)	5.50	.42	.15
1800	15¢ Christmas Ornament	(100) 39.50 (12)	5.50	.42	.15
1801	15¢ Will Rogers	21.00 (12)	6.00	.45	.15
1802	15¢ Vietnam Veterans	26.50 (10)	5.95	.55	.15

1980 Commemoratives (See also 1795-98)

1803   1804

1779-82   1783-86

Scott's No.		Mint Sheet	Plate Block	F-VF NH	F-VF Used
1773	15¢ John Steinbeck	19.00	1.80	.42	.15
1774	15¢ Albert Einstein	19.00	1.80	.42	.15
1775-78	15¢ PA Toleware, attd	(40) 18.00 (10)	5.00	1.90	1.50
1775-78	Set of 4 Singles	...	...	1.80	.60
1779-82	15¢ Architecture, attd	(48) 22.50	2.50	2.00	1.75
1779-82	Set of 4 Singles	...	...	1.90	.60
1783-86	15¢ Endangered Flowers, attd	22.75 (12)	6.50	1.90	1.50
1783-86	Set of 4 Singles	...	...	1.80	.60

1787   1788   1789

1805-10

1790   1791-94

1803-10,21-43 Set of 31		...	...	14.65	3.95
1803	15¢ W.C. Fields	21.00 (12)	6.00	.45	.15
1804	15¢ Benjamin Banneker	19.50 (12)	5.50	.42	.15
1805-10	15¢ Letter Writing, attd	(60) 29.50 (36)	19.50	2.95	2.75
1805-10	Set of 6 Singles	...	...	2.75	1.00

1980-81 Regular Issues

1813   1816   1818/1820

Scott's No.		Mint Sheet	Plate Block	F-VF NH	F-VF Used
1811	1¢ Inkwell & Quill, Coil .... Line Pr.		.40	.20	.15
1811v	1¢ Dry Gum .... Line Pr.		.65	.20	...
1813	3.5¢ Two Violins, Coil .... Line Pr.		.95	.20	.15
1813a	3.5¢ Bureau Precancel .... Line Pr.		2.75	.20	.18
1816	12¢ Conscience, Coil (1981) .... Line Pr.		1.95	.35	.20
1816a	12¢ Bureau Precancel .... Line Pr.		57.50	1.50	.75
1818	(18¢) "B" & Eagle, Perf. 11x10½				
	.... (100) 47.50		2.25	.50	.15
1819	(18¢) "B" & Eagle, Perf. 10, Booklet Single.............................	...	...	.50	.15
1819a	(18¢) Booklet Pane of 8 ('81)........	...	...	3.95	3.50
1820	(18¢) "B" & Eagle Coil ('81) .... Line Pr.		1.50	.55	.15

1980 Commemoratives (continued)

1821   1822   1823

1824   1825   1826

1827-30   1834-37

1980 Commemoratives (continued)

1831   1832   1833   1842

1838-41   1843

Scott's No.		Mint Sheet	Plate Block	F-VF NH	F-VF Used
1821	15¢ Frances Perkins	21.00	1.95	.45	.15
1822	15¢ Dolley Madison .... (150)	57.50	1.80	.42	.15
1823	15¢ Emily Bissell..........................	19.50	1.80	.42	.15
1824	15¢ H. Keller/A. Sullivan	19.50	1.80	.42	.15
1825	15¢ Veterans Administration..........	19.50	1.80	.42	.15
1826	15¢ Gen. Bernardo de Galvez	19.50	1.80	.42	.15
1827-30	15¢ Coral Reefs, attd....................	20.50 (12)	6.00	1.85	1.35
1827-30	Set of 4 Singles............................	...	...	1.70	.60
1831	15¢ Organized Labor	19.50 (12)	5.50	.42	.15
1832	15¢ Edith Wharton	21.75	2.00	.45	.15
1833	15¢ Education in America..............	27.50 (6)	3.50	.60	.15
1834-37	15¢ Pacific Northwest Indian Masks, attd..................... (40)	23.50 (10)	7.00	2.20	1.50
1834-37	Set of 4 Singles............................	...	...	2.00	.60
1838-41	15¢ Am. Architecture, attd .... (40)	22.50	2.50	2.25	1.95
1838-41	Set of 4 Singles............................	...	...	2.00	.60
1842	15¢ Christmas Madonna................	19.50 (12)	5.50	.42	.15
1843	15¢ Christmas Toys	21.50 (20)	10.00	.48	.15

ZIP, MAIL EARLY & COPYRIGHT BLOCKS
Due to space limitations, we do not list prices for zip code, mail early, copyright and other Inscription Blocks. With a few exceptions, these are usually priced at the total price of the single stamps plus one additional stamp. For example, if the stamp retailed for 45¢, a zip block of 4 would be priced at $2.25 (5 x .45).

1980-85 Great Americans Series,
Perforated II (Sheets of 100)

1844	1845	1846	1847
1848	1849	1850	1851
1852	1853	1854	1855
1856	1857	1858	1859
1860	1861	1862	1863
1864	1865	1866	1867
1868	1869		

Scott's No.		Mint Sheet	Plate Block	F-VF NH	F-VF Used
1844-69	Set of 26..	...	...	**12.75**	**3.50**
1844	1¢ Dix, Bullseye Perfs. Pf.11.2 ('83)	8.75 (20)	2.75	.20	.15
1844c	1¢ Dix, Line Pfs. Pf. 10.8 (1983).....	7.50 (20)	2.00	.20	.15
1845	2¢ Igor Stravinsky (1982)	7.50	.45	.20	.15
1846	3¢ Henry Clay (1983)	12.50	.65	.20	.15
1847	4¢ Carl Schurz (1983)	12.50	.65	.20	.15
1848	5¢ Pearl Buck (1983)	13.50	.70	.20	.15
1849	6¢ Walter Lippmann (1985)	18.00 (20)	4.15	.20	.15
1850	7¢ Abraham Baldwin (1985)...........	20.00 (20)	4.50	.22	.15
1851	8¢ Gen. Henry Knox (1985)............	21.50	1.25	.24	.15
1852	9¢ Sylvanus Thayer (1985)............	25.00 (20)	6.00	.27	.15
1853	10¢ R. Russell (1984)....................	28.50 (20)	7.25	.30	.15
1854	11¢ Alden Partridge (1985)............	30.00	1.60	.32	.15
1855	13¢ Crazy Horse (1982)	42.00	2.10	.45	.15
1856	14¢ Sinclair Lewis (1985)	42.00 (20)	9.75	.45	.15
1857	17¢ Rachel Carson (1981)	47.50	2.15	.50	.15
1858	18¢ George Mason (1981)	47.50	2.50	.50	.15
1859	19¢ Sequoyah	55.00	2.65	.60	.15
1860	20¢ Dr. Ralph Bunche (1982)..........	65.00	3.50	.70	.15
1861	20¢ Thomas Gallaudet (1983)........	65.00	3.50	.70	.15
1862	20¢ Harry Truman, Line Pfs. (1984)	62.50 (20)	13.00	.65	.15
1862a	20¢ Truman, Perf 11.2, Lg.Block Tag.	67.50 (4)	4.50	.70	.30
1862b	20¢ Pf. 11.2, Overall Tagging (1990)	72.50	5.75	.75	.50
1862d	20¢ Pf. 11.2, Shiny Gum	77.50	5.50	.80	...

1980-85 Great Americans Series, (cont.)
Perforated II (Sheets of 100)

Scott's No.		Mint Sheet	Plate Block	F-VF NH	F-VF Used
1863	22¢ Audubon, Line Pfs. ('85)	72.50 (20)	16.50	.75	.15
1863d	22¢ Bullseye Perfs, Perf 11.2.........	72.50 (4)	5.75	.75	.20
1864	30¢ F.C. Laubach, Line Pfs. ('84) ...	85.00 (20)	19.75	.90	.15
1864a	30¢ Perf. 11.2, Large Block	87.50	5.75	.90	.20
1864b	30¢ Perf. 11.2, Overall Tagging......	...	24.75	2.00	1.00
1865	35¢ Dr. Charles Drew ('81)	100.00	5.00	1.10	.15
1866	37¢ R. Millikan ('82)	100.00	4.75	1.10	.15
1867	39¢ Grenville Clark, Line Pfs. ('85) .	100.00 (20)	24.50	1.10	.15
1867c	39¢ Bullseye Perfs, Perf 11.2	100.00 (4)	6.75	1.10	.20
1868	40¢ L. Gilbreth, Line Pfs. ('84)	110.00 (20)	25.00	1.20	.15
1868a	40¢ Bullseye Perfs, Perf 11.2	110.00	6.75	1.20	.15
1869	50¢ Admiral Nimitz, Line Pfs. ('85) .	160.00 (4)	10.00	1.70	.15
1869a	50¢ Perf. 11.2, Block Tagging	150.00	8.25	1.60	.20
1869d	50¢ Perf.11.2,Overall Tag. Dull Gum	195.00	12.50	2.10	.35
1869ds	50¢ Pf.11.2,Overall Tag. Shiny Gum	165.00	10.00	1.75	...

1981 Commemoratives

| 1874 | 1875 | 1876-79 |

		Mint Sheet	Plate Block	F-VF NH	F-VF Used
1874-79,1910-45	Set of 42	...	...	25.50	5.50
1874	15¢ Everett Dirksen	19.50	1.80	.42	.15
1875	15¢ Whitney Young	19.50	1.80	.42	.15
1876-79	18¢ Flowers, attd .... (48)	26.75	2.60	2.30	1.75
1876-79	Set of 4 Singles	...	...	2.10	.60

1981-82 Regular Issues

| 1890 | 1891 |

| 1889a | 1892 | 1893 | 1894-96 |

		Mint Sheet	Plate Block	F-VF NH	F-VF Used
1880-89	18¢ Wildlife Bklt. Singles	...	...	8.50	1.50
1889a	Wildlife Bklt., Pane of 10	...	...	9.00	5.00
1890	18¢ Flag & "Amber Waves" ..... (100)	52.50 (20)	11.50	.55	.15
1891	18¢ Flag "Sea", Coil .... (Pl. # Strip)	6.75 (5)	5.00 (3)	.55	.15
1892	6¢ Circle of Stars, Bklt. Sgl.	...	...	.65	.20
1893	18¢ Flag & "For Purple" Bklt. Sgl.	...	...	.50	.15
1892-93	6¢ & 18¢, Vertical Pair................	...	...	1.15	1.10
1893a	Bklt Pn of 8 (2 #1892, 6 #1893) ...	...	...	3.75	3.50
1894	20¢ Flag over Supreme Court, Line Pf. 11, Dry Gum .... (100)	95.00 (20)	21.00	1.00	.15
1894e	20¢ Bullseye Pf. 11.2...................	57.50 (20)	12.50	.60	.15
1895	20¢ Flag over S.C., Coil ...... Pl. # Strip	5.25 (5)	2.75 (3)	.55	.15
1895e	20¢ Flag, Precancelled........ Pl. # Strip	90.00 (5)	85.00 (3)	1.30	.75
1896	20¢ Flag over S.C., Bk. Sgl	...	...	.60	.15
1896a	20¢ Booklet Pane of 6	...	...	3.25	3.00
1896b	20¢ Booklet Pane of 10 (1982)....	...	...	5.50	4.75

NOTE: Modern booklet panes are glued into booklets and prices listed are for panes without selvedge or with partial selvedge and, usually, folded. Limited quantities exist unfolded with full selvedge—these are usually priced anywhere from 1½ to 4 times these prices when available.

1981-91 Transportation Coil Series

11¢ RR Untagged Issue not included in Set.
<u>Pl. #s must appear on center stamp</u>

| 1897 | 1897A | 1898 | 1898A |

| 1899 | 1900 | 1901 | 1902 |

| 1903 | 1904 | 1905 | 1906 |

| 1907 | 1908 |

Scott's No.		Pl# Strip of 5	Pl# Strip of 3	F-VF NH	F-VF Used
1897-1908	**Mint (14 values)**	115.00	47.50	4.00	1.85
1897	1¢ Omnibus (1983)	.60	.50	.20	.15
1897A	2¢ Locomotive (1982)	.65	.55	.20	.15
1898	3¢ Handcar (1983)	.90	.75	.20	.15
1898A	4¢ Stagecoach (1982)	1.25	1.00	.20	.15
1899	5¢ Motorcycle (1983)	1.10	.90	.20	.15
1900	5.2¢ Sleigh (1983)	10.75	5.50	.20	.15
1901	5.9¢ Bicycle (1982)	19.00	6.00	.22	.18
1902	7.4¢ Baby Buggy (1984)	12.75	7.00	.24	.18
1903	9.3¢ Mail Wagon	17.50	6.75	.30	.18
1904	10.9¢ Hansom Cab (1982)	42.50	10.75	.50	.18
1905	11¢ RR Caboose (1984)	5.25	3.50	.35	.15
1905b	11¢ Untagged, not precanc. ('91)	3.25	2.75	.35	.25
1906	17¢ Electric Car	2.65	1.75	.50	.15
1907	18¢ Surrey	3.50	2.25	.60	.15
1908	20¢ Fire Pumper	3.50	2.25	.60	.15

#1897-97A: See #2225-26 for designs without "¢" signs.
#1898A: See #2228 for "B" Press

1981-91 Transportation Coil Series
Precancelled Stamps

Scott's No.		Pl# Strip of 5	Pl# Strip of 3	F-VF NH	F-VF Used
1898Ab/1906a	**Precancelled (8 values)**	115.00	107.50	2.60	1.60
1898Ab	4¢ Stagecoach (1982)	7.50	6.75	.20	.15
1900a	5.2¢ Sleigh (1983)	15.00	13.50	.20	.15
1901a	5.9¢ Bicycle (1982)	39.50	38.50	.28	.22
1902a	7.4¢ Baby Buggy (1984)	6.50	5.95	.30	.22
1903a	9.3¢ Mail Wagon	4.50	3.75	.33	.20
1904a	10.9¢ Hansom Cab (1982)	39.50	37.50	.50	.25
1905a	11¢ RR Caboose (1984)	4.75	4.25	.40	.22
1906a	17¢ Electric Car, Type "A"	4.75	3.75	.50	.35
1906ab	17¢ Type "B"	31.50	29.50	1.50	.75
1906ac	17¢ Type "C"	14.50	12.75	1.00	.50

Type "A" - "Presorted" 11.5mm Length
Type "B" - "Presorted" 12.5mm Length
Type "C" - "Presorted" 13.5mm Length

1983 Express Mail Issue

1909

Scott's No.		Mint Sheet	Plate Block	F-VF NH	F-VF Used
1909	$9.35 Eagle, Booklet Single	...	...	28.50	22.50
1909a	$9.35 Booklet Pane of 3	...	...	82.50	...

1981 Commemoratives (continued)

| 1910 | 1911 | 1920 |

1912-19

1921-24

1910	18¢ American Red Cross	28.75	2.80	.60	.15
1911	18¢ Savings & Loan	25.00	2.50	.55	.15
1912-19	18¢ Space Achievement, attd (48)	32.50 (8)	6.00	5.50	3.75
1912-19	Set of Singles	...	...	5.25	1.50
1920	18¢ Professional Management	25.00	2.40	.55	.15
1921-24	18¢ Wildlife Habitats, attd	25.00	2.50	2.30	1.50
1921-24	Set of 4 Singles	...	...	2.10	.60

1925   1926   1927

1928-31

1932   1934   1933

1935   1936   1939

1937-38   1940

Scott's No.		Mint Sheet	Plate Block	F-VF NH	F-VF Used
1925	18¢ Disabled Persons	25.00	2.40	.55	.15
1926	18¢ Edna St. Vincent Millay	25.00	2.40	.55	.15
1927	18¢ Alchoholism	57.50 (20)	40.00	.65	.15
1928-31	18¢ Architecture, attd .... (40)	27.50	3.00	2.75	2.00
1928-31	Set of 4 Singles	...	...	2.50	.60
1932	18¢ Babe Didrikson Zaharias	39.50	4.00	.85	.15
1933	18¢ Bobby Jones	80.00	7.75	1.75	.15
1934	18¢ F. Remington Sculpture	25.00	2.40	.55	.15
1935	18¢ James Hoban	25.00	2.40	.55	.15
1936	20¢ James Hoban	26.00	2.50	.55	.15
1937-38	18¢ Yorktown - Capes, attd	27.50	3.00	1.40	.90
1937-38	Set of Singles	...	...	1.30	.30
1939	(20¢)Christmas Madonna .... (100)	50.00	2.50	.55	.15
1940	(20¢)Christmas-Teddy Bear	26.00	2.50	.55	.15

1941   1942-45

Scott's No.		Mint Sheet	Plate Block	F-VF NH	F-VF Used
1941	20¢ John Hanson	26.50	2.50	.55	.15
1942-45	20¢ Desert Plants, attached .... (40)	26.00	3.25	2.75	1.50
1942-45	Set of 4 Singles	...	...	2.50	.60

1981-82 Regular Issues

1946-1948   1949

1946	(20¢) "C" & Eagle, Pf. 11x10½ .. (100)	52.50	2.50	.55	.15
1947	(20¢) "C" & Eagle, Coil .... Line Pr.		2.15	.85	.15
1948	(20¢) "C" & Eagle,Perf.10,Bklt. Sgl.	...	...	.60	.15
1948a	(20¢)Booklet Pane of 10	...	...	5.95	5.00
1949	20¢ Ty. I,Bighorn Sheep,Bklt. Sgl...	...	...	.70	.15
1949a	20¢ Ty. I, Booklet Pane of 10	...	...	7.25	5.00
1949c	20¢ Type II, Bklt Single	...	...	1.50	.50
1949d	20¢ Ty. II, Booklet Pane of 10	...	...	14.50	...

* Ty. I is 18¾ mm wide and has overall tagging.
Ty. II is 18½ mm wide and has block tagging.

1982 Commemoratives

1950   1951   1952

1950-52,2003-4,2006-30 Set of 30		...	...	21.75	3.65
1950	20¢ Franklin D. Roosevelt .... (48)	26.50	2.50	.55	.15
1951	20¢ "LOVE", Perf. 11 x 10½	45.00	5.50	.95	.25
1951a	20¢ Perf. 11	36.50	3.25	.75	.15
1952	20¢ George Washington	28.50	2.75	.60	.15

1982 State Birds & Flowers Issue

1953	Alabama	1970	Louisiana	1987	Ohio
1954	Alaska	1971	Maine	1988	Oklahoma
1955	Arizona	1972	Maryland	1989	Oregon
1956	Arkansas	1973	Massachusetts	1990	Pennsylvania
1957	California	1974	Michigan	1991	Rhode Island
1958	Colorado	1975	Minnesota	1992	South Carolina
1959	Connecticut	1976	Mississippi	1993	South Dakota
1960	Delaware	1977	Missouri	1994	Tennessee
1961	Florida	1978	Montana	1995	Texas
1962	Georgia	1979	Nebraska	1996	Utah
1963	Hawaii	1980	Nevada	1997	Vermont
1964	Idaho	1981	New Hampshire	1998	Virginia
1965	Illinois	1982	New Jersey	1999	Washington
1966	Indiana	1983	New Mexico	2000	West Virginia
1967	Iowa	1984	New York	2001	Wisconsin
1968	Kansas	1985	North Carolina	2002	Wyoming
1969	Kentucky	1986	North Dakota		

1982 State Birds & Flowers Issue

| | 1957 | 1961 | 1966 | 1972 |

Scott's No.		Mint Sheet	Plate Block	F-VF NH	F-VF Used
1953-2002	20¢ 50 States, attd, Pf. 10½ x 11	45.00	...	...	...
1953a-2002a	20¢ 50 States, attd., Pf. 11	47.50	...	...	...
1953-2002	Set of Singles,	...	...	42.50	17.50
1953-2002	20¢ Individual Singles....	...	...	1.10	.50

NOTE: Sets of singles may contain mixed perforation sizes.

1982 Commemoratives (continued)

| 2003 | 2004 | 2005 |

2003	20¢ U.S. & Netherlands	32.50 (20)	13.95	.60	.15
2004	20¢ Library of Congress	26.50	2.50	.55	.15

1982 Consumer Education Coil

| 2005 | 20¢ Clothing Label .... (Pl# Strip) | 135.00(5) | 25.00(3) | 1.00 | .15 |

1982 Commemoratives (continued)

| 2006-09 | 2010 |

| 2012 | 2011 | 2013 |

2006-09	20¢ Knoxville Fair, attd	32.50	3.25	2.80	1.50
2006-09	Set of 4 Singles	...	...	2.70	.60
2010	20¢ Horatio Alger	26.50	2.50	.55	.15
2011	20¢ "Aging Together"	26.50	2.50	.55	.15
2012	20¢ Arts - The Barrymores	26.50	2.50	.55	.15
2013	20¢ Mary Walker, Surgeon	30.00	3.00	.65	.15

1982 Commemoratives (continued)

| 2015 | 2014 | 2016 |

| 2019-22 | 2017 |
| | 2018 |

| 2023 | 2024 | 2025 |

| 2026 | 2027-30 |

Scott's No.		Mint Sheet	Plate Block	F-VF NH	F-VF Used
2014	20¢ Peace Garden	26.50	2.50	.55	.15
2015	20¢ Libraries of America	26.50	2.50	.55	.15
2016	20¢ Jackie Robinson	115.00	10.75	2.50	.15
2017	20¢ Touro Synagogue	31.50 (20)	13.75	.65	.15
2018	20¢ Wolf Trap Farm Park	26.50	2.50	.55	.15
2019-22	20¢ Architecture, attached ..... (40)	32.50	4.25	3.50	2.50
2019-22	Set of 4 Singles	...	...	3.25	.60
2023	20¢ St. Francis of Assisi	28.50	2.75	.60	.15
2024	20¢ Ponce de Leon	35.00 (20)	16.00	.75	.15
#2025-30	Christmas Issues				
2025	13¢ Christmas, Kitten & Puppy	20.00	1.95	.45	.15
2026	20¢ Christmas, Tiepolo Madonna	29.50 (20)	13.75	.60	.15
2027-30	20¢ Christmas Winter Scenes, attd	39.50	4.00	3.50	1.60
2027-30	Set of 4 Singles	...	...	3.30	.60

1983 Commemoratives

2032-35

2036   2031   2037

2039   2038   2040

2041   2042   2043

2044   2045   2046   2047

1983 Commemoratives (cont.)

2048-51

2052   2053   2054

2055-58

2059-62

2063   2064   2065

Scott's No.		Mint Sheet	Plate Block	F-VF NH	F-VF Used
2031-65	Set of 35	...	...	22.75	4.65
2031	20¢ Sciences & Industry	26.50	2.50	.55	.15
2032-35	20¢ Ballooning, attached.......... (40)	26.00	3.00	2.75	1.50
2032-35	Set of 4 Singles...........................	...	...	2.50	.60
2036	20¢ Sweden, B. Franklin	26.50	2.50	.55	.15
2037	20¢ Civilian Conservation Corp....	26.50	2.50	.55	.15
2038	20¢ Joseph Priestley....................	31.00	3.00	.65	.15
2039	20¢ Voluntarism	31.75	(20) 13.95	.65	.15
2040	20¢ German Immigration..............	26.50	2.50	.55	.15
2041	20¢ Brooklyn Bridge.....................	26.50	2.50	.55	.15
2042	20¢ Tennessee Valley Authority ..	31.75	(20) 13.95	.65	.15
2043	20¢ Physical Fitness	31.75	(20) 13.95	.65	.15
2044	20¢ Scott Joplin...........................	31.00	3.00	.65	.15
2045	20¢ Medal of Honor.............. (40)	27.50	3.00	.70	.15
2046	20¢ Babe Ruth	105.00	9.75	2.25	.15
2047	20¢ Nathaniel Hawthorne.............	26.50	2.50	.55	.15

Scott's No.		Mint Sheet	Plate Block	F-VF NH	F-VF Used
2048-51	13¢ Summer Olympics, attd........	29.50	3.75	3.00	1.50
2048-51	Set of 4 Singles	...	...	2.90	.80
2052	20¢ Treaty of Paris .... (40)	23.50	2.75	.60	.15
2053	20¢ Civil Service..........................	31.75	(20) 13.95	.65	.15
2054	20¢ Metropolitan Opera...............	29.50	2.75	.60	.15
2055-58	20¢ Inventors, attd......................	35.00	4.25	3.35	1.75
2055-58	Set of 4 Singles	...	...	3.00	.60
2059-62	20¢ Streetcars, attd.....................	29.50	3.75	3.00	1.75
2059-62	Set of 4 Singles	...	...	2.90	.60
#2063-64 Christmas Issues					
2063	20¢ Christmas, Raphael Madonna	26.50	2.50	.55	.15
2064	20¢ Christmas, Santa Claus........	30.00	(20) 13.95	.60	.15
2065	20¢ Martin Luther	26.50	2.50	.55	.15

2066   2067-70   2071

2072   2073   2074   2075

2076-79

2080   2081   2086

2082-85

2087   2091   2092

2088   2089   2090   2093

2094   2095   2096   2097

Scott's No.		Mint Sheet	Plate Block	F-VF NH	F-VF Used
2066-2109	Set of 44	...	...	32.95	5.75
2066	20¢ Alaska Statehood	26.50	2.50	.55	.15
2067-70	20¢ Winter Olympics, attd	40.00	4.25	3.50	1.75
2067-70	Set of 4 Singles	...	...	3.25	.60
2071	20¢ Fed. Deposit Insurance	26.50	2.50	.55	.15
2072	20¢ Love, Hearts	32.50 (20)	14.50	.65	.15
2073	20¢ Carter G. Woodson	29.50	2.75	.60	.15
2074	20¢ Soil & Water Conservation .	26.50	2.50	.55	.15
2075	20¢ Credit Union Act	26.50	2.50	.55	.15
2076-79	20¢ Orchids, attached ....(48)	30.00	3.50	2.75	1.75
2076-79	Set of 4 Singles	...	...	2.50	.60
2080	20¢ Hawaii Statehood	29.50	2.75	.65	.15
2081	20¢ National Archives	29.50	2.75	.65	.15

Scott's No.		Mint Sheet	Plate Block	F-VF NH	F-VF Used
2082-85	20¢ Summer Olympics, attd	47.50	5.50	4.65	2.25
2082-85	Set of 4 Singles	...	...	4.50	.60
2086	20¢ Louisiana World's Fair .....(40)	23.50	2.75	.60	.15
2087	20¢ Health Research	31.50	3.00	.65	.15
2088	20¢ Douglas Fairbanks..............	35.00 (20)	17.50	.65	.15
2089	20¢ Jim Thorpe..........................	33.50	3.00	.70	.15
2090	20¢ John McCormack...............	26.50	2.50	.55	.15
2091	20¢ St. Lawrence Seaway.........	26.50	2.50	.55	.15
2092	20¢ Waterfowl Preservation	45.00	4.50	1.00	.15
2093	20¢ Roanoke Voyages	31.00	2.80	.65	.15
2094	20¢ Herman Melville.................	26.50	2.50	.55	.15
2095	20¢ Horace Moses	37.50 (20)	17.00	.75	.15
2096	20¢ Smokey Bear	32.50	3.00	.70	.15
2097	20¢ Roberto Clemente	130.00	12.75	2.75	.15

1984 Commemoratives (cont.)

2098-2101   2102

2103   2104   2105

2106   2107   2108   2110

2109

Scott's No.		Mint Sheet	Plate Block	F-VF NH	F-VF Used
2098-2101	20¢ Dogs, attd......................(40)	29.50	4.25	3.50	2.50
2098-2101	Set of 4 Singles........................	...	...	3.00	.60
2102	20¢ Crime Prevention..................	26.50	2.50	.55	.15
2103	20¢ Hispanic Americans...........(40)	21.50	2.50	.55	.15
2104	20¢ Family Unity........................	40.00	(20) 17.75	.85	.15
2105	20¢ Eleanor Roosevelt ....(48)	25.00	2.50	.55	.15
2106	20¢ Nation of Readers................	32.50	2.95	.70	.15
#2107-8	Christmas Issues				
2107	20¢ Madonna & Child	26.50	2.50	.55	.15
2108	20¢ Santa Claus	26.50	2.50	.55	.15
2109	20¢ Vietnam Memorial..............(40)	35.00	4.25	.90	.15

1985 Commemoratives

2110,2137-47,52-66	Set of 27...................	...	...	36.75	4.35
2110	22¢ Jerome Kern	31.50	3.00	.65	.15

1985-87 Regulars

2111-2113   2114-2115   2115b   2116

2111	(22¢) "D" Stamp.......................(100)	90.00	(20) 32.50	.75	.15
2112	(22¢) "D" Coil.................. (Pl# Strip)	9.25	(5) 6.50 (3)	.70	.15
2113	(22¢) "D" Booklet Sgl..............	...	...	1.00	.15
2113a	(22¢) "D" Bklt. Pane of 10........	...	...	9.75	5.00
2114	22¢ Flag over Capitol..........(100)	60.00	3.00	.65	.15
2115	22¢ Flag over Cap. Coil.. (Pl# Strip)	4.00	(5) 3.00 (3)	.65	.15
2115b	Flag "T" Test Coil ('87).... (Pl# Strip)	5.50	(5) 4.25 (3)	.65	.15
#2115b has a tiny "T" below capitol building					
2116	22¢ Flag over Cap. Bklt. Sgl....	...	...	.85	.15
2116a	22¢ Booklet Pane of 5	...	...	4.25	2.50

1985-89 Regulars

2117-21

2122

Scott's No.		Mint Sheet	Plate Block	F-VF NH	F-VF Used
2117-21	22¢ Seashells, Strip of 5......................	...	...	3.25	1.75
2117-21	Set of 5 Singles	...		3.15	.90
2121a	22¢ Bklt. Pane of 10	...	...	5.95	5.00
2122	$10.75 Express Mail, Eagle & Moon, Booklet Single, Type I	...	...	27.50	8.95
2122a	$10.75 Bklt. Pane of 3 (Pl. #11111)	...	...	80.00	...
2122b	$10.75 Ty. II, Bklt. Sgl (1989).......	...	...	37.50	11.95
2122c	$10.75 Ty. II Bklt.Pane of 3(Pl.#22222) ...	...	...	110.00	...

* Ty. I: washed out appearance; "$10.75" is grainy.
* Ty. II: brighter colors; "$10.75" is smoother and less grainy.

1985-89 TRANSPORTATION COIL SERIES II

School Bus 1920s 3.4 USA	Buckboard 1880s 4.9 USA	Star Route Truck 5.5 USA 1910s	Tricycle 1880s 6 USA
2123	2124	2125	2126
Tractor 1920s 7.1 USA	Ambulance 1860s 8.3 USA	Tow Truck 1920s 8.5 USA	Oil Wagon 1890s 10.1 USA
2127	2128	2129	2130
Stutz Bearcat 1933 11 USA	Stanley Steamer 1909 12 USA	Pushcart 1880s 12.5 USA	Iceboat 1880s 14 USA
2131	2132	2133	2134
Dog Sled 1920s 17 USA	Bread Wagon 1880s 25 USA		
2135	2136		

1985-89 TRANSPORTATION COIL SERIES II

* Pl. #s must appear on center stamp. Sets do not include "B" press issue.

Scott's No.		Pl.# Strip of 5	Pl.# Strip of 3	F-VF NH	Used
2123-36	Mint (14 values)......................	36.75	28.50	4.25	1.95
2123	3.4¢ School Bus	1.20	1.00	.20	.15
2124	4.9¢ Buckboard	1.15	.90	.20	.18
2125	5.5¢ Star Route Truck ('86)	2.00	1.60	.20	.15
2126	6¢ Tricycle	1.85	1.50	.20	.15
2127	7.1¢ Tractor (1987)..................	2.95	2.50	.22	.18
2128	8.3¢ Ambulance	1.85	1.50	.25	.15
2129	8.5¢ Tow Truck ('87)................	4.00	3.50	.25	.15
2130	10.1¢ Oil Wagon.....................	3.25	2.30	.30	.15
2131	11¢ Stutz Bearcat	1.85	1.30	.32	.15
2132	12¢ Stanley Steamer, Type I.....	2.95	2.50	.40	.15
2133	12.5¢ Pushcart	3.50	2.75	.35	.20
2134	14¢ Iceboat, Type I	2.75	2.25	.40	.15
2134b	14¢ "B" Press (no line) Ty.II ('86)	5.00	4.25	.50	.20
2135	17¢ Dog Sled (1986)	4.25	3.00	.55	.15
2136	25¢ Bread Wagon (1986).........	4.75	3.25	.75	.15

NOTE: #2134 17½ MM WIDE, #2134B 17¼ MM WIDE

PRECANCELLED COILS

Scott's No.		Pl.# Strip of 5	Pl.# Strip of 3	F-VF NH	Used
2123a/33a	Precanc. (12 values)	35.75	30.75	2.90	2.10
2123a	3.4¢ School Bus	6.75	6.50	.20	.15
2124a	4.9¢ Buckboard	2.10	1.85	.20	.18
2125a	5.5¢ Star Route Truck ('86)	1.95	1.60	.20	.15
2126a	6¢ Tricycle	2.15	1.75	.20	.15
2127a	7.1¢ Tractor ('87)	3.95	3.50	.22	.18
2127av	7.1¢ Zip + 4 Precancel ('89)	2.65	2.25	.22	.18
2128a	8.3¢ Ambulance	1.85	1.50	.25	.18
2129a	8.5¢ Tow Truck ('87)................	3.65	3.15	.25	.18
2130a	10.1¢ Oil Wagon, Black Prec. ...	3.25	2.75	.30	.22
2130av	10.1¢ Oil Wagon,Red Prec.('88)	2.90	2.25	.30	.22
2132a	12¢ Stanley Steamer, Type I.....	3.00	2.50	.40	.25
2132b	12¢ "B" Press,Ty.II (no line) ('87)	28.75	27.50	1.20	.50
	#2132, 2132a "Stanley Steamer 1909" 18mm.				
	#2132b "Stanley Steamer 1909" 17½ mm.				
2133a	12.5¢ Pushcart	3.50	3.00	.35	.25

1985 Commemoratives (cont.)

2137   **2138-41**

2142   **2143**   **2144**

2145   **2146**   **2147**

Scott's No.		Mint Sheet	Plate Block	F-VF NH	F-VF Used
2137	22¢ Mary Mcleod Bethune	32.50	3.25	.70	.15
2138-41	22¢ Duck Decoys, attached	95.00	12.00	9.50	3.25
2138-41	Set of 4 Singles	...	...	8.50	.70
2142	22¢ Winter Spec. Olympics ...... (40)	25.00	2.95	.65	.15
2143	22¢ Love.................................	33.50	3.25	.70	.15
2144	22¢ Rural Electrification Ad.	55.00	(20) 32.50	.80	.15
2145	22¢ Ameripex '86, Chicago ...... (48)	27.50	2.75	.60	.15

2149   **2150**   **2152**

2153   **2159**   **2154**

2155-58

2160-63   **2165**

2164   **2166**   **2167**

1985 Commemoratives (cont.)

Scott's No.		Mint Sheet	Plate Block	F-VF NH	F-VF Used
2146	22¢ Abigail Adams......................	28.50	2.75	.60	.15
2147	22¢ Frederic A. Bartholdi.............	28.50	2.75	.60	.15

1985 Regular Issue Coil Stamps

Scott's No.		Mint Sheet	Plate Block	F-VF NH	F-VF Used
2149	18¢ Wash. Pre-Sort Coil.. (Pl#Strip)	3.75 (5)	2.75 (3)	.60	.15
2149a	18¢ Precancelled.............(Pl# Strip)	4.25 (5)	3.50 (3)	.55	.35
2149b	18¢ Precan., Dry Gum ....(Pl# Strip)	5.50 (5)	4.75 (3)	.65	...
2150	21.1¢ Envelope Coil ....(Pl# Strip)	4.75 (5)	3.50 (3)	.65	.15
2150a	21.1¢ Zip + 4 Precancel ..(Pl# Strip)	5.00 (5)	4.00 (3)	.65	.35

1985 Commemoratives (continued)

Scott's No.		Mint Sheet	Plate Block	F-VF NH	F-VF Used
2152	22¢ Korean War Vetrans	36.50	3.50	.75	.15
2153	22¢ Social Security Act	28.50	2.75	.60	.15
2154	22¢ World War I Vetrans	36.50	3.50	.75	.15
2155-58	22¢ Horses, attached .... (40)	115.00	15.00	13.00	6.50
2155-58	Set of 4 Singles	...	...	11.00	1.00
2159	22¢ Public Education	72.50	6.50	1.50	.15
2160-63	22¢ Int'l. Youth Year, attd	59.50	7.95	5.25	3.00
2160-63	Set of 4 Singles	...	...	4.00	.90
2164	22¢ Help End Hunger	31.50	3.00	.65	.15
#2165-66	Christmas				
2165	22¢ Madonna and Child	28.50	2.75	.60	.15
2166	22¢ Poinsettia Plants..................	28.50	2.75	.60	.15

Scott's No.	Mint Sheet	Plate Block	F-VF NH	F-VF Used
2167,2202-04,2210-11, 2220-24,2235-45 Set of 22 (1986)	...	...	16.95	3.50
2167 22¢ Arkansas Statehood	31.50	3.00	.65	.15

2168	2169	2170	2171
2172	2173	2175	2176
2177	2178	2179	2180	2181
2182,2197	2183	2184	2185	2186
2187	2188	2189	2190	2191
2192	2193	2194	2195	2196

1986-94 Great Americans
(Sheets of 100)

Scott's No.	Mint Sheet	Plate Block	F-VF NH	F-VF Used
2168/96 Set of 28	...	160.00	35.00	5.95
2168 1¢ Margaret Mitchell	6.00	.45	.20	.15
2169 2¢ Mary Lyon (1987)	6.75	.50	.20	.20
2169u 2¢ Untagged (1996)	6.75	.50	.20	.15
2170 3¢ Dr.Paul Dudley White,Dull Gum	10.00	.60	.20	.15
2170g 3¢ Glossy Gum (1995)	10.00	.60	.20	...
2171 4¢ Father Flanagan	11.75	.75	.20	.15
2171a 4¢ Untagged	11.75	.75	.20	.18
2172 5¢ Hugo Black	14.50	.85	.20	.15
2173 5¢ Luis Munoz Marin (1990)	18.50	1.00	.20	.15
2173v 5¢ Marin, Pl No &Zip Blk of 4 Combo,LL or LR	1.25	...	...	...
2173a 5¢ Marin, Untagged (1991)	18.00	.95	.20	.15
2175 10¢ Red Cloud, Lake('87)	40.00	1.95	.45	.15
2175a 10¢ Overall Tagging (1990)	47.50	2.50	.50	.35
2175b 10¢ Untagged	32.50	1.65	.35	.18
2175d 10¢ Carmine, Phosphored Paper.	32.50	1.65	.35	.15
2176 14¢ Julia Ward Howe (1987)	35.00	1.85	.38	.15
2177 15¢ Buffalo Bill Cody (1988)	90.00	5.95	.95	.20
2177a 15¢ Overall Tagging (1990)	37.50	2.30	.40	.15
2178 17¢ Belva Ann Lockwood	47.50	2.25	.50	.15
2179 20¢ Virginia Agpar (1994)	41.50	3.00	.45	.15

1986-94 Great Americans
(Sheets of 100)

Scott's No.	Mint Sheet	Plate Block	F-VF NH	F-VF Used
2180 21¢ Chester Carlson (1988)	57.50	3.25	.60	.18
2181 23¢ Mary Cassatt (1988)	55.00	3.50	.60	.15
2181a 23¢ Overall Tagging	75.00	4.75	.80	.30
2181b 23¢ Phosphored, Dull Gum	65.00	3.85	.70	.20
2181bs 23¢ Phosphored, Shiny Gum	65.00	3.85	.70	...
2182 25¢ Jack London, Perf. 11	60.00	3.00	.65	.15
2182a 25¢ Bkt. Pn/10, Perf. 11 (1988)	...	...	6.75	5.00
2183 28¢ Sitting Bull (1989)	75.00	4.00	.80	.18
2184 29¢ Earl Warren (1992)	75.00	3.85	.80	.15
2185 29¢ Thomas Jefferson (1993)	75.00	3.85	.80	.15
2185 Jefferson, Plate Block of 8	...	7.50	...	...
2186 35¢ Dennis Chavez (1991)	70.00	5.00	.75	.18
2187 40¢ Gen'l. Claire Chennault ('90)	90.00	5.00	1.00	.18
2187a 40¢ Phosphored, Dull Gum	120.00	6.00	1.25	.25
2187as 40¢ Phosphored, Shiny Gum	100.00	5.50	1.10	...
2188 45¢ Dr. H. Cushing (1988)	125.00	6.00	1.30	.15
2188a 45¢ Overall Tagging (1990)	220.00	11.75	2.35	.50
2189 52¢ Hubert Humphrey, Dull ('91)	160.00	8.50	1.70	.18
2189s 52¢ Shiny Gum (1993)	125.00	7.75	1.35	...
2190 56¢ John Harvard	150.00	7.50	1.60	.18
2191 65¢ Gen. "Hap" Arnold (1988)	150.00	8.00	1.60	.18
2192 75¢ Wendell Willkie, Dull (1992)	160.00	8.75	1.75	.18
2192s 75¢ Shiny Gum	160.00	8.75	1.75	...
2193 $1 Dr. Bernard Revel	350.00	16.75	3.75	.25
2194 $1 Johns Hopkins (1989) (20)	55.00	12.75	2.75	.20
2194b $1 Overall Tagging (1990) (20)	55.00	12.75	2.75	.20
2194d $1 Phosphored, Dull Gum (20)	43.50	10.75	2.35	.20
2194ds $1 Phosphored, Shiny Gum (20)	43.50	10.75	2.35	...
2195 $2 William Jennings Bryan	450.00	20.00	4.75	.55
2196 $5 Bret Harte, Blk.Tag. ('87) (20)	215.00	49.50	11.50	1.95
2196b $5 Surface Tagged (1992) (20)	190.00	41.50	10.00	1.95
2197 25¢ J. London Bklt. Sgl., Pf.10 ('88)	...	...	.75	.15
2197a 25¢ Bklt. Pane of 6 (1988)	...	...	4.50	3.00

NOTE: SETS CONTAIN OUR CHOICE OF TAGGED OF UNTAGGED, ETC.

1986 Commemoratives (cont.)

2201a

2202	2203	2204	2211

2205-09	2210

Scott's No.	Mint Sheet	Plate Block	F-VF NH	F-VF Used
2198-2201 22¢ Stamp Coll. Bklt. Set of 4 Singles	...	...	2.60	.75
2201a 22¢ Booklet Pane of 4	...	...	2.75	2.50
2202 22¢ Love, Puppy	35.00	3.25	.75	.15
2203 22¢ Sojourner Truth	37.50	3.50	.80	.15
2204 22¢ Texas, 150th Anniv.	35.00	3.50	.75	.15
2205-09 22¢ Fish Set of 5 Booklet Sgls	...	...	8.50	.90
2209a 22¢ Booklet Pane of 5	...	...	8.75	3.75
2210 22¢ Public Hospitals	35.00	3.25	.70	.15
2211 22¢ Duke Ellington	31.50	3.00	.65	.15

| 2216a | 2216d | 2217g |

2220-23

| 2225 | 2224 | 2226 |

Scott's No.		Mint Sheet	Plate Block	F-VF NH	F-VF Used
2216-19	22¢ Ameripex '86, Set of 4 Miniature Sheets of 9	...	...	20.75	20.75
2216a-19i	Presidents, Set of 36 Sgls	...	...	19.75	13.75
2220-23	22¢ Arctic Explorers, attd	60.00	8.00	5.50	3.75
2220-23	Set of 4 Singles	...	...	4.50	.80
2224	22¢ Statue of Liberty	31.50	3.00	.65	.15

1986-96 Transportation "B" Press Coils

Scott's No.		Pl.# Strip of 5	Pl.# Strip of 3	F-VF NH	F-VF Used
2225-31	Set of 4....................................	10.50	8.95	1.25	.60
2225	1¢ Omnibus,Dull Gum("B" Press)	.80	.70	.20	.15
2225a	1¢ Untagged, Dull (1991)	.80	.70	.20	.18
2225s	1¢ Shiny Gum (1996)	7.50	6.75	.25	...
2225sv	1¢ Shiny, Untagged (1996)	1.20	1.10	.20	...
2226	2¢ Locomotive (1987)	.90	.75	.20	.15
2226a	2¢ Untagged (1994)...................	.90	.75	.20	.18
2228	4¢ Stagecoach, Block Tagging .	1.65	1.35	.20	.18
2228a	4¢ Overall Tagging (1990)........	15.00	14.50	.50	.25
2231	8.3¢ Ambulance, Precancel	7.50	6.50	.80	.20

4¢ Stagecoach:
1898A: "Stagecoach 1890s" is 19½ mm. long
2228: "Stagecoach 1890s" is 17 mm. long

8.3¢ Ambulance:
2128: "Ambulance 1860s" is 18½ mm. long
2231: "Ambulance 1860s" is 18 mm. long

1986 Commemoratives (continued)

2235-38

2240-43

| 2239 | 2244 | 2245 |

Scott's No.		Mint Sheet	Plate Block	F-VF NH	F-VF Used
2235-38	22¢ Navajo Art, attd......................	37.50	4.25	3.25	2.75
2235-38	Set of 4 Singles	...	...	3.00	.80
2239	22¢ T.S. Eliot	28.50	2.75	.60	.15
2240-43	22¢ Woodcarved Figurines., attd.	37.50	4.50	3.25	2.75
2240-43	Set of 4 Singles	...	...	3.00	.80
2244-45	Christmas Issues				
2244	22¢ Madonna & Child .... (100)	55.00	2.75	.60	.15
2245	22¢ Village Scene.................... (100)	55.00	2.75	.60	.15

1987 Commemoratives

| 2246 | 2247 | 2248 |

| 2249 | 2250 | 2251 |

2246-51,75,2336-38,2349-54,2360-61,2367-68 Set of 20 ...			15.95	2.85
2246	22¢ Michigan Statehood	28.50	2.75	.60	.15
2247	22¢ Pan American Games...........	28.50	2.75	.60	.15
2248	22¢ Love, Heart ....(100)	55.00	2.75	.60	.15
2249	22¢ Jean Baptiste, Pointe du Sable	32.50	3.25	.70	.15
2250	22¢ Enrico Caruso	28.50	2.75	.60	.15
2251	22¢ Girl Scouts	32.50	3.25	.70	.15

2252	2253	2254	2255
2256	2257	2258	2259
2260	2261	2262	2263
2264	2265	2266	

Scott's No.		Pl.# Strip of 5	Pl.# Strip of 3	F-VF NH	Used
2252-66	Set of 15 Different Values	55.00	45.00	5.75	2.95
2252	3¢ Conestoga Wagon ('88)........	.90	.80	.20	.15
2252a	3¢ Untagged, Dull Gum (1992)..	1.45	1.30	.20	.18
2252b	3¢ Untagged, Shiny Gum	1.60	1.40	.20	...
2253	5¢ Milk Wagon..........................	1.40	1.20	.20	.15
2254	5.3¢ Elevator, Prec. (1988)........	2.40	1.95	.20	.18
2255	7.6¢ Carretta, Prec. (1988)........	2.85	2.50	.22	.18
2256	8.4¢ Wheelchair, Prec. (1986)...	2.40	2.00	.22	.18
2257	10¢ Canal Boat, Block Tagging .	2.25	1.80	.28	.15
2257a	10¢ Overall Tagged (1992).........	4.00	3.50	.35	.25
2257ad	10¢ Overall Tagged, dull gum ('91)	6.25	5.75	.35	...
2258	13¢ Police Wagon, Prec. ('88)..	4.85	4.25	.40	.20
2259	13.2¢ R.R. Coat Car, Prec. ('88)	3.65	3.00	.35	.20
2260	15¢ Tugboat, Block Tagging ('88)	3.25	2.50	.45	.15
2260a	15¢ Overall Tagging (1990).......	5.00	4.25	.50	.25
2260b	15¢ Untagged	POR	POR	4.25	...
2261	16.7¢ Popcorn Wagon, Prec.('88)	3.75	3.25	.45	.25
2262	17.5¢ Marmon Wasp	5.00	4.25	.50	.20
2262a	17.5¢ Precancelled..................	5.50	4.75	.55	.28
2263	20¢ Cable Car (1988)	4.15	3.35	.55	.20
2263b	20¢ Overall Tagged (1990)........	7.00	6.00	.80	.35
2264	20.5¢ Fire Engine, Prec. (1988)	4.75	3.85	.60	.35
2265	21¢ R.R. Mail Car, Prec. (1988)	5.00	3.95	.60	.25
2266	24.1¢ Tandem Bic., Prec. ('88)..	5.75	4.75	.65	.35

1987 Special Occasions Issue

2267-74

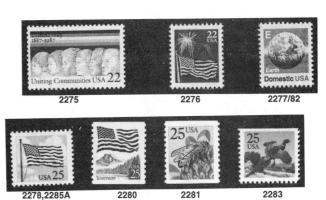

2275	2276	2277/82

2278,2285A	2280	2281	2283

2284	2285

2286			

2286-2335 Examples

Scott's No.		Mint Sheet	Plate Block	F-VF NH	F-VF Used
1987 Special Occasions Issue					
2267-74	22¢ Spec. Occ. Bklt. Sgls. (8)......	...	...	13.50	2.95
2274a	22¢ Bklt. Pane of 10	...	...	16.50	12.00
1987 Commemoratives (cont)					
2275	22¢ United Way	28.50	2.75	.60	.15
1987-89 Regular Issues					
2276	22¢ Flag & Fireworks...............(100)	57.50	3.00	.60	.15
2276a	22¢ Fireworks B. Pane of 20	...	...	11.50	11.00
2277	(25¢) "E" Earth Issue ('88) ....(100)	70.00	3.50	.75	.15
2278	25¢ Flag & Clouds ('88) ....(100)	67.50	3.25	.70	.15
2279	(25¢) "E" Earth Coil ('88) .. Pl# Strip 4.50 (5)		3.50 (3)	.70	.15
2280	25¢ Flag/Yosem Coil ('88)... Pl# Strip 4.25 (5)		3.35 (3)	.70	.15
2280v	25¢ Phosphor Paper ('89)... Pl# Strip 4.25 (5)		3.35 (3)	.70	.15
2281	25¢ Honeybee Coil .... Pl# Strip 4.50 (5)		3.25 (3)	.75	.15
2282	(25¢) "E" Bklt. Sgl. ('88)	...	...	.80	.15
2282a	(25¢) Bklt. Pane of 10	...	...	7.75	6.00
2283	25¢ Pheas. Bk. Sgl., **red & blue sky** ('88)	...	...	.80	.15
2283a	25¢ Bklt. Pane of 10	...	...	7.75	6.00
2283b	25¢ Blue Sky, **(red omitted)**, bklt. sgl. ('89)	...	...	8.75	.50
2283c	25¢ Bklt. Pn. 10 **(Pl# A3111,A3222)**	...	...	85.00	...
2284	25¢ Grosbeak Bklt. Sgl. ('88).......	...	...	.70	.15
2285	25¢ Owl Bklt. Sgl. ('88)	...	...	.70	.15
2284-85	Attached Pair	...	...	1.40	.15
2285b	25¢ Bklt. Pn. (5 ea. #2284,2285) .	...	...	6.75	5.75
2285A	25¢ Flag/Cloud Bk. Sgl. ('88).......	...	...	.75	.15
2285Ac	25¢ Bklt. Pn. 6	...	...	4.25	4.00
1987 North American Wildlife Series					
2286-2335	22¢ American Wildlife...............	69.50	...	...	...
2286-2335	Set of 50 Singles.....................	...	...	65.00	22.50
2286-2335	22¢ Individual Singles...............	...	...	1.50	.55

2286 Barn Swallow	2303 Blackbird	2320 Bison
2287 Monarch Butterfly	2304 Lobster	2321 Snowy Egret
2288 Bighorn Sheep	2305 Jack Rabbit	2322 Gray Wolf
2289 Hummingbird	2306 Scarlet Tanager	2323 Mountain Goat
2290 Cottontail	2307 Woodchuck	2324 Deer Mouse
2291 Osprey	2308 Spoonbill	2325 Prairie Dog
2292 Mountain Lion	2309 Bald Eagle	2326 Box Turtle
2293 Luna Moth	2310 Brown Bear	2327 Wolverine
2294 Mule Deer	2311 Iiwi	2328 American Elk
2295 Gray Squirrel	2312 Badger	2329 Sea Lion
2296 Armadillo	2313 Pronghorn	2330 Mockingbird
2297 Eastern Chipmunk	2314 River Otter	2331 Raccoon
2298 Moose	2315 Ladybug	2332 Bobcat
2299 Black Bear	2316 Beaver	2333 Ferret
2300 Tiger Swallowtail	2317 Whitetailed Deer	2334 Canada Goose
2301 Bobwhite	2318 Blue Jay	2335 Red Fox
2302 Ringtail	2319 Pika	

2336   2337   2338   2339

2340   2341   2342   2343

2344   2345   2346   2347

2348   2349   2350

1987-90 Ratification of the Constitution Bicentennial

Scott's No.		Mint Sheet	Plate Block	F-VF NH	F-VF Used
2336-48	Set of 13	465.00	45.00	9.75	1.65
2336	22¢ Delaware.	31.50	3.00	.65	.15
2337	22¢ Pennsylvania	40.00	3.95	.85	.15
2338	22¢ New Jersey.......................	35.75	3.50	.75	.15
2339	22¢ Georgia ('88).....................	35.75	3.50	.75	.15
2340	22¢ Connecticut ('88)	35.75	3.50	.75	.15
2341	22¢ Massachusetts ('88)...........	35.75	3.50	.75	.15
2342	22¢ Maryland ('88)	35.75	3.50	.75	.15
2343	25¢ South Carolina ('88)...........	40.00	3.95	.85	.15
2344	25¢ New Hampshire ('88)..........	40.00	3.95	.85	.15
2345	25¢ Virginia ('88).....................	40.00	3.95	.85	.15
2346	25¢ New York ('88)...................	40.00	3.95	.85	.15
2347	25¢ North Carolina ('89)............	40.00	3.95	.85	.15
2348	25¢ Rhode Island ('90)	40.00	3.95	.85	.15

1987 Commemoratives (cont.)

2351-54

1987 Commemoratives (cont'd.)

2355-59 Ex.   2360   2361

2362-66 Ex.   2367   2368

Scott's No.		Mint Sheet	Plate Block	F-VF NH	F-VF Used
2349	22¢ U.S.-Morocco Relations	28.50	2.75	.60	.15
2350	22¢ William Faulkner.................	28.50	2.75	.60	.15
2351-54	22¢ Lacemaking, attd............. (40)	35.00	5.00	3.50	2.50
2351-54	Set of 4 Sgls............................	...	...	3.35	.80
2355-59	22¢ Drafting of Constitution, Bklt. Sgls. (5)	...	...	3.95	.90
2359a	22¢ Bklt. Pane of 5	...	...	4.25	3.50
2360	22¢ Signing the Constitution	31.75	3.25	.70	.15
2361	22¢ Cert. Public Accounting......	160.00	15.00	3.50	.15
2362-66	22¢ Locomotives Bklt. Sgls. (5).	...	...	3.75	.90
2366a	22¢ Bklt. Pane of 5	...	...	3.95	3.50
#2367-68 Christmas Issues					
2367	22¢ Madonna & Child............ (100)	55.00	2.75	.60	.15
2368	22¢ Ornaments..................... (100)	55.00	2.75	.60	.15

1988 Commemoratives

2369   2370   2371

2372-75   2376

Scott's No.		Mint Sheet	Plate Block	F-VF NH	F-VF Used
2339-46,69-80,86-93,99-2400	Set of 30 .	...	...	26.50	4.35
2369	22¢ 1988 Winter Olympics	32.50	3.25	.75	.15
2370	22¢ Australia Bicent .... (40)	24.00	2.75	.60	.15
2371	22¢ J.W. Johnson	31.50	3.00	.70	.15
2372-75	22¢ Cats, attd........................ (40)	39.50	5.75	4.50	2.50
2372-75	Set of 4 Sgls............................	...	...	4.25	.80
2376	22¢ Knute Rockne...................	38.50	3.95	.80	.15

2377   2378   2379   2380

2381-85

2386-89

2390-93

Scott's No.		Mint Sheet	Plate Block	F-VF NH	F-VF Used
2377	25¢ Francis Ouimet..................	55.00	5.75	1.20	.15
2378	25¢ Love, Roses .... (100)	67.50	3.25	.70	.15
2379	45¢ Love, Roses	65.00	5.75	1.35	.15
2380	25¢ Summer Olympics..............	36.00	3.50	.80	.15
2381-85	25¢ Classic Cars, Bklt. Sgls.	...	...	9.50	.90
2385a	25¢ Bk. Pn. 5.......................	...	...	10.00	3.75
2386-89	25¢ Antarctic Exp., attd.............	56.75	7.95	5.25	3.00
2386-89	Set of 4 Singles........................	...	...	4.75	.80
2390-93	25¢ Carousel, attd....................	55.00	6.00	5.25	3.00
2390-93	Set of 4 Singles........................	...	...	4.75	.80

2394

2395-98

2399   2400

1988 Express Mail Issue

Scott's No.		Mint Sheet	Plate Block	F.VF NH	F.VF Used
2394	$8.75 Eagle .... (20)	475.00	110.00	25.75	7.75

1988 Special Occasions Issue

2395-98	25¢ Special Occasions, Bklt. Sgls.	...	...	3.75	.80
2396a	25¢ Happy Birthday & Best Wishes B. Pn. of 6 (3&3) w/gutter..........	...	...	5.00	4.00
2398a	25¢ Thinking of You & Love You B. Pn. of 6 (3&3) w/gutter..........	...	...	5.00	4.00

1988 Christmas Issues

2399	25¢ Madonna & Child................	31.50	3.00	.65	.15
2400	25¢ Horse & Sleigh	31.50	3.00	.65	.15

2401   2402   2403

2404   2405-09 Examples

2410 2411 2412 2413

2417 2416 2418

2419 2420 2421

2422-25 2426

1989 Commemoratives

Scott's No.		Mint Sheet	Plate Block	F-VF NH	F-VF Used
2347,2401-04,10-18,20-28,34-37	Set of 27	...	...	23.95	3.95
2401	25¢ Montana Sthd. Cent	40.00	4.00	.90	.15
2402	25¢ A. Philip Randolph..............	39.50	3.75	.85	.15
2403	25¢ North Dakota Sthd. Cent	31.50	3.00	.65	.15
2404	25¢ Washington Sthd. Cent	35.00	3.50	.75	.15
2405-09	25¢ Steamboats, Bklt. Sgls	...	...	3.60	.90
2409a	25¢ Bklt. Pane of 5	(Unfolded 8.25)	...	3.75	3.50
2410	25¢ World Stamp Expo	31.50	3.00	.65	.15
2411	25¢ Arturo Toscanini	35.00	3.50	.75	.15
2412-15	Constitution Bicent., Set of 4	150.00	15.00	3.25	.55
2412	25¢ House of Representatives ..	37.50	3.75	.80	.15
2413	25¢ U.S. Senate	37.50	3.75	.80	.15
2414	25¢ Exec. Branch/G.W. Inaug...	40.00	4.25	.90	.15
2415	25¢ U.S. Supreme Court (1990)	38.50	4.00	.85	.15
2416	25¢ South Dakota Sthd. Cent....	31.50	3.00	.65	.15
2417	25¢ Lou Gehrig........................	52.50	5.25	1.10	.15
2418	25¢ Ernest Hemingway	31.50	3.00	.65	.15

1989 Priority Mail Issue

2419	$2.40 Moon Landing...............(20)	125.00	28.50	6.75	2.50

1989 Commemoratives (cont.)

2420	25¢ Letter Carriers ....(40)	25.00	3.00	.65	.15
2421	25¢ Drafting Bill of Rights..........	50.00	5.50	1.10	.15
2422-25	25¢ Prehistoric Animals, attd..(40)	50.00	5.75	5.25	2.75
2422-25	Set of 4 Singles	...	...	4.85	.80
2426	25¢ Pre-Columbian Customs	31.50	3.00	.65	.15

2427 2428,2429 2431

1989 Christmas Issues

Scott's No.		Mint Sheet	Plate Block	F-VF NH	F-VF Used
2427	25¢ Madonna & Child................	31.50	3.00	.65	.15
2427v	Madonna, Booklet Single	...	...	.75	.18
2427a	25¢ Bklt. Pane of 10	(Unfolded 15.00)		7.50	5.50
2428	25¢ Sleigh & Presents..............	31.50	3.00	.65	.15
2429	25¢ Sleigh, Bklt. Single	...	...	.90	.18
2429a	25¢ Bklt. Pane of 10	(Unfolded 19.50)		8.25	5.50

1989 Regular Issue

2431	25¢ Eagle & Shield, self adhesive	...	...	.90	.30
2431a	25¢ Pane of 18	...	...	15.95	...
2431v	25¢ Eagle & Shield, Coil...........	Strip of 3	2.70	.90	...

1989 World Stamp Expo '89, Washington, DC

The classic 1869 U.S. Abraham Lincoln stamp is reborn in these four larger versions commemorating World Stamp Expo'89, held in Washington, D.C. during the 20th Universal Postal Congress of the UPU. These stamps show the issued colors and three of the trial proof color combinations.
©USPS 1988

2433

2434-37

2438

2433	90¢ World Stamp Expo S/S of 4..	...	...	19.50	15.00
2434-37	25¢ Traditional Mail Deliv., attd (40)	45.00	6.00	5.00	3.25
2434-37	Set of 4 Singles	...	...	4.70	1.00
2438	25¢ Traditional Mail S/S of 4	...	...	6.50	5.00
	See also #C122-26				

2439   2440,2441   2442   2443

2444

2449

2445-48

1990 Commemoratives

Scott's No.	Mint Sheet	Plate Block	F-VF NH	F-VF Used
2348,2439-40,2442,44-49,96-2500,2506-15 Set of 25	...	...	26.95	3.75
2439 25¢ Idaho Sthd. Centenary........	31.50	3.00	.65	.15
2440 25¢ Love, Doves........................	31.50	3.00	.65	.15
2441 25¢ Love, Bklt. Single................	...	...	.75	.18
2441a 25¢ Booklet Pane of 10 .... (Unfolded 55.00)			7.50	6.50
2442 25¢ Ida B. Wells	38.50	3.75	.80	.15

1990 Regular Issue

2443 15¢ Beach Umbrella, Bklt. Sgl...	...	...	.45	.15
2443a 15¢ Booklet Pane of 10 .... (Unfolded 8.95)		...	4.35	3.95

1990 Commemoratives (continued)

2444 25¢ Wyoming Sthd. Centenary..	40.00	3.85	.85	.15
2445-48 25¢ Classic Films, attd ....(40)	85.00	10.00	9.00	5.00
2445-48 Set of 4 Singles	...	...	8.75	1.00
2449 25¢ Marianne Moore	31.50	3.00	.65	.15

1990-95 Transportation Coils IV

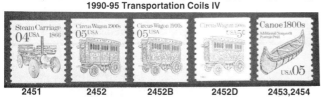

2451   2452   2452B   2452D   2453,2454

2457   2458   2463

2464   2466   2468

Scott's No.	Pl# Strip of 5	Pl# Strip of 3	F-VF NH	FVF Used
2451/2468 Set of 12 values	42.75	33.50	4.95	2.00
2451 4¢ Steam Carriage (1991)	1.10	.90	.20	.15
2451b 4¢ Untagged	1.20	1.00	.20	.18
2452 5¢ Circus Wagon, Engraved......	1.35	1.10	.20	.15
2452a 5¢ Untagged	1.50	1.20	.22	.18
2452B 5¢ Circus Wagon, Gravure ('92)	1.35	1.10	.20	.15
2452D 5¢ Circus Wagon(¢ sign) ('95)...	1.50	1.20	.20	.18

1990-95 Transportation Coils (continued)

Scott's No.	Pl#Strip of 5	Pl#Strip of 3	F-VF NH	F-VF Used
2453 5¢ Canoe, Brown (1991)............	1.50	1.25	.20	.15
2454 5¢ Canoe, Red (1991)	1.60	1.30	.20	.18
2457 10¢ Tractor Trailer, Intaglio ('91)	3.00	2.50	.25	.18
#2457"Additional Presort Postage Paid" In Gray.				
2458 10¢ Tractor Trailer, Gravure ('94)	2.75	2.25	.25	.18
#2458 "Additional, etc." in black. Whiter paper.				
2463 20¢ Cog Railway (1995)	5.50	4.75	.40	.18
2464 23¢ Lunch Wagon (1991)	4.50	3.65	.60	.15
2464p 23¢ Phosphored, Dull Gum	6.75	5.75	.70	.35
2464ps 23¢ Phosphored, Shiny Gum	6.75	5.75	.70	...
2466 32¢ Ferryboat, Shiny (1995)......	7.25	6.00	.70	.15
2466v 32¢ Low Gloss Gum	8.75	7.50	.85	...
2468 $1.00 Seaplane, Dull Gum	13.95	9.50	2.10	.50
2468s $1.00 Shiny Gum	13.95	9.50	2.10	...

Circus Wagon: #2452 Short letters and date, #2452B Taller, thinner letters and date

2470-74

2475

1990 Commemorative Booklet Pane

Scott's No.	Mint Sheet	Plate Block	F-VF NH	F-VF Used
2470-74 25¢ Lighthouse Bklt. Singles			4.75	.90
2474a 25¢ Booklet Pane of 5 .... (Unfolded 6.95)			4.95	3.50

1990 Flag Regular Issue

2475 25¢ ATM Self Adhesive, Plastic Stamp	...	...	.85	.60
2475a 25¢ Pane of 12	...	...	9.95	...

1990-95 Flora and Fauna

2476   2477   2478   2479

2476-82 Set of 7	...	31.50	6.50	1.95
2476 1¢ Kestrel (1991) .... (100)	4.50	.45	.20	.15
2477 1¢ Redesign with "¢" sign (1995)(100)	4.50	.45	.20	.15
2478 3¢ Bluebird (1991) .... (100)	7.50	.65	.20	.15
2479 19¢ Fawn (1991)..................... (100)	47.50	2.50	.50	.15

2480   2481   2482

2480 30¢ Cardinal (1991) .... (100)	55.00	4.00	.65	.20
2481 45¢ Pumpkinseed Sunfish('92) (100)	95.00	5.75	1.00	.30
2482 $2.00 Bobcat............................ (20)	75.00	18.00	3.95	1.10

1991-95 Flora and Fauna Booklet Stamps

2483	2484,2485	2486	2487,2493, 2495	2488,2494, 2495A

Scott's No.		F-VF NH	F-VF Used
2483	20¢ Blue Jay, Booklet Single ('95) ...	.45	.15
2483a	20¢ Booklet Pane of 10 .... (Unfolded 6.95) ...	5.75	4.95
2484	29¢ Wood Duck, BEP bklt sgl Pf 10 ...	.90	.18
2484a	29¢ BEP Bklt Pane of 10 ('91)..... (Unfolded 10.95) ...	7.95	7.75
2485	29¢ Wood Duck, KCS bklt sgl Pf 11 ...	1.00	.18
2485a	29¢ KCS Bklt Pane of 10 ('91) .... (Unfolded 12.75) ...	8.75	8.95
2486	29¢ African Violet	.85	.18
2486a	29¢ Booklet Pane of 10 (1993).... (Unfolded 9.95) ...	8.50	7.50
2487	32¢ Peach, booklet single	.75	.18
2488	32¢ Pear, booklet single	.75	.18
2487-88	32¢ Peach & Pear, Attached Pair ...	1.50	1.10
2488a	32¢ Booklet Pane of 10 (1995).. (Unfolded 9.95) ...	8.50	7.50

1993-96 Self Adhesive Booklets & Coils

2489	2490	2491	2492

Scott's No.				F-VF NH	F-VF Used
2489	29¢ Red Squirrel, ...	...	...	.90	.40
2489a	29¢ Pane of 18	...	...	14.95	11.75
2489v	Squirrel Coil .... Strip of 3	2.70		.90	...
2490	29¢ Rose	...	...	.90	.40
2490a	29¢ Pane of 18	...	...	14.95	...
2490v	Rose coil .... Strip of 3	2.70		.90	...
2491	29¢ Pine Cone	...	...	.90	.40
2491a	29¢ Pane of 18 ('93)	...	...	14.95	...
2491v	Pine Cone coil .... Pl. #Strip (5) 8.00		(3) 6.75	.90	...
2492	32¢ Pink Rose	...	...	.80	.30
2492a	32¢ Pane of 20 (1995)	...	...	15.95	...
2492v	32¢ Pink Rose, Coil ...... Pl.#Strip (5) 7.25		(3) 5.95	.80	...
2492b	32¢ Pink Rose, Folded Pane of 15 ('96)	...	...	10.75	...
2492e	32¢ Pink Rose, Folded Pane of 14 ('96)	...	...	10.75	...
2492f	32¢ Pink Rose, Folded Pane of 16 ('96)	...	...	12.50	...
2492r	32¢ Pane of 20 with Die-cut "Time to Reorder" (1995)	...	...	16.75	...
2493	32¢ Peach, Self-adhesive single .	...	...	.85	.30
2494	32¢ Pear, Self-adhesive single....	...	...	.85	.30
2493-94	32¢ Peach & Pear, Attached Pair...	...	...	1.70	...
2494a	32¢ Pane of 20, Self-adhesive ('95)	...	...	15.75	...
2495	32¢ Peach, Coil, Self-adhesive ...	...	...	.85	...
2495A	32¢ Pear, Coil, Self-adhesive	...	...	.85	...
2495-95A	32¢ Peach & Pear, Coil Pair ('95) Pl # Strip	(5) 7.25	(3) 5.95	1.70	...

1990 Commemoratives (continued)

2496-2500

Scott's No.		Mint Sheet	Plate Block	F-VF NH	F-VF Used
2496-2500	25¢ Olympians,Strip of 5 .... (35)	38.50	(10)12.50	5.75	4.35
2496-2500	Set of 5 Singles	...	...	5.50	1.00
2496-2500	Tab singles, attd, Top or Bot	...	...	6.75	5.75

1990 Commemoratives (continued)

2501-05

2506-07

2508-11

2512   2513

2514, 2514v   2515,2516

Scott's No.		Mint Sheet	Plate Block	F-VF NH	F-VF Used
2501-05	25¢ Indian Headdresses bklt. sgls.	...	...	4.50	.90
2505a	25¢ Booklet Pane of 10 (2 ea.) .... (Unfolded 14.95) ...			8.95	7.50
2506-07	25¢ Micronesia/Marshall Isl., attd	39.50	3.85	1.75	.90
2506-07	Set of 2 Singles	...		1.60	.35
2508-11	25¢ Sea Creatures, attd .... (40)	33.50	3.95	3.50	2.50
2508-11	Set of 4 Singles	...		3.25	.70
2512	25¢ America, Grand Canyon	31.50	3.00	.65	.15
2513	25¢ Dwight Eisenhower .... (40)	42.50	5.00	1.10	.15
2514	25¢ Christmas Madonna & Child .	31.50	3.00	.65	.15
2514v	25¢ Madonna, Booklet Single	...	...	.80	.18
2514a	25¢ Booklet Pane of 10 .... (Unfolded 14.95)...			7.95	5.95
2515	25¢ Christmas Tree, Perf. 11	31.50	3.00	.65	.15
2516	25¢ Tree, Bklt. Sgl., Perf. 11½x11	...	...	.90	.18
2516a	25¢ Booklet Pane of 10 .... (Unfolded 18.95) ...			8.95	5.95

2517-2520   **2521**   **2522**

2523   **2523A**   **2524**   **2526**

2528   **2529**   **2530**   **2531**   **2531A**

Scott's No.		Mint Sheet	Plate Block	F-VF NH	F-VF Used
2517	(29¢) "F" Flower Stamp .... (100)	70.00	3.50	.75	.15
2518	(29¢) "F" Flower Coil............ Pl# Strip	4.75 (5)	3.50 (3)	.80	.15
2519	(29¢) "F" Flower, BEP bklt. sgl. ...	...	...	.85	.18
2519a	(29¢)Bklt.Pane of 10,BEP,bullseye perfs ...			8.50	6.95
2520	(29¢) "F" Flower, KCS bklt. sgl. ...	...	...	2.75	.25
2520a	(29¢) Bklt. Pane of 10, KCS	...	...	26.95	19.95

#2519: Bullseye perforations (11.2). Horizontal and vertical perforations meet exactly in stamp corners.
#2520: Normal (line) perforations, Perf. 11

2521	(4¢) Non-Denom. "make-up" ...(100)	12.50	.60	.20	.15
2522	(29¢) "F" Flag Stamp, ATM self adhes. ...			.85	.60
2522a	(29¢) Pane of 12	...	...	9.95	...
2523	29¢ Flag/Mt. Rushmore Intaglio Coil				
	.... Pl# Strip	4.75 (5)	3.50 (3)	.80	.25
2523c	29¢ Toledo Brown................. Pl# Strip	P.O.R.	P.O.R.	3.25	...
2523A	29¢ Flag, Gravure,............... Pl# Strip	5.75 (5)	4.50 (3)	.80	.25

* On #2523A, "USA" & "29" are not outlined in white.

2524	29¢ Flower, Perf. 11 .... (100)	75.00	4.25	.80	.18
2524a	29¢ Flower, Perf. 12½x13 .... (100)	80.00	5.00	.85	.20
2525	29¢ Flower Coil, rouletted, Pl# Strip	5.50 (5)	4.25 (3)	.80	.18
2526	29¢ Flower Coil, perf ('92) Pl# Strip	5.50 (5)	4.25 (3)	.80	.15
2527	29¢ Flower Bklt. Sgl			.85	.18
2527a	29¢ Booklet Pane of 10 .... (Unfolded 9.75)		8.25	5.95
2528	29¢ Flag with Olympic Rings, bklt. sgl.	...		.80	.18
2528a	29¢ Booklet Pane of 10 .... (Unfolded 9.50)		8.00	5.95
2529	19¢ Fishing Boat Coil, Ty. I Pl# Strip	4.15 (5)	3.35 (3)	.55	.15
2529a	19¢ Boat Coil, Ty. II ('93) Pl# Strip	4.15 (5)	3.35 (3)	.55	.18
2529b	19¢ Type II, Untagged .... Pl# Strip	12.50 (5)	10.00 (3)	.90	.55
2529C	19¢ Boat Coil, Ty. III (94) ... Pl# Strip	6.00 (5)	5.00 (3)	.55	.18

Type I: Darker color & large color cells, Perf. 10
Type II: Lighter color & small color cells, Perf. 10
Type III: Numerals and U.S.A. taller and thinner, only one loop of rope around piling, Perf. 9.8

2530	19¢ Hot-Air Balloons, bklt. sgl	...	...	.50	.20
2530a	19¢ Booklet Pane of 10 .... (Unfolded 6.95)		4.75	4.50
2531	29¢ Flags/Mem. Day Anniv .....(100)	70.00	3.50	.75	.15
2531A	29¢ Liberty & Torch, ATM self adh ...	...	...	.90	.30
2531Ab	29¢ Pane of 18, Original back	...	...	14.75	...
2531Av	29¢ Pane of 18, Revised back.....	...	...	14.95	...

1991 Commemoratives

2533   **2532**   **2534**

2532-35,37-38,50-51,53-58,60-61,67,78-79 Set of 19			...	16.35	2.85
2532	50¢ Switzerland joint issue ....(40)	52.50	6.50	1.30	.35
2533	29¢ Vermont Bicentennial	36.50	3.50	.75	.15
2534	29¢ Savings Bond, 50th Anniv	41.50	3.95	.85	.15

1991 Issues (cont.)

2535,2536   **2537**   **2538**

Scott's No.		Mint Sheet	Plate Block	F-VF NH	F-VF Used
2535	29¢ Love Stamp, Pf. 12½x13.......	37.50	3.75	.80	.15
2535a	Same, Perf. 11	47.50	5.00	1.00	.25
2536	29¢ Booklet Sgl., Pf. 11 on 2-3 sides	...	...	.85	.15
2536a	Booklet Pane of 10 ....(Unfolded 9.95)	...	8.50	5.75

NOTE: "29" is further from edge of design on #2536 than on #2535.

2537	52¢ Love Stamp, two ounces	60.00	5.75	1.30	.30
2538	29¢ William Saroyan	36.50	3.50	.75	.15

1991-96 Regular Issues

2539   **2540**   **2541**

2542   **2543**

2544   **2544A**

2539	$1.00 USPS Logo&Olym. Rings .(20)	52.50	12.50	2.75	.60
2540	$2.90 Priority Mail, Eagle ....(20)	150.00	35.00	7.95	2.25
2541	$9.95 Express Mail, Domestic......(20)	465.00	105.00	24.50	10.75
2542	$14.00 Express Mail, Internat'l. ...(20)	585.00	130.00	30.00	19.50
2543	$2.90 Priority Mail, Space ('93) ....(40)	265.00	29.50	6.95	2.50
2544	$3 Challng.Shuttle,Pr.Mail('95) ....(20)	115.00	25.00	5.95	2.75
2544v	$3 with 1996 Date ('96) ....(20)	115.00	25.00	5.95	2.75
2544A	$10.75 Endvr.Shtl.,Exp.Mail('95) ..(20)	395.00	92.50	21.00	7.95

1991 Commemoratives (continued)

2545-49

2545-49	29¢ Fishing Flies, bklt. singles.	...	...	5.25	.90
2549a	29¢ Booklet Pane of 5 ....(Unfolded 9.75)	...	5.50	3.25

2550   2551   2552

2553-57

2558   2561   2560

2559

Scott's No.		Mint Sheet	Plate Block	F-VF NH	F-VF Used
2550	29¢ Cole Porter	38.50	3.75	.85	.15
2551	29¢ Desert Shield/Desert Storm..	35.00	3.50	.75	.15
2552	29¢ Desert Storm, Bklt. Sgl., ABNCo	...	...	.85	.20
2552a	29¢ Booklet Pane of 5	(Unfolded 6.50)		4.25	4.25
2553-57	29¢ Summer Olympics, attd ..... (40)	35.00 (10)	9.75	4.75	3.00
2553-57	Set of 5 Singles			4.50	.90
2558	29¢ Numismatics	47.50	4.50	1.00	.15
2559	29¢ World War II S/S of 10 .... (20)	15.95	...	8.25	6.75
2559a-j	Set of 10 Singles		...	8.00	4.50
2559s	Se-Tenant Center Block of 10		...	9.50	8.95

2562-66

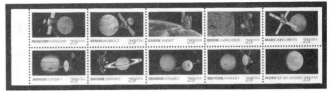

2568-77

2567   2578   2579   2580-81

2582-85

Scott's No.		Mint Sheet	Plate Block	F-VF NH	F-VF Used
2560	29¢ Basketball, 100th Anniversary	47.50	4.50	1.00	.15
2561	29¢ District of Columbia Bicent ...	35.00	3.50	.75	.15
2562-66	29¢ Comedians, bklt. sgls	...	...	4.25	.90
2566a	29¢ Booklet Pane of 10 (2 each) . (Unfolded 10.75)			8.50	6.95
2567	29¢ Jan Matzeliger	40.00	4.25	.85	.15
2568-77	29¢ Space Exploration bklt. sgls .	...	...	8.50	2.50
2577a	29¢ Booklet Pane of 10 .... (Unfolded 10.75)8.75			6.95	
1991 Christmas Issues					
2578	(29¢) Christmas, Madonna & Child	35.00	3.50	.75	.15
2578v	(29¢) Madonna, Booklet single....			.85	.18
2578a	(29¢) Booklet Pane of 10............. (Unfolded 10.75)			8.50	6.50
2579	(29¢) Christmas, Santa & Chimney	35.00	3.50	.75	.15
2580-85	(29¢) Santa & Chimney, Set of 6 Booklet Singles	...	...	12.50	1.75
2580-81	(29¢) Bklt. Singles, Ty. I & II, attd	...	...	10.00	...
* Ty. II, the far left brick from the top row of the chimney is missing from #2581					
2582-85	Booklet Singles, Set of 4	...	...	3.00	.70
2581b-2585a	Bklt. Panes of 4, Set of 5 ...... (Unfolded 35.00)			24.95	22.50

2587   2590   2592

2593,2594   2595-97   2598   2599

1994-95 Definitives Designs of 1869 Essays

2587	32¢ James S. Polk (1995) .... (100)	60.00	3.25	.65	.15
2590	$1 Surrender of Burgoyne .... (20)	38.75	9.00	1.95	.75
2592	$5 Washington & Jackson .... (20)	190.00	45.00	9.75	3.50

1992-93 Pledge of Allegiance

Scott's No.		Mint Sheet	Plate Block	F-VF NH	F-VF Used
2593	29¢ **black** denom. bklt.sgl.,Perf.10		...	.80	.15
2593a	29¢ Booklet Pane of 10, Perf. 10. (Unfolded 8.75)		...	7.50	5.95
2593b	29¢ Black denom.,bklt.sgl.,Perf.11x10	...		1.25	.85
2593c	29¢ Bklt. Pane of 10, Perf. 11x10	...	...	11.95	8.50
2594	29¢,**red** denom,bklt.sgl.('93)..........			.80	.15
2594a	29¢ Booklet Pane of 10 ....(Unfolded 9.95)		...	7.75	6.75

1992 Eagle & Shield Self-Adhesive Stamps

2595	29¢ **"Brown"** denomination	...	...	.90	.30
2595a	29¢ "Brown" denomination, Pane of 17 ...		...	13.75	...
2596	29¢ **"Green"** denomination	...	...	.90	.30
2596a	29¢ "Green" denomination, Pane of 17	...	...	13.75	...
2597	29¢ **"Red"** denomination.............	...	...	.90	.30
2597a	29¢ "Red" denomination, Pane of 17	...	...	13.75	...

1992 Eagle & Shield Self-Adhesive Coils

2595v	29¢ "Brown" denomination .... Strip of 3		2.70	.90	...
2596v	29¢ "Green" denomination .... Strip of 3		2.70	.90	...
2597v	29¢ "Red" denomination............. Strip of 3		2.70	.90	...

1994 Eagle Self-Adhesive Issue

2598	29¢ Eagle, self-adhesive	...	...	.90	.30
2598a	29¢ Pane of 18	...	...	13.75	...
2598v	29¢ Eagle Coil, self-adhesive Pl#Strip..	(5) 8.00	(3) 6.75	.95	...

1994 Statue of Liberty Self-Adhesive Issue

2599	29¢ Statue of Liberty, self-adhesive	...	...	.90	.30
2599a	29¢ Pane of 18	...	...	13.75	...
2599v	29¢ Liberty Coil, Self-adhesive Pl#Strip..	(5) 8.00	(3) 6.75	.95	...

1991-93 Coil Issues

2602 **2603,2604,2907** **2605**

2606 **2607** **2608** **2609**

1991-93 Coil Issues

Scott's No.		Pl# Strip of 5	Pl# Strip of 3	F-VF NH	F-VF Used
2602	(10¢) Eagle, Bulk rate	2.65	2.25	.28	.18
2603	(10¢) Eagle,Bulk rate, **BEP** (1993)	2.75	2.35	.28	.18
2603v	(10¢) Dull Gum.............................	4.25	3.50	.30	...
2603b	(10¢) Tagged................................	16.75	15.75	.50	.35
2604	(10¢) Eagle, Blk rate, **Stamp Venturers**	3.75	3.25	.28	.18

#2603 Orange yellow & multicolored, #2604 Gold & multicolored.

2605	23¢ Flag, Pre-sort First Class	4.75	3.75	.65	.30
2606	23¢ USA, Pre-sort 1st Cl., **ABNCo**('92)	4.75	3.75	.65	.30
2607	23¢ USA, Pre-sort 1st Cl., **BEP** ..('92)	6.00	5.00	.65	.30
2607v	23¢ Dull Gum	6.25	5.25	.75	...
2607t	23¢ Tagged	POR	POR	2.65	...
2608	23¢ USA, Pre-sort 1st Cl., **S.V.** ....('93)	6.50	5.50	.70	.30

#2606 Light blue at bottom, "23" 6 mm wide, "First Class" 9½ mm wide.
#2607 Dark blue at bottom, "23" 7 mm wide, "First Class" 9½ mm wide.
#2608 Violet blue, "23" 6 mm wide, "First Class" 8½ mm wide.

2609	29¢ Flag/White House ('92)	5.50	4.25	.75	.15

1992 Commemoratives

2611-15

2616 **2617** **2618** **2619**

Scott's No.		Mint Sheet	Plate Block	F-VF NH	F-VF Used
2611-23,2630-41,2698-2704,2710-14,2720 Set of 38			...	33.75	7.50
2611-15	29¢ Winter Olympics, attd ....(35)	35.00	(10) 9.75	4.75	3.50
2611-15	Set of 5 Singles	...	...	4.50	.90
2616	29¢ World Columbian Expo.........	35.00	3.50	.75	.15
2617	29¢ W.E.B. DuBois, Black Heritage	37.50	3.75	.80	.15
2618	29¢ Love, Envelope....................	35.00	3.50	.75	.15
2619	29¢ Olympic Baseball.................	52.50	4.75	1.10	.18

2596a Sample of Self-Adhesive Pane

2620-23

2624-29

Scott's No.		Mint Sheet	Plate Block	F-VF NH	F-VF Used
2620-23	29¢ Voyage of Columbus, attd . (40)	37.50	4.75	4.25	3.00
2620-23	Set of 4 Singles	...	...	4.00	.70
2624-29	1¢-$5 Columbian Expo S/S, Set of 6	...	...	39.50	37.50
2624a-29	1¢-$5 Set of 16 Singles	...	...	38.50	35.00
#2624	1¢, 4¢, $1	1893 Designs			
#2625	2¢, 3¢, $4	1893 Designs			
#2626	5¢, 30¢, 50¢	1893 Designs			
#2627	6¢, 8¢, $3	1893 Designs			
#2628	10¢, 15¢, $2	1893 Designs			
#2629	$5	1893 Design			

2631-34

2630   2635   2636

2637-41

2642-46

2647-96 Examples

2697

2698   2699   2704

2700-03

Scott's No.		Mint Sheet	Plate Block	F-VF NH	F-VF Used
2630	29¢ New York Stock Exchange (40)	28.00	3.50	.75	.15
2631-34	29¢ Space Accomplishments, attd	43.50	4.50	4.00	2.75
2631-34	Set of 4 Singles	...	...	3.75	.70
2635	29¢ Alaska Highway.....................	35.00	3.50	.75	.15
2636	29¢ Kentucky Statehood	35.00	3.50	.75	.15
2637-41	29¢ Summer Olympics, attd ..... (35)	31.50 (10)	10.00	4.75	3.95
2637-41	Set of 5 Singles	...	...	4.35	.90
2642-46	29¢ Hummingbirds, Set of 5 bklt. sgls.	...	...	4.35	.90
2646a	29¢ Booklet Pane of 5 ....(Unfolded 5.50)			4.50	3.50

Scott's No.		Mint Sheet	Plate Block	F-VF NH	F-VF Used
2647-96	29¢ Wildflowers, Pane of 50 diff ..	42.50	...	...	...
2647-96	Set of 50 Singles.........................	...	...	39.50	29.75
2647-96	29¢ Individual Singles....................	...	...	1.00	.60
2697	29¢ World War II S/S of 10 ....(20)	15.95	...	8.25	6.75
2697a-j	Set of 10 Singles.........................	...	...	8.00	4.50
2697s	Se-Tenant Center Block of 10	...	...	9.50	8.95
2698	29¢ Dorothy Parker, Literary Arts	35.00	3.50	.75	.15
2699	29¢ Dr. Theodore von Karman	35.00	3.50	.75	.15
2700-03	29¢ Minerals, attd ....(40)	37.50	4.50	4.00	3.00
2700-03	Set of 4 Singles..........................	...	...	3.75	.70
2704	29¢ Juan Rodriguez Cabrillo	35.00	3.50	.75	.15

2705-09

2719

2710	2711-14,15-18	2720

Scott's No.		Mint Sheet	Plate Block	F-VF NH	F-VF Used
2705-09	29¢ Wild Animals, bklt. sgls.........	...	...	4.50	.90
2709a	29¢ Booklet Pane of 5	(Unfolded 6.00)		4.75	3.50
#2710-19a Christmas Issues					
2710	29¢ Madonna & Child.................	35.00	3.50	.75	.15
2710a	29¢ Booklet Pane of 10	(Unfolded 10.75)		7.95	7.50
2711-14	29¢ Toys, **offset**, attd.	41.50	4.25	3.75	3.00
2711-14	Set of 4 Singles	...	...	3.50	.70
2715-18	29¢ Toys, **gravure**, 4 bklt. sgls	...	...	3.50	.70
2718a	29¢ Booklet Pane of 4	(Unfolded 4.75)		3.75	3.50
2719	29¢ Locomotive, ATM, self adhes. sgl.	...	...	.80	.40
2719a	29¢ Locomotive, ATM, pane of 18	...	...	14.50	...
2720	29¢ Happy New Year .... (20)	17.50	3.95	.90	.15

1993 Commemoratives

2721	2722	2723

Scott's No.		Mint Sheet	Plate Block	F-VF NH	F-VF Used
2721-30,2746-59,2766,2771-74,2779-89,2791-94,					
2804-06	Set of 47	...	...	40.75	7.95
2721	29¢ Elvis Presley ....(40)	28.00	3.50	.75	.15
2722	29¢ "Oklahoma!" ....(40)	28.00	3.50	.75	.15
2723	29¢ Hank Williams, Perf. 10......(40)	28.00	3.50	.75	.15
2723a	Same, Perf. 11.2 x 11.4	...	150.00	23.95	9.95

2724-30,31-37

2724-30	29¢ Rock 'n Roll, R & B attd .....(35)	35.00 (8)	7.95	6.95	6.50
2724-30	Top Horiz. Plate Block of 10	...	9.95	...	...
2724-30	Rock 'n Roll, R & B, set of 7 sgls .	...	...	...	1.90
2731-37	29¢ Rock 'n Roll, R & B, 7 bklt. sgls.	...	...	6.25	1.90
2737a	29¢ Booklet Pane of 8.................(Unfolded 8.95)			6.75	6.50
2737b	29¢ Booklet Pane of 4.................(Unfolded 4.95)			4.00	3.85

2745a

2747	2746	2748

2749	2754	2755

2750-53

Scott's No.		Mint Sheet	Plate Block	F-VF NH	F-VF Used
2741-45	29¢ Space Fantasy, bklt. sgls......	...	...	4.35	.90
2745a	29¢Booklet Pane of 5	(Unfolded 5.50)		4.50	3.75
2746	29¢ Percy Lavon Julian	40.00	4.00	.85	.15
2747	29¢ Oregon Trail.........................	35.00	3.50	.75	.15
2748	29¢ World University Games.......	40.00	4.00	.85	.15
2749	29¢ Grace Kelly	35.00	3.50	.75	.15
2750-53	29¢ Circus, attd ....(40)	35.00 (6)	6.75	3.75	3.00
2750-53	Set of 4 Singles	...	...	3.60	.80
2754	29¢ Cherokee Strip...................(20)	14.50	3.50	.75	.15
2755	29¢ Dean Acheson	35.00	3.50	.75	.15

2756-59

2764a

2765

| 2766 | 2783-84 | 2806 |

2771-74, 2775-78

| 2767-70 | 2779-82 |

| 2785-88 | 2791-94, 2795-98, 2799-2802 |

| 2789, 2790 | 2803 | 2804 | 2805 |

Scott's No.		Mint Sheet	Plate Block	F-VF NH	F-VF Used
2756-59	29¢ Sporting Horses, blk. of 4.....(40)	39.50	4.25	4.00	3.00
2756-59	Set of 4 Singles	...	...	3.80	.60
2760-64	29¢ Spring Garden Flowers, 5 bklt. sgls.	...	...	4.35	.75
2764a	29¢ Booklet Pane of 5 ....(Unfolded 5.50)...			4.50	3.50
2765	29¢ World War II S/S of 10 ....(20)	15.95	...	8.25	6.75
2765a-j	Set of 10 Singles	...	...	8.00	4.50
2765s	Se-Tenant Center Block of 10.......	...	...	9.50	8.95
2766	29¢ Joe Louis	47.50	4.75	1.00	.15
2767-70	29¢ Broadway Musicals, 4 bklt. sgls .	...	...	3.35	.80
2770a	29¢ Booklet Pane of 4 ....(Unfolded 4.95) ...			3.50	3.35
2771-74	29¢ Country Music, Block attd ....(20)	16.50	3.95	3.50	3.00
2771-74	Horizontal Strip of 4......................	...	...	3.50	3.00
2771-74	Horiz. Pl. Block of 8 with Label......	...	7.50	...	...
2771-74	Set of 4 Singles	...	...	3.35	.80
2775-78	29¢ Country Music, 4 bklt. sgls.	...	...	3.35	.80
2778a	29¢ Booklet Pane of 4 ....(Unfolded 4.95) ...			3.50	3.35
2779-82	29¢ Nat'l. Postal Museum, Block (20)	18.00	4.25	3.75	3.75
2779-82	Horizontal Strip of 4......................	...	...	3.75	3.75
2779-82	Set of 4 Singles	...	...	3.60	.80
2783-84	29¢ Deaf Communication, pair....(20)	16.50	3.95	1.80	1.25
2783-84	Set of 2 Singles	...	...	1.70	.35
2785-88	29¢ Children's Classics, Black ....(40)	39.50	4.50	4.00	3.00
2785-88	Horizontal Strip of 4......................	...	...	4.00	3.00
2785-88	Set of 4 Singles	...	...	3.80	.80

Scott's No.		Mint Sheet	Plate Block	F-VF NH	F-VF Used
2789	29¢ Christmas Madonna	35.00	3.50	.75	.15
2790	29¢ Madonna, Booklet Single	...	...	.80	.18
2790a	29¢ Booklet Pane of 4 ....(Unfolded 4.95)			3.50	2.75
2791-94	29¢ Christmas Designs, block of 4...	45.00	4.50	4.00	3.50
2791-94	Strip of 4	...	...	4.00	3.50
2791-94	Set of 4 Singles	...	...	3.85	.70
2795-98	29¢ Christmas Designs, set of 4 bklt. sgls.	...	...	3.50	.80
2798a	29¢ Booklet Pane of 10 (3 Snowmen)(Unfolded 11.75)			9.50	7.50
2798b	29¢ Booklet Pane of 10 (2 Snowmen)(Unfolded 11.75)			9.50	7.50
2799-2802	29¢ Christmas Designs, self adhes.,4 sgls	...		3.75	1.80
2802a	29¢ Pane of 12, self-adhesive..........	...	...	10.75	...
2799-2802 var.	Coil, self-adhesive .. Plate Strip of 8	9.95		4.00	...
2803	29¢ Christmas Snowman, self adhes.	...	...	.90	.35
2803a	29¢ Pane of 18, self adhesive..........	...	...	14.75	...
2804	29¢ No. Mariana Is. Comm'nwlth .. (20)	14.50	3.50	.75	.15
2805	29¢ Columbus at Puerto Rico	35.00	3.50	.75	.15
2806	29¢ AIDS Awareness, Perf.11.2	40.00	3.95	.85	.15
2806a	29¢ AIDS Booklet Single, Perf.11	...	...	.90	.18
2806b	29¢ Booklet Pane of 5 ....(Unfolded 5.75)			4.50	3.75

2807-11

| 2812 | 2813 | 2814,2814C | 2815 |

Scott's No.		Mint Sheet	Plate Block	F-VF NH	F-VF Used
2807-12,2814C-28,2834-36,2839, 2848-68,2871-72,2876 **Set of 49**		...	...	25.75	10.95
2807-11	29¢ Winter Olympics, attd..........(20)	14.50	(10)9.50	4.50	4.00
2807-11	Set of 5 Singles			4.35	1.00
2812	29¢ Edward R. Murrow	35.00	3.50	.75	.15
2813	29¢ Love & Sunrise, self adhesive ...	...	...	.85	.30
2813a	29¢ Pane of 18	...	...	14.75	...
2813v	29¢ Love Coil, self adhesive Pl# Strip	(5) 8.00	(3) 6.75	.85	...
2814	29¢ Love & Dove, Booklet Single	...	...	.80	.18
2814a	29¢ Booklet Pane of 10 ....(Unfolded 8.95)			7.95	5.95
2814C	29¢ Love & Dove, sheet stamp........	35.00	3.50	.75	.15
2815	52¢ Love & Doves	63.50	6.75	1.35	.35

| 2816 | 2817 | 2818 |

2833a

| 2834 | 2835 | 2836 |

2837

Scott's No.		Mint Sheet	Plate Block	F-VF NH	F-VF Used
2829-33	29¢ Summer Garden Flowers, set of 5 bklt. sgls.	...	...	4.15	1.00
2833a	29¢ Booklet Pane of 5 ....(Unfolded 5.50)			4.25	3.00
2834	29¢ World Cup Soccer..................(20)	15.00	3.75	.80	.18
2835	40¢ World Cup Soccer..................(20)	19.50	5.25	1.10	.35
2836	50¢ World Cup Soccer..................(20)	24.50	6.25	1.30	.50
2837	29¢,40¢,50¢ World Cup Soccer, Souvenir Sheet of 3	...	...	3.75	3.00

2838

2838	29¢ World War II S/S of 10 ....(20)	15.95	...	8.25	6.75
2838a-j	Set of 10 Singles	...	...	8.00	4.50
2838v	Se-Tenant Center Block of 10	...	...	9.50	8.95

2816	29¢ Dr. Allison Davis .... (20)	16.00	4.00	.85	.15
2817	29¢ Chinese New Year, Dog ...... (20)	15.00	3.65	.80	.15
2818	29¢ Buffalo Soldiers................... (20)	16.00	4.00	.85	.15
2819-28	29¢ Silent Screen Stars, attd...... (40)	32.50 (10)	8.95	8.50	7.25
2819-28	Half-Pane of 20 with selvedge.......	...	...	16.75	14.75
2819-28	Set of 10 singles	...	...	8.25	2.50

2819-28

2840

| 2839 | 2841a | 2842 | 2848 |

2843-47

Scott's No.		Mint Sheet	Plate Block	F-VF NH	F-VF Used
2839	29¢ Norman Rockwell...........................	35.00	3.50	.75	.18
2840	50¢ N. Rockwell, Souvenir Sheet of 4 ..	...	...	5.95	4.95
1994 Moon Landing, 25th Anniversary					
2841	29¢ Moon Landing Miniature Sheet of 12	...	...	8.95	7.50
2841a	29¢ Single Stamp from sheet	...	...	.80	.25
2842	$9.95 Moon Landing Express Mail ... (20)	425.00	95.00	22.50	9.75
1994 Commemoratives (continued)					
2843-47	29¢ Locomotives, set of 5 bklt.singls	...	...	4.15	1.00
2847a	29¢ Booklet Pane of 5	(Unfolded 5.50)		4.25	3.50
2848	29¢ George Meany	35.00	3.50	.75	.18

2849-53

Scott's No.		Mint Sheet	Plate Block	F-VF NH	F-VF Used
2849-53	29¢ Popular Singers, attd............. (20)	16.00	(6)5.75	4.25	3.25
2849-53	Top Plate Block of 12		10.95	...	...
2849-53	Set of 5 Singles	...	...	4.15	1.30

2854-61

2854-61	29¢ Blues & Jazz Artists, attd. ...... (35)	26.75 (10)	8.95 (10)	7.95	6.95
2854-61	Top Plate Block of 10 with Label......		9.50	...	...
2854-61	Set of 8 Singles	...	...	6.75	3.00

Note: Because of Sheet layout there are no blocks of eight possible.

| 2862 | 2867-68 |

2863-66

2862	29¢ James Thurber..............................	35.00	3.50	.75	.18
2863-66	29¢ Wonders of the Sea, attd........ (24)	19.95	3.85	3.50	2.50
2863-66	Set of 4 Singles	...	...	3.35	.90
2867-68	29¢ Cranes, attd. .... (20)	14.95	3.65	1.60	1.10
2867-68	Set of 2 Singles	...	...	1.55	.40

SE-TENANT NOTE: Many modern se-tenants are issued in "staggered" form. Stamp designs in blocks and plate blocks will not always follow "Scott Order" but will vary depending upon their location in sheet.

2869

2870

1994 Legends of the West Miniature Sheet

Scott's No.		Mint Sheet	Plate Block	F-VF NH	F-VF Used
2869	29¢ Revised Sheet of 20 .... (6)	95.00	...	15.95	13.95
2869a-t	Set of 20 Singles	...	...	15.00	8.95
2869a/t	Horiz. Gutter Block of 10	...	...	13.95	...
2869a/t	Vert. Gutter Block of 8	...	...	11.95	...
2869a/t	Set of 4 Vert.Gutter Pairs	...	...	10.95	...
2869a/t	Set of 5 Horiz. Gutter Pairs	...	...	12.95	...
2869a/t	Center Gutter Block of 4	...	...	14.95	...
2869a/t	Cross Gutter Block of 20	...	...	17.75	...
2869a/t	Block of 24 with Vertical Gutter.......	...	...	20.95	...
2869a/t	Block of 25 with Horiz. Gutter	...	...	21.95	...
2870	29¢ Original (recalled) sheet of 20 ...	...	...	265.00	...

| 2871 | 2872 | 2873 | 2874 |

1994 Commemoratives (continued)

Scott's No.		Mint Sheet	Plate Block	F-VF NH	F-VF Used
#2871-74a Christmas Issues					
2871	29¢ Madonna & Child	35.00	3.50	.75	.15
2871a	29¢ Madonna & Child, Bklt. Single	...	...	.80	.18
2871b	29¢ Booklet Pane of 10	(Unfolded 8.95)		7.75	6.35
2872	29¢ Christmas Stocking	35.00	3.50	.75	.15
2872v	29¢ Stocking Booklet Single	...	...	.80	.20
2872a	29¢ Booklet Pane of 20	(Unfolded 19.50)		16.50	12.50
2873	29¢ Santa Claus, self-adhesive	...	...	.85	.25
2873a	29¢ Pane of 12, self-adhesive	...	...	9.95	7.50
2873v	29¢ Santa Claus Coil, self-adhesive Pl# Strip.........	(5) 8.25	(3) 7.00	.85	...
2874	29¢ Cardinal in Snow, self-adhesive	...	...	.80	.25
2874a	29¢ Pane of 18, self-adhesive	...	...	13.95	11.00

2875

2876

2875	$2 Bureau of Engraving Centennial Souvenir Sheet of 4	...	...	18.75	14.50
2875a	$2 Madison, Single Stamp from S/S.....	...	...	4.75	3.50
2876	29¢ Year of the Boar, New Year........ (20)	14.00	3.50	.75	.18

| 2877,2878 | 2879,2880 | 2881-87,2889-92 | 2888 | 2893 |

1994-95 Interim Regular Issues

Scott's No.		Mint Sheet	Plate Block	F-VF NH	F-VF Used
2877	(3¢) Dove, ABN, Light Blue.............. (100)	8.50	.75	.20	.15
2878	(3¢) Dove, SVS, Darker Blue .... (100)	8.50	.75	.20	.15
	#2877 Thin, taller letters. #2878 Heavy, shorter letters.				
2879	(20¢)"G", Postcard Rate, BEP,Black "G".............................. (100)	47.50	2.95	.50	.18
2880	(20¢) "G", Postcard Rate, SVS,Red "G"................................ (100)	52.50	4.95	.55	.18
2881	(32¢) "G",BEP, Black "G"............. (100)	82.50	4.50	.90	.18
2881v	(32¢) Black "G" Booklet Single	...	...	.90	.20
2881a	(32¢) Booklet Pane of 10, Perf. 11	...	...	8.95	7.95
2882	(32¢) "G", SVS, Red "G" .... (100)	82.50	4.25	.90	.18
2883	(32¢) "G", BEP, Black "G", bklt. sgl.	...	...	.90	.18
2883a	(32¢) Booklet Pane of 10, BEP, Perf. 10 ...	...	...	8.95	7.95
2884	(32¢) "G", ABN, Blue "G", bklt. sgl.	...	...	.90	.18
2884a	(32¢) Booklet Pane of 10, ABN	...	...	8.95	7.95
2885	(32¢) "G", KCS, Red "G", bklt. sgl.	...	...	.90	.18
2885a	(32¢) Booklet Pane of 10, KCS..........	...	...	8.95	7.95
2886	(32¢) "G", Surface Tagged, self-adhesive ...	...	...	1.00	.30
2886a	(32¢) Pane of 18, self-adhesive	...	...	16.50	...
2886v	(32¢) "G", Coil, self-adhesive Pl.# Strip	(5)8.25	(3) 7.00	.85	...
2887	(32¢) "G", Overall Tagging, self-adhesive ...	...	...	1.00	.30
2887a	(32¢) Pane of 18, self-adhesive, thin paper ...	...	...	16.50	...
	#2886 Limited amount of blue shading in the white stripes below field of stars.				
	#2887 Stronger blue shading in the white stripes.				

Scott's No.		Pl.Strip of 5	Pl.Strip of 3	F-VF NH	F-VF Used
2888	(25¢) "G" Presort, Coil	6.95	5.95	.75	.25
2889	(32¢) "G" Coil, BEP, Black "G"	8.75	7.50	.80	.18
2890	(32¢) "G" Coil, ABN, Blue "G"	6.50	5.25	.90	.18
2891	(32¢) "G" Coil, SVS, Red "G"	6.50	5.25	.85	.18
2892	(32¢) "G" Coil, SVS, Rouletted	7.75	6.50	.90	.18
2893	(5¢) "G" Non-Profit, green (1995)	2.30	2.00	.20	.15

BEP=Bureau of Engraving and Printing ABN=American Bank-Note Co.
SVS=Stamp Venturers KCS=KCS Industries

| 2897,2913-16 | 2902,2902B | 2903-4B | 2905,7 | 2908-10 |

| 2911-12B | 2919 | 2920-21 |

Scott's No.		Mint Sheet	Plate Block	F-VF NH	F-VF Used
2897	32¢ Flag over Porch, Dull gum.....(100)	62.50	3.95	.70	.15
2897s	32¢ Shiny Gum..........................(100)	62.50	3.95	.70	...

1995-96 Moisture-Activated Coils

Scott's No.		Pl.Strip of 5	Pl.Strip of 3	F-VF NH	F-VF Used
2902	(5¢) Butte	1.75	1.50	.20	.15
2903	(5¢) Mountain, BEP (1996)	2.25	1.95	.20	.15
2904	(5¢) Mountain, SVS (1996)	2.25	1.95	.20	.15
	NOTE: #2903 Letters outlined in purple. #2904 No outline on letters.				
2905	(10¢) Automobile	2.90	2.50	.28	.18
2908	(15¢) Auto Tail Fin, BEP	4.50	3.75	.40	.25
2909	(15¢) Auto Tail Fin, SVS	3.75	3.00	.40	.25
2911	(25¢) Juke Box, BEP	6.25	5.25	.65	.40
2912	(25¢) Juke Box, SVS	5.25	4.25	.65	.40
	NOTE: The SVS varieties of the above 15¢ & 25¢ coils are fainter than the BEP varieties which are sharp and darker.				
2913	32¢ Flag over Porch, BEP, ...	6.25	5.25	.75	.15
2913a	32¢ Dull Gum	6.25	5.25	.75	...
2914	32¢ Flag over Porch, SVS,.................	5.75	4.75	.80	.15
	NOTE: The SVS variety is fainter/duller than the BEP variety.				

1996-97 Self-Adhesive Coil Stamps

2902B	(5¢) Butte	2.00	1.75	.20	.18
2904A	(5¢) Mountain, Die-Cut 11.5	1.95	1.70	.20	.18
2904B	(5¢) Mountain, Die-Cut 9.8 (1997)	1.95	1.70	.20	.18
2906	(10¢) Eagle & Shield (Design of 1993)..	2.95	2.65	.25	.25
2907	(10¢) Automobile..................................	2.95	2.65	.25	.25
2910	(15¢) Auto Tail Fin	3.50	3.00	.35	.30
2912A	(25¢) Juke Box, Die-Cut 11.5...........	4.85	4.00	.55	.30
2912B	(25¢) Juke Box, Die-Cut 9.8 (1997)	4.85	4.00	.55	.30
2915	32¢ Flag over Porch, Die-Cut 8.7 Vert..	7.95	6.75	.80	.30
2915A	32¢ Flag over Porch, Die-Cut 9.7 vert...	8.95	7.50	.95	.30
2915B	32¢ Flag over Porch, Die-Cut 11.5 vert..	7.95	6.75	.80	.30
2915C	32¢ Flag over Porch, Die-Cut 10.9........	10.75	8.75	1.50	.50
2915D	32¢ Flag over Porch, Die-Cut 9.8, Stamps separate on backing (1997)	7.95	6.75	.80	.30

1995-97 Booklets and Panes

Scott's No.		Mint Sheet	Plate Block	F-VF NH	F-VF Used
2916	32¢ Flag over Porch, booklet single......	...	...	.80	.20
2916a	32¢ Booklet Pane of 10.........................(Unfolded 9.75)		7.95	6.95
2919	32¢ Flag over Field, self-adhesive sgl...	...	...	.90	.30
2919a	32¢ Pane of 18, Self-adhesive	...	...	14.50	...
2920	32¢ Flag over Porch, self-adhesive single large date Die-Cut 8.8	...	...	.90	.30
2920a	32¢ Pane of 20, Self-adhesive, large "1995" ...		...	17.50	...
2920b	32¢ Flag over Porch, self adhesive single, small date Die-Cut 8.8.......................	...	...	1.95	.60
2920c	32¢ Pane of 20, self-adhesive,small "1995" ...		...	37.50	...
2920d	32¢ Flag over Porch, self-adhesive, "1996" date (1996) Die-Cut 11.3	...	...	.80	.30
2920e	32¢ Pane of 10, self-adhesive................	...	...	7.50	...
2920f	32¢ Flag over Porch, folded bklt of 15('96) ...		...	9.95	...
2921	32¢ Flag over Porch, self-adhesive booklet single	...	...	.80	.30
2921a	32¢ Booklet Pane of 10, self-adhesive Die-Cut 9.8 (1996) ....(Unfolded 8.50)		7.50	...
2921b	32¢ Booklet Pane of 5, self-adhesive Die-Cut 9.8 (1997)	...	...	3.95	...

| 2933 | 2934 | 2938 | 2940 | 2943 |

Scott's No.		Mint Sheet	Plate Block	F.V.F NH	F.V.F Used
2933-43 Set of 5..		...	24.50	4.75	.95
2933	32¢ Milton S. Hershey.................. (100)	62.50	3.75	.65	.18
2934	32¢ Cal Farley (1996).................... (100)	62.50	3.75	.65	.18
2938	46¢ Ruth Benedict...................... (100)	90.00	4.75	.95	.25
2940	55¢ Alice Hamilton, MD.............. (100)	105.00	5.50	1.10	.20
2943	78¢ Alice Paul, Dull gum.............. (100)	155.00	7.95	1.60	.25
2943g	78¢ Shiny gum (1996).................. (100)	155.00	7.95	1.60	...

1995 Commemoratives

| 2948 | 2949 | 2950 | 2955 |

| 2951-54 | 2956 |

Scott's No.		Mint Sheet	Plate Block	F-VF NH	F-VF Used
2948,2950-58,2961-68,2974,2976-80, 2982-92,2998-99,3001-7,3019-23 Set of 49 ...		...	...	36.95	10.75
2948	(32¢) Love & Cherub	36.00	3.50	.75	.18
2949	(32¢) Love & Cherub, Self-adhesive	...	...	.80	.25
2949a	(32¢) Pane of 20, Self-adhesive............	...	...	15.75	...
2950	32¢ Florida Statehood ....(20)	13.50	3.50	.70	.18
2951-54	32¢ Earth Day/Kids Care, attd........(16)	13.00	3.95	3.50	2.00
2951-54	Set of 4 Singles...................................	...	...	3.25	.90
2955	32¢ Richard Nixon...............................	36.00	3.50	.75	.18
2956	32¢ Bessie Coleman, Black Heritage Series.......................	36.00	3.50	.75	.18

| 2957,2959 | 2958 | 2960 |

2957	32¢ Love Cherub...................................	36.00	3.50	.75	.18
2958	55¢ Love Cherub...................................	62.50	5.75	1.30	.60
2959	32¢ Love Cherub, booklet single...........	...	...	.80	.18
2959a	32¢ Booklet Pane of 10.........................(Unfolded 9.95)		7.95	5.95
2960	55¢ Love Cherub, Self-Adhesive single	...	...	1.35	.65
2960a	55¢ Pane of 20, Self-Adhesive..............	...	...	25.95	...
2960d	55¢ Pane of 20 with Die-cut "Time to Reorder" (1996)	...	...	25.95	...

2961-65

2966   2967   2968

2973a

2975

2981

Scott's No.		Mint Sheet	Plate Block	F-VF NH	F-VF Used
2961-65	32¢ Recreational Sports Strip	15.75	(10)8.50	3.95	2.95
2961-65	Set of 5 Singles	...	...	3.75	1.20
2966	32¢ POW & MIA	(20) 14.50	3.50	.75	.18
2967	32¢ Marilyn Monroe	...	3.50	.75	.18
2967	M. Monroe Miniature Sheet of 20	(6) 87.50	...	14.50	13.75
2967	Block of 8 with Vertical Gutter	...	...	13.75	...
2967	Cross Gutter Block of 8	...	...	16.75	...
2967	Vertical Pair with Horizontal Gutter	...	...	3.95	...
2967	Horizontal Pair with Vertical Gutter	...	...	4.95	...
2968	32¢ Texas Statehood	(20) 14.50	3.50	.75	.18
2969-73	32¢ Great Lakes Lighthouses 5 booklet singles	...	...	3.85	1.00
2973a	32¢ Booklet Pane of 5	(Unfolded 4.95)		3.95	3.50

Scott's No.		Mint Sheet	Plate Block	F-VF NH	F-VF Used
2974	32¢ United Nations	(20) 14.50	3.50	.75	.18
1995 Civil War Miniature Sheet					
2975	32¢ Civil War, Miniature Sheet of 20	(6) 95.00	...	15.95	13.95
2975a-t	Set of 20 Singles	...	...	15.75	9.95
2975a/t	Horizontal Gutter, Block of 10	...	...	11.95	...
2975a/t	Vert. Gutter, Block of 8	...	...	9.95	...
2975a/t	Set of 4 Vert. Gutter Pairs	...	...	8.95	...
2975a/t	Set of 5 Horiz. Gutter Pairs	...	...	10.95	...
2975a/t	Center Gutter Block of 4	...	...	13.50	...
2975a/t	Cross Gutter Block of 20	...	...	18.50	...
2975a/t	Block of 24 with Vertical Gutter	...	...	21.95	...
2975a/t	Block of 25 with Horiz. Gutter	...	...	22.95	...
1995 Commemoratives (cont.)					
2976-79	32¢ Carousel Horses, attd	(20) 15.00	3.65	3.25	2.50
2976-79	Set of 4 Singles	...	...	3.00	.80
2980	32¢ Woman Suffrage	(40) 28.75	3.50	.75	.18
2981	32¢ World War II S/S of 10	(20) 15.95	...	8.25	6.75
2981a-j	Set of 10 Singles	...	...	8.00	4.50
2981v	Se-Tenant Center Block of 10	...	...	9.50	8.95

2974

2980

2976-79

2982   2983   2984

2985   2986   2987

1995 Commemoratives (continued)

2988	2989	2990

2991	2992

2997a

2998	2999

Scott's No.		Mint Sheet	Plate Block	F-VF NH	F-VF Used
2982	32¢5 Louis Armstrong .... (20)	14.50	3.50	.75	.18
2983-92	32¢ Jazz Musicians, attd .... (20)	15.00 (10)	8.50	7.75	6.95
2983-92	Set of 10 Singles	...	...	7.50	3.00
2993-97	32¢ Fall Garden Flowers, 5 bklt.Sgls.	...	...	3.85	.90
2997a	32¢ Booklet Pane of 5 .... (Unfolded 5.25)			3.95	2.95
2998	60¢ Eddie Rickenbacker	62.50	5.95	1.30	.50
2999	32¢ Republic of Palau	36.00	3.50	.75	.18

3000

1995 Comic Strips Miniature Sheet

Scott's No.		Mint Sheet	Plate Block	F-VF NH	F-VF Used
3000	32¢ Comic Strips, Min. Sheet of 20 .... (6)	87.50	...	14.95	13.95
3000a-t	Set of 20 Singles	...	...	14.75	9.95
3000a/t	Horiz. Gutter Block of 8	...	...	10.75	...
3000a/t	Vert. Gutter Block of 10	...	...	12.75	...
3000a/t	Set of 5 Vert. Gutter Pairs	...	...	11.95	...
3000a/t	Set of 4 Horiz. Gutter Pairs	...	...	9.50	...
3000a/t	Center Gutter Block of 4	...	...	13.50	...
3000a/t	Cross Gutter Block of 20	...	...	17.50	...
3000a/t	Block of 25 with Vertical Gutter	...	...	21.75	...
3000a/t	Block of 24 with Horiz. Gutter	...	...	20.75	...

1995 Commemoratives (continued)

3001	3003	3002

3004,3010,3016	3005,3009,3015	3006,3011,3017	3007,3008,3014

3012,3018

Scott's No.		Mint Sheet	3013 Plate Block	F-VF NH	F-VF Used
3001	32¢ U.S. Naval Academy .... (20)	14.50	3.50	.75	.18
3002	32¢ Tennessee Williams .... (20)	14.50	3.50	.75	.18
#3003-18 Christmas Issues					
3003	32¢ Madonna and Child	36.00	3.50	.75	.15
3003a	32¢ Madonna and Child, Bklt.Single	...	...	.75	.15
3003b	32¢ Booklet Pane of 10 .... (Unfolded 9.50)			7.50	5.95
3004-7	32¢ Santa & Children	36.00	3.50	3.00	2.50
3004-7	Strip of 4	...	...	3.00	2.50
3004-7	Set of 4 Singles	...	...	2.90	.80
3007b	32¢ Booklet Pane of 10, 3 each .... (Unfolded 9.50)			7.50	5.95
	#3004-5, 2 each #3006-7				
3007c	32¢ Booklet Pane of 10, 2 each .... (Unfolded 9.50)			7.50	5.95
	#3004-5, 3 each #3006-7				
Self-Adhesive Stamps					
3008-11	32¢ Santa & Children, Block of 9	...	...	6.95	...
3008-11	Set of 4 Singles	...	...	3.20	1.80
3011a	32¢ Pane of 20	...	...	15.00	...
3012	32¢ Midnight Angel	...	...	.80	.45
3012a	32¢ Pane of 20	...	...	15.00	...
3012c	Folded Block of 15 in Booklet	...	...	10.75	...
3013	32¢ Children Sledding	...	...	.80	.45
3013a	32¢ Pane of 18	...	...	14.00	...
Self-Adhesive Coil Stamps					
3014-17	32¢ Santa & Children .... Pl.Strip 8	...	7.50	3.25	...
3014-17	Set of 4 Singles	...	...	3.20	1.80
3018	32¢ Midnight Angel .... Pl.# Strip (5) 6.95		(3) 5.75	.80	.45

3019-23

3019-23	32¢ Antique Automobiles, Strip ...... (25)	18.50	(10) 8.75	3.75	3.00
3019-23	Set of 5 Singles	...	...	3.65	1.00

1996 Commemoratives

3024

3030

3029a

Scott's No.		Mint Sheet	Plate Block	F-VF NH	F-VF Used
3024,3030,3058-67,3069-70,3072-88					
3090-3104,3106-11,3118 Set of 53		...	...	38.95	9.95
3024	32¢ Utah Statehood	36.00	3.50	.75	.18
3024v	Folded Block of 15 in Booklet(BK 245) .	...	...	11.75	...
3025-29	32¢ Winter Garden Flowers, 5 Bklt Sgls	...		3.70	1.00
3029a	32¢ Booklet Pane of 5	(Unfolded 4.95)		3.75	2.95
3030	32¢ Love Cherub, Self-adhesive single	...	...	.85	.30
3030a	32¢ Pane of 20, Self-adhesive	...	...	16.50	...
3030b	32¢ Folded Pane of 15 + Label	...	...	9.95	...
3030c	32¢ Folded Pane of 14	...	...	9.30	...
3030d	32¢ Folded Pane of 16	...	...	10.65	...

NOTE: PRICES ON ABOVE 3 ITEMS ARE TENTATIVE.

1996-97 Flora and Fauna Series

	3032		3033		3044		3048,3053		3049		
3032	2¢ Red-headed Woodpecker	(100)	4.75	.50	.20	.15
3033	3¢ Eastern Bluebird	(100)	6.75	.55	.20	.15
3044	1¢ Kestrel, Coil	(PS5)	.75	(PS3) .60	.20	.15
3048	20¢ Blue Jay, Self-adhesive Bklt Single	...	...		.45	.25
3048a	20¢ Booklet Pane of 10	...	...		4.50	...
3049	32¢ Yellow Rose, Self-adhesive Single	...	...		.75	.25
3049a	32¢ Pane of 20	...	...		13.95	...
3049b	32¢ Booklet Pane of 4	...	...		2.90	...
3049c	32¢ Booklet Pane of 5 + Label	...	...		3.60	...
3049d	32¢ Booklet Pane of 6	...	...		4.30	...
3053	20¢ Blue Jay Coil	(PS5)4.65	(PS3)3.95		.40	.20

1996 Commemoratives (continued)

3059	3058	3060

3061-64   3065

1996 Commemoratives (continued)

3066   3067

Scott's No.		Mint Sheet	Plate Block	F-VF NH	F-VF Used
3058	32¢ Ernest E. Just	(20) 14.50	3.50	.75	.18
3059	32¢ Smithsonian Institution	(20) 14.50	3.50	.75	.18
3060	32¢ Year of the Rat	(20) 14.50	3.50	.75	.18
3061-64	32¢ Pioneers of Communication	(20) 14.50	3.50	3.00	2.25
3061-64	32¢ Strip of 4	...	...	3.00	2.25
3061-64	Set of 4 singles	...	...	2.90	.80
3065	32¢ Fulbright Scholarships	36.00	3.50	.75	.18
3065v	Folded Block of 15 in Booklet (BK246) .	...	...	11.75	...
3066	50¢ Jacqueline Cochran	53.50	5.00	1.10	.40
3067	32¢ Marathon	(20) 14.50	3.50	.65	.18

1996 Atlanta '96 Summer Olympics Miniature Sheet

3068

Scott's No.		Mint Sheet	Plate Block	F-VF NH	F-VF Used
3068	32¢ Centen. Olympic Games, Mini Sht/20(6)	83.50	...	13.95	13.75
3068a-t	Olympics Set of 20 Singles	...	...	13.75	9.95
3068a/t	Vert. Gutter Block of 8	...	...	9.95	...
3068a/t	Horiz. Gutter Block of 10	...	...	11.95	...
3068a/t	Set of 4 Vert. Gutter Pairs	...	...	8.75	...
3068a/t	Set of 5 Horiz. Gutter Pairs	...	...	10.75	...
3068a/t	Center Gutter Block of 4	...	...	12.95	...
3068a/t	Center Gutter Block of 20	...	...	16.50	...
3068a/t	Block of 24 with Vertical Gutter	...	...	18.75	...
3068a/t	Block of 25 with Horiz. Gutter	...	...	19.75	...

1996 Commemoratives (cont.)

3069	3070	3071

3069	32¢ Georgia O'Keeffe	(15) 10.00	3.25	.70	.18
3069v	Folded Block of 15 in Booklet (BK247) .	...	...	11.75	...
3070	32¢ Tennessee Statehood	33.75	3.50	.70	.18
3070v	Folded Block of 15 in Booklet (BK248) .	...	...	11.75	...
3071	Tennessee Self-adhesive single	...	...	.85	.30
3071a	Tennessee Self-adhesive Pane of 20 ...	...	...	15.95	...

3072-76

3096-99

3091-95 **3100-3**

3077-80   **3081**

Scott's No.		Mint Sheet	Plate Block	F-VF NH	F-VF Used
3072-76	32¢ American Indian Dances, 5 Designs,Strip............................(20)	13.75	(10)7.95	3.50	2.95
3072-76	Indian Dancers Set of 5 singles.........			3.40	1.00
3072-76v	Folded Block of 15 in Booklet (BK249)	...	...	11.75	...
3077-80	32¢ Prehistoric Animals, 4 Designs, attd, Block. ....(20)	13.75	3.25	2.85	2.25
3077-80	32¢ Strip of 4	...	...	2.85	2.25
3077-80	Prehistoric Animals Set of 4 singles ..			2.80	.80
3081	32¢ Breast Cancer............................(20)	13.75	3.25	.70	.18

Scott's No.		Mint Sheet	Plate Block	F-VF NH	F-VF Used
3088	32¢ Iowa Statehood	33.75	3.50	.70	.18
3088v	Folded Block of 15 in Booklet (BK253) .	...	...	11.75	...
3089	Iowa Self-Adhesive single	...	...	.85	.30
3089a	Iowa Self-Adhesive Pane of 20	...	...	15.95	...
3090	32¢ Rural Free Delivery ....(20)	13.75	3.25	.70	.18
3090v	Folded Block of 15 in Booklet (BK254) .	...	...	11.75	...
3091-95	32¢ Riverboats, self-adhesive, attd. (20)	13.95	(10)7.95	3.60	2.95
3091-95	Riverboats, Set of 5 singles			3.50	1.00
3091-95v	Riverboats, Set of 15 in Booklet (BK255)	...	...	11.75	...
3096-99	32¢ Big Band Leaders, Block ....(20)	13.75	3.25	2.85	2.25
3096-99	32¢ Strip of 4	...	...	2.85	2.25
3096-99	32¢ Horiz. Pl. Block of 8 with selvedge	...	6.75		
3096-99	Big Band Leaders set of 4 singles			2.80	.80
3100-3	32¢ Songwriters Block ....(20)	13.75	3.25	2.85	2.25
3100-3	32¢ Strip of 4	...	...	2.85	2.25
3100-3	32¢ Horiz. Pl. Block of 8 with selvedge	...	6.75	...	...
3100-3	Songwriters set of 4 singles			2.80	.80
3104	23¢ F. Scott Fitzgerald	26.50	2.75	.55	.18

1996 Endangered Species Miniature Sheet

3105

3105	32¢ Endangered Species Miniature Sheet of 15	...	...	10.75	9.75
3105a-o	Set of 15 singles	...	...	10.50	5.95
3105v	Folded Block of 15 in Booklet (BK256) .	...	...	11.75	...

NOTE: S.A.=Self Adhesive stamps which don't require moisture-activation.

3082   **3083-86**   **3087**

3082	32¢ James Dean ....(20)	13.75	3.25	.70	.18
3082	Block of 8 with Vertical Gutter..............	...	...	13.75	...
3082	Cross Gutter Block of 8	...	...	16.50	...
3082	Vert. Pair with Horiz. Gutter	...	...	3.75	...
3082	Horiz. Pair with Vert. Gutter	...	...	4.75	...
3082v	Folded Block of 15 in Booklet (BK250) .	...	...	11.75	...
3083-86	32¢ Folk Heroes, 4 Designs, Block. (20)	13.75	3.25	2.85	2.25
3083-86	32¢ Strip of 4	...	...	2.85	2.25
3083-86	Folk Heroes Set of 4 singles...............			2.80	.80
3083-86v	Folded Block of 15 in Booklet (BK251)	...	...	11.75	...
3087	32¢ Olympic Games, Discobolus.......(20)	13.75	3.25	.70	.18
3087v	Folded Block of 15 in Booklet (BK252) .	...	...	11.75	...

3090   **3088-89**   **3104**

1996 Commemoratives (cont.)

3106

3108-11, 3113-16

3107, 3112

3118

3119

Scott's No.		Mint Sheet	Plate Block	F-VF NH	F-VF Used
3106	32¢ Computer Technology ....(40)	26.50	3.75	.70	.18
#3107-3117a Christmas Issues					
3107	32¢ Madonna and Child	33.75	3.50	.70	.15
3107v	Folded Block of 15 in Booklet (BK257) .	...	...	11.75	..
3108-11	32¢ Family Scenes, Block	33.75	3.50	2.85	2.25
3108-11	32¢ Strip of 4	...	...	2.85	2.25
3108-11	Family Scenes set of 4 singles	...	...	2.80	.80

Self-Adhesive Stamps Booklet

3112	32¢ Madonna and Child Single	...	...	.80	.30
3112a	32¢ Pane of 20	...	...	14.95	...
3113-16	32¢ Family Scenes	...	...	3.20	...
3116a	32¢ Pane of 20	...	...	14.95	...
3117	32¢ Skaters single	...	...	.80	.30
3117a	32¢ Pane of 18	...	...	13.95	...

1996 Commemoratives (cont.)

3118	32¢ Hanukkah, Self-adhesive ....(20)	13.75	3.25	.70	.25
3118v	Folded Block of 15 in Booklet (BK258) .	...	...	11.75	...
3119	50¢ Cycling Souvenir Sheet of 2	...	...	2.50	2.25
3119a-b	Set of 2 Singles....................................	...	...	2.40	1.20

3120

3121

3122

1997 Commemoratives

Scott's No.			Mint Sheet	Plate Block	F-VF NH	F-VF Used
3120	32¢ Chinese Year of the Ox	(20)	13.75	3.25	.70	.18
3121	32¢ Benjamin O. Davis, Sr.	(20)	12.95	2.95	.65	.18

1997 Self-Adhesive Regular Issue

3122	32¢ Statue of Liberty, Single	...	...	.70	.20
3122a	32¢ Pane of 20	...	...	12.95	...
3122b	32¢ Booklet Pane of 4	...	...	2.70	...
3122c	32¢ Booklet Pane of 5 + Label	...	...	3.35	...
3122d	32¢ Booklet Pane of 6	...	...	3.95	...

3123

3124

3125

1997 Commemoratives (continued)

3123	32¢ Love, Swans, SA Single	...	...	.70	.20
3123a	32¢ Pane of 20, SA	...	...	12.95	...
3124	55¢ Love, Swans, SA Single	...	...	1.15	.50
3124a	55¢ Pane of 20, SA	...	...	20.75	...
3125	32¢ Helping Children Learn, SA.......	(20)	12.95	2.95	.65	.20

3126 3127 3128 3129

1997 Merian Botanical Prints Booklets, SA

#3126-27a Serpentine Die Cut 10.9 x 10.2 on 2,3,4 sides					
3126	32¢ Citron Moth, booklet single........	...	...	.70	.20
3127	32¢ Flowering Pineapple, Cockroaches, bklt sgle	...	...	.70	.20
3127a	32¢ Booklet Pane of 20	...	...	12.95	...
#3128-29b Serpentine Die Cut 11.2 x 10.8 on 2 or 3 sides					
3128	32¢ Citron Moth, booklet single........	...	...	.70	.20
3128a	32¢ Large perforation on right side...	...	...	1.00	.40
3128b	32¢ Booklet Pane of 5, 2-#3128-29, 1-#3128a	...	...	3.50	...
3129	32¢ Flowering Pineapple, Cockroaches, bklt sgle	...	...	.70	.20
3129a	32¢ Large Perforations on right side	...	...	1.25	.50
3129b	32¢ Booklet Pane of 5, 2-#3129-29, 1-#3129a	...	...	3.75	...
3128-29	32¢ Attached Pair	...	...	1.40	...

3130

3131

1997 Pacific '97 Commemoratives

3130	32¢ Clipper Ship.............................	...	...	.65	.18
3131	32¢ Stagecoach...............................	...	...	.65	.18
3130-31	32¢ Pair.......................................	(16)	10.25	2.95	1.30	.90
3131a	32¢ Uncut Sheet of 96....................	69.50	...	...	...
3131a	32¢ Block of 32.............................	...	...	27.50	...
3131a	32¢ Vert. Pair with Horizontal Gutter	...	...	2.75	...
3131a	32¢ Cross Gutter Block of 16	...	...	16.50	...

Note: SA=Self-Adhesive stamps which do not require moisture-activation.

3132   **3133**   **3134**

1997 Linerless Coil Stamps

Scott's No.		Pl.Strip of 5	Pl.Strip of 3	F-VF NH	F-VF Used
3132	(25¢) Juke Box, SA	4.95	3.95	.55	...
3133	32¢ Flag over Porch, SA	5.50	4.25	.70	...

1997 Commemoratives (continued)

Scott's No.		Mint Sheet	Plate Block	F-VF NH	F-VF Used
3134	32¢ Thornton Wilder	(20) 12.95	2.95	.65	.18

3135   **Bugs Bunny**   **Marshall Plan**

3136

Pacific '97 50¢ Benjamin Franklin

Pacific '97 60¢ George Washington

1997 Commemoratives (continued)

Scott's No.		Mint Sheet	Plate Block	F-VF NH	F-VF Used
3135	32¢ Raoul Wallenberg	(20) 12.95	2.95	.65	.18
3136	32¢ World of Dinosaurs, Miniature Pane of 15	...	...	9.75	9.50
3136a-o	Dinosaurs Set of 15 singles	...	...	9.65	6.95

1997 Bugs Bunny Self-Adhesive Special Edition

.....	32¢ Souvenir Sheet of 10	...	...	6.50	...
.....	32¢ Top Half Press Sheet of 6 Panes	39.50	...	...	...
.....	32¢ Bottom Half Press Sheet of 6 Panes	39.50	...	...	...
.....	32¢ Single stamp	...	...	.70	.20
.....	32¢ Souvenir Sheet of 10 with special Die-cut, perfed through liner	...	...	7.50	...

1997 Pacific '97 Souvenir Sheet

.....	50¢ Benjamin Franklin Sheet of 12	...	...	12.95	...
.....	50¢ single stamp from souvenir sheet	...	...	1.15	.95
.....	60¢ George Washington Sheet of 12	...	...	14.95	...
.....	60¢ single stamp from souvenir sheet	...	...	1.30	1.10

1997 Commemoratives (continued)

.....	32¢ Marshall Plan	(20) 12.95	2.95	.65	.18
.....	32¢ Humphrey Bogart	(20) 12.95	2.95	.65	.18
.....	32¢ Humphrey Bogart uncut sht of 120	79.95	...	...	...
.....	32¢ Classic American Aircraft, Miniature Sheet of 20	(6) 79.95	...	12.95	12.50
.....	Aircraft Set of 20 Singles	...	...	12.75	8.95
.....	32¢ Legendary Football Coaches, attached, 4 designs	(20) 12.95	2.95	2.60	2.25
.....	32¢ Coaches, set of 4 singles	...	...	2.55	.90
.....	32¢ Vince Lombardi	(20) 12.95	2.95	.65	.18
.....	32¢ Bear Bryant	(20) 12.95	2.95	.65	.18
.....	32¢ Pop Warner	(20) 12.95	2.95	.65	.18
.....	32¢ George Halas	(20) 12.95	2.95	.65	.18
.....	32¢ American Dolls, Miniature Sht of 15	...	...	9.75	9.50
.....	32¢ American Dolls, set of 15 singles	...	...	9.65	6.95
.....	32¢ Opera Singers, 4 designs	(20) 12.95	2.95	2.60	2.25
.....	32¢ Opera Singers, set of 4 singles	...	...	2.55	.90
.....	32¢ Conductors and Composers	(20) 12.95 (8)	5.95	5.20	4.75
.....	32¢ Conmductors, set of 8 singles	...	...	5.15	1.80
.....	32¢ U.S. Air Force	(20) 12.95	2.95	.65	.18
.....	32¢ Classic Movie Monsters	(20) 12.95 (10)	6.95	3.25	2.75
.....	32¢ Monsters, set of 5 singles	...	...	3.20	1.15

1997 Regular Issues

.....	32¢ Stars and Stripes Forever	31.75	3.00	.65	.18
.....	32¢ Yellow Rose, SA Coil	PS5 5.25	PS3 3.95	.65	.20

MINT COMMEMORATIVE YEAR SETS

Year	Scott's No.	Qty.	F-VF NH
1935	772-75	4	.70
1936	776-84	6	3.70
1937	795-802	8	2.15
1938	835-38	4	1.00
1939	852-58	7	4.15
1940	894-902	9	2.10
1941-3	903-08	6	1.50
1944	922-26	5	1.00
1945	927-38	12	1.95
1946	939-44	6	.90
1947	945-52	8	1.80
1948	953-80	28	4.25
1949	981-86	6	.90
1950	987-97	11	1.65
1951	998-1003	6	.90
1952	1004-16	13	1.95
1953	1017-28	12	1.80
1954	1029,60-63	5	.75
1955	1064-72	9	1.50
1956	1073-85	13	3.95
1957	1086-99	14	2.25

Year	Scott's No.	Qty.	F-VF NH
1958	1100,04-23	21	3.50
1959	1124-38	15	2.35
1960	1139-73	35	5.50
1961	1174-90	17	4.50
1962	1191-1207	17	2.60
1963	1230-41	12	2.15
1964	1242-60	19	3.95
1965	1261-76	16	2.95
1966	1306-22	17	3.25
1967	1323-37	15	4.30
1968	1339-40,42-64	25	6.35
1969	1365-86	22	7.95
1970	1387-92,1405-22	24	6.75
1971	1423-45	23	5.50
1972	1446-74	29	6.85
1973	1475-1508	34	8.25
1974	1525-52	28	8.50
1975	1553-80	28	7.95
1976	1629-32,83-85 1690-1703	21	8.95
1977	1704-30	27	10.00

Year	Scott's No.	Qty.	F-VF NH
1978	1731-33,44-69	29	14.25
1979	1770-1802	33	14.85
1980	1803-10,21-43	31	14.65
1981	1874-79,1910-45	42	25.50
1982	1950-52,2003-4, 2006-30	30	21.75
1983	2031-65	35	22.75
1984	2066-2109	44	32.95
1985	2110,37-47,52-66	27	36.75
1986	2167,2202-4,10-11, 2220-24,2235-2245.		16.95
1987	2246-51,75, 2336-38,2349-54, 2360-61,2367-68	20	15.95
1988	2339-46,69-80, 86-93,2399-2400	30	26.50
1989	2347,2401-04, 10-18,20-28,34-37	27	23.95
1990	2348,2349-40,2442, 44-49,96-2500, 2506-15	25	26.95

Year	Scott's No.	Qty.	F-VF NH
1991	2532-35,37-38,50-51, 2553-58,60-61,67, 2578-79	19	16.35
1992	2611-23,30-41,98-99, 2700-04,10-14,20	38	33.75
1993	2721-30,46-59,65-66, 2771-74,79-89,91-94, 2804-06	47	40.75
1994	2807-12,14C-28,2834-36, 39,48-68,2871-72, 75,76	49	25.75
1995	2948,50-58,61-68,74 76-80,82-92,98-99 3001-7,19-23	49	36.95
1996	3024,30,58-67,69-70 3072-88,90-3104, 3106-11,18	53	38.95

USPS MINT SETS

Commemoratives and Definitives
These are complete with folder or hard cover albums as produced by the U.S. Postal Service

Commemoratives

Year	Scott's Nos.	# Stamps	Price
1968 (1)	"Cover #334-890", #1339-40, 1342-64,C74	26	175.00
1968 (2)	"Cover #369-245", Contents same as (1)		150.00
1969	#1365-86,C76	23	120.00
1970	#1387-92,1405-22	24	175.00
1971 (1)	"Mini Album" #1396,1423-45	24	40.00
1971 (2)	With black strips, Contents same as (1)		120.00
1972	#1446-74,C84-85	31	18.00
1973	#1475-1504,1507-08,C86	33	18.00
1974	#1505-06,1525-51	29	13.50
1975	#1553-80	28	17.50
1976	#1629-32,1633/82 (1 single), 1683-85,1690-1702	21	27.50
1977	#1704-30	27	15.00
1978	#1731-33,44-56,58-69	28	17.50
1979	#1770-94,1799-1802,C97	30	18.50
1980	#1795-98,1803-04,21,23-43	28	23.50
1981	#1874-79,1910-26,28-45	41	30.00
1982	#1950,52,1953/2002 (1 single), 2003-04,06-24,26-30	29	26.50
1983	#2031-65,C101-12	47	45.00
1984	#2066-71,73-2109	43	36.75
1985	#2110,37-47,52-66	27	35.00
1986	#2167,2201a,2202-04,2209a, 2210-11,2216a-9i (1 single), 2220-24,35-45	25	29.50

Year	Scott's Nos.	# Stamps	Price
1987	Soft Cover, #2246-51,2274a,75, 2286/2335 (1 single), 2336-38, 2349-54,59a,60-61,66a,67-68	24	42.50
1987	Hard Cover, Same contents		52.50
1988	Soft Cover, #2339-46,69-80, 85a,86-93,95-99,2400,C117	37	42.50
1988	Hard Cover, Same contents		57.50
1989	#2347,2401-04,09a,10-14, 2416-18,20-28	22	45.00
1990	#2348,2415,39-40,42,44-49,74a, 2496-2515	32	50.00
1991	#2532-35,37-38,49a,50-51,53-67, 2577a,78,80 or 81,82-85, C130-31	33	57.50
1992	Hard Cover, #2611-23,30-41,46a, 2647/96 (1 single), 2697-99, 2700-04,2709a,10-14	41	49.75
1993	Hard Cover, #2721-23,31-37,45a, 2746-59,64a,65-66,70a,78a,79-89, 2791-94,2804-05	47	59.50
1994	Hard Cover, #2807-12,2814-28, 2833a,34-36,38-40,2841a,2847a, 2848-69,71-72	52	69.50
1995	Hard Cover, #2587,2876,2948, 2950-58,61-68,73a,74-92,97a, 2999-3007,3019-23	55	79.50
1996	Hard Cover #3024-29,58-65,67-70 3072-88,90-3111,3118-19	59	69.50

Year	Scott's Nos.	# Stamps	Price
1996	Soft Cover,#3024,3025-29(1), 3058-60,61-64(1),65,67,68a-t(1), 3069-70,72-76(1),77-80(1),81-82, 3083-86(1),87-88,90,91-95(1), 3096-99(1),3100-3(1),3104,3105a-o(1) 3106-7,3108-11(1),18,19a-b(1)	29	29.50

Definitives & Stationery

Year	Scott's Nos.	# Stamps	Price
1980	#1738-42,1805-11,13,22,59,C98-100, U590,U597-99,UC53,UX82-86	27	55.00
1981	#1582b,1818,1819-20 PRS,57-58, 65,89a,90,91 PR,93a,94,95 PR, 96a,1903 PR,1906-08 PRS,1927, 46,47-48 PRS	22	37.50
1982	#1615v PR,1845,55,60,66,97A PR, 1698A PR,1901 PR,1904 PR,49a, 1951,2005 PR,2025,U591,U602-03, UC55,UX94-97,UXC20	22	25.00
1983	#1844,46-48,61,97 PR,98 PR,99 PR, 1900 PR,O127-29,O130,32,35 PR, U604-05,UC56-57,UO73,UX98-100, UXC21,UZ2	25	17.50
1984	#1853,62,64,68,1902 PR,1905 PR, 2072,U606,UX101-04	12	12.50
1987-88	#2115b,2127,29,30av,69,76-78,80, 2182,83,88,92,2226,52-66,C118-19, O138A-B,40-41	35	50.00
1989-90	#2127av,73,84,86,94A,2280v,2419, 2431 (6),43a,52,75a,76,O143,U611, U614-18,UC62,UO79-80,UX127-38, UX143-48,UX150-52	44	62.50

81

U.S. ARROW AND CENTER LINE BLOCKS

NOTE: VF HINGED (#285/329) ARE AVAILABLE AT A DISCOUNT OF 35%
NOTE: VF HINGED (#314/CE2) ARE AVAILABLE AT A DISCOUNT OF 25%

Scott's No.		ARROW BLOCKS NH VF	ARROW BLOCKS NH F-VF	ARROW BLOCKS Unused F-VF	CENTER LINE BLKS. NH VF	CENTER LINE BLKS. NH F-VF	CENTER LINE BLKS. Unused F-VF
	1898-1907 Commemoratives, Perf. 12						
285	1¢ Trans-Miss.	200.00	130.00	87.50	...	...	...
286	2¢ Trans-Miss.	185.00	115.00	77.50	...	...	...
294	1¢ Pan-American	150.00	100.00	67.50	...	...	...
295	2¢ Pan-American	150.00	100.00	67.50	...	...	...
323	1¢ Louisiana	195.00	135.00	90.00	...	...	...
324	2¢ Louisiana	180.00	115.00	80.00	...	...	...
328	1¢ Jamestown	190.00	115.00	75.00	...	...	...
329	2¢ Jamestown	240.00	150.00	97.50	...	...	...
	1906-09 Imperforates, D.L. Wmk.						
314	1¢ Franklin	165.00	120.00	85.00	225.00	175.00	140.00
320	2¢ Washington	155.00	120.00	85.00	215.00	165.00	135.00
343	1¢ Franklin	45.00	35.00	27.50	60.00	47.50	37.50
344	2¢ Washington	55.00	42.50	32.50	75.00	57.50	45.00
345	3¢ Washington	120.00	95.00	70.00	160.00	120.00	100.00
346	4¢ Washington	215.00	160.00	125.00	275.00	210.00	170.00
347	5¢ Washington	300.00	235.00	175.00	375.00	295.00	225.00
368	2¢ Lincoln Mem.	170.00	125.00	95.00	220.00	170.00	135.00
371	2¢ Alaska-Yukon	250.00	190.00	130.00	300.00	230.00	160.00
373	2¢ Hudson-Fulton	275.00	210.00	150.00	375.00	285.00	200.00
	1911-12 Imperforate, S.L. Wmk.						
383	1¢ Franklin	25.00	19.50	15.00	42.50	32.50	24.00
384	2¢ Wash. "Two"	42.50	30.00	21.50	75.00	55.00	40.00
408	1¢ Washington	9.75	7.50	5.25	15.00	11.50	8.50
409	2¢ Wash. "2"	11.50	8.75	6.25	17.50	13.50	10.00
	1916-20 Imperforates, Unwatermarked						
481	1¢ Washington	7.50	6.00	4.25	12.50	10.00	7.00
482	2¢ Washington	11.00	9.00	6.25	13.50	10.50	7.75
483	3¢ Wash., Type I	100.00	82.50	60.00	120.00	97.50	70.00
484	3¢ Wash., Type II	80.00	65.00	45.00	95.00	77.50	55.00
531	1¢ Offset	72.50	59.00	41.00	95.00	75.00	55.00
532	2¢ Offset, Type IV	250.00	200.00	140.00	300.00	240.00	190.00
533	2¢ Offset, Type V	1250.00	1000.00	750.00	1375.00	1100.00	850.00
534	2¢ Offset, Type Va	82.50	65.00	50.00	97.50	77.50	60.00
534A	2¢ Offset, Type VI	235.00	185.00	135.00	275.00	225.00	175.00
535	3¢ Offset	67.50	53.50	37.50	75.00	59.50	42.50
	1923-31 Perforated Issues						
571	$1 Lincoln Mem.	350.00	250.00	185.00	...	...	...
572	$2 Capitol	775.00	625.00	425.00	...	...	...
573	$5 Freedom	1450.00	1100.00	825.00	1600.00	1200.00	875.00
620	2¢ Norse	32.50	23.50	18.00	40.00	32.50	26.00
621	5¢ Norse	130.00	100.00	75.00	165.00	135.00	100.00
651	2¢ G.R. Clark	4.15	3.15	2.50	...	...	...
702	2¢ Red Cross	1.50	1.10	.85	...	...	...
703	2¢ Yorktown	2.95	2.25	1.75	3.25	2.50	1.95
	1923-26 Imperforate Issues						
575	1¢ Franklin	55.00	40.00	30.00	65.00	47.50	35.00
576	1½¢ Harding, Flat	11.00	8.50	6.25	17.50	13.50	10.00
577	2¢ Washington	14.00	11.00	8.00	25.00	20.00	16.00
611	2¢ Harding Mem.	47.50	37.50	27.50	95.00	75.00	55.00
631	1½¢ Harding, Rotary	16.50	12.50	9.50	32.50	25.00	18.00
	1938 Presidential Series						
832	$1 Wilson	52.50	45.00	...	57.50	50.00	...
833	$2 Harding	150.00	125.00	...	160.00	120.00	...
834	$5 Coolidge	600.00	500.00	...	685.00	575.00	...
	1918-38 Airmail Issues						
C1	6¢ Curtiss Jenny	495.00	360.00	265.00	550.00	400.00	300.00
C2	16¢ Curtiss Jenny	650.00	475.00	350.00	775.00	575.00	425.00
C3	24¢ Curtiss Jenny	650.00	475.00	350.00	775.00	575.00	425.00
C11	5¢ Beacon	36.50	25.00	19.50	...	...	...
C23	6¢ Eagle	3.00	2.50	2.00	3.35	2.75	2.25
CE2	16¢ Air Special	3.00	2.50	2.00	3.35	2.75	2.25

EARLY U.S. MINT SHEETS

All F-VF Never Hinged.

Scott's No.			NH F-VF
	1923-1929		
610	2¢ Harding	(100)	95.00
632	1¢ Franklin	(100)	19.50
634	2¢ Washington	(100)	19.50
643	2¢ Vermont	(100)	195.00
644	2¢ Burgoyne	(50)	260.00
645	2¢ Valley Forge	(100)	165.00
646	2¢ Molly Pitcher	(100)	165.00
649	2¢ Aeronautics	(50)	82.50
650	5¢ Aeronautics	(50)	385.00
651	2¢ G.R. Clark	(50)	40.00
653	½¢ N. Hale	(100)	15.00
654	2¢ Edison, Flat	(100)	125.00
655	2¢ Edison, Rotary	(100)	135.00
657	2¢ Sullivan	(100)	120.00
680	2¢ Fallen Timbers	(100)	140.00
681	2¢ Ohio Canal	(100)	110.00
	1930-1932		
682	2¢ Mass. Bay	(100)	145.00
683	2¢ Carolina	(100)	175.00
684	1½¢ Harding	(100)	30.00
685	4¢ Taft	(100)	125.00
688	2¢ Braddock	(100)	140.00
689	2¢ Von Steuben	(100)	75.00
690	2¢ Pulaski	(100)	37.50
702	2¢ Red Cross	(100)	22.50
703	2¢ Yorktown	(50)	25.00
704	½¢ Bicentennial	(100)	15.00
705	1¢ Bicentennial	(100)	19.50
706	1½¢ Bicentennial	(100)	65.00
707	2¢ Bicentennial	(100)	15.00
708	3¢ Bicentennial	(100)	75.00
709	4¢ Bicentennial	(100)	40.00
710	5¢ Bicentennial	(100)	210.00
712	7¢ Bicentennial	(100)	40.00
	1932-1934		
716	2¢ Winter Olympics	(100)	60.00
717	2¢ Arbor Day	(100)	26.50
718	3¢ Olympics	(100)	195.00
719	5¢ Olympics	(100)	275.00
720	3¢ Washington	(100)	25.00
724	3¢ Penn	(100)	50.00
725	3¢ Webster	(100)	75.00
726	3¢ Georgia	(100)	50.00
727	3¢ Newburgh	(100)	22.50
728	1¢ Chicago	(100)	16.50
729	3¢ Chicago	(100)	21.00
732	3¢ N.R.A.	(100)	18.50
733	3¢ Byrd	(50)	50.00
734	5¢ Kosciuszko	(100)	100.00
736	3¢ Maryland	(100)	30.00
737	3¢ Mother's, Rot	(50)	10.00
738	3¢ Mother's, Flat	(50)	15.00
739	3¢ Wisconsin	(50)	15.00
	1934 National Parks		
740-49	1¢-10¢ Set of 10		625.00
740	1¢ Yosemite	(50)	8.75
741	2¢ Grand Canyon	(50)	10.00
742	3¢ Mt. Rainier	(50)	12.50
743	4¢ Mesa Verde	(50)	32.50
744	5¢ Yellowstone	(50)	57.50
745	6¢ Crater Lake	(50)	85.00
746	7¢ Acadia	(50)	55.00
747	8¢ Zion	(50)	120.00
748	9¢ Glacier	(50)	115.00
749	10¢ Great Smoky	(50)	210.00
	1935 Farley Issue		
752	3¢ Newburgh	(400)	375.00
753	3¢ Byrd	(200)	575.00
754	3¢ Mother's Day	(200)	195.00
755	3¢ Wisconsin	(200)	195.00
756-65	1¢-10¢ Parks Set		3950.00
756	1¢ Yosemite	(200)	65.00
757	2¢ Grand Canyon	(200)	77.50
758	3¢ Mt. Rainer	(200)	170.00
759	4¢ Mesa Verde	(200)	295.00
760	5¢ Yellowstone	(200)	495.00
761	6¢ Crater Lake	(200)	615.00
762	7¢ Acadia	(200)	495.00
763	8¢ Zion	(200)	575.00
764	9¢ Glacier	(200)	595.00
765	10¢ Great Smoky	(200)	950.00
766	1¢ Chicago SS	(9)	450.00
767	3¢ Chicago SS	(9)	495.00
768	3¢ Byrd SS	(25)	575.00
769	1¢ Park SS	(20)	250.00
770	3¢ Park SS	(20)	650.00
771	16¢ Air Special	(200)	795.00
	1932-1938 Airmails		
C17	8¢ Winged Globe	(50)	175.00
C19	6¢ Winged Globe	(50)	165.00
C20	25¢ China Clipper	(50)	90.00

AIR MAIL STAMPS

C1   C4   C5   C6

1918 First Issue VF Used + 35% (B)

Scott's No.		NH		Unused		Used
		VF	F-VF	VF	F-VF	F-VF
C1-3	Set of 3	395.00	295.00	285.00	210.00	98.50
C1	6¢ Curtiss Jenny, Orange	115.00	85.00	80.00	60.00	28.50
C2	16¢ Green	155.00	115.00	110.00	80.00	35.00
C3	24¢ Carmine Rose & Blue	155.00	115.00	110.00	80.00	40.00

1923 Second Issue VF Used + 35% (B)

		VF	F-VF	VF	F-VF	F-VF
C4-6	Set of 3	350.00	265.00	245.00	185.00	65.00
C4	8¢ Propeller, Dark Green	43.50	32.50	30.00	22.50	12.50
C5	16¢ Emblem, Dark Blue	155.00	115.00	110.00	80.00	27.50
C6	24¢ Biplane, Carmine	175.00	130.00	120.00	90.00	27.50

C7   C10

C11   C12,C16

1926-27 Map & Mail Planes VF Used + 30% (B)

		VF	F-VF	VF	F-VF	F-VF
C7-9	Set of 3	24.75	18.75	18.50	13.95	4.15
C7	10¢ Map, Dark Blue	4.95	3.70	3.60	2.75	.40
C8	15¢ Map, Brown	5.75	4.35	4.25	3.25	2.25
C9	20¢ Map, Green (1927)	15.00	11.75	11.50	8.75	1.75

1927 Lindbergh Tribute VF + 30% (B)

Scott's No.		NH		Unused		Used
		VF	F-VF	VF	F-VF	F-VF
C10	10¢ Lindbergh, Dark Blue	13.00	10.00	9.75	7.50	1.95
C10a	Booklet Pane of 3	140.00	110.00	110.00	85.00	...

1928 Beacon VF Used + 30% (B)

C11	5¢ Carmine & Blue	8.00	5.50	5.95	4.25	.60

1930 Winged Globe, Flat Press, Perf. 11 VF Used + 30% (B)

C12	5¢ Violet	16.50	12.50	12.75	9.50	.40

1918-30 PLATE BLOCKS

	NH		Unused				NH		Unused
	VF	F-VF	F-VF				VF	F-VF	F-VF
C1 (6)	1150.00	850.00	650.00			C10 (6)	235.00	180.00	135.00
C2 (6)	2100.00	1550.00	1150.00			C11 (6)	70.00	52.50	40.00
C3 (12)	2350.00	1850.00	1350.00			C11 Double "TOP"			
C4 (6)	475.00	350.00	250.00			Plate of 6	170.00	125.00	90.00
C5 (6)	3250.00	2500.00	1850.00						
C6 (6)	3750.00	2850.00	2100.00			C11 No "TOP"			
C7 (6)	65.00	50.00	37.50			Plate of 8	295.00	225.00	175.00
C8 (6)	80.00	60.00	45.00						
C9 (6)	175.00	130.00	100.00						

1930 GRAF ZEPPELIN ISSUE VF Used + 20% (B)

C13   C15   C14

		VF	F-VF	VF	F-VF	F-VF
C13-15	Set of 3	2650.00	2175.00	2075.00	1750.00	1250.00
C13	65¢ Zeppelin, Green	450.00	375.00	365.00	300.00	225.00
C14	$1.30 Zeppelin, Brown	900.00	750.00	725.00	600.00	400.00
C15	$2.60 Zeppelin, Blue	1375.00	1150.00	1100.00	925.00	675.00

1931-32 Rotary Press, Perf. 10½x11, Designs of #C12 VF Used + 30% (B)

Scott's No.		NH		Unused		Used
		VF	F-VF	VF	F-VF	F-VF
C16	5¢ Winged Globe, Violet............	9.00	6.75	6.85	5.25	.50
C17	8¢ Winged Globe (1932)	3.75	2.85	2.85	2.25	.30

C18   **C20**

1933 Century of Progress VF Used + 20% (B)

C18	50¢ Graf Zeppelin, Green......	135.00	110.00	110.00	85.00	70.00

1934 Winged Globe, Design of #C12 VF Used + 30% (B)

C19	6¢ Orange.................................	3.75	3.00	3.15	2.50	.20

ZEPPELIN & WINGED GLOBE PLATE BLOCKS

	NH		Unused			NH		Unused
	VF	F-VF	F-VF			VF	F-VF	F-VF
C13 (6)	3950.00	3250.00	2650.00		C17	60.00	45.00	35.00
C14 (6)	8000.00	6700.00	5650.00		C18 (6)	1075.00	900.00	750.00
C15 (6)	13000.00	10750.00	8650.00		C19	37.50	28.50	21.75
C16	150.00	115.00	90.00					

1935-37 Trans-Pacific Issue (VF + 25%)

Scott's No.		Plate Blocks		F-VF		F-VF
		NH	Unused	NH	Unused	Used
C20-22	Clipper Set of 3	315.00	265.00	24.50	19.50	5.95
C20	25¢ China Clipper.......... (6)	27.50	22.50	1.50	1.25	1.00
C21	20¢ China Clipper (1937)(6)	135.00	110.00	12.00	9.50	1.50
C22	50¢ China Clipper ('37).. (6)	135.00	110.00	12.00	9.50	4.00

C23   **C24**

1938 Eagle (VF + 30%)

C23	6¢ Dark Blue & Carmine............	9.50	7.50	.50	.40	.15

1939 Trans-Atlantic Issue (VF + 30%)

C24	30¢ Winged Globe, Blue (6)	180.00	150.00	11.50	8.75	1.40

C25   **C32**   **C33**

1941-44 Transport Plane

Scott's No.		Mint Sheet	Plate Block	F-VF NH	F-VF Used
C25-31	**Set of 7 ....**	...	130.00	21.50	4.35
C25	6¢ Carmine	11.00	1.00	.20	.15
C25a	6¢ Booklet Pane of 3.......	...	...	2.95	3.00
C26	8¢ Olive Green (1944).........	13.00	1.85	.24	.15
C27	10¢ Violet	70.00	10.00	1.30	.20
C28	15¢ Brown Carmine	135.00	11.50	2.50	.35
C29	20¢ Bright Green	115.00	11.50	2.25	.35
C30	30¢ Blue	125.00	13.00	2.50	.40
C31	50¢ Orange	675.00	85.00	12.00	3.25

1946-1948 Issues

C32	5¢ DC-4 Skymaster.............	7.50	.65	.20	.15
C33	5¢ Small Plane (1947)............ (100)	15.00	.65	.20	.15

C34   **C38**   **C40**

C34	10¢ Pan-Am Building (1947)	13.75	1.35	.30	.15
C34a	10¢ Dry Printing..........................	28.50	2.65	.60	.25
C35	15¢ New York Skyline (1947)......	22.50	2.00	.45	.15
C35b	15¢ Dry Printing..........................	33.50	3.00	.70	.25
C36	25¢ Oakland Bay Bridge (1947) ..	52.50	4.75	1.10	.15
C36a	25¢ Dry Printing..........................	72.50	6.50	1.50	.30

1948-49 Issues

		Mint Sheet	Plate Block	F-VF NH	F-VF Used
			Line Pair		
C37	5¢ Small Plane, Coil		8.50	.85	.80
			Plate Blocks		
C38	5¢ New York City Jubilee .... (100)	18.75	3.95	.20	.15
C39	6¢ Plane (Design of C33) ('49) (100)	18.50	.70	.20	.15
C39a	6¢ Booklet Pane of 6	...	...	11.00	7.50
C39b	6¢ Dry Printing....................... (100)	75.00	3.50	.80	.30
C39c	6¢ Bk. Pane of 6, Dry Printing......	...	...	24.50	...
C40	6¢ Alexandria Bicentennial ('49) ..	9.00	.75	.20	.15
			Line Pair		
C41	6¢ Small Plane, Coil (1949)	...	13.75	3.25	.15

C43   **C45**   **C46**

C42-44	**Univ. Postal Un., Set of 3 (1949)**	...	8.75	1.35	1.10
C42	10¢ Post Office Building.................	14.50	1.40	.30	.25
C43	15¢ Globe & Doves	19.75	1.80	.40	.35
C44	25¢ Stratocruiser & Globe	37.50	6.00	.75	.55
C45	6¢ Wright Brothers Flight (1949) ..	11.50	1.15	.25	.15

1952 Hawaii Issue

C46	80¢ Diamond Head	265.00	29.50	5.50	1.35

1953-58 Issues

C47   **C48**   **C49**   **C51,C52,C60,C61**

C47	6¢ Anniv. of Powered Flight.........	8.50	.75	.20	.15
C48	4¢ Eagle in Flight (1954) ....(100)	12.75	1.80	.20	.15
C49	6¢ Air Force 50th (1957)..............	11.75	.85	.20	.15
C50	5¢ Eagle (as C48) (1958) ....(100)	16.00	1.65	.20	.15
C51	7¢ Jet Silhouette, Blue (1958) .(100)	19.50	.90	.20	.15
C51a	7¢ Booklet Pane of 6	...	...	11.75	6.75
			Line Pair		
C52	7¢ Jet Blue Coil, LargeHoles (1958)	...	17.50	1.85	.15
C52	7¢ Small Holes	...	140.00	9.75	...

1959-60 Issues

C53   **C54**   **C55**

C57   **C56**   **C58**

C53	7¢ Alaska Statehood	11.75	.95	.25	.15
C54	7¢ Balloon Jupiter........................	11.75	.95	.25	.15
C55	7¢ Hawaii Statehood	11.75	.95	.25	.15
C56	10¢ Pan-Am Games, Chicago.....	14.75	1.40	.30	.30
C57	10¢ Liberty Bell (1960)	70.00	7.00	1.50	.80
C58	15¢ Statue of Liberty (1959)	23.50	2.25	.50	.15

1960-67 Issues

C59   C63   C64,C65

Scott's No.		Mint Sheet	Plate Block	F-VF NH	F-VF Used
C59	25¢ Abraham Lincoln....................	35.00	3.25	.70	.15
C59a	25¢ Tagged (1966)	45.00	4.00	.90	.35
C60	7¢ Jet Silh., Carmine ....(100)	19.00	.90	.20	.15
C60a	7¢ Bk. Pane of 6	...	...	12.50	7.75
C61	7¢ Jet, Carmine Coil ....Line Pair	40.00	4.00		.30
C62	13¢ Liberty Bell (1961).................	22.50	2.00	.45	.15
C62a	13¢ Tagged (1967)......................	77.50	15.00	1.35	.65
C63	15¢ Liberty, Re-engraved (1961).	22.50	1.95	.45	.15
C63a	15¢ Tagged (1967)	25.00	2.30	.50	.25

#C58 has wide border around statue, #C63 is divided in center.

C64	8¢ Jet over Capitol (1962)........(100)	22.50	1.00	.24	.15
C64a	8¢ Tagged (1963) ....(100)	26.50	1.15	.27	.20
C64b	8¢ B. Pane of 5, Sl. 1, "Your Mailman"	...	...	4.50	2.75
C64b	8¢ B. Pane of 5, Sl. 2, "Use Zone Numbers"	...		67.50	...
C64b	8¢ B. Pane of 5, Sl. 3, "Always Use Zip"	...		13.75	...
C64c	8¢ Pane/5, Tagged, Slogan 3	...	...	1.65	1.25
C65	8¢ Capitol & Jet Coil (1962).........Line Pair	6.50		.50	.15
C65a	8¢ Tagged...................................Line Pair	2.75		.35	.15

1963-68 Issues

C66   C67   C68

C70   C69   C71

C72,C73   C74   C75

C66	15¢ Montgomery Blair..................	32.50	3.00	.70	.60
C67	6¢ Bald Eagle ....(100)	18.50	1.75	.20	.15
C67a	6¢ Tagged (1967)	...	85.00	3.95	3.25
C68	8¢ Amelia Earhart	15.00	1.40	.32	.15
C69	8¢ Robert H. Goddard (1964)	21.50	2.00	.45	.15
C70	8¢ Alaska Purchase (1967)	14.50	1.70	.30	.18
C71	20¢ Columbia Jays (1967)...........	50.00	4.35	1.00	.15
C72	10¢ 50-Star Runway (1968).....(100)	28.50	1.35	.30	.15
C72b	10¢ Booklet Pane of 8	...	...	2.35	2.25
C72c	10¢ B. Pane of 5 with Sl. 4 or Sl. 5	...	...	3.50	3.25
C72v	10¢ Congressional Precancel......	...	110.00	1.35	...
C73	10¢ 50-Star Runway Coil (1968) . Line Pair	1.85		.35	.15
C74	10¢ Air Mail Service 50th Anniv ('68)	18.50	2.50	.35	.15
C75	20¢ "USA" and Jet (1968)............	29.50	2.75	.60	.15

1969-76 Issues

C76   C77   C78,C82

C79,C83   C80   C81

C85   C84   C86

C87   C88   C89

Scott's No.		Mint Sheet	Plate Block	F-VF NH	F-VF Used
C76	10¢ Moon Landing ....(32)	12.75	1.65	.40	.20
C77	9¢ Delta Wing Plane Silh. ('71).. (100)	23.50	1.20	.25	.20
C78	11¢ Jet Airliner Silhouette ('71).. (100)	27.50	1.35	.30	.15
C78a	11¢ Booklet Pane of 4	...	...	1.20	1.15
C78b	11¢ Congressional Precancel........	...	25.75	.50	...
C79	13¢ Winged Envelope (1973) .... (100)	33.50	1.50	.35	.15
C79a	13¢ Booklet Pane of 5	...	...	1.60	1.50
C79b	13¢ Congressional Precancel........	...	10.50	.40	...
C80	17¢ Statue of Lib. Head (1971)......	24.50	2.15	.50	.20
C81	21¢ "USA" and Jet (1971).............	28.75	2.50	.60	.15
C82	11¢ Jet Silhouette Coil (1971) .... Line Pair	.80		.35	.15
C83	13¢ Winged Env. Coil (1973)......... Line Pair	1.00		.40	.15
C84	11¢ City of Refuge Park ('72)	15.75	1.50	.32	.15
C85	11¢ Olympic Games - Skiing ('72) .	15.75	(10)3.50	.32	.15
C86	11¢ Electronics (1973)	14.75	1.30	.30	.15
C87	18¢ Statue of Liberty (1974)	24.50	2.25	.50	.45
C88	26¢ Mt. Rushmore Memorial (1974)	33.50	3.00	.70	.15
C89	25¢ Plane & Globes (1976)	33.50	3.00	.70	.18
C90	31¢ Plane, Globe and Flag (1976).	38.50	3.50	.80	.15

1978-79 Issues

C91-92   C93-94   C95-96   C97

C91-92	31¢ Wright Bros., attd .... (100)	85.00	3.95	1.80	1.50
C91-92	Set of 2 Singles.............................	...	...	1.70	.80
C93-94	21¢ Octave Chanute, attd. ('79). (100)	85.00	4.75	1.70	1.50
C93-94	Set of 2 Singles.............................	...	...	1.60	.90
C95-96	25¢ Wiley Post, attd. ('79).......... (100)	150.00	9.00	3.00	2.00
C95-96	Set of 2 Singles.............................	...	...	2.80	1.20
C97	31¢ Olympics - High Jump ('79)	45.00	(12)12.50	.90	.35

1980 Airmails

C99   C98   C100

Scott's No.		Mint Sheet	Plate Block	F-VF NH	F-VF Used
C98	40¢ Philip Mazzei, Perf. 11...........	55.00	(12) 13.50	1.10	.25
C98a	40¢ Perf. 10½x11 (1982).............	...	(12) 125.00	6.00	1.50
C99	28¢ Blanche Scott	38.50	(12) 10.50	.80	.25
C100	35¢ Glenn Curtiss........................	47.50	(12) 12.50	.95	.25

1983 Los Angeles Olympic Issues

C101-04

C105-08

C109-12

C101-4	28¢ Summer Olympics, attd.........	62.50	6.00	5.50	3.00
C101-4	Set of 4 Singles	...	...	5.25	1.20
C105-8	40¢ Summer Olympics,				
	Bullseye Perfs Pf. 11.2, attd.........	60.00	6.00	5.25	4.00
C105-8	Set of 4 Singles	...	...	5.00	1.60
C105a-8a	40¢ Line Perfs Pf. 11, attd	110.00	12.75	8.75	7.50
C105a-8a	Set of 4 Singles	...	...	8.50	2.60
C109-12	35¢ Summer Olympics, attd	75.00	10.00	6.50	4.50
C109-12	Set of 4 Singles...........................	...	...	6.25	2.40

1985-1989 Issues

C113   C114   C115

C116   C117   C118

C119   C120   C121

Scott's No.		Mint Sheet	Plate Block	F-VF NH	F-VF Used
C113	33¢ Alfred Verville......................	45.00	4.25	.95	.25
C114	39¢ Sperry Brothers....................	50.00	5.25	1.10	.35
C115	44¢ Transpacific Airmail..............	57.50	5.75	1.20	.30
C116	44¢ Father Junipero Serra	72.50	10.00	1.50	.50
C117	44¢ New Sweden (1988).............	62.50	8.75	1.25	.40
C118	45¢ Samuel Langley (1988).......	65.00	5.75	1.30	.25
C118a	45¢ Overall Tagging...................	165.00	38.50	3.00	1.50
C119	36¢ Igor Sikorsky (1988)...........	48.50	4.50	1.00	.35
C120	45¢ French Revolution ('89)... (30)	36.50	5.75	1.25	.30
C121	45¢ Pre-Columbian Customs ('89)	60.00	5.75	1.25	.25

1989 Universal Postal Congress Issues

C122-125

C126

Scott's No.		Mint Sheet	Plate Block	F-VF NH	F-VF Used
C122-25	45¢ Futuristic Mail Deliv., Attd (40)	65.00	7.50	6.25	4.50
C122-25	Set of 4 Singles	...	...	6.00	3.00
C126	$1.80 Future Mail Delivery Souvenir				
	Sheet, Imperforate	...	...	6.25	6.00

1990-93 Airmail Issues

C127   C128   C129

C130   C131   C132

Scott's No.		Mint Sheet	Plate Block	F-VF NH	F-VF Used
C127	45¢ America, Caribbean Coast	62.50	6.75	1.30	.25
C128	50¢ Harriet Quimby, Pf. 11 (1991)	65.00	7.00	1.35	.35
C128b	H. Quimby, Perf. 11.2 ('93).........	67.50	7.50	1.40	.40
C129	40¢ William T. Piper (1991).........	55.00	5.50	1.20	.40
C130	50¢ Antarctic Treaty (1991).........	65.00	6.50	1.35	.55
C131	50¢ America (1991).....................	65.00	6.50	1.35	.45
C132	40¢ W.T. Piper, new design ('93) .	65.00	6.50	1.30	.40

#C129: Blue sky clear along top of design, Perf. 11
#C132: Piper's hair is touching top of design, Bullseye Perf. 11.2

1934-36 AIR MAIL SPECIAL DELIVERY VF + 20%

CE1,CE2

Scott's No.		Mint Sheet	Plate Block NH	F-VF NH	F-VF Used
CE1	16¢ Great Seal, Dark Blue	55.00 (6)	22.50	.80	.80
CE2	16¢ Seal, Red & Blue..................	35.00	9.50	.55	.30

SPECIAL DELIVERY STAMPS

E1   E2,E3   E4,E5

1885 "At A Special Delivery Office", Unwmkd., Perf. 12 (VF Used+60%)(C)

Scott's No.		NH Fine	Unused Fine	Unused Ave.	Used Fine	Used Ave.
E1	10¢ Messenger, Blue 300.00	300.00	200.00	115.00	35.00	20.75

1888-93 "At Any Post Office", No Line Under "TEN CENTS" Unwatermarked, Perf. 12 VF + 60% (C)

Scott's No.		NH Fine	Unused Fine	Unused Ave.	Used Fine	Used Ave.
E2	10¢ Blue 290.00	290.00	195.00	120.00	11.00	6.75
E3	10¢ Orange (1893) 185.00	185.00	125.00	75.00	15.00	9.50

1894 Line Under "TEN CENTS", Unwmkd., Perf. 12 VF + 60% (C)

Scott's No.		NH Fine	Unused Fine	Unused Ave.	Used Fine	Used Ave.
E4	10¢ Blue 650.00	650.00	450.00	275.00	20.00	11.75

1895 Line Under "TEN CENTS, Double Line Wmk. Perf. 12 VF + 50% (C)

Scott's No.		NH Fine	Unused Fine	Unused Ave.	Used Fine	Used Ave.
E5	10¢ Blue 150.00	150.00	100.00	65.00	2.50	1.60

E6,E8-11   E7

NOTE: PRICES THROUGHOUT THIS LIST ARE SUBJECT TO CHANGE WITHOUT NOTICE IF MARKET CONDITIONS REQUIRE. MINIMUM MAIL ORDER MUST TOTAL AT LEAST $20.00.

Scott's No.		NH VF	NH F-VF	Unused VF	Unused F-VF	Used F-VF
	1902-08 Double Line Watermark VF Used + 50% (B)					
E6	10¢ Ultramarine, Perf. 12	160.00	110.00	105.00	70.00	2.95
E7	10¢ Mercury, Green (1908) ...	110.00	75.00	72.50	50.00	29.50
	1911-14 Single Line Watermark VF Used + 50% (B)					
E8	10¢ Ultramarine, Perf. 12	170.00	115.00	110.00	75.00	4.00
E9	10¢ Ultra., Perf. 10 (1914).....	300.00	200.00	200.00	135.00	5.00
	1916-17 Unwatermarked VF Used + 50% (B)					
E10	10¢ Pale Ultra., Perf. 10	450.00	325.00	335.00	225.00	19.50
E11	10¢ Ultra., Perf. 11 (1917).......	30.00	20.00	19.50	13.75	.45

E12-13,E15-18   E14,E19

1922-1925 Flat Press Printings, Perf. 11 VF Used + 30% (B)

Scott's No.		NH VF	NH F-VF	Unused VF	Unused F-VF	Used F-VF
E12	10¢ Motorcycle, Gray Violet	39.50	28.00	27.50	21.50	.25
E13	15¢ Deep Orange (1925).........	35.00	25.00	24.00	18.50	.95
E14	20¢ P.O. Truck, Black (1925)	3.85	3.00	3.00	2.25	1.50

PLATE BLOCKS

Plate Blocks	NH VF	NH F-VF	Unused F-VF	Plate Blocks	NH VF	NH F-VF	Unused F-VF
E11 (6)	295.00	200.00	150.00	E13 (6)	285.00	200.00	150.00
E12 (6)	450.00	350.00	250.00	E14 (6)	60.00	47.50	32.50

1927-1951 Rotary Press Printings, Perf. 11x10½ VF Used + 20%

Scott's No.		Pl# Blk. NH VF	Pl# Blk. NH F-VF	NH VF	NH F-VF	F-VF Used
E15	10¢ Motorcycle, Gray Violet	8.50	6.75	1.10	.85	.15
E16	15¢ Orange (1931)	5.75	4.75	1.15	.90	.18
E17	13¢ Blue (1944)	5.00	4.00	.90	.75	.18
E18	17¢ Orange Yellow (1944)	33.50	26.50	4.35	3.50	2.75
E19	20¢ P.O. Truck, Black (1951) ..	10.00	8.25	2.20	1.75	.20

E20,E21   E22,E23

1954-1971

Scott's No.		Mint Sheet	Plate Block NH	F-VF NH	F-VF Used
E20	20¢ Letter & Hands	32.50	3.00	.60	.15
E21	30¢ Letter & Hands (1957)	37.50	3.50	.75	.15
E22	45¢ Arrows (1969)	67.50	5.75	1.40	.35
E23	60¢ Arrows (1971)	75.00	6.75	1.50	.25

F1   FA1

1911 REGISTRATION VF Used + 40% (B)

Scott's No.		NH VF	NH F-VF	Unused VF	Unused F-VF	Used F-VF
F1	10¢ Eagle, Ultramarine..........	130.00	90.00	85.00	60.00	4.75

1955 CERTIFIED MAIL

Scott's No.		Sheet F-VF NH	Pl.Block NH	F-VF NH	F-VF Used
FA1	15¢ Postman, Red......................	22.50	5.00	.45	.35

POSTAGE DUE STAMPS

J1/J22 J29/61 J35/65

1879 Perforated 12 (NH + 50%, VF OG & Used + 75%, VF NH + 125%) (C)

Scott's No.		Unused Fine	Ave.	Used Fine	Ave.
J1	1¢ Brown	33.50	20.00	6.50	3.75
J2	2¢ Brown	210.00	125.00	6.00	3.50
J3	3¢ Brown	27.50	17.00	3.50	2.10
J4	5¢ Brown	325.00	200.00	32.50	19.50
J5	10¢ Brown	350.00	215.00	18.75	11.50
J6	30¢ Brown	175.00	110.00	39.50	25.00
J7	50¢ Brown	250.00	150.00	46.50	27.50
1884-1889, Same Design Perf. 12 (NH + 50%, VF OG & Used + 75%, VF NH + 125%)					
J15	1¢ Red Brown	32.50	19.50	3.25	1.95
J16	2¢ Red Brown	39.50	23.50	3.75	2.25
J17	3¢ Red Brown	575.00	350.00	110.00	65.00
J18	5¢ Red Brown	260.00	150.00	17.50	10.75
J19	10¢ Red Brown	260.00	150.00	13.50	8.50
J20	30¢ Red Brown	115.00	70.00	37.50	22.50
J21	50¢ Red Brown	950.00	575.00	135.00	82.50

*** Red Brown issues can be distinguished from Bright Claret issues by placing the stamps under long wave UV light. Bright Clarets give off a warm orange glow, Red Browns do not.**

1891-1893 Same Design Perf. 12 (NH + 50%, VF OG & Used + 75%, VF NH + 125%)

J22	1¢ Bright Claret	15.00	8.75	.75	.45
J23	2¢ Bright Claret	17.50	10.50	.75	.45
J24	3¢ Bright Claret	35.00	21.50	6.00	3.65
J25	5¢ Bright Claret	41.50	25.00	6.00	3.65
J26	10¢ Bright Claret	72.50	42.50	13.75	8.25
J27	30¢ Bright Claret	250.00	150.00	110.00	65.00
J28	50¢ Bright Claret	275.00	165.00	110.00	65.00

1894-95 Unwatermarked, Perf. 12 VF Used + 60% (C)

Scott's No.		NH VF	NH F-VF	Unused VF	Unused F-VF	Used F-VF
J29	1¢ Vermilion	2000.00	1300.00	1375.00	875.00	225.00
J30	2¢ Vermilion	875.00	525.00	575.00	350.00	75.00
J31	1¢ Claret	55.00	32.50	36.50	21.50	4.95
J32	2¢ Claret	52.50	29.50	32.50	19.50	3.00
J33	3¢ Claret (1895)	200.00	125.00	130.00	80.00	25.00
J34	5¢ Claret (1895)	295.00	170.00	190.00	115.00	27.50
J35	10¢ Claret	295.00	170.00	190.00	115.00	20.00
J36	30¢ Claret (1895)	500.00	295.00	350.00	200.00	70.00
J36b	Pale Rose	485.00	285.00	325.00	190.00	65.00
J37	50¢ Claret (1895)	1475.00	750.00	875.00	500.00	195.00
J37a	Pale Rose	1375.00	700.00	825.00	465.00	185.00
1895-97, Double Line Watermark, Perf. 12 VF Used + 60% (C)						
J38	1¢ Claret	13.75	7.75	8.25	5.00	.50
J39	2¢ Claret	13.75	7.75	8.25	5.00	.45
J40	3¢ Claret	85.00	50.00	55.00	32.50	1.40
J41	5¢ Claret	90.00	55.00	60.00	35.00	1.35
J42	10¢ Claret	95.00	57.50	62.50	37.50	2.75
J43	30¢ Claret (1897)	825.00	500.00	550.00	325.00	37.50
J44	50¢ Claret (1896)	475.00	275.00	300.00	180.00	30.00
1910-12, Single Line Watermark, Perf. 12 VF Used + 60% (C)						
J45	1¢ Claret	45.00	28.50	31.50	18.50	2.50
J46	2¢ Claret	45.00	28.50	31.50	18.50	.75
J47	3¢ Claret	875.00	550.00	575.00	350.00	22.50
J48	5¢ Claret	135.00	85.00	90.00	55.00	5.25
J49	10¢ Claret	175.00	110.00	115.00	70.00	9.75
J50	50¢ Claret (1912)	1375.00	900.00	975.00	575.00	90.00
1914-16, Single Line Watermark, Perf. 10 VF Used + 50% (C)						
J52	1¢ Carmine	90.00	56.50	57.50	37.50	8.00
J53	2¢ Carmine	70.00	45.00	46.50	30.00	.40
J54	3¢ Carmine	975.00	550.00	675.00	395.00	29.50
J55	5¢ Carmine	56.50	36.50	36.00	23.50	1.85
J56	10¢ Carmine	90.00	56.50	57.50	37.50	1.50
J57	30¢ Carmine	315.00	210.00	210.00	140.00	13.50
J58	50¢ Carmine	...	...	...	5500.00	500.00
J59	1¢ Rose (No Watermark) (1916)	...	...	1850.00	1100.00	230.00
J60	2¢ Rose(No Watermark)('16)	225.00	135.00	140.00	90.00	15.00
1917-25 Unwatermarked, Perf. 11 VF Used + 50% (B)						
J61	1¢ Carmine Rose	4.50	3.00	2.75	1.85	.20
J62	2¢ Carmine Rose	4.00	2.60	2.50	1.65	.20
J63	3¢ Carmine Rose	19.00	12.00	11.50	7.75	.20
J64	5¢ Carmine Rose	19.00	12.00	11.50	7.75	.20
J65	10¢ Carmine Rose	27.50	17.50	17.00	11.50	.30
J66	30¢ Carmine Rose	140.00	92.50	90.00	60.00	.60
J67	50¢ Carmine Rose	180.00	115.00	120.00	75.00	.25
J68	½¢ Dull Red (1925)	1.60	1.10	1.10	.75	.20

J69,J79 J77,J87 J88 J101

1930-31 Flat Press, Perf. 11 VF Used + 40% (B)

Scott's No.		NH VF	NH F-VF	Unused VF	Unused F-VF	Used F-VF
J69	½¢ Carmine	6.75	5.00	5.25	3.75	1.10
J70	1¢ Carmine	4.75	3.35	3.50	2.50	.20
J71	2¢ Carmine	5.50	4.00	4.00	3.00	.25
J72	3¢ Carmine	42.50	28.50	28.50	20.00	1.35
J73	5¢ Carmine	32.50	22.50	22.50	16.00	2.00
J74	10¢ Carmine	90.00	52.50	50.00	35.00	.75
J75	30¢ Carmine	185.00	125.00	120.00	85.00	1.50
J76	50¢ Carmine	295.00	165.00	160.00	115.00	.55
J77	$1 Carmine or Scarlet	42.50	30.00	27.50	20.00	.20
J78	$5 Carmine or Scarlet	60.00	42.50	38.50	27.50	.25

1931-56 Rotary Press, Perf. 11x10½ or 10½x11

Scott's No.		Mint Sheet	Pl.Blk NH	F-VF NH	F-VF Used
J79	½¢ Carmine	(100) 125.00	27.50	1.00	.18
J80	1¢ Carmine	(100) 13.75	2.00	.20	.15
J81	2¢ Carmine	(100) 14.75	2.00	.20	.15
J82	3¢ Carmine	(100) 24.50	3.00	.25	.15
J83	5¢ Carmine	(100) 42.50	4.50	.45	.15
J84	10¢ Carmine	(100) 110.00	8.50	1.10	.15
J85	30¢ Carmine	...	67.50	8.00	.15
J86	50¢ Carmine	...	75.00	11.50	.20
J87	$1 Red ('56)	...	285.00	42.50	.20
1959-85 Rotary Press, Perf. 11x10½					
J88	½¢ Carmine Rose & Black	(100) 325.00	215.00	1.25	1.75
J89	1¢ Carmine Rose & Black	(100) 5.00	.50	.20	.15
J90	2¢ Carmine Rose & Black	(100) 6.50	.50	.20	.15
J91	3¢ Carmine Rose & Black	(100) 8.75	.50	.20	.15
J92	4¢ Carmine Rose & Black	(100) 11.50	.90	.20	.15
J93	5¢ Carmine Rose & Black	(100) 13.75	.85	.20	.15
J94	6¢ Carmine Rose & Black	(100) 15.75	1.10	.20	.15
J95	7¢ Carmine Rose & Black	(100) 22.50	2.00	.22	.15
J96	8¢ Carmine Rose & Black	(100) 19.75	1.25	.22	.15
J97	10¢ Carmine Rose & Black	(100) 25.00	1.50	.25	.15
J98	30¢ Carmine Rose & Black	(100) 72.50	3.95	.75	.15
J99	50¢ Carmine Rose & Black	(100) 120.00	5.25	1.25	.15
J100	$1 Carmine Rose & Black	(100) 240.00	11.75	2.50	.15
J101	$5 Carmine Rose & Black	...	49.50	11.75	.20
J102	11¢ Carmine Rose & Blk. ('78)	(100) 28.50	3.50	.30	.35
J103	13¢ Carmine Rose & Blk. ('78)	(100) 33.50	2.00	.35	.35
J104	17¢ Carmine Rose & Blk. ('85)	(100) 79.50	39.50	.45	.60

U.S. OFFICES IN CHINA

K1 K2 K13 K17

**1919 U.S. Postal Agency in China
VF Used + 50% (B)**

Scott's No.		NH VF	NH F-VF	Unused VF	Unused F-VF	Used F-VF
K1	2¢ on 1¢ Green (on #498)	39.50	27.50	26.00	18.00	22.50
K2	4¢ on 2¢ Rose (on #499)	39.50	27.50	26.00	18.00	22.50
K3	6¢ on 3¢ Violet (#502)	75.00	47.50	45.00	32.50	50.00
K4	8¢ on 4¢ Brown (#503)	90.00	57.50	52.50	37.50	50.00
K5	10¢ on 5¢ Blue (#504)	100.00	62.50	60.00	42.50	50.00
K6	12¢ on 6¢ Red Orange(#506)	125.00	77.50	75.00	52.50	75.00
K7	14¢ on 7¢ Black (#507)	130.00	80.00	77.50	55.00	85.00
K8	16¢ on 8¢ Olive Bister (#508)	100.00	62.50	60.00	42.50	55.00
K8a	16¢ on 8¢ Olive Green	95.00	60.00	57.50	40.00	45.00
K9	18¢ on 9¢ Salmon Red (#509)	100.00	62.50	60.00	42.50	55.00
K10	20¢ on 10¢ Or. Yellow (#510)	95.00	60.00	57.50	40.00	50.00
K11	24¢ on 12¢ Brn. Carm. (#512)	110.00	67.50	62.50	45.00	57.50
K11a	24¢ on 12¢ Claret Brown	160.00	97.50	92.50	65.00	90.00
K12	30¢ on 15¢ Gray (#514)	135.00	82.50	77.50	55.00	95.00
K13	40¢ on 20¢ Deep Ultra (#515)	195.00	120.00	115.00	80.00	140.00
K14	60¢ on 30¢ Or. Red (#516)	175.00	110.00	105.00	75.00	125.00
K15	$1 on 50¢ Lt. Violet (#517)	750.00	475.00	450.00	325.00	425.00
K16	$2 on $1 Vlt. Brown (#518)	600.00	375.00	375.00	275.00	335.00
1922 Surcharged in Shanghai, China						
K17	2¢ on 1¢ Green (#498)	190.00	110.00	115.00	80.00	80.00
K18	4¢ on 2¢ Carmine (#528B)	175.00	97.50	105.00	70.00	70.00

OFFICIAL DEPARTMENTAL STAMPS

O3,O95   O12   O16,O97   O27,O106   O40

1873 Continental Bank Note Co. - Thin Hard Paper
(NH + 75%, VF OG & Used + 50%, VF NH + 150%) (C)

AGRICULTURE

Scott's No.		Unused Fine	Ave.	Used Fine	Ave.
O1	1¢ Yellow	95.00	57.50	75.00	45.00
O2	2¢	85.00	50.00	32.50	18.75
O3	3¢	65.00	40.00	6.00	3.65
O4	6¢	80.00	47.50	25.00	15.00
O5	10¢	150.00	90.00	85.00	52.50
O6	12¢	195.00	120.00	100.00	60.00
O7	15¢	160.00	95.00	95.00	57.50
O8	24¢	160.00	95.00	85.00	50.00
O9	30¢	225.00	135.00	115.00	70.00

EXECUTIVE

O10	1¢ Carmine	335.00	195.00	200.00	120.00
O11	2¢	210.00	125.00	100.00	60.00
O12	3¢	260.00	155.00	100.00	60.00
O13	6¢	400.00	240.00	275.00	165.00
O14	10¢	350.00	210.00	300.00	180.00

INTERIOR

O15	1¢ Vermilion	21.00	12.50	5.25	3.15
O16	2¢	16.50	10.00	3.25	2.00
O17	3¢	28.00	16.50	3.00	1.75
O18	6¢	21.00	12.00	3.15	1.85
O19	10¢	19.50	11.50	6.25	3.75
O20	12¢	31.75	18.50	4.75	2.65
O21	15¢	47.50	27.50	9.75	5.75
O22	24¢	36.50	20.00	8.25	5.00
O23	30¢	47.50	27.50	8.25	5.00
O24	90¢	115.00	67.50	21.50	12.75

JUSTICE

O25	1¢ Purple	62.50	36.00	46.50	27.50
O26	2¢	100.00	60.00	50.00	30.00
O27	3¢	100.00	60.00	9.75	5.75
O28	6¢	95.00	55.00	15.75	9.50
O29	10¢	110.00	65.00	35.00	18.00
O30	12¢	82.50	50.00	21.50	12.75
O31	15¢	160.00	90.00	75.00	45.00
O32	24¢	425.00	250.00	165.00	100.00
O33	30¢	375.00	225.00	95.00	55.00
O34	90¢	550.00	325.00	240.00	140.00

NAVY

O35	1¢ Ultramarine	42.50	25.00	21.50	13.50
O36	2¢	32.50	19.50	10.00	6.00
O37	3¢	35.00	20.00	5.00	3.00
O38	6¢	35.00	20.00	8.25	4.95
O39	7¢	210.00	125.00	85.00	50.00
O40	10¢	47.50	28.50	17.50	10.75
O41	12¢	55.00	32.50	14.75	8.75
O42	15¢	100.00	60.00	30.00	18.50
O43	24¢	100.00	60.00	33.50	20.00
O44	30¢	80.00	47.50	16.50	10.00
O45	90¢	425.00	250.00	105.00	65.00

O49,O108   O60   O74,O109   O83,O114

POST OFFICE

O47	1¢ Black	7.00	4.25	3.25	1.85
O48	2¢	8.50	5.00	2.75	1.55
O49	3¢	2.75	1.65	.90	.50
O50	6¢	8.75	5.25	2.10	1.25
O51	10¢	40.00	24.00	20.00	12.00
O52	12¢	20.00	11.50	5.50	3.00
O53	15¢	26.50	17.00	8.50	5.00
O54	24¢	35.00	20.00	10.50	6.00
O55	30¢	35.00	20.00	10.00	5.50
O56	90¢	50.00	30.00	10.00	6.00

OFFICIAL DEPARTMENTAL STAMPS (continued)

STATE

Scott's No.		Unused Fine	Ave.	Used Fine	Ave.
O57	1¢ Green	62.50	35.00	22.75	13.50
O58	2¢	130.00	75.00	40.00	24.50
O59	3¢	47.50	27.50	9.50	5.25
O60	6¢	47.50	27.50	11.50	6.50
O61	7¢	90.00	55.00	23.50	13.00
O62	10¢	70.00	37.50	16.00	9.00
O63	12¢	115.00	70.00	50.00	29.50
O64	15¢	125.00	80.00	32.50	19.50
O65	24¢	250.00	150.00	90.00	55.00
O66	30¢	225.00	130.00	65.00	40.00
O67	90¢	450.00	270.00	140.00	85.00
O68	$2 Green & Black	525.00	300.00	400.00	240.00
O69	$5 Green & Black	4250.00	2600.00	1800.00	1250.00
O70	$10 Green & Black	2800.00	1575.00	1400.00	950.00
O71	$20 Green & Black	1950.00	1100.00	950.00	525.00

TREASURY

O72	1¢ Brown	21.50	12.75	2.65	1.60
O73	2¢	26.00	16.00	2.65	1.60
O74	3¢	16.50	9.75	1.25	.75
O75	6¢	21.50	12.75	2.25	1.35
O76	7¢	52.50	30.00	13.50	7.95
O77	10¢	55.00	32.50	5.25	3.00
O78	12¢	55.00	32.50	3.75	2.25
O79	15¢	52.50	30.00	5.00	2.75
O80	24¢	250.00	150.00	42.50	23.50
O81	30¢	82.50	50.00	5.50	3.00
O82	90¢	85.00	51.50	6.00	3.50

WAR

O83	1¢ Rose	80.00	47.50	4.25	2.50
O84	2¢	70.00	41.50	6.25	3.50
O85	3¢	67.50	38.50	1.75	1.00
O86	6¢	250.00	150.00	4.00	2.25
O87	7¢	70.00	41.50	42.50	25.00
O88	10¢	23.50	14.00	6.75	4.00
O89	12¢	80.00	48.50	5.50	3.00
O90	15¢	19.00	11.00	6.75	4.00
O91	24¢	19.00	11.00	4.00	2.35
O92	30¢	21.50	13.00	4.00	2.35
O93	90¢	52.50	31.00	25.00	14.50

1879 American Bank Note Co. - Soft Porous Paper
(NH + 60%, VF OG & Used + 50%, VF NH + 135%) (C)

O94	1¢ Agric. Dept. (Issued w/o gum)	1400.00	800.00	...	...
O95	3¢	175.00	100.00	40.00	24.00
O96	1¢ Interior Department	125.00	70.00	115.00	70.00
O97	2¢	2.25	1.20	1.00	.60
O98	3¢	1.95	1.10	.75	.40
O99	6¢	3.00	1.80	3.25	1.95
O100	10¢	40.00	24.00	32.50	19.50
O101	12¢	80.00	45.00	52.50	32.50
O102	15¢	160.00	95.00	140.00	85.00
O103	24¢	1795.00	1100.00	...	...
O106	3¢ Justice Department	52.50	28.50	35.00	21.00
O107	6¢	110.00	60.00	95.00	57.50
O108	3¢ Post Office Department	8.50	4.50	3.00	1.80
O109	3¢ Treasury Department	27.50	15.75	4.00	2.25
O110	6¢	52.50	28.50	19.50	11.50
O111	10¢	75.00	45.00	22.50	13.50
O112	30¢	750.00	435.00	160.00	95.00
O113	90¢	975.00	575.00	160.00	95.00
O114	1¢ War Department	2.00	1.20	1.65	1.00
O115	2¢	3.00	1.80	1.80	1.10
O116	3¢	3.00	1.75	.95	.55
O117	6¢	3.00	1.65	.90	.50
O118	10¢	22.50	14.00	18.00	11.00
O119	12¢	16.50	9.50	6.00	3.75
O120	30¢	45.00	26.50	39.50	23.75

1910-11 Official Postal Savings VF Used + 50% (B)

O122   O123   O124

Scott's No.		NH VF	F-VF	Unused VF	F-VF	Used F-VF
O121	2¢ Black, D.L. Wmk	23.00	14.50	13.75	8.75	1.25
O122	50¢ Dark Green, D.L. Wmk	235.00	140.00	145.00	95.00	30.00
O123	$1 Ultramarine, D.L. Wmk	225.00	135.00	135.00	90.00	9.00
O124	1¢ Dark Violet, S.L. Wmk	12.50	7.75	7.50	5.00	1.15
O125	2¢ Black, S.L. Wmk	65.00	40.00	42.50	27.50	3.75
O126	10¢ Carmine, S.L. Wmk	22.50	15.00	14.00	9.50	1.10

O127   O133   O135   O138   O139

1983-85 Official Stamps

Scott's No.		Mint Sheet	Pl# Blk. F-VF NH	F-VF NH	F-VF Used
O127	1¢ Eagle .... (100)	7.50	.50	.20	.15
O128	4¢ Eagle .... (100)	12.50	.70	.20	.25
O129	13¢ Eagle .... (100)	37.50	1.95	.40	.75
O129A	14¢ Eagle (No Pl.#) ('85) ...... (100)	42.50	...	.45	.55
O130	17¢ Eagle .... (100)	45.00	2.35	.50	.40
O132	$1 Eagle($1.00) .... (100)	270.00	12.50	2.75	1.50
O133	$5 Eagle	...	40.00	9.75	5.50
O135	20¢ Eagle, Coil .... **(Pl.# Strip)**	85.00(5)	15.00(3)	.75	1.10
O136	22¢ Eagle (No Pl.#) ('85)	...	...	1.25	1.25
O138	(14¢) "D" Postcard rate ('85) ... (100)	365.00	37.50	4.00	3.00
O139	(22¢) "D" Coil ('85)............ **(Pl.# Strip)**	90.00(5)	47.50(3)	3.50	2.50

O138A   O138B   O140   O143   O144

O146   O152   O154   O155   O156

1988-95 Official Stamps
(Sheets and Coils do not have Plate #s)

O138A	15¢ Coil ('88)	...	...	.55	.60
O138B	20¢ Coil (No ¢ sign) ('88)............	...	...	.70	.80
O140	(25¢) "E" Coil ('88)	...	...	1.20	1.70
O141	25¢ Coil ('88)	...	...	.90	.45
O143	1¢ Offset (No ¢ sign) ('89) .... (100)	9.50	...	.20	.25
O144	(29¢) "F" Coil ('91)	...	...	1.65	1.00
O145	29¢ Coil ('91)	...	...	.90	.40
O146	4¢ Make-up rate ('91) .... (100)	10.75	...	.20	.30
O146A	10¢ Eagle (1993) .... (100)	25.00	...	.27	.50
O147	19¢ Postcard rate ('91) .... (100)	52.50	...	.55	.55
O148	23¢ 2nd Ounce rate ('91)......... (100)	65.00	...	.70	.50
O151	$1 Eagle ($1)(1993)................ (100)	200.00	...	2.10	1.75
O152	(32¢) "G" Coil (94)	...	...	.70	1.00
O153	32¢ Eagle, Coil (1995)................	...	...	.70	.95
O154	1¢ "¢" Sign added,No "USA"('95)(100)	7.50	...	.20	.20
O155	20¢ Sheet Stamp (1995) .... (100)	39.50	...	.42	.50
O156	23¢ Reprint, Line above "23"('95)(100)	45.00	...	.50	.60

Q1   QE1   JQ1

1913 PARCEL POST STAMPS VF Used + 40% (B)

Scott's No.		NH VF	NH F-VF	Unused VF	Unused F-VF	Used F-VF
Q1	1¢ Post Office Clerk..................	6.50	4.50	4.00	2.75	1.10
Q2	2¢ City Carrier	7.50	5.25	4.50	3.25	.95
Q3	3¢ Railway Clerk.......................	13.75	9.50	8.75	6.00	4.00
Q4	4¢ Rural Carrier	42.50	26.50	25.00	16.50	2.25
Q5	5¢ Mail Train	42.50	26.50	25.00	16.50	1.50
Q6	10¢ Steamship & Tender..........	67.50	45.00	40.00	27.50	2.25
Q7	15¢ Automobile Service...........	100.00	65.00	60.00	42.50	7.75
Q8	20¢ Airplane Carrying Mail ...	200.00	125.00	115.00	82.50	15.00
Q9	25¢ Manufactured	100.00	65.00	57.50	40.00	4.50
Q10	50¢ Dairying	380.00	260.00	250.00	180.00	30.00
Q11	75¢ Harvesting	115.00	75.00	70.00	50.00	23.50
Q12	$1 Fruit Growing	475.00	350.00	315.00	225.00	18.00

1925-1955 SPECIAL HANDLING STAMPS VF + 30% (B)

QE1	10¢ Yellow Green, Dry (1955) ...	2.25	1.65	1.60	1.25	.90
QE1a	10¢ Wet Printing (1928)	4.00	2.90	2.75	2.25	1.00
QE2	15¢ Yellow Green, Dry (1955) ...	2.25	1.75	1.65	1.25	.90
QE2a	15¢ Wet Printing (1928)............	4.75	3.50	3.25	2.60	1.00
QE3	20¢ Yellow Green, Dry (1955) ...	3.65	2.65	2.50	1.90	1.50
QE3a	20¢ Wet Printing (1928)............	5.50	3.75	3.75	3.00	1.65
QE4	25¢ Yellow Green (1929).........	28.50	22.50	21.00	16.50	7.50
QE4a	25¢ Deep Green (1925)...........	42.50	31.50	29.50	22.50	5.25

1912 PARCEL POST DUE VF + 40% (B)

JQ1	1¢ Dark Green	13.75	9.00	8.00	5.75	3.50
JQ2	2¢ Dark Green	110.00	75.00	70.00	50.00	13.00
JQ3	5¢ Dark Green	20.00	13.50	12.50	8.50	3.25
JQ4	10¢ Dark Green	250.00	160.00	160.00	110.00	35.00
JQ5	25¢ Dark Green	160.00	90.00	90.00	62.50	3.50

PLATE BLOCKS

	NH VF	NH F-VF	Unused F-VF		NH VF	NH F-VF	Unused F-VF
Q1 (6)	160.00	110.00	75.00	QE1 (6)	23.75	17.50	13.50
Q2 (6)	175.00	115.00	85.00	QE2 (6)	37.50	18.50	22.50
Q3 (6)	300.00	200.00	150.00	QE3 (6)	42.50	32.50	25.00

SAVINGS STAMPS (B) PS & WS (NH + 20%) VF + 30%, S (NH + 10%) VF + 20%

PS8   PS14   S2   S7   WS8

Scott's No.		F-VF Unused
	1911-41 Postal Savings	
PS1	10¢ Orange	6.75
PS2	10¢ Orange, Card.......	140.00
PS4	10¢ D. Blue, Pf. 12	4.00
PS5	10¢ Dp, Blue, Card.......	85.00
PS6	10¢ Blue, Perf. 11 ('36) ..	4.00
PS7	10¢ Ultramarine (1940)	13.75
PS8	25¢ Carmine Rose ('40)	16.50
PS9	50¢ Blue Green ('40)....	45.00
PS10	$1 Gray Black (1940) .	125.00
PS11	10¢ Rose Red (1941)........	.60
PS11	Plate Block of 4	7.50
PS11b	Bklt. Pane of 10	45.00
PS12	25¢ Blue Green ("41) .	1.75
PS12	Plate Block of 4	18.75
PS12b	Bklt. Pane of 10	55.00
PS13	50¢ Ultramarine ('41)	6.50
PS13	Plate Block of 4	45.00
PS14	$1 Gray Black ('41).......	11.00
PS15	$5 Sepia (1941)............	35.00
	1954-61 Savings	
S1	10¢ Rose Red	.45
S1	Plate Block of 4	3.00
S1a	Bklt. Pane of 10	140.00
S2	25¢ Blue Green	6.00
S2	Plate Block of 4	30.00
S2a	Bklt. Pane of 10	775.00
S3	50¢ Ultramarine ('56)......	7.50

Scott's No.		F-VF Unused
S3	50¢ Plate Block of 4 ......47.50	
S4	$1 Gray Black (1957) 21.50	
S5	$5 Sepia (1956) 75.00	
S6	25¢ 48 Star Flag (1958) ..1.60	
S6	Plate Block of 4 ....8.00	
S6a	Bklt. Pane of 10 ....67.50	
S7	25¢ 50 Star Flag (1961) ..1.20	
S7	Plate Block of 4 ....9.00	
S7a	Bklt. Pane of 10 ....275.00	
	1917-45 War Savings	
WS1	25¢ Thrift Stamp 12.00	
WS2	$5 Washington 75.00	
WS4	$5 Franklin ('19) 270.00	
WS7	10¢ Rose Red (1942)........45	
WS7	Plate Block of 4 ....4.75	
WS7b	Bklt. Pane of 10............45.00	
WS8	25¢ Blue Green (1942) ...1.00	
WS8	Plate Block of 4 ....8.00	
WS8b	Bklt. Pane of 10............45.00	
WS9	50¢ Ultramarine (1942)...3.75	
WS9	Plate Block of 4 ....21.50	
WS10	$1 Gray Black (1942) 10.00	
WS10	Plate Block of 4 ....65.00	
WS11	$5 Violet Brown (1945) .45.00	
WS12	10¢ Rose Red, Coil ('43).2.25	
WS12	Line Pair........................9.50	
WS13	25¢ Blue Green,Coil '43).4.00	
WS13	Line Pair.......................18.50	

PLATE NUMBER COIL STRIPS

1897

2127

Scott No.	F-VF,NH	Pl.Strip of 5	Pl.Strip of 3
1897	**1¢ Omnibus**		
	Pl# 1,2,5,6	.60	.50
	Pl# 3,4	1.00	.80
2225	**1¢ Omnibus "B" Press**		
	Pl# 1,2	.80	.70
2225a	Pl# 2,3 untagged	.80	.70
2225s	Pl# 3 Shiny, Tag..........	7.50	6.75
2225sv	Pl# 3 Shiny, Untag	1.20	1.10
3044	**1¢ Kestrel**		
	Pl # 1111	1.15	1.00
1897A	**2¢ Locomotive**		
	Pl# 2,6	.85	.70
	Pl# 3,4,8,10	.65	.55
2226	**2¢ Locomotive "B" Press**		
	Pl# 1	.90	.75
2226a	Pl# 2 untagged	.90	.75
1898	**3¢ Handcar**		
	Pl# 1-4	.90	.75
2252	**3¢ Conestoga Wagon**		
	Pl# 1	.90	.80
2252a	Pl# 2,3 untagged	1.45	1.30
2252b	Pl# 3 Shiny Gum	1.60	1.40
	Pl# 6 Shiny Gum	2.50	2.25
2123	**3.4¢ School Bus**		
	Pl# 1,2	1.20	1.00
2123a	Pl# 1,2	6.75	6.50
1898A	**4¢ Stagecoach**		
	Pl# 1,2,3,4	1.25	1.00
	Pl# 5,6	3.25	2.50
1898Ab	Pl# 3,4,5,6	7.50	6.75
2228	**4¢ Stagecoach "B"**		
	Pl# 1	1.65	1.35
2228a	Pl# 1, overall tag ...	15.00	14.50
2451	**4¢ Steam Carriage**		
	Pl# 1	1.10	.90
2451b	Pl# 1, untagged	1.20	1.00
2124	**4.9¢ Buckboard**		
	Pl# 3,4	1.15	.90
2124a	Pl# 1-6	2.10	1.85
1899	**5¢ Motorcycle**		
	Pl# 1-4	1.10	.90
2253	**5¢ Milk Wagon**		
	Pl# 1	1.40	1.20
2452	**5¢ Circus Wagon, Engr.**		
	Pl# 1	1.35	1.10
2452a	Pl# 1, untagged	1.50	1.20
2452B	**5¢ Circus Wagon, Gravure**		
	Pl# A1,A2	1.35	1.10
	Pl# A3 Hi-Brite........	3.95	3.50
2452D	**5¢ Circus Wagon (¢ sign)**		
	Pl# S1,S2	1.50	1.20
2453	**5¢ Canoe, Brown, Engr.**		
	Pl# 1,2,3	1.50	1.25
2454	**5¢ Canoe, Red, Gravure**		
	Pl# S11	1.60	1.30
2893	**(5¢) "G" Non-Profit**		
	Pl# A11111,A21111	2.30	2.00
2902	**(5¢) Butte**		
	Pl# S111.................	1.75	1.50
2903	**(5¢) Mountain,BEP**		
	Pl#11111	2.25	1.95
2904	**(5¢) Mountain,SVS**		
	Pl# S111	2.25	1.95
1900	**5.2¢ Sleigh**		
	Pl# 1,2	10.75	5.50
	Pl# 3,5	225.00	165.00
1900a	Pl# 1-6	15.00	13.50
2254	**5.3¢ Elevator, Precancel**		
	Pl# 1	2.40	1.95
2125	**5.5¢ Star Route Truck**		
	Pl# 1	2.00	1.60
2125a	Pl# 1,2	1.95	1.60
1901	**5.9¢ Bicycle**		
	Pl# 3,4	19.00	6.00
1901a	Pl# 3,4	39.50	38.50
	Pl# 5,6	90.00	85.00
2126	**6¢ Tricycle**		
	Pl# 1	1.85	1.50
2126a	Pl# 1	2.15	1.75
	Pl# 2	8.75	8.00

Scott No.	F-VF,NH	Pl.Strip of 5	Pl.Strip of 3
2127	**7.1¢ Tractor**		
	Pl# 1	2.95	2.50
2127a	Pl# 1	3.95	3.50
2127av	Zip + 4		
	Pl# 1	2.65	2.25
1902	**7.4¢ Baby Buggy**		
	Pl# 2	12.75	7.00
1902a	Pl# 2	6.50	5.95
2255	**7.5¢ Carreta, Precancel**		
	Pl# 1,2	2.85	2.50
	Pl# 3	6.50	6.00
2128	**8.3¢ Ambulance**		
	Pl# 1,2	1.85	1.50
2128a	Pl# 1,2	1.85	1.50
	Pl# 3,4	6.50	5.50
2231	**8.3¢ Ambul."B" Press,Precancel**		
	Pl# 1	7.50	6.50
	Pl# 2	9.50	8.00
2256	**8.4¢ Wheel Chair, Precancel**		
	Pl# 1,2	2.40	2.00
	Pl# 3	15.00	14.00
2129	**8.5¢ Tow Truck**		
	Pl# 1	4.00	3.50
2129a	Pl# 1	3.65	3.15
	Pl# 2	13.50	12.50
1903	**9.3¢ Mail Wagon**		
	Pl# 1,2	17.50	6.75
	Pl# 3,4	45.00	37.50
	Pl# 5,6	375.00	335.00
1903a	Pl# 1,2	16.50	14.50
	Pl# 3	37.50	33.50
	Pl# 4	25.00	22.50
	Pl# 5,6	4.50	3.75
	Pl# 8	225.00	200.00
2257	**10¢ Canal Boat**		
	Pl# 1	2.25	1.80
2257a	Pl# 1,2 overall tag...	4.00	3.50
2257ad	Pl# 1, o.t., dull gum.	6.25	5.75
2457	**10¢ Tractor Trailer,intaglio**		
	Pl# 1	3.00	2.50
2458	**10¢ Tractor Trailer, Gravure**		
	Pl#11	7.75	7.00
	Pl# 22	2.75	2.25
2602	**(10¢) Eagle &Shield**		
	A11111,A11112,A21112,		
	A22112,A22113,A33333,		
	A43334,A43335,A53335	2.65	2.25
	A12213	27.50	25.00
	A21113,A33335,		
	A43324,A43325,A43326,		
	A43426,A54444,A54445	3.25	2.75
	A34424,A34426, ...	6.50	5.75
	A32333	P.O.R	P.O.R.
	A33334	97.50	90.00
	A77777,A88888,A88889,		
	A89999,A99998,A99999	3.00	2.50
	A1010101010,A1110101010,		
	A1011101011,etc.	4.00	3.00
	A111010101011	14.00	13.00
2603	**(10¢) Eagle & Shield (BEP)**		
	Pl# 11111,22221,		
	22222	2.75	2.35
2603v	(10¢) Dull Gum,		
	Pl# 22222,33333	4.25	3.50
2603b	(10¢) Tagged		
	Pl# 11111, 22221 ...	16.75	15.75
2604	**(10¢) Eagle & Shield (SV)**		
	Pl# S11111,S22222.......	3.75	3.25
2905	**(10¢) Automobile**		
	Pl# S111,S222,S333	2.90	2.50
2130	**10.1¢ Oil Wagon**		
	Pl# 1	3.25	2.30
2130a	Pl# 1,2	3.25	2.75
2130av	Pl# 2,3 **Red Prec**....	2.90	2.25
1904	**10.9¢ Hansom Cab**		
	Pl# 1,2	42.50	10.75
1904a	Pl# 1,2	39.50	37.50
	Pl# 3,4	365.00	325.00

Scott No.	F-VF,NH	Pl.Strip of 5	Pl.Strip of 3
1905	**11¢ Caboose**		
	Pl# 1	5.25	3.50
1905b	Pl# 2, untagged.......	3.25	2.75
1905a	Pl# 1	4.75	4.25
2131	**11¢ Stutz Bearcat**		
	Pl# 1-4	1.85	1.30
2132	**12¢ Stanley Steamer**		
	Pl# 1,2	2.95	2.50
2132a	Pl# 1,2	3.00	2.50
2132b	12¢ "B" Press, Prec.		
	Pl# 1	28.75	27.50
2133	**12.5¢ Pushcart**		
	Pl# 1,2	3.50	2.75
2133a	Pl# 1,2	3.50	3.00
2258	**13¢ Patrol Wagon, Prec.**		
	Pl# 1	4.85	4.25
2259	**13.2¢ Coal Car, Prec.**		
	Pl# 1,2	3.65	3.00
2134	**14¢ Iceboat**		
	Pl# 1-4	2.75	2.25
2134b	"B" Press		
	Pl# 2	5.00	4.25
2260	**15¢ Tugboat**		
	Pl# 1,2	3.25	2.50
2260a	Pl# 2, overall tag ...	5.00	4.25
2908	**(15¢) Auto Tail Fin, BEP**		
	Pl# 11111	4.50	3.75
2909	**(15¢) Auto Tail Fin, SVS**		
	Pl# S11111	3.75	3.00
2261	**16.7¢ Popcorn Wagon, Prec.**		
	Pl# 1,2	3.75	3.25
1906	**17¢ Electric Car**		
	Pl# 1-5	2.65	1.75
	Pl# 6	18.75	17.50
	Pl# 7	7.00	6.25
1906a	Pl# 3A-5A	4.75	3.75
	Pl# 6A,7A................	19.50	17.00
1906ab	Pl# 3B,4B................	31.50	29.50
	Pl# 5B,6B................	36.00	33.50
1906ac	Pl# 1C,2C,3C,4C	14.50	12.75
	Pl# 5C,7C................	37.50	35.00
2135	**17¢ Dog Sled**		
	Pl# 2	4.25	3.00
2262	**17.5¢ Marmon Wasp**		
	Pl# 1	5.00	4.25
2262a	Pl# 1	5.50	4.75
1891	**18¢ Flag**		
	Pl# 1	450.00	85.00
	Pl# 2	50.00	25.00
	Pl# 3	1075.00	225.00
	Pl# 4	10.00	6.00
	Pl# 5	6.75	5.00
	Pl# 6	P.O.R.	P.O.R.
	Pl# 7	37.50	32.50
1907	**18¢ Surrey**		
	Pl# 1	110.00	100.00
	Pl# 2,5,6,8...............	3.50	2.25
	Pl# 3,4	70.00	65.00
	Pl# 7	40.00	35.00
	Pl# 9,10	15.00	13.50
	Pl# 11,12,15,16..........	15.75	14.50
	Pl# 13-14,17-18	8.75	6.50
2149	**18¢ GW Monument**		
	Pl# 1112,3333...........	3.75	2.75
2149a	Pl# 11121,33333.........	4.25	3.50
2149b	Pl# 33333 Dry Gum	5.50	4.75
	Pl# 43444 Dry Gum	11.50	10.00
2529	**19¢ Fishing Boat, Ty. I**		
	Pl# A1111,A1212,A2424	4.50	3.75
	Pl# A1112	14.75	13.50
2529a	Ty. II, Andreotti Gravure		
	Pl# A5555,A5556,		
	A6667,A7667,A7679		
	A7766,A7779.............	4.50	3.75
2529b	Type II,untagged		
	A5555...................	12.50	10.00
2529C	Type III, S111................	6.00	5.00

PLATE NUMBER COIL STRIPS

1908

0135

Scott No.	F-VF,NH	Pl.Strip of 5	Pl.Strip of 3
1895	20¢ Flag		
	Pl# 1	95.00	8.50
	Pl# 2,11,12	9.75	7.00
	Pl# 3,5,9-10,13-14	5.25	2.75
	Pl# 4	775.00	45.00
	Pl# 6	185.00	90.00
	Pl# 8	15.00	7.50
1895e	Pl# 14	90.00	85.00
1908	20¢ Fire Pumper		
	Pl# 1	175.00	32.50
	Pl# 2	950.00	160.00
	Pl# 3,4,13,15,16	5.25	3.00
	Pl# 5,9,10	3.50	2.25
	Pl# 6	42.50	35.00
	Pl# 7,8	165.00	110.00
	Pl# 11	80.00	40.00
	Pl# 12,14	7.95	5.00
2005	20¢ Consumer		
	Pl# 1,2	175.00	30.00
	Pl# 3,4	135.00	25.00
2263	20¢ Cable Car		
	Pl# 1,2	4.15	3.35
2263b	Pl# 2, overall tag	7.00	6.00
2463	20¢ Cog Railway		
	Pl# 1,2	5.50	4.75
2264	20.5¢ Fire Engine, Prec.		
	Pl# 1	4.75	3.85
2265	20.5¢ RR Mail Car, Prec.		
	Pl# 1,2	5.00	3.95
2150	21.1¢ Pre-Sort		
	Pl# 111111	4.75	3.50
	Pl# 111121	5.75	4.25
2150a	Pl# 111111	5.50	4.50
	Pl# 111121	6.25	5.00
2112	(22¢) "D" Eagle Coil		
	Pl# 1,2	9.25	6.50
2115	22¢ Flag/Capitol		
	Pl# 1	13.75	9.75
	Pl# 2,8,10,12	4.00	3.00
	Pl# 3	55.00	13.00
	Pl# 4,5,6,11	7.50	6.00
	Pl# 7,13	15.00	12.50
	Pl# 14	33.50	27.50
	Pl# 15,19,22	4.00	3.00
	Pl# 16,17,18,20,21	8.75	7.50
2115b	22¢ Flag Test Coil		
	Pl# T1	5.50	4.25
2464	23¢ Lunch Wagon		
	Pl# 2,3	4.50	3.65
2464p	23¢ Phosphored, Dull Gum		
	Pl# 3	6.75	5.75
2464ps	23¢ Phosphored, Shiny Gum		
	Pl# 3	6.75	5.75
2605	23¢ Flag, Bulk Rate		
	Pl# A111,A212, A222 (FAT)	4.75	3.75
	Pl# A112,A122,A333, A222(THIN)	5.25	4.25
2606	23¢ USA Pre-sort, ABNCo.		
	Pl# A1111,A2222,A2232, A2233,A3333,A4443, A4444,A4453,A4364	4.75	3.75

Scott No.	F-VF,NH	Pl.Strip of 5	Pl.Strip of 3
2607	23¢ USA Pre-sort, BEP		
	Pl# 1111	6.00	5.00
2607v	23¢ Dull Gum #1111	6.25	5.25
2608	23¢ USA Pre-sort, S.V.		
	Pl# S1111	6.50	5.50
2266	24.1¢ Tandem Bike, Prec.		
	Pl# 1	5.75	4.75
2136	25¢ Bread Wagon		
	Pl# 1-5	4.75	3.25
2279	(25¢) "E" Series		
	Pl# 1111,1222	4.50	3.50
	Pl# 1211	6.00	5.00
	Pl# 2222	7.50	6.50
2280	25¢ Yosemite Block tagged		
	Pl# 1,7	8.50	7.50
	Pl# 2-5,8	4.25	3.35
	Pl# 9	13.75	12.50
2280v	25¢ Yosemite Phos. tag.		
	Pl# 1	55.00	52.50
	Pl# 2-3,7-11,13-14	4.25	3.35
	Pl# 5,15	8.50	7.50
	Pl# 6	15.75	14.00
2281	25¢ Honeybee		
	Pl# 1,2	4.50	3.25
2888	(25¢) "G"		
	Pl# S11111	6.95	5.95
2911	(25¢) Juke Box, BEP		
	Pl# 111111,212222, 222222,332222	6.25	5.25
2912	(25¢) Juke Box, SVS		
	Pl# S11111,S22222	5.25	4.25
2518	(29¢) "F" Flower		
	Pl# 1111,1222,2222	4.75	3.50
	Pl# 1211	25.00	22.50
	Pl# 2211	7.50	6.25
2523	29¢ Flag/Mt. Rushmore		
	Pl# 1-7	4.75	3.50
	Pl# 8	7.50	6.25
	Pl# 9	15.00	13.50
2523A	29¢ Rushmore/Gravure		
	Pl# A11111,A22211	5.75	4.50
2525	29¢ Flower, rouletted		
	Pl# S1111,S2222	5.50	4.25
2526	29¢ Flower, perforated		
	Pl# S2222	5.50	4.25
2609	29¢ Flag/White House		
	Pl# 1-8	5.50	4.25
	Pl# 9-16,18	6.75	5.50
2889	(32¢) Black "G"		
	Pl# 1111, 2222	8.75	7.50
2890	(32¢) Blue "G"		
	Pl# A1111,A1112,A1113, A1211,A1212,A1311,A1313 A1314,A1324,A1417,A1433 A2211,A2212,A2213,A2214, A2223,A3113,A3314,A3315 A3323,A3324,A3423,A3433 A3435,A3436,A4426,A4427, A5327,A5417,A5427, A5437	6.50	5.25
	Pl# A1222,A3114,A3426	9.00	7.75
	Pl# A4435	170.00	165.00

Scott No.	F-VF,NH	Pl.Strip of 5	Pl.Strip of 3
2891	(32¢) Red "G"		
	Pl# S1111	6.50	5.25
2892	(32¢) "G" Rouletted		
	Pl# S1111,S2222	7.75	6.50
2466	32¢ Ferry Boat,Shiny		
	Pl# 2,3,4,5	7.75	6.75
2466v	32¢ Low Gloss Gum		
	Pl# 3,5	7.75	6.75
	Pl# 4	21.75	19.75
2913	32¢ Flag over Porch, BEP		
	Pl# 11111,22222,33333, 44444, 45444,66646 66666,77767,78767, 99969	6.25	5.25
	Pl# 22322	49.95	47.95
2913a	32¢ Dull Gum		
	Pl# 11111,22221,22222	6.25	5.25
2914	32¢ Flag over Porch, SVS		
	Pl# S11111	5.75	4.75
2468	$1 Seaplane, Dull Gum		
	Pl# 1	13.95	9.50
2468s	32¢ Shiny Gum		
	Pl# 3	13.95	9.50
O135	20¢ Official		
	Pl# 1	85.00	15.00
O139	(22¢) "D" Official		
	Pl# 1	90.00	47.50
	VARIABLE RATE COILS		
CV31	29¢ Shield, Dull Gum		
	Pl# 1	10.75	9.75
CV31a	29¢ Shiny Gum		
	Pl# 1	10.75	9.75
CV31b	32¢ Dull Gum		
	Pl# 1	14.75	12.75
CV31c	32¢ Shiny Gum		
	Pl# 1	13.75	11.75
CV32	29¢ Vertical Design		
	Pl# A11	9.75	8.75
CV33	32¢ Vertical Design		
	Pl# 11	9.75	8.75

2913

CV31

WHEN IT'S TIME
TO SELL YOUR STAMPS ...

Remember that you can deal with confidence with the
dealer who has been serving your philatelic needs.
Contact your dealer to discuss the disposition of
your collection.

SELF-ADHESIVE PLATE NUMBER COIL STRIPS

2873v

2902B

Scott N.	F-VF, NH	Pl. Strip of 5	Pl. Strip of 3
2431v	25¢ Eagle & Shield	No Plate #	
2489v	29¢ Red Squirrel	No Plate #	
2490v	29¢ Rose.......................	No Plate #	
2491v	29¢ Pine Cone		
	Pl# B1	8.00	6.75
2492v	32¢ Pink Rose		
	Pl# 5111	7.25	5.95
2495-95Av	32¢ Peach & Pear		
	Pl# V11111	7.25	5.95
2595v-97v	29¢ Eagle & Shield	No Plate #	
2598v	29¢ Eagle		
	Pl# 111	8.00	6.75
2599v	Statue of Liberty		
	Pl# D1111....................	8.00	6.75
2799-2802v	29¢ Christmas		
	Pl#V1111111..............	(8) 9.95	...
2813v	29¢ Love		
	Pl# B1	8.00	6.75
2873v	29¢ Santa Claus		
	Pl# V1111	8.25	7.00
2886v	(32¢) "G"		
	Pl# V11111	8.25	7.00

Scott N.	F-VF, NH	Pl. Strip of 5	Pl. Strip of 3
2902B	(5¢) Butte		
	Pl# S111	2.00	1.75
2904A	(5¢) Mountain, 11.5		
	Pl# V222222, V333323,		
	V333333, V333342,		
	V333343	1.95	1.70
2904B	(5¢) Mountain, 9.8		
	Pl# 1111......................	1.95	1.70
2906	(10¢) Eagle & Shield		
	Pl# S111	2.95	2.65
2907	(10¢) Automobile		
	Pl# S11111	2.95	2.65
2910	(15¢) Auto Tail Fin		
	Pl# S11111	3.50	3.00
2912A	(25¢) Juke Box, 11.5		
	Pl# S11111	4.85	4.00
2912B	(25¢) Juke box, 9.8		
	Pl# 111111..................	4.85	4.00
2915	32¢ Flag over Porch, 8.7		
	Pl# V11111	7.95	6.75

Scott N.	F-VF, NH	Pl. Strip of 5	Pl. Strip of 3
2915A	32¢ Flag over Porch, 9.7		
	Pl# 66666,78777,		
	87888,87898,88888,		
	89878,89888,97898		
	99899,99999...............	8.95	7.50
2915B	32¢ Flag over Porch, 11.5		
	Pl# S11111	7.95	6.75
2915C	32¢ Flag over Porch, 10.9		
	PL# 55555,66666	7.95	6.75
2915D	32¢ Flag over Porch, 9.8,		
	Stamps Separate		
	Pl# 11111	7.95	6.75
3014-17	32¢ Santa & Children		
	Pl# V1111	(8)7.50	...
3018	32¢ Midnight Angel		
	Pl# B1111	6.95	5.75
3053	20¢ Blue Jay		
	Pl# S1111	4.65	3.95
3132	(25¢) Juke Box,		
	Linerless Pl #M11111.......	4.95	3.95
3133	32¢ Flags over Porch		
	Linerless Pl #M11111.......	5.50	4.25

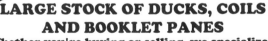

SELF-ADHESIVE PANES AND BOOKLETS

2490a

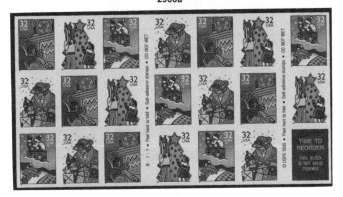

2960a

3116a

Scott N.	Description	F-VF,NH
2431a	25¢ Eagle & Shield (18)	
	Pl# A1111	15.95
2475a	25¢ Flag, Plastic (12)	9.95
2489a	29¢ Red Squirrel (18)	
	Pl# D11111,D22211,D23133	14.95
	Pl#D22221,D22222	18.95
2490a	29¢ Rose (18)	
	Pl# S111	14.95
2491a	29¢ Pine Cone (18)	
	Pl# B3-4,B6-7,B9-11,B13-14,B16.	14.95
	Pl# B2,B5,B8,B12,B15	16.75
	Pl# B1	18.75
2492a	32¢ Pink Rose (20)	
	Pl# S111,S112,S333	15.95
2492r	32¢ Die-Cut "Time to Reorder"	
	S444	16.75
2494a	32¢ Peach & Pear (20)	
	Pl# V11111,V11132, V12131, V12132, V12211, V22212, V22221,V33323, V33333, V33353, V44424, V44454	15.75
	Pl# V11131, V12221, V22222, V33142, V33143, V33243, V33343	19.75
2522a	(29¢) "F" Flag (12)	9.95
2531Ab	29¢ Liberty & Torch (18)	14.75
2531Av	29¢ Revised back	14.95
2595a	29¢ Eagle, Brown (17)	
	Pl# B1111-1,B1111-2,B3434-1 B4344-1,B4444-1,B4444-3	13.75
	Pl# B2226-1,B2222-2,B3333-1 B3333-3,B3434-3	17.50
2596a	29¢ Eagle, Green (17)	
	Pl# D11111,D21221,D22322, D32322,D54561,D54673	13.75
	Pl# D23322,D43352,D43452, D43453,D54563,D54571, D54573,D65784	15.95
	Pl# D32342,D61384	19.50
2597a	29¢ Eagle, Red (17)	
	Pl# S1111	13.75
2598a	29¢ Eagle (18)	
	Pl# M1111,M1112	13.75
2599a	29¢ Statue of Liberty (18)	
	Pl# D1111,D1212	13.75
2719a	29¢ Locomotive (18)	
	Pl# V11111	14.50
2802a	29¢ Christmas (12)	
	Pl# V111-1111,V222-1222, V222-2122,V222-2122,V222-2221, V222-2222,V333-3333	10.75
2803a	29¢ Snowman (18)	
	Pl# V11111	14.75
	Pl# V22222	17.50

Scott N.	Description	F-VF,NH
2813a	29¢ Love & Sunrise (18)	
	Pl# B111-1,B111-2,B111-3,B111-4, B121-5,B222-4,B222-5,B222-6, B333-9,B333-10,B333-11,B333-12, B333-17,B344-12,B344-13,B444-8, B444-9,B444-10,B444-13,B444-14, B444-15,B444-17,B444-18,B444-19, B555-20,B555-21	14.75
	Pl# B221-5,B444-7,B444-16	17.50
	Pl# B333-5,B333-7,B333-8	22.50
	Pl# B344-11	50.00
2873a	29¢ Santa Claus (12)	
	Pl# V1111	9.95
2874a	29¢ Cardinal in Snow (18)	
	Pl# V1111,V2222	13.95
2886a	(32¢) "G" Surface (18)	
	Pl# V11111,V22222	16.50
2887a	(32¢) "G" Overall (18)	
	No Plate Number	16.50
2919a	32¢ Flag over Field (18)	
	Pl# V1111	14.50
2920a	32¢ Flag over Porch, Large "1995"(20)	
	Pl# V12211,V12212,V12312,V12321, V12322,V13322,V22211,V23322, V23422,V45554,V56665	17.50
2920c	32¢ Flag over Porch, Small "1995"(20)	
	Pl# V11111	37.50
2920e	32¢ Flag over Porch, 11.3 (10)	
	Pl# V11111,V12111,V23222, V31121,V32111	7.50
2920f	32¢ Flag over Porch (15)	9.95
	BK226A $4.80 (1 Pane)	10.95
	BK227 $9.60 (2 Panes)	19.95
2921a	32¢ Flag over Porch, 9.8 (10)	
	Pl# P21221	8.50
	BK228 $6.40 (2 Panes)	16.00
2921b	32¢ Flag over Porch (5) No #	3.95
	BK227A $4.80,#2921a(1),2921b(1)	
	Pl# 11111	11.75
	BK228A $9.60,#2921a(2),2921b(2)	
	Pl# 11111	21.75
2949a	(32¢) Love & Cherub (20)	
	Pl# B1111-1,B2222-1 B2222-2,B3333-2	15.75
2960a	55¢ Love Cherub (20)	
	Pl# B1111-1,B2222-1	25.95
3011a	32¢ Santa & Children (20)	
	Pl# V1111,V1211,V1212, V3233,V3333,V4444	15.00
3012a	32¢ Midnight Angel (20)	
	Pl# B1111,B2222	15.00
3012c	32¢ Midnight Angel (15)	10.75
	BK233A $4.80(1)	10.75
	BK233B $9.60 (2 Panes)	21.75

Scott N.	Description	F-VF,NH
3013a	32¢ Children Sledding (20)	
	Pl# V1111	14.00
3030a	32¢ Love Cherub (20)	
	Pl#B1111-1,B1111-2 B2222-1,B2222-2	16.50
3030b	32¢ Love Cherub (15)	9.95
	BK235 $4.80 (1 Pane)	10.50
	BK236 $9.60 (2 Panes)	21.50
3048a	20¢ Blue Jay (10)	4.50
3049a	32¢ Yellow Rose (20)	
	Pl# S1111	13.95
3049b	32¢ Yellow Rose (4) No#	2.90
3049c	32¢ Yellow Rose (5)	
	Pl#S1111	3.60
3049d	32¢ Yellow Rose (6) No#	4.30
	BK241 $4.80 (1 ea. #3049b,c,d)	10.75
	BK242 $9.60 (5 #3049d)	21.00
3071a	32¢ Tennessee (20)	
	Pl# S11111	15.95
3089a	32¢ Iowa (20)	15.95
3112a	32¢ Madonna (20)	
	Pl# 11111	14.95
3116a	32¢ Family Scenes (20)	
	Pl# B3333	14.95
3117a	32¢ Skaters (18)	
	Pl# V1111	13.95
3122a	32¢ Liberty & Torch (20)	
	Pl# V2122	14.95
3122b	32¢ Liberty (4) No#	2.70
3122c	32¢ Liberty (5)	
	Pl# V1111	3.35
3122d	32¢ Liberty (6) No#	3.95
	BK259 $4.80 (1 ea. #3122b,c,d)	9.85
	BK260 $9.60 (5 #3122d)	19.50
3123a	32¢ Love & Swans (20)	
	Pl# B2222	14.95
3124a	55¢ Love & Swans (20)	
	Pl#B3333	24.95
3127c	32¢ Merian Botanical Prints (20) Pl# S11111	12.95
3128b	32¢ Merian Botanical (2 ea. 3128-29,1-3128a) Pl# S11111	3.50
3129b	32¢ Merian Botanical (5 (2 ea. 3128-29,1-3129a) Pl# S11111	3.75
	BK261 $4.80 #3128b (2), 3129b (1) Pl# S11111	10.50

BK58

BK113

Scott No.	Cover Value, Pane No. and Description(Number of Panes)	F-VF NH
1914 Flat Press, Perf. 10, Single-Line Wtmk.		
BK41	25¢ #424d,1¢ Washington (4)	275.00
BK42	97¢ #424d,1¢ Washington (16)	115.00
BK43	73¢ #424d,1¢(4) + #425e,2¢ (4)	300.00
BK44	25¢ #425e,2¢ Washington (2)	400.00
1916 Flat Press, Perf. 10, Unwatermarked		
BK47	25¢ #462a,1¢ Washington (4)	575.00
BK48	97¢ #462a 1¢ Washington(16)	425.00
BK50	25¢ #463a,2¢ Washington (2)	550.00
1917-23 Flat Press, Perforated 11		
BK53	25¢ #498e,1¢ Wash.,"POD"(4)	275.00
BK54	97¢ #498e,1¢ Washington(16)	65.00
BK55	25¢ #498e,1¢ "City Carrier"(4)	75.00
BK56	73¢ #498e,1¢(4) + #499e,2¢(4)	77.50
BK57	73¢ #498e,1¢(4) + #554c,2¢(4)	100.00
BK58	25¢ #499e,2¢ Washington (2)	225.00
BK59	49¢ #499e,2¢ Washington (4)	425.00
BK60	97¢ #499e,2¢ Washington(8)	575.00
BK62	37¢ #501b,3¢ Wash.,Type I(2)	575.00
BK63	37¢ #502b,3¢ Wash., Type II(2)	175.00
1923 Flat Press, Perforated 11		
BK66	25¢ #552a,1¢ Franklin(4)	65.00
BK67	97¢ #552a,1¢ Franklin(16)	550.00
BK68	73¢ #552a,1¢(4) + #554c,2¢(4)	100.00
BK69	25¢ #554a,2¢ Washington (2)	400.00
BK70	49¢ #554a,2¢ Washington (4)	110.00
1926 Rotary Press, Perforated 10		
BK72	25¢ #583a,2¢ Washington (2)	400.00
BK73	49¢ #583a,2¢ Washington (4)	550.00
1927-32 Rotary Press, Perf. 11 x 10½		
BK75	25¢ #632a,1¢ Franklin(4)	82.50
BK76	97¢ #632a,1¢ "P.O.D."cvr.(16)	565.00
BK77	97¢ #632a,1¢ "Postrider"cvr.(16)	550.00
BK79	73¢ #632a,1¢(4) + #634a,2¢(4) "Postrider" Cover	85.00
BK80	25¢ #634d,2¢ Washington (2)	9.00
BK81	49¢ #634d,2¢ Washington (4)	14.50
BK82	97¢ #634d,2¢ "Postrider"cvr.(8)	52.50
BK84	37¢ #720b,3¢ Washington (2)	115.00
BK85	73¢ #720b,3¢ Washington (4)	295.00
1939 Presidential Series - 3mm Gutters		
BK86	25¢ #804bv,1¢ Washington(4)	55.00
BK87	97¢ #804bv,1¢ Washington(16)	550.00
BK89	73¢ #804bv,1¢(4) + #806bv,2¢(4)	165.00
BK94	97¢ #806bv,2¢ John Adams(8)	
BK100	37¢ #807av,3¢ Jefferson(2)	95.00

Scott No.	Cover Value, Pane No. and Description(Number of Panes)	F-VF NH
1942 Presidential Series - 2½mm Gutters		
BK90	25¢ #804b,1¢ Washington(4)	9.00
BK91	97¢ #804b,1¢ "P.O.D."cvr(16)	550.00
BK92	73¢ #804b,1¢(4) + #806b,2¢(4) "Postrider" cover	32.50
BK93	73¢ #804b,1¢(4) + #806b,2¢(4)] "P.O. Seal" cover	40.00
BK96	25¢ #806b,2¢ Adams "Postrider"(2)	18.50
BK97	25¢ #806b,2¢ Adams "P.O.Seal"(2)	110.00
BK98	49¢ #806b,2¢ Adams "Postrider"(4)	65.00
BK99	49¢ #806b,2¢ Adams "P.O. Seal"(4)	60.00
BK102	37¢ #807a,3¢ Jefferson(2)	21.50
BK103	73¢ #807a,3¢ Jefferson(4)	45.00
1954-58 Liberty Series		
BK104	37¢ #1035a,3¢ Liberty, Wet(2)	20.00
BK104a	37¢ #1035f,3¢ Dry Printing(2)	22.50
BK105	73¢ #1035a,3¢ Liberty, Wet(4)	35.00
BK105a	73¢ #1035f,3¢ Dry Printing(4)	37.50
BK106	97¢ on 37¢ #1036a,4¢ Lincoln(4)	75.00
BK107	97¢ on 73¢ #1036a,4¢ Lincoln(4)	42.50
BK108	97¢ "Yellow" paper #1036a(4)	100.00
BK109	97¢ "Pink" paper #1036a(4)	14.50
1962-64 George Washington Issue		
BK110	$1 #1213a,5¢ Slog.1 "Mailman"(4)	35.00
BK111	$1 #1213a,5¢ Slogan 2 "Zone"(4) "Postrider" Cover	130.00
BK112	$1 #1213a,5¢ Slogan 2 "Zone"(4) "Mr. Zip" Cover	110.00
BK113	$1 #1213a,5¢ Slogan 3 "Zip"(4)	17.50
BK114	$1 #1213c,5¢ Tagged, Slogan 2(4)	350.00
BK115	$1 #1213c,5¢ Tagged, Slogan 3(4)	5.75
1967-78 Regular Issues		
BK116	$2 #1278a,1¢(1) + 1284b,6¢(4)	7.50
BK117	$1 #1280c,2¢(1) + #1284c,6¢(3)	6.00
BK117A	$3.60 #1288Bc,15¢ Holmes(3)	11.00
BK117B	$2 #1278a,1¢(1) + #1393a,6¢(4) "P.O. Seal" Cover	12.75
BK118	$2 #1278a,1¢(1) + #1393a,6¢(4) "Eisenhower" Cover	7.50
BK119	$2 #1278ae,1¢(1) + #1393ae,6¢(4) Dull Gum,"Eisenhower"Cover	7.25
BK120	$1 #1280a,2¢(1) + #1393b,6¢(3)	5.75
BK121	$1.92 #1395a,8¢ Eisenhower-8(3)	7.00
BK122	$1 #1278b,1¢(1) + #1395b,8¢(2)	4.75
BK123	$2 #1395c,8¢(1) + #1395d,8¢(3)	9.25
BK124	$1 #1510b,10¢ Jeff. Meml. - 5(2)	4.25
BK125	$4 #1510c,10¢ Jeff. Meml. - 8(5)	13.00
BK126	$1.25 #1510d,10¢(1)+#C79a,13¢(1)	9.75

Scott No.	Cover Value, Pane No. and Description(Number of Panes)	F-VF NH
1975-80 Regular Issues		
BK127	90¢ #1280c,2¢(1) +1595a,13¢(1)	3.95
BK128	$2.99 #1595b,13¢(1)+#1595c,13¢(2)	8.25
BK129	$1.30 #1595d,13¢ Liberty Bell-5(2)	5.50
BK130	$1.20 #1598a,15¢ Fort McHenry Flag-8(1)	5.25
BK131	$1 #1623a,9¢ + 13¢, Pf. 11x10½(1)	2.95
BK132	$1 #1623c,9¢ + 13¢, Perf. 10(1)	30.75
BK133	$3.60 #1736a,(15¢) "A"(3)	8.95
BK134	$2.40#1737a,15¢ Roses(2)	6.95
BK135	$3 #1742a,15¢ Windmills(2)	9.95
BK136	$4.32 #1819a,(18¢) "B"(3)	11.75
1981-83 Regular Issues		
BK137	$3.60 #1889a,18¢ Wildlife(2)	18.50
BK138	$1.20 #1893a,6¢ + 18¢ Flag(1)	3.75
BK139	$1.20 #1896a,20¢ Flag - S.C. -6(1)	3.50
BK140	$2 #1896b,20¢ Flag - S. Court - 10(1)	5.75
BK140A	$4 #1896b,20¢ Flag - S. Court - 10(2)	11.50
BK140B	$28.05 #1909a,$9.35 Exp. Mail(1)	83.50
BK141	$4#1948a,(20¢) "C"(2)	11.95
BK142	$4 #1949a,20¢ Bighorn Sheep(2)	14.50
BK142a	$4 #1949d,20¢ Sheep, Type II(2)	29.50
1985-89 Regular Issues		
BK143	$4.40 #2113a,(22¢) "D"(2)	21.50
BK144	$1.10 #2116a,22¢ Flag - Capitol(1)	5.00
BK145	$2.20 #2116a,22¢ Flag - Capitol(2)	10.00
BK146	$4.40 #2121a,22¢ Seashells(2) Multi-Seashells Cover (7 covers needed for all 25 shells)	12.75
BK147	$4.40 #2121a,22¢(2)"Beach"Cover	11.95
BK148	$32.25 #2122a,$10.75 Express Mail Type I(1)	82.50
BK149	$32.25 #2122c, Type II(1)	115.00
BK150	$5 #2182a, 25¢ Jack London-10(2)	13.50
BK151	$1.50 #2197a,25¢ Jack London-6(1)	4.75
BK152	$3 #2197a,25¢ Jack London-6(2)	9.25
1986 Commemoratives		
BK153	$1.76 #2201a,22¢ Stamp Coil(2)	5.50
BK153a	$1.76 #2201b Black Missing(2)	160.00
BK154	$2.20 #2209a,22¢ Fish(2)	17.75
1987-88 Regular Issues		
BK155	$2.20 #2274a,22¢ Sp. Occasions(1)	16.50
BK156	$4.40 #2276a,22¢ Flag-Fireworks(1)	12.00
BK157	$5 #2282a,(25¢) "E"(2)	16.00
BK158	$5 #2283a,25¢ Pheasant(2)	16.00
BK159	$5 #2283c Bluer sky(2)	170.00
BK160	$5 #2285b,25¢ Owl-Grosbeak(2)	13.50
BK161	$3 #2285Ac,25¢ Flag-Clouds(2)	8.50

BK215

BK191

BKC19

BK202

Scott No.	Cover Value, Pane No. and Description(Number of Panes)	F-VF NH
	1987-90 Commemoratives	
BK162	$4.40 #2359a,22¢ Constitution (4)	16.95
BK163	$4.40 #2366a,22¢ Locomotives (4)	15.95
BK164	$5 #2385a,25¢ Classic Cars(4)	39.95
BK165	$3 #2396a(1),2398a(1),	
	25¢ Special Occasions	10.00
BK166	$5 #2409a,25¢ Steamboats(4)	14.95
BK167	$5 #2427a,25¢ 1989 Madonna(2)	15.00
BK168	$5 #2429a,25¢ Sleigh(2)	16.50
BK169	$5 #2441a,25¢ Love,Doves(2)	14.95
	1990 Regular Issue	
BK170	$3 #2443a,15¢ Beach Umbrella(2)	8.75
	1990 Commemorative	
BK171	$5 #2474a,25¢ Lighthouses(4)	19.75
	1991-96 Flora and Fauna Regular Issues	
BK172	$2 #2483a,20¢ Blue Jay(1)	5.75
BK173	$2.90 #2484a,29¢ Duck,BEP(1)	8.50
BK174	$5.80 #2484a,29¢ Duck,BEP(2)	15.95
BK175	$5.80 #2485a,29¢ Duck,KCS(2)	17.50
BK176	$2.90 #2486a,29¢ African Violet(1)	8.50
BK177	$5.80 #2486a,29¢ African Violet(2)	16.95
BK178	$6.40 #2488a,32¢ Peach-Pear(2)	16.95
BK178B	$9.60 #2492e (1), 2492f(1),	
	32¢ Pink Rose	22.95
	1990 Commemoratives	
BK179	$5 #2505a,25¢ Indian Headdress(2)	17.95
BK180	$5 #2514a,25¢ Madonna(2)	15.95
BK181	$5 #2516a,25¢ Christmas Tree(2)	17.95
	1991 Regular Issues	
BK182	$2.90 #2519a,(29¢) "F",BEP(1)	8.50
BK183	$5.80 #2519a,(29¢) "F",BEP(2)	17.00
BK184	$2.90 #2520a,(29¢) "F",KCS(1)	27.50
BK185	$5.80 #2527a,29¢ Flower(2)	16.50
BK186	$2.90 #2528a,29¢ Olympic(1)	8.00
BK186A	$2.90 #2528a, WCSE Ticket Cover	11.95
BK187	$3.80 #2530a,19¢ Balloons(2)	9.50
	1991 Commemoratives	
BK188	$5.80 #2536a,29¢ Love(2)	16.95
BK189	$5.80 #2549a,29¢ Fishing Flies(4)	21.95
BK190	$5.80 #2552a,29¢ Desert Storm(2)	16.95
BK191	$5.80 #2566a,29¢ Comedians(2)	16.95
BK192	$5.80 #2577a,29¢ Space(2)	17.50
	1991 Commemoratives (cont.)	
BK193	$5.80 #2578a,(29¢) Madonna(2)	16.95
BK194	$5.80 #2581b-85a,(29¢) Santa	
	& Chimney(5 Panes, 1 each)	25.00

Scott No.	Cover Value, Pane No. and Description(Number of Panes)	F-VF NH
	1992-93 Regular Issues	
BK195	$2.90 #2593a,29¢ Pledge,Pf.10(1)	9.95
BK196	$5.80 #2593a,29¢ Pledge,Pf.10(2)	14.95
BK197	$5.80 #2593c,29¢ Perf. 11x10(2)	23.95
BK198	$2.90 #2594a,29¢ Pledge, Red(1)	10.95
BK199	$5.80 #2594a,29¢ Pledge, Red(2)	15.75
	1992 Commemoratives	
BK201	$5.80 #2646a 29¢ Hummingbirds(4)	17.95
BK202	$5.80 #2709a,29¢ Wild Animals(4)	18.95
BK202A	$5.80 #2710a,29¢ Madonna(2)	15.95
BK203	$5.80 #2718a,29¢ Toys(5)	18.75
	1993 Commemoratives	
BK204	$5.80 #2737a(2),2737b(1)	
	29¢ Rock'n Roll, Rythym & Blues	17.50
BK207	$5.80 #2745a,29¢ Space Fantasy(4)	17.95
BK208	$5.80 #2764a,29¢ Garden Flowers(4)	17.95
BK209	$5.80 #2770a,29¢ Broadway(5)	17.50
BK210	$5.80 #2778a,29¢ Country Music(5)	17.50
BK211	$5.80 #2790a,29¢ Madonna(5)	17.50
BK212	$5.80 #2798a(1),2798b(1)	
	29¢ Christmas Designs	18.95
BK213	$2.90 #2806b,29¢ AIDS(2)	8.95
	1994 Commemoratives	
BK214	$5.80 #2814a,29¢ Love & Dove(2)	15.95
BK215	$5.80 #2833a,29¢ Garden Flowers(4)	16.95
BK216	$5.80 #2847a,29¢ Locomotives(4)	16.95
BK217	$5.80 #2871b,29¢ Madonna(2)	15.50
BK218	$5.80 #2872a,29¢ Stocking(1)	16.50
	1994 "G" Regular Issues	
BK219	$3.20 #2881a,(32¢) BEP,Pf.11(1)	8.95
BK220	$3.20 #2883a,(32¢) BEP,Pf.10(1)	8.95
BK221	$6.40 #2883a,(32¢)BEP,Pf.10(2)	17.95
BK222	$6.40 #2884a,(32¢) ABN,Blue(2)	17.95
BK223	$6.40 #2885a,(32¢)KCS,Red(2)	17.95
	1995-97 Regular Issues	
BK225	$3.20 #2916a,32¢ Flag-Porch(1)	7.95
BK226	$6.40 #2916a,32¢ Flag-Porch(2)	13.95
BK226A	$4.80 #2920f 32¢ Flag-Porch (1)	9.95
BK227	$9.60 #2920f 32¢ Flag-Porch (2)	17.95
BK227A	$4.80 #2921a(1), 2921b(1)	
	32¢ Flag-Porch	11.50
BK228	$6.40 2921a 32¢ Flag-Porch (2)	14.95
BK228A	$9.60 2921a 32¢ Flag-Porch (3)	22.50
	1995 Commemoratives	
BK229	$6.40 #2959a,32¢ Love (2)	15.95
BK230	$6.40 #2973a,32¢ Great Lakes	
	Lighthouses(4)	15.75
BK231	$6.40 #2997a,32¢ Garden Flowers(4)	15.75

Scott No.	Cover Value, Pane No. and Description(Number of Panes)	F-VF NH
	1995 Commemoratives (cont.)	
BK232	$6.40 #3003a,32¢ Madonna(2)	14.95
BK233	$6.40 #3007a(1),3007b(1),	
	32¢ Santa & Children	14.95
	1996 Commemoratives	
BK234	$6.40 #3029a,32¢ Winter	
	Garden Flowers(4)	14.95
BK235	$4.80 3030b 32¢ Love (1)	9.95
BK236	$9.60 3030b 32¢ Love (2)	19.85
	1996-97 Issues	
BK241	$4.80 3049b (1), 3049c (1), 3049d (1)	
	32¢ Yellow Rose	10.75
BK242	$9.60 3049c 32¢ Yellow Rose (5)	17.95
BK259	$4.80 3122b (1), 3122c (1), 3122d (1)	
	32¢ Statue of Liberty	10.75
BK260	$9.60 3122c 32¢ Statue of Liberty(5)	17.95
BK261	$4.80 3128b (2), 3129b (1),	
	32¢ Merian Botanical Prints	10.75
	1927-60 Airmail Issues	
BKC1	61¢ #C10a.10¢ Lindbergh(2)	265.00
BKC2	37¢ #C25a,6¢ Transport(2)	8.50
BKC3	73¢ #C25a,6¢ Transport(4)	16.75
BKC4	73¢ #C39a,6¢ Small Plane, Wet(2)	25.00
BKC4a	73¢ #C39c,6¢ Small Plane, Dry(2)	49.50
BKC5	85¢ on 73¢ #C51a,7¢ Blue Jet(2)	45.00
BKC6	85¢ #C51a,7¢ Blue Jet(2)	29.50
BKC7	85¢ #C60a,7¢ Red Jet(2),Blue Cvr.	30.00
BKC8	85¢ #C60a,7¢ Red Jet(2),Red Cvr.	40.00
	1962-64 Jet over Capitol	
BKC9	80¢ #C64b,8¢ Slog.1,"Mailman"(2)	15.00
BKC10	$2 #C64b,8¢ Slog.1,"Mailman"(5)	25.00
BKC11	80¢ #C64b,8¢ Slogan 3,"Zip"(2)	25.00
BKC12	$2 #C64b,8¢ Slogan 2, "Zone"(5)	
	"Wings" Cover	385.00
BKC13	$2 #C64b,8¢ Slog.2(5) Mr. Zip Cvr.	375.00
BKC15	$2 #C64b,8¢ Slogan 3, "Zip"(5)	100.00
BKC16	80¢ #C64c,8¢ Tagged Slogan 3(2)	38.75
BKC18	$2 #C64c,8¢ Tagged, Sl.3,Pink(5)	395.00
BKC19	$2 #C64c,8¢ Tagged, Sl.3,Red(5)	8.50
	1968-73 Airmail Issues	
BKC20	$4 #C72c,10¢ 50-Star Runway-8(5)	12.00
BKC21	$1 #C72c,10¢ 50-Star Runway-5(2)	8.95
BKC22	$1 #1280c,2¢(1) + #C78a,11¢(2)	4.75
BKC23	$1.25 #1510d,10¢(1)+#C79a,13¢(1)	7.50
	1965-81 Postal Insurance Booklets	
QI1	(10¢) "Insured P.O.D. V"	125.00
QI2w	(20¢) "Insured U.S.Mail" White Cvr.	6.00
QI2b	(20¢) "Insured U.S.Mail" Black Cvr.	4.50
QI3	(40¢) "Insured U.S.Mail" Black	4.00
QI4	(50¢) "Insured U.S.Mail" Green	3.50
QI5	(45¢) "Insured U.S.Mail" Red	4.50

Scott N.	Description	F-VF,NH
2409a	25¢ Steamboats, Pl#1	8.25
	Pl# 2	22.50
2427a	25¢ Madonna (10) Pl# 1	15.00
2429a	25¢ Sleigh (10) Pl# 1111	8.25
	Pl#2111..............................	12.75
2441a	25¢ Love (10), Pl# 1211	55.00
2474a	25¢ Lighthouse (5) Pl# 3,5	6.95
	Pl# 1,2................................	8.95
2483a	20¢ Blue Jay (10) Pl#S1111......	6.95
2484a	29¢ Wood Duck, BEP(10) Pl#1111	10.95
2485a	29¢ Wood Duck, KCS (10)	
	Pl#K11111..........................	12.75
2486a	29¢ African Violet (10) Pl# K1111	9.95
2488a	32¢ Peach & Pear (10) Pl#11111	9.95
	Pl# 1111 Without Perf. Hole..	11.95
2505a	25¢ Indian Headresses (10)	
	Pl# 1,2..............................	14.95
2514a	25¢ Madonna (10) Pl# 1	14.95
2516a	25¢ Christmas Tree (10) Pl#1211	18.95
2527a	29¢ Flower (10) Pl# K1111........	9.75
2528a	29¢ Olympic Rings (10) Pl# K11111	9.50
2530a	19¢ Hot-Air Balloons (10) Pl# 1111	6.95
2536a	29¢ Love (10) Pl# 1111,1112	9.95
2549a	29¢ Fishing Flies (5) Pl# A23213	9.75
	Pl# A23133............................	13.50
	Pl# A23124............................	57.50
	pl# A33225,A33233..............	27.50
2552a	29¢ Desert Storm (5)	
	Pl# A11121111.....................	6.50
2566a	29¢ Comedians (10) Pl#1..........	10.75
2577a	29¢ Space (10) Pl# 111111......	10.75
2578a	(29¢) Madonna (10) Pl# 1	10.75
2581b-85a	(29¢) Santa, set of 5	
	Panes of 4, Pl# A11111	35.00
2593a	29¢ Pledge, black (10) Pl# 1111	8.75
2594a	29¢ Pledge, red (10) Pl# K1111	9.95
2646a	29¢ Hummingbirds (5)	
	Pl# A2212112,A2212122,A2222222	5.50
	Pl# A1111111, A2212222..........	9.95

2833a

Scott N.	Description	F-VF,NH
2709a	29¢ Wild Animals (5) Pl# K1111	6.00
2710a	29¢ Madonna (10)Pl#1	10.75
2718a	29¢ Toys (4) Pl# A111111,	
	A222222................................	4.75
2737a	29¢ Rock'n Roll (8) Pl#A22222	8.95
2737b	29¢ Rock'n Roll (4) Pl#A22222	4.95
2745a	29¢ Space Fantasy (5)	
	Pl# 1111,1211.....................	5.50
2764a	29¢ Garden Flowers (5) Pl# 1.	5.50
2770a	29¢ Broadway Musicals (4)	
	Pl# A11121,A22222	4.95
	Pl# A11111.........................	7.95
2778a	29¢ Country Music (4)	
	Pl# A222222......................	4.95
2790a	29¢ Madonna (4)	
	Pl# K1-11111, K1-44444	4.95
	Pl# K1-33333.....................	7.50
2798a	29¢ 3 Snowmen (10) Pl#111111	11.75

Scott N.	Description	F-VF,NH
2798b	29¢ 2 Snowmen (10) Pl#111111	11.75
2806b	29¢ AIDS (5) Pl# K111............	5.75
2814a	29¢ Love & Dove (10) Pl# A11111	8.95
2833a	29¢ Garden Flowers (5) Pl# 2.	5.50
2847a	29¢ Locomotives (5) Pl# S11111	5.50
2871b	29¢ Madonna (10) Pl# 1,2	8.95
2872a	29¢ Stocking (20)	
	Pl# P11111,P44444	19.50
	Pl# P22222,P33333	27.50
2916a	32¢ Flag over Porch (10)	
	Pl# 11111	9.75
2959a	32¢ Love Cherub (10) Pl# 1	9.95
2973a	32¢ Great Lakes Lighthouses (5)	
	Pl# S11111........................	4.95
2997a	32¢ Garden Flowers (5) Pl# 2.	5.25
3003b	32¢ Madonna (10) Pl# 1	9.50
3007b	32¢ Santa (10) Pl# P11111.....	9.50
3007c	32¢ Santa (10) Pl# P11111.....	9.50
3029a	32¢ Garden Flowers (5) Pl# 1.	4.95

U.S. AUTOPOST ISSUES
Computer Vended Postage

Type I

Type II

Washington, D.C., Machine 82	
CV1a	25¢ First Class, Ty. 1 ...
CV2a	$1.00 3rd Class, Ty. 1 ....
CV3a	$1.69 Parcel Post, Ty. 1..
CV4a	$2.40 Priority Mail, Ty. 1 ...
CV5a	$8.75 Express Mail, Ty. 1..
Set of 5 .... **$95.00**	

Kensington, MD, Machine 82	
CV11a	25¢ First Class, Ty. 1 ...
CV12a	$1.00 3rd Class, Ty. 1 .....
CV13a	$1.69 Parcel Post, Ty. 2..
CV14a	$2.40 Priority Mail, Ty. 1 .
CV15a	$8.75 Express Mail, Ty. 1
Set of 5 .... **$67.50**	

Washington, D.C., Machine 83	
CV6a	25¢ First Class, Ty. 1 ...
CV7a	$1.00 3rd Class, Ty. 1 ....
CV8a	$1.69 Parcel Post, Ty. 2..
CV9a	$2.40 Priority Mail, Ty. 1 ...
CV10a	$8.75 Express Mail, Ty. 1 .
Set of 5 .... **$67.50**	

Kensington, MD, Machine 83	
CV16a	25¢ First Class, Ty. 1 ......
CV17a	$1.00 3rd Class, Ty. 1
CV18a	$1.69 Parcel Post, Ty. 2..
CV19a	$2.40 Priority Mail, Ty. 1
CV20a	$8.75 Express Mail, Ty. 1
Set of 5 .... **$67.50**	

CV31,CV31a **CV32,CV33**

1992-96 Variable Rate Coils

Scott's No.		Pl# Strip of 5	Pl# Strip of 3	F-VF NH	F-VF Used
CV31	29¢ Shield, horiz.design, Dull Gum	10.75	9.75	1.50	.50
CV31a	29¢ Shield, Shiny Gum	10.75	9.75	1.50	...
CV31b	32¢ Shield, Dull Gum (1995)........	14.75	12.75	1.50	.50
CV31c	32¢ Shield, Shiny Gum (1995)......	13.75	11.75	1.50	...
CV32	29¢ Shield, vertical design (1994)	9.75	8.75	1.00	.50
CV33	32¢ Shield, Vertical Design ('96)..	9.75	8.75	.95	.50

NOTE: #CV31- CV32 come in a number different denominations but the first class rate of 29¢ and 32¢ are the only rates regularly available.

U.S. TEST COILS

11 etc. **31etc.** **41 etc.** **SV1**

Scott's No.		Line Pair	Pair	F-VF Used
	Blank Coils			
11	Imperforate.....................................	...	55.00	27.50
15	Perforated 10, Shiny Gum............	...	1.00	.50
16	Perforated, 10½	...	3.50	1.75
17	Perforated 11	...	9.00	4.50
18	Perf. 10, Tagged, Dull Gum	65.00	11.50	5.75
21	Perf. 10, Two Horiz. Red Lines	...	2.80	1.40
	1938-60 Solid Design Coil			
31	Purple...	30.00	11.00	5.50
32	Carmine (1954)	...	...	...
33	Red Violet, Large Holes (1960)....	25.00	6.00	3.00
33s	Red Violet, Small Holes	...	10.00	5.00
	1962-88 "FOR TESTING PURPOSES ONLY"			
41	Black, untagged, shiny gum	6.75	2.20	1.10
41a	Black, tagged, shiny gum	5.50	1.60	.80
41b	Black, tagged, pebble-surfaced gum	5.50	1.60	.80
41d	Black, tagged, dull gum...............	19.50	11.00	5.50
41e	Black, untagged, dull gum............	8.75	2.20	1.10
42	Carmine, tagged (1970)	...	...	...
43	Green, tagged	...	170.00	85.00
43c	Green, untagged	...	170.00	85.00
44	Brown, untagged	32.50	4.00	2.00
45	Black, "B" Press, 19mm wide (1988)	...	1.70	.85

STAMP VENTURERS TEST COILS

SV1	Eagle, Perforated	...	2.20	1.10
SV2	Eagle, Rouletted...........................	...	6.50	3.25

MODERN ERRORS

Due to the increasing popularity of modern errors, listings of this nature, formerly scattered throughout the catalogue, have been consolidated in an effort to provide a more useful format. Several new listings have been included as well.

While the listing is not intended to be complete, additions will be considered for subsequent editions of this catalogue.

1519a   **1895a**

IMPERFORATE MAJOR ERRORS

Scott's No.		F-VF NH
525c	1¢ Washington, horiz. pair, Imperf. Between	95.00
554a	2¢ Washington, horiz. pair, Imperf. Vert.	225.00
744a	5¢ Yellowstone, horiz. pair, imperf. vert	550.00
805b	1.5¢ M. Washington, horiz. pair, imperf. between	170.00
805b	1.5¢ M. Washington, horiz. pair, imperf. between, precancelled	25.00
899b	1¢ Defense, Horizontal Pair, Imperf. Between	45.00
900a	2¢ Defense, Horizontal Pair, Imperf. Between	47.50
901a	3¢ Defense, Horizontal Pair, Imperf. Between	32.50
966a	3¢ Palomar, vert. pair, imperf. between	625.00
1055b	2¢ Jefferson, coil pair, imperf., precancelled	500.00
1055c	2¢ Jefferson, coil pair, imperf.	600.00
1058a	4¢ Lincoln, Coil Pair, Imperf	115.00
1058a	4¢ Same, Line Pair.	225.00
1059Ac	25¢ Revere, Coil Pair, Imperf.	50.00
1059Ac	Same, Line Pair.	90.00
1125a	4¢ San Martin, Horizontal Pair, Imperf. between	1350.00
1138a	4¢ McDowell, Vert. Pair, Imperf. between.	450.00
1138b	4¢ McDowell, vert. pair, imperf. horizontal	325.00
1151a	4¢ SEATO, vertical pair, imperf. between	175.00
1229b	5¢ Washington, Coil Pair, Imperf	350.00
1297a	3¢ Parkman, Coil Pair, Imperf	27.50
1297a	Same, Line Pair.	55.00
1297c	Same, Precancelled	10.00
1297c	Same, Precancelled, Line Pair	25.00
1299b	1¢ Jefferson, Coil Pair, Imperf.	30.00
1299b	Same, Line Pair.	65.00
1303b	4¢ Lincoln, Coil Pair, Imperf.	895.00
1304b	5¢ Washington, Coil Pair Imperf	200.00
1304e	Same, Precancelled	425.00
1305a	6¢ FDR, Coil Pair, Imperf	95.00
1305a	Same, Line Pair.	150.00
1305Eg	15¢ Holmes, Coil Pair, Imperf	40.00
1305Eg	Same, Line Pair.	100.00
1305Ej	Holmes, Type II, Dry Gum, Coil Pair, Imperf	85.00
1305Ej	Same, Line Pair.	300.00
1338k	6¢ Flag, vert. pair, imperf. between	550.00
1338Ab	6¢ Flag, Coil Pair, Imperf.	500.00
1338De	6¢ Flag, horiz. pair, imperf. between	165.00
1338Fi	8¢ Flag, Vert. Pair, Imperf	50.00
1338Fj	8¢ Flag, horiz. pair, imperf. between	45.00
1338Gh	8¢ Flag, Coil Pair.	60.00
1355b	6¢ Disney, Vert. Pair, imperf. horiz	875.00
1355c	6¢ Disney, Imperf. Pair.	900.00
1362a	6¢ Waterfowl, vertical pair, imperf. between	600.00
1363b	6¢ Christmas, imperf. pair, tagged	250.00
1363d	6¢ Christmas, imperf. pair, untagged.	350.00
1370a	6¢ Grandma Moses, horiz. pair, imperf. between	265.00
1402a	8¢ Eisenhower, Coil Pair, Imperf	60.00
1402a	Same, Line Pair.	95.00
1484a	8¢ Gershwin, vert. pair, imperf. horiz	265.00
1485a	8¢ Jefferson, vert. pair, imperf. horiz	275.00
1487a	8¢ Cathers, vert. pair, imperf. horiz	300.00
1503a	8¢ Johnson, horiz. pair, imperf. vert	325.00
1508a	8¢ Christmas, vert. pair, imperf. between	400.00
1509a	10¢ Flags, Horiz. Pair, Imperf. Between	55.00
1510e	10¢ Jefferson Memorial, Vert. Pair, imperf. horiz	475.00
1518b	6.3¢ Bell Coil Pair, Imperf	300.00
1518b	Same, Line Pair.	675.00
1518c	Same, Precancelled Pair.	125.00
1518c	Same, Line Pair.	325.00
1519a	10¢ Flag Coil Pair, Imperf.	42.50
1520b	10¢ Jefferson Memorial, Coil Pair, Imperf	45.00
1520b	Same, Line Pair.	80.00
1563a	10¢ Lexington-Concord, vert. pair, imperf. horiz	500.00
1579a	10¢ Madonna, Imperf. Pair.	125.00
1580a	10¢ Prang, Imperf. Pair.	125.00
1596a	13¢ Eagle & Shield, Imperf. Pair.	50.00
1597a	15¢ Flag (from Sheet), Imperf. Pair.	20.00
1615b	7.9¢ Drum, Coil, Pair, Imperf.	650.00
1615Ce	8.4¢ Piano, Coil, Precancelled Pr., Imperf. Between	55.00
1615Cf	8.4¢ Piano, Coil, Precancelled Pair, Imperf.	17.50
1615Cf	Same, Line Pair.	35.00
1616a	9¢ Capitol, Coil Pair, Imperf. (VG)	75.00
1616a	Same, Line Pair (VG)	175.00
1616a	Same, Pair F-VF.	180.00

IMPERFORATE MAJOR ERRORS (cont.)

Scott's No.		F-VF NH
1616a	Same, Line Pair F-VF	475.00
1617b	10¢ Petition, Coil Pair, Imperf	65.00
1617b	Same, Line Pair.	150.00
1617bv	Same, Pair, dull finish gum	65.00
1618b	13¢ Liberty Bell, Coil Pair, Imperf	30.00
1618b	Same, Line Pair.	75.00
1618Cd	15¢ Flag, Coil Pair, Imperf.	25.00
1618Ce	Same, Strip of 4, middle pair imperf. between	175.00
1622a	13¢ Flag, Horiz. Pair, Imperf. Between	50.00
1622d	Same, Imperf. Pair	175.00
1625a	13¢ Flag, Coil Pair, Imperf.	25.00
1695-98b	13¢ Winter Olympics, Imperf. Block of 4	850.00
1699a	13¢ Maass, horiz. pair, imperf. vert	425.00
1701a	13¢ Nativity, Imperf. Pair.	125.00
1702a	13¢ Currier & Ives, Imperf. Pair.	135.00
1703a	13¢ Currier & Ives, Imperf. Pair.	135.00
1704a	13¢ Princeton, Horiz. Pair, Imperf. Vert	550.00
1711a	13¢ Colorado, Horiz. Pair, Imperf. between	535.00
1711a	13¢ Colorado, Horizontal Pair, Imperf. Vertically	950.00
1729a	13¢ G.W. at Valley Forge, Imperf. Pair	90.00
1730a	13¢ Christmas Mailbox, Imperf. Pair.	295.00
1734a	13¢ Indian Head Penny, Horiz. Pair, Imperf. Vert	350.00
1735a	(15¢) "A" Eagle, Vert. Pair, Imperf.	95.00
1735b	(15¢) "A" Eagle, Vert. Pair, Imperf. horiz.	675.00
1743a	(15¢) "A" Eagle, Coil Pair, Imperf.	100.00
1768a	15¢ Christmas Madonna, Imperf. Pair.	100.00
1769a	15¢ Hobby Horse, Imperf. Pair.	125.00
1783-86b	15¢ Flora, Block of 4, Imperf	675.00
1787a	15¢ Seeing Eye Dog, Imperf. Pair.	475.00
1789c	Same, Perf. 12, vert. pair, imperf. horiz.	210.00
1789d	Same, Perf. 11, vert. pair, imperf. horiz.	165.00
1799a	15¢ 1979 Madonna & Child, Imperf. Pair.	110.00
1801a	15¢ Will Rogers, Imperf. Pair.	275.00
1804a	15¢ B. Banneker, Horiz. Pair, Imperf. Vert.	850.00
1811a	1¢ Quill Pen, Coil Pair, Imperf.	175.00
1811a	Same, Line Pair.	325.00
1813b	3.5¢ Violin, Coil Pair, Imperf. (VG)	120.00
1813b	Same, F-VF.	265.00
1813b	Same, F-VF Line Pair.	450.00
1816b	12¢ Torch, Coil Pair, Imperf	200.00
1816b	Same, Line Pair.	400.00
1820a	(18¢) "B" Eagle, Coil Pair, Imperf	120.00
1823a	15¢ Bissell, vert. pair, imperf. horiz	400.00
1825a	15¢ Veterans, horiz. pair, imperf. vert	525.00
1831a	15¢ Organized Labor, Imperf. Pair.	390.00
1833a	15¢ Learning, horiz. pair, imperf. vert.	265.00
1842a	15¢ 1980 Madonna, Imperf. Pair.	100.00
1843a	15¢ Toy Drum, Imperf. Pair.	100.00
1844a	1¢ Dorothea Dix, Imperf. Pair.	400.00
1856a	14¢ S. Lewis, Vert. Pair, Imperf. Horiz	175.00
1856b	14¢ S. Lewis, Horizontal Pair, Imperf. Between.	12.50
1867a	39¢ Clark, vert. pair, imperf. horiz	675.00
1890a	18¢ "Amber" Flag, Imperf. Pair.	120.00
1891a	18¢ "Shining Sea", Coil Pair, Imperf	22.50
1893b	6¢/18¢ Booklet, Imperf. Vertical Between, Perfs at Left	95.00
1894a	20¢ Flag, Vert. Pair, Imperf	50.00
1895a	20¢ Flag, Coil Pair, Imperf.	12.50
1897b	1¢ Omnibus, Imperf. Pair	750.00
1897Ae	2¢ Locomotive, Coil Pair, Imperf	50.00
1898Ac	4¢ Stagecoach, Imperf. Pair, Precancelled	750.00
1898Ad	4¢ Stagecoach, Imperf. Pair.	850.00
1901b	5.9¢ Bicycle, Precancelled Coil Pair, Imperf.	225.00
1903b	9.3¢ Mail Wagon, Precancelled Coil Pair, Imperf.	150.00
1904b	10.9¢ Hansom Cab, Prec. Coil Pair, Imperf.	175.00
1906b	17¢ Electric Car, Coil Pair, Imperf.	190.00
1906c	Same, Precancelled Coil Pair, Imperf.	875.00
1907a	18¢ Surrey, Coil Pair, Imperf.	135.00
1908a	20¢ Firepumper, Coil Pair, Imperf.	125.00
1908a	Same, Line Pair.	325.00
1927a	18¢ Alcoholism, Imperf. Pair.	400.00
1934a	18¢ Remington, vert. pair, imperf. between	265.00
1939a	20¢ 1981 Madonna, Imperf. Pair.	115.00
1940a	20¢ Teddy Bear, Imperf. Pair.	275.00
1949b	20¢ Ram Bklt. (2 Panes) Vert. Imperf. Btwn., Perfs at Left	175.00
1951b	20¢ Love, Imperf. Pair.	325.00
2003a	20¢ Netherlands, Imperf. Pair.	375.00
2005a	20¢ Consumer, Coil Pair, Imperf	120.00
2015a	20¢ Libraries, vert. pair, imperf. horiz	350.00
2024a	20¢ Ponce de Leon, Imperf. Pair.	650.00
2025a	13¢ Christmas, Imperf. Pair.	675.00
2026a	20¢ Madonna & Child, Imperf. Pair.	160.00
2039a	20¢ Voluntarism, Imperf. Pair.	850.00
2044a	20¢ Joplin, Imperf. Pair.	500.00
2064a	20¢ 1983 Santa Claus, Imperf. Pair.	185.00
2072a	20¢ Love, horiz. pair, imperf. vert.	200.00
2092a	20¢ Waterfowl, horiz. pair, imperf. vert.	475.00
2096a	20¢ Smokey Bear, horiz. pair, imperf. between	350.00
2096b	Same, vert. pair, imperf. between.	250.00
2104a	20¢ Family Unity, horiz. pair, imperf. vert.	600.00
2108a	20¢ Santa Claus, Horiz. Pair, Imperf. Vert.	975.00
2111a	(22¢) "D" Eagle, Vert. Pair, Imperf	65.00
2112a	(22¢) "D" Eagle, Coil Pair, Imperf.	57.50
2115a	22¢ Flag, Coil Pair, Imperf.	14.00
2126b	6¢ Tricycle, Precancelled Coil Pair, Imperf	225.00
2130b	10.1¢ Oil Wagon, Black Precancel, Coil Pair, Imperf	125.00

Scott's No.		F-VF NH
2130b var	10.1¢ Oil Wagon, Red Precancel, Coil Pair, Imperf	20.00
2133b	12.5¢ Pushcart, Precancelled Coil Pair, Imperf	50.00
2134a	14¢ Iceboat, Coil Pair, Imperf	125.00
2135a	17¢ Dogsled, Coil Pair, Imperf. Miscut	650.00
2136a	25¢ Bread Wagon, Coil Pair, Imperf	15.00
2142a	22¢ Winter Olympics, vert. pair, imperf. horiz	700.00
2146a	22¢ A. Adams, Imperf. Pair	325.00
2165a	22¢ 1985 Madonna, Imperf. Pair	120.00
2166a	22¢ Poinsettia, Imperf. Pair	150.00
2210a	22¢ Public Hospitals, vert. pair, imperf. horiz	325.00
2228b	4¢ Stagecoach "B" Press, Coil Pair, Imperf	350.00
2259a	13.2¢ Coal Car, Coil Pair, Imperf	110.00
2261a	16.7¢ Popcorn Wagon Pair, Imperf	250.00
2263a	20¢ Cable Car, Coil Pair, Imperf	95.00
2265a	21¢ Railway Car, Coil Pair, Imperf	80.00
2279a	(25¢) "E" Earth, Coil Pair, Imperf	100.00
2280a	25¢ Flag Over Yosemite, Coil Pair, Block Tagged, Imperf	25.00
2280a var	25¢ Flag Over Yosemite, Coil Pair, Prephosphor paper, Impf	15.00
2281a	25¢ Honeybee Coil, Imperf. Pair	70.00
2440a	25¢ Love, Imperf. Pair	900.00
2451a	4¢ Steam Carriage, Imperf. Pair	750.00
2453a	5¢ Canoe, Coil Pair, Imperf	425.00
2457a	10¢ Tractor Trailer, Coil Pair, Imperf	550.00
2464a	23¢ Lunch Wagon, Coil Pair, Imperf	200.00
2517a	(29¢) Flower, Imperf. Pair	800.00
2518a	(29¢) "F" Coil, Imperf. Pair	37.50
2521a	4¢ Non-denominated, vert. pair, imperf. horiz	150.00
2523b	29¢ Mt. Rushmore, Coil Pair, Imperf	25.00
2550a	29¢ Cole Porter, vert. pair, imperf. horiz	675.00
2579a	(29¢) Santa in Chimney, horiz. pair, imperf. vertically	500.00
2579b	(29¢) Santa in Chimney, Vert. Pair, Imperf. Horiz	600.00
2594b	29¢ Pledge Allegiance, Imperf. Pair	950.00
2603a	(10¢) Eagle & Shield, Coil Pair, Imperf	35.00
2607c	23¢ USA Pre-sort, Coil Pair, Imperf	110.00
2609a	29¢ Flag over White House, Coil Pair, Imperf	20.00
2609b	Same, Pair, Imperf. Between	95.00
2897a	32¢ Flag over Porch, Imperf. Pair	325.00
2902a	(5¢) Butte Coil Imperf. Pair	950.00
2913a	32¢ Flag over Porch Coil, Imperf. Pair	65.00

AIRMAILS & SPECIAL DELIVERY

C23a	6¢ Eagle Vertical Pair, Imperf. Horizontal	350.00
C73a	10¢ Stars, Coil Pair, Imperf	850.00
C82a	11¢ Jet, Coil Pair, Imperf	350.00
C82a	Same, Line Pair	450.00
C83a	13¢ Winged Env., Coil Pair, Imperf	110.00
C83a	Same, Line Pair	185.00
C113	33¢ Verville, Imperf. Pair	850.00
C115	44¢ Transpacific, Imperf. Pair	850.00
E15c	10¢ Motorcycle, horiz. pair, imperf. between	325.00

COLOR ERRORS & VARIETIES

499 var.	2¢ Washington, "Boston Lake", with PFC	175.00
1895 var.	20¢ Flag, Blue "Supreme Court" color var	175.00
2115 var.	22¢ Flag, Blue "Capitol Bldg." color var	12.00
C23c	6¢ Ultramarine & Carmine	200.00

COLOR OMITTED - MAJOR ERRORS

1271a	5¢ Florida, ochre omitted	500.00
1331-32 var.	5¢ Space Twins, red stripes of capsule flag omitted, single in block of 9	195.00
1355a	6¢ Disney, ochre omitted	750.00
1362b	6¢ Waterfowl, red & dark blue omitted	1050.00
1363c	6¢ Christmas, 1968, light yellow omitted	95.00
1370b	6¢ Grandma Moses, black and prussian blue omitted	950.00
1381a	6¢ Baseball, black omitted	1250.00
1384c	6¢ Christmas, 1969, light green omitted	20.00
1414b	6¢ Christmas, 1970, black omitted	700.00
1420a	6¢ Pilgrims, orange & yellow omitted	975.00
1432a	8¢ Revolution, gray & black omitted	795.00
1436a	8¢ Emily Dickinson, black & olive omitted	1000.00
1444a	8¢ Christmas, gold omitted	575.00
1471a	8¢ Christmas, 1972, pink omitted	225.00
1501a	8¢ Electronics, black omitted	750.00

Scott's No.		F-VF NH
1506a	10¢ Wheat Fields, black & blue omitted	950.00
1509b	10¢ Crossed Flags, blue omitted	175.00
1511a	10¢ Zip, yellow omitted	60.00
1542a	10¢ Kentucky, dull black omitted	950.00
1547a	10¢ Energy Conservation, blue & orange omitted	800.00
1547b	10¢ Energy Conservation, orange & green omitted	800.00
1547c	10¢ Energy Conservation, green omitted	950.00
1551a	10¢ Christmas, buff omitted	40.00
1555a	10¢ D.W. Griffith, brown omitted	800.00
1557a	10¢ Mariner, red omitted	650.00
1559a	8¢ Ludington, green inscription on gum omitted	300.00
1560a	10¢ Salem Poor, green inscription on gum omitted	250.00
1561a	10¢ Salomon, green inscription on gum omitted	300.00
1561b	10¢ Salomon, red color omitted	275.00
1596a	13¢ Eagle & Shield, yellow omitted	225.00
1597a	15¢ McHenry Flag, gray omitted	675.00
1608a	50¢ Lamp, black color omitted	400.00
1610a	$1.00 Lamp, brown color omitted	325.00
1610b	$1.00 Lamp, tan, yellow & orange omitted	375.00
1618Cf	15¢ Flag Coil, grey omitted	45.00
1690a	13¢ Franklin, light blue omitted	325.00
1800a	15¢ Christmas, green & yellow omitted	700.00
1800b	15¢ Christmas, yellow, green & tan omitted	775.00
1826a	15¢ de Galvez, red, brown & blue omitted	850.00
1894c	20¢ Flag, dark blue omitted	100.00
1894d	20¢ Flag, black omitted	350.00
1895b	20¢ Flag Coil, black omitted	65.00
1926a	18¢ Millay, black omitted	525.00
1934b	18¢ Remington, brown omitted	600.00
1937-38b	18¢ Yorktown, se-tenant pair, black omitted	500.00
1951c	20¢ Love, blue omitted	225.00
2014a	20¢ Peace Garden, black, green & brown omitted	250.00
2045a	20¢ Medal of Honor, red omitted	325.00
2055-58b	20¢ Inventors, Block of 4, black omitted	490.00
2059-62b	20¢ Streetcars, Block of 4, black omitted	550.00
2145a	22¢ Ameripex, black, blue & red omitted	250.00
2201b	22¢ Stamp Collecting, cplt. bklt. of 2 panes, black omitted	160.00
2235-38b	22¢ Navajo Art, black omitted	425.00
2281b	25¢ Honeybee, black (engraved) omitted	75.00
2281c	25¢ Honeybee, Black (litho) omitted	550.00
2349a	22¢ U.S./Morocco, black omitted	350.00
2361a	22¢ CPA, black omitted	950.00
2399a	25¢ Christmas, 1988, gold omitted	40.00
2421a	25¢ Bill of Rights, black (engraved) omitted	365.00
2474b	25¢ Lighthouse bklt., white omitted, cplt. bklt. of 4 panes	350.00
	Same, Individual Pane	90.00
2481a	45¢ Sunfish, black omitted	600.00
2482a	$2 Bobcat, black omitted	350.00
2561a	29¢ Washington, DC Bicentennial, black "USA 29¢" omitted	200.00
2635a	29¢ Alaska Highway, black omitted	800.00
2764b	29¢ Garden Flowers, booklet pane, black omitted	450.00
2833b	29¢ Garden Flowers, booklet pane, black omitted	450.00
C76a	10¢ Man on the Moon, red omitted	450.00
C76 var.	10¢ Man on the Moon, patch only omitted	250.00
C91-92b	31¢ Wright Bros., ultramarine & black omitted	850.00
J89a	1¢ Postage Due, Black Numeral omitted	350.00

POSTAL STATIONERY ENTIRES

U571a	10¢ Compass, brown omitted	150.00
U572a	13¢ Homemaker, brown omitted	150.00
U573a	13¢ Farmer, brown omitted	150.00
U575a	13¢ Craftsman, brown omitted	150.00
U583b	13¢ Golf, black & blue omitted	550.00
U584d	13¢ Conservation, black & red omitted	450.00
U586a	15¢ Star, black surcharge omitted	350.00
U587a	15¢ Auto Racing, black omitted	150.00
U595 var.	15¢ Veterinarians, brown & grey omitted	125.00
U596a	15¢ Olympics, red & green omitted	250.00
U596b	15¢ Olympics, black omitted	250.00
U596c	15¢ Olympics, black & green omitted	250.00
U597a	15¢ Bicycle, black omitted	95.00
U599a	15¢ Honeybee, brown omitted	165.00
U611a	25¢ Stars, dark red omitted	100.00
U612a	8.4¢ Constellation, black omitted	625.00
UX50a	4¢ Customs, blue omitted	450.00

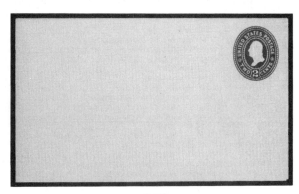

U 362

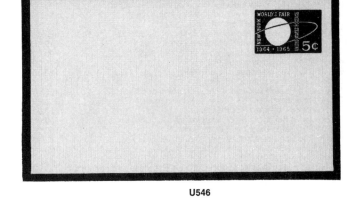

U546

Scott's No.		Mint Entire
1886 Grant Letter Sheet		
U293	2¢ Green, folded	21.50
1887-94 Issues		
U294	1¢ Blue	.95
U295	1¢ Dark blue	11.00
U296	1¢ Blue, amber	5.25
U297	1¢ Dk. blue, amber	57.50
U300	1¢ Blue, manila	1.00
W301	1¢ Blue, wrapper	1.00
U302	1¢ Dk. blue, manila	29.50
W303	1¢ Dk. blue, wrapper	22.50
U304	1¢ Blue, amber manila	7.50
U305	2¢ Green, die 1	20.00
U306	2¢ Green, amber	27.50
U307	2¢ Green, oriental buff	90.00
U311	2¢ Green, die 2	.55
U312	2¢ Green, amber	.60
U313	2¢ Green, oriental buff	1.10
U314	2¢ Green, blue	1.10
U315	2¢ Green, manila	2.50
W316	2¢ Green, wrapper	7.00
U317	2¢ Green,amber manila	5.50
U324	4¢ Carmine	3.25
U325	4¢ Carmine, amber	4.75
U326	4¢ Carmine,oriental buff	9.00
U327	4¢ Carmine, blue	7.00
U328	4¢ Carmine, manila	9.00
U329	4¢ Carmine,amber manila	9.00
U330	5¢ Blue, die 1	7.00
U331	5¢ Blue, amber	9.00
U332	5¢ Blue, oriental buff	11.00
U333	5¢ Blue, blue	11.50
U334	5¢ Blue, die 2	13.75
U335	5¢ Blue, amber	15.00
U336	30¢ Red brown	50.00
U337	30¢ Red brown,amber	57.50
U338	30¢ Red brown, oriental buff	52.50
U339	30¢ Red brown,blue	52.50
U340	30¢ Red brown,manila	50.00
U341	30¢ Red brown, amber manila	57.50
U342	90¢ Purple	80.00
U343	90¢ Purple, amber	95.00
U344	90¢ Purple,oriental buff	95.00
U345	90¢ Purple, blue	110.00
U346	90¢ Purple, manila	110.00
U347	90¢ Purple, amber manila	115.00
1893 Columbian Issue		
U348	1¢ Deep Blue	3.00
U349	2¢ Violet	2.50
U350	5¢ Chocolate	15.00
U351	10¢ Slate Brown	60.00
1899 Issues		
U352	1¢ Green	1.50
U353	1¢ Green, amber	7.75
U354	1¢ Green, or. buff	13.50
U355	1¢ Green, blue	12.75
U356	1¢ Green, manila	6.50
W357	1¢ Wrapper	8.75
U358	2¢ Carmine	8.50
U359	2¢ Carmine, amber	26.75

Scott's No.		Mint Entire
U360	2¢ Carmine, or. buff	29.75
U361	2¢ Carmine, blue	75.00
U362	2¢ Carmine	.65
U363	2¢ Carmine, amber	3.25
U364	2¢ Carmine, or. buff	2.75
U365	2¢ Carmine, blue	3.50
W366	2¢ Wrapper	12.50
U367	2¢ Carmine	9.50
U368	2¢ Carmine, amber	22.50
U369	2¢ Carmine, or. buff	33.50
U370	2¢ Carmine, blue	22.50
U371	4¢ Brown	28.75
U372	4¢ Brown, amber	29.50
U374	4¢ Brown	25.00
U375	4¢ Brown, amber	50.00
W376	4¢ Wrapper	23.75
U377	5¢ Blue	13.75
U378	5¢ Blue, amber	20.75
1903-04 Issues		
U379	1¢ Green	1.10
U380	1¢ Green, amber	18.75
U381	1¢ Green, or. buff	16.50
U382	1¢ Green, blue	19.50
U383	1¢ Green, manila	4.35
W384	1¢ Wrapper	2.00
U385	2¢ Carmine	.85
U386	2¢ Carmine, amber	3.65
U387	2¢ Carmine, or. buff	2.50
U388	2¢ Carmine, blue	3.25
W389	2¢ Wrapper	21.50
U390	4¢ Chocolate	26.50
U391	4¢ Chocolate, amber	26.50
W392	4¢ Wrapper	25.00
U393	5¢ Blue	25.00
U394	5¢ Blue, amber	25.00
U395	2¢ Carmine (1904)	1.00
U396	2¢ Carmine, amber	11.75
U397	2¢ Carmine, or. buff	7.50
U398	2¢ Carmine, blue	5.75
W399	2¢ Wrapper	22.50
1907-16 Issues		
U400	1¢ Green	.50
U401	1¢ Green, amber	1.10
U402	1¢ Green, or. buff	5.95
U403	1¢ Green, blue	5.95
U404	1¢ Green, manila	4.50
W405	1¢ Wrapper	.65
U406	2¢ Brown red	1.75
U407	2¢ Brown red, amber	8.50
U408	2¢ Brown red, or. buff	10.75
U409	2¢ Brown red, blue	6.75
W410	2¢ Wrapper	57.50
U411	2¢ Carmine	.60
U412	2¢ Carmine, amber	.95
U413	2¢ Carmine, or. buff	.65
U414	2¢ Carmine, blue	.85
W415	2¢ Wrapper	9.50
U416	4¢ Black	10.00
U417	4¢ Black, amber	12.50
U418	5¢ Blue	12.50
U419	5¢ Blue, amber	21.00
1916-32 Issues		
U420	1¢ Green	.30

Scott's No.		Mint Entire
U421	1¢ Green, amber	.60
U422	1¢ Green, or. buff	2.75
U423	1¢ Green, blue	.85
U424	1¢ Green, manila	9.50
W425	1¢ Wrapper	.60
U428	1¢ Green, brown	12.50
U429	2¢ Carmine	.35
U430	2¢ Carmine, amber	.45
U431	2¢ Carmine, or. buff	4.50
U432	2¢ Carmine, blue	.60
W433	2¢ Wrapper	.50
U436	3¢ Dark violet	.70
U436f	3¢ Purple (1932)	.50
U437	3¢ Dark violet, amber	6.75
U437a	3¢ Purple, amber (1932)	.75
U438	3¢ Dark violet, buff	32.50
U439	3¢ Dark violet, blue	10.75
U439a	3¢ Purple, blue (1932)	.70
U440	4¢ Black	3.25
U441	4¢ Black, amber	5.50
U442	4¢ Black, blue	5.50
U443	5¢ Blue	6.50
U444	5¢ Blue, amber	6.75
U445	5¢ Blue, blue	8.75
1920-21 Surcharge Issues		
U446	2¢ on 3¢ (U436)	18.50
U447	2¢ on 3¢ (U436)	9.50
U448	2¢ on 3¢ (U436)	3.50
U449	2¢ on 3¢ (U437)	7.75
U450	2¢ on 3¢ (U438)	21.50
U451	2¢ on 3¢ (U439)	14.75
U458	2¢ on 3¢ (U436)	.70
U459	2¢ on 3¢ (U437)	4.75
U460	2¢ on 3¢ (U438)	6.50
U461	2¢ on 3¢ (U439)	6.75
U468	2¢ on 3¢ (U436)	1.00
U469	2¢ on 3¢ (U437)	5.50
U470	2¢ on 3¢ (U438)	7.75
U471	2¢ on 3¢ (U439)	11.00
U472	2¢ on 4¢ (U390)	30.00
U473	2¢ on 4¢ (U391)	27.50
1925 Issues		
U481	1½¢ Brown	.65
U482	1½¢ Brown, amber	1.80
U483	1½¢ Brown, blue	2.25
U484	1½¢ Brown, manila	12.50
W485	1½¢ Wrapper	1.20
U490	1½¢ on 1¢ (U400)	7.50
U491	1½¢ on 1¢ (U401)	14.50
U495	1½¢ on 1¢ (U420)	.75
U496	1½¢ on 1¢ (U421)	25.00
U497	1½¢ on 1¢ (U422)	7.00
U498	1½¢ on 1¢ (U423)	2.25
U499	1½¢ on 1¢ (U424)	22.50
U500	1½¢ on 1¢ (U428)	75.00
U501	1½¢ on 1¢ (U426)	75.00
U508	1½¢ on 1¢ (U353)	75.00
U509	1½¢ on 1¢ (U380)	27.50
U509B	1½¢ on 1¢ (U381)	70.00
U510	1½¢ on 1¢ (U400)	4.00
U512	1½¢ on 1¢ (U402)	12.50
U513	1½¢ on 1¢ (U403)	8.50
U514	1½¢ on 1¢ (U404)	37.50

Scott's No.		Mint Entire
U515	1½¢ on 1¢ (U420)	.70
U516	1½¢ on 1¢ (U421)	65.00
U517	1½¢ on 1¢ (U422)	5.50
U518	1½¢ on 1¢ (U423)	5.50
U519	1½¢ on 1¢ (U424)	32.50
U521	1½¢ on 1¢ (U420)	5.75
1926-58 Issues		
U522	2¢ Sesquicent	2.75
U522a	Same, Die 2	13.50
U523	1¢ Wash. Bicent. ('32)	2.50
U524	1½¢ Wash. Bicent	3.75
U525	2¢ Wash. Bicent	.70
U526	3¢ Wash. Bicent	4.00
U527	4¢ Wash. Bicent	30.00
U528	5¢ Wash. Bicent	6.50
U529	6¢ Orange	9.75
U530	6¢ Orange, amber	17.50
U531	6¢ Orange, blue	17.50
U532	1¢ Franklin (1950)	9.00
U533	2¢ Washington	1.35
U534	3¢ Washington	.55
U535	1½¢ Washington (1952)	6.50
U536	2¢ Franklin (1958)	1.10
U537	2¢ + 2¢ Sur., Circle	4.75
U538	2¢ + 2¢ Sur., Oval	1.00
U539	3¢ + 1¢ Sur., Circle	18.00
U540	3¢ + 1¢ Sur., Oval	.65
1960-74 Issues		
U541	1¼¢ Franklin	.90
U542	2½¢ Washington	1.10
U543	4¢ Pony Express	.70
U544	5¢ Lincoln (1962)	1.10
U545	4¢ + 1¢ Sur., Frank	1.65
U546	5¢ NY World's Fair ('64)	.80
U547	1¼¢ Liberty Bell (1965)	1.00
U548	1-4/10¢ Liberty Bell ('68)	1.00
U548A	1-6/10¢ Liberty Bell ('69)	1.00
U549	4¢ Old Ironsides ('65)	1.10
U550	5¢ Eagle	1.00
U551	6¢ Liberty Head (1968)	.90
U552	4¢ + 2¢ Surcharge	4.50
U553	5¢ + 1¢ Surcharge	4.25
U554	6¢ Moby Dick (1970)	.65
U555	6¢ Brotherhood (1971)	.95
U556	1-7/10¢ Liberty Bell	.55
U557	8¢ Eagle	.55
U561	6¢ + 2¢ Liberty	1.15
U562	6¢ + 2¢ Brotherhood	2.75
U563	8¢ Bowling	.65
U564	8¢ Aging	.75
U565	8¢ Transpo. '72 (1972)	.90
U566	8¢ + 2¢ Sur., Eagle ('73)	.50
U567	10¢ Liberty Bell	.50
U568	1-8/10¢ Volunteer ('74)	.35
U569	10¢ Tennis	.55
1975-82 Issues		
U571	10¢ Seafaring	.50
U572	13¢ Homemaker (1976)	.60
U573	13¢ Farmer (1976)	.60
U574	13¢ Doctor (1976)	.60
U575	13¢ Craftsman (1976)	.60
U576	13¢ Liberty Tree (1975)	.50
U577	2¢ Star & Pinwheel ('76)	.35

MINT POSTAL STATIONERY ENTIRES

U597

UC17

Scott's No.		Mint Entire
U578	2.1¢ Hexagon (1977)	.40
U579	2.7¢ U.S.A (1978)	.40
U580	(15¢) "A" & Eagle	.55
U581	15¢ Uncle Sam..............	.55
U582	13¢ Bicentennial (1976) .	.50
U583	13¢ Golf (1977)	.60
U584	13¢ Conservation	.55
U585	13¢ Development............	.55
U586	15¢ on 16¢ Surch ('78)...	.55
U587	15¢ Auto Racing.............	.55
U588	15¢ on 13¢ Tree.............	.55
U589	3.1¢ Non Profit	.30
U590	3.5¢ Violins....................	.35
U591	5.9¢ Circle (1982)...........	.35
U592	(18¢) "B" & Eagle (1981)	.55
U593	18¢ Star........................	.55
U594	(20¢) "C" & Eagle	.55
U595	15¢ Veterinary (1979)	.55
U596	15¢ Soccer....................	.90
U597	15¢ Bicycle (1980)	.60
U598	15¢ America's Cup.........	.60
U599	15¢ Honeybee................	.55
U600	18¢ Blinded Veteran.......	.60
U601	20¢ Capitol Dome	.55
U602	20¢ Great Seal (1982)....	.55
U603	20¢ Purple Heart............	.55
1983-89 Issues		
U604	5.2¢ Non Profit	.45
U605	20¢ Paralyzed Vets........	.55
U606	20¢ Small Business ('84)	.70
U607	(22¢) "D" & Eagle (1985)	.65
U608	22¢ Bison	.60
U609	6¢ Old Ironsides.............	.45
U610	8.5¢ Mayflower (1986) ...	.50
U611	25¢ Stars (1988)	.70
U612	8.4¢ USS Const.............	.50
U613	25¢ Snowflake...............	.80
U614	25¢ Philatelic Env. ('89) .	.65
U615	25¢ Stars Security Env ..	.60
U616	25¢ Love	.60
U617	25¢ WSE Space Sta	.65
1990-94 Issues		
U618	25¢ Football	.65
U619	29¢ Star (1991)	.85
U620	11.1¢ Non Profit	.40
U621	29¢ Love	.75
U622	29¢ Magazine Industry...	.75
U623	29¢ Stars & Bars...........	.75
U624	29¢ Country Geese........	.75

Scott's No.		Mint Entire
U625	29¢ Space Station ('92)..	.75
U626	29¢ Western Americana.	.75
U627	29¢ Environmen............	.75
U628	19.8¢ Bulk Rate.............	.55
U629	29¢ Disabled Americans	.75
U630	29¢ Kitten (1993)............	.75
U631	29¢ Football (1994)	.75
1995-96 Issues		
U632	32¢ Liberty Bell	.80
U633	(32¢) "G"......................	.80
U634	(32¢) "G", Security Envelope	.80
U635	(5¢) Sheep	.40
U636	(10¢) Eagle..................	.45
U637	(32¢) Spiral Heart	.80
U638	32¢ Liberty Bell, Security Envelope	.80
U639	32¢ Space Shuttle.........	.80
U640	32¢ Environment ('96)....	.75
U641	32¢ Paralympics ('96) .	.75
AIR MAIL ENTIRES		
1929-44 Issues		
UC1	5¢ Blue, Die 1...............	5.25
UC2	5¢ Blue, Die 2..............	16.50
UC3	6¢ Orange, Die 2a (1934)	1.75
UC3v	6¢ No Border................	2.10
UC4	6¢ Orange, Die 2b (1942)	57.50
UC4v	6¢ No Border................	4.95
UC5	6¢ No Border, Die 2c (1944).........	1.10
UC6	6¢ Orange, Die 3 ('42).	2.25
UC6v	6¢ No Border................	2.50
UC7	8¢ Olive Green ('32)....	18.50
1945-47 Issues		
UC8	6¢ on 2¢ Sur., Wash. ..	1.65
UC9	6¢ on 2¢ Wash. Bic...	100.00
UC10	6¢ on 6¢ Orange Die 2a (1946)	4.00
UC11	5¢ on 6¢ Or. Die 2b.....	11.00
UC12	5¢ on 6¢ Or. Die 2c.....	1.50
UC13	5¢ on 6¢ Or. Die 3......	1.10
UC14	5¢ Plane, Die 1............	1.25
UC15	5¢ Plane, Die 2............	1.25
UC17	5¢ CIPEX (1947)........	.65
1950-58 Issues		
UC18	6¢ Skymaster..............	.65

Scott's No.		Mint Entire
UC19	6¢ on 5¢, Die 1 ('51)..	1.40
UC20	6¢ on 5¢, Die 2..........	1.30
UC21	6¢ on 5¢, Die 1 ('52)..	35.00
UC22	6¢ on 5¢, Die 2..........	5.50
UC25	6¢ FIPEX (1956)	1.10
UC26	7¢ Skymaster (1958)...	1.10
UC27	6¢ + 1¢ Or., Die 2a..	300.00
UC28	6¢ + 1¢ Or., Die 2b..	100.00
UC29	6¢ + 1¢ Or., Die 2c..	50.00
UC30	6¢ + 1¢ Skymaster......	1.25
UC31	6¢ + 1¢ FIPEX............	1.50
UC33	7¢ Jet, Blue	.80
1960-73 Issues		
UC34	7¢ Jet, Carmine..........	.80
UC36	8¢ Jet Airliner (1962)...	.90
UC37	8¢ Jet, Triangle (1965)	.55
UC37a	Same, Tagged (1967) .	2.00
UC40	10¢ Jet, Triangle ('68) .	.90
UC41	8¢ + 2¢ Surcharge.......	1.00
UC43	1¢ Three Circles ('71)..	.65
UC45	10¢ + 1¢ Triangle	2.00
UC47	13¢ Bird in Flight ('73) .	.45
AIRLETTER SHEETS		
1947-71 Issues		
UC16	10¢ DC3, 2 Lines	8.50
UC16a	10¢ 4 Lines Letter (1951)	17.50
UC16c	10¢ Aero., 4 Lines (1953)	52.50
UC16d	10¢ Aero., 3 Lines (1955)	8.00
UC32	10¢ Jet, 2 Lines ('59)...	7.00
UC32a	10¢ Jet, 3 Lines ('58)...	11.50
UC35	11¢ Jet & Globe ('61) ..	3.25
UC38	11¢ J.F. Kennedy (1965)	3.75
UC39	13¢ J.F. Kennedy (1967)	3.35
UC42	13¢ Human Rights (1968)	9.75
UC44	15¢ Birds,Letter ('71)...	1.65
UC44a	15¢ w/"Aerogramme"...	1.65
1973-81 Issues		
UC46	15¢ Ballooning	.85
UC48	18¢ "USA" (1974).........	.95
UC49	18¢ NATO	.95
UC50	22¢ "USA" (1976).........	.95
UC51	22¢ "USA" (1978)	.95

Scott's No.		Mint Entire
UC52	22¢ Moscow Olym. ('79)	1.65
UC53	30¢ "USA", Blue, Red & Brown (1980)	.85
UC54	30¢ "USA", Yel., Bl.&Blk (1981)........ .	.85
1982-95 Issues		
UC55	30¢ World Trade	.85
UC56	30¢ Comm. Year (1983)	.85
UC57	30¢ Olympics	.85
UC58	36¢ Landsat Satellite (85)	.85
UC59	36¢ Travel....................	.85
UC60	36¢ Mark Twain/ Halley's Comet........	.85
UC61	39¢ Styl. Aero (1988)...	.90
UC62	39¢ Mont. Blair (1989) .	.90
UC63	45¢ Eagle,blue paper (1991).....................	1.10
UC63a	Eagle, white paper........	1.10
UC64	50¢T.Lowe (1995)........	1.20
POSTAL SAVINGS OFFICIAL ENVELOPES		
U070	1¢ Green (1911)..........	75.00
U071	1¢ Green, Oriental buff (1911)...........225.00	
U072	2¢ Carmine (1911).......	17.50
OFFICIAL MAIL ENTIRES		
UO73	20¢ Eagle ('83)	1.25
UO74	22¢ Eagle ('85)	1.00
UO75	22¢ Bond Env. ('87)	1.00
UO76	(25¢) "E" Bond Env ('88)	1.10
UO77	25¢ Eagle....................	.95
UO78	25¢ Bond Env	.95
UO79	45¢ Passport 2 oz ('90)	1.50
UO80	65¢ Passport env.3 oz .	1.80
UO81	45¢ Self-sealing 2 oz ...	1.30
UO82	65¢ Self-sealing 3 oz ...	1.80
UO83	(29¢) "F" Sav. Bond (91)	1.25
UO84	29¢ Official Mail	.95
UO85	29¢ Sav. Bond Env.......	.95
UO86	52¢ Consular Service ..	4.50
UO86a	52¢ Reprint (1994).......	1.50
UO87	75¢ Consular Service (1992).....................	9.95
UO87a	75¢ Reprint (1994).......	2.75
UO88	32¢ Official Mail (1995)	.95

Note: Reprints have copyright date.

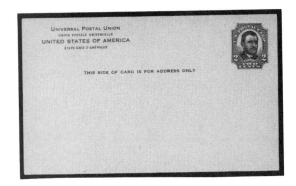

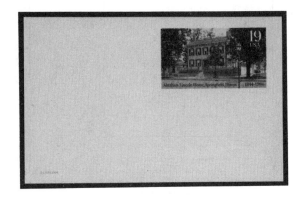

UX 25

UX 174

Scott's No.	Mint Card
1873-98 Issues	
UX1	1¢ Liberty, brown, large watermark 335.00
UX3	Same, small watermark 75.00
UX5	1¢ Liberty, black, "Write" (1875)........................... 65.00
UX6	2¢ Liberty, blue on buff (1879).......................... 28.50
UX7	1¢ Liberty, black, "Nothing" (1881)........................... 57.50
UX8	1¢ Jefferson,brown (85) 50.00
UX9	1¢ Jeff., black (1886) ... 16.50
UX10	1¢ Grant, black (1891) . 32.50
UX11	Same, blue................. 15.00
UX12	1¢ Jeff., black, small wreath (1894)............... 40.00
UX13	2¢ Liberty, blue on cream (1897)............... 155.00
UX14	1¢ Jeff., black, large wreath 27.50
UX15	1¢ Adams, black (1898) 42.50
UX16	2¢ Liberty, black, "No Frame" (1898) 11.50
1902-18 Issues	
UX18	1¢ McKinley, oval......... 12.00
UX19	1¢ McKinley ('07) 40.00
UX20	1¢ Correspond Space at L (1908) 50.00
UX21	1¢ McKnly,shaded ('10) 100.00
UX22	Same, White backgrd... 15.00
UX23	1¢ Lincoln, red ('11) 9.50
UX24	1¢ McKinley, red 12.00
UX25	2¢ Grant, red................ 1.65
UX26	1¢ Lincoln, green ('13) . 11.50
UX27	1¢ Jeff, Die 1 (1914) .... .35
UX28	1¢ Lincoln, green ('17) . .75
UX29	2¢ Jeff, Die 1 .... 40.00
UX30	2¢ Jeff, Die 2 (1918) ... 28.50
1920-64 Issues	
UX32	1¢ on 2¢ red, die 1 ...... 52.50
UX33	1¢ on 2¢ red, die 2 ...... 13.50
UX37	3¢ McKinley (1926)...... 5.00
UX38	2¢ Franklin (1951)........ .40
UX39	2¢ on 1¢ Jeff, green ('52) .65
UX40	2¢ on 1¢ Linc., grn ...... .75
UX41	2¢ on 1¢ Jeff, dk grn ... 5.50
UX42	2¢ on 1¢ Linc, dk grn ... 5.75
UX43	2¢ Liberty, carmine...... .40
UX44	2¢ FIPEX (1956) .... .30
UX45	4¢ Liberty 1.60
UX46	3¢ Liberty (1958)......... .55
UX46c	Precancelled ('61) 4.25
UX48	4¢ Linc., precan ('62) ... .30
UX48a	Same, Tagged ('66) ..... .65

Scott's No.	Mint Card
UX49	7¢ "USA" (1963) 4.50
UX50	4¢ Customs (1964) ...... .55
UX51	4¢ Social Security........ .45
1965-73 Issues	
UX52	4¢ Coast Guard .... .40
UX53	4¢ Census................... .40
UX54	8¢ "USA" (1967) 4.25
UX55	5¢ Lincoln (1968) .... .32
UX56	5¢ Women Marines...... .40
UX57	5¢ Weather (1970)....... .35
UX58	6¢ Paul Revere (1971). .35
UX59	10¢ "USA" 4.75
UX60	6¢ Hospitals .... .35
UX61	6¢ Constellation ('72)... 1.00
UX62	6¢ Monument Valley .... .50
UX63	6¢ Gloucester .... .50
UX64	6¢ John Hanson .... .30
UX65	6¢ Liberty (1973).......... .30
UX66	8¢ Samuel Adams .... .40
1974-79 Issues	
UX67	12¢ Visit USA .... .40
UX68	7¢ Thomson (1975) ...... .40
UX69	9¢ Witherspoon............ .35
UX70	9¢ Rodney (1976) .... .35
UX71	9¢ Galveston (1977) .... .40
UX72	9¢ Nathan Hale .... .35
UX73	10¢ Music Hall (1978).. .40
UX74	(10¢) John Hancock...... .40
UX75	10¢ John Hancock .... .35
UX76	14¢ Cutter "Eagle" ...... .45
UX77	10¢ Molly Pitcher .... .35
UX78	10¢ G.R. Clark (1979).. .35
UX79	10¢ Pulaski .... .35
UX80	10¢ Olympics .... .65
UX81	10¢ Iolani Palace .... .35
1980-83 Issues	
UX82	14¢ Winter Olympics.... .70
UX83	10¢ Salt Lake Temple... .35
UX84	10¢ Rochambeau .... .35
UX85	10¢ King's Mt .... .35
UX86	19¢ Golden Hinde......... .80
UX87	10¢ Cowpens (1981) .... .35
UX88	(12¢) Eagle .... .40
UX89	12¢ Isaiah Thomas ...... .35
UX90	12¢ N. Greene .... .35
UX91	12¢ Lewis & Clark .... .35
UX92	(13¢) Morris .... .35
UX93	13¢ Morris .... .35
UX94	13¢ F. Marion (1982) ... .35
UX95	13¢ LaSalle.................. .35
UX96	13¢ Music Academy ..... .35
UX97	13¢ St. Louis P.O......... .35
UX98	13¢ Georgia (1983)...... .35
UX99	13¢ Old P. Office .... .35

Scott's No.	Mint Card
UX100	13¢ Yachting .... .35
1984-88 Issues	
UX101	13¢ Maryland .... .35
UX102	13¢ Olympics .... .35
UX103	13¢ Baraga................. .35
UX104	13¢ Rancho S.Pedro... .35
UX105	(14¢) Charles Carroll(85) .35
UX106	14¢ Charles Carroll ..... .55
UX107	25¢ Flying Cloud .... .75
UX108	14¢ George Wythe ...... .35
UX109	14¢ Conn. Anniv.......... .35
UX110	14¢ Stamp Coll (1986) .35
UX111	14¢ Francis Vigo .... .35
UX112	14¢ Rhode Island .... .35
UX113	14¢ Wisconsin Ty........ .35
UX114	14¢ Nat'l. Guard .... .35
UX115	14¢ Steel Plow (1987). .35
UX116	14¢ Const. Conv .... .35
UX117	14¢ U.S. Flag .... .35
UX118	14¢ Pride in America... .35
UX119	14¢ Timberline Ldg ..... .35
UX120	15¢ Am. the Beaut ('88) .35
UX121	15¢ Blair House........... .35
UX122	28¢ Yorkshire.............. .70
UX123	15¢ Iowa Terr.............. .35
UX124	15¢ NW/Ohio Terr....... .35
UX125	15¢ Hearst Castle .... .35
UX126	15¢ Fed. Papers.......... .35
1989-92 Issues	
UX127	15¢ The Desert .... .35
UX128	15¢ Healy Hall .... .35
UX129	15¢ Wetlands.............. .35
UX130	15¢ Oklahoma............. .35
UX131	21¢ Can. Geese/Mtns. .60
UX132	15¢ Seashore.............. .35
UX133	15¢ Woodlands .... .35
UX134	15¢ Hull House............ .35
UX135	15¢ Independence Hall .35
UX136	15¢ Balt. Inner Harbor .35
UX137	15¢ 59th St.Bridge,NY .35
UX138	15¢ Capitol Bldg.......... .35
UX139-42	15¢ Cityscape sheet of 4 postcards............ 11.95
UX143	15¢ The White House ... 1.10
UX144	15¢ Jefferson Memorial 1.10
UX145	15¢ Papermaking ('90) .35
UX146	15¢ World Literacy Yr. .35
UX147	15¢ Geo. Bingham Art 1.10
UX148	15¢ Isaac Royall House .45
UX150	15¢ Stanford Univ .... .45
UX151	15¢ DAR/Const. Hall. 1.25
UX152	15¢ Chicago Orch.Hall .45
UX153	19¢ Flag (1991)........... .50
UX154	19¢ Carnegie Hall .... .50

Scott's No.	Mint Card
UX155	19¢ "Old Red", U of TX .50
UX156	19¢ Bill of Rights Bicent .50
UX157	19¢ Notre Dame .... .50
UX158	30¢ Niagara Falls .... .80
UX159	19¢ Old Mill, U of VT . .50
UX160	19¢ Wadsw'th Athen (92) .50
UX161	19¢ Cobb Hall, U of Chi .50
UX162	19¢ Waller Hall .... .50
UX163	19¢ America's Cup 1.10
UX164	19¢ Columbia River.... .50
UX165	19¢ Grt. Hall, Ellis Island .50
1993-94 Issues	
UX166	19¢ National Cathedral .50
UX167	19¢ Wren Building ..... .50
UX168	19¢ Holocaust Mem'l. 1.10
UX169.	19¢ Ft. Recovery .... .50
UX170	19¢ Playmaker's Theater .50
UX171	19¢ O'Kane Hall .... .50
UX172	19¢ Beecher Hall .... .50
UX173	19¢ Massachusetts Hall .50
UX174	19¢ Lincoln Home ('94) .50
UX175	19¢ Myers Hall........... .50
UX176	19¢ Canyon de Chelly . .50
UX177	19¢ St. Louis Station . .50
UX178-97	19¢ Legends of the West (20) 17.95
1995-96 Issues	
UX198	20¢ Red Barn .... .50
UX199	(20¢) "G" .... .50
UX200-19	20¢ Civil War (20).. 18.95
UX220	20¢ Clipper Ship .... .45
UX221-40	20¢ Comic Strip (20) 15.95
UX241	20¢ Winter Farm Scene (1996)............ .45
UX242-61	20¢ Atlanta Olympics (20)(1996).......... 25.95
UX262	20¢ McDowell Hall (96) .45
UX263	20¢ Alexander Hall (96) .45
UX264-78	20¢ Endangered Species (15) (1996)... 22.95
UX279	20¢ Love-Swans 1.25
	Same, Package of 12 13.95

Note: UX279 is sold in packages of 12 with 8 different stamp designs without values.

	Mint Card
.....	20¢ City College of New York....... .45
.....	20¢ Golden Gate Bridge .45
.....	50¢ Golden Gate Bridge 1.10
.....	20¢ Bugs Bunny 1.25
.....	20¢ Bugs Bunny Booklet of 10.... 11.95
.....	20¢ Fort McHenry....... .45

UXC 24

UZ 2

UY 29

Scott's No.		Mint Card
AIRMAIL POSTAL CARDS		
UXC1	4¢ Eagle....................	.60
UXC2	5¢ Eagle (1958)	2.00
UXC3	5¢ Eagle, redrawn (60)	6.50
UXC4	6¢ Bald Eagle ('63) ...	.75
UXC5	11¢ SIPEX, Travel (66)	.70
UXC6	6¢ Virgin Islands ('67)	.50
UXC7	6¢ Boy Scouts...........	.50
UXC8	13¢ Travel USA.........	1.60
UXC9	8¢ Eagle, Precan ('68)	.70
UXC9a	Same, Tagged ('69) ..	2.65
UXC10	9¢ Eagle, Precan ('71)	.60
UXC11	15¢ Travel USA.........	2.25
UXC12	9¢ Grand Canyon ('72)	.55
UXC13	15¢ Niagara Falls......	.70
UXC14	11¢ Mail Early (1974)	.75
UXC15	18¢ Visit USA............	.90
UXC16	21¢ Visit USA (1975)	.85
UXC17	21¢ Curtiss Jenny ('78)	.80
UXC18	21¢ Olympics (1979).	1.10
UXC19	28¢ Trans-Pacific ('81)	1.00
UXC20	28¢ Soaring (1982) ...	1.00
UXC21	28¢ Speedskating ('83)	.90
UXC22	33¢ China Clipper ('85)	.90
UXC23	33¢ Ameripex (1986)	.85
UXC24	36¢ DC-3 (1988)	.95
UXC25	40¢ Yankee Clipper (91)	1.00
UXC26	50¢ Eagle (1995)	1.15

Scott's No.		Mint Card
OFFICIAL POSTAL CARDS		
UZ2	13¢ Emblem (1983)	.80
UZ3	14¢ Emblem ('85)...........	.80
UZ4	15¢ Emblem ('88)...........	.80
UZ5	19¢ Emblem ('91)...........	.80
UZ6	20¢ Emblem ('95)	.60
"POSTAL BUDDY" CARDS		
PB1	15¢ (1990).....................	8.00
	Sheet of 4	32.50
PB2	19¢ (1991).....................	3.75
	Sheet of 4	15.00
PB3	19¢ (1992) Plain	7.50
	Sheet of 4	32.50
	(1992) With Logo	11.00
PB4	19¢ New Back...............	75.00
	Sheet of 4	300.00

Scott's No.		Mint Card
POSTAL REPLY CARDS		
1892-1920 Issues		
Unsevered Cards-Folded		
UY1	1¢ Grant, black..........	37.50
UY2	2¢ Liberty, blue ('93) .	18.50
UY3	1¢ Grant, no frame(98)	70.00
UY4	1¢ + 1¢ Sherman	
	and Sheridan (1904) .	48.50
UY5	1¢ + 1¢ M&G Wash.,	
	Blue (1910)................	150.00
UY6	Same, Green (1911) .	150.00
UY7	Same,sgl.frm. line ('15)	1.50
UY8	2¢ + 2¢ M&G Wash.,	
	red (1918)...................	80.00
UY9	1¢ on 2¢ + 1¢ on 2¢,	
	red (1920).................	20.00
1924-68		
Unsevered cards-Unfolded		
UY11	2¢ + 2¢ Liberty, red...	3.00
UY12	3¢ + 3¢ McKinley ('26)	15.00
UY13	2¢ + 2¢ M&G Wash.(51)	1.75
UY14	2¢ on 1¢ + 2¢ on 1¢	
	M&G Wash (1952)	1.75
UY15	2¢ on 1¢ + 2¢ on 1¢,	
	green	135.00
UY16	4¢ + 4¢ Liberty ('56) ..	1.50
UY17	3¢ + 3¢ Liberty ('58) ..	3.95
UY18	4¢ + 4¢ Lincoln ('62) .	4.50
UY19	7¢ + 7¢ "USA" (1963)	3.00
UY20	8¢ + 8¢ "USA" (1967)	3.50
UY21	5¢ + 5¢ Lincoln (1968)	1.75

Scott's No.		Mint Card
1971-95		
Unsevered Cards-Unfolded		
UY22	6¢ + 6¢ Revere	1.25
UY23	6¢ + 6¢ Hanson (1972)	1.35
UY24	8¢ + S. Adams (1973)..	1.10
UY25	7¢ + 7¢ Thomson ('75) .	1.10
UY26	9¢ + 9¢ Witherson	1.10
UY27	9¢ + 9¢ Rodney (1976)	1.10
UY28	9¢ + 9¢ Hale (1977)	1.10
UY29	(10¢+10¢) Hancock (78)	10.75
UY30	10¢ + 10¢ Hancock......	1.10
UY31	(12¢ + 12¢) Eagle ('81)	1.10
UY32	12¢ + 12¢ Thomas.......	1.30
UY33	(13¢ + 13¢) Morris	2.25
UY34	13¢ + 13¢ Morris..........	1.10
UY35	(14¢ + 14¢) Carroll ('85)	3.25
UY36	14¢ + 14¢ Carroll	1.10
UY37	14¢ + 14¢ Wythe	1.10
UY38	14¢ + 14¢ U.S. Flag ('87)	1.10
UY39	15¢+15¢ Am./Beaut ('88)	1.10
UY40	19¢ + 19¢ Flag (1991) .	1.25
UY41	20¢ + 20¢ Red Barn ('95)	1.15

UNITED STATES REVENUES

| R15 | R24c | R36c | R44c | R60c |

| R71c | R82c | R85c |

1862-71 (All Used) (C)

Scott's No.		Imperforate(a) Fine	Ave.	Part Perforate(b) Fine	Ave.	Perforated(c) Fine	Ave.
R1	1¢ Express	47.50	25.00	37.50	21.00	1.00	.60
R2	1¢ Play Cards	795.00	450.00	550.00	335.00	90.00	52.50
R3	1¢ Proprietary	575.00	325.00	95.00	52.50	.45	.25
R4	1¢ Telegraph	375.00	200.00	...	...	8.50	5.00
R5	2¢ Bank Ck.,Blue	1.10	.70	1.10	.70	.20	.15
R6	2¢ Bank Ck.,Orange ...	...	...	75.00	42.50	.20	.15
R7	2¢ Certif.,Blue	9.50	5.00	...	...	22.50	12.00
R8	2¢ Certif.,Orange	...	...	...	...	22.50	13.00
R9	2¢ Express,Blue	9.50	5.00	15.00	8.50	.25	.15
R10	2¢ Express,Orange	...	...	...	...	5.50	3.25
R11	2¢ Ply.Cds.,Blue	...	...	125.00	75.00	3.00	1.50
R12	2¢ Ply.Cds.,Orange.....	...	...	...	...	25.00	14.00
R13	2¢ Propriet.,Blue	275.00	200.00	100.00	57.50	.40	.25
R14	2¢ Propriet.,Orange	...	...	...	...	30.00	16.00
R15	2¢ U.S.I.R.	...	...	...	...	.20	.15
R16	3¢ Foreign Exchange...	...	...	200.00	115.00	2.75	1.50
R17	3¢ Playing Cards.........	...	...	...	...	90.00	52.50
R18	3¢ Proprietary	...	...	225.00	140.00	1.85	1.00
R19	3¢ Telegraph	47.50	25.00	16.50	9.50	2.35	1.25
R20	4¢ Inland Exchange	...	...	...	...	1.50	1.00
R21	4¢ Playing Cards	...	...	...	...	350.00	175.00
R22	4¢ Proprietary	...	...	165.00	95.00	5.00	3.00
R23	5¢ Agreement	...	...	...	...	.25	.15
R24	5¢ Certificate..............	2.25	1.25	9.00	5.00	.20	.15
R25	5¢ Express	3.75	2.25	4.25	2.60	.30	.17
R26	5¢ Foreign Exch	...	...	...	...	.30	.17
R27	5¢ Inland Exch	3.85	2.35	3.25	1.95	.20	.15
R28	5¢ Playing Cards.........	...	...	...	...	12.50	7.50
R29	5¢ Proprietary	...	...	...	...	17.00	9.50
R30	6¢ Inland Exch	...	...	...	...	1.35	.80
R32	10¢ Bill of Lading	42.50	25.00	170.00	95.00	.85	.50
R33	10¢ Certificate..............	95.00	52.50	150.00	85.00	.25	.15
R34	10¢ Contract,Blue	...	...	130.00	75.00	.30	.17
R35	10¢ For.Exch.,Blue	...	...	...	...	6.00	4.00
R36	10¢ Inland Exch	150.00	85.00	3.25	1.95	.22	.15
R37	10¢ Power of Atty.....	400.00	225.00	18.50	11.00	.35	.20
R38	10¢ Proprietary	...	...	...	...	12.50	7.50
R39	15¢ Foreign Exch	...	...	...	...	12.00	7.00
R40	15¢ Inland Exch	25.00	14.00	10.00	5.50	1.10	.65
R41	20¢ Foreign Exch	38.50	21.50	...	...	26.50	15.00
R42	20¢ Inland Exch	13.00	7.50	15.00	8.50	.35	.20
R43	25¢ Bond	115.00	65.00	5.25	3.15	1.90	1.10
R44	25¢ Certificate.............	7.50	4.25	5.00	2.75	.20	.15
R45	25¢ Entry Goods	15.00	8.50	47.50	27.50	.55	.28
R46	25¢ Insurance	8.00	5.00	9.00	5.00	.25	.15
R47	25¢ Life Insurance	28.50	16.00	165.00	95.00	6.00	4.00
R48	25¢ Power of Atty.......	5.50	3.25	22.50	13.75	.25	.15
R49	25¢ Protest.................	20.00	11.00	200.00	115.00	6.50	4.00
R50	25¢ Wareh'se. Rct......	36.00	20.00	175.00	100.00	19.50	10.50
R51	30¢ Foreign Exch	60.00	36.50	800.00	450.00	33.50	18.50
R52	30¢ Inland Exch	23.00	13.00	51.50	28.75	2.50	1.50
R53	40¢ Inland Exch	450.00	265.00	5.00	3.00	2.50	1.50
R54	50¢ Convey,Blue.........	10.50	5.95	1.10	.65	.20	.15
R55	50¢ Entry of Goods	...	...	10.00	5.50	.25	.15
R56	50¢ Foreign Exch	33.50	18.50	31.50	18.50	4.75	3.00
R57	50¢ Lease	19.50	11.00	50.00	27.50	6.25	4.00
R58	50¢ Life Insurance	25.00	14.00	47.50	26.00	.75	.42
R59	50¢ Mortgage.............	9.50	5.25	2.10	1.20	.35	.20
R60	50¢ Orig.Process	2.65	1.50	450.00	325.00	.30	.17
R61	50¢ Passage Ticket	60.00	32.50	115.00	65.00	.50	.30
R62	50¢ Probate of Will.....	28.50	16.00	47.50	26.50	15.00	8.50
R63	50¢ Sty. Bond,Blue ...	125.00	70.00	2.35	1.30	.25	.15
R64	60¢ Inland Exch	70.00	38.50	40.00	22.00	5.25	3.00
R65	70¢ Foreign Exch........	265.00	150.00	75.00	42.50	6.00	3.50
R66	$1 Conveyance	9.50	5.25	365.00	200.00	3.25	1.85
R67	$1 Entry of Goods	26.50	15.00	...	...	1.40	.80
R68	$1 Foreign Exch	55.00	30.00	...	...	.65	.37
R69	$1 Inland Exch	10.50	6.00	250.00	140.00	.45	.25
R70	$1 Lease	29.50	16.00	...	...	1.65	1.00
R71	$1 Life Insurance	125.00	72.50	...	...	5.00	3.00
R72	$1 Manifest	40.00	22.50	...	...	21.50	12.50
R73	$1 Mortgage..............	16.50	9.75	...	...	125.00	67.50
R74	$1 Passage Ticket	210.00	120.00	...	...	140.00	70.00
R75	$1 Power of Atty.......	62.50	35.00	...	...	1.60	.90
R76	$1 Probate of Will........	55.00	27.50	...	...	30.00	16.50

Scott's No.		Imperforate(a) Fine	Ave.	Part Perforate(b) Fine	Ave.	Perforated(c) Fine	Ave.
R77	$1.30 Foreign Exch	...	...	...	...	45.00	25.00
R78	$1.50 Inland Exch	19.00	10.50	...	...	2.85	1.75
R79	$1.60 Foreign Exch ...	775.00	425.00	...	...	80.00	42.50
R80	$1.90 Foreign Exch	...	1650.00	...	...	55.00	30.00
R81	$2 Conveyance	80.00	45.00	1100.00	650.00	2.25	1.25
R82	$2 Mortgage..............	80.00	45.00	...	...	2.25	1.25
R83	$2 Probate of Will......	...	1500.00	...	...	42.50	22.50
R84	$2.50 Inland Exch	1750.00	950.00	...	...	3.25	2.00
R85	$3 Charter Party.........	95.00	55.00	...	...	4.25	2.50
R86	$3 Manifest	90.00	50.00	...	...	19.00	10.50
R87	$3.50 Inland Exch	...	1250.00	...	...	40.00	22.50
R88	$5 Charter Party........	200.00	115.00	...	...	5.75	3.50
R89	$5 Conveyance	30.00	16.50	...	...	5.75	3.50
R90	$5 Manifest	90.00	50.00	...	...	75.00	41.50
R91	$5 Mortgage..............	85.00	47.50	...	...	15.00	8.25
R92	$5 Probate of Will......	375.00	215.00	...	...	15.00	8.25
R93	$10 Charter Party......	450.00	250.00	...	...	19.00	10.50
R94	$10 Conveyance	75.00	42.50	...	...	50.00	27.50
R95	$10 Mortgage............	300.00	165.00	...	...	19.00	10.50
R96	$10 Probate of Will....	950.00	525.00	...	...	19.00	10.50
R97	$15 Mortgage,Blue.....	800.00	435.00	...	...	90.00	57.50
R98	$20 Conveyance	95.00	57.50	...	...	42.50	30.00
R99	$20 Probate of Will....	975.00	550.00	...	...	875.00	575.00
R100	$25 Mortgage	775.00	435.00	...	...	85.00	50.00
R101	$50 U.S.I.R	160.00	95.00	...	...	70.00	40.00
R102	$200 U.S.I.R.	1150.00	650.00	...	...	475.00	275.00

1ST ISSUE HANDSTAMPED CANCELLATIONS ARE GENERALLY AVAILABLE FOR A 20% PREMIUM.

1871 SECOND ISSUE (C)

| R104,R135 | R107,R137 | R113,R140 | R118,R144 |

R103 through R131 have blue frames and a black center.

Scott's No.		Used Fine	Ave.	Scott's No.		Used Fine	Ave.
R103	1¢ 32.50		16.50	R118	$1 ....2.75		1.50
R104	2¢ 1.10		.55	R119	$1.30 ....230.00		125.00
R105	3¢ 13.00		8.00	R120	$1.50 ....10.00		5.50
R106	4¢ 47.50		27.50	R121	$1.60 ....250.00		140.00
R107	5¢ 1.30		.70	R122	$1.90 ....140.00		80.00
R108	6¢ 70.00		37.50	R123	$2 ....12.75		7.00
R109	10¢ 80		.45	R124	$2.50 ....22.50		12.75
R110	15¢ 20.00		11.50	R125	$3 ....25.00		14.00
R111	20¢ 5.00		2.75	R126	$3.50 ....125.00		70.00
R112	25¢ 60		.33	R127	$5 ....15.00		8.50
R113	30¢ 52.50		30.00	R128	$10 ....85.00		50.00
R114	40¢ 32.50		18.75	R129	$20 ....265.00		165.00
R115	50¢ 50		.33	R130	$25 ....265.00		165.00
R116	60¢ 77.50		45.00	R131	$50 ....325.00		200.00
R117	70¢ 28.50		17.50				

Note : Cut cancels are priced at 25% to 50% of above prices.

1871-72 Third Issue - Same Designs as Second Issue (C)
R134 through R150 have black centers.
1874 Fourth Issue (C)

Scott's No.		Used	Scott's No.		Used
	Fine	Ave.		Fine	Ave.
R134	1¢ Claret..........25.00	14.00	R143	70¢ Green......32.50	17.50
R135	2¢ Orange 20	.15	R144	$1 Green........1.35	.75
R136	4¢ Brown..........30.00	16.50	R145	$2 Vermillion..18.00	9.50
R137	5¢ Orange 25	.15	R146	$2.50 Claret..28.50	16.00
R138	6¢ Orange 28.50	16.00	R147	$3 Green........28.50	16.00
R139	15¢ Brown.......10.50	6.50	R148	$5 Vermillion..16.00	9.50
R140	30¢ Orange......13.00	8.50	R149	$10 Green......60.00	35.00
R141	40¢ Brown......26.50	15.00	R150	$20 Orange..425.00	235.00
R142	60¢ Orange 50.00	28.75			

Note : Cut cancels are priced at 40% to 60% of the above prices.

Scott's No.		Uncancelled		Used
		Fine	Ave.	Fine	Ave.
R151	2¢ Orange and Black, Green Paper	...	...	.20	.15

1875-78 Fifth Issue (C)

		Fine	Ave.	Fine	Ave.
R152a	2¢ Liberty, Blue, Silk Paper	1.50	.90	.20	.15
R152b	2¢ Blue, Watermarked	1.50	.90	.20	.15
R152c	2¢ Blue, Rouletted, Watermarked ...	...	...	28.50	14.50

* 1898 Postage Stamps Overprinted "I.R." (C)
* 1898 Newspaper Stamps Surcharged "INT. REV./$5/DOCUMENTARY" (C)

		Fine	Ave.	Fine	Ave.
R153	1¢ Green, Small I.R. (#279).......	2.50	1.50	2.75	1.65
R154	1¢ Green, Large I.R. (#279).......	.25	.20	.20	.15
R154a	1¢ Green, Inverted Surcharge ...	17.50	10.00	15.00	8.50
R155	2¢ Carmine, Large I.R. (#267) ...	.25	.20	.20	.15
R159	$5 Blue, Surcharge down (#PR121)	210.00	130.00	140.00	85.00
R160	$5 Blue, Surcharge up (#PR121)	90.00	50.00	60.00	35.00

* Used prices are for stamps with contemporary cancels.

R163   R174   R197,R208   R219

1898 Documentary "Battleship" Designs (C)
(Rouletted 5½)

R161	½¢ Orange.............................	2.00	1.25	5.50	3.50
R162	½¢ Dark Gray	.30	.20	.20	.15
R163	1¢ Pale Blue	.25	.20	.20	.15
R163p	1¢ Hyphen Hole Perf. 7	.35	.22	.30	.20
R164	2¢ Carmine	.25	.20	.20	.15
R164p	2¢ Hyphen Hole Perf. 7	.35	.22	.30	.20
R165	3¢ Dark Blue	1.10	.60	.20	.15
R165p	3¢ Hyphen Hole Perf. 7	8.50	5.25	.50	.35
R166	4¢ Pale Rose	.75	.45	.20	.15
R166p	4¢ Hyphen Hole Perf. 7	3.75	2.25	1.00	.60
R167	5¢ Lilac	.25	.20	.20	.15
R167p	5¢ Hyphen Hole Perf. 7	3.75	2.25	.30	.20
R168	10¢ Dark Brown	1.00	.60	.20	.15
R168p	10¢ Hyphen Hole Perf. 7	3.25	1.95	.30	.20
R169	25¢ Purple Brown	1.10	.60	.20	.15
R169p	25¢ Hyphen Hole Perf. 7	5.00	3.00	.35	.25
R170	40¢ Blue Lilac (cut .25)	90.00	50.00	1.80	1.00
R170p	40¢ Hyphen Hole Perf. 7	140.00	85.00	24.00	15.00
R171	50¢ Slate Violet.......................	9.00	5.50	.20	.15
R171p	50¢ Hyphen Hole Perf. 7	16.50	10.75	.30	.20
R172	80¢ Bistre (cut .15)	52.50	32.50	.35	.20
R172p	80¢ Hyphen Hole Perf. 7	140.00	85.00	27.50	16.50

Commerce Design (C) (Rouletted 5½)

R173	$1 Commerce, Dark Green.......	6.50	3.75	.20	.15
R173p	1¢ Hyphen Hole Perf. 7	14.50	9.00	.70	.45
R174	$3 Dark Brown (cut .18)	12.50	7.50	.75	.45
R174p	3¢ Hyphen Hole Perf. 7 (cut .30)	19.50	12.00	2.50	1.50
R175	$5 Orange Red Perf. 7 (cut .20)	16.50	10.75	1.35	.80
R176	$10 Black Perf. 7 (cut .60)	50.00	32.50	2.50	1.50
R177	$30 Red Perf. 7 (cut 35.00).......	160.00	95.00	80.00	50.00
R178	$50 Gray Brown Perf.7(cut 1.80)	75.00	43.50	5.50	3.50

1899 Documentary Stamps Imperforated (C)

R179	$100 Marshall, Brn. & Blk.(cut 17.50)	85.00	53.50	25.00	16.00
R180	$500 Hamilton,Car.Lk/Blk(cut 210.00)	550.00	350.00	400.00	250.00
R181	$1000 Madison, Grn&Blk (cut 95.00)	550.00	350.00	300.00	240.00

1900 Documentary Stamps (C) (Hyphen Hole Perf 7)

R182	$1 Commerce, Carmine (cut .15)	12.75	7.50	.50	.30
R183	$3 Lake (cut 7.50)	95.00	55.00	40.00	24.50

1900 Surcharged Large Black Numerals (C)

Scott's No.		Uncancelled		Used	
		Fine	Ave.	Fine	Ave.
R184	$1 Gray (cut .15)	8.50	5.00	.20	.15
R185	$2 Gray (cut .15)	7.50	4.25	.20	.15
R186	$3 Gray (cut $2.00)	42.50	22.50	10.50	6.00
R187	$5 Gray (cut $1.00)	33.50	20.00	6.50	3.95
R188	$10 Gray (cut 3.35)	57.50	35.00	15.00	9.00
R189	$50 Gray (cut 70.00)	550.00	300.00	325.00	185.00

1902 Surcharged Ornamental Numerals (C)

R190	$1 Green (cut .25)	15.00	8.50	3.25	1.95
R191	$2 Green (cut .15)	13.50	7.50	1.30	.80
R192	$5 Green (cut $4.00)	110.00	65.00	26.50	16.50
R193	$10 Green (cut 45.00)	265.00	150.00	130.00	70.00
R194	$50 Green (cut 210.00)	875.00	495.00	725.00	400.00

1914 Documentary Single Line Watermark "USPS" (40%) (B)

R195	½¢ Rose	6.25	3.85	3.00	1.85
R196	1¢ Rose	1.25	.70	.20	.15
R197	2¢ Rose	1.65	.95	.20	.15
R198	3¢ Rose	40.00	21.50	25.00	14.50
R199	4¢ Rose	10.75	6.50	1.75	1.00
R200	5¢ Rose	3.50	1.95	.20	.15
R201	10¢ Rose	3.00	1.65	.20	.15
R202	25¢ Rose	24.75	15.75	.60	.35
R203	40¢ Rose	15.00	9.00	.85	.50
R204	50¢ Rose	5.00	3.00	.20	.15
R205	80¢ Rose	75.00	45.00	9.00	5.50

1914 Documentary Double Line Watermark "USIR" (40%) (B)

R206	½¢ Rose	1.20	.65	.50	.30
R207	1¢ Rose	.25	.20	.20	.15
R208	2¢ Rose	.25	.20	.20	.15
R209	3¢ Rose	1.35	.70	.20	.15
R210	4¢ Rose	3.25	1.85	.40	.25
R211	5¢ Rose	1.60	.90	.25	.18
R212	10¢ Rose	1.00	.65	.20	.15
R213	25¢ Rose	4.00	2.40	1.10	.65
R214	40¢ Rose (cut .50)	55.00	31.75	11.00	6.50
R215	50¢ Rose	12.50	8.00	.25	.18
R216	80¢ Rose (cut .90)	80.00	43.50	16.00	8.75
R217	$1 Liberty, Green (cut .15).........	23.50	14.00	.25	.18
R218	$2 Carmine (cut .15)	35.00	21.50	.45	.30
R219	$3 Purple (cut .20)	45.00	25.00	2.00	1.10
R220	$5 Blue (cut .60)	42.50	23.00	2.50	1.50
R221	$10 Orange (cut .90)	95.00	55.00	4.50	2.65
R222	$30 Vermillion (cut 2.00)	180.00	110.00	9.75	6.00
R223	$50 Violet (cut 275.00)...............	1000.00	575.00	700.00	385.00

1914-15 Documentary stamps - Perforated 12, without gum (B)

R224	$60 Lincoln, Brown (cut 42.50) ..	...	...	100.00	60.00
R225	$100 Wash., Green (cut 16.50)..	...	...	37.50	20.00
R226	$500 Hamilton, Blue (cut 185.00)	...	...	450.00	250.00
R227	$1000 Madison, Orange (cut 185.00)	...	...	450.00	250.00

R228,R251   R240   R733

1917-33 Documentary Stamps - Perf. 11 (20%) (B)

R228	1¢ Rose...................................	.25	.20	.20	.15
R229	2¢ Rose...................................	.25	.20	.20	.15
R230	3¢ Rose...................................	1.20	.70	.30	.20
R231	4¢ Rose...................................	.40	.25	.20	.15
R232	5¢ Rose...................................	.25	.20	.20	.15
R233	8¢ Rose...................................	1.65	1.00	.30	.20
R234	10¢ Rose.................................	.35	.25	.20	.15
R235	20¢ Rose.................................	1.00	.60	.20	.15
R236	25¢ Rose.................................	1.00	.60	.20	.15
R237	40¢ Rose.................................	1.35	.80	.35	.25
R238	50¢ Rose.................................	1.75	1.10	.20	.15
R239	80¢ Rose.................................	4.25	2.25	.20	.15
R240	$1 Green, Without Date	5.00	3.00	.20	.15
R241	$2 Rose...................................	9.50	5.75	.20	.15
R242	$3 Violet (cut .15).....................	26.50	16.00	.65	.35
R243	$4 Brown (cut .15)....................	20.00	12.00	1.50	.90
R244	$5 Blue (cut .15).......................	12.50	7.00	.25	.18
R245	$10 Orange (cut .15).................	25.00	15.00	.85	.50

1917 Documentary Stamps - Perforated 12, Without Gum (B)

R246	$30 Grant, Orange (cut 1.25)......	40.00	25.00	8.50	5.25
R247	$60 Lincoln, Brown (cut .85)......	47.50	30.00	6.50	4.00
R248	$100 Wash., Green (cut .40)......	25.00	15.00	1.10	.65
R249	$500 Hamilton, Blue (cut 9.00) ..	175.00	120.00	30.00	17.50
R250	$1000 Madison, Orange (cut 4.25)	110.00	62.50	13.00	7.50

1928-29 Documentary Stamps - Perf. 10 (20%) (B)

Scott's No.		Unused Fine	Unused Ave.	Used Fine	Used Ave.
R251	1¢ Carmine Rose.........	1.90	1.15	1.30	.80
R252	2¢ Carmine Rose.........	.50	.30	.20	.15
R253	4¢ Carmine Rose.........	5.50	3.00	3.75	2.25
R254	5¢ Carmine Rose.........	1.00	.45	.55	.35
R255	10¢ Carmine Rose.........	1.50	.90	1.10	.70
R256	20¢ Carmine Rose.........	5.75	3.25	5.00	3.00
R257	$1 Green (cut 4.50).........	75.00	45.00	25.00	15.00
R258	$2 Rose.........	28.50	16.50	2.25	1.30
R259	$10 Orange (cut 20.00).........	95.00	60.00	37.50	22.50

1929-30 Documentary Stamps - Perf. 11x10 (20%) (B)

		Fine	Ave.	Fine	Ave.
R260	2¢ Carmine Rose.........	2.75	1.50	2.50	1.40
R261	5¢ Carmine Rose.........	1.75	1.10	1.75	1.10
R262	10¢ Carmine Rose.........	7.50	4.00	6.50	4.00
R263	20¢ Carmine Rose.........	16.50	10.00	8.50	5.00

#R264-R732 1940-1958 Documentary Stamps (Dated)
We will be glad to quote prices on any of these items we have in stock.

1962-1963 Documentary Stamps

Scott's No.		Plate Block	F.VF NH	F.VF Used
R733	10¢ Internal Revenue Bldg	12.75	2.50	.40
R734	10¢ Bldg., Without Date (1963)........	23.50	3.25	.40

RB1   RB12   RB33,RB45   RB66

1871-74 Proprietary (All Used) (C)

Scott's No.		Violet Paper(a) Fine	Violet Paper(a) Ave.	Green Paper(b) Fine	Green Paper(b) Ave.
RB1	1¢ Green and Black.........	4.25	2.65	6.50	4.00
RB2	2¢ Green and Black.........	4.75	2.75	13.00	7.75
RB3	3¢ Green and Black.........	12.50	7.50	40.00	22.50
RB4	4¢ Green and Black.........	8.25	4.75	12.50	7.50
RB5	5¢ Green and Black.........	120.00	70.00	125.00	75.00
RB6	6¢ Green and Black.........	30.00	18.00	75.00	41.50
RB7	10¢ Green and Black.........	250.00	150.00	40.00	22.50
RB8	50¢ Green and Black.........	525.00	300.00	825.00	450.00

1875-81 Proprietary (All Used) (C)

Scott's No.		Silk Paper(s) Fine	Silk Paper(s) Ave.	Watermarked(b) Fine	Watermarked(b) Ave.	Rouletted(c) Fine	Rouletted(c) Ave.
RB11	1¢ Green.........	1.65	1.00	.40	.25	50.00	27.50
RB12	2¢ Brown.........	2.25	1.30	1.35	.75	70.00	42.50
RB13	3¢ Orange.........	10.75	5.75	4.00	2.50	70.00	42.50
RB14	4¢ Red Brown.........	5.25	3.00	5.25	2.95	...	...
RB15	4¢ Red.........	...	...	4.00	2.25	100.00	60.00
RB16	5¢ Black.........	87.50	50.00	75.00	37.50	...	...
RB17	6¢ Violet Blue.........	21.50	13.00	16.00	9.50	200.00	120.00
RB18	6¢ Violet.........	...	...	25.00	16.00	...	...
RB19	10¢ Blue.........	...	...	265.00	160.00	...	...

1898 Proprietary Stamps (Battleship) (C) (Roulette 5½)

Scott's No.		Uncancelled Fine	Uncancelled Ave.	Used Fine	Used Ave.
RB20	1/8¢ Yellow Green.........	.25	.20	.20	.15
RB20p	1/8¢ Hyphen Hole Perf 7.........	.25	.20	.20	.15
RB21	1/4¢ Pale Brown.........	.25	.20	.20	.15
RB21p	1/4¢ Hyphen Hole Perf 7.........	.25	.20	.20	.15
RB22	3/8¢ Deep Orange.........	.25	.20	.20	.15
RB22p	3/8¢ Hyphen Hole Perf 7.........	.30	.20	.20	.15
RB23	5/8¢ Deep Ultramarine.........	.25	.20	.20	.15
RB23p	5/8¢ Hyphen Hole Perf 7.........	.30	.20	.20	.15
RB24	1¢ Dark Green.........	.80	.50	.30	.20
RB24p	1¢ Hyphen Hole Perf 7.........	23.50	14.75	14.50	9.00
RB25	1¼¢ Violet.........	.25	.20	.20	.15
RB25p	1¼¢ Hyphen Hole Perf 7.........	.30	.20	.20	.15
RB26	1 1/8¢ Dull Blue.........	6.25	4.00	1.10	.70
RB26p	1 1/8¢ Hyphen Hoe Perf 7.........	18.75	11.00	6.50	4.25
RB27	2¢ Violet Brown.........	.60	.40	.20	.15
RB27p	2¢ Hyphen Hole Perf 7.........	3.85	2.25	.30	.20
RB28	2½¢ Lake.........	2.10	1.25	.20	.15
RB28p	2½¢ Hyphen Hole Perf 7.........	2.40	1.50	.25	.18
RB29	3¾¢ Olive Gray.........	25.00	16.50	6.50	4.50
RB29p	3¾¢ Hyphen Hole Perf 7.........	47.50	27.50	14.50	8.50
RB30	4¢ Purple.........	6.25	4.00	.85	.50
RB30p	4¢ Hyphen Hole Perf 7.........	47.50	27.50	14.50	8.50
RB31	5¢ Brown Orange.........	6.00	3.75	.75	.45
RB31p	5¢ Hyphen Hole Perf 7.........	47.50	27.50	7.50	4.50

1914 Black Proprietary Stamps - S.L. Wmk. "USPS" (40%) (B)

Scott's No.		Unused Fine	Unused Ave.	Used Fine	Used Ave.
RB32	1/8¢ Black.........	.25	.20	.20	.15
RB33	¼¢ Black.........	1.50	.90	1.10	.65
RB34	3/8¢ Black.........	.25	.20	.20	.15
RB35	5/8¢ Black.........	3.00	1.80	2.25	1.35

1914 Black Proprietary Stamps - S.L. Wmk. "USPS" (40%) (continued)

Scott's No.		Unused Fine	Unused Ave.	Used Fine	Used Ave.
RB36	1¼¢ Black.........	2.10	1.40	1.10	.70
RB37	1 7/8¢ Black.........	30.00	17.50	15.00	9.50
RB38	2½¢ Black.........	6.00	3.75	2.35	1.50
RB39	3 1/8¢ Black.........	70.00	40.00	42.50	25.00
RB40	3¼¢ Black.........	30.00	18.50	20.00	12.50
RB41	4¢ Black.........	42.50	25.00	23.50	14.00
RB42	4 3/8¢ Black.........	...	695.00	...	...
RB43	5¢ Black.........	95.00	57.50	60.00	35.00

1914 Black Proprietary Stamps - D.L. Wmk. "USIR" (40%) (B)

RB44	1/8¢ Black.........	.25	.20	.20	.15
RB45	¼¢ Black.........	.25	.20	.20	.15
RB46	3/8¢ Black.........	.55	.33	.30	.18
RB47	½¢ Black.........	3.25	1.95	2.25	1.40
RB48	5/8¢ Black.........	.25	.20	.20	.15
RB49	1¢ Black.........	4.50	2.50	3.25	1.90
RB50	1¼¢ Black.........	.40	.25	.35	.22
RB51	1½¢ Black.........	3.25	1.90	2.00	1.10
RB52	1 7/8¢ Black.........	1.10	.65	.65	.40
RB53	2¢ Black.........	5.50	3.50	3.25	1.95
RB54	2½¢ Black.........	1.10	.65	1.10	.65
RB55	3¢ Black.........	3.75	2.10	2.25	1.35
RB56	3 1/8¢ Black.........	5.00	3.00	2.50	1.50
RB57	3¾¢ Black.........	9.00	5.50	8.00	4.75
RB58	4¢ Black.........	.50	.30	.20	.15
RB59	4 3/8¢ Black.........	12.00	7.00	7.00	4.25
RB60	5¢ Black.........	2.65	1.50	2.50	1.40
RB61	6¢ Black.........	47.50	29.50	36.50	21.75
RB62	8¢ Black.........	15.00	9.00	11.00	6.75
RB63	10¢ Black.........	9.00	5.50	7.50	4.50
RB64	20¢ Black.........	18.75	11.50	16.00	9.75

1919 Proprietary Stamps (30%) (B)

RB65	1¢ Dark Blue.........	.25	.20	.20	.15
RB66	2¢ Dark Blue.........	.25	.20	.20	.15
RB67	3¢ Dark Blue.........	1.10	.65	.65	.40
RB68	4¢ Dark Blue.........	1.10	.65	.55	.30
RB69	5¢ Dark Blue.........	1.35	.80	.65	.40
RB70	8¢ Dark Blue.........	11.50	7.00	9.00	5.50
RB71	10¢ Dark Blue.........	4.25	2.75	2.10	1.30
RB72	20¢ Dark Blue.........	6.25	4.00	3.25	1.95
RB73	40¢ Dark Blue.........	40.00	25.00	10.50	6.50

1918-34 Future Delivery Stamps (20%) (B)

RC1	2¢ Carmine Rose.........	2.75	1.75	.20	.15
RC2	3¢ Carmine Rose (cut 10.75)	25.00	15.00	20.00	12.50
RC3	4¢ Carmine Rose.........	5.00	3.00	.20	.15
RC3A	5¢ Carmine Rose.........	57.50	35.00	6.50	3.75
RC4	10¢ Carmine Rose.........	9.50	6.00	.20	.15
RC5	20¢ Carmine Rose.........	12.50	7.50	.20	.15
RC6	25¢ Carmine Rose (cut .15)	30.00	18.00	.75	.45
RC7	40¢ Carmine Rose (cut .15)	35.00	21.50	.85	.50
RC8	50¢ Carmine Rose.........	7.50	4.50	.35	.20
RC9	80¢ Carmine Rose (cut .85)	62.50	38.50	8.00	5.00
RC10	$1 Green (cut .15).........	25.00	15.00	.25	.18
RC11	$2 Rose (cut .15).........	30.00	18.00	.25	.18
RC12	$3 Violet (cut .20).........	70.00	40.00	2.25	1.30
RC13	$5 Dark Blue (cut .15).........	42.50	25.00	.50	.25
RC14	$10 Orange (cut .20).........	70.00	40.00	1.00	.60
RC15	$20 Olive Bistre (cut .50)	125.00	75.00	5.00	3.00
RC16	$30 Vermillion (cut 1.50).......	65.00	40.00	3.25	1.95
RC17	$50 Olive Green (cut .55)	50.00	28.50	1.10	.65
RC18	$60 Brown (cut .80).........	65.00	35.00	2.10	1.30
RC19	$100 Yellow Green (cut 5.75)....	70.00	38.50	22.50	13.50
RC20	$500 Blue (cut 4.50).........	65.00	37.50	10.50	6.25
RC21	$1000 Orange (cut 1.65)...........	65.00	37.50	5.25	3.25
RC22	1¢ Carm. Rose, Narrow Overprt.	1.10	.70	.20	.15
RC23	80¢ Narrow Overprint (cut .30) ..	50.00	35.00	3.00	1.80
RC25	$1 Self Overprint (cut .15)	22.50	15.00	.75	.45
RC26	$10 Self Overprint (cut 8.75)	80.00	50.00	15.00	10.00

1918-29 Stock Transfer Stamps, Perf. 11 or 12 (20%) (B)

RD1	1¢ Carmine Rose.........	.80	.45	.20	.15
RD2	2¢ Carmine Rose.........	.25	.20	.20	.15
RD3	4¢ Carmine Rose.........	.25	.20	.20	.15
RD4	5¢ Carmine Rose.........	.25	.20	.20	.15
RD5	10¢ Carmine Rose.........	.25	.20	.20	.15
RD6	20¢ Carmine Rose.........	.50	.30	.20	.15
RD7	25¢ Carmine Rose (cut .15)	1.25	.70	.25	.20
RD8	40¢ Carmine Rose (cut .15)	1.25	.70	.20	.15
RD9	50¢ Carmine Rose.........	.55	.35	.20	.15
RD10	80¢ Carmine Rose (cut .15)	2.50	1.50	.30	.20
RD11	$1 Green, Red Overprint (cut 4.00)	57.50	33.50	16.50	10.00
RD12	$1 Green, Black Overprint	2.10	1.25	.25	.20
RD13	$2 Rose.........	2.10	1.25	.20	.15
RD14	$3 Violet (cut .22).........	15.00	8.50	3.75	2.30
RD15	$4 Brown (cut .15).........	7.50	4.25	.25	.18
RD16	$5 Blue (cut .15).........	5.00	3.00	.25	.18
RD17	$10 Orange (cut .15).........	13.00	8.00	.30	.20
RD18	$20 Bistre (cut 3.00).........	65.00	40.00	18.00	11.00
RD19	$30 Vermillion (cut 2.00)..........	16.00	9.75	4.25	2.50
RD20	$50 Olive Green (cut 17.50)	95.00	52.50	52.50	28.75
RD21	$60 Brown (cut 7.75).........	95.00	52.50	20.00	13.00
RD22	$100 Green (cut 2.00).........	21.50	13.00	5.25	3.00
RD23	$500 Blue (cut 60.00)	285.00	190.00	100.00	65.00
RD24	$1000 Orange (cut 26.75).........	150.00	95.00	65.00	40.00

1928-32 Transfer Stamps, Pf. 10 (20%)

Scott's No.		Fine Unused	Used
RD25	1¢ Carm rose	2.10	.25
RD26	4¢ Carm rose	2.10	.25
RD27	10¢ Carm rose	1.80	.25
RD28	20¢ Carm rose	2.50	.25
RD29	50¢ Carm rose	3.00	.25
RD30	$1 Green	25.00	.20
RD31	$2 Carm rose	25.00	.20
RD32	$10 Orng (cut .15)	27.50	.30

1920-28 Transfers, Serif Ovpts. (20%)
RD33-38, Pf. 11; RD39-41, Pf. 10

RD33	2¢ Carm rose	6.25	.60
RD34	10¢ Carm rose	1.00	.25
RD35	20¢ Carm rose	1.00	.25
RD36	50¢ Carm rose	2.50	.25
RD37	$1 Green (cut .25)	35.00	8.50
RD38	$2 Rose (cut .25)	30.00	8.50
RD39	2¢ Carm rose	5.00	.45
RD40	10¢ Carm rose	1.10	.45
RD41	20¢ Carm rose	2.00	.25

We will be glad to quote on any of the following Revenue categories:
1940-58 Dated Documentaries
Wine Stamps & Playing Card Stamps

SILVER TAX STAMPS

The Silver Purchase Act of 1934 imposed a 50% tax on the net profit resulting from the transfer of silver bullion. The Silver Tax Stamps, authorized by Congress on Feb. 20, 1934, were to be affixed to the transfer documents as payment of the tax.

RG 1

RG 111

1934 Documentary Stamps of 1917 Overprinted, D.L. Wmk., Perf. 11

Scott's No.		F-VF Unused	Used
RG1	1¢ Carm rose	1.00	.75
RG2	2¢ Carm rose	1.50	.25
RG3	3¢ Carm rose	1.50	.75
RG4	4¢ Carm rose	2.00	1.50
RG5	5¢ Carm rose	3.25	1.50
RG6	8¢ Carm rose	4.25	2.50
RG7	10¢ Carm rose	4.50	1.75
RG8	20¢ Carm rose	6.50	3.00
RG9	25¢ Carm rose	6.75	3.50
RG10	40¢ Carm rose	7.25	5.00
RG11	50¢ Carm rose	6.50	6.00
RG12	80¢ Carm rose	12.50	8.50
RG13	$1 Green	20.00	10.00
RG14	$2 Rose	20.00	13.50
RG15	$3 Violet	47.50	23.50
RG16	$4 Yellow brn	40.00	16.00
RG17	$5 Dark blue	40.00	16.00
RG18	$10 Orange	57.50	16.00

Without Gum, Perf. 12

RG19	$30 Vermillion	100.00	40.00
	Cut cancel	...	17.50
RG20	$60 Brown	115.00	62.50
	Cut cancel	...	25.00
RG21	$100 Green	110.00	25.00
RG22	$500 Blue	335.00	195.00
	Cut cancel	...	85.00
RG23	$1000 Orange	...	90.00
	Cut cancel	...	52.50

1936 Same Ovpt., 11 mm between words "SILVER TAX"

RG26	$100 Green	150.00	60.00
RG27	$1000 Orange	...	450.00

1940 Documentary Stamps of 1917 D.L. Wmk., Perf. 11, Overprinted
SERIES 1940

SILVER
TAX

RG37	1¢ Rose pink	14.00	...
RG38	2¢ Rose pink	14.00	...
RG39	3¢ Rose pink	14.00	...
RG40	4¢ Rose pink	15.00	...
RG41	5¢ Rose pink	8.00	...

Silver Tax (cont.)

Scott No.		F-VF Unused	Used
RG42	8¢ Rose pink	15.00	...
RG43	10¢ Rose pink	14.00	...
RG44	20¢ Rose pink	15.00	...
RG45	25¢ Rose pink	15.00	...
RG46	40¢ Rose pink	22.50	...
RG47	50¢ Rose pink	22.50	...
RG48	80¢ Rose pink	22.50	...
RG49	$1 Green	90.00	...
RG50	$2 Rose	145.00	...
RG51	$3 Violet	195.00	...
RG52	$4 Yellow brn	375.00	...
RG53	$5 Dark blue	475.00	...
RG54	$10 Orange	525.00	...

Ovpt in Blk. SERIES OF 1941 **pf.11 (Gray)**

RG58	1¢ Hamilton	3.00	...
RG59	2¢ Wolcott, Jr	3.00	...
RG60	3¢ Dexter	3.00	...
RG61	4¢ Gallatin	4.50	...
RG62	5¢ Campbell	5.25	...
RG63	8¢ Dallas	6.50	...
RG64	10¢ Crawford	7.50	...
RG65	20¢ Rush	10.00	...
RG66	25¢ Ingham	13.00	...
RG67	40¢ McLane	23.00	...
RG68	50¢ Duane	27.50	...
RG69	80¢ Taney	47.50	...
RG70	$1 Woodbury	60.00	25.00
RG71	$2 Ewing	150.00	45.00
RG72	$3 Forward	125.00	55.00
RG73	$4 Spencer	175.00	65.00
RG74	$5 Bibb	150.00	65.00
RG75	$10 Walker	240.00	85.00
RG76	$20 Meredith	425.00	265.00

Without Gum, Perf. 12

RG77	$30 Corwin	225.00	125.00
	Cut cncl	...	65.00
RG79	$60 Cobb	...	175.00
	Cut cncl	...	85.00
RG80	$100 Thomas	...	275.00
	Cut cncl	...	90.00

#RG58-82 Overprinted SERIES OF 1942

RG83	1¢ Hamilton	2.00	...
RG84	2¢ Wolcott, Jr	2.00	...
RG85	3¢ Dexter	2.00	...
RG86	4¢ Gallatin	2.00	...
RG87	5¢ Campbell	2.00	...
RG88	8¢ Dallas	4.50	...
RG89	10¢ Crawford	5.00	...
RG90	20¢ Rush	7.50	...
RG91	25¢ Ingham	15.00	...
RG92	40¢ McLane	17.50	...
RG93	50¢ Duane	17.50	...
RG94	80¢ Taney	50.00	...
RG95	$1 Woodbury	60.00	...
RG96	$2 Ewing	60.00	...
RG97	$3 Forward	110.00	...
RG98	$4 Spencer	110.00	...
RG99	$5 Bibb	120.00	...
RG100	$10 Walker	325.00	...
RG101	$20 Meredith	425.00	...

1944 Silver Stamps of 1941 w/o ovpt.

RG108	1¢ Hamilton	1.00	...
RG109	2¢ Wolcott, Jr	1.00	...
RG110	3¢ Dexter	1.00	...
RG111	4¢ Gallatin	1.00	...
RG112	5¢ Campbell	2.10	...
RG113	8¢ Dallas	3.15	...
RG114	10¢ Crawford	3.15	...
RG115	20¢ Rush	6.50	...
RG116	25¢ Ingham	8.25	...
RG117	40¢ McLane	12.75	...
RG118	50¢ Duane	12.75	...
RG119	80¢ Taney	18.50	...
RG120	$1 Woodbury	35.00	12.50
RG121	$2 Ewing	52.50	30.00
RG122	$3 Forward	60.00	22.50
RG123	$4 Spencer	75.00	55.00
RG124	$5 Bibb	80.00	25.00
RG125	$10 Walker	110.00	45.00
	Cut cncl	...	13.50
RG126	$20 Meredith	425.00	350.00

Without Gum, Perf. 12

RG127	$30 Corwin	225.00	110.00
	Cut cncl	...	50.00
RG128	$50 Gutherie	525.00	500.00
	Cut cncl	...	285.00
RG129	$60 Cobb	...	350.00
	Cut cncl	...	150.00
RG130	$100 Thomas	...	32.50
	Cut cncl	...	12.50
RG131	$500 Dix	...	400.00
	Cut cncl	...	225.00
RG132	$1000 Chase	...	135.00
	Cut cncl	...	65.00

CIGARETTE TUBE STAMPS

On Feb. 26, 1926, a law was enacted placing a tax on Cigarette Tubes at the rate of 1¢ per 50, or fraction thereof. The tax on tubes, which a smoker would use to make his own cigarettes, was collected by means of 1¢ & 2¢ stamps, which were affixed to the packages.

RH 1
Doc. Stamp of 1917 ovpt., D.L. Wmk.

Scott No.		F-VF Unused	Used
RH1	1¢ Carm rose ('19)	.50	.25
	Perf. 11		
RH2	1¢ Carm rose ('29)	27.50	9.50

RH4

RH3	1¢ Rose (1933)	2.25	.90
RH4	2¢ Rose (1933)	6.75	1.75

POTATO TAX STAMPS

Potato Tax Stamps were issued to comply with the Agricultural Adjustment Act of Dec. 1, 1935. The tax of ¾¢ per pound was to be paid by potato growers who grew more than their official allotments. The Supreme Court declared the Act unconstitutional.

RI 1

Issue of 1935

Scott's No.		F-VF Unused
RI1	¾¢ Carm rose	.25
RI2	1¼¢ Black brn	.50
RI3	2¼¢ Yellow grn	.50
RI4	3¢ Light Violet	.50
RI5	3¾¢ Olive Bistre	.50
RI6	7½¢ Orange brn	1.35
RI7	11¼¢ Deep orange	1.65
RI8	18¾¢ Violet brn	4.00
RI9	37½¢ Red orange	4.00
RI10	75¢ Blue	4.00
RI11	93¾¢ Rose lake	6.50
RI12	$1.12½¢ Green	11.50
RI13	$1.50 Yellow brn	10.50

TOBACCO SALE TAX STAMPS

The Kerr-Smith Tobacco Control Act, effective June 29, 1934, created the need for these tax stamps. The tax was to apply to the sale of tobacco in excess of officially established quotas and was to be paid in stamps. The Supreme Court declared the Act unconstitutional.

TOBACCO SALE TAX STAMPS
1934 Doc. Issue of 1917, Ovpt. D.L. Wmk., pf. 11

RJ 1

RJ 7

Scott's No.		F-VF Unused	Used
RJ1	1¢ Carm rose	.35	.15
RJ2	2¢ Carm rose	.35	.20
RJ3	5¢ Carm rose	1.25	.35
RJ4	10¢ Carm rose	1.50	.35
RJ5	25¢ Carm rose	4.00	1.50
RJ6	50¢ Carm rose	4.00	1.50
RJ7	$1 Green	8.50	1.75
RJ8	$2 Rose	16.00	1.75
RJ9	$5 Dark blue	22.50	3.75
RJ10	$10 Orange	32.50	10.00
RJ11	$20 Olive bistre	80.00	12.50

NARCOTIC TAX STAMPS

Narcotic Tax Stamps were issued as a result of the Revenue Act of 1918 which imposed a tax on narcotics and narcotic derivatives. Narcotic Tax Stamps were affixed to the drug containers to indicate payment of the 1¢ per ounce tax.

It is interesting to note that around 1929, the Federal Government discouraged their collecting by forbidding dealers to trade in the stamps. Listings in the Scott catalog, which were dropped after 1929, were restored after the use of the stamps was discontinued in 1971.

1919 Doc. Issue of 1914, D.L. Wmk., pf. 10, Handstamped "NARCOTIC" in Magenta, Blue or Black

Scott's No.		Fine Unused	Used
RJA1	1¢ Rose	75.00	50.00

1919 Doc. Issue of 1917, D.L. Wmk.,
perf. 11, Handstamped "NARCOTIC," "Narcotic," "NARCOTICS," or "ACT/NARCOTIC/1918"
in Magenta, Blue, Black, Violet or Red

Scott's No.		F-VF Unused	Used
RJA9	1¢ Carm rose	1.75	1.00
RJA10	2¢ Carm rose	4.50	2.75
RJA11	3¢ Carm rose	25.00	20.00
RJA12	4¢ Carm rose	9.00	5.00
RJA13	5¢ Carm rose	12.75	9.50
RJA14	8¢ Carm rose	10.50	8.00
RJA15	10¢ Carm rose	45.00	8.50
RJA16	20¢ Carm rose	50.00	40.00
RJA17	25¢ Carm rose	37.50	26.50
RJA18	40¢ Carm rose	80.00	62.50
RJA19	50¢ Carm rose	17.50	15.00
RJA20	80¢ Carm rose	95.00	65.00
RJA21	$1 Green	85.00	35.00

RJA 33

1919 Doc. Issue of 1917, D.L. Wmk., perf. 11, Overprinted
NARCOTIC
17½ mm wide

RJA33	1¢ Carm rose	1.00	.50
RJA34	2¢ Carm rose	1.50	1.00
RJA35	3¢ Carm rose	32.50	22.50
RJA36	4¢ Carm rose	5.00	3.00
RJA37	5¢ Carm rose	12.00	9.00
RJA38	8¢ Carm rose	21.50	16.50
RJA39	10¢ Carm rose	3.00	3.00
RJA40	25¢ Carm rose	24.00	16.50

Overprint Reading Up

RJA41	$1 Green	35.00	17.50

Narcotic Issues of 1919-1970,D.L. Wmk.

RJA44b

Scott's No.		F-VF Used a.Impf.	b.roult.
RJA42	1¢ Violet..............	4.25	.25
RJA43	1¢ Violet..............	.50	.25
RJA44	2¢ Violet..............	1.00	.50
RJA45	3¢ Violet..............	...	90.00
RJA46	1¢ Violet..............	2.25	.75
RJA47	2¢ Violet..............	1.75	.75
RJA49	4¢ Violet..............	...	7.00
RJA50	5¢ Violet..............	38.50	6.50
RJA51	6¢ Violet..............	...	1.50
RJA52	8¢ Violet..............	6.00	3.00
RJA53	9¢ Violet..............	75.00	8.50
RJA54	10¢ Violet.............	25.00	.50
RJA55	16¢ Violet.............	52.50	4.00
RJA56	18¢ Violet.............	100.00	8.50
RJA57	19¢ Violet.............	135.00	20.00
RJA58	20¢ Violet.............	350.00	175.00

"Cents" below value

RJA59	1¢ Violet..............	50.00	10.00
RJA60	2¢ Violet..............	...	18.50
RJA61	4¢ Violet..............	42.50	32.50
RJA62	5¢ Violet..............	...	25.00
RJA63	6¢ Violet..............	65.00	22.50
RJA64	8¢ Violet..............	...	40.00
RJA65	9¢ Violet..............	21.50	17.00
RJA66	10¢ Violet.............	12.50	14.00
RJA67	16¢ Violet.............	15.00	12.50
RJA68	18¢ Violet.............	350.00	400.00
RJA69	19¢ Violet.............	10.00	...
RJA70	20¢ Violet.............	350.00	195.00
RJA71	25¢ Violet.............	...	23.50
RJA72	40¢ Violet.............	425.00	...
RJA73	$1 Green...............		1.00
RJA74	$1.28 Green...........	25.00	10.50

Imperf.

1963 Denom. added in blk. by rubber plate (similar to 1959 Postage Dues)

		Unused	Used
RJA76	1¢ Violet...............	75.00	75.00

1964 Denomination on Stamp Plate

RJA77	1¢ Violet...............	...	5.50

CONSULAR SERVICE FEE STAMPS

U.S. Consular Service Fee Stamps went into use on June 1, 1906 at U.S. consulates throughout the world. The stamps were affixed to documents to show that a fee for services had been paid. The revenue was to be used to defray the expense of maintaining the consular services.

RK 5   **RK 36**

1906 "Consular Service" Pf. 12

Scott No.		Fine Used
RK1	25¢ Dark green..............	35.00
RK2	50¢ Carmine..................	47.50
RK3	$1 Dark violet................	5.00
RK4	$2 Brown	4.25
RK5	$2.50 Dark blue	1.30
RK6	$5 Brown red	13.00
RK7	$10 Orange....................	47.50

Perf. 10

RK8	25¢ Dark green..............	35.00
RK9	50¢ Carmine..................	37.50
RK10	$1 Dark violet.................	225.00
RK11	$2 Brown	52.50
RK12	$2.50 Dark blue	10.75
RK13	$5 Brown red	70.00

Consular Service, Pf. 11

Scott No.		Fine Used
RK14	25¢ Dark green..............	42.50
RK15	50¢ Carmine.................	70.00
RK16	$1 Dark violet	1.50
RK17	$2 Brown	2.25
RK18	$2.50 Dark blue	.50
RK19	$5 Brown red	3.25
RK20	$9 Gray.........................	10.00
RK21	$10 Orange....................	19.50

1924 "Foreign Service" Pf. 11

RK22	$1 Dark violet	47.50
RK23	$2 Brown	60.00
RK24	$2.50 Dark blue	8.75
RK25	$5 Brown red	40.00
RK26	$9 Gray.........................	165.00

Issue of 1925-52 Perf. 10

RK27	$1 Violet	17.00
RK28	$2 Brown	43.50
RK29	$2.50 Ultramarine	1.35
RK30	$5 Carmine....................	8.00
RK31	$9 Gray.........................	30.00

Perf. 11

RK32	25¢ Green	47.50
RK33	50¢ Orange	47.50
RK34	$1 Violet	2.50
RK35	$2 Brown	2.50
RK36	$2.50 Blue	.50
RK37	$5 Carmine....................	3.25
RK38	$9 Gray.........................	12.00
RK39	$10 Blue gray	57.50
RK40	$20 Violet	65.00

CUSTOMS FEES

Customs Fees Stamps were issued in 1887 to indicate payment of fees to the U.S. Customs House, N.Y. They were affixed to documents and cancelled with a "PAID" handstamp.

RL 5

		F-VF Used
RL1	20¢ Dull Rose	1.00
RL2	30¢ Orange	1.75
RL3	40¢ Green	2.00
RL4	50¢ Dark blue	3.75
RL5	60¢ Red violet	1.75
RL6	70¢ Brown violet.............	27.50
RL7	80¢ Brown......................	67.50
RL8	90¢ Black.......................	80.00

MOTOR VEHICLE USE STAMPS

Motor Vehicle Use Stamps were authorized by the Revenue Act of 1941. The annual tax amounted to $5.00, extending from July 1 to June 30, the government's fiscal year. Since the tax was to be reduced 1/12 of $5.00 each month after July, it was necessary to produce 12 stamps, each with a different dennomination and each decreasing in face value by 1/12 of the annual fee.

MOTOR VEHICLE USE STAMPS

RV 6   **RV 42**

1942 Gum on Back

		F-VF Unused
RV1	$2.09 Light green	1.00

Gum on Face, Inscription on Back

RV2	$1.67 Light green	12.00
RV3	$1.25 Light green	10.00
RV4	84¢ Light green	12.00
RV5	42¢ Light green	10.00

1942 Gum and Control # on Face

RV6	$5.00 Rose red..............	2.50
RV7	$4.59 Rose red..............	20.00
RV8	$4.17 Rose red..............	25.00
RV9	$3.75 Rose red..............	25.00
RV10	$3.34 Rose red..............	25.00
RV11	$2.92 Rose red..............	25.00

1943

RV12	$2.50 Rose red..............	25.00
RV13	$2.09 Rose red..............	20.00
RV14	$1.67 Rose red..............	15.00
RV15	$1.25 Rose red..............	15.00
RV16	84¢ Rose red.................	15.00
RV17	42¢ Rose red.................	15.00
RV18	$5.00 Yellow..................	2.50
RV19	$4.59 Yellow..................	25.00
RV20	$4.17 Yellow..................	35.00
RV21	$3.75 Yellow..................	35.00
RV22	$3.34 Yellow..................	42.50
RV23	$2.92 Yellow..................	50.00

1944

RV24	$2.50 Yellow..................	52.50
RV25	$2.09 Yellow..................	36.50
RV26	$1.67 Yellow..................	25.00
RV27	$1.25 Yellow..................	25.00
RV28	84¢ Yellow....................	21.00
RV29	42¢ Yellow....................	21.00

Gum on Face Control # and Inscription on Back

RV30	$5.00 Violet	2.50
RV31	$4.59 Violet	41.50
RV32	$4.17 Violet	30.00
RV33	$3.75 Violet	30.00
RV34	$3.34 Violet	25.00
RV35	$2.92 Violet	25.00

1945

RV36	$2.50 Violet	25.00
RV37	$2.09 Violet	20.00
RV38	$1.67 Violet	20.00
RV39	$1.25 Violet	20.00
RV40	84¢ Violet	15.00
RV41	42¢ Violet	12.50

1945 Bright blue green & Yellow green

RV42	$5.00	2.50
RV43	$4.59	30.00
RV44	$4.17	30.00
RV45	$3.75	26.50
RV46	$3.34	25.00
RV47	$2.92	20.00

1946 Bright blue green & Yellow green

RV48	$2.50	20.00
RV49	$2.09	20.00
RV50	$1.67	14.50
RV51	$1.25	12.50
RV52	84¢	12.50
RV53	42¢	9.50

Add the next 12 issues to your collection!
Subscribe to Scott Stamp Monthly

Every month you'll get an entertaining, informative look at the world of stamp collecting from some of the hobby's most talented writers. Enjoy a wide variety of articles and regular features on U.S., foreign stamps, covers and more. In-depth stories, time-saving hints, incredible stamp discoveries plus the very latest information on the new stamp issues from around the world, you'll find it all in Scott Stamp Monthly.

As a subscriber you get what many people consider the most original and thought-provoking read in philately today.

You get all this and more every month!

Favorite Find - Stories about stamp discoveries in some of the most unlikely places. Learn how you too can make finds.

Catalogue Update - The #1 source for new issue news. Each month you get Scott numbers and illustrations for hundreds of stamps. The By Topic column organizes stamps by subject matter.

Amazing Stamp Stories - A new stamp story every month done in the classic-illustrated style of Ripley's Believe It Or Not.

Hungry Mind - A just for fun trivia quiz that tests your stamp knowledge.

Spotlight - Written by Ken Lawrence, one of philately's top journalists, the column zeros-in and explores a different topic every month.

Free-For-All - It's your chance to get free stamps or related collectable simply by sending in stamped addressed envelope. It's fun, It's easy, but best of all it's FREE!

Stamp Traveler - Explore some of stampdom's most famous places and the chance stamp encounter that made the trip memorable.

Stars & Stripes, Judaica and **Passage To Asia** are in-depth articles covering specific areas of interest in the stamp kingdom. Each column is written by some of the hobby's best writers like Gary Griffith, Stanley Piller and Zhao Wenyi

Stamp Pub Flubs - Surprising mistakes and hilarious goofs from the the stamp press.

Catalogue Column - A behind-the-scenes look at key Scott Catalogue editorial decisions.

To Err Is Divine - A lighthearted look at stamp designs goofs and gaffes.

Tip Of The Hat - Tips and techniques for the busy collector.

Return coupon to: Scott Publishing Co. Box 828 Sidney OH 45365-0828

**Trial Offer
6 Issues Only
$9.95**

Subscribe today!
You can use the order form or call our toll free number,

1-800-572-6885
SCOTT

Yes! Please start my subscription to *Scott Stamp Monthly*. (Please allow 4 weeks for delivery.)

☐ 12 Issues $17.95   ☐ 6 Issues $9.95

☐ New   ☐ Renewal

Name _____

Address _____   ABRKMN

City_____ ST_____ ZIP_____

Canada surface mail, add $8 (U.S. Funds) per year.
Outside the U.S. and Canada, add $23 (U.S. Funds) per year for foreign surface mail.

Save $18.00 Off the Cover Price!

DISTILLED SPIRITS

Distilled Spirits Stamps were used to indicate payment of a tax on all whiskey held in bonded warehouses that had been on hand for four years or longer. Upon payment of the tax, the stamps were **stapled** to documents.

RX 18

Inscribed "STAMP FOR SERIES 1950"
Yellow, Green & Black

Scott's No.		F-VF Unused	Used
RX1	1¢	27.50	22.50
RX2	3¢	90.00	85.00
RX3	5¢	18.50	15.00
RX4	10¢	16.50	13.50
RX5	25¢	9.50	7.50
RX6	50¢	9.50	7.50
RX7	$1	2.50	2.00
RX8	$3	20.00	16.50
RX9	$5	6.50	5.00
RX10	$10	3.00	2.50
RX11	$25	13.50	11.50
RX12	$50	7.50	6.50
RX13	$100	5.50	4.00
RX14	$300	25.00	22.50
RX15	$500	16.50	12.50
RX16	$1000	9.50	7.50
RX17	$1500	52.50	42.50
RX18	$2000	5.50	4.50
RX19	$3000	23.50	17.50
RX20	$5000	23.50	17.50
RX21	$10,000	27.50	22.50
RX22	$20,000	35.00	28.50
RX23	$30,000	75.00	55.00
RX24	$40,000	75.00	55.00
RX25	$50,000	85.00	75.00

DISTILLED SPIRITS
Inscription
"STAMP FOR SERIES 1950"
omitted

Yellow, Green & Black

		F-VF Punch Cancel
RX28	5¢	35.00
RX29	10¢	4.00
RX30	25¢	15.00
RX31	50¢	11.50
RX32	$1	1.75
RX33	$3	21.50
RX34	$5	23.50
RX35	$10	1.75
RX36	$25	9.50
RX37	$50	23.50
RX38	$100	2.25
RX39	$300	7.50
RX40	$500	32.50
RX41	$1000	6.50
RX42	$1500	57.50
RX43	$2000	57.50
RX44	$3000	...
RX45	$5000	38.50
RX46	$10,000	65.00

FIREARMS TRANSFER TAX STAMPS

Firearms Transfer Tax Stamps are applied to licenses issued by the Bureay of Alcohol, Tobacco and Firearms to indicate the registration of special classes of firearms. The $200 stamp is usually used with machine guns and is often referred to as the "Tommy Gun" stamp.

**Documentary Stamp of 1917
Overprinted Vertically in Black**

NATIONAL FIREARMS ACT

		F-VF Unused
RY1	$1 Green	300.00

**RY 2,4,6
Without Gum
$200 Face Value**

		Unused
RY2	Dark blue & red Serial #1-1500	1250.00
RY4	Dull blue & red Serial #1501-3000	500.00
RY6	Dull blue & red Serial #3001 & up	225.00

FIREARMS TRANSFER TAX STAMPS

RY 3

With Gum

		F-VF Unused
RY3	$1 Green	75.00
RY5	$5 Red	20.00

RECTIFICATION TAX STAMPS

Rectification Tax Stamps were for the use of rectifiers in paying tax on liquor in bottling tanks. **Used stamps have staple holes.**

RZ12

		F-VF Unused	Used
RZ1	1¢	7.50	3.00
RZ2	3¢	25.00	8.50
RZ3	5¢	16.50	2.50
RZ4	10¢	16.50	2.50
RZ5	25¢	16.50	3.00
RZ6	50¢	20.00	5.00
RZ7	$1	20.00	5.00
RZ8	$3	...	17.50
RZ9	$5	37.50	10.00
RZ10	$10	30.00	3.25
RZ11	$25	...	10.50
RZ12	$50	...	8.00
RZ13	$100	...	9.50
RZ14	$300	...	9.50
RZ15	$500	...	9.50
RZ16	$1000	...	15.00
RZ17	$1500	...	40.00
RZ18	$2000	...	75.00

HUNTING PERMIT STAMPS

RW 1   **RW 26**

On each stamp the words "Void After ..." show a date 1 year later than the actual date of issue.
Even though RW1 has on it "Void After June 30, 1935," the stamp was issued in 1934.
RW1-RW25, RW31 Plate Blocks of 6 Must Have Margins on Two Sides

RW1-RW10 VF Used + 50% (B)

Scott's No.		NH VF	NH F-VF	Unused VF	Unused F-VF	Used F-VF
RW1	1934, $1 Mallards	800.00	575.00	495.00	350.00	115.00
RW2	1935, $1 Canvasbacks	750.00	525.00	450.00	325.00	135.00
RW3	1936, $1 Canada Geese	395.00	290.00	240.00	170.00	65.00
RW4	1937, $1 Scaup Duck	325.00	250.00	160.00	120.00	45.00
RW5	1938, $1 Pintails	375.00	250.00	175.00	130.00	45.00
RW6	1939, $1 Teal	210.00	140.00	120.00	85.00	40.00
RW7	1940, $1 Mallards	210.00	140.00	120.00	85.00	40.00
RW8	1941, $1 Ruddy Ducks	210.00	140.00	120.00	85.00	40.00
RW9	1942, $1 Baldplates	210.00	140.00	125.00	90.00	35.00
RW10	1943, $1 Ducks	85.00	57.50	60.00	45.00	35.00

RW10-RW12 VF Used + 50%   RW13-RW15 VF Used + 40%

RW11	1944, $1 Geese	95.00	55.00	55.00	40.00	25.00
RW12	1945, $1 Shovellers	70.00	45.00	42.50	30.00	20.00
RW13	1946, $1 Redheads	50.00	35.00	40.00	30.00	13.50
RW14	1947, $1 Snow Geese	50.00	35.00	30.00	30.00	13.50
RW15	1948, $1 Buffleheads	60.00	43.00	35.00	28.00	13.50

Plate Blocks	NH VF	NH F-VF	Unused F-VF	Plate Blocks	NH VF	NH F-VF	Unused F-VF
RW10 (6)	625.00	425.00	350.00	RW13 (6)	350.00	300.00	225.00
RW11 (6)	675.00	450.00	350.00	RW14 (6)	350.00	300.00	225.00
RW12 (6)	450.00	300.00	225.00	RW15 (6)	350.00	300.00	225.00

1949-58 Issues VF Used + 40%

Scott's No.		Pl# Blocks F-VF NH	VF NH	F-VF NH	F-VF Unus.	Used F-VF
RW16	1949, $2 Goldeneyes	(6) 350.00	72.50	52.50	35.00	12.00
RW17	1950, $2 Swans	(6) 400.00	82.50	60.00	40.00	10.00
RW18	1951, $2 Gadwalls	(6) 400.00	82.50	60.00	40.00	10.00
RW19	1952, $2 Harlequins	(6) 400.00	82.50	60.00	40.00	7.50
RW20	1953, $2 Teal	(6) 400.00	85.00	60.00	40.00	7.50
RW21	1954, $2 Ring-neckeds	(6) 400.00	82.50	60.00	40.00	7.50
RW22	1955, $2 Blue Geese	(6) 400.00	82.50	60.00	40.00	7.50
RW23	1956, $2 Merganser	(6) 400.00	85.00	60.00	40.00	7.50
RW24	1957, $2 Eider	(6) 400.00	82.50	60.00	40.00	7.50
RW25	1958, $2 Canada Geese	(6) 400.00	82.50	60.00	40.00	7.50

1959-71 Issues VF Used + 30%

RW26	1959, $3 Retriever	375.00	110.00	85.00	55.00	7.50
RW27	1960, $3 Redhead Ducks	350.00	100.00	75.00	50.00	7.50
RW28	1961, $3 Mallard	375.00	110.00	80.00	52.50	7.50
RW29	1962, $3 Pintail Ducks	400.00	120.00	85.00	60.00	9.00
RW30	1963, $3 Brant Landing	400.00	120.00	85.00	60.00	9.00
RW31	1964, $3 Hawaiian Nene	(6)2000.00	120.00	85.00	60.00	9.00
RW32	1965, $3 Canvasback Ducks	400.00	120.00	85.00	60.00	9.00
RW33	1966, $3 Whistling Swans	400.00	120.00	85.00	60.00	9.00
RW34	1967, $3 Old Squaw Ducks	400.00	120.00	85.00	60.00	9.00
RW35	1968, $3 Hooded Mergansers	280.00	70.00	55.00	37.50	9.00
RW36	1969, $3 White-winged Scooters	280.00	70.00	55.00	37.50	7.00
RW37	1970, $3 Ross's Geese	280.00	70.00	55.00	35.00	7.00
RW38	1971, $3 Cinnamon Teals	155.00	47.50	35.00	25.00	7.00

1972-95 Issues VF Used + 25%

Scott's No.		F-VF Pl# Blk	NH VF	NH F-VF	Used F-VF
RW39	1972, $5 Emperor Geese	125.00	30.00	22.50	7.00
RW40	1973, $5 Steller's Eiders	100.00	27.50	20.00	7.00
RW41	1974, $5 Wood Ducks	90.00	23.75	18.00	7.00
RW42	1975, $5 Decoy & Canvasbacks	62.50	18.75	14.00	7.00
RW43	1976, $5 Canada Geese	62.50	18.75	14.00	7.00
RW44	1977, $5 Pair of Ross's Geese	62.50	18.75	14.00	7.00
RW45	1978, $5 Hooded Merganser Drake	62.50	18.75	14.00	7.00
RW46	1979, $7.50 Green-winged Teal	75.00	22.50	17.50	7.00
RW47	1980, $7.50 Mallards	75.00	22.50	17.50	7.00
RW48	1981, $7.50 Ruddy Ducks	75.00	22.50	17.50	7.00
RW49	1982, $7.50 Canvasbacks	75.00	22.50	17.50	7.00
RW50	1983, $7.50 Pintails	75.00	22.50	17.50	7.00
RW51	1984, $7.50 Wigeon	75.00	22.50	17.50	7.00
RW52	1985, $7.50 Cinnamon Teal	75.00	22.50	17.50	7.00
RW53	1986, $7.50 Fulvous Whistling Duck	75.00	22.50	17.50	7.00
RW54	1987, $10 Red Head Ducks	90.00	25.00	20.00	10.00
RW55	1988, $10 Snow Goose	90.00	25.00	20.00	10.00
RW56	1989, $12.50 Lesser Scaups	100.00	28.00	22.50	10.00
RW57	1990, $12.50 Blk-Bellied Whistl. Duck	100.00	28.00	22.50	10.00
RW58	1991, $15.00 King Eiders	135.00	32.50	27.50	12.50
RW59	1992, $15.00 Spectacled Eider	135.00	32.50	27.50	12.50
RW60	1993, $15.00 Canvasbacks	135.00	32.50	27.50	12.50
RW61	1994, $15.00 Redbreasted Merganser	135.00	32.50	27.50	12.50
RW62	1995, $15.00 Mallards	135.00	32.50	27.50	12.50
RW63	1996, $15.00 Surf Scoter	135.00	32.50	27.50	12.50
RW64	1997, $15.00 Canada Goose	135.00	32.50	27.50	12.50

Michael Jaffe is Your Total Duck Dealer

111

STATE DUCK STAMPS

State Duck Stamps provide a natural area for the person who wishes to expand his or her field of interest beyond the collecting of Federal Ducks. In 1971, California became the first state to issue a pictorial duck stamp. Other states followed with the sales providing a much needed source of revenue for wetlands. By 1994, all 50 states will have issued duck stamps.

Similar to Federal policy, many states hold an art competition to determine the winning design. Other states commission an artist. Beginning in 1987, some states started to issue a "Governor's" stamp. These stamps with high face values were designed to garner additional wetland funds. In 1989, the Crow Creek Sioux Tribe of South Dakota became the first Indian Reservation to issue a pictorial duck stamp.

Hunter or Agent stamps generally come in booklets with a tab attached to the stamp, or specific serial numbers on the stamp issued in sheet format that allows collectors' orders to be filled more easily. Many of these stamps exist with plate numbers in the margin. The items illustrated below represent just a sampling of the interesting varieties which have been produced by the various states.

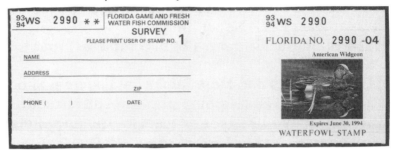

FL 15T SURVEY TAB

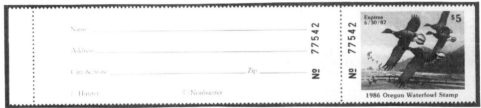

OR 3A HUNTER TYPE WITH TAB

WA 6AN MINI SHEET

MT 4A HZ. PAIR WITH SIDE MARGINS

AR 12 PROOF PAIR, IMPERF.

TN 1A NON-RES. LICENSE

TN 14B 3 PART CARD

STATE HUNTING PERMIT STAMPS

No.	Description	F-VF NH

ALABAMA

AL 1

No.	Description	F-VF NH
AL 1	'79 $5 Wood Ducks	10.00
AL 2	'80 $5 Mallards	10.00
AL 3	'81 $5 Canada Geese	10.00
AL 4	'82 $5 Grn Winged Teal	10.00
AL 5	'83 $5 Widgeon	10.00
AL 6	'84 $5 Buffleheads	10.00
AL 7	'85 $5 Wood Ducks	14.00
AL 8	'86 $5 Canada Geese	14.00
AL 9	'87 $5 Pintails	14.00
AL 10	'88 $5 Canvasbacks	10.00
AL 11	'89 $5 Hooded Mergan	10.00
AL 12	'90 $5 Wood Ducks	10.00
AL 13	'91 $5 Redheads	10.00
AL 14	'92 $5 Cinnamon Teal	10.00
AL 15	'93 $5 Grn Winged Teal	10.00
AL 16	'94 $5 Canvasbacks	10.00
AL 17	'95 $5 Canda Geese	10.00
AL 18	'96 $5 Wood Ducks	10.00
AL 19	'97 $5 Snow Goose	10.00

Alabama Set 1979-97 (19)............ 195.00

ALASKA

AK 1

No.	Description	F-VF NH
AK 1	'85 $5 Emperor Geese	10.00
AK 2	'86 $5 Steller's Elders	10.00
AK 3	'87 $5 Spectacled Elders	10.00
AK 3A	'87 $5 Hunted Full Tab	10.00
AK 4	'88 $5 Trumpeter Swan	10.00
AK 4A	'88 $5 Hunter/Full Tab	10.00
AK 5	'89 $5 Goldeneyes	9.00
AK 5A	'89 $5 Hunter/Full Tab	10.00
AK 6	'90 $5 Oldsquaw	9.00
AK 6A	'90 $5 Hunter/Full Tab	9.50
AK 7	'91 $5 Snowgeese	9.00
AK 7A	'91 $5 Hunter/Full Tab	9.50
AK 8	'92 $5 Canvasbacks	9.00
AK 8A	'92 $5 Hunter/Full Tab	9.50
AK 9	'93 $5 Wh. Fronted Geese	9.00
AK 9A	'93 $5 Hunter/Full Tab	9.50
AK 10	'94 $5 Harlequin	9.00
AK 10A	'94 $5 Hunter/Full Tab	9.50
AK 11	'95 $5 Pacific Brant	9.00
AK 11A	'95 $5 Hunter w/ Full Tab	9.50
AK 12	'96 $5 Aleutian Canada Geese	9.00
AK 12A	'96 $5 Hunter w/ Full Tab	9.50
AK 13	'97 $5 King Eiders	9.00
AK 13A	'97 $5 Hunter w/ Full Tab	9.50

NOTE: Governor's stamps available upon request.

Alaska Set 1985-9 (13) 117.00
Alaska Hunter type, cplt. set (11) 76.00

ARIZONA

AZ 1

No.	Description	F-VF NH
AZ 1	'87 $5.50 Pintails	11.00
AZ 1A	'87 $5.50 Hunter w/tab	11.00

No.	Description	F-VF NH
	ARIZONA (cont.)	
AZ 2	'88 $5.50 Grn. Winged Teal	11.00
AZ 2A	'88 $5.50 Hunter w/tab	11.00
AZ 3	'89 $5.50 Cinnamon Teal	11.00
AZ 3A	'89 $5.50 Hunter w/tab	11.00
AZ 4	'90 $5.50 Canada Geese	11.00
AZ 4A	'90 $5.50 Hunter w/tab	11.00
AZ 5	'91 $5.50 Bl. Winged Teal	9.50
AZ 5A	'91 $5.50 Hunter w/tab	11.00
AZ 6	'92 $5.50 Buffleheads	9.50
AZ 6A	'92 $5.50 Hunter w/tab	11.00
AZ 7	'93 $5.50 Mexican Duck	9.50
AZ 7A	'93 $5.50 Hunter w/tab	11.00
AZ 8	'94 $5.50 Mallards	9.50
AZ 8A	'94 $5.50 Hunter w/tab	11.00
AZ 9	'95 $5.50 Wigeon	9.50
AZ 9A	'95 $5.50 Hunter w/tab	11.00
AZ 10	'96 $5.50 Canvasback	9.50
AZ 10A	'96 $5.50 Hunter w/ Tab	9.50
AZ 11	'97 $5.50 Gadwall	9.50
AZ 11A	'97 $5.50 Hunter w/ Tab	9.50

NOTE: Governor's stamps available upon request.

Arizona Set 1987-97 (11) 105.00
Arizona Hunter type, cplt. set ... 105.00

ARKANSAS

AR 1

No.	Description	F-VF NH
AR 1	'81 $5.50 Mallards	40.00
AR 1B	'81 Hunter (S# 110,001-200,000)	50.00
AR 1P	'81 Imperf Proof Pair	20.00
AR 2	'82 $5.50 Wood Ducks	40.00
AR 2B	'82 Hunter (S# 110,001-200,000)	50.00
AR 2P	'82 Imperf Proof Pair	25.00
AR 3	'83 $5.50 Grn.Wngd Teal	55.00
AR 3B	'83 Hunter (S# 70,001-160,000)	1000.00
AR 3P	'83 Imperf Proof Sgl	67.50
AR 4	'84 $5.50 Pintails	25.00
AR 4B	'84 Hunter (S# 25,001-100,000)	34.00
AR 4P	'84 Imperf Proof Pair	20.00
AR 5	'85 $5.50 Mallards	14.00
AR 5B	'85 Hunter (S# 25,001-100,000)	28.00
AR 5P	'85 Imperf Proof Pair	20.00
AR 6	'86 $5.50 Blk. Swamp Mallards	12.00
AR 6B	'86 Hunter (S# 25,001-100,000)	17.00
AR 6P	'86 Imperf Proof Pair	20.00
AR 7	'87 $7 Wood Ducks	12.00
AR 7A	'87 $5.50 Wood Ducks	13.00
AR 7B	'87 Hunter (S# 25,001-100,000)	14.00
AR 7P	'87 Imperf Proof Pair	20.00
AR 8	'88 $7 Pintails	11.00
AR 8A	'88 $5.50 Pintails	13.00
AR 8B	'88 Hunter (S# 25,001-100,000)	14.00
AR 8P	'88 Imperf Proof Pair	23.00
AR 9	'89 $7 Mallards	11.00
AR 9B	'89 Hunter (S# 30,001-100,000)	12.00
AR 9P	'89 Imperf Proof Pair	23.00
AR 10	'90 $7 Blk Duck/Mallards	11.00
AR 10B	'90 Hunter (S# 30,001-100,000)	12.00
AR 10P	'90 Imperf Proof Pair	23.00
AR 11	'91 $7 Widgeons	11.00
AR 11B	'91 Hunter (S# 30,001-100,000)	11.00
AR 11P	'91 Imperf Proof Pair	17.00
AR 12	'92 $7 Shovelers	11.00
AR 12B	'92 Hunter (S# 30,001-100,000)	11.00
AR 12P	'92 Imperf Proof Pair	17.00
AR 13	'93 $7 Mallards	11.00
AR 13B	'93 Hunter (S# 30,001-100,000)	11.00
AR 13P	'93 Imperf Proof Pair	17.00

No.	Description	F-VF NH
	ARKANSAS (cont.)	
AR 14	'94 $7 Canada Geese	11.00
AR 14B	'94 Hunter (S# 25,001-100,000)	11.00
AR 14P	'94 Imperf Proof Pair	16.00
AR 15	'95 $7 Mallard	11.00
AR 15B	'95 Hunter (S# 25,001-100,000)	11.00
AR 15P	'95 Imperf Proof Pair	16.00
AR 16	'96 $7.00 Black Lab	11.00
AR 16B	Hunter (SN# 13,001-100,000)	11.00
AR 16P	'96 Imperfered Pair	16.00
AR 17	'97 $7.00 Chocolate Lab	11.00
AR 17B	Hunter (SN# 13,001-100,000)	11.00

Arkansas Set 1981-97 (19) 320.00
Arkansas Hunter, cplt (17) 1250.00
Arkansas Imperfs, cplt (17)..... 330.00

CALIFORNIA

CA 8

No.	Description	F-VF NH
CA 1	'71 $1 Pintails Original Backing	825.00
CA 1	'71 $1 Unsigned w/o Orig. Backing	165.00
CA 2	'72 $1 Canvasback Original Backing	3200.00
CA 2	'72 $1 Unsigned w/o Orig. Backing	300.00
CA 3	'73 $1 Mallards	12.00
CA 4	'74 $1 Wh. Fronted Geese	3.00
CA 5	'75 $1 Grn. Winged Teal Clear Wax Back	165.00
CA 5R	'75 $1 Same, Ribbed Back	40.00
CA 6	'76 $1 Widgeon	18.00
CA 7	'77 $1 Cinnamon Teal	45.00
CA 7A	'78 $1 Cinnamon Teal	10.00
CA 8	'78 $5 Hooded Mergans	150.00
CA 9	'79 $5 Wood Ducks	9.00
CA 9P	'79 Imperf Proof Pair	55.00
CA 10	'80 $5 Pintails	9.00
CA 10P	'80 Imperf Proof Pair	55.00
CA 11	'81 $5 Canvasbacks	9.50
CA 12	'82 $5 Widgeon	9.50
CA 13	'83 $5 Grn.Winged Teal	9.50
CA 14	'84 $7.50 Mallard Decoy	12.00
CA 15	'85 $7.50 Ring Neck Duck	12.00
CA 16	'86 $7.50 Canada Goose	12.00
CA 17	'87 $7.50 Redheads	12.00
CA 18	'88 $7.50 Mallards	12.00
CA 19	'89 $7.50 Cinnamon Teal	12.00
CA 20	'90 $7.50 Canada Goose	12.00
CA 21	'91 $7.90 Gadwalls	12.00
CA 22	'92 $7.90 Wh.Frntd Goose	12.00
CA 23	'93 $10.50 Pintails	14.50
CA 24	'94 $10.50 Wood Ducks	14.50
CA 25	'95 $10.50 Snow Geese	14.50
CA 26	'96 $10.50 Mallard	14.50
CA 27	'97 $10.50 Pintails	14.50

California Set (1973-97) (26) 600.00

COLORADO

CO 1

No.	Description	F-VF NH
CO 1	'90 $5 Canada Geese	12.00
CO 1A	'90 $5 Hunter w/tab	12.00
CO 2	'91 $5 Mallards	18.00

No.	Description	F-VF NH
	COLORADO (cont.)	
CO 2A	'91 $5 Hunter w/tab	12.00
CO 3	'92 $5 Pintails	9.00
CO 3A	'92 $5 Hunter w/tab	11.00
CO 4	'93 $5 Grn. Winged Teal	9.00
CO 4A	'93 $5 Hunter w/tab	9.50
CO 5	'94 $5 Wood Ducks	9.00
CO 5A	'94 $5 Hunter w/tab	9.00
CO 6	'95 $5 Buffleheads	9.00
CO 6A	'95 $5 Hunter w/tab	9.50
CO 7	'96 $5.00 Cinnamon Teal	9.00
CO 7A	'96 $5.00 Hunter w/Tab	9.50
CO 8	'97 $5.00 Widgeon	9.50
CO 8A	'97 $5.00 Hunter w/tab	9.50

NOTE: Governor's stamps available upon request.

Colorado Set 1990-97 (8)............ 80.00
Colorado Hunter Set 1990-97 (8) 80.00

CONNECTICUT

CT 2

No.	Description	F-VF NH
CT 1	'93 $5 Black Ducks	9.00
CT 1A	'93 $5 Hunter Hz. Pair	18.00
CT 1M	'93 Commem. Sht. of 4	75.00
CT 2	'94 $5 Canvasbacks	8.50
CT 2A	'94 $5 Hunter Horiz. Pair	17.00
CT 2M	'94 Commem Sheet of 4	39.00
CT 3	'95 $5 Mallards	8.50
CT 3A	'95 $5 Hunter Horiz. Pair	17.00
CT 4	'96 $5 Old Squaw	8.50
CT 4A	'96 $5 Hunter Horiz. Pair	17.00
CT 5	'97 $5 Green Winged Teal	8.50
CT 5A	'97 $5 Hunter Horiz. Pair	17.00

NOTE: Governor's stamps available upon request.

Connecticut Set 1993-97 (5)......... 42.00
Ct. Hunter Prs. (5) 84.00

DELAWARE

DE 2

No.	Description	F-VF NH
DE 1	'80 $5 Black Ducks	95.00
DE 2	'81 $5 Snow Geese	65.00
DE 3	'82 $5 Canada Geese	65.00
DE 4	'83 $5 Canvasbacks	40.00
DE 5	'84 $5 Mallards	15.00
DE 6	'85 $5 Pintail	12.00
DE 7	'86 $5 Widgeon	12.00
DE 8	'87 $5 Redheads	12.00
DE 9	'88 $5 Wood Ducks	10.00
DE 10	'89 $5 Buffleheads	9.50
DE 11	'90 $5 Green Winged Teal	9.50
DE 12	'91 $5 Hooded Mergans	9.50
DE 12A	'91 Hunter-SN# on Back	11.00
DE 13	'92 $5 Bl. Wngd. Teal	9.50
DE 13A	'92 Hunter-SN# on Back	9.50
DE 14	'93 $5 Goldeneyes	9.50
DE 14A	'93 Hunter-SN# on Back	9.50
DE 15	'94 $5 Blue Goose	9.50
DE 15A	'94 Hunter-SN# on back	9.50
DE 16	'95 $5 Scaup	9.00
DE 16A	'95 Hunter-SN# on back	9.50
DE 17	'96 $6 Gadwall	9.00
DE 17A	'96 Hunter-SN# on back	9.50
DE 18	'97 $6 Wh. Winged Scoter	9.00
DE 18A	'97 Hunter-SN# on back	9.50

NOTE: Governor's stamps available upon request.
Delaware Set 1980-97 (18)......... 395.00
Delaware Hunters (7).................. 65.00

STATE HUNTING PERMIT STAMPS

FLORIDA

FL 5

No.	Description	F-VF NH
FL 1	'79 $3.25 Grn Wngd Teal	160.00
FL 1T	'79 $3.25 Full Tab Attd	185.00
FL 2	'80 $3.25 Pintails	18.00
FL 2T	'80 $3.25 Full Tab Attd	24.00
FL 3	'81 $3.25 Widgeon	15.00
FL 3T	'81 $3.25 Full Tab Attd	24.00
FL 4	'82 $3.25 Ring-Neck Duck	24.00
FL 4T	'82 $3.25Full Tab Attd	35.00
FL 5	'83 $3.25 Buffleheads	50.00
FL 5T	'83 $3.25Full Tab Attd	60.00
FL 6	'84 $3.25 Hooded Merg	12.00
FL 6T	'84 $3.25 Full Tab Attd	18.00
FL 7	'85 $3.25 Wood Ducks	12.00
FL 7T	'85 $3.25 Full Tab Attd	10.00
FL 8	'86 $3.00 Canvasbacks	11.00
FL 8T	'86 $3.00 Survey Tab Attd	18.00
FL 9	'87 $3.50 Mallards	9.50
FL 9T	'87 $3.50 Survey Tab Attd	25.00
FL 10	'88 $3.50 Redheads	9.50
FL 10T	'88 $3.50 Survey Tab Attd	23.00
FL 11	'89 $3.50 Bl. Winged Teal	7.50
FL 11T	'89 $3.50 Survey Tab Attd	23.00
FL 12	'90 $3.50 Wood Ducks	7.50
FL 12T	'90 $3.50 Survey Tab Attd	23.00
FL 13	'91 $3.50 Northern Pintail	7.50
FL 13T	'91 $3.50 Survey Tab Attd	17.00
FL 14	'92 $3.50 Ruddy Duck	7.50
FL 14T	'92 $3.50 Survey Tab Attd	14.00
FL 15	'93 $3.50 Amer. Widgeon	7.00
FL 15T	'93 $3.50 Survey Tab Attd	14.00
FL 16	'94 $3.50 Mottled Duck	6.50
FL 16T	'94 $3.50 Survey Tab Attd.	14.00
FL 17	'95 $3.50 Fulvous Whistling Duck	6.50
FL 17T	'95 $3.50 Survey Tab Attd.	12.00
FL 18	'96 $3.50 Goldeneyes	6.50
FL 18T	'96 $3.50 Survey Tab Attchd.	12.00
FL 19	'97 $3.50 Hooded Mergansers	6.50
FL 19T	'97 $3.50 Survey Tab Attchd.	12.00

Florida Set 1979-97 (19) 370.00
Florida Tabs Set 1979-97 (19) 550.00

GEORGIA

GA 5

No.	Description	F-VF NH
GA 1	'85 $5.50 Wood Ducks	11.00
GA 2	'86 $5.50 Mallards	8.50
GA 3	'87 $5.50 Canada Geese	8.50
GA 4	'88 $5.50 Ring Neck Ducks	8.50
GA 5	'89 $5.50 Duckling/Puppy	8.50
GA 6	'90 $5.50 Wood Ducks	8.50
GA 7	'91 $5.50 Grn. Winged Teal	8.50
GA 8	'92 $5.50 Buffleheads	8.50
GA 9	'93 $5.50 Mallards	8.50
GA 10	'94 $5.50 Ringnecks	8.50
GA 11	'95 $5.50 Widgeons/Blk Lab.	8.50
GA 12	'96 $5.50 Black Ducks	8.50
GA 13	'97 $5.50 Lesser Scaup	8.50

Georgia Set 1985-97 (13) 110.00

HAWAII

HA 1

No.	Description	F-VF NH
HI 1	'96 $5 Nene Geese	9.00
HI 1A	'96 $5 Hunter Type	9.00
HI 1M	'96 $5 Mini Sheet of 4	40.00
HI 2	'97 $5 Hawaiian Duck	8.50
HI 2A	'97 $5 Hunter Type	9.00

IDAHO

ID 1

No.	Description	F-VF NH
ID 1	'87 $5.50 Cinnamon Teals.	15.00
ID 1A	'87 $5.50 Bklt. sgl. w/Tab	11.00
ID 2	'88 $5.50 Grn. Winged Teal	13.00
ID 2A	'88 $5.50 Bklt. sgl. w/Tab	13.00
ID 3	'89 $6 Bl. Winged Teal	11.00
ID 3A	'89 $6 Bklt. sgl. w/Tab	11.00
ID 4	'90 $6 Trumpeter Swan	17.00
ID 4A	'90 $6 Bklt. sgl. w/Tab	11.00
ID 5	'91 $6 Amer. Widgeons	9.50
ID 5A	'91 $6 Bklt. sgl. w/Tab	11.00
ID 5X	'91 $6 Provisional	110.00
ID 6	'92 $6 Canada Geese	9.50
ID 6A	'92 $6 Bklt. sgl. w/Tab	9.50
ID 7	'93 $6 Com'n Goldeneye	10.00
ID 7A	'93 $6 Bklt. sgl. w/Tab	9.50
ID 8	'94 $6 Harlequin	9.50
ID 8A	'94 $6 Bklt. sgl. w/Tab	9.50
ID 9	'95 $6 Wood Ducks	9.50
ID 9A	'95 $6 Bklt. Sgl. w/tab	9.50
ID 10	'96 $6 Mallard	9.50
ID 10A	'96 $6 Booklet Sgl.w/Tab	9.50
ID 11	'97 $6.50 Shovelers	9.50

Idaho Set 1987-97 (11) 110.00
Idaho Bklt. Set 1987-95 (9) 90.00

ILLINOIS

IL 1

No.	Description	F-VF NH
IL 1	'75 $5 Mallard	650.00
IL 2	'76 $5 Wood Ducks	290.00
IL 3	'77 $5 Canada Goose	195.00
IL 4	'78 $5 Canvasbacks	100.00
IL 5	'79 $5 Pintail	100.00
IL 6	'80 $5 Grn. Winged Teal	100.00
IL 7	'81 $5 Widgeon	110.00
IL 7A	'81 $5 G.W. Teal Error	585.00
IL 8	'82 $5 Black Ducks	67.50
IL 9	'83 $5 Lesser Scaup	67.50
IL 10	'84 $5 Bl. Winged Teal	67.50
IL 11	'85 $5 Red Head	15.00
IL 11T	'85 $5 Full Tab Attd	20.00
IL 12	'86 $5 Gadwalls	15.00
IL 12T	'86 $5 Full Tab Attd	17.00
IL 13	'87 $5 Buffleheads	12.00
IL 13T	'87 $5 Full Tab Attd	14.00
IL 14	'88 $5 Com'n Goldeneye	12.00
IL 14T	'88 $5 Full Tab Attd	14.00
IL 15	'89 $5 Ring Neck Duck	10.00
IL 15T	'89 $5 Full Tab Attd	11.00
IL 16	'90 $10 Lesser Snow Gs.	16.00
IL 16T	'90 $10 Full Tab Attd	17.00
IL 17	'91 $10 Blk. Lab/Can. Gs.	15.00

ILLINOIS (cont.)

No.	Description	F-VF NH
IL 17T	'91 $10 Full Tab Attd	17.00
IL 18	'92 $10 Retvr./Mallards	15.00
IL 18T	"92 $10 Full Tab Attd	17.00
IL 19	'93 $10 Puppy/Decoy	15.00
IL 19T	'93 $10 Full Tab Attd	17.00
IL 20	'94 $10 Chessies & Canvasbacks	15.00
IL 20T	'94 $10 Full Tab Attd	16.00
IL 21	'95 $10 Green Winged Teal/C. Lab	14.50
IL 21T	'95 $10 Full Tab Attd.	16.00
IL 22	'96 $10 Wood Ducks	14.50
IL 22T	'96 $10 Full Tab Attd	16.00
IL 23	'97 $10 Canvasbacks	14.50

NOTE: Governor's stamps available upon request.

Illinois Set 1975-97 Without Error (23) 1850.00

INDIANA

IN 1

No.	Description	F-VF NH
IN 1	'76 $5 Grn. Winged Teal	9.00
IN 2	'77 $5 Pintail	9.00
IN 3	'78 $5 Canada Geese	9.00
IN 4	'79 $5 Canvasbacks	9.00
IN 5	'80 $5 Mallard Ducklings	9.00
IN 6	'81 $5 Hooded Mergans	9.00
IN 7	'82 $5 Bl. Winged Teal	9.00
IN 8	'83 $5 Snow Geese	9.00
IN 9	'84 $5 Redheads	9.00
IN 10	'85 $5 Pintail	9.00
IN 10T	'85 $5 Full Tab Attd	12.00
IN 11	'86 $5 Wood Duck	9.00
IN 11T	'86 $5 Full Tab Attd	12.00
IN 12	'87 $5 Canvasbacks	9.00
IN 12T	'87 $5 Full Tab Attd	12.00
IN 13	'88 $6.75 Redheads	11.00
IN 13T	'88 $6.75 Full Tab Attd	12.00
IN 14	'89 $6.75 Canada Goose	11.00
IN 14T	'89 $6.75 Full Tab Attd	12.00
IN 15	'90 $6.75 Bl. Winged Teal	11.00
IN 15T	'90 $6.75 Full Tab Attd	12.00
IN 16	'91 $6.75 Mallards	11.00
IN 16T	'91 $6.75 Full Tab Attd	12.00
IN 17	'92 $6.75 Grn. Winged Tl.	11.00
IN 17T	'92 $6.75 Full Tab Attd	12.00
IN 18	'93 $6.75 Wood Ducks	11.00
IN 18T	'93 $6.75 Full Tab Attd	12.00
IN 19	'94 $6.75 Pintail	11.00
IN 19T	'94 $6.75 Full Tab Attd	12.00
IN 20	'95 $6.75 Goldeneyes	11.00
IN 20T	'95 $6.75 Full Tab Attd.	12.00
IN 21	'96 $6.75 Black Ducks	11.00
IN 21T	'96 $6.75 Full Tab Attchd.	12.00
IN 22	'97 $6.75 Canada Geese.	11.00
IN 22T	'97 $6.75 Full Tab Attchd.	12.00

Indiana Set 1976-97 (22) 210.00

IOWA

IA 9

No.	Description	F-VF NH
IA 1	'72 $1 Mallards	195.00
IA 2	'73 $1 Pintails	45.00
IA 3	'74 $1 Gadwalls	95.00
IA 4	'75 $1 Canada Geese	125.00

IOWA (cont.)

No.	Description	F-VF NH
IA 5	'76 $1 Canvasbacks	25.00
IA 6	'77 $1 Lesser Scaup	21.00
IA 7	'78 $1 Wood Ducks	50.00
IA 8	'79 $5 Buffleheads	420.00
IA 9	'80 $5 Redheads	30.00
IA 10	'81 $5 Grn. Winged Teal.	30.00
IA 11	'82 $5 Snow Geese	18.00
IA 12	'83 $5 Widgeon	17.00
IA 13	'84 $5 Wood Ducks	40.00
IA 14	'85 $5 Mallard & Decoy	23.00
IA 15	'86 $5 Bl. Wngd. Teal	16.00
IA 16	'87 $5 Canada Goose	14.00
IA 17	'88 $5 Pintails	12.00
IA 18	'89 $5 Bl. Winged Teal	12.00
IA 19	'90 $5 Canvasback	8.00
IA 19A	'90 Serial #26001-80000.	12.00
IA 20	'91 $5 Mallards	8.00
IA 21	'92 $5 Blk. Lab/Ducks	9.50
IA 22	'93 $5 Mallards	9.50
IA 23	'94 $5 Grn. Winged Teal.	9.00
IA 24	'95 $5 Canada Geese	9.00
IA 25	'96 $5 Canvasbacks	12.00
IA 26	'97 $5 Canada Geese	9.00

Iowa Set 1972-97 (26) 1200.00

KANSAS

KS 1AS

No.	Description	F-VF NH
KS 1	'87 $3 Grn. Winged Teal.	8.50
KS 1	'87 $3 Horiz. Pair	17.00
KS 1AD	'87 Hunter sgl. with DD in Serial Number	8.50
KS 1AD	'87 Horiz. Pair with DD in Serial Number	17.00
KS 1AS	'87 Hunter sgl. with SS in Serial Number	8.50
KS 1AS	'87 Horiz. Pair with SS in Serial Number	17.00
KS 2	'88 $3 Canada Geese	6.50
KS 2A	'88 Hunter sgl.	8.50
KS 2A	'88 $3 Horiz. Pair	17.00
KS 3	'89 $3 Mallards	6.50
KS 3A	'89 Hunter sgl.	7.00
KS 3A	'89 $3 Horiz. Pair	14.00
KS 4	'90 $3 Wood Ducks	6.50
KS 4A	'90 Hunter sgl.	7.00
KS 4A	'90 $3 Horiz. Pair	12.50
KS 5	'91 $3 Pintail	6.00
KS 5A	'91 Hunter sgl.	7.00
KS 5A	'91 $3 Horiz. Pair	12.50
KS 6	'92 $3 Canvasbacks	6.00
KS 7	'93 $3 Mallards	6.00
KS 8	'94 $3 Blue Winged Teal.	6.00
KS 9	'95 $3 Barrow's Goldeneyes	6.00
KS 10	'96 $3 Wigeon	6.00

Kansas Set 1987-96 (10) 62.00
Kansas Hunters Pairs Set 1987-91 (5) 85.00

KENTUCKY

KY 7

No.	Description	F-VF NH
KY 1	'85 $5.25 Mallards	14.00
KY 1T	'85 $5.25 Full Tab Attd	15.00

STATE HUNTING PERMIT STAMPS

KENTUCKY (cont.)

No.	Description	F-VF NH
KY 2	'86 $5.25 Wood Ducks	9.50
KY 2T	'86 $5.25 Full Tab Attd	12.00
KY 3	'87 $5.25 Black Ducks	9.50
KY 3T	'87 $5.25 Full Tab Attd	12.00
KY 4	'88 $5.25 Canada Goose	9.50
KY 4T	'88 $5.25 Full Tab Attd	12.00
KY 5	'89 $5.25 Cnvsbk/Retrvr	9.50
KY 5T	'89 $5.25 Full Tab Attd	12.00
KY 6	'90 $5.25 Widgeons	9.50
KY 6T	'90 $5.25 Full Tab Attd	12.00
KY 7	'91 $5.25 Pintails	9.50
KY 7T	'91 $5.25 Full Tab Attd	12.00
KY 8	'92 $5.25 Grn.Winged Teal	12.00
KY 8T	'92 $5.25 Full Tab Attd	12.00
KY 9	'93 $5.25 Canvasbk/Decoy	15.00
KY 9T	'93 $5.25 Full Tab Attd	16.00
KY 10	'94 $5.25 Canada Goose	9.50
KY 10T	'94 $5.25 Full Tab Attd	10.00
KY 11	'95 $7.50 Ringnecks/ Black Lab	11.50
KY 11T	'95 $7.50 Full tab attd.	12.00
KY 12	'96 $7.50 Bl. Winged Teal	11.50
KY 13	'97 $7.50 Shovelers	11.50

Kentucky Set 1985-97 (13)........ 139.00

LOUISIANA

LA 2

No.	Description	F-VF NH
LA 1	'89 $5 Bl. Winged Teal	12.00
LA 1A	'89 $7.50 Non-Resident	16.00
LA 2	'90 $5 Grn. Winged Teal	9.00
LA 2A	'90 $7.50 Non-Resident	13.00
LA 3	'91 $5 Wood Ducks	9.50
LA 3A	'91 $7.50 Non-Resident	13.00
LA 4	'92 $5 Pintails	8.50
LA 4A	'92 $7.50 Non-Resident	11.75
LA 5	'93 $5 Amer. Widgeons	8.50
LA 5A	'93 $7.50 Non-Resident	11.75
LA 6	'94 $5 Mottled Duck	8.50
LA 6A	'94 $7.50 Non-Resident	11.50
LA 7	'95 $5 Speckled Belly Goose	8.50
LA 7A	'95 $7.50 Non-Resident	11.50
LA 8	'96 $5 Gadwall	8.50
LA 8A	'96 $7.50 Gadwall	11.50
LA 9	'97 $5 Ring Necked Duck	8.50
LA 9A	'97 $7.50 Ring Necked Duck	11.50

NOTE: Governor's stamps available upon request.

Louisiana Set Resident & Non-Res. 1989-97 (18)..................... 165.00

MAINE

ME 1

No.	Description	F-VF NH
ME 1	'84 $2.50 Black Ducks	25.00
ME 2	'85 $2.50 Common Eiders	50.00
ME 3	'86 $2.50 Wood Ducks	8.50
ME 4	'87 $2.50 Buffleheads	8.50
ME 5	'88 $2.50 Grn Winged Teal	8.50
ME 6	'89 $2.50 Goldeneyes	6.00
ME 7	'90 $2.50 Canada Geese	6.00
ME 8	'91 $2.50 Ring Neck Duck	6.00
ME 9	'92 $2.50 Old Squaw	6.00

MAINE (cont.)

No.	Description	F-VF NH
ME 10	'93 $2.50 Hooded Mergans	6.00
ME 11	'94 $2.50 Mallards	6.00
ME 12	'95 $2.50 White Winged Scoter	6.00
ME 13	'96 $2.50 Blue Winged Teal	6.00
ME 14	'97 $2.50 Greater Scuap	6.00

Maine Set 1984-97 (14) 140.00

MARYLAND

MD 7

No.	Description	F-VF NH
MD 1	'74 $1.10 Mallards	12.00
MD 2	'75 $1.10 Canada Geese	12.00
MD 3	'76 $1.10 Canvasbacks	12.00
MD 4	'77 $1.10 Greater Scaup	12.00
MD 5	'78 $1.10 Redheads	12.00
MD 6	'79 $1.10 Wood Ducks	12.00
MD 7	'80 $1.10 Pintail Decoy	12.00
MD 8	'81 $3 Widgeon	7.00
MD 9	'82 $3 Canvasbacks	10.00
MD 10	'83 $3 Wood Duck	14.00
MD 11	'84 $6 Black Duck	12.00
MD 12	'85 $6 Canada Geese	11.00
MD 13	'86 $6 Hooded Mergan	11.00
MD 14	'87 $6 Redheads	11.00
MD 15	'88 $6 Ruddy Duck	11.00
MD 16	'89 $6 Bl. Wngd. Teal	12.00
MD 17	'90 $6 Lesser Scaup	10.00
MD 18	'91 $6 Shovelers	10.00
MD 19	'92 $6 Bufflehead	10.00
MD 20	'93 $6 Canvasbacks	10.00
MD 21	'94 $6 Redheads	10.00
MD 22	'95 $6 Mallards	10.00
MD 23	'96 $6 Canada Geese	10.00
MD 24	'97 $6 Canvasbacks	10.00

Maryland Set 1974-97 (24)........ 250.00

MASSACHUSETTS

MA 18

No.	Description	F-VF NH
MA 1	'74 $1.25 Wood Duck	16.00
MA 2	'75 $1.25 Pintail	12.00
MA 3	'76 $1.25 Canada Goose	12.00
MA 4	'77 $1.25 Goldeneye	12.00
MA 5	'78 $1.25 Black Duck	12.00
MA 6	'79 $1.25 Ruddy Turnstone	12.00
MA 7	'80 $1.25 Old Squaw	12.00
MA 8	'81 $1.25 Rd Brstd Mrgnsr	10.00
MA 9	'82 $1.25 Grtr. Yellowlegs	10.00
MA 10	'83 $1.25 Redhead	9.50
MA 11	'84 $1.25 Wh. Ringed Scooter	9.50
MA 12	'85 $1.25 Ruddy Duck	9.50
MA 13	'86 $1.25 Preening Bluebill	9.50
MA 14	'87 $1.25 Amer. Widgeon	9.50
MA 15	'88 $1.25 Mallard Drake	9.00
MA 16	'89 $1.25 Brant	6.00
MA 17	'90 $1.25 Whistler Hen	6.00
MA 18	'91 $5 Canvasback	8.50
MA 19	'92 $5 Blk-Bellied Plover	8.50
MA 20	'93 $5 Rd Breasted Merg	8.50
MA 21	'94 $5 Wh. Winged Scoter	8.50
MA 22	'95 $5 Hooded Merganser	8.50
MA 23	'96 $5 Eider Decoy	8.50
MA 24	'97 $5 Curlew Shorebird	10.00

Massachusetts Set 1974-97 (24) 225.00

MICHIGAN

MI 6

No.	Description	F-VF NH
MI 1	'76 $2.10 Wood Duck	5.00
MI 2	'77 $2.10 Canvasbacks	330.00
MI 3	'78 $2.10 Mallards	28.00
MI 3T	'78 $2.10 Full Tab	50.00
MI 4	'79 $2.10 Canada Geese	50.00
MI 4T	'79 $2.10 Full Tab	67.50
MI 5	'80 $3.75 Lesser Scaup	23.00
MI 5T	'80 $3.75 Full Tab	34.00
MI 6	'81 $3.75 Buffleheads	28.00
MI 7	'82 $3.75 Redheads	28.00
MI 8	'83 $3.75 Wood Ducks	28.00
MI 9	'84 $3.75 Pintails	28.00
MI 10	'85 $3.75 Ring Neck Duck	28.00
MI 11	'86 $3.75 Com'n Gldneyes	21.00
MI 12	'87 $3.85 Grn. Winged Teal	12.00
MI 13	'88 $3.85 Canada Goose	10.00
MI 14	'89 $3.85 Widgeon	8.00
MI 15	'90 $3.85 Wood Ducks	8.00
MI 16	'91 $3.85 Bl. Wngd. Teal	7.00
MI 17	'92 $3.85 Rd Breasted Merg	7.00
MI 18	'93 $3.85 Hooded Mergan	7.00
MI 19	'94 $3.85 Black Duck	7.00
MI 20	'95 $4.35 Blue Winged Teal	8.00
MI 21	'96 $4.35 Canada Geese	8.00
MI 22	'97 $5 Canvasbacks	8.00

Michigan Set 1976-97 (22)........ 660.00

MINNESOTA

MN 1

No.	Description	F-VF NH
MN 1	'77 $3 Mallards	17.00
MN 2	'78 $3 Lesser Scaup	11.00
MN 3	'79 $3 Pintails	11.00
MN 4	'80 $3 Canvasbacks	11.00
MN 5	'81 $3 Canada Geese	10.00
MN 6	'82 $3 Redheads	11.00
MN 7	'83 $3 Bl & Snow Geese	11.00
MN 8	'84 $3 Wood Ducks	11.00
MN 9	'85 $3 Wh. Front Geese	9.00
MN 10	'86 $5 Lesser Scaup	10.00
MN 11	'87 $5 Goldeneyes	12.00
MN 11T	'87 $5 Full Tab	14.50
MN 12	'88 $5 Buffleheads	11.00
MN 12T	'88 $5 Full Tab	14.50
MN 13	'89 $5 Amer. Widgeons	11.00
MN 13T	'89 $5 Full Tab	14.50
MN 14	'90 $5 Hooded Mergan	17.00
MN 14T	'90 $5 Full Tab	21.50
MN 15	'91 $5 Ross' Goose	9.00
MN 15T	'91 $5 Full Tab	9.50
MN 16	'92 $5 Barrow's Gold'eye	9.00
MN 16T	'92 $5 Full Tab	9.50
MN 17	'93 $5 Bl. Winged Teal	9.00
MN 17T	'93 $5 Full Tab	9.50
MN 18	'94 $5 Ring Necked Duck	9.00
MN 18T	'94 $5 Full Tab	9.50
MN 19	'95 $5 Gadwalls	9.00
MN 19T	'95 $5 Full Tab	9.50
MN 20	'96 $5 Scaup	9.00
MN 20T	'96 $5 Full Tab	9.50
MN 21	'97 $5 Shoveler w/Decoy	9.00
MN 21T	'97 $5 Full Tab	9.50

Minnesota Set 1977-97 (21)...... 219.00

MISSISSIPPI

MS 2

No.	Description	F-VF NH
MS 1	'76 $2 Wood Duck	23.00
MS 1B	'76 $2 Full Comput. Card	28.00
MS 2	'77 $2 Mallards	9.00
MS 3	'78 $2 Grn. Winged Teal	9.00
MS 4	'79 $2 Canvasbacks	9.00
MS 5	'80 $2 Pintails	9.00
MS 5	'81 $2 Redheads	9.00
MS 6	'82 $2 Canada Geese	8.00
MS 7	'82 $2 Canada Geese	9.00
MS 8	'83 $2 Lesser Scaup	9.00
MS 9	'84 $2 Black Ducks	9.00
MS 10	'85 $2 Mallards	9.00
MS 10A	'85 Serial # Error-No Hz#	165.00
MS 10B	'85 Serial # Var.- No Silver Bar	500.00
MS 11	'86 $2 Widgeon	9.00
MS 12	'87 $2 Ring Neck Ducks	9.00
MS 13	'88 $2 Snow Geese	9.00
MS 14	'89 $2 Wood Ducks	6.50
MS 15	'90 $2 Snow Geese	14.00
MS 16	'91 $2 Blk. Lab/ Canvasbk Decoy	5.50
MS 17	'92 $2 Grn. Winged Teal	5.00
MS 18	'93 $5 Mallards	8.00
MS 19	'94 $5 Canvasbacks	8.00
MS 20	'95 $5 Blue Winged Teal	8.00
MS 21	'96 $5 Hooded Merganser	8.00
MS 22	'97 $5 Pintails	9.00

NOTE: Governor's stamps available upon request.

Mississippi Set 1976-97 (22)....... 195.00

MISSOURI

MO 2

No.	Description	F-VF NH
MO 1	'79 $3.40 Canada Geese	695.00
MO 1T	'79 $3.40 Full Tab Attd	895.00
MO 2	'80 $3.40 Wood Ducks	120.00
MO 2T	'80 $3.40 Full Tab Attd	145.00
MO 3	'81 $3 Lesser Scaup	55.00
MO 3T	'81 $3 Full Tab Attd	70.00
MO 4	'82 $3 Buffleheads	60.00
MO 4T	'82 $3 Full Tab Attd	75.00
MO 5	'83 $3 Bl. Wngd. Teal	50.00
MO 5T	'83 $3 Full Tab Attd	60.00
MO 6	'84 $3 Mallards	40.00
MO 6T	'84 $3 Full Tab Attd	60.00
MO 7	'85 $3 Widgeon	20.00
MO 7T	'85 $3 Full Tab Attd	25.00
MO 8	'86 $3 Hooded Mergans	15.00
MO 8T	'86 $3 Full Tab Attd	18.00
MO 9	'87 $3 Pintails	12.00
MO 9T	'87 $3 Full Tab Attd	15.00
MO 10	'88 $3 Canvasbacks	11.00
MO 10T	'88 $3 Full Tab Attd	12.00
MO 11	'89 $3 Ring Neck Ducks	8.50
MO 11T	'89 $3 Full Tab Attd	9.50
MO 12	'90 $3 Redheads	8.00
MO 12T	'90 $3 Full Tab Attd	10.00
MO 13	'91 $5 Snow Geese	8.00
MO 13T	'91 $5 Full Tab Attd	11.00
MO 14	'92 $5 Gadwalls	8.00
MO 14T	'92 $5 Full Tab Attd	11.00
MO 15	'93 $5 Grn. Winged Teal	8.00
MO 15T	'93 $5 Full Tab Attd	10.00
MO 16	'94 $5 Wh Fronted Geese	8.00
MO 16T	'94 $5 Full Tab Attd	9.00
MO 17	'95 $5 Goldeneyes	8.00
MO 17T	'95 $5 Full Tab Attached	9.00
MO 18	'96 $5 Black Duck	8.00

MISSOURI (cont.)

NOTE: Governor's stamps available upon request.

No.	Description	F-VF NH
Missouri Set 1979-96 (18)		**1100.00**
Missouri Tab Set 1979-95 (17)		**1450.00**

MONTANA

MT 1

No.	Description	F-VF NH
MT 1	'86 $5 Canada Geese	12.00
MT 1A	'86 $5 Horiz. Pair w/ Side Margins	2800.00
MT 2	'87 $5 Redheads	17.00
MT 2A	'87 $5 Hz.Pr./side mgns	35.00
MT 3	'88 $5 Mallards	14.00
MT 3A	'88 $5 Hz.Pr./side mgns	25.00
MT 4	'89 $5 Blk. Lab & Pintail	9.00
MT 4A	'89 $5 Hz.Pr./side mgns	34.00
MT 5	'90 $5 Cinn & Bl.Wng.Teal	8.50
MT 5A	'90 $5 Hz.Pr./side mgns	22.00
MT 6	'91 $5 Snow Geese	8.50
MT 6A	'91 $5 Hz.Pr./side mgns	23.00
MT 7	'92 $5 Wood Ducks	8.50
MT 7A	'92 $5 Hz.Pr./side mgns	23.00
MT 8	'93 $5 Harlequin	8.50
MT 8A	'93 $5 Hz.Pr./side mgns	23.00
MT 9	'94 $5 Widgeon	8.50
MT 9A	'94 $5 Hz.Pr./side mgns.	23.00
MT 10	'95 $5 Tundra Swans	8.50
MT 10A	'95 $5 Horz. Pr/side mgns.	23.00
MT 11	'96 $5 Canvasbacks	8.50
MT 11A	'96 $5 Horz.Pr./side MgNS.	23.00
MT 12	'97 $5 Golden Retriever	9.00
MT 12A	'97 $5 Horz.Pr./side MgNS.	23.00

NOTE: Governor's stamps available upon request.

Montana Set 1986-97 (12) 110.00

NEBRASKA

NE 2

No.	Description	F-VF NH
NE 1	'91 $6 Canada Goose	11.00
NE 2	'92 $6 Pintails	9.00
NE 3	'93 $6 Canvasbacks	9.00
NE 4	'94 $6 Mallard	9.00
NE 5	'95 $6 Wood Ducks	9.00

NOTE: Governor's stamps available upon request.

Nebraska Set 1991-95 (5) 45.00

NEVADA

NV1

No.	Description	F-VF NH
NV1	'79 $2 Canvasbks/Decoy	45.00
NV 1T	'79 $2 Serial # Tab Attd.	55.00
NV 2	'80 $2 Cinnamon Teal	6.00
NV 2T	'80 $2 Serial # Tab Attd.	7.00
NV 3	'81 $2 Whistling Swans	7.00
NV 3T	'81 $2 Serial # Tab Attd.	9.00

NEVADA (cont.)

No.	Description	F-VF NH
NV 4	'82 $2 Shovelers	7.00
NV 4T	'82 $2 Serial # Tab Attd.	9.00
NV 5	'83 $2 Gadwalls	12.00
NV 5T	'83 $2 Serial # Tab Attd.	14.00
NV 6	'84 $2 Pintails	12.00
NV 6T	'84 $2 Serial # Tab Attd.	14.00
NV 7	'85 $2 Canada Geese	15.00
NV 7T	'85 $2 Serial # Tab Attd.	17.00
NV 8	'86 $2 Redheads	14.00
NV 8T	'86 $2 Serial # Tab Attd.	15.00
NV 9	'87 $2 Buffleheads	12.00
NV 9T	'87 $2 Serial # Tab Attd.	14.00
NV 10	'88 $2 Canvasback	12.00
NV 10T	'88 $2 Serial # Tab Attd.	14.00
NV 11	'89 $2 Ross' Geese	8.00
NV 11T	'89 $2 Serial # Tab Attd.	11.00
NV 11A	'89 Hunter Tab #50,001-75,000	21.00
NV 12	'90 $5 Grn. Winged Teal	9.00
NV 12T	'90 $5 Serial # Tab Attd.	12.00
NV 12A	'90 Hunter Tab #50,001-75,000	16.00
NV 13	'91 $5 Wh. Faced Ibis	19.00
NV 13T	'91 $5 Serial # Tab Attd.	12.00
NV 13A	'91 Hunter Tab #50,001-75,000	13.00
NV 14	'92 $5 Amer. Widgeon	8.50
NV 14T	'92 $5 Serial # Tab Attd.	9.00
NV 14A	'92 Hunter Tab #50,001-75,000	12.00
NV 15	'93 $5 Com'n Goldeneye	8.50
NV 15T	'93 $5 Serial # Tab Attd.	9.00
NV 15A	'93 Hunter Tab #50,001-75,000	9.00
NV 16	'94 $5 Mallard	8.50
NV 16T	'94 $5 Serial # Tab Attd	9.00
NV 16A	'94 Hunter Tab #50,001-75,000	9.00
NV 17	'95 $5 Wood Ducks	8.50
NV 17T	'95 $5 Serial # Tab Attd.	9.00
NV17A	'95 Hunter Tab #50,001-75,000	9.00
NV 18	'96 $5 Ring Necked Duck	8.50
NV 18T	'96 $5 Serial# Tab Attd.	9.00
NV 18A	'96 Hunter Tab #50,001-75,000	9.00
NV 19	'97 $5 Ruddy Duck	8.50
NV 19T	'97 $5 Serail # Tab Attd.	9.00
NV 19A	'97 Hunter TAb #50,001-75,000	9.00

Nevada Set 1979-97 (19) 215.00
Nevada Tab Set 1979-94 (16).... 240.00

NEW HAMPSHIRE

NH 9

No.	Description	F-VF NH
NH 1	'83 $4 Wood Ducks	150.00
NH 1A	'83 3 Part Bklt. Type	150.00
NH 2	'84 $4 Mallards	105.00
NH 2A	'84 3 Part Bklt. Type	200.00
NH 3	'85 $4 Bl. Wngd. Teal	100.00
NH 3A	'85 3 Part Bklt. Type	110.00
NH 4	'86 $4 Mergansers	25.00
NH 4A	'86 3 Part Bklt. Type	30.00
NH 5	'87 $4 Canada Geese	12.00
NH 5A	'87 3 Part Bklt. Type	14.00
NH 6	'88 $4 Buffleheads	8.50
NH 6A	'88 3 Part Bklt. Type	12.00
NH 7	'89 $4 Black Ducks	8.50
NH 7A	'89 3 Part Bklt. Type	12.00
NH 8	'90 $4 Grn. Winged Teal	8.00
NH 8A	'90 3 Part Bklt. Type	9.00
NH 9	'91 $4 Gldn Retr/Mallard	8.00
NH 9A	'91 3 Part Bklt. Type	10.00
NH 10	'92 $4 Ring Neck Ducks	8.00
NH 10A	'92 3 Part Bklt. Type	9.00
NH 11	'93 $4 Hooded Mergans	8.00
NH 11A	'93 3 Part Bklt. Type	8.00
NH 12	'94 $4 Common Gldneyes	8.00
NH 12A	'94 3 Part Bklt. Type	8.00
NH 13	'95 $4 Pintails	8.00
NH 13A	'95 3 Part Bklt. Type	8.00
NH 14	'96 $4 Surf Scoters	8.00
NH 14A	'96 3 Part Booklet Type.	8.00
NH 15	'97 $4 Old Squaws	8.00

NEW HAMPSHIRE (cont.)

No.	Description	F-VF NH
NH 15A	'97 $4 - 3 Part Booklet Type	8.00

NOTE: Governor's stamps available upon request.

New Hampshire Set '83-'97 (15) 460.00
NH Bklt. Type Set '83-'97 (15) .. 575.00

NEW JERSEY

NJ 6

No.	Description	F-VF NH
NJ 1	'84 $2.50 Canvasbacks	45.00
NJ 1A	'84 $5.00 Non-Resident	60.00
NJ 1B	'84 $2.50 Hunter Bklt. Sgl	65.00
NJ 2	'85 $2.50 Mallards	15.00
NJ 2A	'85 $5.00 Non-Resident	20.00
NJ 2B	'85 $2.50 Hunter Bklt. Sgl	30.00
NJ 3	'86 $2.50 Pintails	12.00
NJ 3A	'86 $5.00 Non-Resident	15.00
NJ 3B	'86 $2.50 Hunter Bklt. Sgl	12.00
NJ 4	'87 $2.50 Canada Geese	12.00
NJ 4A	'87 $5.00 Non-Resident	12.00
NJ 4B	'87 $2.50 Hunter Bklt. Sgl	12.00
NJ 4AB	'87 $5.00 Hunter Bklt. Sgl	12.00
NJ 5	'88 $2.50 Grn. Winged Teal	8.50
NJ 5A	'88 $5.00 Non-Resident	10.00
NJ 5B	'88 $2.50 Hunter Bklt. Sgl	10.00
NJ 5AB	'88 $5.00 Hunter Bklt. Sgl	12.00
NJ 6	'89 $2.50 Snow Geese	6.00
NJ 6A	'89 $5.00 Non-Resident	10.00
NJ 6B	'89 $2.50 Hunter Bklt. Sgl	7.00
NJ 6AB	'89 $5.00 Hunter Bklt. Sgl	10.00
NJ 7	'90 $2.50 Wood Ducks	6.00
NJ 7A	'90 $5.00 Non-Resident	9.50
NJ 7B	'90 $2.50 Hunter Bklt. Sgl	6.00
NJ 7AB	'90 $5.00 Hunter Bklt. Sgl	10.00
NJ 8	'91 $2.50 Atlantic "Brandt"	6.00
NJ 8A	'91 $5.00 Non-Resident	9.50
NJ 8B	'91 $2.50 Hunter Bklt. Sgl	6.00
NJ 8AB	'91 $5.00 Hunter Bklt. Sgl	10.00
NJ 8AV	'91 $5.00 Atlantic "Brandt"	30.00
NJ 8V	'91 $2.50 Atlantic "Brandt"	16.00
NJ 9	'92 $2.50 Bluebills	6.00
NJ 9A	'92 $5.00 Non-Resident	8.50
NJ 9B	'92 $2.50 Hunter Bklt. Sgl	6.00
NJ 9AB	'92 $5.00 Hunter Bklt. Sgl	10.00
NJ 10	'93 $2.50 Buffleheads	6.00
NJ 10A	'93 $5.00 Non-Resident	8.50
NJ 10B	'93 $2.50 Hunter Bklt. Sgl	6.00
NJ 10AB	'93 $5.00 Hunter Bklt. Sgl	10.00
NJ 10M-NJ 10AM	Comm.Shts.of 4	57.50
NJ 11	'94 $2.50 Black Ducks	6.00
NJ 11A	'94 $5.00 Black Ducks	8.00
NJ 11B	'94 $2.50 Hunter Bklt. Sgl	6.00
NJ 11AB	'94 $5.00 Hunter Bklt. Sgl	10.00
NJ 12	'95 $2.50 Widgeon	6.00
NJ 12A	'95 $5 Widgeon	8.00
NJ 12B	'95 $2.50 Hunter Bklt. Sgl.	6.00
NJ 12AB	'95 $5 Hunter Bklt. Sgl.	10.00
NJ 13	'96 $2.50 Goldeneyes	8.00
NJ 13B	'96 $2.50 Hunter Bklt.Sgl.	10.00
NJ 13A	'96 $5 Goldeneyes	15.00
NJ 13AB	'96 $5 Hunter Bklt.Singl.	15.00
NJ 13C	'96 $2.50 Goldeneyes	6.00
NJ 14	'97 $5 Old Squaws	8.50
NJ 14A	'97 $10 Old Squaws	15.00
NJ 14AB	'97 $10 Hunter Bklt Single	15.00
NJ 14B	'97 $5 Hunter Bklt Single	8.50

NOTE: Governor's stamps available upon request.

New Jersey Set 1984-97 (29).... 350.00
NJ Bklt. Type Set '84-'97 (25).... 315.00

NEW MEXICO

NM 1

No.	Description	F-VF NH
NM 1	'91 $7.50 Pintails	11.00
NM 1A	'91 $7.50 Booklet sgl	12.00
NM 2	'92 $7.50 Amer. Widgeon	11.00
NNM 2A	'92 $7.50 Booklet sgl	12.00
NM 3	'93 $7.50 Mallards	11.00
NM 3A	'93 $7.50 Booklet sgl	12.00
NM 3M	'93 Commem. Sheet of 4	55.00
NM 3MI	'93 Imperf. Commem. Sheet of 4	75.00
NM 4	'94 $7.50 Grn.Wngd.Teal	11.00
NM 4A	'94 $7.50 Booklet sgl	12.00
NM 4A	'94 Strip of 4 different attd	48.00
NM 4M	'94 Commem. Sheet of 4	50.00
NM 4MI	'94 Imperf. Commem. Sheet of 4	100.00

NOTE: Governor's stamps available upon request.

New Mexico Set 1991-94 (7)........ 73.00
N.M. Hunter Set 1991-94 (7)........ 75.00

NEW YORK

NY 1

No.	Description	F-VF NH
NY 1	'85 $5.50 Canada Geese	15.00
NY 2	'86 $5.50 Mallards	9.00
NY 3	'87 $5.50 Wood Ducks	9.00
NY 4	'88 $5.50 Pintails	9.00
NY 5	'89 $5.50 Greater Scaup	9.00
NY 6	'90 $5.50 Canvasbacks	9.00
NY 7	'91 $5.50 Redheads	8.50
NY 8	'92 $5.50 Wood Duck	8.50
NY 9	'93 $5.50 Bl. Wngd. Teal	8.50
NY 10	'94 $5.50 Canada Geese	8.50
NY 11	'95 $5.50 Canada Geese	8.50
NY 12	'96 $5.50 Common Loon	8.50
NY 13	'97 $5.50 Hooded Merganser	8.50

New York Set 1985-97 (13)........... 105.00

NORTH CAROLINA

NC 1

No.	Description	F-VF NH
NC 1	'83 $5.50 Mallards	75.00
NC 2	'84 $5.50 Wood Ducks	50.00
NC 3	'85 $5.50 Canvasbacks	25.00
NC 4	'86 $5.50 Canada Geese	18.00
NC 5	'87 $5.50 Pintails	15.00
NC 6	'88 $5 Grn. Winged Teal	10.00
NC 7	'89 $5 Snow Geese	10.00
NC 8	'90 $5 Redheads	10.00
NC 9	'91 $5 Bl. Wngd. Teal	8.50
NC 10	'92 $5 Amer. Widgeon	8.50
NC 11	'93 $5 Tundra Swan	8.50
NC 12	'94 $5 Buffleheads	8.50
NC 13	'95 $5 Brant	8.50
NC 14	'96 $5 Pintails	8.50
NC 15	'97 $5 Wood Ducks	

North Carolina Set '83-'97 (15).... 260.00

NORTH DAKOTA

ND 1

STATE HUNTING PERMIT STAMPS

No.	Description	F-VF NH

NORTH DAKOTA

*North Dakota Hunter Stamps have the
following serial #'s:*
1982-86 #20,001-150,000
1987-95 #20,0011-140,000

No.		Description	F-VF NH
ND 1	'82	$9 Canada Geese	130.00
ND 1A	'82	$9 Hunter Type with Selvedge	2500.00
ND 2	'83	$9 Mallards	75.00
ND 2A	'83	$9 Hunter Type with Selvedge	3900.00
ND 3	'84	$9 Camvasbacks	35.00
ND 3A	'84	$9 Hunter Type	3000.00
ND 4	'85	$9 Blue Bills	24.00
ND 4A	'85	$9 Hunter Type	4500.00
ND 5	'86	$9 Pintails	20.00
ND 5A	'86	$9 Hunter Type	900.00
ND 6	'87	$9 Snow Geese	20.00
ND 6A	'87	$9 Hunter Type	50.00
ND 7	'88	$9 Wh.Wngd.Scooter	15.00
ND 7A	'88	$9 Hunter Type	34.00
ND 8	'89	$6 Redheads	12.00
ND 8A	'89	$6 Hunter Type	17.00
ND 9	'90	$6 Blk Labs/Mallards	12.00
ND 9A	'90	$6 Hunter Type	17.00
ND 10	'91	$6 Grn. Winged Teal	11.00
ND 10A	'91	$6 Hunter Type	14.50
ND 11	'92	$6 Bl. Winged Teal	9.00
ND 11A	'92	$6 Hunter Type	14.00
ND 12	'93	$6 Wood Ducks	9.00
ND 12A	'93	$6 Hunter Type	11.00
ND 13	'94	$6 Canada Geese	9.00
ND 13A	'94	$6 Hunter Type	12.00
ND 14	'95	$6 Widgeon	9.00
ND 14A	'95	$6 Hunter Type	12.00
ND 15	'96	$6 Mallards	9.00
ND 15A	'96	$6 Hunter Type	12.00
ND 16	'97	$6 White Fronted Geese	9.00
ND 16A	'97	$6 Hunter Type	12.00

North Dakota Set 1982-97 (16).   395.00

OHIO

OH 4

No.		Description	F-VF NH
OH 1	'82	$5.75 Wood Ducks	75.00
OH 2	'83	$5.75 Mallards	75.00
OH 3	'84	$5.75 Grn.Winged Teal	75.00
OH 4	'85	$5.75 Redheads	35.00
OH 5	'86	$5.75 Canvasbacks	30.00
OH 6	'87	$5.75 Bl.Winged Teal	12.00
OH 7	'88	$5.75 Goldeneyes	12.00
OH 8	'89	$5.75 Canada Geese	12.00
OH 9	'90	$9 Black Ducks	14.00
OH 10	'91	$9 Lesser Scaup	14.00
OH 11	'92	$9 Wood Ducks	13.00
OH 12	'93	$9 Buffleheads	13.00
OH 13	'94	$11 Mallard	16.00
OH 14	'95	$11 Pintails	16.00
OH 15	'96	$11 Hooded Mergansers	16.00
OH 16	'97	$11 Widgeons	16.00

Ohio Set 1982-97 (16).............. 425.00

OKLAHOMA

OK 4

No.		Description	F-VF NH
OK 1	'80	$4 Pintails	65.00
OK 2	'81	$4 Canada Goose	25.00
OK 3	'82	$4 Grn.Wngd.Teal	10.00
OK 4	'83	$4 Wood Ducks	10.00
OK 5	'84	$4 Ring Neck Ducks	10.00
OK 5T	'84	$4 Same, with Tab	10.00
OK 6	'85	$4 Mallards	7.50
OK 6T	'85	$4 Full Tab Attd	9.00
OK 7	'86	$4 Snow Geese	7.50
OK 7T	'86	$4 Full Tab Attd	9.00

No.		Description	F-VF NH

OKLAHOMA (cont.)

OK 8	'87	$4 Canvasbacks	7.50
OK 8T	'87	$4 Full Tab Attd	9.00
OK 9	'88	$4 Widgeons	7.50
OK 9T	'88	$4 Full Tab Attd	9.00
OK 9TV	'88	$4 Full Tab Attd. Serial #>30,000	18.00
OK 10	'89	$4 Redheads	7.50
OK 10A	'89	$4 Hunter Ty. w/Tab	9.00
OK 11	'90	$4 Hood'd Mergans'r	7.50
OK 11A	'90	$4 Hunter Ty., w/Tab	9.00
OK 12	'91	$4 Gadwalls	7.50
OK 12A	'91	$4 Hunter Ty., w/Tab	9.00
OK 13	'92	$4 Lesser Scaup	7.00
OK 13A	'92	$4 Hunter Ty.,w/ Tab	9.00
OK 14	'93	$4 Wh. Frnt'd Geese	7.00
OK 14A	'93	$4 Hunter Ty.,w/Tab	8.00
OK 15	'94	$4 Widgeon	7.00
OK 15A	'94	$4 Hunter Ty.,w/Tab	7.00
OK 16	'95	$4 Ruddy Ducks	7.00
OK 16A	'95	$4 Hunter Ty.,w/ Tab	7.00
OK 17	'96	$4 Buffleheads	7.00
OK 17A	'96	$4 Hunter Type w/Tab	7.00
OK 18	'97	$4 Goldeneyes	7.00
OK 18A	'97	$4 Hunter Type w/Tab	7.00

NOTE: Governor's stamps available upon request.

Oklahoma Set 1980-97 (18) 195.00

OREGON

OR 2

No.		Description	F-VF NH
OR 1	'84	$5 Canada Geese	25.00
OR 2	'85	$5 Snow Geese	35.00
OR 2A	'85	$5 Hunter Ty. w/Tab	660.00
OR 2A	'85	$5 Same, w/o Tab	105.00
OR 3	'86	$5 Pacific Brant	15.00
OR 3A	'86	$5 Hunter Ty. w/Tab	18.00
OR 3A	'86	$5 Same, w/o Tab	11.00
OR 4	'87	$5 Wh. Frnt'd Geese	10.00
OR 4A	'87	$5 Hunter Ty. w/Tab	14.00
OR 4A	'87	$5 Same, w/o Tab	10.00
OR 5	'88	$5 Grt. Basin Geese	10.00
OR 5A	'88	$5 Hunter Ty (89X197mm)	17.00
OR 6	'89	$5 Blk. Lab/Pintail	9.00
OR 6A	'89	$5 Hunter Ty (89X197mm)	14.00
OR 6YB	'89	$5 Provisional Issue, Black Serial #	28.00
OR 6VR	'89	$5 Provisional Issue, Red Serial #	12.50
OR 7	'90	$5 Gldn. Retr/Mallard	12.00
OR 7A	'90	$5 Hunter Ty (89X197mm)	12.00
OR 8	'91	$5 Ch'pk Bay Retrvr	8.50
OR 8A	'91	$5 Hunter Ty. w/Tab	12.00
OR 9	'92	$5 Grn. Winged Teal	8.50
OR 9A	'92	$5 Hunter Ty(216X152mm)	11.00
OR 10	'93	$5 Mallards	8.50
OR 10A	'93	$5 Hunter Type	12.00
OR 10M	'93	Mini. Sheet of 2	25.00
OR 10MI	'93	Same, Imperf.	170.00
OR 11	'94	$5 Pintails	10.00
OR 11A	'94	$5 Hunter Ty(216X152mm)	12.00
OR 11AN	'94	$25 Hunter Type	40.00
OR 12	'95	$5 Wood Ducks	10.00
OR 12A	'95	$5 Hunter Type	12.00
OR 13	'96	$5 Mallard/Widgeon/ Pintail	10.00
OR 13B	'96	$5 Mallards..in Folder	10.00
OR 13AN	'96	$25 Hunter Booklet	60.00
OR 14	'97	$5 Canvasbacks	10.00
OR 14AN	'97	$25 Hunter Booklet	35.00
OR 14B	'97	$5 Canvasbacks in Fldr	10.00

NOTE: Governor's stamps available upon request.

Oregon Set 1984-97 (14).......... 175.00

No.		Description	F-VF NH

PENNSYLVANIA

PA 1

PA 1	'83	$5.50 Wood Ducks	18.00
PA 2	'84	$5.50 Canada Geese	15.00
PA 3	'85	$5.50 Mallards	10.00
PA 4	'86	$5.50 Bl. Winged Teal	10.00
PA 5	'87	$5.50 Pintails	10.00
PA 6	'88	$5.50 Wood Ducks	10.00
PA 7	'89	$5.50 Hood'd Mergans'r	9.00
PA 8	'90	$5.50 Canvasbacks	9.00
PA 9	'91	$5.50 Widgeon	9.00
PA 10	'92	$5.50 Canada Geese	9.00
PA 11	'93	$5.50 North'n Shovelers	8.50
PA 12	'94	$5.50 Pintails	8.50
PA 13	'95	$5.50 Buffleheads	8.50
PA 14	'96	$5.50 Black Ducks	8.50
PA 15	'97	$5.50 Hooded Merganser	8.50

Pennsylvania Set '83-'97 (15)... 145.00

RHODE ISLAND

RI 1

RI 1	'89	$7.50 Canvasbacks	12.00
RI 1A	'89	$7.50 Hunter Type	17.00
RI 2	'90	$7.50 Canada Geese	12.00
RI 2A	'90	$7.50 Hunter Type	15.00
RI 3	'91	$7.50 Blk. Lab/Wd Dks	13.00
RI 3A	'91	$7.50 Hunter Type	14.50
RI 4	'92	$7.50 Bl. Winged Teal	12.00
RI 4A	'92	$7.50 Hunter Type	12.00
RI 5	'93	$7.50 Pintails	11.00
RI 5A	'93	$7.50 Hunter Type	12.00
RI 5M	'93	Commem. Sheet of 4	55.00
RI 5MI	'93	Same, Imperf.	75.00
RI 6	'94	$7.50 Wood Duck	11.00
RI 6A	'94	$7.50 Hunter Type	12.00
RI 7	'95	$7.50 Hooded Mergan.	11.00
RI 7A	'95	$7.50 Hunter Type	12.00
RI 8	'96	$7.50 Harlequin	11.00
RI 8A	'96	$7.50 Hunter Type	12.00
RI 9	'97	$7.50 Black Ducks	11.00
RI 9A	'97	$7.50 Hunter Type	12.00

NOTE: Governor's stamps available upon request.

Rhode Island Set 1989-97 (9).   99.00
RI Hunter Type Set 1989-97 (9) 110.00

SOUTH CAROLINA

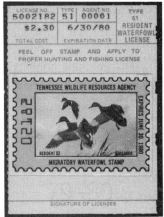

SC 1

SC 1	'81	$5.50 Wood Ducks	65.00
SC 2	'82	$5.50 Mallards	100.00
SC 2A	'82	Hunter-Ser'l # on Rev	550.00
SC 3	'83	$5.50 Pintails	100.00
SC 3A	'83	Hunter-Ser'l # on Rev	500.00
SC 4	'84	$5.50 Canada Geese	65.00
SC 4A	'84	Hunter-Ser'l # on Rev	220.00
SC 5	'85	$5.50 Grn. Winged Teal	65.00
SC 5A	'85	Hunter Ser'l # on Rev	115.00
SC 6	'86	$5.50 Canvasbacks	25.00
SC 6A	'86	Hunter-Ser'l # on Rev	45.00
SC 7	'87	$5.50 Black Ducks	20.00
SC 7A	'87	Hunter-Ser'l # on Rev	25.00

No.		Description	F-VF NH

SOUTH CAROLINA (cont.)

SC 8	'88	$5.50 Spaniel/Widg'n	20.00
SC 8A	'88	Hunter-Ser'l # on Rev	40.00
SC 9	'89	$5.50 Bl. Wingd. Teal	10.00
SC 9A	'89	Hunter-Ser'l # on Rev	15.00
SC 10	'90	$5.50 Wood Ducks	10.00
SC 10A	'90	Hunter-Ser'l # on Rev	10.00
SC 11	'91	$5.50 Blk. Lab/Pintails	9.00
SC 11A	'91	Hunter-Ser'l # on Rev	9.00
SC 12	'92	$5.50 Buffleheads	9.00
SC 12A	'92	Hunter-Ser'l # on Front	9.00
SC 13	'93	$5.50 Lesser Scaup	8.50
SC 13A	'93	Hunter-Ser'l # on Front	9.00
SC 14	'94	$5.50 Canvasbacks	8.50
SC 14A	'94	Hunter-Ser'l # on Front	9.00
SC 15	'95	$5.50 Shovelers	8.50
SC 15A	'95	Hunter, Serial # on Front	9.00
SC 16	'96	$5.50 Redhds/Lighthouse	8.50
SC 16A	'96	Hunter-Serial# on Front	9.00
SC 17	'97	$5.50 Old Squaws	8.50
SC 17A	'97	Hunter-Serial# on Front	9.00

NOTE: Governor's stamps available upon request.

South Carolina Set 1981-97 (17). 525.00
SC Hunter Type Set '81-'97 (16) ... 1530.00

SOUTH DAKOTA

SD 1

SD 1	'76	$1 Mallards	34.00
SD 1V	'76	Small Serial # Variety	67.50
SD 2	'77	$1 Pintails	23.00
SD 3	'78	$1 Canvasbacks	14.00
SD 4	'86	$2 Canada Geese	10.00
SD 5	'87	$2 Blue Geese	8.00
SD 6	'88	$2 Wh. Fronted Geese	6.00
SD 7	'89	$2 Mallards	6.00
SD 8	'90	$2 Bl. Winged Teal	5.00
SD 9	'91	$2 Pintails	5.00
SD 10	'92	$2 Canvasbacks	5.00
SD 11	'93	$2 Lesser Scaup	5.00
SD 12	'94	$2 Redhead	5.00
SD 13	'95	$2 Wood Ducks	5.00
SD 14	'96	$2 Canada Goose	5.00
SD 15	'97	$2 Widgeons	5.00

South Dakota Set 1976-97 (15).. 135.00

TENNESSEE

TN 1

TN 1	'79	$2.30 Mallards	140.00
TN 1A	'79	$5.30 Non-Resident	1000.00
TN 2	'80	$2.30 Canvasbacks	60.00
TN 2A	'80	$5.30 Non-Resident	400.00
TN 2B	'80	$2.30 3 Part Card	895.00
TN 3	'81	$2.30 Wood Ducks	40.00
TN 3B	'81	$2.30 3 Part Card	...
TN 4	'82	$6.50 Canada Geese	60.00
TN 5	'83	$6.50 Pintails	60.00
TN 5B	'83	$6.50 3 Part Card	75.00
TN 6	'84	$6.50 Black Ducks	60.00

STATE HUNTING PERMIT STAMPS

TENNESSEE (cont.)

No.	Description	F-VF NH
TN 6B	'84 $6.50 3 Part Card	75.00
TN 7	'85 $6.50 Bl. Winged Teal	25.00
TN 7B	'85 $6.50 3 Part Card	50.00
TN 8	'86 $6.50 Mallards	15.00
TN 8B	'86 $6.50 3 Part Card	50.00
TN 9	'87 $6.50 Canada Geese	12.00
TN 9B	'87 $6.50 3 Part Card	18.00
TN 10	'88 $6.50 Canvasbacks	14.00
TN 10B	'88 $6.50 3 Part Card	23.00
TN 11	'89 $6.50 Grn Wngd Teal	12.00
TN 11B	'89 $6.50 3 Part Card	14.00
TN 12	'90 $13 Redheads	18.00
TN 12B	'90 $13 3 Part Card	22.00
TN 13	'91 $13 Mergansers	18.00
TN 13B	'91 $13 3 Part Card	22.00
TN 14	'92 $14 Wood Ducks	18.50
TN 14B	'92 $14 3 Part Card	22.00
TN 15	'93 $14 Pintail/Decoy	18.50
TN 15B	'93 $14 3 Part Card	22.00
TN 16	'94 $16 Mallard	21.00
TN 16B	'94 $16 3 Part Card	22.50
TN 17	'95 $16 Ring Nckd Ducks	22.00
TN 17B	'95 $16 3 Part Card	22.50
TN 18	'96 $18 Black Ducks	24.00
TN 18B	'96 $18 3 Part Card	25.00

Tennessee Set 1979-96 (20)...... 1950.00
Tennessee Set 1979-96 (18) w/o Non-Res.................... 600.00

TEXAS

TX 1

No.	Description	F-VF NH
TX 1	'81 $5 Mallards	50.00
TX 2	'82 $5 Pintails	30.00
TX 3	'83 $5 Widgeon	175.00
TX 4	'84 $5 Wood Ducks	30.00
TX 5	'85 $5 Snow Geese	10.00
TX 6	'86 $5 Grn. Winged Teal	10.00
TX 7	'87 $5 Wh. Frnt'd Geese	10.00
TX 8	'88 $5 Pintails	10.00
TX 9	'89 $5 Mallards	10.00
TX 10	'90 $5 Widgeons	8.50
TX 11	'91 $7 Wood Duck	10.00
TX 12	'92 $7 Canada Geese	10.00
TX 13	'93 $7 Bl. Wngd. Teal	10.00
TX 14	'94 $7 Shovelers	10.00
TX 15	'95 $7 Buffleheads	10.00
TX 16	'96 $20 Book of 8 Different	20.00
TX 17	'97 $20 Book of 8 Different	20.00

Texas Set 1981-97 (17).............. 410.00

UTAH

UT 6

No.	Description	F-VF NH
UT 1	'86 $3.30 Whistling Swans	10.00
UT 2	'87 $3.30 Pintails	8.00
UT 3	'88 $3.30 Mallards	8.00
UT 4	'89 $3.30 Canada Geese	7.00
UT 5	'90 $3.30 Canvasbacks	7.00
UT 5A	'90 $3.30 Bklt, sgl. w/Tab	8.00
UT 6	'91 $3.30 Tundra Swans	6.50
UT 6A	'91 $3.30 Bklt. sgl w/Tab	7.00
UT 7	'92 $3.30 Pintails	6.50
UT 7A	'92 $3.30 Bklt. sgl w/Tab	7.00
UT 8	'93 $3.30 Canvasbacks	6.50
UT 8A	'93 $3.30 Bklt. sgl w/Tab	7.00
UT 9	'94 $3.30 Chesepeake	6.50
UT 9A	'94 $3.30 Bklt. sgl. w/Tab.	7.00
UT10	'95 $3.30 Grn Winged Teal	6.50
UT 10A	'95 $3.30 Bklt. Sgl. w/Tab	7.00
UT 11	'96 $7.50 Wh.Fronted Goose	13.00

NOTE: Governor's stamps available upon request.

UTAH (cont.)

Utah Set 1986-96 (11)................ 82.00
Utah Set Bklt. Sgl. 1990-95 (6). 40.00

VERMONT

VT 2

No.	Description	F-VF NH
VT 1	'86 $5 Aut'mn Wd Ducks	12.00
VT 2	'87 $5 Wintr Goldeneyes	9.00
VT 3	'88 $5 Spring Blk. Ducks	9.00
VT 4	'89 $5 Summer Canada Geese	9.00
VT 5	'90 $5 Grn Wngd Teal	9.00
VT 6	'91 $5 H'ded Mergans'r	8.00
VT 7	'92 $5 Snow Geese	8.00
VT 8	'93 $5 Mallards	8.00
VT 9	'94 $5 Ring Necked Duck	8.00
VT 10	'95 $5 Bufflehead	8.00
VT 11	'96 $5 Bluebills	8.00
VT 12	'97 $5 Pintail	8.00

Vermont Set 1986-97 (12)......... 99.00

VIRGINIA

VA 2

No.	Description	F-VF NH
VA 1	'88 $5 Mallards	12.00
VA 1A	'88 $5 Bklt. Single	15.00
VA 1A	'88 $5 Hz. pr./side mgns	25.00
VA 2	'89 $5 Canada Geese	17.00
VA 2A	'89 $5 Bklt. Single	14.50
VA 2A	'89 $5 Hz. pr./side mgns	28.00
VA 3	'90 $5 Wood Ducks	9.00
VA 3A	'90 $5 Bklt. Single	12.00
VA 3A	'90 $5 Hz. pr./side mgns	23.00
VA 4	'91 $5 Canvasbacks	9.00
VA 4A	'91 $5 Bklt. Single	12.00
VA 4A	'91 $5 Hz. pr./side mgns	23.00
VA 5	'92 $5 Buffleheads	9.00
VA 5A	'92 $5 Bklt. Single	12.00
VA 5A	'92 $5 Hz. pr./side mgns	23.00
VA 6	'93 $5 Black Ducks	8.50
VA 6A	'93 $5 Bklt. Single	8.50
VA 6A	'93 $5 Hz. pr./side mgns	17.00
VA 7	'94 $5 Lesser Scaup	8.00
VA 7A	'94 $5 Hz. pr./side mgns.	17.00
VA 8	'95 $5 Snow Geese	8.00
VA 8A	'95 $5 hz. pr./side Mgns.	17.00
VA 9	'96 $5 Hooded Merganser	8.00

Virginia Set 1988-96 (9)............ 92.00
VA Hunter Pairs Set 1988-95 (8) 165.00

WASHINGTON

WA 2

No.	Description	F-VF NH
WA 1	'86 $5 Mallards	9.00
WA 1A	'86 $5 Hunter Type (77X82MM)	15.00
WA 2	'87 $5 Canvasbacks	15.00
WA 2A	'87 $5 Hunter Type (77X82MM)	10.00
WA 3	'88 $5 Harlequin	9.00
WA 3A	'88 $5 Hunter Type (77X82MM)	10.00

WASHINGTON (cont.)

No.	Description	F-VF NH
WA 4	'89 $5 Amer. Widgeon	9.00
WA 4A	'89 $5 Hunter Type (77X82MM)	10.00
WA 5	'90 $5 Pintails/Sour Duck	9.00
WA 5A	'90 $5 Hunter Type (77X82MM)	10.00
WA 6	'91 $5 Wood Duck	9.00
WA 6A	'91 $5 Hunter Type (77X82MM)	10.00
WA 6V	'91 $6 Wood Duck	12.00
WA 6AN	'91 $6 Mini Sheet/ No Staple Holes	40.00
WA 6AV	'91 $6 Hunter Type (77X82MM)	10.00
WA 7	'92 $6 Puppy/Can. Geese	10.00
WA 7N	'92 $6 Mini Sheet/ No Staple Holes	40.00
WA 7A	'92 $6 Hunter Type (77X82MM)	10.00
WA 8	'93 $6 Snow Geese	9.00
WA 8N	'93 $6 Mini Sheet/ No Staple Holes	17.00
WA 8A	'93 $6 Hunter Type (77X82MM)	10.00
WA 9	'94 $6 Black Brent	9.00
WA 9A	'94 $6 Hunter Type (77X82MM)	10.00
WA 9N	'94 $6 Mini Sheet, No staple holes	17.00
WA 10	'95 $6 Mallards	9.00
WA 10A	'95 $6 Hunter Type (77 x 82 MM)	10.00
WA 10N	'95 $6 Mini Sheet No staple holes	17.00
WA 11	'96 $6 Redheads	9.00
WA 11A	'96 $6 Hunter Type (77x82MM)	10.00
WA 11N	'96 $6 Mini Sheet No staple holes	17.00
WA 12	'97 $6 Canada Geese	9.00
WA 12A	'97 $6 Hunter Type (77x82MM)	9.00
WA 12AN	'97 $6 Mini Sheet No staple holes	18.00

Washington Set 1986-97 (13)... 120.00
WA Hunter Set 1986-97 (13)..... 125.00

WEST VIRGINIA

WV 4A

No.	Description	F-VF NH
WV 1	'87 $5 Can. Geese/Res	15.00
WV 1A	'87 $5 Non-Resident	15.00
WV 1B	'87 $5 Bklt. sgl-Resident	45.00
WV 1AB	'87 Same, Non-Res	45.00
WV 2	'88 $5 Wood Ducks/Res	12.00
WV 2A	'88 $5 Non-Resident	12.50
WV 2B	'88 $5 Bklt. sgl-Resident	28.00
WV 2AB	'88 Same, Non-Res	28.00
WV 3	'89 $5 Decoys/Res	12.50
WV 3A	'89 $5 Non-Resident	12.50
WV 3B	'89 $5 Bklt. sgl-Resident	13.00
WV 3AB	'89 Same, Non-Res	13.00
WV 4	'90 Lab/Decoys/Res	12.00
WV 4A	'90 $5 Non-Resident	12.00
WV 4B	'90 $5 Bklt. sgl-Resident	12.00
WV 4AB	'90 Same, Non-Res	12.00
WV 5	'91 $5 Mallards/Res	8.50
WV 5A	'91 $5 Non-Resident	8.50
WV 5B	'91 $5 Bklt. sgl-Resident	12.00
WV 5AB	'91 Same, Non-Res	12.00
WV 5S	'91 WV Ohio Riv. Sht of 6	55.00
WV 6	'92 $5 Can. Geese/Res.	9.50
WV 6A	'92 $5 Non-Resident	9.50
WV 6B	'92 $5 Bklt. sgl-Resident	9.50
WV 6AB	'92 Same, Non-Res	9.50
WV 7	'93 $5 Pintails/Res	9.00
WV 7A	'93 $5 Non-Resident	9.00
WV 7B	'93 $5 Bklt. sgl-Resident	9.00
WV 7AB	'93 Same, Non-Res	9.00
WV 8	'94 $5 Grn. Winged Teal	8.50
WV 8A	'94 Same, Non-Res	8.50
WV 8B	'94 $5 Pintails-Hunter	9.00
WV 8AB	'94 Same, Non-Res	9.00
WV 9	'95 $5 Wood Duck	8.50
WV 9A	'95 Same, Non-Resident	8.50
WV 9B	'95 $5 Hunter Type	9.00

WEST VIRGINIA (cont.)

No.	Description	F-VF NH
WV 9AB	'95 Same, Non-Resident	9.00
WV 10	'96 $5 American Widgeons	8.50
WV 10A	'96 $5 Widgeon Non-Res.	8.50
WV 10B	'96 $5 Widgeon Hunter Typ	9.00
WV 10AB	'96 $5 Widgeon NR Hunter	9.00

NOTE: Governor's stamps available upon request.

West Virginia Set 1987-96 (20)....210.00
WV Hunter Ty.Set 1987-96 (20) 275.00

WISCONSIN

WI 1

No.	Description	F-VF NH
WI 1	'78 $3.25 Wood Ducks	115.00
WI 2	'79 $3.25 Buffleheads	30.00
WI 3	'80 $3.25 Widgeon	12.00
WI 4	'81 $3.25 Lesser Scaup	10.00
WI 5	'82 $3.25 Pintails	8.00
WI 5T	'82 $3.25 Full Tab Attd	10.00
WI 6	'83 $3.25 Bl. Winged Teal	8.50
WI 6T	'83 $3.25 Full Tab Attd	12.00
WI 7	'84 $3.25 Hd'd Mergans'r	8.50
WI 7T	'84 $3.25 Full Tab Attd	12.00
WI 8	'85 $3.25 Lesser Scaup	10.00
WI 8T	'85 $3.25 Full Tab Attd	12.00
WI 9	'86 $3.25 Canvasbacks	10.00
WI 9T	'86 $3.25 Full Tab Attd	12.00
WI 10	'87 $3.25 Canada Geese	6.50
WI 10T	'87 $3.25 Full Tab Attd	8.00
WI 11	'88 $3.25 Hd'd Mergans'r	6.50
WI 11T	'88 $3.25 Full Tab Attd	8.00
WI 12	'89 $3.25 Cm'n Gldneye	6.50
WI 12T	'89 $3.25 Full Tab Attd	8.00
WI 13	'90 $3.25 Redheads	6.50
WI 13T	'90 $3.25 Full Tab Attd	8.00
WI 14	'91 $5.25 Grn. Wngd. Teal	8.50
WI 14T	'91 $5.25 Full Tab Attd	9.50
WI 15	'92 $5.25 Tundra Swans	8.50
WI 15T	'92 $5.25 Full Tab Attd	9.50
WI 16	'93 $5.25 Wood Ducks	8.50
WI 16T	'93 $5.25 Full Tab Attd	9.50
WI 17	'94 $5.25 Pintails	8.50
WI 17A	'94 $5.25 Full Tab Attd	9.50
WI 18	'95 $5.25 Mallards	8.50
WI 18A	'95 $5.25 Full Tab Attd	9.50
WI 19	'96 $5.25 Gr. Winged Teal	8.50
WI 19T	'96 $5.25 Full Tab Attchd.	9.50
WI 20	'97 $7 Canada Goose	8.50
WI 20T	'97 $7 Full Tab Attchd.	9.50

Wisconsin Set 1978-97 (20).........280.00

WYOMING

WY 2

No.	Description	F-VF NH
WY 1	'84 $5 Meadowlark	40.00
WY 2	'85 $5 Canada Geese	40.00
WY 3	'86 $5 Prnghrn Antelope	40.00
WY 4	'87 $5 Sage Grouse	40.00
WY 5	'88 $5 Cut-Throat Trout	40.00
WY 6	'89 $5 Mule Deer	45.00
WY 7	'90 $5 Grizzly Bear	40.00
WY 8	'91 $5 Big Horn Sheep	40.00
WY 9	'92 $5 Bald Eagle	25.00
WY 10	'93 $5 Elk	13.00
WY 11	'94 $5 Bobcat	10.00
WY 12	'95 $5 Moose	10.00
WY 13	'96 $5 Turkey	10.00
WY 14	'97 $5 Rocky Mntn Goats	10.00

Wyoming Set 1984-97 (11) 395.00

NOTE: SEE PAGE 224 FOR CANADA FEDERAL AND PROVINCIAL DUCK STAMPS.

INDIAN RESERVATION STAMPS

NEW MEXICO - JICARILLA

**NORTH DAKOTA
STANDING ROCK SIOUX**

CHEYENNE RIVER SIOUX

CROW CREEK SIOUX

FORT PECK TRIBES

PINE RIDGE - OGLALA SIOUX

LAKE TRAVERSE

MONTANA - CROW

ROSEBUD

MONTANA - FLATHEAD

No.	Description	F-VF NH
	MONTANA CROW	
1992	Waterfowl	110.00
1993	Waterfowl, undated	12.00
	FLATHEAD	
1987	Bird	1450.00
1988	Bird/Fish	900.00
1989	Bird/Fish Pr w/ Duplicate ..	18.00
1990	Bird/Fish Pr w/ Duplicate ..	18.00
1991	Joint Bird	11.00
1992	Bird Annual	10.00
1992	Bird 3-Day	9.00
1993	Bird Annual	9.00
1993	Bird 3-Day	9.00
1994	Bird Annual	9.00
1994	Bird 3-Day	8.00
	FORT PECK	
1975	Bird	1500.00
1976	Bird	110.00
1978	Bird	340.00

No.	Description	F-VF NH
	NEW MEXICO JICARILLA	
1988	Wildlife Stamp	15.00
	NORTH DAKOTA STANDING ROCK SIOUX TRIBE: .	
1992	Waterfowl	17.00
1993	Waterfowl	12.00
1994	Waterfowl	11.00
1995	Waterfowl	13.00
1996	Waterfowl	13.00
	SOUTH DAKOTA CHEYENNE RIVER SIOUX TRIBE	
1983-91	Birds&Small Game,Mem.	500.00
1983-91	Same,Non-Member	395.00
1989-94	Birds & Small Game,Mem.	15.00
1989-94	Same, Non-Member	30.00
1989-94	Member, Shiny Paper	30.00
1989-94	Non-Member, Shiny Paper	55.00
1994	Waterfowl, Member	20.00
1994	Same, Non-Member	30.00

No.	Description	F-VF NH
	CROW CREEK SIOUX TRIBE	
1989	$10 Canada Geese Reservation......................	600.00
1989	$30 SD Resident..............	...
1989	$65 Non-Resident..........	1500.00
1990	$10 Canada Geese Reservation......................	425.00
1990	$30 SD Resident.............	350.00
1990	$65 Non-Resident..........	1400.00
1989-1990	**Sportsman Set (8 stamps) ($770 Face Val.).....**	**4200.00**
1994	$5 Tribal Member.............	40.00
1994	$15 Resident..................	60.00
1994	$30 Non-Resident Daily	90.00
1994	$75 Non-Resident............	160.00
1995	$5 Tribal Member, $15 Resident Member, $30 Non-Resident Daily, $75 Non-Resident, Set of 4	295.00
1996	Set of 4	295.00

No.	Description	F-VF NH
	LOWER BRULE	
1995	Set of 5 Waterfowl..............	50.00
1996	Set of 3 Waterfowl..............	35.00
	LAKE TRAVERSE INDIAN RESERVATION (SISSETON-WAHPETON)	
1986	Game Bird.......................	180.00
1991	Waterfowl - Bright Green.....	100.00
1992	Wood Duck......................	17.00
1993	Waterfowl - Bright Red........	25.00
1994	Waterfowl - Yellow Orange .	10.00
1995	Waterfowl	12.00
	PINE RIDGE (OGLALA SIOUX)	
1988-92	$4 Waterfowl, Rouletted ...	375.00
1988-92	$4 Waterfowl, Perforated..	25.00
1992	$4 Canada Geese	12.50
1993	$6 Canada Geese	12.50
1994	$6 1994 ovrprntd on 1993	15.00

Welcome to First Day Cover Collecting!

by Barry Newton, Editor *FIRST DAYS*, the official journal of the American First Day Cover Society

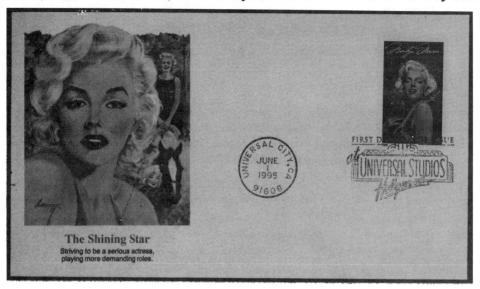

A First Day Cover (FDC) is an envelope or card with a stamp postmarked on the day the stamp was sold. The postmark may be pictorial, like the one shown above, or it can simply have the slogan "FIRST DAY OF ISSUE" (FDOI) between the killer bars of the cancel. Most new stamps are first sold in a city related to the subject of the stamp. Sometimes a stamp subject will be considered so popular or important that it is issued in every PO all across the county on the First Day (FD).

A cachet (pronounced ka-shay) is the design on the envelope. It usually shows something more about the new stamp and is usually on the left side of the envelope. Some cachets cover the entire face of the envelope with the design.

What Should I Collect?

Some people try to collect a FDC for every stamp issued by the Post Office. However, many collectors prefer to start with a collection of FDCs on a subject that is of interest specifically to them. Some examples: History, space exploration, famous people, cars, trains, planes, ships, Boy Scouts, Girl Scouts, the arts, music, science, wildlife, sports, swimming, fishing, horses, dogs, cats, flags, flowers, trees or Christmas.

The best way to obtain advance information about new stamps coming out is to subscribe to weekly philatelic publications such as *Linn's Stamp News, McKeel's or Stamp Collector.* These periodicals provide all the details for impending issues and provide instructions on how to obtain FDOI cancellations by mail. Information is also available in U.S. Post Offices. On the other hand, for those who do not wish to "do it themselves," subscriptions to new issue services are available from many dealers.

Are You Looking for More Information?

"A Handbook for First Day Cover Collectors" is now in its fourth edition. The author, Monte Eiserman, has been the Membership Secretary of the AFDCS for over thirty-five years, and answers dozens of letters each month from FDC collecting beginners. This book covers the kinds of questions asked by beginners. It contains over 40 chapters on many different FDC specialties, plus a complete glossary of FDC terms and is fully illustrated, with over 95 photos.

Mrs. Eiserman will be glad to send you more information about her book and answer your questions about FDC collecting. She can also supply information about the American First Day Cover Society. You can contact her at the address below.

Mrs. Monte B. Eiserman
AFDCS Membership Secretary
14359 Chadbourne, Houston, TX 77079

Making Combination or Combo FDCs

Combination FDCs can be made on any subject. All you need to do is some research into a new stamp you like. Then find some inexpensive stamps that helps to tell the full story of the stamp. Many stamps going all the way back into the 1940s will be inexpensive enough to put on your combination FDC. The *Combo* shown on the opposite page has eight stmaps from the Black Heritage series issued by the US Postal Service.

Having Fun with FDC Collecting!

Attending a First Day Ceremony for a new stamp is always great fun. At the First Day of the Florida Statehood stamp in January 1995, two alligators were guests of honor that day.

Most FD Ceremonies have a special gift for those who attend—a First Day Ceremony Program presented without charge. Most Programs contain the new stamp and a First Day postmark. Collectors who went to the FD Ceremony for the $10.75 Express Mail stamp had a special treat. In addition to a free $10.75 stamp inside the FD Ceremony Program, they could also wait in line to get the autographs of those who spoke at the ceremony, including NASA Astronaut Janice Voss.

Every issue of *FIRST DAYS,* the official journal of the American First Day Cover Society, contains FD Reports, written by collectors from all across the US about their experiences at a First Day Event. I hope the next FD Report that goes into the magazine is from a new AFDCS Member—*you!*

If You Are Building A Prize Collection Or Ready To Part With Your Prize Collection

We're Your Best Source !

"OUR MAN BOB" has spent nearly 40 years specializing in covers. From a million covers to individual covers that sell for many thousands of dollars, Brookman/Barrett & Worthen leads the field. Now that all our stamp orders are handled by our sister company, (Brookman Stamp Co., Vancouver, Washington), we at Brookman/Barrett & Worthen are able to devote our full attention just to covers. Traveling all over the country, we carry want lists for those collectors who want items so scarce that even we don't have them in stock. With a broad base of buyers we are able to pay the fairest prices in the market. Just this year alone we have purchased over 750,000 covers!!! While covers are our business, our customers are our 1st priority.

For Help - Call :

"Our Man Bob"

1-800-332-3383

**40 Years And Still No Difference
Being Fair With Both Buyers & Sellers**

10 Chestnut Drive
Bedford, NH 03110

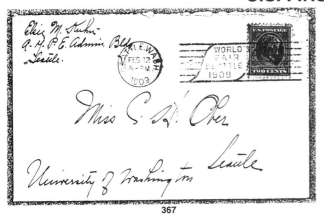

367

564

FDC's will be addressed from #10-952 and unaddressed from 953 to date
Cacheted prices are for FDC's with common printed cachets. From #704 all
FDC's will be cacheted. Multiples are generally priced @ 1.25x for blocks & 2x for
plate blks. or line pairs

Scott #	Description	Uncacheted
	1851-1890	
5A	1¢ Franklin, Blue, Type 1b, 7/1/1851 Any City	135,000.00
7	1¢ Franklin, Blue, Type II 7/1/1851 Any City	4500.00
10	3¢ Washington, Orange Brown 7/1/1851 Any City	17,500.00
64B	3¢ Washington, Rose Pink 8/17/1861 Any City	26,000.00
79	3¢ Washington "A" Grill 8/13/1867 Any City	15,000.00
183	2¢ Jackson, Vermillon 2/4/1879 Any City	500.00
210	2¢ Washington, Red Brown 10/1/1883 Any City	2000.00
210-211	2¢ Wash., 4¢ Jackson on one cvr, 10/1/1883	40,000.00
219D	2¢ Washington, Lake 2/22/1890 Any City	17,500.00
	1893 COLUMBIAN ISSUE	
230	1¢ Columbian 1/2/1893 Any City	5000.00
	Salem, MA 12/31/1892	15,000.00
231	2¢ Columbian 1/2/1893 Any City	3750.00
	New York, NY or Boston, MA 1/1/1893	7500.00
	Salem, MA 12/31/1892	15,000.00
232	3¢ Columbian 1/2/1893 Any City	10,000.00
233	4¢ Columbian 1/2/1893 Any City	10,500.00
234	5¢ Columbian 1/2/1893 Any City	17,500.00
235	6¢ Columbian 1/2/1893 Any City	22,500.00
237	10¢ Columbian 1/2/1893 Any City	25,000.00
	East Lexington, MA 12/31/92 bkstp	25,000.00
242	$2.00 Columbian 1/2/1893 New York, NY	65,000.00
265	2¢ Washington 5/2/1895 Any City	9500.00
279	1¢ Franklin, Deep Green 1/25/1898 New York, NY	700.00

*** Since Jan. 1, 1893 was a Sunday and few post offices were open,
both Jan. 1 and Jan. 2 covers are considered FDC's by collectors.**

Scott #	Description	Uncacheted
	1898 TRANS-MISSISSIPPI ISSUE	
285	1¢ Trans-Mississippi 6/17/1898 Any City	12,500.00
286	2¢ Trans-Mississippi 6/17/1898 DC	11,500.00
	6/17/1898 Pittsburgh, PA	12,500.00
287	4¢ Trans-Mississippi 6/17/1898 Any City	20,000.00
288	5¢ Trans-Mississippi 6/17/1898 DC	20,000.00
289	8¢ Trans-Mississippi 6/17/1898 DC	25,000.00
290	10¢ Trans-Mississippi 6/17/1898 Any City	30,000.00
291	50¢ Trans-Mississippi 6/17/1898 DC	35,000.00
292	$1 Trans-Mississippi 6/17/1898 DC	60,000.00
	1901 PAN AMERICAN ISSUE	
294	1¢ Pan-American 5/1/01 Any City	5000.00
295	2¢ Pan-American 5/1/01 Any City	2750.00
296	4¢ Pan-American 5/1/01 Any City	8500.00
297	5¢ Pan-American 5/1/01 Any City	16,000.00
298	8¢ Pan-American 5/1/01 Any City	16,000.00
298,296	4¢ & 8¢ on one FDC Boston, MA	16,500.00
294-299	1¢-10¢ Pan-American, cplt. set on one FDC, Any City	27,500.00
	1904 LOUISIANA PURCHASE 1907 JAMESTOWN ISSUES	
323	1¢ Louisiana Purchase 4/30/04 Any City	6500.00
324	2¢ Louisiana Purchase 4/30/04 Any City	5000.00
325	3¢ Louisiana Purchase 4/30/04 Any City	18,000.00
326	5¢ Louisiana Purchase 4/30/04 Any City	26,000.00
327	10¢ Louisiana Purchase 4/30/04 Any City	27,500.00
323-327	1¢-10¢ Louisiana Purchase, complete set on 1 FDC	100,000.00
328	1¢ Jamestown Expedition 4/26/07 Any City	10,000.00
329	2¢ Jamestown Expedition 4/26/07 Any City	12,000.00
330	5¢ Jamestown Expedition 5/10/07 Norfolk, VA (eku)	17,500.00
331a	1¢ Franklin, bklt. sgl. 12/2/08 DC	20,000.00
332a	2¢ Washington, bklt. sgl. 11/16/08 DC	35,000.00
	1909 COMMEMORATIVES	
367	2¢ Lincoln 2/12/09 Any City (600-800 known)	500.00
367	2¢ Lincoln 2/12/09 Any City on Lincoln-related post-card.	600.00
368	2¢ Lincoln Imperf. 2/12/09 Canton, OH	17,000.00
370	2¢ Alaska-Yukon 6/1/09 Any City	4500.00
372	2¢ Hudson-Fulton, 9/25/09, Any City, (100-200 Known)	800.00
372	2¢ Hudson-Fulton, 9/25/09 Lancaster,PA, on 2-part Hudson-Fulton post-card	1100.00
373	2¢ Hudson-Fulton Imperf. 9/25/09 Any City	7500.00

Scott #	Description	Uncacheted
	1913 PAN-PACIFIC ISSUE	
397	1¢ Pan-Pacific Expo 1/1/13 Any City	5000.00
398	2¢ Pan-Pacific Expo 1/18/13 Washington, D.C.	2000.00
399	5¢ Pan-Pacific Expo 1/1/13 Any City	22,000.00
400	10¢ Pan-Pacific Expo 1/1/13 Any City	17,500.00
403	5¢ Pan-Pacific Expo, Perf. 10, 2/6/15 Chicago, Ill.	6000.00
397,399,400	1¢,5¢ & 10¢ Pan-Pacific on one FDC, SF, CA	30,000.00
497	10¢ Franklin Coil 1/31/22 DC (all are Hammelman cvrs)	5300.00
526	2¢ Offset Ty. IV 3/15/20 Any City (eku)	825.00
537	3¢ Victory 3/3/19 Any City	800.00
542	1¢ Rotary Perf. 10 x 11 5/26/20 Any City	2000.00
	1920 PILGRIM TERCENTENARY	
548	1¢ "Mayflower" Pair 12/21/20 DC	1000.00
549	2¢ "Landing of the Pilgrims" 12/21/20 DC	1000.00
	12/21/20 Philadelphia, PA	2000.00
	12/21/20 Plymouth, MA	2500.00
548-50	1¢-5¢ Complete set on one cover, Phila., PA	2850.00
	Complete set on one cover, DC	3200.00
	1922-25 FLAT PLATE PERF. 11	
551	½¢ Hale (Block of 4) 4/4/25 DC	18.00
	New Haven, CT	23.00
	Unofficial Clty	150.00
	551 & 576 on one FDC 4/4/25 DC	125.00
552	1¢ Franklin 1/17/23 DC	22.50
	Philadelphia, PA	45.00
	Unofficial City	175.00
553	1½¢ Harding 3/19/25 DC	25.00
554	2¢ Washington 1/15/23 DC	35.00
555	3¢ Lincoln 2/12/23 DC	35.00
	Hodgenville, KY	225.00
	Unofficial City	250.00
556	4¢ Martha Washington 1/15/23 DC	70.00
557	5¢ Teddy Roosevelt 10/27/22 DC	115.00
	New York, NY	175.00
	Oyster Bay, NY	1350.00
558	6¢ Garfield 11/20/22 DC	250.00
559	7¢ McKinley 5/1/23 DC	150.00
	Niles, OH	210.00
560	8¢ Grant 5/1/23 DC	160.00
561	9¢ Jefferson 1/15/23 DC	160.00
562	10¢ Monroe 1/15/23 DC	160.00
	562,554,556 & 561 on one FDC	2000.00
563	11¢ Hayes 10/4/22 DC	650.00
	Fremont, OH	2200.00
564	12¢ Cleveland 3/20/23 DC	175.00
	Boston, MA	250.00
	Caldwell, NJ	175.00
565	14¢ Indian 5/1/23 DC	375.00
	Muskogee, OK	1800.00
	565 & 560 on one FDC, DC	1500.00
566	15¢ Statue of Liberty 11/11/22 DC	550.00
567	20¢ Golden Gate 5/1/23 DC	550.00
	Oakland, CA	8000.00
	San Francisco, CA	3500.00
568	25¢ Niagara Falls 11/11/22 DC	650.00
569	30¢ Bison 3/20/23 DC	800.00
	569 & 564 on one FDC, DC	2500.00
570	50¢ Arlington 11/11/22 DC	1500.00
	570,566 & 568 on one FDC	3500.00
571	$1 Lincoln Memorial 2/12/23 DC	5000.00
	Springfield, IL	5500.00
	571 & 555 on one FDC, DC	7000.00
572	$2 U.S. Capitol 3/20/23 DC	17,500.00
573	$5 Freedom Statue 3/20/23 DC	32,500.00
	1925-26 ROTARY PRESS PERF. 10	
576	1½¢ Harding Imperf. 4/4/25 DC	50.00
581	1¢ Franklin, unprecancelled 10/17/23 DC	7000.00
582	1½¢ Harding 3/19/25 DC	45.00
583a	2¢ Washington bklt pane of 6, 8/27/26 DC	1400.00

* eku: earliest known use

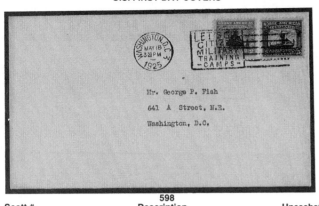

598

Scott #	Description	Uncacheted
584	3¢ Lincoln 8/1/25 DC	60.00
585	4¢ Martha Washington 4/4/25 DC	60.00
586	5¢ T. Roosevelt 4/4/25 DC	65.00
587	6¢ Garfield 4/4/25 DC	65.00
588	7¢ McKinley 5/29/26 DC	70.00
589	8¢ Grant 5/29/26 DC	80.00
590	9¢ Jefferson 5/29/26 DC	80.00
	590, 588 & 589 on one FDC	275.00
591	10¢ Monroe 6/8/25 DC	100.00

Scott #	Description	Uncacheted	Line Pairs
	1923-25 COIL ISSUES		
597	1¢ Franklin 7/18/23 DC	550.00	1750.00
598	1½¢ Harding 3/19/25 DC	55.00	175.00
*599	2¢ Washington 1/15/23 DC (37 known)	2000.00	3500.00

* These are the eku from DC and prepared by Phil Ward.
Other covers are known date 1/10, 1/11 & 1/13.

600	3¢ Lincoln 5/10/24 DC	125.00	275.00
602	5¢ T. Roosevelt 3/5/24 DC	100.00	275.00
603	10¢ Monroe 12/1/24 DC	110.00	350.00
604	1¢ Franklin 7/19/24 DC	85.00	225.00
605	1½¢ Harding 5/9/25 DC	75.00	175.00
606	2¢ Washington 12/31/23 DC	150.00	450.00
	1923 Issues		
610	2¢ Harding 9/1/23 DC	30.00	...
	Marlon, OH	20.00	...
	George W. Linn cachet (1st modern cachet)	...	1000.00
611	2¢ Harding Imperf. 11/15/23 DC	90.00	...
612	2¢ Harding Perf. 10 9/12/23 DC	110.00	...

Scott #	Description	Uncacheted	Cacheted
	1924 HUGENOT-WALLOON ISSUE		
614	1¢ Hugenot-Walloon 5/1/24 DC	40.00	...
	Albany, NY	40.00	...
	Allentown, PA	40.00	...
	Charleston, SC	40.00	...
	Jacksonville, FL	40.00	...
	Lancaster, PA	40.00	...
	Mayport, FL	40.00	...
	New Rochelle, NY	40.00	...
	New York, NY	40.00	...
	Philadelphia, PA	40.00	...
	Reading, PA	40.00	...
	Unofficial City	100.00	...
615	2¢ Hugenot-Walloon 5/1/24 DC	60.00	...
	Albany, NY	60.00	...
	Allentown, PA	60.00	...
	Charleston, SC	60.00	...
	Jacksonville, FL	60.00	...
	Lancaster, PA	60.00	...
	Mayport, FL	60.00	...
	New Rochelle, NY	60.00	...
	New York, NY	60.00	...
	Philadelphia, PA	60.00	...
	Reading, PA	60.00	...
	Unofficial City	125.00	...
616	5¢ Hugenot-Walloon 5/1/24 DC	85.00	...
	Albany, NY	85.00	...
	Allentown, PA	85.00	...
	Charleston, SC	85.00	...
	Jacksonville, FL	85.00	...
	Lancaster, PA	85.00	...
	Mayport, FL	85.00	...
	New Rochelle, NY	85.00	...
	New York, NY	85.00	...
	Philadelphia, PA	85.00	...
	Reading, PA	85.00	...
	Unofficial City	150.00	...
614-16	1¢-5¢ Comp. set on 1 cover, any official city	175.00	...
614-16	Same, Any Unofficial City	300.00	...
	1925 LEXINGTON-CONCORD ISSUE		
617	1¢ Lexington-Concord 4/4/25 DC	30.00	125.00
	Boston, MA	30.00	125.00
	Cambridge, MA	30.00	125.00
	Concord, MA	30.00	125.00
	Concord Junction, MA	35.00	...
	Lexington, MA	35.00	125.00
	Unofficial City	75.00	...

Scott #	Description	Uncacheted	Cacheted
618	2¢ Lexington-Concord 4/4/25 DC	35.00	125.00
	Boston, MA	35.00	125.00
	Cambridge, MA	35.00	125.00
	Concord, MA	35.00	125.00
	Concord Junction, MA	40.00	...
	Lexington, MA	40.00	125.00
	Unofficial City	100.00	...
619	5¢ Lexington-Concord 4/4/25 DC	80.00	175.00
	Boston, MA	80.00	175.00
	Cambridge, MA	80.00	175.00
	Concord, MA	80.00	175.00
	Concord Junction, MA	90.00	...
	Lexington, MA	90.00	175.00
	Unofficial City	125.00	...
617-19	1¢-5¢ **1st Jackson cachet** (see above listings for prices)		
617-19	1¢-5¢ Lexington-Concord, cplt. set on one cover	150.00	...
	Same, Concord-Junction or Lexington	175.00	...
	Same, Any Unofficial City	250.00	...
	1925 NORSE-AMERICAN ISSUE		
620	2¢ Norse-American 5/18/25 DC	20.00	...
	Algona, IA	20.00	...
	Benson, MN	20.00	...
	Decorah, IA	20.00	...
	Minneapolis, MN	20.00	...
	Northfield, MN	20.00	...
	St. Paul, MN	20.00	...
	Unofficial City	60.00	...
621	5¢ Norse-American 5/18/25 DC	30.00	...
	Algona, IA	30.00	...
	Benson, MN	30.00	...
	Decorah, IA	30.00	...
	Minneapolis, MN	30.00	...
	Northfield, MN	30.00	...
	St. Paul, MN	30.00	...
	Unofficial City	90.00	...
620-21	2¢-5¢ Norse-Amer., one cover 5/18/25 DC	50.00	275.00
	2¢-5¢ Algona, IA	50.00	275.00
	2¢-5¢ Benson, MN	50.00	275.00
	2¢-5¢ Decorah, IA	50.00	275.00
	2¢-5¢ Minneapolis, MN	50.00	275.00
	2¢-5¢ Northfield, MN	50.00	275.00
	2¢-5¢ St. Paul, MN	50.00	275.00
	Unofficial City	150.00	...
	1st Ernest J. Weschcke cachet	...	275.00
	1st A.C. Roessler cachet	...	300.00
622	13¢ Harrison 1/11/26 DC	15.00	...
	Indianapolis, IN	25.00	...
	North Bend, OH	150.00	...
	Unofficial City	200.00	...
623	17¢ Wilson 12/28/25	20.00	275.00
	New York, NY	20.00	275.00
	Princeton, NJ	30.00	275.00
	Staunton, VA	25.00	275.00
	Unofficial City	125.00	...
	1st Nickles cachet	...	275.00
627	2¢ Sesquicentennial 5/10/26 DC	10.00	65.00
	Boston, MA	10.00	65.00
	Philadelphia, PA	10.00	65.00
	1st Griffin cachet	...	150.00
	1st Baxter cachet	...	60.00
628	5¢ Ericsson Memorial 5/29/26 DC	25.00	450.00
	Chicago, IL	25.00	450.00
	Minneapolis, MN	25.00	450.00
	New York, NY	25.00	450.00
629	2¢ White Plains 10/18/26 New York, NY	8.00	70.00
	New York, NY Int. Phil. Ex. Agency	8.00	70.00
	White Plains, NY	8.00	70.00
630a	2¢ White Plains S/S, sgl. 10/18/26 NY, NY	12.00	75.00
	New York, NY Int. Phil. Ex. Agency	12.00	75.00
	White Plains, NY	12.00	75.00
630	Complete Sheet 10/18/26	1700.00	...
630	10/28/26	1300.00	...
631	1½¢ Harding Rotary Imperf. 8/27/26 DC	50.00	...
	1926-27 ROTARY PRESS PERF. 11 X 10½		
632	1¢ Franklin 6/10/27 DC	42.50	...
632a	Bklt. Pane of 6 11/27	3500.00	...
633	1½¢ Harding 5/17/27 DC	42.50	...
634	2¢ Washington 12/10/26 DC	45.00	...
634EE	Experimental Electric Eye 3/28/35	1200.00	...
635	3¢ Lincoln 2/3/27 DC	45.00	...
635a	3¢ Lincoln Re-issue 2/7/34 DC	25.00	45.00
636	4¢ Martha Washington 5/17/27 DC	55.00	...
637	5¢ T. Roosevelt 3/24/27 DC	55.00	...
638	6¢ Garfield 7/27/27 DC	65.00	...
639	7¢ McKinley 3/24/27 DC	60.00	...
639, 637	on one FDC	300.00	...
640	8¢ Grant 6/10/27 DC	65.00	...
	640, 632 on one FDC	300.00	...
641	9¢ Jefferson 5/17/27 DC	70.00	...
	641, 633, & 636 on one FDC	350.00	...
642	10¢ Monroe 2/3/27 DC	85.00	...

127

650

Scott #	Description	Uncacheted	Cacheted
	1927		
643	2¢ Vermont 8/3/27 DC	6.00	55.00
	Bennington, VT	6.00	55.00
	1st Joshua Gerow cachet	...	200.00
	1st Harris Hunt cachet	...	150.00
	1sr Kirkjian cachet	...	175.00
644	2¢ Burgoyne 8/3/27 DC	12.00	60.00
	Albany, NY	12.00	60.00
	Rome, NY	12.00	60.00
	Syracuse, NY	12.00	60.00
	Utica, NY	12.00	60.00
	1st Ralph Dyer cachet	...	300.00
	Any Official City	25.00	90.00
	1928		
645	2¢ Valley Forge 5/26/28 DC	5.00	50.00
	Cleveland, OH	60.00	140.00
	Lancaster, PA	5.00	50.00
	Norristown, PA	5.00	50.00
	Philadelphia, PA	5.00	50.00
	Valley Forge, PA	5.00	50.00
	West Chester, PA	5.00	50.00
	Cleveland Midwestern Phil. Sta	5.00	50.00
	1st J.W. Stoutzenberg cachet	...	275.00
	1st Adam K. Bert cachet	...	75.00
	1st Egolf cachet		90.00
646	2¢ Molly Pitcher 10/20/28 DC	12.50	85.00
	Freehold, NJ	12.50	85.00
	Red Bank, NJ	12.50	85.00
647	2¢ Hawaii 8/13/28 DC	15.00	110.00
	Honolulu, HI	17.50	110.00
648	5¢ Hawaii 8/13/28 DC	20.00	125.00
	Honolulu, HI	22.50	125.00
647-48	Hawaii on one cover	40.00	250.00
	1st F.W. Reid Cachet	...	325.00
649	2¢ Aeronautics Conf., green pmk. 12/12/28 DC	6.00	40.00
	Black pmk.	10.00	40.00
650	5¢ Aeronautics Conf., green pmk. 12/12/28 DC	10.00	50.00
	Black pmk.	12.50	50.00
649-50	Aero. Conf., one cover, green pmk	15.00	70.00
	One cover, black pmk	17.50	75.00
	1929		
651	2¢ Clark 2/25/29 Vinncennes, in	5.00	30.00
	1st Harry loor cachet	...	175.00
653	½¢ Hale (block of 4) 5/25/29 DC	30.00	...
	Unofficial City	150.00	...
654	2¢ Electric Lt., flat press 6/5/29 Menlo Park, NJ	10.00	40.00
	1st Klotzbach cachet	...	200.00
655	2¢ Electric Light, rotary press 6/11/29 DC	100.00	200.00
656	2¢ Electric Light, coil 6/11/29 DC	100.00	225.00
656	Coil Line Pair	150.00	275.00
655-56	Rotary & Coil sgls. on one FDC	175.00	375.00
657	2¢ Sullivan 6/17/29 Auburn, NY	4.00	27.50
	Binghamton, NY	4.00	27.50
	Canajoharie, NY	4.00	27.50
	Canandaigua, NY	4.00	27.50
	Elmira, NY	4.00	27.50
	Geneva, NY	4.00	27.50
	Geneseo, NY	4.00	27.50
	Horseheads, NY	4.00	27.50
	Owego, NY	4.00	27.50
	Penn Yan, NY	4.00	27.50
	Perry, NY	4.00	27.50
	Seneca Falls, NY	4.00	27.50
	Waterloo, NY	4.00	27.50
	Watkins Glen, NY	4.00	27.50
	Waverly, NY	4.00	27.50
	1st Robert Beazell cachet	...	400.00
	1st A.C. Elliot cachet	...	75.00

Scott #	Description	Uncacheted	Cacheted
	KANSAS OVERPRINTS		
658-68	Kansas Set of11 covers	1250.00	...
658	1¢ Franklin 5/1/29 DC	50.00	...
	4/15/29 Newton, KS	450.00	...
659	1½¢ Harding 5/1/29 DC	60.00	...
660	2¢ Washington 5/1/29 DC	60.00	75.00
661	3¢ Lincoln 5/1/29 DC	75.00	...
662	4¢ Martha Washington 5/1/29 DC	100.00	...
663	5¢ T. Roosevelt 5/1/29 DC	100.00	150.00
664	6¢ Garfield 5/1/29 DC	125.00	...
	4/15/29 Newton, KS	650.00	...
665	7¢ McKinley 5/1/29 DC	150.00	...
666	8¢ Grant 5/1/29 DC	150.00	...
	4/15/29 Newton, KS	650.00	...
667	9¢ Jefferson 5/1/29 DC	150.00	...
668	10¢ Monroe 5/1/29 DC	200.00	...
658-68	1¢-10¢ Kansas cplt. set on one FDC 5/1/29 DC	1300.00	...
	NEBRASKA OVERPRINTS		
669-79	Nebraska Set of 11 Covers	1250.00	...
669	1¢ Franklin 5/1/29 DC	50.00	...
	4/15/29 Beatrice, NE	400.00	...
670	1½¢ Harding 5/1/29 DC	60.00	...
	4/15/29 Hartington, NE	350.00	...
671	2¢ Washington 5/1/29 DC	60.00	...
	4/15/29 Auburn, NE	350.00	...
	4/15/29 Beatrice, NE	350.00	...
	4/15/29 Hartington, NE	350.00	...
672	3¢ Lincoln 5/1/29 DC	75.00	...
	4/15/29 Beatrice, NE	350.00	...
	4/15/29 Hartington, NE	350.00	...
673	4¢ Martha Washington 5/1/29 DC	100.00	...
	4/15/29 Beatrice, NE	350.00	...
	4/15/29 Hartington, NE	350.00	...
674	5¢ T. Roosevelt 5/1/29 DC	100.00	...
	4/15/29 Beatrice, NE	375.00	...
	4/15/29 Hartington, NE	375.00	...
675	6¢ Garfield 5/1/29 DC	125.00	...
676	7¢ McKinley 5/1/29 DC	150.00	...
677	8¢ Grant 5/1/29 DC	150.00	...
678	9¢ Jefferson 5/1/29 DC	150.00	...
679	10¢ Monroe 5/1/29 DC	200.00	...
669-79	1¢-10¢ Nebraska cplt. set on one FDC 5/1/29 DC	1300.00	...
658-79	all 22 values on 1 cover	3500.00	...
680	2¢ Fallen Timbers 9/14/29 Erie, PA	3.00	35.00
	Maumee, OH	3.00	35.00
	Perrysburgh, OH	3.00	35.00
	Toledo, OH	3.00	35.00
	Waterville, OH	3.00	35.00
681	2¢ Ohio River 10/19/29 Cairo, IL	3.00	35.00
	Cincinnati, OH	3.00	35.00
	Evansville, IN	3.00	35.00
	Homestead, PA	3.00	35.00
	Louisville, KY	3.00	35.00
	Pittsburgh, PA	3.00	35.00
	Wheeling, WV	3.00	35.00
	1930-31		
682	2¢ Mass. Bay Colony 4/8/30 Boston, MA	3.00	35.00
	Salem, MA	3.00	35.00
683	2¢ Carolina-Charleston 4/10/30 Charleston, SC	3.00	35.00
684	1½¢ Harding 12/1/30 Marion, OH	4.00	45.00
685	4¢ Taft 6/4/30 Cincinnati, OH	6.00	60.00
686	1½¢ Harding, coil 12/1/30 Marion, OH	5.00	60.00
686	Coil Line Pair	15.00	90.00
687	4¢ Taft, coil 9/18/30 DC	25.00	95.00
687	Coil Line Pair	50.00	150.00
688	2¢ Braddock 7/9/30 Braddock, PA	4.00	30.00
689	2¢ Von Steuben 9/17/30 New York, NY	4.00	30.00
690	2¢ Pulaski 1/16/31 Brooklyn, NY	4.00	30.00
	Buffalo, NY	4.00	30.00
	Chicago, IL	4.00	30.00
	Cleveland, OH	4.00	30.00
	Detroit, MI	4.00	30.00
	Gary, IN	4.00	30.00
	Milwaukee, WI	4.00	30.00

680

U.S. FIRST DAY COVERS

707

Scott #	Description	Uncacheted	Cacheted
690	New York, NY	4.00	30.00
	Pittsburgh, PA	4.00	30.00
	Savannah, GA	4.00	30.00
	South Bend, IN	4.00	30.00
	Toledo, OH	4.00	30.00
	1st Truby cachet	...	**90.00**

1931 ROTARY PRESS HI-VALUES

692	11¢ Hayes 9/4/31 DC	125.00	...
693	12¢ Cleveland 8/25/31 DC	125.00	...
694	13¢ Harrison 9/4/31 DC	125.00	...
695	14¢ Indian 9/8/31 DC	125.00	...
696	15¢ Statue of Liberty 8/27/31 DC	140.00	...
697	17¢ Wilson 7/27/31 DC	400.00	...
	7/25/31 Brooklyn, NY	3000.00	...
698	20¢ Golden Gate 9/8/31 DC	300.00	...
699	25¢ Niagara Falls 7/27/31 DC	400.00	...
	7/25/31 Brooklyn, NY	1500.00	...
	697, 699 on one FDC, Brooklyn, NY	4000.00	...
700	30¢ Bison 9/8/31 DC	300.00	...
701	50¢ Arlington 9/4/31 DC	450.00	...

1931

702	2¢ Red Cross 5/21/31 DC	3.00	30.00
	Dansville, NY	3.00	30.00
	1st Edward Hacker cachet	...	**150.00**
703	2¢ Yorktown 10/19/31 Wethersfield, CT	3.00	45.00
	Yorktown, VA	3.00	45.00
	Any Predate	200.00	...
	Unofficial City	45.00	...
	1st Crosby cachet	...	**400.00**
	1st Aeroprint cachet	...	**125.00**

1932 WASHINGTON BICENTENNIAL ISSUE

704-15	Bicentennial Set of 12 Covers		220.00
704	½¢ olive brown 1/1/32 DC		17.50
705	1¢ green 1/1/32 DC		17.50
706	1½¢ brown 1/1/32 DC		17.50
707	2¢ carmine rose 1/1/32 DC		17.50
708	3¢ deep violet 1/1/32 DC		17.50
709	4¢ light brown 1/1/32 DC		17.50
710	5¢ blue 1/1/32 DC		17.50
711	6¢ red orange 1/1/32 DC		17.50
712	7¢ black 1/1/32 DC		20.00
713	8¢ olive bistre 1/1/32 DC		20.00
714	9¢ pale red 1/1/32 DC		20.00
715	10¢ orange yellow 1/1/32 DC		20.00
	1st Rice cachet (on any single)		**25.00**
	1st Raley cachet (on any single)		**40.00**
704-15	Wash. Bicent. on one cover		250.00

1932

716	2¢ Winter Olympic Games 1/25/32 Lake Placid, NY		25.00
	1st Beverly Hills cachet		**250.00**
717	2¢ Arbor Day 4/22/32 Nebraska City, NE		15.00
	1st Linnprint cachet		**40.00**
718	3¢ Summer Olympics 6/15/32 Los Angeles, CA		25.00
719	5¢ Summer Olympics 6/15/32 Los Angeles, CA		25.00
718-19	Summer Olympics cplt. set on one FDC		40.00
720	3¢ Washington 6/16/32 DC		40.00
720b	3¢ Booklet Pane 7/25/32 DC		200.00
721	3¢ Washington, coil, vert. 6/24/32 DC		50.00
721	Coil Line Pair		90.00
722	3¢ Washington, coil, horiz. 6/24/32 DC		50.00
722	Coil Line Pair		90.00
723	6¢ Garfield, coil 8/18/32 Los Angeles, CA		60.00
723	Coil Line Pair		95.00
724	3¢ William Penn 10/24/32 New Castle, DE		17.50
	Chester, PA		17.50
	Philadelphia, PA		17.50
725	3¢ Daniel Webster 10/24/32 Franklin, NH		17.50
	Exeter, NH		17.50
	Hanover, NH		17.50

1933-34

726	3¢ Gen'l Oglethorpe 2/12/33 Savannah, GA		17.50
	1st Anderson cachet		**150.00**
727	3¢ Peace Proclamation 4/19/33 Newburgh, NY		17.50
	1st Grimsland cachet		**350.00**
728	1¢ Century of Progress 5/25/33 Chicago, IL		17.50
729	3¢ Century of Progress 5/25/33 Chicago, IL		17.50

U.S. FIRST DAY COVERS

Scott #	Description	Cacheted
728-29	Progress on one cover	22.50
730	1¢ Amer. Phil. Soc., sht. of 25 8/25/33 Chicago, IL	200.00
730a	1¢ Amer. Phil. Soc., single 8/25/33 Chicago, IL	15.00
731	3¢ Amer. Phil. Soc., sht. of 25 8/25/33 Chicago, IL	200.00
731a	3¢ Amer. Phil. Soc., single 8/25/33 Chicago, IL	15.00
730a-31a	Amer. Phil. Soc. on one cover	22.50
732	3¢ National Recovery Act 8/15/33 DC	17.50
	Nira, IA 8/17/33, unofficial	20.00
733	3¢ Byrd Antarctic 10/9/33 DC	25.00
734	5¢ Kosciuszko 10/13/33 Boston, MA	17.50
	Buffalo, NY	17.50
	Chicago, NY	17.50
	Detroit, MI	17.50
	Pittsburgh, PA	50.00
	Kosciuszko, MS	17.50
	St. Louis, MO	17.50
735	3¢ Nat'l Exhibition, sht. of 6 2/10/34 New York, NY	75.00
735a	3¢ National Exhibition, single 2/10/34 New York NY	15.00
736	3¢ Maryland 3/23/34 St. Mary's City, MD	15.00
	1st Torkel Gundel cachet	**300.00**
	1st Don Kapner cachet	**25.00**
	1st Louis Nix cachet	**250.00**
	1st Top Notch cachet	**25.00**
737	3¢ Mothers of Am., rotary 5/2/34 any city	15.00
738	3¢ Mothers of Am., flat 5/2/34 any city	15.00
737-38	Mothers of Am. on one cover	35.00
739	3¢ Wisconsin 7/7/34 Green Bay, WI	15.00

1934 NATIONAL PARKS ISSUE

740-49	National Parks set of 10 covers	100.00
740-49	On 1 Cover 10/8/34	150.00
740	1¢ Yosemite 7/16/34 Yosemite, CA	10.00
	DC	10.00
741	2¢ Grand Canyon 7/24 34 Grand Canyon, AZ	10.00
	DC	10.00
742	3¢ Mt. Rainier 8/3/34 Longmire, WA	10.00
	DC	10.00
743	4¢ Mesa Verde 9/25/34 Mesa Verde, CO	10.00
	DC	10.00
744	5¢ Yellowstone 7/30/34 Yellowstone, WY	10.00
	DC	10.00
745	6¢ Crater Lake 9/5/34 Crater Lake, OR	10.00
	DC	10.00
746	7¢ Acadia 10/2/34 Bar Harbor, ME	10.00
	DC	10.00
747	8¢ Zion 9/18/34 Zion, UT	10.00
	DC	10.00
748	9¢ Glacier Park 8/27/34 Glacier Park, MT	10.00
	DC	10.00
749	10¢ Smoky Mts. 10/8/34 Sevierville, TN	10.00
	DC	10.00
750	3¢ Amer. Phil. Soc., sheet of 6 8/28/34 Atlantic City, NJ..	75.00
750a	3¢ Amer. Phil. Soc., single 8/28/34 Atlantic City, NJ	20.00
751	1¢ Trans-Miss. Phil. Expo., sht. of 6 10/10/34 Omaha, NE	75.00
751a	1¢ Trans-Miss. Phil. Expo., single 10/10/34 Omaha, NE..	20.00

Scott #	Description	Center Gutter or Line Blk	Gutter or Line Pair	Singles
	1935 FARLEY SPECIAL PRINTING			
752-71	Set of 20 covers	...	...	500.00
752-71	Set on 1 cover 3/15/35	...	...	450.00
752-55,766a-71	10 varieties on 1 cover 3/15/35	...	...	250.00
752	3¢ Peace Proclamation 3/15/35 DC	150.00	50.00	35.00
753	3¢ Byrd 3/15/35 DC	175.00	50.00	35.00
754	3¢ Mothers of America 3/15/35 DC	150.00	45.00	35.00
755	3¢ Wisconsin 3/15/35 DC	150.00	45.00	35.00
756-65	Parks set of 10 covers	1750.00	400.00	300.00
756-65	Set on 1 cover 3/15/35	...	...	175.00
756	1¢ Yosemite 3/15/35 DC	150.00	40.00	30.00
757	2¢ Grand Canyon 3/15/35 DC	150.00	40.00	30.00
758	3¢ Mount Rainier 3/15/35	150.00	40.00	30.00
759	4¢ Mesa Verde 3/15/35 DC	150.00	40.00	30.00
760	5¢ Yellowstone 3/15/35 DC	150.00	40.00	30.00
761	6¢ Crater Lake 3/15/35 DC	150.00	40.00	30.00
762	7¢ Acadia 3/15/35 DC	150.00	40.00	30.00
763	8¢ Zion 3/15/35 DC	150.00	40.00	30.00
764	9¢ Glacier Park 3/15/35 DC	150.00	40.00	30.00
765	10¢ Smoky Mountains 3/15/35 DC	150.00	40.00	30.00
766	1¢ Century of Progress 3/15/35, DC Imperf, pane of 25,	...	500.00	...
766a	Strip of 3	150.00	50.00	40.00
767	3¢ Century of Progress 3/15/35, DC Imperf, pane of 25	...	500.00	...
767a	Single	150.00	50.00	40.00
768	3¢ Byrd 3/15/35 DC Imperf, pane of 25	...	500.00	...
768a	Single	175.00	70.00	40.00
769	1¢ Yosemite 3/15/35 DC Imperf, pane of 6	...	500.00	...
769a	Strip of 3	150.00	55.00	40.00
770	3¢ Mount Rainier 3/15/35 Imperf, pane of 6	...	500.00	...
770a	Single	150.00	55.00	40.00
771	16¢ Air Mail-Spec. Del. 3/15/35 DC	175.00	60.00	40.00

793

Scott #	Description	Cacheted
	1935-36	
772	3¢ Connecticut 4/26/35 Hartford, CT	10.00
	1st Winfred Grandy cachet	**30.00**
773	3¢ Calif. Exposition 5/29/35 San Diego, CA	12.00
	1st W. Espenshade cachet	**30.00**
774	3¢ Boulder Dam 9/30/35 Boulder City, NV	15.00
775	3¢ Michigan 11/1/35 Lansing, MI	12.00
	1st Risko Art Studio cachet	**200.00**
776	3¢ Texas 3/2/36 Gonzales, TX	15.00
	1st John Sidenius cachet	**60.00**
1st Walter Czubay cachet		**75.00**
777	3¢ Rhode Island 5/4/36 Providence, RI	10.00
	1st J.W. Clifford cachet	**30.00**
778	3¢ TIPEX sheet 5/9/36 New York, NY	17.50
	1st House of Farnam cachet	**500.00**
778a-78d	Single from sheet	5.00
782	3¢ Arkansas 6/15/36 Little Rock, AK	10.00
783	3¢ Oregon 7/14/36 Astoria, OR	8.00
	Daniel, WY	8.00
	Lewiston, ID	8.00
	Missoula, MT	8.00
	Walla Walla, WA	8.00
784	3¢ Susan B. Anthony 8/26/36 DC	10.00
	1st Historic Arts cachet	**25.00**

Scott #	Description	Price
	1936-37 ARMY - NAVY	
785-94	Army-Navy set of 10 covers	70.00
785	1¢ Army 12/15/36 DC	7.50
786	2¢ Army 1/15/37 DC	7.50
787	3¢ Army 2/18/37 DC	7.50
	1st William Von Ohlen cachet	**75.00**
788	4¢ Army 3/23/37 DC	7.50
789	5¢ Army 5/26/37 West Point, NY	7.50
	#785-89, Army set on one cover, 5/26/37	35.00
790	1¢ Navy 12/15/36 DC	7.50
791	2¢ Navy 1/15/37 DC	7.50
792	3¢ Navy 2/18/37 DC	7.50
793	4¢ Navy 3/23/37 DC	7.50
794	5¢ Navy 5/26/37 Annapolis, MD	7.50
	#790-94, Navy set on one cover, 5/26/37	35.00
	#785-94, Army-Navy set on one cover, 5/26/37	75.00

Scott #	Description	Price
	1937	
795	3¢ Ordinance of 1787 7/13/37 Marietta, OH	8.00
	New York, NY	8.00
	1st Cachet Craft cachet	**60.00**
	1st Linto cachet	**150.00**
796	5¢ Virginia Dare 8/18/37 Manteo, NC	9.00
797	10¢ S.P.A. sheet 8/26/37 Asheville, NC	9.00
798	3¢ Constitution 9/17/37 Philadelphia, PA	8.00
	1st Pilgrim cachet	**90.00**
	1st Fidelity Stamp Co. cachet	**15.00**
799-802	Territory set of 4 covers	60.00
799-802	On 1 Cover 12/15/37	40.00
799	3¢ Hawaii 10/18/37 Honolulu, HI	20.00
800	3¢ Alaska 11/12/37 Juneau, AK	15.00
801	3¢ Puerto Rico 11/25/37 San Juan, PR	15.00
802	3¢ Virgin Islands 12/15/37 Charlotte Amalie, VI	15.00

Scott #	Description	Price
	1938-1954 PRESIDENTIAL SERIES	
803-34	Presidents set of 32 covers	525.00
803-31	Presidents set of 29 covers	135.00
803	½¢ Franklin 5/19/38 Philadelphia, PA	3.00
804	1¢ Washington 4/25/38 DC	3.00
804b	booklet pane 1/27/39 DC	15.00
805	1½¢ Martha Washington 5/5/38 DC	3.00
806	2¢ J. Adams 6/3/38 DC	3.00
806b	booklet pane 1/27/39 DC	15.00
807	3¢ Jefferson 6/16/38 DC	3.00
807a	booklet pane 1/27/39 DC	15.00
	#804b, 806b, 807a Bklt. set on one cover, 1/27/38 DC	60.00
808	4¢ Madison 7/1/38 DC	3.00
809	4½¢ White House 7/11/38 DC	3.00
810	5¢ Monroe 7/21/38 DC	3.00
811	6¢ J.Q. Adams 7/28/38 DC	3.00

Scott #	Description	Price
812	7¢ Jackson 8/4/38 DC	3.00
813	8¢ Van Buren 8/11/38 DC	3.00
814	9¢ Harrison 8/18/38 DC	3.00
815	10¢ Tyler 9/2/38 DC	3.00
816	11¢ Polk 9/8/38 DC	5.00
817	12¢ Taylor 9/14/38 DC	5.00
818	13¢ Fillmore 9/22/38 DC	5.00
819	14¢ Pierce 10/6/38 DC	5.00
820	15¢ Buchanan 10/13/38 DC	5.00
821	16¢ Lincoln 10/20/38 DC	6.00
822	17¢ Johnson 10/27/38 DC	6.00
823	18¢ Grant 11/3/38 DC	6.00
824	19¢ Hayes 11/10/38 DC	6.00
825	20¢ Garfield 11/10/38 DC	6.00
	#824-825 on one FDC	40.00
826	21¢ Arthur 11/22/38 DC	7.00
827	22¢ Cleveland 11/22/38 DC	7.00
	#826-827 on one FDC	40.00
828	24¢ Harrison 12/2/38 DC	8.00
829	25¢ McKinley 12/2/38 DC	8.00
	#828-829 on one FDC	40.00
830	30¢ Roosevelt 12/8/38 DC	10.00
831	50¢ Taft 12/8/38 DC	15.00
	#830-831 on one FDC	40.00
832	$1 Wilson 8/29/38 DC	65.00
832c	$1 Wilson, dry print 8/31/54 DC	30.00
833	$2 Harding 9/29/38 DC	125.00
834	$5 Coolidge 11/17/38 DC	210.00

Scott #	Description	Price
	PRESIDENTIAL ELECTRIC EYE FDC's	
803-31EE	Presidents set of 29 Covers	550.00
803EE	½¢ Electric Eye 9/8/41 DC	10.00
804EE	1¢ Electric Eye 9/8/41 DC	10.00
	#803, 804, E15 on one FDC	30.00
805EE	1½¢ Electric Eye 1/16/41 DC	10.00
806EE	2¢ Electric Eye (Type I) 6/3/38 DC	15.00
806EE	2¢ Electric Eye (Type II) 4/5/39 DC	8.00
807EE	3¢ Electric Eye 4/5/39 DC	8.00
	#806-807 on one FDC 4/5/39	15.00
807EE	3¢ Electric Eye convertible 1/18/40	12.50
808EE	4¢ Electric Eye 10/28/41 DC	17.50
809EE	4½¢ Electric Eye 10/28/41 DC	17.50
810EE	5¢ Electric Eye 10/28/41 DC	17.50
811EE	6¢ Electric Eye 9/25/41 DC	15.00
812EE	7¢ Electric Eye 10/28/41 DC	17.50
813EE	8¢ Electric Eye 10/28/41 DC	17.50
814EE	9¢ Electric Eye 10/28/41 DC	17.50
815EE	10¢ Electric Eye 9/25/41 DC	15.00
	#811, 815 on one FDC	25.00
816EE	11¢ Electric Eye 10/8/41 DC	20.00
817EE	12¢ Electric Eye 10/8/41 DC	20.00
818EE	13¢ Electric Eye 10/8/41 DC	20.00
819EE	14¢ Electric Eye 10/8/41 DC	20.00
820EE	15¢ Electric Eye 10/8/41 DC	20.00
	#816-820 on one FDC	30.00
821EE	16¢ Electric Eye 1/7/42 DC	25.00
822EE	17¢ Electric Eye 10/28/41 DC	25.00
	#808-10, 812-14, 822 on one FDC	60.00
823EE	18¢ Electric Eye 1/7/42 DC	25.00
824EE	19¢ Electric Eye 1/7/42 DC	25.00
825EE	20¢ Electric Eye 1/7/42 DC	25.00
	#824-825 on one FDC	30.00
826EE	21¢ Electric Eye 1/7/42 DC	25.00
	#821, 823-26 on one FDC	60.00
827EE	22¢ Electric Eye 1/28/42 DC	35.00
828EE	24¢ Electric Eye 1/28/42 DC	35.00
829EE	25¢ Electric Eye 1/28/42 DC	40.00
830EE	30¢ Electric Eye 1/28/42 DC	40.00
831EE	50¢ Electric Eye 1/28/42 DC	50.00
	#827-831 on one FDC	75.00
	1938	
835	3¢ Ratification 6/21/38 Philadelphia, PA	9.00
836	3¢ Swedes and Finns 6/27/38 Wilmington, DE	9.00
	1st Staehle cachet	**50.00**
837	3¢ NW Territory 7/15/38 Marietta, OH	9.00
838	3¢ Iowa Territory 8/24/38 Des Moines, IA	9.00

832

U.S. FIRST DAY COVERS

855

1939 PRESIDENTIAL COILS

Scott #	Description	Line Pr	Price
839-51	Presidents set of 13 covers	...	75.00
839	1¢ Washington, pair 1/20/39 DC	12.00	5.00
840	1½¢ M. Wash., pair 1/20/39 DC	12.00	5.00
841	2¢ J. Adams, pair 1/20/39 DC	12.00	5.00
842	3¢ Jefferson 1/20/39 DC	12.00	5.00
842	Same, pair.	...	7.00
843	4¢ Madison 1/20/39 DC	12.00	6.00
844	4½¢ White House 1/20/39 DC	12.00	6.00
845	5¢ Monroe 1/20/39 DC	15.00	6.00
846	6¢ J.Q. Adams, vert. 1/20/39 DC	17.50	7.00
847	10¢ Tyler 1/20/39 DC	20.00	10.00
839-847	On 1 Cover.	125.00	60.00
848	1¢ Washington, pair, vert. coil 1/27/39 DC	12.00	6.00
849	1½¢ M. Wash., pair, vert. coil 1/27/39 DC12.00ea	12.00	6.00
850	2¢ J. Adams, pair, vert. coil 1/27/39 DC	12.00	6.00
851	3¢ Jefferson 1/27/39 DC	12.00	6.00
848-51	On 1 Cover.	75.00	40.00
839-51	On 1 cover	200.00	110.00

1939

Scott #	Description	Price
852	3¢ Golden Gate 2/18/39 San Francisco, CA	10.00
853	3¢ World's Fair 4/1/39 New York, NY	12.00
	1st Artcraft cachet	**300.00**
854	3¢ Wash. Inauguration 4/30/39 NY, NY	9.00
855	3¢ Baseball 6/12/39 Cooperstown, NY	40.00
856	3¢ Panama Canal 8/15/39 USS Charleston	10.00
857	3¢ Printing Tercent. 9/25/39 NY, NY	8.00
858	3¢ 50th Anniv. 4 States 11/2/39 Bismarck, ND..............	7.50
	11/2/39 Pierre, SD	7.50
	11/8/39 Helena, MT	7.50
	11/11/39 Olympia, WA	7.50

1940 FAMOUS AMERICANS

Scott #	Description	Price
859-93	**Famous Americans set of 35 covers**	**175.00**
859	1¢ Washington Irving 1/29/40 Terrytown, NY	4.00
860	2¢ James Fenimore Cooper 1/29/40 Cooperstown, NY ...	4.00
861	3¢ Ralph Waldo Emerson 2/5/40 Boston, MA	4.00
862	5¢ Louisa May Alcott 2/5/40 Concord, MA	5.00
863	10¢ Samuel Clemens 2/13/40 Hannibal, MO	9.00
859-63	Authors on one cover 2/13/40	40.00
864	1¢ Henry W. Longfellow 2/16/40 Portland, ME	4.00
865	2¢ John Greenleaf Whittier 2/16/40 Haverhill, MA..........	4.00
866	3¢ James Russell Lowell 2/20/40 Cambridge, MA	4.00
867	5¢ Walt Whitman 2/20/40 Camden, NJ	5.00
868	10¢ James Whitcomb Riley 2/24/40 Greenfield, IN	6.00
864-68	Poets on one cover 2/24/40	40.00
869	1¢ Horace Mann 3/14/40 Boston, MA	4.00
870	2¢ Mark Hopkins 3/14/40 Williamstown, MA	4.00
871	3¢ Charles W. Eliot 3/28/40 Cambridge, MA	4.00
872	5¢ Frances E. Willard 3/28/40 Evanston, IL	5.00
873	10¢ Booker T. Washington 4/7/40 Tuskegee Inst., AL	12.00
869-73	Educators on one cover 4/7/40	45.00
874	1¢ John James Audubon 4/8/40 St. Francesville, LA	5.00
875	2¢ Dr. Crawford W. Long 4/8/40 Jefferson, GA	5.00
876	3¢ Luther Burbank 4/17/40 Santa Rosa, CA	4.00
877	5¢ Dr. Walter Reed 4/17/40 DC	5.00
878	10¢ Jane Addams 4/26/40 Chicago, IL	6.00
874-78	Scientists on one cover 4/26/40	40.00
879	1¢ Stephen Collins Foster 5/3/40 Bardstown, KY..........	4.00
880	2¢ John Philip Sousa 5/3/40 DC	4.00
881	3¢ Victor Herbert 5/13/40 New York, NY	4.00
882	5¢ Edward A. MacDowell 5/13/40 Peterborough, NH	5.00
883	10¢ Ethelbert Nevin 6/10/40 Pittsburgh, PA	6.00
879-83	Composers on one cover 6/10/40	40.00
884	1¢ Gilbert Charles Stuart 9/5/40 Narragansett, RI.........	4.00
885	2¢ James A. McNeill Whistler 9/5/40 Lowell, MA	4.00
886	3¢ Augustus Saint-Gaudens 9/16/40 New York, NY	4.00
887	5¢ Daniel Chester French 9/16/40 Stockbridge, MA	5.00
888	10¢ Frederic Remington 9/30/40 Canton, NY...............	6.00
884-88	Artists on one cover 9/30/40	40.00
889	1¢ Eli Whitney 10/7/40 Savannah, GA	4.00
890	2¢ Samuel F.B. Morse 10/7/40 NY, NY	4.00
891	3¢ Cyrus Hall McCormick 10/14/40 Lexington, VA..........	4.00
892	5¢ Elias Howe 10/14/40 Spencer, MA	5.00
893	10¢ Alexander Graham Bell 10/28/40 Boston, MA	7.00

U.S. FIRST DAY COVERS

Scott #	Description	Price
889-93	Inventors on one cover 10/28/40	40.00
859-93	Famous American set on one cover 10/28/40	200.00

1940-43

Scott #	Description	Price
894	3¢ Pony Exxpress 4/3/40 St. Joseph, MO	7.00
	Sacramento, CA	7.00
	1st Aristocrats cachet	**15.00**
895	3¢ Pan American Union 4/14/40 DC.............................	6.00
896	3¢ Idaho Statehood 7/3/40 Boise, ID	6.00
897	3¢ Wyoming Statehood 7/10/40 Cheyenne, WY	6.00
	1st Spartan cachet	**40.00**
898	3¢ Coronado Expedition 9/7/40 Albuquerque, NM	6.00
899	1¢ National Defense 10/16/40 DC............................	5.00
900	2¢ National Defense 10/16/40 DC............................	5.00
901	3¢ National Defense 10/16/40 DC............................	5.00
899-901	National Defense on one cover	10.00
902	3¢ 13th Amend. 10/20/40 World's Fair, NY	9.00
903	3¢ Vermont Statehood 3/4/41 Montpelier, VT	8.00
	1st Fleetwood cachet	**90.00**
	1st Dorothy Knapp hand painted cachet	**1600.00**
904	3¢ Kentucky Statehood 6/1/42 Frankfort, KY	6.00
	1st Signed Fleetwood cachet	**75.00**
905	3¢ Win the War 7/4/42 DC	5.00
906	5¢ China Resistance 7/7/42 Denver, CO	10.00
907	2¢ United Nations 1/14/43 DC	5.00
908	1¢ Four Freedoms 2/12/43 DC	5.00

1943-44 OVERRUN NATIONS (FLAGS)

Scott #	Description	Name Blks.	Singles
909-21	**Flags set of 13 covers**........................	130.00	50.00
909	5¢ Poland 3/22/43 Chicago, IL	10.00	6.00
	DC..	10.00	6.00
	1st Penn Arts cachet	...	**20.00**
	1st Smartcraft cachet		**15.00**
910	5¢ Czechoslovakia 7/12/43 DC	10.00	5.00
911	5¢ Norway 7/27/43 DC	10.00	5.00
912	5¢ Luxembourg 8/10/43 DC	10.00	5.00
913	5¢ Netherlands 8/24/43 DC	10.00	5.00
914	5¢ Belgium 9/14/43 DC	10.00	5.00
915	5¢ France 9/28/43 DC	10.00	5.00
916	5¢ Greece 10/12/43 DC	10.00	5.00
917	5¢ Yugoslavia 10/26/43 DC	10.00	5.00
918	5¢ Albania 11/9/43 DC	10.00	5.00
919	5¢ Austria 11/23/43 DC	10.00	5.00
920	5¢ Denmark 12/7/43 DC	10.00	5.00
	#909-920 on one cover, 12/7/43	...	70.00
921	5¢ Korea 11/2/44 DC	10.00	6.00
	#909-921 on one cover, 11/2/44	...	85.00

1944

Scott #	Description	Price
922	3¢ Railroad 5/10/44 Ogden, UT	7.00
	Omaha, NE	7.00
	San Francisco, CA	7.00
923	3¢ Steamship 5/22/44 Kings Point, NY	7.00
	Savannah, GA	7.00
924	3¢ Telegraph 5/24/44 DC	7.00
	Baltimore, MD	7.00
925	3¢ Corregidor 9/27/44 DC	7.00
926	3¢ Motion Picture 10/31/44 Hollywood, CA	7.00

1945

Scott #	Description	Price
927	3¢ Florida 3/3/45 Tallahassee, FL	9.00
928	5¢ UN Conference 4/25/45 San Francisco, CA	9.00
929	3¢ Iwo Jima 7/11/45 DC	15.00
930	1¢ Roosevelt 7/26/45 Hyde Park, NY	4.00
931	2¢ Roosevelt 8/24/45 Warm Springs, GA	4.00
932	3¢ Roosevelt 6/27/45 DC	4.00
	1st Fluegel cachet	**75.00**
933	5¢ Roosevelt 1/30/46 DC	3.00
	#930-933 on one cover 1/30/46 DC	12.00
934	3¢ Army 9/28/45 DC	8.00
935	3¢ Navy 10/27/45 Annapolis, MD	8.00
936	3¢ Coast Guard 11/10/45 New York, NY	8.00
937	3¢ Alfred E. Smith 11/26/45 New York, NY	5.00
938	3¢ Texas Centennial 12/29/45 Austin, TX	6.00

921

976

Scott #	Description	Price
	1946	
939	3¢ Merchant Marine 2/26/46 DC	7.00
	#929, 934-36, 939 on one cover 2/26/46	30.00
940	3¢ Honorable Discharge 5/9/46 DC	7.00
	1st Artmaster cachet	**20.00**
	#929, 934-36, 939-940 on one cover 5/9/46	35.00
941	3¢ Tennessee Sthd. 6/1/46 Nashville, TN	3.00
942	3¢ Iowa Statehood 8/3/46 Iowa City, IA	3.00
943	3¢ Smithsonian 8/10/46 DC	3.00
944	3¢ New Mexico 10/16/46 Santa Fe, NM	3.00
	1947	
945	3¢ Thomas A. Edison 2/11/47 Milan, OH	4.00
946	3¢ Joseph Pulitzer 4/10/47 New York, NY	3.00
947	3¢ Stamp Centenary Sheet 5/17/47 New York, NY	3.00
	1st Fulton cachet (10 different)	**30.00**
948	5¢-10¢ Stamp Centenary Sheet 5/19/47 New York, NY	4.00
949	3¢ Doctors 6/9/47 Atlantic City, NJ	7.00
950	3¢ Utah Cent. 7/24/47 Salt Lake City, UT	3.00
951	3¢ Constitution 10/21/47 Boston, MA	3.50
	1st C.W. George cachet	**75.00**
	1st Suncraft cachet	**25.00**
952	3¢ Everglades 12/5/47 Florida City, FL	3.00
	1948	
953	3¢ G. Washington Carver 1/5/48 Tuskegee Inst., AL	4.50
	1st Jackson cachet	**35.00**
954	3¢ Discovery of Gold 1/24/48 Coloma, CA	2.00
955	3¢ Mississippi 4/7/48 Natchez, MS	2.00
956	3¢ Four Chaplains 5/28/48	2.50
957	3¢ Wisconsin Cent. 5/29/48 Madison, WI	2.00
958	5¢ Swedish Pioneers 6/4/48 Chicago, IL	2.00
959	3¢ Women's Prog. 7/19/48 Seneca Falls, NY	2.00
960	3¢ William A. White 7/31/48 Emporia, KS	2.00
961	3¢ US-Canada 8/2/48 Niagara Falls, NY	2.00
962	3¢ Francis Scott Key 8/9/48 Frederick, MD	2.25
963	3¢ Youth of America 8/11/48 DC	2.00
964	3¢ Oregon Terr. 8/14/48 Oregon City, OR	2.00
965	3¢ Harlan Fisk Stone 8/25/48 Chesterfield, NH	2.00
966	3¢ Palomar Observatory 8/30/48 Palomar Mt., CA	2.25
967	3¢ Clara Barton 9/7/48 Oxford, MA	3.50
968	3¢ Poultry Industry 9/9/48 New Haven, CT	2.00
969	3¢ Gold Star Mothers 9/21/48 DC	2.00
970	3¢ Fort Kearny 9/22/48 Minden, NE	2.00
971	3¢ Fireman 10/4/48 Dover, DE	4.00
972	3¢ Indian Centennial 10/15/48 Muskogee, OK	2.00
973	3¢ Rough Riders 10/27/48 Prescott, AZ	2.00
974	3¢ Juliette Low 10/29/48 Savannah, GA	4.00
975	3¢ Will Rogers 11/4/48 Claremore, OK	2.00
	1st Kolor Kover cachet	**100.00**
976	3¢ Fort Bliss 11/5/48 El Paso, TX	3.00
977	3¢ Moina Michael 11/9/48 Athens, GA	2.00
978	3¢ Gettysburgh Address 11/19/48 Gettysburg, PA	2.50
979	3¢ Amer. Turners 11/20/48 Cincinnati, OH	2.00
980	3¢ Joel Chandler Harris 12/9/48 Eatonton, GA	2.00
	1949	
981	3¢ Minnesota Terr. 3/3/49 St. Paul, MN	2.00
982	3¢ Washington & Lee Univ. 4/12/49 Lexington, VA	2.00
983	3¢ Puerto Rico 4/27/49 San Juan, PR	2.00
984	3¢ Annapolis 5/23/49 Annapolis, MD	2.00
985	3¢ G.A.R. 8/29/49 Indianapolis, IN	2.00
986	3¢ Edgar Allan Poe 10/7/49 Richmond, VA	2.50
	1950	
987	3¢ Bankers 1/3/50 Saratoga Springs, NY	2.00
988	3¢ Samuel Gompers 1/27/50 DC	2.00
989	3¢ Statue of Freedom 4/20/50 DC	2.00
990	3¢ White House 6/12/50 DC	2.00
991	3¢ Supreme Court 8/2/50 DC	2.00
992	3¢ Capitol 11/22/50 DC	2.00
	#989-992 on one cover 11/22/50	7.50
993	3¢ Railroad Engineers 4/29/50 Jackson, TN	5.00
994	3¢ Kansas City 6/3/50 Kansas City, MO	2.00

Scott #	Description	Price
995	3¢ Boy Scouts 6/30/50 Valley Forge, PA	4.50
996	3¢ Indiana Terr. 7/4/50 Vincennes, IN	2.00
997	3¢ California Sthd. 9/9/50 Sacramento, CA	2.00
	1951	
998	3¢ Confederate Vets. 5/30/51 Norfolk, VA	2.00
999	3¢ Nevada Territory 7/14/51 Genoa, NY	2.00
1000	3¢ Landing of Cadillac 7/24/51 Detroit, MI	2.00
1001	3¢ Colorado Statehood 8/1/51 Minturn, CO	2.50
1002	3¢ Amer. Chem. Assoc. 9/4/51 New York, NY	2.00
1003	3¢ Battle of Brooklyn 12/10/51 Brooklyn, NY	2.00
	1st Velvatone cachet	**75.00**
	1952	
1004	3¢ Betsy Ross 1/2/52 Philadelphia, PA	2.50
	1st Steelcraft cachet	**30.00**
1005	3¢ 4-H Clubs 1/15/52 Springfield, OH	2.00
1006	3¢ B. & O. Railroad 2/28/52 Baltimore, MD	5.00
1007	3¢ Am. Automobile Assoc. 3/4/52 Chicago, IL	2.00
1008	3¢ NATO 4/4/52 DC	2.00
1009	3¢ Grand Coulee Dam 5/15/52 Grand Coulee, WA	2.00
1010	3¢ Lafayette 6/13/52 Georgetown, SC	2.00
1011	3¢ Mount Rushmore 8/11/52 Keystone, SD	2.00
1012	3¢ Civil Engineers 9/6/52 Chicago, IL	2.00
1013	3¢ Service Women 9/11/52 DC	2.00
1014	3¢ Gutenberg Bible 9/30/52 DC	2.00
1015	3¢ Newspaper Boys 10/4/52 Phila., PA	2.00
1016	3¢ Red Cross 11/21/52 New York, NY	3.00
	1953	
1017	3¢ National Guard 2/23/53 DC	2.00
1018	3¢ Ohio Statehood 3/2/53 Chillicothe, OH	2.00
	1st Boerger cachet	**25.00**
1019	3¢ Washington Terr. 3/2/53 Olympia, WA	2.00
1020	3¢ Louisiana Pur. 4/30/53 St. Louis, MO	2.00
1021	3¢ Opening of Japan 7/14/53 DC	2.00
	1st Overseas Mailers cachet	**75.00**
1022	3¢ Amer. Bar Assoc. 8/24/53 Boston, MA	4.00
1023	3¢ Sagamore Hill 9/14/53 Oyster Bay. NY	2.00
1024	3¢ Future Farmers 10/13/53 KS City, MO	2.00
1025	3¢ Trucking Ind. 10/27/53 Los Angeles, CA	2.00
1026	3¢ General Patton 11/11/53 Fort Knox, NY	2.00
1027	3¢ Founding of NYC 11/20/53 New York, NY	2.00
1028	3¢ Gadsden Purchase 12/30/53 Tucson, AZ	2.00
	1954	
1029	3¢ Columbia Univ. 1/4/54 New York, NY	2.00
	1954-61 LIBERTY SERIES	
1030-53	Liberty set of 27	110.00
1030	½¢ Franklin 10/20/55 DC	1.75
1031	1¢ Washington 8/26/54 Chicago, IL	1.75
1031A	1¼¢ Palace 6/17/60 Santa Fe, NM	1.75
1032	1½¢ Mt. Vernon 2/22/56 Mt. Vernon, VA	1.75
1033	2¢ Jefferson 9/15/54 San Francisco, CA	1.75
1034	2½¢ Bunker Hill 6/17/59 Boston, MA	1.75
1035	3¢ Statue of Liberty 6/24/54 Albany, NY	1.75
1035a	booklet pane 6/30/54 DC	4.00
1035b	Luminescent 7/6/66 DC	30.00
1035b & 1225a	Luminescent, combo	40.00
1036	4¢ Lincoln 11/19/54 New York, NY	1.75
1036a	booklet pane 7/31/58 Wheeling, WV	3.00
1036b	Luminescent 11/2/63 DC	100.00
1037	4½¢ Hermitage 3/16/59 Hermitage, TN	1.75
1038	5¢ Monroe 12/3/54 Fredericksburg, VA	1.75
1039	6¢ Roosevelt 11/18/55 New York, NY	1.75
1040	7¢ Wilson 1/110/56 Staunton, VA	1.75
1041	8¢ Statue of Liberty 4/9/54 DC	1.75
1042	8¢ Stat. of Lib. (Giori Press) 3/22/58 Cleveland, OH	1.75
1042A	8¢ Pershing 11/17/61 New York, NY	2.25
1043	9¢ The Alamo 6/14/56 San Antonio, TX	2.00
1044	10¢ Independence Hall 7/4/56 Phila., PA	2.00
1044b	Luminescent 7/6/66	30.00
1044A	11¢ Statue of Liberty 6/15/61 DC	2.50
1044Ac	Luminescent 1/11/67	30.00
1045	12¢ Harrison 6/6/59 Oxford, OH	2.00
1045a	Luminescent 5/6/68	30.00
1045a & 1055a	Luminescent, combo	40.00
1046	15¢ John Jay 12/12/58 DC	2.50
1046a	Luminescent 5/6/68	35.00

1053

1107

Scott #	Description	Price
	1958-59	
1100	3¢ Horticulture 3/15/58 Ithaca, NY	1.75
1104	3¢ Brussels Exhibit. 4/17/58 Detroit, MI	1.75
1105	3¢ James Monroe 4/28/58 Montross, VA	1.75
1106	3¢ Minnesota Sthd. 5/11/58 St. Paul, MN	1.75
1107	3¢ Int'l. Geo. Year 5/31/58 Chicago, IL	1.75
1108	3¢ Gunston Hall 6/12/58 Lorton, VA	1.75
1109	3¢ Mackinaw Bridge 6/25/58 Mackinaw Bridge, MI	1.75
1110	4¢ Simon Bolivar 7/24/58 DC	1.75
1111	8¢ Simon Bolivar 7/24/58 DC	1.75
1110-11	Bolivar on one cover	2.50
1112	4¢ Atlantic Cable 8/15/58 New York, NY	1.75
1113	1¢ Lincoln 2/12/59 Hodgenville, NY	1.75
1114	3¢ Lincoln 2/27/59 New York, NY	1.75
1115	4¢ Lincoln & Douglas 8/27/58 Freeport, IL	1.75
1116	4¢ Lincoln Statue 5/30/59 DC	1.75
1113-16	On 1 Cover	8.00
1117	4¢ Lajos Kossuth 9/19/58 DC	1.75
1118	8¢ Lajos Kossuth 9/19/58 DC	1.75
1117-18	Kossuth on one cover	2.50
1119	4¢ Freedom of Press 9/22/58 Columbia, MO	1.75
1120	4¢ Overland Mail 10/10/58 San Fran., CA	1.75
	1958 (cont.)	
1121	4¢ Noah Webster 10/16/58 W. Hartford, CT	1.75
1122	4¢ Forest Conserv. 10/27/58 Tucson, AZ	1.75
1123	4¢ Fort Duquesne 11/25/58 Pittsburgh, PA	1.75
	1959	
1124	4¢ Oregon Sthd. 2/14/59 Astoria, OR	1.75
1125	4¢ Jose de San Martin 2/25/59 DC	1.75
1126	8¢ Jose de San Martin 2/25/59 DC	1.75
1125-26	San Martin on one cover	2.50
1127	4¢ NATO 4/1/59 DC	1.75
1128	4¢ Arctic Explorers 4/6/59 Cresson, PA	1.75
1129	8¢ World Trade 4/20/59 DC	1.75
1130	4¢ Silver Cent. 6/8/59 Virginia City, NV	1.75
1131	4¢ St. Lawrence Seaway 6/26/59 Massena, NY	2.00
1131	Combo w/Canada	10.00
1131	Combo w/Canada, dual cancel	250.00
1132	4¢ 49-Star Flag 7/4/59 Auburn, NY	1.75
1133	4¢ Soil Conserv. 8/26/59 Rapid City, SD	1.75
1134	4¢ Petroleum Ind. 8/27/59 Titusville, PA	2.00
1135	4¢ Dental Health 9/14/59 New York, NY	5.00
1136	4¢ Ernst Reuter 9/29/59 DC	1.75
1137	8¢ Ernst Reuter 9/29/59 DC	1.75
1136-37	Reuter on one cover	2.50
1138	4¢ Dr. McDowell 12/3/59 Danville, KY	1.75
	1960	
1139	4¢ Washington Credo 1/20/60 Mt. Vernon, VA	1.75
1140	4¢ Franklin Credo 3/31/60 Phila., PA	1.75
1141	4¢ Jefferson Credo 5/18/60 Charlottesville, VA	1.75
1142	4¢ Francis Scott Key Credo 9/14/60 Baltimore, MD	1.75
1143	4¢ Lincoln Credo 11/19/60 New York, NY	1.75
1144	4¢ Patrick Henry Credo 1/11/61 Richmond, VA	1.75
	#1139-1144 on one cover, 1/11/61	6.00
1145	4¢ Boy Scouts 2/8/60 DC	3.50
1146	4¢ Winter Olympics 2/18/60 Olympic Valley, CA	1.75
1147	4¢ Thomas G. Masaryk 3/7/60 DC	1.75
1148	8¢ Thomas G. Masaryk 3/7/60 DC	1.75
1147-48	Masaryk on one cover	2.50
1149	4¢ World Refugee Year 4/7/60 DC	1.75
1150	4¢ Water Conservation 4/18/60 DC	1.75
1151	4¢ SEATO 5/31/60 DC	1.75
1152	4¢ American Women 6/2/60 DC	2.00
1153	4¢ 50-Star Flag 7/4/60 Honolulu, HI	1.75
1154	4¢ Pony Express Centennial 7/19/60 Sacramento, CA	2.25
1155	4¢ Employ the Handicapped 8/28/60 New York, NY	1.75
1156	4¢ World Forestry Co. 8/29/60 Seattle, WA	1.75
1157	4¢ Mexican Indep. 9/16/60 Los Angeles, CA	1.75
1157	Combo w/Mexico	20.00
1157	Combo w/Mexico, dual cancel	375.00
1158	4¢ US-Japan Treaty 9/28/60 DC	1.75
1159	4¢ Paderewski 10/8/60 DC	1.75
1160	8¢ Paderewski 10/8/60 DC	1.75
1159-60	Paderewski on one cover	2.50
1161	4¢ Robert A. Taft 10/10/60 Cincinnati, OH	1.75

Scott #	Description	Price
	1954-61 LIBERTY SERIES (con't.)	
1047	20¢ Monticello 4/13/56 Charlottesville, VA	2.50
1048	25¢ Paul Revere 4/118/58 Boston, MA	2.50
1049	30¢ Robert E. Lee 9/21/55 Norfolk, VA	3.00
1050	40¢ John Marshall 9/24/55 Richmond, VA	4.00
1051	50¢ Susan Anthony 8/25/55 Louisville, KY	6.00
1052	$1 Patrick Henry 10/7/55 Joplin, MO	10.00
1053	$5 Alex Hamilton 3/19/56 Patterson, NJ	50.00
	1954-65 LIBERTY SERIES COILS	
1054	1¢ Washington 10/8/54 Baltimore, MD	1.75
1054A	1¼¢ Palace 6/17/60 Santa Fe, NM	1.75
1055	2¢ Jefferson 10/22/54 St. Louis, MO	1.75
1055a	Luminescent 5/6/68 DC	20.00
1055a & 1045a	Luminescent, combo	40.00
1056	2½¢ Bunker Hill 9/9/59 Los Angeles, CA	1.75
1057	3¢ Statue of Liberty 7/20/54 DC	1.75
1057b	Luminescent 5/12/67 DC	50.00
1058	4¢ Lincoln 7/31/58 Mandan, ND	1.75
1059	4½¢ Hermitage 5/1/59 Denver, CO	1.75
1059A	25¢ Paul Revere 2/25/65 Wheaton, MD	2.50
1059b	Luminescent 4/3/73 NY, NY	25.00
1060	3¢ Nebraska Ter. 5/7/54 Nebraska City, NE	1.75
1061	3¢ Kansas Terr. 5/31/54 Fort Leavenworth, KS	1.75
1062	3¢ George Eastman 7/12/54 Rochester, NY	1.75
1063	3¢ Lewis & Clark 7/28/54 Sioux City, IA	1.75
	1955	
1064	3¢ Fine Arts 1/15/55 Philadelphia, PA	1.75
1065	3¢ Land Grant Colleges 2/12/55 East Lansing, MI	2.50
1066	3¢ Rotary Int. 2/23/55 Chicago, IL	2.75
1067	3¢ Armed Forces Reserve 5/21/55 DC	2.00
1068	3¢ New Hampshire 6/21/55 Franconia, NH	1.75
1069	3¢ Soo Locks 6/28/55 Sault St. Marie, MI	1.75
1070	3¢ Atoms for Peace 7/28/55 DC	1.75
1071	3¢ Fort Ticonderoga 9/18/55 Ticonderoga, NY	1.75
1072	3¢ Andrew W. Mellon 12/20/55 DC	1.75
	1956	
1073	3¢ Benjamin Franklin 1/17/56 Phila., PA	1.75
	Poor Richard Station	1.75
1074	3¢ Booker T. Washington 4/5/56	
	Booker T. Washington Birthplace, VA	2.50
1075	11¢ FIPEX Sheet 4/28/56 New York, NY	5.00
1076	3¢ FIPEX 4/30/56 New York, NY	1.75
1077	3¢ Wild Turkey 5/5/56 Fond du Lac, WI	2.50
1078	3¢ Antelope 6/22/56 Gunnison, CO	2.00
1079	3¢ King Salmon 11/9/56 Seattle, WA	2.00
1080	3¢ Pure Food and Drug Laws 6/27/56 DC	1.75
1081	3¢ Wheatland 8/5/56 Lancaster, PA	1.75
1082	3¢ Labor Day 9/3/56 Camden, NJ	1.75
1083	3¢ Nassau Hall 9/22/56 Princeton, NJ	1.75
1084	3¢ Devils Tower 9/24/56 Devils Tower, NY	1.75
1085	3¢ Children 12/15/56 DC	1.75
	1957	
1086	3¢ Alex Hamilton 1/11/57 New York, NY	1.75
1087	3¢ Polio 1/15/57 DC	2.00
1088	3¢ Coast & Geodetic Survey 2/11/57 Seattle, WA	1.75
1089	3¢ Architects 2/23/57 New York, NY	2.25
1090	3¢ Steel Industry 5/22/57 New York, NY	1.75
1091	3¢ Naval Review 6/10/57 USS Saratoga, Norfolk, VA	1.75
1092	3¢ Oklahoma Statehood 6/14/57 Oklahoma City, OK	1.75
1093	3¢ School Teachers 7/1/57 Phila., PA	2.25
	"Philadelpia" error cancel	7.50
1094	4¢ American Flag 7/4/57 DC	1.75
1095	3¢ Shipbuilding 8/15/57 Bath, ME	1.75
1096	8¢ Ramon Magsaysay 8/31/57 DC	1.75
1097	3¢ Lafayette 9/6/57 Easton, PA	1.75
	Fayetteville, NC	1.75
	Louisville, KY	1.75
1098	3¢ Whooping Crane 11/22/57 New York, NY	1.75
	New Orleans, LA	1.75
	Corpus Christi, TX	1.75
1099	3¢ Religious Freedom 12/27/57 Flushing, NY	1.75

1152

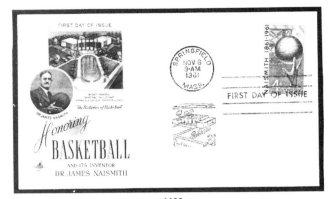

1189

Scott #	Description	Price
	1960 (cont.)	
1162	4¢ Wheels of Freedom 10/15/60 Detroit, MI	1.75
1163	4¢ Boys Clubs 10/18/60 New York, NY	1.75
1164	4¢ Automated P.O. 10/20/60 Providence, RI	1.75
1165	4¢ Gustav Mannerheim 10/26/60 DC	1.75
1166	8¢ Gustav Mannerheim 10/26/60 DC	1.75
1165-66	Mannerheim on one cover	2.50
1167	4¢ Camp Fire Girls 11/1/60 New York, NY	2.50
1168	4¢ Guiseppe Garibaldi 11/2/60 DC	1.75
1169	8¢ Guiseppe Garibaldi 11/2/60 DC	1.75
1168-69	Garibaldi on one cover	2.50
1170	4¢ Walter F. George 11/5/60 Vienna, GA	1.75
1171	4¢ Andrew Carnegie 11/25/60 New York, NY	1.75
1172	4¢ John Foster Dulles 12/6/60 DC	1.75
1173	4¢ Echo 1 12/15/60 DC	3.00
	1961-65	
1174	4¢ Mahatma Gandhi 1/26/61 DC	1.75
1175	8¢ Mahatma Gandhi 1/26/61 DC	1.75
1174-75	Gandhi on one cover	2.50
1176	4¢ Range Cons. 2/2/61 Salt Lake City, UT	1.75
1177	4¢ Horace Greeley 2/3/61 Chappaqua, NY	1.75
1178	4¢ Fort Sumter 4/12/61 Charleston, SC	3.50
1179	4¢ Battle of Shiloh 4/7/62 Shiloh, TN	3.50
1180	5¢ Battle of Gettysburg 7/1/63 Gettysburg, PA	3.50
1181	5¢ Battle of Wilderness 5/5/64 Fredericksburg, VA	3.50
1182	5¢ Appomattox 4/9/65 Appomattox, VA	3.50
1178-82	Civil War on 1 cover 4/9/65	10.00
1183	4¢ Kansas Statehood 5/10/61 Council Grove, KS	1.75
1184	4¢ George Norris 7/11/611 DC	1.75
1185	4¢ Naval Aviation 8/20/61 San Diego, CA	2.00
1186	4¢ Workmen's Comp. 9/4/61 Milwaukee, WI	1.75
1187	4¢ Frederic Remington 10/4/61 DC	2.00
1188	4¢ Sun Yat-Sen 10/10/61 DC	5.00
1189	4¢ Basketball 11/6/61 Springfield, MA	8.00
1190	4¢ Nursing 12/28/61 DC	12.00
	1962	
1191	4¢ New Mexico Sthd. 1/6/62 Santa Fe, NM	2.25
1192	4¢ Arizona Sthd. 2/14/62 Phoenix, AZ	2.25
	1st Glory cachet	**35.00**
1193	4¢ Project Mercury 2/20/62 Cape Canaveral, FL	3.00
	1st Marg cachet	**25.00**
1194	4¢ Malaria Eradication 3/30/62 DC	2.00
1195	4¢ Charles Evans Hughes 4/11/62 DC	1.75
1196	4¢ Seattle Fair 4/25/62 Seattle, WA	1.75
1197	4¢ Louisiana 4/30/62 New Orleans, LA	1.75
1198	4¢ Homestead Act 5/20/62 Beatrice, NE	1.75
1199	4¢ Girl Scouts 7/24/62 Burlington, VT	3.50
1200	4¢ Brien McMahon 7/28/62 Norwalk, CT	1.75
1201	4¢ Apprenticeship 8/31/62 DC	1.75
1202	4¢ Sam Rayburn 9/16/62 Bonham, TX	1.75
1203	4¢ Dag Hammarskjold 10/23/62 NY, NY	1.75
1204	4¢ Hammarskjold Invert. 11/16/62 DC	5.00
1205	4¢ Christmas 11/1/62 Pittsburgh, PA	2.00
1206	4¢ Higher Education 11/14/62 DC	2.25
1207	4¢ Winslow Homer 12/15/62 Gloucester, MA	2.25
	1962-63 REGULAR ISSUES	
1208	5¢ 50-Star Flag 1/9/63 DC	1.75
1208a	5¢ Luminescent 8/25/66 DC	25.00
1209	1¢ Andrew Jackson 3/22/63 New York, NY	1.75
1209a	Luminescent 7/6/66 DC	25.00
1213	5¢ Washington 11/23/62 New York, NY	1.75
1213a	Booklet Pane 11/23/62 New York, NY	3.00
1213b	Luminescent 10/28/63 Dayton, OH	25.00
1213c	Luminescent bklt. pair 10/28/63 Dayton, OH	40.00
1213c	Luminescent bklt. pane 10/28/63 Dayton, OH	100.00
	DC	125.00
1225	1¢ Jackson, coil 5/31/63 Chicago, IL	1.75
1225a	Luminescent 7/6/66 DC	20.00
1225a & 1035b	Luminescent combo	40.00
1229	5¢ Washington, coil 11/23/62 New York, NY	1.75
1229a	Luminescent 10/28/63 Dayton, OH	30.00
	DC	30.00
1229a,1213b, & 1213c	On one FDC 10/28/63 Dayton, OH	60.00

U.S. FIRST DAY COVERS

Scott #	Description	Price
	1963	
1230	5¢ Carolina Charter 4/6/63 Edenton, NC	1.75
1231	5¢ Food for Peace 6/4/63 DC	1.75
1232	5¢ W. Virginia Sthd. 6/20/63 Wheeling, WV	1.75
1233	5¢ Emancipation Proc. 8/16/63 Chicago, IL	2.50
1234	5¢ Alliance for Progress 8/17/63 DC	1.75
1235	5¢ Cordell Hull 10/5/63 Carthage, TN	1.75
1236	5¢ Eleanor Roosevelt 10/11/63 DC	1.75
1237	5¢ Science 10/14/63 DC	2.00
1238	5¢ City Mail Delivery 10/26/63 DC	2.00
1239	5¢ Red Cross 10/29/63 DC	2.50
1240	5¢ Christmas 11/1/63 Santa Claus, IN	2.00
1240a	5¢ Luminescent 11/2/63 DC	60.00
1241	5¢ Audobon 12/7/63 Henderson, KY	2.00
	1964	
1242	5¢ Sam Houston 1/10/64 Houston, TX	2.00
1243	5¢ Charle Russell 3/19/64 Great Falls, MT	2.50
1244	5¢ NY World's Fair 4/22/64 World's Fair, NY	2.00
	1st Sarzin Metallic cachet	**20.00**
1245	5¢ John Muir 4/29/64 Martinez, CA	1.75
1246	5¢ John F. Kennedy 5/29/64 Boston, MA	2.50
	1st Cover Craft cachet	**40.00**
1247	5¢ New Jersey Terc. 6/15/64 Elizabeth, NJ	1.75
1248	5¢ Nevada Sthd. 7/22/64 Carson City, NV	1.75
1249	5¢ Register & Vote 8/1/64 DC	1.75
1250	5¢ Shakespeare 8/14/64 Stratford, CT	2.00
1251	5¢ Doctors Mayo 9/11/64 Rochester, MN	5.00
1252	5¢ American Music 7/2/65 New York, NY	2.50
1253	5¢ Homemakers 10/26/64 Honolulu, HI	1.75
1254-57	5¢ Christmas attd. 11/9/64 Bethlehem, PA	4.00
1254-57	Christmas set of 4 singles	10.00
1254-57a	Luminescent Christmas attd 11/10/64 Dayton, OH	60.00
1254-57a	Luminescent Christmas set of 4 singles	80.00
1258	5¢ Verrazano-Narrows Bridge 11/21/64 Stat. Is., NY	1.75
1259	5¢ Fine Arts 12/2/64 DC	1.75
1260	5¢ Amateur Radio 12/15/64 Anchorage, AK	2.50
	1965	
1261	5¢ Battle of New Orleans 1/8/65 New Orleans, LA	1.75
1262	5¢ Physical Fitness 2/15/65 DC	2.00
1263	5¢ Cancer Crusade 4/1/65 DC	3.50
1264	5¢ Winston Churchill 5/13/65 Fulton, MO	2.00
1265	5¢ Magna Carta 6/15/65 Jamestown, VA	1.75
1266	5¢ Int'l. Cooperation Year 6/26/65 San Francisco, CA	1.75
1267	5¢ Salvation Army 7/2/65 New York, NY	1.75
1268	5¢ Dante 7/17/65 San Francisco, CA	1.75
1269	5¢ Herbert Hoover 8/10/65 West Branch, IA	1.75
1270	5¢ Robert Fulton 8/19/65 Clermont, NY	1.75
1271	5¢ 400th Anniv. of FL 8/28/65 St. Augustine, FL	1.75
1271	Combo w/Spain	90.00
1271	Combo w/Spain, dual cancel	450.00
1272	5¢ Traffic Safety 9/3/65 Baltimore, MD	1.75
1273	5¢ John Copley 9/17/65 DC	1.75
1274	11¢ Int'l. Telecomm. Union 10/6/65 DC	1.75
1275	5¢ A. Stevenson 10/23/65 Bloominton, IL	1.75
1276	5¢ Christmas 11/2/65 Silver Bell, AZ	1.75
1276a	Luminescent 11/16/65 DC	50.00
	1965-68 PROMINENT AMERICANS SERIES	
1278	1¢ Jefferson 1/12/68 Jeffersonville, IN	1.75
1278a	bklt. pane of 8 1/12/68 Jeffersonville, IN	2.00
1278a	bklt. pane of 8, dull gum 3/1/71 DC	90.00
1278a & 1393a Combo, 3/1/71		150.00
1278b	booklet pane of 4 5/10/71 DC	15.00
1279	1¼¢ Gallatin 1/30/67 Gallatin, MO	1.75
1280	2¢ Wright 6/8/66 Spring Green, WI	1.75
1280a	booklet pane of 5 1/8/68 Buffalo, NY	3.00
1280c	booklet pane of 6 5/7/71 Spokane, WA	15.00
1280c var.	bklt. pane of 6, dull gum 10/31/75 Cleveland, OH	100.00
1281	3¢ Parkman 9/16/67 Boston, MA	1.75
1282	4¢ Lincoln 11/19/65 New York, NY	1.75
1282a	Luminescent 12/1/65 Dayton, OH	40.00
	DC	45.00
1283	5¢ Washington 2/22/66 DC	1.75
1283a	Luminescent 2/23/66 Dayton, OH	100.00
	DC	27.50
1283B	5¢ Washington, redrawn 11/17/67 New York, NY	1.75

1285

1309

Scott #	Description	Price
	1965-68 PROMINENT AMERICANS SERIES (con't.)	
1284	6¢ Roosevelt 1/29/66 Hyde Park, NY	1.75
1284a	Luminescent 12/29/66	20.00
1284b	booklet pane of 8 12/28/67 DC	2.50
1284bs	booklet single	1.75
1284c	booklet pane of 5 1/9/68 DC	125.00
1285	8¢ Einstein 3/14/66 Princeton, NJ	2.00
1285a	Luminescent 7/6/66 DC	20.00
1286	10¢ Jackson 3/15/67 Hermitage, TN	1.75
1286A	12¢ Ford 7/30/68 Greenfield Village, MI	2.50
1287	13¢ Kennedy 5/29/67 Brookline, MA	2.50
1288	15¢ Holmes 3/8/68 DC	1.75
1288B	booklet single 6/14/78 Boston, MA	1.75
1288Bc	15¢ bklt. pane of 8 6/14/78 Boston, MA	3.50
1289	20¢ Marshall 10/24/67 Lexington, VA	2.00
1289a	Luminescent 4/3/73 New York, NY	25.00
1290	25¢ Douglass 2/14/67 DC	3.50
1290a	Luminescent 4/3/73 DC	25.00
1291	30¢ Dewey 10/21/68 Burlington, VT	2.50
1291a	Luminescent 4/3/73 New York, NY	25.00
1292	40¢ Paine 1/29/68 Philadelphia, PA	3.00
1292a	Luminescent 4/3/73 New York, NY	25.00
1293	50¢ Stone 8/13/68 Dorchester, MA	4.00
1293a	Luminescent 4/3/73 New York, NY	30.00
1294	$1 O'Neill 10/16/67 New London, CT	7.00
1294a	Luminescent 4/3/73 New York, NY	40.00
1295	$5 Moore 12/3/66 Smyrna, DE	40.00
1295a	Luminescent 4/3/73 New York, NY	100.00
	#1295 & 1295a on one cover 4/3/73	225.00
	1966-81 PROMINENT AMERICAN COILS	
1297	3¢ Parkman 11/4/75 Pendleton, OR	1.75
1298	6¢ Roosevelt, vert. coil 12/28/67 DC	1.75
1299	1¢ Jefferson 1/12/68 Jeffersonville, IN	1.75
1303	4¢ Lincoln 5/28/66 Springfield, IL	1.75
1304	5¢ Washington 9/8/66 Cincinnati, OH	1.75
1304C	5¢ Washington re-engraved 3/31/81 DC	25.00
1305	6¢ Roosevelt, horiz. coil 2/28/68 DC	1.75
1305E	15¢ Holmes 6/14/78 Boston, MA	1.75
1305C	$1 O'Neill 1/12/73 Hampstead, NY	4.00
	1966	
1306	5¢ Migratory Bird 3/16/66 Pittsburgh, PA	2.50
1307	5¢ Humane Treatment 4/9/66 New York, NY	2.00
1308	5¢ Indiana Sthd. 4/16/66 Corydon, IN	1.75
1309	5¢ Circus 5/2/66 Delevan, WI	2.50
1310	5¢ SIPEX 5/21/66 DC	1.75
1311	5¢ SIPEX sheet 5/23/66 DC	2.00
1312	5¢ Bill of Rights 7/1/66 Miami Beach, FL	1.75
1313	5¢ Polish Millenium 7/30/66 DC	1.75
1314	5¢ Nat'l. Park Service 8/25/66 Yellowstone Nat'l. Park	2.00
1314a	Luminescent 8/26/66	35.00
1315	5¢ Marine Corps Reserve 8/29/66 DC	2.50
1315a	Luminescent 8/29/66 DC	35.00
1316	5¢ Women's Clubs 9/12/66 New York, NY	2.00
1316a	Luminescent 9/13/66 DC	35.00
1317	5¢ Johnny Appleseed 9/24/66 Leominster, MA	1.75
1317a	Luminescent 9/26/66 DC	35.00
1318	5¢ Beautification 10/5/66 DC	1.75
1318a	Luminescent 10/5/66 DC	35.00
1319	5¢ Great River Road 10/21/66 Baton Rouge, LA	1.75
1319a	Luminescent 10/22/66 DC	35.00
1320	5¢ Savings Bonds 10/26/66 Sioux City, IA	1.75
1320a	Luminescent 10/27/66 DC	35.00
1321	5¢ Christmas 11/1/66 Christmas, MI	1.75
1321a	Luminescent 11/2/66	35.00
1322	5¢ Mary Cassatt 11/17/66 DC	2.00
1322a	Luminescent 11/17/66 DC	35.00
	1967	
1323	5¢ National Grange 4/17/67 DC	1.75
1324	5¢ Canada Centenary 5/25/67 Montreal, CAN	1.75
1325	5¢ Erie Canal 7/4/67 Rome, NY	1.75
1326	5¢ Search for Peace 7/5/67 Chicago, IL	1.75
1327	5¢ Henry Thoreau 7/12/67 Concord, MA	1.75

Scott #	Description	Price
1328	5¢ Nebraska Statehood. 7/29/67 Lincoln, NE	1.75
1329	5¢ Voice of America 8/1/67	1.75
1330	5¢ Davy Crockett 8/17/67 San Antonio, TX	1.75
1331-32	5¢ Space Twins attd. 9/29/67 Kennedy Space Ctr., FL	10.00
1331-32	Space Twins set of 2 singles	10.00
1333	5¢ Urban Planning 10/2/67 DC	1.75
1334	5¢ Finland Indep. 10/6/67 Finland, MI	1.75
1335	5¢ Thomas Eakins 11/2/67 DC	2.00
1336	5¢ Christmas 11/6/67 Bethlehem, GA	2.00
1337	5¢ Mississippi Statehood 12/11/67 Natchez, MS	1.75
	1968-71 REGULAR ISSUES	
1338	6¢ Flag & White House 1/24/68 DC	1.75
1338A	6¢ Flag & W.H., coil 5/30/69 Chicago, IL	1.75
1338D	6¢ Flag & W.H. (Huck Press) 8/7/70 DC	1.75
1338F	8¢ Flag & White House 5/10/71 DC	1.75
1338G	8¢ Flag & White House, coil 5/10/71 DC	1.75
	1968	
1339	6¢ Illinois Statehood 2/12/68 Shawneetown, IL	1.75
1340	6¢ Hemis Fair '68 3/30/68 San Antonio, TX	1.75
1341	$1 Airlift 4/4/68 Seattle, WA	7.50
1342	6¢ Support Our Youth 5/1/68 Chicago, IL	1.75
1343	6¢ Law and Order 5/17/68 DC	3.00
1344	6¢ Register and Vote 6/27/68 DC	2.50
1345-54	6¢ Historic Flags attd. 7/4/68 Pittsburgh, PA	10.00
1345-54	Historic Flags set of 10 singles	40.00
1355	6¢ Walt Disney 9/11/68 Marceline, MO	35.00
1356	6¢ Marquette 9/20/68 Sault Ste. Marie, MI	1.75
1357	6¢ Daniel Boone 9/26/68 Frankfort, KY	1.75
1358	6¢ Arkansas River 10/1/68 Little Rock, AR	1.75
1359	6¢ Leif Ericson 10/9/68 Seattle, WA	1.75
1360	6¢ Cherokee Strip 10/15/68 Ponca, OK	1.75
1361	6¢ John Trumbull 10/18/68 New Haven, CT	2.00
1362	6¢ Waterfowl Cons. 10/24/68 Cleveland, OH	2.00
1363	6¢ Christmas, tagged 11/1/68 DC	2.00
1363a	6¢ Not tagged 11/2/68 DC	15.00
1364	6¢ American Indian 11/4/68 DC	2.00
	1969	
1365-68	6¢ Beautification attd. 1/16/69 DC	5.00
1365-68	Beautification set of 4 singles	10.00
1369	6¢ American Legion 3/15/69 DC	1.75
1370	6¢ Grandma Moses 5/1/69 DC	2.00
1371	6¢ Apollo 8 5/5/69 Houston, TX	3.00
1372	6¢ W.C. Handy 5/17/69 Memphis, TN	2.00
1373	6¢ California 7/16/69 San Diego, CA	1.75
1374	6¢ John W. Powell 8/1/69 Page, AZ	1.75
1375	6¢ Alabama Sthd. 8/2/69 Huntsville, AL	1.75
1376-79	6¢ Botanical Congress attd. 8/23/69 Seattle, WA	6.00
1376-79	Botanical Congress set of 4 singles	10.00
1380	6¢ Dartmouth Case 9/22/69 Hanover, NH	1.75
1381	6¢ Baseball 9/24/69 Cincinnati, OH	15.00
1382	6¢ Football 9/26/69 New Brunswick, NJ	7.00
1383	6¢ Eisenhower 10/14/69 Abilene, KS	1.75
1384	6¢ Christmas 11/3/69 Christmas, FL	2.00
1384a	6¢ Christmas - Precancel 11/4/69 Atlanta, GA	175.00
	Baltimore, MD	175.00
	Memphis, TN	175.00
	New Haven, CT	175.00
1385	6¢ Hope for Crippled 11/20/69 Columbus, OH	2.00
1386	6¢ William Harnett 12/3/69 Boston, MA	1.75
	1970	
1387-90	6¢ Natural History attd. 5/6/70 NY, NY	4.00
1387-90	Natural History set of 4 singles	8.00
1391	6¢ Maine Statehood 7/9/70 Portland, ME	1.75
1392	6¢ Wildlife - Buffalo 7/20/70 Custer, SD	1.75
	1970-74 REGULAR ISSUES	
1393	6¢ Eisenhower 8/6/70 DC	1.75
1393a	booklet pane of 8 8/6/70 DC	2.50
1393a	booklet pane of 8, dull gum 3/1/71 DC	75.00
1393a & 1278a	Combo, 3/1/71	150.00
1393b	booklet pane of 6 8/6/70 DC	3.00
1393bs	booklet single, 8/6/70	1.75
1393D	7¢ Franklin 10/20/72 Philadelphia, PA	1.75
1394	8¢ Eisenhower 5/10/71 DC	1.75
1395	8¢ Eisenhower, claret 5/10/71 DC	2.00

1410-13

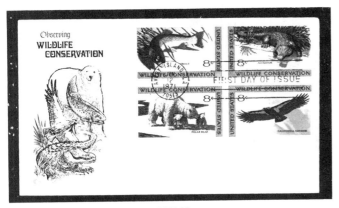

1427-30

Scott #	Description	Price
	1970-74 REGULAR ISSUE (con't.)	
1395a	booklet pane of 8 5/10/71 DC	2.50
1395b	booklet pane of 6 5/10/71 DC	2.50
1395c	bklt. pane of 4 1/28/72 Casa Grande, AZ	2.00
1395cs	Booklet Single 1/28/72 Casa Grande, AZ	1.75
1395d	bklt. pane of 7 1/28/72 Casa Grande, AZ	2.00
1395ds	Booklet Single 1/28/72 Casa Grande, AZ	1.75
1396	8¢ Postal Service Emblem 7/1/71 any city	1.75
1397	14¢ LaGuardia 4/24/72 New York, NY	1.75
1398	16¢ Ernie Pyle 5/7/71 DC	2.50
1399	18¢ Eliz. Blackwell 1/23/74 Geneva, NY	2.00
1400	21¢ Giannini 6/27/73 San Mateo, CA	2.25
1401	6¢ Eisenhower, coil 8/6/70 DC	1.75
1402	8¢ Eisenhower, coil 5/10/71 DC	1.75
	1970	
1405	6¢ Edgar Lee Masters 8/22/70 Petersburg, IL	1.75
1406	6¢ Woman Suffrage 8/26/70 Adams, MA	1.75
1407	6¢ South Carolina 9/12/70 Charleston, SC	1.75
1408	6¢ Stone Mountain 9/19/70 Stone Mt., GA	1.75
1409	6¢ Ft. Snelling 10/17/70 Ft. Snelling, MT	1.75
1410-13	6¢ Anti-Pollution attd. 10/28/70 San Clemente, CA	5.00
1410-13	Anti-Pollution set of 4 singles	8.00
1414	6¢ Christmas - Religious 11/5/70 DC	1.75
1414a	6¢ Christmas Precancel 11/5/70 DC	3.00
1415-18	6¢ Christmas Toys attd. 11/5/70 DC	6.00
1415-18	Christmas Toys set of 4 singles	10.00
1415a-18a	Christmas Toys-Precancel attd. 11/5/70 DC	20.00
1415a-18a	Christmas Toys-Precancel set of 4 singles	60.00
1414a-18a	Religious & Toys (5) on one FDC 11/5/70 DC	30.00
1419	6¢ UN 25th Anniv. 11/20/70 New York, NY	1.75
1420	6¢ Pilgrims' Landing 11/21/70 Plymouth, MA	1.75
1421-22	6¢ Disabled Vets - US Servicemen attd.	
	11/24/40 Cincinnati or Montgomery	2.00
1421-22	D.A.V. - Serv. set of 2 singles	3.50
	1971	
1423	6¢ Wool Industry 1/19/71 Las Vegas, NV	1.75
	1st Bazaar cachet	**30.00**
	1st Colorano Silk cachet	**300.00**
1424	6¢ MacArthur 1/26/71 Norfolk, VA	2.00
1425	6¢ Blood Donor 3/12/71 New York, NY	1.75
1426	6¢ Missouri 5/8/71 Independence, MO	1.75
1427-30	8¢ Wildlife Conservation attd. 6/12/71 Avery Island, LA	4.00
1427-30	Wildlife set of 4 singles	8.00
1431	8¢ Antarctic Treaty 6/23/71 DC	1.75
1432	8¢ American Revolution Bic. 7/4/71 DC	1.75
	1st Medallion cachet	**30.00**
1433	8¢ John Sloan 8/2/71 Lock Haven, PA	1.75
1434-35	8¢ Space Achievement Decade attd. 8/2/71	
	Kennedy Space Center, FL	2.50
	Houston, TX	2.50
	Huntsville, AL	2.50
1434-35	Space Achievement set of 2 singles	
	Kennedy Space Center, FL	3.50
	Houston, TX	3.50
	Huntsville, AL	3.50
1436	8¢ Emily Dickinson 8/28/71 Amherst, MA	1.75
1437	8¢ San Juan 9/12/71 San Juan, PR	1.75
1438	8¢ Drug Abuse 10/4/71 Dallas, TX	1.75
1439	8¢ CARE 10/27/71 New York, NY	1.75
1440-43	8¢ Historic Preservation attd. 10/29/71 San Diego, CA	4.00
1440-43	Historic Preservation set of 4 singles	8.00
1444	8¢ Christmas - Religious 11/10/71 DC	2.00
1445	8¢ Christmas - Partridge 11/10/71 DC	2.00
1444-45	Christmas on one cover	2.50
	1972	
1446	8¢ Sidney Lanier 2/3/72 Macon, GA	1.75
1447	8¢ Peace Corps 2/11/72 DC	1.75
1448-51	2¢ Cape Hatteras 4/5/72 Hatteras, NC	1.75
1452	6¢ Wolf Trap Farm 6/26/72 Vienna, VA	1.75
1453	8¢ Yellowstone 3/1/72 DC	1.75
	Yellowstone Nat'l. Park, WY	1.75
1454	15¢ Mt. McKinley 7/28/72 Mt. McKinley Nat'l. Park, AK	1.75
1448-54,C84	Parks on one cover 7/28/72	6.00

Scott #	Description	Price
	1972 (cont.)	
1455	8¢ Family Planning 3/18/72 New York, NY	1.75
1456-59	8¢ Colonial Craftsmen attd. 7/4/72 Williamsburg, VA	4.00
1456-59	Colonial Craftsmen set of 4 singles	8.00
1460	6¢ Olympic - Bicycling 8/17/72 DC	1.75
1461	8¢ Olympic - Bobsledding 8/17/72 DC	1.75
1462	15¢ Olympic - Runners 8/17/72 DC	1.75
1460-62,C85	Olympics on one cover	4.00
1463	8¢ P.T.A. 9/15/72 San Francisco, CA	1.75
1464-67	8¢ Wildlife attd. 9/20/72 Warm Springs, OR	4.00
1464-67	Wildlife set of 4 singles	8.00
1468	8¢ Mail Order 9/27/72 Chicago, IL	1.75
1469	8¢ Osteopathic Medicine 10/9/72 Miami, FL	2.50
1470	8¢ Tom Sawyer 10/13/72 Hannibal, MO	2.50
1471	8¢ Christmas - Religious 11/9/72 DC	1.75
1472	8¢ Christmas - Santa Claus 11/9/72 DC	1.75
1471-72	Christmas on one cover	2.50
1473	8¢ Pharmacy 11/10/72 Cincinnati, OH	10.00
1474	8¢ Stamp Collecting 11/17/72 NY, NY	2.00
	1973	
1475	8¢ Love 1/26/73 Philadelphia, PA	2.25
1476	8¢ Pamphleteer 2/16/73 Portland, OR	1.75
1477	8¢ Broadside 4/13/73 Atlantic City, NJ	1.75
1478	8¢ Post Rider 6/22/73 Rochester, NY	1.75
1479	8¢ Drummer 9/28/73 New Orleans, LA	1.75
1480-83	8¢ Boston Tea Party attd. 7/4/73 Boston, MA	4.00
1480-83	Boston Tea Party set of 4 singles	8.00
1484	8¢ Geo. Gershwin 2/28/73 Beverly Hills, CA	1.75
1485	8¢ Robinson Jeffers 8/13/73 Carmel, CA	1.75
1486	8¢ Henry O. Tanner 9/10/73 Pittsburgh, PA	2.00
1487	8¢ Willa Cather 9/20/73 Red Cloud, NE	1.75
1488	8¢ Nicolaus Copernicus 4/23/73 DC	2.00
1489-98	8¢ Postal People attd. 4/30/73 any city	7.00
1489-98	Postal People set of 10 singles	20.00
1499	8¢ Harry Truman 5/8/73 Independence, MO	2.00
1500	6¢ Electronics 7/10/73 New York, NY	1.75
1501	8¢ Electronics 7/10/73 New York, NY	1.75
1502	15¢ Electronics 7/10/73 New York, NY	1.75
1500-02,C86	Electronics on one cover	7.00
1503	8¢ Lyndon B. Johnson 8/27/73 Austin, TX	1.75
1504	8¢ Angus Cattle 10/5/73 St. Joseph, MO	1.75
1505	10¢ Chautauqua 8/6/74 Chautauqua, NY	1.75
1506	10¢ Wheat 8/16/74 Hillsboro, KS	1.75
1507	8¢ Christmas - Madonna 11/7/73 DC	1.75
1508	8¢ Christmas - Tree 11/7/73 DC	1.75
1507-08	Christmas on one cover	2.75
	1973-74 REGULAR ISSUES	
1509	10¢ Crossed Flags 12/8/73 San Fran., CA	1.75
1510	10¢ Jefferson Memorial 12/14/73 DC	1.75
1510b	booklet pane of 5 12/14/73 DC	2.00
1510bs	booklet pane single, 12/14/73	1.75
1510c	booklet pane of 8 12/14/73 DC	2.25
1510d	booklet pane of 6 8/5/74 Oakland, CA	5.25
1510ds	booklet pane single, 8/5/74	1.75
1511	10¢ Zip Code 1/4/74 DC	1.75
1518	6.3¢ Liberty Bell, coil 10/1/74 DC	1.75
1518	Untagged, 10/2/74 DC	5.00
1519	10¢ Crossed Flags, coil 12/8/73 San Francisco, CA	1.75
1520	10¢ Jefferson Memorial, coil 12/14/73 DC	1.75
	1974	
1525	10¢ Veterans of Foreign Wars 3/11/74 DC	1.75
1526	10¢ Robert Frost 3/26/74 Derry, NH	1.75
1527	10¢ EXPO '74 4/18/74 Spokane, WA	1.75
1528	10¢ Horse Racing 5/4/74 Louisville, KY	3.00
1529	10¢ Skylab 5/14/74 Houston, TX	2.00
1530-37	10¢ UPU Centenary attd. 6/6/74 DC	5.00
1530-37	UPU Centenary set of 8 singles	20.00
1538-41	10¢ Mineral Heritage attd. 6/13/74 Lincoln, NE	4.00
1538-41	Mineral Heritage set of 4 singles	8.00
1542	10¢ Fort Harrod 6/15/74 Harrodsburg, KY	1.75
1543-46	10¢ Continental Congr. attd. 7/4/74 Philadelphia, PA	4.00
1543-46	Continental Congress set of 4 singles	8.00
1547	10¢ Energy Conserv. 9/23/74 Detroit, MI	1.75
1548	10¢ Sleepy Hollow 10/10/74 North Tarrytown, NY	2.00

1565-68

1612

Scott #	Description	Price
	1974 (cont.)	
1549	10¢ Retarded Children 10/12/74 Arlington, TX	1.75
1550	10¢ Christmas - Angel 10/23/74 NY, NY	1.75
1551	10¢ Christmas - Currier & Ives 10/23/74 NY, NY	1.75
1550-51	Christmas on one cover	2.25
1552	10¢ Christmas - Weathervane 11/15/74 New York, NY	3.00
1550-52	Christmas, dual cancel	5.00
	1975	
1553	10¢ Benjamin West 2/10/75 Swarthmore, PA	1.75
1554	10¢ Paul Dunbar 5/1/75 Dayton, OH	1.75
1555	10¢ D.W. Griffith 5/27/75 Beverly, Hills, CA	1.75
1556	10¢ Pioneer - Jupiter 2/28/75 Mountain View, CA	1.75
1557	10¢ Mariner 10 4/4/75 Pasadena, CA	1.75
1558	10¢ Collective Bargaining 3/13/75 DC	1.75
1559	8¢ Sybil Ludington 3/25/75 Carmel, NY	1.75
1560	10¢ Salem Poor 3/25/75 Cambridge, MA	1.75
1561	10¢ Haym Salomon 3/25/75 Chicago, IL	1.75
1562	18¢ Peter Francisco 3/25/75 Greensboro, NC	1.75
1559-62	Contributions on one cover, any city	8.00
1563	10¢ Lexington-Concord 4/19/75 Lexington, MA	1.75
	Concord, MA	1.75
1564	10¢ Bunker Hill 6/17/75 Charlestown, MA	1.75
1565-68	10¢ Military Uniforms attd. 7/4/75 DC	4.00
1565-68	Military Uniforms set of 4 singles	8.00
1569-70	10¢ Apollo-Soyuz attd. 7/15/75 Kennedy Sp. Ctr., FL	3.00
1569-70	Apollo-Soyuz set of 2 singles	4.00
1569-70	Apollo-Soyuz, combo, dual cancel	450.00
1571	10¢ Women's Year 8/26/75 Seneca Falls, NY	1.75
1572-75	10¢ Postal Serv. Bicent. attd. 9/3/75 Philadelphia, PA	4.00
1572-75	Postal Service set of 4 singles	8.00
1576	10¢ World Peace through Law 9/29/75 DC	2.00
1577-78	10¢ Banking - Commerce attd. 10/6/75 New York, NY	2.00
1577-78	Banking-Commerce set of 2 singles	3.00
1579	(10¢) Christmas - Madonna 10/14/75 DC	1.75
1580	(10¢) Christmas - Card 10/14/75 DC	1.75
1579-80	Christmas on one cover	2.50
	1975-81 AMERICANA SERIES REGULAR ISSUES	
1581	1¢ Inkwell & Quill 12/8/77 St. Louis, MO	1.75
1582	2¢ Speaker's Stand 12/8/77 St. Louis, MO	1.75
1584	3¢ Ballot Box 12/8/77 St. Louis, MO	1.75
1585	4¢ Books & Eyeglasses 12/8/77 St. Louis, MO	1.75
1581-85	4 values on one cover	3.00
1590	9¢ Capitol Dome, bklt. single perf. 11 x 10½ 3/11/77 New York, NY	10.00
1590a	9¢ Capitol Dome, bklt. single perf. 10 3/11/77 New York, NY	15.00
1591	9¢ Capitol Dome 11/24/75 DC	1.75
1592	10¢ Justice 11/17/77 New York, NY	1.75
1593	11¢ Printing Press 11/13/75 Phila., PA	1.75
1594	12¢ Liberty's Torch 4/8/81 Dallas, TX	1.75
1595	13¢ Liberty Bell, bklt. sgl. 10/31/75 Cleveland, OH	1.75
1595b	bklt. pane of 6 10/31/75 Cleveland, OH	2.25
1595c	bklt. pane of 7 10/31/75 Cleveland, OH	2.50
1595c	bklt. pane of 8 10/31/75 Cleveland, OH	2.75
1595d	bklt. pane of 5 4/2/76 Liberty, MO	2.00
1595ds	bklt. pane single, 4/2/76	1.75
1596	13¢ Eagle & Shield 12/1/75 Juneau, AK	1.75
1597	15¢ Ft. McHenry Flag 6/30/78 Baltimore, MD	1.75
1598	15¢ Ft. McHenry Flag,bklt. sgl. 6/30/78 Baltimore, MD	1.75
1598a	booklet pane of 8 6/30/78 Baltimore, MD	2.75
1599	16¢ Statue of Liberty 3/31/78 NY, NY	1.75
1603	24¢ Old North Church 11/14/75 Boston, MA	1.75
1604	28¢ Ft. Nisqually 8/11/78 Tacoma, WA	1.75
1605	29¢ Lighthouse 4/14/78 Atlantic City, NJ	1.75
1606	30¢ School House 8/27/79 Devils Lake, ND	1.75
1608	50¢ Betty Lamp 9/11/79 San Juan, PR	2.00
1610	$1 Rush Lamp 7/2/79 San Francisco, CA	3.50
1611	$2 Kerosene Lamp 11/16/78 New York, NY	7.00
1612	$5 Railroad Lantern 8/23/79 Boston, MA	13.50

Scott #	Description	Price
	1975-79 AMERICANA SERIES COILS	
1613	3.1¢ Guitar 10/25/79 Shreveport, LA	1.75
1614	7.7¢ Saxhorns 11/20/76 New York, NY	1.75
1615	7.9¢ Drum 4/23/76 Miami, FL	1.75
1615C	8.4¢ Grand Piano 7/13/78 Interlochen, MI	1.75
1616	9¢ Capitol Dome 3/5/76 Milwaukee, WI	1.75
1617	10¢ Justice 11/4/77 Tampa, FL	1.75
1618	13¢ Liberty Bell 11/25/75 Allentown, PA	1.75
1618C	15¢ Ft. McHenry Flag 6/30/78 Baltimore, MD	1.75
1619	16¢ Statue of Liberty 3/31/78 NY, NY	1.75
	1975-77 REGULAR SERIES	
1622	13¢ Flag over Ind. Hall 11/15/75 Philadelphia, PA	1.75
1623	13¢ Flag over Capitol, bklt. single perf. 11 x 10½ 3/11/77 NY, NY	2.50
1623a	13¢ & 9¢ booklet pane of 8 (7 #1623 & 1 #1590) perf. 11 x 10½ 3/11/77 NY, NY	25.00
1623b	13¢ Flag over Capitol, bklt. single perf. 10 3/11/77 New York, NY	2.00
1623c	13¢ & 9¢ booklet pane of 8 (7 #1623b & 1 #1590a) perf. 10 3/11/77 New York, NY	15.00
1625	13¢ Flag over Ind. Hall, coil 11/15/75 Phila., PA	1.75
	1976	
1629-31	10¢ Spirit of '76 attd. 1/1/76 Pasadena, CA	3.00
1629-31	Spirit of '76 set of 3 singles	5.75
1632	13¢ Interphil '76 1/17/76 Phila., PA	1.75
	1976 STATE FLAGS	
1633-82	13¢ State Flags 2/23/76 set of 50 DC	75.00
	State Capitals	100.00
	State Capital & DC cancels, set of 50 combo FDC's	150.00
1682a	Full sheet on one FDC (Uncacheted)	40.00
1683	13¢ Telephone 3/10/76 Boston, MA	1.75
1684	13¢ Aviation 3/19/76 Chicago, IL	2.00
1685	13¢ Chemistry 4/6/76 New York, NY	1.75
1686-89	13¢-31¢ Bicent. Souv. Shts. 5/29/76 Philadelphia, PA	30.00
1686a-89e	Set of 20 singles from sheets	90.00
1686a-89e	Set of 20 singles on 4 covers	40.00
1690	13¢ Franklin 6/1/76 Philadelphia, PA	1.75
1690	U.S. & Canada joint issue	5.00
1690	U.S. & Canada joint issue, dual cancel	15.00
1691-94	13¢ Decl. of Indep. attd. 7/4/76 Philadelphia, PA	4.00
1691-94	Decl. of Indep. set of 4 singles	8.00
1695-98	13¢ Olympics attd. 7/16/76 Lake Placid, NY	4.00
1695-98	Olympics set of 4 singles	8.00
1699	13¢ Clara Maass 8/18/76 Belleville, NJ	2.00
1700	13¢ Adolph S. Ochs 9/18/76 New York, NY	1.75
1701	13¢ Nativity 10/27/76 Boston, MA	1.75
1702	13¢ "Winter Pastime" 10/27/76 Boston, MA	1.75
1701-02	Christmas on one cover	2.00
1703	13¢ "Winter Pastime", Grav.-Int. 10/27/76 Boston, MA	2.00
1701,03	Christmas on one cover	2.25
1702-03	Christmas on one cover	2.50
1701-03	Christmas on one cover	3.00
	1977	
1704	13¢ Washington 1/3/77 Princeton, NJ	1.75
	1st Carrollton cachet	**20.00**
1705	13¢ Sound Recording 3/23/77 DC	2.00
1706-09	13¢ Pueblo Pottery attd. 4/13/77 Santa Fe, NM	4.00
1706-09	Pueblo Pottery set of 4 singles	8.00
1710	13¢ Lindbergh 5/20/77 Roosevelt Field Sta., NY	2.50
	1st Doris Gold cachet	**50.00**
	1st GAMM cachet	**50.00**
	1st Spectrum cachet	**25.00**
	1st Tudor House cachet	**20.00**
	1st Z-Silk cachet	**20.00**
1711	13¢ Colorado Sthd. 5/21/77 Denver, CO	1.75
1712-15	13¢ Butterflies attd. 6/6/77 Indianapolis, IN	4.00
1712-15	Butterflies set of 4 singles	8.00
	1st Ham cachet	**450.00**
1716	13¢ Lafayette 6/13/77 Charleston, SC	1.75
1717-20	13¢ Skilled Hands attd. 7/4/77 Cincinnati, OH	4.00
1717-20	Skilled Hands set of 4 singles	8.00
1721	13¢ Peace Bridge 8/4/77 Buffalo, NY	1.75
	US and Canadian stamps on one cover	2.50
	Dual US & Canadian FD cancels	7.50
1722	13¢ Herkimer 8/6/77 Herkimer, NY	1.75
1723-24	13¢ Energy Conservation attd. 10/20/77 DC	2.50
1723-24	Energy Conservation set of 2 singles	3.00
1725	13¢ Alta California 9/9/77 San Jose, CA	1.75
1726	13¢ Articles of Confed. 9/30/77 York, PA	1.75
1727	13¢ Talking Pictures 10/6/77 Hollywood, CA	1.75
1728	13¢ Surrender at Saratoga 10/7/77 Schuylerville, NY	1.75
1729	13¢ Christmas - Valley Forge 10/21/77 Valley Forge, PA	1.75
1730	13¢ Christmas - Mailbox 10/21/77 Omaha, NE	1.75
1729-30	Christmas on one cover, either city	2.50
1729-30	Christmas on one cover, dual FD cancels	4.00
	1978	
1731	13¢ Carl Sandburg 1/6/78 Galesburg, IL	1.75
	1st Western Silk cachet	**35.00**
1732-33	13¢ Captain Cook attd. 1/20/78 Honolulu, HI	2.00
	Anchorage, AK	2.00
1732-33	Captain Cook set of 2 singles Honolulu, HI	3.50
	Anchorage, AK	3.50

1749-52

Scott #	Description	Price
	1978 (con't.)	
1732-33	Set of 2 on one cover with dual FD cancels	15.00
	1st K.M.C. Venture cachet (set of 3)	**70.00**
1734	13¢ Indian Head Penny 1/11/78 Kansas City, MO	1.75
	1978-80 REGULAR ISSUES	
1735	(15¢) "A" & Eagle 5/22/78 Memphis, TN	1.75
1736	(15¢) "A", booklet single 5/22/78 Memphis, TN	1.75
1736a	(15¢) Booklet Pane of 8 5/22/78 Memphis, TN	3.00
1737	15¢ Roses, booklet single 7/11/78 Shreveport, LA	1.75
1737a	Booklet Pane of 8 7/11/78 Shreveport, LA	3.50
1738-42	15¢ Windmills set of 5 singles 2/7/80 Lubbock, TX	10.00
1742av	15¢ Windmills, strip of 5	6.00
1742a	Windmills booklet pane of 10	5.00
1743	(15¢) "A" & Eagle, coil 5/22/78 Memphis, TN	1.75
	1st Kribbs Kover cachet	**40.00**
1744	13¢ Harriet Tubman 2/1/78 DC	2.00
1745-48	13¢ American Quilts attd. 3/8/78 Charleston, WV	4.00
1745-48	American Quilts set of 4 singles	8.00
	1st Collins cachet	**450.00**
1749-52	13¢ American Dance attd. 4/26/78 New York, NY	4.00
1749-52	American Dance set of 4 singles	8.00
	1st Andrews cachet	**40.00**
1753	13¢ French Alliance 5/4/78 York, PA	1.75
1754	13¢ Dr. Papanicolaou 5/18/78 DC	1.75
1755	13¢ Jimmie Rodgers 5/24/78 Meridian, MS	1.75
1756	15¢ George M. Cohan 7/3/78 Providence, RI	1.75
1757	13¢ CAPEX Sheet 6/10/78 Toronto, Canada	3.50
1757a-h	CAPEX set of 8 singles	16.00
1758	15¢ Photography 6/26/78 Las Vegas, NV	1.75
1759	15¢ Viking Mission 7/20/78 Hampton, VA	1.75
1760-63	15¢ American Owls attd. 8/26/78 Fairbanks, AK	4.00
1760-63	American Owls set of 4 singles	8.00
1764-67	15¢ Amer. Trees attd. 10/9/78 Hot Springs Nat'l. Park, AR	4.00
1764-67	American Trees set of 4 singles	8.00
1768	15¢ Christmas - Madonna 10/18/78 DC	1.75
1769	15¢ Christmas - Hobby Horse 10/18/78 Holly, MI	1.75
1768-69	Christmas on one cover	2.50
	1979	
1770	15¢ Robert F. Kennedy 1/12/79 DC	2.00
	1st DRC cachet	**75.00**
1771	15¢ Martin Luther King 1/13/79 Atlanta, GA	2.50
1772	15¢ Int'l. Yr. of the Child 2/15/79 Philadelphia, PA	1.75
1773	15¢ John Steinbeck 2/27/79 Salinas, CA	1.75
1774	15¢ Albert Einstein 3/4/79 Princeton, NJ	1.75
1775-78	15¢ Toleware attd. 4/19/79 Lancaster, PA	4.00
1775-78	Toleware set of 4 singles	8.00
1779-82	15¢ Architecture attd. 6/4/79 Kansas City, MO	4.00
1779-82	Architecture set of 4 singles	8.00
1783-86	15¢ Endangered Flora attd. 6/7/79 Milwaukee, WI	4.00
1783-86	Endangered Flora set of 4 singles	8.00
1787	15¢ Seeing Eye Dogs 6/15/79 Morristown, NJ	1.75
1788	15¢ Special Olympics 8/9/79 Brockport, NY	1.75
1789	15¢ John Paul Jones, perf. 11x12 9/23/79 Annapolis, MD	2.00
1789a	15¢ John Paul Jones, perf. 11 9/23/79 Annapolis, MD	2.00
1789,89a	Both Perfs. on 1 Cover	12.00
1790	10¢ Olympic Javelin 9/5/79 Olympia, WA	1.75
1791-94	15¢ Summer Olympics attd. 9/28/79 Los Angeles, CA	4.00
1791-94	Summer Olympics set of 4 singles	8.00
1795-98	15¢ Winter Olympics attd. 2/1/80 Lake Placid, NY	4.00
1795-98	Winter Olympics set of 4 singles	8.00
1799	15¢ Christmas - Painting 10/18/79 DC	1.75
1800	15¢ Christmas - Santa Claus 10/18/79 North Pole, AK	1.75
1799-1800	Christmas on one cover, either city	2.50
1799-1800	Christmas, dual cancel	2.50
1801	15¢ Will Rogers 11/4/79 Claremore, OK	1.75
1802	15¢ Vietnam Vets 11/11/79 Arlington, VA	2.50
	1980	
1803	15¢ W.C. Fields 1/29/80 Beverly Hills, CA	2.50
	1st Gill Craft cachet	**30.00**
	1st Kover Kids cachet	**20.00**
1804	15¢ Benj. Banneker 2/15/80 Annapolis, MD	2.25
1805-06	15¢ Letters - Memories attd. 2/25/80 DC	2.00
1805-06	Letters - Memories set of 2 singles	3.00
1807-08	15¢ Letters - Lift Spirit attd. 2/25/80 DC	2.00
1807-08	Letters - Lift Spirit set of 2 singles	3.00

Scott #	Description	Price
1809-10	15¢ Letters - Opinions attd. 2/25/80 DC	2.00
1809-10	Letters - Opinions set of 2 singles	3.00
1805-10	15¢ Letter Writing attd. 2/25/80 DC	4.00
1805-10	Letter Writing set of 6 singles	7.50
1805-10	Letters, Memories, 6 on 3	5.00
	1980-81 REGULAR ISSUES	
1811	1¢ Inkwell, coil 3/6/80 New York, NY	1.75
1813	3½¢ Violins, coil 6/23/80 Williamsburg, PA	1.75
1816	12¢ Liberty's Torch, coil 4/8/81 Dallas, TX	1.75
1818	(18¢) "B" & Eagle 3/15/81 San Fran., CA	2.00
1819	(18¢) "B" & Eagle, bklt. sngl. 3/15/81 San Francisco, CA.	1.75
1819a	(18¢) Bklt. Pane of 8 3/15/81 San Francisco, CA	4.00
1820	(18¢) "B" & Eagle, coil 3/15/81 San Francisco, CA	1.75
	1980	
1821	15¢ Frances Perkins 4/10/80 DC	1.75
1822	15¢ Dolly Madison 5/20/80 DC	1.75
	1st American Postal Arts Society cachet (Post/Art)	**35.00**
1823	15¢ Emily Bissell 5/31/80 Wilmington, DE	1.75
1824	15¢ Helen Keller 6/27/80 Tuscumbia, AL	2.00
1825	15¢ Veterans Administration 7/21/80 DC	2.00
1826	15¢ Bernardo de Galvez 7/23/80 New Orleans, LA	1.75
1827-30	15¢ Coral Reefs attd. 8/26/80 Charlotte Amalie, VI	4.00
1827-30	Coral Reefs set of 4 singles	5.00
1831	15¢ Organized Labor 9/1/80 DC	1.75
1832	15¢ Edith Wharton 9/5/80 New Haven, CT	1.75
1833	15¢ Education 9/12/80 Franklin, MA	2.00
1834-37	15¢ Indian Masks attd. 9/25/80 Spokane, WA	4.00
1834-37	Indian Masks set of 4 singles	8.00
1838-41	15¢ Architecture attd. 10/9/80 New York, NY	4.00
1838-41	Architecture set of 4 singles	8.00
1842	15¢ Christmas - Madonna 10/31/80 DC	1.75
1843	15¢ Christmas - Wreath & Toys 10/31/80 Christmas, MI	1.75
1842-43	Christmas on one cover	2.50
1842-43	Christmas, dual cancel	3.00
	1980-85 GREAT AMERICANS SERIES	
1844	1¢ Dorothea Dix 9/23/83 Hampden, ME	1.75
1845	2¢ Igor Stravinsky 11/18/82 New York, NY	1.75
1846	3¢ Henry Clay 7/13/83 DC	1.75
1847	4¢ Carl Shurz 6/3/83 Watertown, WI	1.75
1848	5¢ Pearl Buck 6/25/83 Hillsboro, WV	1.75
1849	6¢ Walter Lippman 9/19/85 Minneapolis, MN	1.75
1850	7¢ Abraham Baldwin 1/25/85 Athens, GA	1.75
1851	8¢ Henry Knox 7/25/85 Thomaston, ME	1.75
1852	9¢ Sylvanus Thayer 6/7/85 Braintree, MA	2.00
1853	10¢ Richard Russell 5/31/84 Winder, GA	1.75
1854	11¢ Alden Partridge 2/12/85 Norwich Un., VT	2.00
1855	13¢ Crazy Horse 1/15/82 Crazy Horse, SD	1.75
1856	14¢ Sinclair Lewis 3/21/85 Sauk Centre, MN	1.75
1857	17¢ Rachel Carson 5/28/81 Springdale, PA	1.75
1858	18¢ George Mason 5/7/81 Gunston Hall, VA	1.75
1859	19¢ Sequoyah 12/27/80 Tahlequah, OK	1.75
1860	20¢ Ralph Bunche 1/12/82 New York, NY	2.00
1861	20¢ Thomas Gallaudet 6/10/83 West Hartford, CT	2.00
1862	20¢ Harry S. Truman 1/26/84 DC	2.00
1863	22¢ John J. Audubon 4/23/85 New York, NY	2.00
1864	30¢ Frank Laubach 9/2/84 Benton, PA	1.75
1865	35¢ Charles Drew 6/3/81 DC	2.50
1866	37¢ Robert Millikan 1/26/82 Pasadena, CA	1.75
1867	39¢ Grenville Clark 3/20/85 Hanover, NH	2.00
1868	40¢ Lillian Gilbreth 2/24/84 Montclair, NJ	2.00
1869	50¢ Chester W. Nimitz 2/22/85 Fredericksburg, TX	3.00
	1981	
1874	15¢ Everett Dirksen 1/4/81 Pekin, IL	1.75
1875	15¢ Whitney Moore Young 1/30/81 NY, NY	2.50
1876-79	15¢ Flowers attd. 4/23/81 Ft. Valley, GA	4.00
1876-79	Flowers set of 4 singles	8.00
1880-89	18¢ Wildlife set of 10 sgls. 5/14/81 Boise, ID	17.50
1889a	Wildlife booklet pane of 10	6.00
	1981-82 REGULAR ISSUES	
1890	18¢ Flag & "Waves of Grain" 4/24/81 Portland, ME	1.75
1891	18¢ Flag & "Sea" coil 4/24/81 Portland, ME	1.75
1892	6¢ Circle of Stars, bklt. sngl. 4/24/81 Portland, ME	2.00
1893	18¢ Flag & "Mountain", bklt. sgl. 4/24/81 Portland, ME	1.75

1822

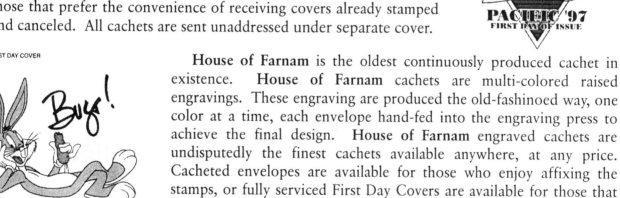

1928-31

Scott #	Description	Price
	1981-82 REGULAR ISSUES (con't.)	
1892-93	6¢ & 18¢ Booklet Pair 4/24/81 Portland, ME	3.75
1893a	18¢ & 6¢ B. Pane of 8 (2 #1892 & 6 #1893) 4/24/81 Portland, ME	5.00
1894	20¢ Flag over Supreme Court 12/17/81 DC	1.75
1895	20¢ Flag, coil 12/17/81 DC	1.75
1896	20¢ Flag, bklt. single 12/17/81 DC	1.75
1896a	Flag, bklt. pane of 6 12/17/81 DC	4.00
	#1894, 1895 & 1896a on one FDC	7.00
1896b	Flag, bklt. pane of 10 6/1/82 DC	6.00
1896bv	Flag, booklet single from pane of 20 11/17/83 DC	1.75
1896bv	Reissue-Flag bklt single, 11/17/83, NY	2.50
1896bv	Reissue-Flag, pane of 10 from 20, 11/17/83, NY	20.00
	1981-84 TRANSPORTATION COIL SERIES	
1897	1¢ Omnibus 8/19/83 Arlington, VA	2.00
1897A	2¢ Locomotive 5/20/82 Chicago, IL	2.00
1898	3¢ Handcar 3/25/83 Rochester, NY	2.00
1898A	4¢ Stagecoach 8/19/82 Milwaukee, WI	2.00
1899	5¢ Motorcycle 10/10/83 San Francisco, CA	2.00
1900	5.2¢ Sleigh 3/21/83 Memphis, TN	2.00
1900a	Precancelled	150.00
1901	5.9¢ Bicycle 2/17/82 Wheeling, WV	2.00
1901a	Precancelled	200.00
1902	7.4¢ Baby Buggy 4/7/84 San Diego, CA	2.00
1902a	Precancelled	300.00
1903	9.3¢ Mail Wagon 12/15/81 Shreveport, LA	2.00
1903a	Precancelled	300.00
1904	10.9¢ Hansom Cab 3/26/82 Chattanooga, TN	2.00
1904a	Precancelled	300.00
1905	11¢ Caboose 2/3/84 Rosemont, IL	2.50
1906	17¢ Electric Car 6/25/81 Greenfield Village, MI	2.00
1907	18¢ Surrey 5/18/81 Notch, MO	2.00
1908	20¢ Fire Pumper 12/10/81 Alexandria, VA	2.00
1909	$9.35 Express Mail, single 8/12/83 Kennedy Sp. Ctr., FL	70.00
1909a	Express Mail, booklet pane of 3	200.00
	1981 Commemoratives (continued)	
1910	18¢ American Red Cross 5/1/81 DC	2.00
1911	18¢ Savings and Loans 5/8/81 Chicago, IL	1.75
1912-19	18¢ Space Ach. attd. 5/21/81 Kennedy Sp. Ctr., FL	6.00
1912-19	Space Achievement set of 8 singles	16.00
1920	18¢ Professional Management 6/18/81 Philadelphia, PA.	1.75
1921-24	18¢ Wildlife Habitats attd. 6/26/81 Reno, NV	4.00
1921-24	Wildlife Habitats set of 4 singles	8.00
1925	18¢ Disabled Persons 6/29/81 Milford, MI	1.75
1926	18¢ Edna St. Vincent Millay 7/10/81 Austeritz, NY	1.75
1927	18¢ Alcoholism 8/19/81 DC	3.00
1928-31	18¢ Architecture attd. 8/28/81 DC	4.00
1928-31	Architecture set of 4 singles	8.00
1932	18¢ Babe Zaharias 9/22/81 Pinehurst, NC	8.00
1933	18¢ Bobby Jones 9/22/81 Pinehurst, NC	12.00
1932-33	Zaharias & Jones on one cover	15.00
1934	18¢ Frederic Remington 10/9/81 Oklahoma City, OK	1.75
1935	18¢ James Hoban 10/13/81 DC	1.75
1936	20¢ James Hoban 10/13/81 DC	1.75
1935-36	Hoban on one cover	3.50
1935-36	Combo w/Irish Stamp-(US cancel)	3.00
1935-36	Combo w/Irish Stamp-(Ireland cancel)	9.00
1937-38	18¢ Battle of Yorktown attd. 10/16/81 Yorktown, VA	2.00
1937-38	Battle of Yorktown set of 2 singles	3.00
1939	(20¢) Christmas - Madonna 10/28/81 Chicago, IL	1.75
1940	(20¢) Christmas - Teddy Bear 10/28/81 Christmas Valley, OR	1.75
1939-40	Christmas on one cover	2.50
1939-40	Christmas, dual cancel	3.00
1941	20¢ John Hanson 11/5/81 Frederick, MD	1.75
1942-45	20¢ Desert Plants attd. 12/11/81 Tucson, AZ	4.00
1942-45	Desert Plants set of 4 singles	8.00
	1st Pugh cachet	**75.00**
	1981-82 REGULAR ISSUES	
1946	(20¢) "C" & Eagle 10/11/81 Memphis, TN	1.75
1947	(20¢) "C" Eagle, coil 10/11/81 Memphis, TN	1.75
1948	(20¢) "C" Eagle, bklt. single 10/11/81 Memphis, TN	1.75
1948a	(20¢) "C" Booklet Pane of 10	5.50
1949	20¢ Bighorn Sheep, bklt. single 1/8/82 Bighorn, MT	1.75
	1st New Direxions cachet	**25.00**
1949a	20¢ Booklet Pane of 10	6.00

Scott #	Description	Price
	1982 Commemoratives	
1950	20¢ Franklin D. Roosevelt 1/30/82 Hyde Park, NY	1.75
1951	20¢ Love 2/1/82 Boston, MA	1.75
1952	20¢ George Washington 2/22/82 Mt. Vernon, VA	2.00
	1982 STATE BIRDS AND FLOWERS	
1953-2002	20¢ Birds & Flowers 4/14/82 Set of 50 DC	70.00
	Set of 50 State Capitals	75.00
2002a	Complete pane of 50 (Uncacheted)	45.00
	1982 Commemoratives (continued)	
2003	20¢ US & Netherlands 4/20/82 DC	1.75
...	Combo FDC with Netherland issue	7.50
...	20¢ US & Netherlands-combo, dual cancel	15.00
2004	20¢ Library of Congress 4/21/82 DC	1.75
2005	20¢ Consumer Education, coil 4/27/82 DC	1.75
2006-09	20¢ Knoxville World's Fair, attd. 4/29/82 Knoxville, TN	4.00
2006-09	20¢ Knoxville World's Fair, Knoxville, TN, set of 4 sngls	8.00
2010	20¢ Horatio Alger 4/30/82 Willow Grove, PA	1.75
2011	20¢ "Aging Together" 5/21/82 Sun City, AZ	1.75
2012	20¢ The Barrymores 6/8/82 New York, NY	1.75
2013	20¢ Dr. Mary Walker 6/10/82 Oswego, NY	1.75
2014	20¢ Peace Garden 6/30/82 Dunseith, ND	1.75
2015	20¢ Libraries 7/13/82 Philadelphia, PA	1.75
2016	20¢ Jackie Robinson 8/2/82 Cooperstown, NY	8.00
2017	20¢ Touro Synagogue 8/22/82 Newport, RI	2.00
2018	20¢ Wolf Trap 9/1/82 Vienna, VA	1.75
2019-22	20¢ Architecture attd. 9/30/82 DC	4.00
2019-22	Architecture set of 4 singles	8.00
2023	20¢ St. Francis of Assisi 10/7/82 San Francisco, CA	1.75
2024	20¢ Ponce de Leon 10/12/82 San Juan, PR	1.75
2025	13¢ Christmas - Kitten & Puppy 11/3/82 Danvers, MA	2.00
2026	20¢ Christmas - Madonna & Child 10/28/82 DC	1.75
2027-30	20¢ Christmas - Winter Scene, attd. 10/28/82 Snow, OK	4.00
2027-30	Christmas set of 4 singles	8.00
2026-30	Christmas on one cover either city	3.00
2026-30	Christmas, dual cancel	3.50
	1983 Commemoratives	
2031	20¢ Science & Industry 1/19/83 Chi., IL	1.75
2032-35	20¢ Ballooning 3/31/83 DC	4.00
	Albuquerque, NM	4.00
2032-35	Ballooning set of 4 singles DC	8.00
	Albuquerque, NM	8.00
2036	20¢ Sweden, 3/24/83 Philadelphia, PA	1.75
	20¢ US & Sweden, joint Issue, dual cancel	15.00
	20¢ US & Sweden, joint issue	5.00
	1st Panda Cachet	**25.00**
2036	w/Swedish issue on one cover	5.00
2037	20¢ Civilian Conservation Corps 4/5/83 Luray, VA	1.75
2038	20¢ Joseph Priestley 4/13/83 Northumberland, PA	1.75
2039	20¢ Voluntarism 4/20/83 DC	1.75
2040	20¢ German Immigration 4/29/83 Germantown, PA	1.75
2040	w/German Issue, dual cancel	8.00
2041	20¢ Brooklyn Bridge 5/17/83 Brooklyn, NY	2.00
2042	20¢ Tennessee Valley Authority 5/18/83 Knoxville, TN	1.75
2043	20¢ Physical Fitness 5/14/83 Houston, TX	2.00
2044	20¢ Scott Joplin 6/9/83 Sedalia, MO	2.00
2045	20¢ Medal of Honor 6/7/83 DC	4.00
2046	20¢ Babe Ruth 7/6/83 Chicago, IL	7.00
2047	20¢ Nathaniel Hawthorne 7/8/83 Salem, MA	1.75
2048-51	13¢ Summer Olympics attd. 7/28/83 South Bend, IN	4.00
2048-51	Summer Olympics set of 4 singles	8.00
2052	20¢ Treaty of Paris 9/2/83 DC	1.75
2053	20¢ Civil Service 9/9/83 DC	1.75
2054	20¢ Metropolitan Opera 9/14/83 NY, NY	1.75
2055-58	20¢ Inventors attd. 9/21/83 DC	4.00
2055-58	Inventors set of 4 singles	8.00
2059-62	20¢ Streetcars attd. 10/8/83 Kennebunkport, ME	4.00
2059-62	Streetcars set of 4 singles	8.00
2063	20¢ Christmas - Madonna & Child 10/28/83 DC	1.75
2064	20¢ Christmas - Santa Claus 10/28/83 Santa Claus, IN	1.75
2063-64	Christmas on one cover either city	2.50
2063-64	Christmas, dual cancel	3.00
2065	20¢ Martin Luther 11/11/83 DC	1.75
2065	w/German Issue, dual cancel	7.50

2046

2123

Scott #	Description	Price
	1984 Commemoratives	
2066	20¢ Alaska Sthd. 1/3/84 Fairbanks, AK	1.75
2067-70	20¢ Winter Olympics attd. 1/6/84 Lake Placid, NY	4.00
2067-70	Winter Olympics set of 4 singles	8.00
2071	20¢ Fed. Deposit Ins. Corp. 1/12/84 DC	1.75
2072	20¢ Love 1/31/84 DC	1.75
2073	20¢ Carter Woodson 2/1/84 DC	2.00
2074	20¢ Soil & Water Cons. 2/6/84 Denver, CO	1.75
2075	20¢ Credit Union Act 2/10/84 Salem, MA	1.75
2076-79	20¢ Orchids attd. 3/5/84 Miami, FL	4.00
2076-79	Orchids set of 4 singles	8.00
2080	20¢ Hawaii Sthd. 3/12/84 Honolulu, HI	2.00
2081	20¢ National Archives 4/16/84 DC	1.75
2082-85	20¢ Summer Olympics attd. 5/4/84 Los Angeles, CA	4.00
2082-85	Summer Olympics set of 4 singles	8.00
2086	20¢ Louisiana World's Fair 5/11/84 New Orleans, LA	1.75
2087	20¢ Health Research 5/17/84 New York, NY	1.75
2088	20¢ Douglas Fairbanks 5/23/84 Denver, CO	1.75
2089	20¢ Jim Thorpe 5/24/84 Shawnee, OK	5.00
2090	20¢ John McCormack 6/6/84 Boston, MA	1.75
	20¢ John McCormack, combo, dual cancel	15.00
	20¢ John McCormack, combo	5.00
2091	20¢ St. Lawrence Swy. 6/26/84 Massena, NY	1.75
	20¢ St. Lawrence Swy. w/Canada combo	5.00
	20¢ St. Lawrence Swy. w/Canada, combo, dual cancel	15.00
2092	20¢ Waterfowl Preservation 7/2/84 Des Moines, IA	1.75
	1st George Van Natta cachet	**40.00**
2093	20¢ Roanoke Voyages 7/13/84 Manteo, NC	1.75
2094	20¢ Herman Melville 8/1/84 New Bedford, MA	1.75
2095	20¢ Horace Moses 8/6/84 Bloomington, IN	1.75
2096	20¢ Smokey the Bear 8/13/84 Capitan, NM	2.00
2097	20¢ Roberto Clemente 8/17/84 Carolina, PR	12.00
2098-2101	20¢ Dogs attd. 9/7/84 New York, NY	4.00
2098-2101	Dogs set of 4 singles	8.00
2102	20¢ Crime Prevention 9/26/84 DC	2.00
2103	20¢ Hispanic Americans 10/31/84 DC	1.75
2104	20¢ Family Unity 10/1/84 Shaker Heights, OH	1.75
2105	20¢ Eleanor Roosevelt 10/11/84 Hyde Park, NY	1.75
2106	20¢ Nation of Readers 10/16/84 DC	1.75
2107	20¢ Christmas - Madonna & Child 10/30/84 DC	1.75
2108	20¢ Christmas - Santa 10/30/84 Jamaica, NY	1.75
2107-08	Christmas on one cover, either city	2.50
2107-08	Christmas, dual cancel	3.00
2109	20¢ Vietnam Memorial 11/10/84 DC	2.50
	1985 REGULARS & COMMEMS.	
2110	22¢ Jerome Kern 1/23/85 New York, NY	1.75
2111	(22¢) "D" & Eagle 2/1/85 Los Angeles, CA	1.75
2112	(22¢) "D" coil 2/1/85 Los Angeles, CA	1.75
2113	(22¢) "D" bklt. single 2/1/85 L.A., CA	1.75
2111-13	(22¢) "D" Stamps on 1	5.00
2113a	(22¢) Booklet Pane of 10	7.00
2114	22¢ Flag over Capitol 3/29/85 DC	1.75
2115	22¢ Flag over Capitol, coil 3/29/85 DC	1.75
2115b	Same, Phosphor Test Coil 5/23/87 Secaucus, NJ	2.50
2116	22¢ Flag over Capitol, bklt. single 3/29/85 Waubeka, WI	1.75
2116a	Booklet Pane of 5	3.00
2117-21	22¢ Seashells set of 5 singles 4/4/85 Boston, MA	10.00
2121a	Seashells, booklet pane of 10	7.00
2122	$10.75 Express Mail, bklt. sgl. 4/29/85 San Francisco, CA	60.00
2122a	Express Mail, booklet pane of 3	150.00
2122b	$10.75 Re-issue, bklt. sgl. 6/19/89 DC	250.00
2122c	Re-issue, booklet pane of 3	700.00
	1985-89 TRANSPORTATION COILS	
2123	3.4¢ School Bus 6/8/85 Arlington, VA	1.75
2123a	Precancelled 6/8/85 (earliest known use)	250.00
2124	4.9¢ Buckboard 6/21/85 Reno, NV	1.75
2124a	Precancelled 6/21/85 DC (earliest known use)	250.00
2125	5.5¢ Star Route Truck 11/1/86 Fort Worth, TX	1.75
2125a	Precancelled 11/1/86 DC	5.00
2126	6¢ Tricycle 5/6/85 Childs, MD	1.75

Scott #	Description	Price
2127	7.1¢ Tractor 2/6/87 Sarasota, FL	1.75
2127a	Precancelled 2/6/87 Sarasota, FL	5.00
2127av	Zip + 4 Prec., 5/26/89 Rosemont, IL	1.75
2128	8.3¢ Ambulance 6/21/85 Reno, NV	1.75
2128a	Precancelled 6/21/85 DC (earliest known use)	250.00
2129	8.5¢ Tow Truck 1/24/87 Tucson, AZ	1.75
2129a	Precancelled 1/24/87 DC	5.00
2130	10.1¢ Oil Wagon 4/18/85 Oil Center, NM	1.75
2130a	Black Precancel 4/18/85 DC (earliest known use)	250.00
2130a	Red. Prec. 6/27/88 DC	1.75
2131	11¢ Stutz Bearcat 6/11/85 Baton Rouge, LA	1.75
2132	12¢ Stanley Steamer 4/2/85 Kingfield, ME	1.75
2132b	"B" Press cancel 9/3/87 DC	60.00
	1985-89 TRANSPORTATION COILS (cont.)	
2133	12.5¢ Pushcart 4/18/85 Oil Center, NM	1.75
2134	14¢ Iceboat 3/23/85 Rochester, NY	1.75
2135	17¢ Dog Sled 8/20/86 Anchorage, AK	1.75
2136	25¢ Bread Wagon 11/22/86 Virginia Bch., VA	1.75
	1985 (cont.)	
2137	22¢ Mary McLeod Bethune 3/5/85 DC	2.00
2138-41	22¢ Duck Decoys attd. 3/22/85 Shelburne, VT	4.00
2138-41	Duck Decoys set of 4 singles	8.00
2142	22¢ Winter Special Olympics 3/25/85 Park City, UT	1.75
2143	22¢ Love 4/17/85 Hollywood, CA	1.75
2144	22¢ Rural Electrification Admin. 5/11/85 Madison, SD	1.75
2145	22¢ Ameripex '86 5/25/85 Rosemont, IL	1.75
2146	22¢ Abigail Adams 6/14/85 Quincy, MA	1.75
2147	22¢ Frederic A. Bartholdi 7/18/85 NY, NY	1.75
2149	18¢ Washington Pre-Sort, coil 11/6/85 DC	1.75
2149a	18¢ Washington, Precanceled, pair w/2149	5.00
2150	21.1¢ Zip + 4, coil 10/22/85 DC	1.75
2150a	21.1¢ Zip + 4, Precanceled, pair w/2150	5.00
2152	22¢ Korean War Veterans 7/26/85	2.00
2153	22¢ Social Security Act 8/14/85 Baltimore, MD	1.75
2154	22¢ World War I Vets 8/26/85 Milwaukee, WI	2.00
2155-58	22¢ Horses attd. 9/25/85 Lexington, KY	4.00
2155-58	Horses set of 4 singles	8.00
2159	22¢ Public Education 10/1/85 Boston, MA	2.00
2160-63	22¢ Int'l. Youth Year attd. 10/7/85 Chicago, IL	4.00
2160-63	Set of 4 singles	8.00
2164	22¢ Help End Hunger 10/15/85 DC	1.75
2165	22¢ Christmas - Madonna 10/30/85 Detroit, MI	1.75
2166	22¢ Christmas - Poinsettia 10/30/85 Nazareth, MI	1.75
2165-66	Christmas on one cover, either city	2.50
	1986	
2167	22¢ Arkansas Sthd. 1/3/86 Little Rock, AR	1.75
	1986-94 GREAT AMERICANS SERIES	
2168	1¢ Margaret Mitchell 6/30/86 Atlanta, GA	2.50
2169	2¢ Mary Lyon 2/28/87 South Hadley, MA	1.75
2170	3¢ Dr. Paul Dudley White 9/15/86 DC	1.75
2171	4¢ Father Flanagan 7/14/86 Boys Town, NE	1.75
2172	5¢ Hugo L. Black 2/27/86 DC	1.75
2173	5¢ Luis Munoz Marin 2/18/90 San Juan, PR	1.75
2175	10¢ Red Cloud 8/15/87 Red Cloud, NE	2.00
2176	14¢ Julia Ward Howe 2/12/87 Boston, MA	1.75
2177	15¢ Buffalo Bill Cody 6/6/88 Cody, WY	1.75
2178	17¢ Belva Ann Lockwood 6/18/86 Middleport, NY	1.75
2179	20¢ Virginia Agpar 10/24/94 Dallas, TX	1.75
2180	21¢ Chester Carlson 10/21/88 Rochester, NY	1.75
2181	23¢ Mary Cassatt 11/4/88 Phila., PA	1.75
2182	25¢ Jack London 1/11/86 Glen Ellen, CA	2.00
2182a	Bklt. Pane of 10 Perf, 11 5/3/88 San Francisco, CA	8.00
2182as	Perf. 11 bklt. single 5/3/88 San Francisco, CA	2.00
2183	28¢ Sitting Bull 9/14/89 Rapid City, SD	2.25
2184	29¢ Earl Warren 3/9/92 DC	2.00
2185	29¢ Thomas Jefferson 4/13/93 Charlottesville, VA	2.00
2186	35¢ Dennis Chavez 4/3/91 Albuquerque, NM	2.00
2187	40¢ General Claire Chennault 9/6/90 Monroe, LA	2.00
2188	45¢ Dr. Harvey Cushing 6/17/88 Cleveland, OH	2.00
2189	52¢ Hubert H. Humphrey 6/3/91 Minneapolis, MN	2.00
2190	56¢ John Harvard 9/3/86 Cambridge, MA	2.00
2191	65¢ General "Hap" Arnold 11/5/88 Gladwyne, PA	2.50
2192	75¢ Wendell Wilkie 2/16/92 Bloomington, IN	3.00
2193	$1 Dr. Bernard Revel 9/23/86 NY, NY	4.00
2194	$1 Johns Hopkins 6/7/89 Baltimore, MD	5.00
2195	$2 William Jennings Bryan 3/19/86 Salem, IL	7.00
2196	$5 Bret Harte 8/25/87 Twain Harte, CA	15.00
2197	25¢ Jack London, perf. 10 bklt. sgl. 5/3/88 San Fran., CA	1.75
2197a	Bklt. Pane of 6	4.00

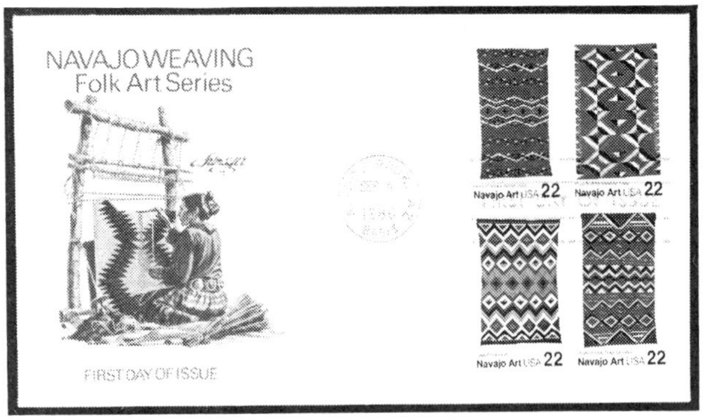
NAVAJO WEAVING
Folk Art Series
FIRST DAY OF ISSUE

2235-38

Scott #	Description	Price
	1986 (cont.)	
2198-2201	22¢ Stamp Coll. set of 4 1/23/86 State College, PA	8.00
2201a	Stamp Collecting, bklt. pane of 4	5.00
2201b	Color error, Black omitted on #2198 & 2201	300.00
2201b	Same, set of 4 singles	300.00
2202	22¢ Love 1/30/86 New York, NY	1.75
2203	22¢ Sojourner Truth 1/4/86 New Paltz, NY	2.00
2204	22¢ Texas 3/2/86 San Antonio, TX	1.75
	Washington-on-the-Brazos, TX	1.75
2205-09	22¢ Fish set of 5 singles 3/21/86 Seattle, WA	10.00
2209a	Fish, booklet pane of 5	6.00
2210	22¢ Public Hospitals 4/11/86 NY, NY	1.75
2211	22¢ Duke Ellington 4/29/86 New York, NY	2.25
2216-19	22¢ U.S. Presidents 4 sheets of 9 5/22/86 Chicago, IL	24.00
2216a-19a	US President set of 36 singles	63.00
2220-23	22¢ Explorers attd. 5/28/86 North Pole, AK	4.00
2220-23	22¢ Explorers set of 4 singles	8.00
2224	22¢ Statue of Liberty 7/4/86 NY, NY	2.00
2224	w/French Issue, combo	5.00
2224	22¢ Statue of Liberty w/French combo, dual cancel	15.00
2225	1¢ Omnibus Coil Re-engraved 11/26/86 DC	1.75
2226	2¢ Locomotive Coil Re-engraved 3/6/87 Milwaukee, WI	1.75
2228	4¢ Stagecoach Coil "B" Press 8/15/86 DC (eku)	150.00
2231	8.3¢ Ambulance Coil "B" Press 8/29/86 DC (eku)	150.00
2235-38	22¢ Navajo Art attd. 9/4/86 Window Rock, AZ	4.00
2235-38	Set of 4 singles	8.00
2239	22¢ T.S. Eliot 9/26/86 St. Louis, MO	1.75
2240-43	22¢ Woodcarved Figurines attd. 10/1/86 DC	4.00
2240-43	Set of 4 singles	8.00
2244	22¢ Christmas - Madonna & Child 10/24/86 DC	2.00
2245	22¢ Christmas Village Scene 10/24/86 Snow Hill, MD	2.00
	1987	
2246	22¢ Michigan Statehood 1/26/87 Lansing, MI	1.75
2247	22¢ Pan American Games 1/29/87 Indianapolis, IN	1.75
2248	22¢ Love 10/30/87 San Francisco, CA	1.75
2249	22¢ Jean Baptiste Point du Sable 2/20/87 Chicago, IL	1.75
2250	22¢ Enrico Caruso 2/27/87 NY, NY	1.75
2251	22¢ Girl Scouts 3/12/87 DC	3.00
	1987-88 TRANSPORTATION COILS	
2252	3¢ Conestoga Wagon 2/29/88 Conestoga, PA	1.75
2253	5¢ Milk Wagon 9/25/87 Indianapolis, IN	1.75
2254	5.3¢ Elevator, Prec. 9/16/88 New York, NY	1.75
2255	7.6¢ Carretta, Prec. 8/30/88 San Jose, CA	1.75
2256	8.4¢ Wheelchair, Prec. 8/12/88 Tucson, AZ	1.75
2257	10¢ Canal Boat 4/11/87 Buffalo, NY	1.75
2258	13¢ Police Patrol Wagon, Prec. 10/29/88 Anaheim, CA	1.75
2259	13.2¢ RR Car, Prec. 7/19/88 Pittsburgh, PA	1.75
2260	15¢ Tugboat 7/12/88 Long Beach, CA	1.75
2261	16.7¢ Popcorn Wagon, Prec. 7/7/88 Chicago, IL	1.75
2262	17.5¢ Marmon Wasp 9/25/87 Indianapolis, IN	1.75
2262a	Precancelled	5.00
2263	20¢ Cable Car 10/28/88 San Francisco, CA	1.75
2264	20.5¢ Fire Engine, Prec. 9/28/88 San Angelo, TX	2.00
2265	21¢ R.R. Mail Car, Prec. 8/16/88 Santa Fe, NM	1.75
2266	24.1¢ Tandem Bicycle, Prec. 10/26/88 Redmond, WA	1.75
	1987-88 REGULAR & SPECIAL ISSUES	
2267-74	22¢ Special Occasions, bklt. sgls. 4/20/87 Atlanta, GA	16.00
2274a	Booklet Pane of 10	7.00
2275	22¢ United Way 4/28/87 DC	1.75
2276	22¢ Flag and Fireworks 5/9/87 Denver, CO	1.75
2276a	Booklet Pane of 20 11/30/87 DC	12.00
2277	(25¢) "E" Earth Issue 3/22/88 DC	1.75
2278	25¢ Flag & Clouds 5/6/88 Boxborough, MA	1.75
2279	(25¢) "E" Earth Coil 3/22/88 DC	1.75
2280	25¢ Flag over Yosemite Coil 5/20/88 Yosemite, CA	1.75
2280 var.	Phosphor paper 2/14/89 Yosemite, CA	1.75
2281	25¢ Honeybee Coil 9/2/88 Omaha, NE	1.75
2282	(25¢) "E" Earth Bklt. Sgl. 3/22/88 DC	1.75
2282a	Bklt. Pane of 10	7.50
2283	25¢ Pheasant Bklt. Sgl. 4/29/88 Rapid City, SD	1.75
2283a	Bklt. Pane of 10	8.00

U.S. FIRST DAY COVERS

Scott #	Description	Price
	1987-88 REGULAR & SPECIAL ISSUES	
2284	25¢ Grosbeak Bklt. Sgl. 5/28/88 Arlington, VA	1.75
2285	25¢ Owl Bklt. Sgl. 5/28/88 Arlington, VA	1.75
2284-85	attached pair	3.50
2285b	Bklt. Pane of 10 (5 of ea.)	8.00
2285A	25¢ Flag & Clouds bklt. sgl. 7/5/88 DC	1.75
2285Ac	Bklt. Pane of 6	4.50
2286-2335	22¢ American Wildlife 6/13/87 Toronto, Canada	
	Set of 50 singles	87.50
2335a	Complete Pane of 50	40.00
	RATIFICATION OF CONSTITUTION	
	STATE BICENTENNIAL ISSUES 1987-90	
2336	22¢ Delaware Statehood Bicent. 7/4/87 Dover, DE	2.00
2337	22¢ Pennsylvania Bicent. 8/26/87 Harrisburg, PA	2.00
2338	22¢ New Jersey Bicent. 9/11/87 Trenton, NJ	2.00
2339	22¢ Georgia Bicent. 1/6/88 Atlanta, GA	2.00
2340	22¢ Connecticut Bicent. 1/9/88 Hartford, CT	2.00
2341	22¢ Massachusetts Bicent. 2/6/88 Boston, MA	2.00
2342	22¢ Maryland Bicent. 2/15/88 Annapolis, MD	2.00
2343	25¢ South Carolina Bicent. 5/23/88 Columbia, SC	2.00
2344	25¢ New Hampshire Bicent. 6/21/88 Concord, NH	2.00
2345	25¢ Virginia Bicent. 6/25/88 Williamsburg, VA	2.00
2346	25¢ New York Bicent. 7/26/88 Albany, NY	2.00
2347	25¢ North Carolina Bicent. 8/22/89 Fayetteville, NC	2.00
2348	25¢ Rhode Island Bicent. 5/29/90 Pawtucket, RI	2.00
2349	22¢ US & Morocco, combo w/Morocco, Dual cancel	15.00
2349	22¢ US & Morocco, combo w/Morocco	5.00
2336-48	Set of 13 on one cover, each with a different FD cancel	100.00
2349	22¢ U.S.-Morocco Relations 7/17/87 DC	1.75
2349	22¢ U.S.-Morocco, Combo w/Morocco, Dual Cancel	15.00
2349	22¢ U.S.-Morocco, Combo w/Morocco	5.00
2349	**1st Anagram cachet**	**25.00**
2350	22¢ William Faulkner 8/3/87 Oxford, MS	1.75
2351-54	22¢ Lacemaking attd. 8/14/87 Ypsilanti, MI	4.00
2351-54	Set of 4 singles	8.00
2355-59	22¢ Drafting of Constitution bklt. sgls. (5) 8/28/87 DC	10.00
2359a	Booklet Pane of 5	5.00
2360	22¢ Signing the Constitution 9/17/87 Philadelphia, PA	2.00
2361	22¢ Certified Public Accounting 9/21/87 NY, NY	10.00
2362-66	22¢ Locomotives, bklt. sgls. (5) 10/1/87 Baltimore, MD	10.00
2366a	Booklet Pane of 5	4.00
2367	22¢ Christmas - Madonna & Child 10/23/87 DC	2.00
2368	22¢ Christmas Ornaments 10/23/87 Holiday, CA	2.00
	1988	
2369	22¢ 1988 Winter Olympics 1/10/88 Anchorage, AK	1.75
2370	22¢ Australia Bicentennial 1/26/88 DC	1.75
2370	22¢ Australia Bicentennial combo, dual cancel	15.00
2370	22¢ Australia Bicentennial combo	5.00
2371	22¢ James Weldon Johnson 2/2/88 Nashville, TN	2.00
2372-75	22¢ Cats attd. 2/5/88 New York, NY	8.00
2372-75	Set of 4 singles	12.00
2376	22¢ Knute Rockne 3/9/88 Notre Dame, IN	4.00
2377	25¢ Francis Ouimet 6/13/88 Brookline, MA	6.50
2378	25¢ Love, 7/4/88 Pasadena, CA	1.75
2379	45¢ Love, 8/8/88 Shreveport, LA	2.00
2380	25¢ Summer Olympics 8/19/88 Colo. Springs, CO	1.75
2381-85	25¢ Classic Cars, Bklt. Sgls. 8/25/88 Detroit, MI	10.00
2385a	Bklt. Pane of 5	4.00
2386-89	25¢ Antarctic Explorers attd. 9/14/88 DC	4.00
2386-89	Set of 4 singles	8.00
2390-93	25¢ Carousel Animals attd. 10/1/88 Sandusky, OH	4.00
2390-93	Set of 4 singles	8.00
2394	$8.75 Eagle 10/4/88 Terra Haute, IN	30.00
2395-98	25¢ Sp. Occasions Bklt. Sgls. 10/22/88 King of Prussia, PA	7.00
2396a	Happy Birthday & Best Wishes, Bklt. Pane of 6	5.00
2398a	Thinking of You & Love You, Bklt. Pane of 6	5.00
2399	25¢ Christmas Madonna & Child 10/20/88 DC	2.00
2400	25¢ Christmas Sleigh & Village 10/20/88 Berlin, NH	2.00
	1989	
2401	25¢ Montana Statehood 1/15/89 Helena, MT	2.00
2402	25¢ A. Philip Randolph 2/3/89 New York, NY	2.00
2403	25¢ North Dakota Statehood 2/21/89 Bismarck, ND	1.75
2404	25¢ Washington Statehood 2/22/89 Olympia, WA	1.75
2405-09	25¢ Steamboats, Bklt. Sgls. 3/3/89 New Orleans, LA	10.00
2409a	Bklt. Pane of 5	4.00
2410	25¢ World Stamp Expo 3/16/89 New York, NY	1.75
2411	25¢ Arturo Toscanini 3/25/89 New York, NY	1.75
2412	25¢ U.S. House of Representatives 4/4/89 DC	2.00
2413	25¢ U.S. Senate 4/6/89 DC	2.00

2440

Scott #	Description	Price
	1989 (cont.)	
2414	25¢ Exec. Branch & George Washington Inaugural 4/16/89 Mt. Vernon, VA	2.00
2415	25¢ U.S. Supreme Court 2/2/90 DC	2.00
2416	25¢ South Dakota Statehood 5/3/89 Pierre, SD	1.75
2417	25¢ Lou Gehrig 6/10/89 Cooperstown, NY	6.00
2418	25¢ Ernest Hemingway 7/17/89 Key West, FL	1.75
2419	$2.40 Moon Landing, Priority Mail, 7/20/89 DC	7.00
2420	25¢ Letter Carriers 8/30/89 Milwaukee, WI	2.00
2421	25¢ Drafting the Bill of Rights 9/25/89 Philadelphia, PA	1.75
2422-25	25¢ Prehistoric Animals attd. 10/1/89 Orlando, FL	5.00
2422-25	Set of 4 singles	10.00
2426, C21(1)	25¢ Pre-Columbian w/45¢ Air Combo	7.50
2426	25¢ Pre-Columbian Customs 10/12/89 San Juan, PR	1.75
2427	25¢ Christmas Madonna & Child 10/19/89 DC	1.75
2427a	Booklet Pane of 10	8.00
2428	25¢ Christmas Sleigh & Presents 10/19/89 Westport, CT	1.75
2429	25¢ Christmas Sleigh, bklt. sgl. Westport, CT	1.75
2429a	Booklet Pane of 10	8.00
2431	25¢ Eagle & Shield, self-adhes. 11/10/89 Virginia Bch., VA	1.75
2431a	Booklet Pane of 18	15.00
2433	90¢ World Stamp Expo S/S of 4 11/17/89 DC	16.50
2434-37	25¢ Traditional Mail Transportation attd. 11/19/89 DC	4.00
2434-37	Set of 4 singles	8.00
2438	25¢ Traditional Mail Transportation, S/S of 4 11/28/89 DC	4.50
	1990	
2439	25¢ Idaho Statehood 1/6/90 Boise, ID	2.00
2440	25¢ Love 1/18/90 Romance, AR	2.00
2441	25¢ Love, bklt. sgl. 1/18/90 Romance, AR	1.75
2441a	Booklet Pane of 10	8.00
2442	25¢ Ida B. Wells 2/1/90 Chicago, IL	2.00
2443	15¢ Beach Umbrella, bklt. sgl. 2/3/90 Sarasota, FL	1.75
2443a	Booklet Pane of 10	6.00
2444	25¢ Wyoming Statehood 2/23/90 Cheyenne, WY	1.75
2445-48	25¢ Classic Films attd. 3/23/90 Hollywood, CA	7.50
2445-48	Set of 4 singles	12.00
2449	25¢ Marianne Moore 4/18/90 Brooklyn, NY	2.00
	1990-95 TRANSPORTATION COILS	
2451	4¢ Steam Carriage 1/25/81 Tucson, AZ	1.75
2452	5¢ Circus Wagon 8/31/90 Syracuse, NY	1.75
2452B	5¢ Circus Wagon, Gravure 12/8/92 Cincinnati, OH	1.75
2452D	5¢ Circus Wagon, Reissue (5¢) 3/20/95, Kansas City, MO	1.90
2453	5¢ Canoe, brown 5/25/91 Secaucus, NJ	1.75
2454	5¢ Canoe, red, Gravure print 10/22/91 Secaucus, NJ	1.75
2457	10¢ Tractor Trailer, Intaglio 5/25/91 Secaucus, NJ	1.75
2458	10¢ Tractor Trailer, Gravure 5/25/94 Secaucus, NJ	1.75
2463	20¢ Cog Railway Car 6/9/95 Dallas, TX	1.90
2464	23¢ Lunch Wagon 4/12/91 Columbus, OH	1.75
2466	32¢ Ferry Boat 6/2/95 McLean, VA	1.90
2468	$1.00 Seaplane 4/20/90 Phoenix, AZ	3.00
	1990-93	
2470-74	25¢ Lighthouse bklt. sgls. 4/26/90 DC	10.00
2474a	Booklet Pane of 5	4.00
2475	25¢ Flag Stamp, ATM self-adhes. 5/18/90 Seattle, WA	1.75
2475a	Pane of 12	10.00
2476	1¢ Kestrel 6/22/91 Aurora, CO	1.75
2477	1¢ Reprint 5/10/95 Aurora,CO w "¢" sign	1.75
2478	3¢ Bluebird 6/22/91 Aurora, CO	1.75
2479	19¢ Fawn 3/11/91 DC	1.75
2480	30¢ Cardinal 6/22/91 Aurora, CO	1.75
2481	45¢ Pumpkinseed Sunfish 12/2/92 DC	2.00
2482	$2 Bobcat 6/1/90 Arlington, VA	7.00
2483	20¢ Blue Jay, Bklt.sgl. 6/15/95 Kansas City, MO	1.90
2483a	Booklet Pane of 10	8.50
2484	29¢ Wood Duck, BEP bklt. single 4/12/91 Columbus, OH	1.75
2484a	BEP Booklet Pane of 10	9.00
2485	29¢ Wood Duck, KCS bklt. single 4/12/91 Columbus, OH	1.75
2485a	KCS Booklet Pane of 10	9.00
2486	29¢ African Violet, Bklt. Sgl. 10/8/93 Beaumont, TX	1.75
2486a	Booklet Pane of 10	8.00
2487	32¢ Peach, Bklt. sgl. 7/8/95 Reno, NV	1.90
2488	32¢ Pear, Bklt. sgl. 7/8/95 Reno, NV	1.90

Scott #	Description	Price
	1990-93 (cont.)	
2487-88	32¢ Peach & Pear, Attached Pair	2.50
2488A	Booklet Pane of 10	8.50
	1993-95 SELF ADHESIVE BOOKLETS & COILS	
2489	29¢ Red Squirrel, Self adhesive,sgl. 6/25/93 Milwaukee, WI	1.75
2489a	Pane of 18	14.00
2490	29¢ Rose, Self adhesive sgl. 8/19/93 Houston, TX	1.75
2490a	Pane of 18	14.00
2491	29¢ Pine Cone, Self adhesive sgl. 11/5/93 Kansas City, MO	1.75
2491a	Pane of 18	14.00
2492	32¢ Pink Rose, Self-adhesive 6/2/95 McLean, VA	1.90
2492a	Pane of 20, Self-adhesive	15.50
2493	32¢ Peach, self-adhesive 7/8/95 Reno, NV	1.90
2494	32¢ Pear, self-adhesive 7/8/95 Reno, NV	1.90
2493-94	32¢ Peach & Pear, attd	2.50
2494a	Pane of 20, self-adhesive	15.50
2495	32¢ Peach, Coil, Self adhesive 7/8/95 Reno, NV	1.90
2495A	32¢ Pear, Coil, Self-adhesive 7/8/95 Reno, NV	1.90
2495-95A	Peach & Pear, Coil Pair	2.50
	1990 COMMEMORATIVES (cont.)	
2496-2500	25¢ Olympians attd. 7/6/90 Minneapolis, MN	5.00
2496-2500	Set of 5 singles	10.00
2496-2500	Olympians with Tab singles attd.	8.00
2496-2500	Set of 5 singles with Tabs	12.00
2501-05	25¢ Indian Headdresses bklt. singles 8/17/90 Cody, WY	10.00
2505a	Booklet Pane of 5	8.00
2506-07	25¢ Micronesia & Marshall Isles joint issue 9/28/90 DC	3.00
2506-07	Set of 2 singles	4.00
2506-07	25¢ Micronesia & Marshall Isles, combo, dual cancel	15.00
2506-07	25¢ Micronesia & Marshall Isles, combo	5.00
2508-11	25¢ Sea Creatures attd. 10/3/90 Baltimore, MD	5.00
2508-11	Set of 4 singles	10.00
2508-11	25¢ Sea Creatures attd, combo, dual cancel	15.00
2508-11	25¢ Sea Creatures attd, combo	5.00
2512	25¢ Pre-Columbian Customs 10/12/90 Grand Canyon, AZ	2.00
2513	25¢ Dwight D. Eisenhower 10/13/90 Abilene, KS	2.00
2514	25¢ Christmas Madonna & Child 10/18/90 DC	2.00
2514a	Booklet Pane of 10 10/18/90 DC	6.50
2515	25¢ Christmas Tree 10/18/90 Evergreen, CO	2.00
2516	25¢ Christmas Tree bklt. sgl. 10/18/90 Evergreen, CO	2.00
2516a	Booklet Pane of 10 10/18/90	6.50
	1991-94	
2517	(29¢) "F" Flower stamp 1/22/91 DC	1.75
2518	(29¢) "F" Flower coil 1/22/91 DC	1.75
2519	(29¢) "F" Flower, BEP bklt. single 1/22/91 DC	1.75
2519a	Bklt. Pane of 10, BEP	7.50
2520	(29¢) "F" Flower, KCS bklt. single 1/22/91 DC	1.75
2520a	Bklt. Pane of 10, KCS	9.50
2521	(4¢) Make-up rate stamp 1/22/91 DC, non-denom.	1.75
2522	(29¢) "F" Flag stamp, ATM self-adhes. 1/22/91 DC	1.75
2522a	Pane of 12	10.00
2523	29¢ Flag over Mt. Rushmore Coil 3/29/91 Mt. Rushmore,SD	1.75
2523A	29¢ Same, Gravure print 7/4/91 Mt. Rushmore, SD	1.75
* On #2523A "USA" and "29" are **not** outlined in white		
2524	29¢ Flower 4/5/91 Rochester, NY	1.75
2525	29¢ Flower coil, rouletted 8/16/91 Rochester, NY	1.75
2526	29¢ Flower coil, perforated 3/3/92 Rochester, NY	1.75
2527	29¢ Flower, bklt. single 4/5/91 Rochester, NY	1.75
2527a	Booklet Pane of 10	7.50
2528	29¢ Flag with Olympic Rings, bklt. sgl. 4/21/91 Atlanta, GA	1.75
2528a	Booklet Pane of 10	7.50
2529	19¢ Fishing Boat, coil 8/8/91 DC	1.75
2529C	19¢ Fishing Boat, coil, Type III 6/25/94 Arlington, VA	1.75
2530	19¢ Ballooning, bklt. sgl. 5/17/91 Denver, CO	1.75
2530a	Booklet Pane of 10	7.00
2531	29¢ Flags/Memorial Day, 125th Anniv. 5/30/91 Waterloo,NY	1.75
2531A	29¢ Liberty Torch, ATM self-adhes. 6/25/91 New York, NY	1.75
2531Ab	Pane of 18	14.00
	1991 COMMEMORATIVES	
2532	50¢ Switzerland, joint issue 2/22/91 DC	2.00
2532	50¢ Switzerland, combo, dual cancel	15.00
2532	50¢ Switzerland, combo	5.00
2533	29¢ Vermont Statehood 3/1/91 Bennington, VT	2.25
2534	29¢ Savings Bonds 4/30/91 DC	1.75
2535	29¢ Love 5/9/91 Honolulu, HI	1.75
2536	29¢ Love, Booklet Sgl. 5/9/91 Honolulu, HI	1.75
2536a	Booklet Pane of 10	7.50
2537	52¢ Love, 2 ounce rate 5/9/91 Honolulu, HI	2.00
2538	29¢ William Saroyan 5/22/91 Fresno, CA	2.25
2538	29¢ William Saroyan, combo, dual cancel	15.00
2538	29¢ William Saroyan, combo	5.00

2540

Scott #	Description	Price
	1991-95 REGULAR ISSUES	
2539	$1.00 USPS & Olympic Rings 9/29/91 Orlando, FL	3.00
2540	$2.90 Priority Mail 7/7/91 San Diego, CA	9.00
2541	$9.95 Express Mail,Domestic rate 6/16/91 Sacramento,CA	25.00
2542	$14.00 Express Mail,Internat'l rate 8/31/91 Indianapolis,IN	32.50
2543	$2.90 Priority Mail, Space 6/3/93 Titusville, FL	7.50
2544	$3 Challenger Shuttle, Priority Mail 6/22/95 Anaheim, CA	7.75
2544A	$10.75 Endeavor Shuttle Express Mail 8/4/95 Irvine, CA	25.00
	1991 COMMEMORATIVES (continued)	
2545-49	29¢ Fishing Flies, bklt. sgls. 5/31/91 Cudlebackville, NY	10.00
2549a	Booklet Pane of 5	5.00
2550	29¢ Cole Porter 6/8/91 Peru, IN	1.75
2551	29¢ Desert Shield / Desert Storm 7/2/91 DC	2.00
2552	29¢ Desert Shield / Desert Storm bklt. sgl. 7/2/91 DC	2.00
2552a	29¢ Booklet Pane of 5	4.50
2553-57	29¢ Summer Olympics,strip of 5 7/12/91 Los Angeles, CA	4.50
2553-57	Set of 5 singles	10.00
2558	29¢ Numismatics 8/13/91 Chicago, IL	2.00
2559	29¢ World War II S/S of 10 9/3/91 Phoenix, AZ	12.00
2559a-j	Set of 10 singles	30.00
2560	29¢ Basketball 8/28/91 Springfield, MA	3.00
2561	29¢ District of Columbia Bicent. 9/7/91 DC	1.75
2562-66	29¢ Comedians bklt. sgls. 8/29/91 Hollywood, CA	10.00
2566a	Booklet Pane of 10	7.50
2567	29¢ Jan Matzeliger 9/15/91 Lynn, MA	1.75
2568-77	29¢ Space Exploration bklt. sgls. 10/1/91 Pasadena, CA	20.00
2577a	Booklet Pane of 10	8.00
2578	(29¢) Christmas, Madonna & Child 10/17/91 Santa, ID	1.75
2578a	Booklet Pane of 10	8.00
2579	(29¢) Christmas, Santa & Chimney 10/19/91 Santa, ID	1.75
2580-85	(29¢) Christmas, bklt. pane sgls. 10/17/91 Santa, ID	12.00
2581b-85a	Booklet Panes of 4, set of 5	20.00
	1994-95 DEFINITIVES DESIGNS OF 1869 ESSAYS	
2587	32¢ James S. Polk 11/2/95 Columbia, TN	1.90
2590	$1 Surrender of Burgoyne 5/5/94 New York, NY	3.00
2592	$5 Washington & Jackson 8/19/94 Pittsburgh, PA	13.50
	1992-93 REGULAR ISSUES	
2593	29¢ "Pledge" Black denom., bklt. sgl. 9/8/92 Rome, NY	1.75
2593a	Booklet Pane of 10	7.00
	1992 Eagle & Shield Self-Adhesives Stamps (9/25/92 Dayton, OH)	
2595	29¢ "Brown" denomination, sgl	2.00
2595a	Pane of 17 + label	12.00
2596	29¢ "Green" denomination, sgl	2.00
2596a	Pane of 17 + label	12.00
2597	29¢ "Red" denomination, sgl	2.00
2597a	Pane of 17 + label	12.00
	1992 Eagle & Shield Self-Adhesive Coils	
2595v	29¢ "Brown" denomination, pair with paper backing	2.25
2596v	29¢ "Green" denomination, pair with paper backing	2.25
2597v	29¢ "Red" denomination, pair with paper backing	2.25
	1994 Eagle Self-Adhesive Issues	
2598	29¢ Eagle, single 2/4/94 Sarasota, FL	1.75
2598a	Pane of 18	12.50
2598v	29¢ Coil Pair with paper backing	2.25
	1994 Statue of Liberty Self-Adhesive Issue	
2599	29¢ Statue of Liberty, single 6/24/94 Haines, FL	1.75
2599a	Pane of 18	12.50
2599v	29¢ Coil pair with paper backing	2.25
	1991-93 Coil Issues	
2602	(10¢) Eagle & Shield, bulk-rate 12/13/91 Kansas City, MO	1.75
2603	(10¢) Eagle & Shield, **BEP** 5/29/93 Secaucus, NJ	1.75
2604	(10¢) Eagle & Shld., **Stamp Venturers** 5/29/93 Secaucus, NJ	1.75
2605	23¢ Flag, First Class pre-sort 9/27/91 DC	1.75
2606	23¢ USA, 1st Cl, pre-sort, **ABNCo.** 7/21/92 Kansas City, MO	1.75
2607	23¢ USA, 1st Cl, pre-sort, **BEP** 10/9/92 Kansas City, MO	1.75
2608	23¢ USA, 1st Cl, p.s., **Stamp Venturers** 5/14/93 Denver, CO	1.75
2609	29¢ Flag over White House 4/23/92 DC	1.75

U.S. FIRST DAY COVERS

Scott #	Description	Price
	1992 Commemoratives	
2611-15	29¢ Winter Olympics, strip of 5 1/11/92 Orlando, FL	5.00
2611-15	Set of 5 singles	10.00
2616	29¢ World Columbian Expo 1/24/92 Rosemont, IL	1.75
2617	29¢ W.E.B. DuBois 1/31/92 Atlanta, GA	2.25
2618	29¢ Love 2/6/92 Loveland. CO	1.75
2619	29¢ Olympic Baseball 4/3/92 Atlanta, GA	4.00
	1992 Columbus Commemoratives	
2620-23	29¢ First Voyage of Columbus 4/24/92 Christiansted, VI	4.00
2620-23	Set of 4 singles	8.00
2620-23	Joint Issue	15.00
2620-23	Joint Issue w/Italy, Dual cancel	450.00
2624-29	1¢-$5.00 Voyages of Columbus S/S 5/22/92 Chicago, IL	50.00
2624a-29	Set of 16 singles	90.00
	1992 Commemoratives (cont.)	
2630	29¢ New York Stock Exchange 5/17/92 New York, NY	2.00
2631-34	29¢ Space: Accomplishments 5/29/92 Chicago, IL	4.00
2631-34	Set of 4 singles	10.00
2635	29¢ Alaska Highway 5/30/92 Fairbanks, AK	1.75
2636	29¢ Kentucky Statehood Bicent. 6/1/92 Danville, KY	1.75
2637-41	29¢ Summer Olympics, strip of 5 6/11/92 Baltimore, MD	5.00
2637-41	Set of 5 singles	10.00
2642-46	29¢ Hummingbirds, bklt. sgls. 6/15/92 DC	10.00
2646a	Booklet Pane of 5	5.00
2647-96	29¢ Wildflowers, set of 50 singles 7/24/92 Columbus, OH	87.50
2697	29¢ World War II S/S of 10 8/17/92 Indianapolis, IN	10.00
2697a-j	Set of 10 singles	25.00
2698	29¢ Dorothy Parker 8/22/92 West End, NJ	1.75
2699	29¢ Dr. Theodore von Karman 8/31/92 DC	1.75
2700-03	29¢ Minerals 9/17/92 DC	4.00
2700-03	Set of 4 singles	8.00
2704	29¢ Juan Rodriguez Cabrillo 9/28/92 San Diego, CA	1.75
2705-09	29¢ Wild Animals, bklt. sgls. 10/1/92 New Orleans, LA	10.00
2709a	Booklet Pane of 5	5.00
2710	29¢ Christmas, Madonna & Child 10/22/92 DC	2.00
2710a	Booklet Pane of 10 10/22/92 DC	8.00
2711-14	29¢ Christmas Toys,offset, 10/22/92 Kansas City, MO	4.00
2711-14	Set of 4 singles	10.00
2715-18	29¢ Christmas Toys,gravure,bklt.sgls.10/22/92 Kansas City,MO	10.00
2718a	Booklet Pane of 4	4.00
2719	29¢ Christmas Train self-adhes. ATM 10/28/92 NY, NY	1.75
2719a	Pane of 18	14.00
2720	29¢ Happy New Year 12/30/92 San Francisco, CA	3.00
	1993 Commemoratives	
2721	29¢ Elvis Presley 1/8/93 Memphis, TN	2.00
2722	29¢ Oklahoma! 3/30/93 Oklahoma City, OK	1.75
2723	29¢ Hank Williams 6/9/93 Nashville, TN	1.75
2724-30	29¢ R 'n' R/R & B 6/16/93 on one cover Cleveland, OH & Santa Monica, CA (same cancel ea. city)	7.00
2724-30	Set of 7 singles on 2 covers	9.00
2724-30	Set of 7 singles	14.00
2731-37	29¢ R 'n' R/R & B, Set/7 bklt. sgls. 6/16/93 Cleveland, OH & Santa Monica, CA (same cancel ea. city)	14.00
2731-37	Set of 7 singles of 2 covers	9.00
2737a	Booklet Pane of 8	7.00
2737b	Booklet Pane of 4	4.00
2737a,2737b	Booklet Panes on 1 cover	10.00
2741-45	29¢ Space Fantasy, bklt. sgls. 1/25/93 Huntsville, AL	10.00
2745a	Booklet Pane of 5	5.00
2746	29¢ Percy Lavon Julian 1/29/93 Chicago, IL	2.00
2747	29¢ Oregon Trail 2/12/93 Salem, OR	1.75
2748	29¢ World University Games 2/25/93 Buffalo, NY	2.00
2749	29¢ Grace Kelly 3/24/93 Hollywood, CA	1.75
2750-53	29¢ Circus 4/6/93 DC	4.00
2750-53	Set of 4 singles	10.00
2754	29¢ Cherokee Strip 4/17/93 Enid, OK	1.75
2755	29¢ Dean Acheson 4/21/93 DC	1.75
2756-59	29¢ Sport Horses 5/1/93 Louisville, KY	4.00
2756-59	Set of 4 singles	10.00
2760-64	29¢ Garden Flowers, bklt. sgls. 5/15/93 Spokane, WA	10.00
2764a	Booklet Pane of 5	5.00
2765	29¢ World War II S/S of 10 5/31/93 DC	10.00
2765a-j	Set of 10 singles	25.00
2766	29¢ Joe Louis 6/22/93 Detroit, MI	3.00
2767-70	29¢ Broadway Musicals, bkt. sgls. 7/14/93 New York, NY	8.00
2770a	Booklet Pane of 4	4.00
2771-74	29¢ Country Music attd. 9/25/93 Nashville, TN	4.00
2771-74	Set of 4 singles	8.00
2775-78	29¢ Country Music, bklt. sgls. 9/25/93 Nashville, TN	8.00
2778a	Booklet Pane of 4	4.00
2779-82	29¢ National Postal Museum 7/30/93 DC	4.00
2779-82	Set of 4 singles	10.00
2783-84	29¢ Deaf Communication, pair 9/20/93 Burbank, CA	2.25
2783-84	Set of 2 singles	4.00
2785-88	29¢ Children's Classics, block of 4 10/23/93 Louisville, KY	4.00
2785-88	Set of 4 singles	10.00
2789	29¢ Madonna & Child 10/21/93 Raleigh, NC	1.75
2790	Booklet Single	1.75
2790a	Booklet Pane of 4	4.00
2791-94	29¢ Christmas Designs attd. 10/21/93 New York, NY	4.00
2791-94	Set of 4 singles	10.00
2795-98	29¢ Contemp. Christmas, 4 bklt.singles 10/21/93 NY, NY	10.00
2798a	Booklet Pane of 10 (3 snowmen)	8.00
2798b	Booklet Pane of 10 (2 snowmen)	8.00
2799-2802	29¢ Contemp. Christmas, self-adhes. (4) 10/28/93 NY, NY	9.00
2802a	Pane of 12	10.00
2803	29¢ Snowman, self-adhesive 10/28/93 New York, NY	1.75

2817

Scott #	Description	Price
	1993 Commemoratives (cont.)	
2803a	Pane of 18	14.00
2804	29¢ Northern Mariana Isles 11/4/93 DC	1.75
2805	29¢ Columbus-Puerto Rico 11/19/93 San Juan, PR	1.75
2806	29¢ AIDS Awareness 12/1/93 New York, NY	1.75
2806a	29¢ AIDS, booklet single 12/1/93 New York, NY	1.75
2806b	Booklet Pane of 5	5.00
	1994 Commemoratives	
2807-11	29¢ Winter Olympics, Strip of 5, 1/6/94 Salt Lake City, UT	5.00
2807-11	Set of 5 Singles	10.00
2812	29¢ Edward R. Murrow 1/21/94 Pullman, WA	1.75
2813	29¢ Love & Sunrise, self-adhesive sgl. 1/27/94 Loveland, OH	1.75
2813a	Pane of 18	14.00
2813v	Coil Pair with paper backing	2.25
2814	29¢ Love & Dove, booklet single 2/14/94 Niagara Falls, NY	1.75
2814a	Booklet Pane of 10	7.00
2814C	29¢ Love & Doves, Sheet Stamp 6/11/94 Niagara Falls, NY	1.75
2815	52¢ Love & Doves 2/14/94 Niagara Falls, NY	2.00
2816	29¢ Dr. Allison Davis 2/1/94 Williamstown, MA	2.00
2817	29¢ Chinese New Year, Dog 2/5/94 Pomona, CA	2.50
2818	29¢ Buffalo Soldiers 4/22/94 Dallas, TX	2.00
2819-28	29¢ Silent Screen Stars, attd. 4/27/94 San Francisco, CA	8.00
2819-28	Set of 10 Singles	20.00
2819-28	Set of 10 on 2 covers	9.50
2829-33	29¢ Summer Garden Flowers 4/28/94 Cincinnati, OH	5.00
2833a	Set of 5 Singles	10.00
2834	29¢ World Cup Soccer 5/26/94 New York, NY	1.75
2834-36	29¢, 40¢, 50¢ Soccer on 1 cover	3.00
2834-36	29¢, 40¢, 50¢ Soccer on 3 covers	5.75
2835	40¢ World Cup Soccer 5/26/94 New York, NY	2.00
2836	50¢ World Cup Soccer 5/26/94 New York, NY	2.00
2837	29¢,40¢,50¢ Soccer Souvenir Sheet of 3 5/26/94 NY,NY	3.50
2838	29¢ World War II Souvenir Sht of 10 6/6/94 U.S.S. Normandy	10.00
2838a-j	Set of 10 Singles	25.00
2839	29¢ Norman Rockwell 7/1/94 Stockbridge, MA	1.75
2840	50¢ Norman Rockwell, S/S of 4 7/1/94 Stockbridge, MA	5.75
2840A-D	Singles from Souvenir Sheet	8.00
	1994 Moon Landing, 25th Anniversary	
2841	29¢ Moon Landing Souvenir Sheet of 12 7/20/94 DC	10.75
2841a	Single from Souvenir Sheet	1.75
2842	$9.95 Moon Landing, Express Mail 7/20/94 DC	25.00
	1994 Commemoratives (continued)	
2843-47	29¢ Locomotives, booklet singles 7/28/94 Chama, NM	10.00
2847a	Booklet Pane of 5	5.00
2848	29¢ George Meany 8/16/94 DC	1.75
2849-53	29¢ Popular Singers 9/1/94 New York, NY	5.00
2849-53	Set of 5 Singles	10.00
2854-61	29¢ Blues & Jazz Artists 9/17/94 Greenville, MI	8.00
2854-61	Set of 8 on 2 covers	9.00
2854-61	Set of 8 Singles	16.00
2862	29¢ James Thurber 9/10/94 Columbus, OH	1.75
2863-66	29¢ Wonders of the Sea 10/1/94 Honolulu, HI	4.00
2863-66	Set of 4 Singles	8.00
2867-68	29¢ Cranes, attd. 10/9/94 DC	2.25
2867-68	Set of 2 Singles	4.00
2867-68	Joint Issue	5.00
2867-68	Joint Issue - Dual Cancel	15.00
	1994 Legends of the West Miniature Sheet	
2869	29¢ Legends of the West, Pane of 20 10/8/94 Tucson, AZ, Laramie, WY and Lawton, OK	20.00
2869a-t	Set of 20 Singles	40.00
2869a-t	Set of four covers, 2 blocks of 4 and 2 blocks of 6	22.50
	1994 Commemoratives (continued)	
2871	29¢ Madonna & Child 10/20/94 DC	1.75
2871a	Booklet single	1.75
2871b	Booklet Pane of 10	8.50
2872	29¢ Christmas Stocking 10/20/94 Harmony, MN	1.75
2872a	Booklet Pane of 20	15.50
2872v	Booklet single	1.75
2873	29¢ Santa Claus, self-adhesive 10/20/94 Harmony, MN	1.75
2873a	Pane of 12	10.00
2873v	Coil pair on paper backing	2.25
2874	29¢ Cardinal in Snow, self-adhesive 10/20/94 Harmony, MN .	1.75
2874a	Pane of 18	14.00

Scott #	Description	Price
	1994 Commemoratives (continued)	
2875	$2 Bureau of Engraving Centennial Souvenir sheet of 4 11/3/94 New York, NY	18.50
2875a	$2 Madison single from souvenir sheet	5.50
2876	29¢ Year of the Boar 12/30/94 Sacramento, CA	2.50
	1994-95 Interim Regular Issues	
2877	(3¢) Dove, ABN, Light blue 12/13/94 DC	1.90
2878	(3¢) Dove, SVS, Darker blue 12/13/94 DC	1.90
2879	(20¢) "G" Postcard Rate, BEP, Black "G" 12/13/94 DC	1.95
2880	(20¢) "G" Postcard Rate, SVS, Red "G" 12/13/94 DC	1.95
2881	(32¢) "G" BEP, Black "G" 12/13/94 DC	1.90
2881a	Booklet Pane of 10	8.50
2882	(32¢) "G" SVS, Red "G" 12/13/94 DC	1.90
2881-82	(32¢) "G" Combo 12/13/94 DC	2.75
2883	(32¢) "G" BEP, Black "G", Booklet Single 12/13/94 DC	1.90
2883a	Booklet Pane of 10, BEP	8.50
2884	(32¢) "G" ABN, Blue "G", Booklet Single 12/13/94 DC	1.90
2884a	Booklet Pane of 10, ABN	8.50
2885	(32¢) "G" KCS, Red "G", Booklet Single 12/13/94 DC	1.90
2885a	Booklet Pane of 10, KCS	8.50
2886	(32¢) "G"Surface Tagged,self-adh.,strip format 12/13/94 DC ...	1.90
2886a	Pane of 18, Self-Adhesive	15.00
2887	(32¢) "G" Overall Tagging, self-adhesive 12/13/94 DC	1.90
2887a	Pane of 18, self-adhesive	15.00
2888	(25¢) "G" Presort, Coil 12/13/94 DC	1.90
2888,2393	(25¢) "G" Presort and (5¢) "G" Non-profit Combo 12/13/94 DC	2.40
2889	(32¢) "G" Coil, BEP, Black "G" 12/13/94 DC	1.90
2890	(32¢) "G" Coil, ABN, Blue "G" 12/13/94 DC	1.90
2891	(32¢) "G" Coil, SVS, Red "G" 12/13/94 DC	1.90
2892	(32¢) "G" Coil, Rouletted, Red "G" 12/13/94 DC	1.90
2893	(5¢) "G" Non-Profit, Green, 12/13/94 date, available for mail order sale 1/12/95 DC	1.90
2897	32¢ Flag over Porch, sheet stamp 5/19/95 Denver, CO	1.90
2902	(5¢) Butte 3/10/95 State College, PA	1.90
2902B	(5¢) Butte - S/A Coil 6/15/96 State College, PA	1.90
2903	(5¢) Mountain, Coil, BE (Letters outlined in purple) 3/16/96, San Jose, Ca	1.90
2904	(5¢) Mountain, Coil, SV, (outlined letters) 3/16/96 San Jose, Ca.	1.90
2904A	(5¢) Mountain, S/A, Coil, 6/15/96	1.90
2904B	(5¢) Mountain, S/A, BEP, 1/24/97	1.90
2905	(10¢) Automobile 3/10/95 State College, PA	1.90
2906	(10¢) Auto, S/A. Coil, 6/15/96	1.90
2907	(10¢) Eagle & Shield, S/A, Coil, 5/21/96	1.90
2908	(15¢) Auto Tail Fin, BEP 3/17/95 New York, NY	1.90
2909	(15¢) Auto Tail Fin, SVS 3/17/95 New York, NY	1.90
2908-9	(15¢) Auto Tail Fin, Combo with BEP and SVS Singles	2.25
2910	(15¢) Auto Tail Fin, S/A, Coil, 6/15/96, New York, NY	1.90
2911	(25¢) Juke Box, BEP 3/17/95 New York, NY	1.90
2912	(25¢) Juke Box, SVS 3/17/95 New York, NY	1.90
2912A	(25¢) Juke Box, S/A, Coil, 6/15/96, New York, NY	1.90
2912B	(25¢) Juke Box, S/A, 1/24/97	1.90
2911-12	(25¢) Juke Box, Combo with BEP and SVS singles	2.35
2913	32¢ Flag over Porch, BEP, coil 5/19/95 Denver, CO	1.90
2914	32¢ Flag over Porch, SVS, coil 5/19/95 Denver, CO	1.90
2913-14	32¢ Flag over Porch, Combo with BEP and SVS singles	2.50
2915	32¢ Flag over Porch, self-adhesive strip format 4/18/95 DC	2.00
2915A	32¢ Flag over Porch, S/A, Coil, 5/21/96	1.90
2915B	32¢ Flag over Porch, S/A, Coil, (serpentine diecut 11.5 vert.) SV, 6/15/96, San Antonio, TX	1.90
2915D	32¢ Flag over Porch, S/A, Coil, BEP, 1/24/97	1.90
2916	32¢ Flag over Porch, booklet single 5/19/95 Denver, CO	1.90
2916a	Booklet Pane of 10	8.50
2919	32¢ Flag over Field, self-adhesive 3/17/95 New York, NY	1.90
2919a	Pane of 18, Self-adhesive	14.50
2920	32¢ Flag over Porch, self-adhesive 4/19/95 DC	4.00
2920a	Pane of 20, self-adhesive	15.50
2920b	Large Date	1.90
2920d	Serpentine die cut 11.3, S/A, Single, 1/20/96	1.90
2920e	Booklet Pane of 10, S/A, 1/20/96	8.50
2921	32¢ Flag over Porch, S/A, Booklet Single, (Serpentine die cut 9.8), 5/21/96	1.90
2921a	Booklet Pane of 10, 5/21/96	8.50
	1995 Great American Series	
2933	32¢ Milton S. Hershey 9/13/95 Hershey, PA	1.90
2934	32¢ Cal Farley 4/26/96 Amarillo, TX	1.90
2938	46¢ Ruth Benedict 10/20/95 Virginia Beach, VA	2.25
2940	55¢ Alice Hamilton, M.D. 7/11/95 Boston, MA	2.25
2943	78¢ Alice Paul 8/18/95 Mount Laurel, NJ	2.75
	1995 Commemoratives	
2948	(32¢) Love & Cherub 2/1/95 Valentines, VA	1.90
2949	(32¢) Love & Cherub, self-adhesive 2/1/95 Valentines, VA	1.90
2949a	Pane of 20, self-adhesive	15.50
2950	32¢ Florida Statehood 3/3/95 Tallahassee, FL	1.90
2951-54	32¢ Earth Day/Kids Care attd. 4/20/95 DC	4.35
2951-54	Set of 4 singles	8.00
2955	32¢ Richard Nixon 4/26/95 Yorba Linda, CA	1.90
2956	32¢ Bessie Coleman 4/27/95 Chicago, IL	1.90
2957	32¢ Love-Cherub 5/12/95 Lakeville, PA	1.90
2958	55¢ Love-Cherub 5/12/95 Lakeville, PA	2.25
2959	32¢ Love-Cherub, booklet single	1.90
2959a	Booklet Pane of 10	8.50
2960	55¢ Love-Cherub, self-adhesive single 5/12/95 Lakevilla, PA .	2.25
2960a	55¢ Pane of 20, self-adhesive	21.50
2961-65	32¢ Recreational Sports, Strip of 5 5/20/95 Jupiter, FL	5.50
2961-65	Set of 5 singles	10.00
2966	32¢ POW & MIA 5/29/95 DC	1.90

2933

Scott #	Description	Price
2967	32¢ Marilyn Monroe 6/1/95 Hollywood, CA	4.00
2967a	Pane of 20 on one cover	16.50
2968	32¢ Texas Statehood 6/16/95 Austin, TX	1.90
2969-73	32¢ Great Lakes Lighthouses, bklt. sgls. 6/17/95 Cheboygan, MI	10.00
2973a	Booklet Pane of 5	5.50
2974	32¢ United Nations 6/26/95 San Francisco, CA	1.90
2975	32¢ Civil War, Miniature Sht. of 20, 6/29/95 Gettysburg, PA	20.00
2975a-t	Set of 20 singles	40.00
2976-79	32¢ Carousel Horses attd. 7/21/95 Lahaska, PA	4.35
2976-79	Set of 4 singles	8.00
2980	32¢ Women's Suffrage 8/26/95 DC	1.90
2981	32¢ World War II s/s of 10 9/2/95 Honolulu, HI	10.00
2981a-j	Set of 10 singles	25.00
2982	32¢ Louis Armstrong 9/1/95 New Orleans, LA	2.25
2983-92	32¢ Jazz Musicians 9/16/95 Monterey, CA	8.50
2983-92	Set of 10 singles	20.00
2993-97	32¢ Fall Garden Flowers, bklt. sgls. 9/19/95 Encinitas, CA	10.00
2997a	Booklet Pane of 5	5.50
2998	60¢ Eddie Rickenbacker 9/25/95 Columbus, OH	2.25
2999	32¢ Republic of Palau 9/29/95 Agana, Guam	1.90
3000	32¢ Comic Strips, Min. Sheet of 20 10/2/95 Boca Raton, FL	20.00
3000a-t	Set of 20 Singles	40.00
3000a-t	Set of 5 combos (incl. Plate Block)	15.00
3001	32¢ U.S. Naval Academy, 150 Anniv. 10/10/95 Annapolis, MD	1.90
3002	32¢ Tennessee Williams 10/13/95 Clarksdale, MS	1.90
3003	32¢ Madonna and Child 10/19/95 Washington, DC	1.90
3003a	Booklet Single	1.90
3003b	Booklet Pane of 10	8.50
3004-7	32¢ Santa + Children 9/30/95 North Pole, NY, set of 4	8.00
3007a	32¢ Christmas (secular) sheet, 9/30/95, North Pole, NY	3.50
3007b	Booklet Pane of 10 (3 ea. of 3004+3005, 2 ea. of 3006+3007)	8.50
3007c	Booklet Pane of 10 (2 ea. of 3004+3005, 3 ea. of 3006+3007)	8.50

1995 Self-Adhesive Stamps

Scott #	Description	Price
3008-11	32¢ Santa + Children 9/30/95 North Pole, NY	3.50
3008-11	Set of 4 Singles	7.00
3011a	Pane of 20	15.50
3012	32¢ Midnight Angel 10/19/95 Christmas, FL	1.90
3012a	Pane of 20	15.50
3013	32¢ Children Sledding 10/19/95 Christmas, FL	1.90
3013a	Pane of 18	14.00

1995 Self-Adhesive Coil Stamps

Scott #	Description	Price
3014-17	32¢ Santa + Children 9/30/95 North Pole, NY	3.50
3014-17	Set of 4 Singles	7.00
3018	32¢ Midnight Angel 10/19/95 Christmas, FL	1.90

1995 Commemoratives (continued)

Scott #	Description	Price
3019-23	32¢ Antique Automobiles 11/3/95 New York, NY	3.75
3019-23	Set of 5 Singles	8.50

1996 Commemoratives

Scott #	Description	Price
3024	32¢ Utah Statehood 1/4/96 Salt Lake City, UT	1.90
3025-29	32¢ Winter Garden Flowers Bklt. Singles 1/19/96 Kennett Square, PA	10.00
3029a	Booklet Pane of 5	5.50
3030	32¢ Love Cherub, Self-adhesive 1/20/96 New York, NY	1.90
3030a	Booklet Pane of 20	15.50

1996 Flora and Fauna Series

Scott #	Description	Price
3032	2¢ Red-headed Woodpecker 2/2/96 Sarasota, FL	1.90
3033	3¢ Eastern Bluebird 4/3/96 DC	1.90
3044	1¢ Kestrel, Coil 1/20/96 New York, NY	1.90
3048	20¢ Blue Jay, S/A, 8/2/96 St. Louis, MO	1.90
3048a	Booklet Pane of 10	8.50
3048 + 53	Combo - Blue Jays, 8/2/96, St. Louis, MO	5.00
3049	32¢ Yellow Rose, single, 10/24/96, Pasadena, Ca.	1.90
3049a	Booklet Pane of 20, S/A	15.50
3053	20¢ Blue Jay, Coil, S/A, 8/2/96, St. Louis, MO	1.90

1996 Commemoratives (continued)

Scott #	Description	Price
3058	32¢ Ernest E. Just 2/1/96 DC	2.25
3059	32¢ Smithsonian Institution 2/5/96 DC	1.90
3060	32¢ Year of the Rat 2/8/96 San Francisco, CA	1.90
3061-64	32¢ Pioneers of Communication Set of 4 2/22/96 NY, NY	7.00
3061-64a	Block of 4 on one cover	3.50
3065	32¢ Fulbright Scholarship 2/28/96 Fayetteville, AR	1.90
3066	50¢ Jacqueline Cochran 3/9/96 Indio, CA	2.25
3067	32¢ Marathon 4/11/96 Boston, MA	1.90

Scott #	Description	Price
	1996 Commemoratives (continued)	
3068	32¢ Centennial Olympic Games, Min. Sheet of 20 5/2/96 DC	13.00
3068a-t	Set of 20 Singles	35.00
3068a-t	Set of 20 on 4 covers	13.00
3069	32¢ Georgia O'Keeffe 5/23/96 Santa Fe, NM	1.90
3069	Souvenir Sheet of 15	11.50
3070	32¢ Tennessee Statehood 5/31/96 Nashville, Knoxville or Memphis, TN	1.90
3071	32¢ Tennessee Statehood, Self-adhesive single	1.90
3071a	Booklet Pane of 20	13.00
3076a	32¢ American Indian Dances, 5 designs attached 6/7/96 Oklahoma City, OK	4.00
3072-76	Set of 5 Singles	8.50
3077-80	32¢ Prehistoric Animals, 4 designs attached 6/8/96 Toronto, Canada	3.50
3077-80	Set of 4 Singles	7.00
3081	32¢ Breast Cancer Awareness 6/15/96 DC	1.90
3082	32¢ James Dean 6/24/96 Hollywood, CA	1.90
3083-86	32¢ Folk Heroes, 4 designs attached 7/11/96 Anaheim, CA	3.50
3083-86	Set of 4 Singles	7.00
3087	32¢ Olympic Games, Discobolus 7/19 /96	1.90
3088	32¢ Iowa Statehood 8/1/96 Dubuque, IA	1.90
3089	Self-adhesive Single	1.90
3089a	Self-adhesive Pane of 20	15.50
3090	32¢ Rural Free Delivery 8/6/96 Charleston, WV	1.90
3091-95	32¢ River Boats, S/A, 8/22/96, (5), Orlando, Fl.	10.00
3095a	Strip of 5	5.50
3096-99	32¢ Big Band Leaders, set of 4, 9/11/96, New York, NY	8.00
3099a	32¢ Big Band Leaders, (4), 9/11/96, New York, NY	4.25
3100-03	32¢ Songwriters, set of 4, 9/11/96, New York, NY	8.00
3103a	32¢ Songwriters, (4), 9/11/96, New York, NY	4.25
3104	23¢ F. Scott Fitzgerald, 9/27/96, St. Paul, MN	2.00
3105	32¢ Endangered Species, pane of 15,10/2/96, San Diego, Ca.	14.50
3105a-o	Set of 15 covers	30.00
3106	32¢ Computer Tech., 10/8/96, Aberdeen Proving Ground, MD	2.00
3107	32¢ Madonna & Child, 11/1/96, Richmond, Va.	2.00
3108-11	32¢ Christmas Family Scenes, (4), 10/8/96, North Pole, AK	8.00
3111a	Block or strip of 4	4.25
3112	32¢ Madonna & Child, single, 11/1/96, Richmond, Va.	2.00
3112a	Pane of 20, S/A	15.50
3116a	Booklet Pane of 20, S/A	15.50
3113-16	32¢ Christmas Family Scene, set of 4, Bklt Pane Singles	8.00
3117	32¢ Skaters - for ATM, 10/8/96, North Pole, AK	2.00
3117a	Booklet Pane of 18, S/A	14.75
3118	32¢ Hanukkah, S/A, 10/22/96, Washington, DC	2.00
3118	32¢ Hanukkah, Combo	5.00
3118	32¢ Hanukkah, Combo w/Dual Cancel	15.00
3119	50¢ Cycling, sheet of 2, 11/1/96, New York, NY	3.75
3119	50¢ Cycling, sheet of 2, 11/1/96, Hong Kong	3.75
3119	50¢ Cycling, set of 2, 11/1/96, New York, NY	4.50
3119	50¢ Cycling, set of 2, 11/1/96, Hong Kong	4.50
	1997 Commemoratives	
3120	32¢ Lunar New Year (Year of the Ox), 1/5/97	2.10
3121	32¢ Benjamin O' Davis Sr., S/A, 1/28/97, Wash. DC	2.00
3122	32¢ Statue of Liberty, S/A, Bklt Single, 2/1/97	2.00
3122a	Pane of 20 w/Label	15.50
3122c	Pane of 5 w/Label	5.50
3122d	Pane of 6	6.00
3123	32¢ Love Swan, S/A, Single, 2/4/97	2.00
3123a	Booklet Pane of 20 w/Label	15.50
3124	55¢ Love Swan, S/A, Single, 2/4/97	2.00
3124a	Booklet Pane of 20 w/Label	15.50
3125	32¢ Helping Children Learn, S/A, 2/18/97	2.00
3126-27	Citron Moth & Flowering Pinaeapple, attd, 3/3/97, Wash. DC	2.50
3126-27	Pane of 20	15.50
3126-27	Set of 2	5.00
3128-29	Booklet pane of 5, Vendor Bklt, From booklet of 15	5.50
3128-29	Slightly smaller than 3126-27, (1)	5.00
3130-31	32¢ Pacific '97 Stagecoach & Ship, 3/13/97, New York, NY	2.50
3130-31	Set of Singles	4.00
3134	32¢ Thornton Wilder, 4/16/97, Hamden, Ct.	2.00
3135	32¢ Raoul Wallenberg, 4/24/97, Wash. DC	2.00
...	32¢ Bugs Bunny, S/A, pane of 10, 5/22/97	11.00
...	32¢ Bugs Bunny, S/A, Single, 5/22/97	2.00
...	50¢ Pacific '97 - 1847 Franklin, 5/29/97, S.F., Ca.	2.00
...	Sheet of 12	24.00
...	60 Pacific '97 - 1847 Washington, 5/30/97, S.F., Ca.	2.00
...	Sheet of 12	24.00
3136	32¢ The World of Dinosaurs, set of 15, 5/1/97	30.00
3136a-o	15 on 1 miniature pane	.
...	32¢ Humphrey Bogart, Legends of Hollywood series, 7/31/97	
...	32¢ Classic American Aircraft, set of 20, 7/19/97, Dayton, OH	40.00
...	Sheet of 20	15.50
...	32¢ Classic American Dolls, set of 15, 7/28/97, Anaheim, Ca.	30.00
...	Sheet of 15	12.00
...	32¢ Legendary Football Coaches, set of 4, 7/25/97	8.00
...	Set of 4 on 1 cover	
...	Sheet of 20, 5 of each design	15.50
...	Same in individual panes of 20, ea. stamp has add. red bar	15.50
...	32¢ Stars & Stripes Forever, 8/21/97, Milwaukee, WI	2.00
...	32¢ U.S. Air Force, 9/18/97	2.00
...	32¢ Classical Composers & Conductors, (1), 9/ /97	11.00
...	Set of 8	16.00
...	32¢ Opera Singers, (1), 9/ /97	4.25
...	Set of 4	8.00
...	Classic Movie Monsters, (1), 9/30/97	5.50
...	Set of 5	10.00

1901

The listing below omits prices on FDC's which are extremely rare or where sufficient pricing information is not available. *Due to market volatility, prices are subject to change without notice.* Prices are for unaddressed FDC's with common cachets and cancels which do not obscure the Pl. #. Strips of 3 must have a plate # on the center stamp.

Scott #	Description	Pl# Pr.	Pl# Str of 3
1897	1¢ Omnibus 8/19/83		
	Pl # 1,2	8.50	12.50
2225	1¢ Omnibus Re-engraved 11/26/86		
	Pl# 1	6.50	12.50
1897A	2¢ Locomotive 5/20/82		
	Pl# 3,4	12.50	20.00
2226	2¢ Locomotive Re-engraved 3/6/87		
	Pl# 1	...	8.50
1898	3¢ Handcar 3/25/83		
	Pl# 1,2,3,4	10.00	20.00
2252	3¢ Conestoga Wagon 2/29/88		
	Pl# 1	...	7.50
2123	3.4¢ School Bus 6/8/85		
	Pl# 1,2	6.50	10.00
1898A	4¢ Stagecoach 8/19/82		
	Pl# 1,2,3,4	10.00	18.50
2228	4¢ Stagecoach, "B" Press 8/15/86 (eku)		
	Pl# 1	...	260.00
2451	4¢ Steam Carriage 1/25/91		
	Pl# 1	...	6.50
2124	4.9¢ Buckboard 6/21/85		
	Pl# 3,4	7.50	13.50
1899	5¢ Motorcycle 10/10/83		
	Pl# 1,2	10.00	15.00
	Pl# 3,4	...	...
2253	5¢ Milk Wagon 9/25/87		
	Pl# 1	...	7.50
2452	5¢ Circus Wagon 8/31/90		
	Pl# 1	...	6.50
2452B	5¢ Circus Wagon, Gravure 12/8/92		
	Pl# A1,A2	...	6.50
2452D	5¢ Circus Wagon, SV 3/20/95		
	Pl# S1	...	6.50
2453	5¢ Canoe 5/25/91		
	Pl# 1	...	6.50
2454	5¢ Canoe, Gravure Print 10/22/91		
	Pl# S11	...	6.50
2902	5¢ Butte 3/10/95		
	Pl# S111	...	6.50
1900	5.2¢ Sleigh 3/21/83		
	Pl# 1,2	15.00	30.00
1900a	Pl# 1,2	...	...
2254	5.3¢ Elevator 9/16/88		
	Pl# 1	...	7.50
2125	5.5¢ Star Route Truck 11/1/86		
	Pl# 1	7.50	12.50
2125a	Pl# 1	...	40.00
1901	5.9¢ Bicycle 2/17/82		
	Pl# 3,4	15.00	25.00
1901a	Pl# 3,4	...	...
2126	6¢ Tricycle 5/6/85		
	Pl# 1	6.50	10.00
2126a	Pl# 1	...	...
2127	7.1¢ Tractor Coil 2/6/87		
	Pl# 1	7.50	12.50
2127a	Pl# 1	...	35.00
2127a	7.1¢ Zip + 4 Pl# 1 5/26/89	...	7.50
1902	7.4¢ Baby Buggy 4/7/84		
	Pl# 2	10.00	20.00
2255	7.6¢ Carreta 8/30/88		
	Pl# 1	...	7.50
2128	8.3¢ Ambulance 6/21/86		
	Pl# 1,2	7.50	12.50
2128a	Pl# 1,2	...	...
2231	8.3¢ Ambulance, "B" Press 8/29/86 (eku)		
2256	8.4¢ Wheelchair 8/12/88		
	Pl# 1	...	7.50

Scott #	Description	Pl#Pr.	Pl#Str of 3
2129	8.5¢ Tow Truck 1/24/87		
	Pl# 1	6.50	10.00
2129a	Pl# 1	...	17.50
1903	9.3¢ Mail Wagon 12/15/81		
	Pl# 1,2	20.00	37.50
	Pl# 3,4	...	...
2257	10¢ Canal Boat 4/11/87		
	Pl# 1		8.50
2457	10¢ Tractor Trailer 5/25/91		
	Pl# 1		6.50
2604	10¢ Eagle & Shield, **ABNCo** 12/13/91		6.50
	Any Pl# (except A12213 & A32333)	...	6.50
	Pl# A12213	...	27.50
	Pl# A32333	...	125.00
2605	10¢ Eagle & Shield, **BEP** 5/29/93		
	Pl# 11111	...	6.50
2606	10¢ Eagle & Shield, **SV**		
	Pl# S11111		6.50
2903	10¢ Auto, 3/10/95		
	Pl # S111	...	7.50
2130	10.1¢ Oil Wagon 4/18/85		
	Pl# 1	7.50	12.50
2130a	10.1¢ Red Prec. Pl# 2 6/27/88	...	8.50
1904	10.9¢ Hansom Cab 3/26/82		
	Pl# 1,2	17.50	35.00
1904a	Pl# 1,2	...	...
1905	11¢ Caboose 2/3/84		
	Pl# 1	15.00	35.00
1905a	11¢ Caboose, "B" Press 9/25/91		
	Pl#2	...	...
2131	11¢ Stutz Bearcat 6/11/85		
	Pl# 3,4	...	12.50
2132	12¢ Stanley Steamer 4/2/85		
	Pl# 1,2	7.50	12.50
2132a	Pl# 1	...	...
2133	12.5¢ Pushcart 4/18/85		
	Pl# 1	7.50	12.50
2258	13¢ Patrol Wagon 10/29/88		
	Pl# 1	...	7.50
2259	13.2¢ Coal Car 7/19/88		
	Pl# 1	...	7.50
2134	14¢ Iceboat 3/23/85		
	Pl# 1,2	10.00	15.00
2260	15¢ Tugboat 7/12/88		
	Pl# 1	...	7.50
2908	15¢ Auto Tail Fin, BEP, 3/17/95		
	Pl# 11111	...	7.50
2909	15¢ Auto Tail Fin, SV, 3/17/95		
	Pl# S11111	...	7.50
2261	16.7¢ Popcorn Wagon 7/7/88		
	Pl# 1	...	7.50
1906	17¢ Electric Car 6/25/82		
	Pl# 1,2	17.50	30.00
2135	17¢ Dog Sled 8/20/86		
	Pl# 2	7.50	12.50
2262	17.5¢ Racing Car 9/25/87		
	Pl# 1	...	8.50
2262a	Pl# 1	...	10.00
1891	18¢ Flag 4/24/81		
	Pl# 1	75.00	120.00
	Pl# 2	180.00	340.00
	Pl# 3	260.00	420.00
	Pl# 4	160.00	280.00
	Pl# 5	125.00	...
1907	18¢ Surrey 5/18/81		
	Pl# 1	30.00	...
	Pl# 2	20.00	45.00
	Pl# 3,4,7,9,10	...	...
	Pl# 5	100.00	...
	Pl# 6,8	100.00	...
2149	18¢ GW Monument 11/6/85		
	Pl# 1112,3333	20.00	35.00
2149a	Pl# 11121	45.00	...
	Pl# 33333	45.00	...

2259/1

2005

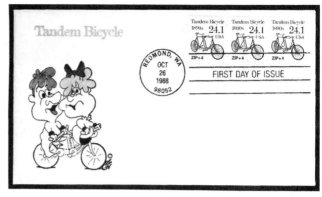

2266

Scott #	Description	Pl# Pr.	Pl# Str of 3
2529	19¢ Fishing Boat 8/8/91		
	Pl# 1111,1212	...	7.50
2529c	19¢ Fishing Boat 6/25/94		
	Pl# S11	...	7.50
1895	20¢ Flag 12/17/81		
	Pl# 1	20.00	40.00
	Pl# 2	100.00	160.00
	Pl# 3	160.00	320.00
1908	20¢ Fire Pumper 12/10/81		
	Pl# 1,7,8	...	...
	Pl# 2	150.00	240.00
	Pl# 3,4	15.00	40.00
	Pl# 5,6	100.00	175.00
2005	20¢ Consumer 4/27/82		
	Pl# 1,2,3,4	25.00	...
2263	20¢ Cable Car 10/28/88		
	Pl# 1	...	7.50
	Pl# 2	...	60.00
2264	20.5¢ Fire Engine 9/28/88		
	Pl# 1	...	7.50
2463	20¢ Cog Railroad 6/9/95		
	Pl#1	...	7.50
2265	21¢ Railroad Mail Car 8/16/88		
	Pl# 1	...	7.50
	Pl# 2	...	...
2150	21.1¢ Pre-Sort 10/22/85		
	Pl# 111111	15.00	25.00
2150a	Pl# 111111	35.00	...
2112	(22¢) "D" Coil 2/1/85		
	Pl# 1,2	10.00	17.50
2115	22¢ Flag over Capitol 3/29/85		
	Pl# 1	35.00	65.00
	Pl# 2	15.00	22.50
2115b	22¢ Test Coil 5/23/87		
	Pl# T1	...	12.50
2464	23¢ Lunch Wagon 4/12/91		
	Pl# 2	...	8.50
	Pl# 3	...	7.50
2607	23¢ Flag, First Class pre-sort 9/27/91	...	7.50
2608	23¢ "USA" First Class pre-sort **ABNCo**, 7/21/92		
	Pl# A1111, A2222	...	7.50
2608A	23¢ "USA" First Class pre-sort **BEP**, 10/9/92		
	Pl# 1111	...	7.50
2608B	23¢ "USA" First Class pre-sort **SV**, 5/14/93		
	Pl# S111	...	7.50
2266	24.1¢ Tandem Bicycle 10/26/88		
	Pl# 1	...	7.50
2136	25¢ Bread Wagon 11/22/86		
	Pl# 1	7.50	12.50
2279	(25¢) "E" & Earth 3/22/88		
	Pl# 1111,1222	...	7.50
	Pl# 1211	...	10.00
	Pl# 2222	...	25.00
2280	25¢ Flag over Yosemite 5/20/88		
	Pl# 1,2	...	10.00
	Pl# 3,4	...	125.00
2280v	Pre-Phosphor Paper 2/14/89		
	Pl# 5	...	17.50
	Pl# 6,9	...	35.00
	Pl# 7,8	...	8.50
	Pl# 10	...	...
2281	25¢ Honeybee 9/2/88		
	Pl# 1	...	10.00
	Pl# 2	...	30.00
2911	25¢ Juke Box, BEP 3/17/95		
	Pl# 111111	...	7.50
2912	25¢ Juke Box, 3/17/95		
	Pl# 111	...	7.50
2518	(29¢) "F" & Flower 1/22/91		
	Pl# 1111,1222,2222	...	10.00
	Pl# 1211	...	...
	Pl# 2211	...	25.00

Scott #	Description	Pl# Pr.	Pl# Str of 3
2523	29¢ Flag over Mt. Rushmore 3/29/91		
	Pl# 1-7	7.50	...
2523A	29¢ Mt. Rushmore, Gravure Print 7/4/91		
	Pl# 11111	...	7.50
2525	29¢ Flower, rouletted 8/16/91		
	Pl# S1111	...	7.50
2526	29¢ Flower, perforated 3/3/92		
	Pl# 2222	7.50	...
2609	29¢ Flag over White House 4/23/92	...	6.00
	Pl# 1-7	...	6.00
	Pl# 8	...	...
2480	29¢ Pine Cone (self-adhesive) 11/5/93		
	Pl# B1	...	10.00
2598	29¢ Statue of Liberty (self-adhesive) 6/24/94		
	Pl# D1111	...	10.00
2799-2809	29¢ Christmas (self-adhesive) 10/28/93		
	Pl# V1111111	...	10.00
2813	29¢ Love (self-adhesive) 1/27/94		
	Pl# B1	...	10.00
2873	29¢ Santa (self-adhesive) 10/20/94		
	Pl# V1111	...	10.00
2466	32¢ Ferryboat 6/2/95		
	Pl# 2-3	...	7.50
	Pl# 4	...	15.00
	Pl# 5	...	35.00
2492	32¢ Rose (self-adhesive) 7/8/95		
	Pl# V11111	...	10.00
2495A	32¢ Peaches and Pears (self-adhesive) 7/8/95		
	Pl# V11111	...	10.00
2888	(32¢) "G" Flag 12/13/94		
	Pl# S11111	...	7.50
2886	(32¢) "G" Flag (self-adhesive) 12/13/94		
	Pl# V11111	...	7.50
2899	(32¢) "G" Flag 12/13/94		
	Pl# 1111, 2222	...	7.50
2890	(32¢) "G" Flag 12/13/94		
	Pl# A1111, A1112, A1113, A1211, A1212, A1222, A1311, A1313, A1314, A1324, A1417, A1433, A2211, A2212, A2213, A2214, A2223, A2313, A3113, A3114, A3315, A3323, A3423, A3324, A3426, A3433, A3435, A3536, A4426, A4427, A5327, A5417, A5427, A5437	...	7.50
2890	(32¢) "G" Flag 12/13/94		
	A4435	...	200.00
2891	(32¢) "G" Flag 12/13/94		
	Pl# S1111	...	7.50
2892	(32¢) "G" Flag 12/13/94		
	Pl# S1111	...	7.50
2893	(32¢) "G" Flag 12/13/94		
	Pl# A11111, A21111	...	7.50
2913	32¢ Flag over Porch 4/18/95		
	Pl# 11111,22222,33333,44444,S11111	...	7.50
	Pl# 22221	...	15.00
	Pl# 45444,66646	...	35.00
3017	32¢ Christmas (self-adhesive) 9/30/95		
	Pl# V1111	...	10.00
3018	32¢ Christmas Angel (self-adhesive) 10/31/95		
	Pl# B1111	...	10.00
2468	$1.00 Seaplane 4/20/90		
	Pl# 1	...	10.00
OFFICIAL STAMPS			
O135	20¢ Official, Pl# 1	27.50	75.00
O139	(22¢) "D" Official, Pl# 1	32.50	75.00
COMPUTER VENDED POSTAGE			
CV31	29¢ Variable Rate Coil 8/20/92		
	Pl# 1	...	7.50
CV31	29¢ Variable Rate 8/20/92, 1st Print		
	Pl# 1	...	7.50
CV31b	29¢ Variable Rate 8/20/92, 2nd Print		
	Pl# 1	...	7.50
CV32	29¢ Variable Rate 8/20/92		
	Pl# A11	...	7.50

C23

Cacheted prices are for FDC's with common printed cachets.
From #C4 - C31, FDC's will usually be addressed.
Prices and Dates for #C1-3 are for First Flight Covers, AND FDC's.

Scott #	Description	Uncacheted	Cacheted
C1	6¢ Jenny 12/10/18 Washington, DC FDC	25000.00	...
C1	6¢ Jenny 12/16/18 NYC; Phila.,PA; DC FFC	2500.00	...
C2	16¢ Jenny 7/11/18 Washington, DC FDC	25000.00	...
C2	16¢ Jenny 7/15/18 NYC; Phila.,PA; DC FFC	800.00	...
C3	24¢ Jenny 5/15/18 NYC; Phila.,PA; DC FFC	800.00	...
C4	8¢ Propeller 8/15/23 DC	375.00	...
C5	16¢ Air Service Emblem 8/17/23 DC	600.00	...
C6	24¢ DeHavilland Biplane 8/21/23 DC	750.00	...
C7	10¢ Map 2/13/26 DC	80.00	...
	Chicago, IL	90.00	...
	Detroit, MI	90.00	...
	Cleveland, OH	120.00	...
	Dearborn, MI	120.00	...
	Unofficial city	175.00	...
C8	15¢ Map 9/18/26 DC	90.00	...
C9	20¢ Map 1/25/27 DC	100.00	...
	New York, NY	110.00	...
	1st Albert E. Gorham cachet	...	250.00
C10	10¢ Lindbergh 6/18/27 DC	30.00	175.00
	St. Louis, MO	30.00	175.00
	Detroit, MI	40.00	175.00
	Little Falls, MN	40.00	175.00
	Air Mail Field, Chicago, unofficial	150.00	...
	Unofficial city (other than AMF Chicago)	175.00	...
	1st Milton Mauck cachet	...	250.00
C10a	10¢ **Booklet Single** 5/26/28 DC	100.00	150.00
	Booklet Sgl., Cleveland Midwest Phil. Sta.	100.00	150.00
	#C10a sgl. & 645 Cleveland Midwest Sta.	150.00	175.00
C10a	10¢ **Booklet Pane of 3** 5/26/28 DC	875.00	1000.00
	B. Pane of 3, Cleveland Midwest Sta.	825.00	1000.00
	#C10a & 645 on one FDC, Clev. Midwest.	900.00	1100.00
	Booklet Pane w/o tab, DC or Cleveland	425.00	750.00
C11	5¢ Beacon, pair 7/25/28 DC	60.00	250.00
	Single on FDC	200.00	...
	Single on FDC with postage due	250.00	...
	Unofficial city (pair)	250.00	...
	Predate	750.00	...
C12	5¢ Winged Globe 2/10/30 DC	12.00	90.00
C13	65¢ Graf Zeppelin 4/19/30 DC	1400.00	2500.00
C13	On flight cover, any date	295.00	...
C14	$1.30 Graf Zeppelin 4/19/30 DC	1000.00	2500.00
C14	On flight cover, any date	525.00	...
C15	$2.60 Graf Zeppelin 4/19/30 DC	1150.00	2500.00
C15	On flight cover, any date	800.00	...
C13-15	Graf Zeppelin, cplt. set on one cover	14000.00	...
C16	5¢ Winged Globe, Rotary 8/19/31 DC	175.00	...
C17	8¢ Winged Globe 9/26/32 DC	16.50	45.00
C17	Combo with UC7	60.00	...
C18	50¢ Zeppelin 10/2/33 New York, NY	175.00	250.00
	Akron, OH 10/4/33	250.00	400.00
	DC 10/5/33	225.00	425.00
	Miami, FL 10/6/33	200.00	325.00
	Chicago, IL 10/7/33	250.00	400.00
C18	On flight cover, any date	110.00	...
C19	6¢ Winged Globe 6/30/34 Baltimore, MD	200.00	600.00
	New York, NY	1250.00	1750.00
	First Day of Rate 7/1/34 DC	20.00	40.00
C19	Combo with UC3	60.00	...

1935-39

C20	25¢ China Clipper 11/22/35 DC		45.00
	San Francisco, CA		45.00
C21	20¢ China Clipper 2/15/37 DC		55.00
C22	50¢ China Clipper 2/15/37 DC		60.00
C21-22	China Clipper on one cover		125.00
C23	6¢ Eagle Holding Shield 5/14/38 Dayton, OH		15.00
	St. Petersburg, FL		15.00
C24	30¢ Winged Globe 5/16/39 New York, NY		50.00

Scott #	Description	Price
C25	6¢ Plane 6/25/41 DC	5.00
C25a	Booklet Pane of 3 (3/18/43) DC	30.00
	Booklet single	10.00
C26	8¢ Plane 3/21/44 DC	5.00
C27	10¢ Plane 8/15/41 Atlantic City, NJ	7.50
C28	15¢ Plane 8/19/41 Baltimore, MD	7.50
C29	20¢ Plane 8/27/41 Philadelphia, PA	10.00
C30	30¢ Plane 9/25/41 Kansas City, MO	15.00
C31	50¢ Plane 10/29/41 St. Louis, MO	30.00
C25-31,C25a	Transport Plane set of 8 covers	100.00

From #C32 - Date, prices are for unaddressed FDC's & common cachets.

1946-59

C32	5¢ DC-4 Skymaster 9/25/46 DC	1.75
C33	5¢ Small Plane (DC-4) 3/26/47 DC	1.75
C34	10¢ Pan Am. Building 8/30/47 DC	1.75
C35	15¢ New York Skyline 8/20/47 NY, NY	2.00
C36	25¢ Bay Bridge 7/30/47 San Francisco, CA	2.50
C37	5¢ Small Plane, coil 1/15/48 DC	1.75
C38	5¢ NY City Jubilee 7/31/48 New York, NY	2.00
C39	6¢ DC-4 Skymaster 1/18/49 DC	1.75
C39a	Booklet Pane of 6 11/18/49 NY, NY	12.00
C39as	Booklet Pane, single,	4.00
C40	6¢ Alexandria 5/11/49 Alexandria, VA	2.00
C41	6¢ DC-4 Skymaster 8/25/49 DC	1.75
C42	10¢ Post Office Bldg. 11/18/49 New Orleans, LA	1.75
C43	15¢ Globe & Doves 10/7/49 Chicago, IL	3.00
C44	25¢ Boeing 11/30/49 Seattle, WA	4.00
C45	6¢ Wright Brothers 12/17/49 Kitty Hawk, NC	2.00
C46	80¢ Diamond Head 3/26/52 Honolulu, HI	15.00
C47	6¢ Powered Flight 5/29/53 Dayton, OH	2.00
C48	4¢ Eagle in Flight 9/3/54 Phila., PA	1.75
C49	6¢ Air Force 8/1/57 DC	2.00
C50	5¢ Eagle 7/31/58 Colorado Springs, CO	1.75
C51	7¢ Blue Jet 7/31/58 Philadelphia, PA	1.75
C51a	Booklet Pane of 6 7/31/58 San Antonio, TX	7.00
C51as	Booklet Pane, single,	4.00
C52	7¢ Blue Jet, coil 7/31/58 Miami, FL	1.75
C53	7¢ Alaska 1/3/59 Juneau, AK	1.75
C54	7¢ Balloon 8/17/59 Lafayette, IN	1.75
C55	7¢ Hawaii Sthd. 8/21/59 Honolulu, HI	2.00
C56	10¢ Pan Am Games 8/27/59 Chicago, IL	1.75

1959-68

C57	10¢ Liberty Bell 6/10/60 Miami, FL	1.75
C58	15¢ Statue of Liberty 11/20/59 NY, NY	1.75
C59	25¢ Lincoln 4/22/60 San Francisco, CA	1.75
C59a	Luminescent 12/29/66 DC	30.00
C60	7¢ Red Jet 8/12/60 Arlington, VA	1.75
C60a	Booklet Pane of 6 8/19/60 St. Louis, MO	8.00
C60as	Booklet Pane, single,	4.00
C61	7¢ Red Jet, coil 10/22/60 Atlantic City, NJ	1.75
C62	13¢ Liberty Bell 6/28/61 New York, NY	1.75
C62a	Luminescent 2/15/67 DC	30.00
C63	15¢ Statue of Liberty 1/31/61 Buffalo, NY	1.75
C63a	Luminescent 1/11/67 DC	30.00
C64	8¢ Jet over Capitol, single 12/5/62 DC	1.75
C64a	Luminescent 8/1/63 Dayton, OH	1.75
C64b	Booklet Pane of 5 12/5/62 DC	1.75
C64bs	Booklet Pane, single,	4.00
C65	8¢ Jet over Capitol, 12/5/62 DC, single	1.75
C65a	Luminescent 1/14/65 New Orleans, LA	30.00
C66	15¢ Montgomery Blair 5/3/63 Silver Springs, MD	2.50
C67	6¢ Bald Eagle 7/12/63 Boston, MA	1.75
C67a	Luminescent 2/15/67 DC	50.00
C68	8¢ Amelia Earhart 7/24/63 Atchinson, KS	3.00
C69	8¢ Robert Goddard 10/5/64 Roswell, NM	2.50
C70	8¢ Alaska Purchase 3/30/67 Sitka, AK	1.75
C71	20¢ Columbia Jays 4/26/67 New York, NY	2.50
C72	10¢ 50-Star Runway 1/5/68 San Fran., CA	1.75
C72	Precancelled, 5/19/71, Wash, DC	75.00
C72b	Bklt. Pane of 8 1/5/68 San Fran., CA	3.00
C72bs	Booklet Pane, single,	4.00
C72c	Bklt. Pane of 5 1/6/68 DC	125.00
C73	10¢ 50-Star Runway, coil 1/5/68 San Francisco, CA	1.75

C46

C91-92

Scott #	Description	Price
	1969-91	
C74	10¢ Jenny 5/15/68 DC	2.00
C75	20¢ "USA" & Jet 11/22/68 New York, NY	1.75
C76	10¢ First Man on Moon 9/9/69 DC	5.00
C77	9¢ Delta Plane 5/15/71 Kitty Hawk, NC	1.75
C78	11¢ Jet Silhouette 5/7/71 Spokane, WA	1.75
C78	Precancel, 5/19/71, Wash, DC	75.00
C78a	Booklet Pane of 4 5/7/71 Spokane, WA	3.00
C78as	Booklet Pane Single	4.00
C79	13¢ Winged Envelope 11/16/73 NY, NY	1.75
C79	Precancel, 3/4/74, Wash, DC	75.00
C79a	Bklt. Pane of 5 12/27/73 Chicago, IL	3.00
C79as	Bklt.Pane, single	4.00
C80	17¢ Statue of Liberty 7/13/71 Lakehurst, NJ	1.75
C81	21¢ "USA" & Jet 5/21/71 DC	1.75
C82	11¢ Jet Silhouette, coil 5/7/71 Spokane, WA	1.75
C83	13¢ Winged Envelope, coil 12/27/73 Chicago, IL ..	1.75
C84	11¢ City of Refuge 5/3/72 Honaunau, HI	1.75
C85	11¢ Olympics 8/17/72 DC	1.75
C86	11¢ Electronics 7/10/73 New York, NY	1.75
C87	18¢ Statue of Liberty 1/11/74 Hampstead, NY	1.75
C88	26¢ Mt. Rushmore 1/2/74 Rapid City, SD	1.75
C89	25¢ Plane and Globe 1/2/76 Honolulu, HI	1.75
C90	31¢ Plane, Globe & Flag 1/2/76 Honolulu, HI	1.75
C89-90	On one FDC	3.00
C91-92	31¢ Wright Bros. attd. 9/23/78 Dayton, OH	2.50
C91-92	Wright Bros. set of 2 singles	3.50
C93-94	21¢ Octave Chanute attd. 3/29/79 Chanute, KS	2.50
C93-94	Octave Chanute set of 2 singles	3.50
C95-96	25¢ Wiley Post attd. 11/20/79 Oklahoma City, OK ..	2.50
C95-96	Wiley Post set of 2 singles	3.50
C97	31¢ Olympic - High Jump 11/1/79 Col. Springs, CO ..	1.75
C98	40¢ Philip Mazzel 10/13/80 DC	1.75
C99	28¢ Blanche Scott 12/30/80 Hammondsport, NY	1.75
C100	35¢ Glenn Curtiss 12/30/80 Hammondsport, NY ...	1.75
C99-100	Scott & Curtiss on one cover	3.50
C101-04	28¢ Olympics attd. 6/17/83 San Antonio, TX	4.00
C101-04	Olympics set of 4 singles	8.00
C105-08	40¢ Olympics attd. 4/8/83 Los Angeles, CA	4.50
C105-08	Olympics set of 4 singles	8.00
C109-12	35¢ Olympics attd. 11/4/83 Colorado Springs, CO ..	4.50
C109-12	Olympics set of 4 singles	8.00
C113	33¢ Alfred Verville 2/13/85 Garden City, NY	1.75
C114	39¢ Sperry Bros. 2/13/85 Garden City, NY	1.75
C115	44¢ Transpacific Airmail 2/15/85 San Francisco, CA ..	2.50
C116	44¢ Junipero Serra 8/22/85 San Diego, CA	2.00
C117	44¢ New Sweden, 350th Anniv. 3/29/88 Wilmington, DE .	2.00
C118	45¢ Samuel P. Langley 5/14/88 San Diego, CA	2.00
C119	36¢ Igor Sikorsky 6/23/88 Stratford, CT	2.00
C120	45¢ French Revolution 7/14/89 DC	2.00
C121	45¢ Pre-Columbian Customs 10/12/89 San Juan, PR ..	2.00
C122-25	45¢ Future Mail Transportation attd. 11/27/89 DC ..	8.00
C122-25	Set of 4 singles	10.00
C126	$1.80 Future Mail Trans. S/S of 4, imperf. 11/24/89 DC ..	7.00
C127	45¢ America, Caribbean Coast 10/12/90 Grand Canyon, AZ	2.00
C128	50¢ Harriet Quimby 4/27/91 Plymouth, MI	2.00
C129	40¢ William T. Piper 5/17/91 Denver, CO	2.00
C130	50¢ Antarctic Treaty 6/21/91 DC	2.00
C131	50¢ America 10/12/91 Anchorage, AK	2.00
	1934-36 AIRMAIL SPECIAL DELIVERY ISSUES	
CE1	16¢ Great Seal, blue 8/30/34 Chic., IL (AAMS Conv. Sta.)	30.00
CE2	16¢ Great Seal, red & blue 2/10/36 DC	25.00

Scott #	Description	Uncacheted	Cacheted
	1885-1931 SPECIAL DELIVERY		
E1	10¢ Messenger 10/1/85 Any City	8500.00	...
E12	10¢ Motorcycle,Flat plate,perf.11 7/12/22 DC	375.00	...
E13	15¢ Motorcycle,Flat plate,perf.11 4/11/25 DC	225.00	...
E14	20¢ Truck, Flat plate, perf.11 4/25/25 DC	110.00	...
E15	10¢ Motorcycle, Rotary 11/29/27 DC	95.00	...
E15EE	Electric Eye 9/8/41 DC	...	25.00
E16	15¢ Motorcycle, Rotary 8/6/31 Easton, PA	1000.00	...
	Motorcycle, Rotary 8/13/31 DC	125.00	...

Scott #	Description	Uncacheted	Cacheted
	1944-1971 SPECIAL DELIVERY		
E17	13¢ Motorcycle 10/30/44	...	10.00
E18	17¢ Motorcycle 10/30/44	...	10.00
E17-18	Motorcycles on one cover	...	15.00
E19	20¢ Post Office Truck, Rotary 11/30/51 DC	...	4.50
E20	20¢ Letter & Hands 10/13/54 Boston, MA	...	2.00
E21	30¢ Letter & Hands 9/3/57 Indpls., IN	...	2.00
E22	45¢ Arrows 11/21/69 New York, NY	...	2.25
E23	60¢ Arrows 5/10/71 Phoenix, AZ	...	2.50
	1911 REGISTERED MAIL		
F1	10¢ Eagle, blue 12/1/11 Any city..............	12500.00	...
	1955 CERTIFIED MAIL		
FA1	15¢ Postman, red 6/6/55 DC	...	2.00
	POSTAGE DUE		
	1925		
J68	½¢ P. Due (4/15/25 EKU) FDC unknown	500.00	...
	1959		
J88	½¢ Red & Black 6/19/59 Any city	75.00	...
J89	1¢ Red & Black 6/19/59 Any city	75.00	...
J90	2¢ Red & Black 6/19/59 Any city	75.00	...
J91	3¢ Red & Black 6/19/59 Any city	75.00	...
J92	4¢ Red & Black 6/19/59 Any city	75.00	...
J93	5¢ Red & Black 6/19/59 Any city	115.00	...
J94	6¢ Red & Black 6/19/59 Any city	115.00	...
J95	7¢ Red & Black 6/19/59 Any city	115.00	...
J96	8¢ Red & Black 6/19/59 Any city	115.00	...
J97	10¢ Red & Black 6/19/59 Any city	115.00	...
J98	30¢ Red & Black 6/19/59 Any city	115.00	...
J99	50¢ Red & Black 6/19/59 Any city	115.00	...
J100	$1 Red & Black 6/19/59 Any city	125.00	...
J101	$5 Red & Black 6/19/59 Any city	125.00	...
	1978-85		
J102	11¢ Red & Black 1/2/78 Any city	...	5.00
J103	13¢ Red & Black 1/2/78 Any city	...	5.00
	#J102-103 on one FDC	...	7.50
J104	17¢ Red & Black 6/10/85 Any city	...	5.00
	1983-95 OFFICIAL STAMPS		
O74	3¢ Treasury 7/1/1873 Washington, DC	5000.00	...
O127	1¢ Eagle 1/12/83 DC	...	1.75
O128	4¢ Eagle 1/12/83 DC	...	1.75
O129	13¢ Eagle 1/12/83 DC	...	1.75
O129A	14¢ Eagle 5/15/85 DC	...	2.00
O130	17¢ Eagle 1/12/83 DC	...	1.75
O132	$1 Eagle 1/12/83 DC	...	5.00
O133	$5 Eagle 1/12/83 DC	...	15.00
O136	22¢ Eagle 5/15/85 DC	...	1.75
O138	(14¢) "D" Eagle 2/4/85 DC	...	1.75
O143	1¢ Eagle, Offset Printing, No ¢ sign 7/5/89 DC .	...	1.75
O146	4¢ Official Mail 4/6/91 Oklahoma City, OK	...	1.75
O146A	10¢ Official Mail 10/19/93	...	1.75
O147	19¢ Official Postcard rate 5/24/91 Seattle, WA ...	...	1.75
O148	23¢ Official 2nd oz. rate 5/24/91 Seattle, WA ...	...	1.75
...	1¢ Eagle, with ¢ sign 5/9/95 DC	...	1.90
...	20¢ Eagle, postcard rate 5/9/95 DC	...	1.90
...	23¢ Eagle, 2nd oz. rate 5/9/95 DC	...	1.90
...	1¢, 20¢, 23¢, 32¢ Coil Combo cover, 5/9/95 DC ..	...	2.50
	1983-95 OFFICIAL COILS		
O135	20¢ Eagle, with ¢ sign 1/12/83 DC	...	1.75
	#O127-129,O130-135 on one FDC	...	15.00
O138A	15¢ Official Mail 6/11/88 Corpus Christi, TX	...	1.75
O138B	20¢ Official Mail, No ¢ sign 5/19/88 DC	...	1.75

0138B

SPECIAL SERVICE FIRST DAY COVERS

RW49

Scott #	Description	Uncacheted	Cacheted
O139	(22¢) "D" Eagle 2/4/85 DC	...	1.75
O140	(25¢) "E" Official 3/22/88 DC	...	1.75
O141	25¢ Official Mail 6/11/88 Corpus Christi, TX	...	1.75
O144	(29¢) "F" Official 1/22/91 DC	...	1.75
O145	29¢ Official Mail 5/24/91 Seattle, WA	...	1.75
O152	(32¢) "G" Official 12/13/94 DC	...	1.90
...	32¢ Official Mail 5/9/95 DC	...	1.90

POSTAL NOTES

Scott #	Description	Uncacheted	Cacheted
PN1-18	1¢-90¢ Black, cplt. set on 18 forms	750.00	...
PN1	1¢ Black 2/1/45 on cplt 3 part M.O. form, any city	45.00	...
PN2	2¢ 2/1/45 on cplt 3 part M.O. form, any city	45.00	...
PN3	3¢ 2/1/45 on cplt 3 part M.O. form, any city	45.00	...
PN4	4¢ 2/1/45 on cplt 3 part M.O. form, any city	45.00	...
PN5	5¢ 2/1/45 on cplt 3 part M.O. form, any city	45.00	...
PN6	6¢ 2/1/45 on cplt 3 part M.O. form, any city	45.00	...
PN7	7¢ 2/1/45 on cplt 3 part M.O. form, any city	45.00	...
PN8	8¢ 2/1/45 on cplt 3 part M.O. form, any city	45.00	...
PN9	9¢ 2/1/45 on cplt 3 part M.O. form, any city	45.00	...
PN10	10¢ 2/1/45 on cplt 3 part M.O. form, any city	45.00	...
PN11	20¢ 2/1/45 on cplt 3 part M.O. form, any city	45.00	...
PN12	30¢ 2/1/45 on cplt 3 part M.O. form, any city	45.00	...
PN13	40¢ 2/1/45 on cplt 3 part M.O. form, any city	45.00	...
PN14	50¢ 2/1/45 on cplt 3 part M.O. form, any city	45.00	...
PN15	60¢ 2/1/45 on cplt 3 part M.O. form, any city	45.00	...
PN16	70¢ 2/1/45 on cplt 3 part M.O. form, any city	45.00	...
PN17	80¢ 2/1/45 on cplt 3 part M.O. form, any city	45.00	...
PN18	90¢ 2/1/45 on cplt 3 part M.O. form, any city	45.00	...

POSTAL SAVINGS

Scott #	Description	Uncacheted	Cacheted
PS11	10¢ Minuteman, red 5/1/41 Any city	175.00	...

Scott #	Description	4th Class (1/1/13)	1st Class (7/1/13)
	PARCEL POST		
Q1	1¢ Post Office Clerk, any city	3500.00	2500.00
Q2	2¢ City Carrier, any city	4500.00	2500.00
Q3	3¢ Railway Postal Clerk, any city	...	3500.00
Q4	4¢ Rural Carrier, any city	...	3500.00
Q5	5¢ Mail Train, any city	7500.00	3500.00
	1925-28 SPECIAL HANDLING		
QE1	10¢ Yellow Green 6/25/28 DC	50.00	...
QE2	15¢ Yellow Green 6/25/28 DC	50.00	...
QE3	20¢ Yellow Green 6/25/28 DC	50.00	...
	1925-28 SPECIAL HANDLING		
QE1-3	Set of 3 on one FDC	250.00	...
QE4a	25¢ Deep Green 4/11/25 DC	225.00	...

FEDERAL DUCK STAMP FIRST DAY COVERS

Scott #	Description	Uncacheted	Cacheted
RW47	$7.50 Mallards 7/1/80 DC		150.00
RW48	$7.50 Ruddy Ducks 7/1/81 DC		75.00
RW49	$7.50 Canvasbacks 7/1/82 DC		55.00
RW50	$7.50 Pintails 7/1/83 DC		55.00
RW51	$7.50 Widgeons 7/2/84 DC		50.00
RW52	$7.50 Cinnamon Teal 7/1/85 DC		45.00
RW53	$7.50 Fulvous Whistling Duck 7/1/86		45.00
RW54	$10.00 Red Head Ducks 7/1/87		45.00
RW55	$10.00 Snow Goose 7/1/88 Any city		45.00
RW56	$12.50 Lesser Scaups 6/30/89 DC		45.00
RW57	$12.50 Black-Bellied Whistling Duck 6/30/90 DC		45.00
RW58	$15.00 King Elders 6/30/91 DC		45.00
RW59	$15.00 Spectacled Elder 6/30/92 DC		45.00
RW60	$15.00 Canvasbacks 6/30/93 DC		35.00
RW60	Same, Mound, MN		35.00
RW61	$15.00 Redbreasted Merganser 6/30/94 DC		35.00
RW62	$15.00 Mallard 6/30/95 DC		35.00
RW63	$15.00 Surf Scoter 6/27/96 DC		35.00
RW64	$15.00 Canada Goose 6/21/97 DC		35.00

POSTAL STATIONERY FIRST DAY COVERS

Prices are for standard 6¾ size envelopes, unless noted otherwise.

Scott #	Description	Uncacheted	Cacheted
	1925-32		
U436a	3¢ G. Washington, white paper, extra quality 6/16/32 DC, size 5, die 1, wmk. 29	75.00	...
	Size 8, die 1, wmk. 29	18.00	...
U436e	3¢ G. Washington, white paper, extra quality 6/16/32 DC, size 5, die 7, wmk. 29	12.00	30.00
U436f	3¢ G. Washington, white paper, extra quality 6/16/32 DC, size 5, die 9, wmk. 29	12.00	50.00
	Size 12, die 9, wmk. 29	18.00	...
U437a	3¢ G. Washington, amber paper, standard qual. 7/13/32 DC, size 5, wmk. 28	50.00	...
	7/19/32 DC, size 5, wmk. 29, extra qual.	35.00	...
U439	3¢ G. Washington, blue paper, standard qual. 7/13/32, size 5, wmk. 28	40.00	...
	Size 13, die 9, wmk. 28	65.00	...
	9/9/32 DC, size 5, wmk. 28	85.00	...
U439a	3¢ G. Washington, blue paper, extra quality 7/19/32 DC, size 5, die 29	40.00	...
U481	1½¢ G. Wash. 3/19/25 DC, size 5, wmk. 27	35.00	...
	Size 8, wmk. 27	70.00	...
	Size 13, wmk. 26	50.00	...
	Size 5, wmk. 27 with Sc#553, 582 & 598	150.00	...
	Size 8, wmk. 27 with Sc#553, 582 & 598	125.00	...
	Size 13, wmk. 26 with Sc#553	60.00	...
U495	1½¢ on 1¢ B. Franklin 6/1/25 DC, size 5	50.00	...
	6/3/25 DC, size 8	65.00	...
	6/2/25 DC, size 13	60.00	...
U515	1½¢ on 1¢ B. Franklin 8/1/25 Des Moines, IA size 5, die 1	50.00	...
U521	1½¢ on 1¢ B. Franklin 10/22/25 DC size 5, die 1, watermark 25	100.00	...
U522a	2¢ Liberty Bell 7/27/26 Philadelphia, PA		
	Size 5, wmk. 27	20.00	30.00
	Size 5, wmk. 27 DC	22.50	32.50
	Unofficial city, Size 5, wmk. 27	35.00	45.00
	WASHINGTON BICENTENNIAL ISSUE		
U523	1¢ Mount Vernon 1/1/32 DC, size 5, wmk. 29	10.00	32.50
	Size 8, 29	12.50	37.50
	Size 13, wmk. 29	10.00	32.50
U524	1½¢ Mount Vernon 1/1/32 DC, size 5, wmk.29	10.00	32.50
	Size 8, 29	12.50	37.50
	Size 13, wmk. 29	10.00	32.50
U525	2¢ Mount Vernon 1/1/32 DC, size 5, wmk. 29	8.00	30.00
	Size 8, 29	10.00	30.00
	Size 13, wmk. 29	8.00	30.00
U526	3¢ Mount Vernon 6/16/32, size 5, wmk.29	18.00	40.00
	Size 8, 29	25.00	80.00
	Size 13, wmk. 29	20.00	60.00
U527	4¢ Mount Vernon 1/1/32 DC, size 5, wmk. 29	30.00	80.00
U528	5¢ Mount Vernon 1/1/32 DC, size 5, wmk. 29	18.00	40.00
	Size 8, 29	20.00	45.00
	Size 13, wmk. 29	10.00	32.50
	1932-71		
U529	6¢ G. Washington, white paper, 8/18/32		
	Los Angeles, CA, size 8, wmk 29	15.00	...
	8/19/32 DC, size 7, wmk 29	20.00	...
	8/19/32 DC, size 9, wmk 29	20.00	...
U530	6¢ G. Washington, amber paper, 8/18/32		
	Los Angeles, CA, size 8, wmk 29	15.00	...
	8/19/32 DC, size 7, wmk 29	20.00	...
	8/19/32 DC, size 9, wmk 29	20.00	...
	size 8, wmk 29 with Sc#723 pair	40.00	...
U531	6¢ G. Washington, blue paper, 8/18/32		
	Los Angeles, CA, size 8, wmk 29	15.00	...
	8/19/32 DC, size 7, wmk 29	20.00	...
	8/19/32 DC, size 9, wmk 29	20.00	...
U532	1¢ Franklin 11/16/50 NY, NY, size 13, wmk 42.	...	1.75
U533a	2¢ Wash. 11/17/50 NY, NY, size 13, wmk 42	...	1.75
U534a	3¢ Wash.,die 1 11/18/50 NY,NY,size 13,wmk 42	...	1.75
U534b	3¢ Wash.,die 2 11/19/50 NY,NY,size 8,wmk 42	...	4.00

U532

U543

Scott #	Description	Uncacheted	Cacheted
U536	4¢ Franklin 7/31/58 Montpelier, VT		1.75
	Size 8, wmk 46	60.00	...
	Size 12, wmk 46	60.00	...
	Size 13, window		...
	Wheeling, WV, size 6¾, wmk 46, w/#1036a.....	35.00	...
U540	3¢+1¢ G.Washington (U534c) 7/22/58 Kenvil, NJ		
	Size 8, wmk 46, die 3 (earliest known use)......	50.00	...
U541	1¼¢ Franklin 6/25/60 Birmingham, AL		1.75
U542	2½¢ Washington 5/28/60 Chicago, IL		1.75
U543	4¢ Pony Express 7/19/60 St. Joseph, MO		1.75
	Sacramento, CA		3.50
U544	5¢ Lincoln 11/19/62 Springfield, IL		1.75
U546	5¢ World's Fair 4/22/64 World's Fair, NY		1.75
U547	1¼¢ Liberty Bell 1/6/65 DC		1.75
	1/8/65 DC, size 10, wmk 48		15.00
U548	1.4¢ Liberty Bell 3/26/68 Springfield, MA		1.75
	3/27/68 DC, size 10, wmk 48		8.00
U548A	1.6¢ Liberty Bell 6/16/69 DC		1.75
	Size 10, wmk 49		1.75
U549	4¢ Old Ironsides 1/6/65 DC		1.75
	1/8/65, window		15.00
	Size 10		15.00
	Size10, window		15.00
U550	5¢ Eagle 1/5/65 Williamsburg, PA		1.75
	1/8/65, window		15.00
	Size 10		15.00
	Size 10, window		15.00
U550a	5¢ Eagle, tagged 8/15/67 DC, wmk 50		1.75
	Dayton, OH..		5.00
	Wmk 48		5.00
	Size 10, wmk 48		5.00
	Size 10, wmk 49, Dayton, OH only		7.50
	Size 10, wmk 49, window		5.00
U551	6¢ Liberty 1/4/68 New York, NY		1.75
	1/5/68 DC, window		3.00
	Size 10, wmk 47		3.00
	Size 10, window, wmk 49		3.00
	11/15/68 DC, shiny plastic window, wmk 48		5.00
U552	4 + 2¢ Old Ironsides, revalued 2/5/68 DC, wmk 50...........		7.50
	Window, wmk 48		7.50
	Size 10, wmk 47		7.50
	Size 10, window, wmk 49		7.50
U553	5 + 1¢ Eagle, revalued 2/5/68 DC		7.50
			7.50
U553a	5 + 1¢ Eagle, revalued, tagged 2/5/68 DC, wmk 48........		7.50
	Size 10, wmk 47 or 49		7.50
	Size 10, window, wmk 49		7.50
U554	6¢ Moby Dick 6/7/70 New Bedford, MA		1.75
U554	**1st Colonial Cachet**		**30.00**
U555	6¢ Youth Conf. 2/24/71 DC		1.75
U556	1.7¢ Liberty Bell 5/10/71 Balt., MD, wmk 48A		1.75
	5/10/71 DC, wmk 49 with #1394		15.00
	5/10/71 Phoenix, AZ, wmk 48A with #E23		30.00
	5/10/71 DC, with #1283		3.00
	5/11/71 DC, size 10, wmk 47 or 49		12.00
	5/11/71 DC, size 10, wmk 48A		6.00

Scott #	Description	Price
	1971-78	
U557	8¢ Eagle 5/6/71 Williamsburg, PA, wmk 48A	1.75
	Wmk 49	2.50
	5/7/71 DC, window, wmk 48A	3.50
	Size 10, wmk 49	3.50
	Size 10, window, wmk 47	3.50
U561	6 + 2¢ Liberty Bell, revalued 5/16/71 DC, wmk 47........	3.00
	Wmk 48A	25.00
	Wmk 49	4.00
	Window, wmk 47	3.00
	Size 10, wmk 48A	3.00
	Size 10, wmk 49	6.00
	Size 10, window, wmk 47	3.00
	Size 10, window, wmk 49	5.00
U562	6 + 2¢ Youth Conf., revalued 5/16/71 DC, wmk 49	3.00
	Wmk 47	30.00

Scott #	Description	Price
U563	8¢ Bowling 8/21/71 Milwaukee, WI	2.50
	Size 10	2.00
U564	8¢ Aging Conference 11/15/71 DC	1.75
U565	8¢ Transpo '72 5/2/72 DC, wmk 49	1.75
	Wmk 47	3.00
U566	8 + 2¢ Eagle, revalued 12/1/73 DC..................	2.50
	Window, wmk 48A........................(uncacheted)	7.50
	Window, wmk 49	4.50
	Size 10, wmk 47	4.50
	Size 10, window, wmk 47	4.50
U567	10¢ Liberty Bell 12/5/73 Phila., PA knife depth 58 mm...	1.75
	Knife depth 51 mm	1.75
U568	1.8¢ Volunteer 8/23/74 Cincinnati, OH	1.75
	Size 10	1.75
U569	10¢ Tennis 8/31/74 Forest Hills, NY	3.00
	Size 10	3.00
	9/3/74 DC, window	4.00
	Size 10, window	4.00
U571	10¢ Seafaring 10/13/75 Minneapolis, MN	1.75
	Size 10	1.75
U572	13¢ Homemaker 2/2/76 Biloxi, MS	1.75
	Size 10	1.75
U573	13¢ Farmer 3/15/76 New Orleans, LA	1.75
	Size 10	1.75
U574	13¢ Doctor 3/30/76 Dallas, TX	2.50
	Size 10	3.00
U575	13¢ Craftsman 8/6/76 Hancock, MA	1.75
	Size 10	1.75
U576	13¢ Liberty Tree 11/8/75 Memphis, TN	1.75
	Size 10	1.75
U577	2¢ Star & Pinwheel 9/10/76 Hempstead, NY	1.75
	Size 10	1.75
U578	2.1¢ Non-Profit 6/3/77 Houston, TX	1.75
	Size 10	1.75
U579	2.7¢ Non-Profit 7/5/78 Raleigh, NC	1.75
	Size 10	1.75
U580	(15¢) "A" Eagle 5/22/78 Memphis, TN, wmk 47	2.00
	Wmk 48A	1.75
	Window, wmk 47 or 48A	2.50
	Size 10	1.75
	Size 10, window	2.50
	Size 6¾, wmk 48A with sheet, coil & bklt. pane	10.00
U581	15¢ Uncle Sam 6/3/78 Williamsburg, PA	1.75
	Window	2.50
	Size 10	1.75
	Size 10, window	2.50
U582	13¢ Bicentennial 10/15/76 Los Angeles, CA, wmk 49	1.75
	Wmk 49, dark green	7.50
	Wmk 48A	3.00
	Size 10	1.75
U583	13¢ Golf 4/7/77 Augusta, GA	7.00
	Size 10	7.50
	4/8/77 DC, Size 6¾, window	9.50
	Size 10, window	9.50
	1977-85	
U584	13¢ Conservation 10/20/77 Ridley Park, PA	1.75
	Window	2.50
	Size 10	1.75
	Size 10, window	2.50
U585	13¢ Development 10/20/77 Ridley Park, PA	1.75
	Window	2.50
	Size 10	1.75
	Size 10, window	2.50
U586	15¢ on 16¢ Surcharged USA 7/28/78 Williamsburg, PA...	1.75
	Size 10	1.75
U587	15¢ Auto Racing 9/2/78 Ontario, CA	1.75
	Size 10	1.75
U588	13 + 2¢ Lib. Tree, revalued 11/28/78 Williamsburg, PA....	1.75
	Size 10	1.75
	11/29/78 DC, size 6¾, window	2.00
	Size 10, window	2.00
U589	3.1¢ Non-Profit 5/18/79 Denver, CO	1.75
	Size 6¾, window	2.00
	Size 10	1.75
	Size 10, window	2.00

U583

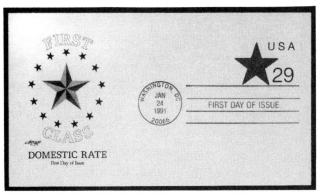

U619

Scott #	Description	Price
U590	3.5¢ Non-Profit 6/23/80 Williamsburg, PA	1.75
	Size 10	1.75
U591	5.9¢ Non-Profit 2/17/82 Wheeling, WV	1.75
	Size 6¾, window	2.00
	Size 10	1.75
	Size 10, window	2.00
U592	(18¢) "B" Eagle 3/15/81 Memphis, TN	1.75
	Size 6¾, window	2.00
	Size 10	1.75
	Size 10, window	2.00
U593	18¢ Star 4/2/81 Star City, IN	1.75
	Size 10	1.75
U594	(20¢) "C" Eagle 10/11/81 Memphis, TN	1.75
U595	15¢ Veterinary Med. 7/24/79 Seattle, WA	1.75
	Size 10	1.75
	7/25/79 Seattle, WA, size 6¾, window, ... **(uncacheted)**	4.00
	Size 10 .... **(uncacheted)**	4.00
U596	15¢ Olympics 12/10/79 E. Rutherford, NJ	1.75
	Size 10	1.75
U597	15¢ Bicycle 5/16/80 Baltimore, MD	1.75
	Size 10	1.75
U598	15¢ America's Cup 9/15/80 Newport, RI	1.75
	Size 10	1.75
U599	15¢ Honey Bee 10/10/80 Paris, IL	1.75
	Size 10	1.75
U600	18¢ Blinded Veteran 8/13/81 Arlington, VA	1.75
	Size 10	1.75
U601	20¢ Capitol Dome 11/13/81 Los Angeles, CA	1.75
	Size 10	1.75
U602	20¢ Great Seal 6/15/82 DC	1.75
	Size 10	1.75
U603	20¢ Purple Heart 8/6/82 DC	2.00
	Size 10	2.00
U604	5.2¢ Non-Profit 3/21/83 Memphis, TN	1.75
	Size 6¾, window	1.75
	Size 10	1.75
	Size 10, window	1.75
U605	20¢ Paralyzed Vets 8/3/83 Portland, OR	1.75
	Size 10	1.75
U606	20¢ Small Business 5/7/84 DC	1.75
	Size 10	1.75
U607	(22¢) "D" Eagle 2/1/85 Los Angeles, CA	1.75
	Size 6¾, window	1.75
	Size 10	1.75
	Size 10, window	1.75
U608	22¢ Bison 2/25/85 Bison, SD	1.75
	Size 6¾, window	1.75
	Size 10	1.75
	Size 10, window	1.75

Scott #	Description 1985-96	Cacheted
U609	6¢ Old Ironsides, Non-Profit 5/3/85 Boston, MA	1.75
	Size 10	2.00
U610	8.5¢ Mayflower 12/4/86 Plymouth, MA	1.75
	Size 10	2.00
U611	25¢ Stars 3/26/88 Star, MS	1.75
	Size 10	2.00
U612	9.4¢ USS Constellation 4/12/88 Baltimore, MD	1.75
	Size 10	2.00
U613	25¢ Snowflake 9/8/88 Snowflake, AZ	1.75
U614	25¢ Philatelic Mail Return Env. 3/10/89 Cleveland, OH	1.75
U615	25¢ Security Envelope 7/10/89 DC	1.75
U616	25¢ Love 9/22/89 McLean, VA	1.75
U617	25¢ Space Hologram, World Stamp Expo 12/3/89 DC	1.75
U618	25¢ Football 9/9/90 Green Bay, WI	4.00
U619	29¢ Star 1/24/91 DC	1.75
U620	11.1¢ Non-Profit 5/3/91 Boxborough, MA	1.75
U621	29¢ Love 5/9/91 Honolulu, HI	1.75
U622	29¢ Magazine Industry 10/7/91 Naples, FL	1.75
U623	29¢ USA & Star, Security Envelope 7/20/91 DC	1.75
U624	29¢ Country Geese 11/8/91 Virginia Beach, VA	1.75
U625	29¢ Space Station Hologram 1/21/92 Virginia Beach, VA...	1.75

Scott #	Description	Cacheted
U626	29¢ Western Americana 4/10/92 Dodge City, KS................	1.75
U627	29¢ Protect the Environment 4/22/92 Chicago, IL	1.75
U628	19.8¢ Bulk-rate, third class 5/18/92 Las Vegas, NV	1.75
U629	29¢ Disabled Americans 7/22/92 DC................	1.75
U630	29¢ Kitten 10/2/93 King of Prussia, PA................	1.75
	Size 10	2.00
U631	29¢ Football size 10 9/17/94 Canton, OH	3.00
U632	32¢ Liberty Bell 1/3/95 Williamsburg, VA	2.00
U633	(32¢) Old Glory 12/13/94 Cancel, released 1/12/95	2.00
U634	(32¢) Old Glory, Security Envelope	2.00
U635	(5¢) Sheep 3/10/95 State College, PA.......................	2.00
U636	(10¢) Eagle 3/10/95 State College,PA.......................	2.00
U637	32¢ Spiral Heart 5/12/95 Lakeville, PA.......................	2.00
U638	32¢ Liberty Bell Security Size 9 5/15/95 DC	2.00
U639	32¢ Space Hologram (Legal size only) 9/22/95 Milwaukee, WI........................	2.00
U640	32¢ Environment 4/20/96 Chicago, IL	2.00
U641	32¢ Paralympics 5/2/96 DC	2.00

Scott #	Description AIRMAIL POSTAL STATIONERY 1929-46	Uncacheted
UC1	5¢ Blue 1/12/29 DC, size 13	40.00
	2/1/29, DC, size 5	45.00
	2/1/29, DC, size 8	65.00
UC3	6¢ Orange 7/1/34, size 8	25.00
	Size 13	14.00
UC3	Combo with C19	60.00
UC7	8¢ Olive green 9/26/32, size 8	30.00
	Size 13	11.00
UC7	Combo with C17	60.00
UC10	5¢ on 6¢ Orange 10/1/46 Aiea Hts, HI die 2a	100.00
UC11	5¢ on 6¢ Orange 10/1/46 Aiea Hts, HI die 2b	150.00
UC12	5¢ on 6¢ Orng. 10/1/46 Aiea Hts, HI, APO & NY, NY die 2c	75.00
UC13	5¢ on 6¢ Orng. 10/1/46 Aiea Hts, HI, die 3	75.00

Scott #	Description 1946-67	Cacheted
UC14	5¢ Skymaster 9/25/46 DC	2.25
UC16	10¢ Air Letter 4/29/47 DC	5.00
UC17	5¢ CIPEX, Type 1 5/21/47 New York, NY	2.50
UC17a	5¢ CIPEX, Type 2 5/21/47 New York, NY	2.50
UC18	6¢ Skymaster 9/22/50 Philadelphia, PA	1.75
UC20	6¢ on 5¢ 9/1/51 U.S. Navy Cancel	400.00
UC22	6¢ on 5¢ die 2 (UC15) 8/29/52 Norfolk, VA .. **(uncacheted)**	20.00
	Cacheted	30.00
UC25	6¢ FIPEX 5/2/56 New York, NY, "short clouds"	1.75
	"Long clouds"	1.75
UC26	7¢ Skymaster 7/31/58 Dayton, OH, "straight left wing"	1.75
	"Crooked left wing"	3.00
	Size 8 .... **(uncacheted)**	35.00
UC32a	10¢ Jet Air Letter 9/12/58 St. Louis, MO.......................	2.00
UC33	7¢ Jet, blue 11/21/58 New York, NY	1.75

Scott #	Description	Cacheted
UC34	7¢ Jet, red 8/18/60 Portland, OR	1.75
UC35	11¢ Jet Air Letter 6/16/61 Johnstown, PA.......................	1.75
UC36	8¢ Jet 11/17/62 Chantilly, VA.......................	1.75
UC37	8¢ Jet Triangle 1/7/65 Chicago, IL	1.75
	Size 10	15.00
UC37a	8¢ Jet Triangle, tagged 8/15/67 DC	7.50
	Dayton, OH	7.50
	Size 10	7.50

	1965-95	
UC38	11¢ Kennedy Air Letter 5/29/65 Boston, MA................	1.75
UC39	13¢ Kennedy Air Letter 5/29/67 Chic., IL	1.75
UC40	10¢ Jet Triangle 1/8/68 Chicago, IL	1.75
	1/9/68 DC, size 10	7.50
UC41	8 + 2¢ revalued UC37 2/5/68 DC	10.00
	Size 10	10.00
UC42	13¢ Human Rights Air Letter 12/3/68 DC	1.75
UC43	11¢ Jet & Circles 5/6/71 Williamsburg, PA	1.75
	Size 10	6.00

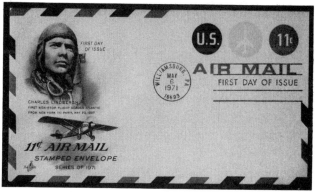

UC43

UX48

Scott #	Description	Cacheted
UC44	15¢ Birds Air Letter 5/28/71 Chicago, IL	1.75
UC44a	15¢ AEROGRAMME 12/13/71 Phila., PA	1.75
UC45	10¢+1¢ revalued UC40 6/28/71 DC	5.00
	Size 10	10.00
UC46	15¢ Balloon Air Letter 2/10/73 Albuquerque, NM	1.75
UC47	13¢ Dove 12/1/73 Memphis, TN	1.75
	1/5/74, size 10, earliest known use	5.00
UC48	18¢ USA Air Letter 1/4/74 Atlanta, GA	1.75
UC49	17¢ NATO Air Letter 4/4/74 DC	1.75
UC50	22¢ USA Air Letter 1/16/76 Tempe, AZ	1.75
UC51	22¢ USA Air Letter 11/3/78 St. Petersburg, FL	1.75
UC52	22¢ Olympics 12/5/79 Bay Shore, NY	1.75
UC53	30¢ USA 12/29/80 San Francisco, CA	1.75
UC54	30¢ USA 9/21/81 Honolulu, HI	1.75
UC55	30¢ USA & Globe 9/16/82 Seattle, WA	1.75
UC56	30¢ Communications 1/7/83 Anaheim, CA	1.75
UC57	30¢ Olympics 10/14/83 Los Angeles, CA	1.75
UC58	30¢ Landsat Sat. 2/14/85 Goddard Flight Ctr., MD	1.75
UC59	36¢ Travel 5/21/85 DC	1.75
UC60	36¢ Twain / Halley's Comet 12/4/85 DC	1.75
UC61	39¢ Stylized Aerogramme 5/9/88 Miami, FL	1.75
UC62	39¢ Montgomery Blair 11/20/89 DC	1.75
UC63	45¢ Eagle 5/17/91 Denver, CO	2.00
UC64	50¢ Thaddeus Lowe Aero 9/23/95 Tampa, FL	2.25

OFFICIAL POSTAL STATIONERY
1983-95

Scott #	Description	Cacheted
UO73	20¢ Eagle 1/12/83 DC, size 10	2.00
	Window	3.00
UO74	22¢ Eagle 2/26/85 CD, size 10	1.75
	Window	2.00
UO75	22¢ Savings Bond Env. 3/2/87 DC	3.00
	Window	4.00
UO76	(25¢) Official "E" Savings Bond Env. 3/22/88 DC	1.75
	Window	2.00
UO77	25¢ Official Mail 4/11/88 DC	1.75
	Window	2.00
UO78	25¢ Savings Bond Env. 4/14/88 DC	1.75
	Window	2.00
UO79	45¢ Passport Envelope (2 oz.) 3/17/90 Springfield, VA	2.00
UO80	65¢ Passport Envelope (3 oz.) 3/17/90 Springfield, VA	2.50
UO81	45¢ "Stars" clear, "Official" 14.5 mm long, 8/10/90 DC	2.00
UO82	65¢ "Stars" clear, "Official" 14.5 mm long, 8/10/90 DC	2.50
UO83	(29¢) "F" Savings Bond Env. 1/22/91 DC	1.75
UO84	29¢ Official Mail 4/6/91 Oklahoma City, OK	1.75
UO85	29¢ Savings Bond Env. 4/17/91 DC	1.75
UO86	52¢ U.S. Consular Service, Passport Env. 7/10/92 DC	2.25
UO87	75¢ U.S. Consular Service, Passport Env. 7/10/92 DC	2.75
UO88	32¢ Eagle (Legal size only) 5/9/95 DC	2.00

Scott #	Description	Uncacheted	Cacheted
	1873-1966		
UX1	1¢ Liberty 5/13/1873 Boston, NY, or DC	3000.00	...
UX37	3¢ McKinley 2/1/26 DC	250.00	...
UX38	2¢ Franklin 11/16/51 New York, NY		1.75
UX39	2¢ on 1¢ Jefferson (UX27) 1/1/52 DC	12.50	25.00
UX40	2¢ on 1¢ Lincoln (UX28) 3/22/82 DC	100.00	250.00
UX43	2¢ Lincoln 7/31/52 DC	...	1.75
UX44	2¢ FIPEX 5/4/56 New York, NY	...	1.75
UX45	4¢ Liberty 11/16/56 New York, NY	...	1.75
UX46	3¢ Liberty 8/1/58 Philadelphia, PA	...	1.75
UX46a	Missing "I"/"N God We Trust"	175.00	250.00
UX46c	Precancelled 9/15/61	50.00	...
UX48	4¢ Lincoln 11/19/62 Springfield, IL	...	1.75
UX48a	4¢ Lincoln, tagged 6/25/66 Bellevue, OH	25.00	30.00
	7/6/66 DC	1.50	2.50
	Bellevue, OH	7.50	12.50
	Cincinnati, OH	4.50	7.50
	Cleveland, OH	6.00	10.00
	Columbus, OH	7.50	12.50
	Dayton, OH	3.50	6.00
	Indianapolis, IN	7.50	12.50
	Louisville, KY	7.50	12.50
	Overlook, OH	4.50	7.50
	Toledo, OH	7.50	12.50

Scott #	Description	Cacheted
	1963-80	
UX49	7¢ USA 8/30/63 New York, NY	1.75
UX50	4¢ Customs 2/22/64 DC	1.75
UX51	4¢ Social Security 9/26/64 DC	1.75
	Official Gov't. Printed Cachet	12.00
	Blue hand cancel and gov't. cachet	20.00
UX52	4¢ Coast Guard 8/4/65 Newburyport, MA	1.75
UX53	4¢ Census Bureau 10/21/65 Phila, PA	1.75
UX54	8¢ USA 12/4/67 DC	1.75
UX55	5¢ Lincoln 1/4/68 Hodgenville, KY	1.75
UX56	5¢ Women Marines 7/26/68 San Fran., CA	1.75
UX57	5¢ Weathervane 9/1/70 Fort Myer, VA	1.75
UX58	6¢ Paul Revere 5/15/71 Boston, MA	1.75
UX59	10¢ USA 6/10/71 New York, NY	1.75
UX60	6¢ America's Hospitals 9/16/71 NY, NY	1.75
UX61	6¢ US Frigate Constellation 6/29/72 Any City	1.75
UX62	6¢ Monument Valley 6/29/72 Any City	1.75
UX63	6¢ Gloucester, MA 6/29/72 Any City	1.75
UX64	6¢ John Hanson 9/1/72 Baltimore, MD	1.75
UX65	6¢ Liberty Centenary 9/14/73 DC	1.75
UX66	8¢ Samuel Adams 12/16/73 Boston, MA	1.75
UX67	12¢ Ship's Figurehead 1/4/74 Miami, FL	1.75
UX68	7¢ Charles Thomson 9/14/75 Bryn Mawr, PA	1.75
UX69	9¢ J. Witherspoon 11/10/75 Princeton, NJ	1.75
UX70	9¢ Caeser Rodney 7/1/76 Dover, DE	1.75
UX71	9¢ Galveston Court House 7/20/77 Galveston, TX	1.75
UX72	9¢ Nathan Hale 10/14/77 Coventry, CT	1.75
UX73	10¢ Music Hall 5/12/78 Cincinnati, OH	1.75
UX74	(10¢) John Hancock 5/19/78 Quincy, MA	1.75
UX75	10¢ John Hancock 6/20/78 Quincy, MA	1.75
UX76	14¢ Coast Guard Eagle 8/4/78 Seattle, WA	1.75
UX77	10¢ Molly Pitcher 9/8/78 Freehold, NJ	1.75
UX78	10¢ George R. Clark 2/23/79 Vincennes, IN	1.75
UX79	10¢ Casimir Pulaski 10/11/79 Savannah, GA	1.75
UX80	10¢ Olympics 9/17/79 Eugene, OR	1.75
UX81	10¢ Iolani Palace 10/1/79 Honolulu, HI	2.00
UX82	14¢ Olympic Skater 1/15/80 Atlanta, GA	1.75
UX83	10¢ Mormon Temple 4/5/80 Salt Lake City, UT	1.75
UX84	10¢ Count Rochambeau 7/11/80 Newport, RI	1.75
UX85	10¢ King's Mountain 10/7/80 King's Mountain, NC	1.75
UX86	19¢ Golden Hinde 11/21/80 San Rafael, CA	1.75
	1981-87	
UX87	10¢ Battle of Cowpens 1/17/81 Cowpens, SC	1.75
UX88	(12¢) "B" Eagle 3/15/81 Memphis, TN	1.75
UX89	12¢ Isaiah Thomas 5/5/81 Worcester, MA	1.75
UX90	12¢ Nathaniel Greene 9/8/81 Eutaw Springs, SC	1.75
UX91	12¢ Lewis & Clark 9/23/81 St. Louis, MO	1.75
UX92	(13¢) Robert Morris 10/11/81 Memphis, TN	1.75
UX93	13¢ Robert Morris 11/10/81 Phila., PA	1.75
UX94	13¢ Frances Marion 4/3/82 Marion, SC	1.75
UX95	13¢ LaSalle 4/7/82 New Orleans	1.75
UX96	13¢ Philadelphia Academy 6/18/82 Philadelphia, PA	1.75
UX97	13¢ St. Louis P.O. 10/14/82 St. Louis, MO	1.75
UX98	13¢ Oglethorpe 2/12/83 Savannah, GA	1.75
UX99	13¢ Old Washington P.O. 4/19/83 DC	1.75
UX100	13¢ Olympics - Yachting 8/5/83 Long Beach, CA	1.75
UX101	13¢ Maryland 3/25/84 St. Clemente Island, MD	1.75
UX102	13¢ Olympic Torch 4/30/84 Los Angeles, CA	1.75
UX103	13¢ Frederic Baraga 6/29/84 Marquette, MI	1.75
UX104	13¢ Rancho San Pedro 9/16/84 Compton, CA	1.75
UX105	(14¢) Charles Carroll 2/1/85 New Carrollton, MD	1.75
UX106	14¢ Charles Carroll 3/6/85 Annapolis, MD	1.75
UX107	25¢ Flying Cloud 2/27/85 Salem, MA	1.75
UX108	14¢ George Wythe 6/20/85 Williamsburg, VA	1.75
UX109	14¢ Settling of CT 4/18/86 Hartford, CT	1.75
UX110	14¢ Stamp Collecting 5/23/86 Chicago, IL	1.75
UX111	14¢ Frances Vigo 5/24/86 Vincennes, IN	1.75
UX112	14¢ Rhode Island 6/26/86 Providence, RI	1.75
UX113	14¢ Wisconsin Terr. 7/3/86 Mineral Point, WI	1.75
UX114	14¢ National Guard 12/12/86 Boston, MA	1.75
UX115	14¢ Steel Plow 5/22/87 Moines, IL	1.75
UX116	14¢ Constitution Convention 5/25/87 Philadelphia, PA	1.75
UX117	14¢ Flag 6/14/87 Baltimore, MD	1.75
UX118	14¢ Pride in America 9/22/87 Jackson, WY	1.75
UX119	14¢ Historic Preservation 9/28/87 Timberline, OR	1.75
	1988-91	
UX120	15¢ America the Beautiful 3/28/88 Buffalo, NY	1.75
UX121	15¢ Blair House 5/4/88 DC	1.75
UX122	28¢ Yorkshire 6/29/88 Mystic, CT	1.75
UX123	15¢ Iowa Territory 7/2/88 Burlington, IA	1.75
UX124	15¢ Northwest/Ohio Territory 7/15/88 Marietta, OH	1.75
UX125	15¢ Hearst Castle 9/20/88 San Simeon, CA	1.75
UX126	15¢ Federalist Papers 10/27/88 New York, NY	1.75
UX127	15¢ The Desert 1/13/89 Tucson, AZ	1.75
UX128	15¢ Healy Hall 1/23/89 DC	1.75
UX129	15¢ The Wetlands 3/17/89 Waycross, GA	1.75
UX130	15¢ Oklahoma Land Run 4/22/89 Guthrie, OK	1.75
UX131	21¢ The Mountains 5/5/89 Denver, CO	1.75
UX132	15¢ The Seashore 6/19/89 Cape Hatteras, NC	1.75
UX133	15¢ The Woodlands 8/26/89 Cherokee, NC	1.75
UX134	15¢ Hull House 9/16/89 Chicago, IL	1.75
UX135	15¢ Independence Hall 9/25/89 Philadelphia, PA	1.75
UX136	15¢ Baltimore Inner Harbor 10/7/89 Baltimore, MD	1.75
UX137	15¢ Manhattan Skyline 11/8/89 New York, NY	1.75

POSTAL CARD FIRST DAY COVERS

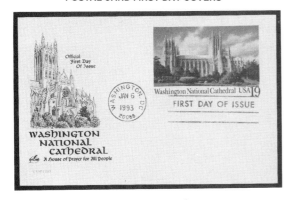

UX166

Scott #	Description	Cacheted
UX138	15¢ Capitol Dome 11/26/89 DC	1.75
UX139-42	15¢ Cityscapes sheet of 4 diff.views,rouletted 12/1/89 DC	7.00
UX139-42	Cityscapes, set of 4 different, rouletted	8.00
UX143	(15¢) White House, Picture PC (cost 50¢)	1.75
UX144	(15¢) Jefferson Mem. Pict. PC (cost 50¢) 12/2/89 DC	1.75
UX145	15¢ American Papermaking 3/13/90 New York, NY	1.75
UX146	15¢ Literacy 3/22/90 DC	1.75
UX147	(15¢)Geo. Bingham Pict.PC (cost 50¢)5/4/90 St.Louis,MO	1.75
UX148	15¢ Isaac Royall House 6/16/90 Medford, MA	1.75
UX150	15¢ Stanford University 9/30/90 Stanford, CA	1.75
UX151	15¢ DAR Mem., Continental/Constitution 10/11/91 DC	1.75
UX152	15¢ Chicago Orchestra Hall 10/19/91 Chicago, IL	1.75
UX153	19¢ Flag 1/24/91 DC	1.75
UX154	19¢ Carnegie Hall 4/1/91 New York, NY	1.75
UX155	19¢ "Old Red" Bldg., U.of Texas 6/14/91 Galveston, TX	1.75
UX156	19¢ Bill of Rights Bicent. 9/25/91 Notre Dame, IN	1.75
UX157	19¢ Notre Dame Admin. Bldg. 10/15/91 Notre Dame, IN	1.75
UX158	30¢ Niagara Falls 8/21/91 Niagara Falls, NY	1.75
UX159	19¢ Old Mill, Univ. of Vermont 10/29/91 Burlington, VT	1.75

1992-96

Scott #	Description	Cacheted
UX160	19¢ Wadsworth Atheneum 1/16/92 Hartford, CT	1.75
UX161	19¢ Cobb Hall, Univ. of Chicago 1/23/92 Chicago, IL	1.75
UX162	19¢ Waller Hall 2/1/92 Salem, OR	1.75
UX163	19¢ America's Cup 5/6/92 San Diego, CA	1.75
UX164	19¢ Columbia River Gorge 5/9/92 Stevenson, WA	1.75
UX165	19¢ Great Hall, Ellis Island 5/11/92 Ellis Island, NY	1.75
UX166	19¢ National Cathedral 1/6/93 DC	1.75
UX167	19¢ Wren Building 2/8/93 Williamsville, VA	1.75
UX168	19¢ Holocaust Memorial 3/23/93 DC	2.25
UX169	19¢ Ft. Recovery 6/13/93 Fort Recovery, OH	1.75
UX170	19¢ Playmaker's Theater 9/14/93 Chapel Hill, NC	1.75
UX171	19¢ O'Kane Hall 9/17/93 Worcester, MA	1.75
UX172	19¢ Beecher Hall 10/9/93 Jacksonville, IL	1.75
UX173	19¢ Massachusetts Hall 10/14/93 Brunswick, ME	1.75
UX174	19¢ Lincoln Home 2/12/94 Springfield, IL	1.75
UX175	19¢ Myers Hall 3/11/94 Springfield, OH	1.75
UX176	19¢ Canyon de Chelly 8/11/94 Canyon de Chelly, AZ	1.75
UX177	19¢ St. Louis Union Station 9/1/94 St. Louis, MO	1.75
UX178-97	19¢ Legends of the West, set of 20 10/18/94 Tucson, AZ Lawton, OK or Laramie, WY	35.00
UX198	20¢ Red Barn 1/3/95 Williamsburg, PA	1.75
UX199	(20¢) "G" Old Glory, 12/13/94 cancel, released 1/12/95	1.75
UX200-219	20¢ Civil War Set of 20 6/29/95 Gettysburg, PA	35.00
UX220	20¢ Clipper Ship 9/23/95 Hunt Valley, MD	1.75
UX221-240	20¢ Comic Strips Set of 20 10/1/95 Boca Raton, FL	35.00
UX241	20¢ Winter Farm Scene 2/23/96 Watertown, NY	1.75
UX242-261	20¢ Olympics, Set of 20 5/2/96 DC	35.00
UX262	20¢ McDowell Hall, Hist.Pres.Series 6/1/96, Anapolis, Md	1.75
UX263	20¢ Alexander Hall, Hist.Pres.Series 9/20/96,Princeton, NJ	1.75
UX264-278	20¢ Endangered Species, Set of 15, 10/2/96, San Diego, Ca.	35.00
UX279	20¢ Love Swan Stamp 2/4/97	1.75
....	20¢ City College of NY, Hist.Pres.Series, NY,NY 5/7/97	1.75
....	20¢ Pacific '97, Golden Gate in Daylight 6/2/97 S.F.,Ca.	1.75
....	40¢ Pacific '97, Golden Gate at Sunset 6/2/97 S. F., Ca.	1.75
....	20¢ Fort McHenry, Hist. Pres. Series 9/97	1.75

AIRMAIL POST CARDS
1949-95

Scott #	Description	Cacheted
UXC1	4¢ Eagle 1/10/49 DC, round "O" in January 10	2.00
	Oval "O" in January 10	5.00
UXC2	5¢ Eagle 7/31/58 Wichita, KS	2.00
UXC3	5¢ Eagle w/border 6/18/60 Minneapolis, MN	2.00
	"Thin dividing line" at top	5.00
UXC4	6¢ Bald Eagle 2/15/63 Maitland, FL	2.00
UXC5	11¢ Visit the USA 5/27/66 DC	1.75
UXC6	6¢ Virgin Islands 3/31/67 Charlotte Amalie, VI	1.75
UXC7	6¢ Boy Scouts 8/4/67 Farragut State Park, ID	1.75
UXC8	13¢ Visit the USA 9/8/67 Detroit, MI	1.75
UXC9	8¢ Eagle 3/1/68 New York, NY	1.75
UXC9a	8¢ Eagle, tagged 3/19/69 DC	15.00
UXC10	9¢ Eagle 5/15/71 Kitty Hawk, NC	1.75
UXC11	15¢ Visit the USA 6/10/71 New York, NY	1.75

AIRMAIL POST CARDS (continued)

Scott #	Description	Cacheted
UXC12	9¢ Grand Canyon 6/29/72 any city	1.75
UXC13	15¢ Niagara Falls 6/29/72 any city	1.75
UXC13a	Address side blank ...... (uncacheted)	600.00
UXC14	11¢ Modern Eagle 1/4/74 State College, PA	1.75
UXC15	18¢ Eagle Weathervane 1/4/74 Miami, FL	1.75
UXC16	21¢ Angel Weathervane 12/17/75 Kitty Hawk, NC	1.75
UXC17	21¢ Jenny 9/16/78 San Diego, CA	1.75
UXC18	21¢ Olympic-Gymnast 12/1/79 Fort Worth, TX	1.75
UXC19	28¢ First Transpacific Flight 1/2/81 Wenatchee, WA	1.75
UXC20	28¢ Soaring 3/5/82 Houston, TX	1.75
UXC21	28¢ Olympic-Speedskating 12/29/83 Milwaukee, WI	1.75
UXC22	33¢ China Clipper 2/15/85 San Fran., CA	1.75
UXC23	33¢ AMERIPEX '86 2/1/86 Chicago, IL	1.75
UXC24	36¢ DC-3 5/14/88 San Diego, CA	2.00
UXC25	40¢ Yankee Clipper 6/28/91	2.00
UXC26	50¢ Eagle 8/24/95 St. Louis, MO	2.25

1892-1956 POSTAL REPLY CARDS

Scott #	Description	Uncacheted	Cacheted
UY1	1¢ + 1¢ U.S. Grant 10/25/1892 any city	350.00	...
UY12	3¢ + 3¢ McKinley 2/1/26 any city	250.00	...
UY13	2¢ + 2¢ Washington 12/29/51 DC	...	1.75
UY14	2¢ on 1¢ + 2¢ on 1¢ G. Wash. 1/1/52 any city	50.00	75.00
UY16	4¢ + 4¢ Liberty 11/16/56 New York, NY	...	1.75
UY16a	Message card printed on both halves	75.00	100.00
UY16b	Reply card printed on both halves	50.00	75.00

1958-75

Scott #	Description		Cacheted
UY17	3¢ + 3¢ Liberty 7/31/58 Boise, ID		1.75
UY18	4¢ + 4¢ Lincoln 11/19/62 Springfield, IL		1.75
UY18a	4¢ + 4¢ Lincoln, Tagged 3/7/67 Dayton, OH		500.00
UY19	7¢ + 7¢ USA 8/30/63 New York, NY		1.75
UY20	8¢ + 8¢ USA 12/4/67 DC		1.75
UY21	5¢ + 5¢ Lincoln 1/4/68 Hodgenville, KY		1.75
UY22	6¢ + 6¢ Paul Revere 5/15/71 Boston, MA		1.75
UY23	6¢ + 6¢ John Hanson 9/1/72 Baltimore, MD		1.75
UY24	8¢ + 8¢ Samuel Adams 12/16/73 Boston, MA		1.75
UY25	7¢ + 7¢ Charles Thomson 9/14/75 Bryn Mawr, PA		1.75
UY26	9¢ + 9¢ John Witherspoon 11/10/75 Princeton, NJ		1.75

POSTAL CARD FIRST DAY COVERS
1976-95

Scott #	Description	Cacheted
UY27	9¢ + 9¢ Caeser Rodney 7/1/76 Dover, DE	1.75
UY28	9¢ + 9¢ Nathan Hale 10/14/77 Coventry, CT	1.75
UY29	(10¢ + 10¢) John Hancock 5/19/78 Quincy, MA	2.50
UY30	10¢ + 10¢ John Hancock 6/20/78 Quincy, MA	1.75
UY31	(12¢ + 12¢) "B" Eagle 3/15/81 Memphis, TN	1.75
UY32	12¢ + 12¢ Isaiah Thomas 5/5/81 Worcester, MA	1.75
UY32a	"Small die"	5.00
UY33	(13¢ + 13¢) Robert Morris 10/11/81 Memphis, TN	1.75
UY34	13¢ + 13¢ Robert Morris 11/10/81 Philadelphia, PA	1.75
UY35	(14¢ + 14¢) Charles Carroll 2/1/85 New Carrollton, MD	1.75
UY36	14¢ + 14¢ Charles Carroll 3/6/85 Annapolis, MD	1.75
UY37	14¢ + 14¢ George Wythe 6/20/85 Williamsburg, PA	1.75
UY38	14¢ + 14¢ American Flag 9/1/87 Baltimore, MD	1.75
UY39	15¢ + 15¢ America the Beautiful 7/11/88 Buffalo, NY	1.75
UY40	19¢ + 19¢ American Flag 3/27/91 DC	2.00
UY41	20¢+20¢ Red Baron 1/3/95 Williamsburg, PA	2.25

OFFICIAL POSTAL CARDS
1983-95

Scott #	Description	Cacheted
UZ2	13¢ Eagle 1/12/83 DC	1.75
UZ3	14¢ Eagle 2/26/85 DC	1.75
UZ4	15¢ Eagle (4 colors) 6/10/88 New York, NY	1.75
UZ5	19¢ Eagle 5/24/91 Seattle, WA	1.75
UZ6	20¢ Eagle 5/9/95 DC	1.75

"POSTAL BUDDY" CARDS

PB1	15¢ 7/5/90 Merrifield, VA	2.50
PB2	19¢ 2/3/91 Any city	...
PB3	19¢ Stylized Flag 11/13/92 Any city	27.50

CHRISTMAS SEAL FIRST DAY COVERS

Beginning in 1936, Santa Claus, Indiana has been used as the First Day City of U.S. National Christmas Seals. In 1936 the Postmaster would not allow the seal to be tied to the front of the cover and seals for that year are usually found on the back. Since 1937, all seals were allowed to be tied on the front of the FDC's.

All prices are for cacheted FDC's.

YEAR	PRICE	YEAR	PRICE	YEAR		
1936 (500 processed)	55.00	1956	10.00	1976	6.00	
1937	35.00	1957	10.00	1977	6.00	
1938	35.00	1958	10.00	1978	10.00	
1939	35.00	1959	10.00	1979	6.00	
1940	35.00	1960	20.00	1980	5.00	
1941	30.00	1961	10.00	1981	5.00	
1942	40.00	1962	10.00	1982	5.00	
1943	25.00	1963	10.00	1983	10.00	
1944	30.00	1964	40.00	1984	5.00	
1945	12.00	1965	10.00	1985	5.00	
1946	12.00	1966	10.00	1986	5.00	
1947	12.00	1967	20.00	1987	5.00	
1948	20.00	1968	10.00	YEAR	PERF	IMPERF
1949	12.00	1969	10.00	1988	7.50	30.00
1950	12.00	1970	6.00	1989	7.50	30.00
1951	15.00	1971	6.00	1990	5.00	20.00
1952	12.00	1972	6.00	1991	5.00	20.00
1953	10.00	1973	6.00	1992	7.50	35.00
1954	10.00	1974	6.00	1993	5.00	20.00
1955	10.00	1975	7.00	1994	5.00	20.00
				1995	5.00	20.00

WORLD WAR II PATRIOTIC EVENT COVERS

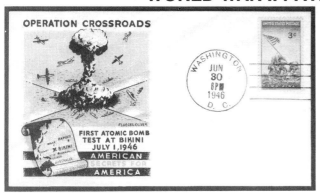

OPERATION CROSSROADS

FIRST ATOMIC BOMB
TEST AT BIKINI
JULY 1, 1946
AMERICAN
SECRETS FOR
AMERICA

6/30/46

The listing below features the dates of significant patriotic events of World War II. The values listed are for standard size covers bearing related, printed cachets, and cancelled on the appropriate date.

Cachets produced by Minkus and others, which feature general patriotic themes such as "Win the War" are valued at 75¢ unused and $2.00 used.

Covers with Naval cancels, when available, usually sell for twice the listed prices.

From 1943 to date, prices are for unaddressed covers.

WORLD WAR II EVENT	CACHETED COVER
Pearl Harbor 12/7/41	100.00
U.S. Declares War on Japan 12/8/41	75.00
Germany and Italy Declare War on U.S. 12/11/41	75.00
U.S. Declares War on Germany and Italy 12/11/41	75.00
Churchill Arrives at the White House 12/22/41	60.00
Manila and Cavite Fall 1/2/42	60.00
Roosevelt's Diamond Jubilee Birthday 1/30/42	60.00
Singapore Surrenders 2/15/42	60.00
Japan Takes Java 3/10/42	60.00
Marshall Arrives in London 4/8/42	60.00
Dedication of MacArthur Post Office 4/15/42	60.00
Doolittle Air Raid on Tokyo 4/18/42	60.00
Fort Mills Corregidor Island Surrenders 5/6/42	60.00
Madagascar Occupied by U.S. 5/9/42	60.00
Mexico at War with Axis 5/23/42	60.00
Bombing of Cologne 6/6/42	60.00
Japan Bombs Dutch Harbor, AK 6/3/42	60.00
Six German Spies Sentenced to Death 8/7/42	60.00
Brazil at War 8/22/42	60.00
Battle of El Alamein 10/23/42	70.00
Operation Torch (Invasion of North Africa) 11/8/42	50.00
Gas Rationing in U.S. 12/1/42	50.00
The Casablanca Conference 1/14/43	50.00
The Casablanca Conference (You must remember this!) 1/22/43	40.00
Point Rationing 3/1/43	50.00
Battle of the Bismarck Sea 3/13/43	40.00
U.S. Planes Bomb Naples 4/5/43	50.00
Bizerte & Tunis Occupied 5/8/43	40.00
Invasion of Attu 5/11/43	40.00
Siciliy Invaded 7/14/43	35.00
Italy Invaded 9/3/43	40.00
Italy Surrenders 9/8/43	40.00
The Quebec Conference 8/14/43	40.00
Italy Surrenders 9/8/43	35.00
Mussolini Escapes 9/18/43	35.00
U.S. Drives Germans out of Naples 10/2/43	35.00
Italy Declares War on Germany 10/13/43	35.00
Hull, Eden, Stalin Conference 10/25/43	35.00
U.S. Government takes over Coal Mines 11/3/43	35.00
The Cairo Meeting 11/25/43	40.00
The Teheran Meeting 11/28/43	40.00
Roosevelt, Churchill, Kai-Shek at Cairo 12/2/43	40.00
FDR, Stalin, Churchill Agree on 3 fronts 12/4/43	40.00
Soviets Reach Polish Border 1/4/44	35.00
Marshalls Invaded 2/4/44	35.00
U.S. Captures Cassino 3/15/44	35.00
Invasion of Dutch New Guinea 4/24/44	35.00
Rome Falls 6/4/44	35.00
D-Day Single Face Eisenhower 6/6/44	100.00
D-Day: Invasion of Normandy 6/6/44	35.00
B29's Bomb Japan 6/15/44	35.00
Cherbourg Surrenders 6/7/44	40.00
Paris Revolts 6/23/44	35.00
Caen Falls to Allies 7/10/44	35.00
Marines Invade Guam 7/21/44	35.00
Yanks Enter Brest, etc. 8/7/44	35.00
U.S. Bombs Phillipines 8/10/44	35.00
Invasion of Southern France 8/16/44	25.00
Liberation of Paris 8/23/44	30.00
Florence Falls to Allies 8/23/44	30.00
Liberation of Brussels 9/4/44	25.00
We Invade Holland, Finland Quits 9/5/44	30.00
Soviets Invade Yugoslavia 9/6/44	30.00
Russians Enter Bulgaria 9/9/44	30.00

WORLD WAR II EVENT	CACHETED COVER
Liberation of Luxembourg 9/10/44	25.00
Albania Invaded 9/27/44	35.00
Phillipines, We Will Be Back 9/27/44	25.00
Greece Invaded 10/5/44	35.00
Liberation of Athens 10/14/44	25.00
Liberation of Belgrade 10/16/44	25.00
Russia Invades Czechoslovakia 10/19/44	30.00
Invasion of the Philippines 10/20/44	25.00
The Pied Piper of Leyte-Philippine Invasion 10/21/44	35.00
Invasion of Norway 10/25/44	25.00
Liberation of Tirana 11/18/44	25.00
100,000 Yanks Land on Luzon 1/10/45	25.00
Liberation of Warsaw 1/17/45	30.00
Russians Drive to Oder River 2/2/45	25.00
Liberation of Manila 2/4/45	25.00
Yalta Conference 2/12/45	25.00
Liberation of Budapest 2/13/45	25.00
Corregidor is Ours 2/17/45	25.00
Turkey Wars Germany and Japan 2/23/45	25.00
Yanks Enter Cologne 3/5/45	25.00
Cologne is Taken 3/6/45	20.00
Historical Rhine Crossing 3/8/45	20.00
Bombing of Tokyo 3/10/45	25.00
Russia Crosses Oder River 3/13/45	25.00
Capture of Iwo Jima 3/14/45	20.00
Battle of the Inland Sea 3/20/45	20.00
Crossing of the Rhine 3/24/45	20.00
Danzig Invaded 3/27/45	25.00
Okinawa Invaded 4/1/45	20.00
Japanese Cabinet Resigns 4/7/45	20.00
Liberation of Vienna 4/10/45	20.00
We Invade Bremen, etc. 4/10/45	25.00
FDR Dies - Truman becomes President 4/12/45	50.00
Liberation of Vienna 4/13/45	25.00
Patton Invades Czechoslovakia 4/18/45	25.00
Berlin Invaded 4/21/45	25.00
Berlin Encircled 4/25/45	20.00
"GI Joe" and "Ivan" Meet at Torgau-Germany 4/26/45	20.00
Mussolini Executed 4/28/45	35.00
Hitler Dead 5/1/45	35.00
Liberation of Italy 5/2/45	20.00
Berlin Falls 5/2/45	25.00
Liberation of Rangoon 5/3/45	20.00
5th and 7th Armies Meet at Brenner Pass 5/4/45	20.00
Liberation of Copenhagen 5/5/45	20.00
Liberation of Amsterdam 5/5/45	25.00
Liberation of Oslo 5/8/45	25.00
Liberation of Prague 5/8/45	25.00
V-E Day 5/8/45	35.00
Atomic Bomb Test 5/16/45	25.00
Invasion of Borneo 6/11/45	25.00
Eisenhower Welcomed Home 6/18/45	20.00
Okinawa Captured 6/21/45	25.00
United Nations Conference 6/25/45	25.00
American Flag Raised over Berlin 7/4/45	25.00
Big Three Meet at Potsdam 8/1/45	25.00
Atomic Bomb Dropped on Hiroshima 8/6/45	65.00
Russia Declares War on Japan 8/8/45	25.00
Japan Capitulates 8/14/45	25.00
Japan Signs Peace Treaty 9/1/45	50.00
Liberation of China 9/2/45	35.00
V-J Day 9/2/45	35.00
Liberation of Korea 9/2/45	35.00
Flag Raising over Tokyo - Gen. MacArthur Takes Over 9/8/45	25.00
Gen. Wainwright Rescued from the Japanese 9/10/45	25.00
Nimitz Post Office 9/10/45	25.00
Marines Land in Japan 9/23/45	40.00
Nimitz Day-Washington 10/5/45	25.00
War Crimes Commission 10/18/45	25.00
Premier Laval Executed as Traitor 10/15/45	25.00
Fleet Reviewed by President Truman 10/27/45	35.00
Trygue Lie Elected 1/21/46	25.00
2nd Anniversary of D-Day 6/6/46	25.00
Operation Crossroads 6/30/46	100.00
Bikini Atomic Bomb Test 7/1/46	125.00
Philippine Republic Independence 7/3/46	25.00
Atomic Age 7/10/46	25.00
Victory Day 8/14/46	25.00
Opening of UN Post Office at Lake Success 9/23/46	25.00
Goering Commits Suicide 10/16/46	40.00
Opening Day of UN in Flushing, NY 10/23/46	25.00
Marshall is Secretary of State 1/21/47	25.00
Moscow Peace Conference 3/10/47	25.00

JOHN F. KENNEDY

**Prices are for covers with PRINTED CACHETS and Wash, D.C. cancels.
Covers with cancels from other cities, except as noted, sell for somewhat less.**

1929	Hoover 3/4/29 **(Uncacheted)**	150.00
1933	Roosevelt 3/4/33	50.00
1937	Roosevelt 1/20/37	225.00
1941	Roosevelt 1/20/41	225.00
1945	Roosevelt 1/20/45	250.00
1945	Truman 4/12/45	250.00
1949	Truman 1/20/49	60.00
1953	Eisenhower 1/20/53	16.00
1957	Eisenhower 1/21/57	12.00
1961	Kennedy 1/20/61	20.00
1963	Johnson 11/22/63 Dayton, OH or New York, NY	90.00

DWIGHT D. EISENHOWER

1965	Johnson 1/20/65	8.00
1969	Nixon 1/20/69	10.00
1973	Nixon 1/20/73	8.00
1974	Ford 8/9/74	6.00
1977	Carter 1/20/77	4.00
1981	Reagan 1/20/81	3.00
1985	Reagan 1/20/85	3.00
1989	Bush 1/20/89	3.00
1993	Clinton 1/20/93	3.00
1997	Clinton 1/20/97	3.00

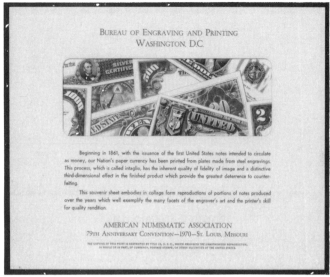

B 7

SCCS#s are used with the express permission of the Souvenir Card Collectors Society. Anyone interested in additional information should write to: **Souvenir Card Collectors Society c/o Dana Marr, P.O. Box 4155, Tulsa, OK 74159-0155.**

Cancelled prices are for cards with First Day of Show or Issue postmarks applied by the USPS or BEP Visitors Center, unless designated **(SC)** or **(F)**.

(SC) Show cancel other than First Day

(F) First Day postmark applied by foreign post office.

SCCS No.	Description	Printer	FD Show/ Issue	Mint Card	Cancelled Card
	1939-1969				
FPS 1939Aa	Truck with Gum	USPS	...	65.00	...
FPS 1939Ab	Truck without Gum	USPS	...	10.00	...
F 1945A	Nat'l. Phil. Museum '54	USPS	3/13/54	1875.00	...
PS 1	Barcelona '60	USPS	3/26/60	450.00	425.00(SC)
F 1966A	SIPEX Scenes '66	BEP	5/21/66	150.00	185.00
SO 1	SIPEX Miner	USBNC	5/21/66	10.00	95.00(SC)
PS 2	EFIMEX '68	USPS	11/1/68	3.00	10.00
B 1	SANDIPEX	BEP	7/16/69	60.00	125.00
B 2	ANA '69	BEP	8/12/69	75.00	...
B 3	Fresno	BEP	10/2/69	500.00	...
B 4	ASDA '69	BEP	11/21/69	22.50	100.00
	1970				
B 5	INTERPEX '70	BEP	3/13/70	55.00	150.00
B 6	COMPEX '70	BEP	5/29/70	12.50	150.00
B 7	ANA 1970	BEP	8/18/70	95.00	...
PS 3	PHILYMPIA	USPS	9/18/70	2.25	12.00(SC)
B 8	HAPEX	BEP	11/5/70	13.00	...
	1971				
B 9	INTERPEX '71	BEP	3/12/71	1.75	50.00
B 10	WESTPEX	BEP	4/23/71	1.75	130.00
B 11	NAPEX '71	BEP	5/12/71	2.25	125.00
B 12	ANA '71	BEP	8/10/71	4.50	...
B 13	TEXANEX	BEP	8/26/71	2.25	250.00
PS 4	EXFILIMA	USPS	11/6/71	1.25	50.00
B 14	ASDA '71	BEP	11/19/71	3.50	37.50
B 15	ANPHILEX	BEP	11/26/71	1.25	...
	1972				
B 16	INTERPEX '72	BEP	3/17/72	1.25	12.50
B 17	NOPEX	BEP	4/6/72	1.50	150.00
PS 5	BELGICA	USPS	6/24/72	1.25	30.00(SC)
B 18	ANA '72	BEP	8/15/72	4.50	100.00
PS 6	Olympia Phil. Munchen	USPS	8/18/72	1.25	32.50
PS 7	EXFILBRA	USPS	8/26/72	1.25	75.00
PS 8	Postal Forum	USPS	8/28/72	1.25	25.00
B 19	SEPAD '72	BEP	10/20/72	1.25	37.50
B 20	ASDA '72	BEP	11/17/72	1.25	12.50
B 21	Stamp Expo '72	BEP	11/24/72	1.50	35.00
	1973				
B 22	INTERPEX '73	BEP	3/9/73	1.50	13.00
PS 9	Postal People (11x14") (with minor creases)	USPS	...	110.00	250.00
PS10	IBRA '73	USPS	5/11/73	1.75	16.00
F 1973B	Washington Statues (4)	PPU	5/21/73	12.00	70.00
B 23	COMPEX '73	BEP	5/25/73	3.50	50.00
PS 11	APEX	USPS	7/4/73	2.00	32.50
B 24	ANA '73	BEP	8/23/73	7.00	30.00
PS 12	POLSKA	USPS	8/19/73	1.75	150.00
B 25	NAPEX '73	BEP	9/14/73	1.75	50.00
B 26	ASDA '73	BEP	11/16/73	1.25	10.00
B 27	Stamp Expo '73	BEP	12/7/73	2.00	20.00

SCCS No.	Description	Printer	FD Show/ Issue	Mint Card	Cancelled Card
	1974				
PS 13	Hobby Show Chicago	USPS	2/3/74	2.25	20.00
B 28	MILCOPEX '74	BEP	3/8/74	2.00	12.50
PS 14	INTERNABA '74	USPS	6/6/74	3.50	17.50
B 29	ANA '74	BEP	8/13/74	9.00	40.00
PS 15	STOCKHOLMIA '74	USPS	9/21/74	3.25	18.00/22.50/F
PS 16	EXFILMEX '74	USPS	10/26/74	3.25	37.50(SC)
	1975				
F 1975Ba	$3 Lewiston Falls Banknote	ABNC	5/-/75	50.00	...
F 1975Bb	Declar. of Indep./Portraits	ABNC	5/-/75	29.00	...
PS 17	ESPANA '75	USPS	4/4/75	1.50	47.50/ 75.00/F
B 30	NAPEX '75	BEP	5/9/75	6.75	22.50
PS 18	ARPHILA '75	USPS	6/6/75	2.75	35.00
B 31	IWY (with folder)	BEP	5/2/75	22.50	250.00
B 32	ANA '75	BEP	8/19/75	9.00	50.00
B 33	ASDA '75 (G. Washington)	BEP	11/21/75	27.50	60.00
	1976				
PS 19	WERABA '76	USPS	4/1/76	3.00	5.50
B 34	INTERPHIL '76 (Jefferson)	BEP	5/29/76	6.50	18.50
B 35	Card from INTERPHIL Prog.	BEP	5/29/76	7.50	75.00
SO 2	INTERPHIL "America"	ABNC	5/29/76	60.00	100.00
SO 3	INTERPHIL "Lincoln"	ABNC	5/29/76	75.00	100.00
SO 4	INTERPHIL Banquet Card	ABNC	6/5/76	150.00	300.00
SO 5	INTERPHIL Banquet Menu	ABNC	6/5/76	275.00	400.00
B 36	Science BEP	BEP	5/30/76	6.50	150.00
PS 20	Science USPS	USPS	5/30/76	3.00	6.00
B 37	Stamp Expo '76	BEP	6/11/76	6.50	60.00
PS 21	Colorado Statehood	USPS	8/1/76	3.00	5.00
PS 22	HAFNIA '76	USPS	8/20/76	3.00	5.00
B 38	ANA '76	BEP	8/24/76	6.50	37.50
PS 23	ITALIA '76	USPS	10/14/76	3.00	5.00 40.00/F
PS 24	NORDPOSTA '76	USPS	10/30/76	3.00	4.00
	1977				
B 39	MILCOPEX '77	BEP	3/4/77	3.00	20.00
B 40	ROMPEX '77	BEP	5/20/77	2.25	11.00
PS 25	AMPHILEX '77	USPS	5/26/77	3.00	5.00
B 41	ANA '77	BEP	8/23/77	4.50	15.00
PS 26	San Marino '77	USPS	8/28/77	3.00	5.00
B 42	PURIPEX '77	BEP	9/2/77	2.25	8.50
B 43	ASDA '77	BEP	11/16/77	3.00	8.00
	1978-79				
PS 27	ROCPEX '78	USPS	3/20/78	3.25	100.00
PS 28	NAPOSTA '78	USPS	5/20/78	3.00	5.50/ 22.50/F
B 44	Money Show '78	BEP	6/2/78	4.50	12.00
B 45	CENJEX '78	BEP	6/23/78	3.00	8.50
SO 9	Int'l Paper Money Show	ABNC	6/15/79	40.00	50.00
SO 10	ANA '79	ABNC	7/28/79	10.00	40.00
PS 29	BRASILIANA '79	USPS	9/15/79	4.50	7.00
PS 30	JAPEX '79	USPS	11/2/79	4.50	7.00

B 37

Department of the Treasury
BUREAU OF ENGRAVING AND PRINTING
Washington, D.C.

This engraving, printed from a plate made from the original master die, is a replica of the face of the $10 United States Note, Series 1901. Known as the "Buffalo Bill," with portraits of Meriwether Lewis and William Clark, and the bison in the central design, it was undoubtedly issued to stimulate interest in the Lewis and Clark Centennial Exposition held in Portland, Oregon, in 1905.

The portraits of Lewis and Clark were engraved by G. F. C. Smillie. Marcus W. Baldwin executed the engraving of the bison which was designed by Ostrander Smith based on a wash drawing by Charles R. Knight.

INTERNATIONAL PAPER MONEY SHOW
MEMPHIS COIN CLUB—MEMPHIS, TENNESSEE—JUNE 6-8, 1980

SO 11

SCCS No.	Description	Printer	FD Show/ Issue	Mint Card	Cancelled Card
	1980				
B 46	ANA '80 Albuquerque	BEP	2/15/80	20.00	50.00
PS 31	London '80	USPS	5/6/80	3.50	75.00
B 47	Money Show '80	BEP	6/6/80	13.50	30.00
SO 11	Intil. Paper Money Show	ABNC	6/6/80	30.00	40.00
PS 32	NORWEX '80	USPS	6/13/80	4.00	5.00
B 48	NAPEX '80	BEP	7/4/80	9.00	37.50
SO 12	ANA '80	ABNC	8/13/80	10.00	55.00
SO 13	Bank Note Reporter	ABNC	-/-/80	12.00	500.00
B 49	Visitor Center	BEP	9/8/80	6.00	15.00
B 50	Stamp Festival '80	BEP	9/25/80	12.50	35.00
PS 33	ESSEN '80	USPS	11/15/80	4.00	5.00
	1981				
SO 14	ANA Winter '81	ABNC	2/5/81	15.00	100.00
B 51	Stamp Expo '81	BEP	3/20/81	15.00	47.50
B 52	Visitor Center '81	BEP	4/22/81	7.50	15.00
F 1981B	Embarkation/Pilgrims	PPU	5/17/81	45.00	...
PS 34	WIPA '81	USPS	5/22/81	4.00	5.00
B 53	Money Show '81	BEP	6/19/81	14.50	27.50
SO 15	Int'l Paper Money Show	ABNC	6/19/81	20.00	24.00
SO 16	INTERPAM	ABNC	6/15/81	9.50	100.00
B 54	ANA '81	BEP	7/27/81	12.50	22.50
SO 17	ANA '81	ABNC	7/28/81	16.00	28.00
SO 18	ANA Building Fund	ABNC	7/28/81	22.50	175.00
PS 35	Stamp Coll. Month '81	USPS	10/1/81	3.00	5.00
PS 36	PHILATOKYO '81	USPS	10/9/81	3.00	5.00
PS 37	NORDPOSTA '81	USPS	11/7/81	3.00	5.00
SO 20	Chester CC/Green	ABNC	12/10/81	10.00	95.00
SO 21	Chester CC/Brown	ABNC	12/10/81	10.00	95.00
	1982				
SO 22	FUN '82	ABNC	1/6/82	12.50	300.00
SO 23	ANA/Winter '82	ABNC	2/18/82	11.00	28.00
B 55	MILCOPEX '82	BEP	3/5/82	12.50	25.00
PS 38	CANADA '82	USPS	5/20/82	4.00	5.00
PS 39	PHILEXFRANCE '82	USPS	6/11/82	4.00	5.00
B 56	Money Show '82	BEP	6/18/82	12.00	25.00
SO 24	Int'l Paper Money Show	ABNC	6/18/82	19.50	25.00
F 1982A	NAPEX '82	PPU	7/2/82	14.00	28.00
SO 25	ANA '82	ABNC	8/17/82	13.00	25.00
B 57	ANA '82	BEP	8/17/82	12.50	22.50
F 1982B	BALPEX	PPU	9/4/82	17.50	40.00
PS 40	Stamp Coll. Month '82	USPS	10/1/82	4.00	5.00
B 58	ESPAMER '82	BEP	10/12/82	28.50	85.00
PS 41	ESPAMER '82 USPS	USPS	10/12/82	4.00	5.00
	1983				
B 59	FUN '83	BEP	1/5/83	20.00	42.50
SO 32	ANA Winter	ABNC	1/5/83	14.00	19.50
PS 42	US-Sweden	USPS	3/24/83	3.75	5.00
PS 43	German Settlers	USPS	4/29/83	3.75	5.00
F 1983A	North Berwick Bank	PPU	...	15.00	40.00
PS 44	TEMBAL '83	USPS	5/21/83	3.75	5.00
F 1983C	NAPEX	PPU	6/10/83	15.00	30.00
B 60	TEXANEX-TOPEX	BEP	6/17/83	19.50	30.00
SO 33	Int'l Paper Money Show	ABNC	6/17/83	16.50	20.00
PS 45	BRASILIANA '83	USPS	7/29/83	3.75	5.00
PS 46	BANGKOK '83	USPS	8/4/83	3.75	5.00
B 61	ANA '83	BEP	8/16/83	16.50	25.00
SO 34	ANA '83	ABNC	8/16/83	17.00	25.00
PS 47	Memento '83	USPS	8/19/83	3.00	4.50

SCCS No.	Description	Printer	FD Show/ Issue	Mint Card	Cancelled Card
	1983 (continued)				
F 1983F	BALPEX	PPU	9/3/83	12.00	20.00
PS 48	Stamp Collecting '83	USPS	10/4/83	4.75	6.00
B 62	Philatelic Show, Boston '83	BEP	10/21/83	13.50	35.00
B 63	ASDA '83	BEP	11/17/83	15.00	22.50
	1984				
B 64	FUN '84	BEP	1/4/84	19.50	25.00
B 65	Eagle/Brown	BEP	1/4/84	300.00	425.00
SO 35	ANA Winter	ABNC	2/23/84	22.50	35.00
B 66	ESPANA '84	BEP	4/27/84	14.50	30.00
PS 49	ESPANA '84 USPS	USPS	4/27/84	3.75	6.00
B 67	Stamp Expo '84	BEP	4/27/84	20.00	27.50
B 68	COMPEX '84	BEP	5/25/84	20.00	35.00
SO 37	Int'l Paper Money Show	ABNC	6/15/84	13.50	25.00
B 69	Money Show '84, Memphis	BEP	6/15/84	52.50	55.00
B 70	Eagle/Blue	BEP	6/15/84	350.00	450.00
PS 50	Hamburg '84	USPS	6/19/84	3.75	6.00
F 1984A	NAPEX	PPU	6/24/84	11.50	25.00
PS 51	US-Canada Seaway	USPS	6/26/84	3.75	5.00
SO 38	Statue of Liberty	ABNC	7/4/84	6.50	18.00
B 71	ANA '84	BEP	7/28/84	12.50	20.00
B 72	Eagle/Green	BEP	7/28/84	350.00	425.00
SO 39	ANA '84	ABNC	7/28/84	30.00	40.00
PS 52	AUSIPEX '84	USPS	9/21/84	3.75	5.00
PS 53	Stamp Collecting '84	USPS	10/1/84	3.25	5.00
PS 54	PHILAKOREA '84	USPS	10/22/84	3.75	5.00
B 73	ASDA '84	BEP	11/15/84	14.50	35.00
B 74	Statue of Liberty/Green	BEP	11/15/84	140.00	200.00
	1985				
SO 40	FUN '85	ABNC	1/3/85	10.00	50.00
B 75	Long Beach '85	BEP	1/31/85	13.50	20.00
SO 41	ANA Winter	ABNC	2/21/85	34.00	45.00
PS 55	Memento '85	USPS	2/26/85	3.75	5.00
B 76	MILCOPEX '85	BEP	3/1/85	12.50	30.00
PS 56	OLYMPHILEX	USPS	3/18/85	3.75	5.50
SO 42	Nat'l Assn./Tobacco Distr	ABNC	3/27/85	10.00	...
B 77	Int'l Coin Club, El Paso	BEP	4/19/85	15.00	30.00
B 78	Statue of Liberty/Maroon	BEP	4/19/85	150.00	180.00
F 1985D	Eagle/81st Convention	PPU	5/12/85	35.00	...
PS 57	ISRAPHIL	USPS	5/14/85	3.75	5.50
B 79	Pacific NW Num Assn	BEP	5/17/85	17.50	25.00
B 80	NAPEX '85	BEP	6/7/85	13.50	27.50
B 81	Money Show, Memphis	BEP	6/14/85	13.50	20.00
PS 58	ARGENTINA '85	USPS	7/5/85	3.75	5.50
PS 61	Statue of Liberty	USPS	7/18/85	27.50	25.00
B 82	ANA '85	BEP	8/20/85	13.50	15.00
B 83	Statue of Liberty/Green	BEP	8/20/85	175.00	200.00
PS 59	MOPHILA	USPS	9/11/85	3.75	5.00
PS 60	ITALIA '85	USPS	10/25/85	3.75	5.00
B 84	Money Show '85, Cherry Hill	BEP	11/14/85	15.00	23.50
B85-6	Liberty Bell/Blue	BEP	11/14/85	160.00	200.00

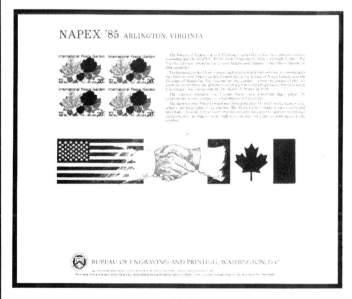

NAPEX '85 ARLINGTON, VIRGINIA

International Peace Garden

BUREAU OF ENGRAVING AND PRINTING, WASHINGTON, D.C.

PS 51

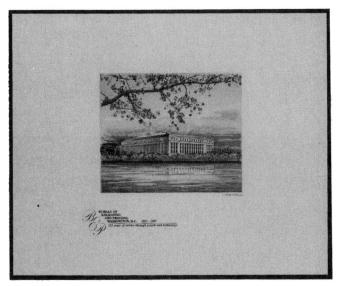

B 101

SCCS No.	Description	Printer	FD Show/Issue	Mint Card	Cancelled Card
	1986				
B 87	FUN '86	BEP	1/2/86	14.00	18.00
B 88	ANA, Salt Lake City	BEP	2/19/86	12.50	20.00
PS 62	Stat.of Liberty,Memento'86	USPS	2/21/86	5.00	6.00
PS 62v	Stat.of Lib.,STAMPEX Ovpt	USPS	8/4/86	15.00	25.00
B 89	Garfield-Perry '86	BEP	3/21/86	13.50	32.50
B 90	AMERIPEX	BEP	5/22/86	12.50	25.00
B 91-92	Liberty Bell/Green	BEP	5/22/86	55.00	100.00
B 93	Money Show '86	BEP	6/20/86	12.50	22.50
B 94	ANA, Milwaukee	BEP	8/5/86	12.50	22.50
B 95-96	Liberty Bell/Brown	BEP	8/5/86	55.00	100.00
PS 63	STOCKHOLMIA '86	USPS	8/28/86	5.00	5.75
B 97	HOUPEX '86	BEP	9/5/86	13.50	25.00
B 98	LOBEX '86	BEP	10/2/86	15.00	22.50
B 99	NW Paper Money Conv	BEP	11/13/86	14.00	27.50
B 100	Dallas Expo	BEP	12/11/86	14.00	22.50
SO 43	SMPC/IBNS Liberty & Holo	ABNC	...	50.00	...
	1987				
B 101	BEP Anniversary	BEP	1/7/87	55.00	70.00
B 101A	Same, "FUN" Embossed	BEP	1/7/87	75.00	120.00
B 101B	Same, ANA Midwinter seals	BEP	2/27/87	100.00	125.00
B 101C	Same, BEP&WMPG seals	BEP	4/9/87	95.00	165.00
B 101D	Same, BEP&IPMS seals	BEP	6/19/87	95.00	120.00
B 101E	Same, BEP&ANA '87 seals	BEP	8/26/87	85.00	125.00
B 101F	Same, BEP&GENA seals	BEP	9/18/87	60.00	120.00
B 102	FUN '87	BEP	1/7/87	14.00	18.50
B 103	ANA Mid-Winter '87	BEP	2/27/87	14.00	18.50
B 104	Ft. Worth Dedication	BEP	4/25/87	20.00	115.00
SO 56	AFL-CIO Trade Show	ABNC	6/19/87	100.00	...
...	200th Anniv. Three States	ABNC	...	15.00	...
PS 64	CAPEX '87	BEP	6/13/87	5.00	5.50
B 105	Money Show '87	BEP	6/19/87	12.50	18.00
SO 54	200th Anniv./Constitution	ABNC	6/19/87	13.00	22.00
B 106	ANA '87 Atlanta, GA	BEP	8/26/87	12.50	18.00
SO 57	$10 Hawaii/ANA	ABNC	8/26/87	16.00	25.00
B 108	Gr. Eastern Num. Assn	BEP	9/18/87	13.50	18.00
B 109	State Shields/Brown	BEP	9/18/87	95.00	170.00
PS 65	HAFNIA '87	USPS	10/16/87	5.00	5.50
B 110	SESCAL '87	BEP	10/16/87	16.50	25.00
SO 58	NWPMC	ABNC	10/29/87	17.00	25.00
B 111	Hawaii State Num. Assn	BEP	11/12/87	19.50	26.50
PS 66	MONTE CARLO	USPS	11/13/87	5.00	5.50
	1988				
B 112	FUN '88	BEP	1/7/88	13.50	19.50
B 113	FUN, State Shields/Green	BEP	1/7/88	95.00	140.00
SO 59	Constitution Anniv./8 states	ABNC	...	12.00	...
F 1988B	Stamporee '88	ABNC	...	30.00	...
B 114	ANA Winter, Little Rock	BEP	3/11/88	13.50	19.50
PS 67	FINLANDIA '88	USPS	6/1/88	5.00	5.50
B 115	Int'l Paper Money Show	BEP	6/24/88	11.50	18.00
SO 60	IPMS	ABNC	6/24/88	17.50	20.00
SO 66	Constitution/3 states	ABNC	...	12.00	...
B 116	ANA Cincinnati	BEP	7/20/88	14.50	18.00
B 117	ANA, State Shields/Blue	BEP	7/20/88	95.00	165.00
SO 61	ANA, $100 Hawaii note	ABNC	7/20/88	15.00	23.00
B 118	APS Detroit	BEP	8/25/88	13.00	26.50
B 119	Illinois Numis. Assn	BEP	10/6/88	13.50	17.50
B 120	MIDAPHIL '88	BEP	11/18/88	11.50	26.50

SCCS No.	Description	Printer	FD Show/Issue	Mint Card	Cancelled Card
	1989				
B 121	FUN	BEP	1/5/89	11.50	17.50
B 122	FUN/American Heritage	BEP	1/5/89	50.00	100.00
SO 62	FUN	ABNC	1/5/89	15.00	25.00
SO 63	Miami Stamp Expo	ABNC	1/27/89	24.00	35.00
B 124	ANA Mid-Winter	BEP	3/3/89	11.50	20.00
SO 64	ANA Museum(SO34 reduced)	ABNC	...	15.00	25.00
SO 65	G. Washington Inaug./Anniv.	ABNC	3/15/89	12.50	...
B 125	Int'l Coin Club of El Paso	BEP	4/28/89	13.50	18.00
B 126	IPMS	BEP	6/23/89	11.50	18.00
B 127	IPMS/Agriculture Proof	BEP	6/23/89	50.00	100.00
SO 67	IPMS	ABNC	6/23/89	15.00	20.00
PS 68	PHILEXFRANCE	USPS	7/7/89	7.50	9.50
B 129	ANA, Pittsburgh, PA	BEP	8/9/89	16.50	19.50
B 130	ANA/Decl.of Indep./Proof	BEP	8/9/89	50.00	100.00
SO 68	ANA	ABNC	8/9/89	15.00	20.00
B 132	APS Anaheim, CA	BEP	8/24/89	11.50	22.50
SO 69	200th Anniv./North Carolina	ABNC	11/2/89	13.00	20.00
PS 69	World Stamp Expo, DC	USPS	11/17/89	7.00	8.00
	1990				
B 133	FUN	BEP	1/4/90	11.50	18.00
B 134	FUN/Ships Proof	BEP	1/4/90	48.00	90.00
SO 71	Miami Stamp Expo	ABNC	1/12/90	23.50	35.00
B 135	ANA Midwinter,San Diego, CA	BEP	3/2/90	11.50	18.00
B 136	CSNS '90, Milwaukee,WI	BEP	4/6/90	11.50	18.00
B 137	CSNS/Ships Proof	BEP	4/6/90	45.00	90.00
B 138	ARIPEX	BEP	4/20/90	11.50	22.50
PS 70	Stamp World London	USPS	5/3/90	7.00	8.00
B 139	DCSE '90, Dallas, TX	BEP	6/14/90	11.50	18.00
SO 72	200th Anniv./Rhode Island	ABNC	6/15/90	15.00	22.00
B 140	ANA National, Seattle, WA	BEP	8/22/90	14.50	18.00
B 141	ANA/Ships Proof	BEP	8/22/90	37.50	90.00
B 142	APS Stampshow	BEP	8/23/90	11.50	21.50
B 143	Westex Num.Exhb,Denver,CO	BEP	9/21/90	13.50	18.00
B 144	HSNA	BEP	11/1/90	15.00	30.00
	1991				
B 145	FUN	BEP	1/3/91	13.50	18.00
B 146	FUN/Statue of Freedom Proof	BEP	1/3/91	45.00	90.00
B 147	ANA, Mid-Winter	BEP	3/1/91	11.50	18.00
B 152	Ft. Worth Facility Dedication	BEP	4/26/91	45.00	175.00
B 148	IPMS, Memphis, TN	BEP	6/14/91	11.50	18.00
SO 74	IPMS	ABNC	6/14/91	17.50	25.00
SO 75	Flag/Hologram	ABNC	6/14/91	17.50	25.00
B 149	ANA, Chicago, IL	BEP	8/13/91	19.50	19.50
B 150	ANA, Intaglio Print	BEP	8/13/91	55.00	82.50
SO 76	ANA	ABNC	8/13/91	16.50	25.00
...	ANA/Capitol Proof	ABNC	8/13/91	40.00	80.00
SO 77	SCCS/10th Anniv.	ABNC	8/13/91	15.00	20.00
B 151	APS Stampshow,Phila.,PA	BEP	8/22/91	12.50	24.00
SO 78	APS	ABNC	8/22/91	15.00	25.00
SO 79	APS/Limited Edition	ABNC	8/22/91	115.00	175.00
SO 80	BALPEX	ABNC	8/31/91	15.00	25.00
SO 81	ASDA	ABNC	11/7/91	15.00	25.00
SO 82	ASDA/Limited Edition	ABNC	11/7/91	110.00	175.00
SO 83	Philadelphia NSE	ABNC	11/15/91	15.00	25.00

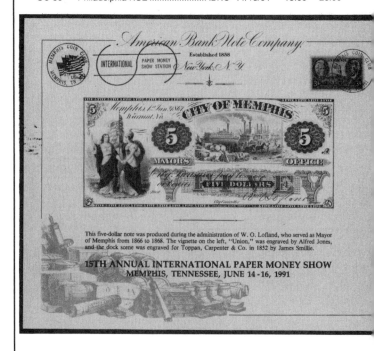

SO 74

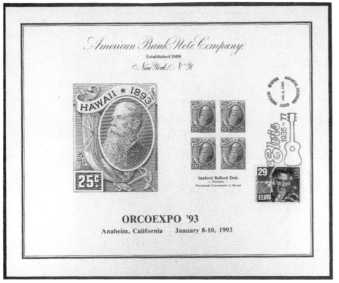

S0109

SCCS No.	Description	Printer	FD Show/ Issue	Mint Card	Cancelled Card
	1992				
B 153	FUN '92	BEP	1/9/92	11.50	18.00
B 154	FUN, Limited Edition	BEP	1/9/92	45.00	85.00
SO 84	FUN '92	ABNC	1/9/92	15.00	25.00
SO 85	Columbus/Hologram	ABNC	1/9/92	17.00	30.00
SO 86	ANA/Early Spring	ABNC	2/27/92	15.00	25.00
SO 87	INTERPEX	ABNC	3/12/92	15.00	25.00
B 155	Central States Numis. Conv.	BEP	4/30/92	13.00	21.50
B 156	World Columbian Stamp Ex	BEP	5/22/92	13.00	22.50
B 157	WCSE/Intaglio Ltd. Edition	BEP	5/22/92	55.00	95.00
SO 88	WCSE/Costa Rica	ABNC	5/22/92	15.00	25.00
SO 89	WCSE/1¢ Columbian	ABNC	5/22/92	15.00	25.00
SO 90	WCSE/Limited Edition	ABNC	5/22/92	110.00	165.00
SO 90A	WCSE/Ltd. Edition Proof	ABNC	5/22/92	...	...
SO 91-96	WCSE/1893 Ticket Reprints	ABNC	5/22/92	165.00	275.00
SO 97	WCSE/Portfolio w/card	ABNC	5/22/92	35.00	45.00
SO 98	WCSE/Columbus	SV	5/22/92	42.50	90.00
SO 99	WCSE/Slania	SV	5/22/92	55.00	80.00
SO 100	WCSE/Bonnie Blair	SV	5/22/92	...	90.00
SO 101	WCSE/Eagle Hologram	SV	5/22/92	50.00	90.00
B 158	Int'l Paper Money Show	BEP	6/19/92	11.50	18.00
SO 102	IPMS	ABNC	6/19/92	15.00	25.00
B 162	Savings Bonds	BEP	6/15/92	12.50	...
B 159	ANA, Orlando	BEP	8/12/92	11.50	18.00
B 160	ANA, Intaglio, Green print	BEP	8/12/92	45.00	85.00
SO 103	ANA, Orlando	ABNC	8/12/92	15.00	35.00
B 161	APS	BEP	8/27/92	11.50	22.50
SO 104	APS	ABNC	8/27/92	15.00	25.00
SO 105	APS/Limited Edition	ABNC	8/27/92	70.00	100.00
SO 105A	APS/Limited Edition Proof	ABNC	8/27/92	...	...
B 163	Columbus Fleet	BEP	10/13/92	40.00	...
SO 106	ASDA, Stamp	ABNC	10/28/92	15.00	25.00
SO 107	ASDA, Historic Event Card	ABNC	10/28/92	15.00	25.00
SO 108	ASDA/Limited Edition	ABNC	10/28/92	100.00	175.00
SO 108A	ASDA/Ltd. Ed. Proof	ABNC	10/28/92	...	...
	1993				
B 165	FUN '93	BEP	1/7/93	15.00	18.00
B 166	American Vistas, 3 views	BEP	1/7/93	45.00	75.00
SO 109	Orcoexpo	ABNC	1/8/93	16.00	25.00
SO 110	Orco Locomotive Hologram	ABNC	1/8/93	17.00	30.00
B 164	CFC,Red Cross Orlando,FL	BEP	1/13/93	11.50	25.00
SO 111	Milcopex, Milwaukee, WI	ABNC	3/5/93	16.00	25.00
F 1993A	GENA, Maple Shade, NJ	PPU	3/5/93	9.50	...
B 167	ANA Colorado Springs	BEP	3/11/93	15.00	18.00
SO 112	ANA Colorado Springs	ABNC	3/11/93	16.00	25.00
SO 113	Plymouth, MI Stamp Show	ABNC	4/24/93	16.00	50.00
B 168	ASDA Mega Event, NYC	BEP	5/5/93	11.50	17.50
SO 114	ASDA Mega Event, NYC	ABNC	5/5/93	16.00	25.00
B 169	Texas Numismatic Assn	BEP	5/6/93	11.50	17.50
B 170	Georgia Numismatic Assn	BEP	5/13/93	15.00	17.50
B 171	IPMS, Memphis, TN	BEP	6/18/93	11.50	17.50
B 172	American Vistas, 3 views	BEP	6/18/93	40.00	75.00
SO 115	IPMS Memphis, TN	ABNC	6/18/93	16.00	25.00
B 173	ANA Baltimore, MD	BEP	7/28/93	11.50	17.50
B 174	American Vistas, 3 Views	BEP	7/28/93	40.00	75.00
SO 116	ANA Baltimore, MD	ABNC	7/28/93	16.00	25.00
SO 117	ANA, Limited Edition	ABNC	7/28/93	80.00	120.00
B 175	Savings Bond	BEP	8/2/93	11.50	30.00
SO 118	APS, Houston, TX	ABNC	8/19/93	16.00	25.00
SO 119	APS, Limited Edition	ABNC	8/19/93	70.00	110.00
B 176	Omaha Philatelic Society	BEP	9/3/93	15.00	23.50
SO 120	ASDA Mega Event, NYC	ABNC	10/28/93	16.50	25.00

SCCS No.	Description	Printer	FD Show/ Issue	Mint Card	Cancelled Card
	1993 (continued)				
SO 121	ASDA Mega, Money vignette	ABNC	10/28/93	16.50	25.00
SO 122	ASDA, Stamp vign., Limited	ABNC	10/28/93	80.00	120.00
SO 122A	ASDA, Stamp vign., Proof	ABNC	10/28/93	...	...
B 178	ASDA Mega Event, NYC	BEP	10/28/93	11.50	17.50
	1994				
B 179	FUN '94, Banknote	BEP	1/6/94	11.50	17.50
B 180	FUN '94, Special	BEP	1/6/94	40.00	75.00
SO 123	ARIPEX, Mesa, AZ	ABNC	1/7/94	16.00	25.00
B 181	SANDICAL, San Diego, CA	BEP	2/11/94	11.50	17.50
B 182	ANA, New Orleans	BEP	3/3/94	11.50	17.50
SO 124	ANA, New Orleans	ABNC	3/3/94	16.00	25.00
SO 125	MILCOPEX, Milwaukee, WI	ABNC	3/4/94	16.00	25.00
SO 126	Garfield-Perry, Cleveland	ABNC	3/18/94	16.00	25.00
SO 127	Central States, Indianapolis	ABNC	4/8/94	16.00	25.00
B 183	EPMB, Maastricht, NL	BEP	4/16/94	11.50	37.50
B 184	IPMS, Memphis, TN	BEP	6/17/94	11.50	17.50
B 185	IPMS, Special	BEP	6/17/94	40.00	60.00
SO 128	IPMS, Memphis, TN	ABNC	6/17/94	16.00	25.00
B 187	ANA, 103rd	BEP	7/27/94	12.50	18.50
B 188	ANA, Special	BEP	7/27/94	70.00	100.00
SO 129	ANA, 103rd	ABNC	7/27/94	16.00	25.00
SO 130	ANA, Hologram	ABNC	7/27/94	20.00	30.00
SO 131	ANA, Limited	ABNC	7/27/94	80.00	120.00
B189	BEP Savings Bond	BEP	8/1/94	15.00	30.00
B 190	APS - 108th, Pittsburgh, PA	BEP	8/18/94	12.50	20.00
SO 132	APS - 90¢, Pittsburgh, PA	ABNC	8/18/94	16.00	25.00
SO 133	APS, Limited	ABNC	8/18/94	80.00	120.00
SO 134	BALPEX, Baltimore, MD	ABNC	9/3/94	16.00	25.00
B 191	ASDA Mega, New York, NY	BEP	11/3/94	12.50	17.50
SO 135	ASDA Mega, 90¢ Lincoln	ABNC	11/3/94	16.00	25.00
SO 136	ASDA Mega, Limited	ABNC	11/3/94	80.00	120.00
SO 137	WPMS, Banknote	ABNC	11/11/94	16.00	25.00
	1995				
B192	FUN '95, Orlando, FL	BEP	1/5/95	13.50	15.00
B193	FUN '95, Special Intaglio	BEP	1/5/95	40.00	60.00
B194	COLOPEX', Columbus, OH	BEP	4/7/95	13.50	15.00
B195	NYINC, New York, NY	BEP	5/5/95	13.50	22.50
B196	IPMS, Memphis, TN	BEP	6/16/95	13.50	20.00
B197	Stamp Centennial, Intaglio Print	BEP	6/30/95	95.00	130.00
B198	Savings Bond '95	BEP	...	13.50	...
B199	ANA, Anaheim, CA	BEP	8/16/95	13.50	20.00
B200	ANA, Special Intaglio	BEP	8/16/95	45.00	55.00
B201	LBN/PE, Long Beach, CA	BEP	10/4/95	13.50	20.00
B202	ASDA, New York, NY	BEP	11/2/95	13.50	20.00
	1996				
B203	FUN'96, Orlando, FL	BEP	1/4/96	13.50	15.00
B204	FUN'96, Special Intaglio	BEP	1/4/96	45.00	...
B205	Suburban Washington-Baltimore Coin	BEP	3/22/96	13.50	15.00
B206	Central States, Kansas City, MO	BEP	4/25/96	13.50	15.00
B207	CAPEX '96, Toronto, Canada	BEP	6/8/96	13.50	15.00
B208	Olymphilex '96, Atlanta, GA	BEP	7/19/96	13.50	15.00
B209	Olymphilex Special Inaglio	BEP	7/19/96	45.00	...
B210	Savings Bond 76	BEP	...	13.50	30.00
B211	ANA, Denver, CO.	BEP	8/14/96	13.50	15.00
B212	ANA, Special Intaglio	BEP	8/14/96	45.00	...
B213	Billings Stamp Club, MT	BEP	10/19/96	13.50	15.00

1266

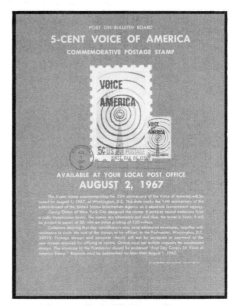

1329

Each Souvenir Page has one or more stamps affixed and cancelled with a "FD of Issue" postmark. Each page also has a picture of the issued stamp(s) and important technical data. Prior to March 1, 1972 these pages were privately distributed. The most prominent servicer was W.C. Bates, who began with Scott #1232 (West Virginia). **These pages were folded twice in order to fit into a #10 envelope.** These are known as "Unofficial" Souvenir Pages.

UNOFFICIAL

Scott No.	Subject	Price
1962-64 Issues		
1232	West Virginia	6.00
1233	Emancipation Proc.	12.50
1234	Alliance/Progress	7.50
1235	Cordell Hull	7.00
1236	Eleanor Roosevelt	9.50
1237	Science	7.50
1238	City Mail	7.00
1239	Red Cross	9.00
1240	Christmas 1963	12.50
1241	Audubon	8.50
1242	Sam Houston	12.00
1243	C.M. Russell	9.50
1244	N.Y. World's Fair	7.00
1245	Muir	15.00
1246	John F. Kennedy	15.00
1247	NJ Tercentenary	7.50
1248	Nevada Statehood	7.50
1249	Register & Vote	7.50
1250	Shakespeare	7.50
1251	Mayo Brothers	7.50
1252	Music	7.50
1253	Homemakers	7.50
1254-57	Christmas 1964	75.00
1258	Verrazano Bridge	9.50
1259	Modern Art	8.00
1260	Radio	8.00
1965 Commemoratives		
1261	Battle/New Orleans	6.00
1262	Sokol Society	7.50
1263	Cancer	7.00
1264	Churchill	7.50
1265	Magna Carta	6.25
1266	Int'l Cooperation Year	6.00
1267	Salvation Army	6.75
1268	Dante	6.00
1269	Herbert Hoover	6.00
1270	Robert Fulton	6.00
1271	St. Augustine, FL	6.00
1272	Traffic Safety	6.00
1273	Copley	7.50
1274	ITU	8.00
1275	Adlai Stevenson	6.00
1276	Christmas 1965	6.00
1965-81 Prominent Americans		
1278	1¢ Jefferson	7.50
1278a	Pane of 8	10.00
1279	1¼¢ Gallatin	7.50
1280	2¢ Wright	7.50

Scott No.	Subject	Price
1965-81 Prominent Americans(cont.)		
1280a	Zip pane of 5	12.50
1280a	Mail early pn. of 5	12.50
1281	3¢ Parkman	7.50
1282	4¢ Lincoln	6.00
1283	5¢ Washington	6.00
1283B	5¢ Wash. re-engr.	9.00
1284	6¢ F.D. Roosevelt	7.00
1285	8¢ Einstein	10.00
1286	10¢ Jackson	6.00
1286A	12¢ Henry Ford	9.50
1287	13¢ J.F. Kennedy	20.00
1288	15¢ Holmes	8.00
1289	20¢ Marshall	9.00
1290	25¢ Douglass	15.00
1291	30¢ Dewey	30.00
1292	40¢ Paine	50.00
1293	50¢ Lucy Stone	45.00
1294	$1 O'Neill	65.00
1295	$5 Moore	150.00
1298	6¢ FDR end coil	7.50
1299	1¢ Jefferson coil	7.50
1303	4¢ Lincoln coil	7.50
1304	5¢ Wash. coil	7.50
1305	6¢ FDR side coil	8.00
1966 Commemoratives		
1306	Migrat. Bird Treaty	8.00
1307	Hum. Treat./Animal	8.00
1308	Indiana Statehood	7.50
1309	Circus	7.50
1310	SIPEX	7.50
1311	SIPEX Souv. Sht	10.00
1312	Bill of Rights	7.50
1313	Polish Millenium	7.50
1314	Nat'l Parks Service	7.50
1315	Marine Reserves	7.50
1316	Women's Clubs	7.50
1317	Johnny Appleseed	8.00
1318	Beautif./America	10.00
1319	Great River Road	7.50
1320	Sav. Bond/Srvcmen	8.00
1321	Christmas 1966	6.00
1322	Mary Cassatt	7.00
1967 Commemoratives		
1323	Nat'l. Grange	7.50
1324	Canada Centenary	6.00
1325	Erie Canal	7.50
1326	Peace/Lions	7.50

Scott No.	Subject	Price
1967 Commemoratives (cont.)		
1327	Thoreau	6.00
1328	NE Statehood	7.50
1329	Voice of America	6.00
1330	Davy Crockett	9.50
1331-32	Space Twins	25.00
1333	Urban Planning	7.50
1334	Finnish Independ.	7.50
1335	Thomas Eakins	7.50
1336	Christmas 1967	7.50
1337	MS Statehood	7.50
1968-71 Regular Issues		
1338	6¢ Flag	6.00
1338A	6¢ Flag coil	7.50
1338D	6¢ Flag huck press	7.50
1338F	8¢ Flag	7.50
1341	$1 Airlift	75.00
1968 Commemoratives		
1339	IL Statehood	7.50
1340	Hemisfair	7.50
1342	Youth/Elks	6.00
1343	Law & Order	6.00
1344	Register and Vote	6.00
1345-54	Historic Flags	100.00
1355	Walt Disney	20.00
1356	Marquette	7.50
1357	Daniel Boone	7.50
1358	AK River Navigation	7.50
1359	Leif Erikson	16.00
1360	Cherokee Strip	9.00
1361	Trumbull Painting	6.00
1362	Waterfowl Conserv.	8.00
1363	Christmas 1968	7.50
1364	Chief Joseph	6.00
1969 Commemoratives		
1365-68	Beautification	20.00
1369	American Legion	7.50
1370	Grandma Moses	6.00
1371	Apollo 8	15.00
1372	W.C. Handy	10.00
1373	CA Settlement	6.00
1374	John Wesley Powell	6.00
1375	AL Statehood	7.50
1376-79	Botanical Congress	27.50
1380	Daniel Webster	7.50
1381	Baseball	150.00
1382	Football	20.00
1383	Eisenhower Memor.	6.00
1384	Christmas 1969	7.50
1385	Hope/Crip. Child	6.00
1386	Harnett Painting	6.00
1970 Commemoratives		
1387-90	Natural History	30.00
1391	Maine Statehood	7.50
1392	Wildlife Conserv.	7.50
1405	Edgar Lee Masters	7.50
1406	Women's Suffrage	5.00

Scott No.	Subject	Price
1970 Commemoratives (cont.)		
1407	SC Founding	6.00
1408	Stone Mountain	6.00
1409	Fort Snelling	6.00
1410-13	Anti-Pollution	20.00
1414	Christmas 1970	10.00
1415-18	Christmas Toys	20.00
1415a-18a	Toys Precancelled	90.00
1419	U.N. 25th Anniv.	7.50
1420	Mayflower	7.50
1421-22	D.A.V./Servicemen	40.00
1970-74 Regular Issues		
1393	6¢ Eisenhower	6.00
1393a	Pane of 8	20.00
1393b	Zip pane of 5	25.00
1939b	Mail early p./5	25.00
1394	8¢ Eisen., multi	6.00
1395a	8¢ Eisen., claret, pane of 8	30.00
1395b	Pane of 6	30.00
1396	8¢ USPS	25.00
1398	16¢ Ernie Pyle	6.00
1401	6¢ Eisen., coil	9.50
1402	8¢ Eisen., coil	10.00
1971 Commemoratives		
1423	American Wool Ind.	8.00
1424	Douglas MacArthur	11.00
1425	Blood Donors	7.50
1426	MO Sesquicent	7.50
Airmails & Special Delivery		
C67	6¢ Eagle	18.00
C68	Amel. Earhart	20.00
C69	Goddard	25.00
C70	Alaska	7.50
C71	Audubon Jays	10.00
C72	10¢ Stars	10.00
C72b	Pane of 8	25.00
C72c	Pane of 5	50.00
C73	10¢ Stars coil	12.00
C74	Air Service	10.00
C75	20¢ USA	20.00
C76	Moon Landing	12.50
C77	9¢ Delta Wing	15.00
C78	11¢ Jet	12.50
C78a	Pane of 4	25.00
C80	17¢ Liberty	25.00
C81	21¢ USA	25.00
C82	11¢ Jet coil	12.50
E22	45¢ Arrows	40.00
E23	60¢ Arrows	25.00

OFFICIAL SOUVENIR PAGES

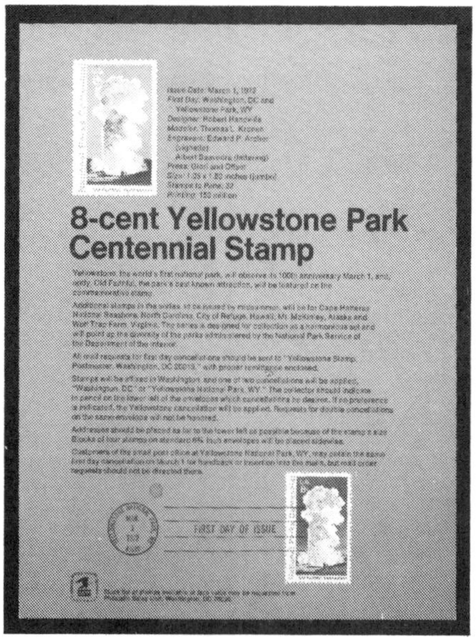

1453

OFFICIAL SOUVENIR PAGES

Since March 1, 1972 the U.S. Postal Service has offered, by subscription, Souvenir Pages with first day cancels. They are known as "Official" Souvenir Pages. **These were issued flat and unfolded.**

Scott No.	Subject	Price
1972-78 Regular Issues		
1297	3¢ Fran. Parkman....	5.00
1305C	$1 O'Neill coil	17.50
1305E	15¢ O.W. Holmes....	3.00
1393D	7¢ B. Franklin..........	8.00
1397	14¢ LaGuardia.........	110.00
1399	18¢ Eliz. Blackwell ..	3.00
1400	21¢ A. Giannini........	6.00
1972 Commemoratives		
1448-51	Cape Hatteras	100.00
1452	Wolf Trap Farm	45.00
1453	Yellowstone Park	125.00
1454	Mt. McKinley...........	30.00
1455	Family Planning.......	750.00
1456-59	Colonial Craftsmen.	20.00
1460-62	C85 Olympics..........	15.00
1463	PTA	9.00
1464-67	Wildlife...................	10.00
1468	Mail Order...............	7.50
1469	Osteopathic Medicine	7.50
1470	Tom Sawyer.............	7.50
1471-72	Christmas 1972	9.00
1473	Pharmacy................	7.50
1474	Stamp Collecting.....	7.50
1973 Commemoratives		
1475	Love........................	10.00
1476	Pamphleteers	7.00
1477	Posting Broadside ...	10.00
1478	Post Rider	7.00
1479	Colonial Drummer ...	6.00
1480-83	Boston Tea Party ...	9.00
1484	George Gershwin	7.50
1485	Robinson Jeffers	6.00
1486	Henry O. Tanner......	7.50
1487	Willa Cather.............	5.00
1488	Copernicus	7.50
1489-98	Postal People	9.00
1499	Harry S. Truman......	6.00
1500-02,C86	Electronics	10.00
1503	Lyndon B. Johnson .	5.00
1504	Angus Cattle............	5.00
1505	Chautauqua.............	3.50
1506	Kansas Wheat.........	3.00
1507-08	Christmas 1973	9.50
1973-74 Regular Issues		
1509	10¢ Crossed Flags ..	4.00
1510	10¢ Jeff. Memor	4.00
1511	10¢ Zip Code...........	6.00
1518	6.3¢ Bulk Rate coil ..	5.00
1974 Commemoratives		
1525	VFW	3.50
1526	Robert Frost	4.00
1527	Expo '74	3.50
1528	Horse Racing	4.50

Scott No.	Subject	Price
1529	Skylab	8.50
1530-37	Univ. Postal Union .	7.00
1538-41	Mineral Heritage.....	7.50
1542	Fort Harrod..............	3.50
1543-46	Cont. Congress	6.00
1547	Energy Conserv	3.00
1548	Sleepy Hollow	4.00
1549	Retarded Children...	3.00
1550-52	Christmas 1974.......	7.50
1975 Commemoratives		
1553	Benjamin West........	3.75
1554	Paul L. Dunbar........	7.50
1555	D.W. Griffith	4.00
1556	Pioneer....................	7.50
1557	Mariner....................	6.00
1558	Coll. Bargaining.......	3.00
1559	Sybil Ludington	4.00
1560	Salem Poor	5.00
1561	Haym Salomon	4.00
1562	Peter Francisco.......	4.75
1563	Lexing. & Concord ..	3.50
1564	Bunker Hill..............	4.00
1565-68	Military Services.....	7.50
1569-70	Apollo Soyuz	7.50
1571	Int'l Women's Year ..	3.00
1572-75	Postal Bicentennial	5.75
1576	Wld. Peace thru Law	3.50
1577-78	Bank & Commerce.	3.50
1579-80	Christmas 1975.......	5.00
1975-81 Americana Issues		
1581-82,84-85	1¢-4¢ Issues .	3.50
1591	9¢ Rt. to Assemble..	3.00
1592	10¢ Petit./Redress ..	3.50
1593	11¢ Free./Press	2.50
1594,1816	12¢ Conscience ..	4.00
1596	13¢ Eagle/Shield.....	3.50
1597,1618C	15¢ Ft. McHenry	4.00
1599,1619	16¢ Liberty	3.00
1603	24¢ Old No. Church	3.00
1604	28¢ Rem. Outpost...	3.00
1605	29¢ Lighthouse	2.75
1606	30¢ Am. Schools.....	4.75
1608	50¢ "Betty" Lamp	6.00
1610	$1 Rush Lamp.........	6.75
1611	$2 Kero. Lamp	7.50
1612	$5 R.R. Lantern.......	17.50
1613	3.1¢ Non Prof coil ...	9.75
1614	7.7¢ Bulk Rate coil ..	4.00
1615	7.9¢ Bulk Rate coil ..	3.00
1615C	8.4¢ Bulk Rate coil ..	4.00
1616	9¢ Assembly coil.....	3.00
1617	10¢ Redress coil	4.00
1618	13¢ Libty. Bell coil...	3.50
1622,25	13¢ Flag/Ind. Hall...	3.00
1623c	$1 Vend bk. p. 10....	25.00

Scott No.	Subject	Price
1976 Commemoratives		
1629-31	Spirit of '76............	5.00
1632	INTERPHIL '76	3.75
1633-82	State Flags (5 pgs.)	50.00
1683	Telephone Cent.	3.00
1684	Commer. Aviation ...	2.75
1685	Chemistry................	2.75
1686-89	Bicentennial S/S (4)	50.00
1690	Benjamin Franklin ...	3.00
1691-94	Dec. of Indepen	6.00
1695-98	Olympics	7.50
1699	Clara Maass...........	2.50
1700	Adolph S. Ochs.......	4.50
1701-03	Christmas 1976......	5.00
1977 Commemoratives		
1704	Wash. at Princeton .	3.00
1705	Sound Recording....	3.00
1706-09	Pueblo Art.............	3.50
1710	Lindbergh Flight......	4.00
1711	CO Centennial	2.75
1712-15	Butterflies..............	3.50
1716	Lafayette	3.00
1717-20	Skilled Hands (4) ...	3.50
1721	Peace Bridge	2.75
1722	Herkimer/Oriskany ..	2.50
1723-24	Energy Conserv.....	2.50
1725	Alta, CA..................	2.75
1726	Art. of Confederation	2.50
1727	Talking Pictures	3.00
1728	Surrender/Saratoga	4.00
1729-30	Christmas, Omaha.	2.75
1729-30	Xmas, Valley Forge	3.00
1978 Issues		
1731	Carl Sandburg.........	2.75
1732-3	Cpt. Cook, Anchor ..	3.75
1732-3	Cpt. Cook/Honolulu.	4.50
1734	13¢ Ind. Hd. Penny.	3.00
1735,43	"A" Stamp (2)..........	7.00
1737	15¢ Rose bklt. sgl ...	3.00
1742a	15¢ Windmills bklt. pane/10 (1980)	6.00
1744	Harriet Tubman.......	5.00
1745-48	American Quilts	4.00
1749-52	American Dance	4.00
1753	French Alliance.......	2.75
1754	Dr. Papanicolaou	3.00
1755	Jimmie Rodgers......	4.50
1756	George M. Cohan ...	3.00
1757	CAPEX '78.............	10.00
1758	Photography	2.75
1759	Viking Missions.......	5.25
1760-63	American Owls.......	3.85
1764-67	American Trees	3.85
1768	Madonna & Child	2.75
1769	Xmas Hobby Horse.	2.75
1979 Commemoratives		
1770	Robert F. Kennedy..	3.00
1771	Martin L. King, Jr.....	5.00
1772	Year of the Child.....	2.75
1773	John Steinbeck	3.00
1774	Albert Einstein.........	3.50
1775-78	PA Toleware	3.85
1779-82	Amer. Architecture .	4.00
1783-86	Endangered Flora ..	4.00
1787	Seeing Eye Dogs....	2.75
1788	Special Olympics	3.00
1789	John Paul Jones	3.85
1790	10¢ Olym. Games...	4.00
1791-94	15¢ Summer Olym.	6.00
1795-98	15¢ Winter Olym(80)	7.50
1799	Virgin & Child.........	3.85
1800	Santa Claus	4.00
1801	Will Rogers	2.75
1802	Vietnam Vets	2.75
1980-81 Issues		
1803	W.C. Fields	3.00
1804	Benjamin Banneker	5.00
1805-10	Letter Writing	3.50
1811	1¢ Quill Pen coil......	2.50
1813	3.5¢ Non Profit coil .	4.00
1818,20	"B" sht./coil stamps .	3.50
1819a	"B" bklt. pane of 8 ...	3.00
1821	Frances Perkins......	2.50
1822	15¢ Dolly Madison ..	4.00
1823	Emily Bissell	2.75
1824	H. Keller/A. Sullivan	3.50
1825	Vet. Administration..	2.50
1826	Gen. B. de Galvez ..	2.50
1827-30	Coral Reefs............	3.00
1831	Organized Labor.....	5.00
1832	Edith Wharton	4.75
1833	Amer. Education	3.75
1834-37	NW Indian Masks...	3.85
1838-41	Amer. Architecture .	3.75
1842	Xmas St. Glass Win.	4.00
1843	Xmas Antique Toys.	4.00

Scott No.	Subject	Price
1980-85 Great Americans		
1844	1¢ Dorothea Dix......	2.75
1845	2¢ I. Stravinsky.......	3.00
1846	3¢ Henry Clay.........	2.50
1847	4¢ Carl Shurz..........	2.50
1848	5¢ Pearl S. Buck.....	2.50
1849	6¢ W. Lippmann	3.00
1850	7¢ A. Baldwin	4.00
1851	8¢ Henry Knox........	2.50
1852	9¢ S. Thayer...........	3.75
1853	10¢ R. Russell	2.50
1854	11¢ A. Partridge......	2.50
1855	13¢ Crazy Horse.....	2.50
1856	14¢ S. Lewis...........	2.75
1857	17¢ R. Carson	2.50
1858	18¢ G. Mason	2.50
1859	19¢ Sequoyah	2.50
1860	20¢ Ralph Bunche ..	6.00
1861	20¢ T. Gallaudet.....	2.50
1862	20¢ Truman	2.50
1863	22¢ Audubon	3.00
1864	30¢ Dr. Laubach.....	2.50
1865	35¢ Dr. C. Drew......	4.00
1866	37¢ R. Millikan........	2.50
1867	39¢ G. Clark	2.50
1868	40¢ L. Gilbreth	2.50
1869	50¢ C. Nimitz..........	3.00
1981-82 Issues		
1874	Everett Dirksen.......	2.50
1875	Whitney M. Young ..	5.00
1876-79	American Flowers ..	3.00
1889a	18¢ Animals bk/10 ..	4.50
1890-91	18¢ Flag.................	4.00
1893a	6¢ & 18¢ Flag & Stars bklt. pn............	3.50
1894-95	20¢ Flag.................	6.00
1896a	20¢ Flag bklt. pn./6.	5.00
1896b	20¢ Flag bklt. pn./10	4.00
1981-84 Transportation Coils		
1897	1¢ Omnibus	4.00
1897A	2¢ Locomotive	5.00
1898	3¢ Handcar.............	5.00
1898A	4¢ Stagecoach........	5.75
1899	5¢ Motorcycle	7.50
1900	5.2¢ Sleigh..............	6.50
1901	5.9¢ Bicycle	9.00
1902	7.4¢ Baby Buggy	5.00
1903	9.3¢ Mail Wagon.....	6.00
1904	10.9¢ Hansom Cab.	6.00
1905	11¢ Caboose	5.00
1906	17¢ Electric Car......	4.50
1907	18¢ Surrey..............	7.50
1908	20¢ Pumper............	8.00
1981-83 Regulars & Commem.		
1909	$9.35 Eagle bklt. sgl.	140.00
1909a	$9.35 Bklt.pane of 3	200.00
1910	Amer. Red Cross.....	2.50
1911	Savings & Loan	2.50
1912-19	Space Achievement	10.00
1920	Prof. Management ..	2.50
1921-24	Wildlife Habitats.....	3.00
1925	Yr. Disable Person.	2.50
1926	E. St. Vincent Millay	3.85
1927	Alcoholism..............	3.75
1928-31	Amer. Architecture.	3.85
1932	Babe Zaharias	7.50
1933	Bobby Jones...........	7.50
1934	Frederic Remington	2.50
1935-36	18¢ & 20¢ J. Hoban	2.50
1937-38	Btl. Yrktwn/V Capes	3.00
1939	Xmas Madonna/Ch.	3.85
1940	Xmas "Teddy Bear"	4.75
1941	John Hanson	2.50
1942-45	U.S. Desert Plants.	3.50
1946-47	"C" sht./coil stamps	4.75
1948a	"C" bklt. pane/10.....	4.00
1949a	20¢ Sheep bk pn/10	3.50
1982 Commemoratives		
1950	F.D. Roosevelt........	2.50
1951	Love........................	2.50
1952	G. Washington........	4.00
1953-2002	Birds&Flowers (5)	90.00
2003	Netherlands	2.50
2004	Library of Congress	2.50
2005	20¢ Consumer Coil.	5.00
2006-09	World's Fair	2.50
2010	Horatio Alger..........	2.50
2011	Aging	2.50
2012	Barrymores.............	4.00
2013	Dr. Mary Walker......	2.50
2014	Int'l Peace Garden ..	2.50
2015	America's Libraries .	2.50
2016	Jackie Robinson	20.00

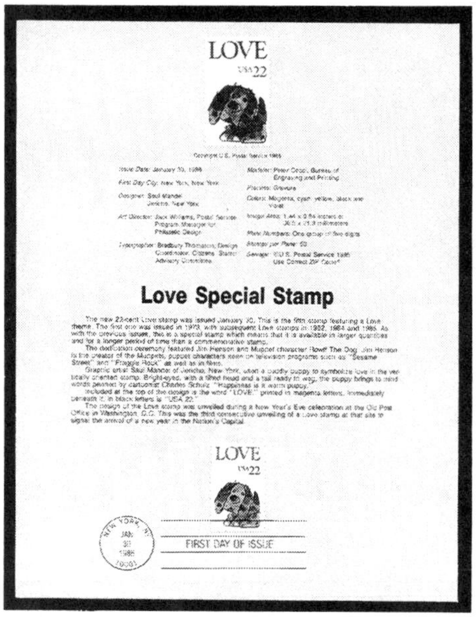

2202

Scott No.	Subject	Price
	1982 Commemoratives (cont.)	
2017	Touro Synagogue	2.50
2018	Wolf Trap	2.50
2019-22	Amer. Architecture	3.00
2023	Francis of Assisi	2.75
2024	Ponce de Leon	2.50
2025	Kitten & Puppy	4.00
2026	Xmas Tiepolo Art	4.00
2027-30	Xmas Snow Scene	4.00
	1983 Commemoratives	
2031	Science & Industry	2.50
2032-35	Balloons	3.00
2036	Sweden/US Treaty	2.75
2037	Civ.Conserv.Corps	2.50
2038	Joseph Priestley	2.50
2039	Volunteerism	2.50
2040	German Immigrants	2.50
2041	Brooklyn Bridge	2.75
2042	Tenn. Valley Auth	2.50
2043	Physical Fitness	2.50
2044	Scott Joplin	4.75
2045	Medal of Honor	4.00
2046	Babe Ruth	15.00
2047	Nath. Hawthorne	2.50
2048-51	13¢ Olympics	4.50
2052	Treaty of Paris	3.00
2053	Civil Service	2.50
2054	Metropolitan Opera	2.50
2055-58	American Inventors	3.00
2059-62	Streetcars	3.50
2063	Xmas Traditional	3.00
2064	Xmas Contemp	3.00
2065	Martin Luther	3.75
	1984 Commemoratives	
2066	Alaska Statehood	2.75
2067-70	Winter Olympics	3.95
2071	FDIC	2.50
2072	Love	2.50
2073	Carter G. Woodson	5.00
2074	Soil/Water Conserv.	2.50
2075	Credit Un.Act/1934	2.50
2076-79	Orchids	3.50
2080	Hawaii Statehood	3.50
2081	Nat'l. Archives	2.50
2082-85	Summer Olympics	5.00
2086	LA World Expo	2.50
2087	Health Research	2.50
2088	Douglas Fairbanks	2.75
2089	Jim Thorpe	10.00
2090	John McCormack	2.75
2091	St. Lawren. Seaway	2.50
2092	Mig. Bird Stamp Act	7.00
2093	Roanoke Voyages	2.50
2094	Herman Melville	2.50
2095	Horace Moses	2.50
2096	Smokey the Bear	5.00
2097	Roberto Clemente	15.00
2098-2101	Dogs	5.00
2102	Crime Prevention	2.75
2103	Hispanic Americans	2.50
2104	Family Unity	4.00

Scott No.	Subject	Price
2105	Eleanor Roosevelt	4.00
2106	Nation of Readers	4.00
2107	Xmas Traditional	3.75
2108	Xmas Santa Claus	3.85
2109	Vietnam Vets Mem.	4.50
	1985-87 Issues	
2110	Jerome Kern	4.00
2111-12	"D" sht./coil stamps	3.00
2113a	"D" bklt. pane/10	4.75
2114-15	22¢ Flag	3.50
2115b	22¢ Flag "T" coil	4.00
2116a	22¢ Flag bklt. bk./5	4.00
2121a	22¢ Seashells bk/10	5.00
2122	$10.75 Eagle bklt.sgl.	55.00
2122a	$10.75 Bklt. pane/3	110.00
	1985-89 Transportation Coils	
2123	3.4¢ School Bus	5.00
2124	4.9¢ Buckboard	5.00
2125	5.5¢ Star Rt. Truck	5.00
2126	6¢ Tricycle	4.75
2127	7.1¢ Tractor	3.00
2127a	7.1¢ Tractor Zip+4	4.00
2128	8.3¢ Ambulance	5.00
2129	8.5¢ Tow Truck	3.50
2130	10.1¢ Oil Wagon	4.00
2130a	10.1¢ Red Prec	4.00
2131	11¢ Stutz Bearcat	5.00
2132	12¢ Stanley Stmr	5.00
2133	12.5¢ Pushcart	4.75
2134	14¢ Iceboat	5.00
2135	17¢ Dog Sled	3.50
2136	25¢ Bread Wagon	5.00
	1985 Issues (cont.)	
2137	Mary M. Bethune	4.50
2138-41	Duck Decoys	4.00
2142	Winter Spec. Olymp.	2.50
2143	Love	5.00
2144	Rural Electrification	2.50
2145	AMERIPEX '86	2.50
2146	Abigail Adams	2.50
2147	Frederick Bartholdi	5.00
2149	18¢ G. Wash. coil	4.00
2150	21.1¢ Zip+4 coil	3.85
2152	Korean War Vets	3.35
2153	Social Security Act	3.00
2154	World War I Vets	3.00
2155-58	American Horses	5.00
2159	Public Education	2.75
2160-63	Int'l. Youth Year	3.75
2164	Help End Hunger	2.75
2165	Xmas Traditional	3.00
2166	Xmas Contemp	3.00
	1986 Issues	
2167	Arkansas Statehood	2.50
	1986-94 Great Americans	
2168	1¢ M. Mitchell	2.50
2169	2¢ Mary Lyon	2.50
2170	3¢ Dr. P.D. White	2.50
2171	4¢ Fr. Flanagan	2.50
2172	5¢ Hugo Black	3.50
2173	5¢ Munoz Marin	3.00
2175	10¢ Red Cloud	2.50

Scott No.	Subject	Price
	1986-94 Great Americans (cont.)	
2176	14¢ Julia W. Howe	2.50
2177	15¢ Buffalo Bill	3.50
2178	17¢ B. Lockwood	3.00
2179	20¢ Virginia Apgar	4.00
2180	21¢ C. Carlson	2.50
2181	23¢ M. Cassatt	2.50
2182	25¢ Jack London	2.50
2182a	Bklt. pn./10	7.00
2183	28¢ Sitting Bull	2.50
2184	29¢ Earl Warren	5.00
2185	29¢ T. Jefferson	5.00
2186	35¢ Dennis Chavez	4.00
2187	40¢ C.L. Chennault	4.50
2188	45¢ Cushing	2.50
2189	52¢ H. Humphrey	4.00
2190	56¢ John Harvard	3.00
2191	65¢ H. Arnold	3.00
2192	75¢ Wendell Wilkie	5.00
2193	$1 Dr. B. Revel	3.00
2194	$1 Johns Hopkins	3.50
2195	$2 W.J. Bryan	5.00
2196	$5 B. Harte	12.50
2197a	25¢ London, bk/6	4.00
	1986 Issues	
2201a	Stamp Col. bk./4	5.75
2202	Love	3.50
2203	Sojourner Truth	4.50
2204	Republic of Texas	2.50
2209a	Fish bklt. pane/5	5.00
2210	Public Hospitals	2.50
2211	Duke Ellington	5.00
2216-19	US Pres. shts.,4 pgs.	25.00
2220-23	Polar Explorers	4.50
2224	Statue of Liberty	5.00
2226	2¢ Locom. re-engr	3.00
2235-38	Navajo Art	3.50
2239	T.S. Elliot	2.50
2240-43	Woodcarved Figs	3.00
2244	Xmas Traditional	2.50
2245	Xmas Contemp	2.50
	1987 Issues	
2246	MI Statehood	3.00
2247	Pan-Amer. Games	3.00
2248	Love	3.00
2249	J. Bap. Pnt. du Sable	7.00
2250	Enrico Caruso	3.00
2251	Girls Scouts	4.75
	1987-88 Transportation Coils	
2252	3¢ Con. Wag	3.50
2253,62	5¢,17.5¢	4.50
2254	5.3¢ Elevator, Prec.	4.00
2255	7.6¢ Carretta, Prec.	4.00
2256	8.4¢ Wheelchair, Prec.	5.00
2257	10¢ Canal Boat	4.00
2258	13¢ Police Wag,Prec.	4.00
2259	13.2¢ RR Car, Prec.	4.00
2260	15¢ Tugboat	4.00
2261	16.7¢ Pop.Wag,Prec.	4.00
2263	20¢ Cbl. Car	3.50
2264	20.5¢ Fire Eng, Prec.	5.00
2265	21¢ RR Mail Car,Prec	4.00
2266	24.1¢ Tandem Bike,Pre	4.00
	1987-89 Issues	
2274a	22¢ Sp. Occ. Bk	6.00
2275	22¢ United Way	2.50
2276	22¢ Flag/Fireworks	2.50
2276a	Bklt. pair	4.00
2277,79	(25¢) "E" sheet/coil	4.50
2278	25¢ Flag/Clouds	2.50
2280	25¢ Flag/Yosem. coil	3.50
2280var	Pre-phos. paper	3.50
2281	25¢ Honeybee coil	4.00
2282a	(25¢) "E" Bklt. Pane/10	6.00
2283a	25¢ Pheasant Bk/10	6.00
2284-85b	25¢ Owl/Grossbk. Bk	5.00
2285Ac	25¢ Flag/Clouds Bk.	5.00
2286-2335	Am. Wildlife (5)	30.00
	1987-90 Bicentennial Issues	
2336	22¢ Delaware	2.75
2337	22¢ Penn	3.00
2338	22¢ New Jersey	4.00
2339	22¢ Georgia	3.00
2340	22¢ Conn	3.00
2341	22¢ Mass	3.50
2342	22¢ Maryland	3.50
2343	25¢ S. Carolina	3.50
2344	25¢ New Hampshire	3.00
2345	25¢ Virginia	3.00
2346	25¢ New York	4.00
2347	25¢ North Carolina	3.00
2348	25¢ Rhode Island	5.00

Scott No.	Subject	Price
	1987-88 Issues	
2349	22¢ U.S.-Moroc. Rel.	2.50
2350	22¢ Faulkner	2.50
2351-54	22¢ Lacemaking	4.50
2359a	22¢ Const. Bklt.	5.00
2360	22¢ Sign. Const	3.00
2361	22¢ CPA	5.00
2366a	22¢ Loco. Bklt	10.00
2367	22¢ Xmas Madon	2.50
2368	22¢ Xmas Orn	2.50
2369	22¢ '88 Wnt. Olym	2.75
2370	22¢ Australia Bicent.	4.00
2371	22¢ J.W. Johnson	4.00
2372-75	22¢ Cats	5.00
2376	22¢ Knute Rockne	6.00
2377	25¢ F. Ouimet	7.50
2378	25¢ Love	3.50
2379	45¢ Love	3.00
2380	25¢ Sum. Olym	3.00
2385a	25¢ Classic Cars bk	6.00
2386-89	25¢ Ant. Expl	4.00
2390-93	25¢ Carousel Anim	4.00
2394	$8.75 Express Mail	30.00
2396a-98a	25¢ Occas.bk.(2)	40.00
2399	25¢ Xmas trad	3.00
2400	25¢ Xmas cont	3.00
	1989-90 Issues	
2401	25¢ Montana Sthd	3.00
2402	25¢ A.P. Randolph	4.50
2403	25¢ N.Dakota Sthd	3.00
2404	25¢ Washington sthd.	3.00
2409a	25¢ Steamboats bklt.	5.00
2410	25¢ Wld. Stamp Expo	3.00
2411	25¢ A. Toscanini	3.00
2412	25¢ House of Reps.	3.00
2413	25¢ U.S. Senate	3.00
2414	25¢ Exec.Branch/GW	3.00
2415	25¢U.S.Sup.Ct.('90)	3.00
2416	25¢ S.Dakota sthd.	3.00
2417	25¢ Lou Gehrig	15.00
2418	25¢ E. Hemingway	3.00
2419	$2.40 Moon Landing	15.00
2420	25¢ Letter Carriers	2.50
2421	25¢ Bill of Rights	2.50
2422-25	25¢ Prehis. Animals	10.00
2426/C21	25¢/45¢ Pre-Columbian Customs	3.50
2427,27a	25¢ Christmas Art, Sht. & Bklt. Pn	9.00
2428,29a	25¢ Christmas Sleigh, Sht. & Bklt. Pn	8.00
2431	25¢ Eagle, self-adhes	4.00
2433	90¢ WSE S/S of 4	10.00
2434-37	25¢ Classic Mail	4.00
2438	25¢ Cl.Mail S/S of 4	6.00
	1990-91 Issues	
2439	25¢ Idaho Sthd	3.00
2440,41a	25¢ Love, sht. & bklt.	7.00
2442	25¢ Ida B. Wells	6.00
2443a	15¢ Bch. Umbr., bklt.	5.00
2444	25¢ Wyoming Sthd	3.00
2445-48	25¢ Classic Films	7.50
2449	25¢ Marianne Moore	3.00
	1990-95 Transportation Coils	
2451	4¢ Steam Carriage	5.00
2452	5¢ Circus Wagon	5.00
2452B	5¢ Wagon, gravure	5.00
2452D	5¢ Circus Wagon, (¢)Sign	6.00
2453,57	5¢/10¢ Canoe/Trailer	5.00
2454	5¢ Canoe, gravure	5.00
2458	10¢ Tractor Trailer	6.00
2463	20¢ Cog Railway	6.00
2464	23¢ Lunch Wagon	4.00
2466	32¢ Ferryboat	6.00
2468	$1.00 Seaplane coil	8.00
	1990-95	
2474a	25¢ Lighthouse bklt	7.50
2475	25¢ ATM Plastic Flag	5.00
2476,78,80	1¢/30¢ Birds	4.00
2477	1¢ Kestrel	5.00
2479	19¢ Fawn	4.00
2481	45¢ Pumpkinseed	4.50
2482	$2 Bobcat	7.50
2483	20¢ Blue Jay	5.00
2484a,85a	29¢ Wood Duck bklts. BEP & KCS	15.00
2486a	29¢ African Violet, booklet pane of 10	8.00
2489	29¢ Red Squirrel	6.00
2490	29¢ Rose	5.00
2491	29¢ Pine Cone	5.00
2492	32¢ Pink Rose	6.00
2496-2500	25¢ Olympics	8.00
2505a	25¢ Indian Headress	9.00
2506-07	25¢ Marsh Is. & Micro. Joint Issue	4.00

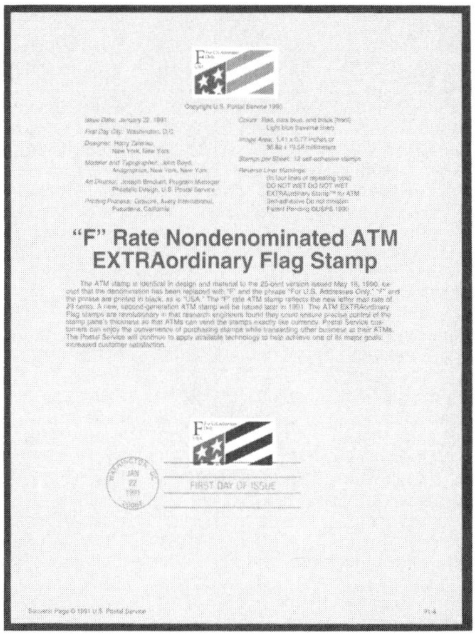
"F" Rate Nondenominated ATM
EXTRAordinary Flag Stamp
FIRST DAY OF ISSUE

2522

Scott No.	Subject	Price
2508-11	25¢ Sea Creatures	7.50
2512/C127	25¢,45¢ America	4.50

1990-94 Issues

Scott No.	Subject	Price
2513	25¢ D.D. Eisenhower	3.00
2514,14a	25¢ Christmas sht. & Bklt. Pn./10	7.50
2515,16a	25¢ Christmas Tree sht. & Bklt. Pn./10	7.50
2517,18	(29¢) "F" Flower, sht. & Coil pr.	5.00
2519a,20a	(29¢) "F" Flower, Bklt. Pns. of 10	15.00
2521	(4¢) Make-up rate	3.50
2522	(29¢) "F" Self Adh.	4.00
2523	29¢ Flag/Rushmore	4.00
2523A	29¢ Mt. Rush, grav.	4.00
2524,27a	29¢ Flower,sht./bklt	9.00
2525	29¢ Flwr. coil,roulette	4.00
2526	29¢ Flower coil,perf.	4.00
2528a	29¢ Flag/Olympic Rings Bklt. pane	9.00
2529	19¢ Fishing Boat coil	4.00
2529C	19¢ Fishing Boat III	5.00
2530a	19¢ Balloons, bklt	7.50
2531	29¢ Flags on Parade	4.00
2531A	29¢ Liberty, ATM	4.00

1991-95 Issues

Scott No.	Subject	Price
2532	50¢ Switzerland	4.00
2533	29¢ Vermont	4.00
2534	29¢ Savings Bonds	4.00
2535,36a,37	29¢,52¢ Love, shts. & Bklt.	15.00
2538	29¢ William Saroyan	4.00
2539	$1.00 USPS & Olym.	6.00
2540	$2.90 Priority Mail	10.00
2541	$9.95 Express Mail	30.00
2542	$14.00 Express Mail	40.00
2543	$2.90 Space P.M.	12.50
2544	$3 Challenger	15.00
2544A	$10.75 Endeavor	30.00
2549a	29¢ Fishing Flies bklt.	7.50
2550	29¢ Cole Porter	4.00
2551	29¢ Desert Storm/ Shield	10.00
2553-57	29¢ Summer Olymp	8.50
2558	29¢ Numismatics	4.00
2559	29¢ WW II S/S	10.00
2560	29¢ Basketball	10.00
2561	29¢ Washington, D.C.	4.00
2566a	29¢ Comedians bklt.	9.00
2567	29¢ Jan Matzeliger	6.50
2577a	29¢ Space bklt.	10.00
2578,78a	29¢ Madonna,sht/bklt	13.50
2579,80, or 81,82-85	29¢ Santa Claus sht./bklt	20.00
2590	$1.00 Burgoyne	7.50
2592	$5.00 Washington	17.50
2593a	29¢ Pledge bklt.	7.50
2595-97	29¢ Eagle & Shield/ Die Cut (3 Pgs.)	7.50
2598	29¢ Eagle S/A	5.00

Scott No.	Subject	Price
2599	29¢ Liberty	5.00
2602	(10¢)Eagle&Shld. coil	4.00
2603-4	(10¢) BEP & SV	6.00
2605	23¢ Flag/Pre-sort	4.00
2606	23¢ USA/Pre-sort	5.00
2607	23¢ Same, BEP	5.00
2608	23¢ Same, SV	5.00
2609	29¢ Flag/W.H. Coil	4.00

1992 Issues

Scott No.	Subject	Price
2611-15	29¢ Winter Olympics	6.00
2616	29¢ World Columbian	4.00
2617	29¢ W.E.B. DuBois	8.00
2618	29¢ Love	4.00
2619	29¢ Olympic BB	15.00
2620-23	29¢ Columb. Voyages	7.50
2624-29	1¢-$5 Columbus S/S	75.00
2630	29¢ NY Stock Exchg.	4.00
2631-34	29¢ Space Accomp	8.00
2635	29¢ Alaska Hwy	4.00
2636	29¢ Kentucky Sthd	4.00
2637-41	29¢ Summer Olymp	8.00
2646a	29¢ Hummingbird Pn.	8.50
2647-96	29¢ Wildflowers (5)	55.00
2697	29¢ WW II S/S	10.00
2698	29¢ Dorothy Parker	4.00
2699	29¢ Dr. von Karman	6.50
2700-03	29¢ Minerals	7.50
2704	29¢ Juan Cabrillo	4.00
2709a	29¢ Wild Animals Bklt.	7.50
2710,10a	29¢ Christmas Trad. Sheet & Bklt.	12.50
2711-14,18a,19	29¢ Toys, sheet bklt.& Die Cut	10.00
2720	29¢ Chinese New Yr.	7.50

1993 Issues

Scott No.	Subject	Price
2721	29¢ Elvis Presley	15.00
2722	29¢ Oklahoma	5.00
2723	29¢ Hank Williams	7.50
2724/30,2737a	29¢ Rock 'n Roll Bklt. & Single	20.00
2745a	29¢ Space Fantasy, Bklt. Pane of 5	10.00
2746	29¢ Perry L. Julian	7.50
2747	29¢ Oregon Trail	5.00
2748	29¢ World Games	5.00
2749	29¢ Grace Kelly	7.50
2750-3	29¢ Circus	7.50
2754	29¢ Cherokee Strip	5.00
2755	29¢ Dean Acheson	5.00
2756-9	29¢ Sports Horses	7.50
2764a	29¢ Garden Flowers, Bklt. Pane of 5	7.50
2765	29¢ WW II S/S	10.00
2766	29¢ Joe Louis	10.00
2770a	29¢ Broadway, Booklet of 4	8.00
2771/4,2778a	Country Music, Booklet & Single	12.50
2779-82	29¢ Postal Museum	6.00
2783-4	29¢ Deaf Commun	5.00
2785-8	29¢ Youth Classics	6.00

Scott No.	Subject	Price
2789,2790a	29¢ Madonna	9.00
2791/4,2798b,2799/2802,2803	29¢ Contem. Xmas	15.00
2804	29¢ N. Marianas	6.00
2805	29¢ Columbus Landing in Puerto Rico	6.00
2806,2806b	29¢ AIDS	10.00

1994 Issues

Scott No.	Subject	Price
2807-11	29¢ Winter Olympics.	7.50
2812	29¢ Edward R.Murrow	6.00
2813	29¢ Sunrise Love	6.00
2814a,15	29¢-52¢ Love	12.50
2814c	29¢ Love	6.00
2816	29¢ Dr. Allison Davis	7.50
2817	29¢ Chinese New Year	7.50
2818	29¢ Buffalo Soldiers	10.00
2819-28	29¢ Silent Scrn. Stars	12.50
2833a	29¢ Garden Flowers, Bklt. Pane of 5	10.00
2834-36	29¢-50¢ Soccer	10.00
2837	Soccer Sv. Sheet	10.00
2838	29¢ WWII S/S	10.00
2839-40	29¢ Rockwell Stamp & S/S	10.00
2841-42	29¢/$9.95 Moon	30.00
2847a	29¢ Locomotive Pn.	8.50
2848	29¢ George Meany	6.00
2849-53	29¢ Pop Singers	10.00
2854-61	29¢ Blues/Jazz	15.00
2862	29¢ J. Thurber	6.00
2863-66	29¢ Wonders-Sea	10.00
2867-68	29¢ Cranes	10.00
2869	29¢ Legends-West	12.50
2871,71b	29¢ Madonna	15.00
2872,72a	29¢ Stocking	12.50
2873-74	29¢ Santa/Cardinal	12.50
2875	$1 BEP S/S	25.00
2876	29¢ Happy New Year	12.50
2877,84,90,93	"G" ABNC	12.00
2878,80,82,85	"G" SVS	12.50
2879,81,83,89	"G" BEP	12.50
2886-87	"G" Self. Adh.	12.00

1995-96 Issues

Scott No.	Subject	Price
2897/2916	32¢ Flag-Porch	12.00
2902	(5¢)Butte Coil	12.00
2902B,4A, 6,10,12A,15B	Coils	11.00
2903-4	(5¢) Mountain Coil	12.00
2905	(10¢) Automobile Coil	12.00
2907,20d,21	Regulars	9.00
2908-9	(15¢) Tail Fin Coil	12.00
2911-12	(25¢) Juke Box Coil	12.00
2919	32¢ Flag - Field, S.A.	10.00
2933	32¢ M. Hershey	12.00
2934	32¢ Cal Farley	11.00
2938	46¢ Ruth Benedict	12.00
2940	55¢ A. Hamilton	12.00
2943	78¢ Alice Paul	12.50
2948-49	(32¢) Love	12.00
2950	32¢ Florida	12.00
2951-54	32¢ Kids Care	12.00
2955	32¢ Richard Nixon	11.00
2956	32¢ Bessie Coleman.	12.00
2957-60	32¢ - 55¢ Angel	12.00
2961-65	32¢ Rec. Sports	12.00
2966	32¢ POW/MIA	12.00
2967	32¢ Marilyn Monroe	13.50
2968	32¢ Texas	12.00
2973a	32¢ Lighthouses Pn.	13.50
2974	32¢ U.N. Nations	12.00
2975	32¢ Civil War	17.50
2976-79	32¢ Carousel	12.00
2980	32¢ Suffrage	11.00
2981	32¢ World War II	13.50
2982	32¢ L. Armstrong	11.00
2983-92	32¢ Jazz	15.00
2997a	32¢ Garden Flowers, Pane of 5	12.50
2998	60¢ E. Rickenbacker.	12.00
2999	32¢ Republic-Palau	11.00
3000	32¢ Comic Strips	20.00
3001	32¢ Naval Academy	11.00
3002	32¢ Tennessee Williams	11.00
3003,3b	32¢ Madonna	14.50
3004-7,8-11	32¢ Christmas	14.50
3012	32¢ Midnight Angel	11.00
3013	32¢ Children Sledding	11.00
3019-23	32¢ Antique Autos	15.00

1996 Issues

Scott No.	Subject	Price
3024	32¢ Utah Statehood	11.00
3029a	32¢ Garden Flowers, Pane of 5	12.50

Scott No.	Subject	Price
3032	2¢ Woodpeckers	11.00
3033	3¢ Bluebird	10.00
3048,53	20¢ Bluejay	11.00
3058	32¢ Ernest Just	11.00
3059	32¢ Smithsonian	11.00
3060	32¢ Chinese New Year	11.00
3061-64	32¢ Communications	13.50
3065	32¢ Fulbright	11.00
3066	50¢ J Cochran	11.50
3067	32¢ Marathon	9.00
3068	32¢ Atlanta Games	15.00
3069	32¢ Georgia O'Keefe	9.00
3070	32¢ Tennessee	9.00
3072-76	32¢ American Indian Dances	13.00
3077-80	32¢ Prehist. Animals.	13.00
3081	32¢ Breast Cancer	9.00
3082	32¢ James Dean	9.00
3083-86	32¢ Folk Heroes	13.00
3087	32¢ Olympic Games	9.00
3088-89	32¢ Iowa	9.00
3090	32¢ Rural Free Delivery	9.00
3091-95	32¢ Riverboats	13.00
3096-99	32¢ Big Band Leaders	13.00
3100-3	32¢ Songwriters	13.00
3104	32¢ F.Scott Fitzgerald	9.00
3105	32¢ Endangered Species	15.00
3106	32¢ Computer Technology	9.00

Airmails (1973-85)

Scott No.	Subject	Price
C79	13¢ Winged Env.	4.00
C83	13¢ Winged Coil	4.00
C84	11¢ City of Refuge	100.00
C87	18¢ Stat. of Liberty	10.00
C88	26¢ Mt. Rushmore	7.50
C89-90	25¢ & 31¢ Airmails	4.00
C91-92	31¢ Wright Brothers	4.00
C93-94	21¢ Octave Chanute	4.00
C95-96	25¢ Wiley Post	5.00
C97	31¢ Olym. Games	6.00
C98	40¢ P. Mazzei	4.00
C99	28¢ Blanche Scott	2.50
C100	35¢ Glenn Curtiss	2.50
C101-04	28¢ Olympics	5.00
C105-08	40¢ Olympics	4.00
C109-12	35¢ Olympics	4.50
C113	33¢ A. Verville	2.50
C114	39¢ L.& E. Sperry	3.00
C115	44¢ Transpacific Flt.	3.00
C116	44¢ Fr.J. Serra	3.00

Airmails (1988-91)

Scott No.	Subject	Price
C117	44¢ New Sweden	3.00
C118	45¢ S.P. Langley	3.00
C119	36¢ Sikorsky	4.00
C120	45¢ French Rev	4.50
C122-25	45¢ Future Mail	6.50
C126	$1.80 Future Mail S/S	8.00
C128	50¢ Harriet Quimby.	4.00
C129	40¢ William Piper	4.00
C130	50¢ Antarctic Treaty	4.75
C131	50¢ America	4.00

1983-95 Official Issues

Scott No.	Subject	Price
O127-29,30-35	1¢/$5 (5 pgs)	25.00
O129A,136	14¢&22¢ Issues	5.00
O138-39	(14¢&22¢)"D" Sht.&Coil	3.00
O138A,141	15¢,25¢ Coils	4.00
O138B	20¢ Coil	3.50
O140	(25¢) "E" Coil	3.50
O143	1¢ Offset	4.50
O144	(29¢) "F" Coil	5.00
O145,47-48	19¢,23¢,29¢ Sgls. & Coil	5.00
O146	4¢ Make-up rate	4.00
O146A	10¢ Official	4.00
0153/56	1¢/32¢ Officials	6.00

1992-94 Variable Rate Coils

Scott No.	Subject	Price
CV31	29¢ Variable Rate	5.00
CV32	29¢ Vert. Design	6.00

AMERICAN COMMEMORATIVE PANELS

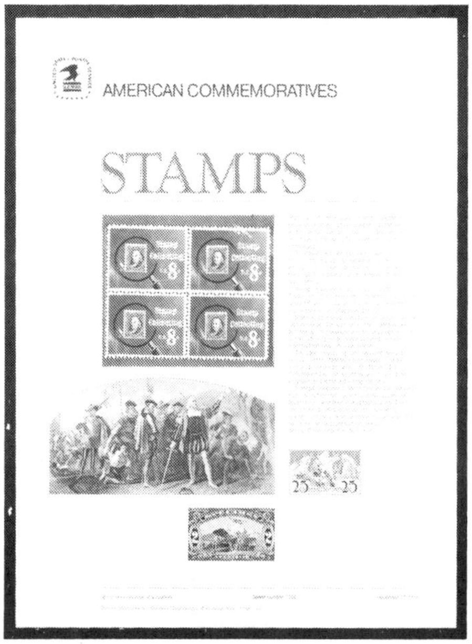

1474

The U.S. Postal Service has provided panels for commemorative and Christmas issues since Scott #1464-67 (Sept. 20, 1972). Each panel features mint stamps along with appropriate steel engravings and interesting stories about the subject.

Scott No.	Subject	Price
	1972 Commemoratives	
1464-67	Wildlife	10.00
1468	Mail Order	9.00
1469	Osteopathic Medicine	9.00
1470	Tom Sawyer	9.00
1471	Christmas 1972	12.50
1472	'Twas Night...Xmas.	12.50
1473	Pharmacy	10.00
1474	Stamp Collecting	9.00
	1973 Commemoratives	
1475	Love	12.50
1476	Pamphleteers	10.00
1477	Posting Broadside	9.00
1478	Post Rider	11.00
1479	Drummer	15.00
1480-83	Boston Tea Party	32.50
1484	George Gershwin	10.00
1485	Robinson Jeffers	10.00
1486	Henry O. Tanner	10.00
1487	Willa Cather	10.00
1488	Copernicus	10.00
1489-98	Postal People	10.00
1499	Harry S. Truman	12.50
1500-02,C86	Electronics	10.00
1503	Lyndon B. Johnson.	12.50
1504	Angus Cattle	10.00
1505	Chautauqua (74)	10.00
1506	Kansas Wheat ..(74)	10.00
1507	Christmas (73)	15.00
1508	Xmas Needlepoint	15.00
	1974 Commemoratives	
1525	Vet. of Foreign Wars	10.00
1526	Robert Frost	10.00
1527	Expo '74	12.50
1528	Horse Racing	12.50
1529	Skylab	12.50
1530-37	Univ. Postal Union	12.50
1538-41	Mineral Heritage	12.50
1542	Fort Harrod	10.00
1543-46	Cont. Congress	12.50
1547	Energy Conserv	10.00
1548	Sleepy Hollow	10.00
1549	Retarded Children	10.00
1550	Xmas Angel Altarpc.	13.00
1551	Xmas "Rd-Winter"	13.00
	1975 Commemoratives	
1553	Benjamin West	10.00
1554	Paul L. Dunbar	11.00
1555	D.W. Griffith	10.00
1556	Pioneer	13.50
1557	Mariner	15.00
1558	Coll Bargaining	10.00

Scott No.	Subject	Price
1559-62	Contrib. to Cause	10.00
1563	Lexing. & Concord	10.00
1564	Bunker Hill	10.00
1565-68	Military Services	10.00
1569-70	Apollo Soyuz	15.00
1571	Int'l Women's Year.	10.00
1572-75	Postal Bicentennial	10.00
1576	Wld. Peace thru Law	10.00
1577-78	Bank & Commerce	11.00
1579	Christmas Madonna	12.50
1580	Christmas Card	14.00
	1976 Commemoratives	
1629-31	Spirit of '76	15.00
1632	INTERPHIL '76	15.00
1633/82	State Flags,Blk.4	30.00
1683	Telephone Cent.	11.00
1684	Commer. Aviation	15.00
1685	Chemistry	13.00
1690	Benjamin Franklin	13.00
1691-94	Dec. of Indepen	12.50
1695-98	Olympics	15.00
1699	Clara Maass	12.00
1700	Adolph S. Ochs	14.50
1701	Copley Nativity	17.50
1702	Currier Winter Past.	17.50
	1977 Commemoratives	
1704	Wash. at Princeton.	17.50
1705	Sound Recording	37.50
1706-09	Pueblo Art	125.00
1710	Lindbergh Flight	125.00
1711	CO Centennial	25.00
1712-15	Butterflies	25.00
1716	Lafayette	21.00
1717-20	Skilled Hands	21.00
1721	Peace Bridge	20.00
1722	Herkimer/Oriskany	20.00
1723-24	Energy Conserv	20.00
1725	Alta, CA	20.00
1726	Art. of Confed	25.00
1727	Talking Pictures	29.50
1728	Surrender/Saratoga	25.00
1729	Xmas/Wash./V. For	30.00
1730	Xmas/Rural Mailbox	45.00
	1978 Issues	
1731	Carl Sandburg	13.50
1732-33	Captain Cook	20.00
1744	Harriet Tubman	16.00
1745-48	American Quilts	27.50
1749-52	American Dance	16.50
1753	French Alliance	16.50
1754	Dr. Papanicolaou	15.00
1755	Jimmie Rodgers	20.00
1756	George M. Cohan	22.50

Scott No.	Subject	Price
1758	Photography	13.00
1759	Viking Missions	60.00
1760-63	American Owls	52.50
1764-67	American Trees	45.00
1768	Madonna & Child	20.00
1769	Xmas Hobby Horse.	22.50
	1979 Commemoratives	
1770	Robert F. Kennedy	13.50
1771	Martin L. King, Jr.	13.00
1772	Year of the Child	12.00
1773	John Steinbeck	12.00
1774	Albert Einstein	13.50
1775-78	PA Toleware	11.50
1779-82	Amer. Architecture.	11.50
1783-86	Endangered Flora	12.50
1787	Seeing Eye Dogs	12.00
1788	Special Olympics	15.00
1789	John Paul Jones	15.00
1790/C97	Olympic Games	16.00
1791-94	15¢ Summer Olym.	17.50
1795-98	15¢ Winter Olym (80)	17.50
1799	Virgin & Child	16.00
1800	Santa Claus	16.00
1801	Will Rogers	15.00
1802	Vietnam Vets	15.00
	1980 Commemoratives	
1803	W.C. Fields	13.50
1804	Benjamin Banneker.	14.00
1821	Frances Perkins	10.00
1823	Emily Bissell	10.00
1824	H. Keller/A. Sullivan	10.00
1825	Vet. Administration	10.00
1826	Gen. B. de Galvez	10.00
1827-30	Coral Reefs	12.50
1831	Organized Labor	10.00
1832	Edith Wharton	10.00
1833	Amer. Education	10.00
1834-37	NW Indian Masks	15.00
1838-41	Amer. Architecture.	12.50
1842	Xmas St. Glass Win.	15.00
1843	Xmas Antique Toys.	15.00
	1981 Commemoratives	
1874	Everett Dirksen	13.00
1875	Whitney M. Young	12.00
1876-79	American Flowers	12.00
1910	Amer. Red Cross	11.00
1911	Savings & Loan	11.00
1912-19	Space Achievement	15.00
1920	Prof. Management	10.00
1921-24	Wildlife Habitats	15.00
1925	Int'l Yr. Disable Per.	10.00
1926	E. St. Vincent Millay	10.00
1928-31	Amer. Architecture.	12.50
1932-33	Jones/Zaharias	37.50
1934	Frederic Remington.	11.00
1935-36	18¢ & 20¢ J. Hoban	10.00
1937-38	Yorktown/V Capes.	10.00
1939	Xmas Madonna/Ch.	15.00
1940	Xmas "Teddy Bear".	15.00
1941	John Hanson	10.00
1942-45	U.S. Desert Plants	14.00
	1982 Commemoratives	
1950	Roosevelt	16.50
1951	Love	18.00
1952	G. Washington	16.50
1953/2002	State Birds/Fl Blk.	50.00
2003	Netherlands	17.50
2004	Library of Congress.	17.50
2006-09	World's Fair	15.00
2010	Horatio Alger	15.00
2011	Aging	18.00
2012	Barrymores	20.00
2013	Dr. Mary Walker	15.00
2014	Int'l Peace Garden	18.00
2015	America's Libraries	16.00
2016	Jackie Robinson	50.00
2017	Touro Synagogue	18.00
2018	Wolf Trap	18.00
2019-22	Amer. Architecture.	20.00
2023	Francis of Assisi	20.00
2024	Ponce de Leon	20.00
2025	Kitten & Puppy	27.50
2026	Xmas Tiepolo Art	25.00
2027-30	Xmas Snow Scene.	25.00
	1983 Commemoratives	
2031	Science & Industry	8.00
2032-35	Balloons	11.00
2036	Sweden/US Treaty	9.00
2037	Civ.Conserv.Corps	8.00
2038	Joseph Priestley	9.00
2039	Voluntarism	9.00
2040	German Immigr	8.00
2041	Brooklyn Bridge	9.00
2042	Tenn. Valley Auth	8.00
2043	Physical Fitness	9.00

Scott No.	Subject	Price
2044	Scott Joplin	13.00
2045	Medal of Honor	11.00
2046	Babe Ruth	40.00
2047	Nath. Hawthorne	9.00
2048-51	13¢ Olympics	15.00
2052	Treaty of Paris	10.00
2053	Civil Service	10.00
2054	Metropolitan Opera.	10.00
2055-58	American Inventors	10.00
2059-62	Streetcars	12.50
2063	Xmas Traditional	15.00
2064	Xmas Contemp	15.00
2065	Martin Luther	12.50
	1984 Commemoratives	
2066	Alaska Statehood	9.00
2067-70	Winter Olympics	10.00
2071	FDIC	8.00
2072	Love	9.00
2073	Carter G. Woodson.	10.75
2074	Soil/Water Conserv.	8.00
2075	Credit Un.Act/1934	8.00
2076-79	Orchids	10.00
2080	Hawaii Statehood	10.00
2081	Nat'l. Archives	9.00
2082-85	Summer Olympics	10.00
2086	Louisiana World Expo	9.00
2087	Health Research	8.00
2088	Douglas Fairbanks	8.00
2089	Jim Thorpe	13.00
2090	John McCormack	8.00
2091	St. Lawren. Seaway	10.00
2092	Mig. Bird Stamp Act	13.00
2093	Roanoke Voyages	8.00
2094	Herman Melville	8.00
2095	Horace Moses	8.00
2096	Smokey the Bear	12.50
2097	Roberto Clemente	52.50
2098-2101	Dogs	10.00
2102	Crime Prevention	10.00
2103	Hispanic Americans	8.00
2104	Family Unity	8.00
2105	Eleanor Roosevelt	9.00
2106	Nation of Readers	9.00
2107	Xmas Traditional	10.00
2108	Xmas Santa Claus	10.00
2109	Vietnam Vets Mem.	13.00
	1985 Issues	
2110	Jerome Kern	10.00
2137	Mary M. Bethune	10.00
2138-41	Duck Decoys	12.50
2142	Winter Spec. Olymp.	10.00
2143	Love	12.00
2144	Rural Electrification.	8.00
2145	AMERIPEX '86	11.50
2146	Abigail Adams	8.00
2147	Auguste Bartholdi	15.00
2152	Korean War Vets	10.00
2153	Social Security Act	8.00
2154	World War I Vets	9.00
2155-58	American Horses	15.00
2159	Public Education	8.00
2160-63	Int'l. Youth Year	12.50
2164	Help End Hunger	9.00
2165	Xmas Traditional	13.00
2166	Xmas Contemp	15.00
	1986 Issues	
2167	Arkansas Statehood	8.00
2201a	Stamp Col. bk./4	12.00
2202	Love	12.50
2203	Sojourner Truth	11.50
2204	Republic of Texas	9.50
2209a	Fish booklet	12.00
2210	Public Hospitals	8.50
2211	Duke Ellington	11.00
2216-19	US Presid., 4 panels	40.00
2220-23	Polar Explorers	11.00
2224	Statue of Liberty	12.50
2235-38	Navajo Art	11.00
2239	T.S. Elliot	9.50
2240-43	Woodcarved Figs	10.00
2244	Xmas Traditional	9.00
2245	Xmas Contemp	9.00
	1987 Issues	
2246	22¢ MI Statehood	9.00
2247	22¢P-Am. Games	9.00
2248	22¢Love	11.00
2249	22¢ J.Bap. Sable	9.00
2250	22¢Enrico Caruso	10.00
2251	22¢Girls Scouts	10.00
2274a	22¢ Sp. Occ. Bk	10.00
2275	22¢ United Way	8.00
2286-2335	22¢ Am.Wildlife(5)	50.00

2381-85

Scott No.	Subject	Price
1987-90 Bicentennial Issues		
2336	22¢ Delaware	12.00
2337	22¢ Penn	10.00
2338	22¢ New Jersey...........	10.00
2239	22¢ Georgia............	11.00
2340	22¢ Conn.............	11.00
2341	22¢ Mass......................	11.00
2342	22¢ Maryland.............	11.00
2343	22¢ S. Carolina............	10.00
2344	25¢ New Hamp.......	11.00
2345	25¢ Virginia	11.00
2346	25¢ New York...........	11.00
2347	25¢ North Carolina.......	12.50
2348	25¢ Rhode Island	12.50
1987 (continued)		
2349	22¢ U.S.-Moroc. Rel....	9.00
2350	22¢ Faulkner	10.00
2351-54	22¢ Lacemaking........	10.00
2359a	22¢ Const. Bklt........	10.00
2360	22¢ Const. Signing........	10.00
2361	22¢ CPA	40.00
2366a	22¢ Locom. Bklt........	12.50
2367	22¢ Xmas Madon	10.00
2368	22¢ Xmas Orn	10.00
1988 Issues		
2369	22¢ '88 Wint. Olym	10.00
2370	22¢ Australia Bicent. ...	10.00
2371	22¢ J.W. Johnson........	12.50
2372-75	22¢ Cats	13.00
2376	25¢ K. Rockne.........	15.00
2377	25¢ F. Ouimet............	35.00
2378-79	25¢-45¢ Love	11.50
2380	25¢ Sum. Olym...........	10.00
2385a	25¢ Classic Cars bk ...	11.50
2386-89	25¢ Ant. Expl.............	12.00
2390-93	25¢ Carousel	12.00
2395-98	25¢ Occasions bk.......	12.50
2399-2400	25¢ Christmas	12.50
1989 Issues		
2401	25¢ Montana.................	10.00
2402	25¢ Randolph	15.00
2403	25¢ N.Dakota...............	10.00
2404	25¢ Wash. Sthd.	10.00

Scott No.	Subject	Price
2409a	25¢ Steamboats bklt.....	12.50
2410	25¢ Wld. Stamp Expo....	10.00
2411	25¢ Arturo Toscanini....	10.00
2412	25¢ House of Reps.......	12.50
2413	25¢ U.S. Senate	12.50
2414	25¢ Exec./GW Inaug.....	12.50
2415	25¢ Supr Court(1990)...	12.50
2416	25¢ S.Dakota Sthd.......	10.00
2417	25¢ Lou Gehrig.........	45.00
2418	25¢ E. Hemingway.......	12.50
2420	25¢ Letter Carriers........	12.50
2421	25¢ Bill of Rights.........	12.50
2422-25	25¢ Prehis. Animals	30.00
2426/C121	25¢/45¢ Pre-Columbian	
	Customs........................	12.50
2427-28	25¢ Christmas	15.00
2434-37	25¢ Classic Mail	12.50
1990 Issues		
2439	25¢ Idaho Sthd	12.50
2440,41a	25¢ Love................	12.50
2442	25¢ Ida B. Wells...........	25.00
2444	25¢ Wyoming Sthd........	10.00
2445-48	25¢ Classic Films	25.00
2449	25¢ Marianne Moore.....	10.00
2474a	25¢ Lighthouse bklt	22.50
2496-2500	25¢ Olympians	20.00
2505a	25¢ Headress Bklt.......	15.00
2506-07	25¢ Marsh Is. & Micro.	
	Joint Issue....................	12.50
2508-11	25¢ Sea Creatures	22.50
2512/C127	25¢,45¢ America.....	15.00
2513	25¢ D.D. Eisenhower.....	15.00
2514,15	25¢ Christmas	15.00
1991 Issues		
2532	50¢ Switzerland...........	14.50
2533	29¢ Vermont...............	12.50
2534	29¢ Savings Bonds	10.00
2535,37	29¢ Love....................	12.50
2538	29¢ William Saroyan.....	12.50
2549a	29¢ Fishing Flies bk ...	17.50
2550	29¢ Cole Porter	12.50
2551	29¢ Desert Shield........	52.50
2553-57	29¢ Summer Olymp ...	15.00

Scott No.	Subject	Price
2558	29¢ Numismatics	15.00
2559	29¢ WW II	20.00
2560	29¢ Basketball	20.00
2561	29¢ Dist.of Columbia ...	12.50
2566a	29¢ Comedians bklt.....	17.50
2567	29¢ Jan Matzeliger	15.00
2577a	29¢ Space bklt.............	17.50
2578-79	29¢ Christmas	15.00
2587	32¢ J. S. Polk(1995)	17.50
1992 Issues		
2611-15	29¢ Winter Olympics .	15.00
2616	29¢ World Columbian..	15.00
2617	29¢ W.E.B. DuBois......	20.00
2618	29¢ Love	15.00
2619	29¢ Olympic Baseball..	60.00
2620-23	29¢ Columb.Voyages .	20.00
2624-29	1¢/$5 Columbus S/S	
	Set of 3 Panels	150.00
2630	29¢ Stock Exchg..........	25.00
2631-34	29¢ Space Accomp	20.00
2635	29¢ Alaska Highway ...	12.50
2636	29¢ Kentucky Sthd	12.50
2637-41	29¢ Summer Olymp....	15.00
2646a	29¢ Humming. B. Pn ...	20.00
2647-96	29¢ Wildflowers (5).....	110.00
2697	29¢ WW II S/S	20.00
2698	29¢ Dorothy Parker......	12.50
2699	29¢ Dr. von Karman.....	15.00
2700-03	29¢ Minerals	20.00
2704	29¢ Juan Cabrillo.........	15.00
2709a	29¢ Wild Animals Pn. .	20.00
2710,14a	29¢ Christmas..........	20.00
2720	29¢ Chinese New Yr....	20.00
1993 Issues		
2721	29¢ Elvis.....................	30.00
2722	29¢ Oklahoma	15.00
2723	29¢ Hank Williams.......	35.00
2737b	29¢ Rock 'n Roll	35.00
2745a	29¢ Space Fantasy......	17.50
2746	29¢ Percy L. Julian......	15.00
2747	29¢ Oregon Trail..........	15.00
2748	29¢ World Games	15.00
2749	29¢ Grace Kelly	25.00
2750-3	29¢ Circus...................	17.50
2754	29¢ Cherokee Strip.......	15.00
2755	29¢ Dean Acheson	18.00
2756-9	29¢ Sports Horses.......	20.00
2764a	29¢ Garden Flowers	20.00
2765	29¢ WW II S/S	20.00
2766	29¢ Joe Louis	30.00
2770a	29¢ Broadway Musicals,	
	Booklet Pane	22.50
2775-8	29¢ Country-West........	28.50
2779-82	29¢ Postal Museum	20.00
2783-4	29¢ Deaf Commun.......	19.50
2785-8	29¢ Youth Classics......	21.00
2789,91-4	29¢ Christmas	20.00
2804	29¢ Nthn.Marianas	17.00
2805	29¢ Columbus Lands	
	in Puerto Rico	18.50
2806	29¢ AIDS	17.50
1994 Issues		
2807-11	29¢ Winter Olympics ...	18.00
2812	29¢ Edward R.Murrow..	12.00
2814a	29¢ Love, Bklt Pane	17.50
2816	29¢ Allison Davis.........	20.00
2817	29¢ Chinese New Year	25.00
2818	29¢ Buffalo Soldiers	24.00
2819-28	29¢ Silent Screen	
	Stars	20.00
2833a	29¢ Garden Flowers,	
	Pane of 5	15.00
2837	29¢,40¢,50¢ World	
	Cup Soccer, S/S of 3 ..	20.00
2838	29¢ WWII S/S	20.00

Scott No.	Subject	Price
2839	29¢ Norman Rockwell .	18.50
2841	29¢ Moon Landing.......	25.00
2847a	29¢ Locomotives,	
	Pane of 5	18.00
2848	29¢ George Meany......	18.00
2849-53	29¢ Pop. Singers	18.00
2854-61	29¢ Jazz/Blues	20.00
2862	29¢ J. Thurber	18.00
2863-66	29¢ Wonders - Sea...	19.50
2867-68	29¢ Cranes	18.00
2871	29¢ Madonna.............	18.00
2872	29¢ Stocking	18.00
2876	29¢ Year of Bear........	20.00
1995 Issues		
2950	32¢ Florida	18.00
2951-54	32¢ Kids Care...........	20.00
2955	32¢ R. Nixon..............	18.00
2956	32¢ B. Coleman..........	20.00
2957-58	32¢-55¢ Love	20.00
2961-65	32¢ Rec. Sports	20.00
2966	32¢ POW/MIA.............	19.50
2967	32¢ M. Monroe............	24.00
2968	32¢ Texas	19.50
2973a	32¢ Lighthouses	23.00
2974	32¢ Un. Nations	17.50
2976-79	32¢ Carousel	23.50
2980	32¢ Women's Suffrage	17.50
2981	32¢ WWII S/S	20.00
2982	32¢ L. Armstrong	20.00
2983-92	32¢ Jazz Mus.	23.50
2997a	32¢ Garden Flowers	
	Pane of 5	17.50
2999	32¢ Palau...................	17.50
3001	32¢ Naval Academy .	17.50
3002	32¢ Tennessee Williams	
	....	17.50
3003	32¢ Madonna.............	17.50
3004-7	32¢ Christmas	18.75
3019-23	32¢ Antique Autos ...	22.50
1996 Issues		
3024	32¢ Utah	17.50
3029a	32¢ Garden Flowers .	22.50
3058	32¢ Ernest E, Just	17.50
3059	32¢ Smithsonian	17.50
3060	32¢ Chinese New Year	17.50
3061-4	32¢ Communications	19.50
3065	32¢ Fulbright..............	17.50
3067	32¢ Marathon.............	17.50
3069	32¢ Georgia O'Keeffe	17.50
3070	32¢ Tennessee	17.50
3071-6	32¢ Indian Dances....	18.50
3077-80	32¢ Prehistoric	
	Animals	17.50
3081	32¢ Breast Cancer......	17.50
3082	32¢ James Dean.........	17.50
3083-86	32¢ Folk Heroes	17.50
3087	32¢ Olympic Games .	17.50
3088	32¢ Iowa	17.50
3090	32¢ Rural Free	
	Delivery...............	17.50
3091-95	32¢ Riverboats........	18.50
3096-99	32¢ Big Band Leaders	17.50
3100-3	32¢ Songwriters........	17.50
3105	32¢ Endangered	
	Species......................	32.50
3118	32¢ Hanukkah...........	16.50
1997 Issues		
3121	32¢ Benjamin Davis..	16.50
Airmails		
C101-04	28¢ Olympics	12.50
C105-08	40¢ Olympics	12.50
C109-12	35¢ Olympics	13.00
C117	44¢ New Sweden	10.00
C120	45¢ French Rev	12.50
C122-25	45¢ Future Mail	15.00
C130	50¢ Antarctic Treaty..	12.50
C131	50¢ America.............	12.50

FREE FROM SCOTT PUBLISHING CO.
The 1997 Scott Product Guide

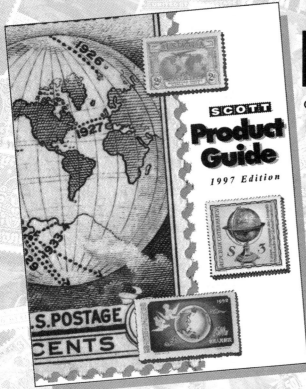

Inside the 1997 edition of the Scott Product Guide you're going to find the largest and most comprehensive line of collecting supplies anywhere.

Highlights include information on changes to the 1998 Scott Catalogues, the latest album and supplement releases and several new products now carried by Scott, including Vario stock pages, and a new Universal binder that will fit virtually every album page and stock sheet sold by Scott. There's all sorts of new album pages, new accessories and they're all inside the 1997 Scott Product Guide.

SEND FOR YOUR FREE COPY TODAY!

For your free copy of the 1997 Scott Product Guide return the coupon on the right to:

**Scott Publishing Co.
P.O. Box 828
Sidney OH 45365-0828**

SCOTT
Serving collectors since 1863

CONFEDERATE STATES OF AMERICA

1,4	2,5	6,7	8

11	12	13	14

1861-62 (OG + 40%) (C)

Scott's No.		Unused		Used	
		Fine	Ave.	Fine	Ave.
1	5¢ Jefferson Davis, Green	165.00	95.00	120.00	70.00
2	10¢ T. Jefferson, Blue	185.00	115.00	135.00	85.00
3	2¢ Andrew Jackson, Green	425.00	250.00	500.00	300.00
4	5¢ Jefferson, Rose	100.00	60.00	75.00	45.00
5	10¢ T. Jefferson, Rose	675.00	400.00	375.00	225.00
6	5¢ J. Davis, London Print, Clear	7.50	4.50	20.00	12.50
7	5¢ J. Davis, Local Print, Coarse	10.75	6.50	15.00	9.00

1862-63 (OG + 40%) (C)

8	2¢ A. Jackson, Brown Red	42.50	26.00	250.00	150.00
9	10¢ J. Davis, Blue "TEN CENTS"	600.00	365.00	425.00	250.00
10	10¢ Blue "TEN CENTS", Frame Line	2500.00	1600.00	1050.00	625.00
11	10¢ Blue, No Frame Line, Die A	8.50	5.50	11.00	6.50
12	10¢ Same, Filled in Corners, Die B	10.00	6.00	12.50	7.50
13	20¢ Washington, Green	27.50	17.00	300.00	185.00
14	1¢ J.C. Calhoun, Orange (unissued)	60.00	37.50	...	...

CANAL ZONE

5	73	84/101	96

1904 U.S. 1902-03 Issue Ovptd. "CANAL ZONE" "PANAMA" VF Used + 50% (C)

Scott's No.		Very Fine		F-VF		F-VF
		NH	Unused	NH	Unused	Used
4	1¢ Frank., Bl. Grn. (#300)	59.50	39.75	40.00	26.50	19.50
5	2¢ Wash., Carmine (#319)	50.00	33.00	32.50	22.50	18.00
6	5¢ Lincoln, Blue (#304)	185.00	120.00	115.00	80.00	60.00
7	8¢ M. Wash., V. Blk. (#306)	345.00	230.00	225.00	150.00	80.00
8	10¢ Webster, Red Brn. (#307)	345.00	230.00	225.00	150.00	80.00

1924-25 U.S. Stamps of 1923-25 Overprinted "CANAL ZONE" (Flat Top "A") Flat Press, Perf. 11 VF Used + 30% (B)

70	½¢ N. Hale (#551)	2.10	1.30	1.50	.95	.65
71	1¢ Franklin (#552)	2.40	1.60	1.70	1.20	.70
71e	1¢ Bklt. Pane of 6 (#552a)	275.00	160.00	175.00	120.00	...
72	1½¢ Harding (#553)	3.00	2.25	2.25	1.65	1.40
73	2¢ Washington (#554)	13.75	9.50	10.00	7.00	1.50
73a	2¢ Bklt. Pane of 6 (#554c)	335.00	250.00	240.00	175.00	...
74	5¢ T. Roosevelt (#557)	33.50	24.00	25.00	18.00	8.00
75	10¢ Monroe (#562)	77.50	53.50	58.50	40.00	20.00
76	12¢ Cleveland (#564)	60.00	40.00	45.00	30.00	27.50
77	14¢ Indian (#565)	50.00	33.75	37.50	25.00	19.50
78	15¢ Liberty (#566)	90.00	60.00	67.50	45.00	32.50
79	30¢ Buffalo (#569)	57.50	37.50	42.50	28.50	19.50
80	50¢ Amphitheater (#570)	110.00	79.50	85.00	60.00	38.50
81	$1 Lincoln Mem. (#571)	425.00	290.00	315.00	215.00	80.00

1925-28 Same as Preceding but with Pointed "A", VF Used + 30% (B)

84	2¢ Washington (#554)	55.00	37.50	40.00	27.50	7.00
84d	2¢ Bklt. Pane of 6 (#554c)	395.00	285.00	275.00	195.00	...
85	3¢ Lincoln (#555)	7.50	5.35	5.50	3.95	2.75
86	5¢ T. Roosevelt (#557)	7.00	5.15	5.25	3.75	1.95
87	10¢ Monroe (#562)	55.00	36.50	40.00	27.50	9.50
88	12¢ Cleveland (#564)	37.50	24.00	27.50	18.50	11.00
89	14¢ Indian (#565)	33.50	22.50	23.50	17.50	14.50
90	15¢ Liberty (#566)	11.50	7.95	8.50	6.00	3.75
91	17¢ Wilson (#623)	7.00	4.85	5.00	3.65	2.75

CANAL ZONE

1925-28 Pointed "A" (cont.)

Scott's No.		Very Fine		F-VF		F-VF
		NH	Unused	NH	Unused	Used
92	20¢ Golden Gate (#567)	10.50	7.00	7.50	5.50	3.00
93	30¢ Buffalo (#569)	8.25	5.95	6.25	4.50	3.75
94	50¢ Amphitheater (#570)	400.00	260.00	285.00	200.00	140.00
95	$1 Lincoln Mem (#571)	190.00	135.00	135.00	100.00	55.00

1926 Sesquicentennial Issue Overprinted "CANAL ZONE"

96	2¢ Liberty Bell (#627)	7.50	5.00	5.50	4.00	3.50

1926-27 Rotary Press, Perf. 10, Overprinted "CANAL ZONE" VF Used + 75% (B)

97	2¢ Washington (#583)	95.00	65.00	52.50	37.50	9.75
98	3¢ Lincoln (#584)	17.50	11.50	10.00	6.75	3.95
99	10¢ Monroe (#591)	31.50	22.50	18.50	13.00	6.00

1927-31 Rotary Press, Perf. 11x10½, Overprinted "CANAL ZONE" VF Used + 30% (B)

100	1¢ Franklin (#632)	3.35	2.50	2.50	1.85	1.20
101	2¢ Washington (#634)	3.85	2.80	2.85	2.10	.90
101a	2¢ Bklt. Pane of 6 (#634d)	350.00	250.00	225.00	160.00	...
102	3¢ Lincoln (#635) (1931)	7.00	4.50	5.00	3.50	2.75
103	5¢ T. Roosevelt (#637)	42.50	30.00	31.50	22.50	9.00
104	10¢ Monroe (#642) (1930)	29.00	18.50	21.75	15.75	10.00

105	107	110	112

1928-40 Flat Plate Printing VF Used + 20% (B)

105-14	Set of 10	12.50	9.00	9.50	7.25	4.95
105	1¢ General Gorgas	.30	.25	.25	.20	.18
106	2¢ General Goethels	.30	.25	.25	.20	.18
106a	2¢ Booklet Pane of 6	27.50	20.00	21.00	15.00	...
107	5¢ Gaillard Cut (1929)	1.50	1.15	1.15	.90	.60
108	10¢ General Hodges (1932)	.45	.35	.37	.28	.20
109	12¢ Colonel Gaillard (1929)	1.50	1.15	1.25	.95	.75
110	14¢ Gen. W.L. Sibert (1937)	1.60	1.20	1.30	1.00	1.00
111	15¢ Jackson Smith (1932)	.75	.60	.60	.45	.45
112	20¢ Adm. Rousseau (1932)	1.00	.85	.85	.65	.25
113	30¢ Col. Williamson (1940)	1.50	1.10	1.20	.90	.85
114	50¢ J. Blackburn (1929)	2.75	2.10	2.30	1.75	.75

PLATE BLOCKS

	NH		Unused		NH		Unused
	VF	F-VF	F-VF		VF	F-VF	F-VF
105 (6)	1.25	1.00	.70	110 (6)	18.50	15.00	11.50
106 (6)	3.50	2.75	2.00	111 (6)	14.50	11.00	7.50
107 (6)	18.50	15.00	9.00	112 (6)	12.50	9.75	7.00
108 (6)	8.50	7.00	5.25	113 (6)	16.50	12.75	9.00
109 (6)	16.50	13.00	10.00	114 (6)	25.00	20.00	15.00

115	117	118	120

1933 Rotary Press, Perf. 11x10½ VF Used + 30% (B)

115	3¢ Washington (#720)	4.65	3.15	3.35	2.35	.30
116	14¢ Indian (#695)	8.75	6.00	6.25	4.50	3.00

1934-39 Issues VF Used + 30% (B)

117	3¢ General Goethals	.35	.28	.25	.20	.18
117a	3¢ Booklet Pane of 6	85.00	60.00	57.50	42.50	...
118	½¢ Franklin (#803) (1939)	.35	.28	.25	.20	.18
119	1½¢ M. Wash. (#805) (1939)	.35	.28	.25	.20	.18

PLATE BLOCKS

	NH		Unused		NH		Unused
	VF	F-VF	F-VF		VF	F-VF	F-VF
115	52.50	40.00	30.00	118	5.25	4.00	3.00
116	100.00	75.00	50.00	119	5.25	4.00	3.00
117 (6)	2.35	1.80	1.40				

CANAL ZONE

1939 25th Anniversary Series VF + 30%

Scott's No.		Plate Blocks F-VF NH	Plate Blocks F-VF Unus.	F-VF NH	F-VF Unus.	F-VF Used
120-35	Set of 16	1475.00	1175.00	110.00	80.00	57.50
120	1¢ Balboa, before................(6)	11.00	9.00	.60	.45	.30
121	2¢ Balboa, after...................(6)	12.00	10.00	.60	.45	.40
122	3¢ Gaillard Cut, before........(6)	11.00	9.00	.60	.45	.22
123	5¢ Gaillard Cut, after..........(6)	18.00	15.00	1.30	.95	.85
124	6¢ Bas Obispo, before ....(6)	38.50	32.50	3.00	2.25	2.35
125	7¢ Bas Obispo, after ....(6)	38.50	32.50	3.00	2.25	2.35
126	8¢ Gatun Locks, before.......(6)	52.50	42.50	4.25	3.15	3.00
127	10¢ Gatun Locks, after........(6)	52.50	42.50	3.75	2.85	2.65
128	11¢ Canal Channel, before .(6)	120.00	100.00	8.50	6.25	6.50
129	12¢ Canal Channel, after ....(6)	100.00	80.00	7.00	5.25	5.50
130	14¢ Gamboa, before ....(6)	110.00	90.00	7.75	5.75	6.25
131	15¢ Gamboa, after ....(6)	135.00	110.00	11.00	8.00	4.75
132	18¢ P. Miguel Locks, before(6)	130.00	105.00	11.00	8.00	7.50
133	20¢ P. Miguel Locks, after....(6)	170.00	135.00	13.50	10.00	6.75
134	25¢ Gatun Spillway, before..(6)	275.00	215.00	19.00	14.00	13.50
135	50¢ Gatun Spillway, after ....(6)	300.00	225.00	24.50	18.00	4.75

137   141   142   146

1946-51 Issues

Scott's No.		Plate Blocks F-VF NH	Plate Blocks F-VF Unus.	F-VF NH	F-VF Unus.	F-VF Used
136-40	Set of 5	21.00	16.50	2.50	2.00	1.50
136	½¢ General Davis (1948)....(6)	2.75	2.25	.35	.28	.25
137	1½¢ Gov. Magoon (1948)...(6)	2.75	2.25	.35	.28	.25
138	2¢ T. Roosevelt (1949)........(6)	.95	.75	.25	.20	.18
139	5¢ J. Stevens, 19x22 mm...(6)	3.50	2.75	.42	.35	.18
140	25¢ J.F. Wallace (1948)......(6)	12.00	9.00	1.25	1.00	.75
141	10¢ Biological Area (1948)..(6)	12.75	8.50	1.65	1.30	.95
142-45	Gold Rush (1949)................	52.50	43.50	5.50	4.25	3.50
142	3¢ "Forty Niners"................(6)	6.50	5.00	.65	.50	.35
143	6¢ Journey to Las Cruces ...(6)	7.00	5.50	.75	.60	.50
144	12¢ Las Cruces Trail...........(6)	19.50	16.50	1.75	1.35	1.00
145	18¢ To San Francisco..........(6)	22.50	18.50	2.50	1.90	1.80
146	10¢ W. Indian Labor(1951) .(6)	27.50	21.50	2.75	2.10	2.00

1955-58 Commemoratives

148   149   150

Scott's No.		Plate Blocks NH	F-VF NH	F-VF Used
147	3¢ Panama Railroad ....(6)	7.50	.70	.50
148	3¢ Gorgas Hospital (1957)...................	4.35	.50	.40
149	4¢ S.S. Ancon (1958)	3.25	.45	.35
150	4¢ T. Roosevelt (1958)	3.50	.50	.40

1960-62 Issues

151   152   153   157

		Plate Blocks NH	F-VF NH	F-VF Used
151	4¢ Boy Scouts.....................	4.50	.50	.40
152	4¢ Administration Bldg.........	1.10	.25	.17

Line Pairs

153	3¢ Goethals, Coil	1.00	.20	.15
154	4¢ Admin. Bldg., Coil	1.15	.20	.18
155	5¢ Stevens, Coil (1962)	1.40	.30	.22

Scott's No.		Plate Blocks NH	F-VF NH	F-VF Used
156	4¢ Girl Scouts (1962)	2.75	.40	.30
157	4¢ Thatcher Ferry Bridge ('62)	3.35	.35	.28

1968-78 Issues

158   159   163   165

		Plate Blocks	F-VF NH	F-VF Used
158	6¢ Goethals Monument Balboa....................	2.25	.35	.25
159	8¢ Fort San Lorenzo (1971)	2.95	.45	.22
160	1¢ Gorgas,Coil,Pf.10 Vert.(1975)...Line Pair	.95	.20	.15
161	10¢ Hodges,Coil,Pf.10 Vert.(1975) Line Pair	4.75	.75	.40
162	25¢ Wallace,Coil,Pf.10 Vert.(1975) Line Pair	19.50	2.75	2.60
163	13¢ Dredge Cascadas (1976)	2.35	.40	.30
163a	13¢ Booklet Pane of 4................................	...	3.00	...
164	5¢ Stevens, Rotary, 19x22½mm (1977)	4.25	.75	.45
165	15¢ Towing Locomotive (1978)....................	2.25	.45	.30

AIR MAIL STAMPS

C3   C5   C6   C17

Scott's No.		Very Fine NH Used	Very Fine NH Unused	F-VF NH Unused	F-VF Used
	1929-31 Surcharges on Issues of 1928-29 VF Used + 30% (B)				
C1	15¢ on 1¢ Gorgas T.I (#105)..	15.00	9.25	12.00	7.50	5.75
C2	15¢ on 1¢ Gorgas T.II (1931).	160.00	115.00	140.00	87.50	87.50
	Type I: Flag "5" points up. Type II: Flag of "5" is curved up.					
C3	25¢ on 2¢ Goethals (#106)	6.00	4.00	4.50	3.00	2.10
C4	10¢ on 50¢ Blackburn (#114).....	14.00	9.00	10.50	7.50	6.50
C5	20¢ on 2¢ Goethals (#106)	11.00	6.75	7.50	5.00	1.85
	1931-49 Series Showing "Gaillard Cut" VF Used + 20% (B)					
C6-14	Set of 9	31.75	22.50	25.50	18.75	6.75
C6	4¢ Red Yellow (1949)	1.10	.85	.90	.70	.75
C7	5¢ Yellow Green	.80	.60	.65	.50	.40
C8	6¢ Yellow Brown (1946)............	1.10	.85	.90	.70	.35
C9	10¢ Orange	1.45	1.10	1.20	.90	.35
C10	15¢ Blue..................................	1.70	1.35	1.40	1.10	.27
C11	20¢ Red Violet	2.95	2.30	2.40	1.90	.30
C12	30¢ Rose Lake (1941)	4.95	3.75	4.00	2.95	1.10
C13	40¢ Yellow	4.95	3.75	4.00	2.95	1.10
C14	$1 Black	13.25	9.75	11.00	8.00	2.50

PLATE BLOCKS

	NH VF	NH F-VF	Unused F-VF		NH VF	NH F-VF	Unused F-VF
C6 (6)	8.50	6.75	5.50	C11 (6)	26.50	21.50	16.50
C7 (6)	6.50	5.00	4.00	C12 (6)	44.00	36.50	27.50
C8 (6)	8.50	6.75	5.50	C13 (6)	44.00	36.50	27.50
C9 (6)	14.75	12.00	9.50	C14 (6)	117.50	97.50	75.00
C10 (6)	15.75	12.75	10.00				

1939 25th Anniversary of Canal Opening VF + 20%

Scott's No.		Plate Blocks NH	Plate Blocks Unused	F-VF NH	F-VF Unused	F-VF Used
C15-20	Set of 6...............................	850.00	650.00	72.50	52.75	42.50
C15	5¢ Plane over Sosa Hill.......(6)	40.00	30.00	4.25	3.25	2.65
C16	10¢ Map of Central America(6)	43.50	32.50	3.75	3.00	2.60
C17	15¢ Fort Amador ....(6)	49.50	37.50	4.50	3.35	1.10
C18	25¢ Cristobal Harbor ....(6)	185.00	135.00	15.00	11.00	8.50
C19	30¢ Gaillaird Cut ....(6)	135.00	110.00	11.50	8.50	7.00
C20	$1 Clipper Landing ....(6)	450.00	350.00	35.00	27.00	23.50

CANAL ZONE

| C21 | C32 | C33 |

1951 "Globe and Wing" Issue

Scott's No.		Plate Blocks NH	Plate Blocks Unus.	F-VF NH	F-VF Unus.	F-VF Used
C21-26	Set of 6	210.00	160.00	24.50	18.75	11.00
C21	4¢ Red Violet ....(6)	7.50	5.75	.80	.60	.40
C22	6¢ Brown ....(6)	5.75	4.25	.65	.50	.35
C23	10¢ Red Orange ....(6)	9.50	7.50	1.15	.90	.50
C24	21¢ Blue.............................(6)	75.00	57.50	8.50	6.50	4.25
C25	31¢ Cerise ....(6)	75.00	57.50	8.50	6.50	4.25
C26	80¢ Gray Black ....(6)	42.50	33.75	5.75	4.50	1.75

1958 "Globe and Wing" Issue

Scott's No.		Plate Blocks F-VF NH	F-VF NH	F-VF Used
C27-31	Set of 5	170.00	24.75	9.00
C27	5¢ Yellow Green	7.00	1.25	.75
C28	7¢ Olive	6.00	1.15	.60
C29	15¢ Brown	30.00	4.50	2.25
C30	25¢ Orange Yellow	90.00	10.75	3.00
C31	35¢ Dark Blue	47.50	8.00	3.25

1961-63 Issues

C32	15¢ U.S. Army Carib. School	13.50	1.50	.95
C33	7¢ Anti-Malaria (1962)	3.50	.60	.50
C34	8¢ Globe & Wing (1963).....................	5.00	.65	.35
C35	15¢ Alliance for Progress (1963)..........	12.50	1.50	.90

1964 50th Anniversary of Canal Opening

C36-41	Set of 6	65.00	12.00	8.75
C36	6¢ Jet over Cristobal........................	2.50	.45	.45
C37	8¢ Gatun Locks	3.00	.55	.45
C38	15¢ Madden Dam	8.00	1.30	.80
C39	20¢ Gaillard Cut...............................	10.50	2.00	1.10
C40	30¢ Miraflores Lock..........................	16.50	3.00	2.50
C41	80¢ Balboa	27.50	5.25	3.75

1965 Seal & Jet Plane

C42-47	Set of 6	28.50	5.75	2.85
C42	6¢ Green & Black	2.25	.40	.30
C43	8¢ Rose Red & Black	2.50	.45	.18
C44	15¢ Blue & Black	2.75	.45	.35
C45	20¢ Lilac & Black	3.00	.70	.45
C46	30¢ Reddish Brown & Black................	5.00	1.00	.50
C47	80¢ Bistre & Black	15.00	3.00	1.25

1968-76 Seal & Jet Plane

C48-53	Set of 6	26.75	4.85	3.00
C48	10¢ Dull Orange & Black	2.00	.40	.20
C48a	10¢ Booklet Pane of 4 (1970)............	...	4.15	...
C49	11¢ Olive & Black (1971)....................	2.25	.45	.25
C49a	11¢ Booklet Pane of 4	...	3.35	...
C50	13¢ Emerald & Black (1974)...............	5.50	1.10	.35
C50a	13¢ Booklet Pane of 4	...	5.50	...
C51	22¢ Violet & Black (1976)..................	5.50	1.10	1.00
C52	25¢ Pale Yellow Green & Black	5.00	.95	.65
C53	35¢ Salmon & Black (1976)................	7.75	1.25	.95

1941-47 OFFICIAL AIRMAIL STAMPS VF Used + 20%
Issue of 1931-46 Overprinted OFFICIAL PANAMA CANAL
"PANAMA CANAL" 19-20 mm long

Scott's No.		Very Fine NH	Very Fine Unused	F-VF NH	F-VF Unused	F-VF Used
CO1-7,14	Set of 8	165.00	125.00	140.00	100.00	45.00
CO 1	5¢ Yellow Green (#C7).............	7.50	5.50	6.00	4.50	2.00
CO 2	10¢ Orange (#C9)...................	14.50	10.50	11.50	8.75	2.50
CO 3	15¢ Blue (#C10)	18.00	12.50	13.50	10.00	3.50
CO 4	20¢ Rose Violet (#C11)	21.00	15.50	17.00	13.00	6.00
CO 5	30¢ Rose Lake (#C12) (1942).	25.50	20.00	21.50	16.50	6.50
CO 6	40¢ Yellow (#C13)	27.50	21.00	22.50	17.00	9.00
CO 7	$1 Black (#C14)....................	40.00	27.50	30.00	22.50	13.50
CO 14	6¢ Yel. Brown (#C8) (1947).....	21.00	14.75	16.50	11.75	5.00

1941 OFFICIAL AIRMAIL STAMPS
Issue of 1931-46 Overprinted OFFICIAL PANAMA CANAL
"PANAMA CANAL" 17 mm long

Scott's No.					Used VF	Used F-VF
CO 8	5¢ Yellow Green (#C7).............	...	...	...	175.00	135.00
CO 9	10¢ Orange (#C9)...................	...	...	...	290.00	225.00
CO 10	20¢ Red Violet (#C11)	...	...	...	215.00	165.00
CO 11	30¢ Rose Lake (#C12)	...	...	...	70.00	55.00
CO 12	40¢ Yellow (#C13)...................	...	...	...	225.00	175.00

NOTE: ON #CO1-CO14 AND O1-9, USED PRICES ARE FOR CANCELLED-TO-ORDER.
POSTALLY USED COPIES SELL FOR MORE.

CANAL ZONE

POSTAGE DUE STAMPS
1914 U.S. Dues Ovptd. "CANAL ZONE", Perf. 12 VF Used + 50% (C)

Scott' No.		Very Fine NH	Very Fine Unused	F-VF NH	F-VF Unused	F-VF Used
J1	1¢ Rose Carmine (#J45a)...	140.00	95.00	95.00	65.00	16.00
J2	2¢ Rose Carmine (#J46a)...	375.00	250.00	250.00	170.00	50.00
J3	10¢ Rose Carmine (#J49a).	...	...	825.00	600.00	50.00

1924 U.S. Dues Ovptd. "CANAL ZONE", Flat "A" VF Used + 40% (B)

J12	1¢ Carmine Rose (#J61).....	230.00	150.00	160.00	110.00	30.00
J13	2¢ Claret (#J62b)...............	140.00	85.00	100.00	60.00	12.00
J14	10¢ Claret (#J65b)..............	525.00	350.00	375.00	250.00	45.00

1925 U.S. Ovptd. "CANAL ZONE POSTAGE DUE" VF Used + 40% (B)

J15	1¢ Franklin (#552)..............	185.00	130.00	130.00	90.00	16.00
J16	2¢ Washington (#554)	45.00	31.50	32.50	22.50	6.75
J17	10¢ Monroe (#562).............	87.50	58.50	62.50	42.50	10.50

1925 U.S. Dues Ovptd. "CANAL ZONE", Sharp "A" VF Used + 40% (B)

J18	1¢ Carmine Rose (#J61).....	18.50	12.00	13.00	8.50	2.75
J19	2¢ Carmine Rose (#J62).....	29.50	19.50	21.00	14.00	4.50
J20	10¢ Carmine Rose (#J65)...	225.00	150.00	160.00	110.00	18.50

1929-30 Issue of 1928 Surcharged "POSTAGE DUE" VF Used + 30% (B)

J21	1¢ on 5¢ Gaillard Cut (#107)	6.50	4.50	5.00	3.50	1.75
J22	2¢ on 5¢ Blue.....................	11.75	7.75	9.00	6.00	3.00
J23	5¢ on 5¢ Blue.....................	11.75	7.75	9.00	6.00	3.50
J24	10¢ on 5¢ Blue...................	11.75	7.75	9.00	6.00	3.50

1932-41 Canal Zone Seal VF + 25% (B) VF Used + 30%

J25-29	Set of 5	6.50	5.00	4.95	3.75	3.25
J25	1¢ Claret	.40	.33	.30	.25	.22
J26	2¢ Claret	.40	.33	.30	.25	.25
J27	5¢ Claret	1.85	.65	.65	.50	.35
J28	10¢ Claret	2.90	2.20	2.25	1.65	1.60
J29	15¢ Claret (1941)	2.15	1.75	1.70	1.35	1.15

1941-47 OFFICIAL STAMPS VF Used + 30% (B)
Issues of 1928-46 Overprinted "OFFICIAL PANAMA CANAL"

O1	1¢ Gorgas, Type 1 (#105)...	3.00	2.25	2.25	1.65	.50
O2	3¢ Goethals, T. 1 (#117).....	5.85	4.35	4.50	3.25	.95
O3	5¢ Gaillard Cut, T. 2 (#107)	...	...	...	...	32.50
O4	10¢ Hodges, Type 1 (#108)..	11.75	8.85	8.75	6.50	2.25
O5	15¢ Smith, Type 1 (#111) ...	20.00	15.00	15.00	11.00	2.50
O6	20¢ Rousseau, T. 1 (#112)..	22.50	16.75	17.00	12.50	3.00
O7	50¢ Blackburn, T. 1 (#114) .	70.00	50.00	50.00	37.50	6.75
O8	50¢ Blackburn, T. 1A (#114)	...	...	...	...	625.00
O9	5¢ Stevens, T. 1 (#139) ('47)	13.00	9.75	9.50	7.00	3.50

Type 1: Ovptd. "10mm", Type 1A: Ovptd. "9mm", Type 2: Ovptd. "19½mm".

CUBA VF + 50% (C)

| 223 | 228 | E2 | J4 |

1899 U.S. Stamps of 1895-98 Surcharged for Use in Cuba

Scott's No.		NH Fine	Unused Fine	Unused Ave.	Used Fine	Used Ave.
221	1¢ on 1¢ Franklin (#279)............	6.00	4.25	2.75	.60	.35
222	2¢ on 2¢ Wash. (#267)	6.75	4.75	2.50	.50	.30
222a	2¢ on 2¢ Wash. (#279B)...........	7.50	5.25	3.00	.50	.30
223	2½¢ on 2¢ Wash. (#279B).........	4.75	3.25	2.10	.60	.35
223a	2½¢ on 2¢ Wash. (#267)	4.35	3.00	1.85	2.40	1.45
224	3¢ on 3¢ Jackson (#268).........	11.00	8.00	5.00	1.50	.90
225	5¢ on 5¢ Grant (#281a)	11.00	8.00	5.00	1.50	.90
226	10¢ on 10¢ Webster (#282C) ..	25.00	17.50	11.50	7.50	4.50

1899 Issues of Republic under U.S. Military Rule

227	1¢ Statue of Columbus	4.65	3.25	1.95	.22	.15
228	2¢ Royal Palms	4.65	3.25	1.95	.22	.15
229	3¢ Allegory "Cuba"	4.65	3.25	1.95	.30	.18
230	5¢ Ocean Liner	5.50	3.75	2.50	.35	.22
231	10¢ Cane Field	14.00	10.00	6.25	.75	.45

1899 SPECIAL DELIVERY

E1	10¢ on 10¢ Blue (#E5)...........	140.00	100.00	65.00	75.00	45.00
E2	10¢ Messenger, Orange..........	55.00	40.00	25.00	12.50	7.50

1899 POSTAGE DUE

J1	1¢ on 1¢ Claret (#J38)............	52.50	35.00	18.50	4.25	2.60
J2	2¢ on 2¢ Claret (#J39)............	52.50	35.00	18.50	4.25	2.60
J3	5¢ on 5¢ Claret (#J41)............	52.50	35.00	18.50	4.25	2.60
J4	10¢ on 10¢ Claret (#J42)........	37.50	25.00	16.50	2.00	1.20

GUAM VF + 60% (C)

| | 1 | 4 | 12 | E1 |

1899 U.S. Stamps of 1895-98 Overprinted "GUAM"

Scott's No.		NH Fine	Unused Fine	Ave.	Used Fine	Ave.
1	1¢ Franklin (#279)	27.50	18.50	12.00	27.50	16.00
2	2¢ Wash. (#267)	25.00	17.50	10.50	26.50	16.00
2a	2¢ Wash. (#279c)	28.50	20.00	13.50	30.00	20.00
3	3¢ Jackson (#268)	150.00	100.00	60.00	135.00	80.00
4	4¢ Lincoln (#280a)	165.00	110.00	65.00	135.00	80.00
5	5¢ Grant (#281a)	35.00	23.50	16.50	35.00	20.00
6	6¢ Garfield (#282)	150.00	100.00	60.00	150.00	90.00
7	8¢ Sherman (#272)	150.00	100.00	60.00	150.00	90.00
8	10¢ Webster (#282C)	55.00	35.00	22.50	55.00	35.00
10	15¢ Clay (#284)	165.00	110.00	65.00	150.00	90.00
11	50¢ Jefferson (#275)	325.00	225.00	135.00	275.00	175.00
12	$1 Perry (#276)	465.00	315.00	190.00	425.00	240.00

1899 SPECIAL DELIVERY

		NH Fine	Unused Fine	Ave.	Used Fine	Ave.
E1	10¢ Blue (on U.S. #E5)	185.00	120.00	72.50	160.00	100.00

HAWAII

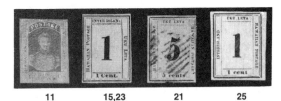

| 11 | 15,23 | 21 | 25 |

1857-68 Issues (OG + 30%) (C)

Scott's No.		Unused Fine	Ave.	Used Fine	Ave.
8	5¢ Kamehameha III, Blue	450.00	275.00	425.00	250.00
9	5¢ Blue, Bluish Paper	185.00	110.00	185.00	110.00
10	5¢ Blue, Reissue	22.50	13.75	...	...
11	13¢ Dull Rose, Reissue	200.00	125.00	...	...
15	1¢ Numeral, Black, Grayish	325.00	200.00	...	...
16	2¢ Black	625.00	395.00	450.00	285.00
19	1¢ Black	350.00	215.00	...	...
20	2¢ Black	475.00	285.00	...	...
21	5¢ Blue, Bluish Paper	500.00	300.00	375.00	230.00
22	5¢ Blue, Interisland	375.00	225.00	600.00	350.00
23	1¢ Black	190.00	110.00	...	...
24	2¢ Black	190.00	110.00	...	...
25	1¢ Dark Blue	190.00	110.00	...	...
26	2¢ Dark Blue	185.00	110.00	...	...

1861-86 Issues (OG + 20%, NH + 100) (C)

| 27-29 | 30 | 32,39,52C | 35,38,43 | 36,46 |

		Fine	Ave.	Fine	Ave.
27	2¢ Kamehameha IV, Pale Rose	165.00	100.00	150.00	90.00
28	2¢ Pale Rose, Vert. Laid Paper	165.00	100.00	110.00	65.00
29	2¢ Red, Thin Wove Paper Reprint	40.00	25.00	...	...
30	1¢ Victoria Kamamalu, Purple	7.50	4.50	5.75	3.50
31	2¢ Kamehameha IV, Vermilion	11.50	7.00	7.00	4.25
32	5¢ Kamehameha V, Blue	110.00	75.00	22.50	13.50
33	6¢ Kamehameha V, Green	18.50	11.00	6.75	4.00
34	18¢ Kekuanaoa, Dull Rose	75.00	42.50	32.50	18.75
35	2¢ Kalakaua, Brown	5.75	3.50	2.40	1.40
36	12¢ Leleiohoku, Black	42.50	25.00	21.50	13.00

HAWAII

1882-91 Issues (OG + 20%) (C)

| 37,42 | 40,44-45 | 41 | 47 | 52 |

Scott's No.		NH Fine	Unused Fine	Ave.	Used Fine	Ave.
37	1¢ Likelike, Blue	7.00	4.50	2.75	7.50	4.75
38	2¢ Kalakaua, Lilac Rose	150.00	95.00	57.50	35.00	21.50
39	5¢ Kamehameha V, Ultra	17.00	10.50	6.50	2.50	1.60
40	10¢ Kalakaua, Black	42.50	27.50	17.50	15.00	9.00
41	15¢ Kapiolani, Red Brown	70.00	42.50	27.50	20.00	12.00
42	1¢ Likelike, Green	3.25	2.10	1.35	1.50	.90
43	2¢ Kalakaua, Rose	4.85	3.00	1.90	.75	.45
44	10¢ Kalakaua, Red Brown	35.00	22.50	14.00	7.50	4.65
45	10¢ Kalakaua, Vermilion	35.00	23.50	14.00	10.50	7.00
46	12¢ Leleiohoku, Red Lilac	95.00	60.00	37.50	26.50	17.50
47	25¢ Kamehameha I, Dk. Viol.	140.00	90.00	55.00	45.00	28.50
48	50¢ Lunalilo, Red	195.00	120.00	75.00	65.00	40.00
49	$1 Kaleleonalani, Rose Red	280.00	175.00	110.00	115.00	70.00
50	2¢ Orange Verm., Imperf	...	130.00	85.00	...	...
51	2¢ Carmine, Imperf	...	22.50	13.50	...	...
52	2¢ Liliuokalani, Dull Violet	7.50	4.00	2.25	1.25	.80
52C	5¢ Kamehameha, V.D. Ind.	150.00	90.00	55.00	100.00	62.50

1893 Issues of 1864-91 Overprinted "Provisional Government 1893" VF + 40% (C)

Red Overprints

53	1¢ Purple (#30)	8.75	5.75	3.50	9.00	5.50
54	1¢ Blue (#37)	7.00	4.50	2.75	9.00	5.50
55	1¢ Green (#42)	2.15	1.35	.75	2.50	1.50
56	2¢ Brown (#35)	11.00	7.50	4.75	15.00	9.50
57	2¢ Dull Violet (#52)	2.10	1.35	.80	1.20	.75
58	5¢ Deep Indigo (#52C)	12.50	8.00	4.75	17.50	11.00
59	5¢ Ultramarine (#39)	7.50	4.75	3.00	3.00	1.75
60	6¢ Green (#33)	17.50	11.50	7.00	18.75	11.50
61	10¢ Black (#40)	11.00	7.00	4.25	11.75	7.50
62	12¢ Black (#36)	10.75	6.75	4.15	13.50	8.00
63	12¢ Red Lilac (#46)	175.00	110.00	65.50	140.00	85.00
64	25¢ Dark Violet (#47)	30.00	18.00	11.00	30.00	18.50

Black Overprint

65	2¢ Rose Vermilion (#31)	80.00	50.00	31.75	55.00	35.00
66	2¢ Rose (#43)	1.85	1.10	.70	2.25	1.35
67	10¢ Vermilion (#45)	18.50	11.50	7.00	23.50	15.75
68	10¢ Red Brown (#44)	8.50	5.50	3.35	9.00	5.50
69	12¢ Red Lilac (#46)	335.00	210.00	135.00	335.00	200.00
70	15¢ Red Brown (#41)	24.00	15.00	9.50	27.50	16.50
71	18¢ Dull Rose (#34)	30.00	19.00	11.00	31.00	18.75
72	50¢ Red (#48)	75.00	47.50	28.50	75.00	45.00
73	$1 Rose Red	140.00	90.00	55.00	130.00	75.00

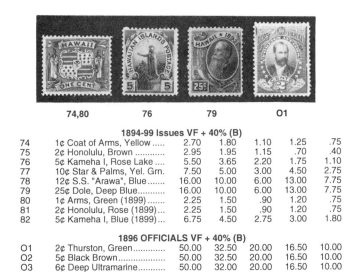

| 74,80 | 76 | 79 | O1 |

1894-99 Issues VF + 40% (B)

74	1¢ Coat of Arms, Yellow	2.70	1.80	1.10	1.25	.75
75	2¢ Honolulu, Brown	2.95	1.95	1.15	.70	.40
76	5¢ Kamehameha I, Rose Lake	5.50	3.65	2.20	1.75	1.10
77	10¢ Star & Palms, Yel. Grn.	7.50	5.00	3.00	4.50	2.75
78	12¢ S.S. "Arawa", Blue	16.00	10.00	6.00	13.00	7.75
79	25¢ Dole, Deep Blue	16.00	10.00	6.00	13.00	7.75
80	1¢ Arms, Green (1899)	2.25	1.50	.90	1.20	.75
81	2¢ Honolulu, Rose (1899)	2.25	1.50	.90	1.20	.75
82	5¢ Kameha I, Blue (1899)	6.75	4.50	2.75	3.00	1.80

1896 OFFICIALS VF + 40% (B)

O1	2¢ Thurston, Green	50.00	32.50	20.00	16.50	10.00
O2	5¢ Black Brown	50.00	32.50	20.00	16.50	10.00
O3	6¢ Deep Ultramarine	50.00	32.00	20.00	16.50	10.00
O4	10¢ Bright Rose	50.00	32.50	20.00	16.50	10.00
O5	12¢ Orange	80.00	50.00	30.00	16.50	10.00
O6	25¢ Gray Violet	100.00	60.00	40.00	20.00	12.50

PHILIPPINE ISLANDS VF + 50% (C)

| | 213 | 226 | E1 | J1 |

1899 U.S. Stamps of 1894-98 Overprinted "PHILIPPINES"

Scott's No.		NH Fine	Unused Fine	Ave.	Used Fine	Ave.
212	50¢ Jefferson (#260)	550.00	350.00	215.00	225.00	140.00
213	1¢ Franklin (#279)	4.50	3.25	1.85	1.00	.60
214	2¢ Wash. (#279d)	2.00	1.25	.80	.75	.45
214a	2¢ Wash. (#267)	2.75	1.75	1.20	1.00	.60
215	3¢ Jackson (#268)	8.75	5.25	2.95	1.95	1.15
216	5¢ Grant (#281)	7.75	5.35	3.15	1.50	.90
217	10¢ Webster Ty. I (#282C) ..	26.00	16.00	9.00	4.25	2.75
217A	10¢ Webster, Ty. II (#283)..	275.00	185.00	115.00	40.00	25.00
218	15¢ Clay (#284)	45.00	32.50	22.50	8.25	4.95
219	50¢ Jefferson (#275)	160.00	120.00	70.00	40.00	25.00

1901 U.S. Stamps of 1895-98 Overprinted "PHILIPPINES"

220	4¢ Lincoln (#280b)	30.00	20.00	13.00	5.25	3.00
221	6¢ Garfield (#282)	37.50	25.00	17.50	7.00	4.25
222	8¢ Sherman (#272)	42.50	28.50	19.50	7.50	4.50
223	$1 Perry, Ty. I (#276)	525.00	350.00	235.00	225.00	140.00
223A	$1 Perry, Ty. II (#276A)	3000.00	2000.00	1375.00	1050.00	650.00
224	$2 Madison (#277a)	700.00	450.00	325.00	300.00	185.00
225	$5 Marshall (#278)	1500.00	950.00	625.00	650.00	425.00

1903-04 U.S. Stamps of 1902-03 Overprinted "PHILIPPINES"

226	1¢ Franklin (#300)	6.00	4.00	2.75	.45	.27
227	2¢ Wash. (#301)	10.50	7.00	3.95	1.85	1.10
228	3¢ Jackson (#302)	95.00	65.00	42.50	16.00	9.00
229	4¢ Grant (#303)	100.00	70.00	47.50	24.00	14.50
230	5¢ Lincoln (#304)	16.00	11.00	6.65	1.40	.85
231	6¢ Garfield (#305)	110.00	75.00	50.00	23.50	13.75
232	8¢ M. Wash. (#306)	60.00	40.00	25.00	15.00	9.00
233	10¢ Webster (#307)	27.50	18.50	12.00	2.75	1.50
234	13¢ Harrison (#308)	45.00	30.00	20.00	16.50	8.75
235	15¢ Clay (#309)	82.50	55.00	32.50	12.50	7.50
236	50¢ Jefferson (#310)	185.00	125.00	85.00	40.00	27.50
237	$1 Farragut (#311)	650.00	400.00	275.00	255.00	150.00
238	$2 Madison (#312)	...	1050.00	700.00	825.00	500.00
239	$5 Marshall (#313)	...	1250.00	850.00	950.00	550.00
240	2¢ Wash. (#319)	7.50	5.00	3.00	2.50	1.50

1901 SPECIAL DELIVERY U.S. #E5 Ovptd. "PHILIPPINES"

E1	10¢ Messenger, Dark Blue .	135.00	90.00	60.00	110.00	65.00

1899-1901 POSTAGE DUES U.S. Dues Ovprd. "PHILIPPINES"

J1	1¢ Deep Claret (#J38)	7.00	4.50	2.75	1.80	1.10
J2	2¢ Deep Claret (#J39)	7.25	4.75	2.85	1.80	1.10
J3	5¢ Deep Claret (#J41)	18.50	11.50	7.00	3.25	1.95
J4	10¢ Deep Claret (#J42)	23.00	15.00	9.15	6.50	4.00
J5	50¢ Deep Claret (#J44)	225.00	155.00	100.00	90.00	60.00
J6	3¢ Deep Claret (#J40)	21.50	13.75	8.25	9.50	5.65
J7	30¢ Deep Claret (#J43)	265.00	175.00	110.00	90.00	60.00

PUERTO RICO VF + 50% (C)

| | 210a | 211 | 212 | 215 | J2 |

1899 U.S. Stamps of 1895-98 Overprinted "PORTO RICO"

210	1¢ Franklin (36 Angle)	9.00	6.00	3.65	1.65	1.00
210a	1¢ (#279) (25 Angle)...........	12.00	8.00	4.85	2.25	1.35
211	2¢ Wash. (36 Angle)	8.00	5.50	3.35	1.50	.90
211a	2¢ (#267) (25 Angle)	10.50	7.50	4.50	1.50	.90
212	5¢ Grant, Blue (#281a)	12.00	8.00	4.85	2.35	1.45
213	8¢ Sherman (36 Angle)	42.50	26.50	15.00	16.00	12.50
213a	8¢ (#272) (25 Angle)	50.00	32.50	18.50	18.50	13.50
214	10¢ Webster (#282C)	28.50	18.50	10.50	5.75	3.50

1900 U.S. Stamps of 1895-98 Overprinted "PUERTO RICO"

215	1¢ Franklin (#279)	8.00	5.75	3.50	1.75	1.05
216	2¢ Wash. (#267)	7.50	5.25	3.25	1.40	.85
216a	2¢ Orange Red (#279d)	9.00	6.00	3.65	1.40	.85

1899 Postage Dues; U.S. Dues Overprinted "PORTO RICO"

J1	1¢ (#J38) (36 Angle)	30.00	20.00	11.00	7.50	4.50
J1a	1¢ Claret (25 Angle)	35.00	23.00	12.00	9.00	5.50
J2	2¢ (#J39) (36 Angle)	20.00	13.50	8.25	6.75	4.00
J2a	2¢ Claret (25 Angle)	26.00	17.50	10.50	7.50	4.50
J3	10¢ (#J42) (36 Angle)........	200.00	135.00	80.00	55.00	32.50
J3a	10¢ Claret (25 Angle)	235.00	165.00	90.00	60.00	35.00

U.S. TRUST TERRITORY OF THE PACIFIC

THE MARSHALL ISLANDS, MICRONESIA, AND PALAU WERE PART OF THE U.S. TRUST TERRITORY OF THE PACIFIC. THE MARSHALL'S BECAME INDEPENDENT IN 1986.

MARSHALL ISLANDS

| | 31 | 35 | 50 |

1984 Commemoratives

Scott's No.		Mint Sheetlet	Plate Block	F-VF NH
31-34	20¢ Postal Service Inaugural, attd........	...	3.50	2.50
50-53	40¢ U.P.U. Congress, attd..................	...	4.00	3.50
54-57	20¢ Ausipex Dolphins, attd..................	...	3.00	2.25
58	20¢ Xmas, 3 Kings, Strip of 4, attd......	(16) 14.00	(8) 8.00	3.75
58	Christmas with tabs, attd.		(8) 8.50	5.75
59-62	20¢ Marshalls Constitution, attd	...	3.50	2.35

1984-85 Maps and Navigational Instruments

35-49A	1¢-$1 Definitives (16)		72.50	14.95
35-38,44,49A	Set 1 1¢-10¢,30¢,$1.00(6)		24.75	4.95
39,41,43,46	Set 2 13¢, 20¢, 28¢, 37¢ (4)		25.95	5.10
39a	13¢ Booklet Pane of 10		...	15.00
41a	20¢ Booklet Pane of 10		...	15.00
41b	13¢/20¢ Bklt. Pane of 10 (5 #39, 5 #41)		...	16.50
40,42,45,47-50	Set 3 14¢, 22¢, 33¢, 39¢, 44¢, 50¢(6)		26.50	5.50
40a	14¢ Booklet Pane of 10		...	12.50
42a	22¢ Booklet Pane of 10		...	12.50
42b	14¢/22¢ Bklt. Pane of 10 (5 #40, 5 #42)		...	13.50

| | 63-64 | |

1985 Commemoratives

63-64	22¢ Audubon, attd	...	3.85	1.65
65-69	22¢ Sea Shells, strip of 5 attd..............	(10) 8.25	2.95
70-73	22¢ Decade for Women, attd...............	...	3.50	2.50
74-77	22¢ Reef and Lagoon Fish, attd	...	3.50	2.75
78-81	22¢ International Youth Year, attd..........	...	3.35	2.65
82-85	14¢,22¢,33¢,44¢ Christmas (4)	...	14.75	2.75
86-90	22¢ Halley's Comet, strip of 5 attd........	(15) 48.75 (10) 19.50	7.50
86-90	Halley's Comet with tabs, attd	...	...	35.00
91-94	22¢ Medicinal Plants, attd	...	3.50	2.50

1986-87 Maps and Navigational Instruments

107	$2 Wotje & Erikub, 1871 Terrestrial Globe	...	30.00	6.75
108	$5 Bikini, Stick Chart	...	75.00	15.75
109	$10 Stick Chart (1987).........................	...	115.00	25.75

| | 110 | 163 |

1986-87 Commemoratives

110-13	14¢ Marine Invertebrates, attd.............	...	3.00	2.21
114	$1 Ameripex S/S (C-54 Globemaster)..	...	...	4.50
115-18	22¢ Operation Crossroads, attd............	...	3.50	2.65
119-23	22¢ Seashells, strip of 5, attd	(10) 7.50	3.50
124-27	22¢ Game Fish, attd	...	3.50	2.95
128-31	22¢ Christmas / Year of Peace, attd.....	...	4.75	3.75
132-35	22¢ Whaling Ships, attd (1987)	...	3.50	2.95
136-41	33¢,39¢,44¢ Pilots (3 pairs)	...	(12)16.50	7.25
142	$1.00 Amelia Earhart / CAPEX S/S......	...	...	3.50
143-51	14¢,22¢,44¢ U.S. Const. Bicent (9)......	(15) 37.50	7.75
152-56	22¢ Seashells, strip of 5, attd..............	(10)7.95	3.75
157-59	44¢ Copra Industry, strip of 3, attd	(6) 7.00	3.25
160-63	14¢,22¢,33¢,44¢ Christmas, Bible Verses (4)	...	14.95	2.95

164 **184**

Scott's No.		Mint Sheetlet	Plate Block	F-VF NH
	1988 Commemoratives			
164-67	44¢ Marine Birds, attd........................	...	5.25	4.50
188	15¢ Olympics, Javelin, Strip of 5	...	(10) 5.25	2.40
189	25¢ Olympics, Runner, Strip of 5.................	...	(10) 6.75	3.15
190	25¢ Robt. Louis Stevenson S/S of 9............	...	...	9.50
191-94	25¢ Colonial Ships and Flags, attd..............	...	3.50	3.00
195-99	25¢ Christmas, strip of 5........................	...	(10) 7.95	3.65
200-04	25¢ John F. Kennedy, Strip of 5	(15) 17.50	...	3.95
205-08	25¢ Space Shuttle, Strip of 4	(12) 9.95	(8) 7.25	3.25
205-08	Space ShuttleTab Strip..........................	...	...	4.25
	1988-89 Fish Definitives			
168-84	1¢-$10.00 Fish (17)	...	260.00	58.75
168/83	Set 1 1¢, 3¢, 14¢, 17¢, 22¢, 33¢, 39¢			
	44¢, 56¢, $1.00, $2.00, $5.00 (12)	...	135.00	29.95
170a	14¢ Booklet Pane of 10	...	...	6.75
173a	22¢ Booklet Pane of 10	...	...	7.75
173b	14¢ & 22¢ Bklt. Pane of 10 (5 ea.)...............	...	...	7.00
171,174,176,179	Set 2 15¢, 25¢, 36¢, 45¢ (4)	...	23.95	5.35
171a	15¢ Booklet Pane of 10	...	...	9.00
174a	25¢ Booklet Pane of 10	...	...	10.50
174b	15¢ & 25¢ Booklet Pane of 10	...	...	9.50
184	$10 Fish Definitive ('89)	...	115.00	26.75
	1989 Commemoratives			

209 **222**

209-12	45¢ Links to Japan, attd................................	...	5.00	4.50
213-15	45¢ Alaska State 30th Anniv., Strip of 3	(9) 13.50	...	3.85
216-20	25¢ Seashells, Strip of 5.........................	...	(10) 7.50	3.65
221	$1.00 Hirohito Memorial S/S......................	...	...	2.95
222-25	45¢ Migrant Birds, attd............................	...	6.50	5.15
226-29	45¢ Postal History, attd...........................	...	6.75	5.65
230	25¢ Postal History, S/S of 6	...	...	12.75
231	$1.00 PHILEXFRANCE, S/S	...	...	12.50
232-38	25¢/$1 Moon Landing, 20th Anniv., Bklt. sgls	...	...	26.75
238a	$2.50 Booklet Pane of 7 (6x25¢,$1)	...	...	26.95
	Also See #341-45			

239 **298**

	* WW II Anniversaries 1939-1989			
239	25¢ Invasion of Poland	(12) 13.50	4.50	.90
240	45¢ Sinking of HMS Royal Oak	(12) 24.50	8.00	1.65
241	45¢ Invasion of Finland...........................	(12) 24.50	8.00	1.65
242-45	45¢ Battle of River Platte, attd...................	(16) 32.50	8.00	6.75
	* WW II Anniversaries 1940-1990			
246-47	25¢ Invas. of Norway & Denmark, attd........	(12) 20.75	4.00	1.85
248	25¢ Katyn Forest Massacre......................	(12) 11.00	3.75	.75
249-50	25¢ Invasion of Belgium, attd	(12) 13.50	4.50	1.80
251	45¢ Churchill Becomes Prime Minister........	(12) 24.50	8.00	1.65
252-53	45¢ Evacuation at Dunkirk	(12) 22.50	7.50	3.25
254	45¢ Occupation of Paris	(12) 25.00	8.00	1.65
255	25¢ Mers-el-Kebir & Burma Rd.	(12) 13.00	4.35	.90
256	25¢ Burma Road...................................	(12) 13.00	4.35	.90
257-60	45¢ U.S. Destroyers for G.B., atd...............	(16) 32.50	8.00	6.50
261-64	45¢ Battle of Britain, attd........................	(16) 32.50	8.00	6.50
265	45¢ Tripartite Pact, 1940.........................	(12) 24.50	8.00	1.65
266	25¢ FDR Elected to Third Term..................	(12) 13.50	4.50	.90
267-70	25¢ Battle of Taranto, attd	(16) 17.75	4.50	3.75

Scott's No.		Mint Sheetlet	Plate Block	F-VF NH
	* WW II Anniversaries 1941-1991			
271-74	30¢ Four Freedoms, attd	(16) 23.50	5.50	4.50
275	30¢ Battle of Beda Fomm.........................	(12) 13.50	4.50	.90
276-77	29¢ German Invasion			
	of Greece & Yugoslavia, attd.........	(12) 16.50	5.50	2.25
278-81	50¢ Sinking of the Bismarck, attd...............	(16) 29.50	10.00	7.50
282	30¢ Germany Invades Russia	(12) 16.50	5.50	1.10
283-84	29¢ Atlantic Charter, attd. pair	(12) 14.50	4.75	2.25
285	29¢ Siege of Moscow	(12) 16.50	5.50	1.10
286-87	30¢ Sinking of the USS Reuben James, attd	(16) 19.50	4.75	2.25
288-91	50¢ Japanese Attack Pearl Harbor, attd......	(16) 35.00	8.95	7.50
288a-91a	50¢ Pearl Harbor Reprint,attd....................	(16) 40.00	9.75	8.00
292	29¢ Japanese Capture Guam.....................	(12) 16.50	5.50	1.10
293	29¢ Fall of Singapore.............................	(12) 16.50	5.50	1.10
294-95	50¢ Flying Tigers, attd............................	(16) 26.50	8.95	3.75
296	29¢ Fall of Wake Island	(12) 16.50	5.50	1.10
	* WW II Anniversaries 1942-1992			
297	29¢ FDR & Churchill at Arcadia Conference	(12) 16.50	5.50	1.10
298	50¢ Japanese enter Manila	(12) 27.75	9.25	1.85
299	29¢ Japanese take Rabaul	(12) 16.50	5.50	1.10
300	50¢ Fall of Java Sea	(12) 27.75	9.25	1.85
301	50¢ Fall of Rangoon	(12) 27.75	9.25	1.85
302	29¢ Battle for New Guinea	(12) 16.50	5.50	1.10
303	29¢ MacArthur Leaves Corregidor..............	(12) 16.50	5.50	1.10
304	29¢ Raid on Saint-Nazaire	(12) 16.50	5.50	1.10
305	29¢ Surrender of Bataan	(12) 16.50	5.50	1.10
306	50¢ Doolittle Raid on Tokyo	(12) 27.75	9.25	1.85
307	29¢ Fall of Corregidor	(12) 16.50	5.50	1.10
308-11	50¢ Battle of the Coral Sea, attd	(12) 35.00	8.95	7.50
308a-11a	50¢ Coral Sea Reprint, attd.......................	(16) 40.00	9.50	8.00
312-15	50¢ Battle of Midway, attd	(16) 35.00	8.95	7.50
316	29¢ Village of Lidice Destroyed.................	(12) 16.50	5.50	1.10
317	29¢ Fall of Sevastopol	(12) 16.50	5.50	1.10
318-19	29¢ Convoy, attd..................................	(12) 16.50	5.00	2.25
320	29¢ Marines Land on Guadalcanal..............	(12)16.50	5.50	1.10
321	29¢ Battle of Savo Island	(12) 16.50	5.50	1.10
322	29¢ Dieppe Raid	(12) 16.50	5.50	1.10
323	50¢ Battle of Stalingrad	(12) 27.50	9.25	1.85
324	29¢ Battle of Eastern Solomons.................	(12) 16.50	5.50	1.10
325	50¢ Battle of Cape Esperance	(12) 27.50	9.25	1.85
326	29¢ Battle of El Alamein	(12) 16.50	5.50	1.10
327-28	29¢ Battle of Barents Sea, attd. pair...........	(12) 16.50	5.50	2.25
	* WW II Anniversaries 1943-1993			
329	29¢ Casablanca Conference	(12) 16.50	5.50	1.10
330	29¢ Liberation of Kharkov	(12) 16.50	5.50	1.10
331-34	50¢ Battle of Bismarck Sea, attd	(16) 35.00	8.95	7.50
335	50¢ Interception of Yamamoto...................	(12) 27.50	9.25	1.85
336-37	29¢ Battle of Kursk	(16) 24.00	6.00	2.50

364 **381** **383**

	1989 Commemoratives (cont.)			
341-44	25¢ Christmas 1989, attd.........................	...	5.50	4.65
345	45¢ Milestones in Space, Sheet of 25 diff. designs	...	...	43.50
	1990-92 Birds Definitives			
346-65A	1¢/$2 Birds (21)	...	225.00	39.50
347,50,53,61	Set 1 5¢, 15¢, 25¢, 50¢ (4)	...	38.50	7.00
357,59-60,65	Set 2 30¢, 36¢, 40¢, $1.00 (4)	...	57.50	9.25
351,54-55,62	Set 3 20¢, 27¢, 29¢, 52¢, (4) (1991)....	...	57.50	9.25
346,49,58,65A	Set 4 1¢, 12¢, 35¢, $2.00 (4)(1991) ..	...	39.50	7.75
356	29¢ Northern Pintail (1992)	...	12.00	2.25
348,52,63-64	Set 5 10¢, 23¢, 65¢, 75¢ (4) (1992).....	...	32.50	6.25
361a	95¢ Essen '90 Min. Sht. of 4 (#347,350,353,361)	...	...	6.25
	1990 Commemoratives			
366-69	25¢ Children's Games, attd	...	5.25	4.50
370-76	25¢,$1 Penny Black, 150th Anniv.,			
	Booklet Singels	...	...	18.75
376a	Booklet Pane of 7 (6x25¢,$1)	...	...	19.50
377-80	25¢ Endangered Sea Turtles, attd..............	...	4.95	4.50
381	25¢ Joint Issue with Micronesia & U.S.	...	11.75	1.30
382	45¢ German Reunification.........................	...	6.75	1.50
383-86	25¢ Christmas, attd...............................	...	5.25	4.50
387-90	25¢ Breadfruit, attd...............................	...	5.25	4.50

399 411

Scott's No.		Mint Sheetlet	Plate Block	F-VF NH
391-94	50¢ US Space Shuttle Flights, 10th Anniv., attd	...	6.50	5.50
395-98	52¢ Flowers, attd	...	8.50	6.75
398a	52¢ Phila Nippon, min. sht. of 4	...	...	6.95
399	29¢ Operation Desert Storm	...	8.75	1.45
400-06	29¢,$1 Birds, set of 7 booklet singles .	...	...	28.75
406a	Booklet Pane of 7 (6x29¢,$1)	...	...	29.50
407-10	12¢,29¢,50¢ (2) Air Marshall Island Aircraft (4)	22.75		4.75
411	29¢ Admission to United Nations........	...	14.50	1.10
412	30¢ Christmas, Peace Dove	...	5.75	1.20
413	29¢ Peace Corps in Marshall Islands..	...	6.50	1.20

425-28

1992 Commemoratives

414-17	29¢ Ships, Strip of 4	...	(8)14.50	6.50
418-24	50¢,$1 Voyages of Discovery, set of 7 booklet sgls	...	...	26.50
424a	Booklet Pane of 7 (6x50¢ + $1)	...	...	27.50
425-28	29¢ Traditional Handcrafts, attd	...	(8) 9.00	4.25
429	29¢ Christmas....................................	...	7.00	1.20

1992 Birds Definitives

430-33	9¢,22¢,28¢,45¢ Birds		31.50	5.95

441 464

1993 Commemoratives

434-40	50¢,$1 Reef Life, 7 booklet sgls..........	...	...	22.50
440a	Booklet Pane of 7 (6x50¢,$1)	...	...	23.00

1993-95 Ship Definitives

441-66B	10¢-$10.00 Ships (28)......................		450.00	83.50
443,47-48,55	Set 1 15¢, 24¢, 29¢, 50¢ (4)..........		27.50	5.50
444,46,56,59	Set 2 19¢, 23¢, 52¢, 75¢ (4)..........		25.95	4.75
441,49,51,65	Set 3 10¢, 30¢, 35¢, $2.90 (4) (1994)		36.50	7.25
445,52-53,57	Set 4 20¢, 40¢, 45¢, 55¢, (4) (1994)		15.75	3.25
450,58,60,66	Set 5 32¢, 60¢, 78¢, $3.00 (4) (1995)		43.50	8.95
463	$1.00 Canoe......................................		23.50	3.50
464	$2.00 Canoe......................................		37.50	5.95
466A	$5.00 Canoe (1994)		100.00	14.50
466B	$10.00 Canoe (1994)		170.00	35.00
466C	15¢-75¢ Sailing Vessels, S/S of 4 (1994)	...	...	5.50

474

Scott's No.		Mint Sheetlet	Plate Block	F-VF NH
	* WW II Anniversaries 1943-1993 (continued)			
467-70	52¢ Invasion of Sicily, attd. blk. of 4 ...	(16)36.50	9.25	7.50
471	50¢ Bombing Raids on Schweinfurt ...	(12)27.50	9.25	1.85
472	29¢ Liberation of Smolensk................	(12)16.50	5.50	1.10
473	29¢ Landing at Bougainville	(12)16.50	5.50	1.10
474	50¢ US Invasion of Tarawa................	(12)27.50	9.25	1.85
475	52¢ Tehran Conference	(12)27.50	9.25	1.85
476-77	29¢ Battle of North Cape, attd. pair....	(12)18.75	6.25	2.60
	* WW II Anniversaries 1944-1994			
478	29¢ Eisenhower Commands SHAEF .	(12)16.50	5.50	1.10
479	50¢ Invasion of Anzio.......................	(12)27.50	9.25	1.85
480	52¢ Siege of Leningrad Ends.............	(12)27.50	9.25	1.85
481	29¢ U.S. Frees Marshall Islands	(12)16.50	5.50	1.10
482	29¢ Japanese Defeat at Truk.............	(12)16.50	5.50	1.10
483	52¢ Bombing of Germany	(12)27.50	9.25	1.85
484	50¢ Rome Falls to Allies	(12)27.50	9.25	1.85
485-88	75¢ D-Day Landings, attd..................	(16)52.50	13.00	11.50
485a-88a	75¢ D-Day, Reprint, attd...................	(16)59.50	16.00	13.00
489	50¢ V-1 Bombs Strike England	(12)27.50	9.25	1.85
490	29¢ Landing on Saipan......................	(12)16.50	5.50	1.10
491	50¢ Battle of Philippine Sea	(12)27.50	9.25	1.85
492	29¢ U.S. Liberates Guam..................	(12)16.50	5.50	1.10
493	50¢ Warsaw Uprising	(12)27.50	9.25	1.85
494	50¢ Liberation of Paris	(12)27.50	9.25	1.85
495	29¢ Marines Land on Peliliu	(12)16.50	5.50	1.10
496	52¢ MacArthur Returns to Philippines	(12)16.50	9.25	1.85
497	52¢ Battle of Leyte Gulf	(12)16.50	9.25	1.85
498-99	50¢ Battleship "Tirpitz" Sunk, attd	(16)36.50	8.75	4.00
500-3	50¢ Battle of the Bulge	(16)37.50	9.25	7.50
	WWII Anniversaries 1945-1995			
504	32¢ Yalta Conference........................	(12)17.50	5.50	1.10
505	55¢ Bombing of Dresden....................	(12)30.00	10.00	2.00
506	$1 Iwo Jima Invaded.........................	(12)49.50	16.50	3.25
507	32¢ Remagen Bridge Taken	(12)18.00	5.50	1.10
508	55¢ Marines Invade Okinawa.............	(12)30.00	10.00	2.00
509	50¢ Death of F.D. Roosevelt..............	(12)28.50	9.50	1.85
510	32¢ US/USSR Troops Link	(12)18.00	5.50	1.10
511	60¢ Soviet Troops Conquer Berlin	(12)36.00	10.75	2.15
512	55¢ Allies liberate concentration camps	(12)35.00	10.50	2.10
513-16	75¢ V.E. Day, Block of 4	(16)55.00	15.75	13.00
517	32¢ United Nations Charter................	(12)18.50	5.75	1.15
518	55¢ Postdam Conference...................	(12)32.50	10.00	2.00
519	60¢ Churchill's Resignati...................	(12)33.75	11.00	2.10
520	$1 Atomic Bomb dropped on Hiroshima	(12)59.50	19.75	4.00
521-24	75¢ V.J. Day, Block of 4	(16)65.00	16.50	13.00

* WW II Anniversary Issues are are available in Tab singles, Tab pairs and Tab blocks for an additional 25%.

1994-95 WWII Anniversary Souvenir Sheets

562	50¢ MacArthur Returns to Philippines, Souvenir Sheet of 2..........................	...	...	3.95
563	$1 U.N. Charter Souvenir Sheet (1995)	...	...	3.95

567 572 576

1993 Commemoratives (continued)

567-70	29¢ Capitol Complex..........................		19.50	2.95
571	50¢ Mobil Oil Tanker, Eagle Souv. Sheet	...	...	1.20
572-75	29¢ Life in 1800's, attd		4.50	3.50
576	29¢ Christmas		6.95	1.15

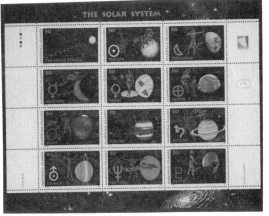

582

1994 Commemoratives

Scott's No.		Mint Sheetlet	Plate Block	F-VF NH
577	$2.90 15th Anniv. Constitution Souv. Sht. (1994)	...	...	5.95
578	29¢ 10th Anniv. Postal Service Souv. Sht. (1994)	...	...	.95
579-80	50¢ Soccer Cup, attd		14.00	6.25
582	50¢ Solar System, sheet of 12		...	18.95
583-86	75¢ Moon Landing, 25th Anniv. attd		8.50	7.50
586b	75¢ Moon Landing, Souv. Sheet of 4		...	7.50
587	29¢, 52¢, $1 Butterflies, Souv. Sheet of 3......		...	5.25
588	29¢ Christmas		5.75	1.00

592 Part   **596 Part**   **599**

1995 Commemoratives

589	50¢ Year of the Boar, Souv. Sheet	...	...	2.20
590	55¢ Underseas Glory, Block of 4		8.75	7.50
591	55¢ John F. Kennedy, Strip of 6	...(12)	12.00	7.25
592	75¢ Marilyn Monroe, Block of 4............	(12) 20.75	8.95	7.50
593	32¢ Cats, Block of 4		5.25	3.65
594	75¢ Mir-Shuttle Docking, Block of 4		7.75	6.75
595	60¢ Game Fish, Block of 8...........	(8)	19.50	15.00
596	32¢ Island Legends, Block of 4		4.00	3.50
597	32¢ Singapore '95 Orchids Souvenir Sheet... Sheet of 4	...	...	3.35
598	50¢ Beijing '95, Suzhou Gardens, Souv. Sheet	...	...	1.25
599	32¢ Christmas		4.25	.80
600	32¢ Jet Fighter Planes, Miniature Sheet of 25........................	...	...	17.00
601	32¢ Yitzhak Rabin	(8) 6.50	4.50	.80

604 Part   **608**   **616**

1996 Commemoratives

602	50¢ Year of the Rat Souvenir Sheet	...	...	1.25
603	32¢ Local Birds, Block of 4		8.95	7.75
604	55¢ Wild Cats, Block of 4		5.95	4.85
605	32¢ Millenium of Navigation, Mini Sht of 25...		...	18.50
606	60¢ Modern Olympics, Block of 4		7.25	6.00
607	55¢ Marshall Island Chronology, Shtlt of 12 ..		...	16.50
608	32¢ Elvis Presley........................	(20) 16.50	(6) 11.00	.85
609	50¢ China '96 Palace Museum Souv. Sheet..		...	1.75
610	32¢ James Dean	(20) 16.50	(6) 11.00	.85
611	60¢ Ford Motor 100th Anniv., S/S of 8		...	11.75
612	32¢ Island Legends, Block of 4		4.25	3.25
613	55¢ Steam Locomotives, sheetlet of 12		...	14.50
614	32¢ Taipei 1996 Souvenir Sheet of 4............		...	2.80
615	$3 Compact with U.S.		30.00	6.50
616	32¢ Christmas Angels	(16) 14.95	...	.75
617	32¢ Biplanes Sheetlet of 25		...	18.50
618	32¢ Handicrafts, Block of 4	...	3.50	2.80

622

1997 Commemoratives

Scott's No.		Mint Sheetlet	Plate Block	F-VF NH
619	60¢ Year of the Ox, Souvenir Sheet...	...	...	1.35
620-21	32¢-60¢ Amata Kabua (2)	(8) 16.50	4.25	2.10
622	32¢ Elvis Presley, Strip of 3	(15) 10.50	(6) 4.75	2.15
623-24	32¢ Hong Kong '97, Souvenir Sheets of 2 (2).................	...	...	2.80
625	60¢ Twelve Apostles, Sheetlet of 12 ..	...	...	15.75
626	$3 Last Supper, Souvenir Sheet	...	...	6.50
......	60¢ 20th Century, 1900-1909 Sheetlet of 15	...	...	19.50
......	50¢-$1 Pacific '97 Booklet (6-50¢, 1-$1 Souvenir Sheet)	...	...	8.95

B1

1996 Semi-Postals

B1	32¢ + 8¢ Operations Crossroads, Sheetlet of 6.......	...	...	5.50

1985-89 Airmails

C1-2	44¢ Audubon, attd....................	...	5.95	2.95
C3-6	44¢ Ameripex - Planes, attd (1986)	...	6.50	5.50
C7	44¢ Operation Crossroads, S/S (1986) ..	...	...	5.75
C8	44¢ Statue of Liberty/Peace Year (1986)	...	6.75	1.50
C9-12	44¢ Girl Scouts, attd (1986)	...	4.50	4.00
C13-16	44¢ Marine Birds, attd (1987).............	...	4.85	4.25

C17   **C22**

C17-20	44¢ Amelia Earhart/CAPEX attd (1987)...............	...	5.50	4.50
C21	45¢ Astronaut and Space Shuttle (1988)................	...	5.75	1.30
C22-25	12¢,36¢,39¢,45¢ Aircraft (1989) (4)	...	23.75	5.25
C22a	12¢ Bklt. Pane of 10....................	...	...	5.50
C23a	36¢ Bklt. Pane of 10....................	...	...	13.00
C24a	39¢ Bklt. Pane of 10....................	...	...	13.75
C25a	45¢ Bklt. Pane of 10....................	...	...	15.75
C25b	36¢-45¢ Bklt. Pane of 10 (5 each)	...	...	14.75

Postal Cards

UX1	20¢ Elvis Presley (1996)	...	...	.60
UX2-5	20¢ Canoes, Set of 4	...	...	2.40
UX6	20¢ Heavenly Angels, Christmas (1996)	...	...	.60
......	32¢ Turtle (1997)...................	...	...	.80

MICRONESIA
MICRONESIA BECAME INDEPENDENT IN 1986

| 1 | 21 | 22 |

| 72 | 102 | 107 |

1984 Commemoratives

Scott's No.		Mint Sheetlet	Plate Block	F-VF NH
1-4	20¢ Postal Service Inaugural, attd	...	3.50	2.95
21,C4-6	20¢,28¢,35¢,40¢ AUSIPEX (4)	...	22.50	4.75
22,C7-9	20¢,28¢,35¢,40¢ Christmas (4)	...	52.50	10.50

1984 Explorers and Views Definitives

5-20	1¢-$5 Definitives (16)	...	110.00	25.75

| 23 | C36 | 45 |

1985 Commemoratives

23,C10-12	22¢,33¢,39¢,44¢ Ships (4)	...	26.50	4.75
24,C13-14	22¢,33¢,44¢ Christmas (3)	...	25.00	4.50
25-28,C15	22¢,44¢ Audubon (5)	...	12.00	5.50
45,C16-18	22¢,33¢,39¢,44¢ Ruins (4)	...	26.50	5.25

1985-88 Definitives

31-39,C34-36	3¢-$10 Definitives & Airs (12)	...	155.00	35.00
39	$10 National Seal	...	110.00	26.00
34	22¢ Senyavin (1986)	...	3.00	.60
31-32,35,C34-36				
	3¢,14¢, 22¢, 33¢, 44¢, $1 Birds (6) (1988)	...	24.75	5.25
33,36,37,38	15¢, 25¢, 36¢, 45¢ Views4 (4) (1988)	...	22.75	4.35
33a	15¢ Booklet Pane of 10	...	...	8.50
36a	25¢ Booklet Pane of 10	...	...	10.00
36b	15¢ & 25¢ Booklet Pane of 10 (5 ea.)	...	...	9.50

| 52 | 58 | 63 |

1986 Commemoratives

46,C19-20	22¢, 44¢ Int'l Peace Year (3)	...	28.00	5.75
48-51	22¢ on 20¢ Postal Service (#1-4), attd	...	3.15	2.85
52,C21-24	22¢,33¢,39¢,44¢ AMERIPEX (4)...	...	27.50	5.75
53	22¢ Passport.................................	...	4.50	1.00
54-5,C26-7	5¢,22¢,33¢,44¢ Christmas Paintings (4)	...	25.95	5.50

1987 Commemoratives

56,C28-30	22¢,33¢,39¢,44¢ Homeless, Events (4)	...	27.50	4.95
57	$1.00 CAPEX Souvenir Sheet.......	...	...	3.95
58,C31-33	22¢,33¢,39¢,44¢ Christmas (4)	(25)150.00	24.75	4.95

1988 Commemoratives

59-62,C37-8	22¢,44¢ Colonial Flags, attd (6).....	...	12.75	7.00
59-62,C37-8	Center Blocks of 8	...	...	25.00
63-66	25¢ Olympics, attd., two pair	...	9.50	4.00
67-70	25¢ Christmas Tree, attd..................	...	3.25	2.95
71	25¢ Truk Lagoon S/S of 18	...	...	13.95

1989 Commemoratives

Scott's No.		Mint Sheetlet	Plate Block	F-VF NH
72-75	45¢ Flowers, attd	...	4.95	4.50
76	$1.00 Hirohito Memorial S/S..............	...	...	2.50
77-80	25¢-45¢ Sharks, attd. two pair..........	...	9.50	3.95
81	25¢ Moon Landing, 20th Anniv., S/S of 9	...	...	6.50
82	$2.40 Moon Landing, 20th Anniv........	...	23.75	5.50
103	25¢ WSE, Fruits & Flowers, Sht. of 18	...	...	13.50
104-05	25¢,45¢ Christmas (2)	...	21.75	4.95

1989 Seashells Definitives

83-102	1¢/$5 Seashell definitives (12)	...	117.50	27.75
85a	15¢ Booklet Pane of 10 (1990)..........	...	...	7.50
88a	25¢ Booklet Pane of 10 (1990)..........	...	...	9.75
88b	15¢ & 25¢ Booklet Pane of 10 (5 ea.)(1990)	...	...	9.50

1990 Commemoratives

106-09	10¢,15¢,20¢,25¢ World Wildlife Fund (4)	...	27.50	4.95
110-113	45¢ Stamp World London '90 Whalers, attd	...	5.50	4.50
114	$1.00 S.W. London '90, Whalers, S/S	...	...	2.75
115	$1.00 Penny Black, 150th Anniv., S/S	...	...	2.75
116-20	25¢ Pohnpei Agric. & School, Strip of 5 (15)	11.95	...	3.95
121	$1.00 Int'l. Garden Expo, Osaka, Japan S/S	...	...	2.50
122-23	25¢,45¢ Loading Mail, Airport & Truk Lagoon (2)	...	8.75	2.60
124-26	25¢ Joint issue w/Marsh. Isl. & U.S....	(12) 12.50	(6) 6.75	2.95
127-30	45¢ Moths, attd.................................	...	5.00	4.65
131	25¢ Christmas, S/S of 9.....................	...	...	6.15

| 134-35 | 142 |

1991 Commemoratives

132	25¢,45¢ New Capital of Micronesia, S/S	...	...	2.50
133	$1 New Capital, S/S	...	...	2.85
134-37	29¢-50¢ Turtles, attd. two pairs	...	18.75	7.75
138-41	29¢ Operation Desert Storm, strip of 4	...	4.00	3.25
142	$2.90 Frigatebird, Flag	...	...	6.25
142a	$2.90 Frigatebird, S/S.......................	...	...	6.35
143	29¢ Phila Nippon '91, min. sht. of 3....	...	...	2.50
144	50¢ Phila Nippon '91, min. sht. of 3....	...	...	4.25
145	$1 Phila Nippon S/S	...	...	2.75
146-48	29¢,40¢,50¢ Christmas (3)	...	...	2.95
149	29¢ Pohnpei Rain Forest, min. sht. of 18	...	...	14.50

1992 Commemoratives

150	29¢ Peace Corps, strip of 5	(15)14.50	...	3.75
151	29¢ Discovery of America, strip of 3...	...	(6) 13.50	5.75
152-53	29¢,50¢ U.N. Membership Anniv (2) ..	...	...	5.75
153a	Same, S/S of 2	...	...	5.95
154	29¢ Christmas	...	19.75	3.95

| 160 | 172 | 179 |

Note: From #151 to date, Plate Blocks have Logos instead of Plate Numbers

Scott's No.		Mint Sheetlet	Plate Block	F-VF NH
1993 Commemoratives				
155	29¢ Pioneers of Flight, se-ten. blk. of 8	...	7.50	6.25
168	29¢ Golden Age of Sail, min. sht. of 12	...	...	19.95
172	29¢ Thomas Jefferson........................		5.75	1.10
173-76	29¢ Pacific Canoes, attd	...	4.50	3.95
177	29¢ Local Leaders, strip of 4.............	(8)	2.25	3.50
178	50¢ Pioneers of Flight, block of 8.......	(8)	10.00	8.50
179-80	29¢-50¢ Pohnpei		11.95	2.85
181	$1 Pohnpei Souvenir Sheet............		...	2.60
182-83	29¢-50¢ Butterflies, two pairs.............		10.00	4.35
184-85	29¢-50¢ Christmas		11.95	2.60
186	29¢ Yap Culture, sheet of 18............		...	16.50
1993-94 Fish Definitives				
157-67	10¢-$2.90 Fish, set of 16..........		105.00	20.95
157,61,64,65	Set 1-19¢, 29¢, 50¢, 1.00, (4).......	...	20.75	4.65
159,62,63,63A	Set 2-22¢,30¢,40¢,45¢ (4).......	...	17.50	3.65
156,58.62A,67	Set 3-10¢,20¢,35¢,$2.90 (4)(94)...	34.00	7.35	
160,64A,64B,66	Set 4-25¢,52¢,75¢,$2.00 (4)(94)	...	37.50	7.50

187	192 Part	202

1994 Commemoratives

187-89	29¢,40¢,50¢ Kosrae	...	13.00	2.95
190	29¢-50¢ Butterflies, Hong Kong, sheet of 4	...	...	5.50
191	29¢ Pioneers of Flight, block of 8		8.95	7.75
192	29¢ Micronesian Games, block of 4 ...		3.75	3.15
193	29¢ Native Costumes, block of 4.......		3.75	3.15
194	29¢ Anniversary of Constitution		4.50	.95
195	29¢ Flowers, Strip of 4	(8)	8.50	3.85
196-97	50¢ World Cup Soccer, attd		12.95	5.95
198	29¢ Postal Service, 10th Anniv., Block of 4		8.75	6.95
199	29¢, 52¢, $1 Philakorea Dinosaurs, Souvenir Sheet of 3........................	...	...	4.95
200	50¢ Pioneers of Flight, Block of 8.......		9.95	8.95
201	29¢ Migratory Birds, Block of 4		10.00	7.75
202-3	29¢-50¢ Christmas (2)......................		26.50	5.50
204-7	32¢ Local Leaders (4)		20.00	5.50

211	236

1995 Commemoratives

208	50¢ Year of the Boar Souvenir Sheet.	...	...	1.85
209	32¢ Chuuk Lagoon, underwater scenes, Blk/4		10.00	7.25
210	32¢ Pioneers of Flight, block of 8.......		6.25	5.75
211	32¢ Dogs of the World, block of 4		3.75	3.15
228	32¢ Hibiscus, Strip of 4	(8)	7.50	3.15
229	$1 United Nations 50th Anniv. Souv. Sheet	...	...	2.40
230	32¢ Singapore '95, Orchids S/S of 4 ..		...	2.85
231	60¢ End of World War II, Block of 4 ...		6.25	5.25
232	50¢ Beijing '95 Souvenir Sheet		...	1.20
233	60¢ Pioneers of Flight, Block of 8.......		11.50	10.50
234-35	32¢-60¢ Christmas (2)......................		11.95	2.20
236	32¢ Yitzhak Rabin	(8)	12.95	.95

1995-96 Fish Definitives

213-26	23¢-$5.00 Fish Set of 9.............		110.00	23.95
214,18,22,25	Set 5 - 32¢,55¢,78¢,$3.00 (4) ...		43.50	9.95
213,19,23,26	Set 6 - 23¢,60¢,95¢,$5.00(4)....		67.50	13.50
217	46¢ Fish, Achilles Tang ('96)		4.85	1.00
227	32¢ Native Fish Shtlt of 25 (96)	...	...	17.00

239

1996 Commemoratives

Scott's No.		Mint Sheetlets	Plate Block	F-VF NH
237	50¢ Year of the Rat Souvenir Sheet...	...	...	1.10
238	32¢ Pioneers of Flight, Block of 8........	...	6.50	5.75
239	32¢ Tourism in Yap, Block of 4.........	...	3.85	3.25
240	55¢ Starfish, Block of 4..................	...	5.85	4.85
241	60¢ Modern Olympics, Block of 4	...	5.95	5.25
242	50¢ China '96 Souvenir Sheet	...	...	1.35
243-44	32¢ Patrol Boats, Pair......................		4.25	1.85
245	55¢ Ford Motor 100th Anniversary, S/S of 8	...	...	9.75
247	32¢ Officer Reza, Police Dog		4.25	.85
248	50¢ Citrus Fruits, strip of 4..................	...	(8) 9.50	4.40
249	60¢ Pioneers of Flight, Block of 8........		12.50	11.00
250	32¢ Taipei '96, Souvenir sheet of 4	...	...	2.75
251-52	32¢-60¢ Christmas (2)		8.95	2.10
253	$3 Compact wtih US		29.50	6.75
1997 Commemoratives				
.....	32¢ Year of the Ox..........................	...	3.50	.70
.....	$2 Year of the Ox, Souvenir Sheet	...	...	4.50
.....	32¢ Pacific '97, Goddesses of the Sea, sheetlet of 6........................	...	...	4.25
.....	60¢ Deng Xiaoping, Sheetlet of 4.......	...	...	5.25
.....	$3 Deng Xiaoping, Souvenir Sheet.....	...	...	6.50

C15	C28	C29

Airmails

C1-3	28¢,35¢,40¢ Aircraft (1984)	...	14.75	3.15
C25	$1.00 Ameripex S/S (1986)	...	...	4.85
C39-42	45¢ Federated State Flags, attd (1989).......	...	4.85	4.50
C43-46	22¢,36¢,39¢,45¢ Aircraft Serving Micronesia ('90)........	...	31.50	6.75
C47-48	40¢,50¢ Aircraft (1992)	...	21.95	4.85
C49	$2.90 Moon Landing Souvenir Sheet (1994)	...	...	6.35

Postal Stationary Entires

U1	20¢ National Flag (1984)	...	...	18.50
U2	22¢ Tall Ship Senyavin (1986)..................	...	...	10.75
U3	29¢ on 30¢ New Capital (1991)	...	...	6.95

Postal Cards

| UX1-4 | 20¢ Scenes, Set of 4 .... | ... | ... | 2.40 |

REPUBLIC OF PALAU
PALAU BECAME INDEPENDENT IN 1994.

1	5	9	21

1983 Commemoratives

Scott's No.		Mint Sheetlet	Plate Block	F-VF NH
1-4	20¢ Postal Service Inaugural, attd......	...	4.50	3.25
5-8	20¢ Birds, attd..................................	...	2.75	2.25
24-27	20¢ Whales, attd...............................	...	3.00	2.25
28-32	20¢ Christmas, Strip of 5	(10) 7.50		3.25
33-40	20¢ Henry Wilson, Block of 8	...	5.00	4.25

1983-84 Marine Definitives

9/21	1¢/$5 Definitives, Set of 13.............		155.00	29.50
9-12,16,19	Set 1 - 1¢, 3¢, 5¢, 10¢, 30¢, $1 (6)	...	24.95	4.85
13-15,17,18	Set 2 - 13¢, 20¢, 28¢, 37¢, 50¢ (5) .	...	22.95	4.50
13a	13¢ Booklet Pane of 10	...	...	12.75
13b	13¢/20¢ Bklt. Pane of 10 (5 #13, 5 #14)	...	...	14.75
14b	20¢ Booklet Pane of 10	...	...	13.75
20-21	Set 3 - $2, $5 (2)...........................		95.00	20.75

59	95	99

1984 Commemoratives

41-50	20¢ Seashells, Block of 10, attd)	...	6.50	5.50
51-54	40¢ 19th UPU Congress....................	...	5.25	4.50
55-58	20¢ Ausipex, attd.............................	...	3.50	2.65
59-62	20¢ Christmas, attd	...	3.50	2.65

1985 Commemoratives

63-66	22¢ Audubon, attd	...	4.50	3.75
67-70	22¢ Shipbuilding, attd......................	...	3.50	2.65
86-89	44¢ International Youth Yr., attd........	...	5.00	4.25
90-93	14¢,22¢,33¢,44¢ Christmas	...	23.50	3.75
94	$1.00 Trans-Pacific Air Anniv. S/S	...	...	3.65
95-98	44¢ Halley's Comet, attd...................	...	5.00	4.25

1985 Marine Definitives

75-85	14¢/$10 Marine Life (7)...................		140.00	30.75
75-77,78-81	Set 4 14¢, 22¢, 25¢, 33¢, 39¢, 44¢ (6)	...	29.50	7.25
75a	14¢ Booklet Pane of 10	...	...	12.50
76a	22¢ Booklet Pane of 10	...	...	16.00
76b	14¢/22¢ Bklt. Pane of 10 (5 #75, 5 #76)	...	...	17.50
85	$10 Spinner Dolphins		115.00	24.50

1986 Commemoratives

99-102	44¢ Songbirds, attd	...	5.25	4.65
103	14¢ AMERIPEX Sea & Reef, Sht of 40	...		50.00
104-08	22¢ Seashells, attd...........................	(10)	8.35	3.85
109-12,C17	22¢ Int'l. Peace Year, attd	...	10.00	4.85
113-16	22¢ Reptiles, attd.............................	...	4.50	3.65
117-21	22¢ Christmas, Strip of 5, attd	(15) 10.50	(10) 5.95	2.75
17-21	Christmas with Tabs		(10) 7.50	3.50

122-123	141

Scott's No.		Mint Sheetlet	Plate Block	F-VF NH

1987 Commemoratives

121B-E	44¢ Butterflies, attd............................	...	5.50	4.85
122-25	44¢ Fruit Bats, attd	...	5.50	4.75
146-49	22¢ CAPEX, attd	...	3.25	2.65
150-54	22¢ Seashells, Strip of 5 attd..............	(10)	7.25	3.25
155-63	14¢,22¢,44¢ U.S. Constitution Bicentennial, attd. (3 strips of 3)..........................	(15) 28.50	...	6.25
164-67	14¢,22¢,33¢,44¢ Japanese Links (4) .	...	16.00	3.25
168	$1 S/S Japanese Links to Palau.........	...	...	2.95
173-77	22¢ Christmas, Strip of 5 attd	(10)	8.50	3.35
178-82	22¢ "Silent Spring" Symb. Species, attd	(15) 12.50	(10) 8.95	3.65

1987-88 Indigenous Flowers Definitives

126-42	1¢ - $10 Flowers (17)......................		250.00	52.50
126-30, 32, 35-36, 38-41	1¢ - 14¢, 22¢, 39¢, 44¢, 50¢-$5 (12) ..	...	125.00	26.50
130a	14¢ Bklt. Pane of 10	...	...	7.75
132a	22¢ Bklt. Pane of 10	...	...	10.00
132b	14¢/22¢ Bklt. Pane of 10 (5 ea.).........	...	...	10.00
131, 33, 34, 37	15¢, 25¢, 36¢, 45¢ (4) (1988)	...	16.50	3.35
131a	15¢ Bklt. Pane of 10 (1988)	...	...	5.00
133a	25¢ Bklt. Pane of 10 (1988)	...	...	7.00
133b	15¢/25¢ Bklt. Pane of 10 (5 ea.) (1988)	...	...	6.75
142	$10 Flower Bouquet (1988)	...	115.00	24.75

191-95

1988 Commemoratives

183-86	44¢ Butterflies & Flowers, attd............	...	5.00	4.35
187-90	44¢ Ground Dwelling Birds, attd.........	...	5.25	4.50
191-95	25¢ Seashells, Strip of 5, attd............	(10)	7.00	3.25
196	25¢ Postal Indep. S/S of 6 (FINLANDIA)	...	...	4.15
197	45¢ USPPS S/S of 6 (PRAGA '88).....	...	...	6.65
198-202	25¢ Christmas, strip of 5....................	(15) 9.50	(8) 7.00	3.35
198-202	Christmas with Tabs	...	(8) 8.75	4.35
198-202	Christmas Sheetlet	...	...	9.50
203	25¢ Palauan Nautilus, S/S of 5...........	...	...	4.15

1989 Commemoratives

204-07	45¢ Endangered Birds, attd...............	...	5.25	4.50
208-11	45¢ Exotic Mushrooms, attd...............	...	5.50	4.75
212-16	25¢ Seashells, strip of 5 ....(10)		7.75	3.65
217	$1 Hirohito Memorial S/S...................	...	...	2.95
218	25¢ Moon Landing, 20 Anniv., S/S of 25	...	...	14.75
219	$2.40 Moon Landing, 20th Anniv	...	28.75	6.35
220	25¢ Literacy, block of 10....................	...	6.95	5.95
221	25¢ World Stamp Expo, Fauna, Min. sheet of 25	...	...	12.95
222-26	25¢ Christmas, Strip of 5, attd	(15)11.00	(10) 7.50	3.65

258

1990 Commemoratives

227-30	25¢ Soft Coral, attd...........................	...	3.25	2.85
231-34	45¢ Forest Birds, attd	...	4.85	4.50
235	25¢ Stamp World London '90, S/S of 9	...	...	5.25
236	$1.00 Penny Black, 150th Anniv. S/S.	...	...	2.65
237-41	45¢ Orchids, strip of 5......................	(15) 16.50	(10) 10.75	4.95
242-45	45¢ Butterflies & Flowers, attd...........	...	4.75	4.25
246	25¢ Lagoon Life, Sheetlet of 25	...	...	16.50
247-48	45¢ Pacifica/Mail Delivery, attd	(10) 19.95	7.75	3.25
249-53	25¢ Christmas, Strip of 5, attd	(15) 8.75	(8) 6.50	3.15
249-53	Christmas with Tabs	...	...	3.50
249-53	Christmas Sheetlet of 15	...	...	7.75
254-57	45¢ U.S. Forces in Palau, 1944, attd..	...	5.25	4.65
258	$1 U.S. Forces in Palau, 1944, S/S....	...	...	2.95

259   266   291

1991 Commemoratives

Scott's No.		Mint Sheetlets	Plate Block	F-VF NH
259-62	30¢ Coral, attd	...	3.50	3.15
263	30¢ Angaur, The Phospate Island, Sheet/16	...	...	11.50
288	29¢ Cent. of Christianity in Palau, Sheet of 6	...	...	4.15
289	29¢ Marine Life, Sheet of 20	...	...	18.95
290	20¢ Desert Shield/Desert Storm, min. Sheet/9	...	...	5.25
291	$2.90 Fairy tern, Yellow/Ribbon	...	...	6.25
292	$2.90 Same, S/S	...	...	6.25
293	29¢ Women's Conf. & Palau,10th Anniv,min sht of 8	...	...	6.25
294	50¢ Giant Clam Cultivation, S/S of 4	...	...	5.50
295	29¢ Pearl Harbor/Pacific Theater Anniv,Shtlt of 6	...	...	4.50
296	$1.00 Phila Nippon S/S	...	...	2.35
297	29¢ Peace Corps in Palau, min. sht. of 6	...	...	4.50
298	29¢ Christmas, strip of 5, attd	(15) 10.50	(10) 7.50	3.50
298	Christmas with Tabs	...	...	4.00
299	29¢ WWII in the Pacific, min. sht. of 10	...	...	8.95

1991-92 Birds Definitives

		Mint Sheetlets	Plate Block	F-VF NH
266/83	1¢-$10 Birds (18)	...	230.00	49.75
267,69,71-76,79-81	4¢, 19¢, 23¢-50¢,95¢-$2 (11)	...	70.00	13.95
269b	19¢ Palau Fantail, Bklt. Pane of 10	...	...	4.50
272a	29¢ Fruit Dove, Bklt. Pane of 10	...	...	6.75
272b	19¢ Fantail & 29¢ Fruit Dove, Bklt. Pane/10(5 ea)	...	...	5.75
266,68,70,77-78,82	1¢, 6¢, 20¢, 52¢, 75¢, $5 (6) ('92)	...	70.00	13.95
287	$10 Bush Warbler ('92)	...	100.00	22.75

300   312

1992 Commemoratives

Scott's No.		Mint Sheetlets	Plate Block	F-VF NH
300	50¢ Butterflies, Block of 4	...	5.00	4.50
301	29¢ Shells, strip of 5	...	(10) 7.50	3.50
302	29¢ Columbus & Age of Discovery, min. sht/20	...	...	13.50
303	29¢ Biblical Creation/Earth Summit, min sht/24	...	...	16.95
304-09	50¢ Summer Olympics, S/S	...	...	7.50
310	29¢ Elvis Presley, min. sht. of 9	...	...	7.50
311	50¢ WWII, Aircraft - Pacific Theater, min sht/10	...	...	11.95
312	29¢ Christmas, strip of 5	(15) 11.50	(10) 8.25	3.95
312	Christmas with Tabs	...	...	4.35

313 Part   315 Part

Scott's No.		Mint Sheetlets	Plate Block	F-VF NH

1993 Commemoratives

Scott's No.		Mint Sheetlets	Plate Block	F-VF NH
313	50¢ Animal Families, block of 4	...	5.00	4.50
314	29¢ Seafood, block of 4	...	...	3.00
315	50¢ Sharks, block of 4	...	...	4.50
316	29¢ WWII, Pacific Theater, min. sheet of 10	...	...	8.75
317	29¢ Christmas, strip of 5	(15) 10.00	(10) 7.75	3.65
318	29¢ Prehistoric & Legendary Sea Creatures, Sheet of 25	...	...	16.50
319	29¢ Indigenous People, sheet of 4	...	...	2.65
320	$2.90 Indigenous People, Souvenir Sheet	...	...	6.25
321	29¢ Jonah and the Whale, sheet of 25	...	...	16.50

323

1994 Commemoratives

Scott's No.		Mint Sheetlets	Plate Block	F-VF NH
322	40¢ Palau Rays, block of 4	...	...	3.95
323	20¢ Crocodiles, block of 4	...	2.35	2.10
324	50¢ Seabirds, block of 4	...	...	4.50
325	29¢ WWII, Pacific Theater, min. sheet of 10	...	...	8.75
326	50¢ WWII, D-Day, min. sheet of 10	...	...	11.75
327	29¢ Baron Pierre de Coubertin	...	...	.90
328-33	50¢, $1, $2 Coubertin and Winter Olympics Stars, Set of 6 Souv. Sheets	...	...	11.95
334-36	29¢, 40¢, 50¢ Philakorea '94 Philatelic Fantasies, Wildlife, 3 Souv. Sheets of 8	...	...	24.95
337	29¢ Apollo XI Moon Landing 25th Anniv., Miniature Sheet of 20	...	...	14.75
338	29¢ Independence Day Strip of 5	...	...	3.65
339	$1 Invasion of Peleliu Souvenir Sheet	...	...	2.25
340	29¢ Disney Tourism Sheetlet of 9	...	...	5.95
341-43	$1, $2.90 Disney Tourism, 3 Souv. Sheets	...	...	10.95
344	20¢ Year of the Family, Min. Sheet of 12	...	...	5.25
345	29¢ Christmas '94 Strip of 5	(15) 10.00	...	3.75
345	Christmas with Tabs	...	...	4.25
346-48	29¢, 50¢ World Cup of Soccer, Set of 3 Sheetlets of 12	...	...	29.95

365   378

1995 Commemoratives

Scott's No.		Mint Sheetlets	Plate Block	F-VF NH
350	32¢ Elvis Presley, Sheetlet of 9	...	...	6.95
368	32¢ Tourism, Lost Fleet, Sheetlet of 18	...	...	14.50
369	32¢ Earth Day '95, Dinosaurs, Shtlt of 18	...	...	13.95
370	50¢ Jet Aircraft, Sheetlet of 12	...	...	14.50
371	$2 Jet Aircraft, Souvenir Sheet	...	...	4.85
372	32¢ Underwater Ships, Sheetlet of 18	...	...	14.50
373	32¢ Singapore '95 Hidden Treasures, Blk of 4	...	3.75	3.25
374	60¢ U.N., FAO 50th Anniv., Block of 4	...	6.25	5.50
375-76	$2 U.N. FAO 50th Anniv., Souv. Sheets	...	...	8.75
377	20¢ Independence, Block of 4	...	2.60	2.10
378	32¢ Independence, Marine Life	...	3.95	.85
379	32¢ End of World War II, Sheetlet of 12	...	...	9.75
380	60¢ End of World War II, Sheetlet of 5	...	...	8.25
381	$3 End of World War II Souvenir Sheet	...	...	6.50
382	32¢ Christmas Strip of 5	(15) 11.50	(10) 8.50	3.75
382	32¢ Christmas with Tabs	...	...	4.25
383	32¢ Life Cycle of the Sea Turtle, Shtlt/12	...	...	11.50
384	32¢ John Lennon	(16) 12.95	...	.85

1995 Fish Definitives

Scott's No.		Mint Sheetlets	Plate Block	F-VF NH
351-64	1¢-$5 Fish Definitives (14)	...	125.00	25.95
365	$10 Fish Definitive	...	100.00	22.50
366	20¢ Fish, Booklet Single	...	...	.50
366a	20¢ Fish, Booklet Pane of 10	...	...	4.25
367	32¢ Fish, Booklet Single	...	...	.80
367a	32¢ Fish, Booklet Pane of 10	...	...	6.65
367b	20¢, 32¢ Fish, Bklt. Pane of 10 (5 each)	...	...	5.50

1996 Commemoratives

387

392A

Scott's No.		Mint Sheetlets	Plate Block	F-VF NH
385	10¢ Year of the Rat Strip of 4	(8) 1.95	...	1.00
386	60¢ Year of the Rat Souvenir Sheet	...	...	2.85
387	32¢ 50th Anniversary of UNICEF Blk/4	(16) 11.50	3.50	2.85
388	32¢ China '96 Underwater Strip of 5	(15) 11.00	...	3.60
389	32¢ Capex '96 Circumnavigators Shtlt/9	...	...	6.50
390	60¢ Capex '96 Air & Space Sheetlet of 9	...	...	11.85
391	$3 Capex '96 Air & Space Souvenir Sheet	...	...	6.65
392	$3 Capex '96 Circumnavigators S/S	...	...	6.65
393	60¢ Disney Sweethearts Sheetlet of 9	...	...	12.15
394-95	$2 Disney Sweethearts Souv. Sheets (2)	...	...	9.00
392A-F	1¢ - 6¢ Disney Sweethearts (6)	...	...	.60
396	20¢ 3000th Anniversary of Jerusalem Shtlt/30	...	...	13.75
397-400	40¢-60¢ Atlanta '96, 2 Pairs	(20) 65.00	11.50	5.50
401	32¢ Atlanta '96, Sheetlet of 20	...	...	13.95
402	50¢ Lagoon Birds, Sheetlet of 20	...	...	22.50
403	40¢ "Spies in the Sky", Sheetlet of 12	...	...	10.50
404	$3 Stealth Bomber, Souvenir Sheet	...	...	6.50
405	60¢ Oddities of the Air, Sheetlet of 12	...	...	7.95
406	$3 Martin Marietta X-24B, Souv. Sheet	...	...	6.50
407-8	20¢ Independence	(16) 6.95	...	.90
409	32¢ Christmas, Strip of 5	(15) 10.00	...	6.50
410	32¢ Voyages to Mars, Sheetlet of 12	...	...	7.95
411-11A	$3 Voyages to Mars, Souvenir Sheet (2)	...	...	12.50

1997 Commemoratives

412	$2 Year of the Ox, Souvenir Sheet	...	...	4.50
413	$1 South Pacific Commission, 50th Anniv., Souvenir Sheet	...	...	2.25

414 425

1997 Pacific '97, Flowers

414-19	1¢-$3 Flowers (6)	...	33.50	6.95
420-21	32¢-50¢ Shoreline Plants, 2 Blocks of 4	(16) 28.50	8.75	7.25

1997 Commemoratives (continued)

422-23	32¢-60¢ Parachutes, Sheetlets of 8 (2)	...	...	14.95
424-25	$2 Parachutes, Souvenir Sheets (2)	...	...	8.50
.....	32¢-60¢ UNESCO, 50th Anniversary, Sheetlets of 8 and 5 (2)	...	...	11.95
.....	$2 UNESCO, Souvenir Sheets (2)	...	...	8.50

B1-2

Scott's No.		Mint Sheetlets	Plate Block	F-VF NH
	1988 Semi-Postals			
B1-4	25¢ + 5¢,45¢ + 5¢ Olympic Sports, 2 pairs	...	10.00	4.85

C5 C10

Airmails

C1-4	40¢ Birds, attd (1984)	...	4.75	3.95
C5	44¢ Audubon (1985)	...	7.50	1.50
C6-9	44¢ Palau-Germany Exchange Cent., attd	...	6.00	4.95
C10-13	44¢ Trans-Pacific Anniv., attd	...	5.50	4.50
C14-16	44¢ Remelik Memorial, Strip of 3 (1986)	(9) 16.50	(6) 9.50	4.50
C14-16	Remelik Mem., with tabs, attd	...	(6) 12.00	5.95
C14-16	Remelik Sheetlet of 9	...	...	15.95
C17	44¢ Peace Year, St. of Liberty	...	7.00	1.35
C18-20	36¢,39¢,45¢ Aircraft (1989)	...	16.95	3.75
C18a	36¢ Bklt. Pane of 10	...	...	8.75
C19a	39¢ Bklt. Pane of 10	...	...	9.50
C20a	45¢ Bklt. Pane of 10	...	...	10.50
C20b	36¢/45¢ Bklt. Pane of 10 (5 each)	...	...	9.50
C21	50¢ Palauan Bai (#293a), self adh (1991)	...	10.50	2.15
C22	50¢ Birds, Block of 4 (1995)	...	...	4.65

Postal Stationery

U1	22¢ Parrotfish (1989)	...	...	4.50
U2	22¢ Spearfishing	...	...	7.95
U3	25¢ Chambered Nautilus (1991)	...	...	4.25
UC1	36¢ Birds (1985)	...	...	11.95
UX1	14¢ Giant Clam (1985)	...	...	3.50

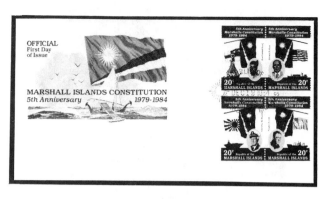

59-62

All Trust Territory FDC's have official cancels and cachets except as noted.
(Marshall Islands #31-57, 107-08 have commercial cachets.)

Scott #	Description	One Cover	Separate Covers
	1984		
31-34	20¢ Postal Service Inaugural attd. 5/2/84	5.00	14.00
35-49A	1¢-$1 Defin. 6/12,12/19/84,6/5/85 (3 FDC's).......	18.75	45.00
39a	13¢ Booklet Pane of 10	21.00	...
40a	14¢ Booklet Pane of 10	14.00	...
41a	20¢ Booklet Pane of 10	21.00	...
41b	13¢,20¢ Booklet Pane of 10 (5 #39, 5 #41)........	23.50	...
42a	22¢ Booklet Pane of 10	14.00	...
42b	14¢,22¢ Booklet Pane of 10 (5 #40, 5 #42)........	17.00	...
50-53	40¢ 19th UPU Congress, attd. 6/19/84	5.00	15.00
50-53	Hamburg FD Cancel...................................	9.00	27.50
54-57	20¢ AUSIPEX Dolphins, attd. 9/5/84............	3.95	14.00
54-57	AUSIPEX FD Cancel...................................	8.50	17.50
58	20¢ Christmas, 3 Kings, Strip of 4 11/7/84	5.50	(16) 57.50
59-62	20¢ Marshalls Constitution, attd. 12/19/84	4.35	14.00
	1985		
63-64/C1-2	22¢/44¢ Audubon, attd. 2/15/85	(2) 8.50	15.00
65-69	22¢ Seashells, attd. 4/17/85......................	6.00	14.00
70-73	22¢ Decade for Women, attd. 6/5/85	5.00	10.00
74-77	22¢ Reef and Lagoon Fish, attd. /15/85	5.00	10.00
78-81	22¢ International Youth Year, attd. 8/31/85.......	5.50	12.50
82-85	14¢,22¢,33¢,44¢ Xmas, 4 Sgls. 10/21/85	6.00	14.00
86-90	22¢ Halley's Comet, attd. 1/21/85................	10.00	32.50
86-90	22¢ Halley's Comet with Tabs, attd.............	37.50	45.00
91-94	22¢ Medicinal Plants, attd. 12/31/85	5.00	12.50
	1986-87		
107-08	$2,$5 Definitives 3/7/86.................................	22.50	25.75
109	$10 Definitive 3/31/87.................................	25.00	...
110-13	14¢ Marine Invertebrates, attd. 3/31/86............	3.25	11.00
114	$1 AMERIPEX S/S (C-54 Globemstr.) 5/22/86...	5.50	...
114	AMERIPEX FD Cancel.................................	7.75	...
115-18	22¢ Operation Crossroads, attd. 7/1/86............	4.75	12.50
115-18	Bikini FD Cancel.................................	8.25	16.50
119-23	22¢ Seashells, attd. 8/1/86........................	4.85	12.50
124-27	22¢ Game Fish, attd. 9/10/86......................	4.50	12.50
128-31	22¢ Christmas/Year of Peace, attd. 10/28/86	4.50	12.50
	1987		
132-35	22¢ Whaling Ships 2/20/87	4.50	12.50
136-41	33¢,39¢,44¢ Pilots 3/12/87 (3 Pairs).................	10.75	19.50
136-41	INTERPEX FD Cancel.................................	16.50	22.50
142	$1 Amelia Earhart / CAPEX S/S 6/15/87	5.00	...
142	CAPEX FD Cancel.................................	13.75	...
143-51	14¢,22¢,44¢ U.S. Const. 7/16/87 (3 Strips of 3) .	10.00	22.50
152-56	22¢ Seashells, attd. 9/1/87........................	4.85	10.50
157-59	44¢ Copra Industry, attd. 12/10/87	4.85	9.00
160-63	14¢,22¢,33¢,44¢ Xmas 12/10/87	4.85	9.50
	1988-89		
164-67	44¢ Marine Birds, attd. 1/27/88	4.85	9.50
168-83	1¢/$5 Fish Def. (16) 3/17,7/19/88 (3 FDC's)	30.00	50.00
184	$10 Blue Jack Definitive 3/31/89	27.50	...
170a	14¢ Bklt. Pane of 10 3/31/88	12.00	...
171a	15¢ Bklt. Pane of 10 12/15/88	10.00	...
173a	22¢ Bklt. Pane of 10 3/31/88	12.00	...
173b	14¢,22¢ Bklt. Pane of 10 (5 ea.) 3/31/88	13.00	...
174a	25¢ Bklt. Pane of 10 12/15/88	10.00	...
174b	15¢,25¢ Bklt. Pane of 10 (5 each) 12/15/88........	11.00	...
188-89	15¢,25¢ Summer Olympics, strips of 5 6/30/88 ..	16.50	23.00
190	25¢ Robert Louis Stevenson S/S of 9 7/19/88	13.50	...
191-94	25¢ Colonial Ships & Flags, attd. 9/2/88	4.00	9.50
195-99	25¢ Christmas, strip of 5 11/7/88	5.00	8.95
200-04	25¢ John F. Kennedy, strip of 5 11/22/88	4.75	11.75
205-08,C21	25¢ (4),45¢ Space Shuttle 12/23/88	6.50	13.50
209-12	45¢ Links to Japan, attd. 1/19/89	5.00	10.00
213-15	45¢ Links to Alaska, attd. 3/31/89	5.00	9.50
216-20	25¢ Seashells, attd. 5/15/89	4.75	10.00
221	$1 Hirohito Memorial S/S 5/15/89	3.75	...

Scott #	Description	One Cover	Separate Covers
222-25	45¢ Migrant Birds, attd. 6/27/89................	4.50	9.00
226-29	45¢ PHILEXFRANCE, attd. 7/7/89................	6.50	11.00
230	25¢ PHILEXFRANCE S/S of 6 7/7/89................	7.50	10.00
230	"FILEX FRANCE Cancel	8.25	11.00
231	$1 PHILEXFRANCE S/S 7/7/89....................	9.00	...
231	FILEX FRANCE Cancel	12.50	...
232-38	25¢,$1 Moon Landing 20th Anniv., set of 7 bklt. sgls. 8/1/89..............................	...	32.50
238a	Bklt. Pane of 7	26.50	...
	WW II Anniversaries 1939-1989		
239	25¢ Invasion of Poland 9/1/89...................	5.50	...
240	45¢ HMS Royal Oak Sinking 10/13/89	6.00	...
241	45¢ Invasion of Finland 11/30/89	6.00	...
242-45	45¢ Battle of the River Plate 12/13/89	...	29.50
	WW II Anniversaries 1940-1990		
246-47	25¢ Invasion of Denmark & Norway 4/9/90..........	...	11.00
248	25¢ Katyn Forest Massacre 4/16/90	5.50	...
249-50	25¢ Invasion of Belgium 5/10/90	...	11.00
251	45¢ Winston Churchill, Prime Minister 5/10/90	6.00	...
252-53	45¢ Evacuation at Dunkirk 6/4/90..................	...	12.00
254	45¢ Occupation of Paris 6/14/90	6.00	...
255	25¢ Battle of Mars-el-Kebir 7/3/90..................	5.50	...
256	25¢ Burma Road 7/18/90	5.50	...
257-60	45¢ U.S. Destroyers for Brit. Bases 9/9/90......	...	23.50
261-64	45¢ Battle of Britain 9/15/90	...	23.50
265	45¢ Tripartite Pact 9/27/90	6.00	...
266	25¢ FDR Elected to Third Term 11/5/90	5.50	...
267-70	25¢ Battle of Taranto 11/11/90	...	27.50
	WW II Anniversaries 1941-1991		
271-74	30¢ Four Freedoms 1/6/91	...	22.50
275	30¢ Battle of Beda Fomm 2/5/91	5.50	...
276-77	29¢ Greek & Yugoslav Invasions 4/6/91	...	11.00
278-81	50¢ Sinking of the Bismarck 5/27/91	...	25.00
282	30¢ German Invasion of Russia 6/22/91	5.50	...
283-84	29¢ Atlantic Charter 8/14/91	...	11.00
285	29¢ Siege of Moscow 10/2/91	5.50	...
286-87	30¢ Sinking of the USS Reuben James 10/31/91 .	...	11.00
288-91	50¢ Japanese Attack Pearl Harbor 12/7/91	...	25.00
292	29¢ Japanese Capture Guam 12/10/91	5.50	...
293	29¢ Fall of Singapore 12/10/91	5.50	...
294-95	50¢ Flying Tigers 12/20/91	...	12.50
296	29¢ Fall of Wake Island 12/23/91	5.50	...
	WW II Anniversaries 1942-1992		
297	29¢ Arcadia Conf., 50th Anniv. 1/1/92	5.50	...
298	50¢ Fall of Manila 1/2/92	6.00	...
299	29¢ Japanese Take Rabaul 1/23/92................	5.50	...
300	29¢ Battle of Java Sea 2/15/92	5.50	...
301	50¢ Fall of Rangoon 3/8/92	6.00	...
302	29¢ Battle for New Guinea 3/8/92	5.50	...
303	29¢ MacArthur Leaves Corregidor 3/11/92	5.50	...
304	29¢ Raid on Saint-Nazaire 3/27/92	5.50	...
305	29¢ Surrender of Bataan 4/9/92	5.50	...
306	50¢ Doolittle Raid on Tokyo 4/18/92	6.00	...
307	29¢ Fall of Corregidor 5/6/92	5.50	...
308-11	50¢ Battle of Coral Sea 5/8/92	...	25.00
312-15	50¢ Battle of Midway 6/4/92	...	25.00
316	29¢ Village of Lidice Destroyed 6/10/92	5.50	...
317	29¢ Fall of Sevastopol 7/3/92	5.50	...
318-19	29¢ Convoy PQ17 Destroyed 7/5/92	...	11.00
320	29¢ Marines Land on Guadalcanal 8/7/92..........	5.50	...
321	29¢ Battle of Savo Island 8/9/92	5.50	...
322	29¢ Dieppe Raid 8/19/92	4.00	...
323	50¢ Battle of Stalingrad 8/19/92	6.00	...
324	29¢ Battle of Eastern Solomons 8/24/92	5.50	...
325	50¢ Battle of Cape Esperance 10/11/92	6.00	...
326	29¢ Battle of El Alamein 10/23/92	5.50	...
327-28	29¢ Battle of Barents Sea 12/31/92	...	11.00
	WW II Anniversaries 1943-1993		
329	29¢ Casablanca Conference 1/14/93	5.50	...
330	29¢ Liberation of Kharkov 2/16/93	5.50	...
331-34	50¢ Battle of Bismarck Sea 3/3/93	...	25.00
335	50¢ Interception of Yamamoto 4/18/93	6.00	...
336-37	29¢ Battle of Kursk 7/5/93	...	11.00
	1989-92 Regulars & Commemoratives		
341-44	25¢ Christmas, attd.10/25/89	...	25.75
345	45¢ Milestones in Space S/S of 25 10/24/89	50.00	...
345/65A	1¢/$2 Birds (21) 10/11/90, 10/11/90, 2/22/91, 3/8/91 11/6/91, 2/3/92, 4/24/92	...	87.50
361a	95¢ ESSEN '90, Min. Sheet of 4 4/19/90	25.00	...
366-69	25¢ Children's Games, attd. 3/15/90	...	23.50
370-76	25¢, $1 Penny Black, 150th Anniv., Bklt. pane of 7 (6x25¢, $1) 4/6/90	...	36.50
377-80	25¢ Sea Turtles, attd. 5/3/90	...	25.75
381	25¢ Joint Issue w/Micronesia & U.S. 9/28/90	5.00	...
382	45¢ German Reunification 10/3/90	7.00	...
383-86	25¢ Christmas, attd., 10/25/90	...	22.50
387-90	25¢ Breadfruit, attd., 12/15/90	...	18.75

OFFICIAL FIRST DAY COVER

REPUBLIC OF THE MARSHALL ISLANDS
JUL 4, 1991
Majuro
FIRST DAY OF ISSUE

To the Heroes of Desert Storm
July 4, 1991

399

Scott #	Description	One Cover	Separate Covers
	1991-92		
391-94	50¢ U.S. Space Shuttle, attd., 4/12/91	...	22.95
395-98	52¢ Flowers, 6/10/91	...	22.95
399	Operation Desert Storm 7/4/91	3.85	...
400-406	29¢,$1 Birds, Bklt. pane of 7 (6x29¢,$1) 7/16/91	...	36.50
407-10	12¢,29¢,50¢ (2) Air Marshall Isl. Aircraft 9/10/91	...	18.75
411	29¢ Admission to U.N. 9/24/91	5.75	...
412	30¢ Christmas 10/25/91	3.75	...
413	29¢ Peace Corps in Marshall Isl. 11/26/91	4.50	...
414-17	29¢ Ships, strip of 4 2/15/92	15.00	15.75
418-24	50¢,$1 Voyages of Discovery, Bklt. Pane of 7 (6x50¢,$1) 5/23/92....................	...	25.00
425-28	29¢ Traditional Handicrafts, strip of 4 9/9/92	6.50	15.00
429	29¢ Christmas 10/29/92	3.00	...
430-33	19¢/45¢ Birds 11/10/92	...	12.50
	1993-95		
434-40	50¢,$1 Reef Life (6x50¢,$1) 5/26/93	...	22.50
443/59	15¢-75¢ Ships, set of 8 6/24/93,10/14/93	...	31.75
441/65	10¢-$2.90 Ships, Set of 4 4/19/94.....................	...	21.50
445/57	20¢-55¢ Ships, Set of 4 9/23/94.......................	...	11.95
450-66	32¢-$3 Ships Definitives, set of 4 5/5/95..........	...	19.75
463	$1 Sailing Vessel 5/29/93.................................	5.50	...
464	$2 Sailing Vessel 8/26/93.................................	7.75	...
466A	$5 Sailing Vessel 3/15/94.................................	12.50	...
466B	$10 Sailing Vessel 8/18/94...............................	35.00	...
	WW II Anniversaries 1943-1993		
467-70	52¢ Invasion of Sicily 7/10/93	...	24.50
471	50¢ Bombing Raids on Schweinfurt 8/17/93.......	6.00	...
472	29¢ Liberation of Smolensk 9/25/93..................	5.50	...
473	29¢ Landing at Bougainville 11/1/93	5.50	...
474	50¢ US Invasion of Tarawa 11/20/93..................	6.00	...
475	52¢ Tehran Conference 12/1/93	6.00	...
476-77	29¢ Battle of North Cape 12/26/93....................	...	11.00
	WW II Anniversaries 1944-1994		
478	29¢ Eisenhower - SHAEF 1/16/94	5.50	...
479	50¢ Invasion of Anzio 1/22/94	6.00	...
480	52¢ Siege of Leningrad Ends 1/27/94................	6.00	...
481	29¢ U.S. Frees Marshall Islands 2/4/94	5.50	...
482	29¢ Japanese Defeat at Truk 2/17/94	5.50	...
483	52¢ Bombing of Germany 2/20/94	6.00	...
484	50¢ Rome Falls to Allies 6/4/94	6.00	...
	WW II Anniversaries 1944-1994 (continued)		
485-88	75¢ D-Day Landings 6/6/94	18.50	27.50
489	50¢ V-1 Bombs Strike England 6/13/94..............	6.00	...
490	29¢ Landing on Saipan 6/15/94	5.50	...
491	50¢ Battle of Philippine Sea 6/19/94	6.00	...
492	29¢ U.S. Liberates Guam 7/21/94......................	5.50	...
493	50¢ Warsaw Uprising 8/1/94	6.00	...
494	50¢ Liberation of Paris 8/25/94	6.00	...
495	50¢ Marines Land on Peliliu 9/15/94	5.50	...
496	52¢ MacArthur Returns to Philippines 10/20/94..	6.00	...
497	52¢ Battle of Leyte Gulf 10/24/94......................	6.75	...
498-99	50¢ German Battleship "Tirpitz" Sunk 11/12/94 ..	...	15.00
500-3	50¢ Battle of the Bulge 12/16/94	...	25.00
562	50¢ MacArthur Returns to Philippines, Souvenir Sheet of 2 10/20/94.............................	7.25	...
	WWII Anniversaries 1945-1995		
504	32¢ Yalta Conference 2/4/95	5.50	...
505	55¢ Bombing of Dresden 2/13/95	6.25	...
506	$1 Iwo Jima Invaded 2/19/95.............................	9.00	...
507	32¢ Remagen Bridge Taken 3/7/95....................	7.00	...
508	55¢ Marines Invade Okinawa 4/1/95...................	6.25	...
509	50¢ Death of F.D. Roosevelt 4/12/95	6.75	...
510	32¢ US/USSR Troops Link 4/25/95	5.95	...
511	60¢ Soviet Troops in Berlin 5/2/95	7.50	...
512	55¢ Allies Liberate Concentration Camps 5/4/95	7.50	...

Scott #	Description	One Cover	Separate Covers
513-16	75¢ V-E Day, Set of 4 5/8/95...........................	18.50	29.50
517	32¢ United Nations Charter 6/26/95...................	6.00	...
518	55¢ Potsdam Conference 7/17/95	6.75	...
519	60¢ Churchill's Resignation 7/26/95	7.00	...
520	$1 Atomic Bomb dropped on Hiroshima 8/6/95...	10.00	...
521-24	75¢ V.J. Day, Set of 4 9/2/95	18.50	24.50
563	$1 United Nations Souv. Sheet 6/26/95	7.00	...
	1993-94		
567-70	29¢ Capitol Complex 8/11/93............................	...	10.75
571	50¢ Mobil Oil Tanker 8/25/93	3.85	...
572-75	29¢ Life in 1800's 9/15/93	...	10.75
576	29¢ Christmas 10/25/93	2.95	...
577	$2.90 Constitution Souvenir Sheet 5/1/94	7.95	...
578	29¢ Postal Service Souvenir Sheet 5/2/94.........	2.95	...
579-80	50¢ World Soccer Cup	...	10.75
582	50¢ Solar System, Set of 12 7/20/94.................	...	36.50
583-86	75¢ Moon Landing, 25th Anniv. 7/20/94............	...	14.50
587	29¢, 52¢, $1 Butterflies Souv. Sht. 8/16/94 (2) ...	13.50	...
588	29¢ Christmas 10/28/94	2.95	...
	1995		
589	50¢ Year of the Boar Souvenir Sheet 1/2/95......	3.75	...
590	55¢ Underseas Glory (4 designs) 3/20/95..........	...	13.00
591	55¢ J.F. Kennedy, set of 6 5/29/95	...	21.75
592	75¢ Marilyn Monroe, set of 4 6/1/95	...	15.75
593	32¢ Cats, set of 4 7/5/95	...	11.50
594	75¢ Mir-Shuttle Set of 5 6/29/95.......................	...	22.75
595	60¢ Game Fish Set of 8 8/21/95	...	27.75
596	32¢ Island Legends Set of 5 8/25/95.................	5.75	17.00
597	32¢ Singapore '95 Set of 2 9/1/95....................	...	6.25
598	50¢ Beijing '95 Set of 2 9/12/95	...	7.75
599	32¢ Christmas 10/31/95	2.95	...
600	32¢ Jet Fighter Planes Set of 5 11/10/95	...	26.50
601	32¢ Yitzhak Rabin 11/30/95	4.75	...
	1996		
602	50¢ Year of the Rat S/S 1/5/96	3.25	...
603	32¢ Local Birds, Set of 4 2/26/96......................	...	13.75
604	55¢ Wild Cats, Set of 4 3/8/96..........................	...	13.75
605	32¢ Millenium of Navigation, Set of 5 Cvrs 4/18/96	...	28.00
606	60¢ Modern Olympics 4/27/96	7.50	...
607	55¢ Marshall Island Chronology 5/2/96 (12)	...	39.50
608	32¢ Elvis Presley 5/5/96...................................	2.95	...
609	50¢ China '96 5/17/96	3.50	...
610	32¢ James Dean 6/1/96	2.95	...
611	60¢ Ford Motor, Set of 8 6/4/96........................	...	28.75
612	32¢ Legends of RMI, Set of 4 7/19/96...............	...	11.50
613	55¢ Steam Locomotives, Set of 12 8/23/96	...	39.75
614	32¢ Taipei '96 Souvenir Sheet 10/21/96	5.25	...
615	$3 Compact with U.S. 10/21/96.........................	8.75	...
616	32¢ Christmas, Madonna 10/31/96	2.95	...
617	32¢ Biplanes, Set of 5 11/1/96..........................	...	28.75
618	32¢ Handicrafts, Set of 4 11/7/96......................	...	11.75
	1997		
619	60¢ Year of the Ox, souvenir Sheet 1/2/97	3.50	...
620-21	32¢-60¢ Amata Kabua 1/27/97..........................	4.25	...
622	32¢ Elvis Presley 1/8/97...................................	8.75	8.75
623-24	32¢ Hong Kong '97, Set of 2 2/12/97	...	7.25
625	60¢ Twelve Apostles, Set of 12 3/28/97	...	43.50
626	$3 Last Supper, Souvenir Sheet 3/28/97	8.75	...
......	60¢ 20th Century, 1900-1909 Set of 15 4/15/97 .	...	52.50
	1996 Semi-Postals		
B1	32¢+8¢ Operations Crossroads, Set of 6 1/1/96.	...	18.50
	Airmails		
C1-2	44¢ Audubon, attd. 2/15/86	4.75	8.00
C3-6	44¢ AMERIPEX Planes, attd. 5/22/86................	6.25	12.75
C7	44¢ Operation Crossroads S/S 7/1/86	4.50	...
C7	Bikini FD Cancel..	6.50	...
C8	44¢ Statue of Liberty/Peace Year 10/28/86	3.50	...
C9-12	44¢ Girl Scouts, attd. 12/8/86..........................	5.00	12.50
C13-16	44¢ Marine Birds, attd. 1/12/87........................	5.00	12.50
C17-20	44¢ Amelia Earhart/CAPEX, attd. 6/15/87	5.50	10.00
C17-20	CAPEX FD Cancel...	7.50	12.50
C22-25	12¢,36¢,39¢,45¢ Aircraft 4/24/89	4.25	8.75
C22a/25b	12¢/45¢ Booklet Panes of 10 (5) 6/10/89..........	...	47.50
	Postal Cards		
UX1	20¢ Elvis Presley 7/8/96..................................	.80	...
UX2-5	20¢ Canoes, Set of 4..	...	2.75
UX6	20¢ Heavenly Angels 9/4/96	.70	...
......	32¢ Turtle 3/7/97...	.95	...

FEDERATED STATES OF MICRONESIA
Hammerhead Shark
Sphyrna zygaena

77-80

Scott #	Description	One Cover	Separate Covers
	1984-1988		
1-4	20¢ Postal Service Inaugural, attd. 7/12/84	7.50	12.50
5-20	1¢/$5 Definitives 7/12/84 (4 FDC's)	...	30.00
21,C4-6	20¢,28¢,35¢,40¢ AUSIPEX 9/21/84	11.50	18.50
22,C7-9	20¢,28¢,35¢,40¢ Christmas 12/20/84	11.50	18.50
23,C10-12	22¢,33¢,39¢,44¢ Ships 8/19/85	11.50	23.75
24,C13-14	22¢,33¢,44¢ Christmas 10/15/85	12.50	22.50
25-28	22¢ Audubon, attd. 10/30/85	11.00	23.75
31-39,C34-36	3¢-$10 Bird Definitives and Airs (6 FDC's) #31-32,35,C34-36 (8/1/88); #34 (4/14/86), #33,36-38 (9/1/88), #39 (10/15/85)	...	40.00
33a	15¢ Bklt. Pane of 10 11/30/88	7.75	...
36a	25¢ Bklt. Pane of 10 11/30/88	9.75	...
36b	15¢,25¢ Bklt. Pane of 10 (5 ea.) 11/30/88	9.50	...
45,C16-18	22¢,33¢,39¢,44¢ Nan Madol Ruins	10.50	25.00
46,C19-20	22¢,44¢ Peace Year,Comet,Nauruans 5/16/86	12.50	25.00
48-51	22¢ on 20¢ (Surcharges on #1-4), attd. 5/19/86	...	43.50
52,C21-24	22¢,33¢,39¢,44¢,75¢ AMERIPEX 5/22/86	11.00	25.00
52,C21-24	AMERIPEX FD Cancel	22.75	35.00
53	22¢ Passport 11/4/86	6.25	...
54-55,C26-27	5¢,22¢,33¢,44¢ Xmas 10/15/86 (2)	16.50	22.50
56,C28-30	22¢,33¢,39¢,44¢ Homeless, Events 6/13/87	14.50	20.00
57	$1 CAPEX S/S 6/13/87	14.50	...
58,C31-33	22¢,33¢,39¢,44¢ Xmas 11/16/87	14.75	25.00
59-62,C37-38	22¢,44¢ Colonial Eras 7/20/88 (2)	12.50	22.50
63-66	25¢,45¢ Summer Olympics, 2 pairs 9/1/88	9.00	13.50
67-70	25¢ Christmas, attd. 10/28/88	5.75	9.50
71	25¢ Truk Lagoon Monument S/S of 18 12/19/88 (3)	22.95	37.50
	1989-1990		
72-75	45¢ Mwarmwarms, attd. 3/31/89	5.75	9.50
76	$1 Emperor Hirohito Memorial S/S 5/15/89	4.50	...
77-80	25¢,45¢ Sharks (2 pairs) 7/7/89	6.50	11.00
81	25¢ 1st Moon Landing, 20th Anniv., S/S of 9 7/20/89 (3)	12.00	11.50
82	$2.40 1st Moon Landing, 20th Anniv. 7/20/89	6.95	...
83/102	1¢/$5 Seashells (12) 9/26/89 (2)	29.95	40.00
85a	15¢ Booklet Pane of 10 9/14/90	9.00	...
88a	25¢ Booklet Pane of 10 9/14/90	11.00	...
88b	15¢,25¢ Booklet Pane of 10 (5 ea.) 9/14/90	10.00	...
	1989-1991		
103	25¢ Kosrae Fruits & Flowers S/S of 18 11/18/89	25.00	40.00
103	Same, World Stamp Expo, DC cancel	30.00	45.00
104-05	25¢,45¢ Christmas 12/14/89	7.50	9.75
106-09	10¢/25¢ Wildlife 2/19/90	6.00	14.50
110-13	45¢ Stamp World London, attd. 5/3/90	6.25	10.00
114	$1 Stamp World London S/S 5/3/90	4.00	...
115	$1 Penny Black, 150th Anniv. 5/6/90	4.00	...
116-20	25¢ Pohnpei Agric. & Trade School, attd. 7/31/90	4.50	9.00
121	$1 Int'l. Garden & Greenery Expo S/S 7/31/90	4.00	...
122-23	25¢,45¢ Mail Plane & Boat 8/24/90	4.00	5.75
124-26	25¢ Jt. Issue Marsh. Isl. & U.S., strip of 3 9/28/90	3.50	6.25
127-30	45¢ Moths, attd. 11/10/90	5.75	8.00
131	25¢ Christmas S/S of 9 11/19/90	7.00	...
132	25¢,45¢ New Capitol of Micronesia S/S 1/15/91	3.50	...
133	$1 New Capitol S/S 1/15/91	4.00	...
134-35	29¢ Turtles, attd. 3/14/91	2.25	4.75
136-37	50¢ Turtles, attd. 3/14/91	3.75	5.25
138-41	29¢ Desert Shield/Desert Storm, strip of 4 7/30/91	4.50	7.75
142	$2.90 Frigatebird, flag 7/30/91	7.95	...
142a	$2.90 Same, S/S 7/30/91	7.95	...
143	29¢ Phila Nippon '91, min. sheet of 3 9/1/91	3.75	...
143a-c	Set of 3 singles	...	5.50
144	50¢ Phila Nippon '91, min. sheet of 3 9/1/91	5.00	...
144a-c	Set of 3 singles	...	6.50
145	$1 Phila Nippon S/S 9/1/91	4.00	...
146-48	29¢,40¢,50¢ Christmas 10/30/91	4.50	6.50
149	29¢ Rain Forest, min. sht. of 18 11/18/91 (3)	17.50	...

Scott #	Description	One Cover	Separate Covers
	1992-1994		
150	29¢ Peace Corps, strip of 5 4/10/92	16.50	...
151	29¢ Discovery of America, Strip of 3 5/23/92	10.95	...
152-53	29¢,50¢ Anniv. of UN Membership 9/24/92	14.50	5.50
153a	Same, S/S of 2	6.50	...
154	29¢ Christmas 12/4/92	3.75	...
155	29¢ Pioneers of Flight, block of 8 4/12/93	8.00	23.50
157/166	10¢-$2.90 Fish, Set of 4 5/20/94	9.50	...
159/65	19¢-$1 Fish, Set of 8 5/14/93,8/26/93 (2)	11.50	...
160A/165A	25¢-$2 Fish, Set of 4 8/5/94	13.50	...
168	29¢ Golden Age of Sail, min. sht. of 12 5/21/93	12.00	30.00
172	29¢ Thomas Jefferson 7/4/93	2.95	...
173-76	29¢ Pacific Canoes, attd. 7/21/93	4.50	...
177	29¢ Local Leaders, strip of 4 9/16/93	5.00	...
178	50¢ Pioneers of Flight, block of 8 9/25/93	10.50	24.75
179-80	29¢-50¢ Pohnpei 10/5/93	4.25	...
181	$1 Pohnpei Souvenir Sheet 10/5/93	4.65	...
182-83	29¢-50¢ Butterflies, two pairs 10/20/93	6.25	...
184-85	29¢-50¢ Christmas 11/11/93	4.50	...
186	29¢ Yap Culture, sheet of 18 12/15/93 (3)	16.75	...
	1994		
187-89	29¢,40¢,50¢ Kosrae 2/11/94	4.50	...
190	29¢-50¢ Butterflies, sheet of 4 2/18/94	14.75	...
191	29¢ Pioneers of Flight, block of 8 3/4/94	7.50	23.75
192	29¢ Micronesian Games, block of 4 3/26/94	4.50	...
193	29¢ Native Costumes, block of 4 3/31/94	4.50	...
194	29¢ Anniversary of Constitution 5/10/94	2.95	...
195	29¢ Flowers, Strip of 4 6/6/94	4.50	5.00
196-97	50¢ World Cup Soccer 6/17/94	7.50	...
198	29¢ Postal Service, 10th Anniv. 7/12/94	6.50	...
199	29¢, 52¢, $1 Philakorea, Dinosaurs, Souvenir Sheet of 3 8/16/95 (2)	13.50	...
200	50¢ Pioneers of Flight, Set of 8 9/20/94	9.50	25.00
201	29¢ Migratory Birds 10/20/94	6.50	...
202-3	29¢-50¢ Christmas 11/2/94	4.75	5.95
204-7	32¢ Local leaders, 4 designs 12/27/94	5.75	...
	1995		
208	50¢ Year of the Boar Souvenir Sheet 1/2/95	3.85	...
209	32¢ Chuuk Lagoon, block of 4 2/6/95	8.00	...
210	32¢ Pioneers of Flight, set of 8 3/4/95	7.75	36.50
211	32¢ Dogs of the World, block of 4 4/5/95	5.25	...
213/226	23¢-$5 Fish Definitives 8/4/95	16.50	...
214/225	32¢-$3 Fish Definitives 5/15/95	11.75	...
227	32¢ Native Fish, Set of 5 Covers	...	28.00
228	32¢ Hibiscus, Strip of 4 6/1/95	5.15	...
229	$1 United Nations Souv. Sheet 6/26/95	4.50	...
230	32¢ Singapore '95 Souv. Sheet, set of 2 9/1/95	...	12.75
231	60¢ End of WWII 9/2/95	7.50	...
232	50¢ Beijing '95 Souv. Sheet, set of 2 9/14/95	...	8.50
233	60¢ Pioneers of Flight, set of 8 9/21/95	13.50	38.50
234-35	32¢-60¢ Christmas 10/30/96	4.25	4.75
236	32¢ Yitzhak Rabin 11/30/96	4.25	...
	1996		
237	50¢ Year of Rat Souv. Sheet 1/5/96	4.25	...
238	32¢ Pioneers of Flight, set of 8 2/21/96	8.25	37.50
239	32¢ Tourism in Yap, block of 4 3/13/96	4.95	...
240	55¢ Starfish 4/26/96	6.75	7.50
241	60¢ Olympics 4/27/96	7.50	8.50
242	50¢ China '96, Souvenir Sheet 5/15/96	3.50	...
243-44	32¢ Patrol Boats 5/3/96	3.95	...
245	55¢ Ford Motor, Set of 8 6/4/96	...	27.50
247	32¢ Officer Reza, Police Dog 7/31/96	2.95	...
248	50¢ Citrus Fruits, Set of 4 8/24/96	...	17.50
249	60¢ Pioneers of Flight, Set of 8 9/15/96	...	37.50
250	32¢ Taipei '96, Souvenir Sheet 10/21/96	5.25	...
251-52	32¢-60¢ Christmas 10/30/96	...	6.50
253	$3 Compact with U.S. 11/3/96	8.75	...

Airmails - Stationery

Scott #	Description	One Cover	Separate Covers
C1-3	28¢,35¢,40¢ Airpost 7/12/84	6.00	12.00
C25	$1 AMERIPEX S/S 5/22/86	10.50	...
C39-42	45¢ Micronesia Flags, attd. 1/19/89	6.25	9.50
C43-46	22¢/45¢ Aircraft Serving Micronesia 7/16/90	5.00	8.00
C47-48	40¢,50¢ Aircraft 3/27/92	3.50	5.25
C49	$2.90 Moon Landing Souvenir Sheet 7/20/94	7.95	...
U1	20¢ National Flag 7/12/84	12.75	...
U3	29¢ on 30¢ 3/3/91	8.75	...

51-54

Scott #	Description	One Cover	Separate Covers
	Palau FDC's (#1-58, 75-81, C1-4) have Commercial Cachets.		
	1983		
1-4	20¢ Postal Service Inaugural 3/10/83	4.95	14.95
1-4	INTERPEX FD Cancel	13.50	25.00
5-8	20¢ Birds 3/16/83	4.25	15.00
9-21	1¢/$5 Definitives (3 covers)	32.50	57.50
13a	13¢ Booklet Pane of 10	22.50	...
13b	13¢/20¢ Booklet Pane of 10 (5 #13, 5 #14)	32.50	...
14b	20¢ Booklet Pane of 10	22.50	...
24-27	20¢ Whales, attd. 9/21/83	4.00	12.50
28-32	20¢ Christmas, attd. 11/18/83	5.00	13.50
33-40	20¢ Capt. Wilson's Voyage, attd. 12/14/83	6.25	19.75
33-40	London FD Cancel	12.75	25.00
	1984-86		
41-50	20¢ Seashells, attd. 3/15/84	9.75	22.95
41-50	INTERPEX FD Cancel	19.50	28.50
51-54	40¢ 19th UPU Congress 6/19/84	6.25	13.75
51-54	Hamburg FD Cancel	10.50	18.50
55-58	20¢ Traditional Fishing attd. 9/6/84	5.00	12.50
55-58	AUSIPEX FD Cancel	7.50	15.00
59-62	20¢ Christmas, attd. 12/5/84	5.00	12.50
63-66/C5	22¢/44¢ Audubon, attd. 2/6/85	7.00	15.00
67-70	22¢ Shipbuilding, attd. 3/27/85	4.00	12.50
75/81	14¢/44¢ Marine Life, Set of 6 6/11/85	7.25	12.50
75a	14¢ Booklet Pane of 10	17.50	...
76a	22¢ Booklet Pane of 10	17.50	...
76b	14¢/22¢ Booklet Pane of 10 (5 #75, 5 #76)	20.00	...
85	$10 Spinner Dolphins 3/31/86	27.50	...
86-89	44¢ International Youth Year, attd. 7/15/85	5.95	15.00
90-93	14¢,22¢,33¢,44¢ Christmas 10/21/85	5.50	12.50
94	$1 Trans-Pacific Air Anniv. S/S 1/21/85	4.50	...
95-98	44¢ Halley's Comet, attd. 12/21/85	6.00	13.50
	1986-88		
99-102	44¢ Songbirds, attd. 2/24/86	6.00	12.50
103	14¢ AMERIPEX Sea & Reef, Sht. of 40 5/22/86	55.00	75.00
104-08	22¢ Seashells, attd. 8/1/86	5.50	12.50
109-12,C17	22¢ International Peace Year 9/19/86	6.00	12.50
113-16	22¢ Reptiles, attd. 10/28/86	4.25	12.50
117-21	22¢ Christmas, attd. 11/26/86	4.50	12.50
121B-E	44¢ Butterflies, attd. 1/5/87	5.75	12.50
122-25	22¢ Fruit Bats, attd. 2/23/87	5.50	12.50
126/45	1¢-$5 Flowers (16) 3/12/87,7/1/88 (2 FDC's)	28.50	38.50
126/45	INTERPEX FD Cancel (12) 3/12/88	28.50	35.00
130a	14¢ Bklt. Pane of 10 3/31/87	9.00	...
131a	15¢ Bklt. Pane of 10 7/5/88	9.00	...
132a	22¢ Bklt. Pane of 10 3/31/87	10.00	...
132b	14¢,22¢ Bklt. Pane of 10 (5 ea.) 3/31/87	10.00	...
133a	25¢ Bklt. Pane of 10 7/5/88	9.50	...
133b	15¢,25¢ Bklt. Pane of 10 (5 ea.) 7/5/88	10.00	...
145A	$10 Flower Bouquet 3/17/88	28.50	...
	1987-88		
146-49	22¢ CAPEX attd. 6/15/87	3.65	10.00
146-49	CAPEX FD Cancel	5.50	12.50
150-54	22¢ Seashells attd. 8/25/87	4.75	12.50
155-63	14¢,22¢,44¢ U.S. Const. Bicent. (3 Strips of 3) 9/17/87 (3 FDC's)	8.50	17.50
164-67	14¢,22¢,33¢,44¢ Japanese Links 10/16/87	5.00	11.00
168	$1 S/S Japanese Links to Palau 10/16/87	5.50	...
173-77	22¢ Christmas attd. 11/24/87	4.25	10.00
178-82	22¢ "Silent Spring" Symb. Spec. atd. 12/15/87	4.25	10.00

Scott #	Description	One Cover	Separate Covers
	1988-90		
183-86	44¢ Butterflies & Flowers, attd. 1/25/88	4.75	8.50
187-90	44¢ Ground Dwelling Birds, attd. 2/29/88	4.75	9.00
191-95	25¢ Seashells (5), attd. 5/11/88	4.25	10.75
196	25¢ Postal Indep. S/S of 6 (FINLANDIA) 6/2/88	6.25	...
197	45¢ U.S. Posses. Phil. Soc. S/S of 6 8/26/88	7.50	...
198-202	25¢ Christmas, attd. 11/7/88	4.25	9.50
203	25¢ Chambered Nautilus S/S of 5 12/23/88	4.65	...
204-07	45¢ Endangered Birds, attd. 2/9/89	5.25	9.00
208-11	45¢ Exotic Mushrooms, attd. 3/16/89	5.25	9.00
212-16	25¢ Seashells, attd. 4/12/89	4.65	8.50
217	$1 Emperor Hirohito Memorial S/S 5/17/89	6.75	...
218	25¢ 1st Moon Landing, 20th Anniv. S/S 7/20/89	17.50	...
219	$2.40 Moon Landing, 20th Anniv. 7/20/89	6.75	...
220	25¢ Literacy, block of 10 10/13/89	6.50	12.00
221	25¢ World Stamp Expo., Sht. of 20 11/20/89	15.75 (4)	...
221	Washington, D.C. cancel	19.75 (4)	...
222-26	25¢ Christmas, attd. 12/18/89	4.25	7.50
227-30	25¢ Soft Coral, attd. 1/3/90	3.75	7.50
231-34	25¢ Forest Birds 3/16/90	5.00	8.00
235	25¢ Prince Lee Boo Visits Engl., S/S of 9 5/6/90	7.00	...
235	London FD Cancel	9.00	...
236	$1 Penny Black, 150th Anniv. S/S 5/6/90	3.50	...
236	London FD Cancel	4.75	...
237-41	45¢ Orchids, attd. 6/4/90	5.75	11.00
242-45	45¢ Butterflies & Flowers, attd. 7/6/90	5.00	10.00
246	25¢ Lagoon Life, Sheetlet of 25 8/10/90	18.00	...
247-48	45¢ Pacifica/Mail Delivery, attd. 8/24/90	3.50	6.25
249-53	25¢ Christmas, attd. 11/28/90	3.65	7.50
254-57	45¢ U.S. Forces in Palau, 1994 attd. 12/7/90	5.00	7.75
258	$1 U.S. Forces in Palau, 1994 S/S 12/7/90	3.50	...
	1991-92		
259-62	30¢ Coral, attd. 3/4/91	4.25	8.00
263	30¢ Angaur, min. sht. of 16 3/4/91	12.50	...
264-286	1¢/$2 Bird Definitives (17) 4/18/91, 1992	...	45.00
287	$10 Bird Definitive 9/10/92	22.75	...
270a	19¢ Palau Fantail, bklt. pane of 10 8/23/91	14.00	...
272a	29¢ Palau, fruit dove, bklt. pane of 10 8/23/91	15.00	...
272b	19¢,29¢ bklt. pane of 10 (5x19¢, 5x29¢) 8/23/91	15.00	...
288	29¢ Christianity in Palau, min. sht. of 6 4/28/91	5.50	...
289	29¢ Marine Life, min. sht. of 6 5/24/91	17.75	...
290	20¢ Desert Shield/Desert Storm, min.sht.of 9 7/2/91	7.75	...
291	$2.90 Desert Shield/Storm 7/2/91	7.75	...
292	$2.90 Desert Shield/Storm S/S 7/2/91	8.25	...
293	29¢ Republic of Palau, 10th Anniv., miniature sheet of 8, 7/9/91	5.50	...
294	50¢ Giant Clams, min. sht. of 5 9/17/91	6.25	...
295	29¢ Japanese Heritage, min. sht. of 6 11/19/91	4.75	...
296	$1 Phila Nippon S/S 11/19/91	3.50	...
297	29¢ Peace Corps in Palau, min. sht. of 6 12/6/91	5.00	...
298	29¢ Christmas, strip of 5, attd. 11/14/91	4.50	...
299	29¢ WWII in the Pacific, min. sht. of 10 12/6/91	11.00	...
300	50¢ Butterflies, blk. of 4 1/20/92	5.50	7.50
301	29¢ Shells, strip of 5 3/11/92	4.50	7.50
302	29¢ Age of Discovery, min. sheet of 20 5/25/92	13.50	...
303	29¢ Biblical Creation, min. sht. of 24 6/5/92	16.50	...
304-09	50¢ Summer Olympics S/S 7/10/92	...	21.00
310	29¢ Elvis Presley, min. sht. of 9 8/17/92	11.00	...
311	50¢ WWII in the Pacific, min. sht. of 10 9/10/92	12.50	...
312	50¢ Christmas, strip of 5 10/1/92	4.50	7.50

PALAU FIRST DAY COVERS

Scott #	Description	One Cover	Separate Covers
	1993-94		
313	50¢ Animal Families, block of 4 7/9/93................	5.50	8.75
314	29¢ Seafood, block of 4 7/22/93..........................	3.50	7.75
315	50¢ Sharks, block of 4 8/11/93...........................	5.50	8.75
316	29¢ WW II, Pacific Theater, min.sht.of 10 9/23/93	10.95	...
317	29¢ Christmas, strip of 5 10/22/93......................	4.50	7.25
318	29¢ Prehistoric and Legendary Sea Creatures, sheet of 25 11/26/93..................................	16.50	...
319	29¢ Indigenous People, sheet of 4 12/8/93..........	3.50	...
320	$2.90 Indigenous People, Souv. Sheet 12/8/93.....	7.50	...
321	29¢ Jonah and the Whale, sheet of 25 12/28/93...	16.50	...
322	40¢ Palau Rays, block of 4 1/28/94.....................	4.50	7.50
323	20¢ Crocodiles, block of 4..................................	2.50	5.25
324	50¢ Seabirds, block of 4 4/12/94........................	5.50	8.95
325	29¢ WW II, Pacific Theater, min.sht. of 10 4/12/94	9.75	...
326	50¢ WW II, D-Day, min.sht.of 10 4/12/94	13.95	...
327	29¢ Baron Pierrede Coubertin 6/15/94.................	1.75	...
328-33	50¢, $1, $2 Coubertin and Winter Olympics Stars, Set of 6 Souv. Sheets 6/15/94...............	16.50	...
334-36	29¢, 40¢, 50¢ Philakorea '94 Philatelic Fantasies, Wildlife, 3 S/S of 8 8/15-25/94........	24.50	...
337	29¢ Apollo XI Moon Landing 25th Anniv. Miniature Sheet of 2 7/7/94...........................	13.50	...
338	29¢ Independence Day strip of 5 10/1/94.............	4.50	...
339	$1 Invasion of Peleliu Souv. Sht 9/15/94..............	4.75	...
340	29¢ Disney Tourism Sheetlet of 9 9/1/94..............	6.50	...
341-43	$1, $2.90 Disney Tourism, 3 Souv. Sheets 9/1/94	...	12.75
344	20¢ Year of the Family, Min. Sheet of 12..............	8.95	...
345	29¢ Christmas '94 Strip of 5 11/1/94...................	4.50	11.00
346-48	29¢, 50¢ World Cup of Soccer, Set of 3 Sheetlets of 12 12/1/94.................................	29.50	...
	1995		
350	32¢ Elvis Presley, Sheetlets of 9 1/26/95..............	9.50	...
351-64	1¢-$5 Fish Definitives (14) 1/2/95 ....(3)	28.50	43.50
365	$10 Fish Definitive 3/1/95..................................	21.00	...
368	32¢ Tourism, Lost Fleet, Sheetlet of 18 3/30/95 ...	13.75	...
369	32¢ Earth Day '95, Sheetlet of 18 3/30/95............	13.75	...
370	50¢ Jet Aircraft, Sheetlet of 12 4/5/95.................	13.75	...
371	$2 Jet Airliner, Souv. Sheet 4/5/95.....................	4.95	...
372	32¢ Underwater Ships, Sheetlet of 18 7/21/95......	13.95	...
373	32¢ Singapore '95 8/15/95.................................	4.25	...
374	60¢ U.N., FAO 50th Anniv. 9/15/95......................	6.75	...
375-76	$2 U.N., FAO 50th Anniv. Souvenir Sheets 9/15/95	11.50	...
377	20¢ Independence 9/15/95.................................	3.50	...
378	32¢ Independence, Marine Life 9/15/95...............	2.30	...
379	32¢ End of WWII, Sheetlet - 12 10/18/95..............	13.75	...
380	60¢ End of WWII, Sheetlet - 5 10/18/95...............	10.00	...
381	$3 End of WWII Souv. Sheet 10/18/95..................	8.00	...
382	32¢ Christmas Strip of 5 10/31/95.......................	4.75	11.75
383	32¢ Sea Turtle, Sheetlet - 12 11/15/95................	9.25	...
384	32¢ John Lennon 12/8/95...................................	3.75	...
	1996		
385	10¢ Year of the Rat Strip-4 2/2/96.......................	2.95	...
386	60¢ Year of Rat Souvenir Sheet 2/2/96.................	3.95	...
387	32¢ UNICEF 3/12/96..	4.50	...
388	32¢ China '96, Marine Life 3/29/96	4.50	...
389	32¢ Circumnavigators 5/3/96	7.50	...
390	60¢ Air & Space 5/3/96	11.50	...
391	$3 Air & Space, Souvenir Sheet 5/3/96.................	7.50	...
392	$3 Cirumnavigators, Souvenir Sheet 5/3/96..........	7.50	...
392A-F	1¢-6¢ Disney Sweethearts 5/30/96	2.75	...
393	60¢ Disney Sweethearts, 5/30/96	11.75	...
394-95	$2 Disney Sweethearts, Souvenir Sheet 5/30/96..	11.75	...
396	20¢ 3000th Anniversary of Jerusalem 6/15/96......	14.95	...
397-98	40¢ Atlanta '96 6/17/96	2.95	...
399-400	60¢ Atlanta '96 6/17/96	3.65	...
401	32¢ Atlanta '96 6/17/96	12.95	...
402	50¢ Lagoon Birds 7/96......................................	22.75	...
403	40¢ Spies in the Sky Sheetlet	12.95	...
404	$3 Stealth Bomber, Souvenir Sheet	7.95	...
405	60¢ Oddities of the Air, Sheetlet	17.95	...
406	$3 Martin Marietta X-24B, Souvenir Sheet...........	7.95	...
407-8	20¢ Independence 10/1/96..................................	2.95	...
409	32¢ Christmas, Strip of 5 10/8/96	4.50	...
410	32¢ Voyages to Mars, Sheetlet	11.00	...
411-12	$3 Voyages to Mars, Souvenir Sheet (2)	...	16.50
	1997		
413	$1 South Pacific, Souvenir Sheet.........................	2.95	...

Scott #	Description	One Cover	Separate Covers
	Semi-Postals		
B1-4	25¢,45¢ Olympic Sports, 2 pairs 8/8/88	7.50	10.95
	Airmails		
C1-4	40¢ Birds, attd. 6/12/84	6.25	13.75
C1-4	Expo '84 FD Cancel..	10.75	18.00
C6-9	44¢ Palau-Germany Exch. Cent. attd. 9/1/85........	6.25	12.50
C10-13	44¢ Trans-Pacific Anniv., attd. 11/21/85..............	5.75	12.50
C14-16	44¢ Remeliik Memorial, attd. 6/30/86..................	6.00	12.50
C17	44¢ Peace Yr., Statue of Liberty 9/19/86..............	2.85	...
C17	Stamp Festival FD Cancel...................................	3.75	...
C18-20	36¢,39¢,45¢ Aircraft 5/17/89.............................	4.25	8.00
C18a/20b	36¢/45¢ Booklet Panes of 10 (4)........................	...	39.50
C21	50¢ Palauan Bai, self adh. (#293a) 7/9/91	2.75	...
C22	50¢ Birds, block of 4 1/26/95.............................	5.50	11.50
	Postal Stationery		
U1	22¢ Parrotfish 2/14/85......................................	2.95	...
U2	22¢ Spearfishing 2/14/85...................................	4.75	...
U3	25¢ Nautilus 1991..	7.75	...
UC1	36¢ Birds 2/14/85...	5.95	...
UX1	14¢ Giant Clam 2/14/85.....................................	2.95	...

UNITED NATIONS

| | | 1 | 2 | 8 | 11 | | |

1951 Regular Issue

Scott's No.		MI Block of 4	F-VF NH	F-VF Used
1-11	1¢-$1 Regular Issue	42.50	8.50	7.50
1	1¢ Peoples, Magenta	.60	.20	.15
2	1½¢ U.N. Hdqtrs. Blue Green	.60	.20	.15
2p	1½¢ Precancelled	...	...	30.00
3	2¢ Peace, Justice, Sec. Purple	.60	.20	.15
4	3¢ Flag, Magenta & Blue	.60	.20	.15
5	5¢ UNICEF, Blue	.60	.20	.15
6	10¢ Peoples, Chocolate	1.25	.25	.20
7	15¢ Flag, Violet & Blue	1.35	.30	.20
8	20¢ World Unity, Dark Brown	3.50	.75	.50
9	25¢ Flag, Olive Gray & Blue	2.75	.60	.50
10	50¢ U.N. Hdqtrs., Indigo	24.50	5.50	4.50
11	$1 Peace, Justice Sec., Red	9.00	2.00	1.50

| | | 13 | 17 | 21 | | |

1952

12	5¢ War Memorial Building, U.N. Charter......	1.00	.20	.20
13-14	3¢-5¢ Human Rights, Flame	2.25	.45	.40

1953

15-16	3¢-5¢ Refugee Family	3.25	.70	.60
17-18	3¢-5¢ Univ. Postal Union......................	5.75	1.25	.95
19-20	3¢-5¢ Technical Assistance	3.25	.70	.60
21-22	3¢-5¢ Human Rights, Hands	9.00	1.85	.75

| | | 23 | 25 | 27 | 30 | | |

1954

23-24	3¢-8¢ Food & Agriculture Org	9.00	1.85	1.15
25-26	3¢-8¢ Int'l. Labor Organization	10.50	2.35	1.15
27-28	3¢-8¢ U.N. European Office, Geneva	16.00	3.50	1.80
29-30	3¢-8¢ Human Rights, Mother and Child	50.00	10.75	3.75

| | | 31 | 35 | 47 | | |

1955

31-32	3¢-8¢ Int'l Civil Aviation Organization...........	18.50	3.75	1.75
33-34	3¢-8¢ UNESCO Emblem	3.00	.60	.55
35-37	3¢, 4¢, 8¢ 10th Anniversary United Nations..	11.75	2.50	1.25
38	3¢, 4¢, 8¢ 10th Anniv. Souv. Sheet of 3......	...	140.00	50.00
38v	3¢, 4¢, 8¢ Second Print, Retouched	...	150.00	60.00
39-40	3¢-8¢ Human Rights, Torch	2.95	.60	.55

NOTE : "MI" REFERS TO MARGINAL INSCRIPTION BLOCKS FROM THE CORNERS OF U.N. MINT SHEETS.

UNITED NATIONS 1956

Scott's No.		MI Block of 4	F-VF NH	F-VF Used
41-42	3¢-8¢ Telecommunications...........................	3.50	.75	.65
43-44	3¢-8¢ World Health Organ...........................	2.95	.60	.55
45-46	3¢-8¢ General Assembly, U.N. Day	1.25	.30	.20
47-48	3¢-8¢ Human Rights, Flame and Globe	1.25	.30	.20

| | | 53 | 55 | 63 | 67 | | |

1957

49-50	3¢-8¢ Meteorological, Weather Balloon	1.25	.30	.20
51-52	3¢-8¢ U.N. Emergency Force......................	1.25	.30	.20
53-54	3¢-8¢ Same, re-engraved...........................	3.00	.60	.40
#53-54 The area around the circles is shaded, giving a halo effect.				
55-56	3¢-8¢ Security Council, Emblem and Globe ..	1.25	.30	.20
57-58	3¢-8¢ Human Rights, Flaming Torch...........	1.25	.30	.20

1958

59-60	3¢-8¢ Atomic Energy Agency	1.25	.30	.20
61-62	3¢-8¢ Central Hall, London	1.25	.30	.20
63-64	4¢-8¢ Regulars, U.N. Seal	1.25	.30	.20
65-66	4¢-8¢ Economic & Social Council	1.25	.30	.20
67-68	4¢-8¢ Human Rights, Hands and Globe	1.25	.30	.20

| | | 69 | 73 | 77 | 86 | | |

1959

69-70	4¢-8¢ Flushing Meadows, Gen. Assembly ...	1.25	.30	.22
71-72	4¢-8¢ Economic Comm. - Europe	1.85	.40	.35
73-74	4¢-8¢ Trusteeship Council..........................	2.00	.45	.30
75-76	4¢-8¢ World Refugee Year	1.25	.30	.20

1960

77-78	4¢-8¢ Chaillot Palace Paris	1.25	.30	.20
79-80	4¢-8¢ Economic Council - Asia & Far East ..	1.25	.30	.20
81-82	4¢-8¢ World Forestry Congress...................	1.25	.30	.20
83-84	4¢-8¢ 15th Anniversary, United Nations.......	1.25	.30	.20
85	4¢-8¢ 15th Anniv. Souvenir Sheet..............	...	1.00	.95
85v	Same broken "v" Variety.............................	...	67.50	65.00
86-87	4¢-8¢ Bank for Reconstruction & Develop. ..	1.25	.30	.20

| | | 88 | 97 | 108 | 112 | | |

1961

88-89	4¢-8¢ Int'l Court of Justice........................	1.25	.30	.20
90-91	4¢-7¢ Monetary Fund	1.25	.30	.20
92	30¢ Regular, Flags	2.25	.50	.40
93-94	4¢-11¢ Economic Council - Latin America ...	2.75	.60	.45
95-96	4¢-11¢ Economic Comm. - Africa...............	2.25	.50	.20
97-99	3¢, 4¢, 13¢ Children's Fund, UNICEF	2.35	.45	.35

1962

100-01	4¢-7¢ Housing & Urban Development..........	1.75	.30	.22
102-03	4¢-11¢ World Health Org., Anti-Malaria	1.90	.40	.27
104-07	1¢, 3¢, 5¢, 11¢ Regulars	3.50	.75	.35
108-09	5¢-15¢ Dag Hammarskjold.........................	2.50	.50	.40
110-11	4¢-11¢ Operations in Congo.......................	2.50	.50	.45
112-13	4¢-11¢ Peaceful Uses of Outer Space	2.10	.45	.40

NOTE: PRICES THROUGHOUT THIS LIST ARE SUBJECT TO CHANGE WITHOUT NOTICE IF MARKET CONDITIONS REQUIRE. MINIMUM MAIL ORDER MUST TOTAL AT LEAST $20.00.

114	119	133	134

192	197	203	209

Scott's No.		MI Block of 4	F-VF NH	F-VF Used
114-15	5¢-11¢ Science & Technology	1.85	.40	.27
116-17	5¢-11¢ Freedom from Hunger	1.85	.40	.27
118	25¢ UN in West New Guinea (UNTEA)	2.50	.55	.30
119-20	5¢-11¢ General Assembly Bldg.,N.York	1.65	.35	.27
121-22	5¢-11¢ Human Rights, Flame	1.90	.40	.27
1964				
123-24	5¢-11¢ Maritime Consultative Org	1.85	.40	.27
125-28	2¢,7¢,10¢,50¢ Regulars	6.95	1.50	.75
129-30	5¢-11¢ Trade & Development	1.85	.40	.30
131-32	5¢-11¢ Control Narcotics	2.35	.50	.40
133	5¢ Ending Nuclear Tests	.80	.20	.15
134-36	4¢,5¢,11¢ Education Progress	2.10	.45	.40

Scott's No.		MI Block of 4	F-VF NH	F-VF Used
192-93	6¢-13¢ Training & Research Inst.	2.10	.45	.35
194-95	6¢-15¢ U.N. Building, Santiago	2.10	.45	.35
196	13¢ Regular "U.N." & Emblem	1.35	.30	.22
197-98	6¢-13¢ Peace Through Law	1.85	.40	.30
199-200	6¢-20¢ Labor & Development	2.10	.45	.40
201-02	6¢-13¢ Art, Tunisian Mosaic	1.65	.35	.30
1970				
203-04	6¢-25¢ Art, Japanese Peace Bell	2.50	.55	.45
205-06	6¢-13¢ Mekong Basin Development.	2.10	.45	.35
207-08	6¢-13¢ Fight Against Cancer	1.60	.35	.30
209-11	6¢,13¢,25¢ 25th Anniversary of U.N.	3.85	.85	.75
212	6¢,13¢,25¢ 25th Anniv. Souv. Sheet of 3	...	.80	.75
213-14	6¢-13¢ Peace, Justice & Progress	2.40	.50	.40

137	139	154	161

215	216	220	224

	1965			
137-38	5¢-11¢ Development Fund	1.85	.40	.25
139-40	5¢-11¢ Peace Keeping Force - Cyprus	1.60	.35	.25
141-42	5¢-11¢ Telecommunications Union	1.85	.40	.25
143-44	5¢-15¢ 20th Anniv. Cooperation Year.	1.60	.35	.30
145	5¢-12¢ 20th Anniv. Souvenir Sheet of 2	...	.50	.45
146-50	1¢,15¢,20¢,25¢,$1 Regulars	16.75	3.50	2.75
151-53	4¢,5¢,11¢ Population Trends	2.10	.45	.35
	1966			
154-55	5¢-15¢ Fed. of U.N. Associations	1.80	.40	.30
156-57	5¢-11¢ W.H.O. Headqtrs. Geneva	1.80	.40	.27
158-59	5¢-11¢ Coffee Agreement	1.80	.40	.27
160	15¢ Peacekeeping - Observers	1.25	.30	.25
161-63	4¢,5¢,11¢ UNICEF 20th Anniv.	2.10	.45	.30

	1971			
215	6¢ Peaceful Uses of the Sea Bed	.85	.20	.15
216-17	6¢-13¢ Support for Refugees	1.65	.35	.30
218	13¢ World Food Program	1.40	.30	.20
219	20¢ U.P.U. Headquarters, Bern	1.85	.40	.35
220-21	8¢-13¢ Racial Discrimination	1.85	.40	.30
222-23	8¢-60¢ Regulars	5.25	1.15	1.00
224-25	8¢-21¢ U.N. Int'l. School	2.50	.55	.50

164	170	185	190

	1967			
164-65	5¢-11¢ Development Program	1.60	.35	.25
166-67	1½¢-5¢ Regulars	1.25	.30	.20
168-69	5¢-11¢ Independent Nations, Fireworks	1.40	.30	.25
170-74	4¢,5¢,8¢,10¢,15¢ Expo '67, Montreal	3.50	.75	.65
175-76	5¢-15¢ Tourist Year	1.60	.35	.27
177-78	6¢-13¢ Disarmament	1.85	.40	.30
179	6¢ Chagall Souvenir Sheet of 6	...	.65	.60
180	6¢ Chagall Window Stamp	.85	.20	.15
	1968			
181-82	6¢-13¢ Secretariat	1.85	.40	.30
183-84	6¢-75¢ Art, Starcke Statue	7.50	1.60	1.30
185-86	6¢-13¢ Industrial Development	1.40	.30	.25
187	6¢ Regular, U.N. Headquarters	.85	.20	.15
188-89	6¢-20¢ World Weather Watch	1.95	.42	.37
190-91	6¢-13¢ Human Rights, Flame	1.95	.42	.37

	1972			
226	95¢ Regular, Letter	10.00	2.10	1.50
227	8¢ No More Nuclear Weapons	.85	.20	.15
228	15¢ World Health Day, Man.	1.40	.30	.25
229-30	8¢-15¢ Human Environment, Stockholm	2.75	.55	.45
231	21¢ Economic Comm. - Europe	2.40	.50	.35
232-33	8¢-15¢ Art, Jose Maria Sert Mural	2.95	.60	.45
	1973			
234-35	8¢-15¢ Disarmament Decade	2.95	.60	.45
236-37	8¢-15¢ Against Drug Abuse	2.95	.60	.45
238-39	8¢-21¢ Volunteer Program	3.25	.65	.50
240-41	8¢-15¢ Namibia, Map of Africa	2.95	.60	.50
242-43	8¢-21¢ Human Rights, 25th Anniv.	2.95	.60	.50

NOTE: PRICES ARE FOR SETS OR SINGLES AS LISTED.

UNITED NATIONS 1974

244	252	256	260

Scott's No.		MI Block of 4	F-VF NH	F-VF Used
244-45	10¢-21¢ ILO Headquarters	3.65	.75	.65
246	10¢ U.P.U. Centenary	1.35	.30	.20
247-48	10¢-18¢ Art, Brazil Peace Mural	3.95	.80	.65
249-51	2¢,10¢,18¢ Regulars	3.75	.75	.60
252-53	10¢-18¢ Population Year	4.25	.85	.75
254-55	10¢-25¢ Law of the Sea	3.95	.80	.65

1975

256-57	10¢-26¢ Peaceful Use of Outer Space	3.95	.80	.70
258-59	10¢-18¢ Women's Year	4.25	.85	.65
260-61	10¢-26¢ 30th Anniversary of U.N.	4.50	.90	.65
262	10¢-26¢ 30th Anniv. Souv. Sheet of 2	...	.90	.80
263-64	10¢-18¢ Namibia, Hand	3.65	.75	.55
265-66	13¢-26¢ Peacekeeping Operations	4.25	.90	.80

272	278	283	289

1976

267-71	3¢,4¢,9¢,30¢,50¢ Regulars	9.75	1.95	1.50
272-73	13¢-26¢ U.N. Associations(WFUNA)	3.50	.75	.60
274-75	13¢-31¢ Trade & Development	3.75	.80	.70
276-77	13¢-25¢ Human Settlement, Habitat	3.75	.80	.75
278-79	13¢-31¢ 25th Postal Anniversary	13.00	2.95	2.25
278-79	Same, Sheetlets of 20	...	50.00	...
280	13¢ World Food Council	1.75	.35	.22

1977

281-82	13¢-31¢ Intellectual Property(WIPO)	3.75	.80	.70
283-84	13¢-25¢ Water Conference	3.50	.75	.65
285-86	13¢-31¢ Security Council	3.75	.75	.70
287-88	13¢-25¢ Racial Discrimination	3.50	.75	.75
289-90	13¢-18¢ Peaceful - Atomic Energy	3.75	.80	.70

296	298	310	312

299	301	302

1978

291-93	1¢,25¢,$1 Regulars	11.00	2.25	1.75
294-95	13¢-31¢ Smallpox-Eradication	3.95	.85	.75
296-97	13¢-18¢ Namibia,Open Handcuff	3.65	.75	.60
298-99	13¢-25¢ Civil Aviation Organ (ICAO)	3.95	.85	.75
300-01	13¢-18¢ General Assembly	3.65	.80	.70
302-03	13¢-31¢ Technical Cooperation	5.50	1.10	.85

UNITED NATIONS

Scott's No.		MI Block of 4	F-VF NH	F-VF Used

1979

304-07	5¢,14¢,15¢,20¢ Regulars	6.00	1.30	1.00
308-09	15¢-20¢ Disaster Relief (UNDRO)	4.25	.75	.60
310-11	15¢-31¢ Year of the Child	4.25	.90	.85
310-11	Same, Sheetlets of 20	...	17.50	...
312-13	15¢-31¢ Namibia, Olive Branch	3.75	.80	.70
314-15	15¢-20¢ Court of Justice, The Hague	4.25	.90	.75

316	325	344	346

1980

316-17	15¢-31¢ New Economic Order	5.25	1.10.	.85
318-19	15¢-20¢ Decade for Women	4.25	.90	.75
320-21	15¢-31¢ Peacekeeping Opererations	5.25	1.10	.90
322-23	15¢-31¢ 35th Anniversary of U.N.	3.75	.80	.70
324	15¢-31¢ 35th Anniv. - Souv. Sheet of 2	...	.75	.75
*325-40	15¢ World Flag Series of 16	13.00	3.25	3.00
325-40	Se-Tenant Block of 4(4)	...	7.50	...

325	Turkey	329	Guinea	333	Jugoslavia	337	Madagascar
326	Luxembourg	330	Surinam	334	France	338	Cameroun
327	Fiji	331	Bangladesh	335	Venezuela	339	Rwanda
328	Vietnam	332	Mali	336	El Salvador	340	Hungary

341-42	15¢-20¢ Economic & Social Council	4.25	.90	.70

1981

343	15¢ Palestinian People	1.60	.35	.30
344-45	20¢-35¢ Disabled Persons	5.75	1.20	1.10
346-47	20¢-31¢ Art, Bulgarian Mural	4.75	1.00	.80
348-49	20¢-40¢ Energy Conference	6.25	1.35	1.25
*350-65	20¢ World Flag Series of 16	19.50	4.75	4.75
350-65	Se-Tenant Blocks of 4(4)	...	11.00	...

350	Djibouti	354	Malta	358	Ukraine	362	U.S.
351	Sri Lanka	355	Czech.	359	Kuwait	363	Singapore
352	Bolivia	356	Thailand	360	Sudan	364	Panama
353	Eq. Guinea	357	Trinidad & T.	361	Egypt	365	Costa Rica

366-67	18¢-28¢ Volunteers Program	5.50	1.20	.80

371	390	394	397

1982

368-70	17¢,28¢,40¢ Regulars	9.75	2.10	1.35
371-72	20¢-40¢ Human Environment	8.00	1.50	1.15
373	20¢ Peaceful Use of Outer Space	4.00	.80	.40
*374-89	20¢ World Flag Series of 16	22.50	5.50	5.25
374-89	Se-Tenant Blocks of 4(4)	...	13.50	...

374	Austria	378	Mozambique	382	Philippines	386	Cape Verde
375	Malaysia	379	Albania	383	Swaziland	387	Guyana
376	Seychelles	380	Dominica	384	Nicaragua	388	Belgium
377	Ireland	381	Solomon Isl.	385	Burma	389	Nigeria

390-91	20¢-28¢ Nature Conservation	6.50	1.35	.90

1983

392-93	20¢-40¢ Communications Year	6.75	1.40	1.00
394-95	20¢-37¢ Safety at Sea	7.25	1.50	1.25
396	20¢ World Food Program	3.00	.60	.50
397-98	20¢-28¢ Trade & Development	6.95	1.50	1.20
*399-414	20¢ World Flag Series of 16	27.00	6.50	5.75
399-414	Se-Tenant Blocks of 4(4)	...	15.00	...

399	U. Kingdom	403	Malawi	407	China	411	Somalia
400	Barbados	404	Byelorussia	408	Peru	412	Senegal
401	Nepal	405	Jamaica	409	Bulgaria	413	Brazil
402	Israel	406	Kenya	410	Canada	414	Sweden

415-16	20¢-40¢ Human Rights, 35th Anniv.	7.50	1.50	1.25
415-16	Same, Sheetlets of 16	...	27.50	...

NOTE: WORLD FLAGS ARE ISSUED IN SHEETS OF 16, EACH WITH 4 DIFFERENT BLOCKS.
SHEETS OF 16 WILL BE SUPPLIED AT MI BLOCK PRICE.

UNITED NATIONS 1984

| | | 417 | | 419 | | 421 | |

Scott's No.		MI Block of 4	F-VF NH	F-VF Used
417-18	20¢-40¢ Population Conference	6.00	1.35	1.15
419-20	20¢-40¢ FAO Food Day	6.00	1.35	1.20
421-22	20¢-50¢ UNESCO World Heritage	7.00	1.50	1.40
423-24	20¢-50¢ Refugee Futures	7.50	1.65	1.35
*425-40	20¢ World Flag Series of 16	55.00	13.00	11.50
425-40	Se-Tenant Blocks of 4(4)	...	22.50	...

425	Burundi	429	Tanzania	433	Poland	437	Paraguay
426	Pakistan	430	United Arab	434	Papua New	438	Bhutan
427	Benin		Emirates		Guinea	439	Central Afric.
428	Italy	431	Ecuador	435	Uruguay		Republic
		432	Bahamas	436	Chile	440	Australia

441-42	20¢-35¢ Youth Year	7.00	1.50	1.25

| | | 466 | | 468 | | 473 | |

1985

443	23¢ ILO-Turin Centre	3.00	.65	.50
444	50¢ U.N. University in Japan	7.50	1.60	1.40
445-46	22¢-$3 Regulars	26.50	5.75	4.50
447-48	22¢-45¢ 40th Anniversary of U.N.	9.50	2.00	1.85
449	22¢-45¢ 40th Anniv. Souvenir Sheet of 2	...	2.40	2.10
*450-65	22¢ World Flag Series of 16	57.50	14.50	12.50
450-65	Se-Tenant Blocks of 4(4)	...	24.50	...

450	Grenada	454	Uganda	458	Liberia	462	Sultanate of
451	Federal Rep.	455	St. Thomas	459	Mauritius		Oman
	of Germ.		& Prince	460	Chad	463	Ghana
452	Saudi Arabia	456	USSR	461	Dominican	464	Sierra Leone
453	Mexico	457	India		Republic	465	Finland

466-67	22¢-33¢ UNICEF Child Survival	6.75	1.50	1.25

1986

468	22¢ Africa in Crisis, Against Hunger	3.25	.70	.65
469-72	22¢ UN Development Program, attd.	10.75	9.75	4.50
469-72	Sheet of 40	...	95.00	...
473-74	22¢-44¢ Philately, Stamp Collecting	8.50	1.85	1.40
475-76	22¢-33¢ International Peace Year	15.00	3.25	1.75
*477-92	22¢ World Flag Series of 16	56.50	13.50	12.50
477-92	Se-Tenant Blocks of 4(4)	...	22.50	...

477	New Zealand	481	Maldives	485	Iceland	489	Romania
478	Lao PDR	482	Ethiopia	486	Antigua &	490	Togo
479	Burkina Faso	483	Jordan		Barbuda	491	Mauritania
480	Gambia	484	Zambia	487	Angola	492	Colombia
				488	Botswana		

493	22¢,33¢,39¢,44¢ WFUNA S/S of 4	...	5.75	5.25

| | | 516 | | 517 | | 518 | |

1987

494	22¢ Trygve Lie, Secretary-General	5.50	1.20	.85
495-96	22¢-44¢ Shelter for the Homeless	11.50	2.50	1.50
497-98	22¢-33¢ Life Yes/Drugs No	11.00	2.40	1.50
*499-514	22¢ 1987 World Flag Series of 16	57.50	13.50	9.50
499-514	Se-Tenant Blocks of 4 (4)	...	23.50	...

499	Comoros	503	Japan	507	Argentina	511	Bahrain
500	DPR Yemen	504	Gabon	508	Congo	512	Haiti
501	Mongolia	505	Zimbabwe	509	Niger	513	Afghanistan
502	Vanuatu	506	Iraq	510	St. Lucia	514	Greece

UNITED NATIONS 1987 (Cont.)

Scott's No.		MI Block of 4	F-VF NH	F-VF Used
515-16	22¢-39¢ U.N. Day	7.75	1.75	1.50
515-16	Miniature Sheets of 12	...	23.50	...
517-18	22¢-44¢ Child Immunization	18.50	3.95	2.00

| | | 519 | | 524 | | 544 | |

1988

519-20	22¢-33¢ World Without Hunger(IFAO)	12.00	2.50	1.50
521	3¢ Regular, UN For a Better World	.90	.20	.15
522-23	25¢-44¢ Forestry, pair	24.75	10.50	9.50
522-23	Miniature Sheet of 12	...	49.50	...
524-25	25¢-50¢ Int'l. Volunteers Day	11.00	2.25	1.50
526-27	25¢-38¢ Health in Sports	12.50	2.75	1.50
*528-43	25¢ World Flag Series of 16	55.00	12.75	9.00
528-43	Se-Tenant Blocks of 4 (4)	...	22.50	...

528	Spain	532	Yemen Arab	536	Qatar	540	Iran
529	St. Vincent		Rep.	537	Zaire	541	Tunisia
	& Gren.	533	Cuba	538	Norway	542	Samoa
530	Ivory Coast	534	Denmark	539	German	543	Belize
531	Lebanon	535	Libya		Dem. Rep.		

544	25¢ Human Rights 40th Anniv.	3.75	1.10	.50
545	$1 Human Rights Anniv. S/S	...	2.95	2.00

1989

546-47	25¢-45¢ World Bank	15.00	3.25	1.65
548	25¢ UN Peace Keeping, Nobel Prize	4.95	.90	.60
549	45¢ Regular UN Headquarters	5.00	1.00	.90
550-51	25¢-36¢ World Weather Watch	15.00	3.50	1.85
552-53	25¢-90¢ UN Offices Vienna, 10th Anniv.	33.50	7.50	2.65
552-53	Sheets of 25	...	225.00	...
*554-69	25¢ World Flags Series of 16	67.50	15.75	9.50
554-69	Se-Tenant Blocks of 4 (4)	...	25.00	...

554	Indonesia	558	South Africa	562	Honduras	566	Algeria
555	Lesotho	559	Portugal	563	Kampucea	567	Brunei
556	Guatemala	560	Morocco	564	Guinea-Bissau	568	St.Kitts-Nevis
557	Netherlands	561	Syrian Arab	565	Cyprus	569	United Nations
			Republic				

570-71	25¢-45¢ Declaration of Human Rights	...	2.50	2.00
570-71	Strips of 3 with Tabs at Bottom	...	7.50	...
570-71	Miniature Sheets of 12	...	29.75	...

| | | 572 | | 580 | | 592 | | 597 | |

1990

572	25¢ International Trade Center	8.25	1.75	.85
573-74	25¢-40¢ Fight Against AIDS	12.75	2.95	1.40
575-76	25¢-90¢ Medicinal Plants	16.50	3.75	2.25
577-78	25¢-45¢ UN 45th Anniversary	23.50	5.25	2.25
579	25¢-45¢ UN 45th Anniversary S/S of 2	...	9.50	8.50
580-81	25¢-36¢ Crime Prevention	19.50	4.25	2.50
582-83	25¢-45¢ Declaration of Human Rights	...	2.50	1.50
582-83	Strips of 3 with Tabs at Bottom	...	7.50	...
582-83	Miniature Sheets of 12	...	29.75	...

1991

584-87	30¢ Europe Econ. Commission attd.	8.00	7.00	3.75
588-89	25¢-50¢ Namibia Independence	16.50	3.50	1.30
590-91	30¢-50¢ Regulars	12.50	2.50	1.40
592	$2 Regular U.N. Headquarters	18.50	3.95	3.25
593-94	30¢-70¢ Children's Rights	19.75	4.25	2.75
595-96	30¢-90¢ Chemical Weapons Ban	29.50	6.75	3.25
597-98	30¢-40¢ UNPA 40th Anniv.	17.50	3.75	1.75
599-600	30¢-50¢ Declaration of Human Rights	...	2.75	1.75
599-600	Strips of 3 with Tabs at Bottom	...	8.00	...
599-600	Miniature Sheets of 12	...	31.00	...

601 611 624

Scott's No.		MI Block of 4	F-VF NH	F-VF Used
601-02	30¢-50¢ World Heritage, UNESCO...........	14.50	3.25	2.00
603-04	29¢ Clean Oceans attd............................	4.75	1.85	1.15
603-04	Miniature Sheet of 12	...	14.75	...
605-08	29¢ UNICED: Earth Summit attd..............	3.75	3.25	2.75
605-08	29¢ UNICED Sheet of 40	...	37.50	...
609-10	29¢ Mission to Planet Earth attd.	27.50	11.00	7.95
609-10	Miniature Sheet of 10	...	55.00	...
611-12	29¢-50¢ Science & Technology	9.00	2.10	1.50
613-15	4¢,29¢,40¢ Regulars	10.00	2.25	1.40
616-17	29¢-50¢ Declaration of Human Rights	...	2.75	2.00
616-17	Strips of 3 with Tabs at Bottom	...	8.00	...
616-17	Miniature Sheet of 12	...	30.00	...

1993

618-19	29¢-52¢ Aging with Dignity.......................	17.50	3.75	2.80
620-23	29¢ Endangered Species attd	3.65	3.25	2.50
620-23	Miniature sheet of 16	...	14.50	...
624-25	29¢-50¢ Healthy Environments	15.00	3.25	1.75
626	5¢ Regular...	.95	.20	.18
627-28	29¢-35¢ Human Rights.............................	...	3.00	1.75
627-28	Strips of 3 with Tabs at Bottom	...	8.75	...
627-28	Miniature Sheets of 12.............................	...	36.50	...
629-32	29¢ Peace Day, attd................................	12.95	11.95	3.75
629-32	29¢ Peace Day, Sheet of 40	...	125.00	...
633-36	29¢ Environment - Climate....................(8)	9.75	4.50	3.25
633-36	Miniature Sheet of 24	...	27.50	...

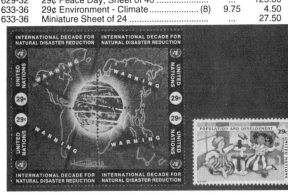

647-50 651

1994

637-38	29¢-45¢ Year of the Family	20.00	4.35	2.00
639-42	29¢ Endangered Species, attd	3.95	3.25	2.50
639-42	Miniature Sheets of 16.............................	...	16.50	...
643	50¢ Refugees	8.50	1.85	1.25
644-46	10¢,19¢,$1 Regulars	14.50	2.95	2.75
647-50	29¢ Natural Disaster, block of 4	12.00	11.00	7.50
647-50	29¢ Natural Disaster, Sheet of 40	...	115.00	...
651-52	29¢-52¢ Population Development	13.00	2.95	2.25
653-54	29¢-50¢ Development Partnership............	10.75	2.30	1.75

655 661 663

1995

655	32¢ U.N. 50th Anniversary	7.00	1.50	.95
656	50¢ Social Summit, Copenhagen..............	6.00	1.35	.95
657-60	32¢ Endangered Species, attd	3.75	3.25	2.50
657-60	Miniature Sheet of 16	...	15.00	...
661-62	32¢-55¢ Youth: Our Future.......................	13.50	2.95	1.95
663-64	32¢-50¢ 50th Anniv. of U.N.	13.50	2.95	1.95
665	82¢ 50th Anniversary Souv. Sheet of 2.....	...	3.95	2.25
666-67	32¢-40¢ Conference on Women	11.75	2.65	1.75
668	20¢ Regular Issue, U.N. Headquarters	2.30	.50	.45
669	32¢ U.N. 50th Anniv. Sheetlet - 12............	...	13.75	...
670	32¢ U.N. 50th Anniv. Souvenir, Booklet of 12...	...	15.00	...

671 672-73

Scott's No.		MI Block of 4	F-VF NH	F-VF Used
671	32¢ WFUNA 50th Anniv.	3.65	.75	.45
672-73	32¢-60¢ Regular Issues	10.50	2.15	1.35
674-77	32¢ Endangered Species	3.35	2.85	2.10
674-77	Miniature Sheet of 16	...	13.50	...
678-82	32¢ City Summit, Strip of 5..................(10)	8.25	3.50	3.00
678-82	Miniature Sheet of 25	...	17.50	...
683-84	32¢-50¢ Sport & Environment	9.50	1.95	1.50
685	32¢-50¢ Sport & Environment Souv. Sheet	...	1.95	1.50
686-87	32¢-60¢ Plea For Peace...........................	10.50	2.25	1.75
688-89	32¢-60¢ UNICEF 50th Anniv.	10.50	2.25	1.75
688-89	Miniature Sheet of 8	...	21.50	...

1997

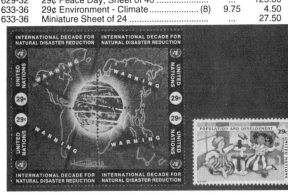

690 698 699

690-97	32¢ Flags of New Countries (8).................	...	5.25	4.25
690-97	Sheetlets of 16 (2)	...	20.75	...
698-99	8¢-55¢ Regulars, Flowers	6.25	1.30	1.10
700-3	32¢ Endangered Species	3.50	2.95	2.10
700-3	Miniature Sheets of 16.............................	...	11.75	...
704-7	32¢ Earth Summit....................................	3.50	2.95	2.10
704-7	Miniature Sheet of 16	...	17.50	...
708	$1 Earth Summit, Souvenir Sheet.............	...	2.25	2.15
709	$1 Pacific "97 Overprint on #708...............	...	2.95	2.75

UNITED NATIONS AIRMAILS

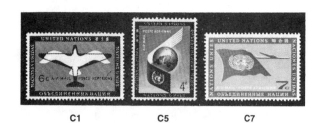

C1 C5 C7

Scott's No.		MI Block of 4	F-VF NH	F-VF Used
	1951 First Airmail Issue			
C1-4	6¢,10¢,15¢,25¢ Airmail Issue	7.50	1.50	1.40
	1957-59			
C5-7	4¢,5¢,7¢ Airmails	1.85	.45	.40

C8 C11 C14

	1963-69			
C8-10	6¢,8¢,13¢ Airmails	2.65	.60	.55
C11-12	15¢ & 25¢ Airmails (1964)	5.50	1.10	.75
C13	20¢ Jet Plane (1968)................................	2.10	.45	.40
C14	10¢ Wings & Envelopes (1969)	1.75	.35	.25

C15 C19 C22

	1972-77			
C15-18	9¢,11¢, 17¢, 21¢ Airmails	5.00	1.10	.90
C19-21	13¢, 18¢, 26¢ Airmails (1974)	5.35	1.15	.95
C22-23	25¢ & 31¢ Airmails (1977)	5.25	1.15	.95

U.N. IN NEW YORK 1951-96

1-689,C1-23	Complete...	...	595.00	...
1/689,C1-23	Without Souvenir Sheet #38	...	475.00	...

**FOR VERY FINE, ADD 20% TO PRICE LISTED.
MINIMUM-10¢ PER STAMP**

UNITED NATIONS POSTAL STATIONERY

U1

UXC 3

Scott's No.		Mint Entire
	ENVELOPE ENTIRES	
U1	3¢ Emblem (1953).......	.90
U2	4¢ Emblem (1958)........	.60
U3	5¢ Wthr. Vane (1963)..	.35
U4	6¢ Wthr. Vane (1969)..	.35
U5	8¢ Hdqtrs (1973)	.50
U6	10¢ Hdqtrs (1975)	.50
U7	22¢ Bouquet (1985).....	12.75
U8	25¢ NY Headqtrs ('89).	3.50
U9	25¢+4¢ Schg on U8 (91)	3.25
U9A	25¢+7¢ Schg on U8 (95)	1.50
U10	32¢ Cripticondina ('97)	.95
U11	32¢ Cripticondina, larger design (1997)	.95
	AIRMAIL ENVELOPE ENTIRES	
UC3	7¢ Flag (1959)	1.95
UC6	8¢ Emblem (1963)	.60
UC8	10¢ Emblem (1969).....	.50
UC10	11¢ Birds (1973)..........	.50
UC11	13¢ Globe (1975)	.55
	AIRLETTER SHEETS	
UC1	10¢ Air Letter (1952) ...	33.95
UC2	10¢ "Air Letter/Aero..." White Border (1954) ...	10.00
UC2a	10¢ Same, No White Border (1958)	8.50
UC4	10¢ Flag (1960)	.90
UC5	11¢ Gull, blue (1961)...	1.00
UC5a	11¢ Greenish (1965) ...	2.00
UC7	13¢ Plane (1968).........	.50
UC9	15¢ Globe (1972)	.90
UC12	18¢ Hdqtrs (1975)	.85
UC13	22¢ Birds (1977)..........	.90
UC14	30¢ Paper Airplane (82)	2.25
UC15	30¢+6¢ Surcharge (87)	57.50
UC16	39¢ NY Headqrtrs (89)	4.95
UC17	39¢+6¢ Surcharge on UC16 (1991)..........	19.50
UC18	45¢ Winged Hand ('92)	3.95
UC19	45¢+5¢ Surcharge on UC18 (95)...............	6.50
UC20	50¢ Cherry Blossom ('97)	1.10

Scott's No.		Mint Entire
	POSTAL CARDS	
UX1	2¢ Hdqtrs (1952)........	.45
UX2	3¢ Hdqtrs (1958)........	.40
UX3	4¢ Map (1963)	.30
UX4	5¢ Post Horn (1969)..	.30
UX5	6¢ "UN" (1973)	.32
UX6	8¢ "UN" (1975)	.75
UX7	9¢ Emblem (1977).....	.75
UX8	13¢ Letters (1982)	.60
UX9-13	15¢ NY HQ Views(89)	7.75
UX14-18	36¢ NY HQ Views (1989)	14.50
UX19	40¢ UN HQ (1992)	2.25
	AIRMAIL POSTAL CARDS	
UXC1	4¢ Wing (1957)...........	.45
UXC2	4¢ + 1¢ Surch (1959).	.50
UXC3	5¢ Wing (1959)..........	.95
UXC4	6¢ Space (1963)	.85
UXC5	11¢ Earth (1966)........	.50
UXC6	13¢ Earth (1968)........	.65
UXC7	8¢ Planes (1969)	.75
UXC8	9¢ Wings (1972)	.50
UXC9	15¢ Planes (1972)	.60
UXC10	11¢ Clouds (1975)...	.55
UXC11	18¢ Pathways ('75)..	.55
UXC12	28¢ Flying Mailman(82)	.70

1   4   8   14

1969-70

Scott's No.		MI Block of 4	F-VF NH	F-VF Used
1-14	5¢,10¢,20¢,30¢,50¢,60¢,70¢,75¢, 80¢,90¢,1fr.,2fr.,3fr.,10 fr. Regular Issue	47.50	9.75	9.50

16   18   22

1971

15	30¢ Peaceful Use of Sea Bed	1.15	.25	.25
16	50¢ Support for Refugees	1.50	.30	.30
17	50¢ World Food Program	1.75	.35	.35
18	75¢ U.P.U. Headquarters	2.40	.50	.50
19-20	30¢-50¢ Racial Discrimination	2.95	.60	.60
21	1.10 fr. U.N. Int'l. School	4.75	.95	.90

1972

22	40¢ Palace of Nations,Geneva	1.40	.25	.25
23	40¢ No Nuclear Weapons	1.95	.40	.40
24	80¢ World Health Day, Man	3.00	.65	.65
25-26	40¢-80¢ Human Environment	4.75	1.00	1.00
27	1.10 fr. Economic Comm. - Europe	6.50	1.35	1.25
28-29	40¢-60¢ Art, Jose Maria Set Mural	6.50	1.35	1.25

36   37   43   45

1973

30-31	60¢-1.10 fr. Disarmament Decade	8.50	1.80	1.70
32	60¢ Against Drug Abuse	3.00	.65	.60
33	80¢ Volunteer Program	2.65	.55	.50
34	60¢ Namibia, Map of Africa	2.70	.55	.50
35-36	40¢-80¢ Human Rights, Flame	5.95	1.20	1.10

1974

37-38	60¢-80¢ ILO Headquarters,Geneva	6.50	1.35	1.30
39-40	30¢-60¢ U.P.U. Centenary	5.25	1.10	1.00
41-42	60¢-1 fr. Art, Brazil Peace Mural	6.50	1.35	1.30
43-44	60¢-80¢ Population Year	8.75	1.85	1.65
45	1.30 fr. Law of the Sea	6.00	1.25	1.10

50   55   59   61

1975

Scott's No.		MI Block of 4	F-VF NH	F-VF Used
46-47	60¢-90¢ Peaceful Use of Outer Space	11.50	2.50	2.25
48-49	60¢-90¢ Women's Year	7.75	1.60	1.50
50-51	60¢-90¢ 30th Anniversary of U.N.	7.00	1.50	1.40
52	60¢-90¢ 30th Anniv. - Souv. Sheet of 2	...	.90	.90
53-54	50¢-1.30 fr. Namibia, Hand	7.00	1.50	1.40
55-56	60¢-70¢ Peacekeeping Operations	7.00	1.50	1.35

1976

57	90¢ U.N. Association (WFUNA)	6.50	1.35	1.20
58	1.10 fr. Trade & Development (UNCTAD)	6.50	1.35	1.20
59-60	40¢-1.50 fr. Human Settlements,Habitat	6.75	1.50	1.35
61-62	80¢-1.10 fr. 25th Postal Anniversary	17.50	3.75	3.25
61-62	Same, Sheetlets of 20	...	65.00	...
63	70¢ World Food Council	3.75	.75	.65

65   71   73   77

1977

64	80¢ Intellectual Property (WIPO)	4.00	.80	.80
65-66	80¢-1.10 fr. Water Conference	8.75	1.85	1.65
67-68	80¢-1.10 fr. Security Council	8.50	1.80	1.60
69-70	40¢-1.10 fr. Racial Discrimination	6.50	1.35	1.20
71-72	80¢-1.10 fr. Peaceful - Atomic Energy	8.00	1.70	1.50

1978

73	35¢ Regular, Tree of Doves	1.30	.25	.25
74-75	80¢-1.10 fr. Smallpox Eradication	8.75	1.85	1.65
76	80¢ Namibia, Handcuffs	5.75	1.25	.65
77-78	70¢-80¢ Civil Aviation Organ (ICAO)	7.25	1.50	1.35
79-80	70¢-1.10 fr. General Assembly	9.75	1.90	1.40
81	80¢ Technical Cooperation	4.75	1.00	.80

82   93   96

1979

82-83	80¢-1.50 fr. Disaster Relief(UNDRO)	9.50	2.00	1.85
84-85	80¢-1.10 fr. Year of the Child	6.25	1.30	1.25
84-85	Same, Sheetlets of 20	...	22.50	...
86	1.10 fr. Namibia, Map	3.75	.80	.75
87-88	80¢-1.10 fr. Court of Justice, The Hague	7.25	1.50	1.40

1980

89	80¢ New Economic Order	5.25	1.10	1.00
90-91	40¢-70¢ Decade for Women	5.75	1.20	1.00
92	1.10 fr. Peacekeeping Operations	5.75	1.15	1.00
93-94	40¢-70¢ 35th Anniversary of U.N.	6.50	1.35	1.25
95	40¢-70¢ 35th Anniv. - Souv. Sheet of 2	...	.90	.90
96-97	40¢-70¢ Economic & Social Council	6.50	1.25	1.10

99   103   105   107

1981

98	80¢ Palestinian People	5.00	.90	.85
99-100	40¢-1.50 fr. Disabled Persons	7.75	1.65	1.60
101	80¢ Art, Bulgarian Mural	5.95	1.20	.95
102	1.10 fr. Energy Conference	6.00	1.25	1.10
103-04	40¢-70¢ Volunteers Program	8.75	1.80	1.60

1982

Scott's No.		MI Block of 4	F-VF NH	F-VF Used
105-06	30¢-1 fr. Regulars.................	7.25	1.50	1.40
107-08	40¢-1.20 fr. Human Environment............	9.50	1.90	1.65
109-10	80¢-1 fr. Peaceful Use of Outer Space ...	9.25	1.85	1.65
111-12	40¢-1.50 fr. Nature Conservation............	10.75	2.30	2.15

113   114   116

1983

113	1.20 fr. Communications Year................	5.75	1.80	1.60
114-15	40¢-80¢ Safety at Sea........................	8.25	1.55	1.35
116	1.50 fr. World Food Program..................	10.50	2.15	2.10
117-18	80¢-1.10 fr. Trade & Development........	9.25	1.90	1.80
119-20	40¢-1.20 fr. Human Rights, 35th Anniv. ..	10.50	2.10	1.95
119-20	Same, Sheetlets of 16..........................	...	32.50	...

121   131   140

1984

121	1.20 fr. Population Conference................	7.50	1.50	1.40
122-23	50¢-80¢ FAO Food Day	7.75	1.50	1.35
124-25	50¢-70¢ UNESCO, World Heritage........	10.75	2.25	2.00
126-27	35¢-1.50 fr. Refugee Futures	10.75	2.25	2.00
128	1.20 fr. Youth Year	7.00	1.50	1.40

1985

129-30	80¢-1.20 fr. ILO - Turin Centre	10.75	2.25	2.10
131-32	50¢-80¢ U.N. Univ. in Japan	10.00	2.10	1.90
133-34	20¢-1.20 fr. Regulars.............................	11.50	2.40	2.00
135-36	50¢-70¢ 40th Anniversary of U.N.	9.00	1.90	1.70
137	50¢-70¢ 40th Anniv. Souvenir Sheet of 2	...	2.75	2.25
138-39	50¢-1.20 fr. UNICEF Child Survival	12.00	2.50	2.00

140   145   154   160

1986

140	1.40 fr. Africa in Crisis, Anti-Hunger........	9.50	2.00	1.50
141-44	35¢ UN Development Program, attd	14.50	12.75	7.50
141-44	Sheet of 40...	...	135.00	...
145	5¢ Regular, Dove & Sun	.80	.20	.15
146-47	50¢-80¢ Philately, Stamp Collecting	9.75	2.00	1.65
148-49	45¢-1.40 fr. Int'l. Peace Year..................	14.50	2.95	2.25
150	35¢,45¢,50¢,70¢ WFUNA S/S	...	6.00	4.75

1987

151	1.40 fr. Trygve Lie, Secretary-General	9.00	2.00	1.90
152-53	90¢-1.40 fr. Bands/Sphere Regulars.......	13.00	2.75	2.65
154-55	50¢-90¢ Shelter for the Homeless...........	11.50	2.50	2.00
156-57	80¢-1.20 fr. Life Yes/Drugs No...............	10.00	2.25	2.25
158-59	35¢-50¢ U.N. Day.................................	9.50	1.95	1.50
158-59	Miniature Sheets of 12	...	24.50	...
160-61	90¢-1.70 fr. Child Immunization	26.75	5.50	4.50

164   171   173   178

Scott's No.		MI Block of 4	F-VF NH	F-VF Used
	1988			
162-63	35¢-1.40 fr. World Without Hunger..........	14.00	2.85	2.25
164	50¢ Regular, UN for a Better World	5.25	1.10	.75
165-66	50¢-1.10 fr. Forest Conservation, pair.....	25.00	11.50	...
165-66	Miniature Sheet of 12	...	57.50	...
167-68	80¢-90¢ Int'l. Volunteers Day	14.50	2.95	2.50
169-70	90¢-1.40 fr. Health in Sports	16.00	3.00	2.25
171	90¢ Human Rights 40th Anniv.................	6.75	1.40	1.30
172	2 fr. Human Rights 40th Anniv. S/S	...	3.65	3.35
	1989			
173-74	80¢-1.40 fr. World Bank.........................	20.75	4.50	3.75
175	90¢ Peace Keeping, Nobel Prize	7.50	1.50	1.25
176-77	90¢-1.10 fr. World Weather Watch..........	22.50	4.75	3.25
178-79	50¢-2 fr. UN Offices in Vienna,10th Anniv	26.50	5.75	4.00
178-79	Miniature Sheets of 25	...	125.00	...
180-81	35¢-80¢ Declaration of Human Rights	...	3.75	1.95
180-81	Strips of 3 with Tabs at Bottom	...	11.50	...
180-81	Miniature Sheets of 12	...	43.50	...

182   184   199

	1990			
182	1.50 fr. International Trade Center	15.00	3.15	2.25
183	5 fr. Regular..	30.00	6.50	5.50
184-85	50¢-80¢ Fight Against AIDS..................	17.50	3.95	3.00
186-87	90¢-1.40 fr. Medicinal Plants.................	19.75	4.35	3.25
188-89	90¢-1.10 fr. UN 45th Anniversary...........	23.75	4.95	3.75
190	90¢-1.10 fr. UN 45th Anniv. S/S of 2	...	8.25	5.50
191-92	50¢-2 fr. Crime Prevention....................	26.00	5.50	4.50
193-94	35¢-90¢ Declaration of Human Rights ...	...	3.50	1.75
193-94	Strips of 3 with Tabs at Bottom	...	10.50	...
193-94	Miniature Sheets of 12	...	42.50	...
	1991			
195-98	90¢ Eur. Econ. Commission, attd...........	8.50	7.50	6.00
195-98	Sheet of 40...	...	80.00	...
199-200	70¢-90¢ Namibia, Independence	24.00	5.00	4.00
201-02	80¢-1.50 fr. Regulars............................	24.00	5.00	4.00
203-04	80¢-1.10 fr. Children's Rights.................	23.50	4.75	3.95
205-06	80¢-1.40 fr. Chemical Weapons Ban	28.50	5.95	4.00
207-08	50¢-1.60 fr. UNPA 40th Anniv	24.00	5.00	3.75
207-08	Miniature Sheets of 25	...	100.00	...
209-10	50¢-90¢ Human Rights	...	3.50	2.25
209-10	Strips of 3 with Tabs at Bottom	...	10.50	...
209-10	Miniature Sheets of 12	...	42.50	...

211   222   232

	1992			
211-12	50¢-1.10 fr. World Heritage	23.75	5.00	3.50
213	3 fr. Regular..	24.50	5.00	3.75
214-15	80¢ Clean Oceans, attd........................	8.50	3.75	2.50
214-15	Miniature Sheet of 12	...	26.50	...
216-19	75¢ UNICED: Earth Summit, attd............	6.95	5.95	4.95
216-19	Sheet of 40...	...	67.50	...
220-21	1.10 fr. Mission to Planet Earth, attd	18.50	7.50	5.00
220-21	Miniature Sheet of 10	...	37.50	...
222-23	90¢-1.60 fr. Science & Technology	23.50	5.25	3.75
224-25	50¢-90¢ Human Rights	...	4.00	3.00
224-25	Strips of 3 with Tabs at Bottom	...	12.00	...
224-25	Miniature Sheets of 12	...	45.00	...

Scott's No.		MI Block of 4	F-VF NH	F-VF Used
	1993			
226-27	50¢-1.60 fr. Aging with Dignity................	24.00	5.00	3.50
228-31	80¢ Endangered Species, attd	6.75	5.95	5.50
228-31	Miniature Sheet of 16.............................	...	25.75	...
232-33	60¢-1 fr. Healthy Environments	25.00	5.50	3.00
234-35	50¢-90¢ Declaration of Human Rights.....	...	4.25	3.75
234-35	Strips of 3 with Tabs at Bottom...............	...	12.50	...
234-35	Miniature Sheets of 12	...	47.50	...
236-39	60¢ Peace Day, attd	11.75	10.75	5.50
236-39	Sheet of 40	...	110.00	...
240-43	1.10 fr. Environment - Climate, attd.... (8)	19.95	8.95	5.75
240-43	Miniature Sheet of 24	...	47.50	...

244	255	258

	1994			
244-45	80¢-1 fr. Year of the Family	21.50	4.75	3.25
246-49	80¢ Endangered Species, attd	6.95	5.95	5.00
246-49	Miniature Sheet of 16..............................	...	24.75	...
250	1.20 fr. Refugees	18.50	3.95	1.75
251-54	60¢ Natural Disaster, Block of 4	9.50	8.25	5.50
251-54	Sheet of 40	...	95.00	...
255-57	60¢,80¢,1.80 fr. Regulars	28.50	5.75	4.25
258-59	60¢-80¢ Population Development	18.95	4.25	3.50
260-61	80¢-1 fr. Development Partnership..........	19.50	3.95	2.50

262	263	268

	1995			
262	80¢ U.N. 50th Anniversary........................	9.25	1.95	1.65
263	1 fr Social Summit....................................	10.75	2.25	1.85
264-67	80¢ Endangered Species, attd	7.95	6.95	5.95
264-67	Miniature Sheet of 16..............................	...	27.50	...
268-69	80¢ 1 fr Youth: Our Future.....................	19.00	3.95	3.75
270-71	60¢-180 fr 50th Anniv. of U.N.	27.50	5.75	4.75
272	2.40 fr 50th Anniv. Souv. Sheet of 2	...	5.95	...
273-74	60¢-1 fr Conference on Women	22.50	4.75	3.50
275	30¢ U.N. 50th Anniv. Sheetlet - 12	...	21.50	...
276	30¢ U.N. 50th Anniv. Souvenir, Booklet of 12...................................	...	21.50	...

280-83

Scott's No.		MI Block of 4	F-VF NH	F-VF Used
	1996			
277	80¢ WFUNA 50th Anniversary................	9.50	1.95	1.50
278-79	40¢-70¢ Regular Issues.........................	10.75	2.25	1.50
280-83	80¢ Endangered Species,attd	7.00	6.00	4.50
280-83	Miniature Sheet of 16.............................	...	23.75	...
284-88	70¢ City Summit, Strip of 5 .... (10)	16.75	6.95	4.95
284-88	Miniature Sheet of 25	...	34.50	...
289-90	70¢-1.10 fr Sport & Environment	17.50	3.75	...
291	70¢-1.10 fr Sport & Environment	...	3.75	...
292-93	90¢-1.10 fr Plea for Peace.....................	17.50	3.75	...
294-95	70¢-1.80 fr UNICEF 50th Anniversary	21.50	4.50	...
294-95	Miniature Sheets of 8	...	25.00	...
I-295	**U.N. in Geneva 1969-96**	...	**435.00**	...

297	298-301

1997

296-97	10¢-1.10 fr Regulars	9.95	2.15	...
298-301	80¢ Endangered Species, attd	6.95	5.95	...
298-301	Miniature Sheet of 16.............................	...	23.75	...
302-5	45¢ Earth Summit	3.50	3.00	...
302-5	Miniature Sheet of 24.............................	...	17.75	...
306	1.10fr Earth Summit, Souvenir Sheet	...	1.90	...

GENEVA POSTAL STATIONARY

UX1

Scott's No.		Mint Entire
	GENEVA AIRLETTER SHEET	
UC1	65¢ Plane (1969)............	1.50
	GENEVA POSTAL CARDS	
UX1	20¢ Post Horn (1969).....	.60
UX2	30¢ Earth (1969)............	.75
UX3	40¢ Emblem (1977)........	.50
UX4	70¢ Ribbons (1977)........	.75

Scott's No.		Mint Entire
	GENEVA POSTAL CARDS	
UX5	50¢ "UN" Emblm (85)	5.50
UX6	70¢ Peace Dove(85)....	5.25
UX7	70¢ + 10¢ Surch (86) ...	2.50
UX8	90¢ Gen Offices (92) ...	1.85
UX9	50¢+10¢ Surch (93)	2.25
UX10	80¢ Palais des Nations (1993)	3.50

| | 5 | 8 | 9 | 12 |

1979 Regular Issue

No.	Description	MI Block of 4	F-VF NH	F-VF Used
1-6	50g,1s,4s,5s,6s,10s Regulars	9.50	1.95	1.95

1980

7	4s New Economic Order ....27.50 (TP)	14.50 (B)	.85	.75
8	2.50s Regular, Dove	1.85	.40	.40
9-10	4s-6s Decade for Women	7.50	1.50	1.50
11	6s Peacekeeping Operations	4.25	.90	.90
12-13	4s-6s 35th Anniversary of U.N.	6.25	1.35	1.35
14	4s-6s 35th Anniv. - Souv. Sheet of 2	...	.80	.80
15-16	4s-6s Economic & Social Council	7.00	1.50	1.40

(TP)= Top Position, (B)=Bottom

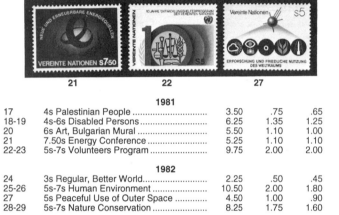

| | 21 | 22 | 27 |

1981

17	4s Palestinian People	3.50	.75	.65
18-19	4s-6s Disabled Persons	6.25	1.35	1.25
20	6s Art, Bulgarian Mural	5.50	1.10	1.00
21	7.50s Energy Conference	5.25	1.10	1.10
22-23	5s-7s Volunteers Program	9.75	2.00	2.00

1982

24	3s Regular, Better World	2.25	.50	.45
25-26	5s-7s Human Environment	10.50	2.00	1.80
27	5s Peaceful Use of Outer Space	4.50	1.00	.90
28-29	5s-7s Nature Conservation	8.25	1.75	1.60

| | 30 | 31 | 33 |

1983

30	4s Communications Year	3.25	.65	.65
31-32	4s-6s Safety at Sea	7.75	1.60	1.50
33-34	5s-7s World Food Program	7.25	1.50	1.40
35-36	4s-8.50s Trade & Development	7.25	1.50	1.40
37-38	5s-7s Human Rights, 35th Anniversary	9.25	1.95	1.65
37-38	Same, Sheetlets of 16	...	32.50	...

1984

39	7s Population Conference	4.75	1.00	.95
40-41	4.50-6s FAO Food Day	7.25	1.50	1.35
42-43	3.50-15s UNESCO, World Heritage	10.75	2.25	2.00
44-45	4.50-8.50s Refugee Futures	11.50	2.50	2.25
46-47	3.50-6.50s Youth Year	8.00	1.75	1.50

| | 48 | 49 | 57 |

Scott's No.		MI Block of 4	F-VF NH	F-VF Used
1985				
48	7.50s ILO - Turin Centre	5.25	1.15	1.10
49	8.50s U.N. Univ. in Japan	5.75	1.25	1.20
50-51	4.50-15s Regulars	17.75	3.75	3.25
52-53	6.50-8.50s 40th Anniversary of U.N.	14.50	2.95	2.50
54	6.50-8.50 40th Anniv. Souvenir Sht of 2	...	3.50	2.75
55-56	4s-6s UNICEF, Child Survival	14.50	2.95	2.25
1986				
57	8s Africa in Crisis, Anti-Hunger	6.00	1.25	1.15
58-61	4.50s UN Dev. Program, attd	15.00	13.50	5.00
58-61	Sheet of 40	...	130.00	...
62-63	3.5s-6.5s Philately, Stamp Collecting	8.50	1.75	1.50
64-65	5s-6s Int'l. Peace Year	12.00	2.50	2.25
66	4s,5s,6s,7s WFUNA S/S of 4	...	5.95	5.75

| | 67 | 70 | 84 |

1987				
67	8s Trygve Lie	6.00	1.25	1.20
68-69	4s-9.50s Shelter for Homeless	11.00	2.25	2.00
70-71	5s-8s Life Yes/Drugs No	12.50	2.50	2.30
72-73	2s-17s Regulars	13.50	3.00	2.75
74-75	5s-6s U.N. Day	12.50	2.75	2.50
74-75	Miniature Sheet of 12	...	35.00	...
76-77	4s-9.50s Child Immunization	17.50	3.75	3.00
1988				
78-79	4s-6s World Without Hunger	12.50	2.65	2.35
80-81	4s-5s Forest Conservation, pair	24.50	10.75	7.50
80-81	Miniature Sheet of 12	...	57.50	...
82-83	6s-7s Int'l. Volunteers Day	16.00	3.25	2.50
84-85	6s-8s Health in Sports	17.00	3.50	2.75
86	5s Human Rights 40th Anniv	5.50	1.10	.95
87	11s Human Rights 40th Anniv. S/S	...	2.65	2.40

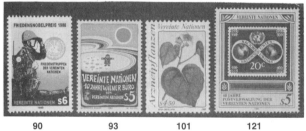

| | 90 | 93 | 101 | 121 |

1989				
88-89	5.50s-8s World Bank	21.50	4.50	3.00
90	6s Peace Keeping, Nobel Prize	7.25	1.50	1.25
91-92	4s-9.50s World Weather Watch	24.00	5.25	3.00
93-94	5s-7.50s UN Offices in Vienna, 10th Anniv.	35.00	7.50	4.50
94-94	Miniature Sheets of 25	...	225.00	...
95-96	4s-6s Human Rights 40th Anniv	...	2.95	1.75
95-96	Strips of 3 with Tabs at Bottom	...	8.85	...
95-96	Miniature Sheets of 12	...	35.00	...
1990				
97	12s International Trade Center	11.00	2.25	2.00
98	1.50s Regular	1.95	.40	.35
99-100	5s-11s Fight Against AIDS	22.50	4.75	3.50
101-02	4.5s-9.5s Medicinal Plants	21.50	4.50	3.00
103-04	7s-9s UN 45th Anniversary	24.00	4.95	3.50
105	7s-9s UN 45th Anniversary S/S of 2	...	7.00	5.00
106-07	6s-8s Crime Prevention	22.50	4.65	3.50
108-09	4.5s-7s Human Rights	...	3.50	2.25
108-09	Strips of 3 with Tabs at Bottom	...	10.50	...
108-09	Miniature Sheets of 12	...	42.50	...
1991				
110-13	5s Europe Econ. Commission, attd	7.50	6.50	4.25
114-15	6s-9.50s Namibia Independence	26.75	5.50	4.25
116	20s Regular	18.75	4.00	3.50
117-18	7s-9s Children's Rights	23.50	5.00	3.75
119-20	5s-10s Chemical Weapons Ban	24.75	5.50	3.75
121-22	5s-8s UNPA 40th Anniv	17.75	4.00	2.75
121-22	Miniature Sheets of 25	...	85.00	...
123-24	4.50s-7s Human Rights	...	3.50	2.25
123-24	Strips of 3 with Tabs at Bottom	...	10.50	...
123-24	Miniature Sheets of 12	...	42.50	...

137   149   150

Scott's No.		MI Block of 4	F-VF NH	F-VF Used
1992				
125-26	5s-9s World Heritage........................	24.50	5.25	4.00
127-28	7s Clean Oceans, attd...........................	5.75	3.75	3.00
127-28	Miniature Sheet of 12	...	29.50	...
129-32	5.5s UNICED: Earth Summit, attd...........	8.50	7.50	4.25
129-32	Sheet of 4	...	75.00	...
133-34	10s Mission to Planet Earth, attd.............	15.75	7.25	5.00
133-34	Miniature Sheet of 10	...	43.50	...
135-36	5.5s-7s Science & Technology...............	17.00	3.65	2.75
137-38	5.5s-7s Regulars	16.50	3.50	2.50
139-40	6s-10s Human Rights	...	4.65	3.00
139-40	Strips of 3 with Tabs at Bottom	...	13.75	...
139-40	Miniature Sheets of 12............................	...	55.00	...
1993				
141-42	5.5s-7s Aging with Dignity	18.75	3.95	3.00
143-46	7s Endangered Species, attd	8.00	6.50	5.50
143-46	Miniature Sheet of 16	...	25.00	...
147-48	6s-10s Healthy Environments	21.00	4.95	3.25
149	13s Regluar, Globe.................................	14.50	3.00	2.25
150-51	5.5s-6s Human Rights	...	3.95	2.75
150-51	Strips of 3 with Tabs at Bottom	...	11.75	...
150-51	Miniature Sheets of 12.........................	...	52.50	...
152-55	5.5s Peace Day, attd	11.00	10.00	5.75
152-55	Sheet of 40	...	110.00	...
156-59	7s Environment - Climate, attd............(8)	18.50	8.50	5.00
156-59	Miniature Sheet of 24	...	50.00	...

162-65   166

1994				
160-61	5.5s-8s Year of the Family........................	21.50	4.50	2.35
162-65	7s Endangered Species, attd	8.00	6.75	5.00
162-65	Miniature Sheet of 16	...	27.50	...
166	12s Refugees	14.50	2.95	2.50
167-69	50g,4s,30s Regulars...............................	29.75	6.25	5.50
170-73	6s Natural Disaster, Block of 4	12.75	11.75	7.50
170-73	Sheet of 40	...	120.00	...
174-75	5.50s-7s Population Development	18.75	3.95	2.95
176-77	6s-7s Development Partnership	18.00	3.75	3.00

180-83

1995				
178	7s U.N. 50th Anniversary	10.50	2.15	1.75
179	14s Social Summit.................................	17.00	3.50	3.00
180-83	7s Endangered Species, attd	8.75	7.50	6.75
180-83	Miniature Sheet of 16	...	37.50	...
184-85	6s-7s Youth: Our Future........................	18.50	3.95	3.25
186-87	7s-10s 50th Anniv. of U.N.	23.50	4.75	4.25
188	17s 50th Anniv. Souv. Sheet of 2	...	5.25	4.75
189-90	5-50s-6s Conference on Women	18.75	3.95	3.00
191	3s U.N. 50th Anniv. Sheetlet - 12...........	...	23.50	...
192	3s U.N. 50th Anniv. Souvenir Booklet of 12	...	24.50	...

193   194-95

1996				
193	7s WFUNA 50th Anniv.	9.50	1.95	1.35
194-95	1s-10s Regular Issues............................	12.00	2.50	1.75
196-99	7s Endangered Species	7.95	6.50	5.25
196-99	Miniature Sheet of 16	...	26.00	...
200-4	6s City Summit, Strip of 5..................(10)	16.75	6.95	...
200-4	Miniature Sheet of 25	...	34.50	...
205-6	6s-7s Sport & Environment	14.50	2.95	...
207	6s-7s Sport & Environment Souv Sheet..	...	2.95	...
208-9	7s-10s Plea for Peace	19.75	4.25	...
210-11	5.50s-8s UNICEF 50th Anniversary	14.50	2.95	...
210-11	Miniature Sheets of 8	...	16.00	...
I-211	**U.N. in Vienna 1979-96**	...	**365.00**	...
1997				
212-13	5s-6s Regulars	10.50	2.30	...
214-17	7s Endangered Species	7.75	6.50	...
214-17	Miniature Sheet of 16	...	25.75	...
218-21	3.50s Earth Summit................................	3.85	3.25	...
218-21	Miniature Sheet of 24	...	19.50	...
222	11s Earth Summit, Souvenir Sheet	...	2.50	...

VIENNA POSTAL STATIONERY

Scott's No.		Mint Entire	Scott's No.		Mint Entire
VIENNA ENVELOPE ENTIRES			**VIENNA POSTAL CARDS**		
U1	6s Vienna Centre (95)....	2.15	UX1	3s Branch (1982).........	1.50
U2	7s Landscape (1995).....	2.40	UX2	5s Glove (1982)...........	1.25
VIENNA AIRLETTER SHEET			UX3	4s Emblem (1985).......	5.25
UC1	9s Bird (1982)	2.75	UX4	5s + 1s Surch (1992)...	22.75
UC2	9s + 2s Surchrg (86)	52.50	UX5	6s Regschek Paint(92)	2.50
UC3	11s Birds in Flight (87)...	3.75	UX6	5s Peoples (1993)	13.50
UC4	11s + 1s Surchrg (92)	57.50	UX7	6s Donaupark (1993)...	4.50
UC5	12s Vienna Offices (92) .	5.25	UX8	5s + 50g (1994)	2.75

UNITED NATIONS SOUVENIR CARDS

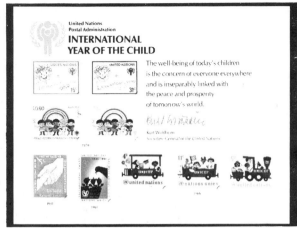

15

33 New York Cancel

		Mint Card	First Day of Issue N.Y.	Geneva	Vienna
1	World Health Day 1st Print............ 4/7/72	.95	18.50	175.00	...
1A	World Health Day 2nd Print........... 4/7/72	8.75	27.50	210.00	...
2	UN Art....................................... 11/17/72	.65	.55	.55	...
3	Disarmament................................ 3/9/73	.75	.60	.60	...
4	Human Rights............................ 11/16/73	1.10	.55	.60	...
5	Univ. Postal Union...................... 3/22/74	1.15	.65	.65	...
6	Population Year........................ 10/18/74	13.75	1.75	1.75	...
7	Outer Space 3/14/75	3.25	1.40	1.30	...
8	Peacekeeping............................ 11/21/75	2.65	1.50	1.40	...
9	WFUNA 3/12/76	5.95	2.50	2.50	...
10	Food Council 11/19/76	3.00	1.85	1.65	...
11	WIPO... 3/11/77	1.95	1.30	1.30	...
12	Combat Racism.......................... 9/19/77	2.10	1.50	1.50	...
13	NAMIBIA 5/5/78	1.20	1.20	1.20	...
14	Civil Aviation............................. 6/12/78	2.25	1.25	1.25	...
15	Year of the Child............................ 5/4/79	.75	.70	.70	...
16	Court of Justice 11/9/79	1.50	1.15	1.15	...
17	Decade of Women........................ 3/7/80	15.00	7.50	6.00	10.75
18	Econ. & Social Council................ 11/7/80	1.25	1.00	1.00	1.20
19	Disabled Persons 3/6/81	.90	1.00	.90	1.10
20	Energy Sources.......................... 5/29/81	1.50	1.25	1.15	1.15
21	Environment 3/19/82	1.50	1.25	1.25	1.40
22	Outer Space 6/11/82	1.65	1.50	1.50	1.50
23	Safety at Sea.............................. 3/18/83	1.95	1.50	1.50	1.50
24	Trade & Development 6/6/83	2.75	2.25	2.25	2.25
25	Population 2/3/84	3.00	2.50	2.00	2.25
26	Youth Year 11/15/84	4.50	3.00	3.00	4.50
27	ILO - Turin Centre 2/1/85	5.75	4.75	4.50	4.75

		Mint Card	First Day of Issue N.Y.	Geneva	Vienna
28	UNICEF 11/22/85	6.00	3.75	3.25	3.25
29	Stamp Collecting........................ 5/22/86	13.50	5.50	5.50	5.50
30	Int'l. Peace Year........................ 6/20/86	5.75	4.00	4.00	4.00
31	Shelter for Homeless 3/13/87	5.75	4.25	4.25	4.50
32	Child Immunization 11/20/87	5.95	5.25	5.00	5.25
33	Int'l. Volunteers Day..................... 5/6/88	9.75	7.50	6.50	7.00
34	WHO/Sports Health 6/17/88	9.75	7.50	6.50	7.00
35	World Bank 1/27/89	9.75	6.00	6.50	7.25
36	World Weather Watch.................. 4/21/89	10.50	7.50	7.75	8.50
37	Fight Against AIDS 3/16/90	12.75	7.50	8.00	8.50
38	Crime Prevention 9/13/90	12.00	8.50	8.50	9.00
39	European Econ. Commission 3/15/91	15.00	8.75	8.50	8.75
40	Children's Rights......................... 6/14/91	18.00	8.95	8.50	8.75
41	Mission to Planet Earth................. 9/4/92	22.50	16.50	14.50	14.50
42	Science And Technology 10/2/92	20.00	13.75	13.50	13.75
43	Healthy Environments...................5/7/93	25.00	14.75	14.50	14.75
44	Peace... 9/21/93	18.50	16.50	16.00	16.00
44A	Peace - Gold Hong Kong overprint..........	22.50	...	...	...
45	Year of the Family......................... 2/4/94	15.00	13.50	13.00	11.75
46	Population - Development 9/1/94	15.00	13.50	13.00	11.75
47	Social Summit............................... 2/3/95	12.50	9.00	8.75	9.95
48	Youth: Our Future 5/26/95	9.50	8.75	8.75	8.75
49	WFUNA 50th Anniversary..............2/2/96	8.75	7.50	7.50	7.50
50	UNICEF 50th Anniversary 9/27/96	6.00	6.00	6.50	6.50

12

Scott #	Description	Separate Covers	One Cover
	NEW YORK		
	1951		
1-11	1¢-$1 Regular Issue 10/24+11/16	75.00	60.00
	1952		
12	5¢ Charter 10/24/52	...	1.10
13-14	3¢-5¢ Human Rights 12/10/52	2.00	2.00
	1953		
15-16	3¢-5¢ Refugee Family 4/24/53	2.25	2.00
17-18	3¢-5¢ Univ. Postal Union 6/12/53	2.50	2.50
19-20	3¢-5¢ Tech. Assistance 10/24/53	2.00	1.50
21-22	3¢-5¢ Human Rights 12/10/54	6.95	5.75
	1954		
23-24	3¢-8¢ F.A.O. 2/11/54	2.00	1.75
25-26	3¢-8¢ Int'l. Labor Organ. 5/10/54	2.50	2.50
27-28	3¢-8¢ U.N. Euro. Office 10/25/54	3.50	3.00
29-30	3¢-8¢ Human Rights 12/10/54	6.95	6.00
	1955		
31-32	3¢-8¢ Int'l. Civil Aviat. 2/9/55	3.50	3.00
33-34	3¢-8¢ UNESCO Emblem 5/11/55	2.00	1.75
35-37	3¢-8¢ 10th Anniv. 10/24/55	3.00	3.00
38	3¢-8¢ 10th Anniversary S/S 10/24/55	...	75.00
39-40	3¢-8¢ Human Rights 12/9/55	2.00	1.75
	1956		
41-42	3¢-8¢ I.T.U 2/17/56	2.00	1.75
43-44	3¢-8¢ W.H.O. 4/6/56	2.00	1.75
45-46	3¢-8¢ General Assembly 10/24/56	1.50	1.00
47-48	3¢-8¢ Human Rights 12/10/56	1.50	1.00
	1957		
49-50	3¢-8¢ Meteor Org. 1/28/57	1.50	1.00
51-52	3¢-8¢ U.N. Emerg. Force 4/8/57	1.50	1.00
55-56	3¢-8¢ Security Council 10/24/57	1.50	1.00
57-58	3¢-8¢ Human Rights 12/10/57	1.50	1.00
	1958		
59-60	3¢-8¢ Atomic Ener. Agency 2/10/58	1.50	1.00
61-62	3¢-8¢ Central Hall London 4/14/58	1.50	1.00
63-64	4¢-8¢ Reg. U.N. Seal 6/2 & 10/24	1.50	1.00
65-66	4¢-8¢ Economic & Social C. 10/24	1.50	1.00
67-68	4¢-8¢ Human Rights 12/10/58	1.50	1.00
	1959		
69-70	4¢-8¢ Flushing Meadows 3/30/59	1.50	1.00
71-72	4¢-8¢ Econ. Comm. Europe 5/18/59	1.00	1.00
73-74	4¢-8¢ Trusteeship Coun. 10/23/59	1.50	1.00
75-76	4¢-8¢ World Refugee Year 12/10/59	1.50	1.00
	1960		
77-78	4¢-8¢ Chalot Palace Paris 2/29/60	1.50	1.00
79-80	4¢-8¢ ECAFE 4/11/90	1.50	1.00
81-82	4¢-8¢ World Forestry Cong. 8/29/60	1.50	1.00
83-84	4¢-8¢ 15th Anniversary 10/24/60	1.50	1.00
85	4¢-8¢ 15th Anniv. S/S 10/24/60	...	3.75
85v	Same broken "v" 10/24	...	120.00
86-87	4¢-8¢ International Bank 12/9/60	1.50	1.00
	1961		
88-89	4¢-8¢ Court of Justice 2/13/61	1.50	1.00
90-91	4¢-7¢ Monetary Fund 4/17/61	1.50	1.00
92	30¢ Regular Flags 6/5/61	...	1.00
93-94	4¢-11¢ Econ. C. Lat. Am. 9/18/61	1.50	1.00
95-96	4¢-11¢ Econ. Comm. Africa 10/24/61	1.50	1.00
97-99	3¢-13¢ Children's Fund 12/14/61	2.25	1.50

Scott #	Description	Separate Covers	One Cover
	NEW YORK		
	1962		
100-01	4¢-7¢ House & Urban Dev. 2/28/62	1.50	1.00
102-03	4¢-11¢ Wld. Health Organ. 3/30/62	1.50	1.00
104-07	1¢-4¢ Regulars 5/25/62	3.00	2.00
108-09	5¢-15¢ Hammarskjold 9/17/62	1.50	1.00
110-11	4¢-11¢ Oper. in Congo 10/24/62	1.50	1.00
112-13	4¢-11¢ Outer Space 12/3/62	1.50	1.00
	1963		
114-15	5¢-11¢ Science & Tech. 2/4/63	1.50	1.00
116-17	5¢-11¢ Freedom from Hung. 3/22/63	1.50	1.00
118	25¢ UNTEA 10/1/63	...	1.00
119-20	5¢-11¢ General Assembly 11/4/63	1.50	1.00
121-22	5¢-11¢ Human Rights 12/10/63	1.50	1.00
	1964		
123-24	5¢-11¢ Maritime Organ. 1/13/64	1.50	1.00
125-27	2¢-10¢ Regulars 5/29/64	2.25	1.25
128	50¢ Reg. Weather Vane 3/6/64	...	1.35
129-30	5¢-11¢ Trade & Develop. 6/15/64	1.50	1.00
131-32	5¢-11¢ Control Narcotics 9/21/64	1.50	1.00
133	5¢ End Nuclear Tests 10/23/64	...	.75
134-36	4¢-11¢ Education Prog. 12/7/64	2.25	1.25
	1965		
137-38	5¢-11¢ Development Fund 1/25/65	1.50	1.00
139-40	5¢-11¢ Peace Force Cyprus 3/4/65	1.50	1.00
141-42	5¢-11¢ Telecomm. Union 5/17/65	1.50	1.00
143-44	5¢-15¢ 20th Anniv. ICY 5/26/65	1.50	1.00
145	5¢-12¢ 20th Anniv. S/S 5/26/65	...	1.50
146-49	1¢-25¢ Regulars 9/20 & 10/25/65	3.00	2.25
150	$1 Regular Emblem 3/25/65	...	2.95
151-53	4¢-11¢ Population 11/29/65	2.25	1.25
	1966		
154-55	5¢-15¢ Fed. U.N. Assoc. 1/31/66	1.50	1.00
156-57	5¢-11¢ W.H.O. Headqtrs. 5/26/66	1.50	1.00
158-59	5¢-11¢ Coffee Agreement 9/19/66	1.50	1.00
160	15¢ Peacekpg. Obsrv. 10/24/66	...	.75
161-63	4¢-11¢ UNICEF 11/28/66	2.25	1.25
	1967		
164-65	5¢-11¢ Develop. Program 1/23/67	1.50	1.00
166-67	1½¢-5¢ Regulars 3/17 & 1/23/67	1.50	1.00
168-69	5¢-11¢ Independ. Nations 3/17/67	1.50	1.00
170-74	4¢-15¢ Expo '67 Montreal 4/28/67	3.50	2.50
175-76	5¢-15¢ Tourist Year 6/19/67	1.50	1.00
177-78	6¢-13¢ Disarmament 10/24/67	1.50	1.00
179	6¢ Chagall S/S 11/17/67	...	1.00
180	6¢ Chagall Window 11/17/67	...	.75
	1968		
181-82	6¢-13¢ Secretariat 1/16/68	1.50	1.00
183-84	6¢-75¢ Art, Starcke Stat. 3/1/68	5.75	5.00
185-86	6¢-13¢ Industrial Dev. 4/18/68	1.50	1.00
187	6¢ Regular, U.N. Hdqtrs. 5/31/68	...	.75
188-89	6¢-20¢ Wld. Weather Watch 9/19/68	1.50	1.00
190-91	6¢-13¢ Human Rights 11/22/68	1.50	1.00
	1969		
192-93	6¢-13¢ Train. & Res. Inst. 2/10/69	1.50	1.00
194-95	6¢-15¢ U.N. Bldg., Chile 3/14/69	1.50	1.00
196	13¢ Regular U.N. & Emblem 3/14/69	...	.75
197-98	6¢-13¢ Peace Through Law 4/21/69	1.50	1.00
199-200	6¢-20¢ Labor & Dev. 6/5/69	1.50	1.00
201-02	6¢-13¢ Tunisian Mosaic 11/21/69	1.50	1.00

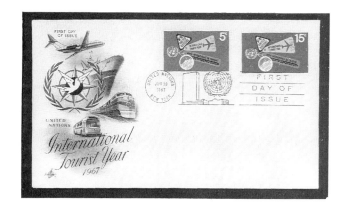

175-76

UNITED NATIONS FIRST DAY COVERS

254-55

Scott #	Description **NEW YORK**	Separate Covers	One Cover
1970			
203-04	6¢-25¢ Art, Peace Bell 3/13/70	1.50	1.00
205-06	6¢-13¢ Mekong Basin Dev. 3/13/70	1.50	1.00
207-08	6¢-13¢ Fight Cancer 5/22/70	1.50	1.00
209-11	6¢-25¢ 25th Anniversary 6/26/70	2.50	1.25
212	6¢-25¢ 25th Anniv. S/S 6/26/70	...	1.25
213-14	6¢-13¢ Peace, Just. & Pro. 5/20/70	1.50	1.00
1971			
215	6¢ Peaceful Uses of the Sea 1/25/71	...	.75
216-17	6¢-13¢ Support Refugees 3/2/71	1.50	1.00
218	13¢ World Food Program 4/13/71	...	.75
219	13¢ U.P.U. Headquarters 5/28/71	...	.75
220-21	8¢-13¢ Racial Discrim. 9/21/71	1.50	1.00
222-23	8¢-60¢ Regulars 10/22/71	2.25	1.85
224-25	8¢-21¢ U.N. Int'l. School 11/19/71	1.50	1.00
1972			
226	95¢ Regular, Letter 1/5/72	...	2.50
227	8¢ No Nuclear Weapons 2/14/72	...	.75
228	15¢ World Health Day, Man. 4/7/72	...	.75
229-30	8¢-15¢ Human Environment 6/5/72	1.50	1.00
231	21¢ Economic Comm. Europe 9/11/72	...	.75
232-33	8¢-15¢ Maria Sert. Mural 11/17/72	1.50	1.00
1973			
234-35	8¢-15¢ Disarmament Decade 3/9/73	1.50	1.00
236-37	8¢-15¢ Against Drug Abuse 4/13/73	1.50	1.00
238-39	8¢-21¢ Volunteer Program 5/25/73	1.50	1.00
240-41	8¢-15¢ Namibia 10/1/73	1.50	1.00
242-43	8¢-21¢ Human Rights 11/16/73	1.50	1.00
1974			
244-45	10¢-21¢ ILO Headquarters 1/11/74	1.50	1.00
246	10¢ U.P.U. Centenary 3/22/74	...	.75
247-48	10¢-18¢ Art, Brazil Mural 5/6/74	1.50	1.00
249-51	2¢-18¢ Regualrs 6/10/74	2.25	1.25
252-53	10¢-18¢ Population Year 10/18/74	1.50	1.00
254-55	10¢-25¢ Law of the Sea 11/22/74	1.50	1.00
1975			
256-57	10¢-26¢ Peaceful-O. Space 3/14/75	1.50	1.00
258-59	10¢-18¢ Women's Year 5/9/75	1.50	1.00
260-61	10¢-26¢ 30th Anniversary 6/26/75	1.50	1.00
262	10¢-26¢ 30th Anniv. S/S 6/26/75	...	1.40
263-64	10¢-18¢ Namibia 9/22/75	1.50	1.00
265-66	13¢-26¢ Peacekpg. Force 11/21/75	1.50	1.00
1976			
267-71	3¢-50¢ Regulars 1/6 & 11/19/76	3.00	2.50
272-73	13¢-26¢ U.N. Assoc. 3/12/76	1.50	1.15
274-75	13¢-31¢ Trade & Dev. 4/23/76	1.50	1.10
276-77	13¢-25¢ Human Settlement 5/28/76	1.50	1.00
278-79	13¢-31¢ 25th Postal Ann. 10/8/76	8.75	7.75
280	13¢ World Food Council 11/18/76	...	.75
1977			
281-82	13¢-31¢ Intellect Prop. 3/11/77	1.50	1.00
283-84	13¢-25¢ Water Conference 4/22/77	1.50	1.00
285-86	13¢-31¢ Security Council 5/27/77	1.50	1.10
287-88	13¢-25¢ Racial Discrim. 9/19/77	1.50	1.00
289-90	13¢-18¢ Atomic Energy 11/18/77	1.50	1.00
1978			
291-93	1¢-$1 Regulars 1/27/78	3.50	3.00
294-95	13¢-31¢ Smallpox-Erad. 3/31/78	1.50	1.10
296-97	13¢-31¢ Namibia 5/5/78	1.50	1.00
298-99	25¢ ICAO 6/12/78	1.50	1.00
300-01	13¢-18¢ General Assembly 9/15/78	1.50	1.00
302-03	13¢-31¢ Technical Coop. 11/17/78	1.50	1.10

Scott #	Description **NEW YORK**	Separate Covers	One Cover
1979			
304-07	5¢-20¢ Regulars 1/19/79	1.85	1.40
308-09	15¢-20¢ Disaster Relief 3/9/79	1.50	1.00
310-11	15¢-31¢ Yr. of the Child 5/4/79	3.50	2.85
312-13	15¢-31¢ Namibia 10/5/79	1.50	1.15
314-15	15¢-20¢ Court of Justice 11/9/79	1.50	1.00
1980			
316-17	15¢-31¢ New Econ. Order 1/11/80	1.50	1.25
318-19	15¢-20¢ Decade for Women 3/7/80	1.50	1.00
320-21	15¢-31¢ Peacekpg. Oper. 5/16/80	1.50	1.25
322-23	15¢-31¢ 35th Anniversary 6/26/80	1.50	1.25
324	15¢-31¢ 35th Anniv. S/S 6/26/80	...	1.30
325-40	15¢ 1980 Flag Series 9/26/80	12.00	...
341-42	15¢-20¢ Econ. & Soc. 11/21/80	1.50	1.00
1981			
343	15¢ Palestinian People 1/30/81	...	.75
344-45	20¢-35¢ Disabled Persons 3/6/81	1.60	1.35
346-47	20¢-31¢ Bulgarian Mural 4/15/81	1.50	1.25
348-49	20¢-40¢ Energy Conf. 5/29/81	1.75	1.50
350-65	20¢ 1981 Flag Series 9/25/81	12.00	...
366-67	18¢-28¢ Volunteers 11/13/81	1.50	1.15
1982			
368-70	17¢-40¢ Definitives 1/22/82	2.35	2.10
371-72	20¢-40¢ Human Environ. 3/19/82	1.80	1.50
373	20¢ Peaceful, Use of Space 6/11/82	...	.80
374-89	20¢ 1982 Wld. Flag Series 9/24/82	12.00	...
390-91	20¢-28¢ Nature Conserv. 11/19/82	1.65	1.40
1983			
392-93	20¢-40¢ Commun. Year 1/28/83	1.95	1.60
394-95	20¢-37¢ Safety at Sea 3/18/83	2.00	1.75
396	20¢ World Food Program 4/22/83	...	.75
397-98	20¢-28¢ Trade & Develop. 6/6/83	1.50	1.30
399-414	20¢ 1983 Flag Series 9/23/83	12.00	...
415-16	20¢-40¢ Human Rights 12/9/83	2.35	2.00
1984			
417-18	20¢-40¢ Population Conf. 2/3/84	2.00	1.75
419-20	20¢-40¢ FAO Food Day 3/15/84	2.00	1.75
421-22	20¢-50¢ UNESCO 4/18/84	2.35	2.00
423-24	20¢-50¢ Refugee Futures 5/29/84	2.15	1.85
425-40	20¢ 1984 Flag Series 9/20/84	13.50	...
441-42	20¢-35¢ Youth Year 11/15/84	2.00	1.75
1985			
443	23¢ ILO-Turin Centre 2/1/85	...	.95
444	50¢ U.N. Univ. in Japan 3/15/85	...	1.50
445-46	22¢-$3 Definitives 5/10/85	7.00	6.00
447-48	22¢-45¢ 40th Anniv. 6/26/85	2.15	1.85
449	22¢-45¢ 40th Anniv. S/S 6/26/85	...	2.00
450-65	22¢ 1985 Flag Series 9/20/85	14.50	...
466-67	22¢-33¢ UNICEF 11/22/85	2.00	1.75
1986			
468	22¢ Africa in Crisis 1/31/86	...	.95
469-72	22¢ UN Dev. & Prog. attd. 3/14/86	...	5.00
469-72	UN Dev. & Prog., set of 4 singles	6.00	...
473-74	22¢-44¢ Philately 5/22/86	2.15	1.85
475-76	22¢-33¢ Int'l. Year of Peace 6/20/86	2.00	1.75
477-92	22¢ 1986 World Flag Series 9-19-86	12.50	...
493	22¢,33¢,39¢,44¢ WFUNA S/S 11/14/86	...	5.50
1987			
494	22¢ Trygve Lie 1/30/87	...	.95
495-96	22¢-44¢ Shelter for the Homeless 3/13/87	2.15	1.85
497-98	22¢-33¢ Life Yes/Drugs No 6/12/87	2.00	1.75
499-514	22¢ 1987 World Flag Series 9/18/87	12.50	...
515-16	22¢-39¢ U.N. Day 10/23/87	2.10	1.80
517-18	22¢-44¢ Child Immunization 11/20/87	2.15	1.85

493

C19-21

Scott #	Description NEW YORK 1988	Separate Covers	One Cover
519-20	22¢-33¢ World Without Hunger 1/29/88	2.00	1.75
521	3¢ UN For a Better World 1/29/88	...	.75
522-23	25¢-50¢ Forest Conservation 3/18/88	8.50	7.50
524-25	25¢-50¢ Int'l. Volunteers Day 5/6/88	2.25	1.95
526-27	25¢-38¢ Health in Sports 6/17/88	2.50	2.15
528-43	25¢ World Flag Series of 16 9/19/88	13.50	...
544-45	25¢,$1 S/S Human Rights Anniv. 12/9/88	3.75	2.75
	1989		
546-47	25¢-45¢ World Bank 1/27/89	2.25	1.85
548	25¢ UN Peace Force, Nobel Prize 3/17/89	...	.95
549	45¢ UN Headquarters 3/17/89	...	1.25
550-51	25¢-36¢ World Weather Watch 4/21/89	2.15	1.85
552-53	25¢-90¢ UN Of. in Vienna Anniv. 8/23/89	3.50	2.50
554-69	25¢ World Flags Series of 16 9/22/89	13.50	...
570-71	25¢-45¢ Human Rights 11/17/89	2.25	1.85
	1990		
572	25¢ International Trade Center 2/2/90	...	2.00
573-74	25¢-40¢ Fight Against AIDS 3/16/90	2.25	1.85
575-76	25¢-90¢ Medicinal Plants 5/4/90	3.50	2.50
577-78	25¢-45¢ UN 45th Anniversary 6/26/90	2.25	2.25
579	25¢-45¢ UN 45th Anniversary S/S	...	4.00
580-81	25¢-36¢ Crime Prevention 9/13/90	2.15	1.85
582-83	25¢-45¢ Human Rights 11/16/90	2.25	1.85
	1991		
584-87	30¢ Eur. Econ. Commission attd. 3/15/91	6.00	3.50
588-89	30¢-50¢ Namibia 5/10/91	3.00	2.35
590-91	30¢-50¢ Definitives 9/11/91	3.00	2.35
592	$2 UN Headquarters Definitive 5/10/91	...	5.00
593-94	30¢-70¢ Children's Rights 6/14/91	3.50	2.75
595-96	30¢-90¢ Chemical Weapons Ban 9/11/91	4.00	3.25
597-98	30¢-40¢ UNPA 40th Anniv. 10/24/91	3.00	2.25
599-600	30¢-50¢ Human Rights 11/20/91	3.00	2.35
	1992		
601-02	30¢-50¢ World Heritage 1/24/92	3.00	2.35
603-04	29¢ Clean Oceans attd. 3/13/92	3.00	2.25
605-08	29¢ UNICED: Earth Summit attd. 5/22/92	6.00	3.50
609-10	29¢ Mission to Planet Earth attd. 9/4/92	4.50	3.75
611-12	29¢-50¢ Science & Technology 10/2/92	3.00	2.35
613-15	4¢,29¢,40¢ Definitives 10/2/92	4.50	2.00
616-17	29¢-50¢ Human Rights S/S 12/10/92	3.00	2.35
	1993		
618-19	29¢-52¢ Aging 2/5/93	3.00	2.35
620-23	29¢ Endangered Species attd. 3/3/93	3.00	2.75
624-25	29¢-50¢ Healthy Environments 5/7/93	3.00	2.35
626	5¢ Definitive 5/7/93	...	.95
627-28	29¢-35¢ Human Rights 6/11/93	3.00	2.35
629-32	29¢ Peace attd. 9/21/93	3.00	3.00
633-36	29¢ Environment - Climate 10/29/93	3.00	3.00
	1994		
637-38	29¢-45¢ Year of the Family 2/4/94	3.00	2.35
639-42	29¢ Endangered Species 3/18/94	3.00	2.75
643	50¢ Refugees 4/29/94	...	1.50
644-46	10¢,19¢,$1 Definitives 4/29/94	3.50	2.65
647-50	29¢ Natural Disaster 5/27/94	3.00	2.75
651-52	29¢-52¢ Population-Development 9/1/94	3.00	2.35
653-54	29¢-50¢ Development Partnership 10/28/94	3.00	2.35
	1995		
655	32¢ U.N. 50th Anniversary 1/1/95	...	1.20
656	50¢ Social Summit 2/3/95	...	1.50
657-60	32¢ Endangered Species 3/24/95	3.20	3.00
661-62	32¢-55¢ Youth: Our Future 5/26/95	3.15	2.50
663-64	32¢-50¢ 50th Anniv. of U.N. 6/26/95	3.10	2.40
665	82¢ 50th Anniv. Souv. Sheet 6/26/95	...	2.40
666-67	32¢-40¢ Conference on Women 9/5/95	3.00	2.25
668	20¢ Definitive 9/5/95	...	1.20
669	32¢ U.N. 50th Anniv. Souv. Sheet 10/24/95	21.00	25.00
670	32¢ U.N. 50th Anniv. Souv. Bklt. of 12 10/24/95	28.00	29.00

Scott #	Description NEW YORK 1996	Separate Covers	One Cover
671	32¢ WFUNA 50th Anniv. 2/2/96	...	1.20
672-73	32¢-60¢ Regular Issues 2/2/96	...	2.50
674-77	32¢ Endangered Species 3/14/96	...	3.00
678-82	32¢ City Summit, Strip of 5 6/3/96	...	3.25
683-84	32¢ - 50¢ Atlanta, GA.	3.45	2.75
683-84	32¢ - 50¢ Sport & Environment	3.10	2.40
686-87	32¢ - 60¢ Plea For Peace	3.20	2.50
688-89	32¢ - 60¢ UNICEF 50th Anniversary	3.20	2.50
	1997		
690-97	32¢ Flags of New Countries (8) 2/12/97	9.00	5.50
698-99	8¢ - 55¢ Regulars, Flowers 2/12/97	3.00	2.80
700-3	32¢ Endangered Species 3/13/97	5.00	2.75
704-7	32¢ Earth Summit 5/30/97	6.75	3.00
708	$1 Earth Summit, S/S 5/30/97	...	2.50
709	$1 Pacific '97 Overprint on #708 5/30/97	...	3.00
	Airmail Issues **1951-59**		
C1-4	6¢-25¢ 1st Airmail Issue 12/14/51	21.50	17.50
C5-7	4¢-7¢ Airmail 5/27/57 & 2/9/59	2.25	...
	1963-69		
C8-10	6¢-13¢ Airmail 6/17/63	2.25	1.25
C11-12	15¢ & 25¢ Airmail 5/1/64	1.50	1.10
C13	20¢ Jet Plane 4/18/68	...	1.00
C14	10¢ Wings & Envelopes 4/21/69	...	.75
	1972-77		
C15-18	9¢-21¢ Airmail 5/1/72	3.00	2.00
C19-21	13¢-26¢ Airmail 9/16/74	2.50	2.00
C22-23	25¢ & 31¢ Airmail 6/27/77	2.25	1.90
	U.N. Postal Stationery **Stamped Envelopes**		
U1	3¢ Emblem 9/15/53	...	4.25
U2	4¢ Emblem 9/22/58	...	.80
U3	5¢ Weather Vane 4/26/63	...	.85
U4	6¢ Weather Vane 4/26/63	...	.75
U5	8¢ Headquarters 1/12/73	...	.75
U6	10¢ Headquarters 1/10/75	...	.85
U7	22¢ Bouquet 5/10/85	...	2.00
U8	25¢ UN Headquarters 3/17/89	...	2.25
U9	25¢ + 4¢ Surcharge on U8 4/15/91	...	2.00
UC3	7¢ Flag and Plane 9/21/59	...	1.50
UC6	8¢ Emblem 4/26/63	...	.90
UC8	10¢ Emblem 1/8/69	...	.85
UC10	11¢ Birds 1/12/73	...	.85
UC11	13¢ Globe 1/10/75	...	.90
	Airletter Sheets		
UC1	10¢ Air Letter 8/29/52	...	6.75
UC2	10¢ Air Letter / Aerogramme 9/14/54	...	60.00
UC4	10¢ Flag 1/18/60	...	1.00
UC5	11¢ Gull, Blue 6/26/61	...	1.00
UC7	13¢ Plane 5/31/68	...	.85
UC9	15¢ Globe 10/16/72	...	.85
UC12	18¢ Headquarters 1/10/75	...	1.25
UC13	22¢ Birds 6/27/77	...	1.10
UC14	30¢ Airplane 4/28/82	...	3.25
UC15	30¢ + 6¢ Surcharge on UC14 7/7/87	...	12.50
UC16	39¢ UN Headquarters 3/17/89	...	2.50
UC17	39¢ + 6¢ Surcharge on UC16 2/12/91	...	2.50
UC18	45¢ Winged Hand 9/4/92	...	2.00
UC20	50¢ Airletter 3/13/97	...	1.75
	Postal Cards		
UX1	2¢ Headquarters 7/18/52	...	1.50
UX2	3¢ Headquarters 9/22/58	...	.90
UX3	4¢ Map 4/26/63	...	.85
UX4	5¢ Post Horn 1/8/69	...	.75
UX5	6¢ "UN" 1/12/73	...	.85
UX6	8¢ "UN" 1/10/75	...	.85
UX7	9¢ Emblem 6/27/77	...	.85
UX8	13¢ Letters 4/28/82	...	.95
UX9-13	15¢ UN Headquarters, 5 Diff. Views 3/17/89	...	1.25 ea.
UX14-18	36¢ UN Headquarters, 5 Diff. Views 3/17/89	...	1.60 ea.
UX19	40¢ U.N. Headquarters 9/4/92	...	1.50
	Airmail Postal Cards		
UXC1	4¢ Wing 5/27/57	...	.75
UXC2	4¢ + 1¢ 6/8/59 (first day of public use)	...	40.00
UXC3	5¢ Wing 5/21/59	...	.75
UXC4	6¢ Space 4/26/63	...	.75
UXC5	11¢ Earth 6/9/66	...	.90
UXC6	13¢ Earth 5/31/68	...	.85
UXC7	8¢ Plane 1/8/69	...	.85
UXC8	9¢ Wing 10/16/72	...	.90
UXC9	15¢ Planes 10/16/72	...	.90
UXC10	11¢ Clouds 1/10/75	...	1.00
UXC11	18¢ Pathways 1/10/75	...	1.10
UXC12	28¢ Mailmen 4/28/82	...	1.25

1

Scott #	Description GENEVA	Separate Covers	One Cover
	1969-70		
1-14	5¢-10¢ fr. Regular 10/4 + 9/22	40.00	...
	1971		
15	30¢ Peaceful Use of Sea 1/25/71	...	.85
16	50¢ Support for Refugees 3/12/71	...	1.00
17	50¢ World Food Program 4/13/71	...	1.25
18	75¢ U.P.O. Headquarters 5/28/71	...	2.65
19-20	30¢-50¢ Racial Discrim. 9/21/71	2.15	1.90
21	1.10 fr. Int'l. School 11/19/71	...	3.35
	1972		
22	40¢ Palace of Nations 1/15/72	...	1.00
23	40¢ No Nuclear Weapons 2/14/72	...	2.00
24	80¢ World Health Day 4/7/72	...	2.00
25-26	40¢-80¢ Human Environment 6/5/72	3.50	3.00
27	1.10 fr. Econ. Comm. Europe 9/11/72	...	3.00
28-29	40¢-80¢ Sert Mural 11/17/72	3.35	3.00
	1973		
30-31	60¢-1.10 Disarm. Decade 3/9/73	3.35	3.00
32	60¢ Against Drug Abuse 4/13/73	...	1.75
33	80¢ Volunteer Program 5/25/73	...	1.85
34	60¢ Namibia 10/1/73	...	1.75
35-36	40¢-80¢ Human Rights 11/16/73	2.50	2.00
	1974		
37-38	60¢-80¢ ILO Headqtrs. 1/11/74	2.65	2.15
39-40	30¢-60¢ UPU Centenary 3/22/74	2.10	1.85
41-42	60¢-1 fr. Brazil Mural 5/6/74	2.75	2.40
43-44	60¢-80¢ Population Year 10/18/74	2.40	2.15
45	1.30 fr. Law of the Sea 11/22/74	...	2.15
	1975		
46-47	60¢-90¢ Peace - Out. Space 3/14/75	2.25	2.00
48-49	60¢-90¢ Women's Year 5/9/75	2.65	2.40
50-51	60¢-90¢ 30th Anniv. 6/26/75	2.15	1.90
52	30¢ Anniv. S/S 6/26/75	...	2.40
53-54	50¢-1.30 fr. Namibia 9/22/75	2.40	2.15
55-56	60¢-70¢ Peacekpg. Force 11/21/75	1.90	1.65
	1976		
57	90¢ U.N. Association 3/12/76	...	1.70
58	1.10 fr. Trade & Develop. 4/23/76	...	1.90
59-60	40¢-1.50 fr. Human Settle. 5/28/76	2.75	2.40
61-62	80¢-1.10 fr. 25th Post Ann. 10/8/76	11.00	10.00
63	70¢ World Food Council 11/19/76	...	1.35
	1977		
64	80¢ Intellect Prop. 3/11/77	...	1.30
65-66	80¢-1.10 fr. Water Conf. 4/22/77	2.75	2.40
67-68	80¢-1.10 fr. Sec. Count. 5/29/77	2.75	2.40
69-70	40¢-1.10 fr. Racial Disc. 9/19/77	2.35	2.10
71-72	80¢-1.10 fr. Atom. Energy 11/18/77	2.80	2.45
	1978		
73	35¢ Regular 1/27/78	...	.80
74-75	80¢-1.10 fr. Smallpox 3/31/78	2.75	2.40
76	80¢ Namibia 5/5/78	...	1.30
77-78	70¢-80¢ Civil Aviat. Org. 6/12/78	2.15	1.90
79-80	70¢-1.10 fr. Gen. Assem 9/15/78	2.85	2.50
81	80¢ Technical Coop. 11/19/78	...	1.30
	1979		
82-83	80¢-1.50 fr. Disaster Relief 3/9/79	2.95	2.60
84-85	80¢--1.10 fr. Year of Child 5/4/79	4.50	3.75
86	1.10 fr. Namibia 10/5/79	...	1.75
87-88	80¢-1.10 fr. Court of Just. 11/9/79	2.85	2.50

Scott #	Description GENEVA	Separate Covers	One Cover
	1980		
89	80¢ New Econ. Organ. 1/11/80	...	1.35
90-91	40¢-70¢ Dec. for Women 3/7/80	1.85	1.60
92	1.10 fr. Peacekpg. Force 5/16/80	...	1.70
93-94	40¢-70¢ 35th Anniv. 6/26/80	1.85	1.60
95	40¢-70¢ 35th Anniv. S/S 6/26/80	...	2.50
96-97	40¢-70¢ Econ. & Social Co. 11/21/80	1.70	1.50
	1981		
98	80¢ Palestinian People 1/30/81	...	1.50
99-100	40¢-1.50 fr. Disabled Persons 3/6/81	2.50	2.25
101	80¢ Bulgarian Mural 4/15/81	...	1.35
102	1.10 fr. Energy Conf. 5/29/81	...	1.50
103-04	40¢-70¢ Volunteers 11/13/81	1.85	1.60
	1982		
105-06	30¢-1 fr. Definitives 1/22/82	1.95	1.70
107-08	40¢-1.20 fr. Human Environ. 3/19	2.25	2.00
109-10	80¢-1 fr. Peac. Use of Space 6/11	2.50	2.25
111-12	40¢-1.50 fr. Nat. Cons. 11/19/82	2.85	2.50
	1983		
113	1.20 fr. Commun. Year 1/28/33	...	1.85
114-15	40¢-80¢ Safety at Sea 3/28/83	1.60	1.40
116	1.50 fr. World Food Prog. 4/22/83	...	2.50
117-18	80¢-1.10 fr. Trade & Dev. 6/6/83	3.00	2.75
119-20	40¢-1.20 fr. Human Rights 12/9	3.25	2.90
	1984		
121	1.20 fr. Population Conf. 2/3/84	...	1.65
122-23	50¢-80¢ FAO Food Day 3/15/84	2.00	1.75
124-25	50¢-70¢ UNESCO 4/18/84	2.35	2.10
126-27	35¢-1.50 fr. Refugee 5/29/84	2.75	2.40
128	1.20 fr. Youth Year 11/15/84	...	1.75
	1985		
129-30	80¢-1.20 fr. ILO-Turin Centre 2/1	2.50	2.25
131-32	50¢-80¢ UN Univ. of Japan 3/15/85	1.75	1.50
133-34	20¢-1.20 fr. Definitives 5/10/85	1.95	1.75
135-36	50¢-70¢ 40th Anniversary 6/26/85	1.75	1.60
137	50¢-70¢ 40th Anniv. S/S 6/26/85	...	2.50
138-39	50¢-4 fr. UNICEF 11/22/85	4.00	3.00
	1986		
140	1.40 fr. Africa in Crisis 1/31	...	1.75
141-44	35¢ UN Dev. attd. 3/14/86	...	7.50
141-44	UN Dev. set of 4 singles	8.50	...
145	5¢ Definitive 3/14/86	...	.95
146-47	50¢-80¢ Philately 5/22/86	1.65	1.45
148-49	45¢-1.40 fr. Int. Peace 6/20/86	2.35	2.10
150	35¢,45¢,50¢,70¢ WFUNA S/S 11/14/86	...	2.75
	1987		
151	1.40 fr. Trygve Lie 1/30/87	...	1.75
152-53	90¢-1.40 fr. Bands/Sphere Definitives 1/30/87	3.00	2.75
154-55	50¢-90¢ Shelter for the Homeless 3/13/87	2.00	1.75
156-57	80¢-1.20 fr. Life Yes/Drugs No 6/12/87	2.50	2.25
158-59	50¢-1.70 fr. U.N. Day 10/23/87	3.00	2.75
160-61	35¢-90¢ Child Immunization 11/20/87	3.00	2.75
	1988		
162-63	35¢-1.40 fr. World Without Hunger 1/29/88	2.50	2.25
164	50¢ UN For a Better World 1/29/88	...	1.00
165-66	50¢-1.40 fr. Forest Conservation 3/18/88	10.50	9.50
167-68	80¢-90¢ Int'l. Volunteers Day 5/6/88	2.50	2.25
169-70	50¢-1.40 fr. Health in Sports 6/17/88	2.50	2.25
171-72	90¢,2 fr. S/S Human Rts. Decl. Anniv. 12/9/88 ...	4.25	3.75
	1989		
173-74	80¢-1.40 fr. World Bank 1/27/89	2.75	2.50
175	90¢ UN Peace Force, Nobel Prize 3/17/89	...	1.25
176-77	90¢-1.10 fr. World Weather Watch 4/21/89	2.50	2.25
178-79	50¢-2 fr. UN Offices in Vienna Anniv. 8/23/89	3.50	3.00
180-181	35¢-80¢ Human Rights 11/17/89	1.65	1.40

119-20

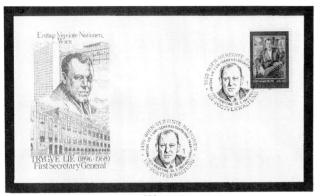

182

UC 1

Scott #	Description	Separate Covers	One Cover
	GENEVA		
	1990		
182	1.50 fr. International Trade Center 2/2/90	...	1.95
183	5 fr. Definitive 2/2/90	...	6.95
184-85	50¢-80¢ Fight Against AIDS 3/16/90	1.95	1.75
186-87	90¢-1.40 fr. Medicinal Plants 5/4/90	3.25	3.00
188-89	90¢-1.10 fr. UN 45th Anniversary 6/26/90	2.75	2.50
190	90¢-1.10 fr. UN 45th Anniversary S/S 6/26/90	...	3.50
191-92	50¢-2 fr. Crime Prevention 9/13/90	3.75	3.25
193-94	35¢-90¢ Human Rights 11/16/90	1.75	1.50
	1991		
195-98	90¢ Eur. Econ. Commission attd. 3/15/91	6.00	5.00
199-200	70¢-90¢ Namibia 5/10/91	3.50	2.75
201-02	80¢-1.50 fr. Definitives 5/10/91	4.50	3.75
203-04	80¢-1.10 fr. Children's Rights 6/14/91	4.00	3.25
205-06	80¢-1.40 fr. Chemical Weapons Ban 9/11/91	4.50	3.75
207-08	50¢-1.60 fr. UNPA 40th Anniv. 10/24/91	4.25	3.50
209-10	50¢-90¢ Human Rights 11/20/91	3.00	2.50
	1992		
211-12	50¢-1.10 fr. World Heritage 1/24/92	3.50	2.75
213	3 fr. Definitive 1/24/92	...	4.95
214-15	80¢ Clean Oceans attd. 3/13/92	3.50	2.75
216-19	75¢ UNICED: Earth Summit attd. 5/22/92	6.00	4.95
220-21	1.10 fr. Mission to Planet Earth attd. 9/4/92	4.25	3.75
222-23	90¢-1.60 fr. Science & Technology 10/2/92	4.50	4.25
224-25	50¢-90¢ Human Rights 12/10/92	3.00	2.50
	1993		
226-27	50¢-1.60 fr. Aging 2/5/93	4.25	3.50
228-31	80¢ Endangered Species, block of 4 3/3/93	7.00	3.75
232-33	60¢-1 fr. Healthy Environments 5/7/93	3.50	2.75
234-35	50¢-90¢ Human Rights 6/11/93	3.00	2.50
236-39	60¢ Peace, block of 4, attd. 9/21/93	5.50	3.75
240-43	1.10 fr. Environment - Climate 10/29/93	6.50	4.50
	1994		
244-45	80¢-1 fr. Year of the Family 2/4/94	4.00	3.00
246-49	80¢ Endangered Species 3/18/94	7.25	5.50
250	1.20 fr. Refugees 4/29/94	...	2.50
251-54	60¢ Natural Disaster 5/24/94 (4)	6.00	4.50
255-57	60¢,80¢,1.80 fr. Definitives 9/1/94	8.00	6.25
258-59	60¢-80¢ Population Development 9/1/94	3.50	2.75
260-61	80¢-1 fr. Development Partnership 10/28/94	4.00	3.25

Scott #	Description	Separate Covers	One Cover
	GENEVA		
	1995		
262	80¢ U.N. 50th Anniversary 1/1/95	...	1.70
263	1 fr Social Summit 2/3/95	...	2.00
264-67	80¢ Endangered Species 3/24/95	7.25	5.50
268-69	80¢-1 fr Youth: Our Future 5/26/95	4.00	3.25
270-71	60¢-1.80 fr 50th Anniv. of U.N. 6/26/95	5.25	4.25
272	2.40 fr 50th Anniv. Souv. Sheet 6/26/95	...	4.25
273-74	60¢-1 fr Conference on Women 9/5/95	3.75	3.00
275	30¢ U.N. 50th Anniv. Souv. Sheet 10/24/95	22.00	30.00
276	30¢ U.N. 50th Anniv. Souv. Bklt. of 12 10/24/95..	23.00	35.00
	1996		
277	80¢ WFUNA 50th Anniversary 2/2/96	...	1.70
278-79	40¢-70¢ Definitives 2/2/96	3.75	3.00
280-83	80¢ Endangered Species 3/14/96	7.25	5.50
284-88	70¢ City Summit Strip of 5 6/3/96	...	1.75
289-90	70¢ - 1.10fr Sport & Environment 7/19/96	3.65	2.95
292-93	90¢ - 1.10fr Plea For Peace 9/17/96	3.80	3.10
294-95	70¢ - 1.80fr UNICEF 50th Anniversary 11/20/96.	3.95	3.25
	1997		
296-97	10¢ - 1.10fr Regulars 2/12/97	3.20	2.50
298-301	80¢ Endangered Species 3/13/97	5.75	3.75
302-5	45¢ Earth Summit 5/30/97	6.75	2.75
306	1.10fr Earth Summit, S/S 5/30/97	...	2.50
	GENEVA AIRLETTER SHEETS		
UC1	65¢ Plane 10/4/69	...	4.75
	GENEVA POSTAL CARDS		
UX1	20¢ Post Horn 10/4/69	...	1.85
UX2	30¢ Earth 10/4/69	...	2.00
UX3	40¢ Emblem 6/27/77	...	1.90
UX4	70¢ Ribbons 6/27/77	...	2.00
UX5	50¢ "UN" 5/10/..	...	1.95
UX6	70¢ Bird 5/10/85	...	2.25
UX7	70¢ + 10¢ Surcharge on UX6 1/2/86	...	8.75
UX8	90¢ Letters 9/4/92	...	2.25
UX9	50¢ + 10¢ Surcharge on UX5 5/7/93	...	2.25
UX10	80¢ Palais des Nations 5/7/93	...	2.00

UNITED NATIONS FIRST DAY COVERS

ERSTTAG

Vereinten Nationen s6

PEACE-KEEPING OPERATIONS IN THE MIDDLE EAST

UNITED NATIONS

Peace-Keeping Operations

1980

11

Scott #	Description	Separate Covers	One Cover
	VIENNA		
1-6	50g-10s Regular Issue 8/24/79	6.00	5.00
	1980		
7	4s Economic Order 1/11/80	...	3.35
8	2.50s Regular, Dove 1/11/80	...	.75
9-10	4s-6s Decade for Women 3/7/80	2.75	2.50
11	6s Peacekeeping Forces 5/16/80	...	1.75
12-13	4s-6s 35th Anniversary 6/26/80	2.85	2.60
14	4s-6s 35th Anniv. S/S 6/26/80	...	3.50
15-16	4s-6s Econ. & Soc. Coun. 11/21/80	2.10	1.85
	1981		
17	4s Palestinian People 1/30/81	...	1.40
18-19	4s-6s Disabled Persons 3/6/81	2.15	1.90
20	6s Art, Bulgarian Mural 4/15/81	...	1.30
21	7.50s Energy Conference 5/29/81	...	1.75
22-23	5s-7s Volunteers 11/13/81	2.75	2.50
	1982		
24	3s Definitive 1/22/81	...	.75
25-26	5s-7s Human Environment 3/19/82	2.25	2.00
27	5s Peaceful Use of Space 6/11/82	...	1.10
28-29	5s-7s Nature Conserv. 11/16/82	2.25	2.00
	1983		
30	4s Communications Yr. 1/28/83	...	.75
31-32	4s-6s Safety at Sea 3/18/83	1.95	1.75
33-34	5s-7s World Food Prog. 4/22/83	2.35	2.10
35-36	4s-8.50s Trade & Dev. 6/6/83	2.50	2.25
37-38	5s-7s Human Rights 12/9/83	2.85	2.50
	1984		
39	7s Population Conf. 2/3/84	...	1.25
40-41	4.50s-6s FAO Food Day 3/15/84	1.95	1.75
42-43	4.50s-8.50s UNESCO 3/15/84	3.00	2.75
44-45	4.50s-8.50s Refugee 3/29/84	2.00	1.75
46-47	3.50s-6.50s Youth Year 11/15/84	2.00	1.75
	1985		
48	7.50s ILO-Turin Centre 2/1/85	...	1.10
49	8.50s UN Univ. of Japan 3/15/85	...	1.20
50-51	4.50s-15s Definitives 5/10/85	2.85	2.50
52-53	6.50s-8.50s 40th Anniv. 6/26/85	2.50	2.25
54	6.50s-8.50s 40th Anniv. S/S 6/26/85	...	3.50
55-56	4s-6s UNICEF 11/22/85	2.25	2.00
	1986		
57	8s African Crisis 1/31/86	...	1.20
58-61	4.50s UN Dev. attd. 3/14/86	...	2.75
58-61	UN Dev. set of 4 singles	4.40	...
62-63	3.50s-6.50s Philately 5/22	1.75	1.50
64-65	6s-7s Int. Year 6/20/86	2.50	2.25
66	3.50s,4s,5s,6s WFUNA S/S 11/14/86	...	5.75
	1987		
67	8s Trygve Lie 1/30/87	...	1.20
68-69	4s-9.50s Shelter for Homeless 3/13/87	2.50	2.25
70-71	5s-8s Life Yes/Drugs No 6/12/87	2.75	2.50
72-73	2s-17s Definitives 6/12/87	3.10	2.85
74-75	5s-6s U.N. Day 10/23/87	2.25	2.00
76-77	4s-9.50s Child Immunization 11/20/87	2.50	2.25
	1988		
78-79	4s-6s World Without Hunger 1/29/88	2.00	1.75
80-81	4s-5s Forest Conservation 3/18/88	9.50	8.00
82-83	6s-7.50s Int'l Volunteers Day 5/6/88	2.10	1.85
84-85	6s-8s Health in Sports 6/17/88	2.50	2.25
86-87	5s-11s Human Rights Decl. Anniv. 12/9/88	4.00	3.50

Scott #	Description	Separate Covers	One Cover
	VIENNA		
	1989		
88-89	5.5s-8s World Bank 1/27/89	2.50	2.25
90	6s UN Peace Force, Nobel Prize 3/17/89	...	1.10
91-92	4s-9.5s World Weather Watch 4/21/89	2.50	2.25
93-94	5s-7.5s UN Offices in Vienna Anniv. 8/23/89	2.25	2.00
95-96	4s-6s Human Rights 11/17/89	2.00	1.75
	1990		
97	12s International Trade Center 2/2/90	...	1.95
98	1.5s Definitive 2/2/90	...	.75
99-100	5s-11s Fight Against AIDS 3/16/90	2.75	2.50
101-02	4.5s-9.5s Medicinal Plants 5/4/90	2.60	2.35
103-04	7s-9s UN 45th Anniversary 6/26/90	2.75	2.50
105	7s-9s UN 45th Anniversary S/S	...	3.50
106-07	6s-8s Crime Prevention 9/13/90	2.50	2.25
108-09	4.5s-7s Human Rights 11/16/90	2.10	1.85
	1991		
110-13	5s Eur. Econ. Commission attd. 3/15/91	5.00	4.00
114-15	6s-9.50s Namibia 5/10/91	4.00	3.25
116	20s Definitive 5/10/91	...	4.25
117-18	7s-9s Children's Rights 6/14/91	4.00	3.25
119-20	5s-10s Chemical Weapons Ban 9/11/91	4.25	3.50
121-22	5s-8s UNPA 40th Anniv. 10/24/91	3.75	3.00
123-24	4.50s-7s Human Rights 11/20/91	3.50	2.75
	1992		
125-26	5s-9s World Heritage 1/24/92	3.75	3.25
127-28	7s Clean Oceans attd. 3/13/92	3.75	3.25
129-32	5.5s UNICED attd. 5/22/92	6.00	4.95
133-34	10s Mission to Planet Earth attd. 9/4/92	4.95	4.50
135-36	5.5s-7s Science & Technology 10/2/92	3.40	3.00
137-38	5.5s-7s Definitives 10/2/92	3.40	3.00
139-40	6s-10s Human Rights 12/10/92	4.50	3.75
	1993		
141-42	5.5s-7s Aging 2/5/93	3.40	3.00
143-46	7s Endangered Species, block of 4 3/3/93	7.00	5.75
147-48	6s-10s Healthy Environments 5/7/93	4.00	3.75
149	13s Definitive 5/7/93	...	2.25
150-51	5s-6s Human Rights 6/11/93	3.25	2.50
152-55	5.5s Peace, block of 4, attd. 9/21/93	6.00	4.95
156-59	7s Environment - Climate 10/29/93	7.50	6.50
	1994		
160-61	5.5s-8s Year of the Family 2/4/94	4.25	3.50
162-65	7s Endangered Species 3/18/94	6.50	5.50
166	12s Refugees 4/29/94	...	2.75
167-69	50g,4s,30s Definitives 4/29/94	8.25	6.75
170-73	6s Natural Disaster 5/24/94 (4)	6.50	4.95
174-75	5.50s-7s Population Development 9/1/94	3.65	2.85
176-77	6s-7s Development Partnership 10/28/94	3.75	2.95
	1995		
178	7s U.N. 50th Anniversary 1/195	...	1.65
179	14s Social Summit 2/3/95	...	3.00
180-83	7s Endangered Species 3/24/95	6.50	5.50
184-85	6s-7s Youth: Our Future 5/26/95	3.75	2.95
186-87	7s-10s 50th Anniv. of U.N. 6/26/95	5.00	3.95
188	17s 50th Anniv. Souv. Sheet 6/2/65	...	3.95
189-90	5.50s-6s Conference on Women 9/5/95	3.50	2.75
191	3s U.N. 50th Anniv. Sheetlet of 12 10/24/95	21.50	35.00
192	3s U.N. 50th Anniv. Souv. Booklet of 12 10/24/95	31.50	35.00
	1996		
193	7s WFUNA 50th Anniversary 2/2/96	...	1.75
194-95	1s-10¢ Regular Issues 2/2/96	4.50	6.00
196-99	7s Endangered Species 3/14/96	6.50	5.50
200-4	6s City Summit, Strip of 5 6/3/96	...	4.50
205-6	6s - 7s Sport & Environment 7/19/96	3.45	2.75
207	6s - 7s Sport & Environment S/S 7/19/96	...	3.00
208-9	7s - 10s Plea For Peace 9/17/96	3.95	3.25
210-11	5.50s - 8s UNICEF 50th Anniversary 11/20/96	2.95	2.25
	1997		
212-13	5s - 6s Regulars 2/12/97	3.20	2.50
214-17s	Endangered Species 3/13/97	5.95	3.85
218-21	3.50s Earth Summit 5/30/97	6.75	2.75
222	11s Earth Summit S/S	...	2.50
	VIENNA AIRLETTER SHEETS		
UC1	9s Bird 4/28/82	...	3.95
UC2	9s + 2s Surcharge on UC1 2/3/86	...	17.50
UC3	11s Birds in Flight 1/30/87	...	3.00
UC5	12s Donaupark 9/4/92	...	3.75
	VIENNA POSTAL CARDS		
UX1	3s Branch 4/28/82	...	2.50
UX2	5s Glove 4/28/82	...	2.50
UX3	4s Emblem 5/10/85	...	2.35
UX4	5s + 1s Surcharge on UX2 1/1/92	...	5.95
UX5	6s Regschek Painting 9/4/92	...	2.50
UX6	5s Peoples 5/7/93	...	1.85
UX7	6s Donaupark 5/7/93	...	2.00

CANADA

1,4 2,5,10 7 8 9

PROVINCE OF CANADA
1851 Laid Paper, Imperforate (OG + 50%) (C)

Scott's No.		Unused		Used	
		Fine	Ave.	Fine	Ave.
1	3p Beaver, Red	...	...	500.00	300.00
2	6p Albert, Grayish Purple	...	...	650.00	375.00

1852-1857 Wove Paper, Imperforate (OG + 50%) (C)

4	3p Beaver, Red, Thick Paper	...	500.00	110.00	75.00
4d	3p Thin Paper	...	575.00	130.00	90.00
5	6p Albert, Slate Gray	...	...	600.00	375.00
7	10p Cartier, Blue	...	...	700.00	400.00
8	½p Victoria, Rose	400.00	240.00	300.00	190.00
9	7½p Victoria, Green	...	...	1300.00	575.00
10	6p Albert, Reddish Purple, Thick	...	...	...	1100.00

1858-59 Wove Paper, Perforated 12 (OG + 50%) (C)

11	½p Victoria, Rose	...	750.00	500.00	325.00
12	3p Beaver, Red	...	1100.00	325.00	200.00
13	6p Albert, Brown Violet	...	...	...	1450.00

14 15 16,17 18 19 20

1859 (OG + 50%) VF + 60% (C)

14	1¢ Victoria, Rose	150.00	90.00	23.50	13.00
15	5¢ Beaver, Vermilion	150.00	90.00	10.75	6.00
16	10¢ Albert, Black Brown	...	...	...	825.00
17	10¢ Red Lilac	375.00	235.00	40.00	25.00

CANADA
1864 (OG + 50%) (VF + 60%) (C)

Scott's No.		Unused		Used	
		Fine	Ave.	Fine	Ave.
18	12½¢ Victoria, Yellow Green	200.00	130.00	32.50	18.50
19	17¢ Cartier, Blue	450.00	240.00	55.00	32.50
20	2¢ Victoria, Rose	225.00	150.00	120.00	80.00

DOMINION OF CANADA
1868-1876 Large "Cents" Issue, Perf. 12 (OG + 30%) VF + 60% (C)

		21	22-23,31	25,33	26	29-30

21	½¢ Victoria, Black	29.50	19.50	25.00	15.00
21a	½¢ Perf. 11½ x 12	32.50	21.50	27.50	16.50
21c	½¢ Thin Paper	35.00	22.50	32.50	21.50
22	1¢ Brown Red	225.00	150.00	37.50	25.00
22a	1¢ Watermarked	...	...	160.00	105.00
22b	1¢ Thin Paper	275.00	175.00	37.50	25.00
23	1¢ Yellow Orange	425.00	275.00	70.00	40.00
24	2¢ Green	250.00	150.00	30.00	15.00
24a	2¢ Watermarked	...	725.00	150.00	100.00
24b	2¢ Thin Paper	300.00	190.00	35.00	19.50
25	3¢ Red	450.00	280.00	11.50	6.00
25a	3¢ Watermarked	1650.00	850.00	135.00	85.00
25b	3¢ Thin Paper	550.00	325.00	15.00	9.50
26	5¢ Olive Green, Perf. 11½ x 12	575.00	325.00	75.00	40.00
27	6¢ Dark Brown	500.00	315.00	40.00	25.00
27b	6¢ Watermarked	...	1250.00	650.00	375.00
27c	6¢ Thin Paper	650.00	375.00	55.00	32.50
28	12½¢ Blue	275.00	165.00	37.50	22.50
28a	12½¢ Watermarked	1125.00	600.00	140.00	90.00
28b	12½¢ Thin Paper	325.00	195.00	52.50	35.00
29	15¢ Gray Violet	35.00	22.50	18.50	11.50
29a	15¢ Perf. 11½ x 12	475.00	250.00	90.00	52.50
29b	15¢ Red Lilac	450.00	300.00	50.00	25.00
29c	15¢ Gray Violet Wmkd	...	1400.00	375.00	210.00
29e	15¢ Gray Violet, Thin Paper	375.00	235.00	65.00	40.00
30	15¢ Gray	30.00	17.50	15.00	10.00
30a	15¢ Perf. 11½ x 12	425.00	250.00	90.00	50.00

1868 Laid Paper, Perf. 12 (OG + 30%) (C)

Scott's No.		NH Fine	Unused Fine	Ave.	Used Fine	Ave.
31	1¢ Brown Red	...	...		1850.00	850.00
33	3¢ Bright Red	...	...		350.00	175.00

34   35   37,41   44   46

1870-1889 Small "Cents" Issue, Perf. 12 (OG + 20%) VF + 60% (C)

No.		Fine	Fine	Ave.	Fine	Ave.
34	½¢ Victoria Black	8.50	4.25	2.40	4.25	2.40
35	1¢ Yellow	28.50	13.50	7.50	.50	.30
35a	1¢ Orange	110.00	50.00	32.50	5.25	3.15
35d	1¢ Orange, Pf. 11½ x 12	190.00	100.00	60.00	8.50	5.50
36	2¢ Green	37.50	18.50	11.75	.90	.55
36d	2¢ Blue Green	67.50	35.00	19.50	2.50	1.50
36e	2¢ Green, Pf. 11½ x 12	225.00	125.00	75.00	12.50	8.00
37	3¢ Dull Red	80.00	37.50	22.50	1.50	.80
37a	3¢ Rose	425.00	225.00	135.00	5.75	3.25
37b	3¢ Copper Red	...	675.00	375.00	25.00	15.00
37c	3¢ Orange Red	75.00	40.00	22.50	1.15	.65
37d	3¢ Cop. Red 12½ x 12	...	...	...	450.00	300.00
37e	3¢ Red, Perf. 11½ x 12	250.00	135.00	75.00	5.75	3.50
38	5¢ Slate Green	375.00	200.00	110.00	9.50	6.50
38a	5¢ Ol. Gr., Pf. 11½ x 12	575.00	295.00	180.00	20.00	13.50
39	6¢ Yellow Brown	350.00	175.00	90.00	9.50	6.50
39b	6¢ Brown, 11½ x 12	600.00	300.00	185.00	20.00	13.50
40	10¢ Dull Rose Lilac	500.00	240.00	140.00	30.00	20.00
40c	10¢ Rose Ll., 11½ x 12	1200.00	500.00	265.00	165.00	95.00

1888-1893 Small "Cents" Issue, Perf. 12 VF + 60% (C)

No.		Fine	Fine	Ave.	Fine	Ave.
41	3¢ Bright Vermilion	24.00	13.50	7.00	.25	.15
41a	3¢ Rose Carmine	425.00	225.00	120.00	5.50	3.65
42	5¢ Gray	60.00	30.00	16.00	2.50	1.50
43	6¢ Red Brown	60.00	30.00	15.75	7.50	4.15
43a	6¢ Chocolate	175.00	85.00	45.00	13.75	8.00
44	8¢ Gray (1893)	75.00	39.50	22.50	2.50	1.40
45	10¢ Brown Red	165.00	90.00	50.00	22.50	12.50
46	20¢ Vermilion (1893)	275.00	150.00	85.00	37.50	22.50
47	50¢ Deep Blue (1893)	300.00	165.00	110.00	27.50	14.75

1897 Jubilee Issue VF Used + 60% (B)

50   55   60

Scott's No.		NH VF	Unused VF	F-VF	Used F-VF
50	½¢ Victoria, Black	140.00	85.00	75.00	45.00	52.50
51	1¢ Orange	15.00	9.00	7.50	4.50	4.00
52	2¢ Green	22.50	13.50	12.50	7.50	7.00
53	3¢ Bright Rose	15.00	9.00	7.50	4.50	1.35
54	5¢ Deep Blue	55.00	32.50	29.50	18.00	13.50
55	6¢ Yellow Brown	225.00	140.00	135.00	80.00	95.00
56	8¢ Dark Violet	55.00	35.00	28.50	17.50	15.00
57	10¢ Brown Violet	135.00	85.00	75.00	45.00	45.00
58	15¢ Steel Blue	240.00	150.00	140.00	87.50	80.00
59	20¢ Vermillion	250.00	160.00	145.00	90.00	90.00
60	50¢ Ultramarine	295.00	180.00	165.00	100.00	90.00
61	$1 Lake	1100.00	675.00	650.00	400.00	375.00
62	$2 Dark Purple	1750.00	1100.00	1000.00	625.00	325.00
63	$3 Yellow Bistre	2000.00	1275.00	1200.00	700.00	575.00
64	$4 Purple	2000.00	1275.00	1200.00	700.00	575.00
65	$5 Olive Green	2100.00	1300.00	1275.00	750.00	550.00

66   74   85-86   87

1897-1898 Issue, Maple Leaves in Four Corners, VF Used + 60% (B)

Scott's No.		VF	NH F-VF	Unused VF	F-VF	Used F-VF
66	½¢ Victoria, Black	9.50	6.25	5.75	3.75	3.50
67	1¢ Blue Green	21.00	12.50	12.50	7.50	.55
68	2¢ Purple	24.50	14.50	14.00	8.50	.90
69	3¢ Carmine (1898)	24.50	14.50	14.00	8.50	.20
70	5¢ Dark Blue	110.00	70.00	57.50	35.00	3.50
71	6¢ Brown	97.50	60.00	53.50	32.50	13.75
72	8¢ Orange	160.00	95.00	85.00	50.00	5.50
73	10¢ Brown Violet (1898)	275.00	170.00	150.00	90.00	40.00

1898-1902 Issue, Numerals in Lower Corners VF Used + 60% (B)

No.		VF	F-VF	VF	F-VF	F-VF
74	½¢ Victoria, Black	3.50	2.10	2.10	1.25	1.00
75	1¢ Gray Green	19.75	12.00	12.50	7.50	.15
76	2¢ Purple	20.00	12.50	12.50	7.50	.15
77	2¢ Carmine, Die I (1898)	25.00	15.00	15.75	9.50	.15
77a	2¢ Carmine, Die II	27.50	16.50	16.50	10.00	.25
78	3¢ Carmine	35.00	21.50	21.50	13.50	.30
79	5¢ Blue	120.00	75.00	72.50	45.00	.70
80	6¢ Brown	165.00	100.00	95.00	57.50	23.50
81	7¢ Olive Yellow (1902)	100.00	60.00	57.50	35.00	10.00
82	8¢ Orange	225.00	135.00	110.00	70.00	11.75
83	10¢ Brown Violet	290.00	180.00	160.00	100.00	10.00
84	20¢ Olive Green (1900)	550.00	350.00	275.00	175.00	45.00

1898 Imperial Penny Post VF Used + 50% (B)

No.		VF	F-VF	VF	F-VF	F-VF
85	2¢ Map, Blk. Lav. Carm	30.00	20.00	18.75	12.50	4.00
86	2¢ Black, Blue, Carmine	30.00	20.00	18.75	12.50	4.00

1899 Surcharges VF Used + 60% (B)

No.		VF	F-VF	VF	F-VF	F-VF
87	2¢ on 3¢ Carmine (on #69)	16.00	9.50	7.50	4.50	3.00
88	2¢ on 3¢ Carmine (on #78)	18.50	11.00	9.50	5.50	2.50

89   96   100

1903-1908 King Edward VII VF Used + 60% (B)

No.		VF	F-VF	VF	F-VF	F-VF
89	1¢ Edward VII, Green	20.00	12.50	12.00	7.50	.15
90	2¢ Carmine	20.00	12.50	12.00	7.50	.15
90a	2¢ Imperforate Pair	52.50	33.75	35.00	22.50	...
91	5¢ Blue	100.00	60.00	60.00	35.00	1.80
92	7¢ Olive Bistre	72.50	45.00	40.00	25.00	2.00
93	10¢ Brown Lilac	200.00	115.00	110.00	65.00	4.00
94	20¢ Olive Green	475.00	295.00	295.00	185.00	15.00
95	50¢ Purple (1908)	750.00	475.00	440.00	275.00	45.00

1908 Quebec Tercentenary VF + 65% (B)

No.		VF	F-VF	VF	F-VF	F-VF
96-103	Set of 8	695.00	415.00	360.00	220.00	190.00
96	½¢ Prince & Princess	7.25	4.25	3.75	2.25	2.25
97	1¢ Cartier & Champlain	14.00	8.25	7.25	4.25	2.40
98	2¢ Alexandria & Edward	18.00	10.50	9.50	5.50	.60
99	5¢ Champlain's Home	67.50	40.00	35.00	21.00	18.00
100	7¢ Montcalm & Wolfe	105.00	62.50	55.00	32.50	22.50
101	10¢ 1700 View of Quebec	120.00	75.00	65.00	39.50	37.50
102	15¢ Champlain Heads West	195.00	110.00	95.00	55.00	52.50
103	20¢ Cartier Arrival	230.00	140.00	125.00	75.00	65.00

104-105   116-118   135   140

1912-1925 "Admiral Issue" Perf. 12 VF Used + 50% (B)

No.		VF	F-VF	VF	F-VF	F-VF
104-22	Set of 18	750.00	495.00	435.00	295.00	23.50
104	1¢ George V. Green	9.50	6.25	5.50	3.50	.15
104a	1¢ Booklet Pane of 6	28.50	19.00	18.75	12.50	...
105	1¢ Yellow (1922)	8.00	5.25	4.50	3.00	.15
105a	1¢ Booklet Pane of 4	57.50	37.50	37.50	25.00	...
105b	1¢ Booklet Pane of 6	45.00	32.50	35.00	22.50	...
106	2¢ Carmine	7.50	5.00	4.50	3.00	.15
106a	2¢ Booklet Pane of 6	38.50	25.50	26.50	17.50	...
107	2¢ Yellow Green (1922)	7.00	4.50	4.00	2.75	.15
107a	2¢ Thin Paper	7.50	4.75	4.50	3.00	1.50
107b	2¢ Booklet Pane of 4	63.50	41.50	41.50	27.50	...
107c	2¢ Booklet Pane of 6	365.00	250.00	260.00	175.00	...
108	3¢ Brown (1918)	9.00	6.00	5.25	3.50	.15
108a	3¢ Booklet Pane of 4	97.50	65.00	67.50	45.00	...
109	3¢ Carmine (1923)	8.00	5.25	4.50	3.00	.15
109a	3¢ Booklet Pane of 4	60.00	40.00	37.50	25.00	...
110	4¢ Olive Bistre (1922)	30.00	20.00	18.50	12.50	1.40
111	5¢ Dark Blue	97.50	65.00	55.00	37.50	.30

1912-1925 "Admiral Issue" Perf. 12, VF Used + 50% (B)

Scott's No.			NH	Unused		Used
		VF	F-VF	VF	F-VF	F-VF
112	5¢ Violet (1922)	18.50	12.00	11.00	7.50	.30
112a	5¢ Thin Paper	20.00	13.50	12.50	8.50	3.75
113	7¢ Yellow Ochre	35.00	23.50	20.00	13.50	1.25
113a	7¢ Olive Bistre	35.00	23.50	20.00	13.50	1.50
114	7¢ Red Brown (1924)	20.00	13.50	11.50	7.50	4.75
115	8¢ Blue (1925)	34.00	22.50	20.00	13.50	4.75
116	10¢ Plum	165.00	110.00	85.00	57.50	.65
117	10¢ Blue (1922)	45.00	30.00	26.50	17.50	.85
118	10¢ Bister Brown (1925)	37.50	25.00	20.00	13.50	.80
119	20¢ Olive Green	72.50	48.50	40.00	27.50	.60
120	50¢ Black Brown (1925)	75.00	50.00	45.00	30.00	1.35
120a	50¢ Black	135.00	90.00	85.00	60.00	3.50
122	$1 Orange (1923)	127.50	85.00	75.00	55.00	5.35

1912 Coil Stamps, Perf. 8 Horizontally VF Used + 50% (B)

123	1¢ Dark Green	97.50	65.00	62.50	42.50	27.50
124	2¢ Carmine	97.50	65.00	62.50	42.50	27.50

1912-1924 Coil Stamps, Perf. 8 Vertically VF Used + 50% (B)

125-30	Set of 6	150.00	105.00	99.50	65.00	9.50
125	1¢ Green	18.00	12.00	11.00	7.50	.55
126	1¢ Yellow (1923)	12.50	8.25	7.50	5.00	3.75
126a	1¢ Block of four	70.00	47.50	45.00	30.00	...
127	2¢ Carmine	26.50	17.50	16.50	11.00	.45
128	2¢ Green (1922)	14.00	9.75	9.00	6.00	.40
128a	2¢ Block of four	70.00	47.50	45.00	30.00	...
129	3¢ Brown (1918)	12.50	8.25	7.50	5.00	.40
130	3¢ Carmine (1924)	77.50	52.50	52.50	35.00	4.50
130a	3¢ Block of four	935.00	625.00	635.00	425.00	...

#126a,128a,130a are from Part.-Perf. Sheets - Pairs are at half block prices.

1915-1924 Coil Stamps, Perf. 12 Horizontally VF Used + 50% (B)

131-34	Set of 4	150.00	99.50	89.50	59.50	49.75
131	1¢ Dark Green	9.00	6.00	5.25	3.50	3.25
132	2¢ Carmine	24.50	16.50	16.50	11.00	6.50
133	2¢ Yellow Green (1924)	115.00	75.00	67.50	45.00	40.00
134	3¢ Brown (1921)	10.00	6.75	6.00	4.00	3.25

1917 Confederation VF Used + 100% (B)

135	3¢ "Fathers of Confed."	45.00	22.50	30.00	15.00	.40

1924 Imperforate VF Used + 20% (B)

136	1¢ Yellow	52.50	42.50	35.00	28.50	28.50
137	2¢ Green	52.50	42.50	35.00	28.50	28.50
138	3¢ Carmine	25.00	20.00	16.50	13.75	13.75

1926 Surcharges on #109 VF Used + 30% (B)

139	2¢ on 3¢ - One Line	65.00	50.00	49.50	32.50	32.50
140	2¢ on 3¢ - Two Lines	26.50	20.00	20.00	13.50	13.50

141	145	146	148

1927 Confederation Issue VF Used + 30% (B)

141-45	Set of 5	38.75	28.50	25.75	19.50	7.35
141	1¢ John A. MacDonald	3.35	2.50	2.25	1.65	.50
142	2¢ "Fathers of Confed."	1.80	1.35	1.10	.85	.15
143	3¢ Parliament Building	9.00	7.00	6.25	4.75	2.95
144	5¢ Sir Wilfrid Laurier	5.75	4.25	3.75	2.75	1.50
145	12¢ Map of Canada	21.50	15.75	13.75	10.50	2.65

1927 Historical Issue VF Used + 30% (B)

146-48	Set of 3	34.75	25.75	22.50	17.75	7.15
146	5¢ Thomas d'Arcy McGee	4.00	3.00	2.60	2.00	1.25
147	12¢ Laurier & MacDonald	10.00	7.50	6.50	5.00	2.75
148	20¢ Baldwin & Lafontaine	22.50	16.50	15.00	11.50	3.50

1928-29 Scroll Series VF Used + 40% (B)

149	154	155	156

149-59	Set of 11	715.00	470.00	415.00	295.00	90.00
149	1¢ George V, Orange	3.00	2.15	1.90	1.35	.20
149a	1¢ Booklet Pane of 6	20.75	14.75	13.50	10.00	...
150	2¢ Green	1.40	1.00	.95	.70	.15
150a	2¢ Booklet Pane of 6	28.50	20.00	18.00	13.00	...
151	3¢ Dark Carmine	23.00	16.50	11.75	8.50	7.50

1928-29 Scroll Series (cont.)

Scott's No.			NH	Unused		Used
		VF	F-VF	VF	F-VF	F-VF
152	4¢ Bistre (1929)	15.00	10.50	10.00	7.00	3.25
153	5¢ Deep Violet	8.50	6.00	4.25	3.00	1.50
153a	5¢ Booklet Pane of 6	140.00	100.00	90.00	65.00	...
154	8¢ Blue	11.75	8.50	7.00	5.00	3.50
155	10¢ Mt. Hurd	13.50	9.50	7.50	5.50	.70
156	12¢ Quebec Bridge (1929)	18.00	13.00	12.50	8.75	4.00
157	20¢ Harvest Wheat (1929)	34.00	25.00	21.00	15.00	6.00
158	50¢ "Bluenose" (1929)	300.00	195.00	175.00	125.00	30.00
159	$1 Parliment (1929)	325.00	210.00	190.00	135.00	35.00

1929 Coil Stamps, Perf. 8 Vertically VF Used + 40% (B)

160	1¢ George V, Orange	27.50	18.75	18.75	13.50	11.50
161	2¢ Green	20.75	15.00	15.00	11.00	1.75

1930-31 King George V & Pictorials VF Used + 40% (B)

162-63	173	174	175

162-77	Set of 16	550.00	375.00	350.00	250.00	40.75
162	1¢ George V. Orange	1.25	.85	.85	.60	.33
163	1¢ Deep Green	1.90	1.50	1.30	.95	.15
163a	1¢ Booklet Pane of 4	125.00	90.00	85.00	60.00	...
163c	1¢ Booklet Pane of 6	25.00	18.00	17.00	12.00	...
164	2¢ Dull Green	1.40	1.00	.90	.65	.15
164a	2¢ Booklet Pane of 6	33.50	24.00	21.00	15.00	...
165	2¢ Deep Red, Die II	2.30	1.65	1.60	1.15	.15
165a	2¢ Deep Red, Die I	1.75	1.25	1.20	.85	.20
165b	2¢ B. Pane of 6, Die I	28.00	20.00	19.00	13.50	...
166	2¢ Dark Br., Die II (1931)	1.75	1.25	1.00	.75	.15
166a	2¢ B. Pane of 4, Die II	130.00	90.00	95.00	67.50	...
166b	2¢ Dark Brown, Die I	6.25	4.50	4.25	3.00	2.50
166c	2¢ B. Pane of 6, Die I	35.00	25.00	25.00	17.50	...
167	3¢ Deep Red (1931)	2.75	1.95	1.75	1.30	.15
167a	3¢ Booklet Pane of 4	35.00	25.00	25.00	17.50	...
168	4¢ Yellow Bistre	12.50	9.00	7.75	5.50	3.00
169	5¢ Dull Violet, Flat Plate	7.00	5.00	4.25	3.00	2.25
169a	5¢ Dull Violet, Rotary	7.00	5.00	4.25	3.00	2.25
170	5¢ Dull Blue	4.00	3.00	2.75	2.00	.15
171	8¢ Dark Blue	21.00	15.00	14.00	10.00	5.00
172	8¢ Red Orange	7.25	5.50	5.00	3.50	2.25
173	10¢ Library of Parliament	10.75	7.75	7.50	5.50	.60
174	12¢ Citadel at Quebec	17.50	12.50	12.00	8.50	3.75
175	20¢ Harvesting Wheat	31.50	22.50	21.00	15.00	.30
176	50¢ Museum-Grand Pre	225.00	150.00	140.00	100.00	8.50
177	$1 Mt. Edith Cavell	250.00	165.00	150.00	110.00	16.50

Die I: Dot of Color in "P" of Postage. Die II: Large Dot in "P".

1930-31 Coil Stamps, Perf. 8½ Vertically VF Used + 40% (B)

178-83	Set of 6	77.50	55.00	46.50	33.50	13.00
178	1¢ George V, Orange	14.00	10.00	9.00	6.50	5.50
179	1¢ Green	8.50	6.00	5.25	3.75	3.50
180	2¢ Dull Green	7.00	5.00	4.50	3.25	2.25
181	2¢ Carmine	17.50	12.50	11.25	8.00	1.75
182	2¢ Dark Brown (1931)	12.50	9.00	7.75	8.00	.50
183	3¢ Deep Red (1931)	21.00	15.00	12.00	8.50	.40

1931 Design of 1912, Perf. 12 x 8 VF Used + 30% (B)

184	3¢ George V Carmine	4.50	3.25	2.50	2.00	1.85

190	192	194	195

1931 Cartier Issue VF + 30% (B)

190	10¢ Sir Georges Cartier	10.75	8.25	7.25	5.50	.18

1932 Surcharges VF + 30% (B)

191	3¢ on 2¢ Deep Red, Die II	1.30	1.00	.85	.65	.18
191a	3¢ on 2¢ Deep Red, Die I	2.60	2.00	1.95	1.50	1.00

1932 Imperial Conference VF + 30% (B)

192-94	Set of 3	16.50	12.50	11.50	9.00	5.15
192	3¢ George V	1.00	.75	.65	.50	.15
193	5¢ Prince of Wales	7.50	5.75	5.25	4.00	1.50
194	13¢ Allegory	9.00	6.75	6.50	5.00	3.75

1932 George V, Medallion, VF Used + 30% (B)

Scott's No.		VF	NH F-VF	Unused VF	F-VF	Used F-VF
195-201	Set of 7....................	115.00	85.00	79.50	62.50	7.50
195	1¢ George V. Dark Green....	1.00	.75	.70	.55	.15
195a	1¢ Booklet Pane of 4	110.00	82.50	80.00	60.00	...
195b	1¢ Booklet Pane of 6	27.00	21.00	21.00	16.00	...
196	2¢ Black Brown....................	1.10	.85	.80	.60	.15
196a	2¢ Booklet Pane of 4	110.00	82.50	80.00	60.00	...
196b	2¢ Booklet Pane of 6	26.50	20.00	19.50	15.00	...
197	3¢ Deep Red........................	1.60	1.20	1.20	.90	.15
197a	3¢ Booklet Pane of 4	27.00	21.00	21.00	16.00	...
198	4¢ Ocher.............................	42.75	33.50	32.50	25.00	3.50
199	5¢ Dark Blue........................	8.75	6.50	5.95	4.50	.15
200	8¢ Red Orange	26.50	20.00	18.50	14.00	2.35
201	13¢ Citadel at Quebec...........	45.00	33.00	30.00	22.50	1.75

202   208   209

1933 Pictorials VF + 30%

202	5¢ U.P.U. Meeting................	8.50	6.50	5.50	4.25	2.00
203	20¢ Grain Exhib. (on #175)......	36.50	27.50	24.00	18.00	8.00
204	5¢ "Royal William"..............	10.00	7.50	6.50	5.00	2.00

1933 Coil Stamps, Perf. Vertically VF + 30% (B)

205	1¢ George V. Dark Green........	18.00	13.50	11.50	8.50	1.50
206	2¢ Black Brown.....................	21.75	16.75	15.00	11.50	.55
207	3¢ Deep Red.......................	14.50	10.50	9.75	7.50	.25

1934 Commemoratives VF + 30%

208	3¢ Cartier at Quebec	3.95	3.00	2.60	2.00	.85
209	10¢ Loyalists Monument..........	21.50	16.50	14.25	11.00	4.75
210	2¢ Seal of New Brunswick........	2.75	2.10	1.85	1.40	1.10

1935 Silver Jubilee VF + 20%

211   213   214   216

Scott's No.		Plate Blocks NH	Unused	F-VF NH	F-VF Unused	Used
211-16	Set of 6	...	...	16.75	12.50	6.95
211	1¢ Princess Elizabeth .... (6)	7.00	5.75	.35	.28	.20
212	2¢ Duke of York .... (6)	8.00	6.25	.60	.45	.15
213	3¢ George V and Mary .... (6)	17.50	13.50	1.70	1.25	.15
214	5¢ Prince of Wales............. (6)	47.50	35.00	4.00	2.75	1.75
215	10¢ Windsor Castle .... (6)	57.50	45.00	5.00	3.75	1.75
216	13¢ Royal Yacht "Brittania" (6)	75.00	55.00	6.75	4.75	3.50

1935 George V & Pictorials VF + 20%

217   222   223   227

Scott's No.		Plate Blocks NH	Unused	F-VF NH	F-VF Unused	Used
217-27	Set of 11	...	...	115.00	82.50	13.00
217	1¢ George V Green .... (8)	3.75	3.00	.25	.20	.15
217a	1¢ Booklet Pane of 4	...	...	50.00	35.00	...
217b	1¢ Booklet Pane of 6	...	...	21.50	15.00	...
218	2¢ Brown..................... (8)	3.75	3.00	.35	.25	.15
218a	2¢ Booklet Pane of 4	...	...	50.00	35.00	...
218b	2¢ Booklet Pane of 6	...	...	17.00	11.50	...
219	3¢ Dark Carmine................ (8)	7.00	5.50	.50	.40	.15
219a	3¢ Booklet Pane of 4	...	...	17.50	12.00	...

1935 George V & Pictorials (cont.)

Scott's No.		Plate Blocks NH	Unused	F-VF NH	F-VF Unused	Used
220	4¢ Yellow.............................(6)	35.00	27.50	2.65	2.00	.35
221	5¢ Blue ....(6)	35.00	27.50	2.25	1.75	.15
222	8¢ Deep Orange..................(6)	35.00	27.50	2.65	2.00	1.30
223	10¢ Mounted Police..............(6)	55.00	42.50	6.50	4.75	.15
224	13¢ Confederation Conf......(6)	55.00	42.50	6.50	4.75	.50
225	20¢ Niagara Falls ....(6)	160.00	120.00	20.00	15.00	.35
226	50¢ Parliament, Victoria......(6)	235.00	175.00	27.50	20.00	3.25
227	$1 Champlain Monument....(6)	500.00	375.00	60.00	42.50	7.00

1935 Coil Stamps, Perf. 8 Vertically VF + 20% (B)

228	1¢ George V, Green	...	...	12.75	8.75	1.60
229	2¢ Brown	...	...	11.00	7.50	.55
230	3¢ Dark Carmine	...	...	11.00	7.50	.25

231   237   241   242

1937 George VI VF + 20% (B)

231-36	Set of 6	...	...	8.25	6.25	.70
231	1¢ George VI, Green	2.25	1.85	.35	.25	.15
231a	1¢ Booklet Pane of 4	...	...	10.50	7.50	...
231b	1¢ Booklet Pane of 6	...	...	1.50	1.10	...
232	2¢ Brown	2.75	2.25	.45	.35	.15
232a	2¢ Booklet Pane of 4	...	...	10.00	7.00	...
232b	2¢ Booklet Pane of 6	...	...	5.75	4.00	...
233	3¢ Carmine	3.50	2.75	.60	.50	.15
233a	3¢ Booklet Pane of 6	...	...	2.00	1.50	...
234	4¢ Yellow	16.50	12.50	2.50	1.85	.15
235	5¢ Blue	15.00	11.00	2.50	1.85	.15
236	8¢ Orange	15.00	11.00	2.50	1.85	.30

1937 Coronation Issue VF + 20% (B)

237	3¢ George VI and Elizabeth....	2.25	1.75	.25	.20	.15

1937 Coil Stamps, Perf. 8 Vertically VF + 20% (B)

238	1¢ George VI, Green...............	...	...	1.60	1.10	.60
239	2¢ Brown..............................	...	...	2.25	1.60	.20
240	3¢ Carmine	...	...	3.75	2.50	.15

1938 Pictorials VF + 20%

241-45	Set of 5	...	...	100.00	67.50	6.75
241	10¢ Memorial Hall	35.00	25.00	5.00	3.75	.15
242	13¢ Halifax Harbor..................	35.00	25.00	7.50	5.25	.30
243	20¢ Ft. Garry Gate, Winnipeg.	90.00	65.00	12.00	8.50	.20
244	50¢ Vancouver Harbor..........	175.00	120.00	20.00	13.50	3.00
245	$1 Chateau de Ramezay........	400.00	275.00	62.50	42.50	3.75

1939 Royal Visit VF + 20%

246   247   248

246-48	Set of 3	3.65	2.90	.55	.50	.30
246	1¢ Elizabeth & Margaret Rose	1.65	1.35	.22	.20	.15
247	2¢ War Memorial, Ottawa	1.65	1.35	.22	.20	.15
248	3¢ George VI and Elizabeth....	1.65	1.35	.22	.20	.15

1942-43 War Set

249   250   253   262

1942-43 War Set

Scott's No.		Plate Blocks NH	Unused	F-VF NH	F-VF Unused	Used
249-62	Set of 14	...	...	115.00	78.50	10.75
249	1¢ George VI, Green..........	1.60	1.25	.25	.20	.15
249a	1¢ Booklet Pane of 4.........	...	...	3.75	2.75	...
249b	1¢ Booklet Pane of 6.........	...	...	1.50	1.10	...
249c	1¢ Booklet Pane of 3.........	...	...	1.20	.85	...
250	2¢ Brown..........................	2.35	1.75	.40	.30	.15
250a	2¢ Booklet Pane of 4.........	...	...	3.75	2.75	...
250b	2¢ Booklet Pane of 6.........	...	...	3.50	2.50	...
251	3¢ Dark Carmine...............	2.35	1.75	.40	.30	.15
251a	3¢ Booklet Pane of 4.........	...	...	1.75	1.25	...
252	3¢ Rose Violet (1943)	2.35	1.75	.40	.30	.15
252a	3¢ Booklet Pane of 4.........	...	...	1.50	1.10	...
252b	3¢ Booklet Pane of 3.........	...	...	2.00	1.50	...
252c	3¢ Booklet Pane of 6.........	...	...	3.00	2.25	...
253	4¢ Grain Elevators	10.00	7.25	1.25	.90	.55
254	4¢ George VI. Carm.(1943)	2.35	1.75	.35	.25	.15
254a	4¢ Booklet Pane of 6.........	...	...	1.90	1.35	...
254b	4¢ Booklet Pane of 3.........	...	...	1.90	1.35	...
255	5¢ George VI, Deep Blue ...	6.75	5.00	1.00	.70	.15
256	8¢ Farm Scene..................	12.50	9.00	1.60	1.10	.35
257	10¢ Parliament Buildings ...	22.50	16.00	3.50	2.50	.15
258	13¢ "Ram" Tank.................	27.50	20.00	4.50	3.25	2.75
259	14¢ "Ram" Tank (1943)......	40.00	30.00	7.00	5.00	.25
260	20¢ Corvette.....................	40.00	30.00	8.00	5.75	.20
261	50¢ Munitions Factory........	140.00	100.00	27.50	20.00	1.50
262	$1 Destroyer.....................	395.00	265.00	67.50	45.00	6.00

1942-43 Coil Stamps, Perf. 8 Vertically

263-67	Set of 5	...	...	9.25	6.50	1.90
263	1¢ George VI, Green..........	...	...	1.00	.70	.35
264	2¢ Brown..........................	...	...	1.35	1.00	.65
265	3¢ Dark Carmine	...	...	1.35	1.00	.65
266	3¢ Rose Violet (1943)	...	...	2.50	1.75	.20
267	4¢ Dark Carmine (1943).....	...	...	3.50	2.50	.18

1946 Reconversion "Peace" Issue

	268		271		273	

268-73	Set of 6	...	...	55.00	37.50	4.50
268	8¢ Farm Scene..................	7.00	5.50	1.20	.90	.40
269	10¢ Great Bear Lake.........	7.00	5.50	1.50	1.10	.15
270	14¢ Hydroelectric Station ...	16.00	12.50	2.70	2.00	.18
271	20¢ Combine.....................	18.00	14.00	3.00	2.25	.15
272	50¢ Logging......................	95.00	60.00	15.00	11.00	1.35
273	$1 Train Ferry...................	200.00	150.00	35.00	25.00	2.50

	274		275		276		283

1947-48 Commemoratives

Scott's No.		Plate Blocks NH	F-VF NH	F-VF Used
274-77,282-83	Set of 6	...	.90	.70
274	4¢ Alexander Graham Bell	.85	.20	.15
275	4¢ Citizenship...................................	.85	.20	.15
276	4¢ Royal Wedding (1948)...................	.85	.20	.15
277	4¢ Parliament (1948)	.75	.20	.15

1948 Coils, Perf. 9½ Vertically

278-81	Set of 4..	...	27.50	11.50
278	1¢ George VI, Green	...	3.00	1.50
279	2¢ George VI, Brown	...	10.75	6.50
280	3¢ George VI, Rose Violet....................	...	6.50	1.85
281	4¢ George VI, Dark Carmine	...	8.50	2.25

1949 Commemoratives

282	4¢ Founding of Newfoundland..............	.95	.20	.15
283	4¢ Halifax Anniversary.........................	.95	.20	.15

1949 George VI with "Postes-Postage" In Design

	284		289		294		302

Scott's No.		Plate Blocks NH	F-VF NH	F-VF Used
284-88	Set of 5..	...	2.10	.60
284	1¢ George VI, Green	.85	.20	.15
284a	1¢ Book. Pane of 3 (1950)...................	...	.60	...
285	2¢ Sepia..	1.10	.25	.15
286	3¢ Rose Violet....................................	1.25	.30	.15
286a	3¢ Book. Pane of 3 (1950)...................	...	1.10	...
286b	3¢ Booklet Pane of 4	...	1.35	...
287	4¢ Dark Carmine................................	1.95	.45	.15
287a	4¢ Book. Pane of 3 (1950)...................	...	7.25	...
287b	4¢ Book. Pane of 6 (1951)...................	...	8.50	...
288	5¢ Deep Blue	4.50	1.00	.15

1950 George VI without "Postes-Postage" In Design

289-93	Set of 5..	...	1.90	1.15
289	1¢ George VI, Green	.65	.20	.15
290	2¢ Sepia..	2.00	.30	.15
291	3¢ Rose Violet....................................	.95	.20	.15
292	4¢ Dark Carmine................................	1.25	.25	.15
293	5¢ Deep Blue	5.25	1.10	.75

1950 Regular Issue

294	50¢ Oil Wells, Alberta	50.00	10.50	1.20

1949-50 Coil Stamps, Perf. 9½ Vertically

295-300	Set of 6..	...	15.00	2.90
	(without "Postes-Postage")			
295	1¢ George VI, Green	...	.50	.25
296	3¢ Rose Violet....................................	...	.75	.50
	(with "Postes-Postage")			
297	1¢ George VI, Green (1950).................	...	.30	.22
298	2¢ Sepia (1950)	...	2.00	1.35
299	3¢ Rose Violet (1950)	...	1.30	.20
300	4¢ Dark Carmine (1950)	...	11.50	.65

1950-1951 Regular Issue

301	10¢ Fur Resources	4.00	.75	.15
302	$1 Fishing (1951).................................	275.00	52.50	9.75

	303		311		314		315

1951-52 Commemoratives

303-4,11-15,17-19	Set of 10	...	4.65	2.50

1951 Commemoratives

303	3¢ Robert L. Borden	1.40	.22	.15
304	4¢ William L. Mackenzie King...............	1.50	.25	.15

1951 Color Changes (with "Postes-Postage")

305	2¢ George VI, Olive Green	.70	.20	.15
306	4¢ Orange Vermillion	1.10	.25	.15
306a	4¢ Booklet Pane of 3	...	2.75	...
306b	4¢ Booklet Pane of 6	...	3.25	...
309	2¢ Ol. Gr., Coil Pf. 9½ Vert.................	...	1.00	.60
310	4¢ Or. Verm., Coil Pf. 9½ Vert............	...	2.40	.70

1951 Int'l. Philatelic Exhibition "CAPEX"

311-14	Set of 4..	...	3.65	1.75
311	4¢ Trains of 1851 & 1951	2.10	.45	.15
312	5¢ Steamships....................................	7.50	1.50	1.20
313	7¢ Plane & Stagecoach	4.50	.90	.30
314	15¢ 1st Canada Stamp	5.00	1.00	.27

1951 Commemoratives

315	4¢ Royal Visit to Canada and U.S.	.95	.20	.15

<u>FROM 1941 TO PRESENT, ADD 20% FOR VERY FINE QUALITY</u>
Minimum of 10¢ per stamp

CANADA

| 316 | 317 | 320 |

1952 Regular Issue

Scott's No.		Plate Blocks NH	F-VF NH	F-VF Used
316	20¢ Paper Industry	7.00	1.35	.15

1952 Commemoratives

317	4¢ Red Cross Conference	1.15	.20	.15
318	3¢ John J.C. Abbott	1.00	.20	.15
319	4¢ Alexander Mackenzie	1.00	.20	.15

1952-53 Regular Issues

320	7¢ Canada Goose	1.50	.30	.15
321	$1 Totem Pole (1953)	55.00	11.00	.70

| 322 | 325 | 330 | 334 |

1953-54 Commemoratives

322-24,35-36,49-50 Set of 7		...	1.75	.95

1953 Wildlife Commemoratives

322	2¢ Polar Bear	1.00	.20	.15
323	3¢ Moose	1.10	.20	.15
324	4¢ Bighorn Sheep	1.25	.23	.15

1953 Queen Elizabeth II Issue

325-29 Set of 5		...	.95	.60
325	1¢ Elizabeth II, Brown	.60	.20	.15
325a	1¢ Booklet Pane of 3	...	.75	...
326	2¢ Green	.60	.20	.15
327	3¢ Carmine Rose	.75	.20	.15
327a	3¢ Booklet Pane of 3	...	1.15	...
327b	3¢ Booklet Pane of 4	...	1.25	...
328	4¢ Violet	1.15	.24	.15
328a	4¢ Booklet Pane of 3	...	1.40	...
328b	4¢ Booklet Pane of 6	...	1.50	...
329	5¢ Ultramarine	1.40	.30	.15

1953 Coronation Issue

330	4¢ Elizabeth II	.85	.20	.15

1953 Queen Elizabeth II Coils, Perf. 9½ Vertically

331	2¢ Elizabeth II, Green	...	1.20	.80
332	3¢ Carmine Rose	...	1.20	.80
333	4¢ Violet	...	2.95	1.35

1953 Regular Issue

334	50¢ Textile Industry	19.00	3.25	.20

| 336 | 337 | 349 | 351 |

1954 Wildlife Commemoratives

335	4¢ Walrus	1.50	.25	.15
336	5¢ Beaver	1.50	.30	.15
336a	5¢ Booklet Pane of 5	...	1.75	...

1954 Queen Elizabeth II Issue

337-43 Set of 7		...	2.10	.75
337	1¢ Elizabeth II, V. Brown	.50	.20	.15
337a	1¢ Booklet Pane of 5 (1956)	...	.75	...
338	2¢ Green	.60	.20	.15
338a	2¢ Min. Pane of 25 (1961)	...	4.00	...
338a	Pack of 2	...	8.00	...
339	3¢ Carmine Rose	.75	.20	.15
340	4¢ Violet	.90	.20	.15
340a	4¢ Booklet Pane of 5 (1956)	...	1.35	...
340b	4¢ Booklet Pane of 6 (1955)	...	3.75	...
341	5¢ Bright Blue	1.10	.20	.15
341a	5¢ Booklet Pane of 5	...	1.35	...
341b	5¢ Min. Pane of 20 (1961)	...	8.00	...

CANADA
1954 Queen Elizabeth II Issue (cont.)

Scott's No.		Plate Blocks NH	F-VF NH	F-VF Used
342	6¢ Orange	1.70	.35	.15
343	15¢ Gannet, Gray	4.50	.95	.15

1954 Elizabeth II Coil Stamps, Perf. 9½ Vertically

345	2¢ Elizabeth II, Green	...	.40	.18
347	4¢ Violet	...	1.25	.20
348	5¢ Bright Blue	...	1.85	.18

1954 Commemoratives

349	4¢ J.S.D. Thompson	1.30	.25	.15
350	5¢ M. Bowell	1.30	.25	.15

1955 Regular Issue

351	10¢ Eskimo in Kayak	1.50	.30	.15

| 352 | 356 | 359 | 360 |

1955 Commemoratives

352-58 Set of 7		...	1.80	.85
352	4¢ Wildlife - Musk Ox	1.25	.25	.15
353	5¢ Whooping Cranes	1.40	.30	.15
354	5¢ Civil Aviation Org	1.40	.30	.15
355	5¢ Alberta - Saskatchewan	1.40	.30	.15
356	5¢ Boy Scout Jamboree	1.40	.30	.15
357	4¢ Richard B. Bennett	1.25	.25	.15
358	5¢ Charles Tupper	1.25	.25	.15

1956 Commemoratives

359-61,364 Set of 4		...	1.05	.50
359	5¢ Ice Hockey	1.25	.25	.15
360	4¢ Wildlife - Caribou	1.35	.30	.15
361	5¢ Mountain Goat	1.35	.30	.15

1956 Regular Issues

362	20¢ Paper Industry	6.00	1.25	.15
363	25¢ Chemistry Industry	7.50	1.50	.15

1956 Commemoratives

364	5¢ Fire Prevention	1.25	.25	.15

1957 Commemoratives

365-74 Set of 10		...	4.15	2.75
365-68	5¢ Outdoor Recreation, attd	1.85	1.50	1.45
365-68	Set of 4 Singles	...	1.20	.80
369	5¢ Wildlife - Loon	1.25	.25	.15
370	5¢ David Thompson	1.25	.25	.15
371	5¢ U.P.U. - Parliament	1.25	.25	.15
372	15¢ U.P.U. - Post Horn	9.00	1.80	1.50
373	5¢ Mining Industry	1.10	.24	.15
374	5¢ Royal Visit	1.10	.24	.15

1958 Commemoratives

| 376 | 378 | 380 | 381 |

375-82 Set of 8		...	1.80	1.00
375	5¢ Newspaper Industry (Blank)	2.50	.25	.18
376	5¢ Int'l. Geophysical Year (Blank)	2.50	.25	.15
377	5¢ British Columbia Cent	2.25	.25	.15
378	5¢ Explorer La Verendrye	1.75	.25	.15
379	5¢ Quebec Anniversary	4.00	.25	.15
380	5¢ National Health	1.50	.25	.15
381	5¢ Petroleum Industry	1.35	.25	.15
382	5¢ 1st Elected Assembly	1.60	.25	.15

CANADA
1959 Commemoratives

383	385	387

Scott's No.		Plate Block	F-VF NH	F-VF Used
383-88	Set of 6..	...	1.35	.75
383	5¢ Golden Anniv. of Flight.......................	1.50	.25	.15
384	5¢ 10th Anniv. of N.A.T.O.	1.35	.25	.15
385	5¢ Country Women of the World............	1.25	.25	.15
386	5¢ Royal Tour.......................................	1.25	.25	.15
387	5¢ St. Lawrence Seaway........................	3.75	.25	.15
388	5¢ Plains of Abraham	1.25	.25	.15

1960-1961 Commemoratives

390	391	393	395

		Plate Block	F-VF NH	F-VF Used
389-95	Set of 7...	...	1.60	.85
389	5¢ Girl Guides Association	1.40	.25	.15
390	5¢ Battle of Long Sault	1.40	.25	.15
391	5¢ Northland Development (1961)	1.40	.25	.15
392	5¢ E. Pauline Johnson (1961).................	1.40	.25	.15
393	5¢ P. Minister A. Meighen (1961)...........	1.40	.25	.15
394	5¢ Colombo Plan (1961).........................	1.40	.25	.15
395	5¢ Resources for Tomorrow (1961)........	1.40	.25	.15

396	398	400	401

1962 Commemoratives

396-400	Set of 5	...	1.10	.65
396	5¢ Education..	1.40	.25	.15
397	5¢ Red River Settlement, Lord Selkirk	1.40	.25	.15
398	5¢ Jean Talon..	1.40	.25	.15
399	5¢ Victoria B.C. Centenary.....................	1.40	.25	.15
400	5¢ Trans-Canadian Highway	1.40	.25	.15

1962-63 Queen Elizabeth Issue

401-05	Set of 5	...	.85	.60
401	1¢ Deep Brown (1963)	.40	.20	.15
401a	1¢ Booklet Pane of 5	...	2.50	...
402	2¢ Green (1963)	3.25	.20	.15
402a	2¢ Miniature Pane of 25 .... (pack of 2)	12.50	6.00	...
403	3¢ Purple (1963)...................................	.70	.20	.15
404	4¢ Carmine (1963).................................	.90	.20	.15
404a	4¢ Booklet Pane of 5	...	3.00	...
404b	4¢ Miniature Pane of 25	...	8.75	...
405	5¢ Violet Blue	1.10	.20	.15
405a	5¢ Booklet Pane of 5 (1963)	...	3.50	...
405b	5¢ Miniature Pane of 20 (1963)	...	10.75	...

1962-63 Coil Stamps, Perf. 9½ Horizontally

406-9	Set of 4...	...	9.75	4.25
406	2¢ Elizabeth, Green (1963)	...	2.75	1.50
407	3¢ Purple (1963)	...	1.80	1.10
408	4¢ Carmine (1963).................................	...	2.85	1.50
409	5¢ Violet Blue	...	2.85	.50

411	413	417

CANADA
1963 Commemoratives

Scott's No.		Plate Block	F-VF NH	F-VF Used
410,412-13	Set of 3..	...	.65	.35
410	5¢ Sir Casimir S. Gzowski......................	1.15	.24	.15

1963 Regular Issues

411	$1 Export Trade, Crate & Map.................	60.00	11.00	1.75

1963 Commemoratives

412	5¢ Explorer M. Frobisher	1.15	.24	.15
413	5¢ First Post Route................................	1.15	.24	.15

1963-1964 Regular Issues

414	7¢ Jet at Ottawa Airport (1964)	1.85	.40	.40
415	15¢ Canada Geese (1963)	10.00	2.00	.20

1964 Commemoratives

416,431-35	Set of 6..	...	1.15	.75
416	5¢ "Peace on Earth"	1.15	.24	.15

418	431	434

1964-1966 Coat of Arms & Flowers

417-29A	Set of 14	14.75	2.75	1.75
417	5¢ Canadian Unity, Maple Leaf	1.00	.20	.15
418	5¢ Ontario, White Trillium	1.00	.20	.18
419	5¢ Quebec, White Garden Lily	1.00	.20	.15
420	5¢ Nova Scotia, Mayflower/1965............	1.00	.20	.15
421	5¢ New Brunswick, Purple Violet ('65)	1.00	.20	.15
422	5¢ Manitoba, Prairie Crocus ('55)...........	1.75	.20	.15
423	5¢ British Columbia, Dogwood ('65)........	1.00	.20	.15
424	5¢ Pr. Edward I., Lady's Slipper ('65)	1.00	.20	.15
425	5¢ Saskatchewan, Prairie Lily ('66)	1.00	.20	.18
426	5¢ Alberta, Wild Rose ('66)	1.00	.20	.15
427	5¢ Newfoundland, Pitcher Plant ('66)	1.75	.20	.15
428	5¢ Yukon, Firewood ('66)	1.00	.20	.18
429	5¢ Northwest Terr., Mountain Avens ('66)	1.00	.20	.15
429A	5¢ Canada, Maple Leaf ('66)	1.00	.20	.15

1964 Regular Issue

430	8¢ on 7¢ Jet Aircraft (on #414) .... (Blank)	1.50	.30	.30

1964 Commemoratives

431	5¢ Charlottestown Conference	1.15	.24	.15
432	5¢ Quebec Conference	1.00	.20	.15
433	5¢ Queen Elizabeth Visit	1.00	.20	.15
434	3¢ Christmas, Family & Star....................	.75	.20	.15
434a	3¢ Miniature Pane of 25 (pack of 2)	12.00	6.00	...
435	5¢ Christmas, Family & Star....................	1.15	.20	.15

1964 Regular Issue

436	8¢ Jet at Ottawa Airport.........................	1.75	.35	.20

1965 Commemoratives

437	440	441	443

437-44	Set of 8......................................	...	1.50	1.00
437	5¢ International Cooperation Year...........	.90	.20	.15
438	5¢ Sir Wilfred Grenfell	.90	.20	.15
439	5¢ National Flag	.90	.20	.15
440	5¢ Sir Winston Churchill	.90	.20	.15
441	5¢ Interparliamentary Union	.90	.20	.15
442	5¢ Ottawa Centennial	.90	.20	.15
443	3¢ Christmas, Gifts of Wise Men............	.70	.20	.15
443a	3¢ Miniature Pane of 25 .... (pack of 2)	11.50	5.75	...
444	5¢ Christmas, Gifts of Wise Men	1.25	.20	.15

	445	448	450	451

Scott's No.		Plate Block	F-VF NH	F-VF Used
445-52	Set of 8...............	...	1.50	1.00
445	5¢ Satellite Alouette II..............	1.00	.20	.15
446	5¢ LaSalle Arrival Tercentary	1.00	.20	.15
447	5¢ Highway Safety...................	1.00	.20	.15
448	5¢ London Conf. Centenary	1.00	.20.	.15
449	5¢ Atomic Energy..............	1.00	.20	.15
450	5¢ Parliamentary Association............	1.00	.20	.15
451	3¢ Christmas, Praying Hands..........	.70	.20	.15
451a	3¢ Miniature Pane of 25 .... (pack of 2)	6.00	3.00	...
452	5¢ Christmas, Praying Hands.............	1.00	.20	.15

1967 Commemoratives

453,469-77	Set of 10...............	...	1.90	1.30
453	5¢ Canadian Centenary.............	1.00	.20	.15

1967-72 Regular Issue, Perf. 12

454	459,460	461	465B

		Plate Block	F-VF NH	F-VF Used
454-65B	Set of 14...........	...	14.50	2.25
454	1¢ Elizabeth & Dog Team, Brown	.70	.20	.15
454a	1¢ Booklet Pane of 5	...	.50	...
454b	B. Pane of 5 (1 #454 & 4 #459), Perf. 10(1968)	...	2.25	...
454c	B. Pane of 10 (5 #454 & 5 #457) Perf.10(1968)	...	2.50	...
454d	1¢ Booklet Single, Perf. 10 (1968)..........	...	.35	.20
454e	1¢ Booklet Single, Perf. 12½ x 12 (1969)	...	.65	.20
455	2¢ Elizabeth & Totem Pole, Green..........	.75	.20	.15
455a	B. Pane of 8 (4 #455, 4 #456)	...	1.75	...
456	3¢ Elizabeth & Combine, Purple...........	1.50	.20	.15
456a	3¢ Booklet Single, Perf. 12½ x 12 (1971)	...	3.75	1.50
457	4¢ Elizabeth & Seaway Lock, Carmine ...	1.50	.20	.15
457a	4¢ Booklet Pane of 5	...	1.30	...
457b	4¢ Miniature Pane of 25	...	18.50	...
457c	4¢ B. Pane of 25, Perf. 10 (1968)............	...	8.50	...
457d	4¢ Booklet Single, Perf. 10(1968)...........	...	.60	.25
458	5¢ Elizabeth & Fishing Port, Blue............	1.25	.20	.15
458a	5¢ Booklet Pane of 5	...	5.75	...
458b	5¢ Miniature Pane of 20	...	25.00	...
458c	5¢ B. Pane of 20, Perf. 10 (1968).........	...	7.50	...
458d	5¢ Booklet Single, Perf. 10 (1968)..........	...	.65	.25
459	6¢ Elizabeth & Trans, Orange, Perf. 10 (1968)	3.00	.30	.15
459a	6¢ B. Pane of 25, Perf. 10 (1968) ...	...	8.00	...
459b	6¢ Orange, Perf. 12½ x 12 (1968)........	3.00	.35	.15
460	6¢ Black, Die I, Perf. 12½ x 12 (1970)	1.75	.20	.15
460a	6¢ Die I, B. Pane of 25, Perf. 10 (1970) ..	...	12.50	...
460g	6¢ Die I, Booklet Single, Perf. 10 (1970).	...	1.35	.35
460b	6¢ Die I, B.Pane of 25, Perf. 12½x12 (1970)	...	16.50	...
460c	6¢ Black, Die II. Perf. 12½ x 12 (1970)	2.00	.25	.15
460d	6¢ Die II, B. Pane of 4, Perf. 12½ x 12 (1970)	...	4.25	...
460e	6¢ Die II, B. Pane of 4, Perf. 10 (1970) ...	...	7.50	...
460h	6¢ Die II Booklet Single, Perf. 10	...	3.50	1.75
460f	6¢ Die II, Perf. 12 (1973)	2.25	.40	.25
461	8¢ "Alaska Highway"	2.50	.30	.15
462	10¢ "The Jack Pine"	1.40	.25	.15
463	15¢ "Bylot Island"	2.75	.40	.15
464	20¢ "The Ferry, Quebec".............	3.25	.55	.15
465	25¢ "The Solemn Land".............	5.75	1.00	.15
465A	50¢ "Summer's Stores"	16.50	3.50	.15
465B	$1 "Oilfield, Edmonton".............	38.75	7.75	.60

#460 has weak shading lines around "6"; #460c has lines strengthened.

1967-70 Coil Stamps, Perf. 9½ or 10 Horiz.

466-68B	Set of 5	...	3.95	2.50
466	3¢ Elizabeth & Oil Rig	...	1.50	1.00
467	4¢ Elizabeth & Canal Lock	...	.70	.60
468	5¢ Elizabeth & Fishing Port	...	1.50	.80
468A	6¢ Elizabeth, Orange (1969)	...	.27	.15
468B	6¢ Elizabeth, Black (1970)............	...	.27	.15

	469	473	476

Scott's No.		Plate Block	F-VF NH	F-VF Used
469	5¢ Expo '67, Montreal...............	1.00	.20	.15
470	5¢ Women's Franchise	1.00	.20	.15
471	5¢ Royal Visit, Elizabeth II.............	1.00	.20	.15
472	5¢ Pan American Games	1.00	.20	.15
473	5¢ Canadian Press	1.00	.20	.15
474	5¢ Georges P. Vanier...............	1.15	.24	.15
475	5¢ Toronto Centennial	1.00	.20	.15
476	3¢ Christmas, Singing Children	.80	.20	.15
476a	3¢ Miniature Pane of 25 .... (pack of 2)	5.50	2.75	...
477	5¢ Christmas, Singing Children	.85	.20	.15

1968 Commemoratives

	479	485	486	488

478-89	Set of 12...............	...	3.85	2.50
478	5¢ Wildlife - Gray Jays...............	3.75	.40	.15
479	5¢ Meteorological Readings	1.00	.20	.15
480	5¢ Wildlife - Narwhal...............	1.00	.20	.15
481	5¢ Int'l. Hydrological Decade	1.00	.20	.15
482	5¢ Voyage of "Nonsuch".............	1.15	.20	.18
483	5¢ Lacrosse Players.............	1.15	.20	.18
484	5¢ George Brown and "Globe"	1.15	.20	.18
485	5¢ Henry Bourassa - Journalist	1.15	.20	.15
486	15¢ World War I Armistice	8.00	1.65	1.20
487	5¢ John McCrae - Poet.............	1.15	.20	.15
488	5¢ Christmas - Eskimo Carving	.75	.20	.15
488a	5¢ Booklet Pane of 10	...	2.75	...
489	6¢ Christmas - Mother & Infant.............	1.10	.22	.15

1969 Commemoratives

	491	496	500	502

490-504	Set of 15...............	...	8.95	6.75
490	6¢ Sports - Curling...............	1.00	.20	.15
491	6¢ Vincent Massey	1.00	.20	.15
492	50¢ Aurele de Fey Suzor-Cote	15.00	3.00	2.25
493	6¢ Int'l. Labor Organization.............	1.00	.20	.15
494	15¢ Non-Stop Atlantic Flight.............	7.50	1.50	1.40
495	6¢ Sir William Osler	1.00	.20	.15
#496-98	Canadian Birds			
496	6¢ White-Throated Sparrow	1.65	.35	.15
497	10¢ Ipswich Sparrow	3.25	.70	.45
498	25¢ Hermit Thrush	8.50	1.75	1.50
499	6¢ Charlottetown Bicentennial.............	1.00	.20	.15
500	6¢ Canada Summer Games	1.00	.20	.15
501	6¢ Sir Isaac Brock	1.00	.20	.15
502	5¢ Christmas, Children Praying	.85	.20	.15
502a	5¢ Booklet Pane of 10	...	3.00	...
503	6¢ Christmas, Children Praying.............	.85	.20	.15
504	6¢ Stephen Leacock.............	1.10	.20	.15

NOTE: STARTING IN 1967, MANY PLATE BLOCKS HAVE IMPRINTS WITHOUT PLATE NUMBERS.

| | | 505 | | 508 | | 513 | |

Scott's No.	Plate Block	F-VF NH	F-VF Used
505-18,531 Set of 15...	...	11.50	9.75
505 6¢ Manitoba Centenary............................	.95	.20	.15
506 6¢ Northwest Territory	.90	.20	.15
507 6¢ Biological Program	.90	.20	.15
508-11 25¢ Expo '70, Osaka, Japan, attd	9.50	8.50	8.50
508-11 Set of 4 Singles.............................	...	7.75	7.75
512 6¢ Henry Kelsey - Explorer.....................	.90	.20	.15
513 10¢ 25th Anniv. of United Nations...........	3.00	.60	.50
514 15¢ 25th Anniv. of United Nations...........	4.50	.90	.70
515 6¢ Louis Riel, Metis Leader....................	.90	.20	.15
516 6¢ Sir A. Mackenzie - Explorer...............	.90	.20	.15
517 6¢ Sir Oliver Mowat...............................	.95	.20	.15
518 6¢ Group of Seven	.95	.20	.15

1970 Christmas - Children's Designs

| | | 519 | | 524 | | 530 | |

519-30 Set of 12 Singles................................	...	3.95	2.50
519-23 5¢ Christmas, attached	(10) 5.75	2.40	2.25
519-23 Set of 5 Singles	...	1.25	.75
524-28 6¢ Christmas, attached	(10) 6.75	2.75	2.50
524-28 Set of 5 Singles	...	1.65	.75
529 10¢ Christ Child in Manger.....................	1.95	.40	.30
530 15¢ Snowmobile & Trees	4.35	.85	.85

1970 Commemoratives (continued)

531 6¢ Donald Alexander Smith	.90	.20	.15

| | | 532 | | 533 | | 535 | | 543 | |

1971 Commemoratives

532-42,552-58 Set of 18	...	5.35	3.95
532 6¢ Emily Carr - Painter........................	.85	.20	.15
533 6¢ Discovery of Insulin........................	.85	.20	.15
534 6¢ Sir Ernest Rutherford	.85	.20	.15
535 6¢ Maple Leaf - Spring........................	1.15	.24	.15
536 6¢ Maple Leaf - Summer......................	1.15	.24	.15
537 7¢ Maple Leaf - Autumn......................	1.15	.24	.15
538 7¢ Maple Leaf - Winter........................	1.15	.24	.15
539 6¢ Louis Papineau	.85	.20	.15
540 6¢ Samuel Hearne	.85	.20	.15
541 15¢ Radio Canada Int'l.........................	7.00	1.50	1.00
542 6¢ Census Centennial	.85	.20	.15

1971-72 Regular Issue

543 7¢ Elizabeth & Transportation, Green...	3.00	.25	.15
543a B. Pane of 5 (1 #454,1 #456,3 #543)	...	3.50	...
543b B. Pane of 20 (4 #454,4 #456,12 #543)	...	8.50	...
544 8¢ Elizabeth & Parliament, Slate..........	2.50	.20	.15
544a B. Pane of 6 (3 #454,1 #460c,2 #544) ..	...	1.75	...
544b B. Pane of 18 (6 #454,1 #460c,11 #544)	...	5.75	...
544c B. Pane of 10 (4 #454,1 #460c,5 #544) (1972)	...	1.80	...
549 7¢ Green, Coil, Perf. 10 Horiz.............	...	.35	.15
550 8¢ Slate, Coil, Perf. 10 Horiz................	...	.28	.15

| | | 554 | | 556 | | 561 | |

Scott's No.	Plate Block	F-VF NH	F-VF Used
552 7¢ British Columbia Centenary..............	.85	.20	.15
553 7¢ Paul Kane - Painter	2.50	.35	.18
554 6¢ Christmas, Snowflake.....................	.85	.20	.15
555 7¢ Christmas, Snowflake.....................	1.00	.20	.15
556 10¢ Christmas, Snowflake.....................	1.40	.30	.30
557 15¢ Christmas, Snowflake.....................	3.00	.65	.60
558 7¢ Pierre Laporte...............................	2.40	.20	.15

1972 Commemoratives

559-61,582-85,606-10 Set of 12	...	7.95	6.50
559 8¢ Figure Skating..............................	1.00	.20	.15
560 8¢ World Health Day	1.40	.30	.18
561 8¢ Frontenac Anniversary	1.00	.20	.15

1972-76 Canadian Indians

| | | 562 | | 564 | | 568 | | 570 | |

1972 Indians of the Plains

562-63 8¢ Plains Indians, attached	1.70	.70	.65
562-63 Set of 2 Singles, Horizontal Design.......	...	.65	.20
564-65 8¢ Plains Indians, attached	1.70	.70	.65
564-65 Set of 2 Singles, Vertical Design...........	...	.65	.20

1973 Algonkian Indians

566-67 8¢ Algonkians, attached.......................	1.50	.60	.55
566-67 Set of 2 Singles, Horizontal Design.......	...	.55	.20
568-69 8¢ Algonkians, attached.......................	1.50	.60	.55
568-69 Set of 2 Singles, Vertical Design...........	...	.55	.20

1974 Pacific Coast Indians

570-71 8¢ Pacific Indians, attached	1.50	.60	.55
570-71 Set of 2 Singles, Horizontal Design.......	...	.55	.20
572-73 8¢ Pacific Indians, attached	1.50	.60	.55
572-73 Set of 2 Singles, Vertical Design...........	...	.55	.20

| | | 576 | | 578 | | 580 | | 582 | |

1975 Subarctic Indians

574-75 8¢ Subarctic, attached........................	1.20	.50	.45
574-75 Set of 2 Singles, Horizontal Design.......	...	.45	.20
576-77 8¢ Subarctic, attached........................	1.20	.50	.45
576-77 Set of 2 Singles, Vertical Design...........	...	.45	.20

1976 Iroquois Indians

578-79 10¢ Iroquois, attached.........................	1.20	.50	.45
578-79 Set of 2 Singles, Horizontal Design.......	...	.45	.20
580-81 10¢ Iroquois, attached.........................	1.20	.50	.45
580-81 Set of 2 Singles, Vertical Design...........	...	.45	.20
562-81 Canadian Indians, set of 20	...*	5.25	1.85

1972 Earth Sciences

582-85 15¢ Sciences, attached........................	(16) 27.50	6.00	6.00
582-85 Set of 4 Singles	...	5.60	5.00

1972-1977 Regular Issue, Perf. 12 x 12½ or 12½ x 12

586 593 594 599

Scott's No.		Plate Block	F-VF NH	F-VF Used
586-601	**Set of 17**	...	**13.75**	**5.65**
	#586-92 Famous People			
586	1¢ Sir John A. MacDonald	.50	.20	.15
586a	B. Pane of 6 (3 #586,1 #591,2 #593) ('74)	...	1.10	...
586b	B. Pane of 18 (6 #586,1 #591,11 #593)('75)	...	1.95	...
586c	B. Pane of 10 (2 #586,4 #587,4 #593c)('76)	...	1.40	...
587	2¢ Sir Wilfred Laurier ('73)	.50	.20	.15
588	3¢ Sir Robert L. Borden ('73)	.60	.20	.15
589	4¢ W.L. Mackenzie King ('73)	.60	.20	.15
590	5¢ Richard B. Bennett ('73)	.80	.20	.15
591	6¢ Lester B. Pearson ('73)	.80	.20	.15
592	7¢ Louis St. Laurent ('74)	.90	.20	.15
593	8¢ Queen Elizabeth II, Perf. 12 x 12½ ('73)	1.00	.20	.15
593b	8¢ Queen Elizabeth II, Perf. 13 x 13½ ('76)	3.25	.60	.20
593A	10¢ Queen Elizabeth II, Perf. 13 x 13½ ('76)	1.10	.22	.15
593c	10¢ Booklet Single, Perf. 12 x 12½ ('76)	...	.30	.25
	#594-601 Scenic Pictorials			
594	10¢ Forests, Tagged, Narrow Side Bars	1.10	.22	.15
594a	10¢ Redrawn, Perf. 13½ ('76)	1.25	.25	.15
595	15¢ Mountain Sheep, Tagged Narrow Bars	1.40	.30	.15
595a	15¢ Redrawn, Perf. 13½ ('76)	1.65	.35	.15
596	20¢ Prairie Mosaic, Tagged Narrow Bars	2.10	.45	.15
596a	20¢ Redrawn, Perf. 13½ ('76)	2.40	.50	.15
597	25¢ Polar Bears, Tagged Narrow Bars	2.50	.50	.15
597a	25¢ Redrawn, Perf. 13½ ('76)	3.00	.65	.15
598	50¢ Seashore	4.75	1.00	.15
598a	50¢ Redrawn, Perf. 13½ ('76)	7.00	1.50	.18
599	$1 Vancouver, Revised ('73)	12.50	2.25	.45
599a	$1 Redrawn, Perf. 13½ ('77)	11.00	2.25	.30
600	$1 Vancouver, Original, Perf. 11	20.00	4.25	1.75
601	$2 Quebec Buildings, Perf. 11	18.00	3.75	2.15
604	8¢ Elizabeth II, Coil, Perf. 10 Vert (1974)	...	.24	.15
605	10¢ Elizabeth II, Coil, Perf. 10 Vert(1976)	...	.30	.15

1972 Commemoratives (continued)

606 608 610

606	6¢ Christmas, Candles	.90	.20	.15
607	8¢ Christmas, Candles	1.00	.20	.15
608	10¢ Christmas, Candles & Fruit	1.95	.40	.35
609	15¢ Christmas, Candles & Prayer Book	2.85	.60	.60
610	8¢ C. Krieghoff, Painter	1.80	.25	.15

1973 Commemoratives

620 623 625

611-28	**Set of 18**	...	**5.15**	**4.25**
611	8¢ Monsignor de Laval	.90	.20	.15
612	8¢ Mounties - G.A. French	.95	.20	.15
613	10¢ Mounties - Spectograph	1.40	.30	.25
614	15¢ Mounties - Municipal Rider	3.15	.65	.60
615	8¢ Jeanne Mance - Nurse	.90	.20	.15
616	8¢ Joseph Howe - Journalist	.90	.20	.15
617	15¢ J.E.H. MacDonald - Painter	2.50	.50	.45

NOTE: STARTING IN 1973, ALL CANADIAN STAMPS ARE TAGGED.

1973 Commemoratives (cont.)

Scott's No.		Plate Block	F-VF NH	F-VF Used
618	8¢ Prince Edward I Centenary	.90	.20	.15
619	8¢ Scottish Settlers Bicentenary	.90	.20	.15
620	8¢ Royal Visit, Elizabeth II	.90	.20	.15
621	15¢ Royal Visit, Elizabeth II	2.75	.60	.50
622	8¢ Nellie McClung, Suffragette	.90	.20	.15
623	8¢ 21st Olympics Publicity	.90	.20	.15
624	15¢ 21st Olympics Publicity	2.25	.50	.45
625	6¢ Christmas - Ice Skate	.70	.20	.15
626	8¢ Christmas - Dove	.90	.20	.15
627	10¢ Christmas - Santa Claus	1.25	.25	.25
628	15¢ Christmas - Shepherd and Star	2.25	.50	.50

1974 Commemoratives

629 634 644

648 650 655

629-55	**Set of 27**	...	**8.75**	**5.50**
629-32	8¢ Summer Olympics, attd	1.50	1.25	.95
629-32	Set of 4 Singles	...	1.20	.70
633	8¢ Winnipeg Centenary	.90	.20	.15
634-39	8¢ Letter Carriers, attached (6)	3.75	3.00	3.00
634-39	Set of 6 Singles	...	2.10	1.80
640	8¢ Agriculture Education	1.00	.22	.15
641	8¢ Telephone Centenary	1.00	.22	.15
642	8¢ World Cycling Champs	1.00	.22	.15
643	8¢ Mennonite Settlement	1.00	.22	.15
644-47	8¢ Winter Olympics, attached	1.50	1.25	.95
644-47	Set of 4 Singles	...	1.20	.70
648	8¢ Universal Postal Union	.90	.20	.15
649	15¢ Universal Postal Union	3.50	.75	.65
650	6¢ Christmas "Nativity"	.70	.20	.15
651	8¢ Christmas "Skaters in Hull"	.85	.20	.15
652	10¢ Christmas "The Ice Cone"	1.45	.30	.25
653	15¢ Christmas "Village"	2.75	.55	.50
654	8¢ Marconi Centenary	.90	.20	.15
655	8¢ William H. Merritt, Welland Canal	.90	.20	.15

1975 Commemoratives

657 662 664 669

658 670 674

216

1975 Commemoratives

Scott's No.		Plate Block	F-VF NH	F-VF Used
656-80	Set of 25...	...	13.50	10.85
656	$1 Olympics "The Sprinter"	11.00	2.25	1.95
657	$2 Olympics "The Plunger"....................	21.50	4.50	4.25
658-59	8¢ Writers,Montgomery,Hemon attached	.95	.40	.35
658-59	Set of 2 Singles	...	.38	.30
660	8¢ Marguerite Bourgeoys	.90	.20	.15
661	8¢ Alphonse Desjardins...........................	.90	.20	.15
662-63	8¢ Religious Leaders,Chown,Cook att	1.10	.45	.40
662-63	Set of 2 Singles	...	.40	.35
664	20¢ Olympics - Pole Vaulting	2.75	.55	.50
665	25¢ Olympics - Marathon Running........	3.15	.65	.55
666	50¢ Olympics - Hurdling	5.50	1.25	1.00
667	8¢ Calgary Centennial "Untamed"..........	1.00	.20	.15
668	8¢ Women's Year	1.00	.20	.15
669	8¢ Supreme Court Centenary..................	1.00	.20	.15
670-73	8¢ Canadian Coastal Ships, attached	1.95	1.50	1.50
670-73	Set of 4 Singles	...	1.40	1.20
674-75	6¢ Christmas, attached............................	.85	.45	.35
674-75	Set of 2 Singles	...	.40	.30
676-77	8¢ Christmas, attached............................	1.00	.45	.35
676-77	Set of 2 Singles	...	.40	.30
678	10¢ Christmas, Gift Box..........................	1.10	.22	.20
679	15¢ Christmas, Tree	1.85	.40	.40
680	8¢ Royal Canadian Legion	1.00	.20	.15

1976 Commemoratives

684   692   697   704

687   700

681-703	Set of 23	...	16.75	12.75
681	8¢ Olympic Ceremonies...........................	.95	.20	.15
682	20¢ Olympic Ceremonies.........................	2.75	.60	.50
683	25¢ Olympic Ceremonies.........................	3.50	.75	.70
684	20¢ Olympics - Communication Arts.....	5.25	1.10	.65
685	25¢ Olympics - Handcraft Tools............	5.75	1.20	.70
686	50¢ Olympics - Performing Arts	9.00	1.95	1.20
687	$1 Olympic Site - Tower and Church	12.00	2.35	1.90
688	$2 Olympic Site - Olympic Stadium.......	23.50	4.50	4.00
689	20¢ Winter Olympic Games	3.25	.75	.65
690	20¢ HABITAT - U.N. Conference	2.00	.45	.45
691	10¢ U.S. Bicentennial - B. Franklin	1.20	.25	.20
692-93	8¢ Royal Military College, attd.	1.00	.45	.40
692-93	Set of 2 Singles	...	.40	.30
694	20¢ Olympiad for Physically Disabled...	2.85	.60	.55
695-96	8¢ Authors,R. Service, G. Guevremont att	1.00	.45	.35
695-96	Set of 2 Singles	...	.40	.30
697	8¢ Xmas - Stained Glass Window.........	.75	.20	.15
698	10¢ Xmas - Stained Glass Window.......	.95	.20	.15
699	20¢ Xmas - Stained Glass Window.......	1.95	.40	.40
700-03	10¢ Canadian Inland Ships, attached ...	1.60	1.25	1.25
700-03	Set of 4 Singles	...	1.20	1.10

1977 Commemoratives

704,732-51	Set of 21..	...	5.50	3.95
704	25¢ Queen Elizabeth II Silver Jubilee ...	2.75	.60	.50

1977-1979 Definitive Issues, Perf. 12 x 12½

707   723   726

1977-1979 Definitive Issues, Perf. 12 x 12½

Scott's No.		Plate Block	F-VF NH	F-VF Used
705-27	Set of 22..	...	13.50	4.50
705	1¢ Wildflower - Bottle Gentian	.50	.20	.15
707	2¢ Wildflower - W. Columbine	.50	.20	.15
708	3¢ Wildflower - Canada Lily.....................	.60	.20	.15
709	4¢ Wildflower - Hepatica.........................	.60	.20	.15
710	5¢ Wildflower - Shooting Star	.60	.20	.15
711	10¢ Wildflower - Lady's Slipper	.90	.22	.15
711a	10¢ Same (1978, Perf. 13).....................	.90	.22	.15
712	12¢ Wildflower - Jewelweed,			
	Pf. 13 x 13½ (1978)	1.50	.30	.20
713	12¢ Elizabeth II, Perf. 13 x 13½	1.20	.25	.15
713a	12¢ Booklet Sngl., Perf. 12 x 12½	...	.35	.25
714	12¢ Houses of Parliament, Perf. 13 ('78).	1.10	.22	.15
715	14¢ Houses of Parliament, Perf. 13 ('78).	1.20	.25	.15
716	14¢ Eliz. II, 13 x 13½ ('78).....................	1.20	.25	.15
716a	14¢ Bklt. Sgl., Perf. 12 x 12½ ('78)..........	...	.35	.15
716b	14¢ B. Pane of 25, Perf. 12 x 12½ ('78) ..	...	5.75	...
717	15¢ Tree - Trembling Aspen, Perf. 13½ ..	1.85	.40	.15
718	20¢ Tree - Doug. Fir, Perf. 13½.............	1.65	.35	.15
719	25¢ Tree - Sugar Maple, Perf. 13½	2.00	.45	.15
720	30¢ Trees - Red Oak, Perf. 13½ ('78)	2.25	.50	.15
721	35¢ Trees - Winter Pine, Perf. 13½ ('79).	2.70	.60	.20
723	50¢ Streets-Prairie Town, Perf.13½ ('78)	4.35	.95	.25
723A	50¢ Same, "1978" on License Plate	4.25	.90	.20
724	75¢ Streets-Row Houses, Perf.13½ ('78)	5.75	1.25	.30
725	80¢ Streets-Maritime, Perf. 13½ ('79)	6.50	1.35	.35
726	$1 Bay of Fundy, Perf. 13½ ('79).............	7.50	1.65	.45
726a	$1 Untagged(1981).................................	8.50	1.85	.55
727	$2 Kluane National Park, Perf.13½ ('79) .	16.00	3.50	1.00
729	12¢ Parliament, Coil, Perf. 10 Vert..........	...	.24	.15
730	14¢ Parliament, Coil, Perf. 10 Vert. ('78).	...	.28	.15
	NOTE: Also see #781-806			

1977 Commemoratives (continued)

733   736   738

741   744   748

732	12¢ Wildlife - Eastern Cougar	1.10	.22	.15
733-34	12¢ Thomson Paintings, attd.................	1.10	.45	.40
733-34	Set of 2 Singles	...	.44	.30
735	12¢ Canadian-born Gov. Generals	1.10	.22	.15
736	12¢ Order of Canada 10th Anniv...........	1.10	.22	.15
737	12¢ Peace Bridge - 50th Anniv..............	1.10	.22	.15
738-39	12¢ Pioneers,Bernier,Fleming att..........	1.10	.45	.40
738-39	Set of 2 Singles	...	.44	.30
740	25¢ Parliamentary Conference..............	3.00	.65	.65
741	10¢ Christmas - Christmas Star	.95	.20	.15
742	12¢ Christmas - Angelic Choir...............	1.10	.22	.15
743	25¢ Christmas - Christ Child	2.20	.45	.40
744-47	12¢ Sailing Ships, attached....................	1.15	.90	.90
744-47	Set of 4 Singles	...	.85	.75
748-49	12¢ Inuit Hunting, attached	1.10	.45	.40
748-49	Set of 2 Singles, Seal, Spear Fishing....	...	.44	.30
750-51	12¢ Inuit Hunting, attached	1.10	.45	.40
750-51	Set of 2 Singles, Caribou, Walrus	...	.44	.30

1978 Commemoratives

752-56,757-79	Set of 28	...	9.75	6.50
752	12¢ Peregrine Falcon	1.10	.24	.15
753	12¢ CAPEX, 12p Queen Victoria	1.00	.22	.15
754	14¢ CAPEX, 10p Cartier	1.20	.25	.15
755	30¢ CAPEX, ½p Queen Victoria	2.50	.55	.40
756	$1.25 CAPEX, 6p Prince Albert	9.00	1.95	.95
756a	$1.69 CAPEX Souvenir Sheet	...	2.85	2.75
757	14¢ Commonwealth Games, Symbol....	1.15	.24	.15
758	30¢ Commonwealth Games, Badminton	2.75	.60	.40

1978 Commemoratives (continued)

| 759 | 765 | 776 |

| 753 | 763 | 768 |

Scott's No.		Plate Block	F-VF NH	F-VF Used
759-60	14¢ Commonwealth Games, attd.............	1.20	.50	.40
759-60	Set of 2 Singles, Stadium,Running	...	.48	.30
761-62	30¢ Commonwealth Games, attd.............	2.50	1.10	1.10
761-62	Set of 2 Singles, Edmonton, Bowls...........	...	1.00	.90
763-64	14¢ Captain Cook, attached.....................	1.20	.50	.40
763-64	Set of 2 Singles	...	.48	.30
765-66	14¢ Resource Development, attd..............	1.20	.50	.40
765-66	Set of 2 Singles	...	.48	.30
767	14¢ Canadian National Exhibition	1.20	.24	.15
768	14¢ Mere d'Youville, Beatified..................	1.20	.24	.15
769-70	14¢ Travels of Inuit, attached....................	1.20	.50	.40
769-70	Set of 2 Singles, Woman Walking,Migration	...	.48	.30
771-72	14¢ Travels of Inuit, attached....................	1.20	.50	.40
771-72	Set of 2 Singles, Plane, Dogteam & Sled ..	...	.48	.30
773	12¢ Christmas, Madonna	.95	.20	.15
774	14¢ Christmas, Virgin & Child	1.15	.24	.15
775	30¢ Christmas, Virgin & Child	2.25	.50	.45
776-79	14¢ Sailing Ice Vessels, attd....................	1.40	1.20	1.10
776-79	Set of 4 Singles	...	1.10	.80

1979 Commemoratives

780,813-20,833-46	Set of 23	...	7.85	4.50
780	14¢ Quebec Winter Carnival	1.25	.25	.15

1977-1983 Definitives, Perf. 13 x 13½
Designs of #705-730 plus new designs

781-792	Set of 11	...	2.90	1.45
781	1¢ Wildflower, Bottle Gentian ('79).............	.50	.20	.15
781a	1¢ Bklt. Sgl., Perf. 12 x 12½	...	.20	.15
781b	B. Pane of 6 (2 #781a & 4 #713a)..............	...	1.25	...
782	2¢ Wildflower, W. Columbine (1979)...........	.50	.20	.15
782a	B. Pane of 7 (4 #782b, 3 #716a) ('78)	...	.90	...
782b	2¢ B. Sgl. Perf. 12 x 12½ ('78)	...	.20	.15
783	3¢ Wildflower-Canada Lily ('79)	.50	.20	.15
784	4¢ Wildflower-Hepatica ('79)	.60	.20	.15
785	5¢ Wildflower-Shooting Star ('79)...............	.60	.20	.15
786	10¢ Wildflower-Lady's Slipper (1979).........	.80	.20	.15
787	15¢ Wildflower-Canada Violet ('79).............	1.40	.30	.15
789	17¢ Elizabeth II ('79)	1.35	.28	.15
789a	B. Sgl. Perf. 12 x 12½ ('79)	...	.65	.50
789b	B. Pane of 25, Perf. 12 x 12½ ('79)............	...	6.75	...
790	17¢ Houses of Parliament / 1979..............	1.35	.28	.15
791	30¢ Elizabeth II (1982)............................	2.25	.50	.15
792	32¢ Elizabeth II (1983)............................	2.50	.55	.15
797	1¢ Parl. B. Sgl. Perf. 12 x 12½ ('79)	...	.35	.20
797a	B. Pane/6 (1 #797,3 #800,2 #789a)	...	.95	...
800	5¢ Parl. B. Sgl. Perf. 12 x 12½ ('79)	...	.20	.15
806	17¢ Parl. Coil, Perf. 10 Vert	...	.32	.15

1979 Commemoratives (continued)

| 813 | 815 | 817 |

1979 Commemoratives (continued)

| 821 | 839 | 843 |

Scott's No.		Plate Block	F-VF NH	F-VF Used
813	17¢ Wildlife, Turtle..................................	1.35	.30	.15
814	35¢ Wildlife, Whale	3.25	.70	.45
815-16	17¢ Postal Code, attached.......................	1.50	.60	.55
815-16	Set of 2 Singles	...	.55	.30
817-18	17¢ Writer F. Grove & Poet E. Nelligan att	1.50	.60	.55
817-18	Set of 2 Singles	...	.55	.30
819-20	17¢ Colonels, De Salaberry & By att........	1.50	.60	.55
819-20	Set of 2 Singles	...	.55	.40
821-32	17¢ Provincial Flags, Set of 12 Singles......	...	3.60	2.40
832a	Sheetlet of Twelve Flags..........................	...	3.75	3.75
833	17¢ Canoe-Kayak Meet............................	1.35	.28	.15
834	17¢ Women's Field Hockey.......................	1.35	.28	.15
835-36	17¢ Inuit, attached.................................	1.45	.60	.55
835-36	Set of 2 Singles, Summer Tent, Igloo	...	.55	.30
837-38	17¢ Inuit, attached.................................	1.45	.60	.55
837-38	Set of 2 Singles, Dance, Two Figures.........	...	.55	.30
839	15¢ Christmas - Antique Toy Train............	1.30	.28	.15
840	17¢ Christmas - Antique Toy Horse...........	1.40	.30	.15
841	35¢ Christmas - Antique Knitted Doll	2.90	.65	.45
842	17¢ Int'l. Year of the Child........................	1.35	.28	.15
843-44	17¢ Flying Boats, attached.......................	1.45	.60	.55
843-44	Set of 2 Singles	...	.55	.30
845-46	35¢ Flying Boats, attached.......................	3.20	1.35	1.25
845-46	Set of 2 Singles	...	1.30	1.00

1980 Commemoratives

849	856	860	870
847-77	Set of 31	...	11.50	6.95
847	17¢ Arctic Islands	1.35	.28	.15
848	35¢ Winter Olympics, Skier.......................	2.85	.60	.55
849-50	17¢ Artists,Harris,Hebert attached	1.45	.60	.55
849-50	Set of 2 Singles	...	.55	.36
851-52	35¢ Artists,Fuller, O'Brien attached	2.95	1.30	1.25
851-52	Set of 2 Singles	...	1.20	1.00
853	17¢ Wildlife Atlantic Whitefish	1.60	.35	.15
854	17¢ Wildlife Greater Prairie Chicken	1.60	.35	.15
855	17¢ Montreal Flower Show	1.35	.28	.15
856	17¢ Rehabilitation Congress	1.35	.28	.15

857	865	873
857-58	17¢ "O Canada" Centenary, attd...............	1.45	.60	.55
857-58	Set of 2 Singles	...	.55	.30
859	17¢ John George Diefenbaker	1.35	.28	.15
860-61	17¢ Musicians, Albani, Willan attached......	1.45	.60	.55
860-61	Set of 2 Singles	...	.55	.35
862	17¢ Ned Hanlan, Oarsman.......................	1.35	.28	.15
863	17¢ Saskatchewan, Wheat Field...............	1.35	.28	.15
864	17¢ Alberta, Strip Mining	1.35	.28	.15
865	35¢ Uranium Resources...........................	3.00	.65	.50
866-67	17¢ Inuit Spirits, attached.......................	1.45	.60	.55
866-67	Set of 2 Singles, Sedna, Return-Sun	...	.55	.30
868-69	35¢ Inuit Spirits, attached.......................	2.95	1.30	1.25
868-69	Set of 2 Singles, Bird Spirit, Shaman	...	1.20	1.00
870	15¢ Christmas, "Christmas Morning"	1.20	.25	.15
871	17¢ Christmas, "Sleigh Ride"....................	1.35	.28	.15
872	35¢ Christmas, "McGill Cab Stand"	2.90	.60	.45
873-74	17¢ Military Aircraft, attached..................	1.50	.65	.55
873-74	Set of 2 Singles	...	.60	.30
875-76	35¢ Military Aircraft, attached..................	2.95	1.30	1.25
875-76	Set of 2 Singles	...	1.20	1.00
877	17¢ E.P. Lachapelle, Physician.................	1.35	.28	.15

1981 Commemoratives

879-82   **889**

Scott's No. 878-906		Plate Block	F-VF NH	F-VF Used
	Set of 29	...	9.35	5.25
878	17¢ 18th Century Mandora	1.35	.28	.15
879-82	17¢ Feminists, attached	1.50	1.25	1.20
879-82	Set of 4 Singles	...	1.20	.70
883	17¢ Endangered Wildlife, Marmot	1.35	.30	.15
884	35¢ Endangered Wildlife, Wood Bison .	3.25	.75	.70
885-86	17¢ Beatified Women, attached...........	1.45	.60	.55
885-86	Set of 2 Singles	...	.55	.30
887	17¢ Marc-Aurele Fortin, Painter	1.35	.28	.15
888	17¢ Frederic H. Varley, Painter............	1.35	.28	.15
889	35¢ Paul-Emile Borduas, Painter.........	2.95	.60	.60
890-93	17¢ Historic Maps, attached strip......... (8)	3.00	1.25	1.20
890-93	Set of 4 Singles	...	1.20	.80
894-95	17¢ Botanists Marie-Victorin, Macoun, att	1.45	.60	.55
894-95	Set of 2 Singles	...	.55	.30
896	17¢ Montreal Rose...........................	1.35	.28	.15
897	17¢ Niagara-on-the-Lake...................	1.35	.28	.15
898	17¢ Acadian Congress Centenary	1.35	.28	.15
899	17¢ Aaron Mosher Labor	1.35	.28	.15
900	15¢ 1781 Christmas Tree...................	1.15	.25	.15
901	15¢ 1881 Christmas Tree...................	1.15	.25	.15
902	15¢ 1981 Christmas Tree...................	1.15	.25	.15
903-04	17¢ Aircraft, attached	1.50	.65	.55
903-04	Set of 2 Singles	...	.60	.30
905-06	35¢ Aircraft, attached	2.95	1.25	1.20
905-06	Set of 2 Singles	...	1.20	1.00

907   **909**   **914**

1981 "A" Interim Definitives

907	(30¢) "A" and Maple Leaf, Perf. 13 x 13½	2.35	.50	.15
908	(30¢) "A" and Maple Leaf, Coil.............	...	.80	.18

1982 Commemoratives

909-13,914-16,954,967-75	Set of 18	...	10.95	6.15
909-13	30¢-60¢ Youth Exhibition, Set of 5........		3.15	2.15
909	30¢ 1851 3d Beaver	2.40	.50	.18
910	30¢ 1908 15¢ Champlain	2.40	.50	.18
911	35¢ 1935 10¢ Mountie	2.85	.60	.55
912	35¢ 1928 10¢ Mt. Hurd	2.85	.60	.55
913	60¢ 1929 50¢ Bluenose	5.75	1.15	.90
913a	$1.90 Exhibition Souvenir Sheet..........	...	3.50	3.50
914	30¢ Jules Leger, Governor-Gen'l	2.40	.50	.15
915	30¢ Marathon of Hope - Terry Fox........	2.40	.50	.15
916	30¢ New Consitution	2.40	.50	.15

1982-89 Regular Issue

917   **923**   **927**   **931**

Scott's No.		Plate Block	F-VF NH	F-VF Used
917-37	Set of 23	...	29.95	9.65
#917-22,927-30,932-33 Artifacts				
917	1¢ Decoy, Perf. 14 x 13½.....................	.50	.20	.15
917a	1¢ Perf. 13 x 13½ (1985)	.50	.20	.15
918	2¢ Fishing Spear, Perf. 14 x 13½.........	.50	.20	.15
918a	2¢ Perf. 13 x 13½ (1984)	.50	.20	.15
919	3¢ Stable Lantern, Perf. 14 x 13½........	.50	.20	.15
919a	3¢ Perf. 13 x 13½ (1985)	.50	.20	.15
920	5¢ Bucket, Perf. 14 x 13½	.60	.20	.15
920a	5¢ Perf. 13 x 13½ (1985)	.60	.20	.15
921	10¢ Weathercock, Perf. 14 x 13½	.90	.20	.15
921a	10¢ Perf. 13 x 13½ (1985)	1.10	.28	.15
922	20¢ Ice Skates...................................	1.75	.38	.15
923	30¢ Maple Leaf, Red & Blue Pf.13x13½	2.30	.50	.15
923a	Bklt. Pane of 20, Pf. 12 x 12½	...	10.75	...
923b	Bklt. Sgl., Pf. 12 x 12½	...	.75	.25
924	32¢ Maple Leaf, Red & Brown on Beige, Pf. 13 x 13½ ('83)	2.30	.55	.15
924a	Bklt. Pane of 25, Pf. 12 x 12½ ('83)	...	14.50	...
924b	Bklt. Sgl., Pf. 12 x 12½ ('83).................	...	.75	.35
925	34¢ Parliament Library ('85)	2.50	.60	.15
925a	Parl. Bklt. Pane of 25 ('85)	...	13.75	...
925b	Bluer sky, Pf. 13½ x 14, bklt. sgl('86)....	...	.95	.25
925c	Same, Bklt. Pane of 25 (1986)	...	14.95	...
926	34¢ Queen Elizabeth II ('85)	2.50	.60	.15
926A	36¢ Queen Elizabeth II ('87)	19.50	3.75	2.25
926B	36¢ Parliamentary Library ('87)	2.75	.60	.15
926Bc	Booklet Pane of 10 ('87)	...	6.00	...
926Bd	Booklet Pane of 25 ('87)	...	14.50	...
926Be	Bklt. Sgl., Perf. 13½ x 14 ('87)	...	.75	.25
927	37¢ Wooden Plow ('83)	3.00	.65	.20
928	39¢ Settle Bed ('85)	3.25	.70	.20
929	48¢ Hand Hewn Cradle ('83)	4.25	.90	.30
930	50¢ Sleigh (1985)	4.00	.85	.25
931	60¢ Ontario Street Scene...................	5.50	1.20	.30
932	64¢ Wood Burning Stove ('83)	5.25	1.10	.35
933	68¢ Spinning Wheel (1985)...................	5.25	1.15	.35
934	$1.00 Glacier National Park ('84)	8.00	1.75	.45
935	$1.50 Waterton Lakes Nat'l. Park..........	12.50	2.75	.60
936	$2.00 Banff National Park ('85)	16.00	3.50	.95
937	$5.00 Point Pelee Nat'l. Park ('83).........	37.50	8.50	2.00

NOTE: Also see #1080-84

Booklet Stamps

938-48	Set of 11	...	4.35	1.80
938	1¢ Parl. East, Bklt. Sgl. ('87)	...	.20	.15
939	2¢ West Parl. Bldg., Booklet Sgl. ('85) ..	...	.20	.15
939a	Slate Green, bklt. sgl. ('89)	...	.20	.15
940	5¢ Maple Leaf, Booklet Single	...	.20	.15
941	5¢ East Parl. Bldg., Booklet Sgl. ('85) ...	...	.35	.15
942	6¢ Parl., West B. Bldg. ('87)	...	.25	.15
943	8¢ Maple Leaf, Bkt. Single ('83)	...	.40	.15
944	10¢ Maple Leaf, Booklet Single	...	.35	.20
945	30¢ Maple Leaf, Red, Bklt. Sgl.	...	.70	.20
945a	Bklt. Pane of 4 (2 #940,#944,#945) Pf. 12 x 12½	...	1.20	...
946	32¢ Maple Leaf, Brown, Bklt. Sgl. ('83) .	...	.60	.20
946b	Bklt. Pane of 4 (2 #941, #943, #946, Pf. 12 x 12½)	...	1.15	...
947	34¢ Center Parl. Bldg., Bklt. Sgl. ('85)...	...	.85	.20
947a	B. Pane of 6 (3 #939,2 #941, #947)	...	1.50	...
948	36¢ Parl. Library, Bklt. Sgl. ('87)............	...	.70	.20
948a	Vend Bklt. of 5 (2 #938,2 #942, #948)...	...	1.10	...

Coil Stamps

950-53	Set of 4	...	2.65	.60
950	30¢ Maple Leaf, Red..........................	...	.80	.20
951	32¢ Maple Leaf, Brown ('83)	...	.65	.15
952	34¢ Parliament Red Brown ('85)	...	.65	.15
953	36¢ Parliament Dark Red ('87)..............	...	.65	.15

1982 Commemoratives (continued)

955   **969**   **973**

954	30¢ Salvation Army	2.40	.50	.15

1982 Canada Day Paintings

955-66	30¢ Canada Day Paintings, Set of 12 Sgls......................................	...	6.60	3.50
966a	Sheetlet of 12 Paintings	...	7.00	7.00

1982 Commemoratives (continued)

Scott's No.		Plate Block	F-VF NH	F-VF Used
967	30¢ Regina Centennial	2.40	.50	.15
968	30¢ Henley Rowing Regatta	2.40	.50	.15
969-70	30¢ Bush Aircraft, attached	2.40	1.10	.90
969-70	Set of 2 Singles	...	1.00	.30
971-72	60¢ Bush Aircraft, attached	5.00	2.00	1.90
971-72	Set of 2 Singles	...	1.95	1.60
973	30¢ Christmas, Nativity	2.40	.50	.15
974	35¢ Christmas, Shepherds	2.75	.60	.45
975	60¢ Christmas, Wise Men	4.75	1.00	.70

1983 Commemoratives

Scott's No.		Plate Block	F-VF NH	F-VF Used
976-82,993-1008 Set of 23		...	**20.50**	**9.50**
976	32¢ Communications Year	2.60	.50	.18
977	$2 Commonwealth Day	35.00	7.50	3.25
978-79	32¢ Poet L. Conan, Author E. Pratt attached	2.60	1.15	1.00
978-79	Set of 2 Singles	...	1.10	.40

	980	981	983

980	32¢ St. John Ambulance	2.80	.55	.18
981	32¢ World University Games	2.80	.55	.18
982	64¢ World University Games	5.50	1.10	.75

1983 Historic Forts Commemorative Booklet

983-92	32¢ Historic Forts, Set of 10 Bklt. Sgls.	...	6.00	4.50
992a	Booklet Pane of 10	...	6.50	6.50

	993	995	996

1983 Commemoratives (continued)

993	32¢ Boy Scout Jamboree	2.50	.55	.18
994	32¢ World Council of Churches	2.50	.55	.18
995	32¢ Sir Humphrey Gilbert	2.50	.55	.18
996	32¢ Discovery of Nickel	2.50	.55	.18
997	32¢ Josiah Henson	2.50	.55	.18
998	32¢ Antoine Labelle	2.50	.55	.18

	999	1003	1004

999-1000	32¢ Steam Locomotives, attd	2.50	1.15	1.10
999-1000	Set of 2 Singles	...	1.10	.50
1001	37¢ Locomotive Samson 0-6-0,	3.00	.65	.55
1002	64¢ Locomotive Adam Brown 4-4-0,	5.50	1.10	.95
1003	32¢ Dalhousie Law School	2.50	.55	.18
1004	32¢ Christmas, Urban Church	2.50	.55	.18
1005	37¢ Christmas, Family	2.75	.60	.45
1006	64¢ Christmas, Rural Church	5.50	1.10	.75
1007-08	32¢ Army Regiment Uniforms, attd	2.50	1.15	1.00
1007-08	Set of 2 Singles	...	1.10	.40

FROM 1941 TO PRESENT, ADD 20% FOR VERY FINE QUALITY
Minimum of 10¢ Per Stamp

1984 Commemoratives

1013	1038

Scott's No.		Plate Block	F-VF NH	F-VF Used
1009-15,1028-39,1040-44 Set of 24		...	**14.50**	**7.50**
1009	32¢ Yellowknife	2.50	.55	.18
1010	32¢ Montreal Symphony	2.50	.55	.18
1011	32¢ Cartier Landing in Quebec	2.50	.55	.18
1012	32¢ Voyage of Tall Ships	2.50	.55	.18
1013	32¢ Red Cross Society	2.50	.55	.18
1014	32¢ New Brunswick	2.50	.55	.18
1015	32¢ St. Lawrence Seaway	2.50	.55	.18

1984 Provincial Landscapes

1016-27	32¢ Canada Day Paintings, Set of 12 Sgls.	...	7.75	2.95
1027a	Sheetlet of Twelve Paintings	...	7.95	7.95

1984 Commemoratives (continued)

1028	32¢ United Empire Loyalists	2.50	.55	.18
1029	32¢ Catholic Church in Newfoundland..	2.50	.55	.22
1030	32¢ Papal Visit	2.50	.55	.22
1031	64¢ Papal Visit	5.25	1.10	.55
1032-35	32¢ Lighthouses, attd	2.50	2.25	1.20
1032-35	Set of 4 Singles	...	2.10	.90
1036-37	32¢ Steam Locomotives, attd	2.50	1.20	1.00
1036-37	Set of 2 Singles	...	1.10	.40
1038	37¢ Locomotive Grand Trunk 2-6-0	3.15	.65	.55
1039	64¢ Locomotive Canadian Pacific 4-6-0	5.75	1.20	1.00
1039a	$1.65 Locomotive Souvenir Sheet	...	3.25	3.25
1040	32¢ Christmas, Annunciation	2.50	.55	.20
1041	37¢ Christmas, Three Kings	2.85	.60	.50
1042	64¢ Christmas, Snow in Bethlehem	5.25	1.10	.75
1043	32¢ Royal Canadian Air Force	2.50	.55	.20
1044	32¢ Newspaper, La Presse	2.50	.55	.20

1985 Commemoratives

1046	1062	1075	1076

Scott's No.		Plate Block	F-VF NH	F-VF Used
1045-49,1060-66,1067-70,1071-76 Set of 22		...	**13.75**	**6.25**
1045	32¢ Int'l. Youth Year	2.50	.55	.20
1046	32¢ Canadian Astronaut	2.50	.55	.20
1047-48	32¢ Decade of Women T. Casgrain, E. Murphy, attd	2.50	1.20	1.00
1047-48	Set of 2 Singles	...	1.10	.40
1049	32¢ Gabriel Dumont, Metis	2.50	.55	.20

1985 Historic Forts Commemorative Booklet

1050-59	34¢ Historic Forts, Set/10 Bklt Sgls	...	6.50	4.50
1059a	Booklet Pane/10	...	7.00	7.00

1985 Commemoratives (continued)

1060	34¢ Louis Hebert	2.75	.60	.20
1061	34¢ Interparliamentary Union	2.75	.60	.20
1062	34¢ Girl Guides 7th Anniv	2.75	.60	.20
1063-66	34¢ Lighthouses, attd	2.95	2.60	2.30
1063-66	Set of 4 Singles	...	2.50	1.00
1066b	$1.36 Lighthouse Souvenir Sheet of 4 ..	...	2.75	2.50
1067	34¢ Christmas, Santa Claus	2.75	.60	.20
1068	39¢ Christmas, Coach	3.25	.65	.50
1069	68¢ Christmas, Tree	5.50	1.15	.75
1070	32¢ Christmas,Polar Float Bklt. Sgl	...	.75	.20
1070a	Christmas Bklt. Pane/10	...	7.00	7.00
1071-72	34¢ Locomotives, attd	2.75	1.20	.50
1071-72	Set of 2 Singles	...	1.15	.40
1073	39¢ Locomotives #010a	3.25	.70	.65
1074	68¢ Locomotives #H4D	5.50	1.15	.90
1075	34¢ Royal Canadian Navy	2.75	.60	.20
1076	34¢ Montreal Fine Arts Museum	2.75	.60	.20

| | 1078 | | 1084 | | 1117 | |

Scott's No.		Plate Block	F-VF NH	F-VF Used
1077-79,1090-1107,1108-15,1116b,1117-21				
	Set of 32	...	22.50	9.50
1077	34¢ 1988 Calgary Winter Olympics, Map	2.75	.60	.20
1078	34¢ EXPO '86 Pavilion...........................	2.75	.60	.20
1079	39¢ EXPO '86 Communications............	3.00	.65	.50

1986-87 Regular Issues

		Plate Block	F-VF NH	F-VF Used
1080-84	Set of 5	...	11.00	2.50
1080	25¢ Artifact Butter Stamp (1987)..........	2.10	.45	.15
1081	42¢ Artifact Linen Chest (1987)	3.75	.75	.20
1082	55¢ Artifact Iron Kettle (1987)	4.50	.95	.30
1083	72¢ Artifact Cart (1987)......................	6.00	1.25	.35
1084	$5 La Maurice Nat'l. Park	37.50	8.50	1.75

1986 Commemoratives (continued)

		Plate Block	F-VF NH	F-VF Used
1090	34¢ Philippe Aubert de Gaspe	2.75	.60	.20
1091	34¢ Molly Brant, Iroquois	2.75	.60	.20
1092	34¢ EXPO '86, Expo Center	2.75	.60	.20
1093	68¢ EXPO '86, Transportation	5.50	1.15	.55
1094	34¢ Canadian Forces Postal Serv	2.75	.60	.20
1095-98	34¢ Indigenous Birds, attd	3.00	2.50	2.25
1095-98	Set of 4 Singles	...	2.40	1.00
1099-1102	34¢ Canada Day,Inventions attd	3.00	2.50	2.25
1099-1102	Set of 4 Singles	...	2.40	.90
1103	34¢ Canadian Broadcasting Corp	2.75	.60	.20
1104-07	34¢ Canada Exploration, attd...............	3.00	2.50	2.00
1104-07	Set of 4 Singles	...	2.40	.90
1107b	$1.36 CAPEX '87, Exploration Souv. Sheet	...	2.75	2.65
1108-09	34¢ Frontier Peacemakers, attd............	2.75	1.20	1.00
1108-09	Set of 2 Singles	...	1.15	.40
1110	34¢ International Peace Year................	2.75	.60	.20
1111-12	34¢ Calgary Winter Olympics, attd........	2.75	1.20	.90
1111-12	Set of 2 Singles, Ice Hockey, Biathlon ..	...	1.15	.40
1113	34¢ Christmas, Angels	2.75	.60	.20
1114	39¢ Christmas, Angels	3.00	.65	.50
1115	68¢ Christmas, Angels	5.50	1.15	.75
1116	29¢ Christmas, Bklt. Sgl. Perf. 12½	...	2.25	.75
1116a	Bklt. Pane of 10, Perf. 12½	...	20.75	...
1116b	Bklt. Sgl., Perf. 13½	...	1.20	.35
1116c	Bklt. Pane of 10, Perf. 13½	...	11.50	...
1117	34¢ John Molson	2.75	.60	.20
1118-19	34¢ Locomotives, attd	2.75	1.20	.90
1118-19	Set of 2 Singles	...	1.15	.40
1120	39¢ Locomotive CN U2a	3.25	.70	.65
1121	68¢ Locomotive CP H1c	5.25	1.10	.90

| | 1122 | | 1130 | | 1134 | |

1987 Commemoratives

		Plate Block	F-VF NH	F-VF Used
1122-25,1126-54	Set of 33	...	20.50	8.95
1122-25	34¢-72¢ CAPEX '87 Set of 4.................	...	3.00	1.85
1122	34¢ 1st Toronto P.O.	2.75	.60	.20
1123	36¢ Nelson-Miramichi P.O.	2.85	.60	.22
1124	42¢ Saint Ours P.O.	3.25	.70	.60
1125	72¢ Battleford P.O.	5.65	1.20	.90
1125A	$1.84 CAPEX S/S	...	3.15	2.95
1126-29	34¢ Exploration,New France, attd.........	3.00	2.50	2.25
1126-29	Set of 4 Singles	...	2.40	.90
#1130-31	1988 Calgary Winter Olympics			
1130	36¢ Speed Skating.............................	2.75	.60	.20
1131	42¢ Bobsledding................................	3.25	.70	.60
1132	36¢ Volunteer Week............................	2.85	.60	.20
1133	36¢ Law Day	2.85	.60	.20
1134	36¢ Engineering Institute	2.85	.60	.20
1135-38	36¢ Canada Day, Communications, attd	3.00	2.50	2.25
1135-38	Set of 4 Singles	...	2.40	.90
1139-40	36¢ Steamships, attd..........................	2.85	1.20	1.00
1139-40	Set of 2 Singles	...	1.15	.45
1141-44	36¢ Underwater Archaeology, attd........	2.85	2.40	2.25
1141-44	Set of 4 Singles	...	2.30	.90

| | 1145 | | 1148 | | 1152-53 | |

Scott's No.		Plate Block	F-VF NH	F-VF Used
1145	36¢ Air Canada 50th Anniv	2.85	.60	.20
1146	36¢ Francophone Int'l. Summit...............	2.85	.60	.20
1147	36¢ Commonwealth Heads of Gov't......	2.85	.60	.20
1148	36¢ Christmas, Poinsettia	2.85	.60	.20
1149	42¢ Christmas, Holly Wreath................	3.25	.70	.60
1150	72¢ Christmas, Mistletoe	5.75	1.25	.85
1151	31¢ Christmas Gifts Bklt. Sgl	...	.75	.25
1151a	Christmas Bklt. Pane of 10...................	...	6.50	...
1152-53	36¢ Calgary Winter Olympics, attd........	2.85	1.20	1.00
1152-53	Set of 2 Singles Skiing, Ski Jumping.....	...	1.15	.45
1154	36¢ Grey Cup 75th Anniv	2.85	.60	.20

1987-91 Regular Issues

| | 1162 | 1165 | 1166 | 1173 | |

		Plate Block	F-VF NH	F-VF Used
1155-83	Set of 30	...	32.75	9.95
#1155-61, 1170-80 Mammals				
1155	1¢ Flying Squirrel, Pf. 13 x 13½ (1988).	.50	.20	.15
1155a	1¢ Perf 13 x 12½ (1991) .... (Blank)	8.75	1.75	1.25
1156	2¢ Porcupine (1988)...........................	.50	.20	.15
1157	3¢ Muskrat (1988)	.50	.20	.15
1158	5¢ Hare (1988)	.60	.20	.15
1159	6¢ Red Fox (1988)..............................	.70	.20	.15
1160	10¢ Skunk, Pf. 13 x 13½ (1988)............	.85	.20	.15
1160a	10¢ Perf. 13 x 12½ (1991) .... (Blank)	15.00	3.00	.50
1161	25¢ Beaver (1988)..............................	2.10	.45	.15
1162	37¢ Elizabeth II.................................	2.95	.65	.15
1163	37¢ Parliament Perf. 13½ x 13.............	2.95	.65	.15
1163a	Booklet Pane of 10 (1163c) ('88)...........	...	6.50	...
1163b	Booklet Pane of 25 (1163c) ('88)...........	...	16.50	...
1163c	Bklt. sgl., Pf. 13½ x 14 ('88)	...	.80	.18
1164	38¢ QE II pf. 13 x 12½ ('88)	3.00	.65	.15
1164a	Bklt. sgl., pf. 13 x 13½ ('88)	...	.90	.50
1164b	Bklt. Pane of 10 + 2 labels (1988)	...	6.50	...
1165	38¢ Parliament Clock Tower ('88)	3.00	.65	.15
1165a	Bklt. Pane of 10 + 2 labels (1988)	...	6.50	...
1165b	Bklt. Pane of 25 + 2 labels (1988)	...	18.75	...
1166	39¢ Flag & Clouds ('89).......................	3.50	.75	.15
1166a	Bklt. Pane of 10 (1989)	...	7.50	...
1166b	Bklt. Pane of 25 (1989)	...	18.75	...
1166c	Perf. 12½ x 13 ('90)............... (Blank)	22.50	4.50	.30
1167	39¢ Elizabeth II, Perf. 13 x 13½ ('90)....	3.25	.70	.15
1167a	Bklt. Pane of 10 (1990)........................	...	6.75	...
1167b	Perf. 13 ('90)......................... (Blank)	37.50	7.50	.40
1168	40¢ Elizabeth II ('90)..........................	3.25	.70	.15
1168a	Bklt. Pane of 10 + 2 labels (1990)	...	6.95	...
1169	40¢ Flag & Mountains ('90)	3.25	.70	.15
1169a	Bklt. Pane of 25 + 2 labels	...	18.50	...
1169b	Bklt. Pane of 10 + 2 labels	...	6.95	...
1170	43¢ Lynx ('88)	3.65	.80	.22
1171	44¢ Walrus Perf. 14½ x 14 ('89)	3.85	.85	.22
1171a	Bklt. Sgl. Perf. 12½ x 13 (1989)	...	1.25	.30
1171b	Perf. 12½ x 13, Bklt. Pane of 5+label....	...	5.95	...
1171c	Perf. 13½ x 13 ('89).................. (Blank)	750.00	150.00	19.50
1172	45¢ Pronghorn ('90) Perf. 14½ x 14 ('90)	3.75	.85	.30
1172f	Bklt. Sgl. Perf. 12½ x 13 ('90)	...	1.10	.35
1172b	Bklt. Pane of 5 + label, Perf. 12½ x 13..	...	5.50	...
1172d	Perf. 13 ('90)......................... (Blank)	55.00	11.75	1.10
1172A	46¢ Wolverine, Perf. 13 ('90)................	3.95	.85	.30
1172Ac	Wolverine,Bklt. Sgl. Perf. 12½ x 13 ('90)	...	.85	.35
1172Ae	Bklt. pn. of 5 + label, Perf. 12½x13 ('91)	...	4.25	...
1172Ag	Wolverine, Perf. 14½ x 14 ('90).............	8.00	1.65	.35
1173	57¢ Killer Whale ('88).........................	4.75	1.00	.35
1174	59¢ Musk-ox Perf. 14½ x 14 ('89)	5.75	1.25	.40
1174a	Perf. 13 ('89)......................... (Blank)	24.50	4.75	.60

1175　　　　　1183　　　　　1185

Scott's No.		Plate Block	F-VF NH	F-VF Used
1175	61¢ Timber Wolf Perf. 14½ x 14 ('90) ...	5.00	1.10	.40
1175a	Perf. 13 ('90).............................(Blank)	150.00	29.50	2.25
1176	63¢ Harbor Porpoise Perf. 14½ x 14 ('90)	5.50	1.15	.40
1176a	Perf. 13 (1990)........................(Blank)	8.75	1.75	.50
1177	74¢ Wapiti ('88)	6.50	1.30	.50
1178	76¢ Grizzly Bear, Perf. 14½ x 14 ('89) ..	6.75	1.35	.40
1178a	Bklt. sgl. perf. 12½ x 13 (1989)	...	2.25	.55
1178b	Bklt. pane of 5 + label, Perf. 12½x13....	...	10.75	...
1178c	Perf. 13 ....(Blank)	135.00	27.50	3.75
1179	78¢ Beluga ('90) Perf. 14½ x 14 ('90) ...	7.00	1.50	.55
1179a	Bklt. Pane of 5, Perf. 12½ x 13	...	13.50	...
1179b	Perf. 13 ('90)........................(Blank)	80.00	17.50	1.85
1179c	Blklt. Sgl. Perf. 12½ x 13 (1990)	...	1.95	.55
1180	80¢ Peary Caribou, Perf. 13 ('90).........	7.50	1.60	.55
1180a	Bklt. Sgl. Perf 12½ x 13 ('90)	...	1.85	.60
1180b	Bklt. Pane of 5+label, Perf. 12½x13 ('91)	...	8.95	...
1180c	Perf. 14½ x 14 ('91)	12.75	2.75	.60
1181	$1 Runnymede Library ('89).................	7.75	1.75	.50
1182	$2 McAdam Train Station ('89).............	15.50	3.50	1.00
1183	$5 Bonsecours Market ('90)	38.50	8.50	2.35

1988-90 Booklet Singles and Panes

1184-90	**Set of 7**		**3.50**	**1.20**
1184	1¢ Flag, Perf. 13½ x 14 (1990)		.20	.15
1184a	1¢ Perf. 12½ x 13 (1990)		5.75	2.25
1185	5¢ Flag, Perf. 13½ x 14 (1990)		.20	.15
1185a	5¢ Perf. 12½ x 13 (1990)		4.50	2.25
1186	6¢ Parliament (1988)......................		.35	.15
1187	37¢ Parl. Library ('88)		.65	.15
1187a	Bklt. Pane of 4 (#938,2 #942,#1187)		.95	...
1188	38¢ Parliament Center, ('89)		.65	.20
1188a	Bklt. pane of 5 (3 #939a, 1186, 1188)		.95	...
1189	39¢ Canadian Flag, ('90)		.80	.25
1189a	Bklt. pn. of 4 (#1184,2 #1185,#1189)		1.25	...
1189b	Perf. 12½ x 13............................		7.00	6.00
1189c	Same, Bklt. pn. of 4 (#1184a,2 #1185v,#1189v)		19.50	...
1190	40¢ Canadian Flag ('90)		.90	.25
1190a	Bklt. pane of 4 (2 #1184,1185,1190)		1.35	...

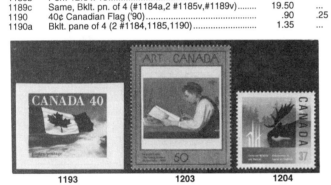

1193　　　　　1203　　　　　1204

1989-91 Self-Adhesive Stamps

1191	38¢ National Flag, bklt. sgl.	.80	.50
1191a	Booklet of 12	9.50	...
1192	39¢ Flag & Landscape, bklt. sgl. ('90) ...	.80	.50
1192a	Booklet of 12	9.50	...
1193	40¢ Flag & Seacoast, bklt. sgl. ('91)	.80	.50
1193a	Booklet of 12	9.50	...

1988-90 Coil Stamps, Perf. 10 Horizontal

1194-94c	**Set of 4**		**2.50**	**.60**
1194	37¢ Parliament Library ('88)		.65	.15
1194A	38¢ Parliament Library ('89)		.65	.15
1194B	39¢ Canadian Flag (1990)		.65	.20
1194C	40¢ Canadian Flag (1990).................		.70	.20

1988 Commemoratives

1195-1228	**Set of 34**.............................	...	**22.75**	**9.95**
1195-96	37¢ Winter Olympics, attd	2.95	1.30	.65
1195-96	Set of 2 Singles Alpine Skiing, Curling...	...	1.25	.45
1197	43¢ Winter Olympics, Figure Skating........	3.50	.75	.60
1198	74¢ Winter Olympics, Luge	5.75	1.30	.85
1199-1202	37¢ 18th Century Explorers, attd..........	2.95	2.65	1.75
1199-1202	Set of 4 Singles	...	2.60	1.00
1203	50¢ Canadian Art, The Young Reader.......	4.25	.95	.95
1204-05	37¢ Wildlife Conservation., attd	2.95	1.30	.90
1204-05	Set of 2 Singles, Duck, Moose	...	1.25	.50

1214　　　　　1215　　　　　1216

Scott's No.		Plate Block	F-VF NH	F-VF Used
1206-09	37¢ Science & Technology, attd	2.95	2.65	2.00
1206-09	Set of 4 Singles	...	2.60	1.00
1210-13	37¢ Butterflies, attd	2.95	2.65	2.00
1210-13	Set of 4 Singles	...	2.60	1.20
1214	37¢ St. John's Newfld. City Cent..........	2.75	.60	.20
1215	37¢ 4-H Clubs Anniversary	2.75	.60	.20
1216	37¢ Les Forges du Saint-Maurice	2.75	.60	.20
1217-20	37¢ Kennel Club Cent. (Dogs) attd	2.95	2.65	2.00
1217-20	Set of 4 Singles	...	2.60	1.20

1221　　　　　1223　　　　　1226　　　　　1228

1221	37¢ Canadian Baseball Sesqui	3.25	.70	.20
#1222-25	Icons of the Eastern Church			
1222	37¢ Christmas, Conception	2.95	.65	.20
1223	43¢ Christmas, Virgin and Child...........	3.95	.85	.65
1224	74¢ Christmas, Virgin and Child...........	5.25	1.25	.85
1225	32¢ Christmas Nativity, bklt. single		.65	.25
1225a	Bklt. Pane of 10..........................	...	6.25	...
1226	37¢ Bishop Charles Inglis	2.75	.60	.20
1227	37¢ Frances Ann Hopkins....................	2.75	.60	.20
1228	37¢ Angus Walters...........................	2.75	.60	.20

1989 Commemoratives

1229　　　　　1241　　　　　1249

1229-63	**Set of 34**	...	**22.95**	**9.50**
1229-32	38¢ Small Craft Series, attd	2.95	2.70	1.75
1229-32	Set of 4 Singles, Canoes and Kayak.....	...	2.60	1.00
1233-36	38¢ Explorers/Canadian North, attd......	2.95	2.70	1.75
1233-36	Set of 4 Singles	...	2.60	1.00
1237-40	38¢ Canada Day Photography, attd....	2.95	2.70	1.75
1237-40	Set of 4 Singles	...	2.60	1.00
1241	50¢ Art, Ceremonial Frontlet	4.50	1.00	.85
1243-44	38¢ Poets, Frechette, Lampman attd.......	2.95	1.35	.75
1243-44	Set of 2 Singles	...	1.30	.45
1245-48	38¢ Mushrooms, attd......................	2.95	2.70	1.75
1245-48	Set of 4 Singles	...	2.60	1.00
1249-50	38¢ Canadian Infantry Regiments, attd.	*225.00	1.50	.90
1249-50	Set of 2 Singles	...	1.45	.60

* Printing difficulties caused a severe shortage of inscription blocks.

| | 1251 | 1252 | 1260 |

Scott's No.		Plate Block	F-VF NH	F-VF Used
1251	38¢ International Trade	2.95	.65	.20
1252-55	38¢ Performing Arts,attd	2.95	2.70	1.25
1252-55	Set of 4 Singles	...	2.60	1.00
1256	38¢ Christmas Landscape, pf. 13 x 13½	3.00	.65	.20
1256a	Bklt. pane of 10, perf. 13 x 12½	...	29.50	...
1256b	Bklt. sgl., perf. 13 x 12½	...	3.25	.75
1257	44¢ Christmas Landscape	3.50	.75	.60
1257a	Bklt. pane of 5 + label	...	17.50	...
1258	76¢ Christmas Landscape	6.00	1.30	.95
1258a	Bklt. pane of 5 + label	...	22.50	...
1259	33¢ Christmas Landscape bklt. sgl	...	.70	.30
1259a	Bklt. Pane of 10	...	7.00	...
1260-63	38¢ WWII Outbreak, 50th Anniv., attd	2.95	2.70	1.25
1260-63	Set of 4 Singles	...	2.60	1.00

1990 Commemoratives

| | 1264 | 1270 | 1271 |

		Plate Block	F-VF NH	F-VF Used
1264-71,1274-1301	Set of 36	...	25.95	11.50
1264-65	39¢ Norman Bethune, attd	3.25	1.45	.85
1264-65	Set of 2 Singles	...	1.40	.50
1266-69	39¢ Small Crafts, attd	3.25	2.90	2.25
1266-69	Set of 4 Singles	...	2.80	1.00
1270	39¢ Multicultural Heritage of Canada	3.00	.65	.25
1271	50¢ Canadian Art, The West Wind	4.25	.90	.75

| 1272-73 | 1278 |

1990 Regular Issues				
1272-73	39¢ Postal Truck bklt. singles	...	1.40	.50
1273a	Bk. pn. of 8 (4 Eng. + 4 Fr. Inscriptions)	...	5.25	...
1273b	Bk. pn. of 9 (4 Eng. + 5 Fr. Inscriptions)	...	8.75	...
1990 Commemoratives (continued)				
1274-77	39¢ Dolls, attd.	3.25	2.90	2.25
1274-77	Set of 4 Singles	...	2.80	1.00
1278	39¢ Canada Day, 25 Anniv. of Flag	3.00	.65	.25
1279-82	39¢ Prehistoric Life, attd	3.25	2.90	2.25
1279-82	Set of 4 Singles	...	2.80	1.00
1283-86	39¢ Forests, World Congress, attd	3.65	3.30	2.25
1283-86	Set of 4 Singles	...	3.20	1.00
1283a-86b	Miniature sheets of 4 (Set of 4)	...	19.50	...

| | 1287 | 1288 | 1293 | 1294 |

Scott's No.		Plate Block	F-VF NH	F-VF Used
1287	39¢ Weather Observations Sesqui.	3.00	.65	.20
1288	39¢ International Literacy Year	3.00	.65	.20
1289-92	39¢ Canadian Lore and Legend, attd	3.25	2.90	2.50
1289-92	Set of 4 Singles, Perf. 12½ x 13	...	2.80	1.80
1289v-92v	39¢ Lore, Perf. 12½ x 12, attd	...	22.50	12.00
1289v-92v	Set of 4 Singles, Perf. 12½ x 12	...	22.00	11.00
1293	39¢ Agnes Macphail, 1st Woman MP	3.00	.65	.20
1294	39¢ Christmas, Virgin Mary	3.00	.65	.20
1294a	Booklet Pane of 10	...	6.50	...
1295	45¢ Christmas, Mother & Child	3.50	.75	.55
1295a	Booklet Pane of 5 + label	...	6.50	...
1296	78¢ Christmas, Children/Raven	6.00	1.35	.75
1296a	Booklet Pane of 5 + label	...	10.75	...
1297	34¢ Christmas, Rebirth, bklt. sgl	...	.60	.20
1297a	Bklt. Pane of 10	...	6.00	...
1298-1301	39¢ WWII, Canada Mobilizes, attd	3.85	3.50	3.25
1298-1301	Set of 4 Singles	...	3.40	2.40

1991 Commemoratives

| | 1302-05 | 1310 | 1316 |

		Plate Block	F-VF NH	F-VF Used
1302-43,1345-48	Set of 45	...	33.50	11.95
1302-05	40¢ Physicians, attd	3.50	3.00	2.25
1302-05	Set of 4 Singles	...	2.90	1.00
1306-09	40¢ Prehistoric Life in Canada, attd	3.50	3.00	2.25
1306-09	Set of 4 Singles	...	2.90	1.00
1310	50¢ Canadian Art, Emily Carr	4.25	.90	.75
1311-15	40¢ Public Gardens, bklt. sgls, strip of 5	...	3.75	2.75
1311-15	Set of 5 Singles	...	3.65	1.25
1315b	Booklet Pane of 10	...	6.95	...
1316	40¢ Canada Day	3.25	.70	.20
1317-20	40¢ Small Craft, attd	3.50	3.00	2.25
1317-20	Set of 4 Singles	...	2.90	1.00
1321-25	40¢ River Heritage, bklt. sgls., strip of 5	...	3.75	2.75
1321-25	Set of 5 Singles	...	3.65	1.25
1325b	Booklet Pane of 10	...	6.95	...
1326-29	40¢ Ukrainian Migration to Canada, attd	3.50	3.00	2.25
1326-29	Set of 4 Singles	...	2.90	1.00
1330-33	40¢ Dangerous Public Service orgs,attd	3.50	3.00	2.25
1330-33	Set of 4 Singles	...	2.90	1.00
1334-37	40¢ Canadian Folktales, attd	3.50	3.00	2.25
1334-37	Set of 4 Singles	...	2.90	1.00

| | 1338 | 1339 | 1345 |

1338	40¢ Queen's University, bklt. single	...	.75	.25
1338a	Booklet Pane of 10	...	6.95	...
1339	40¢ Christmas, Santa at Fireplace	3.25	.75	.20
1339a	Booklet Pane of 10	...	6.95	...
1340	46¢ Christmas,Santa with Tree	3.75	.80	.55
1340a	Booklet Pane of 5	...	4.95	...
1341	80¢ Christmas, Sinterklass & Girl	6.50	1.40	.75
1341a	Booklet Pane of 5	...	8.50	...
1342	35¢ Greet More, Santa Claus, bklt. sgl.	...	.65	.20
1342a	Bklt. Pane of 10	...	6.35	...

1991-96 Regular Issues (continued)

Scott's No.		Plate Block	F-VF NH	F-VF Used
1343	40¢ Basketball Centennial........................	3.25	.70	.25
1344	40¢, 46¢, 80¢ Basketball S/S of 3	...	3.75	3.75
1345-48	40¢ World War II Annic., block or strip	3.50	3.00	2.25
1345-48	Set of 4 Singles	...	2.90	1.20

1991-96 Regular Issues

| 1349 | 1358 | 1359 | 1361 |

1349-78	Set of 28	...	31.50	9.95

#1349-55, 1361-74 Edible Berries

1349	1¢ Blueberry (1992)	.50	.20	.15
1350	2¢ Strawberry (1992)	.50	.20	.15
1351	3¢ Crowberry (1992)	.50	.20	.15
1352	5¢ Rose Hip (1992)	.50	.20	.15
1353	6¢ Black Raspberry (1992)	.60	.20	.15
1354	10¢ Kinnikinnik (1992)	.80	.20	.15
1355	25¢ Saskatoon Berry (1992)	1.80	.42	.20
1358	42¢ Canadian Flag & Rolling Hills	3.25	.70	.20
1358a	Booklet Pane of 10	...	7.50	...
1358b	Booklet Pane of 50	...	36.50	...
1358c	Booklet Pane of 25	...	18.95	...
1359	42¢ QE II, Karsh Portrait	3.25	.70	.20
1359a	Booklet Pane of 10	...	7.50	...
1360	43¢ QE II Karsh Portrait (1992)	3.50	.75	.20
1360a	Booklet Pane of 10	...	7.50	...
1360B	43¢ Flag & Prairie (1992)	3.50	.75	.20
1360Bc	Booklet Pane of 10	...	7.50	...
1360Bd	Booklet Pane of 25	...	18.95	...
1360H	45¢ Elizabeth II ('95)	3.50	.75	.20
1360Hi	Booklet Pane of 10	...	8.50	...
1360J	45¢ Flag Perf. 14½ ('95)	3.50	.75	.20
1360Jk	Booklet Pane of 10	...	7.50	...
1360Jl	Booklet Pane of 25	...	18.50	...
1360Jm	45¢ Flag Perf. 13½ x 13	...	.75	.30
1360Jn	Booklet Pane of 10	...	7.50	...
1360Jo	Booklet Pane of 25	...	18.50	...
1361	48¢ McIntosh Apple Tree, Perf. 13............	3.75	.80	.20
1361a	Bklt. single, Perf. 14½x14 on 3 sides	...	.95	.30
1361b	Booklet Pane of 5	...	4.50	...
1362	49¢ Delicious Apple, Perf. 13 (1992).........	3.85	.80	.20
1362a	Perf. 14½ x 14	...	.95	.30
1362b	Booklet Pane of 5, Perf. 14½ x 14............	...	4.50	...
1362v	Booklet Pane of 5, Perf. 13......................	...	7.95	...
1363	50¢ Snow Apple (1994)	3.95	.85	.25
1363a	Booklet Pane of 5	...	4.75	...
1363b	50¢ Perf. 14½ x 14 (1995)......................	...	1.00	.40
1363c	Booklet Pane of 5, Pf. 14½ x 14	...	4.75	...
1364	52¢ Gravenstein Apple Perf. 13 ('95)	4.25	.90	.25
1364a	Booklet Pane of 5	...	4.50	...
1364b	52¢ Perf. 14 ½ x 14	...	1.10	.35
1364c	Booklet Pane of 5	...	5.25	...
1366	65¢ Black Walnut Tree	4.95	1.10	.40
1367	67¢ Beaked Hazlenut (1992)	5.25	1.15	.40
1368	69¢ Shagbark Hickory (1994)	5.50	1.20	.40
1369	71¢ American Chestnut ('95)	5.95	1.20	.45
1371	84¢ Stanley Plum Tree, Perf. 13	6.50	1.40	.40
1371a	Bklt. single, Perf. 14½x14 on 3 sides	...	1.50	.50
1371b	Booklet Pane of 5	...	7.50	...
1372	86¢ Bartlett Pear, Perf. 13 (1992)............	7.25	1.50	.45
1372a	Perf. 14½ x 14	...	1.60	.50
1372b	Booklet Pane of 5, Perf. 14½ x 14............	...	7.85	...
1372v	Booklet Pane of 5, Perf. 13......................	...	14.95	...
1373	88¢ Westcot Apricot 4 Sides Tagged(1994)	7.00	1.50	.50
1373a	Booklet Pane of 5, 4 Sides Tagged	...	7.50	...
1373b	88¢ Perf. 14½ x 14 (1995)	...	1.60	.55
1373c	Booklet Pane of 5, Pf. 14½ x 14	...	7.85	...
1373p	88¢ 2 Sides and Center Tagged	...	2.95	...
1373ap	Booklet Pane of 5, 2 Sides/Center Tagged	...	14.50	...
1374	90¢ Elberta Peach, Perf. 13 ('95)	7.25	1.50	.45
1374a	Booklet Pane of 5	...	7.50	...
1374b	90¢ Perf 14½ x 14	...	1.60	.65
1374c	Booklet Pane of 5	...	7.85	...

1991-96 Regular Issues (continued)

| 1375 | 1388 | 1395 |

Scotts No.		Plate Block	F-VF NH	F-VF Used
1375	$1 Yorkton Court House (1994)	7.75	1.70	.60
1376	$2 Truro Normal School (1994)	15.00	3.35	.95
1378	$5 Victoria Public Library ('96)	38.75	8.35	2.75

1992 Self-Adhesive Stamps

1388	42¢ Flag & Mountains, bklt. sgl.	...	.80	.40
1388a	Booklet of 12	...	9.50	...
1389	43¢ Flag & Seashore,bklt.sgl.	...	.80	.40
1389a	Booklet of 12	...	9.50	...

1991-95 Coil Stamps, Perf. 10 Horizontal

1394	42¢ Canadian Flag & Rolling Hills	...	.75	.25
1395	43¢ Canadian Flag (1992)........................	...	.75	.25
1396	45¢ Canadian Flag (1995)........................	...	.75	.20

1992 Commemoratives

| 1407 | 1413 | 1419 |

1399-1407,1408-19,1432-55	Set of 45		34.75	12.75
1399-1403	42¢ Winter Olympics, strip of 5 bklt. stamps...		4.00	2.50
1399-1403	Set of 5 Singles	...	3.90	1.50
1403b	Bklt. Pane of 10......................................	...	7.85	...
1404-05	42¢ 350th Anniv. of Montreal, attd. pair ...	3.50	1.50	.80
1404-05	Set of 2 Singles	...	1.45	.50
1406	48¢ Jacques Cartier	3.95	.85	.45
1407	84¢ Christopher Columbus	6.95	1.50	.65
1407a	$2.16 Explorers S/S of 4, regular edition .	...	3.95	2.95
1407a var	Same, special ed., w/Maisonneuve sig. .	...	160.00	...
1408-12	42¢ Rivers, strip of 5 bklt. stamps............	...	3.85	2.75
1408-12	Set of 5 Singles	...	3.75	1.25
1412b	Bklt. Pane of 10......................................	...	7.50	...
1413	42¢ Alaska Highway	3.50	.75	.20
1414-18	42¢ Summer Olympics,strip of 5 bklt.stamps	...	4.00	3.50
1414-18	Set of 5 Singles	...	3.90	1.25
1418b	Bklt. Pane of 10......................................	...	7.85	...
1419	50¢ Art, Red Nasturtiums.........................	4.00	.85	.75
1431a	42¢ Canada Day, min.sht.of 12 paintings	...	8.95	7.50
1420-31	Set of 12 Singles, Provincial Views	...	8.75	5.50

| 1436 | 1441-42 |

1432-35	42¢ Legendary Heroes, attd.....................	3.50	3.00	2.25
1432-35	Set of 4 Singles	...	2.95	1.00
1436-40	42¢ Minerals, strip of 5 bklt. stamps	...	4.00	3.50
1436-40	Set of 5 Singles	...	3.90	1.25
1440b	Bklt. Pane of 10......................................	...	7.85	...
1441-42	42¢ Space Exploration, Pair	3.50	1.60	1.50
1441-42	Set of 2 Singles	...	1.50	1.00

1445	1446-47	1453

Scott's No.		Plate Block	F-VF NH	F-VF Used
1443	42¢ Hockey, Early Years	...	.75	.25
1443a	Skates, sticks, bklt. pane of 8	...	5.95	...
1444	42¢ Hockey, Six-Team Years	...	.75	.25
1444a	Team emblems, bklt. pane of 8	...	5.95	...
1445	42¢ Hockey, Expansion Years	...	.75	.25
1445a	Goalie's mask, bklt. pane of 9	...	7.50	...
1446-47	42¢ Order of Canada & R. Michener, pair	3.95	1.65	1.15
1446	42¢ Order of Canada	...	.75	.25
1447	42¢ Roland Michener	...	.90	.30
1448-51	42¢ WWII, Dark Days Indeed, attd.	3.50	3.00	2.25
1448-51	Set of 4 Singles	...	2.95	1.00
1452	42¢ Christmas, Jouluvana, perf. 12½	3.50	.75	.20
1452a	Perf. 13½	...	.85	.25
1452b	Booklet Pane of 10	...	7.50	...
1453	48¢ Christmas, La Befana	3.75	.80	.40
1453a	Booklet Pane of 5	...	4.35	...
1454	84¢ Christmas, Wehlnachsmann	6.75	1.40	.50
1454a	Booklet Pane of 5	...	6.95	...
1455	37¢ Christmas, Santa Claus, Bklt. Sgl	...	.70	.25
1455a	Booklet Pane of 10	...	6.50	...

1460	1466	1484

1993 Commemoratives

1456-71,1484-89,1491-1506 Set of 38		...	28.50	9.95
1456-59	43¢ Canadian Woman, attd.	3.50	3.00	2.25
1456-59	Set of 4 Singles	...	2.95	1.00
1460	43¢ Stanley Cup Centennial	3.50	.75	.20
1461-65	43¢ Hand-crafted textiles, strip of 5	...	3.75	2.25
1461-65	Set of 5 Singles	...	3.65	1.25
1465b	Booklet Pane of 10	...	7.50	...
1466	86¢ Art, Drawing for the Owl	7.00	1.50	1.00
1467-71	43¢ Historic Hotels, Strip of 5 bklt. sgls	...	3.75	2.75
1467-71	Set of 5 Singles	...	3.65	1.25
1471b	Booklet Pane of 10	...	7.50	...
1483a	43¢ Canada Day, Provincial & Territorial Parks, miniature sheet of 12	...	8.95	7.95
1472-83	Set of 12 Singles	...	8.75	4.95
1484	43¢ Founding of Toronto	3.50	.75	.20

1485-89	1491-94	1495-98

1485-89	43¢ Rivers, Strip of 5 bklt. sgls.	...	3.75	2.50
1485-89	Set of 5 Singles	...	3.65	1.25
1489b	Booklet Pane of 10	...	7.50	...
1490	$3.56 Motor Vehicles, Souv. Sheet of 6	...	7.75	7.50
1490a-f	Set of 6 Singles, 2-43¢,2-49¢,2-86¢	...	...	6.95
1491-94	43¢ Folk Songs, attd.	3.50	3.00	2.25
1491-94	Set of 4 Singles	...	2.95	1.00
1495-98	43¢ Dinosaurs, attd	3.50	3.00	2.25
1495-98	Set of 4 Singles	...	2.95	1.00

Scott's No.		Plate Block	F-VF NH	F-VF Used
1499	43¢ Christmas, Swiety Mikolaj	3.50	.75	.20
1499a	Booklet Pane of 10	...	7.50	...
1500	49¢ Christmas, Ded Moroz	3.95	.85	.40
1500a	Booklet Pane of 5	...	4.25	...
1501	86¢ Christmas, Father Christmas	7.00	1.50	.50
1501a	Booklet Pane of 5	...	7.35	...
1502	38¢ Christmas, Santa Claus, bklt. sgl	...	.75	.20
1502a	Booklet Pane of 10	...	6.95	...
1503-06	43¢ World War II, block or strip	3.50	3.00	2.25
1503-06	Set of 4 Singles	...	2.95	1.00

1509	1510	1511-15

1994 Regular Issues

1507-08	43¢ Greetings, Self-adhesive	...	1.70	1.00
1508a	Booklet Pane of 10 (5 each)	...	7.95	...

1994 Commemoratives

1509-22,1525-26,1528-40 Set of 29		...	22.95	8.25
1509	43¢ Jeanne Sauve with Tab	...	.90	.30
1509	Block of 4 w/4 different tabs	4.25	3.75	2.25
1510	43¢ T. Eaton Company	...	.75	.20
1510a	Prestige Booklet of 10	...	6.95	...
1511-15	43¢ Rivers, Strip of 5 bklt. sgls.	...	3.75	2.65
1511-15	Set of 5 Singles	...	3.65	1.25
1515b	Booklet Pane of 10	...	7.50	...
1516	88¢ Canadian Art, Vera	7.00	1.50	.75

1522	1529-32

1517-22	43¢-88¢ Commonwealth Games(6)	15.00	4.95	1.95
1517-18	43¢ Lawn Bowl and Lacrosse, Pair	3.50	1.50	.80
1517-18	Set of 2 Singles	...	1.45	.50
1519-20	43¢ High Jump and Wheelchair Marathon, Pair	3.50	1.50	.80
1519-20	Set of 2 Singles	...	1.45	.50
1521	50¢ Diving	4.25	.85	.40
1522	88¢ Cycling	7.00	1.50	.75
1523	43¢ Year of the Family, Souv. Sht. of 5	...	3.75	3.75
1524	43¢ Canada Day, Maple Trees, Miniature Sheet of 12	...	8.95	7.95
1524a-l	Set of 12 Singles	...	8.75	4.95
1525-26	43¢ Billy Bishop and Mary Travers, Pair	3.50	1.50	.80
1525-26	Set of 2 Singles	...	1.45	.50
1527	$3.62 Public Service Vehicles, Souvenir Sheet of 6	...	5.95	5.25
1527a-f	Set of 6 Singles, 2-43¢,2-50¢,2-88¢	...	...	4.50
1528	43¢ Civil Aviation, ICAO	3.50	.75	.25
1529-32	43¢ Prehistoric Life, attd.	3.50	3.00	2.25
1529-32	Set of 4 Singles	...	2.95	1.00
1533	43¢ Christmas, Singing Carols	3.50	.75	.20
1533a	Booklet Pane of 10	...	7.50	...
1534	50¢ Christmas, Choir	3.95	.85	.40
1534a	Booklet Pane of 5	...	4.25	...
1535	88¢ Christmas, Caroling	7.00	1.50	.50
1535a	Booklet Pane of 5	...	7.35	...
1536	38¢ Christmas, Soloist, bklt. sgl.	...	.75	.20
1536a	Booklet Pane of 10	...	6.95	...
1537-40	43¢ World War II, block or strip.	3.50	3.00	1.85
1537-40	Set of 4 Singles	...	2.95	1.00

1552

Scott's No.		Plate Block	F-VF NH	F-VF Used
1541-51,1553-58,1562-67,1570-90 Set of 47		...	34.95	11.50
1541-44	43¢ World War II, block or strip.	3.50	3.00	1.85
1541-44	Set of 4 Singles	...	2.95	1.00
1545	88¢ Art, "Floraison"	7.00	1.50	.75
1546	(43¢) Canada Flag 30th Anniv.	3.50	.75	.25
1547-51	(43¢) Fortress of Louisbourg, Strip of 5 Bklt. Singles.	...	3.75	3.25
1547-51	Set of 5 singles	...	3.65	1.25
1551b	Booklet Pane of 10	...	7.50	...
1552	$3.62 Farm and Frontier Vehicles, Souvenir Sheet of 6	...	6.25	4.95
1552a-f	Set of 6 Singles, 2-43¢,2-50¢,2-88¢.......	...	...	4.75
1553-57	43¢ Golf, Strip of 5 Bklt. Sgls.	...	3.75	3.25
1553-57	Set of 5 Singles	...	3.65	1.25
1557b	Booklet Pane of 10	...	7.50	...

| 1558 | 1536-66 | 1562 |

1558	43¢ Lunenburg Academy	3.50	.75	.25
1559-61	43¢ Canada Day, Set of 3 Souvenir Sheets bearing 10 different stamps........	...	7.50	6.95
1559a-c,1560a-d,1561a-c	Set of 10 Singles	...	...	4.50
1562	43¢ Manitoba	3.50	.75	.25
1563-66	43¢ Migratory Wildlife,"Aune" Block of 4 .	3.50	3.00	1.85
1563-66	Set of 4 singles	...	2.95	1.00
1563/67	43¢ Migratory Wildlife revised Inscribed "Faune", Block of 4	3.50	3.00	1.85
1567	43¢ Belted Kingfisher Single "Faune"......	...	...	.30

1568-69

Scotts No.		Plate Block	F-VF NH	F-VF Used
1568-69	45¢ Greetings, Self-adhesive	...	1.95	.70
1569a	Booklet Pane of 10 (5 Each) w/ labels	...	8.95	...
1569c	Booklet Pane of 10 w/ "Canadian Memorial Chiropractic College", covers and labels	...	8.95	...

| 1579 | 1584 | 1585 |

1995 Commemoratives (continued)

1570-73	45¢ Bridges, Block of 4	3.50	3.00	1.85
1570-73	Set of 4 Singles	...	2.95	1.00
1574-78	45¢ Canadian Arctic, Strip of 5 Bklt.Sgls.	...	3.75	3.25
1574-78	Set of 5 Singles	...	3.65	1.25
1578b	Booklet Pane of 10	...	7.50	...
1579-83	45 Comic Books, Strip of 5 Bklt. Singls. ..	...	3.75	3.25
1579-83	Set of 5 Singles	...	3.65	1.25
1583b	Booklet Pane of 10	...	7.50	...
1584	45¢ U.N. 50th Anniversary	3.75	.75	.25
1585	45¢ Christmas,The Nativity	3.75	.75	.20
1585a	Booklet Pane of 10	...	7.50	...
1586	52¢ Christmas,The Annunciation	4.50	.90	.40
1586a	Booklet Pane of 5	...	4.50	...
1587	90¢ Christmas,Flight to Egypt	7.50	1.50	.50
1587a	Booklet Pane of 5	...	7.50	...
1588	40¢ Christmas,Holly, booklet single	...	.70	.20
1588a	Booklet Pane of 10	...	6.95	...
1589	45¢ La Francophonie	3.75	.75	.25
1590	45¢ End of Holocaust	3.75	.75	.25

1996 Commemoratives

1591-98,1602-6,1608-29 Set of 35		...	42.50	...
1591-94	45¢ Birds, Strip of 4	...	3.00	2.25
1591-94	Set of 4 singles	...	2.95	1.00
1591-94d	Diamond Pane of 12	...	11.95	...
1591-94r	Rectangular Pane of 12	...	15.95	...
1591-94	Uncut Sheet of 60	...	110.00	...

1595-98

1595-98	45¢ High Technology Industries, Block of 4 Booklet singles	...	3.00	1.60
1595-98	Set of 4 singles	...	2.95	1.00
1598b	Booklet Pane of 12	...	8.95	...

1996 Regular Issue

1600-1	45¢ Greetings, Self-adhesive	...	1.65	.70
1601a	Booklet Pane of 10 (5 each) with labels ..	...	7.50	...

1996 Commemoratives (continued)

1602	90¢ Art "The Spirit of Haidi Gwali"...........	7.00	1.50	1.00
1603	45¢ Aids Awareness	3.75	.75	.25
1604	$3.74 Industrial and Commercial Vehicles Souvenir Sheet of 6	...	6.50	5.95
1604a-f	Set of 6 singles, 2-45¢,2-52¢,2-90¢	...	...	4.75
1605	5¢ (10), 10¢ (4), 20¢ (10), 45¢ Canadian Vehicles Souvenir Pane of 25	...	5.95	...
1605a-y	Set of 25 Singles	...	...	5.75

NOTE: The above pane pictures all 24 stamps shown on the Vehicles series souvenir sheets of 6 plus one additional vehicle.

1605	Uncut Sheet of 3 Canadian Vehicles Souvenir Panes of 25	...	37.50	...

1996 Commemoratives (continued)

| | 1607 | 1613 | 1614 |

Scott's No.		Plate Block	F-VF NH	F-VF Used
1606	45¢ Yukon Gold Strip of 5	...	3.75	2.00
1606a-e	Yukon Set of 5 Singles	...	3.65	1.25
1606	Yukon MiniaturePane of 10	...	7.50	...
1607	45¢ Canada Day, Maple Leaf in stylized Quilt Design, self-adhesive......	...	.80	.50
1607a	Canada Day Pane of 12	...	9.50	...
1608-12	45¢ Canadian Olympic Gold Medalist, Strip of 5 Booklet Singles	...	3.75	2.25
1608-12	Set of 5 Singles	...	3.65	1.25
1612b	Booklet Pane of 10	...	7.50	...
1613	45¢ British Columbia	3.50	.75	.25
1614	45¢ Canadian Heraldry	3.50	.75	.25
1615-16	45¢ 100 Years of Cinema, Self-adhesive Souvenir Sheets of 5 (2)......	...	7.75	...
1615a-16a	Set of 10 Singles	...	...	4.75

| | 1617 | 1627 | 1630 |

1617	45¢ Edouard Montpetit	3.50	.75	.25
1618-21	45¢ Winnie the Pooh, Block of 4	...	3.35	2.95
1618-21	Set of 4 Singles	...	3.25	1.25
1618-21	Booklet of 16 (4 each design)	...	13.50	...
1621b	45¢ Winnie the Pooh, Souvenir Sheet of 4	...	3.35	3.25
1622-26	45¢ Authors, Booklet Strip of 5......	...	3.75	2.25
1622-26	Set of 5 Singles	...	3.65	1.25
1626b	Booklet Pane of 10	...	7.50	...
1627	45¢ Christmas, Snowshoes, Sled	3.50	.75	.20
1627a	Booklet Pane of 10	...	7.50	...
1628	52¢ Christmas, Skiing	4.25	.90	.40
1628a	Booklet Pane of 5	...	4.50	...
1629	90¢ Christmas, Skating	6.95	1.50	.50
1629a	Booklet Pane of 5	...	7.50	...

1997 Commemoratives

1630	45¢ New Year, Year of the Ox	4.25	.90	.30
1630a	New Year Souvenir Sheet of 2	...	1.95	1.85

| 1631-34 | | | 1636 |

1997 Commemoratives (continued)

Scott's No.		Plate Block	F-VF NH	F-VF Used
1631-34	45¢ Birds, Block or Strip of 4	3.50	3.00	1.60
1631-34	Set of 4 Singles	...	2.90	1.00
1635	90¢ Art, "York Boat on Lake Winnipeg"...	6.95	1.50	1.25
1636	45¢ Canadian Tire, 75th Anniversary	...	.75	.30

| 1637 | Blue Poppy | Victorian Nurses |

1636a	Booklet of 12......	...	8.95	...
1637	45¢ Father Charles-Emile Gadbois	3.50	.75	.25
....	45¢ Quebec Floral Festival, Blue Poppy	...	.75	.25
....	Blue Poppy, Booklet Pane of 12......	...	8.95	...
....	45¢ Victorian Order of Nurses	3.50	.75	.25

| Law | Ocean Water Fish |

....	45¢ Law Society of Upper Canada......	3.50	.75	.25
....	45¢ Ocean Water Fish, Block of 4......	3.50	3.00	1.85
....	Fish, Set of 4 Singles	...	2.90	1.00
....	45¢ Confederation Bridge, Pair	3.50	1.50	.95
....	Bridge, Set of 2 Singles......	...	1.45	.50
....	45¢ Gilles Villeneuve	3.50	.75	.25
....	90¢ Gilles Villeneuve	6.95	1.50	.75
....	45¢-90¢ Gilles Villeneuve, S/S of 8......	...	8.95	...
....	45¢ John Cabot	3.50	.75	.25
....	45¢ Scenic Highways, Block of 4	3.50	3.00	1.85
....	Highways, Set of 4 Singles......	...	2.90	1.00

MINT CANADA COMMEMORATIVE YEAR SETS
All Fine To Very Fine, Never Hinged

Year	Scott Nos.	Qty.	F-VF NH
1947-49	274-77,82-83	6	.90
1951-52	303-04,11-15,17-19	10	4.65
1953-54	322-24,35-36,49-50	7	1.75
1955	352-58	7	1.80
1956	359-61,64	4	1.05
1957	365-74	10	4.15
1958	375-82	8	1.80
1959	383-88	6	1.35
1960-61	389-95	7	1.60
1962	396-400	5	1.10
1963	410,12-13	3	.65
1964	416,431-35	6	1.15
1964-66	417-29A (Coats of Arms & Flowers)	14	2.75
1965	437-44	8	1.50
1966	445-52	8	1.50
1967	453,469-77	10	1.90
1968	478-89	12	3.85
1969	490-504	15	8.95
1970	505-18,531	15	11.50
1970	519-30 (Christmas)	12	3.95
1971	532-42,552-58	18	5.35
1972	559-61,582-85,606-10	12	7.95
1972-76	562-81 (Indians)	20	5.25
1973	611-28	18	5.15
1974	629-55	27	8.75
1975	656-80	25	13.50
1976	681-703	23	16.75
1977	704,732-51	21	5.50
1978	752-56,757-79	28	9.75
1979	780,813-20,833-46	23	7.85
1980	847-77	31	11.50
1981	878-906	29	9.35
1982	909-13,914-16,954,967-75	18	10.95
1983	976-82,993-1008	23	20.50
1984	1009-15,1028-39,1040-4444	24	14.50
1985	1045-49,1060-66,1067-70,1071-76	22	13.75
1986	1077-79,1090-1107,1108-15,1116b,1117-21	32	22.50
1987	1122-25,1126-54	33	20.50
1988	1195-1228	34	22.75
1989	1229-63	34	22.95
1990	1264-71,1274-1301	36	25.95
1991	1302-43,1345-48	45	33.50
1992	1399-1407,1408-19,1432-55	45	34.75
1993	1456-71,1484-89,1491-1506	38	28.50
1994	1509-22,1525-26,1528-40	29	22.95
1995	1541-51,1553-58,1562-67,1570-90	47	34.95
1996	1591-98,1602-6,1608-29	35	42.50

CANADA
SEMI-POSTALS

B1   B4   B7   B10

Scott's No.		Plate Block	F-VF NH	F-VF Used
B1-12	Set of 12	...	4.95	4.95

1974 Olympic Games

B1	8¢+2¢ Olympic Emblem, Bronze	1.40	.30	.30
B2	10¢+5¢ Olympic Emblem, Silver............	2.15	.45	.45
B3	15¢+5¢ Olympic Emblem, Gold	2.85	.60	.60

1975 Olympic Games - Water Sports

B4	8¢+2¢ Swimming....................................	1.40	.30	.30
B5	10¢+5¢ Rowing	2.15	.45	.45
B6	15¢+5¢ Sailing	2.85	.60	.60

1975 Olympic Games - Combat Sports

B7	8¢+2¢ Fencing	1.40	.30	.30
B8	10¢+5¢ Boxing	2.15	.45	.45
B9	15¢+5¢ Judo	2.85	.60	.60

1976 Olympic Games - Team Sports

B10	8¢+2¢ Basketball................................	1.40	.30	.30
B11	10¢+5¢ Vaulting	2.15	.45	.45
B12	20¢+5¢ Soccer	3.25	.70	.70

1996 Literacy Issue

B13

B13	45¢ + 5¢ Literacy Singles.......................	...	.85	.50
B13a	Booklet Pane of 10.................................	...	8.25	...

AIR MAIL STAMPS

C1   C2   C5

1928-1932 Airmail Issues VF + 30% (B)

Scott's No.		NH VF	NH F-VF	Unused VF	Unused F-VF	Used F-VF
C1	5¢ Allegory (1928)	13.75	10.00	9.00	6.75	2.50
C2	5¢ Globe, Brown (1930)	55.00	41.50	36.50	27.50	16.50
C3	6¢ on 5¢ Allegory (1932)	9.00	6.75	6.00	4.50	2.25
C4	6¢ on 5¢ Ottawa (1932)..............	20.75	14.50	13.50	9.75	7.75

C6   C7   C9

1935-46 Airmail Issues VF + 25%

Scott's No.		Plate Blocks NH	Plate Blocks Unused	F-VF NH	F-VF Unused	F-VF Used
C5-9	Set of 5.................................	...	...	8.85	6.95	1.95
C5	6¢ Daedalus, Red Brown...... (6)	16.50	12.50	2.25	1.75	.75
C6	6¢ Steamer (1938)................	13.00	9.75	2.25	1.75	.25
C7	6¢ Student Flyers (1942)......	18.50	14.00	3.50	2.75	.75
C8	7¢ Student Flyers (1943)......	3.50	2.75	.70	.55	.15
C9	7¢ Canada Geese (1946).....	3.25	2.50	.65	.50	.15
C9a	7¢ Booklet Pane of 4	...	...	2.65	2.10	...

CANADA
AIRMAIL SPECIAL DELIVERY 1942-1947

CE1   E1

Scott's No.		Plate Blocks NH	Plate Blocks Unused	F-VF NH	F-VF Unused	F-VF Used
CE1-4	Set of 4............................	...	...	12.50	8.95	8.75
CE1	16¢ Aerial View............................	12.50	9.00	1.65	1.20	1.20
CE2	17¢ Aerial Veiw (1943)	14.00	11.00	2.50	1.80	1.75
CE3	17¢ Plane, Original Die (1946) ...23.00	23.00	18.00	4.50	3.25	3.15
CE4	17¢ Corrected Die (1947)	23.00	18.00	4.50	3.25	3.15

CE3 has circumflex (e) over second "E" of "EXPRESS". CE4 has an accent (e).

AIRMAIL OFFICIAL STAMPS 1949-1950

CO1	7¢ Ovptd. "O.H.M.S." (C9)..........47.50	35.00	10.75	7.95	3.50
CO2	7¢ Ovptd. "G" (#C9) (1950) 75.00	58.50	15.00	11.00	12.50

SPECIAL DELIVERY STAMPS 1898-1933
E1 VF Used + 40% (B) E2-5 VF Used + 30% (B)

E2   E3   E4

Scott's No.		NH VF	NH F-VF	Unused VF	Unused F-VF	Used F-VF
E1	10¢ Blue Green (1898) 100.00	67.50	47.50	30.00	5.50
E2	20¢ Carmine (1922) 80.00	55.00	45.00	30.00	6.00
E3	20¢ Mail Transport (1927) 16.75	11.50	10.75	7.50	6.50
E4	20¢ "TWENTY" (1930) 65.00	45.00	40.00	27.50	11.00
E5	20¢ "20 CENTS" (1933) 59.50	42.50	35.00	25.00	14.00

E6   E7

E10   E11

SPECIAL DELIVERY 1935-1946 VF + 20%

Scott's No.		Plate Blocks NH	Plate Blocks Unused	F-VF NH	F-VF Unused	F-VF Used
E6-11	Set of 6.................................	...	...	41.50	29.50	27.50
E6	20¢ Progress .... (6)	65.00	45.00	6.75	4.50	4.00
E7	10¢ Arms, Green (1939).............	22.50	17.50	4.00	3.25	3.25
E8	20¢ Arms, Carm. (1938)	195.00	140.00	25.00	17.50	17.50
E9	10¢ on 20¢ (#E8) (1939).............	33.50	24.00	4.50	3.25	3.25
E10	10¢ Arms & Flags (1942).............	12.00	8.75	2.00	1.50	1.00
E11	10¢ Arms (1946)	8.75	6.50	1.50	1.15	.75

SPECIAL DELIVERY OFFICIAL STAMPS 1949-1950

EO1	10¢ Ovptd. "O.H.M.S." (#E11)....75.00	55.00	13.00	9.50	9.50
EO2	10¢ Ovptd. "G" (#E11) (1950)...140.00	110.00	22.50	17.50	17.50

NOTE: PRICES THROUGHOUT THIS LIST ARE SUBJECT TO CHANGE WITHOUT NOTICE IF MARKET CONDITIONS REQUIRE. MINIMUM ORDER MUST TOTAL AT LEAST $20.00.

REGISTRATION STAMPS 1875-1888 (OG + 20%) VF + 50% (C)

	F1	J1	J6	J11

Scott's No.		NH Fine	Unused Fine	Unused Ave.	Used Fine	Used Ave.
F1	2¢ Orange, Perf. 12	100.00	50.00	30.00	2.25	1.40
F1a	2¢ Vermillion, Perf. 12	115.00	57.50	35.00	6.50	3.75
F1b	2¢ Rose Carmine, Perf. 12	275.00	140.00	80.00	75.00	42.50
F1d	5¢ Orange, Perf. 12 x 11½	...	250.00	150.00	75.00	42.50
F2	5¢ Dark Green, Perf. 12	140.00	70.00	41.50	2.50	1.50
F2a	5¢ Blue Green, Perf. 12	150.00	75.00	45.00	2.75	1.55
F2b	5¢ Yellow Green, Perf. 12	210.00	110.00	65.00	3.75	2.25
F2d	5¢ Green, Perf. 12 x 11½	...	700.00	400.00	140.00	85.00
F3	8¢ Blue (1876)	...	295.00	185.00	250.00	150.00

POSTAGE DUE STAMPS
1906-1928 VF Used + 40% (B)

Scott's No.		NH VF	NH F-VF	Unused VF	Unused F-VF	Used F-VF
J1-5	**Set of 5**	**147.50**	**105.00**	**92.50**	**65.00**	**21.50**
J1	1¢ Violet	13.00	9.25	8.00	5.50	2.50
J1a	1¢ Thin Paper (1924)	17.75	12.00	11.00	7.50	5.00
J2	2¢ Violet	13.00	9.25	8.00	5.50	.60
J2a	2¢ Thin Paper (1924)	17.75	12.00	11.00	7.50	5.75
J3	4¢ Violet (1928)	70.00	50.00	45.00	32.50	11.00
J4	5¢ Violet	12.75	9.50	8.50	6.00	.90
J4a	5¢ Thin Paper (1928)	11.50	8.25	7.50	5.25	4.75
J5	10¢ Violet (1928)	46.50	32.50	28.00	19.50	7.50

1930-1932 VF Used + 30% (B)

Scott's No.		NH VF	NH F-VF	Unused VF	Unused F-VF	Used F-VF
J6-10	**Set of 5**	**140.00**	**105.00**	**85.00**	**65.00**	**13.50**
J6	1¢ Dark Violet	11.50	8.75	6.75	5.25	2.40
J7	2¢ Dark Violet	7.50	6.00	5.00	3.75	.55
J8	4¢ Dark Violet	15.75	11.50	9.50	7.00	2.15
J9	5¢ Dark Violet (1931)	16.75	12.50	10.00	7.50	3.75
J10	10¢ Dark Violet (1932)	97.50	75.00	59.50	45.00	5.50

1933-1934 VF Used + 30% (B)

Scott's No.		NH VF	NH F-VF	Unused VF	Unused F-VF	Used F-VF
J11-14	**Set of 4**	**49.75**	**38.75**	**30.75**	**23.75**	**10.95**
J11	1¢ Dark Violet (1934)	12.95	9.75	7.75	6.00	3.95
J12	2¢ Dark Violet	5.25	4.00	3.25	2.50	.70
J13	4¢ Dark Violet	12.95	9.75	7.75	6.00	3.95
J14	10¢ Dark Violet	23.00	18.00	14.00	10.75	3.25

	J15	J23	J28	MR1	MR3

POSTAGE DUE STAMPS
1935-1965 VF + 20%

Scott's No.		Plate Block	F-VF NH	F-VF Used
J15-20	**Set of 7**	...	**4.75**	**2.95**
J15	1¢ Dark Violet	1.75	.20	.15
J16	2¢ Dark Violet	1.75	.20	.15
J16B	3¢ Dark Violet ('65)	15.00	2.00	1.10
J17	4¢ Dark Violet	2.25	.25	.15
J18	5¢ Dark Violet ('48)	3.00	.40	.25
J19	6¢ Dark Violet ('57)	12.50	1.65	1.25
J20	10¢ Dark Violet	2.75	.35	.15

1967 Regular Size 20 x 17 mm., Perf. 12

Scott's No.		Plate Block	F-VF NH	F-VF Used
J21-27	**Set of 7**	...	**2.90**	**2.90**
J21	1¢ Carmine Rose	7.00	.20	.20
J22	2¢ Carmine Rose	1.25	.22	.22
J23	3¢ Carmine Rose	1.25	.22	.22
J24	4¢ Carmine Rose	2.50	.35	.35
J25	5¢ Carmine Rose	8.75	1.40	1.40
J26	6¢ Carmine Rose	2.50	.30	.30
J27	10¢ Carmine Rose	2.50	.35	.35

POSTAGE DUE STAMPS (cont.)

Scott's No.		Plate Block	F-VF NH	F-VF Used
	1969-1974 Modular Size 20 x 15¾ mm., Perf. 12			
J28,J31,J32a,J34,J35,J36 Dextrose (6)		...	**20.75**	**20.50**
J28v,J29-30,J31v,J33,J34v,J35v,J36v,J37 White Gum(9)		**2.10**		**1.75**
J28	1¢ Dextrose (Yellow Gum) ('70)	2.50	.40	.35
J28v	1¢ Carmine Rose, White Gum ('74)	1.65	.35	.25
J29	2¢ Carmine Rose White Gum ('73)	1.50	.20	.20
J30	2¢ Carmine Rose White Gum ('74)	1.65	.35	.15
J31	4¢ Dextrose (Yellow Gum) ('69)	1.80	.30	.25
J31v	4¢ Carmine Rose, White Gum ('74)	.95	.20	.15
J32a	5¢ Dextrose (Yellow Gum) ('69)	95.00	19.50	19.50
J33	6¢ Carmine Rose White Gum ('73)	.95	.20	.15
J34	8¢ Dextrose (Yellow Gum)	1.85	.30	.25
J34v	8¢ Carmine Rose, White Gum ('74)	1.10	.20	.20
J35	10¢ Dextrose (Yellow Gum) ('69)	2.25	.50	.15
J35v	10¢ Carmine Rose, White Gum ('73)	1.10	.20	.20
J36	12¢ Dextrose (Yellow Gum) ('69)	3.75	.65	.50
J36v	12¢ Carmine Rose, White Gum ('73)	1.50	.25	.25
J37	16¢ Carmine Rose White Gum('74)	1.75	.30	.30

1977-78 Modular Size 20 x 15¾mm.,Perf. 12½ x 12

Scott's No.		Plate Block	F-VF NH	F-VF Used
J28a-40	**Set of 9**	...	**4.15**	**2.75**
J28a	1¢ Carmine Rose	.50	.20	.15
J31a	4¢ Carmine Rose	.60	.20	.15
J32	5¢ Carmine Rose	.75	.20	.15
J34a	8¢ Carmine Rose (1978)	2.10	.35	.20
J35a	10¢ Carmine Rose	1.10	.22	.22
J36a	12¢ Carmine Rose	10.75	1.40	.65
J38	20¢ Carmine Rose	2.25	.45	.35
J39	24¢ Carmine Rose	2.75	.60	.40
J40	50¢ Carmine Rose	4.00	.80	.70

WAR TAX STAMPS 1915-1916 VF Used + 50% (B)

Scott's No.		NH VF	NH F-VF	Unused VF	Unused F-VF	Used F-VF
MR1	1¢ George V, Green	13.75	8.75	7.25	4.75	.20
MR2	2¢ Carmine	13.75	8.75	7.25	4.75	.25
MR3	2¢ + 1¢ Carm., T.1 ('16)	20.00	13.00	10.75	7.00	.15
MR3a	2¢ + 1¢ Carm., Type II	165.00	110.00	95.00	62.50	2.50
MR4	2¢ + 1¢ Brown, Type II	20.00	13.00	10.75	7.00	.15
MR4a	2¢ + 1¢ Brown, Type I	...	...	240.00	160.00	6.50
MR5	2¢ + 1¢ Carm., Perf. 12 x 8	50.00	32.50	26.50	17.50	15.00
MR6	2¢ + 1¢ Carm., P.8 Vert. Coil.	165.00	110.00	90.00	60.00	4.50
MR7	2¢ + 1¢ Br.,T.II P.8 Vt. Coil.	22.50	14.50	12.00	8.00	.60
MR7a	2¢ + 1¢ Br.,T.I P.8 Vt. Coil.	200.00	135.00	115.00	75.00	4.75

OFFICIAL STAMPS (VF + 30%)

	O1	O12	O16	021

1949-50 Issues of 1942-46 Overprinted O.H.M.S.

Scott's No.		Plate Blocks NH	Plate Blocks Unused	F-VF NH	F-VF Unused	F-VF Used
O1-10	**Set of 9**	...		**235.00**	**170.00**	**145.00**
O1	1¢ George VI, Green (249)	9.50	7.25	1.95	1.50	1.35
O2	2¢ George VI, Brown (250)	100.00	80.00	8.75	6.50	6.50
O3	3¢ George VI, Violet (252)	9.75	7.25	2.00	1.50	1.00
O4	4¢ George VI, Carmine (254)	17.50	12.50	2.35	1.75	.55
O6	10¢ Great Bear Lake (269)	18.75	15.00	3.00	2.25	.45
O7	14¢ Hydroelectric Sta. (270)	26.75	21.75	3.75	2.75	1.85
O8	20¢ Reaper (271)	75.00	55.00	10.00	7.50	2.50
O9	50¢ Lumbering (272)	950.00	700.00	175.00	125.00	110.00
O10	$1 Train Ferry (273)	350.00	250.00	42.50	30.00	30.00

1950 Issues of 1949-50 Overprinted O.H.M.S.

Scott's No.		Plate Blocks NH	Plate Blocks Unused	F-VF NH	F-VF Unused	F-VF Used
O11	50¢ Development (294)	135.00	95.00	25.00	17.50	15.00
O12-15A	**Set of 5**	...		**4.85**	**3.85**	**2.35**
O12	1¢ George VI, Green (284)	3.65	3.00	.30	.25	.25
O13	2¢ George VI, Sepia (285)	4.50	3.50	.95	.75	.55
O14	3¢ G. VI, Rose Violet (286)	5.75	4.50	1.00	.80	.45
O15	4¢ G. VI, Carmine (287)	5.75	4.50	1.00	.80	.15
O15A	5¢ G. VI, Deep Blue (288)	10.75	8.00	1.95	1.50	1.10

NOTE: Number in ( ) indicates catalog number of basic stamp which has not been overprinted.

1950 Issues of 1948-50 Overprinted G

Scott's No.		Plate Blocks NH	Unused	F-VF NH	F-VF Unused	F-VF Used
O16-25	Set of 11	...	...	110.00	82.50	65.00
O16	1¢ George VI, Green (284)..........2.10		1.65	.35	.28	.15
O17	2¢ George VI, Sepia (285) 6.25		5.00	1.25	1.00	.70
O18	3¢ G. VI, Rose Violet (286) 6.25		5.00	1.25	1.00	.15
O19	4¢ G. VI, Carmine (287) 6.25		5.00	1.25	1.00	.15
O20	5¢ G. VI, Deep Blue (288) 13.00		10.75	1.50	1.20	.75
O21	10¢ Great Bear Lake (269)........12.50		10.00	2.25	1.80	.40
O22	14¢ Hydroelectric Sta. (270)......28.50		23.50	5.00	4.00	1.65
O23	10¢ Reaper (271) 87.50		65.00	13.50	9.75	.90
O24	50¢ Oil Development (294) 52.50		40.00	9.00	7.00	4.75
O25	$1 Train Ferry (273).................375.00		300.00	80.00	60.00	60.00
O26	10¢ Fur Trading (301)..................5.95		4.75	1.25	.95	.20

028   033   040   046

1951-53 Issues of 1951-53 Overprinted G

Scott's No.		Plate Blocks NH	Unused	F-VF NH	F-VF Unused	F-VF Used
O27	$1 Fisheries (302)....................375.00		300.00	75.00	60.00	60.00
O28	2¢ G. VI, Olive Green (305).........2.40		1.95	.50	.40	.15
O29	4¢ George VI, Orange (306)..........4.50		3.25	.80	.60	.15
O30	20¢ Forestry Products (316).......10.75		8.00	2.00	1.50	.18
O31	7¢ Canada Goose (320) 14.50		11.00	3.25	2.50	.95
O32	$1 Totem Pole (321)..................77.50		60.00	15.00	11.00	8.50

1953-55 Issues of 1953-55 Overprinted G

Scott's No.		Plate Blocks NH	Unused	F-VF NH	F-VF Unused	F-VF Used
O33-37	Set of 5	...	1.80	1.45		.65
O33	1¢ Queen Elizabeth (325).............1.70		1.40	.30	.25	.15
O34	2¢ Queen Elizabeth (326).............1.70		1.40	.30	.25	.15
O35	3¢ Queen Elizabeth (327).............1.70		1.40	.30	.25	.15
O36	4¢ Queen Elizabeth (328).............2.40		1.95	.50	.40	.15
O37	5¢ Queen Elizabeth (329).............2.40		1.95	.50	.40	.15
O38	50¢ Textile (334)........................24.00		19.50	5.00	4.00	1.00
O38a	50¢ Textile, Flying G (1961) 23.50		18.75	4.75	3.75	1.75
O39	10¢ Eskimo (351) 4.75		3.75	.85	.65	.15
O39a	10¢ Eskimo, Flying G (1962)......12.50		10.00	1.75	1.40	.85

1955-56 Issues of 1955-56 Overprinted G

Scott's No.		Plate Blocks NH	Unused	F-VF NH	F-VF Unused	F-VF Used
O40-44	Set of 4	...	3.65	2.95		.80
O40	1¢ Queen Elizabeth (337).............1.50		1.30	.30	.25	.25
O41	2¢ Queen Elizabeth (337).............1.85		1.60	.40	.35	.15
O43	4¢ Queen Elizabeth (340).............4.50		3.75	.95	.80	.15
O44	5¢ Queen Elizabeth (341).............2.50		1.95	.55	.45	.15
O45	20¢ Paper Industry (362).............8.25		6.75	1.65	1.30	.18
O45a	20¢ Paper, Flying G (1962) 36.50		30.00	6.00	5.00	.50

1963 Issue of 1962-63 Overprinted G

Scott's No.		Plate Block	F-VF NH	F-VF Used
O46-49	Set of 4	...	2.40	2.40
O46	1¢ Queen Elizabeth (401) ....(Blank)	3.00	.65	.65
O47	2¢ Queen Elizabeth (402) ....(Blank)	3.00	.65	.65
O48	4¢ Queen Elizabeth (404) ....(Blank)	7.50	.75	.75
O49	5¢ Queen Elizabeth (405) ....(Blank)	2.75	.50	.50

CANADA "TAGGED" ISSUES

(A) = Wide Side Bars
(B) = Wide Bar in Middle
(C) = Bar at Left or Right
(D) = Narrow Bar in Middle
(E) = Narrow Side Bars - General

Scott's No.		F-VF NH
1962-63 Elizabeth II		
337-41p	1¢-5¢, Set of 5................7.95	
337p	1¢ Violet Brown (A) 1.10	
338p	2¢ Green (A) 1.10	
339p	3¢ Carmine Rose (A) 1.10	
340p	4¢ Violet (B) 2.95	
341p	5¢ Blue (A) 2.50	
401-5p	1¢-5¢, Set of 5................1.90	
401p	1¢ Brown (A) 20	
402p	2¢ Green (A) 20	
403p	3¢ Purple (A) 25	
404p	4¢ Carmine (C) 80	
404pa	4¢ Carmine (D) 90	
404pb	4¢ Carmine (B) 3.75	
405p	5¢ Violet Blue (A) 55	
405q	5¢ Min. Pane of 20 ....42.50	
1964-67		
434p	3¢ Brown (A) 65	
434q	3¢ Min. Pane of 25 ....11.00	
435p	5¢ 1964 Xmas (A) 1.00	
443p	3¢ 1965 Xmas (A) 25	
443q	3¢ Min. Pane of 25 ....8.00	
444p	5¢ 1965 Xmas (A) 30	
451p	3¢ 1966 Xmas (A) 25	
451q	3¢ Min. Pane of 25 ....4.65	
452p	5¢ 1966 Xmas (A) 45	
453p	5¢ Flag over Globe (A) 40	

Scott's No.		F-VF NH
1967-72 Definitives, Pf. 12		
454p	1¢ Brown (A).....................25	
454pa	1¢ Brown (B).....................25	
454pb	1¢ Brown (E).....................20	
454ep	1¢ Booklet single, Perf. 12½ x 12 (E)........25	
455p	2¢ Green (A).....................25	
455pa	2¢ Green (B).....................20	
455pb	2¢ Green (E).....................20	
456p	3¢ Purple (A).....................20	
456pa	3¢ Purple (E) precan 35	
457p	4¢ Carmine (C)..................25	
457pa	4¢ Carmine (B)..................40	
457pb	4¢ Carmine (E)..................55	
458p	5¢ Blue (A)........................55	
458bp	5¢ Min. Pane of 20 ....50.00	
458pa	5¢ Blue (B)........................35	
459p	6¢ Orange, Pf. 10 (A) 50	
459bp	6¢ Orange, Perf. 12½ x 12 (A)........60	
460p	6¢ Black, Die I, Perf. 12½ x 12 (A)........30	
460cp	6¢ Black, Die I, Perf. 12½ x 12 (B)........40	
460cpa	6¢ Black, Bklt. Sgl., Die II (E)....................50	
460fp	6¢ Black, Die I (B) 30	
462p	10¢ Jack Pine (A) 1.00	
462pa	10¢ Jack Pine (E) 75	
463p	15¢ Bylot Island (A) 90	
463pa	15¢ Bylot Island (E) 90	
464p	20¢ Ferry (A) 1.50	

Scott's No.		F-VF NH
465p	25¢ Solemn Land (A)......2.75	
1967-69		
476p	3¢ 1967 Xmas (A)...........25	
476q	3¢ Min. Pane of 25 ....4.50	
477p	5¢ 1967 Xmas (A)...........30	
488p	5¢ 1968 Xmas (B)...........25	
488q	5¢ B. Pane of 10.......3.75	
489p	6¢ 1968 Xmas (A)...........30	
502p	5¢ 1969 Xmas (B)...........20	
502q	5¢ B. Pane of 10.......3.50	
503p	6¢ 1969 Xmas (A)...........25	
1970		
505p	6¢ Manitoba (A) 35	
508-11p	25¢ Expo '70 (A) 11.75	
513p	10¢ UN (A)........................90	
514p	15¢ UN (A).....................1.50	
519-30p	5¢-15¢ Set of 12 sngls..5.95	
519-23p	5¢ Strip of 5 (B) 3.00	
524-28p	6¢ Strip of 5 (B) 3.50	
529p	10¢ Manager (B)...............55	
530p	15¢ Snowmobile (B) 1.00	
1971-72		
541p	15¢ Radio Canada (A)....2.75	
543p	7¢ Green (A)......................60	
544p	8¢ Slate (A).......................35	
544pa	8¢ Slate (E).......................30	
544q	B.Pn.of 6 [#454pb (3), 460cpa (1),544pa (2)].....2.50	
544r	B.Pn.of 18 [#454pb (6), 460cpa (1),544pa (11)]...4.75	

Scott's No.		F-VF NH
544s	B.Pn.of 10 [#454pb (4), 460cpa (1),544pa (5)].....2.50	
550p	8¢ Coil, Slate (E) 30	
554p	6¢ Snowflake (B) 25	
555p	7¢ Snowflake (A) 35	
556p	10¢ Snowflake (A) 50	
557p	15¢ Snowflake (A) 95	
560p	8¢ World Health (E) 60	
561p	8¢ Fronterac (E) 75	
562-63p	8¢ Indians (E) 1.10	
564-65p	8¢ Indians (E) 1.10	
582-85p	15¢ Sciences (E) 11.00	
1972 Pictorials		
594	10¢ Forests (E) 22	
594p	10¢ Forests (E) 1.10	
595	15¢ Mountain Sheep (E)....30	
595p	15¢ Mountain Sheep (A).1.10	
596	20¢ Prairie Mosaic (E).......45	
596p	20¢ Prairie Mosaic (A) 1.60	
597	25¢ Polar Bears (E)..........50	
597p	25¢ Polar Bears (A)........1.85	
1972 Commemoratives		
606p	6¢ Christmas (E)...............25	
606pa	6¢ Christmas (A)...............30	
607p	8¢ Christmas (E)...............30	
607pa	8¢ Christmas (A)...............35	
608p	10¢ Christmas (E)..............60	
608pa	10¢ Christmas (A)..............65	
609p	15¢ Christmas (E)............1.00	
609pa	15¢ Christmas (A)...........1.25	
610p	8¢ Krieghoff (E) 35	

CANADA DUCK STAMPS

No.	Description	F-VF NH
CANADA		
CN 1	'85 $4 Mallards Bklt............	12.00
CN 2	'86 $4 Canvasbks Bklt.......	12.00
CN 2B	'86 Min. Sheet of 16.....	275.00
CN 3	'87 $6.50 Can. G'se Bklt.....	11.00
CN 3B	'87 Min. Sheet of 16.....	275.00
CN 4	'88 $6.50 Pintails Bklt.....	14.00
CN 4B	'88 Min. Sheet of 16.....	275.00
CN 5	'89 $7.50 Snow G'se Bklt...	14.50
CN 5B	'89 Min. Sheet of 16.....	275.00
CN 6	'90 $7.50 Wood Duck Bklt..	13.00
CN 6B	'90 Min. Sheet of 16.....	220.00
CN 7	'91 $8.50 Blk. Duck Bklt	13.00
CN 7B	'91 Min. Sheet of 16.....	220.00
CN 7J	'91 Joint Issue w/US..........	31.50
CN 7JI	'91 J'nt Issue w/US, Impf....	72.50
CN 8	'92 $8.50 Cmn Elders Bklt..	13.00
CN 8B	'92 Min. Sheet of 16.....	220.00
CN 9	'93 $8.50 Hd'd Mergans'r ...	13.00
CN 9B	'93 Min. Sheet of 16.....	220.00
CN 10	'94 $8.50 Ross' Geese.......	13.00
CN10B	'94f Min. Sheet of 16..........	220.00
CN 11	'95 $8.50 Redheads..........	13.00
CN11B	'95 Min. Sheet of 16.....	220.00
CN12	'96 $8.50 Goldeneyes.......	13.00
CN12B	'96 Min. Sheet of 16..........	220.00
ALBERTA		
AB 1	'89 $6 Canada Geese	25.00
AB 2	'90 $7 Mallards..............	20.00
AB 3	'91 $7.71 Pintails.............	18.00
AB 4	'92 $7.90 Snow Geese.......	17.00
AB 5	'93 $7.90 Canvasbacks.......	15.00
AB 6	'94 $8.36 Redheads..........	13.00
AB 7	'95 $8.36 Wh. Fronted Geese	13.00
AB 8	'96 $8.36 Goldeneyes.......	13.00
BRITISH COLUMBIA		
BC 1	'95 $6 Bighorn Sheep	8.00
BC 1B	'95 Same, Booklet.........	10.00
BC 1M	'95 Same, Mini Sheet.......	30.00
BC 2	'96 $6 Elk	8.00
BC 2B	'96 Same, Booklet.........	10.00
BC 2M	'96 Same, Mini Sheet.......	34.00
BC 3	'97 $6 Grizzly Bear..........	8.00
BC 3B	'97 Same, Booklet..........	10.00
BC 3M	'97 Same, Mini Sheet.......	34.00

No.	Description	F-VF NH
MANITOBA		
	Winnipeg Duck Stamp	11.00
	Winnipeg Duck, Flourescent Paper	11.00
MAN 1	'94 $6 Polar Bear..........	8.00
MAN 1B	'94 Same, Booklet	10.00
MAN 1M	'94 Same, Mini Sheet 4 .	34.00
MAN 2	'95 $6 Whitetailed Deer .	8.00
MAN 2B	'95 Same, Booklet	10.00
MAN 2M	'95 Same, Mini Sheet 4 .	34.00
MAN 3	'96 $6 Lynx	8.00
MAN 3B	'96 Same, Booklet	10.00
MAN 3M	'96 Same, Mini Sheet	34.00
NEW BRUNSWICK		
NB 1	'94 $6 White Tail Deer	8.00
NB 1B	'94 Same, Booklet..........	10.00
NB 1M	'94 Same, Mini Sheet of 4	34.00
NB 2	'95 $6 Cougar	8.00
NB 2B	'95 Same, Booklet..........	10.00
NB 2M	'95 Same, Mini Sheet of 4	30.00
NB 3	'96 $6 Moose	8.00
NB 3B	'96 Same, Booklet..........	10.00
NB 3M	'96 Same, Mini Sheet.....	34.00
NB 4	'97 $6 Pheasant..............	8.00
NB 4B	'97 Same, Booklet..........	10.00
NB 4M	'97 Same, Mini Sheet.....	34.00
NEWFOUNDLAND		
NEWF 1	'94 $6 Woodland Caribou	8.00
NEWF 1B	'94 Same, Booklet.......	8.50
NEWF 1M	'94 Same, Mini Sheet. 4..	34.00
NEWF 2	'95 $6 Goldeneyes	8.00
NEWF 2B	'95 Same, Booklet.......	8.50
NEWF 2M	'95 Same, Mini Sheet ..	34.00
NEWF 3	'96 $6 Moose	8.00
NEWF 3B	'96 Same, Booklet.......	10.00
NEWF 3M	'96 Same, Mini Sheet...	34.00
NORTWEST TERRITORIES		
NWT 1	'97 $6 Artic Hare............	8.00
NWT 1B	'97 Same, Booklet.........	10.00
NWT 1M	'97 Same, Mini Sheet	34.00
NOVA SCOTIA		
NS 1	'92 $6 Whitetail Deer.......	12.00
NS 1B	'92 $6 Wh'tail Deer Bklt...	22.00
NS 1M	'92 $6 Mini Sheet of 4	50.00
NS 2	'93 $6 Summer Pheasant.	9.00
NS 2B	'93 $6 Pheasant Bklt........	12.50

No.	Description	F-VF NH
NOVA SCOTIA (cont.)		
NS 2M	'93 $6 Mini Sheet of 4	34.00
NS 3	'94 $6 Wood Duck...........	8.00
NS 3B	'94 Same, Booklet.........	10.00
NS 3M	'94 Same, Mini Sheet of 4	27.00
NS 4	'95 $6 Coyote	8.00
NS 4B	'95 Same, Booklet.........	10.00
NS 4M	'95 Same, Mini Sheet of 4	30.00
NS 5	'96 $6 Osprey...............	8.00
NS 5B	'96 Same, Booklet.........	10.00
NS 5M	'96 Same, Mini Sheet.......	34.00
NS 6	'97 $6 Woodpecker.........	8.00
NS 6B	'97 Same, Booklet.........	10.00
NS 6M	'97 Same, Mini Sheet.......	34.00
ONTARIO		
ON 1	'93 $6 Ruffled Grouse....	11.00
ON 1B	'93 $6 Grouse Bklt.........	9.00
ON 1M	'93 Same, Mini Sheet of 4..	34.00
ON 2	'94 $6 Deer..................	8.00
ON 2B	'94 Same, Booklet.........	9.00
ON 2M	'94 Same, Mini Sheet of 4	34.00
ON 3	'95 $6 Fish..................	8.00
ON 3B	'95 Same, Booklet..........	10.00
ON 3M	'95 Same, Mini Sheet/4 .	30.00
ON 4	'96 $6 Blue Wing Teal ...	8.00
ON 4B	'96 Same, Booklet..........	10.00
ON 4M	'96 Same, Mini Sheet.......	34.00
PRINCE EDWARD ISLAND		
PEI 1	'94 $6 Geese	8.00
PEI 1B	'94 Same, Booklet.........	9.00
PEI 1M	'94 Same, Mini Sheet of 4	34.00
PEI 2	'95 $6 Canada Geese ...	8.00
PEI 2B	'95 Same, Booklet.........	9.00
PEI 2M	'95 Same, Mini Sheet of 4	30.00
PEI 3	'96 $6 Woodcock..........	8.00
PEI 3B	'96 Same, Booklet..........	10.00
PEI 3M	'96 Same, Mini Sheet.....	34.00
PEI 4	'97 $6 Red Fox	8.00
PEI 4B	'97 Same, Booklet..........	10.00
PEI 4M	'97 Same, Mini Sheet	34.00
QUEBEC		
QU 1	'88 $6 Ruffled Grouse....	120.00
QU 1M	'88 $6 Mini Sheet of 4...	225.00
QU 1MI	'88 Imperf. Sheet of 4 .	1100.00
QU 2	'89 $6 Black Ducks	37.50

No.	Description	F-VF N
QUEBEC (cont.)		
QU 2M	'89 $6 Mini Sheet of 4....	140.00
QU 2MI	'89 Imperf. Sheet of 4	350.00
QU 3	'90 $6 Common Loons ..	22.00
QU 3M	'90 $6 Mini Sheet of 4....	135.00
QU 3MI	'90 Imperf. Sheet of 4	350.00
QU 4	'91 $6 Cmn Gldneyes....	16.00
QU 4M	'91 $6 Mini Sheet of 4....	83.40
QU 4MI	'91 Imperf. Sheet of 4	350.00
QU 5	'92 $6.50 Lynx	12.50
QU 5A	'92 $10 Lynx Surcharge.	25.00
QU 5M	'92 $6 Mini Sheet of 4....	90.00
QU 5MI	'92 Imperf. Sheet of 4	280.00
QU 6	'93 $6.50 Pergrn Falcon	12.50
QU 6M	'93 $6.50 Mini Sheet of 4	60.00
QU 6MI	'93 $6.50 Impf Sht. of 4 .	225.00
QU 7	'94 $7 Beluga Whale	13.00
QU 7M	'94 Same, Mini Sheet of 4	45.00
QU 7MI	'94 Same, Imperf. Sht. 4	225.00
QU 8	'95 $7 Moose................	12.00
QU 8M	'95 Same, Mini Sheet of 4	45.00
QU 8MI	'95 Same, Imperf.Sht/4..	225.00
QU 9	'96 $7 Blue Heron........	12.00
QU 10	'97 $8.50 Snow Owl	14.00
SASKATCHEWAN		
SK 1	'88 $5 American Widg'n.	40.00
SK 2	'89 $5 Bull Moose.........	40.00
SK 3	'90 $5 Shp Tail'd Grouse	50.00
SK 4	'93 $6 Mallards	8.00
SK 4B	'93 $6 Mallards Bklt.......	10.00
SK 4M	'93 $6 Mini Sht. of 4.......	34.00
SK 5	'94 $6 Wood Ducks	8.00
SK 5B	'94 Same, Booklet.........	10.00
SK 5M	'94 Same, Mini Sheet/4 .	34.00
SK 6	'95 $6 Antelope	8.00
SK 6B	'95 Same, Booklet.........	9.00
SK 6M	'95 Same, Mini Sheet/4..	30.00
SK 7	'96 $6 Ruddy Duck.......	8.00
SK 7B	'96 Same, Booklet.........	10.00
SK 7M	'96 Same, Mini Sheet	34.00
YUKON TERRITORY		
YT 1	'96 $6 Bald Eagle..........	8.00
YT 1B	'96 Same, Booklet.........	10.00
YT 1M	'96 Same, Mini Sheet	34.00

NEWFOUNDLAND

1,15A-16   3,11A   13,20   23

1857 Imperf. Thick Wove Paper, Mesh (OG + 50%) (C)

Scott's		Unused		Used	
No.		Fine	Ave.	Fine	Ave.
1	1p Crown & Flowers, Brn. Violet	50.00	30.00	100.00	65.00
3	3p Triangle, Green........................	250.00	160.00	300.00	200.00
5	5p Crown & Flowers, Vlt. Brown.......	150.00	90.00	250.00	165.00
8	8p Flowers, Scarlet Vermillion..........	160.00	95.00	225.00	150.00

1860 Imperf. Thin Wove Paper, No Mesh (OG + 50%) (C)

11	2p Flowers, Orange	165.00	110.00	225.00	150.00
11A	3p Triangle, Green...........................	37.50	24.00	75.00	50.00
12	4p Flowers, Orange	...	...	600.00	400.00
12A	5p Crown & Flowers, Vlt. Brown.......	45.00	25.00	100.00	65.00
13	6p Flowers, Orange	...	...	500.00	350.00

1861-62 Imperforate Thin Wove Paper (OG + 50%) (C)

15A	1p Crown & Flowers, Vlt. Brown.......	100.00	60.00	160.00	110.00
17	2p Flowers, Rose.............................	95.00	55.00	130.00	85.00
18	4p Flowers, Rose.............................	23.75	14.50	47.50	27.50
19	5p Crown & Flowers, Red Brown	30.00	17.50	50.00	31.50
20	6p Flowers, Rose.............................	12.50	7.00	38.50	24.50
21	6½ Flowers, Rose.............................	50.00	27.50	120.00	70.00
22	8p Flowers, Rose.............................	45.00	25.00	195.00	120.00
23	1sh Flowers, Rose...........................	25.00	13.75	100.00	65.00

24   28-29   32-32A   35-36

1865-1894 Perf. 12 (OG + 30%, NH + 80%) (C)

24	2¢ Codfish, Green, Yellow Paper.....	40.00	27.50	22.50	12.50
24a	2¢ Green, White Paper.....................	30.00	18.50	16.00	9.00
25	5¢ Harp Seal, Brown	275.00	185.00	200.00	135.00
26	5¢ Harp Seal, Black (1868)	150.00	100.00	85.00	55.00
27	10¢ Prince Albert, Black, Yel. Paper	125.00	80.00	57.50	35.00
27a	10¢ Black, White Paper....................	100.00	65.00	30.00	16.50
28	12¢ Victoria, Red Brown, Yel.Paper.	185.00	125.00	115.00	75.00
28a	12¢ Red Brown, White Paper...........	27.50	15.00	27.50	15.00
29	12¢ Brown, White Paper (1894)........	24.50	14.00	24.50	14.00
30	13¢ Fishing Ship, Orange.................	65.00	40.00	45.00	27.50
31	24¢ Victoria, Blue	20.00	12.50	18.50	11.50

1868-1894 Perf. 12 (OG + 30%, NH + 80%) (C)

32	1¢ Prince of Wales, Violet	24.00	15.00	23.00	14.00
32A	1¢ Brown Lilac (1871).....................	30.00	18.00	30.00	18.00
33	3¢ Victoria, Vermillion (1870)	150.00	90.00	90.00	55.00
34	3¢ Blue (1873)................................	150.00	90.00	16.00	9.00
35	6¢ Victoria, Dull Rose (1870)	8.50	5.00	8.50	5.00
36	6¢ Carmine Lake (1894)..................	10.00	6.25	10.00	6.25

1876-1879 Rouletted (OG + 30%, NH + 80%) (C)

37	1¢ Prince of Wales, Brn. Lilac (1877)	45.00	27.50	17.50	10.00
38	2¢ Codfish, Green (1879).................	65.00	40.00	20.00	14.00
39	3¢ Victoria, Blue (1877)...................	150.00	90.00	7.00	4.75
40	5¢ Harp Seal, Blue	100.00	60.00	7.00	4.75

1880-1896 Perf. 12 (OG + 20%) VF + 50% (C)

41-45   46-48   56-58   59

NEWFOUNDLAND
1880-1896 Perf. 12 (OG + 20%) VF + 50% (C)

Scott's		NH	Unused		Used	
No.		Fine	Fine	Ave.	Fine	Ave.
41	1¢ Prince, Vlt. Brown	16.00	8.00	4.25	6.50	3.25
42	1¢ Gray Brown	16.00	8.00	4.25	6.50	3.25
43	1¢ Brown (1896)	45.00	22.50	12.50	18.50	11.00
44	1¢ Deep Green (1887).................	9.00	5.00	3.00	2.50	1.50
45	1¢ Green (1897)	10.00	5.50	3.50	3.00	1.75
46	2¢ Codfish, Yellow Green...........	20.00	10.00	6.00	9.50	5.00
47	2¢ Green (1896)	35.00	20.00	12.00	14.00	8.50
48	2¢ Red Orange (1887).................	15.00	8.50	4.50	5.25	3.00
49	3¢ Victoria, Blue	29.50	15.00	9.00	3.50	1.95
51	3¢ Umber Brown (1887)	20.00	10.00	6.50	3.00	1.65
52	3¢ Violet Brown (1896)	65.00	35.00	20.00	35.00	20.00
53	5¢ Harp Seal, Pale Blue	250.00	150.00	90.00	7.00	4.25
54	5¢ Dark Blue (1887)	100.00	60.00	35.00	5.25	3.25
55	5¢ Bright Blue (1894)	28.50	15.00	9.00	3.75	2.25

1887-1896 (OG + 20%) VF + 50% (C)

56	½¢ Dog, Rose Red......................	8.50	4.75	2.75	4.00	2.25
57	½¢ Orange Red (1896)..............	45.00	25.00	15.00	24.00	14.00
58	½¢ Black (1894)	8.00	4.50	2.50	3.50	1.85
59	10¢ Schooner, Black	70.00	37.50	22.50	30.00	16.00

60   61   63   69   74

1890 Issue (OG + 20%) VF + 40% (C)

60	3¢ Victoria, Slate	11.50	6.25	3.75	.75	.45

1897 John Cabot Issue VF Used + 30% (B)

Scott's		NH		Unused		Used
No.		VF	F-VF	VF	F-VF	F-VF
61-74	Set of 14..............................	315.00	245.00	170.00	130.00	99.50
61	1¢ Queen Victoria	2.60	2.00	1.45	1.10	1.10
62	2¢ Cabot	3.25	2.50	1.75	1.35	1.10
63	3¢ Cape Bonavista	5.00	3.75	2.60	2.00	1.00
64	4¢ Caribou Hunting...................	6.50	5.00	3.75	2.75	2.25
65	5¢ Mining	8.50	6.50	5.25	4.00	2.25
66	6¢ Logging	8.75	6.50	4.75	3.50	3.00
67	8¢ Fishing	15.00	11.50	8.50	6.50	4.50
68	10¢ Ship "Matthew"	25.00	18.00	13.50	10.00	3.95
69	12¢ Willow Ptarmigan..............	26.00	19.50	14.50	11.00	5.25
70	15¢ Seals.................................	26.00	19.50	14.50	11.00	5.00
71	24¢ Salmon Fishing..................	22.50	17.50	12.50	9.50	6.00
72	30¢ Colony Seal	65.00	45.00	35.00	25.00	25.00
73	35¢ Iceberg..............................	110.00	85.00	60.00	45.00	40.00
74	60¢ King Henry VII	15.00	11.50	8.50	6.50	6.00

1897 Surcharges VF Used + 50% (C)

75	1¢ on 3¢ Type a (#60)	38.50	25.00	22.75	14.00	11.50
76	1¢ on 3¢ Type b (#60)	175.00	120.00	100.00	70.00	80.00
77	1¢ on 3¢ Type c (#60)............	675.00	450.00	450.00	300.00	335.00

78   79-80   81-82   85   86

1897-1901 Royal Family Issue VF Used + 30% (B)

78-85	Set of 8.................................	100.00	79.75	62.50	46.50	14.75
78	½¢ Edward VII as Child............	3.25	2.50	1.95	1.50	1.65
79	1¢ Victoria, Carm. Rose	5.00	3.75	3.25	2.40	2.25
80	1¢ Yellow Green (1898)............	3.35	2.50	2.00	1.50	.18
81	2¢ Prince, Orange	5.75	4.50	3.75	2.75	2.75
82	2¢ Vermillion (1898)	11.00	8.50	6.75	5.00	.45
83	3¢ Princess (1898)	21.50	16.00	12.00	9.00	.45
84	4¢ Duchess (1901)	28.50	21.00	17.00	12.50	3.00
85	5¢ Duke of York (1899)	29.50	25.00	19.00	14.00	2.00

1908 Map Stamp VF Used + 30% (B)

86	12¢ Map of Newfoundland.......	33.50	25.00	19.75	15.00	1.00

NOTE: PRICES THROUGHOUT THIS LIST ARE SUBJECT TO CHANGE WITHOUT NOTICE IF MARKET CONDITIONS REQUIRE. MINIMUM ORDER MUST TOTAL AT LEAST $20.00.

1910 Guy Issue (Lithographed) Perf. 12 except as noted
VF Used + 30% (B)

| 87 | 88 | 91 | 92-92A,98 | 96,102 |

Scott's No.		NH VF	F-VF	Unused VF	F-VF	Used F-VF
87-97	**Normal Set of 12** 465.00	350.00	250.00	175.00	175.00
87	1¢ James I,Pf. 12 x 11 .... 2.60	2.00	1.30	1.00	.80
87a	1¢ Perf. 12 .... 4.50	3.50	2.95	2.25	1.50
87b	1¢ Perf. 12 x 14 .... 4.00	3.00	2.25	1.75	1.25
88	2¢ Company Arms 9.00	7.00	5.25	4.00	.75
88a	2¢ Perf. 12 x 14 .... 8.25	6.50	4.75	3.75	.65
88c	2¢ Perf. 12 x 11½	...	300.00	225.00	225.00
89	3¢ John Guy 14.50	11.00	8.00	6.00	7.00
90	4¢ The "Endeavor" 24.00	17.50	13.75	10.00	7.50
91	5¢ Cupids, Perf. 14 x 12 .... 16.00	12.00	9.50	7.00	2.50
91a	5¢ Perf. 12 .... 20.00	15.00	11.75	9.00	3.75
92	6¢ Lord Bacon Claret (Z Reversed) 100.00	75.00	53.50	40.00	37.50
92A	6¢ Claret (Z Normal) 32.50	24.00	17.50	13.00	15.00
93	8¢ Mosquito, Pale Brown 75.00	55.00	40.00	28.50	28.50
94	9¢ Logging, Ol. Green 75.00	55.00	40.00	28.50	28.50
95	10¢ Paper Mills, Black 75.00	55.00	40.00	28.50	27.50
96	12¢ Edward VII, L. Brown 75.00	55.00	40.00	28.50	28.50
97	15¢ George V, Gray Black 90.00	65.00	50.00	35.00	35.00

1911 Guy Issue (Engraved) Perf. 14 VF Used + 30% (B)

98-103	**Set of 6** 450.00	350.00	240.00	185.00	185.00
98	6¢ Lord Bacon Brown Violet 29.50	22.50	16.50	12.50	12.50
99	8¢ Mosquito, Bistre Brn 75.00	55.00	39.50	30.00	30.00
100	9¢ Logging, Ol. Grn 62.50	47.50	32.50	25.00	25.00
101	10¢ Paper Mills, Vi. Black 120.00	90.00	65.00	50.00	50.00
102	12¢ Edward VII, Red Brn 100.00	75.00	52.50	40.00	40.00
103	15¢ George V, Slate Gr 100.00	75.00	52.50	40.00	40.00

| 104 | 105 | 107 | 115 |

1911 Royal Family Coronation Issue VF Used + 30% (B)

104-14	**Set of 11** 325.00	245.00	175.00	135.00	115.00
104	1¢ Queen Mary 2.85	2.10	1.50	1.15	.18
105	2¢ George V 2.95	2.25	1.65	1.25	.18
106	3¢ Prince of Wales 30.00	22.75	16.00	12.00	12.00
107	4¢ Prince Albert 26.50	20.00	14.50	10.75	9.00
108	5¢ Princess Mary 12.50	9.50	6.50	5.00	1.00
109	6¢ Prince Henry 26.00	19.50	14.50	11.00	11.00
110	8¢ George (color paper) 85.00	65.00	43.50	33.50	31.50
110a	8¢ White Paper 87.50	67.50	45.00	35.00	32.50
111	9¢ Prince John 29.50	22.50	16.50	12.50	12.50
112	10¢ Queen Alexandra 45.00	33.75	25.00	18.50	17.50
113	12¢ Duke of Connaught 41.75	32.50	23.00	17.50	16.50
114	15¢ Seal of Colony 40.00	30.00	21.50	16.50	15.00

1919 Trail of the Caribou Issue VF Used + 30% (B)

115-26	**Set of 12** 255.00	190.00	147.50	110.00	100.00
115	1¢ Suvla Bay 2.00	1.50	1.20	.90	.20
116	2¢ Ubique 2.50	1.90	1.50	1.10	.35
117	3¢ Gueudecourt 3.35	2.50	2.00	1.50	.20
118	4¢ Beaumont Hamel 5.50	4.25	3.00	2.40	.85
119	5¢ Ubique 6.25	4.75	3.65	2.75	.85
120	6¢ Monchy 24.50	18.00	14.00	10.50	10.50
121	8¢ Ubique 24.50	18.00	14.00	10.50	10.50
122	10¢ Steenbeck 13.00	9.75	7.50	5.50	2.50
123	12¢ Ubique 50.00	37.50	30.00	22.50	20.00
124	15¢ Langemarck 40.00	30.00	23.50	17.50	20.00
125	24¢ Cambrai 50.00	37.50	28.50	21.50	21.50
126	36¢ Combles 47.50	35.00	26.50	20.00	20.00

1920 Stamps of 1897 Surcharged VF Used + 30% (B)

127	2¢ on 30¢ Seal (#72) 8.00	5.75	4.75	3.50	3.50
128	3¢ on 15¢ Bars 10½ mm 295.00	210.00	175.00	130.00	135.00
129	3¢ on 15¢ Bars 13½ mm 15.00	11.75	9.00	7.00	7.00
130	3¢ on 35¢ Iceberg (#73) 12.50	9.50	7.75	6.00	6.00

1923-1924 Pictorial Issue VF Used + 30% (B)

| 131 | 132 | 133 | 139 |

Scott's No.		NH VF	F-VF	Unused VF	F-VF	Used F-VF
131-44	**Set of 14** 165.00	125.00	105.00	79.50	72.50
131	1¢ Twin Hills, Tor's Cove 2.25	1.70	1.50	1.10	.20
132	2¢ South West Arm, Trinity 2.25	1.70	1.50	1.10	.18
133	3¢ War Memorial 2.50	1.85	1.60	1.20	.18
134	4¢ Humber River 3.00	2.25	1.95	1.50	1.40
135	5¢ Coast of Trinity 4.65	3.50	3.00	2.25	1.50
136	6¢ Upper Steadies, Humber R. .. 5.00	3.75	3.35	2.50	2.50
137	8¢ Quidi Vidi 4.65	3.50	3.00	2.25	2.15
138	9¢ Caribou Crossing Lake 29.50	21.50	19.00	14.00	14.00
139	10¢ Humber River Canyon 5.50	4.25	3.50	2.75	1.60
140	11¢ Shell Bird Island 9.00	7.00	6.00	4.50	4.50
141	12¢ Mt. Moriah 9.00	7.00	6.00	4.50	4.50
142	15¢ Humber River 10.50	7.50	6.75	5.00	4.50
143	20¢ Placentia (1924) 14.00	10.00	8.75	6.75	4.50
144	24¢ Topsail Falls (1924) 72.50	55.00	45.00	35.00	35.00

| 145,163,172 | 146,164,173 | 148,166,175 | 155 |

1928 Publicity Issue - Unwatermarked - Thin Paper VF Used + 30% (B)

145-59	**Set of 15** 105.00	79.50	68.50	52.00	45.00
145	1¢ Map, Deep Green 1.70	1.30	1.15	.85	.50
146	2¢ "Caribou", Deep Carmine 2.40	1.85	1.60	1.25	.45
147	3¢ Mary & George V, Brown 2.75	2.00	1.80	1.35	.30
148	4¢ Prince, Lilac Rose 3.25	2.50	2.15	1.60	1.35
149	5¢ Train, Slate Green 7.00	5.00	4.50	3.25	2.50
150	6¢ Newfld. Hotel, Ultramarine 5.00	3.75	3.25	2.50	2.25
151	8¢ Heart's Content, Lt. Red Brn 7.00	5.25	4.65	3.50	3.25
152	9¢ Cabot Tower Myrtle Green ... 8.00	6.00	5.25	4.00	3.75
153	10¢ War Mem., Dark Violet 8.00	6.00	5.25	4.00	3.50
154	12¢ P.O., Brown Carmine 5.95	4.50	3.95	3.00	2.50
155	14¢ Cabot Tower, Red Brown ... 8.00	6.00	5.25	4.00	3.25
156	15¢ Nonstop Flight, Dark Blue... 9.00	6.75	6.00	4.50	4.25
157	20¢ Colonial Bldg, Gray Blk 7.75	5.75	5.00	3.75	3.00
158	28¢ P.O., Gray Green 26.50	21.00	17.00	13.50	12.50
159	30¢ Grand Falls, Olive Brown... 8.75	6.50	5.75	4.25	4.50

1929 Stamp of 1923 Surcharged VF Used + 30% (B)

160	3¢ on 6¢ Upper Steadies(#136) 4.50	3.50	2.95	2.25	2.25

1929-31 Publicity Issue Re-engraved -
Like Preceding but Thicker Paper VF Used + 30% (B)
(See your favorite Specialized catalog for details)

163-71	**Set of 9** 125.00	95.00	87.50	66.50	42.75
163	1¢ Green 1.75	1.35	1.25	.95	.35
164	2¢ Deep Carmine 1.75	1.35	1.25	.95	.18
165	3¢ Deep Red Brown 2.15	1.65	1.50	1.15	.18
166	4¢ Magenta 3.15	2.40	2.15	1.65	.75
167	5¢ Slate Green 4.25	3.25	2.95	2.25	.80
168	6¢ Ultramarine 11.50	8.50	7.95	6.00	5.50
169	10¢ Dark Violet 4.65	3.50	3.25	2.50	1.20
170	15¢ Deep Blue (1930) 42.50	32.50	29.50	22.50	21.00
171	20¢ Gray Black (1931) 60.00	45.00	42.50	32.50	15.00

1931 Publicity Issue - Re-engraved - Wmk. Arms VF Used + 30% (B)

172-81	**Set of 11** 220.00	170.00	145.00	110.00	73.50
172	1¢ Green 2.25	1.60	1.45	1.10	.70
173	2¢ Red 3.35	2.60	2.30	1.75	.85
174	3¢ Red Brown 3.35	2.60	2.30	1.75	.70
175	4¢ Rose 3.95	3.00	2.65	2.00	1.00
176	5¢ Greenish Gray 10.50	7.75	7.00	5.25	5.00
177	6¢ Ultramarine 19.50	15.00	13.00	10.00	11.00
178	8¢ Red Brown 19.50	15.00	13.00	10.00	11.00
179	10¢ Dark Violet 14.50	11.00	9.75	7.50	4.75
180	15¢ Deep Blue 45.00	35.00	29.00	22.50	19.50
181	20¢ Gray Black 65.00	50.00	42.50	32.50	5.75
182	30¢ Olive Brown 45.00	35.00	29.50	22.50	16.50

1932-1937 Pictorial Set, Perf. 13½ or 14 VF Used + 20%

183-84,253	190-91,257	199,266	210,264

Scott's No.		NH VF	F-VF	Unused VF	F-VF	Used F-VF
183-99	Set of 17..............................	75.00	61.50	56.50	46.75	31.95
183	1¢ Codfish, Green	1.85	1.50	1.35	1.10	.30
183a	1¢ Booklet Pane of 4	85.00	70.00	60.00	50.00	...
184	1¢ Gray Black.............................	.40	.30	.27	.22	.15
184a	1¢ Bk. Pane of 4, Pf. 13½	65.00	52.50	45.00	37.50	...
184b	1¢ Bk. Pane of 4, Pf. 14..........	80.00	65.00	55.00	45.00	...
185	2¢ George V, Rose....................	1.85	1.50	1.35	1.10	.15
185a	2¢ Bk. Pane of 4	52.50	42.50	36.50	30.00	...
186	2¢ Green....................................	1.15	.95	.90	.75	.15
186a	2¢ Bk. Pane of 4, Pf. 13½	26.00	21.50	20.00	16.50	...
186b	2¢ Bk. Pane of 4, Pf. 14..........	37.50	29.50	26.00	21.00	...
187	3¢ Queen Mary........................	1.20	1.00	.90	.75	.18
187a	3¢ Bk. Pane of 4, Pf. 13½	60.00	50.00	42.50	35.00	...
187b	3¢ Bk. Pane of 4, Pf. 14..........	75.00	60.00	52.50	42.50	...
187c	3¢ Bk. Pane of 4, Pf. 13..........	85.00	70.00	60.00	50.00	...
188	4¢ Prince, Deep Violet..............	5.00	4.00	3.65	3.00	1.25
189	4¢ Rose Lake............................	.65	.50	.50	.40	.15
190	5¢ Caribou V. Brown (I)............	6.00	4.75	4.25	3.50	.70
191	5¢ Deep Violet (II).....................	.95	.75	.75	.60	.15
191a	5¢ Deep Violet (I)......................	10.50	8.50	7.50	6.35	.75
192	6¢ Elizabeth, Dull Blue	10.50	8.50	7.75	6.50	6.50
193	10¢ Salmon, Olive Black	1.15	.95	.90	.75	.50
194	14¢ Dog, Intense Black	2.50	2.00	1.95	1.60	1.50
195	15¢ Seal Pup, Magenta	2.50	2.00	1.95	1.60	1.50
196	20¢ Cape Race, Gray Green.....	2.50	2.00	1.95	1.60	.65
197	25¢ Sealing Fleet, Gray............	2.85	2.35	2.25	1.90	1.40
198	30¢ Fishing Fleet, Ultra	27.50	22.50	20.00	16.50	14.75
199	48¢ Fishing Fleet Red Brown (1937)	11.50	9.25	8.50	7.00	3.50

#191 Antler under "T" higher, #190,191a Antlers are even height.

1932 New Values VF Used + 20%

208	7¢ Duchess, Red Brown............	1.40	1.10	1.10	.85	.85
209	8¢ Corner Brook, Or. Red..........	1.40	1.10	1.10	.85	.65
210	24¢ Bell Island, Light Blue.........	3.00	2.50	2.35	1.95	1.95

1933 "L & S Post" Overprinted on C9 VF + 20%

211	15¢ Dog Sled & Plane	8.75	7.00	6.75	5.50	5.00

1933 Sir Humphrey Gilbert Issue VF + 20%

212	213	216	222

212-25	Set of 14..............................	140.00	115.00	105.00	85.00	79.50
212	1¢ Sir Humphrey Gilbert............	1.00	.80	.75	.60	.50
213	2¢ Compton Castle....................	1.25	1.00	.90	.75	.50
214	3¢ Gilbert Coat of Arms.............	1.90	1.50	1.40	1.15	.45
215	4¢ Eton College.........................	1.90	1.50	1.40	1.15	.35
216	5¢ Token from Queen.................	2.25	1.80	1.65	1.35	.75
217	7¢ Royal Patents	14.00	11.50	10.50	8.50	8.50
218	8¢ Leaving Plymouth.................	8.00	6.75	6.00	5.00	5.00
219	9¢ Arriving St. John's................	9.50	7.75	7.00	5.75	5.75
220	10¢ Annexation..........................	9.50	7.75	7.00	5.75	4.50
221	14¢ Coat of Arms.......................	19.50	15.00	14.00	11.50	10.50
222	15¢ Deck of "Squirrel"	17.50	14.50	13.00	10.75	10.50
223	20¢ 1626 Map of Nwfld.............	12.00	10.00	9.00	7.50	6.50
224	24¢ Queen Elizabeth I	25.00	20.00	18.00	15.00	15.00
225	32¢ Gilbert Statue at Truro	25.00	20.00	18.00	15.00	15.00

1935 Silver Jubilee Issue VF + 20%

226	230	233

Scott's No.		F-VF NH	Unused	F-VF Used
226-29	Set of 4......................................	9.75	7.50	6.50
226	4¢ George V, Bright Rose	.95	.75	.45
227	5¢ Violet..	.95	.75	.65
228	7¢ Dark Blue	2.50	2.00	1.85
229	24¢ Olive Green	5.75	4.50	4.00

1937 Coronation Issue VF + 20%

230-32	Set of 3..	2.75	1.90	1.15
230	2¢ Elizabeth & George VI Deep Green	.75	.55	.35
231	4¢ Carmine Rose	.75	.55	.30
232	5¢ Dark Violet..	1.40	1.10	.60

1937 Coronation Issue (Long Set) VF + 20%

233-43	Set of 11..	24.00	18.50	15.75
233	1¢ Codfish	.40	.30	.20
234	3¢ Map of Newfoundland (I), Fine	1.60	1.25	.70
234a	3¢ Map (II), Coarse	1.40	1.10	.60
235	7¢ Caribou	1.75	1.40	1.10
236	8¢ Corner Brook Paper Mills	1.75	1.40	1.10
237	10¢ Salmon	3.15	2.50	2.25
238	14¢ Newfoundland Dog	2.40	1.90	1.85
239	15¢ Harp Seal Pup	3.00	2.40	2.00
240	20¢ Cape Race	2.25	1.75	1.50
241	24¢ Loading Iron Ore	2.90	2.30	2.10
242	25¢ Sealing Fleet	2.90	2.30	2.00
243	48¢ Fishing Fleet	3.35	2.65	2.25

245	249	252

1938 Royal Family, Perf. 13½ VF + 20%

245-48	Set of 4..	5.25	4.15	1.30
245	2¢ George VI, Green	1.25	1.00	.15
246	3¢ Queen Elizabeth, Dark Carmine................	1.25	1.00	.18
247	4¢ Princess Elizabeth, Light Blue	1.75	1.35	.15
248	7¢ Queen Mother, Ultramarine	1.25	1.00	.90

1939 Royal Visit VF + 20%

Scott's No.		Plate Blocks NH	Unused	F-VF NH	Unused	F-VF Used
249	5¢ George VI - Elizabeth	8.00	6.50	.80	.65	.65

1939 Royal Visit Surcharge VF + 20%

250	2¢ on 5¢ (#249)	11.75	9.50	1.10	.85	.85
251	4¢ on 5¢ (#249)	10.50	8.50	.85	.65	.65

1941 Grenfell Issue VF + 20%

252	5¢ Wilfred Grenfell	2.75	2.25	.30	.25	.25

1941-1944 Pictorial Set, Perf. 12½ VF + 20%

253-66	Set of 14..............................	...	...	12.95	10.50	8.75
253	1¢ Codfish, Dark Gray	2.50	2.00	.25	.20	.15
254	2¢ George VI, Deep Green........	2.50	2.00	.25	.20	.15
255	3¢ Elizabeth, Rose Carm...........	3.75	2.95	.30	.25	.15
256	4¢ Princess Elizabeth, Blue.......	4.95	3.95	.55	.45	.15
257	5¢ Caribou, Violet (I).................	4.95	3.95	.55	.45	.15
258	7¢ Queen Mother (1942)	...	...	.90	.70	.70
259	8¢ Corner Brook, Red...............	6.75	5.25	.70	.55	.55
260	10¢ Salmon, Brown Black	6.75	5.25	.70	.55	.45
261	14¢ Dog, Black	12.50	9.75	1.25	1.00	1.00
262	15¢ Seal Pup, Rose Violet........	12.50	9.75	1.25	1.00	1.00
263	20¢ Cape Race, Green..............	12.50	9.75	1.25	1.00	1.00
264	24¢ Bell Island, Deep Blue	12.50	9.75	1.65	1.35	1.25
265	25¢ Sealing Fleet, Slate	12.50	9.75	1.65	1.35	1.25
266	48¢ Fishing, Red Br. (1944).......	17.50	13.50	2.50	1.95	1.40

| | 267 | | 269 | | 270 | |

1943 University Issue VF + 20%

Scott's No.		Plate Blocks NH	Unused	F-VF NH	F-VF Unused	F-VF Used
267	30¢ Memorial University	8.00	6.50	1.10	.90	.80

1946 Two Cent Provisional VF + 20%

268	2¢ on 30¢ (#267)....................	3.50	3.00	.30	.25	.25

1947 Issues VF + 20%

269	4¢ Princess Elizabeth	2.35	2.00	.30	.25	.15
270	5¢ Cabot in the "Matthew".......	2.75	2.25	.30	.25	.20

AIRMAIL STAMPS

1919-21 Overprint Issues VF Used + 30% (B)

Scott's No.		NH VF	F-VF	Unused VF	F-VF	Used F-VF
C2	$1 on 15¢ "Trans-Atlantic" AIRPOST,1919. ONE DOLLAR (#70)	260.00	195.00	175.00	135.00	135.00
C2a	$1 on 15¢ Without Comma after "Post""	285.00	215.00	200.00	150.00	165.00
C3	35¢ "AIR MAIL to Halifax, N.S. 1921"(#73)	195.00	140.00	130.00	95.00	100.00
C3a	35¢ Period after "1921"..........	215.00	160.00	145.00	110.00	120.00

| C7,C10 | C6,C9 | C8,C11 |

1931 Airs, Unwatermarked VF Used + 30% (B)

			VF	F-VF		
C6-8	Set of 3	100.00	79.50	72.50	55.00	55.00
C6	15¢ Dog Sled & Airplane	8.50	6.50	5.85	4.50	4.50
C7	50¢ Trans-Atlantic Plane..........	23.00	19.00	17.50	13.50	13.50
C8	$1 Flight Routes........................	75.00	57.50	52.50	40.00	40.00

1931 Airs, Watermarked "Coat of Arms" VF Used + 30% (B)

C9-11	Set of 3	157.50	117.50	110.00	80.00	75.00
C9	15¢ Dog Sled & Airplane	8.00	6.00	5.50	4.25	4.25
C10	50¢ Trans-Atlantic Plane..........	42.50	32.50	29.50	22.50	21.50
C11	$1 Flight Routes.....................	115.00	85.00	80.00	60.00	52.50

| | C13 | C19 | J3 | |

1932 DO-X Trans-Atlantic Surcharge VF Used + 30% (B)

Scott's No.		NH VF	F-VF	Unused VF	F-VF	Used F-VF
C12	$1.50 on $1 Routes (#C11).......	315.00	250.00	230.00	175.00	175.00

1933 Labrador Issue VF Used + 20%

C13-17	Set of 5............................	175.00	145.00	125.00	100.00	110.00
C13	5¢ "Put to Flight".....................	11.75	8.75	8.00	6.50	6.50
C14	10¢ "Land of Heart's Delight" ..	18.00	15.00	12.50	10.50	10.50
C15	30¢ "Spotting the Herd"	35.00	28.50	24.00	20.00	22.50
C16	60¢ "News from Home"...........	60.00	50.00	42.50	35.00	40.00
C17	75¢ "Labrador, Land of Gold"..	60.00	50.00	42.50	35.00	40.00

1933 General Balbo Flight VF Used + 20%

C18	$4.50 on 75¢ (#C17)	385.00	325.00	285.00	235.00	235.00

1943 St. John's VF + 20%

Scott's No.		Plate Blocks NH	Unused	F-VF NH	F-VF Unused	F-VF Used
C19	7¢ View of St. John's	3.00	2.50	.35	.30	.25

POSTAGE DUE STAMPS 1939-1949 VF + 20%
Unwatermarked, Perf. 10 x 10½ Unless Otherwise Noted

Scott's No.		F-VF NH	Unused	F-VF Used
J1-6	Set of 6	27.50	19.50	18.50
J1	1¢ Yellow Green	3.75	2.75	2.50
J1a	1¢ Perf. 11 (1949)	3.00	2.25	2.50
J2	2¢ Vermillion	4.00	3.00	2.50
J2a	2¢ Perf. 11 x 9 (1946)	4.25	3.25	2.75
J3	3¢ Ultramarine	4.95	3.50	3.00
J3a	3¢ Perf. 11 x 9 (1949)	5.50	4.00	4.00
J4	4¢ Yellow Orange	9.00	6.50	6.50
J4a	4¢ Perf. 11 x 9 (1949)	7.00	5.00	5.00
J5	5¢ Pale Brown..	3.50	2.50	2.50
J6	10¢ Dark Violet	3.50	2.50	2.50
J7	10¢ Watermarked, Perf. II..............................	9.75	6.75	8.50

NOTE: PRICES THROUGHOUT THIS LIST ARE SUBJECT TO CHANGE WITHOUT NOTICE IF MARKET CONDITIONS REQUIRE. MINIMUM ORDER MUST TOTAL AT LEAST $20.00.

BRITISH COLUMBIA AND VANCOUVER ISLAND

Scott's No.		Unused Fine	Unused Ave.	Used Fine	Used Ave.
2	2½p Victoria, Dull Rose	190.00	90.00	125.00	60.00

1865 Vancouver Island (OG + 50%) (C)

4	10¢ Victoria, Blue, Imperf	1250.00	850.00	850.00	550.00
5	5¢ Victoria, Rose, Perf. 14	225.00	130.00	150.00	85.00
6	10¢ Victoria, Blue, Perf. 14	225.00	130.00	150.00	85.00

1865 British Columbia (OG + 50%) (C)

7	3p Seal, Blue, Perf. 14	70.00	45.00	70.00	45.00

1867-1869 Surcharges on #7 Design, Perf. 14 (OG + 40%) (C)

8	2¢ on 3p Brown (Black Surch)	90.00	55.00	90.00	55.00
9	5¢ on 3p Bright Red (Black)	150.00	90.00	150.00	90.00
10	10¢ on 3p Lilac Rose (Blue)	1100.00	650.00	...	...
11	25¢ on 3p Orange (Violet)................	150.00	90.00	150.00	90.00
12	50¢ on 3p Violet (Red)	475.00	285.00	475.00	285.00
13	$1 on 3p Green (Green)....................	900.00	550.00	...	...

1869 Surcharges on #7 Design, Perf. 12½ (OG + 40%) (C)

14	5¢ on 3p Bright Red (Black)..............	900.00	550.00	900.00	550.00
15	10¢ on 3p Lilac Rose (Blue)	700.00	425.00	675.00	400.00
16	25¢ on 3p Orange (Violet)................	425.00	240.00	425.00	240.00
17	50¢ on 3p Green (Green).................	600.00	350.00	600.00	350.00
18	$1 on 3p Green (Green)....................	1100.00	650.00	1100.00	650.00

NEW BRUNSWICK

Scott's No.		Unused Fine	Unused Ave.	Used Fine	Used Ave.
	1851 Imperforate - Blue Paper - Unwatermarked (OG + 50%) (C)				
1	3p Crown & Flowers, Red.................	950.00	525.00	225.00	140.00
2	6p Olive Yellow.................................	...	1250.00	450.00	275.00
3	1sh Bright Red Violet.......................	...	...	...	1250.00
4	1sh Dull Violet.................................	...	...	...	1600.00

1860-1863 - Perf. 12 - White Paper (OG + 30%, NH + 80%) (C)

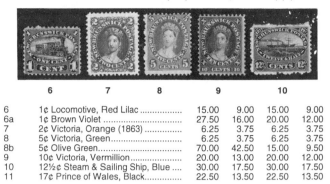

	6	7	8	9	10

6	1¢ Locomotive, Red Lilac	15.00	9.00	15.00	9.00
6a	1¢ Brown Violet	27.50	16.00	20.00	12.00
7	2¢ Victoria, Orange (1863)	6.25	3.75	6.25	3.75
8	5¢ Victoria, Green...........................	6.25	3.75	6.25	3.75
8b	5¢ Olive Green	70.00	42.50	15.00	9.50
9	10¢ Victoria, Vermillion....................	20.00	13.00	20.00	12.00
10	12½¢ Steam & Sailing Ship, Blue	30.00	17.50	30.00	17.50
11	17¢ Prince of Wales, Black..............	22.50	13.50	22.50	13.50

NOVA SCOTIA
1851-1853 - Imperforate - Blue Paper (OG + 50%) (C)

2,3

Scott's No.		Unused Fine	Unused Ave.	Used Fine	Used Ave.
1	1p Victoria, Red Brown	1500.00	900.00	275.00	175.00
2	3p Crown & Flowers, Blue	385.00	220.00	90.00	55.00
3	3p Dark Blue....................................	750.00	450.00	115.00	70.00
4	6p Crown & Flowers,,Yellow Green..	...	1250.00	300.00	185.00
5	6p Dark Green	...	2750.00	525.00	325.00
6	1sh Crown & Flowers, Reddish Violet	...	...	...	1500.00
7	1sh Dull Violet..................................	...	...	...	1500.00

1860-1863 - Perforated 12
(VF + 50%, NH + 25%, #10, 10a NH + 75%) (C)

	8	9	11	12	13

8	1¢ Victoria, Black, White Paper	3.50	2.15	3.50	2.15
8a	1¢ White Paper	3.50	2.15	3.50	2.15
9	2¢ Lilac, White Paper.......................	4.50	3.00	4.50	3.00
9a	2¢ Yellowish Paper..........................	4.50	3.00	4.50	3.00
10	5¢ Blue, White Paper.......................	185.00	115.00	5.00	3.25
10a	5¢ Yellowish Paper..........................	165.00	105.00	5.00	3.25
11	8½¢ Green,Yellowish Paper	3.50	2.25	12.00	7.50
11a	8½¢ White Paper..............................	3.50	2.25	9.00	5.50
12	10¢ Vermillion, White Paper	5.00	3.25	5.00	3.25
12a	10¢ Yellowish Paper.........................	5.00	3.25	5.00	3.25
13	12½¢ Black, Yellowish Paper...........	16.50	10.00	15.00	9.50
13a	12½¢ White Paper...........................	16.50	10.00	15.00	9.50

PRINCE EDWARD ISLAND

	1,5	2,6	9	10

1861 - Perf. 9 - Typographed (OG + 50%)

Scott's No.		Unused Fine	Unused Ave.	Used Fine	Used Ave.
1	2p Victoria, Dull Rose	250.00	160.00	125.00	80.00
2	3p Blue..	465.00	300.00	240.00	150.00
3	6p Yellow Green	750.00	500.00	400.00	260.00

1862-1865 - Perf. 11,11½,12 and Compound - Typographed
(OG + 30%, NH + 80%)

4	1p Victoria, Yellow Orange	15.00	9.50	15.00	9.50
5	2p Rose, White Paper	4.00	2.50	4.00	2.50
5a	2p Yellowish Paper...........................	4.25	2.65	4.25	2.65
6	3p Blue, White Paper........................	5.50	3.25	5.50	3.25
6a	3p Yellowish Paper...........................	7.50	4.65	5.75	3.50
7	6p Yellow Green	45.00	25.00	45.00	25.00
8	9p Violet..	37.50	21.75	37.50	21.75

1868-1870 Issues (OG + 30%, NH + 80%)

9	4p Victoria, Black, White Paper	4.75	2.75	13.50	8.50
9a	4p Yellowish Paper...........................	8.50	5.50	17.50	11.50
10	4½p Brown (1870)	27.50	17.50	32.50	20.00

1872 Issue, Perf. 12,12½ (OG + 20%, NH + 60%)

	11	13	14	15	16

11	1¢ Victoria, Brown Orange	3.00	1.85	5.00	3.25
12	2¢ Ultramarine	8.00	5.25	17.50	11.00
13	3¢ Rose	13.50	8.00	13.50	8.00
14	4¢ Green..	3.50	2.25	8.50	5.50
15	6¢ Black...	3.50	2.25	8.50	5.00
16	12¢ Violet...	3.50	2.25	15.00	9.75

Looking For Those Missing Stamps, Covers & Supplies
And at Bargain Prices Too!!!
Do You Enjoy Great Articles from the Leading Philatelic Writers?
You'll Find the Answer in the

BROOKMAN TIMES

"The Brookman Times" is published 6 times a year and has ads from leading stamp dealers and articles from leading Philatelic writers, such as Les Winick, Marjory Sente & George Griffenhagen. In addition we have added a classified advertisement section. There are bargains galore and of particular note is that only dealer's who advertise in the Brookman Price Guide can advertise in "The Brookman Times." We feel these dealers are the "cream of the crop" and heartily endorse them.

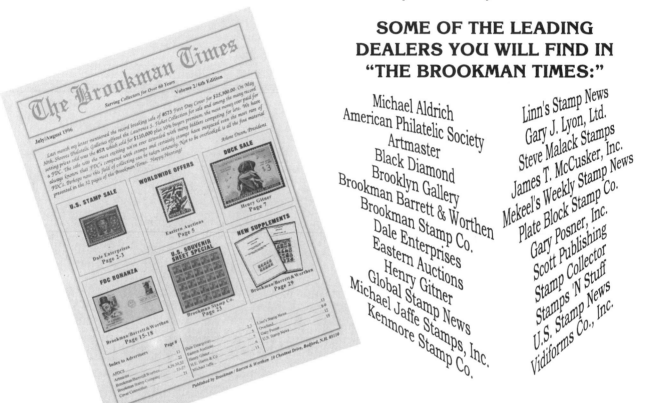

SOME OF THE LEADING DEALERS YOU WILL FIND IN "THE BROOKMAN TIMES:"

Michael Aldrich
American Philatelic Society
Artmaster
Black Diamond
Brooklyn Gallery
Brookman Barrett & Worthen
Brookman Stamp Co.
Dale Enterprises
Eastern Auctions
Henry Gitner
Global Stamp News
Michael Jaffe Stamps, Inc.
Kenmore Stamp Co.

Linn's Stamp News
Gary J. Lyon, Ltd.
Steve Malack Stamps
James T. McCusker, Inc.
Mekeel's Weekly Stamp News
Plate Block Stamp Co.
Gary Posner, Inc.
Scott Publishing
Stamp Collector
Stamps 'N Stuff
U.S. Stamp News
Vidiforms Co., Inc.

Now You Can Get This $9.95 Value FREE!!!

Everyone who purchases a Brookman Price Guide
can *receive the Brookman Times FREE*.
All you have to do is fill out the coupon below (or a copy of coupon).

☐ Please send me 6 issues of the Brookman Times.

I am enclosing $2.00 for Postage and Handling.

BROOKMAN
Barrett & Worthen

DEPT - PG
10 CHESTNUT DRIVE
BEDFORD, NH 03110

Name:_____

Address:_____

_____

_____

NO PHONE ORDERS PLEASE - MAIL ONLY.

$5 THIS COUPON
IS WORTH $5.00 **$5**

Towards any order over $55.00 from
this 1998 Brookman Price Guide

ONE COUPON PER ORDER
Available from:

$5 Brookman, Vancouver,
WA 98666-0090 **$5**

$10 THIS COUPON
IS WORTH $10.00 **$10**

Towards any order over $110.00 from
this 1998 Brookman Price Guide

ONE COUPON PER ORDER

Available from:

$10 Brookman, Vancouver,
WA 98666-0090 **$10**

$10 THIS COUPON
IS WORTH $10.00 **$10**

Towards any order over $110.00 from
this 1998 Brookman Price Guide

ONE COUPON PER ORDER

Available from:

$10 Brookman, Vancouver,
WA 98666-0090 **$10**

$10 THIS COUPON
IS WORTH $10.00 **$10**

Towards any order over $55 from
this 1998 Brookman Price Guide

ONE COUPON PER ORDER

Available from:

$10 Brookman, Vancouver,
WA 98666-0090 **$10**

$25 THIS COUPON
IS WORTH $25.00 **$25**

Towards any order over $275.00 from
this 1998 Brookman Price Guide

ONE COUPON PER ORDER

Available from:

$25 Brookman, Vancouver,
WA 98666-0090 **$25**

$40 THIS COUPON
IS WORTH $40.00 **$40**

Towards any order over $450.00 from
this 1998 Brookman Price Guide

ONE COUPON PER ORDER

Available from:

$40 Brookman, Vancouver,
WA 98666-0090 **$40**

HOW TO WRITE YOUR ORDER—PLEASE USE THE ORDER BLANK

Please send the items listed below for which I enclose: $_____   Date: 9/1/97

SHIP TO: **CREDIT CARD BILLING ADDRESS:**

Name: Brian Williams   1622 Meadow Lane

Address: P.O. Box 4621

City: Louisville   City: Louisville

State: Ky   Zip: 40216   State: Ky   Zip: 40216

Phone: (999) 555-1234   Please charge my: Visa ✓ MasterCard____ ____ Check Enclosed.

Card#: 4620 999 888 777   Expiration Date: 12/98

From Page#	Qty. Wanted	Country and items ordered: Specify Scott Numbers plus first day cover, souvenir card, plate block, mint sheet or other description	Quality Wanted	Unused	Used	Price Each	Leave Blank
4	1	# 229	FVFNH			400.00	
16	1	# 740-49 P.B. Set	FVFNH			160.00	
122	1	# 681 FDC, Louisville, Ky	Cacheted			35.00	
141	1	# 1949 Truman Inaugural				60.00	
154	1	B23 Souvenir Card	Cancelled			50.00	

1. Fill out date, phone#.

2. Print name and address, information including ZIP CODE. Please make sure to include your credit card billing address.

3. Note Minimum order of $20.00.

4. If ordering by Visa or Mastercard, please indicate charge # and expiration date.

5. If paying by check, please make payments in U.S. Funds.

6. Example of how to write up your orders above.

PAY SHIPPING/INSURANCE AS FOLLOWS:

Stamps only - $ 3.50

Other orders:

$20.00 to $49.99 - $ 3.50
$50.00 to $199.99 - $ 5.50
$200.00 & over - $ 8.00

Total this page	705	00
Total from reverse		
Shipping/Insurance (see chart at left)	8	00
SUBTOTAL	713	00
Sales Tax (if any)	—	
Less any discounts, refund checks, (coupons) etc.	<40	00>
TOTAL ENCLOSED	673	00

SATISFACTION GUARANTEED
MINIMUM ORDER MUST TOTAL AT LEAST $20.00
On orders outside the U.S. additional postage will be billed if necessary

EASY ORDER FORM – 1998 EDITION

Please send the items listed below for which I enclose: $_____ Date:_____

SHIP TO: CREDIT CARD BILLING ADDRESS:

Name:_____   _____

Address:_____   _____

_____   _____

City:_____   City:_____

State:_____ Zip:_____   State:_____ Zip:_____

Phone:_____   Please charge my: Visa_____ MasterCard_____ _____Check Enclosed.

Card#:_____   Expiration Date:_____

From Page#	Qty. Wanted	Country and items ordered: Specify Scott Numbers plus first day cover, souvenir card, plate block, mint sheet or other description	Qty. Wanted	Unused	Used	Price Each	Leave Blank

PAY SHIPPING/INSURANCE AS FOLLOWS:		
	Total this page	
	Total from reverse	
Stamps only - $ 3.50	Total from reverse	
Other orders:	Shipping/Insurance (see chart at left	
$20.00 to $49.99 - $ 3.50	**SUBTOTAL**	
$50.00 to $199.99 - $ 5.50	Sales Tax (if any)	
$200.00 & over - $ 8.00	Less any discounts, refund checks, coupons, etc.	
	TOTAL ENCLOSED	

SATISFACTION GUARANTEED
MINIMUM ORDER MUST TOTAL AT LEAST $20.00
On orders outside the U.S. additional postage will be billed if necessary

From Page#	Qty. Wanted	Country and items ordered: Specify Scott Numbers plus first day cover, souvenir card, plate block, mint sheet or other description	Qty. Wanted	Unused	Used	Price Each	Leave Blank
			Total This Page				

EASY ORDER FORM – 1998 EDITION

Please send the items listed below for which I enclose: $_____ Date:_____

SHIP TO: **CREDIT CARD BILLING ADDRESS:**

Name:_____

Address:_____   _____

_____   _____

City:_____   City:_____

State:_____ Zip:_____   State:_____ Zip:_____

Phone: _____ Please charge my: Visa_____ MasterCard_____ _____Check Enclosed.

Card#:_____ Expiration Date:_____

From Page#	Qty. Wanted	Country and items ordered: Specify Scott Numbers plus first day cover, souvenir card, plate block, mint sheet or other description	Qty. Wanted	Unused	Used	Price Each	Leave Blank

PAY SHIPPING/INSURANCE AS FOLLOWS:		
	Total this page	
	Total from reverse	
Stamps only - $ 3.50	Total from reverse	
Other orders:	Shipping/Insurance (see chart at left	
$20.00 to $49.99 - $ 3.50	**SUBTOTAL**	
$50.00 to $199.99 - $ 5.50	Sales Tax (if any)	
$200.00 & over - $ 8.00	Less any discounts, refund checks, coupons, etc.	
	TOTAL ENCLOSED	

SATISFACTION GUARANTEED
MINIMUM ORDER MUST TOTAL AT LEAST $20.00
On orders outside the U.S. additional postage will be billed if necessary

From Page#	Qty. Wanted	Country and items ordered: Specify Scott Numbers plus first day cover, souvenir card, plate block, mint sheet or other description	Qty. Wanted	Unused	Used	Price Each	Leave Blank
		Total This Page					